COMPREHENSIVE HANDBOOK
OF
PERSONALITY AND PSYCHOPATHOLOGY

COMPREHENSIVE HANDBOOK
OF
PERSONALITY AND PSYCHOPATHOLOGY

VOLUME 1
PERSONALITY AND EVERYDAY FUNCTIONING

Jay C. Thomas

Daniel L. Segal

Volume Editors

Michel Hersen

Jay C. Thomas

Editors-in-Chief

WILEY

John Wiley & Sons, Inc.

Library of Congress Cataloging-in-Publication Data:

Comprehensive handbook of personality and psychopathology / Michel Hersen & Jay C. Thomas, editors-in-chief.
    p. ; cm.
   Includes bibliographical references.
  ISBN-13 978-0-471-47945-1 (cloth : alk. paper : set)
  ISBN-10 0-471-47945-4 (cloth : alk. paper : set) —
  ISBN-13 978-0-471-48837-8 (cloth : alk. paper : v. 1)
  ISBN-10 0-471-48837-2 (cloth : alk. paper : v. 1) —
  ISBN-13 978-0-471-48838-5 (cloth : alk. paper : v. 2)
  ISBN-10 0-471-48838-0 (cloth : alk. paper : v. 2) —
  ISBN-13 978-0-471-48839-2 (cloth : alk. paper : v. 3)
  ISBN-10 0-471-48839-9 (cloth : alk. paper : v. 3)
   1. Psychology, Pathological—Handbooks, manuals, etc. 2. Child psychopathology—
Handbooks, manuals, etc. 3. Personality—Handbooks, manuals, etc. 4. Psychology—
Handbooks, manuals, etc. I. Hersen, Michel. II. Thomas, Jay C., 1951–
  [DNLM: 1. Mental Disorders—therapy. 2. Personality. 3. Psychological Theory. WM 400
C737 2006] 1951–
RC456.C66 2006
618.92′89—dc22

                                               2005043981

Printed in the United States of America.

10 9 8 7 6 5 4 3 2 1

Contents

PART ONE
FOUNDATIONS

PART TWO
BROAD-RANGE THEORIES AND SYSTEMS

Handbook Preface

Remarkably, the linkage between personality and psychopathology, although extensive, has not been underscored in the larger tomes on these subjects. In the last decade there have been many books on personality, adult psychopathology, and child psychopathology, but none seems to have related the three in an integrated fashion. In part, this three-volume *Comprehensive Handbook of Personality and Psychopathology* (CHOPP), with the first volume on *Personality and Everyday Functioning,* the second on *Adult Psychopathology,* and the third on *Child Psychopathology,* is devoted to remedying this gap in the literature. Another unique feature of CHOPP appears in the volumes on *Adult Psychopathology* and *Child Psychopathology,* where impact of adult and child psychopathology on family, work, school, and peers is highlighted, in addition to the relation of specific psychopathology to normal development. Given the marked importance of such impact, contributors were asked to delineate the negative impact of psychopathology on the individual's daily environments.

In light of the aforementioned features, we trust that CHOPP is timely and that it will be well received in many quarters in psychology. The work should stand as an entity as a three-volume endeavor. However, given the structure of each volume, we believe that it is possible to break up the set into individual volumes for relevant courses on personality, normal development, adult psychopathology, and child psychopathology.

Volume 1 (*Personality and Everyday Functioning*) contains 23 chapters divided into four parts (Foundations, Broad-Range Theories and Systems, Mid-Range Theories, and Special Applications). This volume is unique in that it encompasses both the broad theories of personality and those theories with a more limited range, known as mid-range theories. Broad-range theories were originally developed to explain the behavior of normal people in everyday situations. But it also is important to have a reference point for those individuals suffering from various sorts of psychopathology. Chapters in this section follow a general format where possible:

A. Statement of the Theory
B. Developmental Considerations
C. Biological/Physiological Relationships
D. Boundaries of the Theory

E. Evidence in Support of and against the Theory
F. Predictions for Everyday Functioning
   1. Family Life
   2. Work or School
   3. Retirement
   4. Recreation

Thus, Volume 1 sets the stage for Volumes 2 and 3 while at the same time standing on its own for understanding everyday life from the personality perspective.

Volume 2 (*Adult Psychopathology*) contains 30 chapters divided into three parts (General Issues, Major Disorders and Problems, Treatment Approaches). Volume 3 (*Child Psychopathology*) contains 27 chapters divided into three parts (General Issues, Major Disorders and Problems, Treatment Approaches). As previously noted, a unique feature in these volumes is mention of the impact of psychopathology on the family, work, school, and peers, often neglected in standard works. In both Volumes 2 and 3, most of the contributors have adhered to a relatively standard format for Part Two. In some instances, some of the authors have opted to combine sections.

A. Description of the Disorder
B. Epidemiology
C. Clinical Picture
D. Etiology
E. Course, Complications, and Prognosis
F. Assessment and Diagnosis
G. Impact on the Environment
   1. Family
   2. Work or School
   3. Peer Interactions
H. Treatment Implications

In addition, authors in Volume 2 include the sections Personality Development and Psychopathology and Implications for Future Personality Development. We trust that the relatively uniform format in Part Two of Volumes 2 and 3 will make for ease of reading and some interchapter comparisons within and across volumes.

Many individuals have worked very hard to bring this series of volumes to fruition. First, we thank our editor at John

Wiley, Tracey Belmont, for once again understanding the import and scope of the project and having confidence in our ability to execute in spite of interfering hurricanes, other natural events, and varied life events. Second, we thank our editors of the specific volumes for planning, recruiting, and editing. Third, we thank our eminent contributors for taking time out from their busy schedules to add yet one more writing task in sharing their expertise. Claire Huismann, our project manager at Apex Publishing, deserves special recognition for her extraordinary efforts, competence, and patience throughout the creation of this series. And finally, but hardly least of all, we thank all at John Wiley and Pacific University, including Carole Londeree, Linda James, Alison Brodhagen, Greg May, and Cynthia Polance, for their excellent technical assistance.

Michel Hersen and Jay C. Thomas
Forest Grove and Portland, Oregon

Preface to Volume 1

People who find the study of psychology fascinating are usually intrigued by personality. This interest stems from recognition that, at its core, personality must describe at least some causes of behavior. Theoretical positions may quibble about whether personality is a direct, indirect, or mediating cause, but, bottom line, it is somehow causally involved with the way people behave. This view contrasts with that of some attribution theorists, who maintain the validity of the Fundamental Error of Attribution (Ross, 1977) and argue that personal dispositions are not necessarily the cause of behavior. This seems to be frequently misinterpreted as meaning that individual characteristics do not cause behavior (Funder & Colvin, 1997), an approach that we may label the *Fundamental Error of Attribution Theorists*. No one today would assert that personality causes all behavior. The interesting issues are when does personality impact behavior, to what extent does it influence behavior, and under what conditions? Personality theories must attempt to answer these questions if they are to be viable explanations of the human situation.

Both of the editors of this volume are not only psychologists, they are applied psychologists. Jay Thomas's training and practice are in industrial and organizational psychology, and Dan Segal's training and practice are in clinical psychology. Our applied focus led to other important questions about personality. We both have had the experience of studying the great and not-so-great systems of personality and wondering what those systems had to do with people in everyday life. How does personality influence family life, work life, recreation, retirement, and so forth? Further, personality and psychopathology would seem to be intimately related, but how? The Freudian system, for example, attempts to answer the latter, but often fails in the former (Dr. Freud, when is a cigar just a cigar?). This led us to ask what we should expect from a theory of personality, and we asked Theodore Millon and Seth D. Grossman in Part One, named "Foundations," to define what the goals of a theory of personality should be. Their answer not only encompasses the questions with which we began, but it also insists that personality psychology be consistent with the other sciences, most notably the evolutionary and biological sciences.

About a quarter century ago the debate over environmental versus personal determinates of behavior finally led to an interactionist perspective (Ekehammar, 1974; Magnussen & Endler, 1977). The interactionist perspective held that behavior was a product of both the person and the situation. Of course a theory that merely predicts behavior based on a current and local combination of person and environment may have some practical value, but it would not be viewed as a solution to the primary problem of how does personality cause behavior. Over time, situations mold personality and personality molds, or chooses, situations. Personality develops within an environmental context; general courses of development along with the local context must be attended to in order to understand both personality and psychopathology. Thus, the developmental systems perspective forms a foundation for understanding personality and psychopathology. This foundation is addressed by Richard M. Lerner, Jacqueline V. Lerner, Jason Almerigi, and Christina Theokas in Chapter 2.

If the environment influences personality development, then, of course, a critical component of that environment is the culture or cultures in which the person is born, develops, and lives. Cultures vary to an extraordinary degree in just about every facet of life. Culture is now seen as a pervasive influence on the development and expression of personality, and no broad system of personality is complete without incorporating it. One of the most interesting and least appreciated is the manner in which different cultures consider and use the construct of time. We asked Richard W. Brislin and Kevin D. Lo to present how culture, personality, and time work together in influencing behavior as the third and final chapter of "Foundations."

Personality is usually studied through broad systems that attempt to explain functioning in all or, at least, most areas of life and, in particular, abnormal behavior. The psychodynamic, behavioral, existential, and other such systems have become so infused into psychology that these same terms and accompanying concepts are used to describe competing approaches to psychotherapy. No handbook would be complete without thorough and incisive presentation of these major systems. In Part Two, named "Broad-Range Theories and Systems," we challenged our authors not only to think critically about the foremost theories of personality and psychopathology but also to flesh out how each approach contributes to our understanding of functioning in everyday life.

Authors of these chapters were given a structured format to follow (data and common sense permitting, of course), including a statement of the theory, developmental considerations, boundaries of the theory, evidence for and against the theory, and predictions for everyday functioning. These chapters include: "Psychodynamic Theories" (David L. Wolitzky), "Trait and Factor Theories" (Paul T. Costa Jr. and Robert R. McCrae), "Developmental Stage Theories" (Bert Hayslip Jr., Craig S. Neumann, Linda Louden, and Benjamin Chapman), "Behavioral Theories" (Madelon Y. Bolling, Christeine M. Terry, and Robert J. Kohlenberg), "Evolutionary Theories" (David A. Beaulieu and Daphne Blunt Bugental), "Cognitive Theories" (David J. A. Dozois, Paul A. Frewen, and Roger Covin), "Existential and Humanistic Theories" (Paul T. P. Wong), and "Constructivist Theories" (Jonathan D. Raskin). Although these experts on the broadband theories had a similar structure to follow, they excelled at providing thoughtful overviews and critiques of the models so that readers can understand the unique strengths and limitations of each major paradigm. Perhaps the greatest diversity among these chapters is the approaches to understanding everyday functioning, with topics as varied and far-ranging as the nature of romantic love, the choosing of one's spouse, success or failure regarding interpersonal relationships, the primal reciprocity of parent-child relationships, the emotional and academic transitions that children make in the school environment, child maltreatment, bullying at school and work, coping with retirement, choosing and valuing leisure interests and recreation, and the role of meaning-making and personal constructions in the major domains of life. These chapters provide numerous provocative and stimulating ideas for clinical intervention and research focus.

Psychologists are sometimes described as having "physics envy" because of our admiration of the success of physicists in quantifying, mathematizing, and empirically validating so many of the phenomena they study. However, even physics, with some of the greatest minds in history at its disposal, has not succeeded with a "theory of everything." So it is in psychology. The classic, broad systems of personality and psychopathology have not gained universal acceptance and sometimes seem inapplicable to many of the problems psychologists face as theoreticians, scientists, and practitioners. This was clear more than a half century ago when Robert Merton (1949) called for middle-range theories that attempted to explain behavior on a more limited scope than the prevailing broad theories of psychologists and sociologists. Even smaller in scope are limited-domain theories (cf. Miner, 1993) that attempt to explain and predict specific forms of behavior under bounded conditions. Our opinion is that the limited-domain theories are usually not as limited in scope

as their authors proclaim, so Part Three is simply denoted Mid-Range Theories. The personality as depicted in these theories is not descriptive of the individual all the time, but rather it explains the situations certain people get themselves into and what they do once there. The prototype mid-range theory is John B. Miner's role motivation theory (Chapter 12), which loosely can be said to maintain that people have a repertoire of roles that they feel comfortable playing, and they tend to seek situations that allow them to play those roles. Think of John Wayne, who effectively played a limited range of characters across his many movies. One shudders to imagine him playing the pensive and indecisive Hamlet or the suave James Bond. John Wayne himself would probably have shuddered at the prospect.

For nearly a century, psychologists and career counselors have encouraged their clients to pursue careers in occupations that match their interests. The successful development of vocational-interest measures was an impetus to the wide use of testing in counseling and employee selection (Hansen & Dik, 2004). In spite of the success of interest measures, for many years there was little agreement about just what interests are and what their place in a taxonomy of human attributes should be. Crites (1969) treated interests separately from personality, although he termed them *dispositional response tendencies*. By 1991, René Dawes generally agreed with Crites but concluded that interests are manifestations or expressions of personality distinct from what is measured by standard personality inventories. Today, interests are firmly fixed as components of personality; one leader in the field even considers clusters of interests as representing personality types (Holland, 1997). Vocational interests are a critical aspect of personality as it influences everyday life, but as K. S. Douglas Low and James Rounds show in Chapter 13 controversy still abounds regarding the universality of the structure of interests.

If interests are part of personality, and because Silvia (2001) showed that interests are also emotions, then what is the relationship between personality and emotion? One current focus of research and theory is positive (PA) and negative (NA) affect and whether these are on opposite poles of a single continuum or represent different constructs altogether. Paul J. Silvia and John B. Warburton take on the PA/NA divide and address whether these are state or trait characteristics in Chapter 14.

The Declaration of Independence declares a right to "Life, Liberty, and the pursuit of Happiness" for all. Presumably the pursuit of happiness includes attaining a sense of well-being, clearly an important facet of everyday life. Removing external barriers to happiness and well-being may be a political process, but internal barriers abound as well. How one thinks about life events, obstacles, and even good fortune seems to have an important impact on feelings of well-being. Following the issue of the relation of emotions to personality we now have to consider how cognition and personality are related. In Chapter 15 Deborah Wise and Johan Rosqvist explain how explanatory style influences well-being and how this may be considered an aspect of personality. Attitudes are largely cognitive constructs and they impact personality as well. Life is stressful. In the extreme case, about 50 percent of adults have been exposed to some form of trauma, but only about 10 percent of women and 5 percent of men (overall about 7 percent) develop post-traumatic stress disorder (PTSD) (Ozer & Weiss, 2004). It is a matter of considerable importance to determine why so many people seem resilient in the face of life's vicissitudes whereas a large minority are not resilient. According to Salvatore R. Maddi, hardiness, or the courage to face a stressful life, is a critical piece of the puzzle, as he discusses in Chapter 16. Finally, for some people the pursuit of happiness involves the pursuit of sensations, of risks. These people may at times appear fearless to the rest of us. In Chapter 17 Genevieve L. Y. Arnaut builds on the earlier work of Marvin Zuckerman (1994) to define sensation seeking as a personality trait and reviews the research of the past decade in establishing sensation seeking as an important and useful mid-range theory of personality.

One unifying characteristic of the mid-range theories is they are both theoretical and immediately practical. Because they are precise about predictions, conditions, and boundaries, their survival is far more subject to the results of empirical tests. Consequently, the chapters in Part Three tend to have an empiricist edge. Theories are presented, research results are provided, and the theories are revised in light of the findings to a greater extent than is the case for the broad-range systems.

Part Four, labeled "Special Applications," obviously includes aspects of personality and everyday life that we believe are important but that do not fit well into the previous sections of the volume. For most of these, the special application means the situation—the work organization. It is noteworthy that all of the authors of these chapters lead double lives as scholars and practitioners. Their academic side leads them to focus on the neatness of theory: internal consistency, relations to other theories, and research support. Their practitioner side demands practicality and a focus on what the theory means in the real world. This has led to some exciting and, we believe, seminal contributions to the relationship between personality and everyday life. Leadership theorists have recently been struck by the notion of the transformational leader, a person whose achievements stem primarily from the ability to establish a common vision and move followers to make that vision a reality. In popular parlance we often say the transformational leader does this through the strength of his or her personality. Is personality really part of transformational leadership? Is transformational leadership part of personality? These issues are addressed by Ram Aditya in Chapter 18 along with an extensive review of the research connecting personality to transformational leadership.

Person-environment fit (P-E fit) is a consistent theme throughout much of psychology. Probably everyone believes that P-E fit is important, but few have considered how to conceptualize how such a fit really comes about and what it means. We challenged John F. Binning, James M. LeBreton, and Anthony J. Adorno to reconceptualize what P-E fit is and how it relates to performance (loosely defined to include any aspect of performance). The result in Chapter 19 is a new theoretical statement that will generate interest and research for the next several years. In Chapter 20 a different permutation of the same authors also wrote on the phenomenon of subclinical psychopaths. Subclinical psychopaths are people who have many of the characteristics of antisocial personality disorder but are not severe enough to warrant a diagnosis. Such individuals are a matter of much concern in organizations, where they can generate considerable disruption and, occasionally, do some good. The very concept of *subclinical* raises interesting issues for the study of personality and psychopathology because it implies a gradation along a continuum rather than a threshold effect in which a person on one side of a line technically is not disordered whereas a person on the other side is disordered. Continuing the P-E fit theme is Daniel J. Svyantek and Jennifer P. Bott's Chapter 21 relating organizational climate, personality, and organizational behavior. This has been an area that has not received the research attention it deserves, partly because such studies are difficult to conceive and implement. As a consequence, much of their chapter is a review of the relevant literature followed by an example of how these issues can be researched.

The final chapters in Part Four change the pace a little to set the stage for the next two volumes of the handbook. In Chapter 22 Paula G. Williams and Heather E. Gunn examine gender differences in personality, particularly in the Big Five personality traits, and gender differences in psychopathology. They also incisively describe and scrutinize possible models that link gender, personality, and psychological adjustment. Finally, in Chapter 23 John D. Mayer closes the volume by explaining how the diagnoses in the most commonly used diagnostic system, the *Diagnostic and Statistical Manual of Mental Disorders,* 4th edition, text revision (*DSM-IV-TR;* American Psychiatric Association, 2000), can be organized based on modern personality theory. Considering the *DSM-IV-TR* was developed from a (purported) atheoretical stance,

Mayer's exposition is an impressive and noteworthy accomplishment. It allows for an informed and systematic transition from *Personality and Everyday Functioning* to personality and psychopathology, the theme of Volumes 2 and 3.

This volume is the product of many people's hands and minds. The chapter authors invested ingenuity and labor to create the body of the book, and we are grateful to them for their contributions. Linda James, Carole Londeree, and Alison Brodhagen were extraordinarily helpful in preparing the manuscript. Tracey Belmont and the staff of John Wiley & Sons were critical in completing this project. Finally, our friend and colleague (and Jay Thomas's coeditor in chief of the series) Michel Hersen has been a tremendous influence on this project from start to finish. Only those who have worked with Michel can appreciate the nature of his contributions.

Jay C. Thomas
Portland, Oregon

Daniel L. Segal
Colorado Springs, Colorado

REFERENCES

American Psychiatric Association. (2000). *Diagnostic and statistical manual of mental disorders* (4th ed., text rev.). Washington, DC: Author.

Crites, J. O. (1969). *Vocational psychology: The study of vocational behavior and development.* New York: McGraw-Hill.

Dawes, R. (1991). Vocational interests, values, and preferences. In M. Dunnette & L. Hough (Eds.), *Handbook of industrial and organizational psychology* (Vol. 2, 2nd ed., pp. 833–872). Palo Alto, CA: Consulting Psychologists Press.

Ekehammar, B. (1974). Interactionism in psychology from a historical perspective. *Psychological Bulletin, 81,* 1026–1048.

Funder, D. C., & Colvin, C. R. (1997). Congruence of other's and self-judgments of personality. In R. Hogan, J. Johnson, & S. Briggs (Eds.), *Handbook of personality psychology* (pp. 617–647). New York: Academic Press.

Hansen, J., & Dik, B. J. (2004). Measures of career interests. In J. C. Thomas (Ed.), *Comprehensive handbook of psychological assessment: Vol. 4. Industrial and organizational assessment* (pp. 166–191). New York: Wiley.

Holland, J. L. (1997). *Making vocational choices: A theory of vocational personalities and work environments* (3rd ed.). Odessa, FL: Psychological Assessment Resources, Inc.

Magnussen, D., & Endler, N. S. (1977). *Personality at the crossroads.* New York: Wiley.

Merton, R. (1949). *Social theory and social structure.* New York: Free Press.

Miner, J. (1993). *Role motivation theories.* London: Routledge.

Ozer, E. J., & Weiss, D. S. (2004). Who develops posttraumatic stress disorder? *Current Directions in Psychological Science, 13,* 169–172.

Ross, L. (1977). The intuitive psychologist and his shortcomings. In L. Berkowitz (Ed.), *Advances in experimental social psychology* (Vol. 10, pp. 174–214). New York: Academic Press.

Silvia, P. J. (2001). Interest and interests: The psychology of constructive capriciousness. *Review of General Psychology, 5,* 270–290.

Zuckerman, M. (1999). *Behavioral expressions and biosocial bases of sensation seeking.* New York: Cambridge University Press.

Contributors

Ram Aditya, PhD
Florida International University
Miami, Florida

Anthony J. Adorno, MS
DeGarmo Group
Bloomington, Illinois

Jason Almerigi, PhD
Tufts University
Medford, Massachusetts

Genevieve L. Y. Arnaut, PsyD, PhD
Pacific University
Portland, Oregon

David A. Beaulieu, BA
University of California at Santa Barbara
Santa Barbara, California

John F. Binning, PhD
Illinois State University
Normal, Illinois

Madelon Y. Bolling, PhD
University of Washington
Seattle, Washington

Jennifer P. Bott, PhD
Ball State University
Muncie, Indiana

Richard W. Brislin, PhD
University of Hawaii at Manoa
Honolulu, Hawaii

Daphne Blunt Bugental, PhD
University of California at Santa Barbara
Santa Barbara, California

Benjamin Chapman, MS
University of North Texas
Denton, Texas

Paul T. Costa Jr., PhD
National Institute on Aging
Baltimore, Maryland

Roger Covin, MA
University of Western Ontario
London, Ontario

David J. A. Dozois, PhD
University of Western Ontario
London, Ontario

Paul A. Frewen, MA
University of Western Ontario
London, Ontario

Seth D. Grossman, PsyD
Institute for Advanced Studies in Personology and
    Psychopathology
Coral Gables, Florida

Heather E. Gunn, BS
University of Utah
Salt Lake City, Utah

Bert Hayslip Jr., PhD
University of North Texas
Denton, Texas

Robert J. Kohlenberg, PhD
University of Washington
Seattle, Washington

James M. LeBreton, PhD
Wayne State University
Detroit, Michigan

Jacqueline V. Lerner, PhD
Boston College
Medford, Massachusetts

Richard M. Lerner, PhD
Tufts University
Medford, Massachusetts

Kevin D. Lo, MBA, MAPS
University of Hawaii at Manoa
Honolulu, Hawaii

Linda Louden, MS
University of North Texas
Denton, Texas

K. S. Douglas Low, MA
University of Illinois at Urbana-Champaign
Champaign, Illinois

Salvatore R. Maddi, PhD
University of California, Irvine
Irvine, California

John D. Mayer, PhD
University of New Hampshire
Durham, New Hampshire

Robert R. McCrae, PhD
National Institute on Aging
Baltimore, Maryland

Theodore Millon, PhD
Institute for Advanced Studies in Personology and
    Psychopathology
Coral Gables, Florida

John B. Miner, PhD
Retired
Eugene, Oregon

Craig S. Neumann, PhD
University of North Texas
Denton, Texas

Jonathan D. Raskin, PhD
State University of New York at New Paltz
New Paltz, New York

Johan Rosqvist, PsyD
Pacific University
Portland, Oregon

James Rounds, PhD
University of Illinois at Urbana-Champaign
Urbana, Illinois

Paul J. Silvia, PhD
University of North Carolina at Greensboro
Greensboro, North Carolina

Daniel J. Svyantek, PhD
Auburn University
Auburn, Alabama

Christeine M. Terry, BA
University of Washington
Seattle, Washington

Christina Theokas, PhD
Tufts University
Medford, Massachusetts

John B. Warburton, MA
University of North Carolina at Greensboro
Greensboro, North Carolina

Paula G. Williams, PhD
University of Utah
Salt Lake City, Utah

Deborah Wise, PhD
Pacific University
Portland, Oregon

David L. Wolitzky, PhD
New York University
New York, New York

Paul T. P. Wong, PhD, CPsych
Trinity Western University
Langley, British Columbia

PART ONE
FOUNDATIONS

CHAPTER 1

Goals of a Theory of Personality

THEODORE MILLON AND SETH D. GROSSMAN

THEORETICAL FUNCTIONS

Kurt Lewin wrote some 70 years ago (1936) that "there is nothing so practical as a good theory." Theory, when properly fashioned, ultimately provides more simplicity and clarity than unintegrated and scattered information. Unrelated knowledge and techniques, especially those based on surface similarities, are a sign of a primitive science, as has been effectively argued by modern philosophers of science. All natural sciences have organizing principles that not only create order but also provide the basis for generating hypotheses and stimulating new knowledge. A good theory not only summarizes and incorporates extant knowledge but is heuristic, that is, has "systematic import," as Hempel has phrased it (1961), in that it originates and develops new observations and new methods. It is unfortunate that the number of theories that have been advanced to explain clinical phenomena is directly proportional to the internecine squabbling found in the literature. Paroxysms of "scientific virtue" and pieties of "methodological purity" rarely are exclaimed by theorists themselves but rather by their less creative disciples.

Of course, formal theory should not be pushed far beyond the data, and its derivations should be linked wherever feasible to established observations. However, even a reasonable speculative framework can be a compelling instrument for helping coordinate and give consonance to complex and diverse observations—if its concepts are linked where possible to relevant facts in the empirical world. By probing beneath surface impressions to inner structures and processes, previously isolated facts and difficult-to-fathom data may yield new relationships and expose clearer meanings. Progress does not advance by brute empiricism alone, that is, by merely piling up more descriptive and more experimental data. What is elaborated and refined in theory is understanding, an ability to see relations more plainly, to conceptualize categories more accurately, and to create greater overall coherence in a subject, that is, to integrate its elements in a more logical, consistent, and intelligible fashion.

Unfortunately, the formal structure of most clinical theories of the past has been haphazard and unsystematic; concepts often were vague, and procedures by which empirical consequences could be derived were tenuous, at best. Instead of presenting an orderly arrangement of concepts and propositions by which hypotheses could be clearly derived, most theorists presented a loosely formulated pastiche of opinions, analogies, and speculations. Brilliant as many of these speculations may have been, they often have left the reader dazzled rather than illuminated. Though many theories in personality generated brilliant deductions and insights, few of these ideas could be attributed to their structure, the clarity of their central principles, the precision of their concepts, or their formal procedures for hypothesis derivation. It is here where the concepts and laws of adjacent sciences may come into play, providing models of structure and derivation that may undergird and parallel the principles and observations of personology.

A unifying theory for personology must coalesce the disparate schools of personality study, not in a haphazard way that merely identifies or records their separate contributions, but in a manner that integrates alternative perspectives at a deeper level, that is, one that synthesizes the several viewpoints intrinsically. Whereas eclectic approaches have as their benefit the advantages of open-mindedness and comprehensiveness, they are likely to generate little more than a measure of illusory psychic comfort. A substantively unifying paradigm will interweave fundamental relationships that exist among the cognitive, biological, intrapsychic, and behavioral elements that inhere in the person. This will, for example, generate synergistic therapeutic strategies such as those that have been demonstrated by employing combinatorial treatment approaches (e.g., cognitive-behavioral therapy [CBT], pharmacologic/family interventions). However, even more synergy is possible and desirable.

Theories that focus their attention on only one level of data (e.g., intrapsychic, cognitive) cannot help but generate formulations that are limited by their narrow preconceptions; their formulations must, inevitably, be constrained by the simple fact that psychological processes are multidetermined and multidimensional in expression. Contrariwise, those who endorse a single-level approach assert that theories that seek to encompass the totality of personality structure and functions will sink in a sea of data that can be neither charted conceptually nor navigated methodologically. Clearly, those who undertake to propose integrative or holistic theories are faced with the formidable task not only of exposing the inadequacies of single-level theories but of providing a convincing alternative that is both comprehensive and systematic. The reader must judge whether such theorists possess the analytic skills necessary not only to penetrate the complex labyrinths of one's mind and behavior but to chart their intricate pathways in a manner that is both conceptually clear and methodologically testable.

In this chapter, we will go beyond current conceptual boundaries in personology and incorporate the contributions of more firmly grounded adjacent sciences. We believe that much of psychology remains adrift, divorced from broader spheres of scientific knowledge, isolated from deeper and more fundamental, if not universal, principles. Psychology has built a patchwork quilt of dissonant concepts and diverse data domains. Preoccupied with but a small part of the larger pie, or fearing accusations of reductionism, we have failed to draw on the rich possibilities that may be found in both historic and adjacent realms of scholarly pursuit. With notable exceptions, there are few cohering concepts that would connect current personologic topics to those of our sister sciences of nature. We seem trapped in (obsessed with?) contemporary fads and horizontal refinements. Integrative schemata and cohesive constructs that link relevant personologic observations to other fields of science are needed. This goal—albeit a rather grandiose one—would be to refashion our patchwork quilt into a well-tailored and cohesive tapestry that interweaves the diverse forms in which nature expresses itself.

No better sphere within the psychological sciences undertakes such a synthesis than the subject matter of personology, the study of persons. Persons are the only organically integrated system in the psychological domain, evolved through the millennia and inherently created from birth as natural entities rather than culture-bound and experience-derived gestalts. The intrinsic cohesion of persons is not merely a rhetorical construction but an authentic substantive unity. Personologic features may be differentiated into normal or pathological and may be partitioned conceptually for pragmatic or scientific purposes, but they are segments of an inseparable biopsychosocial entity. Arguing in favor of establishing explicit links between the several domains of personologic science calls neither for a reductionistic philosophy, a belief in substantive identicality, or efforts to so fashion such links by formal logic. Rather, one should

aspire to their substantive concordance, empirical consistency, conceptual interfacing, convergent dialogues, and mutual enlightenment.

The remainder of this chapter will attempt to address several key questions concerning the nature of personology, its foundations, and future directions.

HOW CAN WE CREATE A SCIENTIFIC STRUCTURE FOR THE SUBSTANTIVE SUBJECT OF PERSONOLOGY?

Integrative consonance such as previously described is not an aspiration limited to the physical sciences but is a worthy goal within personologic science as well. If personology is ever to become a full-fledged science, rather than a potpourri of miscellaneous observations and ideas, the overall and ultimate architecture of the field must be comprehensively structured, that is, given a scaffold or framework within which its diverse elements and principles can be located and coordinated. For example, personality traits or types should not stand alone, unconnected to other realms of scientific discourse. They should be anchored to an empirically supportable theory, on the one hand, and prove instrumental for clinical assessment and pragmatic for therapeutic action, on the other. The overall arrangement of personology should seek to coordinate all of the separate realms that make up its scientific and applied efforts, namely a foundation in the universal laws of nature, a coordinated psychological theory, a derivable taxonomic classification, a series of operational assessment tools, and a flexible yet integrated group of remediation techniques. As recorded in Millon (2000), rather than developing independently and being left to stand as autonomous and largely unconnected functions, a truly mature personologic science, one that is designed to create a synergistic bond between its components, will be structured explicitly to embody the following five elements:

Universal scientific principles, that is, it should be grounded in the ubiquitous laws of nature. Despite varied forms of expression (in physics, chemistry, psychology, for example), these principles should reflect fundamental evolutionary processes and thereby provide an undergirding framework for guiding and constructing subject-oriented theories.

A subject-oriented theory, that is, explanatory and heuristic conceptual schemata of nature's expression in what we call personology and psychopathology. This theory should be consistent with established knowledge in both its own and related sciences (e.g., biology, sociology), and reasonably accurate propositions concerning normal functioning and clinical conditions should be both deduced and understood from it, enabling thereby the development of a formal classification system.

- A *taxonomy of personality patterns and clinical syndromes,* that is, a classification and nosology derived logically from the personology/psychopathology theory. These should provide a cohesive organization within which its major categories can be readily grouped and differentiated, permitting thereby the development of relevant and coordinated assessment instruments.
- *Integrated clinical and personality assessment tools,* that is, instruments that are empirically grounded and quantitatively sensitive. These should enable the theory's propositions and hypotheses to be operationally investigated and evaluated and the categories making up its taxonomy to be readily identified (diagnosed) and measured (dimensionalized), specifying therefrom target areas for interventions.
- *Personalized therapeutic interventions,* that is, coordinated strategies and modalities of treatment. These should be designed in accord with the theory, incorporate and synthesize diverse therapeutic techniques (interpersonal, cognitive, intrapsychic, biochemical), and be oriented to modify both problematic clinical and personologic characteristics, consonant with professional standards and social responsibilities.

The coordination of all five elements (i.e., making them reciprocally enhancing and mutually reinforcing) constitutes the structure of a personologic science. Working together, these components will produce integrated knowledge that is greater than the sum of its individual constituent parts. It is the synthesis of these structural elements that have been disconnected and pursued independently in the twentieth century that is sought. Just as each person is an intrinsic unity, each component of a personologic science should not remain a separate element of a potpourri of unconnected parts. Rather, each facet of our work should be integrated into a gestalt, a coupled and coordinated unity in which the whole becomes more informative and useful than its individual parts.

WHY SHOULD EVOLUTIONARY THEORY SERVE AS THE SUBSTANTIVE BASIS OF UNIVERSAL PRINCIPLES FOR PERSONOLOGY?

In our view, all basic or applied sciences (physics, engineering, personology) are outgrowths of a common conceptual grounding in evolution theory. All disciplines of science, once achieving sufficient maturity, are natural expressions of the operation of evolutionary principles. With reference to the preceding discussion of the structure of a science, each of these disciplines is composed of subject-area theories (e.g., elementary particle physics, personology), formal classification taxonomies (e.g., composition of synaptic neurochemical substances, the International Classification of Diseases [ICD]), operational measuring instruments (e.g., cyclotron apparatus, the Minnesota Multiphasic Personality Inventory (MMPI)), and, when applied, efficacious methods of effecting change (e.g., locomotive engine, cognitive therapy). As noted in prior paragraphs, we believe that only when all of the structural components of a science are articulated and coordinated can a science and its research techniques achieve full empirical validity and instrumental efficacy.

We are reaching a time, we believe, when our knowledge of personology can be structured in a manner akin to our more advanced sciences. By employing universal principles of evolutionary theory as a guide to understanding the components of personality study, we can begin to formulate theoretical conceptual hypotheses that will explain our subject domain. Such principles also will enable us to construct a taxonomic system derived from the theory and assessment tools that can identify the categories and dimensions composing the taxonomy and then point to the clinical characteristics that will serve as therapeutic targets. In effect, a substantive clinical paradigm based on evolutionary principles that is structured in this manner will furnish a guide to where, how, and which research investigations and treatment interventions are wisest to employ. Failing to build a substantive and structured paradigm will keep us on the same scattered and helter-skelter course that has plagued the field of personality study since time immemorial. Assuredly, brilliant theoretical ideas have been proposed in the past, as have classification systems and instruments been generated as well as imaginative therapies developed, but our field remains stuck in a babel of conflicting and confusing perspectives in which little has changed in the past half-century and little has been synthesized or structured logically. Integrating the several structural components that make up a personologic science, aligned with a generative substantive paradigm such as evolutionary theory, will provide us with an overarching framework worthy of our collaborative efforts.

The role of evolution may be most clearly grasped when it is paired with the principles of ecology. So conceived, the procession of evolution in physics, chemistry, and biology represents a series of serendipitous transformations in the structure of a phenomenon (for example, elementary particle, chemical molecule, living organism) that appear to promote survival in both its current and its future environments

(Millon, 1990). Such processions usually stem from the consequences of either random fluctuations (such as mutations) or replicative reformations (for example, recombinant mating) among an infinite number of possibilities—some simpler and others more complex, some more and others less organized, some increasingly specialized and others not. Evolution is defined, then, when these restructurings enable a natural entity (for example, a biological species) or its subsequent variants to survive within present and succeeding ecologic milieus. It is the continuity through time of these fluctuations and reformations that makes up the sequence we characterize as evolutionary progression.

In recent times, we have seen the emergence of *sociobiology,* a new science that explores the interface between human social functioning and evolutionary biology (Cosmides & Tooby, 1987; Daly & Wilson, 1978; Rushton, 1985; Symons, 1992; Wilson 1975, 1978, 1998). Contemporary formulations by psychologists have likewise proposed the potentials and analyzed the problems involved in cohering evolutionary notions, individual differences, and personality traits (e.g., Buss, 1984, 1994). The concept of personology, first formulated by Murray (1938), has been extended in the senior author's writings (Millon, 1990) to parallel the concept of sociobiology. It represents a field of science and study that defines and encompasses the broad subject of personality. It is intended to serve as a conceptual model and formal theory that utilizes evolutionary principles, generates a formal taxonomy, and formulates a basis for clinical assessments and personalized therapies (Millon with Davis, 1996; Millon, 1997, Millon with Grossman, Meagher, Millon, & Everly, 1999).

The common goal among personologic scientists is not only the desire to apply common principles across diverse scientific realms but also to reduce the enormous range of personality concepts that have proliferated through history; this might be achieved by exploring the power of evolutionary theory to simplify and order previously disparate features. For example, all organisms seek to avoid injury, find nourishment, and reproduce their kind if they are to survive and maintain their populations. Each species displays commonalities in its adaptive or survival style. Within each species, however, there are differences in style and differences in the success with which its various members adapt to the diverse and changing environments they face. In these simplest of terms, *personality* would be employed as a term to represent the more or less distinctive style of adaptive functioning that a particular organism of a species exhibits as its relates to its typical range of environments. *Normal personalities,* so conceived, would signify the utilization of species-specific modes of adaptation that are effective in average or expectable environments. Disorders of personality, or what we would pre-

fer to term *pathological personality patterns,* would represent different ways of maladaptive functioning that can be traced to psychic deficiencies, trait imbalances, or internal conflicts that characterize some members of a species as they relate to the environment they routinely face.

During its life history an organism develops an assemblage of traits that contribute to its individual survival and reproductive success, the two essential components of fitness formulated by Darwin. Such assemblages, termed *complex adaptations* and *strategies* in the literature of evolutionary ecology, are close biological equivalents to what we in psychology have conceptualized as *personality styles.* In biology, explanations of a life-history strategy of adaptations refer primarily to biogenic variations among constituent traits, their overall covariance structure, and the nature and ratio of favorable to unfavorable ecologic resources that have been available for purposes of extending longevity and optimizing reproduction. Such explanations are not appreciably different from those used to account for the development of normal and pathological personality styles.

Bypassing the usual complications of analogies, a relevant and intriguing parallel may be drawn between the *phylogenic evolution* of a species genetic composition and the *ontogenic development* of an individual organism's adaptive strategies (that is, its "personality style"). At any point in time, a species will possess a limited set of genes that serve as trait potentials. Over succeeding generations the frequency distribution of these genes likely will change in their relative proportions depending on how well the traits they undergird contribute to the species "fittedness" within its varying ecological habitats. In a similar fashion, individual organisms begin life with a limited subset of their species' genes and the trait potentials they subserve. Over time the salience of these trait potentials—not the proportion of the genes themselves—will become differentially prominent as the organism interacts with its environments, learning from these experiences which of its traits fit best, that is, are optimally suited to its ecosystem. In phylogenesis, then, actual gene frequencies change during the generation-to-generation adaptive process, whereas in ontogenesis it is the salience or prominence of gene-based traits that changes as adaptive learning takes place. Parallel evolutionary processes occur, one within the many generations of life of a species, the other within the limited life of a single organism. What is seen in the individual organism is a shaping of latent potentials in adaptive and manifest styles of perceiving, feeling, thinking, and acting; these learned and distinctive ways of adaptation, engendered by the interaction of biologic endowment and social experience, constitute, in our view, the elements of what are termed personality styles, normal or abnormal. Thus the formative process of a single lifetime parallels gene redistributions among species during their evolutionary history.

It may be a bit presumptuous, but what the senior author has proposed in his recent books and papers may be seen as akin to Sigmund Freud's abandoned *Project for a Scientific Psychology* (1895/1924), to Henry Murray's seminal thesis in his proposal for a field he christened personology (1938), and to Edward Wilson's recent and controversial *Sociobiology* (1975). Each were worthy endeavors to advance our understanding of human nature; this they did by exploring interconnections between scientific disciplines that evolved ostensibly unrelated bodies of research and manifestly dissimilar languages.

Pre-Darwinian theorists such as Linnaeus limited themselves to apparent similarities and differences between animals as a means of constructing their taxonomic categories. Darwin was not seduced by overt appearances. Rather, he sought to understand the principles by which these surface features came about. His classifications were based not only on descriptive qualities but on theoretically explanatory ones. Both the spirit and substance of Darwin's explanatory principles guide the proposals of the theoretical ideas that follow. The principles employed are similar to those that Darwin developed in explicating the origins of species. However, these efforts seek not to derive the origins of species, but the structure and style of each of the normal styles and clinical personality syndromes described in the ICD and *Diagnostic and Statistical Manual of Mental Disorders* (*DSM-IV;* American Psychiatric Association, 1994), each of which were based on psychiatric observation and inference alone. Aspects of the brief formulations recorded here have been elaborated in numerous published books by the senior author (Millon, 1969, 1981, 1990; Millon with Davis, 1996; Millon et al., 1999).

A rough model concerning the styles of clinical and personality patterns may be derived with reference to four spheres in which evolutionary and ecological principles are operative. They have been labeled *existence, adaptation, replication,* and *abstraction.*

Existence relates to the serendipitous transformation of states that are more ephemeral, less organized, or both into those possessing greater stability, greater organization, or both. It pertains to the formation and sustenance of discernible phenomena, to the processes of evolution that enhance and preserve life, and to the psychic polarity that I have termed *pleasure* and *pain. Adaptation* refers to homeostatic processes employed to foster survival in open ecosystems. It relates to the manner in which extant phenomena adapt to their surrounding ecosystems, to the mechanisms employed in accommodating to or in modifying these environments,

and to the psychic polarity termed *passivity* and *activity. Replication* pertains to reproductive styles that maximize the diversification and selection of ecologically effective attributes. It refers to the strategies utilized to replicate ephemeral organisms, to the methods of maximizing reproductive propagation and progeny nurturance, and to the psychic polarity labeled as *self* and *other. Abstraction* incorporates the sources employed to gather knowledge about the experiences of life and the manner in which this information is registered and transformed. Here, we are looking at *styles of cognizing*— differences (first) in what people attend to in order to learn about life and (second) how they process information; that is, what they do cognitively to record this knowledge and make it useful to themselves. They constitute the reflective capacity to transcend the immediate and concrete; how they interrelate and synthesize the diversity of experience; how they represent events and processes symbolically; and how they weigh, reason, and anticipate. In essence, these abstraction powers signify a quantum leap in evolution's potential for human change and adaptation.

As noted, the polarities articulated here in evolutionary terms have forerunners in psychological theory that may be traced back to the early 1900s. A number of pre–World War I theorists proposed a set of three parallel polarities that were used time and again as the raw materials for constructing psychological processes. For example, Freud wrote in 1915 (1925) what many consider to be among his most seminal papers, those on metapsychology and, in particular, the section entitled "Instincts and Their Vicissitudes," speculations that foreshadowed several concepts developed more fully later, both by himself and others. Although he failed to pursue their potentials, the ingredients Freud formulated for his tripartite polarity schema were drawn on by his disciples many decades later, seen prominently in the recent growth of ego psychology, self psychology, and object relations theory (see Millon, 1990, and Millon & Grossman, 2005, for a fuller discussion of this recent history).

WHAT ARE THE ORIGINS OF NORMAL STYLES AND PATHOLOGICAL PATTERNS OF PERSONALITY?

The culling of that which we call personality from a universe of influences takes place through the addition of successive constraints on system functioning. Each child displays a wide variety of behaviors in the first years of life. Although exhibiting a measure of consistency consonant with his or her constitutional disposition, the way in which the child responds to and copes with the environment tends to be largely spontaneous, changeable, and unpredictable. These seemingly random and capricious behaviors serve an important exploratory function. The child is trying out a variety of behavioral alternatives for dealing with his or her environment. Over time the child begins to discern which of these actions enable him to achieve his or her desires and avoid discomforts. Endowed with certain capacities, energies, and temperaments, and through experience with parents, siblings, relatives, and peers, the child learns to discriminate which activities are both permissible and rewarding and which are not.

Tracing this sequence over time, it can be seen that a shaping process has taken place in which the child's initial range of diverse behaviors gradually becomes narrowed, selective, and, finally, crystallized into preferred ways of relating to others and coping with this world. These learned behaviors not only persist but are accentuated as a result of being repetitively reinforced by a limited social environment. Given continuity in constitutional equipment and a narrow band of experiences for learning behavioral alternatives, the child acquires a pattern of traits that are deeply etched and difficult to modify. These characteristics make up his or her personality—that is, ingrained and habitual ways of psychological functioning that emerge from the individual's entire developmental history and that, over time, come to characterize the child's style.

The interaction between biological and psychological factors is not unidirectional such that biological determinants always precede and influence the course of learning; the order of effects may be reversed, especially in early development. Biological maturation is dependent on favorable environmental experience, and the development of the biological substrate itself can be disrupted, even totally arrested, by depriving the maturing organism of stimulation at sensitive periods of neurological growth. Nevertheless, there is an intrinsic continuity throughout life. The authors contend that childhood events are more significant to personality formation than later events and that later behaviors are related in a determinant way to early experience. Despite an occasional disjunction in development, there is an orderly and sequential continuity, fostered by mechanisms of self-perpetuation and social reinforcement, that links the past to the present.

Deeply embedded behavior patterns may arise as a consequence of psychological experiences that affect developing biological structures so profoundly as to transform them into something substantially different from what they might otherwise have been. Circumstances that exert so profound an effect are usually those experienced during infancy and early childhood, a view persuasively articulated in the seminal writings of Freud at the turn of the century. The observations of ethologists on the consequences of early stimulation upon adult animal behaviors add substantial evidence for this position (Rakic, 1985, 1988). Experimental work on early developmental periods also has shown that environmental stimulation is crucial to the neurological maturation of psychological functions. In essence, psychological capacities fail to develop fully if their neurological substrates are subjected to impoverished stimulation; conversely, these capacities may develop to an excessive degree as a consequence of enriched stimulation (Lipton & Kater, 1989).

What evidence is there that serious consequences may result from an inadequate supply of early psychological and psychosensory stimulation? Numerous investigators (e.g., Beach & Jaynes, 1954; Killackey, 1990; Melzick, 1965; Rakic, 1985, 1988; Scott, 1968; Thompson & Schaefer, 1961) have shown that impoverished early environment results in permanent adaptational difficulties. For example, primates reared in isolation tend to be deficient in traits such as emotionality, activity level, social behavior, curiosity, and learning ability. As adult organisms they possess a reduced capacity to cope with their environments, to discriminate essentials, to devise strategies, and to manage stress.

Conversely, intense levels of early stimulation also appear to have effects, at least as experimentally demonstrated in lower mammalian species. Several investigators have demonstrated that enriched environments in early life resulted in measurable changes in brain chemistry and brain weight. Others have found that early stimulation accelerated the maturation of the pituitary-adrenal system, whereas equivalent later stimulation was ineffective. On the behavioral level, enriched environments in animals enhance problem-solving abilities and the capacity to withstand stress. More interesting, however, is the possibility that some kinds of overstimulation may produce detrimental effects. Accordingly, excess stimulation would result in overdevelopments in neurobiological substrates that are disruptive to effective psychological functioning. Just as excess food leads to obesity and physical ill health, so, too, may the psychostimulation of certain neural substrates, such as those subserving emotional reactivity, dispose the organism to overreact to social situations. Thus, when neurological dispositions that subserve potentially problematic personality traits become prepotent, they may disrupt what would otherwise be a more balanced pattern of psychological functioning.

Another and related question to be posed is does the timing of environmental events have any bearing on their effect? The concept of sensitive periods of development states that there are limited time periods during which particular stimuli are necessary for the full maturation of an organism, after which they will have minimal or no effects. Without the requisite stimulation, the organism will suffer various maldevelopments that are irremediable and cannot be compensated for at a later date.

The senior author has proposed four neurodevelopmental stages through which individual human organisms progress that are paralleled by a set of four psychosocial tasks that must be fulfilled to achieve adequate growth in later life. The first three pairings of stages and tasks, and in part the fourth as well, are shared by all mammalian species; they recapitulate the four evolution phases referred to earlier: existence, adaptation, replication, and abstraction. Each evolutionary phase has its ontogenetic parallel; that is, each individual organism moves through neurodevelopmental stages that have functional psychological capacities related to their respective phases of evolution. Within each stage, every individual acquires personologic dispositions representing a balance or predilection toward one of the two polarity inclinations; which inclination emerges as dominant over time results from the inextricable and reciprocal interplay of intraorganismic and extraorganismic factors. Thus, during early infancy, the primary organismic function is to continue to exist. Here, each evolution phase has supplied two contrasting polarity components that orient the infant toward life-enhancing environments (pleasure) and away from life-threatening ones (pain).

Personality development should be coordinated with several fundamental polarity orientations derived from evolutionary principles. These will be briefly noted; they are more extensively discussed in Millon, 1990, Millon with Davis, 1996, and Millon, Grossman, Millon, Meagher, & Ramnath, 2004. Although four seemingly distinct stages of neurodevelopment have been differentiated as sequential stages, it is important to state at the outset that all four stages and their related evolutionary functions begin in utero and continue throughout life, that is, they proceed simultaneously and overlap throughout the ontogenetic process. For example, the elements that give shape to gender identity are underway during the sensory-attachment phase, although at a modest level, as do the elements that give rise to attachment behaviors continue and extend well into puberty. Stages are differentiated only to bring attention to periods of development when certain processes and tasks are prominent and central. The concept of sensitive periods implies that developmental stages are not exclusionary; rather, they merely demarcate a period in life when certain developmental potentialities are salient in their maturation and in their receptivity to relevant life experiences. Note again that each evolutionary phase is related to a different stage of ontogenetic development. For example, life enhancement–life preservation corresponds to the sensory-attachment stage of development in that the latter represents a period when the young child learns to discrim-

inate between those experiences that are enhancing (pleasurable) and those that are threatening (painful).

As evident in the foregoing, it would have been an error to leave the discussion of evolutionary-neuropsychological development with the impression that personality growth was merely a function of stimulation at sensitive maturational periods. Impoverishment and enrichment have their profound effects, but the quality or kind of stimulation the youngster experiences is often of greater importance. The impact of parental harshness or inconsistency, of sibling rivalry or social failure, is more than a matter of stimulus volume and timing. Different dimensions of experience take precedence as the meaning conveyed by the source of stimulation becomes clear to the growing child.

Both neurological and learning concepts can be utilized to describe changes in response probabilities arising from prior stimulus exposure. But, because learning concepts are formulated in terms of behavior-environment interactions, it is reasonable, when discussing the specific properties of qualitatively discriminable stimulus events, to utilize the conceptual language of learning. Moreover, the principles derived from learning theory and research describe subtle features of psychological behavior that cannot begin to be handled intelligently in neurological terms. Moreover, further reason for the stage-specific significance of experience is the observation that children are exposed to a succession of psychosocial tasks that they are expected to fulfill at different points in the neurodevelopmental sequence. These stage-specific tasks are timed to coincide with periods of rapid neurological growth (e.g., the training of bladder control is begun when the child possesses the requisite neural equipment for such control; similarly, children are taught to read when intracortical development has advanced sufficiently to enable a measure of consistent success). In short, a reciprocity appears between periods of rapid neurological growth and exposure to related experiences and tasks. To use Erikson's (1950) terms, the child's newly emerging neurological potentials are challenged by a series of crises with the environment. Children are especially vulnerable at these critical stages because experience both shapes their neurological patterns and results in learning a series of fundamental attitudes about themselves and others. During the sensory-attachment stage, for example, when pleasure and pain discriminations are central, the critical attitude learned deals with one's trust of others. The sensorimotor-autonomy stage, when the progression from passive to active modes of adaptation occurs, is noted by learning attitudes concerning adaptive confidence. During the pubertal gender-identity stage when the separation between self and other roles is sharpened, we see the development of reasonably distinct sexual roles. The intracortical-integrative stage, when the coordination between intellectual and affective processes develops, is characterized by the acquisition of a balance between reason and emotion.

The premise that early experience plays a central role in shaping personality attributes is one shared by numerous theorists. To say the preceding, however, is not to agree as to which specific factors during these developing years are critical in generating particular attributes, nor is it to agree that known formative influences are either necessary or sufficient. There is reason to ask whether developmental analysis is even possible in personality studies in light of the complex and variable character of developmental influences. Can this most fundamental of scientific activities be achieved given that we are dealing with an interactive and sequential chain of causes composed of inherently inexact data of a highly probabilistic nature in which even the very slightest variation in context or antecedent condition often of a minor or random character produces highly divergent outcomes? Because this looseness in the causal network of variables is unavoidable, are there any grounds for believing that such endeavors could prove more than illusory? Further, will the careful study of individuals reveal repetitive patterns of personologic congruence, no less consistency among the origins of such diverse attributes as overt behavior, intrapsychic functioning, and biophysical disposition? And will attribute commonalities and coherence prove to be valid phenomena, that is, not merely imposed upon observed data by virtue of observational expectation or theoretical bias?

The yearning among researchers and theorists of all viewpoints for a neat package of developmental influences simply cannot be reconciled with the complex philosophical issues, methodological quandaries, and difficult-to-disentangle subtle and random factors that give shape to personality. In the main, almost all developmental theses today are, at best, perceptive conjectures that ultimately rest on tenuous empirical grounds, reflecting the views of divergent schools of thought positing their favorite hypotheses. These speculative notions should be conceived as questions that deserve continued evaluation rather than promulgated as the gospel of confirmed fact.

It should be noted that data and inferences concerning past experiences, especially those of early childhood, are of limited, if not dubious, value. For example, events and relationships of the first years of life are notably unreliable, owing to the lack of clarity of retrospective memories. The presymbolic world of infants and young toddlers comprises fleeting and inarticulate impressions that remain embedded in perceptually amorphous and inchoate forms, forms that cannot be reproduced as the growing child's cognitions take on a more discriminative and symbolic character. What is recalled,

then, draws upon a highly ambiguous palette of diffuse images and affects, a source of which recaptured content is readily subject both to direct and to subtle promptings from contemporary sources, for example, a theoretically oriented researcher or therapist.

Arguments pointing to thematic or logical continuities between the character of early experience and later behaviors, no matter how intuitively rational or consonant with established principles they may be, do not provide unequivocal evidence for their causal connections. Different, and equally convincing, developmental hypotheses can be and are posited. Each contemporary explication of the origins of most personality disorders is persuasive yet remains but one among several plausible possibilities.

For pedagogical purposes, personality can be heuristically decomposed into various trait domains. Although these facilitate clinical investigation and experimental research, no such division exists in reality. Personality development represents the complex interplay of elements within and across each of these domains. Not only is there an interaction between person and environment, there also are interactions and complex feedback loops operating within the person as well at levels of organization both biological and psychological.

Because all scientific theories are to some extent simplifications of reality—the map rather than the territory—all theories involve trade-offs between scope and precision. Most modern developmental models are organismic and contextual in character. By embracing a multitrait model we might aspire to completely explain personality development as a totality. However, we must simultaneously accept the impossibility of any such explanation. Thus, we must posit the existence or reality of experimental error, that is, that the interaction of personality variables is often synergistic, combinatorial, and nonlinear rather than simply additive. Certain conceptual gimmicks could be used to recover this imprecision or to present an illusion of precision. We might give an exposition of personality-disorder development from a single-domain perspective, whether cognitive, psychodynamic, or behavioral. Such explanations might increase precision, but this feat would be accomplished only by denying essential aspects of the whole person. Such reductionism with respect to content is incommensurate with a guiding metaphor, that of the total organism. Thus, whereas any one personologic domain could be abstracted from the whole in order to give an exposition of personality development from a particular and narrow perspective, this would not do justice to the entire fabric of the person. Further, the interaction of influences persists over time. The course of later characteristics is related intrinsically to earlier events; an individual's personal history is itself a constraint on future development. Personality development must be viewed, therefore, as a process in which organismic and environmental forces display not only a mutuality and circularity of influence but also an orderly and sequential continuity throughout the life of the individual.

We have contended that childhood experiences are crucially involved in shaping lifelong patterns of behavior. A few words should be said, however, about why early experience should be judged as more important than comparable later experiences. Throughout evolutionary history, early life has been a preparation for later life. Until recently, and except at times of massive environmental upheaval, all species have lived in the same basic ecological niches throughout their history. Under these conditions, the experiences of early life provide an opportunity for the young organism to acquire sensitivities and behaviors that enable it to function more adequately in its environment. It learns to become acquainted with the elements of its habitat, differentiating those components that are gratifying from those that are endangering. It learns to imitate the behavior of its parents, thereby acquiring methods and competencies that would otherwise take appreciably longer, if ever, to learn.

The importance of early learning cannot be overstated for creatures that continue to live in the same environments as had their ancestors. Until recently, this continuity has been true for humans, as well. In recent decades, however, childhood learnings are often inapplicable and inappropriate when carried into adulthood. We are now in a Western society in which few constants persevere, where values and customs are in conflict, and where the styles of human interaction today are likely to change tomorrow. We now see the emergence of a new unstructured and highly fluid personality style that is commonly diagnosed clinically today as the borderline personality. In these adults we find a reflection of the contradictory and changing customs and beliefs of contemporary society. This newest pattern of childhood adaptation leaves the person unable to find the center of him or herself. Such persons have learned *not* to demonstrate consistency and continuity in their behaviors, thoughts, and feelings, no less in their ways of relating to others. These unstable and contradictory cultural patterns impact experiential discontinuities, a new consideration in our study of personality development.

Given the preceding, we would be remiss in our presentation if we failed to stress further that personality development is shaped by the institutions, traditions, and values that make up the cultural context of societal living; these cultural forces serve as a common framework of formative influences that set limits and establish guidelines for members of a social group. The continuity and stability of cultural groups depend largely on the success with which their young are imbued with common beliefs and customs. To retain what has been wrought through history, each group must devise ways of molding its children to fit in, that is, to accept and perpetuate the system of prohibitions and sanctions that earlier group members have developed to meet the persistent tasks of life. Each infant undergoes a process of socialization by which he learns to progressively surrender his impulsive and naive behaviors and to regulate or supplant them with the rules and practices of his group. Despite the coerciveness of this process and the loss of personal freedom that it entails, children learn, albeit gradually, that there are many rewards for cooperative and sharing behaviors. Societal rules enable the child to survive, to predict the behaviors of others, to obtain warmth and security, and to learn acceptable strategies for achieving the rich and diverse rewards of life. It is important to recognize, then, that the traditions of a culture provide its members with a shared way of living by which basic needs are fulfilled for the greater majority with minimal conflict and maximal return.

We must note, once again, that for many children the process of cultural training and inculcation is far from ideal; methods by which societal rules and regulations are transmitted by parents often are highly charged and erratic, entailing affection, persuasion, seduction, coercion, deception, and threat. Feelings of stress, anxiety, and resentment may be generated within the young, leaving pathological residues that are perpetuated and serve to distort their future relationships.

The notion that many of the pathological personality patterns observed today can best be ascribed to the perverse, chaotic, or frayed conditions of our cultural life has been voiced by many commentators of the social scene (Fromm, 1955; Goodman, 1960; Millon, 1987; Millon with Davis, 1996; Reisman, 1950; Wachtel, 1983; Yankelovich, 1981); these conditions have been characterized in phrases such as *the age of anxiety, growing up absurd,* and *the lonely crowd.* It is not within the scope of this chapter to elaborate the themes implied in these slogans; the reader may be interested in an article written by the senior author about two decades ago regarding the effects of contradictory social values and the disintegration of social beliefs and traditions on the emergence of the so-called borderline personality disorder (Millon, 1987).

HOW CAN WE BEST DIFFERENTIATE NORMAL FROM PATHOLOGICAL PERSONALITIES?

Any conception of personality must distinguish pathological patterns not only from their more normal variants but also from other, so-called classical, psychiatric disorders. Pathological patterns of personality are not medical illnesses for which some discrete pathogen can be found or for which exists some underlying unitary cause. The use of *DSM* language, *disorder,* for these pathologies or maladaptive patterns is indeed unfortunate, for these individuals are not disordered at all in the medical sense in that a healthy organism has been upset or undermined. Personality, normal or maladaptive, is best conceptualized as an intrinsic and enduring pattern comprising the entire matrix of the person that functions well or not in an average, expectable environment. Hence, we prefer the terms *pattern* or *style* rather than the implicitly misleading *disorder.* This mislabeling tends to nullify the logic of the multiaxial model, encouraging the view that clinical syndromes and personality disorders are parallels, existing alongside each other in a horizontal relationship. The *DSM* multiaxial model was intended to be a structural innovation, that is, composed to encourage the view that classical clinical syndromes represented a disabling outcome when the more enduring and more stable personality pattern of the patient had been upset or disordered. That is, clinical syndromes (Axis I) signify a disordered state, whereas personality pathologies (Axis II) are persistent and enduring patterns of maladaptation. The organization of personality pathologies is as integrative as those of so-called normal personalities, which is why personality pathologies are so tenacious.

Numerous attempts have been made to develop definitive criteria for distinguishing psychological normality from abnormality. Some of these criteria focus on features that characterize the so-called normal, or ideal, state of mental health, as illustrated in the writings of Offer and Sabshin (1974, 1991). Central to our understanding of normality and abnormality is the recognition that these terms exist as relative concepts; they represent arbitrary points on a continuum or gradient. No sharp line divides normal from pathological behavior. Not only is personality so complex that certain areas of psychological functioning can operate normally while others do not, but environmental circumstances change such that behaviors and strategies that prove adaptive at one time fail to do so at another. Moreover, features differentiating normal from abnormal functioning must be extracted from a complex of signs that not only wax and wane but often develop in an insidious and unpredictable manner. Pathological personality patterns, as previously remarked, are not disorders or diseases at all in the medical sense. Rather, personality pathologies are reified constructs employed to represent varied styles or patterns in which the personality system functions maladaptively in relation to its environment and over time.

When alternative strategies employed to achieve goals, relate to others, and cope with stress are few in number and rigidly practiced (*adaptive inflexibility*); when habitual perceptions, needs, and behaviors perpetuate and intensify pre-existing difficulties (*vicious circles*); and when the person tends to lack resilience under conditions of stress (*tenuous stability*), we speak of a pathological personality pattern. We keep in mind that personality is an interactional concept that admits of degrees, shading gently from normality to clinicality, and has at a latent level no single underlying cause or pathogenicity, but instead is as multidetermined as the personality system itself is multifaceted. The three disorder criteria noted previously are intimately related to the personality pathology taxonomy that we will briefly note in later paragraphs.

In the following paragraphs we will draw upon the first three of the evolutionary polarities touched on previously. The fourth polarity also is worthy of note and relevant to an understanding of personality traits; however, to include this polarity in the following section will take us somewhat afield in this already extensive chapter. Interested readers wishing to review the details of this fourth and cognitively oriented polarity may look into the manual for the *Millon Index of Personality Styles-R* (*MIPS-R;* Millon, Weiss, Millon, & Davis, 2003).

Evolution/Neurodevelopmental Stage I: Aims of Existence: The Pain-Pleasure Polarity

An interweaving and shifting balance between the two extremes that make up the pain-pleasure polarity typifies normality. Both of the following criteria should be met in varying degrees as life circumstances require. In essence, a synchronous and coordinated personal style should have developed to answer the question of whether the person should focus on experiencing only the pleasures of life versus concentrating his or her efforts on avoiding its pains.

Life Preservation: Avoiding Danger and Threat

One might assume that a criterion based on the avoidance of psychic or physical pain would be sufficiently self-evident not to require specification. As is well known, debates have arisen in the literature as to whether mental health/normality reflects the absence of mental disorder, being merely the reverse side of the mental illness/abnormality coin. That there is a relationship between health and disease cannot be questioned; the two are intimately connected, conceptually and physically. On the other hand, to define health solely as the absence of disorder will not suffice. As a single criterion among several, however, features of behavior and experience that signify both the lack of (e.g., anxiety, depression) and an aversion to (e.g., threats to safety and security) pain in its many and diverse forms provide a necessary foundation upon which other, more positively constructed criteria may rest. Substantively, positive normality must comprise elements beyond mere nonnormality or abnormality. And despite the complexities and inconsistencies of personality, from a definitional point of view normality does preclude nonnormality.

It may be of interest next to record some of the psychic pathologies of personality that can be traced to aberrations in meeting this first criterion of normality. For example, among those termed *avoidant personalities* (Millon, 1969, 1981; Millon with Davis, 1996), we see an excessive preoccupation with threats to psychic security, an expectation of and hyper-alertness to the signs of potential rejection that leads these persons to disengage from everyday relationships and pleasures. At the other extreme of the criterion we see a risk-taking attitude, a proclivity to chance hazards and to endanger life and liberty, a behavioral pattern characteristic of those we label *antisocial personalities.* Here there is little of the caution and prudence expected in the normality criterion of avoiding danger and threat; rather, we observe its opposite, a rash willingness to put one's safety in jeopardy, to play with fire, and to throw caution to the wind.

Life Enhancement: Seeking Rewarding Experiences

At the other end of the existence polarity are attitudes and behaviors designed to foster and enrich life, to generate joy, pleasure, contentment, fulfillment, and thereby strengthen the capacity of the individual to remain vital and competent physically and psychically. This criterion asserts that existence/survival calls for more than life preservation alone; beyond pain avoidance is pleasure enhancement.

This criterion asks us to go at least one step further than Freud's parallel notion that life's motivation is chiefly that of reducing tensions (that is, avoiding or minimizing pain), maintaining thereby a steady state, if you will, a homeostatic balance and inner stability. In accord with our view of evolution's polarities, we would assert that normal humans are driven also by the desire to enrich their lives, to seek invigorating sensations and challenges, to venture and explore, all to the end of magnifying if not escalating the probabilities of both individual viability and species replicability.

As before, a note or two should be recorded on the pathological consequences of a failure to meet a criterion. These are seen most clearly in the personality disorders labeled *schizoid* and *avoidant.* In the former there is a marked hedonic deficiency, stemming either from an inherent deficit in affective substrates or the failure of stimulative experience to develop either or both attachment behaviors or affective capacity (Millon, 1981; Millon with Davis, 1996). Among those designated *avoidant personalities,* constitutional sensitivities or abusive life experiences have led to an intense attentional sensitivity to psychic pain and a consequent distrust in either the genuineness or the durability of the pleasures, such that these individuals can no longer permit themselves to experience them. Both of these personalities tend to be withdrawn and isolated, joyless and grim, neither seeking nor sharing in the rewards of life.

Evolution/Neurodevelopmental Stage II: Modes of Adaptation: The Passive-Active Polarity

To maintain their unique structure, differentiated from the larger ecosystem of which they are a part, to be sustained as a discrete entity among other phenomena that make up their environmental field, requires good fortune and the presence of effective modes of functioning. The vast range of behaviors engaged in by humans fundamentally may be grouped in terms of whether initiative is taken in altering and shaping life's events or whether behaviors are reactive to and accommodate those events.

Normal or optimal functioning, at least among humans, appears to call for a flexible balance that interweaves both polar extremes. In the first evolutionary stage, that relating to existence, behaviors encouraging both life enhancement (pleasure) and life preservation (pain avoidance) are likely to be more successful in achieving survival than actions limited to one or the other alone. Similarly, regarding adaptation, modes of functioning that exhibit both ecologic accommodation and ecologic modification are likely to be more successful than either by itself. Normality calls for a synchronous and coordinated personal style that weaves a balanced answer to the question of whether one should accept what the fates have brought forth or take the initiative in altering the circumstances of one's life.

Ecological Accommodation: Abiding Hospitable Realities

On first reflection, it would seem to be less than optimal to submit meekly to what life presents, to adjust obligingly to one's destiny. To illustrate: The evolution of plants is essentially grounded (no pun intended) in environmental accommodation, in an adaptive acquiescence to the ecosystem. Crucial to this adaptive course, however, is the capacity of these surroundings to provide the nourishment and protection requisite to the thriving of a species.

To the extent that the events of life have been and continue to be caring and giving, is it not perhaps wisest, from an evolutionary perspective, to accept this good fortune and let matters be? This accommodating or passive-life philosophy has worked extremely well in sustaining and fostering those complex organisms that make up the plant kingdom. Hence passivity, the yielding to environmental forces, may be in itself not only unproblematic but, where events and circumstances provide the pleasures of life and protect against their pains, positively adaptive and constructive. Where do we find clinical nonnormality that reflects failures to meet the accommodating/abiding criterion?

One example of an inability to leave things as they are is seen in what the *DSM* terms the *histrionic personality*. Their persistent and unrelenting manipulation of events is designed to maximize the receipt of attention and favors as well as to avoid social disinterest and disapproval. They show an insatiable if not indiscriminate search for stimulation and approval. Their clever and often artful social behaviors may give the appearance of an inner confidence and self-assurance; but beneath this guise lies a fear that a failure on their part to ensure the receipt of attention will, in short order, result in indifference or rejection, and hence their desperate need for reassurance and repeated signs of approval. As they are quickly bored and sated, they keep stirring up things, becoming enthusiastic about one activity and then another. There is a restless stimulus-seeking quality in which they cannot leave well enough alone.

At the other end of the polarity are personality pathologies that exhibit an excess of passivity, failing thereby to give direction to their own lives. Several Axis II disorders demonstrate this passive style, although their passivity derives from and is expressed in appreciably different ways. Dependent personalities typically are average on the pleasure/pain polarity. Passivity for them stems from deficits in self-confidence and competence, leading to deficits in initiative and autonomy skills as well as a tendency to wait passively while others assume leadership and guide them. Passivity among obsessive-compulsive personalities stems from their fear of acting independently, owing to intrapsychic resolutions they have made to quell hidden thoughts and emotions generated by their intense self-other ambivalence. Dreading the possibility of making mistakes or engaging in disapproved behaviors, they became indecisive, immobilized, restrained, and passive.

Ecologic Modification: Mastering One's Environment

The active end of the polarity signifies the taking of initiative in altering and shaping life's events. Such persons are best characterized by their alertness, vigilance, liveliness, vigor, and forcefulness, their stimulus-seeking energy and drive.

White (1959, 1960), in his concept of effectance, sees it as an intrinsic motive that activates persons to impose their desires upon environments. In a similar vein, Fromm (1955) proposed a need on the part of humans to rise above the roles

of passive creatures in an accidental if not random world. To him, humans are driven to transcend the state of merely having been created; instead, humans seek to become the creators, the active shapers of their own destiny. Rising above the passive and accidental nature of existence, humans generate their own purposes and thereby provide themselves with a true basis of freedom.

Evolution/Neurodevelopmental Stage III: Strategies of Replication: The Other-Self Polarity

If an organism merely duplicates itself prior to death, then its replica is doomed to repeat the same fate its original suffered. However, if new potentials for extending existence can be fashioned by chance or routine events, then the possibility of achieving a different and conceivably superior outcome may be increased. And it is this co-occurrence of random and recombinant processes that does lead to the prolongation of a species' existence. This third hallmark of evolution's procession also undergirds another of nature's fundamental polarities, that between self and other.

As before, we consider both of the following criteria necessary to the definition and determination of normality. We see no necessary antithesis between the two. Humans can be both self-indulging and other-nurturing, although most persons are likely to lean toward one or the other side. A balance that coordinates the two provides a satisfactory answer to the question of whether one should be devoted to the support and welfare of others or should fashion one's life in accord with one's own needs and desires.

Progeny Nurturance: Constructively Encouraging Others

As described earlier, recombinant replication achieved by sexual mating entails a balanced though asymmetric parental investment in both the genesis and nurturance of offspring. Eloquent proposals related to this criterion have been formulated by the noted psychologist Gordon Allport. One of Allport's (1961) criteria of the mature personality, which he terms a warm relating of self to others, refers to the capability of displaying intimacy and love for a parent, child, spouse, or close friend. Here the person manifests an authentic oneness with the other and a deep concern for his or her welfare. Beyond one's intimate family and friends, there is an extension of warmth in the mature person to humankind at large, an understanding of the human condition, and a kinship with all peoples.

The pathological consequences of a failure to embrace the polarity criterion of others are seen most clearly in the personality pathologies termed *antisocial* and *narcissistic*. Both personalities exhibit an imbalance in their replication strategy; in this case, however, there is a primary reliance on self rather than others. They have learned that reproductive success as well as maximum pleasure and minimum pain is achieved by turning primarily to themselves. In the narcissistic personality, development reflects the acquisition of a self-image of superior worth, learned largely in response to admiring and doting parents. They display manifest confidence, arrogance, and an exploitative egocentricity in social contexts, blithely assuming that others will recognize their specialness. Those exhibiting the antisocial personality act to counter the expectation of pain at the hand of others; this is done by actively engaging in duplicitous or illegal behaviors in which they seek to exploit others for self-gain. Skeptical regarding the motives of others, they desire autonomy and wish revenge for what are felt as past injustices.

Individual Propagation: Indulging Self

The converse of progeny nurturance is not progeny propagation but rather the lack of progeny nurturance. Thus, to fail to encourage others constructively does not assure the indulgence of one's potentials. Both may and should exist in normal or healthy individuals.

Rogers (1963), for example, posited a single, overreaching motive for the normal/healthy person—maintaining, actualizing, and enhancing one's potential. The goal is not that of maintaining a homeostatic balance or a high degree of ease and comfort but rather to move forward in becoming what is intrinsic to self and to enhance further that which one has already become. Believing that humans have an innate urge to create, Rogers stated that the most creative product of all is one's own self.

Where do we see failures in the achievement of self-indulgence, a giving up of self to gain the approbation of others? One personality disorder may be drawn upon to illustrate forms of self-denial. Those with dependent personalities have learned that feeling good, secure, confident, and so on—that is, those feelings associated with pleasure or the avoidance of pain—is provided almost exclusively in their relationship with others. Behaviorally, these persons learn early that they themselves do not readily achieve rewarding experiences; the experiences are secured better by leaning on others. They learn not only to turn to others as their source of nurturance and security but to wait passively for others to take the initiative in providing safety and sustenance.

HOW DOES THE CONCEPT OF PERSONALITY HELP US UNDERSTAND PSYCHOPATHOLOGY?

Personality patterns and their vulnerabilities can be seen as representing each person's psychic immune system, that is,

an individual's longstanding pattern of perceiving and coping with the psychic stressors in his or her mental life. Personality pathologies represent areas of vulnerability; the different personality pathology patterns (e.g., avoidant, dependent) differ in which vulnerabilities they possess. Our task as scientists is to decode these vulnerabilities from a person's behaviors and thoughts and then to do research and therapy, not only to understand their personalities but to resolve their vulnerabilities. Understanding the vulnerabilities—the patient's weakened intrapsychic defenses, neurochemical imbalances, cognitive misinterpretations, and interpersonal difficulties—will enable us to take steps to effect beneficent changes.

For taxonomic purposes, I believe it may be useful to distinguish three prototypal categories of psychopathologies: *complex syndromes, simple reactions,* and *personality patterns.* See Millon et al. (1999) for a full discussion of these distinctions.

Complex syndromes signify difficulties that arise when disruptions occur in a person's characteristic (personality pattern) style of functioning: They signify pathological responses to a situation for which the individual's psychic makeup is notably vulnerable. Hysterical conversions and fugue states would be dramatic examples of complex syndromes in that they usually arise in response to situations that appear rather trivial or innocuous when viewed objectively. Nevertheless, vulnerable patients with a pathology of personality style feel and respond in a manner similar to those of so-called normal persons who face a realistically distressing situation. As a consequence, complex syndromes may fail to make sense and often appear irrational and strangely complicated. To the experienced clinician, however, the response signifies the presence of an unusual vulnerability on the part of the patient; in effect, a seemingly neutral stimulus apparently has touched a painful hidden memory or emotion. Viewed in this manner, complex syndromes arise among individuals encumbered with adverse past experiences. They reflect the upsurge of deeply rooted feelings that press to the surface, override present realities, and become the prime stimulus to which the individual responds. It is this flooding into the present of the reactivated past that gives complex syndromes much of their symbolic, bizarre, and hidden meaning.

At the farthest end of the clinical continuum of pathology are simple reactions; they are highly specific pathological responses that are precipitated by and largely attributable to circumscribed external events or endogenous biochemical dispositions. These simple reactions result when an otherwise normal person is faced with situations to which almost anyone would react pathologically, the demise of one's entire family in a natural disaster, for example. In contrast to complex syndromes, simple reactions are uncomplicated and straightforward. They do not pass through a chain of intricate and circuitous transformations before emerging in manifest form. Uncontaminated by the intrusion of personality vulnerabilities (e.g., distant memories or intrapsychic transformations), simple reactions tend to be rational and understandable in terms of a precipitating external stimulus or endogenous biological weakness. Isolated from a problematic past, a defensive manipulation, or a neurochemical susceptibility, they are expressed in a direct and understandable fashion—unlike complex syndromes, the features of which tend to be highly fluid, wax and wane, taking on different forms at different times.

To elaborate further on the psychopathology continuum, traits that make up the personality patterns have an inner momentum and autonomy; they are expressed with or without inducement or external precipitation. In contrast, responses that make up simple reactions are stimulus specific; that is, they are linked to external or internal precipitants, operating independently of the individual's personality, elicited by events that are objectively troublesome. Complex syndromes are similar to simple reactions in that they are prompted also by distinct external events or unseen biological vulnerabilities, but their interaction with personality weaknesses results in the intrusion of enduring traits that complicate what might otherwise be a response to the environment within the nonclinical range.

WHAT ARE THE PATHOLOGICAL DOMAINS IN WHICH PERSONALITY EXPRESSES ITSELF?

Individuals differ in the degree to which their behaviors are enduring and pervasive. Moreover, each individual displays this durability and pervasiveness only in certain of his or her characteristics; that is, each of us possesses a limited number of attributes that are resistant to changing times and situational influences, whereas other of our attributes are more readily modified. It should be noted also that the features that exhibit this consistency and stability in one person may not be the same features exhibited by others. These core qualities of persistence and extensiveness appear only in characteristics that have become crucial in maintaining the individual's structural balance and functional style. To illustrate: The interpersonal attribute of significance for some is being agreeable, never differing or having conflict; for another, it may be interpersonally critical to keep one's distance from people so as to avoid rejection or the feeling of being humiliated; for a third, the influential interpersonal characteristic may be that of asserting one's will and dominating others. These enduring (stable) and pervasive (broadly ex-

pressed) characteristics are what we search for when we diagnose personality.

In the following paragraphs, we will identify a number of the major domains and attributes of personality that we believe possess theoretical, research, and/or clinical significance. They make up a set of structural and functional characteristics that not only will aid us in differentiating among normal personalities but also will provide us with potential diagnostic criteria for identifying pathological personality prototypes. There are some useful benefits in differentiating the more-or-less-stable or ingrained personality attributes (structures) from those that represent the widely operative and modulating features of personality (functions).

Functional Domain Attributes

Functional characteristics represent dynamic processes that transpire within the intrapsychic world and between the individual and his psychosocial environment. For definitional purposes, we might say that functional personality attributes represent broadly expressed modes of regulatory action, that is, behaviors, cognitions, perceptions, affects, and mechanisms that manage, adjust, transform, coordinate, balance, discharge, and control the give and take of inner and outer life.

Not only are there several modes of regulatory action (e.g., behavioral, cognitive), but there are numerous variations in the way each of these functional modalities are manifested or expressed (e.g., cognitively flighty, cognitively deviant). Every individual employs every modality in the course of his life, but individuals differ with respect to which modalities they enact most frequently and, even more so, diverge in which of the expressive variations of these functions they typically manifest. As Bowers has put it (1977): "The way a person performs a common behavior is sometimes quite revealing. One person ordinarily eats and makes love fastidiously; another person is given to gluttony in both circumstances. The more idiosyncratically expressive a common behavior is . . . [the more it is] attributable to a relatively stable personality and behavioral organization" (p. 75).

Particular modalities and expressive variations characterize certain personalities best, but even the most distinctive of personalities will display several variations of a modality. Dissimilar individuals differ in which modality variations they express most often, but these differences are largely a matter of *quantitative frequency* (dimensionality) and not *qualitative distinctness* (categorality).

Four functional domains relevant to personality will be briefly described. Numerous expressive attribute variations, one associated with each clinical personality prototype, have been specified in other publications (Millon with Davis, 1996); several of these have been formulated as the Grossman Content Scales in a forthcoming elaboration of the Millon Clinical Multiaxial Inventory (in press).

1. *Expressive Behavior Domain.* These relate to the observables of physical and verbal behavior, usually recorded by noting what the person does and how the person does it. Through inference, observations of overt behavior enable us to deduce either what the person unknowingly reveals about him or herself or, often conversely, what he or she wishes us to think or to know about him or her. The range and character of behavioral functions are not only wide and diverse, but they convey both distinctive and worthwhile information, from communicating a sense of personal incompetence to exhibiting general defensiveness to demonstrating a disciplined self-control, and so on.

2. *Interpersonal Conduct Domain.* A person's style of relating to others may be captured in a number of ways, such as the manner in which his or her actions impact on others, intended or otherwise; the attitudes that underlie, prompt, and give shape to these actions; the methods by which he or she engages others to meet his or her needs; or his or her way of coping with social tensions and conflicts. Extrapolating from these observations, the researcher or clinician may construct an image of how the person functions in relation to others, be it antagonistically, respectfully, aversively, secretively, and so on.

3. *Cognitive Style Domain.* How the person perceives events, focuses his or her attention, processes information, organizes thoughts, and communicates his or her reactions and ideas to others are among the most useful indexes to the researcher or clinician of the person's distinctive way of functioning. By synthesizing these signs and symptoms, it may be possible to identify indications of what may be termed an impoverished style, or distracted thinking, or cognitive flightiness, or constricted thought, and so on.

4. *Regulatory Mechanism Domain.* Although mechanisms of self-protection, need gratification, and conflict resolution are consciously recognized at times, those that remain unconscious and thereby avoid reflective appraisal often begin a sequence of events that intensifies the very problems they were intended to circumvent. Mechanisms usually represent internal processes and, hence, are more difficult to discern and describe than processes anchored closer to the observable world. Despite the methodological problems they present, the task of identifying which mechanisms are chosen (e.g., rationalization, displacement, reaction-formation) and the extent to which they are employed is central to a comprehensive personality assessment.

Structural Domain Attributes

These domains represent a deeply embedded and relatively enduring template of imprinted memories, attitudes, needs, fears, conflicts, and so on, that guide the experience and transform the nature of ongoing life events. Psychic structures have an orienting and preemptive effect in that they alter the character of action and the impact of subsequent experiences in line with preformed inclinations and expectancies. By selectively lowering thresholds for transactions that are consonant with either constitutional proclivities or early learnings, future events are often experienced as variations of the past. Significant experiences of early life may never recur again, but their effects remain and leave their mark. Physiologically, we may say they have etched a neurochemical change; psychologically, they are registered as memories, a permanent trace and an embedded internal stimulus. In contrast to the fleeting stimuli of the external world, these memory traces become part and parcel of every stimulus complex that activates behavior. Once registered, the effects of the past are indelible, incessant, and inescapable. They now are intrinsic elements of the individual's makeup; they latch on and intrude into the current events of life, coloring, transforming, and distorting the passing scene. Although the residuals of subsequent experiences may override them, becoming more dominant internal stimuli, the presence of earlier memory traces remains in one form or another. In every thought and action the individual cannot help but carry these remnants into the present. Every current behavior is a perpetuation, then, of the past, a continuation and intrusion of these inner stimulus traces.

For purposes of definition, *structural domain attributes* might be described as cognitive-affective substrates and action dispositions of a quasi-permanent nature. Possessing a network of interconnecting pathways, these structures contain the internalized residues of the past in the form of memories and affects that are associated intrapsychically with conceptions of self and others.

Four structural domains relevant to personality will be briefly described. Numerous variations, one for each clinical personality prototype in *Diagnostic and Statistical Manual of Mental Disorders,* fourth edition (*DSM-IV;* American Psychiatric Association, 1994), have been specified in other publications (Millon with Davis, 1996).

1. *Self-Image Domain.* As the inner world of symbols is mastered through development, the swirl of events that buffet

the young child gives way to a growing sense of order and continuity. One major configuration emerges to impose a measure of sameness upon an otherwise fluid environment, the perception of self-as-object, a distinct, ever-present, and identifiable *I* or *me.* Self-identity provides a stable anchor to serve as a guidepost and to give continuity to changing experience. Most persons have an implicit sense of who they are but differ greatly in the clarity and accuracy of their self-introspections. Few can articulate the psychic elements that make up this image, such as stating knowingly whether they view themselves as primarily alienated, or inept, or complacent, or conscientious, and so on.

2. *Object Representations Domain.* As noted previously, significant experiences from the past leave an inner imprint, a structural residue composed of memories, attitudes, and affects that serve as a substrate of dispositions for perceiving and reacting to life's ongoing events. Analogous to the various organ systems of which the body is composed, both the character and substance of these internalized representations of the past can be differentiated and analyzed for assessment purposes. Variations in the nature and content of this inner world can be associated with one or another personality and can lead us to employ descriptive terms to represent them, such as shallow, vexatious, undifferentiated, concealed, and irreconcilable.

3. *Morphologic Organization Domain.* The overall architecture that serves as a framework for an individual's psychic interior may display weakness in its structural cohesion, exhibit deficient coordination among its components, and possess few mechanisms to maintain balance and harmony, regulate internal conflicts, or mediate external pressures. The concept of intrapsychic morphologic organization refers to the structural strength, interior congruity, and functional efficacy of the personality system. *Organization* is a concept akin to and employed in conjunction with current psychoanalytic notions such as borderline and psychotic levels, but this usage tends to be limited, relating essentially to quantitative degrees of integrative pathology, not to variations neither in normal personality nor to the integrative character or structural configuration of the personality makeup. Stylistic variants of this structural domain have been specified for each of the *DSM-IV* clinical personality prototypes in earlier publications; their distinctive organizational qualities are represented by descriptors such as *inchoate, disjoined,* and *compartmentalized.*

4. *Mood Temperament Domain.* Few observables are more relevant to personologic analysis than the predominant character of an individual's affect and the intensity and frequency with which he or she expresses it. The meaning of extreme and transient emotions is easy to decode. This is not so with the more characteristic and persistent moods and subtle feelings that insidiously and repetitively pervade the person's ongoing relationships and experiences. The structural features of affect are conveyed by terms such as *distraught, labile, fickle,* or *hostile* are often communicated explicitly via self-report, but they are revealed as well, albeit indirectly, in the person's characteristic level of activity, speech quality, and physical appearance.

WHAT MAJOR PERSONALITY TYPES AND SUBTYPES CAN BE GENERATED BY THEORY?

The evolutionary-based principles and concepts of the generative theory have served as a base for deducing and coordinating both normal and pathological personality patterns. The full scope of this schema has been published by the senior author in earlier texts. First identified as a *biosocial-learning theory* (Millon, 1969), it is now cast in evolutionary terms (Millon, 1990; Millon with Davis, 1996) and has served to establish the *DSM* personality categories through formal deduction as well as to show their covariation with other mental disorders.

Though the taxonomy of personality patterns that follows is combinatorially generated, the personologic consequences of a single polar extreme may be usefully noted. For example, a high standing on the pain pole—a position typically associated with a disposition to experience anxiety—will be used for this purpose. The upshot of this singular sensitivity takes different forms depending on a variety of factors that lead to the learning of diverse styles of anxiety-coping. For example, *avoidants* learn to deal with their pervasively experienced anxiety-sensitivity by removing themselves across the board, that is, actively withdrawing from most relationships unless strong assurances of acceptance are given. The *compulsive,* often equally prone to experience anxiety, has learned that there are sanctioned but limited spheres of acceptable conduct; the compulsive reduces anxiety by restricting activities only to those that are permitted by more powerful and by potentially rejecting others, as well as by adhering carefully to rules so that unacceptable boundaries will not be transgressed. And the anxiety-prone *paranoid* has learned to neutralize pain by constructing a semidelusional pseudocommunity (Cameron, 1963), one in which environmental realities are transformed to make them more tolerable and less threatening, albeit not very successfully. In sum, a high standing at the pain pole leads not to one, but to diverse personality outcomes.

Another of the polar extremes will be selected to illustrate the diversity of forms that personality styles may take as a function of covariant polarity positions; in this case reference will be made to a shared position on the passivity pole. Five personality types demonstrate the passive style, but their passivity derives from and is expressed in appreciably different ways that reflect disparate polarity combinations. *Schizoid types,* for example, are passive owing to their relative incapacity to experience pleasure and pain; without the rewards these emotional valences normally activate, they will be devoid of the drive to acquire rewards, leading them to become rather indifferent and passive observers. *Dependent types* typically are average on the pleasure and pain polarity, yet they are usually no less passive than schizoids. Strongly oriented to others, they are notably weak with regard to self. Passivity for them stems from deficits in self-confidence and competence, leading to deficits in initiative and autonomous skills, as well as a tendency to wait passively while others assume leadership and guide them. Passivity among *compulsives,* as noted previously, stems from their fear of acting independently, owing to intrapsychic resolutions they have made to quell hidden thoughts and emotions generated by their intense self-other ambivalence. Dreading the possibility of making mistakes or engaging in disapproved behaviors, they became indecisive, immobilized, restrained, and passive. High on pain, and low on both pleasure and self, the *self-defeating* (masochistic) personality operates on the assumption that they dare not expect, nor do they deserve, to have life go their way; giving up any efforts to achieve a life that accords with their true desires, they passively submit to others' wishes, acquiescently accepting their fate. Finally, *narcissists,* especially high on self and low on others, benignly assume that good things will come their way with little or no effort on their part; this passive exploitation of others is a consequence of the unexplored confidence that underlies their self-centered presumptions.

Specifically, each of the *DSM* disorders should be described and interpreted in terms of a theoretical model, as we will note briefly. Also noted briefly will be a number of the several subtypes of each personality prototype. The effort is made here in recognition of the fact that each pure prototype is merely an anchoring referent about which real persons vary.

The Axis II listings that constitute the body of the *DSM* personality disorders represent derivations based essentially on a series of ideal or pure textbook conceptions of each ostensibly discrete and boundaried category. There are, however, numerous divergences from published descriptive texts that reflect both the results of empirical personologic research and the observation of everyday clinical work. Given the

philosophic and multidimensional complexities of any taxonomic category construct, we must resist the ever-present linguistic compulsion to simplify and separate constructs from their objective reality and then treat them as if these hypothetical constructions were fixed disease entities. Constructs (e.g., clinical or personality prototypes) should be used heuristically, as guidelines to be reformulated or replaced as necessary; it is only the unique way in which the construct is seen in actual and specific persons that should be of primary interest. The *DSM* disorders are nomothetic in that they comprise abstract taxons derived from historical, clinical, or statistical sources (biochemical, intrapsychic). Given the fixed nature in which each of these constructs is promulgated in the *DSM,* it is imperative that researchers and clinicians generate a range of subtypes to represent *trait-constellation variants* that are close to corresponding to the distinctive or idiosyncratic character of actual patients.

Not only is *DSM* not an exhaustive listing of clinical configurations that correspond to many of our patients, but it does not begin to scratch the surface of human individuality and personality variability. *DSM-IV* diagnoses alone, unsupplemented by information from additional descriptive domains, constitute an insufficient basis from which we can articulate the distinctive, complex, and often conflictual trait dynamics of real persons, no less patients. Nomothetic propositions and diagnostic labels are superficialities to be overcome as understanding is gained. Taxonomic systems such as *DSM* and ICD make up a crude first step; they rarely are sufficient for useful research and clinical work and, in fact, if left as they are, should be regarded as prescientific.

All experienced personologists and clinicians know that there is no such thing as a purely homogeneous descriptive group or category; for example, there is no single schizoid (or avoidant, or depressive, or histrionic) personality type. Rather, there are innumerable variations, different forms in which the classical syndrome or prototypal personality manifests itself. Life experiences impact and reshape biological dispositions and early learned behaviors in a variety of ways, taking divergent turns and producing shadings composed of meaningfully discriminable psychological features. The course and character of each person's life experiences are, at the very least, marginally different from all others, producing influences that have sequential effects that generate *recombinant mixtures* of all clinical syndromes and personality types. Some of these mixtures may even result in contrasting inclinations and characteristics within the same person, such as those that stem, for example, from parents who were strikingly different in their child-rearing methods, one rearing pattern conducive to the formation of a so-called avoidant style in a child, the other to an obsessive-compulsive one in the same child. Internal schisms of psychological traits and character, so well understood by our psychoanalytic colleagues, are not at all uncommon, as are discrepancies we see between the overt and covert characteristics in many patients.

The inexact fit between a patient and his or her diagnostic label is a nagging and noisome reminder of the individuality of persons; it reflects the idiographic as contrasted with the nomothetic approach to psychological study. This incessant conceptual trouble has fueled the development of modern multiaxial taxonomies, but these taxonomies are at best only a beginning step in what might come to be an appropriate structure for devising flexible, relevant, and comprehensive taxonomic models. The monotypic categories of the *DSM* are but a crude and global beginning in a march toward specification and the accommodation of a taxonomy of individuality. Although the initial phases of a diagnostic taxonomy must consist of categories of broad bandwidth and little specificity, *DSM* diagnostic categories provide gross distinctions, if not invalid ones. As clinical knowledge and empirical studies accrue, the manifestation of classification groupings must become more sharply delineated, that is, broad diagnostic taxons should be broken down into multiple, narrow taxons of greater specificity and individually descriptive value, as we begin to do when formulating category subtypes. Clinicians and personologists must learn not only classical textbook categories but also subtype mixtures possessing numerous domain attributes that are seen in normal and clinical reality.

Let us briefly record just a few subtype variants among several of the *DSM*-related personality types. Patients recorded as dependent personalities have learned that feeling good, secure, confident, and so on—that is feelings associated with pleasure or the avoidance of pain—is provided almost exclusively in relationships with others. Among the five clinical subtypes recorded in Millon with Davis (1996), we find the *disquieted* variant, a group that in part also displays avoidant features, as seen in their clinging, yet fretful, behaviors. Notable also is an *accommodating* subtype with partial histrionic traits, evidencing both compliant and enticing features. Among the others noted are the *ineffectual,* the *immature,* and the *selfless* dependent subtypes. Still other subtypes will be identified and described in a series of books by the senior author and his colleagues. These will detail *normal* and *healthy* variants of the clinical prototypes included in the *DSM* (Millon, Meagher, Grossman, et al., in press).

Narcissistic personality patterns reflect the acquisition of self-images of superior worth, usually learned in response to admiring and doting parents. They display an inflated sense of self-worth, manifest confidence, arrogance, and an exploitive egocentricity. Among this category's four clinical subtypes are the *elitists,* who fancy themselves as demigods, flaunt their status, and engage in self-promotion. Other notable variants are the *compensatory* type with covert avoidant features, underlying feelings of inferiority, yet public displays of superiority. Noteworthy also are the *amorous* and the *unprincipled* subtypes, as well as a number of nonclinical variants.

Among the antisocial personality group are those who engage in duplicitous or illegal behaviors, evincing a skeptical disregard of the motives of others and a wish to gain revenge for what are felt as past injustices. Among the five clinical subtypes of the antisocial is the *covetous* variant, noted by enviousness, retribution-seeking, and a greedy avariciousness. Also prevalent is a *risk-taking* type, seen in recklessness, impulsivity, and heedless behaviors; other variants include the *nomadic,* the *reputation-defending,* and the *malevolent* subtypes, the latter two seen often in prisons.

Among the borderline personality we find a relative absence of higher self-regulatory processes, evident in an inconsistent and changing view of the world and the self and an intense lability among cognitive, affective, and behavioral controls. Several clinical subtypes are notable. Common is the *self-destructive* variant with depressive traits, parasuicidal behaviors, and a high-strung, inward-turning of moody behaviors. Also prevalent is an *impulsive* type with histrionic and/or antisocial features, seen in their capricious, agitated, irritable, and incipient suicidal behaviors. Two other clinical variants are the *discouraged* and *petulant* subtypes.

CONCLUSION

Our primary aim in this chapter on the goals of theory in personality was to connect the conceptual structure of both normal and abnormal personalities and their stages of neurodevelopment to what we judged to be the omnipresent principles of evolution, a theoretical ambition. A second goal was to utilize the evolutionary theory to create a deductively derived clinical taxonomy, also a conceptual goal. We have bypassed a third and fourth aim, that of linking the taxonomy to newly developed assessment instruments and to outline prescriptions for an integrative or personalized model of psychotherapy, the latter two practical and utilitarian purposes discussed in other papers and books. It is on these foundations that we see a framework for a systematic science of personology.

REFERENCES

Allport, G. (1961). *Pattern and growth in personality.* New York: Holt, Rinehart, and Winston.

American Psychiatric Association (1994). *Diagnostic and statistical manual of neural disorders (DSM-IV)*. Washington, DC: Amerian Psychiatric Press.

Beach, F., & Jaynes, J. (1954). Effects of early experience upon the behavior of animals. *Psychological Bulletin, 51,* 239–262.

Bowers, K. S. (1977). There's more to Iago than meets the eye: A clinical account of personality consistency. In D. Magnusson & N. S. Endler (Eds.), *Personality at the crossroads.* Hillsdale, NJ: Erlbaum.

Buss, D. M. (1984). Evolutionary biology and personality psychology. *American Psychologist, 39,* 1135–1147.

Buss, D. M. (1994). *The evolution of desire: Strategies of human mating.* New York: Basic Books.

Cameron, N. (1963). *Personality and psychopathology.* New York: Houghton Mifflin.

Cosmides, L., & Tooby, J. (1987). From evolution to behavior: Evolutionary psychology as the missing link. In J. Dupre (Ed.), *The latest on the best: Essays on evolution and optimality.* Cambridge, MA: MIT Press.

Daly, M., & Wilson, M. (1978). *Sex, evolution, and behavior.* Boston: Grant Press.

Erikson, E. (1950). *Childhood and society.* New York: Norton.

Freud, S. (1915/1925). The instincts and their vicissitudes. In *Collected Papers* (Vol. 4). London: Hogarth.

Freud, S. (1924). Project for a scientific psychology. In *Standard edition* (Vol. 1, pp. 3–95). London: Hogarth. (Original work published 1895.)

Fromm, E. (1955). *The sane society.* New York: Holt, Rinehart, and Winston.

Goodman, P. (1960). *Growing up absurd: Problems of youth in the organized system.* New York: Random House.

Grossman, S. D. (in press). Content scales. In T. Millon, *Millon Clinical Multiaxial Inventory, III-E.* Minneapolis, MN: Pearson Assessments.

Hempel, C. G. (1961). Introduction to problems of taxonomy. In J. Zubin (Ed.), *Field studies in the mental disorders* (pp. 3–22). New York: Grune & Stratton.

Killackey, H. P. (1990). Neocortical expansion: An attempt toward relating phylogeny and ontogeny. *Journal of Cognitive Neuroscience, 2,* 1–17.

Lewin, K. (1936). *Principles of topographical psychology.* New York: McGraw-Hill.

Lipton, S. A., & Kater, S.B. (1989). Neurotransmitter regulation of neuronal outgrowth, plasticity, and survival. *Trends in Neuroscience, 12,* 265–269.

Melzick, R. (1965). Effects of early experience upon behavior: Experimental and conceptual considerations. In P. Hoch & J. Zubin (Eds.), *Psychopathology of perception.* New York: Grune & Stratton.

Millon, T. (1969). *Modern psychopathology: A biosocial approach to maladaptive learning and functioning.* Philadelphia: Saunders.

Millon, T. (1981). *Disorders of personality: DSM-III, Axis II.* New York: Wiley.

Millon, T. (1987). On the genesis and prevalence of the borderline personality disorder: A social learning thesis. *Journal of Personality Disorders, 1,* 354–372.

Millon, T. (1990). *Toward a new personology: An evolutionary model.* New York: Wiley-Interscience.

Millon, T. (Ed.). (1997). *The Millon inventories: Clinical and personality assessment.* New York: Guilford Press.

Millon, T. (2000). Toward a new model of integrative psychotherapy: Psychosynergy. *Journal of Psychotherapy Integration, 10,* 37–53.

Millon, T. (with Davis, R.). (1996). *Disorders of personality: DSM-IV and beyond.* New York: Wiley.

Millon, T. (with Grossman, S., Meagher, S., Millon, C., & Everly, G.). (1999). *Personality-guided therapy.* New York: Wiley.

Millon, T., & Grossman, S. D. (2005). Personology: A theory based on evolutionary concepts. In M. Lenzenwenger (Ed.), *Major theories of personality disorders* (2nd ed.). New York: Guilford Press.

Millon, T., Grossman, S. D., Millon, C. M., Meagher, S. E., & Ramnath, R. D. (2004). *Personality disorders in modern life* (2nd ed.). New York: Wiley.

Millon, T., Meagher, D., Grossman, S. D., Millon, C. N., Ramnath, R., & Bloom, C. (in press). *Personality Series.* New York: Wiley.

Millon, T., Weiss, L., Millon, C., & Davis, R. (2003). *Millon index of personality styles-R (MIPS-R) manual.* Minneapolis, MN: Pearson Assessments.

Murray, H. A. (Ed.). (1938). *Explorations in personality.* New York: Oxford University Press.

Offer, D., & Sabshin, M. (Eds.). (1974). *Normality.* New York: Basic Books.

Offer, D., & Sabshin, M. (Eds.). (1991). *The diversity of normality.* New York: Basic Books.

Rakic, P. (1985). Limits of neurogenesis in primates. *Science, 227,* 154–156.

Rakic, P. (1988). Specification of cerebral cortical areas. *Science, 241,* 170–176.

Reisman, D. (1950). Authority and liberty in Freud's thought. *University of Chicago Round Table, 638,* 20–32.

Rogers, C. R. (1963). Toward a science of the person. *Journal of Humanistic Psychology, 3,* 79–92.

Rushton, J. P. (1985). Differential K theory: The sociobiology of individual and group differences. *Personality and Individual Differences, 6,* 441–452.

Scott, J. P. (1968). *Early experience and the organization of behavior.* Belmont, CA: Brooks/Cole.

Symons, D. (1992). On the use and misuse of Darwinism in the study of human behavior. In J. Barkow, L. Cosmides, & J. Tooby (Eds.), *The adapted mind* (pp. 137–159). New York: Oxford University Press.

Thompson, W. R., & Schaefer, T. (1961). Early environmental stimulation. In D. Fiske & S. Maddi (Eds.), *Functions of varied experience* (pp. 81–105). Homewood, IL: Dorsey.

Wachtel, P. L. (1983). Integration misunderstood. *British Journal of Clinical Psychology, 22,* 129–130.

White. R. W. (1959). Motivation reconsidered: The concept of competence. *Psychological Review, 66,* 297–323.

White, R. W. (1960). Competence and the psychosexual stages of development. In M. R. Jones (Ed.), *Nebraska symposium on motivation.* Lincoln: University of Nebraska Press.

Wilson, E. O. (1975). *Sociobiology: The new synthesis.* Cambridge, MA: Harvard University Press.

Wilson, E. O. (1978). *On human nature.* Cambridge, MA: Harvard University Press.

Wilson, E. O. (1998). *Consilience: The unity of knowledge.* New York: Knopf.

Yankelovich, D. (1981). New rules: Some implications for advertising. *Journal of Advertising Research, 22,* 9–16.

CHAPTER 2

Dynamics of Individual ←→ Context Relations in Human Development: A Developmental Systems Perspective

RICHARD M. LERNER, JACQUELINE V. LERNER, JASON ALMERIGI, AND CHRISTINA THEOKAS

Understanding of either healthy, positive, or optimal personality functioning and development or, alternatively, variations in functioning or development that might be appropriate to categorize as problematic, maladaptive, or psychopathological, rests on knowledge of what is normative in personality structure, function, and development. Such delineation of the normative is of course a standard component of the nomological requirements of any science, because deviations from normal cannot be identified without such specification. However, normative specification is problematic for scholarship about personality.

The field of personality involves the study of the mental and behavioral characteristics of the individual, and, obviously, the study of personality development involves the appraisal of individual change in these characteristics across the life span. Accordingly, it may seem true by definition that scholars of personality and of personality development adopt, implicitly if not explicitly, a person-centered approach to their theory and research. However, this is not the case. For instance, Magnusson and Stattin (in press) note that "The study of personality has often been defined as the study of individual differences. . . . [Nevertheless,] [r]esults of studying individual differences at the group level often form the basis for conclusions about functioning at the individual level." At least in part this apparently counterintuitive situation occurs because assessing an individual's characteristics and their development is complicated by two key, interrelated conceptual issues.

PROBLEMATIC 1: THE IDIOGRAPHIC-NOMOTHETIC DIMENSION

First, if a focus on the person involves an idiographic assumption, that is, that the laws governing the structure, function, and development of the person are unique to him or her, then normative specification is obviated. For instance, in regard to personality development, the presence of only idiographic laws would necessitate an ipsative (within the person) approach to developmental research in order to identify patterns of intraindividual change defining of and unique to the person (Lerner, 2002b). Such an approach to the study of personality might jeopardize the place of this field of scholarship within normal science.

In the history of the scientific study of personality and personality development, this situation could have led in to a field that was defined as one that studied the modal personality (e.g., see Benedict, 1934; Kardiner & Linton, 1939). However, by and large this did not happen. The exclusive focus on the generic human being did not occur because both theory and research indicate that all individuals possess characteristics that may be partitioned in at least three ways along a dimension defined by the end points of idiographic and nomothetic. Recalling here the Kluckhohn and Murray (1948, p. 35) framework for characterizing this situation, we may note that in certain respects every person is:

1. *Like all other people.* For instance, and consistent with an interest in the modal or normative in regard to development, some theorists believe there are universal stages of personality development (e.g., Erikson, 1959; Freud, 1954). Other theorists posit regulatory principles (e.g., the orthogenetic principle; Werner, 1948, 1957) that describe any person's structural pattern of change. In such theories, interest is in the generic human being (Emmerich, 1968), and individual differences are seen as unimportant for un-

Acknowledgments: The writing of this chapter was supported in part by grants from the National 4-H Council and from the William T. Grant Foundation. Key facets of the chapter are based on Lerner (2002b).

derstanding the fundamental laws of personality or, at best, are regarded as having marginal significance for accounting for variations in personality structure and development;

2. *Like some other people.* For instance, people's personality development may be comparable to those other individuals classifiable into various differential subgroups defined on the basis of sex, race, ethnicity, socioeconomic status, child-rearing experiences, etc. (e.g., Kagan & Moss, 1962). Here, the developmental question is how such differentiation occurs across time (and nature and/or nurture variables have been forwarded as the source of such sorting of individuals into groups), and the key structural issue has been the specification of the foundational types or basic categories (e.g., core traits) constituting human personality.

3. *Like no other person.* For instance, the particular constellation of personality or behavioral attributes possessed by a person may be singular to him or her, for example, in regard to attributes of temperamental individuality (Chess & Thomas, 1999; Thomas & Chess, 1977) or the constellation of behavioral or emotional traits (e.g., Block, 1971).

In short, then, the study of the person must involve at least in part an effort to differentiate those facets of individual functioning and development that are common to some or to all other people and those facets that are unique to the individual. However, even when this tripartite focus is acknowledged, a second conceptual issue arises in the study of personality development, one that complicates the use of idiographic, differential, or nomothetic approaches to personality, especially in regard to the assessment of systematic change across ontogeny (Emmerich, 1968).

PROBLEMATIC 2: THE CONCEPT OF DEVELOPMENT

The very meaning of the term *development* continues to engage scholars in philosophical and theoretical debate (e.g., Collins, 1982; Featherman, 1985; Ford & Lerner, 1992; Harris, 1957; Kaplan, 1983; Lerner, 2002b; Overton, 1998, 2003; Reese & Overton, 1970). The existence of the debate is itself indicative of a key feature of the meaning of the term: Development is not an empirical concept. If it were, inspection of a set of data would indicate to any observer whether development was present. However, different scientists can look at the same data set and disagree about whether development has occurred. The presence of this debate means that scholars of personality development must specify a crite-

rion by which they will differentiate between change and development.

Past concepts of development were predicated on Cartesian philosophical ideas about the character of reality that separated, or split, what was regarded as real from what was relegated to the unreal or epiphenomenal (Overton, 1998, 2003). In human development, major instances of such splitting involved classic debates about nature versus nurture as the source of development, continuity versus discontinuity as an appropriate depiction of the character of the human developmental trajectory, and stability versus instability as an adequate means to describe developmental change. Today, most major developmental theories eschew such splits and use concepts drawn from developmental systems theories (e.g., Lerner, 2002b; Overton, 1998, 2003) to depict the basic developmental process as involving relations, or fusions (Thelen & Smith, 1998; Tobach & Greenberg, 1984), between variables from the multiple levels of organization that make up the ecology of human development (e.g., see Bronfenbrenner, 2001, 2005). In contemporary developmental science, the basic process of development involves mutually influential (that is, bidirectional) relations between levels of organization ranging from biology through individual and social functioning to societal, cultural, physical, ecological, and, ultimately, historical levels of organization (e.g., Baltes, Lindenberger, & Staudinger, 1998; Elder, 1998; Ford & Lerner, 1992).

As a consequence, contemporary developmental theory transcends another split that has characterized the field of human developmental science, a split between basic science and application (Fisher & Lerner, 1994; Lerner, 2002b). The relational character of development means that some degree of change is always possible within the developmental system, as the temporality of history imbues each of the other levels of organization within the developmental system with the potential for change. Temporality means that at least relative plasticity (the potential for systematic change) exists within the integrated (fused) developmental system and that changes in the relations between individuals and their context (which may be represented as changes in individual ←→ context relations) may be instituted by entering the ecology of human development at any of its levels of organization.

Theoretically predicated attempts to change the course of development—the trajectory of individual ←→ context relations—constitute both tests of the basic, relational process of human development and (given ethical mandates to act only to enhance human development) attempts to improve the course of life. Depending on the level of organization on which such interventions into the life course are aimed (e.g., individual, families, communities, or the institutions of society), we may term such actions either programs or policies (Lerner, 2002b). Thus, from the viewpoint of the developmental systems theories that define the cutting edge of contemporary developmental science, there is no necessary distinction between research on the basic, relational process linking individuals to their multitiered ecological systems and applications aimed at promoting positive individual ←→ context relations.

Explanation of the theoretical and empirical reasons that developmental science traversed a conceptual course, from split conceptions of the basis and course of development to integrative concepts and models that emphasize the relational character of human development and the synthesis of basic and applied foci, requires a specification of the defining features of contemporary developmental science. In turn, the features of contemporary developmental science, which involve the specification of one or another variations of developmental systems theories (Lerner, 2002b), afford a means to conceptualize the individual and his or her path to health and thriving or problematic mental and behavioral functioning.

TRANSCENDING THE PROBLEMATICS OF PERSONALITY THEORY

The purpose of this chapter is to describe the development of personality in a manner than transcends the two conceptual problems we have identified. That is, in regard to the idiographic versus nomothetic issue we have described, we will present an approach to personality development that integrates both idiographic and nomothetic dimensions of the person, and thus that enables the field of personality study to remain within normal science and, as well, to embrace the importance of a focus on the person and, potentially, of the significance of the lawful and individual actions of the person in promoting his or her own positive or problematic development.

We are able to offer this integrative conception of personality functioning because, in regard to the issues surrounding the definition of development, we use dynamic, relational models of development. That is, we forward a model of individual ←→ context relations to depict the person as an active agent in his or her own development. Moreover, as we make clear in our discussion of this model, this approach to development results in a positive, indeed an optimistic, view of the potential for healthy human development. Thus, the model suggests that the appropriate way to address issues of developmental psychopathology is not to pursue prevention strategies but, rather, strategies that promote positive human development.

DEVELOPMENTAL SYSTEMS PERSPECTIVES

The power of a developmental systems perspective is constituted by four interrelated, in fact fused (Lerner, 2002b; Tobach & Greenberg, 1984), components of such theories: (1) change and relative plasticity, (2) relationism and the integration of levels of organization, (3) historical embeddedness and temporality, and (4) the limits of generalizability, diversity, and individual differences. Although these four conceptual components frame the contemporary set of developmental systems theories within the field of human development (Lerner, 1998, 2002b), each has a long and rich tradition in the history of the field (Cairns, 1998).

Change and Relative Plasticity

Developmental systems theories stress that the focus of developmental understanding must be on (systematic) change. This focus is required because of the belief that the potential for change exists across (1) the life span and (2) the multiple levels of organization that make up the ecology of humans. Although it is also assumed that systematic change is not limitless (e.g., it is constrained both by past developments and by contemporary ecological, or contextual, conditions), developmental systems theories stress that relative plasticity exists across life (Lerner, 1984).

There are important implications of relative plasticity for understanding the range of intraindividual variation that can exist over ontogeny (Lerner, in press) and for the application of development science. For instance, the presence of relative plasticity legitimates a proactive search across the life span for characteristics of people and of their contexts that, together, can influence the design of policies and programs promoting positive development (Lerner, 2004, in press). For example, the plasticity of intellectual development that is a feature of a systems view of mental functioning provides legitimization for educational policies and school- and community-based programs aimed at enhancing cognitive and social cognitive development (Dryfoos, 1994; Lerner, 2004). Such implications for the design of policies and programs stand in marked contrast to those associated with mechanistic, genetic reductionistic theories that suggest that genetic inheritance constrains intellectual development among particular minority and/or low-income groups (e.g., Hernstein & Murray, 1994; Rushton, 2000).

Relationism and the Integration of Levels of Organization

Developmental systems theories stress that the bases for change, and for both plasticity and constraints in development, lie in the relations that exist between the multiple levels of organization that make up the substance of human life (Schneirla, 1957; Tobach, 1981). These levels range from the inner biological, through the individual/psychological and the proximal social relational (e.g., involving dyads, peer groups, and nuclear families), to the sociocultural level (including key macroinstitutions such as educational, public policy, governmental, and economic systems) and the natural and designed physical ecologies of human development (Bronfenbrenner, 1979, 2001, 2005; Bronfenbrenner & Morris, 1998; Riegel, 1975). These tiers are structurally and functionally integrated, thus underscoring the use of a developmental systems view of the levels involved in human.

A developmental systems perspective promotes a relational unit of analysis as a requisite for developmental analysis: Variables associated with any level of organization exist (are structured) in relation to variables from other levels; the qualitative and quantitative dimensions of the function of any variable are shaped as well by the relations that variable has with ones from other levels. Unilevel units of analysis (or the components of, or elements in, a relation) are not an adequate target of developmental analysis; rather, the relation itself—the interlevel linkage—should be the focus of such analysis (Lerner, 1991; Magnusson, 1999a, 1999b; Magnusson & Stattin, 1998, in press; Riegel, 1975).

Relationism and integration have a clear implication for unilevel theories of development. At best, such theories are severely limited, and inevitably provide a nonveridical depiction of development, due to their focus on what are essentially main effects embedded in higher-order interactions (e.g., see Walsten, 1990). At worst, such theories are neither valid nor useful. Thus, neither nature nor nurture theories provide adequate conceptual frames for understanding human development (see Hirsch, 1970; Lewontin, 1992). Moreover, many nature-nurture interaction theories also fall short in this regard because theories of this type still treat nature and nurture variables as separable entities and view their connection in manners analogous to the interaction term in an analysis of variance (e.g., Bijou, 1976; Erikson, 1959; cf. Gollin, 1981; Gottlieb, Wahlsten, & Lickliter, 1998, in press; Hebb, 1970; Plomin, 2000; Walsten, 1990). Developmental systems theories move beyond the simplistic division of sources of development into nature-related and nurture-related variables or processes; they see the multiple levels of organization that exist within the ecology of human development as part of an inextricably fused developmental system.

Historical Embeddedness and Temporality

The relational units of analysis of concern in developmental systems theories are understood as change units. The change component of these units derives from the ideas that all of the levels of organization involved in human development are embedded in the broadest level of the person-context system: history. That is, all other levels of organization within the developmental system are integrated with historical change. History—change over time—is incessant and continuous and is a level of organization that is fused with all other levels. This linkage means that change is a necessary, and inevitable, feature of variables from all levels of organization. In addition, this linkage means that the structure, as well as the function, of variables changes over time.

Because historical change is continuous and temporality is infused in all levels of organization (Elder, 1998; Elder, Modell, & Parke, 1993), change-sensitive measures of structure and function as well as change-sensitive (i.e., longitudinal) designs are necessitated in contemporary theories of human development (Baltes, Reese, & Nesselroade, 1977; Brim & Kagan, 1980). The key questions vis-à-vis temporality in such research is not whether change occurs but whether the changes that do occur make a difference for a given developmental outcome (Lerner, Skinner, & Sorell, 1980).

Given that the study of these changes will involve appraisal of both quantitative and qualitative features of change, which may occur at multiple levels of organization, there is a need to use both quantitative and qualitative data-collection and analysis methods, ones associated with the range of disciplines having specialized expertise at the multiple levels of organization at which either quantitative or qualitative change can occur (Shweder et al., 1998). In essence, the concepts of historical embeddedness and temporality indicate that a program of developmental research adequate to address the relational, integrated, embedded, and temporal changes involved in human life must involve multiple occasions, methods, levels, variables, and cohorts (Baltes, 1987; Lerner, 1991).

A developmental systems perspective, and the implications it suggests for research, through concepts such as temporality, may seem descriptively cumbersome; inelegant (if not untestable) in regard to explanations of individual and group behavior and development; and, as a consequence, of little use in the formulation of interventions aimed at enhancing individual and social life. However, in the face of the several profound historical changes in the lives of children and their families that have occurred across this century (e.g., see Elder et al., 1993; Hernandez, 1993), it would seem, at best, implausible to maintain that the nature of the human life course has been unaffected by this history. Accordingly, it would seem necessary to adopt some sort of developmental systems perspective in order to incorporate the impact of such historical changes, and of the contemporary diversity it has created, into the matrix of covariation considered in developmental explanations and the interventions that should, at least ideally, be derived from them (Lerner & Miller, 1993).

Yet, it would be traditional in developmental psychology to assert that the historical variation and contemporary diversity of human (individual and group) development was irrelevant to understanding basic processes. Indeed, within developmental science, the conventional view of basic process, whether involving cognition, emotion, personality, or social behavior, is that it is a function generalizable across time and place. However, data such as those presented by Elder et al. (1993) and Hernandez (1993), which document the profound impact of historical change on individual and family life over the course of just the last two centuries, constitute a serious challenge to the ontological presuppositions that have grounded this view of basic process and, as such, of developmental psychology's theory and research about people's ontogenies.

The traditional view of basic process found in developmental psychology (i.e., the prototypical view for much of the last 50 to 60 years) cannot be defended in the face of the historical and contextual variation characterizing U.S. individuals and families across the past century. Indeed, without adequate tests of, and evidence for, its presuppositions about the irrelevance of temporality, context, and diversity for its view of basic process, the field of developmental psychology fails in even an attempt to represent veridically the course of human life (Cairns, 1998).

By weaving historical change and contextual specificities into the matrix of causal covariation that shapes human developmental trajectories, a developmental systems perspective reconstitutes the core process of human development, from a reductionistic and individualistic one to a synthetic, or multilevel integrated, one. Through the seemingly simple step of integrating historical change, contextual variation, and individual developmental change, a developmental systems perspective provides a paradigmatic departure from the psychogenic, biogenic, or reductionistic environmentalist models of causality that have underlain the theories of human development that have been prevalent during most of this century (Gottlieb, 1992; Lerner, 1991).

The Limits of Generalizability, Diversity, and Individual Differences

The temporality of the changing relations between levels of organization means that changes that are seen within one historical period (or time of measurement), and/or with one set of instances of variables from the multiple levels of the ecology of human development, may not be seen at other points in time (Baltes et al., 1977; Bronfenbrenner, 1979). What is seen in one data set may be only an instance of what does or

what could exist. As Magnusson and Stattin (in press) note, however, past personality research "is very ethnocentric; too often, the Western human being is regarded as the model and results are often generalized to the rest of the world, in spite of the fact that the population of the Western countries constitute only one fifth of the globe's population."

Accordingly, in recognition of the implications of the view expressed by Magnusson and Stattin (in press), contemporary theories focus on diversity—of people, of relations, of settings, and of times of measurement (Lerner, 1991, 2002b). Diversity is the exemplary illustration of the presence of relative plasticity in human development (Fisher et al., 1998; Lerner, 1984). Diversity is also the best evidence that exists of the potential for change in the states and conditions of human life (Brim & Kagan, 1980).

For instance, several studies of U.S. adolescents report that pubertal maturation alters negatively the nature of the social interactions between youth and their parents. For example, at the height of pubertal change, more conflict and greater emotional distance is seen (e.g., Steinberg, 1987; Susman & Rogol, 2004). However, these findings have been derived in large part from research with homogeneous, European American samples of adolescents and their families (Brooks-Gunn & Reiter, 1990). When diversity is introduced into the database used for understanding the links between pubertal change and adolescent-parent relationships, a much more complicated—and richer and more interesting—pattern is evident. Among samples of Latino (primarily Mexican American) boys and their families, pubertal maturation brings youth closer to their parents (Molina & Chassin, 1996). The emergence of puberty among these Latino youth is associated with greater parental social support and less intergenerational conflict than is the case either for correspondingly mature European American samples or for Latino youth prior to of after their maturation.

In essence, racial/ethnic, cultural, and developmental diversity must be understood systemically in order to appreciate the nature and variation that exists within and across time in human behavior and development (Lerner, in press; McLoyd, 1998; Spencer, in press). In other words, individual differences arise inevitably from the action of the development system; in turn, they move the system in manners that elaborate diversity further, and that therefore make individuals both more like some other people and more like no other person.

The preceding four components constitute a developmental systems perspective. This perspective leads us to recognize that, if we are to have an adequate and sufficient science of human development, we must integratively study individual and contextual levels of organization in a relational and temporal manner (Bronfenbrenner, 1974; Zigler, 1998). Developmental contextualism is an instance of developmental systems theory. Consistent with the emphases on integrative, or fused, relations between individuals and contexts found in other instances of such systems perspectives, the central idea in developmental contextualism is that changing, reciprocal relations (or dynamic interactions) between individuals and the multiple contexts within which they live make up the essential process of human development (Lerner & Kauffman, 1985).

We consider in the following section this instance of developmental systems theories. In addition, we also review another major example of such an approach to the understanding of human development, the holistic, person ←→ context interaction theory of David Magnusson (1999a, 1999b; Magnusson & Stattin, 1998, in press).

DEVELOPMENTAL CONTEXTUALISM AS AN INSTANCE OF DEVELOPMENTAL SYSTEMS THEORY

Developmental contextualism, an instance of developmental systems theory, emphasizes the integrative, or fused, relations between individuals and contexts that are envisioned in other instances of such systems perspectives. Derived from the work in biological and comparative psychology (e.g., Gottlieb, 1997; Maier & Schneirla, 1935; Schneirla, 1957; Tobach, 1981; Tobach & Greenberg, 1984), the central idea in developmental contextualism is that changing, mutually influential, and reciprocal relations (or dynamic interactions) between individuals and the multiple contexts within which they live make up the essential process of human development (Lerner & Kauffman, 1985).

These bidirectional and mutually influential relations exist between the multiple levels of organization involved in human life (e.g., biology, psychology, social groups, and culture; Bronfenbrenner, 1979; Lerner, 2002b). Each level of organization within the developmental system regulates the structure and function of the other levels in the system. As such, these dynamic relations provide a framework for the structure of human behavior (Ford & Lerner, 1992). When developmental regulations are mutually beneficial they may be termed *adaptive*. Such relations are the basis of positive human development.

The historical context is the superordinate level of organization within the developmental context (Bronfenbrenner, 2001, 2005; Bronfenbrenner & Morris, 1998, in press; Elder, 1998; Elder & Shanahan, in press), and this embeddedness means that all levels within the ecology of human development are dynamically interactive with historical changes.

This temporality provides a change component to human life and provides the basis of the potential that exists across life for systematic change—for plasticity. The presence of plasticity affords an optimistic stance about the possibility of changing the nature and course of individual ←→ context relations and of moving them in positive, healthy directions. Simply, developmental contextualism emphasizes the possibility of promoting positive human development across the life span (Baltes et al., 1998, in press; Lerner, 1984, 2002b, 2004, in press).

Thus, behavioral or mental problems in human life are not fixed or irreversible characteristics of any person or group. Instead, they represent only some portion of the potential instantiation of human development, as it is manifested along a dimension ranging from problematic to positive/healthy. We believe that, in fact, problems of human behavior and development represent only a very small proportion of the variance that exists in human life. The abundant evidence of healthy developmental trajectories between people of diverse racial, ethic, religious, physical ability, sexual preference, and cultural groups (e.g., see Lerner, in press; Lerner, Taylor, & von Eye, 2002; McAdoo, 1995; McLoyd, 1998; Savin-Williams & Diamond, 2004; Spencer, in press) may be interpreted as support for the idea that there exists an impressive array of possible pathways of positive development.

Moreover, developmental contextualism asserts that human beings are active rather than passive. As well, developmental contextualism stresses that the world around the developing person—both the physical world and the social ecology of human life—is active also. Specifically, then, in developmental contextualism the integration of (1) the actions of people in and on their world and (2) the actions of the world on people (3) shape the quality of human behavioral and psychological functioning (Brandtstädter, 1998, 1999, in press; Brandtstädter & Lerner, 1999; Lerner & Busch-Rossnagel, 1981; Lerner, Theokas, & Jelicic, in press). In essence, developmental regulation, plasticity, and optimism (about the possibility of promoting positive human development through enhancing individual ←→ context relations) are the key theoretical ideas associated with the theory—and potential application to individuals and their ecologies—of developmental contextualism.

Sources of Action in Human Development

Where do the actions that propel human development come from? It is clear that in a general sense the only sources of behavior are a person's genetic inheritance (nature) and his or her environmental experience and contextual influences (nurture). However, consistent with its conceptualization of the character of human life—of focusing on the integration of levels of organization—developmental contextualism stresses that the source of the actions involved in human development is derived from dynamic interactions between nature and nurture, that is, from developmental regulations between the levels of organization within the developmental system. That is, the biological (organismic) characteristics of the individual affect the context (e.g., adolescents who look differently as a consequence of contrasting rates of biological growth, earlier versus later maturation, elicit different social behaviors from peers and adults; e.g., Lerner, 2002a; Susman & Rogol, 2004), and, at the same time, contextual variables in the individual's world affect its biological characteristics (e.g., girls growing up in nations or at times in history with better health care and nutritional resources reach puberty earlier than girls developing is less advantaged contexts; Susman & Rogol, 2004; Tanner, 1991).

In other words, the individual has characteristics that act on the environment, and, at the same time, he or she lives in an environment that acts on his or her characteristics. Given that the individual is at the center of these reciprocal actions, he or she, through his or her actions, is a source of his or her own development (Brandtstädter, 1998, 1999, in press; Brandtstädter & Lerner, 1999; Lerner & Busch-Rossnagel, 1981; Lerner et al., in press). In short, in developmental contextualism, there is a third source of development—the individual (cf. Schneirla, 1957).

These dynamic changes may involve both quantitative and qualitative changes in the processes of development. For instance, processes involved with a person's perceptual, motivational, or cognitive development undergo changes in kind, or type (quality), and in amount, frequency, magnitude, or duration (quantity). This conception of change does not deny that there are some aspects of a person that remain the same across life; rather, it asserts that human development is a synthesis between changes and processes and variables that remain constant (Brim and Kagan 1980). Moreover, because of the integration of the levels of organization of human life, developmental contextualism asserts that the laws that govern the functioning of both constancy and change are related both to an organism's biology (e.g., heredity) and to its environment (e.g., experience). Within the relational conception of the actions of levels of organization found in developmental contextualism, these two sets of factors (heredity and environment) are fused in behavioral development.

Logically, there are several possible ways that heredity and environment can be related to each other (Anastasi, 1958; Lerner 2002b; Overton 1973; Schneirla, 1956). It is possible that either heredity or environment might act alone as a source of behavioral development. It may be the case that the contribution of heredity is added to the contribution of the environment. Gottlieb (1997, 1998, 2004; Gottlieb et al., 1998, in press), Hirsch (1997, 2004), and Lerner (2002b, in press) note that these two possible ways in which nature- and nurture-related variables (or levels of organizations) may be related are both conceptually flawed and counterfactual (see also Garcia Coll, Bearer, & Lerner, 2004). Accordingly, these possibilities, which form the basis of both the behavioral genetics (e.g., Plomin, 2000; Rende, 2004; Rowe, 1994) and the sociobiological (e.g., Rushton, 2000) views of human development, may be rejected for the presence of these egregious scientific flaws. As such, another interpretation of the relation between nature and nurture must be sought.

A third possibility is that heredity and environment may be related to each other in a multiplicative, or interactionist, manner. This last alternative is the one pursued within developmental contextualism. However, many different types of interaction may occur. For instance, Lerner and Spanier (1980) and Lerner (2002b) have identified three such types, labeling them weak, moderate, and strong (see also Overton, 1973). Developmental contextualism advances a model of strong interactions, wherein the components of any relation (e.g., between genes and the intraorganism or extraorganism context or between the individual and the context) are part of a superordinate, enmeshed (fused) system; discussion of the parts of the system may be convenient for analytic or methodological reasons (e.g., see Gollin, 1981; Overton, 1998), but the reality of the system is that parts exist only in relation (Thelen & Smith, 1998, in press).

In other words, components cannot exist apart from, and in fact are defined by, their relation to (integration in) the system (Gollin, 1981; Gottlieb, 1997; Tobach & Greenberg, 1984). It is important to discuss the details of this admittedly more complex—but veridical (Gottlieb, 1997, 1998, 2004; Gottlieb et al., 1998, in press)—view of the relations between biological and contextual levels of organization.

Probabilistic Epigenesis: The Conception of Nature ←→ Nurture Relation within Developmental Contextualism

Developmental contextualism takes what Gottlieb (1970, 1992, 1998, 2004) terms a *probabilistic epigenetic* view of biological functioning. Biological and contextual factors are considered to be reciprocally interactive, and developmental changes are probabilistic in respect to normative outcomes due to variation in the timing of the biological, psychological, and social factors (or levels) that provide interactive bases of ontogenetic progressions (e.g., Schneirla, 1957; Tobach, 1981).

The developmental contextual conception of development can be traced to comparative biology (Novikoff, 1945a, 1945b) and comparative psychology (e.g., Gottlieb, 1970, 1992, 1997, 1998; Kuo, 1976; Maier & Schneirla, 1935; Schneirla, 1957). In this literature, the concept of probabilistic epigenesis is not used to emphasize intrinsically predetermined or inevitable time tables and outcomes of development; instead, probabilistic epigenesis stressed that the influence of the changing context on development is to make the trajectory of development less certain with respect to the applicability of norms to the individual (e.g., Gottlieb, 1970, 1997, 1998; Tobach, 1981).

Thus, such a conception emphasizes the probabilistic character of both the directions and outcomes of development, and in so doing it recognizes more plasticity in development than do conceptions that contend that there is a predetermined part to developmental change that is set by a genetically fixed maturational timetable (e.g., Erikson, 1959; Hamburger, 1957). The probabilistic (yet causal) interaction between levels of organization within the ecology of human development (Bronfenbrenner, 1979, 2001, 2005) make both continuity and/or discontinuity a probabilistic feature of developmental change across life periods.

Probabilism in continuity and discontinuity is stressed because, as noted by Gottlieb (1970, p. 123), "behavioral development of individuals within a species does not follow an invariant or inevitable course, and, more specifically, . . . the sequence or outcome of individual behavioral development is probable (with respect to norms) rather than certain." Of course, it is possible to ask whether all instances of continuity and discontinuity have an equal probability of occurrence. As explained by Thelen and Smith (1998; see also Ford & Lerner, 1992), this is not the case. Within a dynamic developmental system, the dialectic between system-changing and system-constraining relations reduces the degrees of freedom available for change; thus the potentially infinite instances of change that could exist within a dynamic, open, and living system are reduced through the self-organizing actions of the system.

Development occurs in a multilevel context. The nature of the changes in this context contributes to the probabilistic character of development; but one needs to appreciate also that the organism as much shapes the context as the context shapes the organism, and that, at the same time, both organism and context constrain, or limit, the other. In other words, the processes that give humans their individuality and their plasticity are the same ones that provide their commonality and constancy (Lerner, 1984, 2002b).

Here, another key point about the developmental contextual view needs to be highlighted. Although, in attempting to explain development, both this conception and mechanistic-behavioral views (e.g., Baer, 1976; Bijou & Baer, 1961; Gewirtz & Stingle, 1968) conceive of the context as enveloping an organism, it is clear that they do so in distinctly different ways. Developmental contextual theorists do not adopt a reductionistic approach to conceptualizing the impact of the context (Tobach, 1981). Instead, there is a focus on organism ←→ context transactions (Sameroff, 1975), a commitment to using an interlevel, or relational, unit of analysis (Lerner, 1984, 2002b), and, as emphasized previously, a concept of the context as composed of multiple, qualitatively different levels (e.g., see Bronfenbrenner, 1979, 2001, 2005; Riegel, 1975).

Moreover, although both the mechanistic and the developmental contextual perspectives hold that changes in the context become part of interindividual changes in the organism's constitution, the concept of organism found in the two perspectives is also quite distinct. The individual in developmental contextualism is not merely the host of the elements of a simplistic environment (e.g., as in Baer, 1976). Instead, the organism is itself a qualitatively distinct level within the multiple, dynamically interacting levels forming the context of life. As such, the organism has a distinct influence on the multilevel context that is influencing it. The organism is an active contributor to its own development (Brandtstädter, 1998, 1999, in press; Lerner, 1982; Lerner & Busch-Rossnagel, 1981; Lerner et al., in press; Lerner & Walls, 1999).

Figure 2.1 presents the developmental contextual view of person ←→ context relations (represented in the figure by child ←→ parent relations) seen from the perspective of this instance of developmental systems theory (Lerner, 2002b, 2004).

As shown in this figure, the inner and outer worlds of a child are fused and dynamically interactive. The same may be said of the parent depicted in the figure and, in fact, of the parent-child relationship. Each of these foci—child, parent, and/or parent-child relationship—is part of a larger, enmeshed system of fused relations between the multiple levels that compose the ecology of human life (Bronfenbrenner, 1979, 2001, 2005; Bronfenbrenner & Morris, 1998, in press). For instance, Figure 2.1 illustrates the idea that both parent and child are embedded in a broader social network and that each person has reciprocal reactions within this network. This set of relationships occurs because both the child and the parent are much more than just people playing only one role in life. The child may also be a sibling, a peer, and a student; the parent may also be a spouse, a worker, and an adult child. All of these networks of relationships are embedded within a particular community, society, and culture. Finally, all of

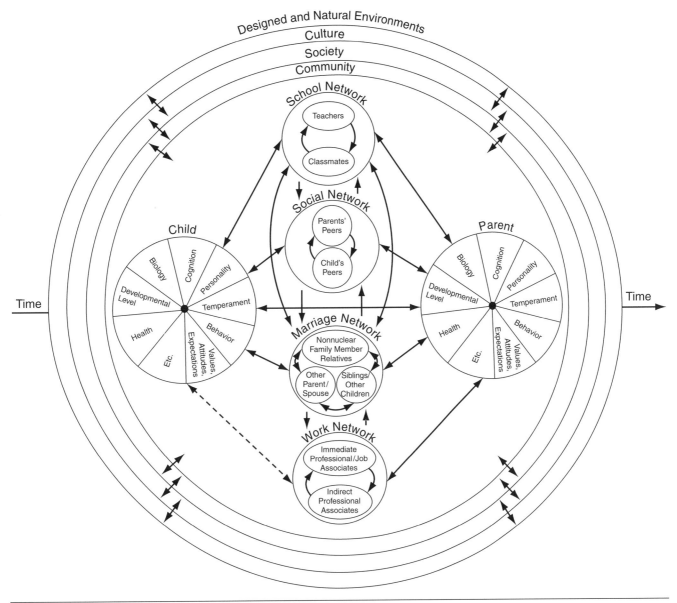

Figure 2.1   A model of the developmental contextual view of human development. The dashed lines between the work network and the child is used to denote that in many contemporary industrialized settings for child development, the young person may not enter the workforce until after the childhood years.

these relationships are continually changing across time and history.

Thus, Figure 2.1 illustrates also that the child-parent relationship and the social networks in which it is located are embedded in still larger community, societal, cultural, and historical levels of organization. Moreover, the arrow of time—history—cuts through all the systems. This feature of the model underscores the idea that, as with the people populating the social systems, change is always occurring. Diversity within time is created as changes across time (across history) occur. As depicted in Figure 2.1, such diversity in-

troduces variation into all the levels of organization involved in the system. As such, the nature of parent-child relationships, of family life and development, and of societal and cultural influences on the child-parent-family system are influenced by both normative and nonnormative historical changes (Baltes, 1987; Baltes et al., 1998) or, in other words, by evolutionary (i.e., gradual) and revolutionary (i.e., abrupt; Werner, 1957) historical changes.

It is useful to illustrate how the developmental contextual theory illustrated in Figure 2.1 may be used to understand the developmental import of the mutually influential individual ←→ context relations that structure the course of the life span. To do this, we discuss one model of individual ←→ context relations that has framed research about the relational bases of positive or problematic outcomes of the process of development.

The Goodness of Fit Model

Just as a child brings his or her characteristics of individuality to a particular social setting there are demands placed on the child by virtue of the social and physical components of the setting. These demands may take the form of: (1) attitudes, values, or stereotypes that are held by others in the context regarding the person's attributes (either his or her physical or behavioral characteristics); (2) the attributes (usually behavioral) of others in the context with whom the child must coordinate, or fit, his or her attributes (also, in this case, usually behavioral) for adaptive interactions to exist; or, (3) the physical characteristics of a setting (e.g., the presence or absence of access ramps for the motorically handicapped) that require the child to possess certain attributes (again, usually behavioral abilities) for the most efficient interaction within the setting to occur.

The child's individuality, in differentially meeting these demands, provides a basis for the specific feedback he or she gets from the socializing environment. For example, considering the demand domain of attitudes, values, or stereotypes, teachers and parents may have relatively individual and distinct expectations about behaviors desired of their students and children, respectively. Teachers may want students who show little distractibility, but parents might desire their children to be moderately distractible, for example, when they require their children to move from television watching to dinner or to bed. Children whose behavioral individuality was either generally distractible or generally not distractible would thus differentially meet the demands of these two contexts. Problems of adjustment to school or to home might thus develop as a consequence of a child's lack of match (or goodness of fit) in either or both settings.

Thomas and Chess (e.g., 1977; Chess & Thomas, 1999) and Lerner and Lerner (e.g., 1983) have forwarded ideas and conducted research pertinent to the role of individual ←→ context fit in moderating positive or negative outcomes of development in childhood and adolescence. Thomas and Chess and Lerner and Lerner have found that if a child's characteristics of individuality provide a good fit (or match) with the demands of a particular setting, adaptive outcomes will accrue in that setting. Those children whose characteristics match most of the settings within which they exist receive supportive or positive feedback from the contexts and

show evidence of the most adaptive behavioral development. In turn, of course, poorly fit, or mismatched, children, those whose characteristics are incongruent with one or most settings, appear to show alternative developmental outcomes.

But what are the precise competencies a child must possess to attain a good fit within and across time? To competently attain an adaptive fit a child must be able to evaluate appropriately: (1) the demands of a particular context, (2) his or her psychological and behavioral characteristics, and (3) the degree of match that exists between the two. In addition, other cognitive and behavioral skills are necessary. The child has to have the ability to select and gain access to those contexts with which there is a high probability of match and to avoid those contexts where poor fit is likely. In addition, in contexts that cannot usually be selected—for example, family of origin or assigned elementary school class— the child has to have the knowledge and skills necessary either to change him or herself to fit the demands of the setting or, in turn, to alter the context to better fit his or her attributes (e.g., Lerner & Lerner, 1983; Mischel, 1977). Moreover, in most contexts multiple types of demands will impinge on the person, and not all of them will provide identical presses. As such, the child needs to be able to detect and evaluate such complexity and to judge which demand it will be best to adapt to when all cannot be met.

This point is underscored by findings reported by Eccles and her colleagues (e.g., Eccles, 1991; Eccles & Harold, 1996; Eccles, Lord, & Buchanan, 1996; Eccles & Midgley, 1989; Eccles, Midgley, et al., 1993; Fuligni, Eccles, & Barber, 1995; Midgley, Feldlaufer, & Eccles, 1989a, 1989b). Through a focus on young adolescents and their transition from elementary school to either junior high or middle school, Eccles and her colleagues have offered a theoretically nuanced and empirically highly productive approach to understanding the significance for development of person ←→ context fit. In particular, they have demonstrated the importance for achievement motivation and academic achievement of goodness of fit between young adolescents and their school environment.

For instance, there may be effects of the transition from elementary school to junior high school or middle school on students' academic performance or on their academic feelings and motivation that may be due in part to the poorness of fit between the students' orientation to learning and the organization and curriculum of the junior high or middle school (Eccles & Midgley, 1989; Eccles et al., 1996; Eccles, Wigfield, Midgley, et al., 1993).

To account for such findings, Eccles et al. (1996) explain that the theory of person-environment fit within which this work is embedded proposes that "behavior, motivation, and mental health are influenced by the fit between the characteristics individuals bring to their social environments and the characteristics of these social environments. Individuals are not likely to do very well, or be very motivated, if they are in social environments that do not fit their psychological needs" (p. 254).

Accordingly, this model of person-context fit leads Eccles et al. (1996) to predict that "If the social environments in the typical junior high school do not fit very well with the psychological needs of adolescents, then person-environment fit theory predicts a decline in the adolescents' motivation, interest, performance, and behavior as they move into this environment" (p. 254). Indeed, Eccles et al. (1996) note that there is considerable "evidence that such a negative change in the school environment occurs with the transition to junior high school" (p. 254) and that "The nature of these environmental changes, coupled with the normal course of individual development, is likely to result in a developmental mismatch so that the 'fit' between the early adolescent and the classroom environment is particularly poor, increasing the risk of negative motivational outcomes, especially for adolescents who are already having difficulty succeeding in school academically" (p. 258).

In sum, as the child develops competency in self-regulation (Brandtstädter, 1998, 1999; Eccles, Early, Frasier, Belansky, & McCarthy, 1997; Heckhausen, 1999), he or she will be able to become an active selector and shaper of the contexts within which he or she develops. Thus, as the child's agency (Bakan, 1966) develops, it will become increasingly true that he or she rears his or her parents as much as they do him or her (Lerner, 2003). More generally, and across contextual settings, individuals, through the mutually influential relations they have with their ecology, act as potent sources of their own development.

Conclusions

Developmental contextualism incorporates the ideas of dynamic interaction, levels of integration, and self-organization associated with other instances of open, living, developmental systems theories of human development (Ford & Lerner, 1992) and emphasizes that through developmental regulations—individual ←→ context relations—potential plasticity may be actualized. As we have emphasized, such possibilities allow both scholars and practitioners to be optimistic that positive or healthy relations (e.g., fits) between individuals and contexts may exist or may be created to prevent problems and to promote positive human development. As such, scholarship framed by such a model eschews reductionism, unilevel assessments of the individual, and time-insensitive and atemporal analyses of human development. Instead, integrative/holistic, relational, and change-oriented research focused on the individual-in-context (e.g., Magnusson, 1985, 1999a, 1999b; Magnusson & Stattin, 1998) research is promoted.

Although the developmental contextual approach represents an important example of the family of developmental systems theories, there are other theories that are also quite influential. One very significant instance of such a theory has been formulated by David Magnusson who, over the course of more than a quarter century, has made innovative and articulate contributions to scholarship about developmental systems and—most centrally—of the importance of adopting a person-centered approach to the study of personality.

DAVID MAGNUSSON'S HOLISTIC PERSON ←→ CONTEXT INTERACTION THEORY

Magnusson's theoretical formulations and research programs have emphasized the fundamental role of context in human behavior and development (e.g., Magnusson, 1995, 1999a, 1999b; Magnusson & Stattin, 1998). His intellectual vision includes a compelling conceptual rationale and substantive basis for internationally contextualized, comparative scholarship (e.g., Magnusson, 1995, 1999a, 1999b) and is built on four conceptual pillars: interactionism, holism, interdisciplinarity, and the longitudinal study of the person.

These themes emerge in Magnusson's theory, which stresses the synthesis, or fusion, of the person-environment system. Magnusson seeks to understand the structures and processes involved in the operation of this system and the way in which the individual behaves and develops within it. Given this integrative emphasis on person and context, Magnusson (1995) terms his theory a *holistic approach*. He states that:

> The individual is an active, purposeful part of an integrated, complex, and dynamic person-environment system. Furthermore, within this person-environment system, the individual develops and functions as an integrated, complex, and dynamic totality. Consequently, it is not possible to understand how social systems function without knowledge of individual functioning, and it is not possible to understand individual functioning and development without knowledge of the environment. (Magnusson & Stattin, 1998, pp. 685–686)

Causality in Holistic Interactionism

To Magnusson, then, as is seen also in respect to the theories of Schneirla (1957), Kuo (1976), Gottlieb (1997), and Thelen and Smith (1998), the cause of development—the emergence of novel forms across life—is an outcome of the coactions of the components of the dynamic, person-context system. This self-organizational source of developmental change stands in contrast either to the unidirectional, single source (nature or nurture) or to the weak or moderate interactional ideas regarding the causes of development.

In what Magnusson terms the modern interactionist perspective, or the holistic interactionist viewpoint, the basis of development lies in two types of interaction: inner interactions, involving bidirectional relationships between biological, psychological, and behavioral characteristics; and outer, person-context interactions, involving continual exchanges between the person and his or her environment. Magnusson explains that holistic interaction builds and extends the ideas of interactionism found in what he terms *classical interactionism* (Magnusson & Stattin, 1998, p. 694).

Holistic interactionism expands upon this classic conception of interaction by, first, placing greater emphasis on the dynamic, integrated character of the individual within the overall person-environment system and, second, stressing both biological and behavioral action components of the system. Thus, and drawing on many of the same literatures relied on by Gottlieb (e.g., in regard to neuropsychology and developmental biology, e.g., Damasio & Damasio, 1996) and by Thelen and Smith (e.g., in regard to chaos and general systems theory, e.g., von Bertalanffy, 1968), and buttressed by what Magnusson (1995, 1999a, 1999b) sees as the growing importance of holistically oriented longitudinal studies of human development (e.g., Cairns & Cairns, 1994), Magnusson and Stattin (1998, p. 694) specify the four basic propositions of holistic interaction:

1. The individual functions and develops as a total, integrated organism.
2. Individual functioning within existing mental, biological, and behavioral structures, as well as development change, can best be described as complex, dynamic processes.
3. Individual functioning and development are guided by processes of continuously ongoing, reciprocal interactions between mental, behavioral, and biological aspects of individual functioning and social, cultural, and physical aspects of the environment.
4. The environment, including the individual, functions and changes as a continuously ongoing process of reciprocal interactions between social, economic, and cultural factors.

Features of the Person-Environment System

The holistic interactionist theory has profound implications for the conduct of developmental science. Indeed, the far-

reaching character of these implications extends even to the role of the concept of variable in developmental research.

Magnusson and Stattin (1998) note that in most approaches to developmental science the concept of variable is embedded within a theoretically reductionistic model of humans. Within this perspective, the variable becomes the unit of analysis in developmental research. However, within the context of what they term the *holistic principle,* Magnusson and Stattin (1998) forward a person-centered view of development and, as such, forward the individual, the whole person, as the core unit of developmental analysis. That is, the holistic principle

> emphasizes an approach to the individual and the person-environment system as organized wholes, functioning as totalities.... The totality derives its characteristic features and properties from the interaction among the elements involved, not from the effect of each isolated part on the totality. (Magnusson & Stattin, 1998, p. 698)

Accordingly, if the totality, the whole person or, better, the person-environment relation, characterizes the essence of developmental change, then developmental analysis that assesses single aspects of the system (single variables, for instance) are necessarily incomplete. Only a distorted view of development can be derived from appraising variables divorced from the context of other, simultaneously acting variables (Magnusson & Stattin, 1998, in press). It is this integration of variables from across the person-environment system that constitutes the core process of human development and, as such, the necessary focus of developmental science.

Indeed, within the holistic interactionist theory the developmental process involves a continual flow of integrated, reciprocally related events. Time becomes a fundamental feature of individual development given that, within the probabilistic epigenetic view taken by Magnusson (1995, 1999a, 1999b) of the interrelation of the constituent events that make up the process of development, the same event occurring at different times in ontogeny will have varying influences on behavior and development. As a consequence, "A change in one aspect affects related parts of the subsystem and, sometimes, the whole organism. At a more general level, the restructuring of structures and processes at the individual level is embedded in and is part of the restructuring of the total person-environment system" (Magnusson & Stattin, 1998, p. 700).

Thus, to Magnusson (1995, 1999a, 1999b; Magnusson & Stattin, 1998, in press), individual development is marked by a continual restructuring of existing patterns and, through the facilitation and constraint of the biological through sociocultural levels of the total person-environment system, the emergence of new structures and processes. In other words, as also specified within the Thelen and Smith (1998) dynamic systems theory, novelty in structures and processes, in forms and patterns, arises through principles of system self-organization. Indeed, self-organization is a guiding principle within the developmental systems theory proposed by Magnusson. Thus, development, novelty, arises in the living world because the parts of the organism produce each other and, as such, through their association create the whole (Magnusson & Stattin, 1998, in press).

Also consistent with the theories of Gottlieb (1997), Thelen and Smith (1998), and others (Lerner, 1991, 2002b; Schneirla, 1957; Tobach & Greenberg, 1984) is Magnusson's view (1995, 1999a, 1999b; Magnusson & Endler, 1977) of the character of the relation between the components of this system: That is, holistic interaction is synonymous with dynamic interaction. Indeed, Magnusson and Stattin (1998, p. 701) note that, "Dynamic interaction among operating factors is a fundamental characteristic of the processes of all living organisms *at all levels* . . . from the interaction that takes place between single cells in the early development of the fetus . . . to the individual's interplay with his or her environment across the lifespan."

Magnusson (1995, 1999a, 1999b; Magnusson & Stattin, 1998) notes that there are two key concepts that are involved in understanding the character of dynamic interaction: reciprocity and nonlinearity. Magnusson and Stattin (1998) point to data on the mutual influences of parents and children (e.g., Lerner, 2003) as the best illustration of reciprocity in the person-environment system. Similar to Schneirla's (1957) idea of circular functions, Magnusson and Stattin note that reciprocity occurs in parent-child interactions as the behavior of each person in the relationship act as an influence on the behavior of the other person and, at the same time, change as a consequence of the influence of the other person's behavior.

As do Thelen and Smith (1998), Magnusson (1995, 1999a, 1999b; Magnusson & Stattin, 1998, in press) notes that non-linearity is the prototypical characteristic of the relationship between constituents of the person-environment system. Nonsystems perspectives typically approach scholarship with the perspective that the relationship between variables is linear and, as well, that linear relations between variables that are identified by appraising differences between people may be generalized to the relations that exist between variables within a person (Magnusson & Stattin, 1998, in press). However, increases (or decreases) in one variable are not always accompanied by proportional increases (or decreases) in another variable, either across people or within individuals.

That is, rather than finding such linear changes to be ubiquitous, changes in one variable may be accompanied by disproportionate changes in another variable. Such relationships are curvilinear in character and, for instance, may take the form of U- or inverted U-shaped functions. For example, low levels of stress may not provide enough impetus to elicit high levels of performance on a given task or skill; high levels of stress may overwhelm the person and produce performance paralysis rather than high-level performance; but moderate levels of stress may be associated with the greatest likelihood of high-level performance (Magnusson & Stattin, 1998, in press; Strauss, 1982).

Together, the notions of reciprocity and nonlinearity associated with dynamic interaction underscore the bidirectional causality involved in the developmental system envisioned by Magnusson (1995, 1999a, 1999b) and return us to the point that his model challenges the key concepts of nonsystems approaches to human development, even insofar as fundamental notions, such as the definition of the concept of variable, are concerned:

> The concepts of independent and dependent variables, and of predictors and criteria, lose the absolute meaning that they have in traditional research, which assumes unidirectional causality. What may function as a criterion or dependent variable at a certain stage of a process may, at the next stage, serve as a predictor or independent variable. (Magnusson & Stattin, 1998, p. 702)

Moreover, Magnusson's theory changes the emphasis in developmental science from one of a search for information that will allow generalizations to be made about how variables function across individuals to one of attempting to understand how variables function within the person. That is, because of the nonlinear relation between variables within the individual, and because the individual's internal distinctiveness is both a product and a producer of his or her distinct pattern of exchanges with the other levels of organization within the total person-environment system, individual differences are a fundamental feature of human development. Indeed, in order to understand the development of the individual, one must identify the particular factors that are pertinent to his or her life and the specific ways these factors are organized and operate within him or her (Magnusson & Stattin, 1998, in press). In short, "developmental changes do not take place in single aspects isolated from the totality. The total individual changes in a lawful way over time; individuals, not variables, develop" (Magnusson & Stattin, 1998, p. 727).

The complexity of this person-centered analysis is underscored when, as Magnusson (1995, 1999a, 1999b; Magnusson & Stattin, 1998, in press) explains, one understands that the contextual component of the person-environment system is as multifaceted and individualistic as are the levels of organization having their primary loci within the individual (e.g., biology, cognition, personality, behavior). That is:

> The total, integrated, and organized system, of which the individual forms a part, consists of a hierarchical system of elements, from the cellular level of the individual to the macro level of environments. . . . In actual operation, the role and functioning of each element in the total person-environment system depends on its context *within each level*. Each level of the system is simultaneously a totality seen in relation to lower levels, and a subsystem in relation to higher levels. Systems at *different levels* are mutually interdependent. (Magnusson & Stattin, 1998, p. 705)

Magnusson and Stattin (1998, in press) depict the complexity of these contextual components of the person-environment system by noting that the environment may be differentiated on the basis of its physical and social dimensions and that a person may be influenced by either the actual or the perceived features of these two dimensions or both. Either dimension may serve as a source of stimulation for behavior and/or a resource for information. In addition, environments may differ in the extent to which they provide an optimal context for healthy development and in regard to the extent to which they serve over time as a basis for developmental change (i.e., as a formative environment; Magnusson & Stattin, 1998) or as a source for a specific behavior at a particular point in time (i.e., as a triggering environment; Magnusson & Stattin, 1998).

In addition, environments may be differentiated on the basis of their proximal or distal relationship to the person. For instance, the family or the peer group may constitute proximal contexts for the person, whereas social policies pertinent to family resources (e.g., policies regarding welfare benefits for poor families) may be part of the distal context of human development (Bronfenbrenner & Morris, 1998).

Conclusions

When the complexity of the environment is coupled with the multiple dimensions of the person (e.g., his or her biology; mental system; subconscious processes; values, norms, motives, and goals; self-structures and self-perceptions; and behavioral characteristics; Magnusson & Stattin, 1998, in press), the need for a holistic, integrated theory of the developmental system is apparent. This system must be engaged in order to understand the course of human development and to enhance or optimize it. Consistent with our earlier discussions of the implications of plasticity for intervention to enhance the course of human life, Magnusson sees the need to

involve all levels of the person and the system to not only design a comprehensive scientific research agenda but to devise strategies to apply developmental science in ways that will integratively promote positive human change:

> The holistic interactionistic view on individual functioning and development, as advocated here, implies that in the development of societal programs for intervention and treatment, the total person-environment system must be considered, not single problems of individual functioning and single risk factors in the social context. . . . Multiple agencies, programs, and initiatives must be integrated if the breadth of the person-context system is to be adequately engaged. (Magnusson & Stattin, 1998, p. 740)

Thus, Magnusson's ideas about holistic interaction underscore the integral connection between science and application involved in a developmental systems perspective. His views of the scientific and societal utility of such theories, which are consistent with, and buttressed by, the ideas of other developmental systems theorists (e.g., Baltes et al., 1998), underscore the importance of transcending the basic science–applied science split and in discussing the integral role that application plays in contemporary theory in human developmental science.

DEVELOPMENTAL SYSTEMS THEORIES AND THE APPLICATION OF DEVELOPMENTAL SCIENCE

A focus on person-context relations underscores the key implications of developmental systems models for research and application pertinent to promoting positive human development. At any given point in ontogenetic and historical time, neither individuals' attributes nor the features of their context per se are the foremost predictors of their healthy functioning. Instead, the relations between the child, the parent, the school, the community, and the other levels of organization within the developmental system are most important in understanding the character of human development and the role of the ecology of human development in a person's ontogeny.

Framed within a developmental systems theoretical perspective, Fisher et al. (1993) summarized the five conceptual components that, together, characterize the core principles of applied developmental science (ADS). Taken together, these conceptual principles make ADS a unique approach to understanding and promoting positive development.

The first conceptual component of ADS is the notion of the temporality, or historical embeddedness, of change pertinent to individuals, families, institutions, and communities. Some components of the context or of individuals remain stable over time and other components may change historically. Because phenomena of human behavior and development vary historically, one must assess whether generalizations across time periods are legitimate. Thus, temporality has important implications for research design, service provision, and program evaluation.

Elder's (1974) research on the children of the Great Depression provides an important example of this first conceptual component of ADS. For instance, Elder found that experiencing the Great Depression during one's childhood affected adult views of the family and of issues about economic security. Accordingly, without a design that embeds a person's development within a historical context, the nature of the challenges they faced would not be adequately understood and programs and policies could not be most effectively designed.

Interventions are aimed at altering the developmental trajectory of within-person changes. To accomplish this aim, the second conceptual feature of ADS is that applied developmental scientists take into account interindividual differences (diversity) among, for instance, racial, ethnic, social class, and gender groups, and intraindividual changes, such as those associated with pubertal maturation or with aging.

An example of the importance of diversity for intervention can be found in the research of Magnusson and Stattin (1998). The impact of puberty on delinquency and norm-breaking behavior varies in relation to individual differences in both timing of puberty and the nature of the peer context in which development is embedded. Specifically, early-maturing girls are more likely to break norms for substance abuse when embedded in peer groups composed of girls older than themselves than when embedded in peer groups composed of girls of the same age.

The third conceptual feature of ADS places an emphasis on the centrality of context. There is a focus on the relations between all levels of organization within the ecology of human development. These levels involve biology, families, peer groups, schools, businesses, neighborhoods and communities, physical/ecological settings, and the sociocultural, political, legal/moral, and economic institutions of society. Together, bidirectional relations between these levels of the developmental system necessitate systemic approaches to research, program and policy design, and program and policy implementation.

A key example of the importance of considering the context in attempts to understand individual development comes from the work of Eccles, Wigfield, and Byrnes (2003), who point to the importance of understanding stage-environment fit when interpreting the impact of school curricula and curricula change on adolescent motivation. Similarly, as noted earlier, considerable data indicate that a goodness of fit between infant or child temperament and the demands for behavior present in the home or school, respectively, provide a basis for infant and child adjustment and positive development (e.g., Chess & Thomas, 1999).

The fourth principle of ADS emphasizes descriptively normative developmental processes, and primary prevention and optimization rather than remediation. Applied developmental scientists emphasize healthy and normative developmental processes and seek to identify the strengths and assets of individuals, groups, and settings rather than focusing on deficits, weaknesses, or problems of individuals, families, or communities. Although not denying that problems exist, or the need to reduce or prevent them, the developmental systems orientation of applied developmental scientists leads to a focus on the relative plasticity of development and to the adoption of the view that problems represent only a proportion (and probably a small one) of the range of outcomes of person-context relations. Accordingly, instead of dwelling on the problems faced by people, applied developmental scientists seek to find combinations of individual and ecological assets associated with thriving among people (e.g., Scales, Benson, Leffert, & Blyth, 2000) and with the Five Cs of positive individual development: competence, confidence, connection, character, and caring/compassion (e.g., Lerner, 2004).

The final principle of applied developmental science is the appreciation of the bidirectional relationship between knowledge generation and knowledge application. By acknowledging bidirectionality, applied developmental scientists recognize the importance of knowledge about life and development that exists among the individuals, families, and communities being served by applied developmental science. For applied developmental scientists, collaboration and co-learning between researchers/universities and communities are essential features of the scholarly enterprise. Such community-collaborative efforts are termed *outreach scholarship* (Lerner & Miller, 1998).

In other words, given the developmental systems perspective on which ADS is predicated, applied developmental scientists assume that:

> there is an interactive relationship between science and application. Accordingly, the work of those who generate empirically based knowledge about development and those who provide professional services or construct policies affecting individuals and families is seen as reciprocal in that research and theory guide intervention strategies and the evaluation of interventions and policies provides the bases for reformulating theory and future research. . . . As a result, applied developmental [scientists] not

only disseminate information about development to parents, professionals, and policy makers working to enhance the development of others, they also integrate the perspectives and experiences of these members of the community into the reformulation of theory and the design of research and interventions. (Fisher & Lerner, 1994, p. 7)

In sum, the developmental systems model specifies that applied developmental scholarship pertinent to understanding and enhancing the life course should focus on the relational process of human development by integrating longitudinally the study both of the actions of the individual and of the actions of parents, peers, teachers, neighbors, and the broader institutional context within which the individual is embedded. Bearing in mind the centrality of this complex relational system, the synthetic research and application agenda seem clear. Applied developmental scientists must continue to educate themselves about the optimal means available to promote positive human development, for example, through enhancing the goodness of fit among the integrations within the developmental system, and they must strive to seek ways to translate this knowledge into policies and programs that enhance the life chances among all individuals and families, but especially among those whose potential for positive contributions to civil society is most in danger of being wasted (Dryfoos, 1990; Hamburg, 1992; Lerner, 2002b, 2004; Schorr, 1997). The key challenge in such efforts is to generate scientifically rigorous evaluations of the usefulness of the policies and the programs associated with the application of developmental science and, as well, to promote the use of such information in the day-to-day operation of programs and the actions of policy makers (e.g., Jacobs, 1988; Jacobs, Wertlieb, & Lerner, 2003).

CONCLUSIONS

The concepts and theories we have reviewed illustrate that the power of developmental systems theories lies in their ability not to be limited by a unidimensional portrayal of the developing person. In developmental systems theories the person is neither biologized, psychologized, nor sociologized. Rather, the individual is systemized, that is, his or her development is embedded within an integrated matrix of variables derived from multiple levels of organization; development is conceptualized as deriving from the dynamic relations between the variables within this multitiered matrix. Development is a matter of individual ←→ context relations, and positive and healthy human development occurs when all components of these relations are benefiting.

Developmental systems theories use the polarities that engaged developmental theory in the past (e.g., nature/nurture, individual/society, biology/culture; Lerner, 2002b) but not to split depictions of developmental processes along conceptually implausible and empirically counterfactual lines (Overton, 1998) or to force counterproductive choices between false opposites; rather, these issues are used to gain insight into the integrations that exist between the multiple levels of organization involved in human development. These theories are certainly more complex than their one-sided predecessors; however, they are also more nuanced, more flexible, more balanced, and less susceptible to extravagant, or even absurd, claims (for instance, that nature, split from nurture can shape the course of human development; that there is a gene for altruism, militarism, intelligence, and even television watching; or that when the social context is demonstrated to affect development the influence can be reduced to a genetic one; e.g., Hamburger, 1957; Lorenz, 1966; Plomin, 2000; Rowe, 1994; Rushton, 2000).

These mechanistic and atomistic views of the past have been replaced by the sorts of theoretical models considered in this chapter. The person—and the attributes of individuality that define his or her personality and that promote its health or psychopathology—derives from a dynamic synthesis of multiple levels of analysis. Developmental systems theories stress that personality and its development are properties of systemic changes in the multiple and integrated levels of organization (ranging from biology to culture and history) that make up human life and its ecology.

The power of these theories lies in the multilevel and, hence, multidimensional design criteria they impose on concepts (and research) pertinent to any content area about, or dimension of, the person. Power lies as well in their potential for advancing simultaneously both the understanding of the bases of human development and of the individual ←→ context relations involved in promoting well-being and thriving across the life span.

Ultimately, it will be this last use—of serving humanity through the science it generates—that will give developmental systems theories a place of importance in the history of developmental science. Such contributions to enhancing personality and its development and, more generally, the human condition will document the wise observation of Kurt Lewin (1943) that there is nothing as practical as a good theory.

REFERENCES

Anastasi, A. (1958). Heredity, environment, and the question "how"? *Psychological Review, 65,* 197–208.

Baer, D. M. (1976). The organism as host. *Human Development, 19,* 87–89.

Bakan, D. (1966). *The duality of human existence.* Chicago: Rand McNally.

Baltes, P. B. (1987). Theoretical propositions of life-span developmental psychology: On the dynamics between growth and decline. *Developmental Psychology, 23,* 611–626.

Baltes, P. B., Lindenberger, U., & Staudinger, U. M. (1998). Life-span theory in developmental psychology. In W. Damon (Ed. in Chief) & R. M. Lerner (Vol. Ed.), *Handbook of child psychology: Vol. 1. Theoretical models of human development* (5th ed., pp. 1029–1144). New York: Wiley.

Baltes, P. B., Reese, H. W., & Nesselroade, J. R. (1977). *Life-span developmental psychology: Introduction to research methods.* Monterey, CA: Brooks/Cole.

Benedict, R. F. (1934). *Patterns of culture.* Boston: Houghton Mifflin.

Benson, P. (1997). *All kids are our kids: What communities must do to raise caring and responsible children and adolescents.* San Francisco: Jossey-Bass.

Bijou, S. W. (1976). *Child development: The basic stage of early childhood.* Englewood Cliffs, NJ: Prentice Hall.

Bijou, S. W., & Baer, D. M. (1961). *Child development: A systemic and empirical theory* (Vol. 1). New York: Appleton-Century-Crofts.

Block, J. (1971). *Lives through time.* Berkeley, CA: Bancroft.

Brandtstädter, J. (1998). Action perspectives on human development. In W. Damon (Ed. in Chief) & R. M. Lerner (Vol. Ed.), *Handbook of child psychology: Vol. 1. Theoretical models of human development* (5th ed., pp. 807–863). New York: Wiley.

Brandtstädter, J. (1999). The self in action and development: Cultural, biosocial, and ontogenetic bases of intentional self-development. In J. Brandtstädter & R. M. Lerner (Eds.), *Action and self-development: Theory and research through the life-span* (pp. 37–65). Thousand Oaks, CA: Sage.

Brandtstädter, J. (in press). Action perspectives on human development. In W. Damon & R. M. Lerner. (Eds. in Chief) & R. M. Lerner (Vol. Ed.), *Theoretical models of human development: Vol. 1. Handbook of child psychology* (6th ed.). New York: Wiley.

Brandtstädter, J., & Lerner, R. M. (Eds.). (1999). *Action and self-development: Theory and research through the life-span.* Thousand Oaks, CA: Sage.

Brim, O. G., Jr., & Kagan, J. (Eds.). (1980). *Constancy and change in human development.* Cambridge, MA: Harvard University Press.

Bronfenbrenner, U. (1974). Developmental research, public policy, and the ecology of childhood. *Child development, 45,* 1–5.

Bronfenbrenner, U. (1977). Toward an experimental ecology of human development. *American Psychologist, 32,* 513–531.

Bronfenbrenner, U. (1979). *The ecology of human development.* Cambridge, MA: Harvard University Press.

Bronfenbrenner, U. (2001). The bioecological theory of human development. In N. J. Smelser & P. B. Baltes (Eds.), *International encyclopedia of the social and behavioral sciences* (pp. 6963–6970). Oxford, England: Elsevier.

Bronfenbrenner, U. (2005). *Making human beings human.* Thousand Oaks, CA: Sage.

Bronfenbrenner, U., & Morris, P. A. (1998). The ecology of developmental process. In W. Damon (Ed. in Chief) & R. M. Lerner (Vol. Ed.), *Handbook of child psychology: Vol. 1. Theoretical models of human development* (5th ed., pp. 993–1028). New York: Wiley.

Bronfenbrenner, U., & Morris, P. A. (in press). The ecology of developmental process. In W. Damon & R. M. Lerner (Eds. in Chief) & R. M. Lerner (Vol. Ed.), *Theoretical models of human development: Vol. 1. Handbook of child psychology* (6th ed.). New York: Wiley.

Brooks-Gunn, J., & Reiter, E. O. (1990). The role of pubertal processes in the early adolescent transition. In S. Feldman & G. Elliott (Eds.), *At the threshold: The developing adolescent* (pp. 16–53). Cambridge, MA: Harvard University Press.

Cairns, R. B. (1998). The making of developmental psychology. In W. Damon (Ed. in Chief) & R. M. Lerner (Vol. Ed.), *Handbook of child psychology: Vol. 1. Theoretical models of human development* (5th ed., pp. 419–448). New York: Wiley.

Cairns, R. B., & Cairns, B. D. (1994). *Lifelines and risks: Pathways of youth in our time.* New York: Cambridge University Press.

Chess, S., & Thomas, A. (1999). *Goodness of fit: Clinical applications from infancy through adult life.* Philadelphia: Brunner/Mazel.

Collins, W. A. (1982). *The concept of development: The Minnesota Symposia on Child Psychology* (Vol. 15). Hillsdale, NJ: Erlbaum.

Damasio, A. R., & Damasio, H. (1996). Making images and creating subjectivity. In R. R. Llinas & P. S. Churchland (Eds.), *The mind-brain continuum: Sensory processes* (pp. 19–27). Cambridge, MA: MIT Press.

Dryfoos, J. G. (1990). *Adolescents at risk: Prevalence and prevention.* New York: Oxford University Press.

Dryfoos, J. G. (1994). *Full service schools: A revolution in health and social services for children, youth, and families.* San Francisco: Jossey-Bass.

Eccles, J. S. (1991). Academic achievement. In R. M. Lerner, A. C. Petersen, & J. Brooks-Gunn (Eds.), *Encyclopedia of adolescence* (Vol. 1, pp. 1–9). New York: Garland.

Eccles, J. S., Early, D., Frasier, K., Belansky, E., & McCarthy, K. (1997). The relation of connection, regulation, and support for autonomy to adolescents' functioning. *Journal of Adolescent Research, 12,* 263–286.

Eccles, J. S., & Harold, R. D. (1996). Family involvement in children's and adolescents' schooling. In A. Booth & J. F. Dunn (Eds.), *Family-school links: How do they affect educational outcomes?* (pp. 3–34). Mahwah, NJ: Erlbaum.

Eccles, J. S., Lord, S., & Buchanan, C. M. (1996). School transitions in early adolescence: What are we doing to your young people? In J. A., Graber, J. Brooks-Gunn, & A. C. Petersen (Eds.), *Transitions through adolescence* (pp. 251–284). Mahwah, NJ: Erlbaum.

Eccles, J. S., & Midgley, C. (1989). Stage-environment fit: Developmentally appropriate classrooms for young adolescents. In C. Ames & R. Ames (Eds.), *Research on motivation in education: Vol. 3. Goals and cognitions* (pp. 139–186). New York: Academic Press.

Eccles, J. S., Midgley, C., Wigfield, A., Buchanan, C. M., Reuman, D., Flanagan, C., & MacIver, D. (1993). Development during adolescence: The impact of stage-environment fit on young adolescents' experiences in schools and in families. *American Psychologist, 48,* 90–101.

Eccles, J. S., Wigfield, A., & Byrnes, J. (2003). Cognitive development in adolescence. In R. M. Lerner, M. A. Easterbrooks, & J. Mistry (Eds.), *Handbook of psychology: Developmental psychology* (Vol. 6, pp. 325–350). New York: Wiley.

Eccles, J. S., Wigfield, A., Midgley, C., Reuman, D., MacIver, D., & Feldlaufer, H. (1993). Negative effects of traditional middle schools on students' motivation. *Elementary School Journal, 93,* 553–574.

Elder, G. H., Jr. (1974). *Children of the great depression.* Chicago: University of Chicago Press.

Elder, G. H., Jr. (1998). The life course and human development. In W. Damon (Ed. in Chief) & R. M. Lerner (Vol. Ed.), *Handbook of child psychology: Vol. 1. Theoretical models of human development* (5th ed., pp. 939–991). New York: Wiley.

Elder, G. H., Modell, J., & Parke, R. D. (1993). Studying children in a changing world. In G. H. Elder, J. Modell, & R. D. Parke (Eds.), *Children in time and place: Developmental and historical insights* (pp. 3–21). New York: Cambridge University Press.

Elder, G. H., Jr., & Shanahan, M. J. (in press). The life course and human development. In W. Damon & R. M. Lerner (Eds. in Chief) & R. M. Lerner (Vol. Ed.), *Theoretical models of human development: Vol. 1. Handbook of child psychology* (6th ed.). New York: Wiley.

Emmerich, W. (1968). Personality development and concepts of structure. *Child Development 39,* 671–690.

Erikson, E. H. (1959). Identity and the life cycle. *Psychological Issues, 1,* 50–100.

Featherman, D. L. (1985). Individual development and aging as a population process. In J. R. Nesselroade & A. von Eye (Eds.), *Individual development and social change: Explanatory analysis* (pp. 213–241). New York: Academic Press.

Fisher, C., & Jackson, J., & Villarruel, F. (1998). The study of African American and Latin American children and youth. In W. Damon (Ed. in Chief) & R. M. Lerner (Vol. Ed.), *Handbook of child psychology: Vol. 1. Theoretical models of human development* (6th ed., pp. 1145–1208). New York: Wiley.

Fisher, C. B., & Lerner, R. M. (1994). Foundations of applied developmental psychology. In C. B. Fisher & R. M. Lerner (Eds.), *Applied developmental psychology* (pp. 3–20). New York: McGraw-Hill.

Fisher, C. B., Murray, J. P., Dill, J. R., Hagen, J. W., Hogan, M. J., Lerner, R. M., Rebok, G. W., Sigel, I., Sostek, A. M., Smyer, M. A., Spencer, M. B., & Wilcox, B. (1993). The national conference on graduate education in the applications of developmental science across the life-span. *Journal of Applied Developmental Psychology, 14,* 1–10.

Ford, D. L., & Lerner, R. M. (1992). *Developmental systems theory: An integrative approach.* Newbury Park, CA: Sage.

Freud, S. (1954). *Collected works, standard edition.* London: Hogarth.

Fuligni, A. J., Eccles, J. S., & Barber, B. (1995). The long-term effects of seventh-grade ability groupings in mathematics. *Journal of Early Adolescence, 15,* 58–89.

Garcia Coll, C., Bearer, E., & Lerner, R. M. (Eds.). (2004). *Nature and nurture: The complex interplay of genetic and environmental influences on human behavior and development.* Mahwah, NJ: Erlbaum.

Gewirtz, J. L., & Stingle, K. G. (1968). Learning of generalized imitation as the basis for identification. *Psychological Review, 75,* 374–397.

Gollin, E. S. (1981). Development and plasticity. In E. S. Gollin (Ed.), *Developmental plasticity: Behavioral and biological aspects of variations in development* (pp. 231–251). New York: Academic Press.

Gottlieb, G. (1970). Conceptions of prenatal behavior. In L. R. Aronson, E. Tobach, D. S. Lehrman, & J. S. Rosenblatt (Eds.), *Development and evolution of behavior: Essays in memory of T. C. Schneirla* (pp. 111–137). San Francisco: Freeman.

Gottlieb, G. (1992). *Individual development and evolution: The genesis of novel behavior.* New York: Oxford University Press.

Gottlieb, G. (1997). *Synthesizing nature-nurture: Prenatal roots of instinctive behavior.* Mahwah, NJ: Erlbaum.

Gottlieb, G. (1998). Normally occurring environmental and behavioral influences on gene activity: From central dogma to probabilistic epigenesis. *Psychological Review, 105,* 792–802.

Gottlieb, G. (2004). Normally occurring environmental and behavioral influences on gene activity: From central dogma to probabilistic epigenesis. In C. Garcia Coll, E. Bearer, & R. M. Lerner (Eds.), *Nature and nurture: The complex interplay of genetic and environmental influences on human behavior and development* (pp. 85–106). Mahwah, NJ: Erlbaum.

Gottlieb, G., Wahlsten, D., & Lickliter, R. (1998). The significance of biology for human development: A developmental psychobiological systems view. In W. Damon (Ed. in Chief) & R. M. Lerner (Vol. Ed.), *Handbook of child psychology: Vol. 1. Theoretical models of human development* (5th ed., pp. 233–273). New York: Wiley.

Gottlieb, G., Wahlsten, D., & Lickliter, R. (in press). Biology and human development. In W. Damon & R. M. Lerner (Eds. in Chief) & R. M. Lerner (Vol. Ed.), *Handbook of child psychology: Vol. 1. Theoretical models of human development* (6th ed.). Hoboken, NJ: Wiley.

Hamburg, D. A. (1992). *Today's children: Creating a future for a generation in crisis.* New York: Time Books.

Hamburger, V. (1957). The concept of development in biology. In D. B. Harris (Ed.), *The concept of development* (pp. 49–58). Minneapolis: University of Minnesota Press.

Harris, D. B. (1957). *The concept of development.* Minneapolis: University of Minnesota Press.

Hebb, D. O. (1970). A return to Jensen and his social critics. *American Psychologist, 25,* 568.

Heckhausen, J. (1999). *Developmental regulation in adulthood: Age-normative and sociocultural constraints as adaptive challenges.* New York: Cambridge University Press.

Hernandez, D. J. (1993). *America's children: Resources for family, government, and the economy.* New York: Russell Sage Foundation.

Hernstein, R. J., & Murray, C. (1994). *The bell curve: Intelligence and class structure in American life.* New York: Free Press.

Hirsch, J. (1970). Behavior-genetic analysis and its biosocial consequences. *Seminars in Psychiatry, 2,* 89–105.

Hirsch, J. (1975). Jensenism: The bankruptcy of "science" without scholarship. *Educational Theory, 25,* 3–27, 102.

Hirsch, J. (1997). The triumph of wishful thinking over genetic irrelevance. *Current Psychology of Cognition, 16,* 711–720.

Hirsch, J. (2004). Uniqueness, diversity, similarity, repeatability, and heritability. In C. Garcia Coll, E. Bearer, & R. M. Lerner (Eds.), *Nature and nurture: The complex interplay of genetic and environmental influences on human behavior and development* (pp. 127–138). Mahwah, NJ: Erlbaum.

Jacobs, F. (1988). The five-tiered approach to evaluation: Context and implementation. In H. B. Weiss & F. Jacobs (Eds.), *Evaluating family programs* (pp. 37–68). Hawthorne, NY: Aldine.

Jacobs, F., Wertlieb, D., Lerner, R. M. (2003). Learning from policy and practice: A view of the issues. In R. M. Lerner, F. Jacobs, & D. Wertlieb (Eds.), *Handbook of applied developmental science: Promoting positive child, adolescent, and family development through research, policies, and programs: Vol. 2. Enhancing the life chances of youth and families: Public service systems and public policy perspectives* (pp. 1–14). Thousand Oaks, CA: Sage.

Kagan, J., & Moss, H. A. (1962). *Birth to maturity.* New York: Wiley.

Kaplan, B. (1983). A trio of trials. In R. M. Lerner (Ed.), *Developmental psychology: Historical and philosophical perspectives* (pp. 185–228). Hillsdale, NJ: Erlbaum.

Kardiner, A., & Linton, R. (1939). *The individual and his society.* New York: Columbia University Press.

Kluckhohn, C., & Murray, H. (1948). Personality formation: The determinants. In C. Kluckhohn & H. Murray (Eds.), *Personality in nature, society, and culture.* New York: Knopf.

Kuo, Z. Y. (1976). *The dynamics of behavior development: An epigenetic view.* New York: Plenum.

Lerner, J. V., & Lerner, R. M. (1983). Temperament and adaptation across life: Theoretical and empirical issues. In P. B. Baltes & O. G. Brim Jr. (Eds.), *Life-span development and behavior* (Vol. 5, pp. 197–231). New York: Academic Press.

Lerner, R. M. (1982). Children and adolescents as producers of their own development. *Developmental Review, 2,* 342–370.

Lerner, R. M. (1984). *On the nature of human plasticity.* New York: Cambridge University Press.

Lerner, R. M. (1991). Changing organism-context relations as the basic process of development: A developmental-contextual perspective. *Developmental Psychology, 27,* 27–32.

Lerner, R. M. (1998). Theories of human development: Contemporary perspectives. In W. Damon (Ed. in Chief) & R. M. Lerner (Vol. Ed.), *Handbook of child psychology: Vol. 1. Theoretical models of human development* (5th ed., pp. 1–24). New York: Wiley.

Lerner, R. M. (2002a). *Adolescence: Development, diversity, context, and application.* Upper Saddle River, NJ: Prentice Hall.

Lerner, R. M. (2002b). *Concepts and theories of human development* (3rd ed.). Mahwah, NJ: Erlbaum.

Lerner, R. M. (2003). "Easy," "difficult," or unique? Improving the parent-child match. In Faculty of Tufts University's Eliot-Pearson Department of Child Development (Eds.), *Proactive parenting: Guiding your child from two to six* (pp. 3–27). New York: Berkley Books.

Lerner, R. M. (2004). *Liberty: Thriving and civic engagement among America's youth.* Thousand Oaks, CA: Sage.

Lerner, R. M. (in press). Diversity in individual ←→ context relations as the basis for positive development across the life span: A developmental systems perspective for theory, research, and application. *Research in Human Development.*

Lerner, R. M., & Busch-Rossnagel, N. A. (1981). *Individuals as producers of their development: A life-span perspective.* New York: Academic Press.

Lerner, R. M., & Kauffman, M. B. (1985). The concept of development in contextualism. *Developmental Review, 5,* 309–333.

Lerner, R. M., & Lerner, J. V. (1983). Temperament-intelligence reciprocities in early childhood: A contextual model. In M. Lewis (Ed.), *Origins of intelligence: Infancy and early childhood* (2nd ed., pp. 399–421). New York: Plenum Press.

Lerner, R. M., & Miller, J. R. (1993). Integrating human development research and intervention for America's children: The Michigan State University model. *Journal of Applied Developmental Psychology, 14,* 347–364.

Lerner, R. M., & Miller, J. R. (1998). Developing multidisciplinary institutes to enhance the lives of individuals and families: Academic potentials and pitfalls. *Journal of Public Service & Outreach, 3*(1), 64–73.

Lerner, R. M., Skinner, E. A., & Sorell, G. T. (1980). Methodological implications of contextual/dialectic theories of development. *Human Development, 23,* 225–235.

Lerner, R. M., & Spanier, G. B. (1980). *Adolescent development: A life-span perspective.* New York: McGraw-Hill.

Lerner, R. M., Taylor, C. S., & von Eye, A. (Eds.). (2002). *Pathways to positive development among diverse youth. New directions for youth development: Theory, practice, and research.* San Francisco: Jossey-Bass.

Lerner, R. M., Theokas, C., & Jelicic, H. (in press). Youth as active agents in their own positive development: A developmental systems perspective. In W. Greve, K. Rothermund, & D. Wentura (Eds.), *The adaptive self: Personal continuity and intentional self-development.* Göttingen, Germany: Hogrefe/Huber Publishers.

Lerner, R. M., & Walls, T. (1999). Revisiting individuals as producers of their development: From dynamic interactions to developmental systems. In J. Brandtstädter & R. M. Lerner (Eds.), *Action and self-development: Theory and research through the life-span* (pp. 3–36). Thousand Oaks, CA: Sage.

Lewin, K. (1943). Psychology and the process of group living. *Journal of Social Psychology, 17,* 113–131.

Lewontin, R. C. (1992). Foreword. In R. M. Lerner (Ed.), *Final solutions: Biology, prejudice, and genocide* (pp. vii–viii). University Park, PA: Penn State Press.

Lorenz, K. (1966). *On aggression.* New York: Harcourt, Brace & World.

Magnusson, D. (1985). Implications of an interactional paradigm for research on human development. *International Journal of Behavioral Development, 8,* 115–137.

Magnusson, D. (1995). Individual development: A holistic integrated model. In P. Moen, G. H. Elder, & K. Lusher (Eds.), *Linking lives and contexts: Perspectives on the ecology of human development* (pp. 19–60). Washington, DC: APA Books.

Magnusson, D. (1999a). Holistic interactionism: A perspective for research on personality development. In L. A. Pervin & O. P. John (Eds.), *Handbook of personality: Theory and research* (2nd ed., pp. 219–247). New York: Guilford Press.

Magnusson, D. (1999b). On the individual: A person-oriented approach to developmental research. *European Psychologist, 4,* 205–218.

Magnusson, D., & Endler, N. S. (1977). Interactional psychology: Present status and future prospects. In D. Magnusson and N. S. Endler (Eds.), *Personality at the crossroads: Current issues in interactional psychology* (pp. 3–31). Hillsdale, NJ: Erlbaum.

Magnusson, D., & Stattin, H. (1998). Person-context interaction theories. In W. Damon (Ed. in Chief) & R. M. Lerner (Vol. Ed.), *Handbook of child psychology: Vol. 1. Theoretical models of human development* (5th ed., pp. 685–759). New York: Wiley.

Magnusson, D., & Stattin, H. (in press). The person in the environment: A holistic-interactionist perspective. In W. Damon &

R. M. Lerner (Series Eds.), *Handbook of child psychology: Vol. 1. Theoretical models of human development* (6th ed.). New York: Wiley.

Maier, N. R. F., & Schneirla, T. C. (1935). *Principles of animal behavior.* New York: McGraw-Hill.

McAdoo, H. P. (1995). Stress levels, family help patterns, and religiosity in middle- and working-class African American single mothers. *Journal of Black Psychology, 21,* 424–449.

McLoyd, V. C. (1998). Children in poverty: Development, public policy, and practice. In W. Damon (Ed.) & I. E. Sigel, & K. A. Renninger (Vol. Eds.), *Handbook of psychology: Child psychology in practice* (Vol. 4). New York: Wiley.

Midgley, C., Feldlaufer, H., Eccles, J. (1989a). Change in teacher efficacy and student self- and task-related beliefs in mathematics during the transition to junior high school. *Journal of Educational Psychology, 81*(2), 247–258.

Midgley, C., Feldlaufer, H., Eccles, J. (1989b). Student/teacher relations and attitudes toward mathematics before and after the transition to junior high school. *Child Development, 60,* 981–992.

Mischel, W. (1977). On the future of personality measurement. *American Psychologist, 32,* 246–254.

Molina, B. S. G., & Chassin, L. (1996). The parent-adolescent relationship at puberty: Hispanic ethnicity and parent alcoholism as moderators. *Developmental Psychology, 32,* 675–686.

Novikoff, A. B. (1945a). The concept of integrative levels of biology. *Science, 101,* 209–215.

Novikoff, A. B. (1945b). Continuity and discontinuity in evolution. *Science, 101,* 405–406.

Overton, W. F. (1973). On the assumptive base of the nature-nurture controversy: Additive versus interactive conceptions. *Human Development, 16,* 74–89.

Overton, W. F. (1998). Developmental psychology: Philosophy, concepts, and methodology. In W. Damon (Ed. in Chief) & R. M. Lerner (Vol. Ed.), *Handbook of child psychology: Vol. 1. Theoretical models of human development* (5th ed., pp. 107–187). New York: Wiley.

Overton, W. F. (2003). Development across the life span: Philosophy, concepts, theory. In B. Weiner (Series Ed.) & R. M. Lerner, M. A. Easterbrooks, & J. Mistry (Vol. Eds.), *Handbook of psychology: Vol. 6. Developmental psychology* (pp. 13–42). New York: Wiley.

Plomin, R. (2000). Behavioural genetics in the 21st century. *International Journal of Behavioral Development, 24,* 30–34.

Reese, H. W., & Overton, W. F. (1970). Models of development and theories of development. In L. R. Goulet & P. B. Baltes (Eds.), *Life-span developmental psychology: Research and theory* (pp. 115–145). New York: Academic Press.

Rende, R. (2004). Beyond Heritability: Biological Process in Social Context. In C. Garcia Coll, E. Bearer, & R. M. Lerner (Eds.), *Nature and nurture: The complex interplay of genetic and en-*

vironmental influences on human behavior and development (pp. 107–126). Mahwah, NJ: Erlbaum.

Riegel, K. F. (1975). Toward a dialectical theory of human development. *Human Development, 18,* 50–64.

Rowe, D. (1994). *The limits of family influence: Genes, experience, and behavior.* New York: Guilford Press.

Rushton, J. P. (2000). *Race, evolution, and behavior* (2nd special abridged ed.). New Brunswick, NJ: Transaction Publishers.

Sameroff, A. (1975). Transactional models in early social relations. *Human Development, 18,* 65–79.

Savin-Williams, R., & Diamond, L. (2004). Sex. In R. M. Lerner & R. Steinberg (Eds.), *Handbook of Adolescent Psychology* (pp. 189–232). New York: Wiley.

Scales, P., Benson, P., Leffert, N., & Blyth, D. A. (2000). The contribution of developmental assets to the prediction of thriving among adolescents. *Applied Developmental Science, 4,* 27–46.

Schneirla, T. C. (1956). Interrelationships of the innate and the acquired in instinctive behavior. In P. P. Grasse (Ed.), *L'instinct dans le comportement des animaux et de l'homme* (pp. 387–452). Paris: Masson et Cie.

Schneirla, T. C. (1957). The concept of development in comparative psychology. In D. B. Harris (Ed.), *The concept of development* (pp. 78–108). Minneapolis: University of Minnesota Press.

Schorr, L. B. (1997). *Common purpose: Strengthening families and neighborhoods to rebuild America.* New York: Doubleday.

Shweder, R. A., Goodnow, J., Hatano, G., LeVine, R., Markus, H., & Miller, P. (1998). The cultural psychology of development: One mind, many mentalities. In W. Damon (Ed. in Chief) & R. M. Lerner (Vol. Ed.), *Handbook of child psychology: Vol. 1. Theoretical models of human development* (5th ed., pp. 865–937). New York: Wiley.

Spencer, M. B. (in press). Phenomenological variant of ecological systems theory (PVEST): A human development synthesis applicable to diverse individuals and groups. In W. Damon & R. M. Lerner (Eds. in Chief) & R. M. Lerner (Vol. Ed.), *Theoretical models of human development: Vol. 1. Handbook of child psychology* (6th ed.). New York: Wiley.

Steinberg, L. (1987). The impact of puberty on family relations: Effects of pubertal status and pubertal timing. *Developmental Psychology, 23,* 833–840.

Strauss, S. (1982). *U-shaped behavioral growth.* New York: Academic Press.

Susman, E. J., & Rogol, A. (2004). Puberty and psychological development. In R. M. Lerner & R. Steinberg (Eds.), *Handbook of Adolescent Psychology* (pp. 15–44). New York: Wiley.

Tanner, J. (1991). Menarche, secular trend in age of. In R. M. Lerner, A. C. Petersen, & J. Brooks-Gunn (Eds.), *Encyclopedia of adolescence* (Vol. 1, pp. 637–641). New York: Garland.

Thelen, E., & Smith, L. B. (1998). Dynamic systems theories. In W. Damon (Ed. in Chief) & R. M. Lerner (Vol. Ed.), *Handbook of child psychology: Vol. 1. Theoretical models of human development* (5th ed., pp. 563–633). New York: Wiley.

Thelen, E., & Smith, L. B. (in press). Dynamic systems theories. In W. Damon & R. M. Lerner (Eds. in Chief) & R. M. Lerner (Vol. Ed.), *Theoretical models of human development: Vol. 1. Handbook of child psychology* (6th ed.). New York: Wiley.

Thomas, A., & Chess, S. (1977). *Temperament and development.* New York: Brunner/Mazel.

Tobach, E. (1981). Evolutionary aspects of the activity of the organism and its development. In R. M. Lerner & N. A. Busch-Rossnagel (Eds.), *Individuals as producers of their development: A life-span perspective* (pp. 37–68). New York: Academic Press.

Tobach, E., & Greenberg, G. (1984). The significance of T. C. Schneirla's contribution to the concept of levels of integration. In G. Greenberg & E. Tobach (Eds.), *Behavioral evolution and integrative levels* (pp. 1–7). Hillsdale, NJ: Erlbaum.

von Bertalanffy, L. (1968). *General systems theory.* New York: Braziller.

Walsten, D. (1990). Insensitivity of the analysis of variance to heredity-environment interaction. *Behavioral and Brain Sciences, 13,* 109–120.

Werner, H. (1948). *Comparative psychology of mental development.* New York: International Universities Press.

Werner, H. (1957). The concept of development from a comparative and organismic point of view. In D. B. Harris (Ed.), *The concept of development* (pp. 125–148). Minneapolis: University of Minnesota Press.

Zigler, E. E. (1998). A place of value for applied and policy studies. *Child Development, 69,* 532–542.

CHAPTER 3

Culture, Personality, and People's Uses of Time: Key Interrelationships

RICHARD W. BRISLIN AND KEVIN D. LO

INTRODUCTION

The purpose of this chapter is to examine relationships among three major influences on people's behavior. One influence is the culture in which people were socialized, as well as other cultures with which they have had contact in roles such as immigrant, international student, or overseas businessperson (Adler, 2002; Brislin, 2000; Triandis & Suh, 2002). A second influence is people's personality, with influences stemming both from genetics and from various personal experiences that take place in people's environments (Hofstede & McCrae, 2004; McCrae & Costa, 1997; Mischel, 2004). A third influence is how people use time, for instance the importance they place on punctuality and planning for the future, or their acceptance of typical time lines that can exist in their cultures (e.g., the age at which people go to college, get married, or retire from work; Brislin & Kim, 2003; Hall, 1959; Levine, 1997). We will examine various relationships among these broad concepts based on various research studies. Although we feel it would be premature to present an integrative theory of culture, personality, and time, we will indicate components of what likely will be central to such a theory.

We also will discuss a major aspect of people's culture. If people interact with culturally similar others, they rarely have to think about their shared culture (Brislin, 2000). Much behavior becomes automatic: what constitutes social skills, what appropriate topics for conversation are, proper ways for college students to approach and to interact with professors, and ways of disagreeing with others in public forums. People

do think about the possibility of cultural influences in well-meaning clashes with people who were socialized in another part of the world. Or, the socialization of the culturally different others can take place within a large and complex nation such as the United States or Canada, as with the experiences of a cultural minority group who congregate in designated parts of big cities (Chinatowns, or Native Americans in geographically isolated areas). Well-meaning clashes refer to interactions among polite and highly educated people who may be models of good social skills within their own culture. In addition, they want to act in a tolerant manner that is accepting of differences. But after many interactions with culturally different others, these socially skilled people conclude that the interactions did not go well. They were not smooth, people clearly were not comfortable, and goals associated with the interaction (either social or task-oriented) were not met. So why did the interactions not go well?

Given the assumption of polite people who want to be tolerant, the reason must involve cultural differences. Very often, researchers who become involved in cross-cultural research do so based on the stimulation experiences in their own intercultural interactions, not all of which were successful (Bochner, 1994; Cushner & Brislin, 1996; Hall, 1959; Hofstede, 2004; Triandis, 2004). As an example considering culture and time, many academics from the United States have been invited to give papers at prestigious meetings in South American countries such as Brazil or Argentina. If the presentations were scheduled at 10:00 A.M., the blood pressure of the Americans rose noticeably if they had not begun speaking by 10:45 or 11:00 A.M. The Americans may or may not notice that their hosts do not seem at all bothered and that the meetings seem to progress smoothly even though clocks seem to be absent or ignored.

Many times, the importance of cross-cultural research becomes apparent if it helps people understand their intercultural interactions and if it helps them advance their goals of

Acknowledgments: We gratefully acknowledge the help of the following people in developing the critical incidents in this chapter that we used to illustrate key points: The Mary Collins incident was suggested by Julia Nikulina Compton; the Frank Williams incident by D. P. S. Bhawuk; the Samsung Electronics incident by Eugene Kim; the Chu Jin incident by Julie Haiyan Chao. The other incidents are from the authors' personal experiences.

tolerance and the acceptance of diversity. In this chapter, we will use various critical incidents that summarize typical intercultural interactions. The use of critical incidents is an approach commonly used in cross-cultural training programs that have the goal of making intercultural interactions smoother, less stressful, and more effective (Brislin & Yoshida, 1994; Landis & Bhagat, 1996).

CULTURAL INFLUENCES ON BEHAVIOR

If the influences of culture are to be discussed, and cross-cultural differences explained, then definitions of terms are clearly needed. Entire volumes have been devoted to definitions of culture (Kroeber & Kluckhohn, 1952; Sperber, 1996), and so we will be emphasizing selected aspects that have assisted researchers in their empirical work. Culture comprises ideals, values, and assumptions that are shared among people and that guide specific behaviors and their interpretations. Most often, the people sharing these values and ideas live in proximity to each other and speak the same language. Important exceptions occur in the case of diasporas, where people become scattered around the world but maintain aspects of a shared culture. Culture refers to the part of the environment that people make. Rainfall is not part of culture, but people's reaction to rainfall (the creation of reservoirs, norms concerning water conservation) are cultural. Cultural values and ideals are passed on generation to generation, from adults to children, and so older people in a culture take on the task of becoming transmitters, and younger people are successful recipients if they become respected and productive members of a culture. Transmitters have different roles depending upon the society of which they are members. Parents are always transmitters, and they can be joined by relatives, teachers, religious figures, respected elders, mentors, and coaches. As part of the intergeneration transmission process, young people have specific experiences that lead to cultural learning. They go to funerals and observe proper etiquette; they learn to defer to certain people who are role models for high-level performance on certain tasks; they learn that the expression of some attitudes is acceptable but that the expression of other sentiments is verboten. When they make mistakes, they are corrected, and memories of these mistakes become the basis of lifelong lessons for acceptable behaviors within their culture.

Once they have learned these acceptable behaviors, people become emotionally upset when their cultural assumptions are violated. In the academic meeting example, speakers did not say, "Isn't this an interesting violation of my cultural expectation that meetings start on time. I'll have to remember this and use it as an example with my students." Instead, they become upset, sometimes angry, and quick to label their preferred behavior as correct and the other culture's behavior as just plain wrong. When considering observed differences, the presence of an emotional reaction is often a good sign that people are dealing with behaviors influenced by their culture. These emotions come to the forefront in well-meaning clashes, as already discussed. People are trying to be tolerant and to be understood, but their interactions with others are not proceeding smoothly. The reason is likely to be cultural. An example, in the form of a critical incident developed to help people in their overseas assignments or other types of extensive intercultural interaction, should be helpful.

Incident: More than One Interaction during the Day

Mary Collins had impressed her superiors during her five years at the Pittsburgh office of a manufacturing firm specializing in farm equipment. Her superiors asked her to accept an assignment in Russia to determine the possibility of joint ventures. A firm in Moscow was identified whose executives agreed to have a series of meetings with Mary. On her first day at the firm, she met Yuri Sakharov who showed her around, introduced her to secretaries, and offered to answer questions as they came up during the next few weeks.

The next morning, Mary saw Yuri in the hall and they greeted each other and had a short conversation. Later in the afternoon, Mary saw Yuri again but he walked by her and did not acknowledge her presence. Mary wondered if she had done or said something offensive earlier in the day.

We can examine this incident with the previous discussion of cultural influences in mind. The cultural issue here involves a difference in workplace norms regarding how people are expected to respond to each other over the course of the day. In the United States, people have developed the informal norm that people acknowledge each other every time they come into contact. As children, they probably were corrected if they did not acknowledge individuals every time they were seen during a day. In Russia, the norm is that once is enough. People greet each other and exchange pleasantries the first time they see each other, but they are not expected to do this upon a second or third meeting during the same day. Mary should not take the lack of a second greeting personally, that is, have an emotional reaction that is common when cultural assumptions are violated. Yuri is behaving quite appropriately according to Russian workplace norms. This incident also introduces another example of people's use of time. In one culture, time is spent on a second or third greeting during the day. In the other, this same time is spent on other, often task-related, activities.

This analysis of a cultural difference was developed during conversations with the University of Hawaii's Julia Nikulina Compton. She is originally from Siberia and also has worked in Moscow. She points to another implication of the American desire to chat at every interaction compared to the once-is-enough norm. Julia has had the opportunity to learn a number of languages in addition to her native Russian. She found English the easiest of these additional languages to learn. She points out that "English speakers, especially Americans, are willing to talk with you and so you have the opportunity to get a lot of practice."

There are many other definitions of culture, and we believe that most give attention to the aspects we have chosen to emphasize. This concise definition is useful (Triandis, Kurowski, Tecktiel, & Chan, 1993, p. 219): Culture is "a set of human made objective and subjective elements that in the past have (a) increased the probability of survival, (b) resulted in satisfaction for the participants in an ecological niche, and thus (c) become shared among those who communicate with each other because they had a common language and lived in the same time-place." To these points we would add the features of transmission generation to generation, emotional attachment to cultural values, and the probability of well-meaning clashes when interacting with people from other cultures.

DIMENSIONS OF CULTURE

Cross-cultural researchers have identified various dimensions that describe major emphases within a culture and give insights into cultural differences (Hofstede, 2001; Osland & Bird, 2000; Triandis, 1995). It is important to remember that these dimensions describe culture and are not meant to be the source of individual difference analyses (Hofstede, 2004). That is, a culture may emphasize a certain dimension, such as individual goal-setting and initiative, but that does not allow analysts to predict the behavior of specific people in that culture. There are cooperative, group-oriented people in all cultures, and this feature of people is better analyzed through the study of personality. We will return to this theme again because the relations between cultural dimensions and individual differences such as personality form the basis of important current research (Markus & Kitayama, 1991, 1998), and the study of these relationships is likely to continue into the future.

Individualism and Collectivism

In individualistic societies, there is an emphasis placed on people's own goals and their pursuit of them. Beyond their nuclear families, there are not groups of people whose members have major influences on any one person's goal-setting. In everyday language, people are expected to do things on their own, and so certain psychological concepts are emphasized. If the emphasis is the individual, then terms such as traits, attitudes, and opinions are commonly discussed both by laypersons and by behavioral scientists. In collectivism, there is emphasis placed on people's membership in groups. Any one person is likely to be attentive to the wishes of significant others in the setting and pursuit of goals. These significant others can come from one's extended family, school, organization, or religious affiliation. Triandis (1995; see also Bhawuk, 2001) has suggested that there are four factors that are especially important in distinguishing individualism from collectivism. In considering the self, there is emphasis on statements that start with *I* (individualism) in contrast to *we* (collectivism). As already discussed, there is a differential emphasis placed on individual or group goals. In making decisions about their behavior, people in individualist nations are likely to emphasize their personal attitudes, and people in collectivist nations are likely to be attentive to group norms. People in individualist nations make decisions based on rational reasoning, with emphasis placed on resources and outcomes involving themselves. People in collectivist nations are more likely to make decisions based on their relationships with others who are somehow involved in the decision-making process. Individualism is found in North America, Western Europe, and in countries where there have been waves of immigration from these parts of the world. The United States is the most individualistic nation in the world. Collectivism in found in Asia, Pacific island cultures, South America, and Africa. A critical incident should be helpful in exploring this important cultural dimension.

Incident: Personal Relationships Can Take Second Place to Contracts

Frank Williams and his family had saved for a vacation in Kathmandu, Nepal, for more than two years. Family members decided to book with a company that offered a packaged tour led by Pearl Bryan. Traveling from Los Angeles, group members arrived in Kathmandu late one evening, passed through customs, settled into their rooms, and started out the next day on a sightseeing trip in and around the city.

Many of the activities involved ground transportation on a tour bus owned by Suresh Shrestha. As a hands-on manager, Suresh often talked with tour group members to make sure that their needs were met. He found that Frank and Pearl were especially interested in the history of Nepal, and he was happy to teach them as much as he could by pointing out important historical sites. The tour was going well, highlighted by a trip to Chitwan National Park to observe elephants and shopping tours to Freak Street in Thamal. One evening, Suresh picked up Pearl and Frank in his car and took them to the site of recent prodemocracy demonstrations.

The next morning, the tour was supposed to leave the hotel at 8:00 A.M. for a trip to a staging area for expeditions to Mount Everest. The bus was late, and it still had not arrived at 9:15 A.M. Frank and Pearl complained to Suresh. Suresh replied that the bus driver might have overslept but that he would be at the hotel soon. Frank and Pearl became visibly upset and pointed to a piece of paper that specified the 8:00 A.M. departure time. Suresh was surprised with the Americans' firm tone of voice and felt betrayed given the positive relationship he had developed with Frank and Pearl.

When problems arise in business dealings, different cultures offer various ways of finding a solution, and many are guided by the distinction between individualism and collectivism. Suresh brings a relational orientation from his collectivist background. He feels that he has developed good personal relations with the Americans, and that difficulties can be handled if people call upon past positive interactions. Americans often bring a more rational orientation to problem solving. "We had an agreement, here it is in writing, and so the bus should be here by now!" People's appeal to the very familiar behaviors of their own culture are more frequent when they are upset and when they feel that their time and money are being wasted.

This incident and analysis developed from conversations with D. P. S. Bhawuk, University of Hawaii College of Business Administration. He points out that the relational orientation is common in cultures such as Nepal where people view themselves as long-term members of permanent groups. The rational orientation is common in cultures such as the United States where people depend upon a strong legal system to protect their individual rights.

Power Distance: High and Low

There is no culture where power is equally distributed among its members. Power distance refers to the relative amount of psychological distance that separates high status and powerful people from lower status people (Hofstede, 2001). In high-power distant cultures (Philippines, Japan, Korea), power is held by relatively few people, and they are given great amounts of respect and deference. Employees are not likely to disagree with executives and company owners in public, and the use of first names when addressing superiors is uncommon or unthinkable. In low-power distant cultures, such as the United States, power is distributed widely, with different people having influence in diverse spheres. In addition, there is not a large psychological distance between leaders and followers such that leaders are seen as better people. People from different status backgrounds sometimes use first names when addressing each other. In fact, in low-power distant cultures, employees say to themselves, "The executives better watch out. In a few years I may have their jobs and they will be working for me!" In low-power distant cultures, powerful people can be the target of jokes. Comedians such as Jay Leno and David Letterman make large sums of money by deflating the powerful.

Incident: Business Cards Aid Discourse in Japan

Ron Olsen worked in Detroit for a large firm that imported automobile replacement parts. He traveled to Japan with the goal of identifying companies that might enter into joint venture agreements. Fortunately, he learned of an upcoming convention in Nagoya whose attendees worked in the automobile industry. He e-mailed his home office, where a Japanese colleague put him in touch with the convention organizers, and they issued an invitation to Ron.

Ron knew that Japanese businesspeople exchange business cards, and so he had some made while still in Detroit. However, he forgot to take them to the convention. Upon meeting people, they would offer him their cards but he would be unable to reciprocate. Ron was surprised that conference participants seemed to have difficulty communicating with him.

Ron knew of the norm that business cards are exchanged but he underestimated its importance. Reflecting its high-power distance, the Japanese language has various stylistic features that are used with people of different status levels compared to the speaker. There is a style for those with higher status, one for those with equal status, and another for those with lower status. A company president in Japan would use one style with government officials of equal status and another style with recent college graduates just starting their careers.

If Ron does not present his business card that gives the name of his organization and his title, then the Japanese have a very difficult time deciding what style to use. Rather than make a mistake, the Japanese might say very little. In contrast to Japanese, English (all English-speaking countries are low-power distant) has an important feature that might be called one style fits all. There is a collection of phrases accompanied by a pleasant voice tone that can be used with many people of varying status levels. In welcoming visitors from other countries, regardless of with whom they are communicating, English speakers frequently find themselves using phrases such as: "How was your trip? Are you over jet lag yet? Have you had a chance to go to do any sightseeing?"

Another implication of high-power distance is that people doing business in Japan frequently engage in title inflation. Salespeople become assistant vice presidents for marketing, and computer specialists become directors of electronic information processing. The belief is that prestigious titles lead to better treatment in Japan. Title inflation is not recommended, however, because the Japanese may overestimate the decision-making powers of the visiting businesspeople and will lose respect if the Americans cannot deliver on promises.

Uncertainty Avoidance: High and Low

We cannot predict the future with certainty. Given this universal fact, cultures react in different ways. In some cultures (e.g., Greece, Korea, Peru) people have tried to maximize predictability by having many norms and insisting that everybody take the norms seriously. These are sometimes called tight cultures (Triandis, 2004). The reaction to uncertainty is to have as much certainty as possible in the form of norms that children must learn so that they take them into their adulthoods. In other cultures (United States, Ireland, Sweden), there is less emphasis placed on multiple norms. They must have some norms to ensure everyday functioning in society (e.g., appropriate topics of conversation when meeting someone for the first time), but there are as few norms as possible and there are not draconian sanctions if norms are broken. Such cultures are said to be loose. In these low uncertainty avoidant cultures, people face the vicissitudes of the future by knowing that there may be many ways to deal with unpredictability. If there is a problem in the future, maybe it can be solved one way, maybe another, and maybe in a way we cannot even foresee today. But people are relatively comfortable with this uncertainty given that they are not locked into one set of norms that are taken seriously.

Incident: Cultural Expectations—Lockstep and Flexible Schedules

Knowing that future plans called for more expansion into North American markets, the divisional director of Samsung Electronics wanted to hire two entry-level managers with good English-language skills. He asked Minho Lee and Phil Harris to review applications, conduct interviews, and make recommendations. Minho was a Korean national and Phil was an American who had lived in Korea for eight years.

Minho was impressed with the application of Junkee Park, who was 26 years old. Junkee had attended Yonsei University

where he took as many English courses as possible, and he had also completed three years of military service. Phil preferred Bob Evans, originally from Phoenix, Arizona, who was 32 years old. Bob had traveled for two years after high school graduation, then went to a community college, and then worked for a construction company. After completing his bachelor's degree, he accepted a position teaching English in Korea. Even though Minho and Phil recommended that both candidates be hired, they were puzzled with each other's level of enthusiasm for their favorite candidate.

The cultural difference is based on expectations of what good job candidates should bring to an interview. In Korea, a relatively tight culture, candidates are impressive if their behavior has been lockstep. They go to high school, start college when 18 years old, have three years of military service, and then present themselves to the job market at age 25 or 26. If they deviate from this lockstep pattern, they may send the message that they are not serious and hardworking people. In the United States, a culture marked by relatively low uncertainty avoidance, expectations about job candidates are more open. People can take a few years off from formal schooling, can obtain work experience, and can develop skills hard to acquire in the classroom. These candidates often communicate desirable qualities such as creativity, independence, and willingness to take risks. Community colleges, in which people can enroll anytime during their adulthood, allow people to move away from lockstep expectations concerning age and formal education.

There are signs that the lockstep system is changing slowly. One of the first challenges occurred with Koreans who traveled to North America for a year of intense English-language instruction. This was frowned upon 10 years ago but is now much more common and is even encouraged by Korean companies interested in candidates with language skills.

Universal and Particular Relationships

In some cultures, people achieve their goals through developing complex sets of social relationships. These are called particular cultures, and the key to moving successfully through society is knowing many influential people (Osland & Bird, 2000). In China, developing such relationships is very complex. One's social networks where a person gives and receives favors is their *guanxi* (Fang, 1998; Luo & Chen, 1996). There is great emphasis places on who you know. In other cultures, there is a value placed on treating everyone alike and giving everyone the same opportunities. Admittedly often set aside, as with the efforts of high status parents to obtain benefits for their children, the value can be seen when people can achieve their goals even though they do not have personal relations with others who might affect goal achievement. There is a greater emphasis placed on what you know, for example, skills that will allow a person to obtain good job interviews because relatives and social networks cannot be the sole source of jobs and job leads.

Incident: Bureaucracies Have Their Attractions

Chu Jin, from Beijing, had traveled to Boston for the purpose of examining joint venture possibilities in the manufacturing of component parts for computers. His counterpart in Boston was Jim Allen. About a month into his stay, Chu Jin found that he needed some paperwork to complete a report that he wanted to send back to his home office in Beijing. He needed one tax form for claims on depreciation of inventory, and he also needed application forms for English as a second language classes at a local public school.

Chu Jin asked Jim if he knew some people who could get these forms for him. Jim said, "No, but I can call the tax office and the local school and talk to people who can send these materials to you." Jim got on the phone, made two calls, and 15 minutes later said that the tax and school forms should be in the mail by the end of the workday. Chu Jin looked stunned and did not know how to respond to Jim's news.

The cultural difference is that in China, people obtain information and official paperwork through their personal connections or through the connections of others whom they know. In the United States, people have insisted on a responsive bureaucracy whose employees are expected to be efficient in the distribution of basic information and paperwork. Americans do not have to know the person at the other end of the phone when they make a request. If the person in the bureaucracy is responsible for dispensing information and paperwork, then this is likely to happen.

We once asked a colleague from Shanghai how she would contact a government official for a basic tax form. She replied, "I wouldn't even try. I would have to ask around and find a friend who knows the government official." People who work with international businesspeople recommend that long-term Chinese visitors be introduced and integrated into a supportive group after they arrive in the United States. Even though these visitors could get on the phone and obtain information and various documents, they are more comfortable doing this through interactions with people they know rather than with strangers in an unseen bureaucracy.

Developing *guanxi* takes years and years. Good *guanxi* is more available to people from influential families than to people from modest backgrounds. Chinese who study in the United States find the ability to develop relations quickly,

and the presence of responsive bureaucracies, to be very attractive. This is one reason why so many want to stay in America, contributing to brain drain from China. This also illustrates another connection between time and culture: the time required to create social networks.

High- and Low-Trust Cultures

In some cultures, given the importance of particular relations, trust is slow to develop when newcomers are met (Fukuyama, 1995). The cultural value seems to be, "We won't trust you until you demonstrate that you can be trusted." This can take a great deal of time as people try to develop a reputation for trustworthiness. People in low-trust cultures feel that there are enemies who are out to do evil to them. In-group ties, developed over many years, are very important in low-trust cultures. In high-trust cultures, people can develop interpersonal relationships much more quickly. The cultural value is, "We will trust you until you demonstrate that you can't be trusted." For example, people can develop a business relationship after knowing each other for only a few months. This would be unimaginable in a low-trust culture.

Incident: Short Business Trips Can Yield Few Benefits

"Let's compare notes on our trips," Susan Nolan suggested to two of her colleagues. Susan, Mike James, and Judy Barth worked for an office supplies company in Atlanta, Georgia. The company both imported products that were manufactured abroad and also sought various international markets for direct sales to various businesses. The three division managers had recently traveled to Venezuela, Indonesia, and Spain. The three agreed that, after meeting potential collaborators and clients in these three countries, it took a long time to get down to business.

They shared other common experiences. They commented that people in the other countries wanted to engage in endless small talk about extraneous matters like families and hobbies. People were wonderful hosts and took the three Americans to some excellent restaurants, but conversations continued to focus on nonbusiness issues. All three managers had to renegotiate with travel agents because they were forced to extend their visits beyond their originally scheduled time frames.

Susan, Mike, and Judy are trying to do business in cultures where trust develops more slowly than in the United States. In these cultures, people view themselves as long-term members of a group, and membership in these groups is often determined by birth. Given strong group affiliations, people benefit from group memberships, but they also have extensive obligations to fellow members and also have the feeling that outsiders may be threatening. With this combination of benefits, obligations, and perceived threats, people do not offer group membership quickly to those not presently in the in-group.

Potential collaborators and clients in the three countries want to learn a great deal about the three Americans. What sorts of people are they? Will they be good business partners? Can we trust them to follow through on commitments? Will they follow through on unwritten agreements that were sealed with a handshake? Answers to these questions come during the many conversations and evening dinners that the Americans found tiring. If they agree to do business with the Americans, the people in the three countries would be offering collective memberships. This is a major step in business negotiations that collectivists take very seriously.

Americans certainly join many groups, but the time frame for membership is often shorter and the obligations are fewer. The three Americans who want to do business overseas have undoubtedly learned a set of social skills that allows them to meet people quickly and to get down to business. But these social skills have to be set aside in cultures where trust develops slowly.

CULTURE AND PERSONALITY

There are great debates regarding the nature of interaction between culture and personality. Some cross-cultural theorists argue that people are inherently different, and culture merely accentuates these differences. Other theorists maintain that people are fundamentally the same, and culture serves to make them different. Regardless of these arguments, however, the fact remains that people within a given culture can exhibit largely disparate tendencies. If we acknowledge that a given culture provides the cues and norms that govern the general nature of people's behavior in that culture, we conclude tentatively that personality serves to differentiate people's behaviors in similar contexts even further than culture alone. Recognizing this difference takes us a step closer to understanding behavioral differences within a certain culture. Having discussed some of the more salient points regarding culture, our analysis now turns us to personality. One caveat we offer from the outset of integrating the literatures on culture, personality, and time is that no single framework can accurately account for all the possible facets of each construct. Rather, we can only suggest what components of each construct are most prominent. Ultimately the interplay between the three can never integrate all individual differences, as there will always be outliers and exceptions no matter how comprehensive a framework is.

Returning to our discussion of personality, the most recent themes in the literature suggest that contextualized patterns of situational behavior strongly govern people's actions, and people behave within cultural norms according to a situational context (Mischel, 2004). Whereas this principle is strongly grounded in theory and corroborated by empirical test results, people often have difficulty accepting that their behaviors are not consistent and that they do not behave the same way in all situations. Consider the following incident that may help to elucidate the reality of behaviors differing according to situational contexts.

Incident: Contextualized Behaviors—What Would You Say?

Lance Robertson is a high school band director and an accomplished saxophone player. Because of his visibility in the local music community, he has been asked to judge the annual High School Solo and Ensemble Band competition. On the day of the competition, Lance hears many band players on different instruments. As primarily a saxophone player, Lance takes particular interest in the playing of the student saxophonists. Of all the students in the program, one young man in particular sticks out in Lance's mind. The young man attempts a popular, yet challenging, piece in the saxophone repertoire. Unfortunately, he plays the piece quite badly with poor tone and intonation, inconsistent tempo, and lack of overall musicianship. He is forced to stop more than once because he loses his place. Although Lance would like to be encouraging, he also feels the need to be honest in his ratings. He assigns a rating of poor to the student and tells him not only that the piece was obviously too difficult for his level of playing but also that he needs to take some serious time to work on the basics of woodwind playing.

The following week, Lance's 10-year-old nephew, Harold, plays "Happy Birthday" for Lance on the saxophone at his 50th birthday party celebration. With Lance's encouragement, Harold has been studying the saxophone at school for the last year. Having studied only for a year, he plays with some random squeaks and missed notes. However, Lance is delighted, gives Harold a warm hug, and tells him how well he played and how proud he is. Harold just beams with pride.

Few people would have difficulty relating to this situation. The variable of family versus stranger aside, there is a strong tendency to behave differently given different situational contexts. Whereas the first situation in the preceding incident necessitated constructive criticism, the second received heartfelt praise even though the playing in both situations was decidedly mediocre.

Rather than assume that people behave in the same manner in all situations, the more stable *if . . . then . . .* patterns of behavior are a more popular explanation than unconditional, decontextualized personality references. In the preceding incident, the context provided cues for Lance's behavior in two similar, yet different, situations. One could characterize Lance as being helpful. Given that characterization, one might describe Lance's behavior using the following *if . . . then . . .* contexts: If Lance is critiquing saxophone playing in a competition, then he is constructively critical. If Lance is listening to his 10-year-old nephew play the saxophone, then he is categorically positive and encouraging. Lance deems both types of feedback as helpful, but his help manifests in two obviously contrasting ways. The inclusion of the contexts differentiates between occasions when Lance behaves differently even though he is being helpful on both occasions. In the same way, saying, "Mary is happy," is not as precise as saying, "If Mary gets her way, then she is happy." This is the specificity of the contextualized reference.

Understanding of this incident underscores the reality that people will not behave in the same way in all situations. Rather, there are certain conditions that influence behavior. This type of *if . . . then . . .* contextual behavior pattern constitutes a behavioral signature of personality. The term *signature* relates to how a person behaves in the majority of like situations (Mischel, 2004). There will be few exceptions to the norms of the behavior pattern because that is the behavioral signature. With this predictive knowledge, it is easier to place an individual into a framework that is more consistently stable because of the knowledge that certain conditions will precipitate certain behaviors. If we accept that people behave according to certain situational contexts, we can now turn our discussion to dimensions of personality.

DIMENSIONS OF PERSONALITY

One of the most popular approaches in the social sciences for categorizing personality is the Five-Factor Model (FFM; McCrae and John, 1992; see also Chapter 5 in this volume). To devise these five factors, the creators combed the dictionary to gather names of personality traits. As such, the Big Five are descriptive and fail to explain the origins of personality (McCrae & Costa, 1989). As merely a taxonomy of personality characteristics, the Big Five have been the subject of much debate as to their universality or etic nature. Whereas it remains highly possible that not all personality constructs have been correctly identified in all cultures, current research directions do include testing the applicability of the FFM in many cultures (Hofstede & McCrae, 2004; McCrae, 2002).

Although more research is necessary in this direction, preliminary findings attest to the etic nature of the FFM. For example, McCrae and Terracciano (2005) found that general personality traits based on observer ratings show evidence of being universal. Coupled with previous research using self-reports, this finding places researchers a step closer to determining the existence of pancultural personality traits.

The five factors in the model are often referred to as the Big Five of personality: Openness to Experience, Conscientiousness, Extraversion, Agreeableness, and Neuroticism. Although these single labels commonly describe the five factors, each factor also can be placed at the extreme of a continuum that creates a dimension of personality similar to the Hofstede dimensions (Hofstede, 2001) in cultural theories discussed in preceding sections. Taken in this manner, each of the personality dimensions becomes: Openness to Experience versus Closed to Experience, Conscientiousness versus Unconscientiousness, Extraversion versus Introversion, Agreeableness versus Antagonism, and Neuroticism versus Emotional Stability.

SUBSETS OF THE BIG FIVE

Under each of these dimensions fall multiple adjectives that further describe the nature of each construct.

Openness to Experience versus Closed to Experience

People who are open to experience are curious and demonstrate a need for variety. At the extreme, they can be radical. People with this personality are usually creative, imaginative, and have a cultivated sense of aesthetic sensitivity. In many cases, they have a wide range of interests.

It is interesting to note that a study of children's personalities as manifested by their behaviors found that Openness to Experience was the only factor among the Big Five that did not correlate systematically or intuitively to expected patterns of behavior for that personality type (Markey, Markey, & Tinsley, 2004). Although more research is needed in this area, it is possible to conclude tentatively that people may develop a broad range of interests over the years leading to increased Openness to Experience. That said, Openness to Experience arguably changes with age more than the other constructs of the Big Five.

Conscientiousness versus Unconscientiousness

Conscientious people are organized and orderly. Scrupulousness and self-discipline characterize their behavior. Conscientious people may also demonstrate greater persistence and a higher need for achievement.

Extraversion versus Introversion

Extraversion is perhaps the most widely debated construct among the Big Five. Questions regarding the precise definition of Extraversion as a personality type have formed the basis for multiple research studies on personality and extraversion. One of the debates surrounding this personality construct is the nature of extraversion as linked to sociability or reward sensitivity. Lucas and colleagues (Lucas, Diener, Grob, Suh, & Shao, 2000) obtained results that argue that extraverts' sociability is a by-product of reward sensitivity. This means that extraverts find social situations rewarding. Therefore, they engage in more social behavior as a means of satisfying their reward need. However, according to the original meaning as put forth by McCrae and John (1992), Extraversion is characterized by sociability, warmth, and gregariousness. Extraverts have tendencies toward assertiveness and even domination. They seek excitement and tend to experience positive emotions.

Agreeableness versus Antagonism

Sympathy, trust, cooperation, and altruism are some of the characteristics of Agreeableness. As a personality construct, Agreeableness might also prove difficult to pinpoint. It is important to remember that an individual with this personality trait will not necessarily say yes to everything that is said and agree with other people. Rather, Agreeableness is a sign of harmony-seeking, not the sign of a pushover or a yes-man.

Neuroticism versus Emotional Stability

Neuroticism is the only construct among the Big Five with negative connotations. As such, Neuroticism describes people with the predisposition to experience negative affects. Some of these affects include anxiety, anger, and depression. Hostility, self-consciousness, impulsiveness, and vulnerability also have been used to describe people with Neuroticism as a dominant personality trait. At the other end of this continuum are emotionally stable people who experience fewer of these difficulties.

Jungian Types as Measured by the Myers-Briggs Type Inventory

Another way of conceptualizing measuring personality types is Jungian types as measured by the Myers-Briggs Type In-

ventory (MBTI). Although the Big Five dominates in academic research as the instrument of choice for measuring personality, the MBTI enjoys great success in popular research and consulting. According to its creators, the MBTI has a solid theoretical basis by which to explain its findings because it takes its roots in Jungian theory (Myers & McCaulley, 1985). Similar to the Big Five, the MBTI uses continua to characterize an individual's predisposition for each of the four following dichotomous preferences: Extraversion (E) versus Introversion (I), Sensing (S) versus Intuiting (N), Thinking (T) versus Feeling (F), and Judging (J) versus Perceiving (P). With MBTI, there is a dominant preference among each pairing, and all preferences are positive. Given a person's dominant preferences on each of these eight characterizations, the MBTI can profile people with one of 16 different personality types.

Rather than explain each of these characterizations of the MBTI, a more prudent use of our limited space is to discuss the existence of a correlation between the Myers-Briggs types and the Big Five constructs. McCrae and Costa (1989) analyzed results of data collected from both instruments and suggested the following correlation between these two conceptualizations of personality as shown in Table 3.1.

Neuroticism versus Emotional Stability from the Big Five is not measured by the MBTI, which is indicative of Jung's omission of any definitions of emotional instability. However, with the exception of Neuroticism, McCrae and Costa found that the remaining four continua of the Big Five match the four pairings of the MBTI with "impressive evidence of convergence" (p. 33). Although respective research disciplines still maintain a preference for one instrument over the other, this correlation is significant in that it lends validity to both instruments as effective measures of personality. Furthermore, discovering the correlation between the Big Five and MBTI is useful for the purposes of this chapter and the

TABLE 3.1 **Expected Relationships between Jungian Types and Big Five Personality Traits**

Jungian Type (from MBTI)	Big 5
Intuitive	Open
Sensing	Closed (not Open)
Feeling	Agreeable
Thinking	Not prioritizing Agreeableness
Judging	High Conscientiousness
Perceiving	Low Conscientiousness
Extraversion	Extraversion
Introversion	Introversion

Note. Adapted from data reported in "Reinterpreting the Myers-Briggs Type Indicator from the Perspective of the Five-Factor Model of Personality," by R. McCrae and P. Costa, 1989, *Journal of Personality, 57,* pp. 17–40. Copyright 1989 by R. McCrae and P. Costa. Adapted with permission of the authors.

attempt to ascertain a relationship between culture, personality, and time because there has been a direct link made between Myers-Briggs types and time orientation. With a correlation not only between the MBTI and time orientations but also between the MBTI and the Big Five, we can now also suppose a relationship between the Big Five and time orientations. With this correlation of MBTI with Big Five personality types, we have a much more comprehensive framework in which to analyze the relationships between culture, personality, and time orientation. However, before examining the relationship between personality (as measured either by MBTI or by the Big Five) and time, it is necessary to discuss some of the dimensions of time.

DIMENSIONS OF TIME

Time, like personality, is one of the more popular research constructs in the cross-cultural field and the social sciences. It has been found that people around the world have different perspectives on time. Anyone who has had a siesta in South America or ran for a train in Japan has experienced some of the different perspectives on time from around the world. Regardless of these differing perspectives, time remains a dominant theme as a universal construct regardless of the culture in which it is found. Also, the work of previous researchers who have related perspectives on time as they related to specific cultures provides us with additional pieces to fit into a comprehensive framework that relates culture, personality, and time. We now turn our attention to some of these findings on time.

Past, Present, and Future

One of the earliest writings on time as a cultural theory came from the anthropologists Kluckhohn and Strodtbeck (1961) who wrote about time as one of five value orientations. According to their research, people's time orientation can be toward the past, present, or future. They write the following regarding each of these time classifications: Cultures with orientations toward the past revere tradition and resist change. They often take pride in having long historical traditions. Reverence for the elderly and traditions are also symbols of past-oriented cultures. Some of the cultures that Kluckhohn and Strodtbeck placed into this category include British, Greek, French, Japanese, and Chinese.

Present-oriented cultures emphasize a spirit of living in the moment. A relaxed, unhurried style is consistent with this spirit. As such, people from these cultures are more likely to be spontaneous. According to Kluckhohn and Strodtbeck, Philippine and Latin American cultures are present-oriented.

Finally, future orientation is most highly characteristic of U.S. culture. Americans are constantly planning for the future and organizing their lives. For most Americans, there is a palpable impatience when they are made to wait beyond an appointed time. Finally, future-oriented cultures embrace change and innovation and have less tolerance for tradition and convention.

Monochronic and Polychronic Time

Another anthropologist, Edward Hall, pointed to the importance of monochronic (M-time) and polychronic time (P-time) (Hall, 1983). According to Hall, polychronic time is synonymous with doing many things at once. A common example of this behavior is a U.S. businessperson who is responding to an e-mail, talking on an international long-distance phone call, and eating lunch simultaneously. Monochronic time, on the other hand, connotes doing one thing at a time and finishing a task before moving on to the next one. Whereas it might seem that P-time is synonymous with the U.S. obsession with multitasking, Hall's original classification actually placed the United States in the M-time category. However, more recent research has suggested not only that the United States is gravitating toward a P-time orientation (Kaufman, Lane, & Lindquist, 1991) but also that organizational cultures can impose P-time orientations on otherwise M-time oriented individuals (Bluedorn, Kaufman, & Lane, 1992). Furthermore, Brislin and Kim (2003) have suggested that it is necessary to examine Hall's M-time and P-time classifications in conjunction with another dimension of time and accordingly suggest clock and event time. With these three caveats, let us examine the clock versus event perspective on time and then consider Brislin and Kim's framework before making any conclusions regarding the U.S. classification as M-time or P-time.

Clock and Event Time

The distinction between clock time and event time is largely as the name implies: Does the clock govern one's perspective on time and the course of events one follows, or does the flow of events and their sequencing determine one's plans? Cultures that pay strict attention to schedules and punctuality, such as the United States, are clock-time cultures. In contrast, cultures such as Latin America tend to be event-time cultures. Interestingly, the distinction between clock time and event time as it relates to a specific culture is not always an absolute. Just as an M-time oriented individual can multitask under certain conditions to meet the demands of a P-time work culture, a single culture can encompass both clock time and event time characteristic properties. The first author has found this to be true in Hawaii. During the weekdays, people in Hawaii maintain adherence to a clock and keep appointments with faithful punctuality that would be acceptable anywhere in the United States. On the weekends, however, punctuality and appointments are set aside in favor of letting events take their natural course. In Hawaii, going to a picnic on the weekend and showing up two hours after the appointed start time is acceptable. However, during the week, showing up two hours late for a business appointment is likely to incur the frustration of the person with whom you are meeting.

In light of the discussion in the section on personality about the if . . . then . . . signatures, it is worthwhile to note that the same structure is applicable to this example of the integration of clock time and event time in Hawaii. In this case, the two signatures would read as follows: If it is a weekday, people in Hawaii are clock-time oriented and maintain appointments punctually. If it is a weekend, people are event-time oriented and let the natural flow of events guide their schedules. Whereas the experiences of both authors suggests that this type of situation works in Hawaii, consider the following example of how integrating clock time and event time norms can be tricky:

Incident: Who to See First?—Clock Time versus Event Time

Ferdinand Valenzuela is originally from Chile and currently works as a professor of Spanish language and South American literature at a prestigious New England college. He is quite a popular professor among the students as evidenced by full classes and busy office hours. He is scheduled to have a meeting with his department head, Professor Dorothy Jennings, next Tuesday afternoon at 2:00 regarding curriculum and classes for the following semester. Because of both individuals' busy schedules, this is the third time that they have rescheduled the meeting.

On Tuesday just as Ferdinand is preparing to meet with Professor Jennings, there is a knock at his office door. When Ferdinand opens the door, he is pleasantly surprised to see an old colleague from Chile, Professor Manuel Ramirez. Professor Ramirez has been in the United States for the past week at a conference in another city and has made a special trip to Ferdinand's university in hopes of seeing him. He has a few hours that afternoon before heading to the airport to take a plane home later that night. Ferdinand is ecstatic to see his old friend, but he remembers also that he has a meeting with Professor Jennings that has already been postponed three times.

Originally coming from an event-time culture in South America, Ferdinand should be used to dropping everything else to spend some precious time with the friend whom he has not seen in some time. In his culture, this is an important event! However, being that he is operating in a clock-time culture, he also understands the importance of maintaining appointments, especially because the upcoming appointment has already been rescheduled three times. This is a tough dilemma for Ferdinand. On one hand he wishes to see his friend and does not want to offend him by running off to another appointment. At the same time, he cannot appear irresponsible or frivolous to his department head by entertaining a last-minute, out-of-town guest, even if it is a long-time friend. Yet this is the difficulty for people with a clock-time orientation living in an event-time culture and vice versa. There are countless cross-cultural misunderstandings that ensue as a result of the seeming incompatibility of these two time perspectives.

With the understanding of both M-time versus P-time and clock time versus event time, we can now take a look at Brislin and Kim's framework for classifying cultures according to both dimensions. Brislin and Kim make the distinction in their framework between fast and slow paces of life. A fast pace of life corresponds to a clock-time orientation; a slow pace of life is more indicative of an event-time orientation. They use this difference in conjunction with the M-time versus P-time difference to categorize countries. Using a standard 2-by-2 matrix, Brislin and Kim make the following four classifications: (1) P-time and clock time: United States, (2) P-time and event time: Latin America and Mediterranean countries, (3) M-time and clock time: East Asian countries, and (4) M-time and event time: nonindustrialized cultures with abundant resources (see Brislin & Kim, 2003, p. 370). With this framework, we have an additional building block in our framework relating culture, time, and personality.

Perhaps the countries in the fourth cell prove most elusive in terms of specific examples because relatively little psychological research has been done in these countries vis-à-vis topics analyzed in this chapter. However, the remaining three classifications should be understandable. Additionally, there are implications from these differences that arise in business and other interactions between people from these cultures. For example, the difference between P-time and M-time in the United States and East Asia, respectively, frequently surfaces in business negotiations. At the same time, U.S. professionals traveling to South America frequently express frustration at locals' lack of punctuality.

One note worth mentioning is that these assignments are not fixed. Just as the United States shows migration from Hall's original classification as an M-time culture to more P-time, other countries might also be showcasing similar shifts.

Future research might be directed at showing how cultures that were originally event time are affected by globalization and the need to do business with clock-time cultures. In addition, the dominance of research from the United States in many social sciences disciplines places a heavy ethnocentric bias on knowledge. A worthwhile study might compare time perspectives between East Asian and South American countries without the United States included, as its absence will force the examination of concepts as they are experienced in these countries without the imposition of U.S. concepts.

One recent indication of such movement from event time to clock time in a South American country was found in a recent popular press article detailing the efforts of Ecuadorian President Lucio Guttierez to be on time particularly to his professional meetings and appointments. President Guttierez's efforts are at the forefront of a national effort to move away from the traditional "Ecuadorian Time" of being routinely late. The president's promise to be more punctual was echoed by promises from a citizens group to keep criticizing the president for his habitual tardiness. This criticism is unusual because typically high-status people do not need to apologize for their tardiness (Brislin & Kim, 2003). Ostensibly, as people come into increasingly more frequent contact with people from other cultures, everyone will need to make adjustments to their indigenous norms regarding time perspectives.

Brislin and Kim reference punctuality as having different cross-cultural implications in terms of the unit of analysis. This term refers to how people organize their days. In terms of punctuality, the reference is to how late one can be without having to apologize or make the other party feel impatient. In the United States, the unit of analysis is five minutes. However, in South American countries, the unit of analysis can be much longer, even extending to hours. Robert Levine alludes to the frustration he experienced teaching at a Brazilian university in *A Geography of Time* (Levine, 1997). He details how students would come to class up to two hours late (after the scheduled dismissal time) and still expected him to stay and answer their questions. To people socialized in North America, such an expectation seems clearly unrealistic. However, in Brazil, this was commonplace. Knowing what the unit of analysis is when traveling to different countries and cultures with different clock-time or event-time orientations is an important key to successful intercultural interactions.

TOWARD INTEGRATING CULTURE, PERSONALITY, AND TIME

Personality and Time

The section on personality not only introduced two popular instruments for measuring personality, it also took a step to-

ward showing how the two instruments correspond to each other. With this knowledge, we can also start to integrate time into the overall framework. One of the first such scales to integrate time and personality is the Zimbardo Time Perspective Inventory.

According to Zimbardo and Boyd (1999), time perspective (TP) is an individual-differences variable that exerts considerable influence on human behavior by allowing individuals to divide their experiences into past, present, and future segments. TP influences decision-making, and, as such, TP biases have predictive characteristics regarding how an individual will react to certain situations.

Zimbardo and Boyd's study used the Zimbardo Time Perspective Inventory (ZTPI) to create individual profiles that have corresponding personality characteristics. However, these personality constructs might not necessarily be the Big Five. If we can relate these constructs to the Big Five, perhaps the Zimbardo framework also will be useful to our framework. The ZTPI asks respondents to make self-assessments using a 5-point Likert scale on the following five items that correspond to TP biases: past-negative, present-hedonistic, future, past-positive, and present-fatalistic. Characteristics of each of these biases are as follows:

- Past-negative: reflects a negative, aversive view of the past.
- Present-hedonistic: risk-taking, carpe diem, orientation with present pleasure.
- Future: delay of gratification, resisting temptation, maturity, striving toward future goals.
- Past-positive: warm, sentimental attitude about the past.
- Present-fatalistic: helplessness toward future and life.

Another measure of validity of the ZTPI involved in-depth interviews with students from Stanford University who scored above the 95th percentile on one of the ZTPI items but below the 95th percentile on the remaining four. The conclusion that Zimbardo and Boyd make is that TP influences a wide array of behavioral characteristics. Some of these behaviors include risk-taking, goal-setting and achievement, sexual behaviors, spirituality, and interacting with other people. Whereas the generalizability of these findings is limited due to the small, student sample, certain findings could potentially contribute to developing a profile that integrates time perspective with personality. Furthermore, these findings reveal implications for training and health care. Because different social settings may require different time perspectives, learning to alter one's perspective based on the requirements of a social setting could be a valuable skill that is teachable through training. One of the main points is that no individual can live exclusively with one single TP bias. Rather, balance between

TPs related to the past, present, and future is the key. Finally, a greater understanding of time perspective may ultimately help to shed some additional light on the Big Five personality dimensions. Additionally, understanding time perspective more intimately may help to reveal additional personality dimensions that are not captured in the Big Five. As current research is testing the etic nature of the Big Five, the ZTPI might be a useful instrument toward this end.

Culture and Time

Brislin and Kim (2003) attempted to provide a piece of this framework that comes from their comparison of cultures as a function of their M-time versus P-time orientations as well as clock-time versus event-time orientations. Although shifts are occurring (e.g., the United States toward a more P-time orientation and event-time cultures toward more clock-time orientations), their framework provides a definitive starting point for future research.

Culture and Personality

Comparing culture as a cultural-level difference and personality as an individual-level difference poses a unique challenge. However, research suggests that certain personality types may appear more frequently in some cultures than in others. For example, Markus and Kitayama (1991) use the terms *independence* and *interdependence* to describe how cultures can be categorized based on the perceptions of self held by people in those cultures. At the most general level, Europeans and Caucasian Americans are independent, whereas Asians are interdependent. People with independent concepts of self, which Markus and Kitayama call self-construals, express their individuality and uniqueness. Conversely, those with interdependent concepts of self emphasize harmony within their in-group over individual uniqueness and aspirations. Markus and Kitayama (1991) argue that these views of the self influence cognition, emotion, and motivation. Thus, we have at least one possible starting point for sifting through differences in personality as a function of culture.

In addition, the concept of priming suggests possibilities for relating personality differences to the cultures in which they are found. People primed with different stimuli might be motivated to act in different ways, thus revealing different parts of their personalities. One of the classic examples is that of a Chinese American person who views images of the Statue of Liberty and the Great Wall of China. Upon seeing the Statue of Liberty, the individual might experience feelings of nationalism and patriotism that are consistent with their socialization in the United States where the Statue of Liberty is a symbol of liberty and freedom. In contrast, the same individual viewing images of the Great Wall of China might experience the same feelings of national pride now directed at China, not the United States.

This individual clearly identifies with two different national cultures. When primed with two different cultural symbols respectively, he or she will experience sentiments specific to that culture. Herein lies yet another example of the if . . . then . . . signature discussed at the beginning of the section on personality. In this instance, the scenarios would read as follows: If a Chinese American person sees pictures of the Statue of Liberty, he or she will experience feelings of American patriotism. If a Chinese American person sees pictures of the Great Wall of China, he or she will experience feelings of Chinese nationalism. Depending on the stimulus, different reactions can be evoked, thus exposing different parts of the personality. This conclusion supports Mischel's (2004) claim that personality is rooted in situational contexts. Furthermore, if more research supports the situational nature of personality, mainstays of attribution theory, namely the fundamental attribution error, might not be made as frequently if people accept that behaviors are largely contextual rather than immutable features of personality (Markus & Kitayama, 1991).

METHODOLOGICAL CONCERNS

We have chosen to present material on culture, personality, and time by discussing research findings and putting them into frameworks that aid in their understanding. We chose not to discuss cross-cultural methodological issues during the presentation of research findings but instead decided to present them in this section. Some colleagues would disagree, feeling that methodological concerns are so important that they must be covered at the same time that tentative research findings are presented. We do not disagree with the importance of discussing methodology, but we felt that the material would flow more smoothly for readers given our decision on how to cover both research findings and research methodology.

The literature on cross-cultural research methods is extensive, and it is required reading for scholars planning research in languages and cultures other than their own. Key references include an overview of methods by Brislin, Lonner, and Thorndike (1973); a book written for researchers to actually bring to other cultures (Lonner & Berry, 1986); one of the volumes of each edition of the *Handbook of Cross-Cultural Psychology* (Triandis & Berry, 1980; Berry, Poortinga, & Panday, 1997); and an *Annual Review of Psychology* chapter with discussion of methodological concerns in cross-cultural personality research (Triandis & Suh, 2002). Given this extensive literature, our limited space allows us to discuss only a few issues. We have decided to discuss conceptual equivalence, familiarity with materials and procedures, translation between languages, and sampling.

Conceptual Equivalence

The basic question in discussion of conceptual equivalence is, "Are the meanings of concepts, and items that measure the presence or absence of those concepts, the same in all the cultures under study?" Another way of asking the question is, "Are researchers imposing concepts from their own culture, usually the culture where the research questions were first raised, on people from other cultures?" Researchers are wise to remember how scales are first developed. Researchers write many items and then administer them to people, often samples of convenience from their own communities, in their own cultures, easily available to the researchers. All items are examined, and many are eliminated based on such criteria as lack of positive correlations with a core of items that do intercorrelate. Thus, items are purified based on the fact that they seem to cluster (sometimes the slang term *hang together* is used) in one culture easily available to the researchers. Items that do not contribute to an interpretable cluster are discarded. It becomes a very reasonable question to ask, "Why should researchers expect a set of purified items that measure a concept, for example in a community within the United States, to measure the same concept in Japan, Nigeria, or India?"

Researchers need to examine the meaning of concepts and their corresponding items meant to measure the concepts. For example, researchers may be interested in the possible universality of introversion and extroversion. Items on published and widely used scales often ask about comfort levels at parties. These could be good items in individualistic countries where extroverts pursue their own interests at parties and circulate among different people trying to find interesting conversationalists. Party-oriented items might not work as well in cultures where people are not expected to circulate. In China, for instance (Wang, Brislin, Wang, Williams, & Chao, 2000), people arrive at a party and start talking with others whom they already know. They stay with these others for the length of the party. If high-status people feel that someone should meet another person, they will interrupt conversational groups and make sure that the introductions take place.

For the concept conscientiousness, items concerning punctuality to meetings may work well in some cultures. But as we have already discussed in our discussion on cross-cultural

research into time, some cultures place less emphasis on clocks in the organization of people's days. In fact, in these cultures people would be considered unconscientious if they failed to help a coworker who needed a little help at 11:25 A.M. given that they had an appointment with a client at 11:30 A.M.

One way to deal with the equivalence is to work with personality concepts that are important within a culture as evidenced by frequency of conversations about the traits, their role in defining people's reputations, and their importance in life decisions such as job hires and approval of children's proposed spouses. Then, items can be written that also reflect how people talk about the concepts. For example, in China, conscientious people can cancel a social outing with a friend if a high-status person suggests a last-minute meeting. Conscientious people are attentive to the wishes of high-status authority figures. They do not even have to present an excuse to the friends with whom they originally had a social engagement. This approach to personality-scale development, working with concepts meaningful within a culture, was utilized by Cheung and her colleagues (Cheung et al., 1996) with their work on the Chinese Personality Assessment Inventory.

Familiarity with Materials and Procedures

Most personality tests were developed in highly industrialized nations and were normed on literate samples whose members had long experience with reading test items, making choices, filling in answer sheets, and so forth. Children in these cultures are familiar with aspects of performance tests such as puzzle completion and finding hidden figures in pictures of forests, cities, and big crows. These experienced test takers also are accustomed to the presence of researchers and testers who enter their lives, ask them to answer some questions about themselves, and then leave, never to be seen again. These are totally unfamiliar behaviors in many cultures around the world. Especially when tests involve performance in terms of how much can be done in a certain amount of time, or how many small figures can be found in large, abstract pictures, researchers are wise to worry whether or not familiarity with tests and research procedures is affecting results. Simply, the concept of thinking about oneself in terms of personality test items, and then responding on various types of scales, is far more familiar to schooled adolescents and adults than it is to preliterate people. Standard cross-cultural practice has long been to allow great amounts of time to familiarize people with test procedures and to make them comfortable with materials (Brislin et al., 1973). Practice tests, time spent manipulating objects, and asking personal questions people are comfortable answering (e.g., kinship ties) are good investments.

Cultural differences can have an impact on people's preferred manner of responding. In semiliterate collective cultures, it can be an odd request if researchers ask people to complete a questionnaire or interview by themselves as in the standard testing situation common in highly industrialized nations. In these collective cultures, people may not have personal opinions or well-developed views of the self. They have group opinions and views about people, including themselves. They may be much more comfortable getting together with members of their collectives and completing the questionnaire or interview as a group effort. This would be a good study. Can the five-factor solution be found in a highly collective culture where people are much more comfortable filling out questionnaires with constant input from members of their in-groups?

Translation between Languages

After careful thought has been given to the types of items that researchers want to work with, as discussed in the preceding, cross-cultural research often demands that measuring instruments in other languages be developed. Based on experiences working with translators who were bilingual in English and one of 10 additional languages, Brislin (1986) developed a set of guidelines for writing English that is likely to lead to good translations. These guidelines include: using short sentences of no more than 16 words, use the active rather than passive voice, repeat nouns instead of using pronouns, avoid metaphors and colloquialisms, add context for key ideas to make sure that translators (and eventual research participants who respond to the items) are clear as to the meaning of items, and use specific terms rather than generic class terms of which the specific is a member.

After item preparation, researchers can consider use of the back-translation procedure (Brislin, 1986). In this method, one bilingual works with the original English material (or other starting language decided upon by the researcher) and prepares a version in the target language. Then, a second bilingual blindly translates back into English. Researchers can then compare the two English versions and can begin to make inferences about the quality and equivalence of the translation. This procedure can continue for additional rounds with additional bilinguals acting as translators, as in this algorithm:

Original language → target language → original → target → original → target → original

If material from the original language can survive these multiple translations, then the third translation is probably both equivalent to the original and is clear to translators and, by extension, eventual research participants. Using a procedure such as this, researchers decenter their translations. No one language is the center of the research project. Instead, aspects of the target language are taken into account. If material in the original language is not readily translatable, it disappears during the multistep back-translation procedure. With decentering, researchers would use the final back-translated version as the wording with original language respondents, because that is the one most equivalent to the target version. For example, items from the Marlowe-Crowne social-desirability inventory (Crowne & Marlowe, 1964) went through the multistep back-translation procedure in attempts to produce a version in the Chamorro language. One of the original items is: "I don't find it particularly difficult to get along with loud-mouthed, obnoxious people." There is not a readily available equivalent of *obnoxious* in Chamorro, and *loud-mouthed* is just enough of an English-language colloquialism to cause difficulties. After the multistep back-translation procedure, the Chamorro version became, "It is not hard for me to talk with people who have a big mouth." In comparing Chamorro and English speakers, this back-translated version was used, given the assumption that it is closest to the Chamorro version (the third target version from the algorithm).

After the translation process, instruments are available in two or more languages. Pretesting is always important to identify difficulties in that actual use of instruments by respondents, such as fatigue, difficulties with item format, local meanings of terms that the translators may have missed, and so forth. After data is gathered, decisions have to be made concerning statistical analyses that follow from the purpose of the research. For example, researchers may want to test the existence of a concept from the five-factor solution, such as open-mindedness in another culture. They could perform a confirmatory factor analysis to determine if the translations of the English-language items cluster together in the same way as they do in the United States.

As with all advice concerning cross-cultural methods, we can introduce only a few key points. The references listed at the beginning of the section "Methodological Concerns" should be consulted during the design of actual research projects.

Sampling of Respondents

Always a problem no matter what the psychological study, the appropriate selection of samples of respondents takes on additional complications in cross-cultural research. Generalizations to populations from selected samples can be very dangerous. If researchers sample college students in an African or Asian country, they must worry about the representativeness of this select sample, given that in many countries very few students go to college. If they use paper-and-pencil tests that demand high levels of literacy, they must worry about generalization to nonliterate people from the country under study. If they sample students in high schools and colleges where the curricula and texts are patterned after models in North America and Europe, they have to worry about whether they are measuring concepts that students learned from reading books or whether they learned the concepts growing up in their cultures. If U.S. or European research is based on multiple samples from multiple regions within countries (e.g., research on the five-factor solution), then it is a mistake for researchers to claim that they are supporting or refuting earlier research based on one sample of respondents from one part of a country.

Even knowing these caveats, given the expense of random surveys of a country's population, and the difficulties of encouraging people randomly chosen to complete personality measures, most research will be based on various samples of convenience. However, researchers sometimes can choose samples that are more appropriate than others. When testing the universality of personality concepts and structures, for example, Triandis and Suh (2002) suggest that samples be chosen that are maximally distinct in terms of the types of cultural dimensions discussed earlier in this chapter. If psychological concepts were developed in highly individualistic nations, sample from collectivistic cultures. If the languages used in early research were Indo-European, sample from distant language-family groups. If there is not an emphasis on tremendous deference between research psychologists and respondents (as in low-power distant countries such as the United States), sample from countries where well-educated researchers attached to universities are revered. Many times, good research can take place when researchers search for additional concepts that may have been missed or underemphasized in previous research carried out in a limited number of countries. In work that had, as one aim, to expand on the five-factor solution, Cheung and her colleagues (1996) felt there could be a factor that involved a respect for tradition. Such a concept is not well captured by the Big Five. From their own socialization and observations, for example, the researchers were familiar with traditions such as respected places in the home devoted to ancestors and the emphasis placed in school on learning the importance of Chinese historical figures and the concepts (e.g., Confucian teachings) passed down over the generations. They found such a con-

cept, and also found that this respect for tradition is not as strong among American respondents.

CONCLUSIONS

People's orientation to time is a cultural universal. People everywhere have to answer questions such as, "What is the best season to perform certain tasks such as farming and hunting? When should young people marry and start families? Should we organize our day around standards (position of the sun, clocks), or should we let events take what seems like a proper amount of time and then move to another event?" In making decisions about these questions, people bring their personality traits to their considerations. Conscientious people will be especially attentive to agreed-upon ways of organizing the day. Extraverted people will look forward to socializing with others.

The role of cultural influences on personality and time orientation is still being debated, but there is no disagreement as to its importance. Certainly, different researchers put emphasis on one set of concepts compared to another, but these differences lead to rich dialogues and healthy debates among scholars who take different positions. Two of the proponents of a universal structure for personality argue, "[Culture] is an essential context for the expression of all personality traits. Just as verbal fluency cannot exist without a learned language in which to be fluent, so Extraversion, Openness, and the other personality factors cannot be manifested except in culturally conditioned thoughts, feelings, and behaviors. Personality is expressed through culture, but so far, there is no good evidence that culture shapes the structure of personality" (Allik & McCrae, 2004, pp. 264–265).

Other researchers, whose primary interest is cultural influences, argue that the jury is still out regarding culture as providing contributions to the structure (in addition to possible universal aspects) of personality (Triandis & Suh, 2002). Research will continue on cultural aspects such as individualism and collectivism, respect for historical tradition, time orientations, and sensitivity to power in interpersonal communication for many reasons. One is to document aspects of the culture where people were socialized to make predictions about behavior. A second is to suggest the situation part of personality-situation signatures because culture determines various important social contexts in which people are expected to behave appropriately. A third reason is to provide guidance for people about to live in a culture other than the one where they were socialized. Knowing about culture dimensions allows people to be on the lookout for differences that they will inevitably encounter when living in another culture (e.g., punctuality, means of organizing the workday). A fourth reason for research on cultural dimensions is to determine if they have an effect on people's personality that explains behavior above and beyond the variance accounted for by models such as the five-factor solution.

REFERENCES

Adler, N. (2002). *International dimensions of organizational behavior* (4th ed.). Boston: PWS-Kent.

Allik, J., & McCrae, R. (2004). Escapable conclusions: Toomela (2003) and the universality of trait structure. *Journal of Personality and Social Psychology, 87,* 261–265.

Berry, J., Poortinga, Y., & Panedy, J. (Eds.), (1997). *Handbook of Cross-Cultural Psychology: Vol. 1. Theory and method.* Needham Heights, MA: Allyn & Bacon.

Bhawuk, D. P. S. (2001). Evolution of culture assimilators: Toward theory-based assimilators. *International Journal of Intercultural Relations, 25,* 141–163.

Bluedorn, A., Kaufman, C., & Lane, P. (1992). How many things do you like to do at once? An introduction to monochronic and polychronic time. *The Academy of Management Executive, 6,* 17–26.

Bochner, S. (1994). Culture shock. In W. Lonner & R. Malpass (Eds.), *Psychology and culture* (pp. 245–251). Needham Heights, MA: Allyn and Bacon.

Brislin, R. (1986). The wording and translation of research instrument. In W. Lonner & J. Berry (Eds.), *Field methods in cross-cultural research* (pp. 137–164). Newbury Park, CA: Sage.

Brislin, R. (2000). *Understanding culture's influence on behavior* (2nd ed.). Fort Worth, TX: Harcourt.

Brislin, R., & Kim, E. (2003). Cultural diversity in people's understanding and use of time. *Applied Psychology: An International Review, 52,* 363–382.

Brislin, R., Lonner, W., & Thorndike, R. (1973). *Cross-cultural research methods.* New York: Wiley.

Brislin, R., & Yoshida, T. (1994). *Intercultural communication training: An introduction.* Thousand Oaks, CA: Sage.

Cheung, F., Leung, K., Fan, R., Song, W., Zhang, J. X., & Zhang, J. P. (1996).Development of the Chinese Personality Assessment Inventory. *Journal of Cross-Cultural Psychology, 27,* 181–189.

Crowne, D., and Marlowe, D. (1964). *The approval motive.* New York: Wiley.

Cushner, K., & Brislin, R. (1996). *Intercultural interactions: A practical guide* (2nd ed.). Thousand Oaks, CA: Sage.

Ecuador President promises to be punctual. (2003, September 8). *Rednova News.* Retrieved April 4, 2004, from http://www .rednova.com/news/display/?id=9536

Fang, T. (1998). *Chinese business negotiating style: A middle kingdom perspective.* Thousand Oaks, CA: Sage.

Fukuyama, F. (1995). *Trust: The social virtues and the creation of prosperity.* New York: Free Press.

Hall, E. (1959). *The silent language.* New York: Fawcett.

Hall, E. (1983). *The dance of life.* Garden City, NY: Anchor Press/ Doubleday.

Hofstede, G. (2001). *Culture's consequences: Comparing values, behaviors, institutions, and organizations across nations* (2nd ed.). Thousand Oaks, CA: Sage.

Hofstede, G. (2004). An interview with Geert Hofstede. *The Academy of Management Executive, 18*(1), 75–79.

Hofstede, G., & McCrae, R. (2004). Personality and culture revisited: Linking traits and dimensions of culture. *Cross-Cultural Research, 38*(1), 52–88.

Kaufman, C., Lane, P., & Lindquist, J. (1991). Exploring more than 24 hours a day: A preliminary investigation of polychronic time use. *Journal of Consumer Research, 18,* 392–401.

Kluckhohn, F., & Strodtbeck, F. (1961). *Variations in value orientations.* Westport, CT: Greenwood.

Kroeber, A., & Kluckhohn, C. (1952). *Culture: A critical review of concepts and definitions* (Peabody Museum Papers, Vol. 47, No. 1). Cambridge, MA: Harvard University Press.

Landis, D., & Bhagat, R. (Eds.). (1996). *Handbook of intercultural training* (2nd ed.). Thousand Oaks, CA: Sage.

Levine, R. (1997). *A geography of time.* New York: Basic Books.

Lonner, W., & Berry, J. (Eds.). (1986). *Field methods in cross-cultural research.* Newbury Park, CA: Sage.

Lucas, R., Diener, E., Grob, A., Suh, E., & Shao, L. (2000). Cross-cultural evidence for the fundamental features of extraversion. *Journal of Personality and Social Psychology, 79,* 452–468.

Luo, Y., & Chen, M. (1996). Managerial implications of *guanxi*-based business strategies. *Journal of International Management, 2,* 293–316.

Markey, P., Markey, C., & Tinsley, B. (2004). Children's behavioral manifestations of the Five-Factor Model of personality. *Personality and Social Psychology Bulletin, 30,* 423–432.

Markus, H., & Kitayama, S. (1991). Culture and the self: Implications for cognition, emotion, and motivation. *Psychological Review, 98,* 224–253.

Markus, H., & Kitayama, S. (1998). The cultural psychology of personality. *Journal of Cross-Cultural Psychology, 29*(1), 63–87.

McCrae, R. (2002). NEO-PI-R data from 36 cultures: Further intercultural comparisons. In R. McCrae & J. Allik (Eds.), *The Five-Factor Model of personality across cultures* (pp. 105–125). New York: Kluwer Academic/Plenum Publishers.

McCrae, R., & Costa, P. (1989). Reinterpreting the Myers-Briggs Type Indicator from the perspective of the Five-Factor Model of personality. *Journal of Personality, 57,* 17–40.

McCrae, R., & Costa, P. (1997). Personality trait structure as a human universal. *American Psychologist, 52,* 509–516.

McCrae, R., & John, O. (1992). An introduction to the five-factor model and its applications. *Journal of Personality, 60,* 175–215.

McCrae, R., & Terracciano, A. (2005). Universal features of personality traits from the observer's perspective: Data from 50 cultures. *Journal of Personality and Social Psychology, 88*(3), 547–561.

Mischel, W. (2004). Toward an integrative science of the person. *Annual Review of Psychology, 55,* 1–22.

Myers, I., & McCaulley, M. (1985). Manual: A guide to the development and use of the Myers-Briggs Type Indicator. Palo Alto, CA: Consulting Psychologists Press.

Osland, J., & Bird, A. (2000). Beyond sophisticated stereotyping: Cultural sensemaking in context. *The Academy of Management Executive, 14*(1), 65–79.

Sperber, D. (1996). *Explaining culture: A naturalistic approach.* Oxford: Blackwell.

Triandis, H. (1995). *Individualism & collectivism.* Boulder, CO: Westview.

Triandis, H. (2004). The many dimensions of culture. *The Academy of Management Executive, 18*(1), 88–93.

Triandis, H., & Berry, J. (Eds.), (1980). *Handbook of cross-cultural psychology: Vol. 2. Methodology.* Boston: Allyn & Bacon.

Triandis, H., Kurowski, L., Tecktiel, A., & Chan, D. (1993). Extracting the emics of cultural diversity. *International Journal of Intercultural Relations, 17,* 217–234.

Triandis, H., & Suh, E. (2002). Cultural influences on personality. *Annual Review of Psychology, 53,* 133–160.

Wang, M., Brislin, R., Wang, W., Williams, D., and Chao, J. (2000). *Turning bricks into jade: Critical incidents for mutual understanding among Chinese and Americans.* Yarmouth, ME: Intercultural Press.

Zimbardo, P., & Boyd, J. (1999). Putting time in perspective: a valid, reliable individual-difference metric. *Journal of Personality and Social Psychology, 77,* 1271–1288.

PART TWO

BROAD-RANGE THEORIES AND SYSTEMS

CHAPTER 4

Psychodynamic Theories

DAVID L. WOLITZKY

INTRODUCTION

First, a few words of clarification about the meaning of the terms *psychodynamic* and *psychoanalytic*. These terms are used interchangeably by some writers whereas others use these terms to differentiate Freudian psychoanalysis from other forms of psychodynamic theory. Some theorists have used new terms to differentiate their psychoanalytic views from Freud's (e.g., Adler's Individual Psychology, Adler, 1927; Jung's Analytic Psychology, Jung, 1968). In this chapter, for ease of exposition, I will use psychoanalytic and psychodynamic interchangeably.

The essential defining characteristic of a psychodynamic approach to personality and psychopathology is a view of mental life from the perspective of inner conflict, particularly conflicts outside of awareness. There are many divergent views that spring from this common ground of emphasizing conflicting forces in the mind.

As is well known, Sigmund Freud (1856–1939) was the founder of psychoanalysis as a theory, as a method of investigating the human mind, and as a method of treatment. As a theory, psychoanalysis was, and remains, the most ambitious, comprehensive, and complex attempt to understand human behavior, both normal and pathological. It aims not only to explain the myriad forms of psychopathology but also is concerned with key cognitive, emotional, and motivational aspects of personality development, including the possible biological bases of these processes. It also ventures into virtually every aspect of human experience, including sexual and aggressive wishes and behaviors; interpersonal functioning; creativity in art, music, and literature; the psychology of humor, dreams, and fantasies; various aspects of memory (including experiences such as déjà vu and so-called screen memories); the repetition of maladaptive patterns of behav-

ior; the meanings of religion, rituals, politics, and international conflict; the psychology of historical figures; reports of alien abduction; psychoanalytic approaches to anthropology, and so on.

Freud changed aspects of his theory many times in his long, productive career, as one can see from a study of the 23 volumes of his collected works, published as the definitive *Standard Edition.* His impact on twentieth-century thought is unrivaled by any other conception of personality. His influence has penetrated our cultural experience to the point that many of his ideas no longer seem radical but commonplace and are part of our implicit conceptions of personality. At the same time, certain of his views remain controversial and objectionable (e.g., the centrality of the Oedipus complex).

In addition to Freud's own changing theories, shortly after the turn of the century several clinicians who were initially attracted to Freud's ideas began to develop divergent views. Carl Jung (1968), Alfred Adler (1927), and Karen Horney (1950) were the main theorists who took issue with what they felt was Freud's excessive emphasis on sexuality in personality development and his insufficient appreciation of sociocultural determinants of personality. These theorists were called neo-Freudians. Freudian analysts at the time claimed that they did not deserve to call their alternative versions psychoanalytic.

Because these theories also focused on conflict and maintained the view that conflicting forces in the mind could give rise to psychopathology and because they also dealt with the phenomena of transference and resistance in the treatment situation, the broader term psychodynamic began to be used. The neo-Freudians, however, claimed that the basis of inner conflict was not to be found in biologically rooted sexual and aggressive instincts but in the context of interpersonal relationships and sociocultural forces. Virtually all so-called deviations from Freud's theory have been based on the objection to his biological emphasis on instinctual drives.

In the last four decades, shifts in the sociohistorical Zeitgeist have influenced what is regarded as psychoanalytic ver-

Acknowledgments: I would like to thank Drs. Morris Eagle and Jerome Wakefield for their helpful comments on an earlier version of this chapter.

sus psychodynamic. Theories that, early in the twentieth century, would have lost their claim to be considered psychoanalytic are now part of mainstream psychoanalytic thought (Eagle, 1987). Given the current state of the field, the issue of whether a given theory is properly designated psychodynamic or psychoanalytic is rarely debated, although as recently as 1999 Westen and Gabbard claimed that the neo-Freudians "... are not, *strictly speaking* [italics added], psychoanalytic" (Westen & Gabbard, 1999, p. 61). Nonetheless, as noted earlier, for present purposes, we will use the terms psychoanalytic and psychodynamic interchangeably.

At the present time, we are living in an age of theoretical pluralism in which the field by and large accepts the theorist's own designation of his or her approach as psychoanalytic or psychodynamic. At the same time, we are more apt to use the term psychoanalytic when referring to theories that are most closely linked to Freud's theories (e.g., contemporary psychoanalytic theory). In addition to the so-called neo-Freudians (Jung, Adler, Horney, Sullivan) whose theories still have influence, we have seen within the evolution of psychoanalysis not only elaborations of Freudian theory (e.g., ego psychology) but two other major theoretical approaches: object-relations theories (both in their British and American versions) and Kohut's (1971) self psychology (Greenberg & Mitchell, 1983). None of these theories has been presented in a comprehensive, systematic set of propositions with clearly testable predictions, nor have we seen any successful efforts to integrate the various psychoanalytic theories. Rapaport (1960) did attempt to synthesize traditional Freudian theory, but that ambitious, elegant effort has been largely neglected.

STATEMENT OF THE THEORIES

As noted previously, there is no single psychoanalytic theory to present but a family of theories whose common core differentiates them from nonpsychoanalytic theories. The common ground of a psychoanalytic perspective on mental life includes an emphasis on the inner life of the individual; the conflicts, particularly the unconscious conflicts, that are associated with maladaptive behavior; the central motives, needs, and wishes of the individual (for Freud, primarily sexual and aggressive wishes) and the compromises made among conflicting tendencies; the basic anxieties and defenses against them; the implications of these factors for the person's interpersonal relationships and for the development of a cohesive sense of self; and the vital influence of childhood experiences with primary caregivers in shaping person-

ality development. These are the major ingredients that characterize psychodynamic thinking. From this point of view, psychopathology of any clinical significance (e.g., phobias) reflects inner conflict and is not simply the result of the person's reinforcement history and exposure to traumatic events or frightening experiences.

The psychoanalytic approach to treatment is to help the patient become aware of and resolve inner conflicts as they are expressed in transference reactions to the therapist. In more recent years, insight has been somewhat displaced as the main therapeutic agent in increased recognition of the healing powers of the relationship, particularly for patients with a history of traumatic relationships characterized by emotionally unavailable primary caregivers.

Psychodynamic theorists have room in their formulations for the kinds of cognitive and learning processes and structures (e.g., schemata) that writers like Beck (1976) and Ellis (1987) emphasize, but they see these as elements in the larger context of complex motivational aspects of behavior. With regard to psychotherapy, although some psychoanalytic clinicians incorporate cognitive-behavioral elements in their work, particularly when they are aiming at the alleviation of symptoms, they regard the cognitive-behavioral understanding of personality and psychopathology as simplistic (e.g., as failing to appreciate the tragic and ironic dimensions of human existence and the power of unconscious conflicts and fantasies).

Basic Freudian Theory

The biological survival of the infant requires that psychic life evolves in the context of interaction with a primary caregiver who serves as the psychobiological regulator of the infant's needs and tension states, a task that previously occurred naturally through the homeostatic regulation of the infant's intrauterine existence. Although Freud recognized this state of affairs, he viewed the infant's attachment to the mother as being secondary to her role in the gratification of the infant's hunger needs. It is on this issue that all significant psychodynamic theories part company from Freud, although some have tried to integrate his emphasis on instinctual drives and an emphasis on interpersonal relationships.

According to Freud, the primary aim of the organism is to reduce tension states. The diminution of excitation is pleasurable whereas the increase of excitation is painful.[1] The aim of the organism is to live according to the pleasure principle. The impossibility of immediate gratification means that the infant has to take reality into account and learn to sacrifice immediate pleasure in the service of finding eventual satisfaction. Thus, a fantasy of eating will bring only partial, temporary gratification compared to finding real food. Survival requires that the pleasure principle give way to the reality principle. In his essay "Beyond the Pleasure Principle," Freud (1920) claimed that there was something even more important than seeking pleasure, namely the need to avoid being rendered helpless by excessive stimulation, as seen in the mastery efforts involved in the repetitive reenactment of traumatic experiences.

The tensions that the organism had to reduce were those based on the instinctual drives of sex (more broadly and accurately thought of as sensual) and aggression. Drives are rooted in the body and make a demand on the mind for psychic work in the service of gratification. The thoughts, impulses, feelings, and fantasies in one's mind are regarded as drive derivatives, the psychic representation of the instinctual drives. We can think of these drive derivatives as wishes. Wishes are psychic experiences that strive toward the fulfillment of the instinctual drives. Technically, they are efforts to reinstate previous experiences of satisfaction. This is a core idea in Freud's theory of motivation (Freud, 1900).

There are four characteristics of an instinctual drive: *source, aim, impetus,* and *object.* The source of the drive is the endogenous, bodily tensions associated with the sexual (libidinal) and aggressive drives. The aim is the discharge of the tension associated with the drive. The impetus is the intensity or force of the drive. The object is the person or thing that will satisfy the drive. It is the most variable aspect of the drive in that there are multiple ways of satisfying the drive. The theory uses the term *object* to indicate that a person or an inanimate object can bring at least partial drive gratification (e.g., a pacifier used to satisfy orality).

The energy that derives from the drives was called psychic energy, and cathexis referred to the amount of psychic energy invested in a particular wish or fantasy. These terms attempted to capture the force and quantitative aspects of behavior but are rarely used today, except as metaphors.

Reality presents serious obstacles to the free expression and gratification of sexual and aggressive wishes, thus presenting the organism with a conflict between inhibiting and attempting to gratify wishes. The concept of intrapsychic conflict became a core notion in Freudian theory; insofar as the person believes that the attempted satisfaction of instinctual wishes are dangerous, an approach-avoidance situation is created, both on the level of thought as well as on behaviors that can be construed as attempts to gratify wishes (Freud, 1926). The principal dangers are, in developmental order, loss of the object (e.g., total abandonment by the mother), loss of the object's love (e.g., maternal rejection), castration,

and guilt. The latter two dangers presuppose loss of the object's love. The anticipation of these dangers gives rise to signal anxiety, which automatically instigates defenses against the potential conscious awareness and/or behavioral expression of the wish in order to stave off the full-blown experience of traumatic anxiety in which the person is overwhelmed with panic. Traumatic anxiety can develop if the wish is too intense and/or the defense against it is too weak, meaning, if the signal function of the ego has failed to trigger an adequate defense. In this model, anxiety leads to repression (and other defenses). (In Freud's earlier toxic theory of anxiety, undischarged drive pressures led to anxiety.) This drive-defense model was used by Freud to explain a variety of psychological phenomena and experiences, including dreams, character traits, jokes, and psychiatric symptoms (Freud, 1933).

Conflict is inevitable. It can occur between wishes and external reality, between competing wishes, and between wishes and the person's judgment about the negative consequences of being aware of and/or expressing one's wishes, including guilt over wishes that are deemed to be wrong or immoral. Actual interpersonal conflicts that threaten to create psychological difficulties are considered to do so because of the intrapsychic conflicts to which they give rise.

In viewing mental life from the perspective of intrapsychic conflict, Freud described three main aspects of the personality—*id, ego,* and *superego*—in what is known as the structural or tripartite model of mental functioning. These are the three aspects of personality that often conflict with one another. The concept of the id refers to the libidinal and aggressive instinctual drives; the ego is the part of the personality that tests reality, that uses perception and judgment to appraise what is safe and what is dangerous, and that institutes the operation of defense mechanisms in an effort to ward off anxiety. Whereas the id operates according to the so-called primary process (i.e., seeks the immediate discharge of excitation), the ego functions according to secondary-process (i.e., makes use of reality-testing, judgment, planning), reality-oriented thinking in the service of allowing the organism as much pleasure as possible and as little pain as possible. The third agency of the psychic apparatus is the superego, the part of the personality that has internalized standards of right and wrong, good and bad, the violation of which arouses feelings of guilt, as well as standards of what the person should strive to live up to (the so-called ego ideal). The id, ego, and superego are hypothetical constructs by which the observer organizes aspects of behavior that often come into conflict with one another. Too often, the psychoanalytic literature reads as if id, ego, and superego are concrete entities doing battle with one another. The main point is that if we look at behavior from the standpoint of conflict, we can say that all behavior, normal and pathological, reflects a compromise formation among the major aspects of personality, particularly the desire for the gratification of one's wishes and the constraints against the immediate, free, and open pursuit of such gratification (Brenner, 1982).

After Freud's strong emphasis on the instinctual drives (sometimes called id psychology) later psychoanalytic theorists paid attention to the functioning of the ego, a period of theorizing referred to as ego psychology. These theorists, principally Hartmann, Kris, and Loewenstein (1946), stressed the idea that not all of mental life was embroiled in conflict and that ego capacities such as memory and cognition, delay of gratification, reality-testing, interests, and so forth have an independent, conflict-free, innate, autonomous basis. In other words, they have a primary autonomy. Ego functions that do get caught up in conflict but then become independent of it were said to have secondary autonomy. These developments balanced Freud's emphasis on instinctual drives with a recognition that not all behavior is always or simply an expression of sexual and aggressive wishes (Hartmann, 1939).

Freudian theory makes room for the influence and interaction of both genetic/constitutional and environmental factors as determinants of behavior (termed by Freud a *complemental series*). The determinants of behavior, both innate and environmental, are complex; the same motive can give rise to myriad behaviors (divergent causality) and a given behavior can be a function of several motives (convergent causality). This principle of multiple determination is sometimes misleadingly referred to as overdetermination.

Freud stressed that the major portion of mental life takes place outside of conscious awareness. This includes not only preconscious ideas that can readily be brought to awareness but, more importantly, unconscious wishes and fantasies that are kept unconscious through mechanisms of defense, most notably repression. Psychiatric symptoms arise when defenses are ineffective in containing the repressed wishes; this is referred to as the return of the repressed (Freud, 1915b, 1915c).

According to Freudian theory, childhood experiences have a profound impact on personality development. The experiences that are most decisive are traumatic events and conflicts associated with the various stages of psychosexual development. The concept of psychosexual stages refers to the psychological experiences associated with the different erogenous zones: mouth, anus, and genitals. In order, the psychosexual stages are *oral, anal, phallic,* and *genital* (Freud, 1905). Gratifications, frustrations, and conflicts at each stage influence the way in which subsequent stages are experienced. Excessive gratification or frustration at a given stage can lead to

fixation or regression. Fixation refers to the persistence of behavior beyond the stage at which it was age appropriate (e.g., thumb sucking in a 10-year-old). Regression refers to the return of stage-related behaviors in reaction to stress or conflict (e.g., the return of bed-wetting in an eight-year-old following the birth of a sibling).

Each psychosexual stage has a characteristic anxiety associated with it. For the oral stage, it is loss of the object, for the anal stage it is loss of the object's love, and for the phallic stage it is castration anxiety. It is during the phallic stage that the Oedipal complex is at its height. As is well known, the Oedipus complex refers to the child's wish for an exclusive relationship with the parent of the opposite sex. The same-sexed parent thus becomes a rival. The resolution of the Oedipus complex involves the identification with the parent of the same sex and the resignation of incestuous wishes toward the parent of the opposite sex. Freud placed enormous explanatory weight on the Oedipus complex as a determinant of neurotic behavior (Freud, 1933).

The concept of identification is central to the psychoanalytic understanding of personality development. Identification refers to the tendency to take on the characteristics of another person. This is the principal means of dealing with separation and loss, but it does not preclude identification on the basis of modeling. For Freud, the ego, at least its personality traits and patterns, can be described as a precipitate of abandoned object cathexis, meaning that the personality characteristics of those with whom one has had a significant relationship become part of his or her personality based on the desire to maintain a bond with the person (Freud, 1914b, 1915a).

A comprehensive psychoanalytic account of behavior should include a detailed consideration of multiple perspectives: *genetic* (i.e., developmental), *adaptive, dynamic, topographical, structural,* and *economic* (Rapaport & Gill, 1959). These terms refer, respectively, to the psychosexual stages of development (described previously); the coping and defensive devices by which the ego mediates between motivational drive pressures, external reality, and superego prohibitions; the nature of the conflicts involved; the relation of mental contents to consciousness; the id, ego, and superego aspects; and the energic and quantitative aspects of the forces in the mind. It has now long been recognized by psychoanalytic theorists that the postulation of psychic energies to explain the economics of mental life is problematic if taken as more than a metaphor, and psychoanalytic writings in the past three decades are increasingly devoid of this so-called metapsychological concept.

Psychoanalytic theorists since Freud either have totally abandoned his drive theory or have tried to integrate it with theories that have a strong emphasis on internalized object relations and on interpersonal relationships as the key building blocks of personality (Greenberg & Mitchell, 1983). A second, important development in psychoanalytic theory has been a focus on the development of the sense of self (Kohut, 1971, 1977), an area not dealt with in traditional Freudian theory. According to Pine (1990), object-relations theories and self psychology followed id psychology and ego psychology as the four main waves of psychoanalytic theorizing.

Ego Psychology

At first, Freud concentrated on the vicissitudes of sexual and aggressive instinctual drives, whose derivatives came to be referred to as wishes. As noted previously, this overriding emphasis was balanced later on by a concern with the person's adaptive functioning and the coping and defensive strategies that facilitated or impaired effective, relatively conflict-free ego functioning. Anna Freud (1936) and Hartmann, Kris, and Lowenstein (1946) were the major theorists who contributed to the flowering of psychoanalytic ego psychology. Hartmann (1939), for example, noted that the infant starts life with innate perceptual capacities (what he called primary ego apparatuses) that are not derivatives of sexual or aggressive conflicts but can become embroiled in conflict (e.g., hysterical blindness), and can emerge with a degree of secondary autonomy, that is, can function in a relatively conflict-free manner. Ego and superego development were conceptualized in the now-anachronistic language of neutralized and deneutralized psychic energy.

Ego psychology, with its emphasis on coping and adaptation, incorporated and went beyond id psychology. Ego interests and creativity, for example, became areas of study in their own right. Kris (1952), for example, advanced the concept of regression in the service of the ego as a way of understanding the creative use of primary process experience in an adaptive manner. The work of G. S. Klein (1976) on cognitive style (stable individual differences in the nature of perceptual and cognitive processing and problem solving) was an outgrowth of the development of ego psychology. Bellak, Hurvich, and Gediman (1973) developed an ego psychological approach to the study of ego functions in schizophrenia. Erikson's (1950) work on psychosocial adaptations, on ego identity, and on the life cycle was a further contribution to the study of ego psychology. The common thread in these works, and others, was a view of mental life from the perspective of executive ego functions that defended against anxiety associated with sexual and aggressive drives in attempting to make an adequate adaptation to an average expectable environment.

Object-Relations Theories

Relational psychoanalysis is a term that has gained popularity in recent years. It is not a systematic set of concepts and treatment techniques. The core notion is that psychic structure derives "... from the individual's relations with other people. This, of course, was intended as an alternative to the prevailing view that innately organized drives and their developmental vicissitudes were, at root, the basis of psychic structure " (Ghent, 2002, p. 5). As Ghent points out, "There is no such thing as *a* relational theory, but there is such a thing as a relational point of view, a relational way of thinking, a relational sensibility . . . ." (p. 5). The impetus for the development of this perspective was the encounter with patients who complained not so much of particular symptoms (e.g., obsessions or compulsions) but of strain, strife, and unhappiness in their intimate relationships and of earlier, traumatic experiences in relation to their parents. These theorists stressed the vital importance of the pre-Oedipal period of personality development, beginning with the innate need for relatedness, nurturance, and a sense of belonging. These needs are seen as primary rather than as derived from the mother's provision of oral gratification. From this perspective, relatedness rather than sensual pleasure are seen as the basic motivational striving of the organism. Traumatic anxiety, in this view, is triggered by fear of loss of the object or the object's love whereas for Freud it is not the object per se that is essential but is capacity to enable the infant not to be overwhelmed by excitation that is not discharged.

The growing infant is assumed to develop an internal working model of relationships in which self and others are mentally represented (in terms of good and bad) as are the interactions between self and others. In this view, the internal working model is assumed to be primarily an accurate representation of the infant's experiences. From a Freudian perspective, the internal working model is in many ways a fantasy-driven construction, although some object-relations theorists (e.g., Melanie Klein [1921–1945/1964]) emphasized the importance of primitive fantasies.

There is no monolithic theory called Object-Relations Theory. Rather this designation refers to a group of theories that bear a family resemblance to one another. What is called Object-Relations Theory is an amalgam of the British object-relations theorists, principally Klein (1921–1945/1964), Fairbairn (1941), Winnicott (1965), Sullivan (1953), Kohut (1971, 1977), and U.S. versions of object-relations theories (e.g., Mitchell, 1988). There is insufficient space to present a detailed account of these various theories. I must restrict myself to a few general comments that will provide the main flavor of this approach.

In general, the object-relations approach to understanding personality and psychopathology starts from the premise that the ". . . libido is object seeking rather than pleasure seeking" (Fairbairn, 1941). That is, the primary aim of the organism is not the satisfaction of instinctual urges but the inherent need for relatedness with others. This aim is not secondary to the object's function as a source of drive gratification, as it is in Freud's theory. Greenberg and Mitchell (1983) feel that this approach represents a paradigm shift and draw (an unnecessarily sharp) distinction between the two views by referring to the Freudian model as a drive-discharge model and the object-relations perspective as a relational model. The relational model places a very heavy emphasis on the vital importance of social interaction as shaping the development of personality. In this regard, relational approaches have a close affinity with Bowlby's (1969, 1973, 1975) attachment theory, which focuses on the development of secure (versus insecure) attachments to primary caregivers, and the representation of these attachment schemata in the person's internal working models of how relationships operate and what the implicit rules, requirements, and expectations are regarding the availability and reliability of trustworthy caregivers. Thus, an important focus of the relational approach is not only to examine the actual interpersonal relationships between people but to consider these interactions in the context of internalized mental representations of self and others and the interactions between self and others. In contrast to Freudian theory, which sees the intensity and degree of resolution of the Oedipus complex as the central childhood experience that decisively influences later relationships, object-relations theorists stress the importance of the early infant-mother interaction in shaping the personality. As applied to the clinical situation, this approach looks closely at what each participant brings to the interaction, whereas in the Freudian model the analyst focuses on the unfolding of the patient's inner conflicts.

Self Psychology

The notion of self and the development of selfhood was neglected in Freudian theory, perhaps because in Freud's time people grappled more with repression of unacceptable sexual and aggressive wishes than with the matter of personal identity. For Kohut (1971, 1977), who started his career as a traditional Freudian, the development of a cohesive sense of self and the actualization of one's talents, skills, ambitions, and ideals are regarded as the best perspectives from which to understand both normal and pathological behavior. At first Kohut applied his theory only to narcissistic pathology, but over time he broadened his theoretical explanations to include all behavior, healthy and pathological, with the concept of self as the central focus.

Central to Kohut's (1971, 1977) conception is the view that healthy development requires that the infant and child have ample experiences of mirroring self-objects and idealized self-objects. Mirroring self-object experiences are those in which the child feels recognized, appreciated, and empathized with by a person who is experienced as a partial extension of the self. An example would be an appreciative, loving gleam in the mother's eye in reaction to some behavior of the child (e.g., building a tower of blocks), a gleam that allows the child to feel "I am good and perfect, and you are validating my feeling through the gleam in your eye." These kind of validating experiences are the building blocks for feeling valued and validated. They lead to a positive sense of self-esteem. An example of an idealized self-object experience would be the momentary sense of pleasure and power that the child feels as he vicariously acquires a sense of strength from his father when his father holds him on his shoulders (as in "you are big, strong, and perfect, and I am part of you"). The development of a solid, cohesive sense of self with healthy ambitions, values, and ideals stems from these kinds of experiences. They depend on the parents' capacity to be empathically attuned to and responsive to these basic psychological needs. Chronic failures in parental empathy are seen as the primary cause of psychopathology. The needs for mirroring and idealized self-objects persist throughout life, but if they were well met during childhood they are less vital, relatively speaking, during adulthood. A person with a more cohesive sense of self can cope better with the inevitable ruptures of empathic attunement, both in therapy and in other relationships.

A major characteristic of object-relations theories and self psychology is the emphasis on the early mother-child relationship as a critical period for the development of secure attachments and stable, secure, integrated, cohesive sense of self. This emphasis, partly the result of treating more disturbed patients, has replaced the primary emphasis given to the vicissitudes of the Oedipus complex as central to the understanding of adult psychopathology.

The Common Ground

We can summarize the discussion thus far by a statement of the main psychoanalytic concepts influencing most dynamically oriented clinicians today:

1. The psychic life of the individual has important unconscious elements.

2. Individuals are motivated to avoid pain and seek pleasure

through the expression of their needs and wishes in relationships with others.

3. Seeking such gratification often is associated with anxiety and guilt, triggering tendencies to defend against the awareness of such desires and to engage in self-deception.

4. People are therefore in conflict (both consciously and unconsciously) between their impulse to seek gratification and their need to inhibit their desire for gratification.

5. Ambivalence, though common, is hard to tolerate, leading people to defensive splitting of mental representations of themselves and others into good and bad.

6. Most behavior can be understood as a compromise formation reflecting the interaction of wishes, needs, anxieties, one's ego ideal, the demands of conscience, anticipated guilt and other negative affects, and the requirements of reality.

7. People seek safety and security, typically in the context of relatedness to others, and develop internal working models that include representations of the nature of relationships (e.g., security of one's attachment to caregivers).

8. Early experiences, particularly traumas, significantly shape personality development and influence adult behavior. The internalization of an ego-supportive environment (in the form of a soothing introject) goes a long way in ensuring the individual's emotional security and self-esteem.

9. There is a dialectic tension (Blatt & Zuroff, 1992) between the tendency toward separateness and autonomy and the need for relatedness (which includes the needs to belong, to be protected, and to be loved).

10. The development of a cohesive sense of self requires empathic attunement from caregivers who serve the child as mirroring and idealized self-objects (Kohut, 1971, 1977). Part of maintaining a cohesive sense of self includes one's sense of identity, which is strongly influenced by the nature of one's identifications with significant others.

11. People have a strong tendency to reenact in their significant relationships their unresolved conflicts and childhood patterns of behavior, often in neurotic vicious cycles in which they perpetuate the very problems that cause them to suffer. The transference patterns seen in therapy, and in other relationships, express unresolved conflicts from childhood.

12. Sociocultural factors must be considered the context that shapes and influences the nature of the individual's principal anxieties and conflicts in relation to others.

13. Sexual and aggressive wishes are particularly apt to become involved in intrapsychic conflict.

These propositions have not been systematically integrated into a contemporary psychoanalytic model. Thus, Holzman (cited in Grunbaum, 1993, p. xvii) regards ". . . psychoanalysis not as a unified theory, but rather as many theories loosely tied together." Creating an integrated theory is problematic in view of the fact that id psychology, ego psychology, object-relations theories, and self psychology, although they are considered useful multiple perspectives from which to approach clinical work (Pine, 1990), are not compatible with regard to their basic assumptions about human nature and basic human motives.

All the theories mentioned thus far have undergone significant extensions and modifications by the generations of clinicians that followed these early- and mid-twentieth-century theorists, changes that deserve a book-length discussion. A highly abbreviated list of major contributors to psychoanalytic theory building in the past half century include Hartmann, Kris, and Loewenstein (1946), Erikson (1950), Brenner (1982), Mahler (1968), Mahler, Pine, and Bergman (1975), Jacobson (1964), Kernberg (1975, 1984), Loewald (1960), Modell (1984), Sandler (1987), Schafer (1976), A. Freud (1936), Gedo (1986), Lichtenberg (1989), Greenberg and Mitchell (1983), and Mitchell (1988). It is difficult to determine the extent to which the contributions of these theorists constitute genuine progress toward cumulative knowledge or whether they mainly reflect changing cultural/historical trends and/or changes in the kind of psychopathology being seen (Eagle, 1987; Eagle & Wolitzky, 1989). Highly cogent critiques of psychoanalytic theory can be found in the writings of Klein (1976), Holt (1976, 1991), Schafer (1976), Gill (1976, 1984), Rubenstein (1976), and Eagle (1984).

The Neo-Freudians

The neo-Freudians, principally Alfred Adler (1927), Carl Gustav Jung (1968), Karen Horney (1950), and, later, Sullivan (1953), would be in general agreement with several of the propositions stated previously, with the common exception of rejecting Freud's overriding emphasis on the importance of sexuality and aggression in favor of an emphasis on the sociocultural and interpersonal determinants of personality development. These theoretical contributions began in the early 1900s, shortly after the birth of psychoanalysis, but did not evolve from Freudian theory the way ego psychology, object-relations theories, and self psychology did. Although it has been more than four decades since each of these theorists published their major work, they each continue to have a sufficient group of adherents, as evidenced by the existence of psychoanalytic training programs and institutes bearing their names (or closely following their approach to psychoanalysis). Although they are an influential part of today's psychoanalytic world, it is not possible to do justice to the contributions of these theorists. The interested reader can refer to Munroe's classic, *Schools of Psychoanalytic Thought* (1955).

DEVELOPMENTAL CONSIDERATIONS

Virtually all psychodynamic theories have a strong developmental perspective in which personality is seen as evolving through a series of stages or phases, with each stage or phase being influenced by the preceding phase or phases and influencing the succeeding ones. Regression to earlier stages and/or fixations at a given stage make the individual vulnerable to developing psychopathology.

Whether cast in psychosexual terms (e.g., Freud's oral, anal, phallic, and genital phases) or in more psychological terms (e.g., Erikson's [1950] notion of the life cycle and his eight stages of man, starting with basic trust versus mistrust), the negotiation of these stages strongly influences the style and degree of pathology of adult functioning. Freud, for example, stressed the importance of the conflicts involved in seeking the gratification of sexual and aggressive wishes, highlighted by the centrality of the Oedipus complex. Later theorists extended Freud's view of psychosexual development to include psychosocial factors (e.g., Erikson's [1950] well-known conception of stages in the life cycle) that parallel Freud's psychosexual stages (e.g., the sense of basic trust versus mistrust that is associated with the oral stage). Erikson went beyond Freud's scheme by postulating adult life stages that are not directly tied to sexuality (e.g., ego identify versus ego diffusion in late adolescence or generativity versus stagnation in adulthood).

The nature of ego functioning in young adulthood also has strong predictive power with respect to the psychological maturity, level of satisfaction and effective coping, and even the longevity of men followed for many years after graduation from college (Vaillant, 1977).

Anna Freud (1965) described a series of developmental lines (e.g., from dependence to independence, from amorality to morality) that each individual traverses in the course of development. The nature of these developments are believed to have important implications for various aspects of ego and superego functioning (e.g., affect regulation, delay of gratification, adequacy of reality testing, etc.).

Other psychodynamic theories emphasize the development of selfhood (e.g., Winnicott's [1965] notions about the development of a false versus a true self, Kohut's [1977] claims about the importance of empathic mirroring and idealized self-objects in the development of a cohesive sense of self, and Mahler's [1968] conception of separation-individuation). Stern's (1985) concept of Representation of Interactions Generalized and Fonagy's (2001) work on mentalizing and the development of reflective self-awareness (see also, Fonagy & Target, 1997) point to other essential features of personality development and interpersonal relationships.

Whatever their different emphases, all psychodynamic theorists have a very strong developmental viewpoint and tend to view personality development as continuous. They vary somewhat in how decisive a role they attribute to the earliest infant-mother interactions as compared with later stages of psychological development (e.g., the Oedipal period).

BIOLOGICAL/PHYSIOLOGICAL RELATIONSHIPS

From the beginning, Freud wanted to link the clinical phenomena he described to a neurobiological model of psychic functioning. He hoped to find out what was going on in the brain when a person was conscious versus unaware of an impulse or when the person was defending against the awareness of an impulse. His most ambitious effort in this direction was his posthumously published "Project for a Scientific Psychology." Written in 1895, but not published until 1950 (Freud, 1895), it presented what by today's standards (Pribram & Gill, 1976) is a remarkably sophisticated neurobiological model of mental functioning. As we know, Freud, recognizing the limited knowledge of brain functioning available at the turn of the century, abandoned the project as a premature effort and went on to concentrate on building a psychological theory. Yet he did not give up the hope that someday his psychology could be rooted in and explained by the structure and biochemical processes of the nervous system.

It was only with the explosion of brain research in the last two decades that an increasing cadre of psychoanalysts and some neuroscientists have become excited about finding the links between brain structure and functioning and the kinds of phenomena that psychoanalysts have been studying purely on the psychological level. There is already a sizable literature on the interface of psychoanalysis and cognitive neuroscience and, more recently, affective neuroscience. Although most training in psychotherapy no longer emphasizes a psychoanalytic approach, recent work in cognitive and affective neuroscience is reviving a keen interest in psychoanalysis as a theory of mental functioning.

Psychoanalysis and Cognitive/Affective Neuroscience

Kandel, a 2000 winner of the Nobel Prize in Physiology and Medicine, notes that in the first half of the twentieth century, "... psychoanalysis revolutionized our understanding of mental life. It provided a remarkable set of new insights about unconscious mental processes, psychic determinism, infantile sexuality, and, perhaps most important of all, about the irrationality of human motivation" (Kandel, 1999, p. 505). He is disappointed that psychoanalysis has not evolved scientifically "... since psychoanalysis still represents the most coherent and intellectually satisfying view of the mind" (Kandel, 1999, p. 505). This lack of scientific progress is one reason that it has fallen out of favor in most clinical psychology training programs.

Kandel hopes that psychoanalysis will be reenergized by forging a closer relationship with cognitive neuroscience. This is consistent with Freud's vision that psychology would presumably one day be based on an organic substructure. Freud developed two theories, a clinical one and a neurobiological one to explain the clinical one (Klein, 1976). Although, as noted previously, he expected that our understanding eventually would rest on neurobiology, he was forced to proceed on a psychological level.

Kandel's (1999) proposed marriage of neurobiology and psychoanalysis is in the process of being consummated. According to Solms, work groups trying to integrate psychoanalysis and neuroscience "have been formed in every major city of the world" (Solms, 2004, p. 84) and are part of the International Neuro-Psychoanalysis Society that publishes a new journal called *Neuro-Psychoanalysis.*

Thus far, apart from controversies concerning Freud's theory of dreams (Hobson, 1988), I am not aware of any neurophysiological evidence that is incompatible with psychoanalytic theory, and there is a great deal of evidence that is consistent with it (Schore, 1994; Solms, 2004). In his *Scientific American* article summarizing developments in neurobiology, Solms (2004) makes a number of points: (1) There is evidence for unconscious motivation in the studies that distinguish explicit and implicit memory systems; (2) unconscious memory systems mediate emotional learning; (3) there is at least a rough correspondence between the limbic system and the id and between the ego/superego and the ventral frontal region of the brain (which is relevant to selective inhibition) and the dorsal frontal area of the brain (which is relevant to self-conscious thought), and the posterior cortex (which is said to represent the outside world); and (4) clinical case

studies with neurologically impaired patients support the idea that the left hemisphere is the seat of the Freudian mechanisms of defense. Solms adduces other neurological evidence in support of Freud's pleasure principle and the wishful thinking to which it gives rise. He views the dopamine-regulated seeking or reward system that has been identified by neuroscientists as bearing "a resemblance to the Freudian libido" (Solms, 2004, p. 87). Whether these analogies will stand up under careful scrutiny remains to be seen, but they do show us that some prominent neuroscientists are attempting to link their findings to the psychoanalytic theory of mind.

Cognitive neuroscience, which came of age since the 1980s, has yielded an explosion of information about brain functioning in relation to various kinds of cognitive processes (e.g., working memory, implicit and explicit memory, etc.). Since the mid-1990s, there have been increasing references to *affective neuroscience,* a term that refers to the study of the neural substrate of emotion, an area closer to psychoanalytic interests. It is in the integration of the cognitive and affective aspects of psychological functioning and the neural networks involved that we probably can learn most about which aspects of psychoanalytic theory are most supported by empirical findings in neuroscience.

The understanding of the neural mechanisms that mediate and regulate emotion will be most relevant to psychoanalytic concepts. For example, the capacity of the left frontal cortex to inhibit the activity of the amygdala is relevant to the issue of gaining rational control over fear. If the reduction of phobic fears is accompanied by lesser amygdala activity and greater activity in regions of the prefrontal cortex, we have identified a neural process that corresponds to a psychoanalytic account of phobic fears (LeDoux, 1995). It should be acknowledged, however, that these brain changes could also be explained from a cognitive-behavioral perspective.

As another example, consider the recent work on the neural mechanisms involved in the suppression of unwanted memories (Anderson et al., 2004). These authors found that deliberate efforts to suppress the recall of experiences are related to the interaction of the hippocampus and the dorsolateral prefrontal cortex. These results are most relevant to the Freudian account of suppression in which there is a conscious, deliberate attempt to keep certain ideas away from focal awareness. If we also can find that the degree of activation in certain areas of the brain corresponds to the subject's nonconscious, motivational goal of preventing an association to a word from entering consciousness, we will be much closer to the neurological basis for repression in which motivated forgetting occurs in the absence of the subject's conscious desire to bar mental contents from awareness. Such a demonstration should finally quiet the critics who deny the presence of the dynamic unconscious (e.g., Kihlstrom, 1999). In this regard, Tomarken and Davidson (1994) reported differential patterns of frontal brain activation in repressors and nonrepressors.

BOUNDARIES OF THE THEORY (CULTURAL EFFECTS AND LIMITATIONS)

Most psychodynamic theories have implied that the phenomena and concepts that they address are universal in nature and thus cut across the boundaries of time and of cultural and ethnic differences. This tendency is perhaps most clearly seen in Jung's (1968) notion of archetypes and the collective unconscious and in Freud's claims concerning the universality of the incest taboo and of incest wishes. At the same time, although it is not given much emphasis, psychodynamic theories usually can accommodate differences in an individual's cultural and socioeconomic background in their understanding of personality and psychopathology. Broad sociocultural changes can explain the decrease in certain forms of psychopathology (e.g., hysteria) and the increase in other types of disorders (e.g., narcissistic disorders). Thus, the cultural emphasis on thinness and body shape among educated females in contemporary U.S. society can help explain the rise in eating disorders over the past several decades while taking into account the intrapsychic and familial conflicts and issues that make some young women more susceptible to anorexia and bulimia than others.

Emphases within psychodynamic theories have shifted over the years in accord with changing cultural and societal factors. For example, in turn-of-the-century Vienna, the repression of sexual and aggressive impulses is what impressed Freud as a leading cause of pathology. Issues of selfhood and ego identity were rarely spoken about and had no formal place in the theory at a time when the culture had fairly well-defined roles for people. Given the post–World War II existential uncertainties and the greater flexibility in life style and career choice, issues of selfhood and ego identity became more prominent clinically and began to be reflected in the theorizing of the time (e.g., Erıkson, 1950; Kohut, 1971). Another example is provided by Eagle (2004). In Freud's Victorian era, agoraphobia was thought to reflect fear of sexual wishes. In recent formulations, it is regarded in attachment-theory terms as related to insecure attachment and fears of separation. Finally, even where there are universal issues that all children must cope with (e.g., attachment and separation), the predominant style in which they cope will differ in different cultures. For example, it has been found that the preponderance of different insecure attachment styles

differs in different cultures, as does the emphasis on selfhood and autonomy versus relatedness and family (Shaver, 2002).

In summary, one can say that psychodynamic theories vary in the extent to which they make explicit provisions for cultural factors within the central propositions of the theory. Perhaps the strongest appreciation of the role of cultural factors is found in Erikson's classic work, *Childhood and Society* (1950), in which he shows quite clearly how personality development and ego identity are shaped by social and cultural factors. His insightful psychobiographies of political and historical figures also present very convincing accounts of the social and cultural forces that shape personality (e.g., Erikson, 1958).

Contemporary psychoanalytic theorists understand that intrapsychic dynamics do not operate in a social vacuum and that family dynamics, as well as political and economic conditions, and cultural forces shape the development and expression of individuality. Thus, not all cultures produce suicide bombers and only a minority of suicide bombers have responded in that particular way to the same social conditions. In the United States, the emphasis on physical appearance (e.g., the weight of the women in *Playboy* centerfolds has declined over the years; Nolen-Hoeksema, 2004) clearly is one factor that contributes to eating disorders. At the same time, the majority of women do not have eating disorders. Although psychoanalytic theorists are cognizant of these broad social influences, they are particularly interested in individual differences in behavior under similar conditions.

There has been a tendency among psychoanalytic theorists to claim that their discoveries constitute universal truths about mankind. Freud was guilty of this in his claims about the Oedipus complex. Although the incest taboo appears to be universal, it is less clear that the Oedipus complex is universal. Some (e.g., Malinowski, 1927, 1929) have argued that it is not universal; others claim that Malinowski's studies of the Trobiander islanders was flawed. In my view, it is not fruitful to debate whether the Oedipus complex is universal. It probably is more accurate to state that there are certain universal generalizations that probably can be made and other universal potentials based on innate tendencies that will be more or less activated depending on environmental conditions. Thus, children raised in communal settings (e.g., on a kibbutz in Israel) might be expected to experience the Oedipal period differently from those raised in a more traditional family structure (Rabin, 1958; see following paragraph). On the other hand, where we are dealing with universal facts, like the biological helplessness of the human infant, some form of attachment to the caregiver has to occur, even though the form is influenced by cultural factors. In other words, it seems reasonable to propose that developmental issues that are less tied to innate tendencies will be more strongly influenced by environmental factors, between or within cultures, communities, and families. Thus, castration anxiety in the boy and penis envy in the girl might be fairly commonly observed phenomena based on innate fears and predispositions, but the extent to which they pass uneventfully or, instead, become complexes in the young child and go on to dominate personality development and psychopathology depends on other aspects of personality, temperament, family dynamics, and cultural factors. For example, factors such as growing up in a male-dominated society and in a family situation in which the father devalues females in favor of males will likely make penis envy more of a salient issue for the developing girl, all else being equal.

These considerations also apply to the Oedipus complex. Freud regarded a poorly resolved Oedipus complex as the central factor in the development of neurosis. Here, Freud overgeneralized from his experience with neurotics in turn-of-the-century Vienna. Some have alleged that his views also were influenced by his need to universalize his own Oedipal strivings. What can we say about the pervasiveness of the Oedipal complex? I think it is useful to distinguish between the Oedipal stage and the Oedipal complex, the former referring to a relatively mild, uneventful rivalry with the father for the mother's affection, the latter to a more intense version of this scenario in which neurotic symptoms might form. In other words, if we consider that jealousy and rivalry are common emotions, then we can say that under conditions where the father makes himself a rival for the affection that mother and child share, the child's Oedipal issues probably will be more intense. If the mother is not emotionally available to her son, the boy will be more likely to resent the father and want an exclusive relationship with the mother. Under these circumstances, the boy is also more likely to develop an Oedipus complex rather than merely pass fairly harmoniously through an Oedipal stage. Thus, whereas the incest taboo is universal, the intensity and pathological potential of incest wishes in a given individual is a more variable factor. Cultural factors play a role as well. For example, in Rabin's (1958) study, Israeli children raised on a kibbutz seemed to have a lesser intensity of Oedipal preoccupations.

In considering the relevance of different family dynamics associated with a greater or lesser significance of Oedipal issues, we need look no further than the original Oedipal story itself. Oedipus (the name means "swell-foot" and derives from a spike that his father, Laius, ordered be driven through his son's foot) was the son of Jocasta and Laius, king of Thebes. Laius, who was himself abandoned and persecuted as a baby, cast his son out and left him to die alone. He had been warned by an oracle that his unborn son would murder

him. The oracle also warned Oedipus that he was destined to murder his father and marry his mother. After Oedipus murdered his father and married his mother, he realized what he had done and proceeded to blind himself. (As Freud put it, "It is the fate of all of us, perhaps, to direct our first sexual impulse toward our mother and our first hatred and our first murderous wish against our father" [1900, pp. 261–264].) So, here we have a parricide by a son with a filicidal father. Sophocles' play depicts a tragic resonance between Laius's acts and Oedipus's deed. Overall, the play depicts the intergenerational transmission of psychopathology and the adverse outcome of generations of bad parenting. The clear implication is that with more benign parenting and intrafamilial dynamics there would not be an attempted resolution of the Oedipus complex through parricide.

EVIDENCE IN SUPPORT OF AND AGAINST THE THEORY

We have reviewed several theories that are grouped under the general rubric of psychoanalytic theory. Each of these theories is complex and comprehensive as each aims to account not simply for a small slice of behavior (e.g., some aspect of memory) but for the nature of person's overall functioning, including the developmental processes that shape the adult personality. Each theory contains core assumptions and numerous hypotheses. It is therefore impossible to present and evaluate all of the relevant evidence, even if there were to be good agreement as to what constitutes the relevant evidence.

Furthermore, psychodynamic theories never were presented in a final, systematic, unified manner. In Freud's case, for example, although there are some core propositions, there are multiple theories to be found in his 23 volumes, often with revisions and diverse with respect to content and level of abstraction (e.g., clinical theories and metapsychological concepts). Thus, there is no monolithic Freudian theory about which one can call valid or invalid. One has to consider the evidence for particular concepts, or what Fisher and Greenberg (1996) call Freud's series of minitheories.

It should be noted that psychoanalytic theory has been attacked from the start as being unscientific. In response, psychoanalysts have made the untenable claim that in conducting treatment they are simultaneously doing research, like any other scientists (Brenner, 1982). They have pointed to the fact that their observations are made under standardized conditions (e.g., the patient lying on the couch and free associating), that the observations are repeated many times in the course of treatment and across cases, and that they have tried to spell out the criteria for the validity of their interpretations (Brenner, 1982).

There have been numerous symposia and articles attacking this position. For example, Grunbaum (1993), in a series of closely reasoned arguments, makes the persuasive point that the psychoanalytic situation is epistemologically contaminated because of the factor of suggestion and that the only relevant evidence for psychoanalytic assertions is to be found in validation efforts outside the clinical situation. In other words, although the case-study method might be a method par excellence for generating insights about the human mind, it fails as an arena for subjecting these insights to rigorous tests. We are talking about the familiar distinction between the context of discovery and the context of justification. Some analysts (e.g., Edelson, 1988; Luborsky & Auerbach, 1969) have made the case that clinical data can have probative value, especially if systematically evaluated. For example, Luborsky and Auerbach's (1969) symptom-context method showed that reports of certain somatic symptoms were more likely to appear in the context of particular psychodynamic themes.

One of the main drawbacks in relying on clinical data is that we have no independent knowledge of the presumed independent variable, for example, inferring that a particular unconscious conflict is causally linked to a particular behavior (e.g., a phobic reaction). In recognition of the limitations of the analytic situation as a scientific laboratory, investigators turned to studies outside the consulting room, almost from the inception of psychoanalysis.

Research on Freudian Theory

By now there have been so many thousands of studies of various psychoanalytic concepts that we have to rely on the book-length evaluations by Kline (1981) and Fisher and Greenberg (1977, 1996). It is a safe bet that more than 90 percent of empirical studies of psychoanalytic hypotheses are based on traditional Freudian theory.

A Sampling of Freudian Concepts

Fisher and Greenberg (1996) review studies in the following areas of Freudian theory: depression, paranoia, orality, anality, the Oedipus complex, and the theory of dreams. Even with this restriction of topics, they could not be expected to cover all the relevant studies. Furthermore, not all relevant aspects of theory in the areas they did survey have been tested and some of those that were tested were not tested adequately.

With these reservations in mind, it is impressive that, with the exception of Freud's dream theory, Fisher and Greenberg

(1996) found that many of Freud's ideas have received a reasonable degree of empirical support. For example, they conclude that Freud's formulations with regard to paranoia and depression have received fairly solid empirical support as have his ideas concerning the oral and anal personality characteristics. Similarly, several aspects of Freud's notions about the Oedipus complex are considered valid. Overall, Fisher and Greenberg are ". . . impressed with how robust many of Freud's minitheories have shown themselves to be. Significant chunks of his theorizing have held up well to probing" (Fisher & Greenberg, 1996, pp. 266–267). They add that "A reservoir of experimental data pertinent to Freud's work currently exists, and . . . offers support for a number of his major ideas and theories" (Fisher & Greenberg, 1996, pp. 284–285).

Fisher and Greenberg (1996) acknowledge that their review of the scientific literature did not focus on unconscious processes and on repression, yet these are the most distinctive of Freud's formulations. Nonetheless, they state that the findings regarding these concepts are generally supportive.

Westen and Gabbard (1999) also have surveyed the academic research literature that is relevant to psychoanalytic views. They concluded that there is evidence for some of the core propositions of contemporary psychodynamic thinking and indicated that the findings have stood the test of time:

1. A considerable portion of mental life, including cognitions, motives, and feelings, takes place outside of conscious awareness.
2. Enduring patterns of personality functioning, particularly those pertaining to interpersonal relationships, have their origins in experiences during childhood.
3. Mental representations of the self and others, and their interaction, influence the nature of interpersonal relationships and the type of psychopathology that one expresses.
4. In the course of personality development individuals move from helplessness and dependency to a mature interdependent state in the course of which they learn to regulate their aggressive and sexual feelings.
5. "Mental processes, including affective and motivational processes, operate in parallel, so that individuals can have conflicting feelings toward the same person or situation that motivate them in opposing ways and often lead to compromise solutions" (Westen & Gabbard, 1999, p. 74).

One might argue that (1) whereas these five propositions are consistent with psychoanalytic theory, it is the first proposition that is both most distinctively psychoanalytic, and the most controversial, and (2) omitted from the list of core propositions are some that have been more central to Freudian theory, for example, the presumed centrality of the Oedipus complex, the theory of dream formation with its postulation of latent and manifest contents, the use of symbolism and displacement in the dream work, and defenses against unacceptable sexual and aggressive wishes.

Empirical Studies of Unconscious Influences

Arguably the most central aspect of Freudian theory is the phenomenon of repression, the phenomenon that Freud (1915b) regarded as the cornerstone of psychoanalysis. Although Westen and Gabbard (1999) refer to unconscious processes, neither they nor Fisher and Greenberg (1996) address the literature on repression.

According to Freud, unconscious ideas, fantasies, and conflicts influence conscious thought. In fact, for Freud (1915b), nonconscious processes are the norm in mental life. In his famous iceberg analogy he described three aspects of mental life: a small portion that is in focal awareness at any one moment; a portion that is preconscious, meaning that a simple effort of will could readily bring the idea to awareness (e.g., if asked to state one's social security number); and an unconscious realm in which mental contents are inaccessible to awareness for motivational reasons. That is, certain mental contents never became conscious in the first place (primal repression) or did briefly but were banned from awareness because they were threatening and unacceptable to the person (repression proper). The mental contents kept out of awareness continue to exert an influence on the person, an influence that could be expressed in the form of symptoms (what Freud called "the return of the repressed").

Until the 1980s, the idea of unconscious influences on cognition and perception was rejected by most academic psychologists. Now, cognitive psychologists readily demonstrate and acknowledge that information can be processed outside of awareness.

Distinctions can be made between a cognitive, emotional, motivational, and dynamic unconscious (Kihlstrom, 1999). The cognitive unconscious can be demonstrated with studies of priming word associates using neutral stimuli (e.g., priming with the word *table* makes it easier to perceive *chair*). It also is seen in the Nisbett and Wilson (1977) study that found that subjects are more likely to think of Tide laundry detergent after having learned the word pair *ocean-moon,* but they had no idea that their activated associative network led to the response *Tide.* Bargh (1997) reported that priming certain concepts can lead to a behavioral effect. For example, the subliminal prime *old age* resulted in subjects walking more slowly when they leave the experimental cubicle!

Actually, in one of the earliest attempts to investigate the influence of the cognitive unconscious, Otto Poetzl (1917/ 1960) used stimuli outside of awareness. Subjects described pictures that were exposed to subjects very briefly. Details omitted from their reports of what they saw, presumably because it did not consciously register, were details that often showed up in their reports of dreams that night, a finding that was taken as offering some support for Freud's notion of the day residue, that is, incidental impressions in waking life around which the dreamer constructs the dream. This study was the inspiration for a series of studies over the past several decades by psychoanalytic investigators that have repeatedly demonstrated the influence of stimuli outside of awareness on conscious thought (e.g., Fisher, 1954; Eagle, 1961; Klein, Spence, Holt, & Gourevitch, 1958).

The emotional unconscious is seen when the tachistoscopic exposure of the words *happy* or *sad* leads to descriptions of a neutral face in accord with the nature of the preceding emotional tone of the word presented (Wolitzky & Wachtel, 1973). Several other studies that used emotionally loaded subliminal stimuli provided evidence for the emotional unconscious (Dixon, 1971, 1981; Wolitzky & Wachtel, 1973). For example, using a priming technique called backward masking, two stimuli are presented briefly in immediate temporal succession (the A-B technique). If the A stimulus is not immediately followed by the B stimulus, the A stimulus would be seen clearly. The B stimulus, which is clearly a supraliminal presentation, masks the A stimulus so that the subject has no awareness that there has been an A stimulus, yet the A stimulus influences reactions to the B stimulus. For example, if the A stimulus is a picture of a man with a dagger (versus a picture of a man holding a birthday cake) and the B stimulus is a neutral figure that the subject has to describe, the trait-adjective descriptions of the B stimulus are affectively toned in line with the affective tone of the A stimulus (Eagle, 1961). Many such studies found that subliminally presented stimuli influenced conscious thought, often in ways different from the impact of the same stimuli presented supraliminally (see especially, Shevrin, Bond, Brakel, Hertel, & Williams, 1996).

One of the problems with backward-masking studies (Wolitzky & Wachtel, 1973) was that when one spoke of subliminal registration, the only evidence of this claim was its impact on behavior. Now, we have direct evidence of subliminal registration in the brain. Kandel (2004), a recent Nobel Prize winner with a keen interest in Freudian theory, reported a study in which backward masking of a menacing face activated areas of the amygdala in the absence of conscious awareness, but only in subjects high on a measure of trait anxiety. Furthermore, the area activated was different from the area activated with supraliminal presentations. This is an impressive demonstration of a neurobiological basis for the unconscious appraisal of threat in those who are already anxious and hyper vigilant and for differences in the processing of stimuli in and outside of awareness.

The motivational unconscious is seen in Silverman's studies (Silverman, Lachman, & Milich, 1982) in which the subliminal activation of psychoanalytic themes (e.g., thoughts of merging with one's mother, e.g., "Mommy and I are one," or competition with father, e.g., "It's okay to beat Dad") led to the predicted outcomes with regard to changes in thinking and behavior. For instance, the subliminal message "It's okay to beat Dad" led to improvements in the accuracy of dart throwing (Silverman et al., 1982; see also Bornstein & Pittman, 1992; Dixon, 1981; and Shevrin & Dickman, 1980).

None of these three types of unconscious influence directly involve the phenomenon of defense per se and therefore do not establish the validity of the Freudian dynamic unconscious, that is, a motivated attempt to avoid awareness of potentially anxiety-laden mental contents, as in the case of repression. Kihlstrom (1999) is therefore correct in claiming that Westen and Gabbard (1999) review evidence that bears primarily if not exclusively on the cognitive, emotional, and motivational unconscious.

Thus, although he is persuaded that there is overwhelming evidence for processing outside of awareness of the first three types, Kihlstrom (1999, p. 435) insists that "THIS IS NOT THE PSYCHOANALYST'S UNCONSCIOUS" because the evidence does not deal with repressed sexual and aggressive urges. Kihlstrom therefore considers it a gambit by Westen to claim that there is evidence for the Freudian unconscious. He believes this is a cop out and that Westen and his psychoanalytic colleagues should be held to what Freud said in his 23 volumes, not what has been written since Freud died. "Culturally, the twentieth century has been the century of Sigmund Freud, not the century of Heinz Kohut or Melanie Klein." Freud's view of the unconscious, according to Kihlstrom has ". . . found little or no support in empirical science" (Kihlstrom, 1999, p. 436).

This is not the place for a detailed debate of what I regard as Kihlstrom's narrow view. The fact is that the Freudian unconscious includes the cognitive, emotional, and motivational unconscious (Shevrin, 2004). At the same time, Kihlstrom is correct in stating that thus far there is less support for the dynamic unconscious than for the cognitive, affective, and motivational unconscious.

It also should be noted that even restricting ourselves to the 23 volumes, as Kihlstrom advises, still allows for a consideration of Freud's broadening of the concept of defense beyond repression as well as the broadening of the kinds of

mental contents defended against. On the latter point, Eagle points out that ". . . both prior to the development of his drive theory and scattered throughout his writings, Freud did not limit the application of the concept of repression to instinctual wishes, but employed it in a much broader context, to refer to any mental contents inimical to or sharply incompatible with the ego and with one's self-image" (Eagle, 2000, pp. 166–167). Thus, it is unnecessarily constraining, even when confined to Freud's writings, to insist that (1) we consider only repression of sexual and aggressive wishes rather than defenses against unacceptable wishes more broadly conceived and that (2) only anxiety associated with conflicted wishes be studied and not other negative affects. It is necessary and legitimate to test meaningful extensions and modifications of Freud's theories.

Repression

Let us turn specifically to Freud's concept of repression, which he regarded as the cornerstone of psychoanalysis. The core of Freud's view of repressive defenses and unconscious conflict can be stated as follows: (1) Repression is the motivated avoidance of awareness of any potentially dysphoric affect state; (2) that which is successfully defended against, that is, kept from awareness, continues to exert an active influence that can be seen in one or more ways—dreams, symptoms, behavior; (3) the person cannot voluntarily access that which has been repressed; (4) defenses include not only intrapsychic mental mechanisms (e.g., repression, projection, isolation of affect) but any patterns of behavior motivated by the desire to avoid conscious awareness of a potentially dysphoric affect state; (5) although Freud stressed the operation of defenses in relation to conflicted sexual and aggressive wishes (because he observed that the ideational content and affects associated with such content were most apt to cause negative affect), there is no theoretical reason to restrict the concept of defense in this manner; and (6) defensive operations require an expenditure of mental energy such that these efforts should have consequences (e.g., behavioral, physiological) for some aspects of behavior.

The essence of defense is self-deception, a desire not to know that which would produce dysphoric affect. Repression (motivated forgetting and motivated inability to retrieve mental contents) are not the only means of promoting self-deception. Thus, it is not always the case that the ideational component of an unacceptable wish is kept out of awareness. For example, in the case of isolation of affect, the person is fully aware of the objectionable idea or wish, but its normally associated affect is not experienced.

Most studies of defense have focused on repression. Searching the literature specifically for studies of repression yields more than four thousand entries, beginning with Rosenzweig's (1934) experimental study. I would estimate that of these four thousand entries about one hundred of them are experimental studies of repression. A review of this body of work by Holmes (1990) led him to the conclusion that there is no convincing evidence for the existence of repression. Most of the studies reviewed by Holmes, however, used methods that failed to capture the phenomenon of repression in an ecologically valid manner. Other authors view the evidence regarding repression as strongly supportive.

Numerous studies, starting in the late 1940s, showed that subjects had heightened perceptual thresholds for so-called threatening or unacceptable stimuli. As part of the New Look in Perception these studies of perceptual defense tried to show that the very act of perception was a process that was influenced by the subject's motives and needs. Many of these studies were criticized on methodological grounds, primarily because it was difficult to prove conclusively that the subject operated without benefit of some partial cues, meaning, partial awareness of the stimuli (Wolitzky & Wachtel, 1973).

Overall, there is adequate evidence that a potentially upsetting stimulus can be detected before it reaches awareness and triggers a defensive delay in perceiving it. At the same time, these studies were not designed to show another aspect of the concept of repression, that is, the persistent influence of such stimuli on other aspects of behavior. Realizing that there is no crucial experiment to be done in this area, it is nonetheless useful to note a few studies that seem to be reasonably good approximations to the terms of the theory, potentially threatening mental contents that activate nonconscious defenses against awareness of them and evidence of their continued influence.

Wolitzky, Klein, and Dworkin (1975) reported an experimental study that meets these criteria. A hypnotic induction of an experience of rejection, compared to an induction with neutral content, led to less recall of the distressing material in the experimental group. At the same time, there was evidence of the continued activation of the rejection theme as manifested in word associations and in physiological indices.

Shevrin and colleagues (1996) made clinical assessments of patients who had phobias and selected words that the patients used that clinicians thought reflected the patient's hypothesized unconscious conflict as well as the patient's conscious experience of the symptom. These words were exposed supraliminally and subliminally. When presented subliminally, frequency features of the recorded brain responses showed similarities between key words only when the stimuli were exposed on a subliminal level. Shevrin and his colleagues have amassed impressive evidence that cortical evoked potentials reflect differences in stimulus content without any awareness on the part of the subject. Theirs is probably the most persuasive experimental evidence thus far for the dynamic unconscious.

The two studies just cited are faithful to the concept of repression in that they demonstrate (1) some kind of defensive activity designed to ward off some kind of dysphoric affect and (2) the continued activation and influence of that which was warded off. For other empirical studies of defenses see Vaillant (1977, 1992) and Singer (1990).

Repressive Style

It is extremely difficult to capture the process of repression in the laboratory. Laboratory analogues aimed at establishing operational definitions and proper controls led to experimental studies that did not resemble real-life clinical phenomena and have not had any impact on any aspects of psychoanalytic theory.

Because it is difficult to find ecologically valid measures of the operation repression in the here and now, investigators have developed measures that assess the chronic, generalized use of repression, in other words, repressive style as a personality characteristic. Investigators then study individual differences in the degree of repressive style and then expose subjects to situations in which tendencies to avoid potentially upsetting stimuli can be studied. Repressive style is measured by a combination of low scores on self-report measures of anxiety and high scores on a self-report measure of tendencies to respond in a socially desirable manner (the Crowne-Marlowe [1964] scale), which is considered a measure of defensiveness, particularly with respect to protecting one's self-image and self-esteem.

This research approach, although not capturing repression as it operates in the moment, is consistent with clinical observations of patients who have the following characteristics: difficulty in accessing memories, particularly emotional memories, poor recall of their early years, a relatively flat level of current emotional experience, and a sense that potentially vivid and important earlier experiences (e.g., their first sexual experience, their wedding, etc.) never registered in an emotionally vibrant manner when those experiences took place. In short, their emotional lives seem barren and bland. One gets the impression that feelings of any kind would rather be minimized or avoided.

Bringing these kinds of experiences into the laboratory in studies of repressive style has yielded a fairly consistent set of findings. The preponderance of the evidence is that those higher in repressive style show more of the expected correlates of this style (Eagle, 2000). For example, those high in repressive style make more errors in forming a concept with aggressive, compared with neutral, content (Eagle, 2000) and show slower reaction times to sentences with sexual and aggressive content, poorer recall of negatively toned affective memories, slower retrieval time in accessing these memories, and more difficulty in accessing early memories (Davis & Schwartz, 1987; Singer, 1990). Repressors also show higher levels of physiological arousal, a decreased immune response to stress, and poorer health outcomes (Singer, 1990).

Freud (1915b, p. 151) noted repression requires "an expenditure of force" and that this work takes its toll on a somatic level. Although the repressive style has the short-term adaptive advantage of sparing the person the experience of negative affect, there are likely to be longer term disadvantages to one's physical health (Eagle, 2000).

The numerous studies of repressive style have greater ecological validity than most studies that try to capture the repressive process as it is happening. Eagle (2000) does not think that it is fruitful to argue whether the work on repressive style reflects the precise meaning of repression intended by Freud and claims that the concept of repressive style ". . . does capture the essence of the repressive process" (Eagle, 2000, p. 167). I agree that this body of work is strongly consistent with Freud's ideas about repression.

If one had to draw an overall conclusion from the considerable number of studies inspired by psychoanalytic concepts, it would be fair to say that the research supports many aspects of the theory, including its distinctive emphasis on unconscious influences and on defense. At the same time, some hypotheses have not been supported and many aspects of the theory have yet to be tested.

PREDICTIONS FOR EVERYDAY FUNCTIONING: A PSYCHOANALYTIC PERSPECTIVE

I believe it is accurate to claim that no competing theory of personality and psychopathology has attempted to explain as broad and diverse an array of human experience as has been offered by psychoanalytic theory. A few key psychoanalytic concepts have been employed by numerous theoreticians to understand domains of psychological experience ranging from dreams, jokes, everyday parapraxes, and psychiatric symptoms to religious beliefs and ritual practices, art, literature, music, cinema, love, violence and war, sports, reports of alien abductions, and the popularity of certain nursery rhymes and children's games,[2] just to mention a few areas. Psychoanalysts also have tried their hand at psychobiography, political psychology, anthropology, the development of

morality, career choice, the nature of romance and marriage, and the nature of treason (Greenacre, 1969), to add but a few more topics. It probably is safe to say that there is not a realm of significant human experience that has been untouched by psychoanalytic theorizing.

Psychoanalysts always have been interested in the darker side of human nature and in mapping the terrain of the unconscious and the irrational motives that drive human action. They are drawn to an examination of the nuances of conscious experiences. Thus, they inquire into such matters as the dynamics of envy compared with awe, of shame versus guilt, and so on.

It is important to acknowledge that few of the topics of everyday functioning that have engaged psychoanalytic writers have been approached from the standpoint of systematic, controlled testing of hypotheses as is the custom in the natural sciences. It is both the strength and the limitation of psychoanalytic theory that it has contributed an interesting, often illuminating, albeit sometimes overly speculative, collection of insights most of which are refractory to attempts at verification through experiment. Because psychoanalytic understandings of everyday experiences rarely have been put to any kind of systematic testing, it is more accurate to speak of psychoanalytic perspectives or implications for everyday functioning rather than predictions.

A General Psychoanalytic Perspective on the Main Domains of Everyday Functioning

Freud is said to have declared that the goals of life are to love and to work. He left out play. Psychoanalysts, based on extrapolation from the consulting room, have had a lot to say about the psychodynamics of everyday life as they pertain to the three broad domains of life: love, work, and play.

Contributions that in one way or another bear on the phenomenon of love include an elucidation of various aspects of family life and interpersonal relationships: forms of love, friendships, marriage and divorce, infidelity, marital interaction, fatherhood and motherhood, sibling relationships, adoption, and the role of parents and grandparents in the child's personality development, the nature of sexuality, and so on.

In the realm of work, psychoanalysts have written about the dynamics involved in such areas as the choice of career, organizational dynamics, the meanings of work, wishes for and fears of failure and success, the meanings of money, and the meanings of psychic work in the analytic situation.

Play is a topic addressed mainly by analysts who by virtue of their work with children observe firsthand the nature of symbolic play and the fantasies associated with it. Much has been written about the development of play in childhood as well as the adult's capacity for play, both within and outside the psychoanalytic situation. The essential point in most writings in this area is that play occupies an intermediate position between reality and fantasy that allows for the expression of wishes and fantasies within some reality constraints and that it contributes to the mastery of childhood fears and anxieties.

Before proceeding to present a psychoanalytic perspective on some aspects of everyday life it would be useful to restate (and to add) a few core propositions that are especially relevant to an understanding of virtually all aspects of daily functioning:

1. The biological helplessness of the infant and the necessity for forming an attachment (preferably a secure one) to the caregiver who serves as a psychobiological regulator of the infant's tension states and who is essential to the infant's survival.

2. The internalization of working models of self, other, and self-other interactions guides behavior and experience, often in an unconscious way.

3. Identifications with significant others are crucial in personality development.

4. Personality development involves strategies of coping, defense, and conflict resolution, which includes attempts to modulate impulses, guilt, anxieties, and moods.

5. Development and maintenance of a cohesive sense of self in the context of negotiating dyadic and triadic (including Oedipal) relationships is a crucial aspect of one's functioning.

6. A flexible, adaptive balance between autonomy and relatedness in a way that permits sustained commitments to love relationships and to work is a basic human striving and challenge in that it often leads to inner conflict and to interpersonal tensions.

7. People are largely unaware of the unacceptable, feeling, fantasies, motives, and conflicts that influence their beliefs, attitudes, and behavior.

8. The concepts of compromise formation and the dynamics of repetitive behavior are important for understanding normal and pathological behavior (Brenner, 1982).

Even though I will not explicitly draw on these propositions and concepts in the discussion that follows, they form an essential backdrop for an appreciation of the psychology of everyday functioning in the domains we shall discuss: personal relationships, work, recreation, and retirement. The discussion that follows will rely mainly on a Freudian perspective, although, space permitting, some of the phenomena addressed could also benefit from insights offered by object-relations theories and by self psychology.

To the extent that developmental tasks and challenges proceed in a nonpathological manner, life experiences such as falling in love, commitment, family life, career, recreation, and retirement should be less fraught with interpersonal conflict and less impaired. In psychoanalytic terms, adaptive behavior reflects adequate sublimation of sexual and aggressive wishes and needs for love and security. Perhaps the clearest evidence for this general proposition comes from the extensive studies by Vaillant (1977), who found that college-age subjects with less mature defenses, compared to those with more mature defenses, had a much poorer level of psychosocial functioning and physical health when followed well into their adult years.

FAMILY LIFE

Although psychoanalysts have written extensively on the dynamics of family life, there is no overall theory or body of research on this topic. Among the issues addressed are: (1) the dynamics of romantic relationships, (2) mother-infant interactions, (3) parent-child relationships, and (4) the dynamics of family life. As space is limited and the latter three topics have received a fair amount of attention, I will restrict myself primarily to a discussion of certain features of romantic relationships.

As a framework for the discussion to follow I would like to outline a developmental perspective from which family life can be understood as a sequence of transitions that activate and deactivate different conflicts and issues among family members. Carter and McGoldrick (1989) presented a series of stages in what they call the family life cycle. Like Erikson's life cycle, each stage highlights certain developmental challenges. The six stages described by Carter and McGoldrick (1989) are: (1) the single adult leaving his or her family of origin, (2) getting married and adapting to new families, (3) having children, (4) dealing with adolescents, (5) coping with children moving on, and (6) adapting to the shift in generational roles. Without taking the space to elaborate, one can see that the psychological issues and conflicts at each stage would be an interactive function of relatively stable personality characteristics and the specific meanings evoked at a given stage in the trajectory of family life. For example, relatively speaking, the ability to differentiate one's self from one's parents and family of origin without undue separation anxiety or separation guilt probably is most central in the first phase in which one leaves home as a single adult. Creating and maintaining a romantic, committed relationship is a central task in the second phase, and so on. From a general psychoanalytic/developmental perspective one would expect that unresolved issues of childhood would present different challenges at different points in the family life cycle. Consider, for example, the challenge of selecting a marriage partner with whom one will not reenact to a maladaptive extent conflicts with one's own parents. Following mate selection there is the challenging task of integrating love and sexual desire. Unresolved Oedipal issues frequently play a role here. For example, several of my male patients show indications of regarding the woman they married as a maternal figure toward whom sexual interest felt taboo, evoking feelings of nausea and disgust. They felt strong affection toward their wives but their sexual interest was directed toward other women. These men acknowledged that sex with their wives felt dirty. From a Freudian perspective, these men either selected women modeled too closely on their mothers or turned them into maternal figures, which then made it difficult for them to regard their wives as sexually appealing.

As an example from the next stage in the family life cycle consider the common maternal preoccupation with new children. For the mother, it is important to know to what extent her own background inclines her to see her new baby as an extension of herself, to what extent she is determined to give her child the nurturance and attention that she failed to receive or make the child suffer the privations she did, to what extent she views the child as interfering with her life, and so on. From the father's perspective one has to consider such factors as his feeling displaced by the new arrival in terms of its emotional resonance with his history of rivalry with siblings and/or with his father.

The point of these examples is that unresolved issues, whether seen from a Freudian, object-relational, or self-psychological perspective, can color and invade various aspects of family life at different stages of the family life cycle. In this regard, the situation is analogous to the outbreak of symptoms (e.g., hysterical blindness, obsessive-compulsive behaviors, eating disorders, etc.) when repressed inner conflicts are not adequately defended against.

I now turn more directly to the four areas listed previously under the heading "Family Life." As noted, my main focus will be on romantic relationships. Given the high divorce rate (50 percent of marriages dissolve within 20 years and 67 percent within 40 years) and the seemingly high rate of unsatisfactory marriages that continue, it seems safe to say that creating and sustaining a romantic relationship is an uphill struggle for many couples (Jacobs, 2004).

The Dynamics of Romantic Relationships

Love, defined in many different ways, generally is acknowledged to be vital to human existence. We all have heard the phrases "Love makes the world go round" and "What is this thing called love?" People are preoccupied with love. "Do you love me?" "Am I lovable?" "How do I know if I'm in love?" "Can I love?" Insofar as popular cultural forms are expressions of our central preoccupations, it is apparent, as one example, how much popular songs focus on love, frequently unrequited love ("Unrequited love's a bore and I've got it pretty bad"; "Celia, you're breaking my heart. . . ."), sometimes on Oedipal yearnings (e.g., "I want a gal just like the gal that married dear old Dad").

Philosophers and poets have described the ecstasy and agony of love in more profound ways than can be achieved in any psychological account. Nonetheless, psychoanalysts have tried their hand at conceptualizing the nature of normal and pathological love. After all, that is what most patients (and nonpatients) talk about most of the time.

Any theory of love would have to account for the development and interaction of the three main components described by Sternberg (1988): commitment, passion, and intimacy. It would have to explain the conditions necessary for these qualities, the motivations to express or inhibit these qualities in the context of a love relationship, and issues and conflicts in each of these three realms and in their attempted integration. For example, what are the factors involved in sexual passion? Why does it sometimes require pain, as in sexual masochism? Why is sexual desire enhanced by mystery and allure, for example, why is seeing cleavage a turn-on or seeing a woman in a negligee rather than naked more inviting, why do some gentlemen prefer blondes, why do some men prefer or insist on big-breasted sexual partners, why do some men prefer masturbation even when they have ready access to an available, willing sexual partner? These are but a brief sample of the dozens of similar questions that come up regularly in the context of psychoanalytic psychotherapy.

I will rely on Sternberg's (1988) triangular theory of love as the starting point. He depicts the three major components to love (passion, intimacy, and commitment) on an equilateral triangle with these components forming the vertices of the triangle, yielding eight subsets created from the different combinations of the three components. These are as follows: If there is intimacy only, then liking is the result; if intimacy is combined with passion, we get romantic love; if we have passion alone, we see infatuation; passion plus commitment leads to fatuous love; intimacy combined with commitment yields companionate love, and commitment alone results in what Sternberg calls empty love. The absence of any of the three components is a state of nonlove. The presence of all three components to a significant degree—passion, intimacy, and commitment—is what he calls consummate love. This is the romantic ideal toward which most people in our culture strive. Most people are more successful in developing than in maintaining this kind of love.

Sternberg considers the different time courses of the three components, the fact that these are not all or none dimensions, the fact that two partners might have different and multiple triangles, and the difference between real and ideal triangles. With regard to the latter, Sternberg notes that discrepancies between real and ideal triangles are related to dissatisfaction with the relationship. This finding is consistent with the findings by Murray, Holmes, and Griffin (1996) that some modicum of idealization is necessary for romantic love to flourish. From a psychoanalytic perspective, the individual is in part looking for someone who, among other things, can fulfill one's own unattained ideals. It is this normal human need that leads to the initial idealization of the love object.

Psychoanalysts would argue that although Sternberg's account is a useful description of the components of love, it does not address the dynamic underpinnings of love. Even though psychoanalysts have not presented a systematic theory of love backed by empirical data other than those from the consulting room, the privacy of that context leads to revelations that are unique to that setting and unavailable to academic psychologists. In the clinical context, psychoanalysts have addressed questions such as the dynamic basis of partner selection, the basis for the discrepancy between real and idealized relationships, the personality factors associated with individual differences in the degree to which a given person stresses one or another of the three components noted by Sternberg, individual difference is the decline of passion, the difficulties in integrating intimacy and passion in relation to the same love partner, and the reasons love is so important in the first place. Clinicians also ask to what extent the patient's insistence on self-sufficiency is motivated by fear of intolerable narcissistic injury in love relationships and/or the conviction that one is unlovable, overly needy and greedy, and undeserving of love. For some promising efforts toward a psychoanalytic theory of love see Bergmann (1987), Kernberg (1995), and Person (1988).

From a psychoanalytic perspective, supplemented by Bowlby's (1969) attachment theory, the nature of adult love can be said to have its origins in the earliest mother-infant relationship that sets the stage for how the child negotiates the psychosexual phases of development. The earliest love relationship forms what Freud (1912a) called a stereotype plate, which means that this first relationship becomes the prototype for all future love relationships. We can assume that the prototype includes the implicit conditions for loving, for example, some notion of the rules of the game: Is my caregiver sensitive, empathic, reliable? Do I face frustration when she is in a bad mood or can she take care of me anyway, and without resentment? Does she encourage or discourage

bids for attention? Does she hold me in a way that is comforting? Does she pick me up when I am too agitated? Of course, the infant is not verbalizing these questions in the language indicated previously. Nonetheless, the growing infant is developing, in Bowlby's (1975) terms, an internal working model (IWM) of how a love relationship is constituted. That is, the growing infant, based on experiences of satisfaction and frustration and the conditions that seem to be associated with each, forms mental representations of himself or herself, of the caregivers, and of the affective quality of interactions with the caregivers. These interactions are positively and/or negatively colored depending on the nature of the actual interaction with the caregiver as influenced by the infant's temperament and by whatever inner fantasies influence the actual interactions (Kernberg, 1975). These mental representations become fundamental constituents of the child's anticipation of the nature of further social interaction. An essential aspect of the IWM is the nature of the child's attachment to the caregiver. In the language of Bowlby (1969, 1973, 1975) and Ainsworth, Blehar, Waters, and Wall (1978), the child can be securely attached or insecurely attached. Insecure attachment takes two main forms: an avoidant attachment style or an anxious/ambivalent attachment style. Recently, a disorganized attachment style has been observed (Main, 1995), a style that has carried a poor prognosis for effective functioning later on.

These attachment styles have been measured in adults and found to predict experiences in a variety of behavioral domains as well as in a variety of relationships, including romantic relationships (Shaver, 2002). For example, avoidant subjects tend to be less invested in relationships, withdraw from relationships in times of stress, feel distant and bored during social interactions, and are reluctant to be personally self-disclosing. They use work to avoid close relationships, seem less grieved by losses, have more one-night-stand sexual encounters, are more likely to fantasize about someone else during sex, and are more likely to poach and be poachable for short-term relationships. In terms of Sternberg's (1988) triangular theory of love, the person with an avoidant attachment style is more likely to seek passion and less likely to seek intimacy and commitment. Anxious/ambivalent subjects would be more apt to "buy" closeness via sex, prefer the cuddly to the directly genital aspects of sex, are more invested in relationships (even though they show a higher rate of breakups), and grieve intensely following a loss. The anxious/ambivalent type tends to become enmeshed in relationships and worries about being unlovable and rejected. In this regard, there is a fear of being known too intimately by the other. The implication is that anxious/ambivalent individuals prefer to avoid passion, use sex in the service of winning their partner, but worry about rejection and abandonment. In

Sternberg's terms, they seek commitment but fear intimacy and passion. In contrast, securely attached subjects appear to be highly invested in relationships, enjoy all aspects of sex (particularly in the context of a long-term relationship), and are more likely to maintain long-term relationships. Their relationships are characterized by trust (a quality that Freudian theorists, especially Erikson, believe is formed during the first year of life). Secure subjects will grieve following a personal loss but seem to be more resilient in that they sooner achieve a constructive resolution of the loss. In Sternberg's terms, those with secure attachment styles would be the most likely to seek and achieve the integration of passion, intimacy, and commitment—what Sternberg call consummate love and which includes romantic love (passion + intimacy).

These (and other) kinds of individual differences in romantic relationships need to be integrated with other aspects of romantic relationships, for example, the relationship between love and sexual desire. Eagle (2004), a psychoanalytic theorist, offers an incisive, illuminating foray into the common clinical as well as everyday observation: the split between love and desire. Many years ago, Freud (1912b) observed that men often seek women who are either sexual objects or someone to love. As Freud (1912b, p. 183) put it, "where they love, they do not desire and where they desire they cannot love." In his view, such men suffered from psychic impotence based on an incestuous fixation. That is, insofar as the object of love has connotations of Oedipal desire, it becomes threatening and unacceptable to seek sexual fulfillment with that person. Freud and others have referred to this not uncommon split as the Madonna/Whore complex.

I will illustrate this phenomenon with two clinical examples from my own work. In the first case, the patient was a man in his late 20s who was having an affair with a woman 15 years his senior. A few months into the relationship, which by all accounts was proceeding smoothly, especially on the sexual level, he spent a weekend with her at his mother's country house. As he began having intercourse with his girlfriend in his mother's bedroom, he experienced a massive panic attack, the first one he ever had. From this experience, accompanied by other associations, it seemed reasonable to assume that the idea of sex with an older woman in his mother's bed activated unacceptable, frightening Oedipal wishes. The second example, concerns another male patient, also in his late 20s, who married a woman who, even prior to their marriage, reminded him somewhat of his mother. She was bland, conservative, nice, but not at all sexy or exciting. Over time, these qualities that he perceived in her took on added intensity, particularly after the birth of their child. Now, he found the very idea of kissing her to be aversive, to the point of inducing nausea. Having sexual intercourse with her

was something he felt he must avoid. Even his growing horniness was insufficient to override his sexual aversion toward her. He preferred to masturbate. Prior to his marriage, the patient dated a succession of highly sexy women. The problem was that they rejected him. The appeal of his nonsexy wife was that she was devoted and reliable, would never leave him, and thereby provided a secure attachment that helped calm him and enabled him to function better at work. The clinical evidence suggested the operation of Oedipal wishes, wishes that were activated and intensified by the wife's similarity to his mother.

Eagle points out that ". . . insofar as one's romantic partner becomes one's attachment figure, she takes on a role that is, in important respects, similar to the role played by mother" (Eagle, 2004, p. 10). He claims that what is triggered or intensified in this situation is not necessarily Oedipal wishes but the incest taboo. That is, if the woman is seen too much like the mother then she becomes off limits as a sexual partner. In Eagle's formulation, it is not that the man really wants to have sex with his mother but that he knows he should not do it. Eagle points out that a taboo does not necessarily presuppose a wish, noting that the fact that there is a taboo against suicide does not automatically mean that there is a universal wish to commit suicide. The counter to this point is that although Oedipal wishes or suicidal wishes need not be universal, the evolution of taboos would seem to serve the social function of inhibiting the expression of such desires in those people who harbor them. It would be a challenging research task to devise studies that would allow us to choose between the Oedipal wish versus the incest-taboo interpretation.

Eagle's (2004) central thesis is that attachment and sexuality are functionally separable systems and to some degree operate in antagonistic ways. He maintains that it is this partial antagonism rather than forbidden incestuous wishes that constitutes the foundation for the commonly observed split between love and desire. He adds that this split will be greater in those who are insecurely attached and presents evidence in support of this claim, including some of the findings mentioned previously.

Eagle notes the general tendency of a contradiction between safety and excitement. And, insofar as the sexual system and the exploratory system operate in concert with one another, they point, more clearly in the male, toward variety and novelty as necessary to foster sexual interest and excitement. Men seem to want more variety in their sexual partners and think more about sex. Relatively speaking, women seem more drawn to intimacy and commitment. Men are more prone to sexual jealousy, women are more likely to experience emotional jealousy. Buss (1994) notes the evolutionary reasons for this gender difference.

Before presenting Bergmann's (1987) treatise on love from a traditional psychoanalytic perspective, it will be useful to state a few key psychoanalytic propositions that are most relevant to understanding the nature of romantic love.

1. The infant's experience contains the precursors of adult sexuality. Sensual experiences are tied to different bodily or erogenous zones (e.g., mouth, anus) that produce bodily sensations (e.g., based on being fed, held, and comforted) that are pleasurable and/or painful.

2. The infant's primary caregiver, usually the mother, becomes the infant's first attachment object and first sexual object. According to Freud, the "... child sucking at his mother's breast has become the prototype of every relation of love. *The finding of an object is in fact a refinding of it* [italics added]" (Freud, 1905, p. 222). Bergmann regards the previous italicized statement as "... Freud's most profound contribution to love" (Bergmann, 1987, p. 159). (See Appendix A for the lyrics of a popular song that, although open to other interpretations, seem to capture this notion quite well.)

3. In normal development, the original object has to be given up as a means of genital pleasure (the Oedipal phase). In adolescence, with the advent of sexual maturity, the person has to find a nonincestuous object. According to Bergmann, "The newly selected person must in some way resemble the old, but must not awaken the guilt feelings associated with the incestuous oedipal object" (Bergmann, 1987, p. 159). In fact, as Eagle (2004) pointed out, there is evidence to suggest that optimal mate selection involves a choice that bears some resemblance to the familiar caregiver of childhood yet is sufficiently different. (Choosing mates of intermediate similarity operates on an animal level as well so that it is insufficient to explain it in humans only on the basis of a compromise solution for Oedipal wishes.) Some people choose partners who are very dissimilar from themselves (e.g., different ethnic or racial backgrounds). It is commonly reported that such partners are more exotic. From a psychoanalytic perspective, such choices often entail a flight from incestuous wishes yet a chance to act out such wishes with a forbidden, taboo object. Part of the problem is that whomever one marries becomes a relative and thereby is in danger of taking on the quality of an incestuous object!

Bergmann, as suggested previously, claims that for Freud "Love is the restoration of happiness that was lost" (Bergmann, 1987, p. 160; i.e., a refinding of the lost object and a desire for union with that object). I think it probably

is more accurate to say that romantic love is not always based on the refinding of an actual lost love object but on a nostalgic yearning, often based on fantasy, for a blissful merger with an object that one imagines will re-create an earlier state that might never have been experienced or might have occurred as momentary states of blissful merger. Thus, it might not be that something actually was lost that one strives to recapture but that one is looking for something special (e.g., the fantasy of eternal bliss) that has felt elusive all along (see Appendix A).

Love that is not burdened or undermined by neurosis requires that the person has not remained fixated on a parent as their love object but, as Freud said, "it should merely take them [parents] as a model, and should make a gradual transition from them on to extraneous people when the time for a final choice for an object arrives" (Freud, 1910b, p. 48). This observation is consistent with the finding that secure attachment is associated with more effective adult love relationships (Shaver, 2002). Presumably, securely attached individuals are less apt to remain fixated on early objects.

4. These considerations are relevant to the split between love and desire and the psychological difficulty of integrating these two tendencies.

5. Operating with a closed-system model of finite psychic energy, Freud believed that libido was divided between love for one's self and love of the other such that the stronger the latter, the weaker the former. Excessive love for the other could lower one's self-esteem unless the now-idealized love object loves one in return. Falling in love entails dealing with one's own sense of dissatisfaction and inadequacy about aspects of one's self by projecting one's ego ideal onto the love object. The love object then becomes idealized (as the parents originally were). This projection allows the person to narrow the gap between his actual and ideal self. There is a contradiction here because rather than lowering self-esteem by idealizing the loved one, this narrowing of the gap between the actual and the ideal self should raise it. In any case, the implication of Freud's formulation is that falling in love is exhilarating and raises one's self-esteem via the projection of the ego ideal and the idealization that accompanies it. There is the further implication that processes of partial merger and identification are involved.

With regard to partner selection, we also need to explain why the choice might be of a more narcissistic nature (e.g., choosing a partner that reminds one of one's self or whom one would like to become). Or, why one might choose a partner in what Freud (1931) called an anaclitic type, that is, modeled on the parent who fed and protected one as a child. Most choices of love partners are admixtures of the two types noted previously, but if any of these elements is overly emphasized the result can be a pathological one.

Kernberg (1995) has addressed these possibilities. He has constructed a hierarchical classification system that has direct implications for love relationships. At the lowest end of the continuum are pathologically narcissistic personalities who either find it difficult to fall in love or, if they do, typically fail in their love relationships. They tend to idealize external aspects of the love object (e.g., fame, wealth, power, beauty). For example, a narcissistic man married to a famous actress is uplifted by the public acclaim accorded his trophy wife, but he can easily be bored to be with her in private. That is, his love rests on what his partner can do for his self-esteem.

Borderline personalities are more prone to initial waves of idealization. But, their tendency toward splitting the other into good and bad means that their relationships will be unstable as their initial enthrallment shifts readily to devaluation. Compared to neurotics, they will also be more preoccupied with fears of separation and abandonment. Neurotic individuals find it hard to integrate sexual desire with love, in part because of fixation at the Oedipal level.

According to Kernberg (1995), the essence of, nonneurotic, mature sexual love is an emotional experience in which the person integrates erotic desire and tenderness. Tenderness requires that in dealing with the ambivalence that is a natural aspect of all human relations, love predominates over aggression. Love entails a "mature form of idealization" of one's partner and a commitment to the relationship and to one's partner (Kernberg, 1995, p. 32). In line with this view, Murray and colleagues (1996) found that positive illusions about their romantic partner were associated with reports of greater love, trust, and satisfaction and less ambivalence and conflict in marital and dating relationships as well as a greater likelihood that the relationship would persist over time.

Even among relatively healthy couples partner selection often is unconsciously guided by efforts to reenact and/or to work out unresolved conflicts originating with significant others in the past. This is one reason that marriages often exert a regressive pull in which the partner is reacted to in a parent-child mode. Another way to put this is that each partner is subject to the transference reactions of the other. Based on his work with married couples, Dicks (1967) noted that spouses tend to project onto each other disowned aspects of themselves, making it difficult to perceive and validate the other's true nature. In the language of object-relations theory, splitting and projective identification are used to transform an internal conflict into an external one that involves the spouse and attempts to coerce the spouse into taking on one

side of the inner conflict. Consider, for example, a husband whose development has led to the internalized belief that it is morally superior to be frugal and, therefore, cannot acknowledge the part of him that wants to spend money more freely, even impulsively. He relies on his wife to enact this part of his conflict, but when she obliges him he becomes upset and critical of her.

I have presented only a limited sampling of psychoanalytic insights about couples, particularly about the nature of romantic love. The fact that my discussion of romantic love has occupied a disproportionate amount of space in this chapter accords well with the fact that love relationships are central preoccupations in everyday life and not only in the consulting room. A more complete account of love from a psychoanalytic point of view would have to include such areas as the love between parents and children and between friends.

Mother-Infant Interactions

There is a substantial psychoanalytic literature on the importance of early mother-infant interactions in shaping the personality of the young child. In recent years, psychoanalytic notions about this period have become increasingly integrated with Bowlby's attachment theory. The mother's sensitive attunement to the infant's mental states is considered important in fostering secure attachment (Osofsky, 1982). One of the more important findings in the literature is that when pregnant women are assessed using the Adult Attachment Interview, their security of attachment to their mothers (as measured by certain qualities in their narrative accounts, e.g., coherence) predicts the security of attachment to their, as yet unborn, infants (Main, 1995). This work gives us some insight into the issue of the intergenerational transmission of personality patterns. In the Adult Attachment Interview, one obviously is not measuring the woman's actual security of attachment when she was an infant but rather what her descriptions and memories of her early experience suggest regarding how well she has come to terms with whatever she recalls having experienced. This kind of self-reflective processing will enable the mother to avoid automatically having her child relive what she experienced. Everyday clinical work, as well as research findings (Fonagy, 2001), strongly suggests that the introspective reexamination of one's past often has beneficial effects on one's children.

Several authors point to the importance of reciprocity (Osofsky, 1982) in the mutual regulatory cycles of mother-infant interaction (Beebe & Lachman, 1988; Fonagy, 2001; Sander, 1980; Stern, 1985) and the implications of these interactive patterns for eventual emotional self-regulation, self-awareness, the development of a sense of self, and mentalization (the awareness of the other person as a separate center of initiative). Fonagy (2001), for example, views the budding awareness that the behavior of others (as well as of the self) is motivated by internal states as a decisive step forward in development, a step taken incompletely by patients who have borderline personality disorder. In general, perhaps more than any other theory, psychoanalytic theory stresses the importance of the quality of mother-infant interactions in the shaping of personality.

Parent-Child Relations

The interaction of parents and children beyond infancy is also considered extremely influential in personality development. As with mother-infant interactions, there is a vast literature on this topic. By and large, the findings from empirical studies are consistent with psychoanalytic observations. Some studies of child psychopathology have focused on the variables of warmth and aversive control. It has been found that mothers who warmly and responsively engage in mutual turn-taking have children who show secure attachment, good school adaptation, and social competence (Sroufe & Fleeson, 1988). That infants with secure attachments to primary caregivers are later characterized by more effective self-regulation is not surprising because an essential aspect of secure attachment is the experience of well-modulated dyadic regulation of emotion and arousal. In other words, in the case of secure attachment, the mother has served as an effective, external psychobiological regulator of the infant's tension and need states. From a psychoanalytic perspective, this enables the child to internalize an ego-supportive environment, or what has been called a soothing introject (Adler, 1993).

Clinical observations are entirely consonant with these views. In the case of repeated traumatic experiences, the child is not protected in a way that would allow for the internalization of a soothing introject. It is said that persons with borderline personality disorder suffer from not having achieved this kind of internalization. From the standpoint of self psychology, one could say that the caregivers failed to provide sufficient experiences of being mirroring self-objects or idealized self-objects, thus depriving the child of opportunities for the development of a cohesive sense of self and a sense of inner strength.

The Dynamics of Family Life

Family therapists have helped us understand some central aspects of family dynamics. If we regard boundaries and hierarchical structure as two essential characteristics of family interaction, then we can look at impaired individual and family functioning in relation to these factors. For example, optimal permeability of boundaries allows for an avoidance of enmeshment on the one hand versus rigid, overcontrol on the other hand (Bowen, 1978).

Bowen (1978) also describes how triangulation contributes to the development of maladaptive family patterns and how it results from the tensions in the couple and is an attempt to decrease those tensions. In an emotional triangle, different coalitions and collusions are possible—for example, the parents lessening their conflicts with one another by uniting against a bad child. Or, if either spouse takes a lover, a triangle is created that might lend some stability to the marriage.

Another important concept developed by Bowen is self-differentiation, that is, the degree to which there are clear boundaries among family members. Difficulties in optimal self-differentiation, in concert with other personality issues, can create a variety of family problems. For example, where the mother and son feel weak in relation to a father perceived as powerful and controlling, a cross-generational coalition of mother and son can develop. Finally, one could say that finding the optimal balance between autonomy and intimacy is perhaps the couple's and the family's greatest challenge. A psychoanalytic perspective would examine the intrapsychic factors in each person (e.g., fear of submerging one's identity) that interfere with finding a suitable balance between intimacy and autonomy.

Applying the concepts of splitting and projective identification to family dynamics, psychoanalytic clinicians (e.g., Dicks, 1967; Scharff & Scharff, 1987) see the so-called identified patient as the carrier of the symptom for the family, that is, as expressing the unacceptable, split-off aspects of other family members. For example, impulsivity on the part of a child might be subtly encouraged and influenced by parents who consciously insist on attitudes of restraint and self-control.

Psychoanalytic theories can shed light on many other aspects of family life (e.g., sibling rivalry, sexual abuse, incest, child abuse and neglect, motivations for parenthood, capacity to parent, extramarital relationships, relationships with in-laws, etc.). The central theme in all these domains would be that unresolved intrapsychic conflicts and personality deficits can invade and impair any and all aspects of family life.

A separate chapter would be required to described the pervasive, profound influence that these deficits and conflicts exert by way of transference reactions, that is, distorted cognitions and inappropriate feelings in current relationships that are reenactments of unresolved issues with significant others in the past (Dicks, 1967; Freud, 1912a). There is now a substantial experimental research literature on transference in everyday life (Andersen & Berk, 1998).

WORK OR SCHOOL

In the area of work and school, psychoanalysts are interested in motivations for these activities: What goes into the choices made, the degree of commitment, the adequacy of one's coping resources in the face of stressful situations in work or school, attitudes toward authority, feelings and fantasies about success and failure, strivings toward activity and passivity, achievement motivation, and competition, to mention only some of the salient issues.

There are a multitude of dynamic issues relevant to all of the previous topics. Broadly speaking, from a Freudian perspective, the extent to which one can function in a relatively conflict-free manner with good ego strength and in a reasonably adaptive manner in school or work depends on such factors as: (1) how brittle one's defenses are, (2) one's level of self-esteem and capacity to tolerate blows to self-esteem (narcissistic injuries) without decompensating, (3) ability to compete in a healthy manner (which includes attitudes toward authority and preoccupation with issues of power and prestige), (4) the match between one's ego interests and the work or academic situation, (5) capacity to delay gratification, (6) the organizational dynamics of the institution as they resonate with an individual's personal issues, (7) one's capacity for sublimation of sexual and aggressive wishes, and (8) freedom from disabling symptoms, notably anxiety and depression, as well as grandiosity or masochistic trends.

Aside from basic abilities and talents, and luck, the quality of a person's work, persistence in the face of frustration, enjoyment of the work, and the sense of fulfillment in doing it will be a joint interaction of the factors noted previously. For example, a patient complained bitterly that he was painfully bored with his work. He had an MBA from a prestigious university but he had no compelling desire to get this degree. He earned excellent grades by being bright but not studying very much. Coworkers who had been with his organization for several years but had not advanced to higher executive positions were regarded by him as losers. The patient hated competition when there was any chance that he might lose. He also resented anyone in authority over him, in large part because he felt inferior to such people. His sense of boredom was a symptomatic expression of the factors noted previously. It was a way of disengaging from the competitive nature of his job. It was akin to getting good grades without studying so as not to face the prospect of not getting an A if he studied. In the work situation, however, this strategy failed

and the patient was fired. One could present numerous clinical examples of how attitudes toward work and the effectiveness of one's work are influenced by unresolved conflicts of various kinds.

Clinical work has led to the formulation of different character types, that is, enduring styles of personality functioning that have implications for interpersonal relationships, for career choice, and career success. Because the clinical situation naturally focuses on maladaptive behavior patterns, the analyst is attuned to the blatant and subtle ways in which people unconsciously undermine their own conscious efforts to succeed. Early on, Freud (1916) wrote about *Those Wrecked by Success,* noting that an unconscious sense of guilt can lead a person to wrest defeat from the jaws of victory. In more recent years, Schafer (1984) offered an illuminating account of the motives that could lead someone to unconsciously pursue and prefer failure rather than success. Many clinicians have noted that factors such as separation guilt, survivor guilt, and guilt about a sense of Oedipal triumph can lead a person to believe that it is wrong for them to surpass their family of origin.

RETIREMENT

The issues involved in deciding whether, when, and how to retire obviously are emotionally loaded. As with any other phase of the life cycle, the meanings of retirement are the key factor in determining the adequacy of the person's functioning during the retirement years. The meanings are likely to be influenced by such factors as (1) whether the retirement was forced or involuntary, (2) the age at which it occurred, (3) the degree of loss of status, income, and other perks of the job, (4) the degree to which the person's identity and sense of worth was linked to the job and the extent to which the person has other interests and resources to embark on new activities, (5) the reactions of family members and of those in the community, (6) the person's ability to cope with whatever physical illnesses or disabilities are accompanying the aging process, (7) general flexibility and adequacy of ego resources, and (8) attitudes toward mortality. In Eriksonian terms, the life cycle phase most relevant to one's typical retirement age is *ego integrity* versus *despair.* In this stage, a positive outcome is one in which the person reflects on his or her life with a sense of fulfillment and satisfaction rather than a sense of despair and regret over lost or missed opportunities or a life not well led. Being at the positive end of this continuum would seem to enable the person to enter the retirement years with a sense of opportunity to cultivate interests and activities that might not have been possible earlier.

In this, as in earlier phases of life, strong ego interests can sustain the person as much as solid interpersonal relationships (Eagle, 1982).

Presented previously are commonsense considerations that are not distinctively psychoanalytic. A psychoanalytic perspective is relevant in that unresolved conflicts, particularly unconscious ones, and self-esteem issues related to narcissistic vulnerabilities can readily influence how one copes with retirement. Here are two brief clinical examples. A 72-year-old man with a history of several major depressive episodes was forced into retirement by a company that employed him for 25 years. He was hired without the credentials ordinarily required for the job, but his determination and talent led him to excel beyond the level of his peers who had the prior training ordinarily required for the job. His job also brought him into frequent contact with famous people. Outside his job when he flashed his ID card he received favored treatment (e.g., in restaurants). The patient had a severely traumatic childhood, marked by humiliating experiences and forced separations in which his mother placed him in foster care. He grew up feeling rejected and abandoned and had chronically low self-esteem. The forced separation from his job was experienced as a serious narcissistic injury that resonated with his feelings that his mother abandoned him. Within a short period of time his functioning deteriorated, marital tensions escalated, and he became so depressed that he required hospitalization and a course of electroconvulsive treatment. In contrast is the case of a 54-year-old man who voluntarily retired from his career as an accountant following the receipt of a substantial inheritance. He had not enjoyed his work, was not motivated to do the work, was leaving work early, and had been fired from several jobs. His sense of identity and feelings of self-worth were not tied to his career. Quitting was a relief. He enjoyed his leisure time (reading and playing sports) and only occasionally had twinges of guilt about not being a productive member of society. Retirement suited him well. Thus, the premorbid personality adjustment plays a significant role in one's reaction to retirement.

RECREATION

A psychoanalytic perspective on recreation and leisure activity would include a focus on the motivation and meanings of different recreational activities. Among the factors involved are: (1) the person's capacity to suspend their working activities in order to enjoy some guilt-free leisure time, (2) the ability to engage in play, that is, to suspend a strict reality orientation and allow an adaptive regression, (3) the ego resources and flexibility to have non-work-related interests,

(4) the capacity for sublimation of instinctual impulse, and (5) the relative absence of depression and anhedonia.

Recreation, of course, can take many forms. For example, one might prefer active participation (e.g., competitive sports, gambling, making furniture) to relatively more passive experiences (e.g., watching TV and movies, reading, going to antiques shows and museums, listening to music). From a psychoanalytic perspective one would view the preferred forms of recreation (e.g., relatively active versus passive) and the preferred content of the activity (e.g., the Friday-night poker game, engaging in a competitive sport) as reflecting the interaction of the person's conflict-free ego interests, temperamental inclination, and underlying, usually unconscious, personality conflicts.

Perhaps the main contribution of a psychoanalytic perspective on recreation and leisure, as well as all aspects of behavior, is the idea of normal compromise formation. Following Brenner (1982), all behavior (whether dreams, psychiatric symptoms, play, and other forms of leisure activity) is a compromise formation in that it is (simultaneously) motivated by the desire for gratification of sexual and aggressive wishes, sometimes openly expressed, but more often defended against to avoid anxiety and other dysphoric affects, and sublimated in conformity with the requirements of one's conscience and ego-ideal and the constraints of reality. Compromise formations also reveal one's ego interests, desires for mastery and pleasure, and interpersonal goals. Of course, temperamental factors also play a role. As a common example, some people can lie on a beach for hours at a time in a kind of reverie whereas others become restless after a few minutes and must engage in some kind of activity (even if it is only reading) to avoid becoming tense and uncomfortable. In some cases, however, this is not simply a difference in temperament. Here I am thinking of patients who are unable to engage in prolonged reverie for fear of the eruption of unwelcome thoughts and fantasies and who need to be active in order to stave off awareness of troubling mental contents.

Play, of course, originates in childhood. It occupies a zone between reality and fantasy. It both expresses and promotes ego development in that it exercises ego functions of planning, imagination, and so forth as well as facilitating interpersonal relatedness when it calls for cooperation and competition. Both interactive and parallel play are important in developing ego capacities (e.g., the growth of symbolic capacity), in providing experiences of ego mastery, and in allowing a balance between gratification and rule-governed behavior.

Socialization experiences force us to shift the balance of our activities from play to work, with the latter often having the connotation of an activity that is onerous. For some work is a necessary but unwelcome impediment to play. For those with an overdeveloped work ethic, and a generally harsh superego, play is an unacceptable escape from reality. To the extent that the individual enjoys his or her work, and has an intrinsic interest in it, it becomes more akin to play, and the discrepancy between work and play is less pronounced.

As noted previously, different forms of adult play and leisure activity can be selected for dynamic reasons. Myers (1989) presents a case in which spelunking was unconsciously motivated and represented a counterclaustrophobic activity based on an attempt to deal with the death of a brother who had fallen from a high place. In a case of the present author, a male patient clearly used leisure activity as a thinly veiled sublimation of his aggressive, competitive strivings. He was down on himself for his lack of career success and did not have a secure sense of his masculinity. He was a decent golfer, and when he played against a friend of his he would chide him for missing an easy shot by calling him *Mrs. Smith* ("Way to go, *Mrs.* Smith!"). This attempt to demasculinize his golf partner led his friend to refuse further golf outings and eventually to a deterioration of the friendship. The patient was unaware of the unconscious sources of his remarks and regarded them as merely playful teasing. Competitive strivings and a strong desire to avert any sense of being a loser can become manifest in varied ways. In one case, a patient did not engage in any competitive sports for fear that he would not win, but when he realized that he could excel at Internet poker he became semiaddicted to that recreational activity.

Patients with strong oral wishes are more prone to become engrossed in passive forms of leisure, as in the TV couch potato. In fact, watching movies and television obviously is a major form of leisure activity for both children and adults. Psychoanalysts have presented many analyses of the appeal of television and the movies. I refer the interested reader to Greenberg's (1993) *Screen Memories* and Gabbard's (1999) *Psychiatry and Cinema* as well as to Gabbard's (2002) analysis of *The Sopranos*.

Let me offer a couple of additional clinical examples of personality dynamics that can influence leisure activities and the way in which one experiences them. A male patient who insisted on frequent golf weekends with his buddies, despite his wife's protestations, seemed motivated by (1) his desire to preserve his sense of his own space and autonomy (Blatt & Zuroff, 1992), (2) his unconscious homoerotic desires to hang out with his buddies on these all-male weekends, and (3) the opportunity to at least flirt with other women when the golf day was done. Another male patient was generally inclined to solitary forms of leisure activity (e.g., watching golf on TV, exercising alone, etc.). On summer vacations at the beach, he would spend hours floating on his surfboard far from shore while his wife was sitting on the beach feeling abandoned. His leisure activity during vacation was very much in line with his generally noninteractive style with his wife during the rest of the year. Put in terms of play, he preferred parallel play while his wife preferred interactive play and, in general, was much more playful than her husband.

As another example, consider the case of a male patient who spends a significant chunk of his leisure time searching the Internet for pictures that match his image of women with perfect breasts. For this patient, perfect breasts are large, round, upright, with small areolae. These pictures are his preferred visual input while masturbating. The activity has a distinctly compulsive quality, and he prefers it to having sex with his wife. In fact, it is his favorite form of leisure activity. It frees him from the pressure of sexual performance and sexual intimacy. Based on his associations, it seemed that the unconscious fantasy underlying this activity was one of blissful merger with a maternal, nurturing figure.

From a psychoanalytic perspective, a central, underlying factor in leisure activity is that it temporarily frees one from the stringent demands of reality and gives freer rein to one's conscious and unconscious fantasy life. This tends to be true even when the leisure activity involves serious intellectual engagement as in appreciating art, literature, and music.

Almost from the start, psychoanalysts have attempted to extend their understanding of the individual psyche as observed in the consulting room to a probing of the dynamics of a variety of other human experiences. Most, but not all, of the work in applied psychoanalysis is based on traditional psychoanalytic theory, sometimes with its ego-psychological emphases (e.g., Erikson, 1950).

The application of psychoanalysis (called applied psychoanalysis) started with Freud's 1910 study of Leonardo da Vinci in which he felt challenged to explain *Mona Lisa*'s enigmatic smile. His excursions into applied analysis extended to the speculations put forth in such works as "Moses and Monotheism" (Freud, 1939), "The Future of an Illusion" (Freud, 1927), "Civilization and Its Discontents" (Freud, 1930), and a number of shorter essays focused mostly on works of art and literature. Freud's approach, continued by numerous theorists, is both illuminating and problematic. The approach has generated insights into vital aspects of the individual psyche and of cultural and historical phenomena, including artistic creations, but it does not readily lend itself to attempts at empirical validation. It has been argued, however, that such an approach commands our interest in that it can deepen our understanding of the essential tendencies of the human mind (Panofsky, 1939).

For purposes of this chapter, the point to be made is that in devoting one's leisure time to experiencing works of art, music, or literature, one is selecting works that have an emotional resonance that often derives from unconscious conflicts or fantasies, many of them of a universal nature. In other words, the enduring appeal of certain works of art, myths, and fairy tales across cultures and generations appears to be based on their capacity to arouse in the audience, viewer, or reader the same (or similar) dynamic issues and themes (e.g., fears of loss and abandonment). There is the further assumption that these dynamic themes also inspired the artists who created works that have stood the test of time. Bettelheim's (1976) treatise on *The Uses of Enchantment* is a stimulating account of why children in each generation are drawn to the same fairy tales (e.g., "Jack and the Beanstalk"). It is a separate but equally interesting issue as to why emotional resonances of this kind are more profound when activated in the context of an esthetic, symbolic experience than when conveyed in more direct, nonartistic forms.

One can cite countless examples of the dynamic impact of art on the esthetic sensibilities of adults. The interested reader might start with Freud's interpretation of the Michelangelo's sculpture *Moses* (Freud, 1914a), which posits that the postural elements evoke in the viewer a sense of inhibited rage (see also Liebert, 1982; Oremland, 1978).

In conclusion, I have attempted to present some essential features of a psychoanalytic view of personality and how it can inform our understanding of everyday behavior, or to paraphrase Freud's (1901) *Psychopathology of Everyday Life,* an account that one might call the "Psychodynamics of Everyday Life," which is really what Freud meant to convey in his title. I have only been able to introduce the topic but I hope the reader appreciates the depth, complexity, and potential for understanding that a psychoanalytic perspective can offer.

APPENDIX A

Where or When

It seems we stood and talked like this before
We looked at each other in the same way then
But I can't remember where or when
The clothes you're wearing are the clothes you wore
The smile you are smiling you were smiling then
But I can't remember where or when

Some things that happened for the first time
Seem to be happening again
And so it seems that we have met before

And laughed before
And loved before
But who knows where or when

Some things that happened for the first time
Seem to be happening again
And so it seems that we have met before
And laughed before
And loved before
But who knows where or when

Lorenz Hart and Richard Rodgers (1936)

NOTES

1. Freud's theory typically is depicted as a quantitatively based drive-reduction theory. Yet, in his paper on masochism (Freud, 1924), he referred to a qualitative factor that also determined pleasure and unpleasure that might have to do with the sequence of stimuli, their rhythm, or the nature of their fluctuation in intensity.
2. Consider the game of peekaboo. Interest in this game is seen as motivated by a desire to master the issue of separation by gaining control over the temporary disappearance and reappearance of the adult.

REFERENCES

Adler, A. (1927). *Understanding human nature.* Greenwich, CT: Fawcett.

Adler, G. (1993). The psychotherapy of core borderline psychopathology. *American Journal of Psychiatry, 47*(2), 194–205.

Ainsworth, M. D. S., Blehar, M. C., Waters, E., & Wall, S. (1978). *Patterns of attachment: A psychological study of the strange situation.* Hillsdale, NJ: Erlbaum.

Andersen, S. M., & Berk, M. S. (1998). Transference in everyday experience: Implications of experimental research for relevant clinical phenomena. *Review of General Psychology, 2*(1), 81–120.

Anderson, M. C., Ochsner, K. N., Kuhl, B., Cooper. J., Roberstson, E., Gabrieli, S. W., et al. (2004). Neural systems underlying the suppression of unwanted memories. *Science, 303,* 232–235.

Bargh, J. (1997). The automaticity of everyday life. In R. S. Wyer Jr. (Ed.), *The automaticity of everyday life: Advances in social cognition* (Vol. 10, pp. 1–61). Mahwah, NJ: Erlbaum.

Beck, A. (1976). *Cognitive therapy and the emotional disorders.* New York: International Universities Press.

Beebe, B., & Lachman, F. (1988). The contribution of mother-infant mutual influence to the origins of self- and object representations. *Psychoanalytic Psychology, 5,* 305–357.

Bellak, L., Hurvich, M., & Gediman, H. (1973). *Ego functions in schizophrenics, neurotics, and normals.* New York: Wiley.

Bergmann, M. S. (1987). *The anatomy of loving.* New York: Columbia University Press.

Bettelheim, B. (1976). *The uses of enchantment: The meaning and importance of fairy tales.* New York: Knopf.

Blatt, S. J., & Zuroff, D. (1992). Interpersonal relatedness and self-definition: Two prototypes for depression. *Clinical Psychology Review, 12,* 527–562.

Bornstein, R. F., & Pittman, T. S. (Eds.). (1992). *Perception without awareness.* New York: Guilford Press.

Bowen, M. (1978). *Family therapy in clinical practice.* New York: Aronson.

Bowlby, J. (1969). *Attachment.* New York: Basic Books.

Bowlby, J. (1973). *Separation: Anxiety and anger.* New York: Basic Books.

Bowlby, J. (1975). *Loss: Sadness and depression.* New York: Basic Books.

Buss, D. (1985). Human mate selection. *American Scientist, 73,* 47–51.

Buss, D. (1994). *The evolution of desire.* New York: Basic Books.

Buss, D. (2000). *The dangerous passion: Why jealousy is as necessary as love and sex.* New York: Free Press.

Brenner, C. (1982). *The mind in conflict.* New York: International Universities Press.

Carter, B., & McGoldrick, M. (1989). *The changing family life cycle* (2nd ed.). Needham Heights, MA: Allyn and Bacon.

Crowne, D. P., & Marlowe, D. (1964). *The approval motive: Studies in evaluative dependence.* New York: Wiley.

Davis, P. J., & Schwartz, G. E. (1987). Repression and the inaccessibility of affective memories. *Journal of Personality and Social Psychology, 52,* 155–162.

Dicks, H. V. (1967). *Marital tensions.* New York: Basic Books.

Dixon, N. F. (1971). *Subliminal perception: The nature of controversy.* New York: McGraw-Hill.

Dixon, N. F. (1981). *Preconscious processing.* London: Wiley.

Eagle, M. (1961). Effects of subliminal stimuli of aggressive content upon conscious cognition. PhD diss., New York University. *Dissertation Abstracts, 21*(12), 3849.

Eagle, M. (1982). Interests as object relations. In J. Masling (Ed.), *Empirical studies in analytic theory* (pp. 159–188). Hillsdale, NJ: Erlbaum.

Eagle, M. (1984). *Recent developments in psychoanalysis.* New York: McGraw-Hill.

Eagle, M. (1987). Theoretical and clinical shifts in psychoanalysis. *American Journal of Orthopsychiatry, 57*(2), 175–184.

Eagle, M. (2000). Repression (Pts. 1 & 2). *Psychoanalytic Review, 87*(1, 2), 1–38, 161–187.

Eagle, M. (2004, April 13). *Attachment and sexuality.* Paper presented at Columbia University, New York City.

Eagle, M., & Wolitzky, D. L. (1989). The idea of progress in psychoanalysis. *Psychoanalysis and contemporary thought* (Vol. 12, pp. 27–72).

Edelson, M. (1988). *Psychoanalysis: A theory in crisis.* Chicago: University of Chicago Press.

Ellis, A. (1987). The impossibility of achieving consistently good mental health. *American Psychologist, 42,* 364–375.

Erikson, E. H. (1950). *Childhood and society.* New York: Norton.

Erikson, E. H. (1958). *Young man Luther.* New York: Norton.

Fairbairn, W. R. D. (1941). A revised psychopathology of psychosis and psychoneurosis. *International Journal of Psychoanalysis, 22,* 250–279.

Fairbairn, W. R. D. (1954). *An object-relations theory of the personality.* New York: Basic Books.

Fisher, C. (1954). Dreams and perception: The role of preconscious and primary modes of perception in dream formation. *Journal of the American Psychoanalytic Association, 2,* 389–445.

Fisher, S., & Greenberg, R. (1977). *The scientific credibility of Freud's theories and therapy.* New York: Columbia University Press.

Fisher, S., & Greenberg, R. (1996). *Freud scientifically reappraised: Testing the theories and therapy.* New York: Wiley.

Fonagy, P. (2001). *Attachment theory and psychoanalysis.* New York: Other Press.

Fonagy, P., & Target, M. (1997). Attachment and reflective function: Their role in self-organization. *Development and Psychopathology, 9,* 679–700.

Freud. A. (1936). *The ego and the mechanisms of defense.* New York: International Universities Press.

Freud, A. (1965). *Normality and pathology in childhood.* Harmondsworth, England: Penguin.

Freud, S. (1895). Project for a scientific psychology. *Standard Edition* (Vol. 1, pp. 281–387). London: Hogarth.

Freud, S. (1900). The interpretation of dreams. *Standard Edition* (Vol. 4, pp. 1–715). London: Hogarth.

Freud, S. (1901). The psychopathology of everyday life. *Standard Edition* (Vol. 6, pp. 1–290). London: Hogarth.

Freud, S. (1905). Three essays on sexuality. *Standard Edition* (Vol. 7, pp. 123–243). London: Hogarth.

Freud, S. (1910a). Leonardo da Vinci and a memory of his childhood. *Standard Edition* (Vol. 11, pp. 59–135). London: Hogarth.

Freud, S. (1910b). A special type of object choice made by men. *Standard Edition* (Vol. 11, pp. 175–190). London: Hogarth.

Freud, S. (1912a). The dynamics of transference. *Standard Edition* (Vol. 12, pp. 97–108). London: Hogarth.

Freud, S. (1912b). On the universal tendency to debasement in the sphere of love. *Standard Edition* (Vol. 11, pp. 178–190). London: Hogarth.

Freud, S. (1914a). The *Moses* of Michelangelo. *Standard Edition* (Vol. 13, pp. 211–236). London: Hogarth.

Freud, S. (1914b). On Narcissism. *Standard Edition* (Vol. 14, pp. 69–102). London: Hogarth.

Freud, S. (1915a). Mourning and melancholia. *Standard Edition* (Vol. 14, pp. 237–258). London: Hogarth.

Freud, S. (1915b). Repression. *Standard Edition* (Vol. 14, pp. 141–158). London: Hogarth.

Freud, S. (1915c). The unconscious. *Standard Edition* (Vol. 14, pp. 159–215). London: Hogarth.

Freud, S. (1916). Some character types met with in psycho-analytic work. *Standard Edition* (Vol. 14, pp. 309–336). London: Hogarth.

Freud, S. (1920). Beyond the pleasure principle. *Standard Edition* (Vol. 18, pp. 3–64). London: Hogarth.

Freud, S. (1924). The economic problem of masochism. *Standard Edition* (Vol. 19, pp. 155–172). London: Hogarth.

Freud, S. (1926). Inhibitions, symptoms, and anxiety. *Standard Edition* (Vol. 20, pp. 87–156). London: Hogarth.

Freud, S. (1927). The future of an illusion. *Standard Edition* (Vol. 21, pp. 1–56). London: Hogarth.

Freud, S. (1930). Civilization and its discontents. *Standard Edition* (Vol. 21, pp. 59–145). London: Hogarth.

Freud, S. (1931). Libidinal types. *Standard Edition* (Vol. 21, pp. 215–220). London: Hogarth.

Freud, S. (1933). New introductory lectures on psychoanalysis. *Standard Edition* (Vol. 22, pp. 1–182). London: Hogarth.

Freud, S. (1939). Moses and monotheism. *Standard Edition* (Vol. 21, pp. 1–138). London: Hogarth.

Gabbard, G. (1999). *Psychiatry and the cinema* (2nd ed.). Washington, DC: American Psychiatric Association.

Gabbard, G. (2002). *The psychology of the Sopranos: Love, death, desire, and betrayal in America's favorite gangster family.* New York: Basic Books.

Gedo, J. E. (1986). *Conceptual issues in psychoanalysis.* Hillsdale, NJ: Analytic Press.

Ghent, E. (2002). Relations: Introduction to the First International Association for Relational Psychotherapy and Psychoanalysis (IARPP) Conference. *IARPP e-Newsletter, 1*(1). Retrieved March 4, 2005, from http://www.iarpp.org/html/resources/newsletter_1_1.cfm#article4

Gill, M. M. (1976). Metapsychology is not psychology. In M. M. Gill & P. S. Holzman (Eds.), Psychology versus metapsychology: Psychoanalytic essays in memory of George S. Klein. *Psychological Issues, 9*(4), Monograph No. 36.

Gill, M. M. (1984). *Psychoanalysis in transition: A personal view.* Hillsdale, NJ: Analytic Press.

Greenacre, P. (1969). The nature of treason and the character of traitors. In P. Greenacre, *Emotional growth* (Vol. 1, pp. 365–396). New York: International Universities Press.

Greenberg, H. R. (1993). *Screen memories: Hollywood cinema on the psychoanalytic couch.* New York: Columbia University Press.

Greenberg, J., & Mitchell, S. (1983). *Object relations in psychoanalytic theory.* Cambridge, MA: Harvard University Press.

Greenspan, S. I. (1981). *Psychopathology and adaptation in infancy and early childhood.* New York: International Universities Press.

Grunbaum, A. (1993). *Validation in the clinical theory of psychoanalysis: A study in the philosophy of psychoanalysis.* Madison, CT: International Universities Press.

Hartmann, H. (1939). *Ego psychology and the problem of adaptation.* New York: International Universities Press.

Hartmann, H., Kris, E., & Loewenstein, R. (1946). Comments on the formation of psychic structure. In A. J. Solnif, R. S. Eissler, A. Freud, & P. B. Neubauer (Eds.), *Psychoanalytic study of the child* (Vol. 2, pp. 11–38). New York: International Universities Press.

Hobson, J. A. (1988). *The dreaming brain.* New York: Basic Books.

Holmes, D. (1990). The evidence for repression: An examination of sixty years of research. In J. L. Singer (Ed.), *Repression and dissociation* (pp. 85–102). Chicago: University of Chicago Press.

Holt, R. R. (1976). Drive or wish? A reconsideration of the psychoanalytic theory of motivation. In M. Gill & P. Holzman (Eds.), Psychology versus metapsychology: Psychoanalytic essays in memory of George S. Klein. *Psychological Issues, 9*(4), Monograph No. 36. New York: International Universities Press.

Holt, R. R. (1991). *Freud reappraised: A fresh look at psychoanalytic theory.* New York: Guilford Press.

Horney, K. (1950). *Neurosis and human growth.* New York: Norton.

Jacobs, J. W. (2004). *All you need is love and other lies about marriage.* New York: HarperCollins.

Jacobson, E. (1964). *The self and the object world.* New York: International Universities Press.

Jung, C. G. (1968). *Analytical psychology: Its theory and practice.* New York: Pantheon.

Kandel, E. R. (1999). Biology and the future of psychoanalysis: A new intellectual framework for psychiatry revisited. *American Journal of Psychiatry, 156*(4), 505–524.

Kandel, E. R. (2004, May 12). Psychoanalysis and neuroscience. Lecture at Columbia University, New York City.

Kernberg, O. F. (1975). *Borderline conditions and pathological narcissism.* New York: Jason Aronson.

Kernberg, O. F. (1984). *Severe personality disorders: Psychotherapeutic strategies.* New Haven, CT: Yale University Press.

Kernberg, O. F. (1995). *Love relations.* New Haven, CT: Yale University Press.

Kihlstrom, J. E. (1987). The cognitive unconscious. *Science, 237,* 1445–1452.

Kihlstrom, J. E. (1999). The psychological unconscious. In L. A. Pervin & O. P. John (Eds.), *Handbook of personality: Theory and research* (2nd ed.). New York: Guilford Press.

Klein, G. S. (1976). *Psychoanalytic theory: An exploration of essentials.* New York: International Universities Press.

Klein, G. S., Spence, D. P., Holt, R. R., & Gourevitch, S. (1958). Cognition without awareness: Subliminal influences upon conscious thought. *Journal of Abnormal and Social Psychology, 54,* 167–170.

Klein, M. (1964). *Contributions to psychoanalysis, 1921–1945.* New York: McGraw-Hill.

Kline, P. (1981). *Fact and fantasy in Freudian theory* (2nd edition). London: Methuen.

Kohut, H. (1971). *The analysis of the self.* New York: International Universities Press.

Kohut, H. (1977). *The restoration of the self.* New York: International Universities Press.

Kris, E. (1952). *Psychoanalytic explorations in art.* New York: International Universities Press.

LeDoux, J. (1995). Emotion: Clues from the brain. *Annual Review of Psychology, 46,* 209–235.

Lichtenberg, J. D. (1989). *Psychoanalysis and motivation.* Hillsdale, NJ: Analytic Press.

Liebert, R. S. (1982). *Michelangelo.* New Haven, CT: Yale University Press.

Loewald, H. (1960). On the therapeutic action of psychoanalysis. *International Journal of Psychoanalysis, 58,* 463–472.

Luborsky, L., & Auerbach, A. H. (1969). The symptom-context method. *Journal of the American Psychoanalytic Association, 17,* 68–99.

Mahler, M. (1968). *On human symbiosis and the vicissitudes of individuation.* New York: International Universities Press.

Mahler, M., Pine, F., & Bergman, A. (1975). *The psychological birth of the human infant.* New York: Basic Books.

Main, M. (1995). Recent studies in attachment: Overview with selected implications for clinical work. In S. Goldberg, R. Muir, & J. Kerr, *Attachment theory: Social, developmental, and clinical perspectives* (pp. 407–474). Hillsdale, NJ: Analytic Press.

Malinowski, B. (1927). *Sex and repression in savage society.* New York: Meridian Books.

Malinowski, B. (1929). *The sexual life of savages in North-Western Melanesaia.* New York: Eugenic.

Mitchell, S. (1988). *Relational concepts in psychoanalysis.* Cambridge, MA: Harvard University Press.

Modell, A. (1984). *Psychoanalysis in a new context.* New York: International Universities Press.

Munroe, R. (1955). *Schools of psychoanalytic thought.* New York: Holt, Rinehart, and Winston.

Murray, S., Holmes, J. G., & Griffin, D. W. (1996). The benefits of positive illusions: Idealization and the construction of satisfaction in close relationships. *Journal of Personality and Social Psychology, 71,* 1155–1180.

Myers, W. (1989). Spelunking as a manifestation of counterclaustrophobia. *Journal of the American Psychoanalytic Association, 37*(3), 727–735.

Nisbett, R., & Wilson, T. (1977). Telling more than we can know: Verbal reports on mental processes. *Psychological Review, 84,* 231–259.

Nolen-Hoeksema, S. (2004). *Abnormal psychology.* New York: McGraw-Hill.

Oremland, J. D. (1978). Michelangelo's Pieta. *Psychoanalytic Study of the Child, 33,* 563–591.

Osofsky, J. (1982). The development of the parent-infant relationship. *Psychoanalytic Inquiry, 1,* 625–642.

Panofsky, E. (1972). *Studies in iconology.* New York: Harper and Row. (Original work published 1923)

Person, E. (1988). *Dreams of love and fateful encounters.* New York: Norton.

Pine, F. (1990). *Drive, ego, object, and self.* New York: Basic Books.

Poetzl, O. (1960). The relationship between experimentally induced dream images and indirect vision. *Psychological Issues, 2,* 41–120. (Original work published 1917)

Pribram, K. H., & Gill, M. M. (1976). *Freud's "Project" reassessed: Preface to contemporary cognitive theory and neuropsychology.* New York: Basic Books.

Rabin, A. I. (1958). The Israeli kibbutz (collective settlement) as a laboratory for testing psychoanalytic hypotheses. *Psychological Record, 7,* 111–115.

Rapaport, D. (1960). The structure of psychoanalytic theory: A systematizing attempt. *Psychological Issues, 2,* Monograph No. 6.

Rapaport, D., & Gill, M. M. (1959). The points of view and assumptions of meta-psychology. *International Journal of Psychoanalysis, 40,* 153–162.

Rosenzweig, S., & Mason, G. (1934). An experimental study of memory in relation to the theory of repression. *British Journal of Psychology, 24,* 247–265.

Rubinstein, B. (1976). On the possibility of a strictly clinical theory: An essay on the philosophy of psychoanalysis. In M. M. Gill & P. S. Holzman (Eds.), Psychology versus metapsychology: Psychoanalytic essays in memory of George S. Klein. *Psychological Issues, 9*(4), Monograph No. 36.

Sander, L. (1980). Investigation of the infant and its caregiving environment as a biological system. In S. I. Greenspan & G. Pollock (Eds.), *The course of life* (Vol. 1, pp. 177–202). Rockville, MD: NIMH.

Sandler, J. (1987). *From safety to superego: Selected papers of Joseph Sandler.* New York: Guilford Press.

Schafer, R. (1976). *A new language for psychoanalysis.* New Haven, CT: Yale Universities Press.

Schafer, R. (1984). The pursuit of failure and the idealization of unhappiness. *American Psychologist, 39*(4), 398–405.

Scharff, D., & Scharff, J. (1987). *Object relations family therapy.* New York: Aronson.

Schore, A. (1994). *Affect regulation and the origin of the self: The neurobiology of emotional development.* Mahwah, N.J.: Erlbaum.

Shaver, P. R. (2002, June). Psychodynamics of adult attachment: A research perspective. Paper presented at the Rapaport-Klein Study Group, Austen-Riggs, MA.

Shevrin, H., & Dickman, S. (1980). The psychological unconscious: A necessary assumption for all psychological theory? *American Psychologist, 35,* 421–434.

Shevrin, H., Bond, J. A., Brakel, L. A. W, Hertel, R. K., & Williams, W. J. (1996). *Conscious and unconscious processes: Psychodynamic, cognitive, and neurophysiological convergences.* New York: Guilford Press.

Silverman, L., Lachman, F., & Milich, R. (1982). *The search for oneness.* New York: International Universities Press.

Singer, J. L. (1990). *Repression and dissociation.* Chicago: University of Chicago Press.

Solms, M. (2004). Freud returns. *Scientific American, 290,* 82–88.

Sroufe, L. A., & Fleeson, J. (1988). The coherence of family relationships. In R. A. Hinde & S. Stevenson-Hinde, *Relationships within families* (pp. 27–47). Oxford, England: Clarendon Press.

Stern, D. (1985). *The interpersonal world of the infant: A view from psychoanalysis and developmental psychology.* New York: Basic Books.

Sternberg, R. (1986). A triangular theory of love. *Psychological Review, 93,* 119–135.

Sternberg, R. (1988). Triangulating Love. In R. J. Sternberg & M. L. Barnes (Eds.), *The psychology of love.* New Haven, CT: Yale University Press.

Sullivan, H. S. (1953). *The interpersonal theory of psychiatry.* New York: Norton.

Szalaim, J. D., & Eagle, M. (1994). The role of deployment of attention in the overlearning reversal effect (ORE) with aggressive and non-aggressive stimuli. *Psychological Reports, 72,* 1195–1201.

Tomarken, A. J., & Davidson, R. J. (1994). Frontal brain activation in repressors and nonrepressors. *Journal of Abnormal Psychology, 103,* 339–349.

Vaillant, G. E. (1977). *Adaptation to life.* Boston: Little Brown.

Vaillant, G. E. (1992). *Ego mechanisms of defense: A guide for clinicians and researchers.* Washington, DC: American Psychiatric Association.

Westen, D., & Gabbard, G. O. (1999). Psychoanalytic approaches to personality. In L. A. Pervin & O. P. John (Eds.), *Handbook of personality: Theory and research* (2nd ed.). New York: Guilford Press.

Winnicott, D. W. (1965). *The maturational process and the facilitating environment.* New York: International Universities Press.

Wolitzky, D. L., Klein, G. S., & Dworkin, S. (1975). An experimental approach to the study of repression: Effects of a hypnotically induced fantasy. In D. P. Spence (Ed.), *Psychoanalysis and contemporary science* (Vol. 4, pp. 211–233). New York: International Universities Press.

Wolitzky, D. L., & Wachtel, P. L. (1973). Personality and perception. In B. Wolman (Ed.), *Handbook of general psychology* (pp. 826–857). Englewood, NJ: Prentice Hall.

CHAPTER 5

Trait and Factor Theories

PAUL T. COSTA JR. AND ROBERT R. MCCRAE

THE TRAIT PERSPECTIVE ON PERSONALITY

The trait perspective is perhaps the oldest approach to an understanding of human personality. The Sumerian *Epic of Gilgamesh*, the earliest surviving narrative in world literature, describes the "courage," "arrogance," and "stormy heart" of its hero, although it also depicts him as "wise, comely, and resolute." These are trait attributions, suggesting that Gilgamesh had distinctive qualities that reliably characterized him. To be sure, the trait psychology of the Sumerians was not what we would consider a scientific approach: Contemporary trait psychologists debate the roles of heredity and environment in trait development, whereas the Sumerians considered Gilgamesh's courage a gift from Adad, the god of the storm.

The trait approach is also the most widespread of personality theories, as attested by the lexicon of trait terms found in every human language (Dixon, 1977). It is apparently natural to the human mind to attribute enduring characteristics such as fearfulness, joviality, curiosity, kindness, and diligence to oneself and other people. Social psychologists who study trait attribution processes have sometimes concluded that people are all too ready to attribute behavior to such traits, even when situational factors may be more important (Ross, 1977). Indeed, in the 1970s, following Mischel's (1968) influential critique, many psychologists thought traits were mere cognitive fictions, as quaintly mythological as Adad, god of the storm.

In the last quarter century, however, rigorous empirical research has clarified the nature, structure, origins, and consequences of personality traits. The data now provide ample justification for humanity's predilection for trait explana-

tions, because traits do indeed explain much of human behavior (McCrae & Costa, 1995).

Phenotypic Definitions of Traits

It is possible to give purely descriptive definitions of personality traits that make no assumptions about their origins or their development over the life course. Such definitions are of two types: *intensive,* which explain what is required to be considered a trait, and *extensive,* which point out the full range of traits. McCrae and Costa defined traits intensively as "dimensions of individual differences in tendencies to show consistent patterns of thoughts, feelings, and actions" (McCrae & Costa, 2003, p. 25). This definition is consistent with most contemporary views of traits, and fits well with their operationalization in personality trait measures. For example, items from the Revised NEO Personality Inventory (NEO-PI-R; Costa & McCrae, 1992a) ask respondents if they "have a wide range of intellectual interests" (a pattern of thoughts), "rarely experience strong emotions" (feelings), and "often try new and foreign foods" (actions).

The terms *rarely* and *often* in these items—like the term *tendencies* in the definition of traits—emphasize the fact that traits have a probabilistic influence on behavior. We should not expect that people who possess a trait will be unfailingly consistent in expressing it—as even the Sumerians understood, who related that courageous Gilgamesh was terrified by a dream sent by the gods. Fleeson (2001) has recently documented the hour-to-hour fluctuations of personality characteristics, while simultaneously showing that people are highly consistent when their behavior is averaged over occasions.

The definition offered previously does not explicitly define the scope of personality traits; it does not provide an extensive definition. Is intelligence a personality trait? It does contribute to consistencies in behavior, but most psychologists regard intelligence as outside the scope of personality traits proper, chiefly because it involves abilities rather than dispositions (cf. Goff & Ackerman, 1992). Again, Gilgamesh

Acknowledgments: We thank Niyada Chittcharat, Department of Psychology, Srinakharinwirot University, Bangkok, Thailand, for providing NEO-PI-R data reported in this chapter, and Cynthia Koenig for advice on introductory psychology texts (see www .lemoyne.edu/OTRP/introtexts.html).

is described as comely, and physical attractiveness is a powerful variable in human interactions, but physical traits are also not normally considered aspects of personality. Very general attitudes such as authoritarianism (Altemeyer, 1981) may be regarded as personality traits, but specific attitudes ("medicinal marijuana should be legalized," "NAFTA should be repealed") are not.

As much as anything, this ambiguity about the scope of personality traits led to divisions among differential psychologists. Some studied needs (Jackson, 1984; Murray, 1938), some psychological types (Jung, 1923/1971; Myers & McCaulley, 1985), some folk concepts (Gough, 1987), some temperaments (Buss & Plomin, 1975), some personality disorders (Millon, 1981). It was not clear for many years whether these different categories of psychological variables were related, or equivalent, to traits or which system most adequately covered the entire territory. Eysenck (1960) had long argued that many commonly used psychological constructs could be subsumed under two broad factors he called Neuroticism (N) and Extraversion (E); Costa and McCrae (1980) suggested the addition of a third factor, Openness to Experience (O).

There was, in fact, widespread (though not universal) agreement among personality psychologists that the solution to this problem lay in the use of factor analysis. Mathematical complexities aside, factor analysis is simply a technique for summarizing data. It begins with correlations between individual variables (for example, the positive correlation of anxiety with depression or the negative correlation of quarrelsomeness with modesty) and seeks to identify clusters of variables that covary, and are unrelated to other clusters of variables. These clusters each define a factor. In the NEO-PI-R, for example, the E factor is defined by scales that measure Warmth, Gregariousness, Assertiveness, Activity, Excitement Seeking, and Positive Emotions.

In principle, then, the organizing taxonomy that would bring order to the field of personality psychology required only the application of factor analysis to a representative sample of personality measures. But representative of what? Needs? Folk concepts? Temperaments? How many scales should be included, and where should the borders be drawn?

Historically, the solution to this problem first came from lexical studies inaugurated in the United States by one of the fathers of trait psychology, Gordon Allport. With a graduate student, Henry Odbert, he produced the first comprehensive listing of traits by consulting an unabridged dictionary (Allport & Odbert, 1936). Lexical researchers have argued that traits exist in natural languages because they are useful in social interactions (we can warn our friends that so-and-so is *deceitful,* or advance our candidate by calling her *hardworking*). If trait information is useful, surely trait names will

have been invented to communicate it over the course of the centuries. Thus, an enumeration of traits in the dictionary should give a comprehensive census of traits.

The first problem with that strategy was that Allport and Odbert had identified more than seventeen thousand trait names, of which at least four thousand appeared to be meaningful descriptions of people—not mere evaluations like *swell* or *objectionable.* Some scheme was necessary to reduce this to a manageable number. Over the years, several were tried; suffice it to say that factoring the reduced sets consistently led to the identification of five factors (John, Angleitner, & Ostendorf, 1988).

But many psychologists were not convinced that these findings had resolved the problem of trait taxonomy. In the first place, it was relatively simple to identify traits that had not, in fact, been encoded in natural language. For example, the English language lacks single terms to express "is sensitive to art and beauty" or "prefers variety" or "has wide interests" (McCrae, 1990). In addition, many researchers believed that trained psychologists, using sophisticated psychological theories and psychometric methods, might identify important traits overlooked by laypersons. The Big Five might suffice for lay vocabulary, but it might be insufficient for a full scientific description of personality traits.

The first test of that hypothesis came when lay-adjective measures of the Big Five were correlated with McCrae and Costa's (1985b) three-factor model. That analysis showed that three of the lexical factors corresponded well to N, E, and O but that two lexical factors, Agreeableness (A) and Conscientiousness (C), appeared to tap new dimensions of personality. A follow-up article included new questionnaire measures of these two factors and showed multitrait, multimethod validation of the Five-Factor Model (FFM; McCrae & Costa, 1987).

A broad consensus on the value of the FFM came as a result of empirical studies showing that needs (Costa & McCrae, 1988), types (McCrae & Costa, 1989), folk concepts (McCrae, Costa, & Piedmont, 1993), temperaments (Angleitner & Ostendorf, 1994), and personality disorders (Costa & McCrae, 2005) were all understandable in terms of the FFM. Although some researchers continue to argue for additional factors (e.g., Cheung & Leung, 1998; Piedmont, 1999), most personality psychologists now agree that the broadest themes in individual differences in personality are described by the factors of the FFM.

STATEMENT OF THE THEORIES

We can now describe traits as relatively enduring dispositions related to five broad factors, N, E, O, A, and C. But how do we explain traits, account for their origins and operation? Although trait psychology is sometimes considered "dustbowl empiricism," there is in fact a strong tradition of theorizing associated with the trait perspective, and it has flourished in recent years (Wiggins, 1996).

Gordon Allport

Understandably, many introductory psychology textbooks devote much of their discussion of traits to the work of Gordon Allport. His 1937 classic, *Personality: A Psychological Interpretation,* established personality psychology as a discipline, and it was largely concerned with personality traits. As recently as 1998, Caspi based a review of personality development on Allport's theorizing, because "by and large, Allport had it right" (Caspi, 1998, p. 312). Allport's theory, however, was essentially an exposition of what a trait was. He noted that traits were relatively enduring dispositions, that they influenced the frequency and intensity of actions and experiences, that they could be expressive or motivational. Perhaps most importantly, he insisted that traits were not mere evaluations, that they were instead real neuropsychological structures that contributed to each individual's action. Far from being static entities, traits are dynamic organizers of behavior in transaction with environmental circumstances. As stated by Caspi, "Personality traits are thus organizational constructs; they influence how individuals organize their behavior to meet environmental demands and new challenges" (Caspi, 1998, p. 312). During the long decades when behaviorism dominated U.S. psychology and B. F. Skinner advocated an empty organism, Allport defended the reality of traits: "the person who confronts us possesses inside his skin generalized action tendencies (or traits) and . . . it is our job scientifically to discover what they are" (Allport, 1966).

Allport was keenly aware of what was to become a perennial criticism of trait psychology, namely, that it offered only circular explanations of behavior: We observe that John acts aggressively, infer that he has a trait of aggression, and explain his behavior as due to his trait. That would, of course, be simplistic, as Allport perfectly well understood. He distinguished between the facile attribution of traits and the difficult science of personality assessment, and he has been followed in this respect by generations of trait psychologists schooled in the concept of construct validity and the practice of psychometrics. Despite this, the view still prevails in many contemporary textbooks that trait explanations are "primarily descriptive" (Morris & Maisto, 2002, p. 462) rather than explanatory or that the explanations they offer have a "circular quality" (Coon, 2004, p. 533). Although this may be true of casual lay attributions of traits, especially first impressions,

it rather cavalierly dismisses the prodigious quantity of thought and research that has gone into the development and validation of contemporary trait-assessment instruments and the evidence that traits are real entities that can be considered true causes of behavior (McCrae & Costa, 1995). Claims that cognitive approaches are needed to help identify "mechanisms that map abstract dispositions onto specific outcomes" (Cantor, 1990, p. 735) were anticipated by Allport: "Personality is and does something. . . . It is what lies behind specific acts and within the individual. The systems that constitute personality are in every sense determining tendencies, and when aroused by suitable stimuli provoke those adjustive and expressive acts by which personality comes to be known" (Allport, 1937, pp. 48–49).

Allport's most distinctive contribution to trait theory was his distinction between *common traits* and *personal dispositions.* The former are those "dimensions of individual differences" that McCrae and Costa noted and correspond to such traits as *aggressive, serious,* and *cautious.* These traits are common not in the sense of being widespread but rather in the sense of being relevant to all people. Everyone can be considered more or less aggressive or serious or cautious. By contrast, personal dispositions are concrete tendencies found in individuals that may not be relevant to any other person. These are discovered by an analysis of single case studies (for example, from a collection of letters; Allport, 1965), and because they are concretely located in the behavior of a single individual, one can be sure that they are real. By contrast, common traits are statistical abstractions from groups of people and may or may not correspond directly to the psychological functioning of any one given individual—just as no family has the statistically average 2.5 children. Allport's preference for personal dispositions that are unique to individuals has recently been championed by Walter Mischel and his colleagues (Mischel, 1999; Mischel & Shoda, 1995), who seek characteristic *dispositional signatures* in profiles of behavior across situations. We will return to a consideration of these alternatives to common traits after introducing Five-Factor Theory.

Hans Eysenck

Eysenck was one of the giants of psychology, a researcher and theorist who made major contributions to the study of intelligence, political psychology, psychopathology, and behavior therapy (Modgil & Modgil, 1986). In the United States, however, he is chiefly regarded as a personality psychologist, famous for two ideas: First, he offered one of the earliest and simplest models of trait structure by noting and demonstrating factor analytically the ubiquity of the two dimensions of N and E—later dubbed the Big Two by Wiggins (1968). Second, he proposed that both of these dispositions reflected individual differences in brain structure and functioning. Most notable was his proposition that E resulted from a chronic lack of cortical arousal: Extraverts sought external stimulation because they lacked internal stimulation (Eysenck, 1967). Such a theory could be tested in the laboratory. For example, Eysenck claimed that introverts—already primed by high cortical arousal—salivate more in response to lemon juice than do extraverts. Subsequent tests of that hypothesis offered support when subjects were tested in the morning but not the afternoon (Deary, Ramsay, Wilson, & Riad, 1989), for girls but not boys (Casey & McManis, 1971), and not at all in Dutch subjects (Ramsay, 1969). In a Columbian study (Rodriguez & de Mikusinski, 1977), extraverts salivated more than introverts.

As this example illustrates, it was not the empirical success of Eysenck's theory that gave it such importance, but the mere fact that it was a testable theory. Empirical studies could verify or falsify its claims, and if there were problems with the theory, it could (in principle) be corrected by the facts. This situation contrasted profoundly with psychoanalytic models of personality that could never be falsified by laboratory tests and with merely descriptive approaches that offered no deep insights into the nature and functioning of traits.

Eysenck's neurophysiological theories were offered at a time when very little was understood about brain functioning. PET scans and MRIs were unheard of, and the importance of neurotransmitters was only beginning to be understood. As a result, the specifics of Eysenck's biological theorizing were primitive by today's standards, and the experimental evidence for his model has been mixed at best (Amelang & Ullwer, 1991). Yet his work was tremendously influential because it attempted to ground the statistical abstractions of factor analysis in biological processes. His work continues to inspire researchers who now have a far more sophisticated understanding of brain processes (e.g., Canli et al., 2001).

Five-Factor Theory

McCrae and Costa (1996, 1999) have recently proposed a new theory of personality, intended to make sense of a large body of findings from studies using the FFM. The empirical findings themselves are generally accepted, but the theoretical interpretation offered by Five-Factor Theory (FFT) is more controversial, and readers need to keep in mind the distinction between FFM and FFT.

The idea of constructing a theory after the facts are known may seem to be cheating: Couldn't anyone come up with post

hoc explanations for known phenomena? But in the history of science, the discovery of facts and the creation of theories is always a dialectical process. In 1887 Michelson and Morley established empirically that the speed of light was the same regardless of the observer's motion, but the interpretation of that fact awaited Einstein's 1905 publication of the Theory of Relativity; that theory subsequently led to many other predictions that have (thus far) confirmed it. In the case of FFT, the crucial data for generating the theory came from longitudinal studies of aging Americans; to date, the most powerful data for confirming the theory have come from cross-cultural studies.

How did longitudinal observations lead to a theory of personality? Before 1980 psychologists had only the vaguest notion about what happened to personality across the life span. Erikson (1950) had offered an elegant progression of life stages, but no one had traced people's progress through those hypothesized stages. If asked, most psychologists would have speculated that personality would change markedly in response to life events such as the birth of a child, divorce, or retirement. It came, therefore, as a great surprise when in the 1970s the first large-scale longitudinal studies showed exceptionally high levels of stability in both mean levels and individual differences (Block, 1977; Costa & McCrae, 1978; Douglas & Arenberg, 1978). As later studies would confirm, personality traits are quite stable in adulthood despite multiple changes in roles, relationships, and health, and the traumatic and triumphant personal experiences of a lifetime (McCrae & Costa, 2003). How could traits be stable when so much else about the individual was changing?

The central idea of FFT is that traits must be distinguished from most of the attributes studied by psychologists—attitudes, beliefs, values, habits, skills, roles, relationships, and so forth. All of these latter attributes can and do change with time and circumstance, whereas traits (by and large) do not. As Costa and McCrae put it, "traits provide the stable structure of personality within which the aging individual copes, adapts, defends, compensates, or adjusts" (Costa & McCrae, 1980, p. 97).

Some 15 years later, this idea led to the distinction between Basic Tendencies (including personality traits) and Characteristic Adaptations (attitudes, beliefs, etc.). As illustrated in Figure 5.1, Characteristic Adaptations form the functioning center of the person (which is why psychologists spend so much time studying them). The arrows in the model indicate the direction of causal influence and show that over the course of a lifetime, Characteristic Adaptations arise and change in response to both Basic Tendencies and External Influences. It is their grounding in enduring Basic Tendencies that makes them characteristic of the individual; it is their

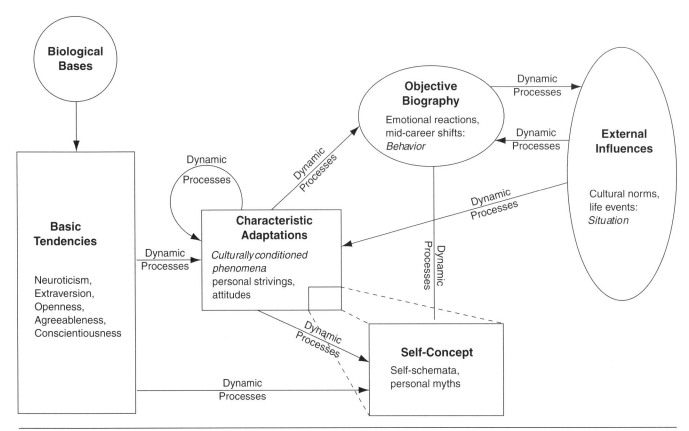

Figure 5.1   A representation of the personality system, with categories of variables, specific examples, and arrows indicating causal pathways. Adapted from McCrae & Costa, 1999.

responsiveness to External Influences that makes them Adaptations. The Self-Concept is a subdivision of Characteristic Adaptations, shaped both by what we truly are and by how others perceive us.

The output of this system is called the Objective Biography; it is the cumulative record of everything we do and experience. At any given moment, the Objective Biography amounts to what psychologists traditionally call *behavior*. By highlighting its integration over time, FFT underlines the fact that personality is better discovered by looking at the whole sweep of a person's life rather than an isolated instance of behavior.

Figure 5.1 shows an arrow from Biological Bases into Basic Tendencies. That is consistent with Eysenck's theorizing, but more importantly, it is consistent with a large body of empirical work showing that traits of the FFM are strongly influenced by genetics (Bouchard & Loehlin, 2001). There are other documented biological influences on personality, including antidepressant medication (Bagby, Levitan, Kennedy, Levitt, & Joffe, 1999) and Alzheimer's disease (Costa & McCrae, 2000).

The idea that personality traits are influenced by biology is certainly not new; even Freud nodded to constitutional factors in personality development (Freud, 1933). FFT, however, distinguishes itself from most other theories of personality because it postulates that only biological factors affect Basic Tendencies. In particular, there are no arrows from External Influences to Basic Tendencies. That would explain why life events such as marriage and retirement have little or no effect on personality trait development. It would also explain why adoptive parents do not seem to shape their children's personalities (Loehlin, Willerman, & Horn, 1985) and why the resemblance between biological parents and their children can be accounted for almost exclusively in terms of the genes they share (Harris, 1998). In a later section we will examine evidence from cross-cultural studies that also supports the claim that traits are not determined by the environment. Readers should bear in mind, however, that theories, especially in the early stages of their development, are intended to be aides to understanding a complex area, and, as such, they are usually oversimplifications. In all likelihood it will turn out that some External Influences do affect personality traits, and a revised version of the FFT would add another arrow and, one hopes, an explanation of why there are specific exceptions to the general rule.

FFT is simplified in another way: Most of the details are unspecified. For example, McCrae and Costa (1996) postulated that there are Dynamic Processes that account for the operation of the personality system, and they listed such examples as operant conditioning, delay of gratification, role-playing, and suppression of affect. But which mechanisms are important for developing Characteristic Adaptations, which for forming the Self-Concept? Do they operate on a conscious or unconscious level? Are there individual differences in the use of different dynamic processes? These details are relatively unimportant from the perspective of FFT, which is intended (at present) chiefly to give a broad overview of the development and operation of personality.

The fundamental distinction between personality traits and Characteristic Adaptations has proven to be useful in a number of contexts. In particular, Harkness and McNulty (2002) have argued that it forms the basis for a reconceptualization of clinical psychology. It is, at best, difficult to change fundamental personality traits, but it is possible to modify the characteristic maladaptations that we recognize as the source of problems in living. A fundamentally antagonistic individual will probably not become a model of loving-kindness as a result of psychotherapy, but he or she might learn to channel antagonism away from intimate relationships and into professional arenas (such as the law) where the same traits can be adaptive (cf. the case of Madeline G.; Costa & McCrae, 2005).

It would also be possible to reinterpret Allport's concept of personal dispositions in FFT terms. Allport's common traits, of course, are conceived within FFT as Basic Tendencies, but personal dispositions might be interpreted as Characteristic Adaptations, the result of the joint operation of common traits and the unique life experiences of the individual. Allport's insistence on understanding the individual at the level of personal dispositions would thus anticipate McAdams's advocacy of "units of personological analysis that are explicitly contextualized" (McAdams, 1992, p. 343), such as personal projects and strivings. Similarly, Thorne's (1989) *conditional patterns* and Mischel's (1999) *if . . . then . . . situation-behavior profiles* can be seen as acquired Characteristic Adaptations.

Both common traits and personal dispositions are compatible with FFT, and both are useful in a full psychology of personality. Personal dispositions are potentially more accurate and useful when applied in the specific context to which they are relevant; common traits are more useful in making global assessments. If personality psychologists have historically favored the common-trait approach, it is probably because it has an established methodology. After many years of psychometric research, we now have a personological armamentarium for the assessment of common traits in all individuals. By contrast, even using established tools such as the Role Construct Repertory Test (Kelly, 1955) or Personal Projects Analysis (Little, 1983), the researcher must start from scratch in formulating the unique personal dispositions of each new case.

FFT can offer some assistance in this endeavor. Because basic personality traits shape the development of Characteristic Adaptations, knowledge of the individual's trait profile can point to classes of personal dispositions (or projects, or strivings) that are likely to be particularly relevant to the individual and can help focus the idiographic interpretation. Widiger, Costa, and McCrae, for example, argued that an understanding of personality pathology could be guided by general personality traits. For example, an individual who scores low on C typically "underachieves; . . . has a poor academic performance relative to ability; disregards rules and responsibilities, . . . is unable to discipline him- or herself" (Widiger, Costa, & McCrae, 2002, p. 442). Some, or all, or none, of these problems may be faced by a particular patient low in C, and that must be established by clinical interview. But an interview that focuses on such problems is more likely to yield useful results quickly than one that searches for problems without guidance.

FFT, then, is a modern trait theory that is consistent with a large body of research on the structure and development of personality, that shares Eysenck's (and Cloninger's, 1994) belief in a biological basis for personality without settling prematurely on specific brain mechanisms, and that can accommodate Allport's personal dispositions as well as common traits.

DEVELOPMENTAL CONSIDERATIONS

Traits are sometimes defined as enduring dispositions, which means that they are to be distinguished from transient moods and situational influences. Traits are characteristics of the individual, and so should show some continuity; but there is no requirement that they be immutable. Physical traits provide a useful analogy. Height is surely a property of the individual, not a momentary mood or a reflection of the situation. Yet height changes dramatically in childhood and adolescence and declines modestly in old age (Friedlander et al., 1977); height can also be affected by diseases (such as osteoporosis) and by pharmacological interventions (e.g., human growth hormone given in childhood). As this example shows, enduring traits can change, either through intrinsic development or through external interventions. The same is, in principle, true of personality traits, and their life-span development must be understood not by definition but by empirical observation.

The Stability of Individual Differences

For the most part, psychologists are interested in two aspects of trait development. The first concerns the relative stability or change of individual differences, and the second concerns stability or change in group means. Stability of individual differences (or rank-order consistency) is usually estimated by measuring traits on two occasions—say, at age 20 and again at age 30. A large correlation implies that rank order has been largely preserved: Those individuals who scored high on the trait at age 20 also scored high at age 30. Early findings of impressively high rank-order stability ($rs \cong .75$; e.g., Costa & McCrae, 1977; Costa, McCrae, & Arenberg, 1980) over intervals of 10 or more years were little short of revelatory: At a time when many psychologists doubted the existence of traits, these data seemed to say that people did indeed have enduring dispositions. Naturally, critical objections were raised. Perhaps these results reflected not real stability but a crystallized self-image oblivious to personality change. Perhaps they were due to stability in the environment. Perhaps they were specific to the relatively well-educated and healthy volunteers who participated in longitudinal studies. Perhaps stability characterized only a small subset of traits.

These and other objections were eventually answered by a series of studies conducted by many researchers (see McCrae & Costa, 2003, for a more detailed account). Today, the notion that personality traits in the FFM show substantial rank-order stability is generally accepted (Roberts & DelVecchio, 2000). There are two qualifications to the assertion that traits are stable. The first is that the degree of stability declines somewhat as the retest interval increases. For example, Costa and McCrae (1992b, p. 181) reported that the median stability coefficient for scales from the Guilford-Zimmerman Temperament Survey (Guilford, Zimmerman, & Guilford, 1976) was .77 over a 6-year interval, .71 over a 16-year interval, and .63 over a 30-year interval. (All of these values, by the way, are underestimates of true stability, because personality tests are not perfectly reliable measuring instruments.)

The second major qualification is that stability coefficients are lower in children and increase with age. In one comparison, the median 4-year stability coefficient for 12-year-olds was .38, whereas it was .60 for college students (McCrae & Costa, 2003). Both of these values are lower than the 30-year data reported by Costa and McCrae (1992b) for individuals initially aged 25 to 57. This general trend is supported by Roberts and DelVecchio's (2000) meta-analysis.

However, there is still some controversy about the age at which peak stability is reached. From their meta-analytic results, Roberts and DelVecchio argued that there is substantial fluidity until age 50; Costa and colleagues (Costa & McCrae, 1994; Terracciano, McCrae, Brant, & Costa, 2004) have provided evidence that personality is largely stable by age 30. It is testimony to the maturation of personality as a scientific discipline that so subtle an issue can be a major point of controversy.

Lifespan Development of Mean Trait Levels

Stability in rank order does not guarantee stability of mean levels. The tall 6-year-old is likely to become a tall 20-year-old, but that does not mean that height is fixed. Instead, there are monotonic increases in height from birth to age 18 or so; a long period of stability is then typically followed by a slow loss of height in old age as the vertebral column settles. The same normative developmental curves could be drawn for personality traits; in fact, one of the giants of personality trait psychology, Raymond Cattell, offered such curves 30 years ago (Cattell, 1973). Costa and McCrae (2002) have updated that work, summarizing a large number of cross-sectional and longitudinal studies. A schematic representation is offered in Figure 5.2; it shows that, from age 12 on, N and E decline whereas A and C increase. O increases into the 20s and thereafter declines. In Figure 5.2, A and C appear flat after age 30; more recent evidence (Terracciano et al., 2004) suggests that A continues to increase at a modest rate throughout adulthood whereas C increases and then declines in old age. All of these changes, however, are rather small in magnitude; after age 30, they amount to about one-half standard deviation of change over an interval of 40 years.

It is of some interest to compare current views with Cattell's (1973) early estimates. His scales only can be mapped roughly onto contemporary constructs of the FFM, but there are some parallels. For example, his scale C (now called Emotional Stability; Conn & Rieke, 1994) is the opposite of N; Cattell showed an increase in C from adolescence to middle adulthood that matches the decline in N shown in Figure 5.2. Similarly, 16PF Q3, Perfectionism, is related to C, and shows a similar increase from adolescence to age 40. Cattell even reported something like the curvilinear trend for O in Figure 5.2; his scale M, Abstractedness or Imagination, increases up to age 40 and then declines.

There are, of course, also differences. Most notably, Cattell's (1973) plots suggest considerable change in mean levels between ages 10 and 20, whereas more recent data

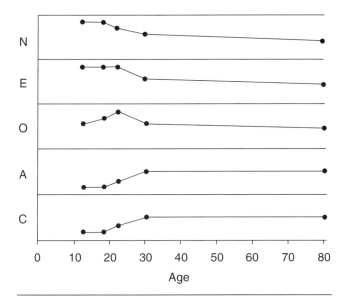

Figure 5.2 A schematic representation of age changes from age 12 to age 80. Each panel reflects the developmental curve of one of the five factors. From Costa & McCrae, 2002.

(McCrae et al., 2002)—including Cattell's own (Cattell, Cattell, & Johns, 1984)—argue for general stability of mean levels during this portion of the life span.

The Causes of Trait Development

Parallels between Cattell's (1973) findings and more recent research offer more than a tribute to the quality of his pioneering work. More profoundly, they suggest that the course of personality-trait development was the same in the middle of the twentieth century as in the latter half. The traits of children who grew up during the deprivations of the 1930s show the same developmental curves as the traits of children who grew up during the rebellions of the 1960s. The advent of television and later of the Internet seems to have had little influence on trait development.

This same phenomenon is seen even more dramatically in cross-cultural studies. Yang, McCrae, and Costa (1998) compared cross-sectional age differences in the United States and the People's Republic of China. From the 1930s on, the Chinese experienced invasion by Japan, civil war, famine in the 1950s, and the Cultural Revolution in the 1960s. More recently, a capitalist economy has emerged, leading to the largest migration in human history from rural China to the industrialized cities. Despite all these tumultuous social and cultural changes that might be expected to leave their mark on successive generations of Chinese, cross-sectional age differences on the personality scales of the California Psychological Inventory (Gough, 1987) closely resembled those found in the United States. In other studies, the age trends

seen in Figure 5.2 have been found in a wide range of countries, from Zimbabwe to Estonia (McCrae & Costa, in press; McCrae et al., 1999).

Trait development thus seems to proceed independently of culture and history—a startling idea that is hard to reconcile with many traditional personality theories. Psychoanalysts (Erikson, 1950), humanistic psychologists (Fromm, 1955), behaviorists (Dollard, Miller, Doob, Mowrer, & Sears, 1939), and multiculturalists (Gergen, Gulerce, Lock, & Misra, 1996) all emphasize the influence of culture and social context on the developing personality. Striking uniformities across starkly different cultures hardly would be predicted by any of them. But this is precisely what FFT predicts. As Figure 5.1 shows, traits, as Basic Tendencies, are influenced by Biological Bases, which are common to the human species, but not by External Influences like history and culture. Erikson, Fromm, and other personality theorists were correct in asserting that culture affects personality, but they failed to specify that this influence is limited to Characteristic Adaptations. Underlying traits appear to operate at a deeper level.

Most personality psychologists today probably regard FFT as too radical a statement; they would argue that environmental influences, perhaps in interaction with genetic predispositions (Caspi et al., 2003), can also influence trait levels. Brent Roberts and colleagues (Roberts & Helson, 1997; Roberts, Helson, & Klohnen, 2002) have been particularly strong advocates of this position, but even Costa and colleagues (Costa, Herbst, McCrae, & Siegler, 2000) have offered tentative evidence of such environmental effects. This issue is at present unresolved; there are no well-replicated findings of environmental effects and no instances in which changes in self-reported personality have been corroborated by observer ratings. This state of affairs contrasts clearly with well-replicated biological effects on personality traits. The effects of Alzheimer's disease (notably, a dramatic decline in C) have been reported by many researchers (see Costa & McCrae, 2000).

THE BIOLOGICAL BASIS OF PERSONALITY TRAITS

The strongest evidence for a biological basis of personality traits comes from behavior genetics. Hundreds of studies now have been reported in which traits from one or more of the FFM factors have been examined in adult samples. Some have studied identical twins reared apart (Tellegen et al., 1988), some have contrasted identical and fraternal twins reared together (Jang, McCrae, Angleitner, Riemann, & Livesley, 1998), some have compared biological and adopted siblings (Loehlin et al., 1985). Studies have been conducted in the United States, Australia, Germany, Poland, and Japan. Almost without exception, the studies have converged on three findings: (a) About half the variance in measures of traits from all five factors appears to be genetic; (b) the common environment (those features that children raised in the same family share, such as parents, neighborhood, religion, diet, etc.) accounts for almost none of the variance; and (c) the remaining variance is attributed to what is called the *nonshared environment,* which is still very much a mystery. Part of the nonshared environment is error of measurement, both random and systematic. Some theorists argue that the rest is chiefly due to peer influences (Harris, 1998) or to random biological events, such as prenatal environment or illness and injury (Pinker, 2002). Efforts to identify specific nonshared influences thus far have been unsuccessful (Loehlin, Neiderhiser, & Reiss, 2003).

Given such solid evidence of a genetic basis for personality traits, one of the most exciting topics of research in the past decade has been the hunt for specific genes associated with traits. Early studies (e.g., Benjamin et al., 1996) reported that genes thought to be involved in the regulation of neurotransmitters were associated with personality traits, especially E and N, but a flurry of attempted replications led to very mixed results (e.g., Vandenbergh, Zonderman, Wang, Uhl, & Costa, 1997). One reason for the limited success in these efforts may be that the effects of single genes on traits are very small; most traits are likely to be determined by many genes, and there is some evidence that the interactions among genes (nonadditive genetic influences) may be more important than the sum of single genes (Loehlin et al., 2003). For this reason, more recent studies have focused on gene/gene interactions (e.g., Ebstein et al., 1998; Williams et al., 2003).

Investigating single, candidate genes for specific personality traits is an appealing way to proceed if one can identify plausible candidates. Neurotransmitter genes certainly would seem to be relevant to psychological traits, but at present our knowledge of genes and brain function is so limited that the selection of any candidate gene is largely a matter of guesswork. An alternative approach utilizes polymorphic markers to perform a whole genome scan, in which the entire genome is divided into regions that are then examined for Quantitative Trait Loci (QTLs) (Botstein, White, Skolnick, & Davis, 1980). Identification of QTLs would enable comparison of individuals who do and do not resemble each other in terms of some personality trait. Especially when conducted in isolated populations (such as Sardinia and Iceland) that have a limited range of allelic variations, this method can lead to the identification of regions where relevant genes are located.

The identification of a gene or genes related to a trait is only one of many steps in discovering the biological basis of personality. Some genes are chiefly involved in development and may have their impact on forming the structure of the brain; others are involved in the ongoing operation of cells and may regulate neurotransmitters. Some genes turn on or off the action of still other genes. The processes by which a gene comes to manifest itself as a personality phenotype are intricate indeed, and much can be learned by studying the intermediate steps. Neuroimaging, using PET scans (Mayberg et al., 2000) and functional MRIs (Canli et al., 2001), can help illuminate these processes.

It is natural to assume that characteristics that are governed by genes must have evolved and thus that there must be an evolutionary explanation for personality traits. Clearly, genes related to personality traits are subject to the laws of natural selection, and one can reasonably conclude that none of the traits in the FFM, at the levels at which we usually find them, is lethal. But there is some controversy over whether personality traits, and particularly individual differences in traits, are evolved adaptations (MacDonald, 1998) or simply genetic noise (Tooby & Cosmides, 1990). However, what is noise from the perspective of survival may be of the highest significance in human life (Buss, Haselton, Shackelford, Bleske, & Wakefield, 1998).

Any evolutionary understanding of personality traits must include a comparison of other species (Gosling, 2001) and especially nonhuman primates. Recent research has suggested that there are replicable personality factors in chimpanzees (King, Weiss, & Farmer, 2005) and orangutans (Weiss, King, Perkins, & Blanke, 2003) that show some resemblance to the FFM factors found in humans. Further, cross-sectional age differences among chimpanzees (which have a life span of about fifty years) also resemble those found in humans (King et al., 2005)—further evidence that trait development is a part of biological maturation.

FFT postulates that personality traits, as basic tendencies, are biologically based. But it would be a mistake to assume that only genetic factors are involved in this biological environment. Intrauterine hormonal influences may affect the subsequent development of traits (Resnick, Gottesman, & McGue, 1993). Alzheimer's disease profoundly alters personality traits as perceived by caregivers (Costa & McCrae, 2000). Antidepressant medication can modify some traits, particularly N and E (Du, Baksih, Ravindran, & Hrdina, 2002). In principle, diet, exercise, chronic infections, and exposure to environmental toxins all might have some impact on trait levels; all these possibilities are worth exploring.

FIVE-FACTOR THEORY: CROSS-CULTURAL EVIDENCE

We now turn from the biological environment to a consideration of the cultural environment. As McCrae (2004) noted, cross-cultural research provides the strongest available test of the accuracy of FFT. Cultures differ dramatically in language, economic structures, child-rearing practices, religions, and many other features, and they cannot fail to have profound influences on attitudes, beliefs, values, and behaviors. By contrast, the members of different cultures are all Homo sapiens, far more similar than different in their fundamental biology and brain structure. If personality traits are Basic Tendencies as FFT proposes, then the FFM should be essentially the same in every culture. By contrast, environmentalists have argued that "different cultures and different languages should give rise to other models that have little chance of being five in number nor of having any of the factors resemble those derived from the linguistic/social network of middle-class Americans" (Juni, 1996, p. 864).

The intuitive appeal of environmentalism is never stronger than when we contemplate the inscrutability of foreign languages, especially those unrelated to our own. Most English speakers could believe that the statement "Kha-pa-chao chop tee ja mee khon jam-nuan mak ma hom-lom" might mean almost anything. Is it really possible that such sounds convey the familiar sentiment "I like to have a lot of people around me"?

But a little thought dispels the illusion that people speaking foreign languages are really foreign to us. Consider the characters in the Chinese film *Crouching Tiger, Hidden Dragon,* who are perfectly intelligible to non-Chinese audiences once they are provided with subtitles. Even more remarkable is *Gilgamesh,* written thousands of years ago in a language apparently unrelated to any existing language family, which still can intrigue and move modern readers.

Factor Structure

Cross-cultural replication of the factor structure of personality-trait measures is one of the most straightforward tests of universality. If traits are indeed universal, then they should covary the same way everywhere, and that covariance is summarized by the factor structure. The most compelling demonstrations of factor generalizability are from the most remote cultures, and few modern societies are more remote culturally from the United States than Thailand. Thai culture has been influenced by India and China as well as the West, but Thailand never came under European colonial control. Currently, Thai-

land is a kingdom with a democratically elected government. In religion, most Thais are Buddhist. The Thai language—a transliterated example was given previously—is a member of the Daic family, which has not been represented previously in studies of the FFM.

Table 5.1 reports the factor structure of college students' ratings of Thai students and adults, collected using a Thai translation of the NEO-PI-R. The factors were rotated to the best alignment with the U.S. normative structure (McCrae, Zonderman, Costa, Bond, & Paunonen, 1996) and evaluated by variable- and factor-congruence coefficients. All five factors and 26 of the 30 variables showed significant agreement with the U.S. pattern; by the usual rules of thumb, four of the factors are clearly replicated; only O is problematic. In this Thai sample, Openness to Fantasy and especially Values are poor indicators of O; this might indicate problems in translation or in the cultural equivalence of the items, or it might suggest a real, if subtle, difference in personality between Americans and Thais. Overall, however, the similarity of factor structures is unmistakable.

Thailand is not an isolated example. Self-report data from some 40 cultures (McCrae & Allik, 2002) convincingly replicate the U.S. structure. New data (McCrae et al., 2005) from a collaborative study of peer ratings of personality (which include the Thai data) confirm the five-factor structure. The clarity of the replication varies somewhat across cultures; however, McCrae and his colleagues showed that this was chiefly a function of the quality of data collected. In non-Western cultures where respondents are less familiar with questionnaires, and in samples using provisional translations of the NEO-PI-R, there is an apparent increase in error of measurement and a small degradation of the factor structure. Increasing sample size correspondingly improves the quality of the replication.

Age and Sex Differences

As noted previously, age differences in personality are pancultural: Older adults are lower in N, E, and O and higher in A and C than young adults (McCrae et al., 1999). These findings have been replicated in cross-cultural studies of both self-reports (McCrae & Allik, 2002) and observer ratings (McCrae et al., 2005), although the effects for N and A are less consistent in observer rating studies. Similarities in patterns of age differences might be due to common features of world history (such as the rise of mass communications in the twentieth century) or to role requirements common to most cultures, such as parents' responsibility to raise chil-

TABLE 5.1 Factor Loadings for Thai Students' Ratings of Students and Adults

	Factor					
NEO-PI-R facet	N	E	O	A	C	VCC[a]
N1: Anxiety	**.76**	.06	−.12	.03	.18	.93*
N2: Angry Hostility	**.51**	.03	−.08	**−.63**	.11	.94**
N3: Depression	**.70**	−.21	.26	.10	−.16	.92*
N4: Self-Consciousness	**.72**	−.24	−.06	.02	−.09	.99**
N5: Impulsiveness	**.49**	.23	.09	−.33	**−.41**	.96**
N6: Vulnerability	**.62**	−.13	−.11	−.17	**−.53**	.95**
E1: Warmth	−.22	**.74**	.15	**.41**	.13	.99**
E2: Gregariousness	.04	**.74**	.08	−.01	−.26	.90*
E3: Assertiveness	−.28	.34	.16	−.50	**.42**	.95**
E4: Activity	−.20	.29	.26	−.33	**.57**	.87*
E5: Excitement Seeking	−.05	**.40**	**.55**	−.20	−.29	.71
E6: Positive Emotions	−.14	**.71**	.30	.36	−.01	.93*
O1: Fantasy	**.42**	**.42**	.20	.08	−.35	.70
O2: Aesthetics	.14	.20	**.68**	.26	−.09	.93*
O3: Feelings	.32	**.48**	.28	−.11	.39	.88*
O4: Actions	−.35	.03	**.55**	−.12	.07	.88*
O5: Ideas	−.13	−.05	**.69**	.07	**.44**	.92*
O6: Values	−.31	.35	.12	.17	.13	.34
A1: Trust	−.24	.33	.18	**.59**	.07	.98**
A2: Straightforwardness	−.08	−.14	−.24	**.67**	.22	.98**
A3: Altruism	−.19	**.48**	.15	**.65**	.29	.96**
A4: Compliance	−.22	−.24	.03	**.74**	−.13	.96**
A5: Modesty	−.02	−.27	.10	**.66**	−.02	.85
A6: Tender-Mindedness	−.06	.37	.33	**.61**	.32	.88*
C1: Competence	−.25	.23	.25	.12	**.74**	.96**
C2: Order	.18	−.12	−.08	.01	**.71**	.91*
C3: Dutifulness	−.12	.12	−.01	.31	**.77**	.97**
C4: Achievement Striving	−.10	.22	.14	−.21	**.81**	.99**
C5: Self-Discipline	−.29	.15	.04	.08	**.80**	.99**
C6: Deliberation	−.24	−.08	.15	.28	**.74**	.92*
Congruence[b]	.94**	.92**	.82**	.95**	.93**	.92**

Note. $N = 210$. These are principal components rotated to the U.S. normative target (Costa & McCrae, 1992). Loadings greater than .40 in absolute magnitude are given in boldface.
[a]Variable congruence coefficient.
[b]Factor/total congruence coefficient with target matrix.
*Congruence higher than that of 95% of rotations from random data.
**Congruence higher than that of 99% of rotations from random data.

dren. But it is also possible that age changes in personality are biological universals, like the graying of hair.

Similarly, there are universal gender differences. Women in almost all cultures score higher than men on measures of anxiety, tender-mindedness, and openness to aesthetics; men score higher on assertiveness, excitement seeking, and openness to ideas (Costa, Terracciano, & McCrae, 2001). These findings, too, are replicated in cross-cultural studies of observer-rated personality (McCrae et al., 2005). Environmentalists might object that this is really evidence of the pervasive effect of sexist attitudes and socialization practices, but if that were so, we would expect the most pronounced sex differences to be found in traditional cultures and the smallest differences in contemporary Western societies that

have worked for some years to erase sexism. Instead, exactly the opposite pattern of results is found, with the largest sex differences in such countries as Belgium and the Netherlands. Costa and his colleagues (2001) speculated that this might be due to the attribution of masculine or feminine behaviors to gender roles rather than to traits in traditional societies. Consistent with FFT, that explanation implies that gender differences themselves are universal, even if they are perceived somewhat differently in different cultures.

Consensual Validation and Other Features of Traits

Over the past 25 years a large body of data in Western cultures has demonstrated the consensual validity of trait assessments across observers (Funder, Kolar, & Blackman, 1995; Riemann, Angleitner, & Strelau, 1997): Self-perceptions of traits agree with others' assessments far beyond chance (though not perfectly). But that agreement might be limited to Western, individualistic cultures, where traits are crucial for understanding oneself and others. It has been proposed that traits are less relevant in collectivistic cultures, where behavior is governed by relationships and the immediate context (Markus & Kitayama, 1991). A recent review and study of that issue, however, found comparable levels of cross-observer agreement in North America and in other countries, including collectivistic cultures such as South Korea and China, and previously collectivized cultures such as Russia and the Czech Republic (McCrae, Costa, et al., 2004).

Traits are heritable in Japan as in the West (Ono et al., 2000); C predicts job performance in Europe as it does in the United States (Salgado, 1997); momentary affect is related to personality traits in similar ways in English and Korean samples (Yik, Russell, Ahn, Fernández Dols, & Suzuki, 2002); personality traits are associated with personality disorders in Chinese psychiatric patients as in U.S. patients (Yang et al., 2002). All these findings suggest that personality traits exist and function in similar ways around the world. Culture, that most potent of environmental forces, seems to have little ability even to moderate trait effects. Such findings provide powerful evidence that FFT's insistence on the biological basis of traits is at least a good first approximation to the truth.

SOME LIMITATIONS OF TRAIT THEORY

Every theory has a range and focus of convenience (Kelly, 1955), a sphere of applicability in which it is maximally useful and beyond which it needs to be supplemented by other theories. The FFM was originally discovered in analyses of observer ratings of adult Americans (Tupes & Christal, 1992), but subsequent studies have shown that it applies as well to self-reports of citizens from Iceland to Australia. The factors are found in parent ratings of children as young as six years old (Mervielde & De Fruyt, 1999), and similar factors even have been reported in studies of animal personality (e.g., Weiss et al., 2003). The scope of traits, and of the FFM in particular, is broad indeed. But there are many other important ways in which people differ, including intelligence, physical attractiveness, and spirituality. Personality traits do not exhaust the range of individual differences.

And individual differences do not provide a complete psychology of personality. If we know an individual's standing on the five factors and 30 facets of the NEO-PI-R we can make a large number of predictions, but they are rather general in nature. We can, for example, tell if the individual is likely to be a religious fundamentalist, but we cannot guess whether he will be a Christian, Hindu, or Muslim fundamentalist because traits lack cultural context. We can predict the kinds of leisure activities she enjoys, but we cannot say how she will schedule them during the week because traits do not describe temporal sequencing. We may be able to anticipate the narrative tone of the individual's life story (McAdams et al., 2004), but we will not be able to discern the nuclear episodes that loom so large in the individual's conception of his or her life because traits are ahistorical.

Even FFT, which tries to locate traits in the full operating system of human personality, is short on details. It predicts that individuals high in N will find ways to be miserable, but it does not specify the cognitive, defensive, and interpersonal mechanisms that make them unhappy. And it is precisely these details that are of interest to counselors and clinicians who try to help people cope with their problems. Clinicians need a detailed understanding of the life context of the patient—actual and potential social supports, acquired skills and deficiencies, situations that evoke or inhibit maladaptive behaviors. And they must find ways to give patients both a better understanding of the risks and rewards they are likely to encounter and new skills for coping with life's problems that cannot be derived simply from understanding traits. But as some insightful clinicians have noted, trait assessments can provide a useful general orientation for this detailed work. Traits point to problems the individual is likely to experience, and they are also useful in selecting the optimal approach to treating them (Miller, 1991) and in deciding whether treatment is even feasible (Stone, 2002).

Elsewhere (Costa & McCrae, 1998) we have argued that psychology should emulate medicine. All physicians, regardless of specialty, must have a working knowledge of anatomy and physiology because the body is an integrated whole in which all major organ systems play interdependent roles. In the same way, psychological perspectives on traits, roles, the self-concept, behavior, and biology are all potentially complementary approaches, and personality psychologists need to master at least the rudiments of all of them.

PERSONALITY TRAITS IN EVERYDAY LIFE

The plan of this handbook as a whole is based on the distinction between everyday (also known as normal) functioning and psychopathology. As an editorial expedient, that distinction is both classic and still serviceable. But one of the major advances of trait psychology since the 1980s has been the growing understanding that the same traits that underlie everyday functioning are powerful determinants of psychopathology, including both Axis I (Bagby et al., 1999) and Axis II (Clarkin, Hull, Cantor, & Sanderson, 1993) disorders, and in children (Asendorpf & Van Aken, 1999) as well as in adults. Thomas Widiger (personal communication, July 18, 2003) has recommended that the constructs measured by the NEO-PI-R be called *general traits* rather than *normal traits* because they characterize all people, regardless of their mental health. For the present purposes, however, we will adhere to the format of this volume and note a few of the many applications of trait psychology to functioning in everyday life. Among the everyday topics we will not discuss are religion (McCrae, 1999), health (Smith & Williams, 1992), and politics (Van Hiel, Kossowska, & Mervielde, 2000).

Family Life

One of the most important decisions any individual can make is the choice of a spouse, and it would seem reasonable to take personality characteristics strongly into account in one's selection. One old hypothesis is that opposites attract; another is that people seek partners who share their interests and values and thus resemble them in personality. The data provide strong support for neither hypothesis.

Behavior geneticists call the phenotypic resemblance between couples *assortative mating;* it is a serious concern for them because it affects the interpretation of resemblance among their offspring. In the United States today there is clear assortative mating on the basis of race and socioeconomic status but not on the basis of personality traits. An exception occurs with regard to O and the political and social values related to it (McCrae, 1996): It is unusual for an extremely closed individual to choose to marry a highly open person. By contrast, introverts marry extraverts, adjusted people marry neurotics, and the highly conscientious may spend their lives with underachievers.

Buss and Barnes (1986) showed that people do take traits into account in mate preferences: Almost everyone prefers agreeable to antagonistic partners. But mate selection is a competition, and to the extent that all people value the same traits, it is a zero-sum competition. As a result, people often marry individuals who have less than ideal traits, and those traits sometimes have consequences for the quality of the relationship.

McCrae, Stone, Fagan, and Costa (1998) measured the quality of marriage in a sample of couples using a scale that assesses satisfaction, cohesion, consensus on values, and affectional expression. They found that it was associated with low N, high C, and especially high A. In a prospective lon-

gitudinal study, Kelly and Conley (1987) showed that men and women who rated high in N were more likely to become divorced; this was also true of men low in C, perhaps because of associated problems with infidelity and alcohol abuse.

Personality traits also affect parent-child and sibling-sibling relationships. Parenting styles are related to personality traits; for example, very closed parents tend to use authoritarian methods of child rearing (McCrae, 1996). But FFT cautions against the commonsense notion that these expressions of parental personality will shape the personality of the child: In the long run, it is the genes parents pass on, not their actions, that shape the personality traits of the child.

But surely it is the case that personality traits help shape the relationship of parent and child. Some research shows that abusive parents are narcissistic and lack impulse control (Wiehe, 2003)—characteristics that suggest low A and C. And many studies have documented that parent-child interactions also are shaped in part by the temperament or personality of the child (e.g., Kochanska, Friesenborg, Lange, & Martel, 2004). The love or resentment that children develop toward their parents during childhood may last a lifetime, so the enduring effects of traits on one of life's most important relationships may be substantial.

Work and School

Personality traits are closely related to occupational interests (De Fruyt & Mervielde, 1997). In particular, extraverts prefer Social and Enterprising vocations, whereas Open men and women prefer Artistic and Investigative occupations. In the real world, it is often not possible to satisfy these preferences, but people do tend to gravitate toward vocations that suit their personality. For example, sculptors (Caraca, Loura, & Martins, 2000) and rock musicians (Gillespie & Myors, 2000) score higher than average on Openness to Experience.

One of the most influential articles in the history of industrial/organizational (I/O) psychology was a meta-analysis of the effects of personality traits on job performance (Barrick & Mount, 1991). After many years in which I/O psychologists had dismissed the contributions of personality to work, this study clearly demonstrated that traits did matter. In particular, C emerged as a strong predictor of performance in almost all kinds of jobs. That analysis opened the door to a host of studies of personality and work, which have shown that N is related to job dissatisfaction (Judge, Heller, & Mount, 2002), that E predicts effective job search behaviors (Kanfer, Wanberg, & Kantrowitz, 2001), and that O leads to midcareer shifts (McCrae & Costa, 1985a).

Two of the five personality factors are theoretically of importance for school performance and academic achievement.

Conscientious individuals are likely to complete assignments neatly and on time; Open students are likely to be more interested in intellectual topics and pursue them with more independent thought. Duff, Boyle, Dunleavy, and Ferguson (2004) showed that O was related to a deep approach to learning, emphasizing a need to acquire a full understanding of a topic, and that C was related to a strategic approach to learning, which is primarily goal-oriented. De Fruyt and Mervielde (1996) showed that several traits predicted academic major and that C was a good predictor of grades. Among adults, years of education is consistently, although modestly, related to O (Costa & McCrae, 1992a), perhaps because a liberal education increases O or perhaps—as FFT would argue—because Open people are predisposed to pursue further education.

Particularly in children, academic achievement is only part of the school experience. Hair and Graziano (2003) reported that A in middle school predicted both self-reports and teacher ratings of classroom behavior. The widespread problem of school bullying is one troubling expression of low A.

Retirement

The feature of personality traits most relevant to retirement is their stability (McCrae & Costa, 2003). After retirement, people retain much the same interests, motives, needs, and styles as they had during the years of their working life (Havighurst, McDonald, Maculen, & Mazel, 1979). Retirement is a life transition, but it does not usually usher in a new stage of personality development. That can be good news or bad news.

The bad news is that retirement itself will do little to solve personal problems. The individual who has complained about her job for 40 years will find something else to complain about after retirement. The poorly organized man who felt there was never time to do what he wanted may discover the problem has been his own lack of initiative and organization all along. Interpersonal friction from an antagonistic spouse may be exacerbated by increased time spent at home.

The good news about personality stability is that it allows one to predict and thus prepare for the future. The people and activities we cherish in our 40s are still likely to appeal to us in our 70s. The open, extraverted individual may plan and enjoy a life of travel; the closed extravert can look forward to more time spent chatting with familiar friends. Conscientious people should ensure that they can remain productive; introverts should safeguard their solitude. For many people, old age brings financial hardships and physical limitations; the years after retirement are not golden for them. But people can make the most of their situation by considering the traits that they carry with them throughout life.

Leisure and Recreation

Because people are generally free to choose the leisure activities they prefer, recreation is usually a better indicator of personality traits than is occupation. NEO-PI-R items ask about reading poetry, watching scary movies, attending parties, vacationing in the woods, and discussing philosophy because such activities are often diagnostic of personality traits.

In view of this close conceptual link, there is surprisingly little empirical evidence on the relation between personality traits and leisure activities. Rentfrow and Gosling noted that "of nearly 11,000 articles published between 1965 and 2002 in the leading social and personality journals, *music* was listed as an index term . . . in only seven articles" (Rentfrow & Gosling, 2003, p. 1236). They went on to show that extraverted people like rap and dance music; agreeable people like pop and religious music; and Open people like classical music and jazz. A scattering of other findings can be mentioned: Motorcycle enthusiasts are aggressive and irresponsible (Jackson & Wilson, 1993); baseball card collectors who are hobbyists are more agreeable than those who are investors (Dodgen & Rapp, 1992); college football players are less conscientious than professionals (Koo, 2003). All of these are sensible if not surprising findings.

Although individual differences in traits are remarkably stable in adulthood, most traits show some changes in mean levels, and these changes can affect recreational choices. In particular, there are pronounced declines in a facet of E, Excitement Seeking, from adolescence onward (cf. Zuckerman, 1979). Activity also declines with age. As a result, older individuals usually abandon skydiving and basketball and gravitate toward more sedate hobbies like gardening and bird-watching. In addition, A and C increase with age, and the self-centered pleasures of youth may be replaced by more altruistic and generative leisure activities like volunteer work.

REFERENCES

Allport, G. W. (1937). *Personality: A psychological interpretation.* New York: Holt, Rinehart, and Winston.

Allport, G. W. (Ed.). (1965). *Letters from Jenny.* New York: Harcourt, Brace & World.

Allport, G. W. (1966). Traits revisited. *American Psychologist, 21,* 1–10.

Allport, G. W., & Odbert, H. S. (1936). Trait names: A psycholexical study. *Psychological Monographs, 47*(211).

Altemeyer, R. A. (1981). *Right-wing authoritarianism.* Winnipeg: University of Manitoba Press.

Amelang, M., & Ullwer, U. (1991). Correlations between psychometric measures and psychophysiological as well as experimental variables in studies on extraversion and neuroticism. In J. Strelau & A. Angleitner (Eds.), *Explorations in temperament: International perspectives on theory and measurement* (pp. 287–316). New York: Plenum Press.

Angleitner, A., & Ostendorf, F. (1994). Temperament and the Big Five factors of personality. In C. F. Halverson, G. A. Kohnstamm, & R. P. Martin (Eds.), *The developing structure of temperament and personality from infancy to adulthood* (pp. 69–90). Hillsdale, NJ: Erlbaum.

Asendorpf, J. B., & van Aken, M. A. G. (1999). Resilient, overcontrolled, and undercontrolled personality prototypes in childhood: Replicability, predictive power, and trait-type issue. *Journal of Personality and Social Psychology, 77,* 815–832.

Bagby, R. M., Levitan, R. D., Kennedy, S. H., Levitt, A. J., & Joffe, R. T. (1999). Selective alteration of personality in response to noradrenergic and serotonergic antidepressant medication in depressed sample: Evidence of non-specificity. *Psychiatry Research, 86,* 211–216.

Barrick, M. R., & Mount, M. K. (1991). The Big Five personality dimensions and job performance: A meta-analysis. *Personnel Psychology, 44,* 1–26.

Benjamin, J., Li, L., Patterson, C., Greenberg, B. D., Murphy, D. L., & Hamer, D. H. (1996). Population and familial association between the D4 dopamine receptor gene and measures of novelty seeking. *Nature Genetics, 12,* 81–84.

Block, J. (1977). Advancing the psychology of personality: Paradigmatic shift or improving the quality of research? In D. Magnusson & N. S. Endler (Eds.), *Personality at the crossroads: Current issues in interactional psychology* (pp. 37–64). Hillsdale, NJ: Erlbaum.

Botstein, D., White, R. L., Skolnick, M., & Davis, R. W. (1980). Construction of a genetic linkage map in man using restriction fragment length polymorphisms. *American Journal of Human Genetics, 32,* 314–331.

Bouchard, T. J., & Loehlin, J. C. (2001). Genes, evolution, and personality. *Behavior Genetics, 31,* 243–273.

Buss, A. H., & Plomin, R. (1975). *A temperament theory of personality development.* New York: Wiley.

Buss, D. M., & Barnes, M. (1986). Preferences in human mate selection. *Journal of Personality and Social Psychology, 50,* 559–570.

Buss, D. M., Haselton, M. G., Shackelford, T. K., Bleske, A. L., & Wakefield, J. C. (1998). Adaptations, exaptations, and spandrels. *American Psychologist, 53,* 533–548.

Canli, T., Zhao, Z., Desmond, J. E., Kang, E., Gross, J., & Gabreli, J. D. E. (2001). An fMRI study of personality influences on brain reactivity to emotional stimuli. *Behavioral Neuroscience, 115,* 33–42.

Cantor, N. (1990). From thought to behavior: "Having" and "doing" in the study of personality and cognition. *American Psychologist, 45,* 735–750.

Caraca, M. L., Loura, L., & Martins, C. (2000). [Personality characteristics in sculptors and scientific researchers]. *Analise Psicologica, 18,* 53–58.

Casey, J., & McManis, D. L. (1971). Salivary response to lemon juice as a measure of introversion in children. *Perceptual and Motor Skills, 33,* 1059–1065.

Caspi, A. (1998). Personality development across the life course. In N. Eisenberg (Ed.), *Handbook of child psychology: Vol. 3. Social, emotional, and personality development* (pp. 311–388). New York: Wiley.

Caspi, A., Sugden, K., Moffitt, T. E., Taylor, A., Craig, I. W., Harrington, H., et al. (2003). Influence of life stress on depression: Moderation by a polymorphism in the 5-HTT gene. *Science, 301,* 386–389.

Cattell, R. B. (1973). *Personality and mood by questionnaire.* San Francisco: Jossey-Bass.

Cattell, R. B., Cattell, M. D., & Johns, E. (1984). *Manual and norms for the High School Personality Questionnaire.* Champaign, IL: Institute for Personality and Ability Testing.

Cheung, F. M., & Leung, K. (1998). Indigenous personality measures: Chinese examples. *Journal of Cross-Cultural Psychology, 29,* 233–248.

Clarkin, J. F., Hull, J. W., Cantor, J., & Sanderson, C. (1993). Borderline personality disorder and personality traits: A comparison of SCID-II BPD and NEO-PI. *Psychological Assessment, 5,* 472–476.

Cloninger, C. R. (1994). Temperament and personality. *Current Opinion in Neurobiology, 4*(2), 266–273.

Conn, S. R., & Rieke, M. L. (Eds.). (1994). *16PF fifth edition technical manual.* Champaign, IL: Institute for Personality and Ability Testing.

Coon, D. (2004). *Introduction to psychology: Gateways to mind and behavior* (10th ed.). Belmont, CA: Wadsworth/Thomson Learning.

Costa, P. T., Jr., Herbst, J. H., McCrae, R. R., & Siegler, I. C. (2000). Personality at midlife: Stability, intrinsic maturation, and response to life events. *Assessment, 7,* 365–378.

Costa, P. T., Jr., & McCrae, R. R. (1977). Age differences in personality structure revisited: Studies in validity, stability, and change. *International Journal of Aging and Human Development, 8,* 261–275.

Costa, P. T., Jr., & McCrae, R. R. (1978). Objective personality assessment. In M. Storandt, I. C. Siegler, & M. F. Elias (Eds.), *The clinical psychology of aging* (pp. 119–143). New York: Plenum Press.

Costa, P. T., Jr., & McCrae, R. R. (1980). Still stable after all these years: Personality as a key to some issues in adulthood and old age. In P. B. Baltes & O. G. Brim Jr. (Eds.), *Life span development and behavior* (Vol. 3, pp. 65–102). New York: Academic Press.

Costa, P. T., Jr., & McCrae, R. R. (1988). From catalog to classification: Murray's needs and the five-factor model. *Journal of Personality and Social Psychology, 55,* 258–265.

Costa, P. T., Jr., & McCrae, R. R. (1992a). *Revised NEO Personality Inventory (NEO-PI-R) and NEO Five-Factor Inventory (NEO-FFI) professional manual.* Odessa, FL: Psychological Assessment Resources.

Costa, P. T., Jr., & McCrae, R. R. (1992b). Trait psychology comes of age. In T. B. Sonderegger (Ed.), *Nebraska Symposium on Motivation: Psychology and aging* (pp. 169–204). Lincoln: University of Nebraska Press.

Costa, P. T., Jr., & McCrae, R. R. (1994). "Set like plaster"? Evidence for the stability of adult personality. In T. Heatherton & J. Weinberger (Eds.), *Can personality change?* (pp. 21–40). Washington, DC: American Psychological Association.

Costa, P. T., Jr., & McCrae, R. R. (1998). Trait theories of personality. In D. F. Barone, M. Hersen & V. B. Van Hasselt (Eds.), *Advanced personality* (pp. 103–121). New York: Plenum Press.

Costa, P. T., Jr., & McCrae, R. R. (2000). Contemporary personality psychology. In C. E. Coffey & J. L. Cummings (Eds.), *Textbook of geriatric neuropsychiatry* (2nd ed., pp. 453–462). Washington, DC: American Psychiatric Press.

Costa, P. T., Jr. & McCrae, R. R. (2002). Looking backward: Changes in the mean levels of personality traits from 80 to 12. In D. Cervone & W. Mischel (Eds.), *Advances in personality science* (pp. 219–237). New York: Guilford Press.

Costa, P. T., Jr., & McCrae, R. R. (2005). A five-factor model perspective on personality disorders. In S. Strack (Ed.), *Handbook of personology and psychopathology* (pp. 257–270). Hoboken, NJ: Wiley.

Costa, P. T., Jr., McCrae, R. R., & Arenberg, D. (1980). Enduring dispositions in adult males. *Journal of Personality and Social Psychology, 38,* 793–800.

Costa, P. T., Jr., Terracciano, A., & McCrae, R. R. (2001). Gender differences in personality traits across cultures: Robust and surprising findings. *Journal of Personality and Social Psychology, 81,* 322–331.

De Fruyt, F., & Mervielde, I. (1996). Personality and interests as predictors of educational streaming and achievement. *European Journal of Personality, 10,* 405–425.

De Fruyt, F., & Mervielde, I. (1997). The five-factor model of personality and Holland's RIASEC interest types. *Personality and Individual Differences, 23,* 87–103.

Deary, I. J., Ramsay, H., Wilson, J. A., & Riad, M. (1989). Stimulated salivation: Correlations with personality and time of day effects. *Personality and Individual Differences, 9,* 903–909.

Dixon, R. M. W. (1977). Where have all the adjectives gone? *Studies in Language, 1,* 19–80.

Dodgen, L., & Rapp, A. (1992). An analysis of personality differences between baseball card collectors and investors based on the Myers-Briggs Personality Inventory. *Journal of Social Behavior and Personality, 7,* 355–361.

Dollard, J., Miller, N. E., Doob, L. W., Mowrer, O. H., & Sears, R. R. (1939). *Frustration and aggression.* New Haven, CT: Yale University Press.

Douglas, K., & Arenberg, D. (1978). Age changes, cohort differences, and cultural change on the Guilford-Zimmerman Temperament Survey. *Journal of Gerontology, 33,* 737–747.

Du, L., Baksih, D., Ravindran, A. V., & Hrdina, P. D. (2002). Does fluoxetine influence major depression by modifying five-factor personality traits? *Journal of Affective Disorders, 71,* 235–241.

Duff, A., Boyle, E., Dunleavy, K., & Ferguson, J. (2004). The relationship between personality, approach to learning and academic performance. *Personality and Individual Differences, 36,* 1907–1920.

Ebstein, R. P., Levine, J., Geller, V., Auerbach, J., Gritsenko, I., & Belmaker, R. H. (1998). Dopamine D4 receptor and serotonin transporter promoter in the determination of neonatal temperament. *Molecular Psychiatry, 3,* 238–246.

Erikson, E. H. (1950). *Childhood and society.* New York: Norton.

Eysenck, H. J. (1960). *The structure of human personality.* London: Methuen.

Eysenck, H. J. (1967). *The biological basis of personality.* Springfield, IL: Charles C Thomas.

Fleeson, W. (2001). Toward a structure- and process-integrated view of personality; Traits as density distributions of states. *Journal of Personality and Social Psychology, 80,* 1011–1027.

Freud, S. (1933). *New introductory lectures in psychoanalysis* (W. J. H. Sprott, Trans.). New York: Norton. (Original work published 1913)

Friedlander, J. S., Costa, P. T., Jr., Bossé, R., Ellis, E., Rhods, J. G., & Stoudth, H. (1977). Longitudinal physique changes among healthy white veterans at Boston. *Human Biology, 49,* 541–558.

Fromm, E. (1955). *The sane society.* New York: Rinehart.

Funder, D. C., Kolar, D. C., & Blackman, M. C. (1995). Agreement among judges of personality: Interpersonal relations, similarity, and acquaintanceship. *Journal of Personality and Social Psychology, 69,* 656–672.

Gergen, K. J., Gulerce, A., Lock, A., & Misra, G. (1996). Psychological science in cultural context. *American Psychologist, 51,* 496–503.

Gillespie, W., & Myors, B. (2000). Personality of rock musicians. *Psychology of Music, 28,* 154–165.

Goff, M., & Ackerman, P. L. (1992). Personality-intelligence relations: Assessment of typical intellectual engagement. *Journal of Educational Psychology, 84,* 537–552.

Gosling, S. D. (2001). From mice to men: What can we learn about personality from animal research? *Psychological Bulletin, 127,* 45–86.

Gough, H. G. (1987). *California Psychological Inventory administrator's guide.* Palo Alto, CA: Consulting Psychologists Press.

Guilford, J. S., Zimmerman, W. S., & Guilford, J. P. (1976). *The Guilford-Zimmerman Temperament Survey Handbook: Twenty-*

five years of research and application. San Diego, CA: Edits Publishers.

Hair, E. C., & Graziano, W. G. (2003). Self-esteem, personality and achievement in high school: A prospective longitudinal study in Texas. *Journal of Personality, 71,* 971–994.

Harkness, A. R., & McNulty, J. L. (2002). Implications of personality individual differences science for clinical work on personality disorders. In P. T. Costa Jr. & T. A. Widiger (Eds.), *Personality disorders and the five-factor model of personality* (2nd ed., pp. 391–403). Washington, DC: American Psychological Association.

Harris, J. R. (1998). *The nurture assumption: Why children turn out the way they do.* New York: Free Press.

Havighurst, R. J., McDonald, W. J., Maculen, L., & Mazel, J. (1979). Male social scientists: Lives after sixty. *The Gerontologist, 19,* 55–60.

Jackson, C., & Wilson, G. D. (1993). Mad, bad or sad? The personality of bikers. *Personality and Individual Differences, 14,* 241–242.

Jackson, D. N. (1984). *Personality Research Form manual* (3rd ed.). Port Huron, MI: Research Psychologists Press.

Jang, K. L., McCrae, R. R., Angleitner, A., Riemann, R., & Livesley, W. J. (1998). Heritability of facet-level traits in a cross-cultural twin sample: Support for a hierarchical model of personality. *Journal of Personality and Social Psychology, 74,* 1556–1565.

John, O. P., Angleitner, A., & Ostendorf, F. (1988). The lexical approach to personality: A historical review of trait taxonomic research. *European Journal of Personality, 2,* 171–203.

Judge, T. A., Heller, D., & Mount, M. K. (2002). Five-factor model of personality and job satisfaction: A meta-analysis. *Journal of Applied Psychology, 87,* 530–541.

Jung, C. G. (1971). *Psychological types* (H. G. Baynes, Trans.; rev. by R. F. C. Hull). Princeton, NJ: Princeton University Press. (Original work published 1923)

Juni, S. (1996). Review of the Revised NEO Personality Inventory. In J. C. Conoley & J. C. Impara (Eds.), *12th Mental Measurements Yearbook* (pp. 863–868). Lincoln: University of Nebraska Press.

Kanfer, R., Wanberg, C. R., & Kantrowitz, T. M. (2001). Job search and employment: A personality-motivational analysis and meta-analytic review. *Journal of Applied Psychology, 86,* 837–855.

Kelly, E. L., & Conley, J. J. (1987). Personality and compatibility: A prospective analysis of marital stability and marital satisfaction. *Journal of Personality and Social Psychology, 52,* 27–40.

Kelly, G. A. (1955). *The psychology of personal constructs: Vols. 1–3.* New York: Norton.

King, J. E., Weiss, A., & Farmer, K. H. (2005). A chimpanzee *(Pan troglodytes)* analogue of cross-national generalization of personality structure: Zoological parks and an African sanctuary. *Journal of Personality, 73,* 389–410.

Kochanska, G., Friesenborg, A. E., Lange, L. A., & Martel, M. M. (2004). Parents' personality and infants' temperament as contributors to their emerging relationship. *Journal of Personality and Social Psychology, 86,* 744–759.

Koo, D. H. (2003). The utility of the Neuroticism Extraversion Openness Five-Factor Inventory (NEO-FFI) as an instrument for profiling the personalities of professional and college football players. *Dissertation Abstracts International, 64*(2-B), 994.

Little, B. R. (1983). Personal projects: A rationale and method for investigation. *Environment and Behavior, 15,* 273–309.

Loehlin, J. C., Neiderhiser, J. M., & Reiss, D. (2003). The behavior genetics of personality and the NEAD study. *Journal of Research in Personality, 37,* 373–387.

Loehlin, J. C., Willerman, L., & Horn, J. M. (1985). Personality resemblances in adoptive families when the children are late-adolescent or adult. *Journal of Personality and Social Psychology, 48,* 376–392.

MacDonald, K. (1998). Evolution, culture, and the five-factor model. *Journal of Cross-Cultural Psychology, 29,* 119–149.

Markus, H. R., & Kitayama, S. (1991). Culture and the self: Implications for cognition, emotion, and motivation. *Psychological Review, 98,* 224–253.

Mayberg, H. S., Brannan, S. K., Tekell, J. L., Silva, J. A., Mahurin, R. K., McGinnis, S., et al. (2000). Regional metabolic effects of fluoxetine in major depression: Serial changes and relationship to clinical response. *Biological Psychiatry, 48,* 830–843.

McAdams, D. P. (1992). The five-factor model in personality: A critical appraisal. *Journal of Personality, 60,* 329–361.

McAdams, D. P., Anyidoho, N. A., Brown, C., Huang, Y. T., Kaplan, B., & Machado, M. A. (2004). Traits and stories: Links between dispositional and narrative features of personality. *Journal of Personality, 72,* 761–784.

McCrae, R. R. (1990). Traits and trait names: How well is Openness represented in natural languages? *European Journal of Personality, 4,* 119–129.

McCrae, R. R. (1996). Social consequences of experiential openness. *Psychological Bulletin, 120,* 323–337.

McCrae, R. R. (1999). Mainstream personality psychology and the study of religion. *Journal of Personality, 67,* 1209–1218.

McCrae, R. R. (2004). Human nature and culture: A trait perspective. *Journal of Research in Personality, 38,* 3–14.

McCrae, R. R., & Allik, J. (Eds.). (2002). *The five-factor model of personality across cultures.* New York: Kluwer Academic/Plenum Publishers.

McCrae, R. R., & Costa, P. T., Jr. (1985a). Openness to experience. In R. Hogan & W. H. Jones (Eds.), *Perspectives in personality* (Vol. 1, pp. 145–172). Greenwich, CT: JAI Press.

McCrae, R. R., & Costa, P. T., Jr. (1985b). Updating Norman's "adequate taxonomy": Intelligence and personality dimensions in natural language and in questionnaires. *Journal of Personality and Social Psychology, 49,* 710–721.

McCrae, R. R., & Costa, P. T., Jr. (1987). Validation of the five-factor model of personality across instruments and observers. *Journal of Personality and Social Psychology, 52,* 81–90.

McCrae, R. R., & Costa, P. T., Jr. (1989). Reinterpreting the Myers-Briggs Type Indicator from the perspective of the five-factor model of personality. *Journal of Personality, 57,* 17–40.

McCrae, R. R., & Costa, P. T., Jr. (1995). Trait explanations in personality psychology. *European Journal of Personality, 9,* 231–252.

McCrae, R. R., & Costa, P. T., Jr. (1996). Toward a new generation of personality theories: Theoretical contexts for the five-factor model. In J. S. Wiggins (Ed.), *The five-factor model of personality: Theoretical perspectives* (pp. 51–87). New York: Guilford Press.

McCrae, R. R., & Costa, P. T., Jr. (1999). A five-factor theory of personality. In L. A. Pervin & O. P. John (Eds.), *Handbook of personality: Theory and research* (2nd ed., pp. 139–153). New York: Guilford.

McCrae, R. R., & Costa, P. T., Jr. (2003). *Personality in adulthood: A five-factor theory perspective* (2nd ed.). New York: Guilford.

McCrae, R. R., & Costa, P. T., Jr. (in press). Cross-cultural perspectives on adult personality trait development. In D. Mroczek & T. Little (Eds.), *Handbook of personality development.* Hillsdale, NJ: Erlbaum.

McCrae, R. R., Costa, P. T., Jr., Lima, M. P., Simões, A., Ostendorf, F., Angleitner, A., et al. (1999). Age differences in personality across the adult life span: Parallels in five cultures. *Developmental Psychology, 35,* 466–477.

McCrae, R. R., Costa, P. T., Jr., Martin, T. A., Oryol, V. E., Rukavishnikov, A. A., Senin, I. G., et al. (2004). Consensual validation of personality traits across cultures. *Journal of Research in Personality, 38,* 179–201.

McCrae, R. R., Costa, P. T., Jr., & Piedmont, R. L. (1993). Folk concepts, natural language, and psychological constructs: The California Psychological Inventory and the five-factor model. *Journal of Personality, 61,* 1–26.

McCrae, R. R., Costa, P. T., Jr., Terracciano, A., Parker, W. D., Mills, C. J., De Fruyt, F., et al. (2002). Personality trait development from 12 to 18: Longitudinal, cross-sectional, and cross-cultural analyses. *Journal of Personality and Social Psychology, 83,* 1456–1468.

McCrae, R. R., Stone, S. V., Fagan, P. J., & Costa, P. T., Jr. (1998). Identifying causes of disagreement between self-reports and spouse ratings of personality. *Journal of Personality, 66,* 285–313.

McCrae, R. R., Terracciano, A., & 78 Members of the Personality Profiles of Cultures Project. (2005). Universal features of personality traits from the observer's perspective: Data from 50 cultures. *Journal of Personality and Social Psychology, 88,* 547–561.

McCrae, R. R., Zonderman, A. B., Costa, P. T., Jr., Bond, M. H., & Paunonen, S. V. (1996). Evaluating replicability of factors in the Revised NEO Personality Inventory: Confirmatory factor analysis versus Procrustes rotation. *Journal of Personality and Social Psychology, 70,* 552–566.

Mervielde, I., & De Fruyt, F. (1999). Construction of the Hierarchical Personality Inventory for Children. In I. Mervielde, I. Deary, F. De Fruyt, & F. Ostendorf (Eds.), *Personality psychology in Europe: Proceedings of the Eighth European Conference on Personality Psychology* (pp. 107–127). Tilburg, Netherlands: Tilburg University Press.

Miller, T. (1991). The psychotherapeutic utility of the five-factor model of personality: A clinician's experience. *Journal of Personality Assessment, 57,* 415–433.

Millon, T. (1981). *Disorders of personality: DSM III: Axis II.* New York: Wiley.

Mischel, W. (1968). *Personality and assessment.* New York: Wiley.

Mischel, W. (1999). Personality coherence and dispositions in a Cognitive-Affective Personality System (CAPS) approach. In D. Cervone & Y. Shoda (Eds.), *The coherence of personality: Social-cognitive bases of consistency, variability, and organization* (pp. 37–60). New York: Guilford Press.

Mischel, W., & Shoda, Y. (1995). A cognitive-affective system theory of personality: Reconceptualizing situations, dispositions, dynamics, and invariance in personality structure. *Psychological Review, 102,* 246–268.

Modgil, S., & Modgil, C. (Eds.). (1986). *Hans Eysenck: Consensus and controversy.* Barcombe, Lewes, Sussex: Falmer.

Morris, C. G., & Maisto, A. A. (2002). *Psychology: An introduction* (11th ed.). Upper Saddle River, NJ: Pearson Education.

Murray, H. A. (1938). *Explorations in personality.* New York: Oxford University Press.

Myers, I. B., & McCaulley, M. H. (1985). *Manual: A guide to the development and use of the Myers-Briggs Type Indicator.* Palo Alto, CA: Consulting Psychologists Press.

Ono, Y., Ando, J., Onoda, N., Yoshimura, K., Kanba, S., Hirano, M., et al. (2000). Genetic structure of the five-factor model of personality in a Japanese twin population. *Keio Journal of Medicine, 49,* 152–158.

Piedmont, R. L. (1999). Does spirituality represent the sixth factor of personality? Spiritual transcendence and the five-factor model. *Journal of Personality, 67,* 985–1013.

Pinker, S. (2002). *The blank slate: The modern denial of human nature.* New York: Penguin Books.

Ramsay, R. W. (1969). Salivary response and introversion-extraversion. *Acta Psychologica, 29,* 181–187.

Rentfrow, P. J., & Gosling, S. D. (2003). The do re mi's of everyday life: The structure and personality correlates of music preferences. *Journal of Personality and Social Psychology, 84,* 1236–1256.

Resnick, S. M., Gottesman, I. I., & McGue, M. (1993). Sensation seeking in opposite-sex twins: An effect of prenatal hormones? *Behavior Genetics, 23,* 323–329.

Riemann, R., Angleitner, A., & Strelau, J. (1997). Genetic and environmental influences on personality: A study of twins reared together using the self- and peer report NEO-FFI scales. *Journal of Personality, 65,* 449–475.

Roberts, B. W., & DelVecchio, W. F. (2000). The rank-order consistency of personality traits from childhood to old age: A quantitative review of longitudinal studies. *Psychological Bulletin, 126,* 3–25.

Roberts, B. W., & Helson, R. (1997). Changes in culture, changes in personality: The influence of individualism in a longitudinal study of women. *Journal of Personality and Social Psychology, 72,* 641–651.

Roberts, B. W., Helson, R., & Klohnen, E. C. (2002). Personality development and growth in women across 30 years: Three perspectives. *Journal of Personality, 70,* 79–102.

Rodriguez, J., & de Mikusinski, E. (1977). [Salivation as a physiological measure of the introversion-extraversion dimension]. *Revista Latinoamericana de Psicologia, 9,* 201–211.

Ross, L. (1977). The intuitive psychologist and his shortcomings: Distortions in the attribution process. In L. Berkowitz (Ed.), *Advances in experimental social psychology* (Vol. 10, pp. 173–220). New York: Academic Press.

Salgado, J. F. (1997). The five-factor model of personality and job performance in the European Community. *Journal of Applied Psychology, 82,* 30–43.

Smith, T. W., & Williams, P. G. (1992). Personality and health: Advantages and limitations of the five-factor model. *Journal of Personality, 60,* 395–423.

Stone, M. H. (2002). Treatment of personality disorders from the perspective of the five-factor model. In P. T. Costa Jr. & T. A. Widiger (Eds.), *Personality disorders and the five-factor model of personality* (2nd ed., pp. 405–430). Washington, DC: American Psychological Association.

Tellegen, A., Lykken, D. T., Bouchard, T. J., Jr., Wilcox, K. J., Segal, N. L., & Rich, S. (1988). Personality similarity in twins reared apart and together. *Journal of Personality and Social Psychology, 54,* 1031–1039.

Terracciano, A., McCrae, R. R., Brant, L. J., & Costa, P. T., Jr. (2004). Hierarchical linear modeling analyses of NEO-PI-R scales in the Baltimore longitudinal study of aging. Manuscript submitted for publication.

Thorne, A. (1989). Conditional patterns, transference, and the coherence of personality across time. In D. M. Buss & N. Cantor (Eds.), *Personality psychology: Recent trends and emerging directions* (pp. 149–159). New York: Springer-Verlag.

Tooby, J., & Cosmides, L. (1990). On the universality of human nature and the uniqueness of the individual: The role of genetics and adaptation. *Journal of Personality, 58,* 17–68.

Tupes, E. C., & Christal, R. E. (1992). Recurrent personality factors based on trait ratings. *Journal of Personality, 60,* 225–251. (Original work published 1961)

Van Hiel, A., Kossowska, M., & Mervielde, I. (2000). The relationship between Openness to Experience and political ideology. *Personality and Individual Differences, 28,* 741–751.

Vandenbergh, D. J., Zonderman, A. B., Wang, J., Uhl, G. R., & Costa, P. T., Jr. (1997). No association between novelty seeking and dopamine D4 receptor (D4DR) exon III seven repeat alleles in Baltimore Longitudinal Study of Aging participants. *Molecular Psychiatry, 2,* 417–419.

Weiss, A., King, J. E., Perkins, L., & Blanke, M. K. (2003, June). *Personality in orangutans (Pongo pygmaeus and Pongo abelii).* Paper presented at the International Society for the Study of Individual Differences, Graz, Austria.

Widiger, T. A., Costa, P. T., Jr., & McCrae, R. R. (2002). A proposal for Axis II: Diagnosing personality disorders using the five-factor model. In P. T. Costa Jr. & T. A. Widiger (Eds.), *Personality disorders and the five-factor model of personality* (2nd ed., pp. 431–456). Washington, DC: American Psychological Association.

Wiehe, V. R. (2003). Empathy and narcissism in a sample of child abuse perpetrators and a comparison sample of foster parents. *Child Abuse and Neglect, 27,* 541–555.

Wiggins, J. S. (1968). Personality structure. *Annual Review of Psychology, 19,* 293–350.

Wiggins, J. S. E. (1996). *The five-factor model of personality: Theoretical perspectives.* New York: Guilford Press.

Williams, R. B., Siegler, I., Marchuk, D., Helms, M., Barefoot, J., Kuhn, C., et al. (2003, December). *An interaction between monoamine oxidase A and serotonin transporter gene polymorphisms is associated with a resilient personality profile (low Neuroticism and high Conscientiousness).* Paper presented at the Convention of the American College of Neuropsychopharmacology, San Juan, Puerto Rico.

Yang, J., Dai, X., Yao, S., Cai, T., Gao, B., McCrae, R. R., et al. (2002). Personality disorders and the five-factor model of personality in Chinese psychiatric patients. In P. T. Costa Jr. & T. A. Widiger (Eds.), *Personality disorders and the five-factor model of personality* (2nd ed., pp. 215–221). Washington, DC: American Psychological Association.

Yang, J., McCrae, R. R., & Costa, P. T., Jr. (1998). Adult age differences in personality traits in the United States and the People's Republic of China. *Journal of Gerontology: Psychological Sciences, 53B,* P375–P383.

Yik, M. S. M., Russell, J. A., Ahn, C.-K., Fernández Dols, J. M., & Suzuki, N. (2002). Relating the five-factor model of personality to a circumplex model of affect: A five language study. In R. R. McCrae & J. Allik (Eds.), *The five-factor model of personality across cultures* (pp. 79–104). New York: Kluwer Academic/Plenum Publishers.

Zuckerman, M. (1979). *Sensation seeking: Beyond the optimal level of arousal.* Hillsdale, NJ: Erlbaum.

CHAPTER 6

Developmental Stage Theories

BERT HAYSLIP JR., CRAIG S. NEUMANN, LINDA LOUDEN, AND BENJAMIN CHAPMAN

INTRODUCTION

This chapter deals with personality across the life span and viewing such changes in the context of stage theories of personality development. It is in this context that we present and critically examine the major tenets of the dominant stage theories of personality, that is, Sigmund Freud's psychosexual approach, Erik Erikson's psychosocial crisis theory, as well as a number of stage approaches whose core stagelike assumptions are similar to those of either Freud or Erikson including the work of Carl Jung, Roger Gould, Daniel Levinson, and Jane Loevinger.

Most stage theories are identified with the organismic metamodel of development and rest upon several key assumptions: (1) that stage-specific functioning rests upon that in previous stages and is preparatory for the subsequent stage, (2) that the stages are qualitatively different from one another and, consequently, are differentiated by distinct organizing principles, (3) that the organization of the individual's functional structures integrates previous structures that were preparatory, and (4) that the sequence of stages is universal and not subject to substantial individual variability, except to the extent that the tempo/timing of each stage may vary across persons (for discussions, see Kuhn, 1962; Langer, 1969; Lerner, 2002). We also examine the age-related and, presumably, maturational basis for the changes in personality functioning purported to exist by the stage theorists discussed here. Ideally, one would expect to see an isomorphic relationship between stages of personality development and the maturationally driven, biological substrata upon which such changes presumably rest; longitudinal data investigating questions of causality are quite valuable in this respect. We also examine, where they exist, cross-cultural findings speaking to the generalizability of conclusions about stage-related personality change based on each theory.

In the larger framework of whether personality changes in a stagelike manner, the answer to this question depends upon one's definition of stability or change over time (e.g., whether we are studying the stability of averages, the stability of individual differences, the stability of individuals per se, or the stability of patterns of traits or behaviors; see Caspi & Roberts, 1999). Most theories of a stagelike nature explore the stability of averages. Such conclusions also rest upon the particular design (e.g., cross-sectional versus longitudinal versus sequential; see Baltes, 1968; Schaie, 1965) utilized to gather data about personality change, the level of personality examined (i.e., socioadaptational versus intrapsychic; see Neugarten, 1977), how personality functioning is assessed (i.e., via self-report, behavioral observations, projective techniques; see Hayslip & Panek, 2002), as well as one's predisposition regarding whether consistency should be found and the mechanisms responsible (see Caspi & Roberts, 1999). Depending upon these factors and their interactions, personality can be at once stable and yet changing over time, to say nothing of the extent to which such changes might be interpreted as stagelike in character. In this respect it is worth noting that despite the wealth of literature derived from trait theory exploring stability and change over time (see Caspi & Roberts, 1999; Roberts & Caspi, 2003), such work is adevelopmental in nature, as it lacks an a priori maturational basis regarding such change and, moreover, is not therefore stagelike in character. However, in this respect, Roberts and Caspi (2003) have attempted to address this issue by evoking identity theory as an explanatory mechanism for trait models of personality continuity and change.

Reflecting the potential link between personality and everyday adjustment, another goal here will be to understand stage theories of personality development in terms of the extent to which they might relate to the functional skills individuals must develop in the context of the necessity to cope with change. Such changes may reflect age-related variations in one's health and ability to think, both predictable and/or normative changes in interpersonal relationships that are both inclusive and exclusive of those in the world of work, and perhaps even those regarding end-of-life questions of survival and the quantity and quality of one's life. Likewise, both idiosyncratic (i.e., nonnormative) life events as well as those events whose occurrence are a direct function of historical change present opportunities for individuals whose personalities differ either to adapt or to fail to adapt to such changes. Thus, the value of stage theories of personality in predicting everyday behavior must be understood in the context of the adaptive demands that normative age-graded, normative history-graded, and nonnormative life events (see Baltes, 1997) make on individuals.

Before moving on, we raise one caveat regarding stage theories of personality. This relates to the observation that any approach to personality development emphasizing developmental stages is more properly viewed as a *descriptive* framework within which to view individual development, rather than as *prescriptive* in nature, the latter of which reflects an understandable desire to predict developmental change. From this perspective, for example, challenges to one's identity are brought about by marker events (birthdays, occupational changes, marriages, births of children, divorces, retirement, the deaths of others), which often elicit intraindividual comparisons with regard to the past and projection into the future (see Bybee & Wells, 2003; Markus & Herzog, 1992). Depending upon the nature of the life event bringing about such evaluative processes and the adaptiveness of one's efforts to cope with that event, a "crisis" (i.e., a failure to adapt) may be experienced. Such changes in personality may or may not be interpreted as stagelike in nature (see Riegel, 1976). In this context, it is also important to emphasize that developmental stages are really attempts to explain the behavior of individuals at a given point in their lives that are exhibited by such persons most of the time (Lerner, 2002). Such behavior may or may not generalize across individuals or across historical contexts. Consequently, as attention to both intraindividual and interindividual variability, and to historical change/cohort effects in developmental research, has, in varying degrees, characterized the study of both child and adolescent development and adult development and aging for several decades (see, e.g., Baltes, Reese, & Nesselroade, 1977; Hetherington & Baltes, 1988; Nelson & Dannefer, 1992), these issues have a direct bearing on the validity of the often-held assumption that stagelike progression is both universal across persons and contexts (see Lerner, 2002) and, therefore, is predictable.

STATEMENT OF THE THEORIES

Freud: Basic Concepts and Psychosexual Development Stages

Psychoanalytic theory, one of the greatest historical influences on the field of psychology, is a necessary starting point when exploring stage theories of personality development. Freud's comprehensive work launched the psychoanalytic movement, and his thinking influenced many personality theorists and popularized the belief that the first few years of life were the most important in the formation of personality (P. H. Miller, 2002). Freud's theory can be viewed as containing four separate but related components: dynamic energy, a structural model, a topographical model, and a developmental stage model (Freud, 1933/1964a; 1940/1964b). As our focus here is to discuss the developmental aspects of Freud's views about personality, we refer the reader to Chapter 4 of this volume, which deals with psychodynamic theory, for an in-depth examination of the dynamic, structural, and topographical aspects of Freud's approach.

Freud used a developmental stage model spanning birth through puberty that incorporates the exchange and allocation of psychic energy as well as the structural and topographical aspects of his theory to explain personality development. Each stage represents a new source of tension and anxiety the child must learn to manage, and the quality and traits of the management style has implications for later personality characteristics. Freud believed that many of the individual differences in adult personality are caused by failure to progress from one stage of development to the next, a phenomenon he referred to as *fixation*. Also, traumatic events or emotional stress may result in a partial regression to an earlier stage's behavioral patterns.

Infants begin life in the *oral stage,* which begins at birth and ends approximately one year later. Freud viewed the primary tasks of infancy, such as eating, sucking, biting, and chewing, as granting sexual pleasure through the release of libidinal energy and the resulting physical sensations in the tongue, lips, and mouth. In this manner, libidinal energy is focused on the oral erogenous zone. Infants, who are essentially all id, are focused solely on instant gratification. However, frustration and anxiety also are experienced, wherein the infant may hunger for a bottle, but the caregiver may be slower than preferred in providing this desired object. Through these experiences of pleasure and pain and interaction with caregivers (most importantly the mother, according to Freud), the groundwork for the infant's personality is laid. Too little gratification of oral needs can lead to frequent anxiety and continuous seeking of oral gratification later in life. Too much gratification of oral needs can complicate the infant's libido shift to the next developmentally appropriate physical area. Without the correct balance of frustration and gratification, fixation at the oral stage occurs. Beginning with Freud's ideas about the oral stage and its effect on personality, Hall (1954) outlined five types of oral behaviors and linked them to later-life personality characteristics. Finding immense pleasure from taking in food contributes to an adult continually seeking knowledge or power. The infant who tries to hold on orally to a nipple or spoon may become determined or stubborn. Biting behavior foreshadows the adult who uses sarcasm, is cynical, dominates others, and who potentially may be destructive. The infant who rejects through spitting may later come to reject others. Rejection, negativity, and introversion find their roots in closing the mouth to offered food or objects. In addition to oral activities, attachment to the mother is a critical event during the oral stage. Traditionally the mother has been the primary source of the infant's oral pleasure, and this relationship is the most important for attachment purposes. Bowlby (1958, 1969) and Ainsworth and her colleagues (Ainsworth, Blehar, Waters, & Wall, 1978) have further elaborated on this attachment's importance, and their work will be considered shortly.

The *anal stage* lasts approximately from age one to three. Libidinal energy shifts away from the mouth and to the anal area, and new sources of tension and conflict are experienced. Toilet training exemplifies the delicate developmental task of balancing personal gratification needs with society's expectations, which aids in developing the ego and self-control. A parent who harshly trains his or her child, begins training too soon, or puts too much pressure on the child may contribute to the anxiety already present in the physical need to defecate. Later life personality traits indicative of difficulty in this stage are disorganization and irresponsibility or obsessive tidiness and stubbornness.

The *phallic stage,* beginning at about three years of age and ending at approximately five, continues the child's efforts to manage anxiety. In this stage, Freud believed the libidinal energy is focused on the opposite-sex parent. For boys, this is labeled the Oedipus complex; for girls, it is called the Electra complex. Emphasis during this stage is upon the growing boy, as Freud thought this stage's conflict was more intense and critical to males. The male child's sexual energy is directed toward the mother, and he aggressively does not want to share her with his father. However, he fears retaliation from his father for this longing and suspects it will come in the form of castration. The successful resolution to this dilemma is the son's identification with his father. Identification is possible only when the son represses his desire for his mother and his hostility toward his father. Successful identification with the father creates the superego and gender-appropriate interests and actions. For girls, desire is directed toward her father, and she envies his penis while blaming her mother for not having one of her own. Resolution for the girl also comes through superego development and identifying with the same-sex parent. Experiences during this stage and the success of the outcome theoretically create the basis for later emotional beliefs, attitudes, and actions regarding the opposite sex.

Latency spans the period from five years of age until the beginning of puberty. This is a period of relative peace for the sexual urges and tensions when compared to the first three stages; the child plays with primarily same-sex children and advances cognitively and socially. However, the superego continues to develop; the libidinal urges still exist but are managed through channeling the energy into social endeavors and improving defenses.

Freud's final stage is the *genital* stage. It begins with puberty, lasts throughout adolescence, and is without a distinct end. Representative of adult sexuality, partners are chosen and the libidinal tensions gain an altruistic flavor. Less focus is placed upon pleasing the self as the child learns to care for others' needs in addition to, and sometimes to the exclusion of, his or her own needs. Partner choice likely reflects the child's experiences in earlier psychosexual stages. For example, a man may choose a woman like his mother to marry, perhaps illustrating his earlier longing for his mother. By this point, ego structure is hopefully strong and the person can adequately balance reality's demands (e.g., needing to work for money) and personal needs (e.g., wanting to play or spend time with a spouse).

Freud: A Continuing Influence in Psychodynamic Thought

Although Freud's work has been quite influential, utilizing multiple criteria such as heuristic value, internal consistency, parsimony, and comprehensiveness (see Hall & Lindzey, 1978), generally speaking, there is little overall evidence for the psychosexual stage model of development (Hunt, 1979), and the theory is implicitly difficult to validate empirically due to its focus on unconscious processes (see P. H. Miller, 2002; Thomas, 2000; Wrightsman, 1994). It is for this reason that evidence specifically tailored to the value of classical psychoanalytic theory in predicting everyday behavior is comparatively sparse.

The Freudian legacy can be seen in the work of Neo-Freudians such as Erik Erikson (1963), who attempted to remedy his overemphasis on biological drives by including social and cultural factors that impact personality development. Erikson, who is discussed in a following section, viewed personality development as continuing throughout the life span rather than restricted to and determined by the first years of life. Equally important, however, are extensions of classical analytic theory to be found in attachment and object relations theories, to which we now turn.

Attachment Theory and Object Relations Theory

Initiated by Freud's explanation of the oral stage, the significance of the infant's relationship with the mother, and the study of ethology, attachment theory postulates that personality is formed though the infant's and child's interactions with important people early in life (see Ainsworth et al., 1978; Bowlby, 1969). From an evolutionary perspective, the attachment between infant and caregiver must be solidified in order for the infant to survive. Smiling, babbling, and reflexive grabbing are all behaviors that encourage infant-parent interaction in support of creating this bond, which is likely to take place during a sensitive period (see Scott, 1962) when the infant is more easily impacted by the reactions of those around him or her. This attachment is at first very general; the infant looks at all people. However, the infant quickly develops a preference for one or two people in particular, typically the mother or other significant caregivers such as the father, and he or she becomes increasingly more social. These attachment-oriented behaviors are complex and reflexive innate signals to the caregiver, and they act as mechanisms to ensure the child is nurtured and protected by encouraging close proximity with this caregiver. The attachment relationships that the child primarily relies upon to meet his or her basic needs instruct him or her about the world. Childhood experiences are vital as they create lifelong patterns of relating to others and enable the child to form internal representations of those relationships, also called *internal working models*. These models are mental representations of the caregiver, the child, and the relationship between the two and greatly influence what the child can come to expect from important others in the future.

Bowlby (1969) found evidence for the bond between child and caregiver in the child's reactions to separation from the caregiver. For example, most infants cry or fuss when parental figures leave and smile when they return, but they do not display this reaction when strangers come and go. Mary Ainsworth (1989) has continued research on attachment relationships, primarily via the Strange Situation paradigm, which illustrates infant attachment to mothers and suggests later life implications for the kind of bond formed (see Ainsworth, 1989). The baby, his or her parent, and an experimenter who is a stranger to the baby progress through scenarios that are designed to be increasingly stressful for the child. Beginning with a low-stress experience (child with the mother) and continuing to a high-stress experience (child with the strange experimenter without the mother present), the child and parent are assessed for their attachment reactions, which determines to which of four attachment categories the parent-child bond belongs and has implications for personality traits and later life experiences with others. *Securely attached* infants are able to explore using the parent as a safe base. The parent is attentive to the child's signals, such as providing appropriate comfort if the child appears distressed and allowing the child to explore when the child appears comfortable and confident. This interaction teaches the child that others are reliable and can competently care for his or her needs. This attachment style influences the development of secure adults, who find it relatively easy to get close to others and are comfortable depending on others and having others depend on them. *Insecure-avoidant* infants do not seek comfort from the parent but often appear to be distressed. This parent and child are typically not as effective as the securely attached parent-child dyad in understanding and appropriately responding to each other's signals. As a result, the child is taught that others are not to be relied upon to meet his or her needs. An avoidant adult continues this pattern and is often uncomfortable being close to others; he or she finds it hard to trust others completely and to depend upon them. *Insecure-ambivalent* attachment styles in infants can contribute to an adult tendency to find that others are reluctant to get as close as they would like. These adults often worry that their partner does not really love them and might abandon them. Appearing to want to "merge" completely with the romantic partner and "needy" or "suffocating" behavior may ironically contribute to the relationship's end. There is empirical evidence to support the assumption that the kind of attachment that people form with their parents in childhood colors their later relationships with adults and even their own children. Hazan and Shaver (1987) have demonstrated that adult romantic relationships follow attachment relationship predictions, whereas Steele, Steele, and Fonagy (1996) found the type of relationship a pregnant woman had with her mother related to the kind of attachment relationship formed with her own infant.

Notable theoretical amendments to classical attachment theory have been presented by Coleman and Watson (2000), who reconceptualized infant attachment in the context of systems theory, and by Crittenden (1997), who redefined insecure attachment styles (i.e., anxious and dismissive or avoidant) as successful attempts by the infant to assess and respond to varying degrees of aversive and/or uncontrollable interpersonal experiences and suggests an ongoing sense of continuity over time into adulthood with regard to attachment style. Whether such styles are indeed consistent over time and/or unmodifiable is debatable at present (Hobdy, Hayslip, Kaminski, & York, under review; Kenny & Barton, 2003).

Object relations theory also gives predominance to relationship interactions, but languages the importance of relationships in a different way. *Object* is in reference to other people, but object relations theory itself has many variants. Kernberg (1976) focuses on libido as the driving force behind finding and maintaining interpersonal relationships, but others such as Fairbairn (1954) dispute this. In general, object relations theory proposes that there is an innate tendency to develop a *self,* which is composed of various images derived from interpersonal relationships (Maddi, 1989). The self develops in stages, the first of which is *autism,* an undifferentiated state during the first few months of life in which the infant is blissfully unaware of interpersonal relationships. The second stage, *symbiosis,* lasts between two and seven months and brings with it a sense of confusion between the self and others in the infant's mind. During this time, the infant is unable to see the self and others as independent of one another. *Differentiation,* stage three, occurs when the infant is able to see the self and others as clearly independent. At approximately two years old, the *integration* stage occurs, during which the self and other representations, while continuing to be seen as independent, are now conceived as in relationship to each other. Differentiation and integration contribute to a sense of emerging personal identity and shape expectations about relationships with others.

Contemporary thinking about personality development and relationships with others has shifted away from searching for direct relationships between early years, stages, and personality traits and toward viewing the early years as only one of many influences upon personality development that continues to unfold throughout life. As Runyan (1988) has stated, "Effects of early life are mediated by intervening experiences and contingencies, and . . . personality and behavior are continually shaped throughout the life cycle" (p. 226). Notably, whereas Freud had little that was substantive to say about development later in life, work by Neugarten (1977) emphasizing increasing interiority (turning inward) with age and work by Hayslip, Panek, and Stoner (1990) that suggests an age-related exploration for changes in defense mechanisms, at least based upon projective test performance across three cohorts of adults, is generally consistent with psychoanalytic theory. Moreover, work by Hayslip, Guarnaccia, Radika, and Servaty (2002) suggests that there is an inverse relationship between overt/conscious and unconscious/covert death fear in adults, supporting the operation of denial as a defense mechanism in the face of anxiety over one's own decline and eventual death.

Jung's Analytical Psychology

Whereas Jung's developmental stages figure somewhat less prominently in his system of analytical psychology than did Freud's in psychoanalytic theory, Jung is noteworthy for his attention to later life development. Unlike Freud, Jung believed that personality continued to evolve as a matter of course well into the second half of life. These extended dynamics of change are due both to analytical psychology's overriding emphasis on the dialectic tension between opposites and to the complexity with which the psyche is represented. The details of Jung's theory are incredibly complicated, and the interested reader is referred to Rychlak (1981) for a thorough summary of his work.

Jung (1954) posited a *Presexual Period* beginning at birth and lasting until age three, four, or five. The Presexual Period seems the first enactment of interplay between opposites with a child's realization of the distinction between *I* and *me.* Next, children begin to place ideas in relations to form more complex notions, such as combining "me" and "mommy" to express a desire to be held. Thus, the first step toward knowledge acquisition is one of differentiating ideas, the second one of relating them. As the name suggests, sexual impulses either are not present or play no significant role in personality development during this time. Beginning somewhere between ages three and five, the *Prepubertal Period* begins, bringing with it emerging sexual instincts. Children also enter the educational system around this time, so consciousness and knowledge develop quickly. Although sexuality emerges during this time, Jung did not believe that children form sexual attachments to their parents or experience incest fantasies as a matter of course. Jung's *Pubertal Period* occurs sometime between age 10 and 13 and is a time of multiple challenges, including maturing sexual instincts, deciding on a career path, and forming satisfying interpersonal relations as well as an identity independent of one's social "mask," to which Jung referred to as the *persona.* Jung warned that overidentification with the persona impaired the development of other aspects of the psyche, such as the self or ego, and often resulted in personality pathology. The pubertal period extended to about age 19 or 20 for women but might last until age 25 for men.

Youth, Jung's next stage, extends to age 35 or 40 and is a time of increasing differentiation from one's family of origin, as well as a time of marriage, child rearing, and competitive strivings for career success. Knowledge continues to increase, as does responsibility, but individuals in this stage still have the energy and vitality to pursue strivings across multiple arenas of life. *Middle Life* begins at about age 40 and for Jung was the beginning of a gradual shift in personality characterizing the second half of life. By Middle Life, most people have established careers and families and are able to reap some of the rewards of hard work in their Youth. However, much of this has been achieved based on strong attention to the external world and to the elements of the conscious. By contrast, Middle Life development involves an increasing attention to inner life and one's unconscious in order to bring about a better psychic balance. Social demands may be lessened as a result of children leaving home and a stable interpersonal network. Greater work seniority usually permits the delegation of onerous work tasks to younger colleagues. Thus, psychic energy is freed up for the process of *Individuation.*

Individuation is a complicated process of intrapsychic differentiation and transformation that occurs throughout the second half of life (Jung, 1960). It involves confronting both the *shadow* and *anima* complexes. The shadow is an element of the unconscious representing all things opposite of the ego, which are typically those impulses, wishes, fears, and desires that people feel are the most disturbing, frightful, and shameful. The anima is an element of the unconscious representing the feminine side of men (an animus exists for women, representing their masculine side). The shadow and anima join and are confronted by the ego through what Jung termed the *transcendent function,* a process of integrating conscious and unconscious contents through the free exchange of libido (psychic energy) across the boundary of consciousness. The result of successful individuation is a more balanced and integrated personality. The self, which Jung posits as a psychic entity separate from the ego, becomes more central to personality than the ego. At a practical level, people who have individuated in the Jungian sense have integrated both masculine and feminine needs and desires, are more aware of the interplay between their conscious and unconscious lives, and may shift what Jung (1946/1971) called *dominant* and *inferior functions.* The dominant function is simply one's primary mode of relating to the world; the inferior function is a separate category that may be implemented in some situations. Thus, someone who is normally an extrovert may become more introverted, and vice versa.

Individuation is an ongoing process that spans Middle Life and extends into Jung's (1960) last period of *Old Age.* For Jung, this begins at age 60 or 65 and represents a time of contemplation and wisdom as a result of life experience. Old Age also involves continued inward focus and a realization and acceptance of eventual death. Related to this, people in Old Age must resolve their beliefs in or their understanding of an afterlife. Jung felt that to deny or ignore death was unhealthy, but to face, accept, and reach some understanding of it represented a major goal or purpose of life's final period. In this respect, the notion of a midlife crisis association with inner reorganization of the self has not, for the most part, been empirically supported, yet some individuals do undergo shifts in the manner by which they define themselves (see Labouvie-Vief & Diehl, 1999).

Loevinger's Stages of Ego Development

In Jane Loevinger's (1976) work, ego development rests at the core of personality development. Loevinger's theory, which has received some empirical support (cf. Hy & Loevinger, 1996), attributes considerable significance to the period of life after adolescence. However, Loevinger (e.g., 1976) eschews the assignment of certain stages to certain ages because "the average stage for a given age is not the same as the average age for a given stage" (p. 13), and mechanical age-stage links produce an inflexible theory that faces problems accommodating individual differences in development. For much the same reason, Loevinger does not number her stages, instead referring to them by name and symbol. It is important to note that although these stages are not tied to specific age ranges, some later stages are clearly impossible in very young children, and some earlier stages of ego development in adults would indicate gross impairment.

Loevinger's *Presocial Stage (I-1)* characterizes infancy and is marked by the development of the infant's ability to differentiate him or herself from the external world. Loevinger considers delay at this stage autism. The *Symbiotic Stage,* also coded I-1, involves the crystallization of self-other differentiation and the baby's eventual realization of his or her separateness in the symbiotic relationship with his or her mother. This process is catalyzed by language development. The exertion of independence and autonomy characterizes the *Impulsive Stage (I-2),* and limits or proscriptions are met with anger. Notions of morality are limited to simple "good" versus "bad" splitting, and such attributions tend to be a function of whether an object is "nice" or "mean" to the child. Understanding and descriptions of emotional states are limited. If intelligence is sufficient, physical causation may be grasped, but rarely can the person in this stage understand other's motivations or abstract causal chains. Loevinger (1976) calls a person delayed in this state *uncontrollable* or *incorrigible.*

The *Self-Protective Stage (ΔΔ)* is named for the guardedness persons feel as they learn that their actions bring both rewards and punishments. Constraint over impulses is internalized but exists mostly in the sense of avoiding punishment rather than abstract moral principles. The person in this stage tends to externalize blame, and individuals who linger in this stage tend to become deceitful, exploitative, and hedonistic and may be preoccupied with material success if adults. The *Conformist (I-3) Stage* is seen as a major improvement in development because persons begin to associate their own success and well-being with that of their family (or a larger group). This is not possible without a basic trust of those around one, however. A lack of trust may relegate an individual to the opportunism of the Self-Protective Stage. In general, individuals in the Conformist Stage are strongly influenced by the norms and opinions of their group, have little tolerance of or understanding for individual differences, have a simplistic grasp of emotions and inner states, and have a relatively mechanical moral code based on group norms. They tend to be concerned with appearance, status, group acceptance, and material things.

There is a transition from the Conformist to Conscientious Stage called the *Self-Aware* or the *Conscientious-Conformist Level (I-3/4)*. Loevinger considers this the most common level of adult ego development in our society but leaves open the issue of whether this transition or level actually constitutes a stage in itself. Although individuals retain many characteristics of the conformist level, there is greater self-awareness as well as greater appreciation for the complex set of possibilities inherent in various situations. Some allowance is made for individual differences, but this allowance still may be couched in a sense of deviation from collective "normality." Inner emotional awareness improves but still may be imprecise or uncertain.

When this transitional level has been negotiated, people move into the *Conscientious Stage (I-4)*. Here, one has internalized rules and developed the ability to evaluate oneself based on an internalized sense of responsibility that goes beyond (or sometimes against) the morality of the group. Loevinger notes that this stage cannot be achieved until about age 13 or 14 at the earliest. Individuals in the Conscientious Stage may pursue achievement for its own sake because they find something intrinsically rewarding, and moral judgment is complex and differentiated from social norms. Inner experiences tend to be rich and more complex, and the ability to take others' perspectives deepens interpersonal relations.

Next is the *Individualistic Level (I-4/5),* which is a transition between the Conscientious and Autonomous Stages. The Individualistic Level is marked by a concern for problems of dependence versus independence; emotional intimacy begins to be seen as a motive conflicting with achievement drive. People at the Individualistic Level also are keenly aware of psychological development and causality and see morals and behaviors in relatively complex terms. The stage is also marked by greater tolerance of oneself and others.

When people acquire the capacity to fully acknowledge and cope with inner conflict, they enter the *Autonomous State (I-5)*. This state is marked by great tolerance for ambiguity, an acknowledgment of others' autonomy, and the inevitability of emotional interdependence. Awareness of psychological causality assumes a greater degree of complexity, such as considering the motives of others, not just in the present context but in the context of their background, idiosyncratic

needs, and motives. Autonomous individuals also may pursue things out of self-fulfillment rather than out of achievement needs.

The *Integrated Stage (I-6)* is the highest level of ego development, and Loevinger (1976) notes that it is difficult to describe because it is rare and it may exceed the ego development (and complete understanding) of the psychologist interested in studying it. The brief guide she does provide is that "the description of the Autonomous Stage holds also for the Integrated Stage. A new element is the consolidation of a sense of identity" (p. 26). She also compares it to Maslow's self-actualizing person, but this remains a somewhat ambiguous element of her theory.

All in all, Loevinger is careful to note that development through these stages may not occur in a linear fashion, or may not occur at all, because the modal stage for adults is considered the Conformist/Conscientious transition level. Indeed, there is some support for an age-related shift is the maturing of one's defenses (see Labouvie-Vief & Diehl, 1999; Vaillant, 1977). However, it is also evident that there are individual and contextual differences in the exact way underlying issues at each stage will be expressed. For instance, some people are likely to be frustrated at a relatively low level of ego development if they are surrounded by others at a similarly low ego level or if their environment is aesthetically, educationally, and interpersonally barren. In other instances, environments rich in social, emotional, and material resources will facilitate ego development.

Erik Erikson's Psychosocial Crisis Theory

To a certain extent, organismic themes of development present in Freud's system are played out in the work of Erikson (1959, 1963, 1980), who sees personality (ego) development in terms of eight *psychosocial crises,* each of which can be resolved positively or negatively. In contrast to Freud, who viewed development in primarily psychosexual terms and for whom the function of the ego was anxiety reduction, Erikson's psychosocial crisis theory takes on a more proactive, positive view of ego development and recasts personality in terms of the interaction between the ego functions and the larger social/interpersonal context that codefines the parameters along which choices with regard to self and others are continually being made. Like that of Freud's theory, however, Erikson's theory is an age-graded approach to ego development and as well emphasizes the importance of difficulties in resolving earlier crises seriously interfering with the resolution of later crises. Furthermore, each crisis, regardless of its resolution, comes to help redefine later crises. For example, trust (characterizing infancy) and industry (characterizing early childhood) are played out several times over one's life in dealing with, respectively, the issues of intimacy (young adulthood) and generativity (middle adulthood; Logan, 1986). Likewise, one's identity (characteristic of adolescence) undergoes several transformations if one marries, has children, divorces, gains and loses a job, retires, or suffers the loss of one's spouse. These crises are *epigenetic* (*epi,* referring to *upon,* and *genesis,* referring to *emergence*) that is, they arise out of a *maturational ground plan,* wherein each stage has its special "time of ascendancy" that comes together to form a "functional whole" organism (Erikson, 1963). Maturation brings about new skills that enhance one's capacity for growth, but with such changes, new demands on the individual are made by others. Whereas the order and essential nature of each psychosocial stage are presumed to be universal, cultures vary in terms of the means available to them either to restrict or to enhance ego development (see the following section).

Whereas earlier forms of identity influence later forms, in Erikson's model, as noted previously, this sense of emergence and redefinition is played out several times, wherein, for example, the *trust-mistrust crisis,* which is relevant to being the infant's being cared for in a timely way, may reemerge in young adulthood, when persons often crystallize their feelings about educational or career goals, ideals, and relationships with the opposite sex. Each of these requires the ability to project oneself into the future and requires trust in one's own skills and abilities as well as trust in others and, more importantly, a sense of trust in time itself; one must have faith that goals will be realized. Likewise, the crisis of *autonomy versus shame and doubt,* representing the ability to walk, talk, and control one's bowels (ages two to four), comes to redefine later crises and to reemerge later in terms of anxiety about being separated from others, feelings of vulnerability, and interactions with authority figures requiring one to respect the limits imposed on him or her by others. This is expressed in terms of whether to hold on to what one has or to let go of what one has come to value (see P. H. Miller, 2002) and the risk of failure and feeling vulnerable in doing so, as might be expressed in leaving home, selecting an occupation, or going on after divorce or the death of others. The *initiative versus guilt crisis* reflects the acquisition of language and increased cognitive skills and further advances in personal mobility brought about by physical maturation. Key here is the importance of further defining oneself in terms of literally taking the initiative and setting goals versus guilt at having been either too aggressive or immoral or not aggressive enough. The crisis central to young adulthood, *intimacy versus isolation,* requires the individual to be able to merge with another person (e.g., a parent, spouse, child) to form a relationship that is built upon mutual trust and love (Logan,

1986); such a relationship is *mutual.* One's ability to form such a relationship is a function of the individual's previous efforts in establishing a stable sense of *ego identity* (versus *identity confusion*) in adolescence. If one's identity is poorly formed or not formed at all, the crisis of intimacy will be perceived as threatening. This inability to commit oneself to another person, or in a sense merge one's identity with that of someone else, is termed *isolation.* Characteristic of middle age is the crisis of *generativity versus stagnation.* To be generative literally means to generate—to produce things or people that symbolize one's continued existence after death—a reexpression of the industry versus inferiority crisis of early childhood. Generativity may be expressed by productivity in one's work (in writing or teaching), personal creativity (in finding a novel solution to a problem, in painting an original picture), or most directly in having children, caring for them, and raising them to become adults. In contrast, stagnation implies a withdrawal from others—being self-indulgent, bitter, and isolated. A change in identity likely will accompany this process as well. Intimacy will be redefined to include relationships with one's children or perhaps a few trusted friends. *Integrity versus despair* characterizes old age and implies a sense of completeness, of having come full circle. Persons who have integrity have been able, through the process of introspection, to integrate a lifetime full of successes and failures to reach a point where they have a "sense of the life cycle" (Erikson, 1959). Despairing individuals fear death as a premature end to a life for which they have not been able to take personal responsibility, whereas those who have a sense of integrity accept death as the inevitable end of having lived. Significantly, Clayton (1975) has argued that a complete resolution of Erikson's last psychosocial crisis is unrealistic and that it is better recast in terms of compromises at not only this last point but at others preceding it as well. Peck (1968) has further elaborated upon Erikson's latter stage, such that a more elaborate set of choices (e.g., valuing wisdom versus valuing physical powers, ego/body transcendence versus ego/body preoccupation, mental/cathectic flexibility versus mental/cathectic rigidity) replace wisdom versus despair.

The major impetus to Erikson's continuing influence is not to be found in Erikson's work per se, but in that of such researchers and theorists as (1) Marcia (1967, 1999), who describes the processes by which identity is formed in terms of identity statuses (i.e., being identity diffused, foreclosed, in moratorium, or identity achieved) based upon the effort and/or perceived consequences of testing the limits of one's identity and/or redefining oneself, (2) McAdams (McAdams, 2001; McAdams & de St. Aubin, 1998), who has redefined the antecedents of generativity and its consequences for human development along multiple parameters, (3) Vaillant (1977,

2002), who, in the context of an extension of Loevinger, describes the continued ego development and sophistication of one's adaptive skills and defense mechanisms, based on a longitudinal study of three cohorts of men followed for multiple decades from 1937 in the Grant Study of Harvard Graduates, and (4) Baltes, who popularized the study of wisdom and its measurement and antecedents (see also Sternberg & Lubart, 2001) as an attribute of integrity (e.g., Baltes & Smith, 1990; Baltes & Staudinger, 1993).

As with other stage theories (see previous sections), we might criticize Erikson on the basis of his failure to specify the processes by which individuals are transformed as they progress through this maturationally determined sequence of psychosocial crises (see Lerner, 2002; P. H. Miller, 2002; Wrightsman, 1994). Although several studies have found moderate support for Erikson's model of personality development (Vaillant & Milosfsky, 1980; Whitbourne, Zuschlag, Elliot, & Waterman, 1992), his work has been criticized as being rooted in the dichotomous style of thinking characteristic of the 1950s and, therefore, not being capable of speaking to individual differences across the continuum of each crisis (i.e., individuals might be better described in terms of degrees to which crises are resolved). Likewise, his work, particularly that relating to intimacy and identity, has been faulted as being too male-oriented in nature (Gilligan, 1982) and, as pointed out by Wrightsman (1994), more generally for deemphasizing outcomes (McAdams, 1987), wherein changes in one's identity take the form of a personal narrative coming to define a life story. These novel elements defining personality recently have been defined in the context of a *six foci of personality* model integrating personality structures (traits, personal action constructs, life stories) and processes (states, self-regulation, self-narration; Hooker, 2002; Hooker & McAdams, 2003).

Whitbourne's Identity Styles

A relatively new approach to personality driven by Eriksonian identity emphasizes the concept of *identity style* (e.g., Whitbourne, 1987; Whitbourne & Connolly, 1999). An individual's identity style is that person's manner of representing and responding to life experiences. As individuals interact with others in the environment, they begin to separate the *self-as-agent* from the *self-as-object*. It is through the particular identity style of the individual that experiences are processed to contribute to our selves. These identity styles can be *assimilative, accommodative,* or *balanced.* In identity assimilation, new experiences are fit into the existing identity of the individual, whereas in identity accommodation, one's identity is changed to fit a new experience. As persons have new experiences or interactions with others, they attempt to

fit these into how they see themselves along those dimensions that are important to them. For example, if it is important to be a loving parent, the experiences with one's children will be processed in a way that reinforces the perception of oneself as a loving father or mother (Whitbourne, 1987). In other words, these new experiences are assimilated into one's existing identity. Likewise, if being productive is an important aspect of the self, then retiring will be processed in a way that complements one's view about oneself as productive. Experiences to which one's identity must be changed (or accommodated) so the individual can cope with them are those that are most discrepant from the individual's views about self. In some cases, assimilation simply is not possible. For example, if divorce separates one from his or her children, or if one is forcibly retired, these experiences cause the person to redefine himself or herself. The self is accommodated or changed to fit these new events in one's life. Successful development or adaptation occurs when there is a balance between identity assimilation and identity accommodation. When one must discipline a child, this experience can be assimilated in one's identity as a loving parent via "I am disciplining my child because I love him." Yet, this same experience may require that one's identity as a loving parent be accommodated to fit the negative experience of being violent, of a child's crying, or of feelings of hurt and guilt at having to discipline one's child. Thus, one's identity may shift to incorporate the necessity for limits on the type of discipline one uses—"I love my child, but maybe I am not the perfect parent. Perhaps I should seek advise from my spouse." Whitbourne (1987) found several forms of both identity assimilation, balance, and identity accommodation among adults; some were more adaptive than others, such as with regard to the healthy use of denial, their impact on health, or in coping with the aging process. For example, regarding being open to new experiences, assimilative persons had a controlling style and needed to win most arguments, whereas accommodative individuals gave in without considering alternatives because they lacked confidence in their ideas or because they needed to please others. Whitbourne et al. (1992) also found some evidence for age-related shifts in identity status over two decades. Such shifts may be a response to idiosyncratic age-related or historically relevant life events requiring adaptation to them if successful development is to continue.

Levinson's Life Structure

Another stage approach to adult personality development, building upon that of Erikson, is that of Levinson, who conducted an intensive study of 40 men aged 35 to 45 to investigate the process by which these men created a *life structure,* defined as a coherent relationship between one's own goals and the roles one plays in various life arenas (e.g., career, family, marriage, social roles; Levinson, 1978, 1986). The life structure evolves through a sequence of distinct periods, is shaped by decisions that each individual makes at varying times in adulthood, and is seen in terms of shifts between structure-building periods of stability and structure-changing periods of transition (Wrightsman, 1994), where certain polarities, such as attachment/separateness, youth/old age, destruction/creation, masculine/feminine, define the discrepancies in their self-images that men who are in a midlife transition must resolve.

The *Early Adult Transition* (approximate ages 17 to 22) links adolescence and early adulthood. The individual reevaluates the preadult world and his role in it. Relationships with one's parents, siblings, extended family members, friends, or teachers either are terminated or altered, and one becomes less dependent upon parental support and authority. This process is never fully complete.

Entering the Adult World (ages 22 to 28) allows one to create a provisional life structure that provides a link to adult society. The young man is entering a *novice* phase where important decisions of what may become a more permanent fixture of his life structure are shaped (e.g., occupational choice, marriage and family, peer relationships, values, life style). Many of these decisions are made within the context of one's *Dream,* for example, being president of one's own company, being a loving father, or simply being good at one's trade. The novice's task is to define more precisely this Dream and to realistically live it out, making sure that the "thread" of this Dream is not lost in revising his life structure.

The *Age Thirty Transition* (ages 28 to 33) enables one to work on the flaws and limitations of the first life structure. This transition is a traumatic one, in that the changes one makes either are out of step with the individual's wishes or abilities or are based on a poorly formed initial life structure. For a minority of men, this transition was a smooth one. In the *Settling-Down Period,* the man reinvests himself in those aspects of his life structure that were somewhat tentative earlier, allowing him to "establish a niche" for himself and to succeed at whatever is most important.

At the end of this period (ages 36 to 40), the individual is *Becoming One's Own Man (BOOM)* and begins to ascend the occupational ladder to become a respected authority. At this point in his life he may assume the role of mentor for someone younger who is just beginning work on his own life structure. Mentors can fulfill a formal role where they serve a guiding, teaching function in helping the novice define his Dream. Alternatively, the mentor also can fill a more informal role that is emotionally supportive, much like that of a parent.

The mentor role will be shed (willingly or not) as that young adult reaches his own *Settling-Down Period* and becomes someone else's mentor. Levinson rarely found men over 40 who still maintained an active mentor relationship with someone their senior.

The *Midlife Transition* (ages 40 to 45) represents a period of soul-searching, questioning, and assessment regarding the extent to which all that has been accomplished within the life structure has any real meaning or not. For some, it is a rather gradual, relatively painless change; for others, it is full of uncertainties and often has an "either-or" quality to it. Either one starts anew or perceives that he has failed in some way to define what is important to him.

Levinson finds the man next *Entering Middle Adulthood,* wherein he must again make choices regarding a new life structure. In some cases, these choices are defined by marker life events: divorce, illness, a shift in occupations, or the death of someone who is close. In other cases, changes are less obvious but nonetheless significant: subtle shifts in enthusiasm for one's work or changes in the quality of his marriage.

Levinson tentatively proposed an *Age Fifty Transition* (ages 50 to 55), which represents an opportunity to further solidify and/or change the life structure established during middle adulthood. For some, it is experienced as the Midlife Transition because they did little to alter the life structure or were not very successful in doing so.

The period from age 55 to 60 is seen as a relatively stable one, analogous to Settling Down, where the life structure is solidified, followed by a *Late Adult Transition* (ages 60 to 65), which terminates middle adulthood and prepares one for older adulthood. Because Levinson did not interview men in their 50s and 60s, his views about these latter life periods are speculative and perhaps somewhat biased. Additionally, empirical support for his views on mentoring have been challenged (Wrightsman, 1994), as has the age-relatedness of his theory, its universality, and its exemplar status as a theory of personality (McCrae & Costa, 1990), though Levinson himself debates this latter point (Levinson, 1979).

Some work suggests that the life structure, and its accompanying personality changes, may also apply to women (Roberts & Newton, 1987). Two cross-sectional studies of women's development (Harris, Elliot, & Holmes, 1986; Reinke, Holmes, & Harris, 1985) generally support the viability of Levinson's work. These studies indicated that the ages 27 to 30 seemed to reflect the most dramatic changes in women's lives, beginning with ages 26 to 30, where personal disruption was a major theme. The second phase began between the ages of 28 and 31 and had as its major thrust a focus on the self and self-development. Women felt less oriented to others, set personal goals, and often experienced separation and divorce at this time. The third period, between ages 30 to 35, reflected a new sense of well-being. The questioning and soul-searching of the two previous periods ceased, and women felt more self-confidence and greater satisfaction with their lives. Rather than an age 40 crisis for men, these studies suggest an age 30 crisis for women. Perhaps this reflects an awareness of their "biological clock," and thus an urgency in beginning a family, or increased autonomy due to greater career opportunities (Wrightsman, 1988). Women aged 45 to 60 experienced increased satisfaction with life and marriage and greater "mellowing, patience, assertiveness, and expressivity" (Harris et al., 1986, p. 415). It may be that the differences in the timing of men's and women's personality development are due to the greater diversity in women's lives (Wrightsman, 1988). In a work he completed shortly before his death in 1994, Levinson explored the applicability of his work to women, intensively studying three groups of women in the early 1980s ranging in age from their teens to their mid-40s: homemakers, women with corporate financial careers, and women with academic careers (Levinson & Levinson, 1996). He found that women go through the same transitions as do men and that these changes were experienced at similar ages. However, he also discovered that *gender splitting* permeated every aspect of these women's lives: how they defined themselves, the choice and availability of careers to them, their roles within marriage, and the perception that it was "unnatural" to be the head of the household, executive, and leader if one was a female. Whereas homemakers struggled with the internal "antitraditional figure"— a secret desire to be more independent—the career women actually attempted to change this traditional pattern, often at the cost of their personal and occupational lives. On the other hand, results by Stewart and Ostrove (1998) suggest that highly educated midlife women are filled with enthusiasm and self-confidence about their lives.

Gould's Transformations

Roger Gould's (1980) ideas, like Erikson's, are stagelike in character. Gould thinks that there is a shift in time perspective across the adult life cycle, from the seeming infinity of time that is available when persons leave high school to a more limited sense of time that leads to winning the "prize"—freedom from restrictions by one's parents. This sense of time becomes more restricted in one's late 20s, and by the late 30s and early 40s, time becomes precious as persons become more aware of their own mortality and begin to question whether the prize was worth it or whether the prize even exists. Gould argues that persons must free themselves of the

illusion of absolute safety, based on four age-graded sets of major false assumptions (i.e., "I will always belong to my parents and believe in their world"; "Doing things my parents' way, with willpower and perseverance, will always bring results"; "Life is simple and controllable; there are no contradictory forces within me"; "There is no evil or death in the world"; see Gould, 1978, 1980a). This involves a series of transformations whereby persons give up the security of the past to form their own ideas, which can be troublesome.

Although Erikson's, Levinson's, and Gould's theories are each stagelike in character, there are important differences between the approaches. Whereas Levinson feels that one begins adulthood with a life structure that is absent, Gould feels that the structure (illusion) that persons have created for themselves must be given up in order for growth to occur. Gould's ideas are childhood-centered, with growth or maturity more or less boiling down to a complete resolution of the separation anxiety in childhood, perhaps precipitated by the deterioration and eventual death of one's parents. Whereas Gould, like Levinson and Erikson, breaks down the adult life span into different sets of issues or tasks that are age-related—in light of what we currently know about occupational development (see Adams & Beehr, 2003; Super, Savickas, & Super, 1996) as well as about adult development and aging, especially regarding bereavement (see Demick & Andreoletti, 2003; Stroebe, Hansson, Stroebe, & Schut, 2001)—there is more potential epistemological potential associated with the systematic testing of the theories of Erikson, Gould, and Levinson to the extent that we will come to know more about age-related changes in how people deal with culturally relevant shifts in the self (career, marriage, family) brought about by and causing changes in one's identity, the life structure, and/or by transformations in the illusion of absolute safety. However, in contrast to Erikson, at least in a descriptive sense, Levinson and Gould had little to say about later life, and whereas Erikson and Levinson advocate positions suggesting *qualitative changes* in adult personality, Gould's position, however, essentially supports a *stability* of personality point of view stemming from transformations in the self that are extensions of childhood separation anxiety. As a developmental stage-oriented approach to personality, the work of Havighurst (1972), emphasizing age-related sets of developmental tasks, and that of Buhler (1982), emphasizing age-graded sets of qualitatively different life tendencies that assume special importance during distinct life periods (see Havighurst, 1973), are descriptively similar to that of Levinson, Gould, and Erikson. In this respect, it is worth noting that developmental tasks may be cohort-specific, and may be confronted and reconfronted several times (Oerter, 1986).

BIOLOGICAL/PHYSIOLOGICAL RELATIONSHIPS

Speculation on a link between personality and biology is certainly one of the oldest areas of inquiry, beginning with the ancient Greeks and the idea that specific bodily humors were associated with certain personality types. In the modern era, conceptions of personality have become increasingly diverse and diffuse. Thus, how one defines personality (e.g., in terms of higher-order traits versus psychosocial adaptations) plays a large role in determining whether it is viewed as stable or malleable (Heatherton & Weinberger, 1994) and the extent to which biology and personality are causally related (Cloninger, 1998; Costa & McCrae, 1994; Plomin, Defries, Craig, & McGuffin, 2003).

Broadly defined, personality can refer to individual differences in such characteristics as traits, goals and motives, emotion and moods, self-evaluative processes, coping strategies, and well-being (Ryff, Kwan, & Singer, 2001). Clearly, biological and physiological processes can be shown to have close links to some of the characteristics listed previously but will have more distant associations to others. Linking certain psychosexual or psychosocial stages of personality development to various biological factors is a particularly challenging endeavor. Nevertheless, in this section of the chapter we briefly discuss research that shows an association between personality and behavior genetics, neurochemistry, and brain structure and function and how this research may reveal some consistency with developmental or stage theories of personality.

Zuckerman (1991) provided a comprehensive discussion on the psychobiology of personality, particularly as it related to the dimensions of neuroticism (or negative emotionality), extroversion (or sociability), and impulsivity/sensation seeking. Moreover, traits such as neuroticism and extroversion are highly stable over time (Costa & McCrae, 1994) and have been shown to be moderately heritable (Ebstein, Benjamin, & Belmaker, 1998). On the other hand, the heritability estimates for personality traits decrease over the life span (Brody, 1994). Consistent with this latter observation, the relationship between neuroticism and daily stress has been shown to increase as a function of age (Mroczek & Almeida, 2004). Thus, despite the fact that certain basic personality dispositions are heritable and stable over time, environmental experiences explain a considerable amount of the variance in personality measures and appear to increase in significance over the life span. In this sense, genetic factors may play more or less of a role in the expression of certain personality features depending on the context and stage of a person's life.

In terms of other characteristics more aligned with stage theories of personality, variance in social support measures have been reported to have significant heritability estimates over a six-year period (Bergeman, Neiderhiser, Pedersen, & Plomin, 2001). Noteworthy is that the investigators of this study also found that nonshared environmental influences made substantial contributions to social support, though they were less stable across three follow-ups compared to the phenotypic correlations (Bergeman et al., 2001). Similarly, Plomin and colleagues have shown that components of self-concept are genetically influenced; however, unique experiences were also important correlates of individual differences in self-concept in adolescents (McGuire et al., 1999). Consistent with these studies, Whitbourne, Zuschlag, Elliott, and Waterman (1992) found that individuals manifested shifts in their identity and intimacy statuses over a 22-year time period. Collectively, the findings suggest a dynamic interplay between genes and environment in the expression of different stages of personality development.

Of course, genes do not code for specific behaviors or personality characteristics (Plomin et al., 2003). In fact, any given gene is likely to influence many different kinds of behaviors, and this phenomenon has been referred to as *pleiotropy* (Zuckerman, 1991). Moreover, genes tend to have a general effect on behavior, and specific environmental experiences shape the genetic effect (Eley, 1997). Finally, genes can turn on and off during particular developmental periods (Helson & Stewart, 1994). Thus, it is possible that different stages of development and life experience may play a role in determining the expression of genetically influenced behaviors.

Perhaps more important than simple additive behavior genetic models are models that typify gene-environment interactions or gene-environment correlations (Plomin et al., 2003; Zuckerman, 1991). Gene-environment interactions occur when individuals with specific genotypes show greater or lesser sensitivity to the environment compared to individuals with other genotypes (Rowe, 2003). For instance, the level of adversity in family functioning has been shown to influence the expression of genetic risk for antisocial behavior (Cadorate, Yates, Troughton, Woodward, & Stewart, 1995) as well as genetic potential for verbal intelligence (Rowe, Jacobson, & Van den Oord, 1999). Gene-environment correlations (Rowe, 2003) are discussed as either passive (genotypes are correlated with family environment such as aggression in both the children and the parents in a family), evocative (individuals with certain genotypes evoke particular reactions from the social environment), or active. In active gene-environment correlations, individuals with certain genotypes play a critical role in the selection or creation of particular environmental circumstances. For instance, selection of friends appears to involve a gene-environment correlation such that individuals choose to associate with other individuals who reinforce their own genetic propensities (Rowe, 2003; Zuckerman, 1991).

Taken together, the findings are consistent with the notion that basic developmental or psychosocial tasks faced by the individuals in their environment will influence the degree to which genetic factors contribute to the expression of certain personality features. Also, certain stages of development or different environmental contexts may trigger the expression of particular developmentally relevant genes.

Of course, genes code for proteins, which in turn are used for building such things as neurotransmitters, hormones, and immune cells (Lesch, 2003). As it turns out, neurochemicals play an important role in the expression of personality. For instance, serotonin has been associated with impulsivity and aggression (Caccaro, 1998), dopamine with novelty seeking (Cloninger, 1998), and norepinephrine with social attachment (Cloninger, 1998). More broadly, and consistent with a psychosocial personality perspective, both norepinephrine and immune-system functioning have been shown to be associated with the level of conflict in intimate relationships (Kiecolt-Glaser et al., 1997). In a sample of older adults, self-esteem was shown to be related to neuroendrocrine functioning (Seeman et al, 1995). To complicate matters, Panksepp and Miller (1996) provided substantial evidence that there is a decline in the neurotransmitter systems with age. Thus, there is a great need for additional research to address how changes in neurophysiology are associated with different stages of psychosocial development.

At a more macrolevel, neurophysiological structure and function also play an important role in motivation, emotion, and personality functioning (Shepard, 1994). Moreover, all levels of brain systems are probably important for many aspects of behavior (e.g., MacLean's [1982] triune conceptualization of brain organization in terms reptilian, paleomammalian, neomammalian systems). However, for psychosocial approaches to personality, the most evolutionarily recent and advanced neocortex is perhaps most relevant (Zuckerman, 1991). In particular, the integrity of the frontal lobes appears to be critical for the expression of mature and responsible personality functioning (Shepard, 1994). This observation may stem, in part, from the fact that frontal-lobe functioning enables a critical psychological function referred to as working memory, which allows individuals to hold "on-line" representations of their environment and the actions of other individuals (Goldman-Rakic, 1991). These representations then allow one to process an ongoing experience with respect to future plans as well as past experiences. Clearly, the level of development of the frontal brain system will play an important role in the ability to develop a self-concept, plan

and engage in industrious activities, or accurately understand the intentions of an intimate partner.

At the same time, however, it is important not to lose sight of the fact that various brain regions do not function in isolation but rather work as parts of a unified system (Luria, 1980). For example, the status of the link between the limbic system (critical for motivation and emotion; Shepard, 1994) and the frontal lobes will influence the psychosocial stage of development. A disconnection between these regions will result in behavioral disinhibition and emotional lability (Lichter & Cummings, 2001). Moreover, the limbic system is critical to the acquisition of complex emotional behaviors and the maturation of its interconnections with frontal regions, a period that extends into early adulthood, and plays a critical role in the integration of cognition with emotion (Benes, 1994). As such, the ability of a person to enter a psychosocial stage of intimacy or generativity, for example, likely will depend on the status of interconnections between the limbic and frontal lobe systems.

In sum, both micro- and macrolevels of neurophysiology are associated with personality functioning not just at the level of basic traits but also in terms of more abstract levels of psychosocial functioning. Nonetheless, it is important to note that, whereas biology clearly influences personality functioning, it is just as likely that psychological experiences play a fundamental role in influencing biological systems (G. A. Miller, 1996). For instance, teaching emotional self-management skills has been shown to affect psychosocial functioning as well as autonomic recovery from stress in middle-school children (McCraty, Atkinson, Tomasino, Goelitz, & Mayrovitz, 1999).

It is worth noting that psychological constructs such as personality are likely to play an important role in understanding individual differences, and these differences cannot be reduced simply to the level of biology. Indeed, understanding of the relationship between biology and personality may be further enhanced by modeling both domains at the level of latent variables (MacCallum & Austin, 2000). Given that latent-variable modeling has been used to explore both behavior genetics (Plomin et al., 2003) and personality (Barnes, Murray, Patton, Bentler, & Anderson, 2000), it would be fruitful to test models that employ both biological and psychological variables. Not only would such models control for measurement error (Bentler, 1980), but good-fitting models could be examined across different age groups. In this way, the structural invariance of a model across ages could be examined, and lack of invariance would provide some support for the notion that biology and personality are related to one another in different ways at different ages. This type of finding would suggest that different processes may operate at different stages of psychosocial personality functioning.

CROSS-CULTURAL VALIDITY OF STAGE THEORIES OF PERSONALITY DEVELOPMENT

Whereas speculation abounds about the application of the preceding stage theories to other cultures, there has been less rigorous systematic empirical investigation from which to draw such conclusions. As noted previously, the core concepts of many theories, particularly those of Freud, Jung, and, to a lesser extent, Erikson, are difficult to operationalize and test empirically. This has led to a large body of theoretical and ethnographic literature on Freudian theory, and the Oedipus complex in particular (psychoanalytic anthropology; see, e.g., Gehrie, 1977), much of which was sparked by Malinowski's (1929/1951) *The Sexual Life of Savages* (*savage* being an accepted technical term during the era). Similarly, Jung's notions on myths and archetypes are rooted in his own qualitative observations of many different cultures. Again, whereas notions such as the collective unconscious elude empirical testing, Jung's theory of types has been examined with the Myers-Briggs Type Inventory, for which an entire journal, the *Journal of Psychological Type,* exists. However, the test is only loosely tied to Jung's theory, and a thorough review of such studies is beyond the scope of this chapter. Instead, this section will limit itself to the small body of contemporary empirical investigations of the validity of these theories in other cultures. Importantly, due to its impact on Freudian theory, the ethnographic-theoretical Malinowski debates will be noted briefly.

Eriksonian Stages

A number of studies simply have compared cultures across Eriksonian stages, on the assumption that the underlying stage framework is itself valid. In an early study, McClain (1975) found that teenagers from Munich, Germany, and Brussels, Belgium, and Anglo-American teenagers from Knoxville, Tennessee, showed greater resolution of the first six Eriksonian crises than did teenagers from France and Spain and African Americans from Knoxville. Across cultures, males showed greater autonomy and industry than females, a result that speaks as much to the generality of instrumental male gender roles as to Eriksonian stages. Wang and Viney (1996) found that Chinese and Australian primary- and secondary-school children showed comparable levels of trust and psychosocial maturity and concluded that Erikson's notion of rations between positive and negative poles in each

conflict was applicable to these two cultures. An earlier study indicated that within Australian culture itself, Anglo- and Greek Australian 9th and 11th graders appeared to be significantly more resolved with respect to the crises of later adolescence than Italian Australians (Rosenthal, Moore, & Taylor, 1983). However, only one study has directly assessed the validity of Erikson's stages themselves in another country.

Ochse and Plug (1986) constructed a scale assessing individual differences along subscales tapping the first seven Eriksonian stages (omitting the eighth, which was not represented in their sample) and examined a number of hypotheses across a wide age range (15 to 60) of Black and White (their labels) South Africans. Results were somewhat mixed with respect to the validity of Erikson's specific stages. Greater resolution on each stage subscale was associated with greater well-being in both Blacks and Whites when the age groups were collapsed, providing some general support for the scale's validity and Erikson's notion that the negotiation of psychosocial crises is important for adjustment. However, an exploratory factor analysis of the scale, which was carefully designed to sample from each Eriksonian stage, did not provide solid support for the existence of the stages themselves in either group of South Africans. In samples (collapsed across age), an initial general factor accounted for about half the variance, tapping "negative feelings about public image" in Whites and "feelings of inadequacy, no confidence" in Blacks (Ochse & Plug, 1986, p. 1245). Ochse and Plug also appear to have extracted seven factors for theoretical reasons, regardless of their eigenvalues, which are not reported. As a result, in the Black sample, the final three factors appear to have accounted for less than 1 percent of the variance, and two were uninterpretable. Only two factors clearly matched the stages: Intimacy versus Isolation was clearly defined in both samples, as was Generativity versus Stagnation in the Black sample. A more limited factor dealing with the positive aspects of Generativity was evident in the White sample. Ochse and Plug interpreted the general first factor as evidence of the overlap between stages. This is to be expected developmentally as each crisis is resolved and ego-integrated, and they argued that the lack of factors reflecting clearly defining childhood stages is the result of the fact that even the youngest members of the sample had already passed through these stages. Both interpretations seem reasonable, although the large communalities necessary for such a general first factor also could have been partly a function of the common response format of the scale, or some general underlying trait-driving item responses, rather than evidence of increasing personality integration with passage through stages.

Ochse & Plug's (1986) data did support their hypothesis of increasing statistical overlap (i.e., integration) between psychosocial stages already passed through, and the mean intercorrelation of all stage-related subscales tended to increase with increasing age groups for White women, reflecting theoretical increases in overall personality integration. This pattern did not hold for White men though, or for Black men or women. The study did replicate prior results in U.S. samples showing higher resolution of Intimacy versus Isolation for women (across ages). In addition, Well-being was associated with higher scores on the subscale reflecting the participant's current stage (e.g., the Intimacy–Well-Being correlation was highest in the 24 to 29 age group, and the Generativity–Well-Being correlation highest in the 25 to 39 age group) for Whites, but the pattern was weaker for Blacks. Thus, there is some support for Erikson's idea that one's current psychosocial crisis is most relevant to Well-Being for Whites but less so for Blacks. Other results were generally consistent with the theory, including that men scored higher on the Autonomy, Initiative, and Industry subscales, and Identity and Intimacy scores were significantly linked for women in their 20s. In general, Ochse and Plug's research supports the idea that prior psychosocial conflicts become more integrated into personality with age in White and Black South Africans. However, the results for Whites were more consistent, and only two of the first seven stages appeared empirically distinguishable in their sample.

Finally, a qualitative study by Chatterjee, Bailey, and Aronoff (2001) asked a group of 12 anthropologists and sociologists who were variously experts on Romanian, New Zealand, Indian, and U.S. cultures to evaluate the applicability of Erikson's stages to both mainstream and marginalized groups within each society. The results of these expert raters suggested that whereas the tasks of infancy and toddlerhood were generally universal, considerable cultural variation emerged after the early adolescent period. In nontechnological cultures and subcultures, entry into the world of work occurred earlier, and the development of self-esteem tended to be unresolved in marginalized subcultures (i.e., the Maori of New Zealand). The tasks of later adolescence also did not clearly characterize African American, Maori, and Indian Lotha and Santal cultures. However, the tasks characterizing early and middle adulthood appeared more universal. Old age was not a relevant stage for technologically unsophisticated cultures, whose members did not typically live past 60. These are interesting findings, and they are important in that they are based on a survey of knowledgeable experts. However, they do not represent direct sampling of the populations in these cultures, and should be understood accordingly.

Overall, extant cross-cultural research suggests some support for Erikson's stage of early adulthood; that is, Ochse & Plug's (1986) otherwise ambiguous factor analyses did reveal reliably an Intimacy-Isolation task across White and Black South Africans. Chatterjee and colleagues (2001) also agreed that such a stage was present in New Zealand, Romania, and Indian cultures and in subcultures within these societies. However, there is no clear evidence about the status of the childhood stages, middle and late adulthood, and old age, as Erikson posited them, in other cultures.

Levinson

Ross (1984) conducted a small-sample study on the validity of some of Levinson's stages (Early Adult Transition, Entering the Adult World, Age 30 Transition, Settling Down, and Midlife Transition) in middle-aged samples of Anglo- and Mexican American men; the latter had immigrated to the United States in their early 20s. Content analyses of taped biographical interviews by independent judges provided ratings of the degree to which elements of Levinson's stages were present for each sample. Both groups of men showed a strong family orientation, although this tended to come as early as the Early Adult Transition for the Mexican American men. Both groups also evidenced a life dream, an Age 30 Transition, niche building, advancement, and a Midlife transition. However, both groups reported the absence of a significant male mentor, an important element in Levinson's theory. Mexican American men showed little evidence of a specific occupational plan.

Ross was at a loss to explain the absence of mentors in the sample, but he interpreted the lack of an occupational dreams or aspirations in the Mexican American men to their more limited education (e.g., 7.3 years formal education versus 13.8 in the Anglo-American sample). Rather than a White, middle-class focus on the status and achievement perspective of work, Mexican American men tended to view work as a means to support their families. After starting families of their own, the Mexican American men also maintained stronger ties to their family of origin and extended family than the Anglo-American men. Both groups showed evidence of significant life transitions as a result of Levinson's marker events, and, not surprisingly, Mexican American men experienced their immigration as a very prominent transition, often sparked by desires of better work and/or family situations. In general, Ross's work supports the applicability of Levinson's stages in Mexican American men, with significant differences pertaining to the meaning of work and the age at which family becomes a primary focus.

Loevinger

Jane Loevinger's theory has been investigated empirically with her (1979) Sentence Completion Test (WU-SCT) in U.S. samples (e.g., Holt, 1980), but cross-cultural work has been scarce. In an early study, Snarey and Blasi (1980) found that Loevinger's stages of ego development were somewhat applicable to an Israeli population but that the WU-SCT tapped a number of culture-dependent constructs. The Israeli participants omitted several items that had no meaning or relevance, and Snarey and Blasi recommended that future cross-cultural researchers consider changing the WU-SCT stems to culture-relevant content when using the instrument in non-U.S. populations. In the only other published cross-cultural study on Loevinger's theory, Ravinder (1986) administered the unmodified WU-SCT to Indian and Australian college students. She found few omissions and no systematic patterns in omissions, suggesting that the sentence-completion stems were relevant at least to her samples. This may constitute at least vague evidence for the validity of the ego-development stages tapped by the test. Ravinder also found that Australian college students' modal ego development was in the Conscientious stage, whereas the modal stage for Indian students was Conscientious-Conformist, consistent with Loevinger's (1979) notion that ego development may be higher in groups of greater socioeconomic status (SES). In contrast, Loevinger (1976) estimated modal ego development (presumably in the United States) at the Conscientious-Conformist level. Therefore, Ravinder's (1986) results indicate either that Australians are more ego-developed than their U.S. counterparts, or, if one assumes the societies to be similar in gross sociopolitical aspects, perhaps Loevinger underestimated ego development in U.S. adults. In this respect, time-of-measurement (period) effects seem unlikely; ego development probably could not advance by a half stage at the population level between the appearance of Loevinger's (1976) book and Ravinder's (1986) study. However, Ravinder did find that most women in the Australian sample were at the Conscientious stage, whereas most men were at the Conscientious-Conformist stage.

Ravinder's (1986) and Snarey's and Blasi's (1980) results provide some support for the generalizability of Loevinger's theory to these cultures but shed no light on more complex issues such as how individuals actually progress through stages or whether they experience all social, emotional, and cognitive characteristics Loevinger posited for each stage. Furthermore, Snarey's and Blasi's (1980) observations indicate that the WU-SCT may need to be modified or refined for other cultures.

Freud

The most famous cross-cultural work in Freudian theory has been that of Bronislaw Malinowski (cf. 1929/1953), who lived among the Trobriand islanders (a tribe of aboriginal Australians) between 1916 and 1918. Based on copious notes and naturalistic observation, Malinowski concluded that the Oedipus complex was absent in Trobrianders because their society is matrilineal. He argued that the biological father plays a less central role because the male authority figure in child rearing is the mother's brother, and so no Oedipal conflicts arise: "The father is a beloved, benevolent friend" to the male child (Malinowski, 1927/1951, p. 10).

Malinowski's work was immediately attacked by Freudians. They argued that because an infant boy sleeps with his mother for his first two years of life and postpartum sex is prohibited during this time, the mother develops an eroticized attachment to the child, who, when his biological father replaces him in his mother's bed after two years, has ample reason to develop feelings of competition (cf. Wax, 2000). Wax (1990, 2000) has argued that Malinowski's own observations can be interpreted as evidence of an Oedipus complex, but that because his work was engagingly written and appealed to an audience beyond academicians, it became so popular as to be impervious to dissenting arguments and evidence. Wax (1990) also claimed that Malinowski's own childhood predisposed him in various ways to interpret his ethnographic data in a manner contradicting Oedipal theory. This debate is philosophically interesting but seems unresolvable because it is characterized mostly by hermeneutic debates about Freud's various expositions on the Oedipus complex and by alternative anthropological readings of ethnographic evidence. The interested reader is referred to Wax (1990, 2000) as a starting point for these issues.

Carroll (1978) made an attempt to test empirically a few relatively specific predictions germane to the Oedipus complex. His study is noteworthy primarily because it included a total of 51 different cultures, using ratings obtained from the Standard Cross Cultural Sample, a sociological database compiled by Murdock and White (1969). Specifically, Carroll hypothesized, based on Freudian theory, that greater father-son contact is associated with less chance of later homosexuality and greater superego development, that offspring sexual attachment to mother is inversely related to later homosexuality, and that the correlation between homosexuality and superego predicted by Freud (through some relatively detailed and convoluted reasoning) actually would be a function of a third variable, father-son contact.

Carroll interpreted several small to moderate one-tailed phi correlations as support for these hypotheses and concluded that Freud's notions about the development of homosexuality are relevant to the 51 cultures included in his analyses. However, he seems overly enthusiastic, given the magnitude of the correlations (e.g., highest in the .3s) and his methodology. Although psychoanalytic processes and constructs are difficult to operationalize in any circumstance, Carroll's choice of variables weakens his conclusions. For instance, the length of postpartum sexual abstinence in a society was used as an index of an offspring's sexual attachment to his mother because "it will be assumed here that a long post-partum sex taboo increases the probability that a mother will unconsciously seduce her son" (Carroll, 1978, p. 262). This assumption is tenuous because it was a post hoc piece of theory modification offered by initial critics of Malinowski and, therefore, deserves to be tested itself rather than taken for granted. Similarly, the aggregate level of superego within a society was operationalized by either the presence or the absence of an institutionalized police force. Clearly, this may represent different constructs than those reflected in the average superego development of a society. Although the use of a large, existing database precluded more precise operationalizations of these constructs, the variables used in this study render its results ambiguous. In the main, the status and meaning of Freud's developmental theory in other cultures has proven remarkably elusive to rigorous empirical inquiry.

Jung

Jungian theory similarly is devoid of rigorous empirical cross-cultural investigation, with the exception of the cross-cultural use of the Myers-Briggs Type Inventory, which has been validated in a Korean sample (Sim & Kim, 1993). As noted previously, the test is only vaguely related to Jungian type theory and not immediately relevant to Jung's stage theories.

At a general level, however, the cross-cultural applicability of analytical psychology is built into Jung's theory. Jung was fascinated by other cultures, and his notion of the collective unconscious entails a universal psychic substrate (the collective unconscious) to which all cultures are bound and from which arise various cultural manifestations of certain universal themes. These come mostly in the forms of *Myths* and *Symbols,* which, whereas they vary in style or manifest content, ultimately express common themes underlying all of humanity. Jung did see variations on universal archetypal themes as significant enough to warrant psychological distinctions between different groups of people. For him, individual expressions of human universals were largely determined by their social and cultural contexts (Jung, 1964). One of his

more sensational claims was that Jews could not understand non-Jewish Europeans without a full understanding of the history of non-Jewish Europeans. This led to further contention with Freud and sparked later claims of anti-Semitism (Rychlak, 1981).

Little attention has been paid specifically to the cross-cultural validity of Jung's developmental stages. Although because his broader theory is couched in terms of universality at fundamental levels of the individual and collective psyche, the applicability of his developmental stages to all people seems implicit. Some cultures probably facilitate Individuation better than others. For instance, Jung (1953) suggests that Roman Catholicism is more conducive than Protestantism to Individuation because it is richer in symbols. Symbols, in analytical psychology, connect the elements of consciousness with those of the unconscious more readily. Empirical investigations of Jung's developmental stages across cultures appear nonexistent, however. This is understandable, given that, like psychoanalysis, the stages of analytical psychology would be extremely difficult to operationalize and test rigorously.

Personality Development in the Context of Sociocultural Change

Although we have focused on the major developmental stage theory approaches to personality, there is a voluminous literature that has emerged in the last decade speaking to the general issue of personality stability and/or consistency and change and the mechanisms by which such change or lack thereof is accomplished (see Caspi & Roberts, 1999; Lachman & Bertrand, 2001; Roberts & Caspi, 2003; Srivastava, John, Gosling, & Potter, 2003), often conducted in the context of an emphasis on trait theory (i.e., the Big Five; see McCrae, 2002). Likewise, there has been increased interest in the intersection of what appear to be age-related changes in personality and historical change, as exemplified in the work of Avshalom Caspi and Glenn Elder (1986; see also Caspi & Bem, 1990; Elder, 1979; Kogan, 1990; Ryff et al., 2001), who compared two cohorts—children of the Oakland Growth sample (1920–1921 cohorts) and those of the Berkeley Guidance sample (1928–1929 cohorts)—in their respective adolescent years (the Great Depression of the 1930s) and again 30 years later. Elder concluded that the earlier the Depression occurred in the lives of boys, the more negative was its impact, whereas the effects of the Depression on girls were opposite. Thirty years later, especially for the father-deprived boys in the Berkeley sample, psychological health was greater. This appeared to be due in part to their experience in the military (World War II, Korea), which caused them to marry later (hence more emotional support) and go on to become college educated (G.I. bill). Caspi and Elder (1986) studied the persons in the Berkeley Guidance sample who were born in 1900 at age 30 and again at age 70 and found that having had more adaptive skills (being good problem solvers, being more emotionally healthy) predicted life satisfaction depending on social class. Stewart and Healy (1989) found that the impact of changing women's roles on women themselves was influenced by when such changes were experienced in the life cycle and by cohort membership. For example, older cohorts of women, whose traditional identities were already formed, were less affected by the women's movement. In contrast, younger cohorts of women, whose identities were still being formed felt more pressure to combine work and family. For the earlier-born cohorts, parental models were most influential in impacting identity development. Research speaking to the importance of cohort effects in adolescent personality development also has been conducted by Baltes and his colleagues (e.g., Baltes & Nesselroade, 1972).

Although these studies certainly do not represent all the published work on the intersection of personality and historical change, they call into question the necessary assumption of the universality of personality development posited by stage theorists, as do the preceding cross-cultural studies. Stage approaches to personality stand in contrast to a sociohistorical, contextual approach to personality development (see Lachman & Bertrand, 2001), which emphasizes the divergence over time of individuals with similar personality characteristics in response to divergent historical or idiosyncratic life event-specific choices and responses, as well as the differential selection of specific environmental contexts as a function of particular personality characteristics or personality styles (see Kogan, 1990; Neugarten, 1977).

PREDICTIONS REGARDING EVERYDAY BEHAVIOR

Family Life

Psychoanalytic theory, which views the elements of personality in the context of their relationship to one another (see discussion by McCrae & Costa, 2003), and its extension, object relations theory, have contributed to our understanding of the dynamics of family functioning. For example, Marsh (1998) discusses personality as one of many variables that influence how the family copes with the mental illness (and by implication, physical illness) of one of its members. In this respect, Marsh argues that special attention be placed on each family member's use of defense mechanisms. The nature and extent of the use of such defenses impact each individual's ability to cope with threats to one's sense of self as well as bring up issues regarding safety and vulnerability in the face of the illness or death (see Nadeau, 2001) of a family member. Analytic theory also frames the work of Hayslip and his colleagues in operationalizing the relationship between conscious and unconscious death fear (see Hayslip et al., 2002) and the work of Cicirelli in exploring the powerful role that personality might play in predicting fear of death (see Cicirelli, 2002), based upon terror management theory (Pyszczynski, Greenberg, & Solomon, 1999). In either respect, death as the ultimate threat to one's personal and social existence likely elicits varying degrees of denial, and, as such, denial is utilized to a greater extent; material that exists at the conscious level of awareness becomes less accessible (Hayslip et al., 2002).

In part based on projective test data, Neugarten (1977) has discussed the intrapsychic adjustments, which she termed *interiority*, that aging individuals make in withdrawing psychic energy from the outside world and reinvesting it to manage one's emotional life. Such changes have a Jungian flavor to them and are consistent with the current interest in the management of one's emotions and in spirituality in later life (see Magai, 2001; McFadden, 1996). In this respect, Vaillant (1977, 2002) has discussed the maturation of one's defenses with age, based on the distinction between mature (e.g., intellectualization, sublimation) and immature (e.g., projection, acting out) defenses. The regulation of anxiety via defenses is a function of ego processes.

Choosing a mate and/or mastering the crisis of intimacy versus isolation is central to early adulthood. Indeed, Erikson argues that to the extent that one's identity is securely defined, such choices can not be made if one's own identity is threatened. Moreover, questions of identity have been explored in the context of changing definitions of adolescence, termed *emerging adulthood*, elongating the process by which a viable identity can be achieved (see Arnett, 1994, 2000). Such an extension of this process of identity formation and stabilization is likely to make the task of intimacy versus isolation somewhat more problematic for younger cohorts, whose transition to adulthood has been redefined. Helson, Pals, and Solomon (1997) also discuss identity as a precursor of the choice of spouse among women, incorporating the interconnection between one's "inner space" (the capacity for reproduction) and its integration with other aspects of the self. As noted previously, identity is a central construct in Whitbourne and Connolly's (1999) process-oriented model of how individuals cope with the aging process. Consequently, one might expect that older persons would cope with disruptions in their family lives in the event of a divorce or the death of a spouse as a function of the extent to which their identity styles were predominantly accommodative or assimilative in nature. In an application of Marcia's work to death and dying, Lavoie and DeVries (2004) found among young adults a positive relationship between identity status (i.e., identity achievement) and death acceptance and contemplation.

Of recent interest is the Eriksonian construct of generativity, represented to a large extent over the last decade by the work of McAdams (2001), who discusses *parental generativity,* in nurturing and guiding children throughout their lives, and *cultural generativity,* where a meaningful symbol system, in terms of ideas or institutions, is created and passed along to the succeeding generation. McAdams (2001) not only develops a theoretical model that explains the development of generativity but also reviews research speaking not only to parental generativity but also to cultural and technical (see following) generativity.

Attachment theory has been utilized in a variety of interpersonal contexts to predict behavior and has been extended to late adolescence and early adulthood to understand not only emotional expressivity but also loneliness (see Kenny & Barton, 2003). Attachment theory also has been employed as a framework within which to understand how persons adjust to stressful family life events (i.e., the empty nest in adulthood; Hobdy & Hayslip, 1997; Mikulincer & Florian, 1998), becoming a parent (Alexander, Feeney, Hohaus, & Noller, 2001), and social support seeking (Simpson, Rholes, & Nelligan, 1992). In these respects, attachment style has been operationalized either via self-report scales or via clinical interviews. Attachment style is likely to be relevant to understanding responses to the renegotiation of one's relationship to another person or to the role of bereaved individual in the context of death (see Shaver & Tancredy, 2001), the transition to kindergarten or first grade, or even to the birth of a child (see Kenny & Barton, 2003). Personality constructs derived from attachment theory as well as both Jungian (e.g., in equating the mandala with a sense of readiness for death) and Eriksonian thought (in exploring the relationship between integrity, wisdom, and purpose in life; see, e.g., Reker, Peacock, & Wong, 1987) hold great promise in understanding the many adjustments dying persons and their families make at the end of life (see Lawton, 2000) in the context of the former's terminal illness, enabling persons not only to transcend pain, loss, and grief but also to reframe their feelings about life, death, and the afterlife in light of the personal and yet universal relationship to death established by millions of other individuals who have preceded them. In this respect, Waskowic and Chartier (2003) found widows and widowers who had been securely attached to a spouse to grieve more adaptively than did those who were insecurely attached.

School

Classical analytic theory, object relations theory, and attachment theory all hold promise in understanding the emotional and academic transitions that children make in the school environment. For example, Mayman (1968) has argued that affective quality, as derived from projective test data, as well as the manner in which one represents his or her relationships to others in terms of richness each differentially predict the capacity for intimacy, which also can be understood in terms of Eriksonian trust. Lewis (1999) uses attachment theory to predict school adjustment in the context of the child's relationship to a depressed mothering figure when the latter was younger. Such children are best described as insecurely attached and are likely to be either overly dependent upon or avoidant regarding the child's interactions with a teacher and are likely to be less socially competent in their interactions with peers. In this respect, Lewis also discusses the possibility that the temporal stability of attachment may be influenced by current parenting behaviors. Such stability is likely to be tested by other life transitions making demands, so to speak, on one's attachment style, such as forced relocation, divorce, or death (see preceding). Taking a strictly analytic perspective, Cramer and Gaul (1988) who studied children in the second and sixth grades, found children who experienced academic failure to utilize more primitive defenses (denial and projection), in contrast to those who experienced success, who used more mature defenses (identification). Such data also are consistent with the maturation of defenses associated with increased academic success.

Work and Retirement

As most of us spend a fair proportion of our lives engaging in work-related pursuits, it would not be surprising to observe that personality impacts our behavior in the context of work. Of course, as discussed previously, identity development both impacts and is impacted by issues at work. In this respect, Helson et al. (1997) discuss identity development as a prerequisite for vocational choice, and Hogan and Ones (1997) target conscientiousness, an outgrowth of superego development, as a predictor of job performance and of the degree to which one can adapt to the work demands of authority figures, wherein persons high in conscientiousness either are unable to resolve conflicts with supervisors or are stubborn, stingy, or dependent. By extension such characteristics, as well as difficulties in resolving the psychosocial crisis of trust-mistrust (see Hartup, 1983; Radke-Yarrow, Zahn, Wahxler, & Chapmen, 1983), may alienate one from peers at school or at work. McNulty, Hogan, and Bordeaux (2002) have conceptualized anger and hostility in the workplace in the context of the "belief that much social behavior is unconsciously motivated" (p. 405), meaning, that one is predisposed toward aggression via his or her psychological makeup, wherein the workplace simply becomes a place in which anger, aggression, and hostility are expressed toward others.

A unique approach to appreciating the relationship between personality and work in adulthood has been discussed by Helson and Stewart (1994), who focus upon the findings of Howard and Bray (1988), who studied managerial candidates over a 20-year period from their 20s onward. Although not framed in Eriksonian terms, these authors found drops in the Ambition factor score (as derived from a self-report measure of personality, the Edwards Personal Preference Schedule), which Helson and Stewart interpret as a function of the realization of the possibilities for promotion. Increases over time in Autonomy, with increases in hostility and decreases in the need for the friendship of others, also were found, which Helson and Stewart interpret in terms of Eriksonian generativity, wherein the salience of individual productivity is emphasized at the expense of nurturance. Continuing the Eriksonian tradition, in contrast to parental and cultural generativity, McAdams (2001) identifies technical generativity, wherein adults teach and model skills to those who need them, as in the case of the adult who serves as a mentor for a younger employee or an apprentice in need of specific training. Hobdy and Hayslip (1997) found attachment style to mediate adults' response to the loss of a job in midlife.

With regard to adjustment to retirement—to the extent that one feels he or she has personal control over events in one's life—the willingness and ability to revise one's identity as a worker and shift to that of a retiree predicts the extent to which retirement preparation is beneficial, the decision to retire, as well as, to a certain extent, retirement adjustment (Abel & Hayslip, 1986, 1987; Barnes-Farrell, 2003). Likewise, middle-aged and older adults who perceive that they have control over the decision to work report greater personal well-being (Heckhausen & Schulz, 1995). Barnes-Farrell (2003) suggests that work attachment reflects a preference for working versus retiring dependent upon the roles in which one is most heavily invested, as specifically reflected in the work of Adams and his colleagues (Adams, 1999; Adams, Presher, Beehr, & Lepisto, 2002). Whereas ideas such as Levinson's suggest a general orientation toward a preference for retirement with increased age, impacting the life structure, Barnes-Farrell (2003) notes that these parallels are somewhat imprecise and that such preferences are heavily influenced,

developmentally speaking, by other variables, such as marital and family values, market considerations, alternatives to working in retirement, and health. Thus, the decision to retire is best seen as an ongoing one, which may be made and remade several times during an individual's working life (see Sterns & Kaplan, 2003).

Leisure

There is some literature to support an interest in linking personality and leisure behavior. For example, Mannell and Kleiber (1997) discuss the relevance of analytic theory to leisure in the context of social forces that influence competitiveness, materialism, neuroticism, and intimacy, which in varying degrees are relevant to the pursuit of leisure in our culture. Likewise, needs for dominance and autonomy, as well as rigidity, all of which could have their origins in psychosexual development, have been associated with leisure interests (see Mannell & Kleiber, 1997). Interestingly, whereas Stebbins (2004) discusses the motivational origins of "serious leisure" (careerlike involvement in a hobby, volunteerism, or amateur activity), its apparent psychodynamic roots are ignored. Yet, serious leisure is defined as coexisting with one's identity, and it is this very centrality that differentiates it from other more casual forms of leisure involvement. Indeed, even casual leisure has been portrayed as serving a hedonistic function (Stebbins, 2001), which seems libidinal in character. Taking an analytic perspective, Kelly and Freysinger (2000) explain gender differences in leisure behavior in terms of the differential psychosexual experiences in early in life revolving around the identification with the same-sex parent for boys and girls, freeing the former to engage in play permitting more "freedom of movement" (p. 151). Other discussions of motivation for leisure (e.g., McCabe, 2000) allude to the relevance of psychodynamic theory in understanding leisure behavior, but there is a paucity of research on this issue.

Conclusions: Predicting Everyday Behavior

Especially with respect to issues of adulthood, it is probably fair to say that—with the exceptions of the applicability of Levinson's theory to the fields of work and retirement, the contribution of attachment theory to dealing with loss and life transitions in the most general sense, and the Eriksonian constructs of identity, generativity, and integrity—most older stage theories (i.e., Freud, Jung, in part because the scientific zeitgeist has shifted away from analytic theory to either trait or contextual models of personality; for discussions, see Lachman & Bertrand, 2001; Ryff et al., 2001) have lost their appeal as models within which to conceptualize personality development, especially in a life-span context (see also Havighurst, 1973). In this context, it is fair to say that it is with regard to specific constructs derived from a theory, rather than the theory per se, that informs us in this manner.

In light of (1) the attention paid to individual differences and sociocultural change/cohort effects in developmental change and the contextual and life-event influences on adjustment across the life span, all of which are consistent with the life-span tradition (see Baltes, 1997; Parke, Ornstein, Reiser, & Zahn-Waxler, 1994); (2) the impact of the social cognitive-behavioral tradition emphasizing the appraisal of life events and the development of coping mechanisms (see Bandura, 2001; Clark & Steer, 1996; Mischel, 1999; Rachman, 1997 for reviews) as key elements in understanding personality; (3) the ease with which constructs derived from trait theory can be operationalized (see McCrae, 2002), leading to a tremendous amount of research over the last decade exploring the consistency of personality in the context of trait models; and (4) the extent of the developmental nature per se of those constructs and associated behaviors deemed to be relevant to prediction via stage theory, it remains to be seen what value stage models of personality will continue to have in the prediction of everyday behaviors.

REFERENCES

Abel, B., & Hayslip, B. (1986). Locus of control and adjustment to retirement. *Journal of Psychology, 120,* 479–488.

Abel, B., & Hayslip, B. (1987). Locus of control and retirement preparation. *Journal of Gerontology, 42,* 165–167.

Adams, G. A. (1999). Career-related variables and retirement age: An extension of Beehr's model. *Journal of Vocational Behavior, 55,* 221–235.

Adams, G. A., & Beehr, T. A. (2003). *Retirement: Reasons, processes, and results.* New York: Springer.

Adams, G. A., Presher, J., Beehr, R. A., & Lepisto, L. (2002). Applying work-role attachment theory to retirement decision making. *International Journal of Aging and Human Development, 54,* 125–137.

Ainsworth, M. D. (1989). Attachments beyond infancy. *American Psychologist, 44,* 709–716.

Ainsworth, M. D., Blehar, M. C., Waters, E., & Wall, S. (1978). *Patterns of attachment: A psychological study of the strange situation.* Hillsdale, NJ: Erlbaum.

Alexander, R., Feeney, J., Hohaus, L., & Noller, P. (2001). Attachment style and coping resources as predictors of coping strategies in the transition to parenthood. *Personal Relationships, 8,* 137–152.

Arnett, J. J. (1994). Are college students adults? Their conceptions of the transition to adulthood. *Journal of Adult Development, 1,* 213–224.

Arnett, J. J. (2000). Emerging adulthood: A theory of development from the late teens through the twenties. *American Psychologist, 55,* 469–480.

Baltes, P. B. (1968). Longitudinal and cross-sectional sequences in the study of age and generation effects. *Human Development, 11,* 145–171.

Baltes, P. B. (1997). On the incomplete architecture of human ontogeny. *American Psychologist, 52,* 366–379.

Baltes, P. B., & Nesselroade, J. R. (1972). Cultural change and adolescent personality development. *Developmental Psychology, 7,* 244–256.

Baltes, P. B., Reese, H. W., & Nesselroade, J. R. (1977). *Life-span developmental psychology: Introduction to research methods.* Hillsdale, NJ: Erlbaum.

Baltes, P. B., & Smith, J. (1990). Toward a psychology of wisdom and its ontogenesis. In R. J. Sternberg (Ed.), *Wisdom: Its nature, origins, and development* (pp. 89–120). New York: Cambridge University Press.

Baltes, P. B., & Staudinger, U. (1993). The search for a psychology of wisdom. *Current Directions in Psychological Science, 3,* 75–80.

Bandura, A. (2001). Social cognitive theory: An agentic perspective. *Annual Review of Psychology, 52,* 1–26.

Barnes, G. E., Murray, R. P., Patton, D., Bentler, P. M., & Anderson, R. E. (2000). *The addiction prone personality: Longitudinal research in the social sciences.* New York: Plenum Publishers.

Barnes-Farrell, J. L. (2003). Beyond health and wealth: Attitudinal and other influences on retirement decision making. In G. Adams & T. Beehr (Eds.), *Retirement: Reasons, processes, and results* (pp. 159–187). New York: Springer.

Benes, F. (1994). Development of the cortical limbic system. In G. Dawson & K. Fischer (Eds.), *Human behavior and the developing brain* (pp. 176–206). New York: Guilford Press.

Bentler, P. M. (1980). Multivariate analysis with latent variables: Causal modeling. *Annual Review of Psychology, 31,* 419–456.

Bentler, P. M. (1995). *EQS structural equations program manual.* Encino, CA: Multivariate Software.

Bergeman, C. S., Neiderhiser, J. M., Pedersen N. L., & Plomin, R. (2001). Genetic and environmental influences on social support in later life: A longitudinal analysis. *International Journal of Aging and Human Development, 53,* 107–135.

Bowlby, J. (1958). The nature of the child's tie to his mother. *International Journal of Psychoanalysis, 39,* 350–373.

Bowlby, J. (1969). *Attachment and loss: Vol. 1. Attachment.* New York: Basic Books.

Brody, N. (1994). +5 or −5: Continuity and change in personal dispositions. In T. F. Heatherton & J. L. Weinberger (Eds.), *Can personality change?* (pp. 59–82). Washington, DC: American Psychological Association.

Buhler, C. (1982). Meaningfulness of the biographical approach. In L. R. Allman & D. Jaffe (Eds.), *Readings in adult psychology: Contemporary perspectives* (pp. 30–37). New York: Harper & Row.

Bybee, J., & Wells, Y. (2003). The development of possible selves during adulthood. In J. Demick & C. Andreoletti (Eds.), *Handbook of adult development* (pp. 257–270). New York: Kluwer.

Caccaro, E. F. (1998). Neurotransmitter function in personality disorders. In K. R. Silk (Ed.), *The biology of personality disorders* (pp. 1–26). Washington, DC: American Psychiatric Press.

Cadorate, R. J., Yates, W. R., Troughton, E., Woodward, G, & Stewart, M. A. (1995). Genetic-environmental interaction in the genesis of aggressivity and conduct disorders. *Archives of General Psychiatry, 52,* 916–924.

Carroll, M. P. (1978). Freud on homosexuality and super-ego: Some cross-cultural tests. *Behavioral Science Research, 4,* 255–271.

Caspi, A., & Bem, D. (1990). Personality continuity and change across the life course. In L. A. Pervin (Ed.), *Handbook of personality: Theory and research* (pp. 549–577). New York: Guilford Press.

Caspi, A., & Elder, G. (1986). Life satisfaction in old age: Linking social psychology and history. *Psychology and Aging, 1,* 18–26.

Caspi, A., & Roberts, B. W. (1999). Personality continuity and change across the life course. In L. A. Pervin & O. P. John (Eds.), *Handbook of personality: Theory and research* (2nd ed., pp. 300–326). New York: Guilford Press.

Chatterjee, P., Bailey, D., & Aronoff, N. (2001). Adolescence and old age in twelve communities. *Journal of Sociology and Social Welfare, 28,* 121–159.

Cicirelli, V. (2002). Fear of death in older adults: Predictions from terror management theory. *Journal of Gerontology: Psychological Sciences, 57*(B), 358–366.

Clark, D., & Steer, R. (1996). Empirical status of the cognitive model of anxiety and depression. In P. Salkovskis (Ed.), *Frontiers of cognitive therapy* (pp. 75–96). New York: Guilford Press.

Clayton, V. (1975). Erikson's theory of human development as it applies to the aged. Wisdom as contraindicative cognition. *Human Development, 18,* 119–128.

Cloninger, C. R. (2003). Completing the psychological architecture of human personality development: Temperament, character, and coherence. In D. M. Staudinger & U. Lindenberger (Eds.), *Understanding human developmental lifespan psychology in exchange with other disciplines* (pp. 159–182). Dodrecht, Netherlands: Kluwer.

Cloninger, R. C. (1998). The genetics and psychobiology of the seven-factor model of personality. In K. R. Silk (Ed.), *Biology of personality disorders* (pp. 63–92). Washington, DC: American Psychiatric Press.

Coccaro, E. F. (1998). Neurotransmitter function in personality disorders. In K. R. Silk (Ed.), *Biology of personality disorders* (pp. 1–26). Washington, DC: American Psychiatric Press.

Coleman, P., & Watson, A. (2000). Infant attachment as a dynamic system. *Human Development, 43,* 295–313.

Costa, P. T., & McCrae, R. R. (1994). Set like plaster? Evidence for the stability of adult personality. In T. F. Heatherton & J. L. Weinberger (Eds.), *Can personality change?* (pp. 21–40). Washington, DC: American Psychological Association.

Cramer, P., & Gaul, R. (1988). The effects of success and failure on children's use of defense mechanisms. *Journal of Personality, 56,* 729–742.

Crittenden, P. M. (1997). The effect of early relationship experiences on relationships in adulthood. In S. Duck (Ed.), *Handbook of personal relationships* (pp. 99–119). Chichester, UK: Wiley.

Demick, J., & Andreoletti, C. (2003). *Handbook of adult development.* New York: Kluwer.

Ebstein, R. P., Benjamin, J., & Belmaker, R. H. (1998). Behavior genetics, genomics, and personality. In R. Plomin, J. C. Defries, I. W. Craig, & P. McGuffin (Eds.), *Behavioral genetics in the postgenomic era* (pp. 363–442). Washington, DC: American Psychological Association.

Elder, G. H. (1979). Historical change in life patterns and personality. In P. Baltes & O. Brim (Eds.), *Life span development and behavior* (Vol. 2, pp. 118–161). New York: Academic Press.

Elder, G. H. (1986). Military times and turning points in men's lives. *Developmental Psychology, 22,* 233–245.

Elder, G. H. (1979). Historical change in life patterns and personality. In P. Baltes & O. Brim (Eds.), *Life span developmental and behavior* (V. 2) (pp. 118–161). New York: Academic Press.

Eley, T. C. (1997). General genes: A new theme in developmental psychopathology. *Current Directions in Psychological Science, 6,* 90–95.

Erikson, E. H. (1959). Identity and the life cycle. *Psychological Issues, 1*(1).

Erikson, E. H. (1963). *Childhood and society* (2nd ed.). New York: Norton.

Erikson, E. H. (1980). *Identity and the life cycle.* New York: Norton.

Fairbairn, W. R. D. (1954). *An object-relations theory of personality.* New York: Basic Books.

Fisher, S., & Greenberg, R. P. (1977). *The scientific credibility of Freud's theories and therapy.* New York: Basic Books.

Freud, S. (1964a). New introductory lectures on psychoanalysis. In J. Strachey (Ed. & Trans.), *The standard edition of the complete psychological works of Sigmund Freud* (Vol. 22). London: Hogarth. (Original work published 1933)

Freud, S. (1964b). An outline of psycho-analysis. In J. Strachey (Ed. & Trans.), *The standard edition of the complete psychological works of Sigmund Freud* (Vol. 23). London: Hogarth. (Original work published 1940)

Gehrie, M. (1977). Psychoanalytic anthropology: A brief review of the state of the art. *American Behavioral Scientist, 20,* 201–209.

Gilligan, C. (1982). *In a different voice: Psychological theory and women's development.* Cambridge, MA: Harvard University Press.

Goldman-Rakic, P. S. (1991). Prefrontal cortical dysfunction in schizophrenia: The relevance of working memory. In B. J. Carroll & J. E. Barrett (Eds.), *Psychopathology and the brain* (pp. 1–23). New York: Raven Press.

Gould, R. (1978). *Transformations: Growth and change in adult life.* New York: Simon & Schuster.

Gould, R. (1980). Transformational tasks in adulthood. In National Institute of Mental Health (Ed.) *The course of life: Vol. 3. Adulthood and aging process* (pp. 55–90). Bethesda, MD: National Institute of Mental Health.

Gould, R. (1980b). Transformations in mid-life. New York *University Education Quarterly, 10,* 2–9.

Hall, C. S. (1954). *A primer of Freudian psychology.* New York: World.

Hall, C. S., & Lindzey, G. (1978). *Theories of personality.* New York: Wiley.

Harris, R. L., Elliot, A. M., & Holmes, D. S. (1986). The timing of psychosocial transitions and changes in women's lives: An examination of women aged 45 to 60. *Journal of Personality and Social Psychology, 51,* 409–416.

Hartup, R. (1983). Peer relations. In P. Mussen (Ed.), *Handbook of child psychology: Vol. 4* (pp. 104–195). New York: Wiley.

Havighurst, R. (1972). *Developmental tasks and education.* New York: David McKay.

Havighurst, R. (1973). History of developmental psychology: Socialization and personality development through the life span. In P. Baltes & K. Schaie (Eds.), *Life span developmental psychology: Personality and socialization* (pp. 1–25). New York: Academic Press.

Hayslip, B. (2003). Death denial: Hiding and camouflaging death. In C. D. Bryant (Ed.), *Handbook of death and dying* (Vol. 1, pp. 34–42). Thousand Oaks, CA: Sage.

Hayslip, B., Guarnaccia, C., Radika, L., & Servaty, H. (2002). Death anxiety: An empirical test of a blended self-report and projective measurement model. *Omega: Journal of Death and Dying, 44,* 277–294.

Hayslip, B., & Panek, P. (2002). *Adult development and aging.* Melbourne, FL: Krieger.

Hayslip, B., Panek, P., and Stoner, S. (1990). Cohort differences in Hand Test performance: A time lagged analysis. *Journal of Personality Assessment, 54,* 704–710.

Hazan, C., & Shaver, P. R. (1987). Romantic love conceptualized as an attachment process. *Journal of Personality and Social Psychology, 52,* 511–524.

Heatherton, T. F., & Weinberger, J. L. (Eds.). (1994). *Can personality change?* Washington, DC: American Psychological Association.

Heckhausen, J., & Schulz, R. (1995). A life span theory of control. *Psychological Review, 102,* 284–304.

Helson, R., Pals, J., & Solomon, M. (1997). Is there adult development distinctive to women? In R. Hogan, J. Johnson, & S. Briggs (Eds.), *Handbook of personality psychology* (pp. 293–317). San Diego, CA: Academic Press.

Helson, R., & Stewart, A. (1994). Personality change in adulthood. In T. F. Heatherton & J. L. Weinberger (Eds.), *Can personality change?* (pp. 201–225). Washington, DC: American Psychological Association.

Hetherington, E. M., & Baltes, P. B. (1988). Child psychology and life span development. In E. M. Hetherington, R. M. Lerner, & M. Perlmutter (Eds.), *Child development in life span perspective* (pp. 1–19). Hillsdale, NJ: Erlbaum.

Hobdy, J., & Hayslip, B. (1997, August). *Attachment style and adjustment to life events in adulthood.* Paper presented at the annual convention of the American Psychological Association, Chicago, IL.

Hobdy, J., Hayslip, B., Kaminski, P., & York, C. *The role of adult attachment style in coping with life events.* Manuscript under review for publication.

Hogan, J., & Ones, D. (1997). Conscientiousness and integrity at work. In R. Hogan, J. Johnson, & S. Briggs (Eds.), *Handbook of personality psychology* (pp. 849–870). San Diego, CA: Academic Press.

Holt, R. R. (1980). Loevinger's measure of ego development: Reliability and national norms for male and female short forms. *Journal of Personality and Social Psychology, 39,* 909–920.

Hooker, K. (2002). New directions for research in personality and aging: A comprehensive model for linking, level, structure, and processes. *Journal of Research in Personality, 36,* 318–334.

Hooker, K., & McAdams, D. P. (2003). The psychological construction of the life span. In J. Birren & K. Schaie (Eds.), *Handbook of the psychology of aging* (pp. 594–618). New York: Van Nostrand Reinhold.

Horney, K. (1967). *Feminine psychology.* New York: Norton.

Howard, A., & Bray, D. (1988). *Managerial lives in transition: Advancing age and changing times.* New York: Guilford Press.

Hunt, J. M. (1979). Psychological development: Early experience. *Annual Review of Psychology, 30,* 103–143.

Hy, L. H., & Loevinger, J. (1996). *Measuring ego development* (2nd ed.). Hillsdale, NJ: Erlbaum.

Jung, C. J. (1953). Psychology and alchemy. In H. Read, M. Fordham, & G. Adler (Eds.), *The collected works of C. G. Jung* (Vol. 12). New York: Pantheon.

Jung, C. J. (1954). The development of the personality. In H. Read, M. Fordham, & G. Adler (Eds.), *The collected works of C. G. Jung* (Vol. 17). New York: Pantheon.

Jung, C. J. (1960). The structure and dynamics of the psyche. In H. Read, M. Fordham, & G. Adler (Eds.), *The collected works of C. G. Jung* (Vol. 8). New York: Pantheon.

Jung, C. J. (1964). Civilization in transition. In H. Read, M. Fordham, & G. Adler (Eds.), *The collected works of C. G. Jung* (Vol. 10). New York: Pantheon.

Kelly, J. R., & Freysinger, V. J. (2000). *21st century leisure: Current issues.* Boston: Allyn & Bacon.

Kenny, M. E., & Barton, C. E. (2003). Attachment theory and research. In J. Demick & C. Andreoletti (Eds.), *Handbook of adult development* (pp. 371–389). New York: Kluwer.

Kernberg, O. F. (1976). *Object relations theory and clinical psychoanalysis.* New York: Aronson.

Kiecolt-Glaser, J. K., Glaser, R., Cacioppo, J. T., MacCallum, R. C., Snydersmith, M., Kim, C., et al. (1997). Marital conflict in older adults: Endocrinological and immunological correlates. *Psychosomatic Medicine, 59,* 339–3349.

Kline, P. (1972). *Fact and fantasy in Freudian theory.* London: Methuen.

Kogan, N. (1990). Personality and aging. In J. E. Birren & K. W. Schaie (Eds.), *Handbook of the psychology of aging* (pp. 330–346). New York: Academic Press.

Kuhn, T. S. (1962). *The structure of scientific revolutions.* Chicago: University of Chicago Press.

Labouvie-Vief, G., & Diehl, M. (1999). Self and personality development. In J. C. Cavanaugh & S. K. Whitbourne (Eds.), *Gerontology: An interdisciplinary perspective* (pp. 238–268). New York: Oxford University Press.

Lachman, M. E., & Bertrand, R. M. (2001). Personality and the self in midlife. In M. E. Lachman (Ed.), *Handbook of midlife development* (pp. 279–309). New York: Wiley.

Langer, J. (1969). *Theories of development.* New York: Holt, Reinhart, and Winston.

Lavoie, J., & DeVries, B. (2004). Identity and death: An empirical investigation. *Omega, 48,* 223–243.

Lawton, M. P. (2000). *The end of life: Scientific and social issues.* New York: Springer.

Lerner, R. M. (2002). *Concepts and theories of human development.* Mahwah, NJ: Erlbaum.

Lesch, K. P. (2003). Neuroticism and serotonin: A developmental genetic perspective. In R. Plomin, J. C. Defries, I. W. Craig, & P. McGuffin (Eds.), *Behavioral genetics in the postgenomic era* (pp. 389–424). Washington, DC: American Psychological Association.

Levinson, D. J. (1978). *The seasons of a man's life.* New York: Knopf.

Levinson, D. J. (1979). Adult development—Or what? *Contemporary Psychology, 24,* 727.

Levinson, D. J. (1986). A conception of adult development. *American Psychologist, 41,* 3–13.

Levinson, D. J., & Levinson, J. (1996). *The seasons of a woman's life.* New York: Ballantine.

Lewis, M. (1999). On the development of personality. In L. A. Pervin & O. P. John (Eds.), *Handbook of personality theory and research* (pp. 327–346). New York: Guilford Press.

Lichter, D. G., & Cummings, J. L. (2001). *Frontal-subcortical circuits in psychiatric and neurological disorders.* New York: Guilford Press.

Loevinger, J. (1976). *Ego development.* San Francisco: Jossey-Bass.

Loevinger, J. (1979). Construct validity of the sentence completion test of ego development. *Applied Psychological Measurement, 3,* 281–311.

Logan, R. (1986). A reconceptualization of Erikson's theory: A repetition of existential and instrumental themes. *Human Development, 29,* 125–136.

Luria, A. R. (1980). *Higher cortical function in man* (2nd ed.). New York: Basic Books.

MacCallum, R. C., & Austin, J. (2000). Applications of structural equation modeling in psychological research. *Annual Review of Psychology, 51,* 201–226.

MacLean, P. D. (1982). On the origin and progressive evolution of the triune brain. In E. Armstrong & D. Falk (Eds.), *Primate brain evolution: Methods and concepts* (pp. 291–316). New York: Plenum Press.

Maddi, S. R. (1989). *Personality theories: A comparative analysis* (5th ed.). Chicago: Dorsey.

Maddi, S. R. (1996). *Personality theories: A comparative analysis.* Pacific Grove, CA: Brooks/Cole.

Magai, C. (2001). Emotions over the life span. In J. Birren & K. W. Schaie (Eds.), *Handbook of the psychology of aging* (pp. 399–426). San Diego, CA: Academic Press.

Malinowski, B. (1951). *Sex and repression in savage society.* New York: Humanities Press. (Original work published 1927)

Malinowski, B. (1953). *The sexual life of savages.* London: Routledge and Kegan Paul. (Original work published 1929)

Mannell, R. C., & Kleiber, D. A. (1997). *A social psychology of leisure.* State College, PA: Venture.

Marcia, J. E. (1967). Ego identity status: Relationship to change in self esteem, general adjustment, and authoritarianism. *Journal of Personality, 1,* 118–133.

Marcia, J. E. (1999). Representational thought in age identity, psychotherapy, and psychosocial developmental theory. In I. E. Sigel (Ed.), *Development of mental representation: Theories and applications* (pp. 234–254). Mahwah, NJ: Erlbaum.

Markus, J. R., & Herzog, A. R. (1992). The role of self concept in aging. *Annual Review of Gerontology and Geriatrics, 11,* 111–143.

Marsh, G. (1998). *Serious mental illness in the family.* New York: Wiley.

Mayman, H. (1968). Early memories and character structure. *Journal of Projective Techniques and Personality Assessment, 32,* 303–316.

McAdams, D. (1987). A life-story model of identity. In R. Hogan & W. Jones (Eds.), *Perspectives on personality* (Vol. 2, pp. 14–50). Greenwich, CT: JAI Press.

McAdams, D., & de St. Aubin, E. (1998). *Generativity and adult development: How and why we care for the next generation.* Washington, DC: American Psychological Association.

McAdams, D. P. (2001). Generativity in midlife. In M. E. Lachman (Ed.), *Handbook of midlife development* (pp. 395–446). New York: Wiley.

McCabe, S. (2000). The problem of motivation in understanding the demand for leisure day visits. In A. Woodside, G. Crouch, J. Mazanec, M. Oppermann, & M. Sakai (Eds.), *Consumer psychology of tourism, hospitality, and leisure* (pp. 211–226). Cambridge, MA: CABI Publishing.

McClain, E. W. (1975). An Eriksonian cross-cultural study of adolescent development. *Adolescence, 10,* 527–541.

McCrae, R. R. (2002). The maturation of personality psychology: Adult personality development and psychological well being. *Journal of Research in Personality, 36,* 307–317.

McCrae, R. R., & Costa, P. T. (1990). *Personality in adulthood.* New York: Guilford Press.

McCrae, R. R., & Costa, P. T. (2003). *Personality in adulthood* (2nd ed.). New York: Guilford Press.

McCraty, R., Atkinson, M., Tomasino, D., Goelitz, J., & Mayrovitz, H. N. (1999). The impact of an emotional self-management skills course on psychosocial functioning and autonomic recovery to stress in middle school children. *Integrative Physiological and Behavioral Science, 34,* 246–268.

McFadden, S. H. (1996). Spirituality and aging. In J. Birren & K. W. Schaie (Eds.), *Handbook of the psychology of aging* (pp. 162–180). San Diego, CA: Academic Press.

McGuire, S., Manke, B., Saudino, K. J., Reiss, D., Hetherington, E. M., & Plomin, R. (1999). Perceived competence and self-worth during adolescence: A longitudinal behavioral genetic study. *Child Development, 70,* 1283–1296.

McNulty, J. L., Hogan, R., & Bordeaux, C. R. (2002). Anger, hostility, and violence in the workplace. In J. C. Thomas & M. Hersen (Eds.), *Handbook of mental health in the workplace* (pp. 401–412). Thousand Oaks, CA: Sage.

Mikulincer, M., & Vlorian, V. (1998). The relationships between adult attachment styles and emotional and cognitive reactions to life events. In J. A. Simpson & W. S. Rholes (Eds.), *Attachment theory in close relationships* (pp. 24–36). New York: Guilford Press.

Miller, G. A. (1996). How we think about cognition, emotion and biology in psychopathology. *Psychophysiology, 33,* 615–628.

Miller, P. H. (2002). *Theories of developmental psychology* (4th ed.). New York: Worth.

Mischel, W. (1999). Personality coherence and dispositions in a cognitive-affective personality system (CAPS) approach. In D. Cervone & Y. Shoda (Eds.), *The coherence of personality: Social-cognitive bases of consistency, variability, and organization* (pp. 37–60). New York: Guilford Press.

Mroczek, D. K., & Almeida, D. M. (2004). The effect of daily stress, personality, and age on daily negative affect. *Journal of Personality, 72,* 355–378.

Murdock, G. P., & White, D. W. (1969). Standard cross-cultural sample. *Ethnology, 8,* 329–369.

Nadeau, J. W. (2001). Meaning making in family bereavement: A family systems approach. In M. S. Stroebe, R. O. Hansson, W. Stroebe, & H. Schut (Eds.), *Handbook of bereavement research* (pp. 329–348). Washington, DC: American Psychological Association.

Nelson, E. A., & Dannefer, D. (1992). Aged heterogeneity: Fact or fiction? The fate of diversity in gerontological research. *Gerontologist, 32,* 17–23.

Neugarten, B. L. (1977). Personality and aging. In J. E. Birren & K. W. Schaie (Eds.), *Handbook of the psychology of aging* (pp. 626–649). New York: Academic Press.

Ochse, R., & Plug, C. (1986). Cross-cultural investigation of the validity of Erikson's theory of personality development. *Journal of Personality and Social Psychology, 50,* 1240–1252.

Oerter, R. (1986). Developmental tasks through the life span: A new approach to an old concept. In P. Baltes, D. Featherman, & R. Leiner (Eds.), *Life-span development and behavior* (Vol. 7, pp. 233–271). Hillsdale, NJ: Erlbaum.

Pankepp, J., & Miller, A. (1996). Emotions and the aging brain: Regrets and remedies. In M. Carol & S. H. McFadder (Eds.), *Handbook of emotion, adult development, and aging* (pp. 3–26). San Diego, CA: Academic Press.

Parke, R. D., Ornstein, P. A., Reiser, J. J., & Zahn-Waxler, C. (1994). The past as prologue: An overview of a century of developmental psychology. In R. D. Park, P. A. Ornstein, J. J. Reiser, & C. Zahn-Waxler (Eds.), *A century of developmental psychology* (pp. 1–72). Washington, DC: American Psychological Association.

Peck, R. C. (1968). Psychological developments in the second half of life. In B. L. Neugarten (Ed.), *Middle age and aging* (pp. 44–49). Chicago: University of Chicago Press.

Plomin, R., Defries, J. C., Craig, I. W., & McGuffin, P. (2003). *Behavioral genetics in the postgenomic era.* Washington, DC: American Psychological Association.

Pyszczynski, T., Greenberg, J., & Solomon, S. (1999). A dual-process model of defense against conscious and unconscious death-related thoughts: An extension of Terror Management Theory. *Psychological Review, 106,* 835–845.

Rachman, S. (1997). The evolution of cognitive behavior therapy. In D. Clark & C. Fairburn (Eds.), *Science and practice of cognitive behaviour therapy* (pp. 3–26). Oxford, UK: Oxford University Press.

Radke-Yarrow, M., Zahn, C., Wahxler, D., & Chapmen, M. (1983). Children's prosocial dispositions and behavior. In P. Mussen (Ed.), *Handbook of child psychology* (Vol. 4, pp. 469–546). New York: Wiley.

Ravidner, S. (1986). Loevinger's sentence completion test of ego development: A useful tool for cross-cultural researchers. *International Journal of Psychology, 21,* 679–684.

Reinke, B. J., Holmes, D. S., & Harris, R. L. (1985). The timing of psychosocial changes in women's lives: The years 25 to 45. *Journal of Personality and Social Psychology, 48,* 1353–1364.

Reker, G. T., Peacock, E. J., & Wong, T. P. (1987). Meaning and purpose in life: A life span investigation. *Journal of Gerontology, 42,* 44–49.

Riegel, K. (1976). The dialectics of human development. *American Psychologist, 31,* 689–700.

Roberts, B. R., & Caspi, A. (2003). The cumulative continuity model of personality development: Striking a balance between continuity and change in personality traits across the life course. In D. M. Staudinger & U. Lindenberger (Eds.), *Understanding human developmental lifespan psychology in exchange with other disciplines* (pp.183–214). Dodrecht, Netherlands: Kluwer.

Roberts, B. R., & DelVichio, W. F. (2000). The rank order consistency of personality from childhood to old age: A quantitative review of longitudinal studies. *Psychological Bulletin, 126,* 3–25.

Roberts, P., & Newton, P. M. (1987). Levinsonian studies of women's adult development. *Psychology and Aging, 12,* 154–163.

Rosenthal, D. A., Moore, S. M., & Taylor M. J. (1983). Ethnicity and adjustment: A study of the self image of Anglo, Greek, and Italian Australians. *Journal of Youth and Adolescence, 12,*117–135.

Ross, D. B. (1984). A cross-cultural comparison of adult development. *The Personnel and Guidance Journal, 62,* 418–421.

Rowe, D. C. (2003). Assessing genotype-environment interactions and correlations in the postgenomic era. In R. Plomin, J. C. Defries, I. W. Craig, & P. McGuffin (Eds.), *Behavioral genetics in the postgenomic era* (pp. 71–86). Washington, DC: American Psychological Association.

Rowe, D. C., Jacobson, J. C., & Van den Oord, E. J. C. D. (1999). Genetic and environmental influences on vocabulary IQ: Parental education as a moderator. *Child Development, 70,* 1151–1162.

Runyan, W. M. (1988). A historical and conceptual background to psychohistory. In W. M. Runyan (Ed.), *Psychology and historical interpretation* (pp. 3–60). New York: Oxford University Press.

Ruth, J., & Coleman, P. (1996). Personality and aging. Coping and the management of the self in later life. In J. E. Birren & K. W. Schaie (Eds.), *Handbook of the psychology of aging* (pp. 308–322). San Diego, CA: Academic Press.

Rychlak, J. F. (1981). *Introduction to personality and psychotherapy: A theory construction approach* (2nd ed.). Dallas, TX: Houghton Mifflin.

Ryff, C. D., Kwan, C., & Singer, B. H. (2001). Personality and aging: Flourishing agenda and future challenges. In J. E. Birren

& K. W. Schaie (Eds.), *Handbook of the psychology of aging* (5th ed., pp. 477–499).

Schaie, K. W. (1965). A general model for the study of developmental problems. *Psychological Bulletin, 64,* 92–107.

Scott, J. P. (1962). Critical periods in behavioral development. *Science, 138,* 949–958.

Seeman, T. E., Berkman, L. F., Gulanski, B. I., Robbins, R. J., Greenspan, S.L., Charpentier, P. A., et al. (1995). Self-esteem and neuroendocrine response to challenge: MacArthur studies of successful aging. *Journal of Psychosomatic Research, 39,* 69–84.

Shaver, P. R., & Tancredy, C. M. (2001). Emotion, attachment, and bereavement. In M. S. Stroebe, R. O. Hansson, W. Stroebe, & H. Schut (Eds.), *Handbook of bereavement research* (pp. 63–88). Washington, DC: American Psychological Association.

Shepherd, G. M. (1994). *Neurobiology* (3rd ed.). New York: Oxford University Press.

Sim, H. S., & Kim, J. T. (1993). The development and validation of the Korean version of the MBTI. *Journal of Psychological Types, 26,* 18–27.

Simpson, J. A., Rholes, W. S., & Nelligan, J. S. (1992). The role of attachment styles. *Journal of Personality and Social Psychology, 62,* 434–446.

Snarey, J. R., & Blasi, J. R. (1980). Ego development among adult kibbutzniks: A cross-cultural application of Loevinger's theory. *Genetic Psychology Monographs, 102,* 117–157.

Srivastava, S., John, O. P., Gosling, S. D., & Potter, J. (2003). Development of personality in early and middle adulthood: Set like plaster or persistent change? *Journal of Personality and Social Psychology, 84,* 1041–1053.

Stebbins, R. A. (2001). *New directions in the theory and research of serious leisure.* Levinston, NY: Mellon Press.

Stebbins, R. A. (2004). *Between work and leisure: The common ground of two separate worlds.* New Brunswick, NJ: Transaction Publishers.

Steele, H., Steele, M., & Fonagy, P. (1996). Associations among attachment classifications of mothers, fathers, and their infants. *Child Development, 67,* 541–555.

Sternberg, R. J., & Lubart, T. I. (2001). Wisdom and creativity. In J. E. Birren & K. W. Schaie (Eds.), *Handbook of the psychology of aging* (pp. 500–522). San Diego, CA: Academic Press.

Sterns, H. L., & Kaplan, J. (2003). Self-management of career and retirement. In G. Adams & T. Beehr (Eds.), *Retirement: Reasons, processes, and results* (pp. 188–213). New York: Springer.

Stewart, A. J., & Healy, J. M. (1989). Linking individual development and social changes. *American Psychologist, 44,* 30–42.

Stewart, A. J., & Ostrove, J. M. (1998). Women's personality in middle age: Gender, history, and midcourse corrections. *American Psychologist, 53,* 1185–1194.

Stroebe, M. S., Hansson, R. O., Stroebe, W., & Schut, H. (2001). *Handbook of bereavement research.* Washington, DC: American Psychological Association.

Sullivan, H. S. (1953). *The interpersonal theory of psychiatry.* New York: Norton.

Super, D., Savickas, M. L., & Super, C. M. (1996). The life span, life space approach to careers. In D. Brown & L. Brook (Eds.), *Career choice and development* (pp. 104–124). San Francisco: Jossey-Bass.

Thomas, R. M. (2000). *Comparing theories of child development.* Belmont, CA: Wadsworth.

Tribich, D., & Messer, S. (1974). Psychoanalytic type and status of authority as determiners of suggestibility. *Journal of Consulting and Clinical Psychology, 42,* 842–848.

Vaillant, G. (1977). *Adaptation to life,* Boston: Little Brown.

Vaillant, G. E. (2002). *Aging well.* Boston: Little Brown.

Vaillant, G., & Milofsky, E. (1980). Natural history of male psychological health: Empirical evidence for Erikson's model of the life cycle. *American Journal of Psychiatry, 137,* 1348–1359.

Wang, W., & Viney, L. L. (1996). A cross cultural comparison of Eriksonian psychosocial development: Chinese and Australian children. *School Psychology International, 17,* 33–48.

Waskowic, T. D., & Chartier, B. M. (2003). Attachment and the experience of grief following the loss of spouse. *Omega, 47,* 77–91.

Wax, M. L. (1990). Malinowski, Freud, and Oedipus. *International Review of Psychoanalysis, 17,* 47–70.

Wax, M. L. (2000). Oedipus as normative? Freud's complex, Hook's query, Malinowski's Trobrianders, Stoller's anomalies. *Journal of the American Academy of Psychoanalysis, 28,* 117–132.

Whitbourne, S. (1987). Personality development in adulthood and old age: Relationships among identity style, health, and well being. In K. W. Schaie & C. Eisdorfer (Eds.), *Annual Review of gerontology and geriatrics* (Vol. 7, pp. 189–216). New York: Springer.

Whitbourne, S., & Connolly, L. (1999). The developing self in mid-life. In S. Willis & J. Reid (Eds.), *Life in the middle: Psychological and social development in middle age* (pp. 25–45). San Diego, CA: Academic Press.

Whitbourne, S. K., Zuschlag, M. K., Elliot, M. B., & Waterman, A. S. (1992). Psychological development in adulthood. *Journal of Personality and Social Psychology, 63,* 260–271.

Wrightsman, L. S. (1988). *Adult personality development: Theories and concepts.* Thousand Oaks, CA: Sage.

Wrightsman, L. S. (1994). *Adult personality development theories and concepts.* Newbury Park, CA: Sage.

Zuckerman, M. (1991). *Psychobiology of personality.* New York: Cambridge University Press.

CHAPTER 7

Behavioral Theories

MADELON Y. BOLLING, CHRISTEINE M. TERRY, AND ROBERT J. KOHLENBERG

STATEMENT OF THE THEORY: BEHAVIORAL THEORIES

The irony of a chapter on behaviorism in a handbook of personality[1] is that behaviorists do not think in terms of personality or personality variables. These are reified constructs, or abstractions that have been given the status of things. When behaviorists detect a reified construct, they look for specific situations and behaviors associated with the use of the term in question (e.g., Biglan, 1995; Cordova & Scott, 2001). Thus, to a behaviorist there is no such thing as narcissism, optimism, introversion, or sadism. Rather, these are behaviors that are called narcissistic, and so forth. These behaviors and their contexts need to be specified before the behaviorist can seek to explain, predict, or change the behavior patterns in question. In this chapter, then, we specify the behaviors and contexts in which the term *personality* is used, with examples of how this approach can help us explain, predict, and/or seek to change those patterns of behavior.

Before attending in depth to matters of personality from an operant viewpoint, we give a brief orientation to basic behaviorist thinking. Two intertwined lines of reasoning and research form the behaviorist theories: respondent (or classical) conditioning and operant (or instrumental) learning. Classical learning theory studies the relations among unconditioned and conditioned stimuli and responses. Operant learning theory adds to this the role of contingencies (consequences) in guiding and influencing behavior. Although the emphases differ, both theories focus on environmental determinants and influences, and this focus sets behaviorist theories apart from others such as cognitive or psychodynamic approaches.

Respondent Theory

Respondent theory (based on classical conditioning) is named for its emphasis on the observable, autonomically mediated (often termed *involuntary*) response of the subject to a specific stimulus. It is sometimes referred to as stimulus-response or S-R psychology. Respondent theorists study behavior that is identified by a particular stimulus preceding it (English & English, 1958). Behavior is seen as directly (automatically) elicited by antecedent stimuli in the environment. The task of psychology in this view is to determine the relationships between specific stimuli and specific responses. Complex behavior is explained in terms of clearly identified, compounded, and interrelated units.

To respondent theorists such as I. P. Pavlov (1849–1936) and J. B. Watson (1878–1958), behavior is to be viewed nonmentalistically, as a reflexive response to the environment. Pavlov's experiments with dogs were an example of respondent theory at work, as were Watson's experiments conditioning a boy to fear small furry animals. Respondent theorists limit the range of study to behaviors that are directly observable either with the naked eye or with the proper instrumentation (such as galvanometers, heart monitors, or plethysmographs). Complex and uniquely human behaviors such as unconscious linguistic responses (Lang, Geer, & Hnatiow, 1963) have been investigated fruitfully by researchers based on a respondent learning paradigm. Though their potential importance is not denied, private events such as creativity, spirituality, or the experience of self remain outside the realm of interest to respondent theorists. There are always elements of respondent learning even in primarily operant learning situations, and their role is acknowledged by operant theorists.

Operant Theory

The operant approach is the centerpiece of the theory and philosophy originated by B. F. Skinner (1953, 1957). Operant theory is named for its emphasis on behavior that is identified by its consequences in the environment (technically termed *contingencies of reinforcement;* English & English, 1958). An operant is a behavior or class of behaviors that in previous similar situations has operated on the environment and thus has a specific consequence for the individual (or, depending

142

on the level of analysis, for the group). If the consequence has the effect of increasing the likelihood of the behavior preceding it (a strengthening of the behavior) under similar circumstances, the consequence is defined as a reinforcer. If the consequence reduces the likelihood of behavior, it is defined as a punisher. Please note that feelings of pleasure or enjoyment are not part of the definition, although humans often do report such feelings when consequences increase the likelihood of the behavior occurring again. Thus, feelings are epiphenomena, not causally related to behavior, though they are of interest for other reasons as described later.

Professionals who follow this theory in their work refer to themselves as *behavior analysts,* and to their work as *behavior analysis,* so we will follow that tradition here. Behavior analysts assume that behavior is to be viewed nonmentalistically and in context; that private events such as thinking, feeling, seeing, hearing, dreaming, and so forth, are behaviors. From this viewpoint, even the most private behavior such as seeing a mental image or thinking can ultimately be traced back to origins in the person's experience of consequences in the past. This past experience is termed *reinforcement history.*

These assumptions provide a concept of human nature and a language that clarifies the interaction between an individual's behavior and the natural (which includes the social) environment. For example, Rasheed leaves school a little early each day, and his teachers are concerned. A behavior analyst would seek to discover the function of such behavior in the student's life through a functional analysis, or identification of the relevant contingencies, a hallmark of behavior analysis. That is, what consequence does leaving early have for Rasheed? Is he avoiding bullies, catching a certain bus, meeting with a girlfriend, going home to watch his little brother, or getting to a job on time? In contrast to respondent theory, the behavior in question is not seen as, say, a conditioned response to a particular position of the hands on the clock face (though this may be part of the behavioral chain). Rather, it is understood as functioning with respect to consequences. Notice that this differs considerably from trait theories that might look for some characteristic such as oppositionalism to explain Rasheed's leaving school early.

Behavior analysis deals pragmatically with complex human behavior. Behaviors are preferably studied idiographically (in the context of the particular circumstances and history of the individual in question) and are frequently multiply determined by a history of several kinds of consequence operating at once. Thus, Rasheed may need to catch a certain bus (on which he has often seen a girl in whom he is interested) in order to get home in time to watch his little brother so that his father will not be angry with him later. This also may spare him unpleasant interactions with the vice principal who patrols the hallways after class. Before turning to our analysis of personality and everyday functioning, we need to present the basics of operant learning in a little more detail.

More about Behavior Analysis

Consequences or Contingencies of Reinforcement. We use the term *contingencies of reinforcement* to refer to all consequences that affect (increase or decrease) the strength (or likelihood) of behavior, including positive reinforcement (presenting a stimulus or state of affairs that increases the likelihood of a given behavior), negative reinforcement (removing a stimulus or state of affairs that subsequently increases the likelihood of a given behavior), and punishment (adding or removing a stimulus that decreases the likely occurrence of a target behavior). Even though a conscious experience of pleasure often accompanies positive reinforcement, relief often accompanies negative reinforcement, and displeasure accompanies punishment, the presence of these feelings is not a necessary part of the process and should not be confused with it.

Contingencies of reinforcement are omnipresent in our daily lives—almost always occurring naturally and rarely the result of someone trying to reinforce another's behavior. The strengthening or weakening of behavior (e.g., increasing or decreasing the probability of doing it again) occurs at an unconscious level. That is, awareness—either of what you are supposed to do or of particular feelings—is not required. In operant theory this strengthening or weakening of the likelihood of behavior constitutes our reinforcement history (itself embedded in contingencies of culture and of survival), which may be viewed as the ultimate cause of our actions.

It is important to note the operant distinction between near-at-hand influences (your present environment, feelings, and/or thinking) and the fundamental cause: reinforcement history. It may be useful or even sufficient at times to view our behavior as resulting from more proximal (near-at-hand) influences such as the current environment, thoughts, and emotions. However, behavior analysts maintain that complete explanations require one to take reinforcement history into account. For example, you might say that you yelled at your friend because you were angry. That is, you explain your yelling as being caused by your anger. This might be a sufficient explanation in a social situation. As a behavioral explanation, however, it is incomplete because it contains no information about the past contingencies that account for (1) your getting angry and (2) your yelling. That is, not everyone would necessarily have become angry under these circumstances, nor does everyone yell when they are angry. A complete (or causal) explanation addresses the history leading to internal states and the reaction to the current situation.

What Constitutes an Explanation?   People have learned to attribute our reactions in various situations to our personality, something we are said to bear within us. But from the operant perspective, personality simply refers to the probability of behaving in a certain way. The way we see it, this merely says that things are as they are, much as T. S. Eliot said of his tomcat:

> For he will do
> As he do do
> And there's no doing anything about it.
>
> (T. S. Eliot, 1940, "The Rum Tum Tugger," p. 19)

This is hardly satisfactory for psychologists, who are often faced with the task of doing something about it.

Operant explanations always give accounts of the behavior of interest in terms of the history of the individual's interactions with others (and/or the physical environment) in addition to the current situation and internal state that triggered the behavior or reaction. Explanations that refer to mental structures as causes of behavior do not seem as satisfactory to the behavior analyst. For example, you see Jeremy putting a coin into a vending machine. This behavior could be explained in different ways: he has a desire for a candy bar; he has regressed to an oral needs stage; he is under the influence of a specific expectancy of success; he is driven by hunger.

These are all explanations of Jeremy's actions. Still, behavior analysts will ask, where did the desire come from? What does it mean to be driven by hunger? How did the specific expectancy come to be? How is it that, having regressed to an oral stage, Jeremy finds and operates a vending machine?

In each of these cases, operant theory inquires after the same three things: history, the current situation, and the internal state. That is, desire, expectancy, or hunger for a candy bar would be seen as a function of:

1. A history of having watched others put coins in such a machine and receive food, plus a history of having eaten a candy bar and finding that it relieves the discomfort of not having eaten (negative reinforcement).

2. Being in the vicinity of a vending machine with sufficient coins in hand (current situation), given this history.

3. The number of hours without eating (history accounting for the internal state).

These are all (at least potentially) publicly observable events (or events in the environment) that account for Jeremy's behavior. They also account for the inferred nonbehavioral entities, such as drive, desire, expectancy, and the manifestation of a breakdown in ego function.

Similarly, if a woman takes off alone in a small boat to circumnavigate the world, the operant explanation would focus on her past experiences, such as the past results (contingencies) of taking risks, sailing alone, and undertaking large challenges. Nonoperant explanations might explain her behavior as being the result of inner strength or having a risk-taker's personality. Operant behaviorists call this *mentalism:* inner, nonbehavioral processes such as willpower, and fear of failure, are given the power to cause other more observable events to come about, just as though a little person named *willpower* or *adventurousness* resided within the individual and caused the individual to do or not do certain things.

This is known as the homuncular problem: attributing agency to some unseen entity (literally like a "little man," or *homunculus*) within the individual. The homunculus originally referred to the seventeenth-century explanation of how an ovum eventually became a full-sized animal. It was postulated that a microscopic miniature human is encased within the sperm and grows into the full-sized organism during gestation. The problem with this explanation is that we now are left with a puzzle to solve that is very much like the one we started out with. Rather than explaining where the full-sized animal came from, we are instead left with trying to explain the origins of the microscopic one.

To review the preceding: Behaviorists consider explanations of behavior to be incomplete if they do not involve tracing the observable antecedents of behavior back as far as possible into the individual's historical environment. These observable antecedents are the variables (termed *controlling variables*) that account for the behavior in question. Many current psychological explanations do little more than specify some inner process as the cause of a particular aspect of behavior. We feel it is only reasonable to ask, in turn, what makes that inner process work as it does.

The Importance of Context and Function.   The search for controlling variables amounts to a deep concern for the context within which the behavior takes place. Context is not only a matter of the local surroundings and events (the current situation) wherein the behavior takes place, but it also necessarily includes the historical surroundings or the past experiences of the person or persons involved. For example, if my friend says, "Wow, it's roasting out today!" and I am puzzled by her remark, it helps to know the current context (an outside temperature of 73° F) and her historical context:

she just arrived in southern California after spending most of the winter in the Aleutian Islands. An incomplete explanation simply would point to her sensitivity to heat. Further, I may consider it pleasantly cool, because I have just returned from two weeks of fighting forest fires in Arizona. An incomplete explanation simply might point to my heat tolerance.

Notice here that the stimulus 73° F is not the same stimulus to my friend as it is to me. That is, there is no inherent quality of the experience of 73-degreeness independent of the context within which the responses to temperature occur. Context is of central importance to operant theory because what we know about a behavior changes when the context of that behavior changes. Context determines the function of a behavior. That is why operant behaviorists' central approach to human behavior is the *functional analysis.*

A functional analysis, according to Skinner (1953), yields "the external variables of which behavior is a function" (p. 35). The analysis consists of three parts: (1) the context or environmental setting, including the person's history, physiological and behavioral state; (2) the response of the individual; and (3) the consequences brought about due to acting on the environment.

You may grasp the importance of context to the analysis of behavior from the following example: Four students are studying late at night for a physics exam. You might say they are all engaged in the same behavior. You could compare the percentage of students studying with the grade point outcome of the exam or with career expectancies and outcomes. There would be a certain truth to these observations and correlations. But now let us do something really different (yet familiar to our everyday thinking) and examine context. (Notice that context is much more than the library location and the time of day.) Adam is studying because he wants his dad to keep paying for school and living expenses. Beth, on the other hand, is working for a 4.0 so she will qualify for a physics honor society. Carl is studying so that Beth will want to go for a walk with him. And Denise finds studying preferable to the chaos at home. In each case, that is, in each context, a different function is served by the same behavior. Knowing what we know now, are we still watching four people engaged in the same behavior? It does look the same at a certain level, but this apparent similarity is due to very different outcomes and so serves very different functions.

Most accounts of personality deal with describing and predicting behavior. As we have just seen, there are two general ways to do this. One approach, the formal or topographical analysis, tells us what behavior looks like: studying late for a physics exam. A different approach, functional analysis, tells us the effect or function of behavior: earning living ex-

penses, seeking accolades, pursuing a relationship, avoiding an aversive situation.

The formal or topographical approach is close to everyday usages in the realm of personality. That is, we ordinarily say such things as, "He is gentle," or "She is the embodiment of politeness, but make no mistake, she's vicious." Notice that this kind of description—and many other more professional psychological terms such as *aggressive, passive, delusional, obsessive, compulsive, sociopathic, inattentive, manic, hyperactive, apathetic, depressed,* and so forth—consists of abstract modifiers of a sort that we naturally tend to turn into nouns: aggression, gentleness, obsessions, mania, depression, and so on. And this, as we mentioned earlier, is reification. We believe such a grammatical turn confuses more than it clarifies.

If we remember that a certain person is not, for instance, an obsessive but a person behaving obsessively, we are more likely to look for the causes of such behaving. What effect does behaving obsessively have in this person's life? What are the consequences of this way of being? What function does it serve in her life?

In seeking explanations of behavior then, operant theorists view themselves as engaged in a search for controlling variables in the environment. Events are considered controlling variables when they are perceived to contribute to the behavioral result or process being observed and when changing such events would change this behavior or process.

Explanation and Verbal Behavior.   Because language—talking, or verbal behavior—seems to take a privileged position as a uniquely human phenomenon encompassing both private and public behaviors, it is the source of much confusion. Talking and other verbal activity, however, is just behavior and as such is under the control of the environment just as is any other behavior.

All verbal behavior, no matter how private its subject matter may appear to be, has its origins in the environment. Although phenomena related to human verbal functioning vary from the most intimately personal to the most publicly social, all meaningful language is shaped into effective form by the action of an environmental verbal community. Thus, when a speaker says she sees an image in her mind's eye, she is using an expression that was taught to her in childhood by others who could not actually see into her mind's eye. These teachers used directly observed events in the teaching process.

What factors are involved in leading the speaker to say what he or she does? To know thoroughly what has caused a person to say something is to understand the significance of what has been said in its very deepest sense (Day, 1969). That is, to know thoroughly is to have identified the controlling variables, an analysis just as relevant to verbal behavior as it is to any other. For example, to understand what a man means when he says he just had an out-of-body experience, we would search for its causes. First, we would want to know about the stimulation in the body that was just experienced (the proximal cause). Then, we would want to know why a particular bodily state is experienced as out of body. Thus, we would look for environmental causes going back into the man's history, including the circumstances he encountered as he was growing up that resulted in his saying *body, out of, just had,* and *I*. As soon as we knew all of these, we would understand thoroughly the significance of what was said.

This then is the reason we begin our operant account of personality by examining commonly held verbal definitions of the term.

A Behavior-Analytic Account of Personality

We have chosen two definitions of personality, one from a textbook on personality and the other from an encyclopedia. These definitions are representative of the term as used both in scholarly contexts and in daily life. First, the textbook definition:

> We define personality as consistent behavior patterns originating within the individual. (Burger, 1993, p. 3)

Next, the encyclopedia definition of personality as given in the 1994 edition of *Encarta:*

> [D]eeply ingrained and relatively enduring patterns of thought, feeling, and behavior. Personality usually refers to that which is unique about a person, the characteristics that distinguish him or her from other people. Thought, emotion, and behavior as such do not constitute a personality, which is, rather, the dispositions that underlie these elements. Personality implies predictability about how a person will act or react under different circumstances.

Certain features are common to both of these definitions. First, there is the notion of *consistency* referred to in the textbook. A similar quality is conveyed in the encyclopedia's reference to *enduring.* Both definitions refer to patterns of behavior. Patterns only can be construed when behavior is consistent or is perceived to recur at various times and under various conditions. Consistency in behavior has everything to do with predictability, which is why we are interested in the study of persons in the first place.

Next, the textbook definition specifies that patterns of behavior originate from within. In the encyclopedia definition this quality is referenced by the descriptors *deeply ingrained*

and *dispositions that underlie* (emphasis added). And finally, although the textbook definition does not directly refer to individual differences, the notion of uniqueness given in the encyclopedia is included later in the textbook's discussion.

We will examine each of these—consistency, the quality within, and uniqueness—from an operant viewpoint to throw some light on the causes of predictability in behavior. As part of the process, we will explain how an individual might come to have, or not have, one or more of these features in order to understand what is meant by not having any personality or having a disturbed personality.

Consistency over Time

Behaving consistently results from a consistent environment with consistent contingencies over time. As we explained previously, if a behavior results in consequences that reduce deprivation or remove aversive stimuli, then the probability is increased that the person will behave that same way again under those circumstances in the future. Those circumstances would be the context of deprivation of reinforcers and a setting in which those reinforcers are available. As long as these conditions occur and the reinforcement is reliable, the behavior will be maintained over time.

Notice how neatly the notion of the probability of a behavior recurring, or the tendency to do it again, fits with the encyclopedia's specification that personality consists of dispositions that underlie behavior. *Disposition* is sometimes defined as "a tendency or inclination, especially when habitual" (Morris, 1978). These dispositions or tendencies refer to the likelihood of behavior, which, as we said, is changed by the consequences of that behavior.

Most of us have experienced a relatively consistent environment. Many factors are involved in accounting for a consistent environment: It is important to the culture, to us as individuals, and to physical survival that we behave consistently. Parents do not usually change drastically from day to day in the way that they treat their children, much less from hour to hour. Social contingencies also select for consistent behavior: Systems such as traffic lights work only so long as people behave consistently with respect to them. We tend to reject or avoid people who regularly say one thing and do another or behave in wildly different ways from day to day or from moment to moment. If we can predict another's behavior, our life is made easier: We can make plans, count on others, avoid unpleasant or dangerous social situations, and in general feel safer and lead more productive lives. For the most part, then, we have relatively consistent experiences.

But not everyone is so lucky. In fact, if a person is not predictable, they may be considered to have a disordered personality. An extreme example of this is borderline personality disorder. People exhibiting this style of behavior are notorious for their unpredictability. Their behaviors can swing dramatically from ingratiating to furious, from frightened to confident. These individuals "frequently vacillate between avoidance of conflict and intense confrontation" (Linehan, 1993, p. 152). In relationships, someone with borderline symptoms will suddenly switch from idealizing the other person to devaluing them. These people show a great need for intimate relationships and attention, but on the other hand, they reject intimacy after a short time and often terminate relationships prematurely. They often show abrupt and dramatic shifts in self-image with concomitant changes in values, opinions, goals, and so on. The history of people with this behavioral style usually includes a very troubled or traumatic childhood. The family environment usually invalidated the individual's needs and/or feelings in some way, was typically quite inconsistent, and often contained contradictory communications, negligence, and abuse.

With this, we need to clarify the use of the term *consistency,* as it is quite clear that we have been describing people who consistently vacillate among extreme behaviors. Even though a person may be predictably unpredictable, the norm for acceptable consistency seems to be more restrictive. People like to be able to pinpoint probable behavior at least within a relatively narrow range of the possible spectrum of behaviors. We would fire a weather forecaster who always predicted "Heavy snow tomorrow, or possibly a mild day with high overcast, that is if we don't have a tornado followed by hail—and yes, it might be another gorgeous hot summer day!"

The point here is that even unpredictable behavior actually has causal antecedents in the environment. People who carry the rather stigmatizing label of borderline personality disorder do not lack personality because they are seen as inconsistent in their responses. It is just that the logic (or inferred causality) of their responses baffles most people and the variability in their behavior precludes accuracy in prediction. Because, apparently, most of their extremely variable responses are in the interpersonal realm, they are experienced as compellingly painful to relate to, which in turn causes them even more trouble and pain.

If, however, you or I had parents who were on occasion very attentive but mostly not at home, who were often distracted by the stress of work and impatient with us; who held impossibly high standards for our behavior and only listened to grievances from us if they were life-threatening, who protested that they loved us dearly, yet who would from time to time beat us severely—we might have similar expectations of other people as we grew up. This would be due to our reinforcement history.

Children naturally pick up on incidental cues in the environment. In this case they do so while trying to find some reliable way to predict the parent's irritability or accessibility. Because the child could not know the actual antecedents of the parent's behavior, these cues might be irrelevant—a certain quality of light, a certain time of day, or the color of clothing the parent wore during a critical incident. Nonetheless, these cues might become part of the setting for puzzling behaviors on the child's part in the presence of intimate others after they grow up. This could account for an unaccountable behavior of frantic avoidance in the friend you meant to meet for coffee. She wanted to meet you, arranged for everything, but when you showed up, she slammed the door, ran and hid and would not come back. You might be wearing a sweater the same color as the one that her mom wore the day she blamed your friend for breaking the dishwasher, beat her with a lamp cord, and locked her in a closet. Remember that such conditioning (in this case, respondent) does not require awareness on the part of the one being conditioned; your friend would probably not be able to explain her actions. Again, even inconsistent or incomprehensible behavior has environmental antecedents.

Consistency across Situations

We have just been talking about consistency (or lack of it) over time. Consistency across different situations is another important feature of personality. Some theories of personality claim that cross-situational consistency indicates that personality traits are at work controlling behavior. Others argue that behavior changes depending on what the situational factors are and therefore the situation is more important than traits. Operant theory takes a different stance and provides an explanation of both consistency and inconsistency across situations, through the use of functional analysis.

To the behaviorist, similar behavior across differing situations does not indicate that a drive or a trait is causing that particular style of behavior, no matter what the situation. Nor do we agree that the situation alone determines behavior. Rather, it is the current situation in combination with an individual's history that determines the probability (but not the necessity) of behavior. A functional analysis of the different situations will reveal contextual similarities that evoke the behavior based on the individual's reinforcement history relative to those stimulus conditions. In other words, people are sensitive to different situations (contexts) based on their past experience with similar settings.

For example, Bill tends to act in outgoing or extroverted ways, such as speaking more loudly than others, dominating social interactions with frequent witty remarks and humor, and dressing more stylishly than most of his acquaintances. But there are other situations when he does not act that way. It turns out that for most of his life, Bill was able to get attention, approval, or just one more cookie from his mother and his friends when he was loud and witty and well dressed, so he is quite likely to act that way now and in the future under similar circumstances.

On the other hand, Bill's father avoided him and criticized him for having a loud mouth while he was growing up. And neither his seventh-grade teacher nor the scout leaders appreciated his brand of humor. From then on, Bill tended to be more restrained when there were men in charge of the situation.

So we may see Bill acting in his loud and funny manner when he is hanging out with friends at a pub, when he is trying to make a new acquaintance into a sweetheart, when he is attending Professor Linda Gromwell's anthropology class, and when he is spending a Sunday afternoon with the college Bible study group. At one glance, these seem to be rather different situations. But they all share stimulus properties with Bill's experience in situations described previously with his mother and his friends.

If we were to see Bill interacting during a meeting at work (where the supervisor bears a distinct resemblance to Mr. Folger of the seventh grade) or discussing his driving speed with Highway Patrolman Bob Greenspan, we would see a different Bill. These situations have stimulus qualities similar to those he ran into with his father, so he is likely to behave in a more restrained fashion under these circumstances.

Andy, on the other hand, was always able to get what he wanted and to get out of uncomfortable predicaments with his parents when he used wit and humor. His teachers and recreation leaders all seemed to appreciate his humor. For him, this behavior is likely even when dealing with Patrolman Greenspan. Though he is Bill's coworker, he did not have Mr. Folger in the seventh grade, so Andy pretty reliably contributes humor during the meetings.

Consistency of behavior (personality), rather than being determined exclusively by the situation or exclusively by biological dispositions or by traits, largely reflects the combined effects of reinforcement history, genetic endowment, and the functional qualities of the situation.

The Quality "Coming from Within" and the Sense of Self

Both actors and observers sense that the tendency to behave a certain way comes from within, whether they call it personality or not. How has this come to be?

From the observer's point of view, supposing two people in the same situation are seen to react differently; where do these reactions come from? The stimuli in the environment were the same. The only observable difference was that the stimuli affected two different bodies, or reached two different people, who then reacted quite differently. The observer's logical conclusion is that the reactions must have come from within the bodies. In contrast, not all behavior is usually attributed to personality nor is it said to come from within. If you were watching a troop of soldiers drilling on the parade grounds, it is highly unlikely that you would say their lock-step precision was due to their personalities, or that the behavior came from within.

A little more difficult to account for is the actor's own experience of his or her reactions. What are the stimuli that are experienced such that a person speaks of his or her behavior as coming from within? Sensations interior to the body (or as we say, private, or within the skin) always accompany one's actions, both public and nonpublic. From here, it is a perfectly logical move to assume that those actions came from within simply because they are inevitably accompanied by sensations not observable by anyone else.

Though there is a certain simple truth to the statement, to say that the behaviors came from within is itself an incomplete explanation similar to our earlier example of saying you yelled at your friend because you were angry. Though one's behavior may be perceived to come from within, largely due to normal development of language and usages of the verbal community, as we will explain shortly, there is no accounting for the particular form of the behavior without tracing it back into its antecedent causes that are always in the environment.

There are instances, however, when a person does not perceive his or her own behavior as coming from within. If your behavior does not come from within, does it mean you do not have a personality? That you are nobody? These are statements that people who say their behavior is not their own or does not come from within are apt to make.

In order to see how such a situation may have come about, let us look at how we learn to attribute behaviors to ourselves, how we learn to say they come from inside, or not, as the case may be.

An Excursus on the Development of the Sense of Self

We learn to say *I* when we first learn to talk. Not only do we learn to make the sound, but we actually learn the acceptable referents for the sound from other people who teach us to talk, primarily our parents and peers but also teachers, relatives, strangers, media figures, and anyone who interacts with us in a given language. Operant behaviorists refer to these people as the *verbal community*. Linguists and developmental psychologists call the period of life from about six months of age to two years the *single-word speech period*. Toward the second year of life, many of these single words actually are two or three-word phrases such as *Mommy hit, juice all gone, beep-beep trucks,* but they serve as single functional units (Kohlenberg & Tsai, 1991, p. 132).

A functional unit is the behavior that occurs between the cue (technically, the discriminative stimulus) and the reinforcer (the consequence that increases the likelihood that the behavior will recur). In language acquisition, the actual size of the functional unit changes with experience and the coaching of the verbal community. That is, most parents will reinforce (with a natural delighted response) any approximation of speech. Whatever is reinforced is likely to recur, and such is the *single functional unit* of early speech. Single functional units also include phrases such as *memorejuice, babyice-cream,* or *meseemama,* which serve as self-referent phrases.

There is evidence that children learn abstractions such as *big* or *red* or self-referent pronouns gradually, after learning them as larger functional units, such as *bigtruck, bigdoll, bigGregor, redball, redshirt, rednose, memorejuice, mebear-bear,* or *Billypiano.* This will not seem so strange if you recall (as I do) thinking that *ellemenopee* was a single unit within the thing called *alphabet,* or that the song phrase *My country tizovthee* ended with *of the icing,* and that it all took some years to straighten out.

Kohlenberg and Tsai (1991) propose that *I* (also *me, my, mine,* one's name, etc.) emerges as a separate functional unit gradually, from the larger functional units that include it, such as those mentioned previously. Thus, *I am hot, I am hungry, I am here,* all have *I am* in common; *I feel sad, I feel icky, I feel happy,* have *I feel* in common; *I want ice cream, I want juice, I want mommy,* have *I want* in common; *I see car, I see mommy, I see fishie,* have *I see* in common, and so forth for all the *I* x-type statements a person may ever make. Keep in mind, of course, that in real life the actual statements from this first stage may be more like *me see mama* or *baby ice cream.* The function is the same, so we use *I* here as the generic form of self-reference.

In the second stage of the emergence of *I,* the smaller functional units such as *I want, I see, I have* emerge as separate. The child then can combine them with new objects, making statements they never have said or have heard before. *I want Yellowstone, I see fireman,* or *I am very unhappy* may be heard at this stage.

In turn, *I am, I feel, I want, I see,* and *I* x all have *I* in common. In the third stage, not only *I* as a functional verbal unit but also *I* as referent and the experience of *I* emerge. The experience of *I* is acquired just as the experience of a football,

ice cream, mommy, or heat was acquired with the learning of each word. These experiences differ from *I,* however, in that they are under the control of specific public stimuli and can be learned separately. *I,* on the other hand, is under the control of a complex private stimulus. What is common to all of the preceding, in addition to the vocable *I* or its equivalents, is perspective, the child's location in space in relation to others. It is where he or she is—right here—as opposed to where he or she is not—over there—and perspective is the only element that is present across all responses containing *I.*

Remember, however, that the real-life processes are much more complex and not as linear as this outline. This amounts to the merest sketch of a very rich continuum of phenomena. (For a more detailed description of this process, see Kohlenberg & Tsai, 1991, 1995; for a slightly different, more technical view, see Hayes, Barnes-Holmes, & Roche, 2001.)

Perspective is the stimulus that remains constant for all the *I want x* and *I see x* type of statements, because the *x* (or object) and the activity (wanting, seeing, etc.) vary from time to time. The public aspects of the stimulus would vary considerably with the particular situation. Sometimes the child may be 5 feet to the left of the parent and at other times may be 50 feet away. Given the wide variation in where *here* versus *there* may be, a private aspect seems likely to gain control. Thus, the response *I* as a unit is under the stimulus control of a locus.

During normal development, this perspective is the physical location of the private activities such as seeing, wanting, and having, so the self is experienced as relatively unchanging, centrally located, and continuous. This is where the sense of *within* develops. The locus of awareness is where the body is, but it also observes the body. *I hurt my finger, I have a tummy ache,* and the like teach us that the *I* possesses the body, but the *I* is not the body. This is consistent with the continuity of self experience, that is, the experience that it was you at your first day of school even though your body is now completely different. Although it is not the body, the *I* observes things that happen inside the body as well as outside. Because this observing has the perspective from behind the eyes as it were, the *I* is experienced as within. Activities under private control then—activities attributed to the *I*—are experienced as coming from within.

Although normal development leads to a large degree of control of the *I* response by private (within the skin) stimuli, maladaptive development involves the opposite: a small degree of control of *I* by private stimuli. That is, a number of *I* x responses have come under public control. What does this mean for real people? It means that some parents (or other early caretakers) inadvertently teach children to take their cues from people or situations outside themselves (public stimuli) rather than from the private events and responses that only the child can access.

For example, little Tammy is in the grocery store with her mom. She says, "I'm hungry! I wanna candy bar." Mom, in a hurry to finish shopping, says, "No you don't. We've got to get home." This teaches Tammy that her private experience is not valid when her mom is in a hurry. Furthermore, it is likely that on other occasions when her mother is in a hurry Tammy will tend to ignore her private experience again. That is, the public stimulus of mom-in-a-hurry is more important than whatever private stimuli may have led to Tammy's statement. If this happens regularly or under punishing circumstances, *I want* may come to be under public control under other circumstances as well, even when Tammy is with other people. That is, she may come to scan the environment for any important person who looks anxious or hurried as the discriminative stimulus for whether she really wants something or not. Behaviorists call this *generalization.*

If similar invalidations of Tammy's other *I x* statements occur, she may eventually come to have a more or less severe psychological problem.

"I feel sick today."
"Nonsense, you're perfectly fine."

"Look, I'm taking giant steps!"
"You call that 'giant steps'?! Quit exaggerating."

"OK, I'm gonna do the shopping for you today."
"You wouldn't know how to do the shopping if your life depended on it."

"He hurt me!"
"Quit whining. Act like a grownup."

This kind of exchange may pervade the history of people who eventually say their actions do not come from within or that they are not doing what they appear to be doing. This still may sound a little far-fetched, but how many times have you heard disclaimers like these?

"Are you writing that paper?"
"No, not really."
"I mean, are you or aren't you?"
"Well I can't really write, so I'm just sorta faking it."

"Do you want to go out tonight?"
"I don't know, do you?"

"Is that your poem on the wall, there?"

"Well, sort of."
"Didn't you write it?"
"Well, not exactly. The words came to me. I just kinda heard 'em and wrote 'em down. It's not, like, my words or anything."

Although the preceding are relatively nonpathological statements, they show self-referent behaviors that are being described as under public control. There is a continuum of possible severity of problems with self, depending on the degree of private control of the functional unit *I*. Keep in mind that we are not referring to someone suppressing a verbal report of known feelings or needs. Rather, we are discussing the developmental antecedents of becoming aware of one's feelings (private stimuli) and needs (reinforcers) at all and how one comes to notice and define them in the first place. When the functional unit *I* is exclusively under public control, the individual is not aware of having private feelings or needs at all.

If the tendency to behave a certain way is consistently blocked by a punishing or invalidating environment, one may come to inhibit those tendencies oneself to avoid punishment or the humiliation of invalidating responses. In this case, one may readily perceive that one's own behavior does not come from within. Indeed, in a sense it does not come from within if it is always (or nearly always) determined by what is going on outside, in other people—that is, if the tendency to behave is under public control. We are not just referring to unassertive people who may know what they would prefer but are reluctant to speak of it. People whose *I* is under public control really do not know what they want, what they can do, what they feel, see, and so on until and unless they find out what significant others want or will allow (see Kanter, Parker, & Kohlenberg, 2001).

It is a short step from this to "I have no personality," if most of what a person does is actually subject to the modifications of others. The statement, "You have no personality," on the other hand, is more in the nature of a put-down than a diagnosis. It means "your behavior does not interest me," or "you are uninteresting." Curiously enough, a person who always defers to the wishes of others may be exactly the kind of person who will receive such a put-down. However, this person still behaves consistently and uniquely (or identifiably). Whether such a person feels that their behavior comes from within or not, other people will still attribute it to them as though it did. In this sense, there is no such thing as having no personality.

Although in normal development we do experience our behavior as originating within ourselves, behavior is always rooted in the environment. Access to private stimuli, the sense of private control, even the experience of within itself, are learned.

Uniqueness

The third factor in the concept of personality is uniqueness, a quality observed by actors and observers alike. What is it that distinguishes one person from another? From the observer's point of view, we notice that in any given situation (under the same stimulus conditions, in behavioral terms), no two people will act exactly the same way.

For example, Ron and DJ, both in their middle twenties, are groundskeepers in an industrial park. The supervisor has assigned a project for the day: trimming all the hedges and clipping the ivy back off the curbs of all the parking lots. So Ron starts the hedger and begins squaring up the hedges. DJ, on the other hand, starts pruning dead twigs out of the maple trees. Then he cuts some old flowers out of the geranium beds. He pulls Johnson grass out of one ivy planting and rakes up some of the hedge trimmings that Ron is still producing steadily. After drinking a can of cola he brought from home, DJ finally picks up his pruners and starts cutting the ivy back from a parking-lot curb.

We could perhaps account for these differences by referring to biological factors (what we usually refer to as *genetic endowment*), such as Ron's higher energy level, or we might say that DJ is a little slow on the uptake. Although it is true that biological factors provide the foundation on which behavior is built, and this foundation can determine certain limits of behavior (it is unlikely that a very short person will become a professional basketball player, or that a tall and heavy person will become a race jockey), biological factors are not the whole story. In fact, there is plenty of evidence that experience actually alters physiology (see Kalb, 1994; Salm, Modney, & Hatton, 1988; Weiler, Hawrylak, & Greenough, 1995).

There are any number of ways of behaving given the same biological foundation (e.g., there is no biological necessity that Ron should have expressed his high energy by starting the work assignment right away; he might equally have done a few handsprings or decided today was the day to take the machete to the thorn bushes behind the dumpster). What we want to do is account for the behavioral differences over and above the biological foundations.

So what accounts for Ron and DJ's differing behavior? If the situation or stimulus conditions are exactly the same and if the actors in question perceive them as the same, must there be an internal structure or personality difference to account for different behavior? Is it that Ron is a diligent, disciplined, no-nonsense worker, whereas DJ is headstrong, somewhat unreliable, a procrastinator? By now you know that these qualities themselves are not causal structures but are descriptions of behavior arising from different reinforcement histories. Thus, the work situation is actually not the same to the two men because of their histories.

When Ron was three years old, his dad praised him for picking up the hairbrush right away when asked. His parents continued to notice and appreciate it whenever Ron responded promptly to requests and carried tasks to completion. As you read in the section on consistency, such a history of positive reinforcement (barring complications, of course) leads to a lasting high probability of behaving the same way. To Ron, this situation at the industrial park was yet another opportunity to receive positive consequences for a job done quickly and well.

To DJ, on the other hand, the situation at work is entirely different. When he was very small, his mom once asked him to hold her coffee cup while she looked at the map in the car to check the route to the hospital. The mug was heavier than he expected and he did not get a good grip, so it slipped and fell, spilling coffee on him and all over the car. Mom was frightened lest he burn himself, DJ was naturally shocked, and to top it all off, his dad who was in the back seat holding his badly cut arm, yelled, "That's the last time we'll ask you to do anything, you useless bastard!" And that was not an isolated incident. They did ask him to do other things, of course. But each time, his dad found something wrong with what he did: he was too slow, too hasty, reckless, careless, not accurate enough. Not once did either parent tell him what was right with what he did. He was raised under a regime of punishment.

Although he had other experiences with playmates and at school, situations like the one at work, where the supervisor lays out tasks to be done, seem to be threatening, promising only negative consequences no matter what he does. DJ is not at all aware of this state of affairs. To him it just seems that a dark cloud always hangs over the work situation; that's the way it is with work, he figures, and a person has to overcome it as best he can. So he tends to do little tasks that were not assigned first, things he knows need doing, but nobody has asked him to do them. If he does enough of these, he feels that at least he has done something, so he can face the main awful task and get on with it. DJ's predicament illustrates some of the complex unintended effects of punishment (which includes criticism, disapproval, blame, and ridicule; Skinner, 1953, p. 190).

Operant theory acknowledges biological endowment as a factor and also accounts for the uniqueness of behavior through the individual's reinforcement history. This history actually will change the experience of the environment; no situation is exactly the same to any two people. Hence their responses will be unique.

There is also an internal or subjective aspect to uniqueness; many people feel unique. In the section on the quality *within,* we mentioned that the sense of self is normally a perspective or the location from which a person sees, hears, speaks, feels, and so forth. Because no two bodies can occupy the same space at the same time, this locus of experience is indeed unique. The subjective feeling of uniqueness is not merely a private experience, then, but is based on physical laws as well as the unique history of which each of us is a product.

Uniqueness, then, from the point of view of the observer is a product of the reinforcement history of the individual. From the point of view of the actor, the sense of uniqueness is based on the private stimuli that are available to no other and on the truly unique perspective, or locus of experience, that each of us has learned to call *I.*

DEVELOPMENTAL CONSIDERATIONS

Because the person's stage of development (including her body) is part of the environment influencing her behavior, proper functional analyses must take this into account. For an example of developmental issues, see the behavior-analytic view of the development of a sense of self in the preceding section and in the section on problems of specific populations.

BIOLOGICAL/PHYSIOLOGICAL RELATIONSHIPS

The importance of genetic endowment is acknowledged in operant theory. Skinner (1953) discusses the contingencies of survival, which are theorized to be the phylogenic characteristics that are passed on, resulting in survival of the species. In keeping with Darwin's theory of evolution, in which adaptive traits are passed on to offspring, Skinner stressed that these contingencies of survival are a part of the individual's history and thus have an influence on the individual's behavior. For example, Breland and Breland (1961) found that it was difficult to train a chicken to play baseball. Indeed, the chicken often would peck the baseball rather than play baseball with it. Although the experimenters used the principles of operant theory to train the chicken, playing baseball was contradictory to inherited survival-strengthening behaviors such as pecking at objects. The same principle applies to humans. Thus, the genetic endowment of the person is an important factor to consider when seeking the causes of behavior from a behavior-analytic perspective.

Although genetic endowment is important in behavior analysis, it does not have a privileged role. Human behaviors are not explained solely as genetically determined. Rather, contingencies of survival, contingencies of culture, and contingencies operating in the individual's history (both proximal and distal) together influence behavior and are thus considered causal. Genetic endowment can be a powerful influence on behavior, but in behavior analysis it is treated as an environmental variable. In this case, the environment is within the individual's skin, specifically in the individual's genes and the structures and patterns determined by the genes. For example, a person with a more sensitive nervous system will react differently than a person with a less sensitive nervous system. This has been supported by research on infant disposition in developmental psychology (Kagan & Snidman, 1991; Thomas & Chess, 1986). Researchers found that certain infants tend to cry more, have more negative reactions to new situations, and startle more easily. Behavior analysis takes into account the observation that these infants are biologically more sensitized to the environment, but it does not accord sole causal status to this fact. Instead, the infant's biology is treated as an environmental variable, which in conjunction with contingencies of culture and of individual history influences the likelihood of particular behaviors and behavioral patterns. This idiographic approach to the explanation of behaviors is termed *functional analysis.* It identifies all relevant environmental variables, including physiology, and specifies their relevance to the behavior or behaviors being analyzed.

Physiological changes and variations in neurotransmitter concentrations that are correlated with behaviors of various kinds (such as crying, despondent thinking, or repetitive nervous actions) and with response to consequences in the environment are acknowledged by behavior analysts but are not viewed as causal. Some exceptions do seem to apply, as in cases of gross head injury or organic brain disease. However, even in these cases we tend to analyze in terms of the history of interactions with the environment. That is, the injury or disease is an important and probably a crucial factor in the individual's behavior, but we also take into account the individual's interactions with the environment (proximal, distal, and cultural) to explain his or her behaviors.

BOUNDARIES OF THE THEORY

Training, research, and intervention programs in behavior analysis now exist worldwide (Malott, 2004). We may conclude, therefore, that the consequences of behavior affect the probability of the recurrence of that behavior regardless of the culture of the persons in question.

Behavior analysts have done empirical work from the smallest specific behavioral units to complex behaviors including creativity (Skinner, 1974), language (Hayes et al., 2001; Skinner, 1957), and spirituality (Hayes, 1984). Although Skinner specified contingencies of survival as a significant factor in behavioral analyses pointing to evolutionary factors in our behavior, these are difficult to research. Studies have necessarily concentrated on more proximal reinforcement histories. Sociocultural phenomena may be viewed ultimately as remote, overarching contingencies of survival (Biglan, 1995; Glenn, 1991; Skinner, 1981). Despite the difficulties of arranging empirical study at this level, behavior analysts also consider cultural change an appropriate arena for applied psychological theory (Biglan, 1995; Lamal, 1991; Lowery & Mattaini, 1999; Malagodi, 1986; Mattaini, 2003; Rakos, 1983). Using operant principles to promote beneficial changes in society was one of Skinner's central interests (see Skinner, 1953, 1969, 1971, 1974, 1986), and work in this area continues to be one of the major concerns of behavioral researchers.

An interesting lacuna, given the passionately held contextualist philosophy behind behavior analysis and Skinner's avowed interest in environmental issues (Skinner, 1953, 1971), is the lack of theory, research, or practice among behavior analysts recognizing systemic or reciprocal relationships of humans with the natural world outside of human society. Some behavior analysts view this as an appropriate direction for the growth of operant theory and application because humans evolved as an integral part of complex ecosystems for thousands of generations before the advent of what we now know as urban life (Kahn & Kellert, 2002). In his assessment of environmental psychology, J. H. Wohlwill (1970) pointed out the relative lack of work in this area. Until recently, psychologists of all theoretical approaches have ignored the functional details of our complex interrelationships with the living nonsocial world (ordinarily termed *nature*) in favor of learning how humans interact with each other and with human-built environments.

One hypothesis is that much of the widespread dysfunction in human society (including our meticulously documented psychological disorders as well as many social ills) may be due in part to our "civilized" ignoring, minimizing, discounting, or shutting down of responses to nature, including conditions of sunlight, weather, seasons, patterns of vegetation, bodies of water, geographical features, and nonhuman animals. Further, survival mechanisms presumably now at work in us may be mismatched to the exclusively human-built environment many of us now inhabit, contrib-

uting to ongoing stress. Well-known practices such as keeping pets and houseplants, gardening, appreciation of natural beauty, and vacationing in unspoiled nature tend to support this view. Interdisciplinary research on beneficial effects of contact with nature (Kaplan & Kaplan, 1989) tends to support this hypothesis, which in clinical applications is referred to as *ecopsychology* (Roszak, Gomes, & Kanner, 1995).

EVIDENCE IN SUPPORT OF AND AGAINST THE THEORY

Pragmatic criteria mark behavioral research agendas, and examination of the practical uses of classical and operant theory reveals their usefulness. We may cite here some well-known behavioral therapies for depression (Martell, Addis, & Jacobson, 2001), anxiety, phobias, and obsessive-compulsive disorder (see Foa & Steketee, 1987). Treatments of phobias especially depend heavily on classical conditioning models. Operant theory has led to successful treatment for autistic children (Lovaas, 1977) as well as behavior problems in confined populations such as schools and mental hospitals. More recently researchers have shown promising results in research on outpatient psychotherapy based on operant theory (Hayes, Strosahl, & Wilson, 1999; Kanter et al., 2001; Kohlenberg, Kanter, Bolling, Parker, & Tsai, 2002; Kohlenberg & Tsai, 1991; Martell et al., 2001; Vandenberghe, Ferro, & da Cruz, 2003), interventions for violence in schools (Mattaini, 2001; Mattaini & Lowery, 1999), and health-intervention research (see Biglan, 1995).

The Issue of Language and Private Behaviors

Although it is commonly held that behaviorism is deficient because it ignores all that makes us human—language, feelings, perceptions, dreams, values, and aspirations—this is mistaken. Skinner himself wrote extensively on the nature and role of these private behaviors (1953, 1957, 1974, 1986), and we have described previously a behavior-analytic view of the sense of self. There are still some methodological (non-Skinnerian) behaviorists who steadfastly refuse to deal with behaviors that they cannot observe. However, there are several behavior analysts whose work with these most-human private behaviors is becoming widely known. They conceptualize private behaviors differently than laypersons and professionals who readily accept cognition as a reified (and therefore potentially causal) entity. Basic and applied research on a detailed operant analysis of verbal behavior is now growing around the world, based on groundbreaking work by S. C. Hayes and colleagues (2001), including work on values-centered interventions (Wilson & Murrell, 2004).

Problems of Specific Populations

Some arguments against operant theory are based on misunderstandings. This may be due to a mechanistic application of the form of behavioral techniques in the absence of a functional understanding of the behaviors in question. Thus, when it is claimed that behavioral approaches would not work with sociopaths, because they seem to be indifferent to punishment and respond differently than most people to reinforcers, this is due to an inadequate functional analysis of the behavior of those individuals rather than to a failure of the theory. Sociopaths do function as a result of consequences, and an adequate functional analysis will locate the variables in the environment (including the neurobiology of the individual) that maintain sociopathic behavior. The old saying, "One man's meat is another man's poison," is a basic assumption that behavior analysts understand particularly well.

Here is an example of inappropriate (in this case, incomplete) functional analysis that might be misunderstood as a failure of the theory when in fact it is due to neglecting the developmental context of the behaviors in question. In certain circumstances it may make sense to attempt to fade or extinguish excess crying behavior in a grown person by ignoring it. The function of crying in infants less than six months old, however, is generally different than it may be in adults because infants are physically helpless. Crying functions to draw an adult to attend to their needs (food, comfort, changing, burping, temperature regulation, protecting eyes from sun, etc.). For this reason, parents who ignore a baby's cries (in a misguided attempt to apply behavioral extinguishing) are not likely to see a lessening of crying until the infant is exhausted. Further, they may well be sabotaging normal development of trusting behavior toward others, setting in motion a lifelong pattern of dysfunctional relationships because their child has now learned that needed help and comfort are not available from others. Once again, awareness of the function or functions that behaviors serve, given a thorough analysis of contextual (including developmental) factors, is essential to any attempt to change them.

Similarly, studies of violence among adolescents using an operant model have shown that violence may serve many functions (Mattaini & Lowery, 2001). A blunt application of punishment (a common understanding of operant intervention) clearly does not lessen violence unless it happens to address the specific function or functions of violence in an individual's life. Even then, punishment is known to suppress but not extinguish behavior (Skinner, 1953, p. 190). Mattaini and Lowery (1999) have documented that violence may be a means of obtaining recognition, approval, and respect, of fending off fear, or of gaining power, as well as a way of resolving conflict or expressing anger. They showed that when these functions were satisfied in other ways, violence lessened significantly in a high school sample. Clearly, identifying behavioral interventions with a one-size-fits-all program of punishment or anger-management training in the case of violent behavior would lead one to believe that the operant model is ineffective. However, the heart of an operant approach is a finely honed, individualized functional analysis leading to effective, tailored interventions that address the function or functions of maladaptive behavior.

Another relevant issue is the problem of cross-cultural understanding: a person's understanding of behavior is based on his or her own cultural conditioning. This does not change the validity of the principle of consequences. However, one may misunderstand the way specific consequences function for a person whose culture differs from our own, and our functional analysis of a behavior may then be invalid. We cannot trace the function of a behavior without taking into account the cultural contexts of both the client and the behavior analyst (Bolling, 2002). We understand culture in this context not as an additional variable but as the shared reinforcement history among communities of people (Glenn, 1991). Taking into account this level of reinforcement history—both for the subject and for the behavior analyst—is integral to a thorough functional analysis.

PREDICTIONS FOR EVERYDAY FUNCTIONING

In the preceding story of Ron and DJ, we refer to positive reinforcement and punishment and illustrate some of the results of these experiences. One of the most useful principles of applied behavior analysis (that is, behavior analysis used to solve real-life problems) is that positive reinforcement is preferable to punishment or coercion. Coercion and punishment have numerous troublesome side effects, as illustrated in DJ's story. But contrary to everyday understanding, punishment is not the only way to decrease or stop unwanted behaviors (see Sidman, 1989; Skinner, 1953, pp. 190). Positive reinforcement of alternative behaviors works better in the long run (for a practical introduction to this principle, see Pryor, 1999). Thus, in the four domains of everyday functioning we predict not only that idiographic analysis of function will reveal relevant reinforcers that may not be apparent to the casual observer but also that techniques of positive reinforcement will have more lasting and desirable effects than punishment or coercion in dealing with undesirable behaviors.

Family Life

Both with regard to raising children and with regard to marital relationships, positive reinforcement, differential reinforcement of alternative behaviors, and negative punishment (in which a reinforcer is taken away) plus positive reinforcement of alternative behavior are widely recommended, based on empirical studies, as effective ways to manage behavioral problems in the family (Gottman & Gottman, 1999; Pryor, 1999). However, these techniques must be used with a clear understanding of the function of the target behavior, otherwise it is possible to reinforce unwanted behaviors and punish wanted behaviors.

Work and School

Skinner (1986) hypothesized that the dissatisfaction of many workers in industrialized society is a result of their separation from the immediate consequences of their behavior (i.e., their work). That is, most workers in an industrialized society no longer contact the consequences of their labor because they are separated from the end product that the company produces. In recent years, self-directed work teams have been found to be effective in increasing worker productivity and satisfaction. A self-directed work team is "a group of people working together in their own ways toward a common goal which the team defines" (Chatfield, n.d., p. 1). Work teams are actively involved in making decisions that affect not only their coworkers but also the end product. Thus, workers come into direct contact with the consequences of their behavior, and this has a powerful effect on their experience as well as future behavior. Work teams are "30–50 percent more productive than their conventional counterparts"; quality and productivity increases, operating costs decrease, employee commitment and retention increases (Williams, 1995, pp. 1–2). These findings would be expected from a behavior-analytic point of view because work teams entail increased contact with the consequences of behavior, decreased instances of coercion and punishment, and most likely increased occurrence of positive reinforcement.

Regarding school life, interventions that use negative punishment and positive reinforcement of alternative behaviors have been advocated to decrease problem behaviors and improve school performance (e.g., Meyer, 1999; Northup et al., 1994). However, behavior analysts generally advocate using positive reinforcement rather than any form of punishment (negative or positive) to change problematic behaviors

(Pryor, 1999; Sidman, 1989; Skinner 1986). We mentioned previously the success of this strategy (detecting and positively reinforcing functionally relevant alternative behaviors) in decreasing violence in a high school (Mattaini & Lowery, 1999).

Retirement

Persons reaching retirement age face significant changes in their environment: physical aging, loss of the structure of the workplace (sense of being useful), loss of family and friends, and often reduction of income. This loss of availability of accustomed contingencies may lead retired people to a sense of being at loose ends, not sure how to structure time. When sources of contingent reinforcement are limited, it may lead to depression (Lewinsohn, Biglan, & Zeiss, 1976). If one has access to or ways of developing alternative activities, leading to a sense of usefulness (having an effect on the world, being valued by others), the risk of depression may be averted (Follette, Bach, & Follette, 1993). Thus many retirees engage in volunteer work: campaigning for valued issues, tutoring, involvement with church, temple, or retirement center, and so forth. Those who elect to enjoy passive entertainments (watching TV, reading, attending plays, listening to music) that they were unable to enjoy while employed may feel relief from the coercive aspects of employment (Sidman, 1989; Skinner, 1953). But unless they are also actively engaged with others or with activities that have some effect in the world (creating or repairing something, maintaining a pet or a garden, helping the less fortunate), they are likely to feel a lack of the meaningfulness that would be available from such engagement. That is, in Skinnerian terms, they would not be in contact with relevant controlling variables (Skinner, 1953, pp. 87–89).

Recreation

Because context and reinforcement history determine the likelihood of future behavior, it is no mystery to behavior analysts that one person's recreation may be another person's torture. Risk-taking behaviors and their opposites, for instance, would be predicted on an individual basis from context (including physiological constitution) and reinforcement history.

CONCLUSION

Though its assumptions differ considerably from those in common use, operant theory can be turned toward explaining the phenomena referred to as personality. Reinforcement history has been shown to account for consistency in behavior, for the sense that behavior comes from within, and for the uniqueness of behavior both from the objective and from the subjective points of view.

One of the most difficult areas to approach through behavior theory is the interiority of the sense of self. Though we did this in an abbreviated fashion, we have demonstrated that operant theory can deal with issues of the self and private experience, though it is reputed not to do so. Because it is a theory of change, operant theory helps us not only to perceive the sources of current behavior but also to discern ways to change it through finding the function of that behavior in its context. Hence, one of the strengths of this approach is in helping people with difficulties in living. We hope this chapter has shed some light on our view of the roots of the phenomena referred to as personality.

NOTE

1. Portions of this chapter are adapted from "Operant Theory of Personality," by C. R. Parker, M. Y. Bolling, and R. J. Kohlenberg, 1998, in D. F. Barone, M. Hersen, and V. B. van Hasselt (Eds.), *Advanced Personality* (pp. 155–171). New York: Plenum. Copyright 1998 by Plenum Press. Adapted with permission.

REFERENCES

Biglan, A. (1995). *Changing cultural practices: A contextualist framework for intervention research.* Reno, NV: Context Press.

Bolling, M. Y. (2002). Research and representation: A conundrum for behavior analysts. *Behavior and Social Issues, 12,* 19–28.

Breland, K., & Breland, M. (1961). The misbehavior of organisms. *American Psychologist, 16,* 681–684.

Burger, J. M. (1993). *Personality: Theory and research.* Pacific Grove, CA: Brooks/Cole.

Chatfield, M. M. (n.d.). Self-directed and self-managed teams. Retrieved August 24, 2004, from http://irism.com/selfteam.htm

Cordova, J. V., & Scott, R. L. (2001). Intimacy: A behavioral interpretation. *The Behavior Analyst, 24,* 75–86.

Day, W. F. (1969). Radical behaviorism in reconciliation with phenomenology. *Journal of the Experimental Analysis of Behavior, 12,* 315–328.

Eliot, T. S. (1940). *Old Possum's book of practical cats.* London: Faber and Faber.

Encarta complete multimedia encyclopedia. (1994). CD-ROM. Microsoft.

English, H. B., & English, A. C. (1958). *A Comprehensive dictionary of psychological and psychoanalytical terms: A guide to usage.* New York: David McKay.

Foa, E. B., & Steketee, G. (1987). Behavioral treatment of phobics and obsessive-compulsives. In N. S. Jacobson (Ed), *Psychotherapists in clinical practice: Cognitive and behavioral perspectives* (pp. 78–120). New York: Guilford Press.

Follette, W. C., Bach, P. A., & Follette, V. M. (1993). A behavior-analytic view of psychological health. *The Behavior Analyst, 16,* 303–316.

Glenn, S. S. (1991). Contingencies and metacontingencies: Relations among behavioral, cultural and biological evolution. In P. A. Lamal (Ed.), *Behavioral analysis of societies and cultural practices* (pp. 39–73). New York: Hemisphere.

Gottman, J. M., & Gottman, J. S. (1999). The marriage survival kit: A research-based marital therapy. In R. Berger & M. T. Hannah (Eds.), *Preventive approaches in couples therapy* (pp. 304–330). Philadelphia: Bunner/Mazel.

Hayes, S. C. (1984). Making sense of spirituality. *Behaviorism, 12,* 99–110.

Hayes, S. C., Barnes-Holmes, D., & Roche, B. (2001). *Relational frame theory: A post-Skinnerian account of human language and cognition.* New York: Kluwer Academic/Plenum.

Hayes, S. C., Strosahl, K. D., & Wilson, K. G. (1999). *Acceptance and commitment therapy: An experiential approach to behavior change.* New York: Guilford Press.

Kagan, J., & Snidman, N. (1991). Infant predictors of inhibited and uninhibited profiles. *Psychological Science, 2,* 40–44.

Kahn, P. H., Jr., & Kellert, S. R. (Eds.). (2002). *Children and nature: Psychological, sociocultural, and evolutionary investigations.* Cambridge, MA: MIT Press.

Kalb, R. G. (1994). Regulation of motor neuron dendrite growth by NMDA receptor activation. *Development, 120*(11), 3063–3071.

Kanter, J. W., Parker, C. R., & Kohlenberg, R. J. (2001). Finding the self: A behavioral measure and its clinical implications. *Psychotherapy: Theory, Research and Practice, 38,* 198–211.

Kaplan, R., & Kaplan, S. (1989). *The experience of nature: A psychological perspective.* New York: Cambridge University Press.

Kohlenberg, R. J., Kanter, J. W., Bolling, M. Y., Parker, C. R., & Tsai, M. (2002). Enhancing cognitive therapy for depression with functional analytic psychotherapy: Treatment guidelines and empirical findings. *Cognitive and Behavioral Practice, 9,* 213–229.

Kohlenberg, R. J., & Tsai, M. (1991). *Functional analytic psychotherapy: Creating intense and curative therapeutic relationships.* New York: Plenum Press.

Kohlenberg, R. J., & Tsai, M. (1995). I speak, therefore I am: A behavioral approach to understanding problems of the self. *The Behavior Therapist, 18*(6), 113–116.

Lamal, P. A., (Ed.). (1991). *Behavioral analysis of societies and cultural practices.* New York: Hemisphere.

Lang, P. K., Geer, J., & Hnatiow, M. (1963). Semantic generalization of conditioned autonomic responses. *Journal of Experimental Psychology, 65,* 552–558.

Lewinsohn, P.M., Biglan, T., & Zeiss, A. (1976). Behavioral assessment of depression. In P. Davidson (Ed.), *Behavioral management of anxiety, depression, and pain* (pp. 91–146). New York: Brunner/Mazel.

Linehan, M. (1993). *Cognitive-behavioral treatment of borderline personality disorder.* New York: Guilford Press.

Lovaas, O. I. (1977). *The autistic child: Language development through behavior modification.* New York: Irvington.

Lowery, C. T., & Mattaini, M. A. (1999). The science of sharing power: Native American thought and behavior analysis. *Behavior and Social Issues, 9,* 3–23.

Malagodi, E. F. (1986). On radicalizing behaviorism: A call for cultural analysis. *The Behavior Analyst, 9,* 1–17.

Malott, M. E. (2004). Toward the globalization of behavior analysis. *The Behavior Analyst, 27,* 25–32.

Martell, C. R., Addis, M. E., & Jacobson, N. S. (2001). *Depression in context: Strategies for guided action.* New York: Norton.

Mattaini, M. A. (2001). Constructing cultures of non-violence: The PEACE POWER! strategy. *Education and Treatment of Children, 24,* 430–447.

Mattaini, M. A. (2003). Understanding and reducing collective violence. *Behavior and Social Issues, 12,* 90–108.

Mattaini, M. A., & Lowery, C. T. (1999). Youth violence prevention: The state of the science. Retrieved August 25, 2004, from http://www.bfsr.org/violence.html

Mattaini, M. A., & Lowery, C. T. (2001). Constructing community: The applied science of youth violence prevention. In D. S. Sandhu (Ed.), *Faces of violence: Psychological correlates, concepts and intervention strategies* (pp. 439–453). Commack, NY: Nova Science.

Meyer, K. A. (1999). Functional analysis and treatment of problem behavior exhibited by elementary school children. *Journal of Applied Behavior Analysis, 32*(2), 229–232.

Morris, W. (Ed.). (1978). *The American heritage dictionary of the English language* (New College ed.). Boston: Houghton Mifflin.

Northup, J., Wacker, D. P., Berg, W. K., Kelly, L., Sasso, G., & DeRaad, A. (1994). The treatment of severe behavior problems in school settings using a technical assistance model. *Journal of Applied Behavior Analysis, 27,* 33–48.

Pryor, K. (1999). *Don't shoot the dog! The new art of teaching and training* (Rev. ed.). New York: Bantam Books.

Rakos, R. F. (1983). Behavior analysis as a framework for a multi-disciplinary approach to social change. *Behaviorists for Social Action Journal, 4,* 12–16.

Roszak, T., Gomes, M. E., & Kanner, A. D. (Eds.). (1995). *Ecopsychology: Restoring the earth, healing the mind.* San Francisco: Sierra Club Books.

Salm, A. K., Modney, B. K., & Hatton, G. I. (1988). Alterations in supraoptic nucleus ultrastructure of maternally behaving virgin rats. *Brain Research Bulletin, 21*(4), 685–691.

Sidman, M. (1989). *Coercion and its fallout.* Boston: Authors Cooperative.

Skinner, B. F. (1945). The operational analysis of psychological terms. *Psychological Review, 52*(5), 270–277.

Skinner, B. F. (1953). *Science and human behavior.* New York: Macmillan.

Skinner, B. F. (1957). *Verbal behavior.* New York: Appleton-Century-Crofts.

Skinner, B. F. (1969). *Contingencies of reinforcement: A theoretical analysis.* New York: Appleton-Century-Crofts.

Skinner, B. F. (1971). *Beyond freedom and dignity.* New York: Knopf.

Skinner, B. F. (1974). *About behaviorism.* New York: Knopf.

Skinner, B. F. (1981). Selection by consequences. *Science, 213,* 501–504.

Skinner, B. F. (1983). *A matter of consequences.* New York: Knopf.

Skinner, B. F. (1986). What is wrong with daily life in the Western world? *American Psychologist, 41*(5), 568–574.

Thomas, A., & Chess, S. (1986). The New York Longitudinal Study: From infancy to early adult life. In R. Plomin & J. Dunn (Eds.), *The study of temperament: Changes, continuities, and challenges* (pp. 39–52). New York: Brunner/Mazel.

Vandenberghe, L., Ferro, C. L. B., & da Cruz, A. C. F. (2003). FAP-enhanced group therapy for chronic pain. *The Behavior Analyst Today, 4,* 369–375.

Weiler, I. J., Hawrylak, N., & Greenough, W. T. (1995). Morphogenesis in memory formation: Synaptic and cellular mechanisms. 69th Titisee Conference: The neurobiology of memory formation in vertebrates: Neuronal plasticity and brain function (1994, Titisee, Germany). *Behavioural Brain Research, 66*(1–2), 1–6.

Williams, R. (1995). Self-directed work teams. Retrieved August 24, 2004, from http://www.qualitydigest.com/nov95/html/self-dir.html

Wilson, K. G., & Murrell, A. R. (2004). Values work in acceptance and commitment therapy: Setting a course for behavioral treatment. In S. C. Hayes, V. M. Follette, & M. Linehan (Eds.), *Mindfulness and acceptance: Expanding the cognitive-behavioral tradition* (pp. 120–151). New York: Guilford Press.

Wohlwill, J. H. (1970). The emerging discipline of environmental psychology. *American Psychologist, 25,* 303–312.

CHAPTER 8

Evolutionary Theories

DAVID A. BEAULIEU AND DAPHNE BLUNT BUGENTAL

INTRODUCTION

Evolutionary psychology is a theoretical approach concerned with the processes by which humans evolved to solve reoccurring problems in our evolutionary past. However, the natural selection of adaptive behavior in our evolutionarily past does not guarantee that such behavior will be adaptive in our current environment. In fact, many people show social responses that seem to be harmful to both self and others in today's world (e.g., intergroup aggression) but may have served an adaptive function in our evolutionary past (e.g., defending shared resources from out-group competitors).

In this chapter, we discuss the ways in which evolutionarily ancient adaptations continue to influence us in our modern world. We begin by introducing the basic tenets of evolutionary psychology. We then ask how evolutionary psychology views the role of (1) development and (2) physiological processes within its formulations. We move on to consider the boundaries and controversies concerning the application of evolutionary psychology to human behavior. Finally, we explore the predictions that have been (or might be) made about human functioning within everyday experience. Within this final section we consider both the adaptive and maladaptive processes (as understood from an evolutionary perspective) that operate in the areas of family life, work and school, retirement, and recreation.

STATEMENT OF THEORY

Given the focus on evolutionary theory, a quick overview is provided of (1) the principles of evolution, (2) the focus of explanatory processes in evolutionary psychology, and (3) the products of evolution. We end this section with examples of how evolutionary theory is applied to psychopathology.

The Principles of Evolution

Fossil records undeniably demonstrate that life-forms on Earth have undergone tremendous changes over time (in-creasing in both diversity and complexity). Today, only one unifying scientific theory explains this historical process: evolution. At the foundation of this explanation lie three principles: (1) the principle of variation (i.e., organisms demonstrate phenotypic differences in morphology and behavior), (2) the principle of inheritance (some phenotypic differences are heritable), and (3) the principle of adaptation (some phenotypic characteristics are better able to solve problems associated with survival and reproduction). The logical consequence of these premises is evolution (Dunbar, 1982). More specifically, out of phenotypic variance, traits and characteristics are selected based on their ability to solve adaptive problems. In this way, organisms become specialized problem solvers within their particular ecology, and through this process life on Earth has branched out into every possible terrestrial niche.

The Focus of Explanatory Processes in Evolutionary Psychology

The burden that all social scientists willingly accept is the burden of *Why?* Why do sociopaths feel no obligation to social norms (especially those concerning reciprocity)? Why would some caregivers be moved to abandon, abuse, or neglect their offspring? Why are certain romantic partners morbidly vigilant of cues that may indicate infidelity? Why? Why? Why?!? Like an incessantly curious child the social scientist never stops asking: Why? Whereas social scientists do not differ in their inquisitiveness, they do differ in the perspective they choose to utilize in answering such questions.

The levels of analysis (or differing perspectives) used by social scientists today evolved out of heated debates concerning the different methods of analysis first outlined and elaborated upon by animal researchers in the early 1960s (Mayr, 1961; Tinbergen, 1963). During this time much misunderstanding and controversy among scholars was occurring because academics were not fully acknowledging that in explaining the same behavior there existed different (but complementary) perspectives of analysis. For instance, in answering the question, "Why are children with medical problems more likely to be targeted for abuse?" one can explain the behavior by referring to *proximate* causes (e.g., social stigma associated with being a parent of a medically at-risk child may lead to the festering of resentment directed toward one's offspring), or one can equally refer to *ultimate* causes (e.g., parents may have evolved psychological mechanisms that would have aided them in making decisions concerning parental investment based upon the survival and/or reproductive potential of one's offspring). Within evolutionary psychology, the focus of interest has been on ultimate explanations. Thus, it offers an approach that works together with other theoretical perspectives to provide a full accounting of human behavior.

In explaining the origin of behavior, proximate explanations focus on ontogeny. Ontogeny refers to the developmental trajectory of a specific individual; ontogenetic explanations take into consideration how genetic inheritance/makeup interacts with one's particular life history in producing behavior. As such, ontogenetic explanations include explanations of behavior that make reference to socialization, development, or even genetic inheritance. Whereas proximate explanations focus on the relatively recent ontogenetic trajectory of an individual, ultimate explanations focus on the evolutionarily ancient trajectory of an organism. In utilizing the evolutionary trajectory to explain the origin of behavior, social scientists can examine both (1) the phylogenetic history of a behavior (by looking across and within species) and (2) the functional advantage conferred by a behavior in an organism's evolutionary past (as discussed here, a functional advantage would refer to any biological advantage that would have increased an organism's chances of survival and/or reproduction). Proximate explanations and ultimate explanations are not competing alternatives, but instead they encompass a much-needed complete explanation of behavior (Dewsbury, 1999).

The Products of Evolution

Out of the three principles of evolution, three products arise: adaptations, by-products, and noise.

Adaptations

The hallmark of an adaptation is the existence of design features that serve to solve a particular adaptive problem. Adaptations are recognizable by the high degree of complexity, economy, and efficiency utilized in solving a specific problem associated with survival or reproduction (Williams,

1966). The way an adaptation fits a particular problem is the same way a key fits a lock. As noted by Buss (1999, p. 47), "just as the shape of the key must be coordinated to fit the internal features of the lock, the shape of design features of a psychological mechanism must be coordinated with the features required to solve an adaptive problem of survival or reproduction." In this way, adaptations demonstrate a level of design that makes it difficult to argue that their outcome (i.e., adaptive solution to an adaptive problem) is due to chance or fortuitous effects (Williams, 1966).

By-Products

Adaptations exist as the result of the active selection of characteristics based on their ability to solve adaptive problems. On the other hand, a by-product exists based solely on the strength of its chance association with adaptive characteristics. For instance, the belly button is a by-product of the umbilical cord (i.e., an adaptation whose function is to provide the developing fetus with nutrients; Buss, 1999). The belly button itself does not have an adaptive function (i.e., belly buttons neither increase nor decrease an organism's chances of survival or reproduction).

It should be noted, however, that by-products can lose their neutral status. In fact, theoretically, many complex adaptations seen today may be examples of beneficial by-products that either (1) have been incorporated within the originally associated adaptation or (2) have obtained their own evolutionary function (distinct from the adaptation with which it was originally associated). For instance, many animal researchers interested in avian evolution propose that avian feathers first arose in response to adaptive problems associated with body-temperature regulation (Ostrom, 1974). However, the selection of feathers for their insulation properties also led to the selection of incidental by-products, including the streamlining of avian morphology, which led to increased aerodynamics and ultimately flight (Bock, 2000).

Noise

Whereas the belly button is a by-product, the variation that exists among belly buttons (e.g., small, large, flat, round, oval, etc.) represents another product of evolution: noise (Buss, 1999). Unlike by-products, characteristics described as noise may or may not be systematically associated with adaptations. In fact, noise is better described as involving random effects. The conception of noise as random variation in morphological and behavioral characteristics constitutes one of the central foundations of the evolutionary process, that is, the principle of variation.

Random variation can continue to exist for a number of reasons. One reason concerns the potential neutrality of variation. Like by-products, noise may have no impact on the survival and/or reproduction of an organism, and such neutral noise may simply be tolerated. A second reason variation may continue to be an elementary part of an organism's constitution relates to whether or not the organism in question engages in sexual recombination. Among organisms that undergo sexual recombination, a degree of variation between one generation and the next is inevitable. Finally, variation arises out of unpredictable mutations, deviations in development, and unprecedented changes in the environment (e.g., individual differences in susceptibility to schizophrenia as the result of exposure to radiation from the atomic bomb; Inamura, Nakane, Ohta, & Kondo, 1999).

Distinguishing between Adaptations, By-Products, and Noise

Evolutionary social scientists focus the bulk of their energy on attempting to map out the psychological adaptations of the human psyche. As such, this perspective is often referred to as an adaptationist approach. However, as mentioned previously, adaptations are not the only product of the evolutionary process. Before evolutionary psychologists can be confident that a particular behavior is an adaptation, they must first rule out the alternative conclusion that the behavior in question is not a by-product or simply noise in the psychological machinery. But how does one tell the difference between psychological adaptations, by-products, and noise?

Let us take the design features associated with social-exchange processes as an example of an adaptation. Cosmides and Tooby (1992) have proposed (and provided experimental evidence to support) that social-exchange processes make use of evolved social contract reasoning. Because the survival and reproductive interest of our kin indirectly increases our own reproductive success, it is easy to see how cooperation with kin would have evolved. However, because nonkin do not share reproductive interests, an adaptive problem arises when such cooperation occurs between unrelated individuals. One means by which this adaptive problem can be solved is via reciprocity (i.e., cooperation in service of mutual benefit). However, this requires social-exchange mechanisms that ensure that exchange partners both provide and receive benefits; if either partner cheats, the process fails. Thus the design features associated with a social-exchange adaptation include psychological mechanisms that (1) estimate the cost and benefit of exchange items (from both one's own perspective and the perspective of one's social-exchange partner), (2) detect cheaters (i.e., individuals who take a benefit without incur-

ring a cost), and (3) store information about past exchanges in order to avoid cheaters and seek out cooperators (for a more exhaustive list of social-exchange design features, see Cosmides and Tooby, 1992).

At the same time, one can also see evidence of by-products of this adaptation. By-products of these design features include the ability to navigate a modern world composed of the New York Stock Exchange, e-commerce (e.g., eBay), and other aspects of a free-market economy. That is, these modern competencies did not arise directly from adaptive problems faced in our evolutionary past (e.g., hunter-gatherers were not concerned with the diversity of their portfolios). As such, these competencies do not have design features of their own but instead borrow their structure from an adaptation designed to deal with social exchanges faced by our hunter-gatherer ancestors.

Individual differences in the design features associated with social exchange constitute noise. For instance, individuals may vary in their ability to estimate the value of exchange items from the perspective of their exchange partners or may vary on the thresholds they use in determining whether or not a exchange partner is a perpetual cheater. Those who have a strong belief in a just world may underestimate the possibility that others may cheat, whereas those who are wary of the motives of others may overestimate the possibility that others may cheat.

Psychopathology: An Evolutionary Approach

In recent years there has been a growing movement to apply an evolutionary framework in explaining the origins of psychopathology (e.g., Baron-Cohen, 1997; Gilbert, 1998). Fundamentally, this endeavor has led to a number of explanations concerning the manifestation of modern psychopathologies, including those based on evolutionary tolerability, modern mismatches, and the miscalibration of ancient adaptations.

Evolutionarily Tolerable Psychopathologies

Genetically heritable characteristics responsible for psychopathology can be passed on to future generations as long as those characteristics do not drastically impede an individual's survival or reproduction. For example, schizophrenia, with its adult onset, does not drastically hinder an individual's ability to reach reproductive age and have progeny. As such, genes responsible for schizophrenia can be passed on to subsequent generations. However, even if a particular psychopathology does not have a late adult onset, other factors may prevent susceptibility to psychopathology from having a negative impact on the ultimate survival and reproductive success of an organism. Specifically, the genetic factors responsible for psychopathology can prosper in the gene pool simply because, more often than not, those genes are not expressed in the form of psychopathology. In the case of psychopathologies thought to be caused by recessive genes (e.g., autism, schizophrenia, Tourette's syndrome), certain mental illness may remain essentially dormant across generations and as such be tolerated by evolution.

Evolutionarily Novel Mismatches

Adaptive characteristics are selected over evolutionary time in response to reoccurring obstacles to survival and reproduction. The greater the obstacle associated with an adaptive problem, the greater the selection pressures that are placed upon the organism to solve that adaptive problem. The exact amount of time needed before an adaptive problem leads to the selection and fixation of an adaptive solution is unknown. However, once a particular adaptation has reached fixation within an organism, the design features of that adaptation will remain essentially unchanged unless strong selection pressures arise that modify or reverse its features. This process of adaptive fixation is believed to be a slow one (occurring over many generations). In order for an adaptive solution to be selected, the conditions associated with an adaptive problem must remain consistent and unchanged over many generations. Absent such consistency, the selection pressures associated with such an adaptive problem would either fluctuate or disappear, and the fixation of an adaptive solution would not be possible (Tooby & Cosmides, 1992).

Given the evolutionary time course by which adaptations reach fixation within an organism, evolutionary social scientists have come to the conclusion that our modern skulls house stone-age minds (Tooby & Cosmides, 1992). Because modern advances in technology (e.g., agriculture, the industrial revolution, the computer age) have led to many unpredictable changes, there are also many potential mismatches between the adaptiveness of a mechanism in evolutionarily distant times and the adaptiveness of that same mechanism in today's world. For example, the human sweet tooth is an adaptive solution to the problem of selecting relatively scarce high-energy packets of food as an important source of nutrition. However, a sweet tooth in today's world—where refined mass-produced sugar is abundant—leads to the negative consequences of obesity, heart disease, and tooth decay. In other words, there exists a mismatch between the adaptive problem faced today (i.e., selecting healthy items for consumption) and the adaptive solution selected for in our evolutionary past (i.e., selecting food based on its associated sweetness; Symons, 1992).

Modern mismatches between adaptive problems and adaptive solutions may explain to some extent the psychopathologies we observe today. For example, Jensen and colleagues (1997) argue that attention-deficit/hyperactivity disorder (ADHD) may represent an adaptive response to an evolutionary harsh environment. In this argument the characteristic symptoms of ADHD (hyperactivity, inattention, and impulsivity) are reconceptualized in terms of response readiness. This response readiness manifests itself as (1) increased exploration of one's environment for potential threats and opportunities (i.e., increased motor activity/hyperactivity), (2) hypervigilance for signs of danger (i.e., rapid-scanning and attentional shifts), and (3) quick responses to environmental stimuli (i.e., impulsivity). During impoverished times, where threats were plentiful and opportunities scarce, such a response-ready individual may have been better able to (1) avoid dangers and (2) quickly seize fleeting benefits. As such, the selection of genes responsible for ADHD may have occurred in our evolutionary past. However, the behavioral manifestation of the genes today is maladaptive and disruptive in a number of modern environments, including work and school.

Miscalibration of Ancient Adaptations

As is well known, the immune system acts to protect the body from external threats (e.g., viruses, bacteria). Within the immune system, miscalibrations concerning self-recognition lead to autoimmune diseases like multiple sclerosis, and miscalibrations concerning the potential threat of a substance lead to a variety of allergic reactions. Just as miscalibrations in the immune system can lead to maladaptive immune responses, miscalibrations in the psychological architecture of the human mind can lead to maladaptive behavior.

Phobias often occur in response to stimuli that posed some reasonable threat in our evolutionary past (e.g., spiders, snakes, heights). Agoraphobia, as another example, is the fear of finding oneself in a situation where it would be difficult to escape or impossible to find help. Arguably, such concerns may have served an adaptive function in our evolutionary past by motivating individuals to avoid such situations (Marks & Nesse, 1994). However, this social anxiety quickly can become maladaptive if the threshold for anxiety is set too low, the fear response is too intense, the recovery process is too long, or if an individual becomes increasingly sensitized to the fear-invoking event with repetition. Additionally, post-traumatic stress disorder may reflect an originally adaptive fear reaction that fails to turn off and continues past the point that the fear-eliciting events are still occurring.

DEVELOPMENTAL CONSIDERATIONS

One of the greatest misconceptions concerning psychological adaptations is the belief that the relevant competencies must be present at birth if they are to be viewed as involving evolutionary design. This false belief stems from a widely used but arcane conceptualization of innateness that dictates that evolutionary competencies must be experience-independent (i.e., derived solely from the biological constitution of the brain and independent from experience). However, from an evolutionary perspective, the brain is not solely experience-independent, nor is it solely experience-dependent. It is, in fact, both. As a caveat, however, the central focus of evolutionary thought has been with the experience-expectant brain.

An experience-expectant brain is one that anticipates a particular set of environmental inputs and responds to these environmental inputs in a reliably adaptive fashion. Across development, different experience-expectant adaptations come online in a clocklike fashion. The earliest developmentally activated adaptations are those associated with infant attachment.

In order for an infant to survive, he or she must be efficient at eliciting care from a primary caregiver. In solving the problem of eliciting care from one's primary caregiver, the quick identification and later recognition of one's caregiver is paramount. Over evolutionary time, infants solved this adaptive problem by taking advantage of the reliable features associated with their species. For example, infants can anticipate that their primary caregiver will have two eyes, a nose, and a mouth. Evidence that infants take advantage of these reliable features comes from research demonstrating that newborn infants focus particular interest on these aspects of the human face (e.g., Maurer & Salapatek, 1976) and show a strong preference for these facial features in their correct orientation (e.g., Goren, Sarty, & Wu, 1975). That is, infants not only expect these features to be part of the human face but they expect them to be in a particular configuration.

Given the experience-expectant nature of the human mind, what happens if the experiences one expects do not occur? For some adaptations, sensitive periods exist during which the focus is on key environmental inputs. If key inputs are missing during these sensitive periods, the activation of particular adaptations may be impeded, leading to pathology that cannot be repaired as a result of later processes. For instance, during language acquisition the child anticipates exposure to predictable linguistic environmental inputs. However, when access to these environmental inputs is hindered by early hearing loss, pathologies associated with speech will arise (Geers & Moog, 1987). If cochlear implants are introduced at a later age, the same speech benefits will not be found as when the child receives a cochlear implant at a younger age (e.g., NiParko, 2004).

Similarly, in early infancy, if children lack responsive parental care, attachment disorders may develop (Bowlby, 1969). A good illustration of this process has been provided in the work of Rutter and his research team (e.g., Rutter & O'Connor, 2004) on the long-term outcomes of children adopted from Romanian orphanages in which they had experienced an extreme level of interpersonal deprivation. Although children adopted into well-functioning homes showed a high level of recovery, they also showed persistent deficits (deficits that were not shown by children from less socially deprived backgrounds adopted into similar families). In other words, later experiences failed to fully compensate for deficits that occurred during a sensitive period that had passed.

BIOLOGICAL/PHYSIOLOGICAL PROCESSES

Evolutionary psychology is biological in its origins in that it draws its basic concepts from evolutionary biology. It also borrows from neuroendocrinology in the mediating processes that are involved. For example, it also is concerned with the hormonal regulatory processes that are activated in response to the evolutionary design of humans.

Although it is implicit within evolutionary psychology, it is not always clearly specified that evolutionary design is implemented at the level of the central nervous system. Genes contain the blueprints. Neurotransmitters and neurohormones act as the messengers. However, the brain is not simply an organizer of receptivity to experience; it also is characterized by a high degree of plasticity (Bruer & Greenough, 2001). This plasticity is made possible by the dynamic processes that exist between genes, neurotransmitters, and neurohormones. For instance, as a child gains experience, hormonal responses lead ultimately to the relocation of genes to more active sites within relevant brain cells, which, in turn, leads to heightened expression of the effects of those genes (Lamond & Earnshaw, 1998). The implementation of these processes involves the complex subject matter of concern to developmental neuroscientists. However, the basic platform for those processes involves evolutionary design.

BOUNDARIES OF THE THEORY (INCLUDING CULTURAL EFFECTS AND LIMITATIONS)

The application of evolution to human behavior has proven insightful in many areas of human psychology, including perception (e.g., Shepard, 1992), cognition (e.g., Cosmides & Tooby, 1992), development and socialization (e.g., Bjorklund & Pellegrini, 2000; Bugental & Beaulieu, 2003), social psychology (e.g., Kenrick, Neuberg, Zierk, & Krones, 1994), and psychopathology (e.g., Baron-Cohen, 1997). Nevertheless, boundaries do exist.

Evolutionary psychology can provide only limited insight into historically novel adaptive problems. Literacy represents an example of a historically novel competence for which there is no preexisting adaptation. Learning to read and write are critical adaptive problems faced by a large portion of the world, yet humans are not prepared for this task by their evolutionary history. The ways in which evolutionarily novel adaptive problems are solved often involves bootstrapping; that is, a novel problem is solved by use of evolved adaptations that act in the service of some other problem. For example, the use of written language bootstraps off the capacity to acquire spoken language and to engage in abstract thought. At the same time, the absence of an evolved adaptation poses costs. For example, the prevalence of reading problems among the young is a great deal higher than the prevalence of speech problems. That is, we easily acquire competence in spoken language in that it makes use of an adaptation; however, acquiring competence in written language (which borrows from other adaptations) does not come easily.

At the most general level, evolution accounts for the basic capacity to acquire and integrate knowledge from many different sources. However, evolutionary theory has little to contribute toward our understanding of abstract levels of thought that had no counterpart in ancient times; for example, it cannot help in explaining how individuals engage in the level of abstract thinking required to understand calculus, string theory, or genetic drift.

Another limitation in the explanatory power of evolutionary psychology involves the specific content of some types of socially acquired knowledge. As an example, the specific ability to learn social conventions appears to represent an adaptation; that is, there are sensitive periods for learning about social conventions, and there is a high degree of receptivity to such knowledge at that time (Emde, Biringen, Clyman, & Oppenheim, 1991). Nonetheless, there is a great deal of latitude with respect to the content of social conventions. Cultures vary widely in the content of their rituals, style of dress, eating routines, and so forth. Whereas the basic functions of social conventions may act in the service of evolutionary adaptations, the specific forms of these conventions is not entirely specified by evolutionary processes.

EVIDENCE IN SUPPORT OF AND AGAINST EVOLUTIONARY THEORY

Evolutionary theory has provided a central framework in understanding many processes that cannot easily be accounted for by other theories. The integrated thought of such research-

ers as Harlow (1973) and Bowlby (1969) led to the early recognition that the relationship between mothers and infants involved an evolutionary design that was universal in nature and that made use of mechanisms that could not be explained by the traditional tenets of learning theory. Evolutionary psychology also helped to account for universal processes in sexually dimorphic play styles. It became apparent that boys and girls tended to show high levels of sex differences in play styles—often despite the influence of socializing agents (e.g., Geary, 1998). As another example, the characteristics found to be attractive in a potential mate showed some characteristic differences between the sexes that were broadly shared across cultures—differences that appeared to serve as adaptations (Buss, 1989).

There have been a number of controversies on the evolutionary design of some aspects of human nature, however. A contemporary example of such a controversy involves the extent to which males and females differ in their experiences of sexual and emotional jealousy. It has been argued from an evolutionary position (Buss, 1992) that sexual jealousy is more common in males and emotional jealousy more common in females. The rationale for this position is that males are necessarily more uncertain than are females with respect to the paternity of offspring and thus are more invested in guarding mates against sexual contact with other males. Females, on the other hand, have greater need of protection and support for dependent offspring and thus guard against their partner's emotional investment in another female. Within the empirical literature the strongest support for the existence of these sex differences comes from a forced-choice methodology whereby participants are asked to choose which of two types of infidelities (sexual or emotional) would cause them to feel the most upset (Buss, Larsen, Westen, & Semmelroth, 1992). As predicted from an evolutionary perspective, men reported greater upset to sexual infidelity than did women, and women reported greater upset to emotional infidelity than did men. In addition, a meta-analysis including 32 samples of forced-choice participants also reconfirmed the existence of these sex differences (Harris, 2003). Finally, Buss et al. (1992) showed that men demonstrate greater electrodermal activity in response to imagined sexual infidelity (compared to imagined emotional infidelity), and women demonstrate a greater reactivity to imagined emotional infidelity (compared to imagined sexual infidelity).

Serious doubts have been raised about the robustness of these findings, however. Whereas force-choice methodology often replicates this sex difference, other self-report data has demonstrated limited support and contradictory findings (e.g., for review, see Harris, 2003). For instance, a continuous scale found no evidence for sex difference in the experience of sexual and emotional jealousy (DeSteno, Bartlett, Braverman, &

Salovey, 2002). Furthermore, whereas the psychophysiological reactions reported by Buss et al. (1992) seems to provide compelling evidence in support of an evolutionary account of romantic jealousy, subsequent attempts to replicate and extend these findings have failed.

Even though we end this section with a current controversy, the fact remains that the application of evolution to human behavior adheres to the Lakatosian philosophy of science (Ketelaar & Ellis, 2000). That is, evolutionary theory not only provides novel predictions and explanations that can be subjected to rigorous scientific testing but also demonstrates the ability to provide insights into areas of the human condition when other competing theories have been baffled. As such, strong support exists concerning the continued utilization of evolutionary theory in the social sciences.

PREDICTIONS FOR EVERYDAY LIFE

Having considered the theoretical tenets and organizing features of evolutionary psychology, we now move on to consider how it may be utilized in considering the processes that operate within everyday life. In doing so, we consider both (1) the ways in which evolutionary psychology views (or might view) the adaptive processes that operate within family life, work and school, retirement, and recreation, and (2) the ways in which evolutionary psychology views (or might view) psychopathology (or maladaptive processes) within these areas of life.

Family Life

Everyday Adaptations in Family Life

In our discussion of the role of evolutionary psychology in accounting for everyday family processes, we focus on those mechanisms that usually serve us well in the relationships between caregivers and the young and between mated partners. It is not surprising that some of the clearest examples of evolutionary design should be found in such relationships in that they include the strongest motives for social connection with others.

Parent-Child Relationships. The evolutionary design of mother-offspring relationships is apparent across cultures and across species (among mammals). Among mammals, the young are born as dependent organisms unable to care for themselves. As a result, their successful survival is contingent upon the care provided by those individuals who are invested in them (i.e., individuals who will gain reproductive benefits as a result of providing parental care).

Bowlby's (1969) notion of attachment provides an evolutionary framework for understanding the processes that operate within caregiving relationships early in life. Given the level of dependence demonstrated by the young, the dyadic system of attachment is based upon the parental provisioning and maintenance of safety. Although parents also provide other benefits (e.g., provision of food), the attachment system is designed fundamentally to maintain proximity between caregiver and offspring and thus maintain the safety of the young (which is also experienced as relief from distress; Bugental & Grusec, in press).

The basic design features of parental care are further accounted for within evolutionary psychology by parental investment theory. First proposed by Trivers (1974), and expanded by Wilson and Daly (1994), the basic idea is that parents invest in their offspring to the extent that those offspring will increase the parent's own reproductive success. This requires that the young are healthy and grow up to parent successfully their own healthy children (thus replicating shared genes). However, parental investment involves trade-offs. The more a parent invests in one child, the less he or she is able to invest in other offspring or potential offspring (or engage in other personal activities). Therefore, evolutionary mechanisms operate to provide cues to the relative value of individual children—cues that are available at birth or soon after birth. Such cues are used in parental investment decisions (processes that operate automatically and need not involve conscious reflective thought). Cues may include the child's apparent health, the child's responsiveness to others (suggesting their receptivity to socialization), as well as cues to their biological relatedness (important for putative fathers who, unlike mothers, can never be completely certain that a child is their own).

Although the various factors that are involved in parental care and attachment have filled many scholarly volumes, we can summarize the most distinctive features of their evolutionary design among humans as follows:

1. Humans are designed to show a positive interest in infant faces (e.g., Zebrowitz, Kendall-Tackett, & Fafel, 1991) and activation of concern in response to infant cries (e.g., Ostwald, 1963; Zebrowitz, 1997).

2. Infants are designed to show heightened attention to social stimuli (e.g., looking at faces) in the first few hours of life (e.g., Johnson, Dziurawiec, Ellis, & Morton, 1991).

3. Infants are designed to learn easily the identity of their own parents (e.g., DeCasper & Fifer, 1987; Field, Cohen, Garcia, & Greenberg, 1984).

4. Humans are designed to engage in a particular style of

communication (infant-directed speech) that facilitates their relationship with infants (e.g., it is responded to positively by the young) and increases the ability of the young to acquire language (Fernald et al., 1989; Kitamura, Thanavishuth, Burnham, & Luksaneeyanawin, 2002).

5. Infants are designed to manifest distress in response to stimuli that suggest danger (or would have suggested danger in our evolutionary past), for example, unfamiliar humans (in particular, unfamiliar males; Skarin, 1977) and animal-type stimuli, potential predators in our evolutionary past (Scarr & Salapatak, 1970).

6. The hormonal-response system of mothers is designed to prepare them for the provision of parental care. Across the course of pregnancy, women show changes in the presence of certain hormones (e.g., estradiol, prolactin, and cortisol). Some of these hormonal changes are important for the birthing process itself; others are important as sources of influence on the interest the mothers shows and the level of care she provides to the child (Fleming, 1990). For example, new mothers rate infant odor cues (general body, urine, and feces) more positively than do nonmothers (Fleming et al., 1993). In addition, they demonstrate higher levels of arousal to infant cries than do nonmothers (Boukydis & Burgess, 1982).

7. The hormonal changes shown by fathers during the pregnancy of their partners prepares them for the provision of parental care. Men show many changes during the pregnancy of their partner that mirror those shown by the prospective mother (e.g., increases in prolactin, a change that is associated with increased interest in infant stimuli; Fleming, Corter, Stallings, & Steiner, 2002). In addition they show other changes (reduced levels of testosterone) that prepare them for reduced aggression (Gray, Kahlenberg, Barrett, Lipson, & Ellison, 2002).

Within all these processes, evidence has been found for evolutionary design. That is, the processes involved typically make use of biased (but unlearned) attentional processes, privileged acquisition of information, and privileged learning. In addition, the processes involved are typically regulated by prenatal hormonal processes and are universal in nature.

Mating Relationships.   Among species that are cooperative breeders (i.e., species in which fathers share in the care of the young), there are many complex processes that serve as adaptations. If a mated relationship is to serve the reproductive interests of both parties, it is necessary that the outcome of that pairing increase the reproductive success of both. Just as with parental investment, the selective investment in a

mated relationship has trade-offs—in particular for males. For example, males can invest their efforts differentially in mating activity or in the maintenance of a continuing relationship. If, on the one hand, a male invests in mating activity, he is likely to sire a large number of children but will resultingly be unable to provide care for all (a quantity strategy). If, on the other hand, a male invests in a long-term relationship with a partner, the smaller number of progeny produced are more likely to survive and flourish (a quality strategy). Even in the present time, children who are reared in a family that includes their biological father (but not stepfather) show many consistent benefits, even when controlling for such related factors as differential access to economic resources. For example, boys are more likely to show hormonal patterns that are consistent with intermale competitive success (Flinn, Quinlan, Decker, Turner, & England, 1996) and are less likely to engage in deviant behavior (Dornbusch et al., 1985); girls are less likely to show precocial interest in sexual activity that will limit their future long-term opportunities (Belsky, Steinberg, & Draper, 1991).

The trade-offs experienced in the mating game differ across context. It has been suggested that investment in short-term mating activity as opposed to investment in long-term relationships (that includes care of the young) follows from cues within the immediate environment. That is, there are cues present in the early life of the child that are diagnostic with respect to the type of world to which they are born. When the young are born to a world that is uncertain or has cues to danger (e.g., the father is absent), those children are more likely to grow up fast (in terms of their actual sexual maturation) and follow a short-term mating strategy that insures that they will at least have some progeny (Belsky et al., 1991). If, on the other hand, early environmental cues suggest safety (e.g., a positive-harmonious family relationship), children are more likely to grow up to follow a long-term mating strategy (Ellis, McFadyen-Ketchum, Dodge, Pettie, & Bates, 1999).

As with parental care relationships, mating relationships manifest the operation of adaptive mechanisms, including:

1. Selection of mates that show cues to health (e.g., symmetry) and probable reproductive success (e.g., dominance in males, youth in females; Buss, 1992; Ellis, 1992; Fink & Penton-Voak, 2002).

2. Maintenance of exclusive access to the benefits available within the relationship. This includes both exclusive sexual access to the partner and exclusive access to the partner's investment in care and protection of self and shared progeny. As discussed earlier, this process plays out as romantic jealousy (e.g., Buss, 1992).

3. Increased levels of gentleness among mated males. Just as males show decreasing levels of testosterone during their partner's pregnancy, they also show decreasing levels of testosterone when they become committed to a romantic relationship (Burnham et al., 2003), thus ensuring reductions in levels of aggression and increases in levels of interest in nurturance.

Psychopathology in Family Life

Just as adaptive processes can ordinarily be seen in the operation of family life, psychopathology can be seen under some circumstances. Psychopathology may occur when the safeguards that served to prevent destructive responses in our ancient evolutionary past are absent in our modern environment. In addition, some of the behaviors that we currently refer to as psychopathologies may have been acceptable behavior in our evolutionary past. That is, what is considered psychopathology is partially in the eye of beholder. Thus, processes that reflected adaptations in evolutionary ancient times (some of which are still seen as acceptable in traditional cultures) are often seen as immoral or pathological (as well as illegal) in contemporary Western culture. Infanticide provides a classic example.

First, let us consider some of the safeguards to lethal aggression to family members that were present in distant evolutionary times (and that may still be present in some small communities). In communities in which individuals are well known to each other, and the presence of kin is common, harm threatened to kin will lead to mobilization of their protective efforts (consistent with their shared reproductive interests). Figueredo and his colleagues (2001) explored the effects of local density of male and female kin on spousal abuse in Madrid, Spain, and Sonora, Mexico. The results showed that in both cultures a high presence of male kin (but not female kin) protected women from spousal abuse. Although there is physical evidence (from ancient gravesites) of injuries consistent with spousal battery (e.g., nonlethal facial injury), there is virtually no evidence of child injuries that are consistent with physical abuse (a process that is distinct from infanticide, which usually involves abandonment; Walker, 2001). It may be that lethal harm to children arose at the point that there was increased isolation between family units, that is, with the advent of the industrial revolution. At this point, families increasingly lived behind closed doors away from an extended family. The privacy and isolation that characterizes today's industrialized world prevents the easy opportunity for kin to intervene to prevent abuse or to provide needed support (Gabarino, 1977), a supposition that is supported by empirical evidence showing that child abuse is significantly more likely to be prevented by kin support than other kinds of support (Albarracin, Repetto, Albarracin, 1997).

Second, the definition of psychopathology is to some extent flexible. Some of the aberrant practices in families (e.g., child abandonment or infanticide) may be definable as adaptive in our distant evolutionary past (in the absence of cultural norms against such practices). Infanticide tends to be associated with two different factors: (1) cues to health problems in the infant and (2) the current inability of the parent to care for the young. If the rules of parental investment were to operate outside the constraints of cultural norms, parental reproductive interests would have been served (in our distant evolutionary past) when investment was withheld from a child who was unlikely to survive to adulthood or who would demand levels of care that exceed the parents' current capacities. Although this seems inhumane and primitive, similar practices exist informally in today's world in terms of failure to provide medical care to infants who are handicapped (e.g., Turnbull, 1986).

Despite the moral unacceptability of such practices as infanticide in today's world, evolutionary design has led to processes that still reflect this adaptation. Mothers are more likely to maltreat (physically abuse or neglect) their infants if they either lack resources (economic or social) or if they have low perceived power as caregivers (translatable as low perceived resources; Bugental & Happaney, 2004). Mothers with low perceived power—in particular when they give birth to a child with medical complications—are more likely to abuse or neglect their child in the first year of life. This negative outcome is, in turn, mediated by the presence of maternal depression. It has been suggested (Hagen, 1999) that maternal depression in response to an at-risk child reflects an evolutionary design for seeking support from others when the demands of the current environment exceed the individual's capacity to cope with them. In this way, depression (as with some other types of psychopathology) may represent adaptive efforts to alter or eliminate a situation that is a threat to one's own reproductive interests (Gilbert, 2001; Leahy, 2002).

School and Work

Everyday Adaptations in School and Work

Many aspects of contemporary school and work life had no direct counterparts in our distant evolutionary past. However, both of these areas did have distant counterparts in the social processes that occurred within coalitional groups. In this first section, we consider some of the adaptive processes that continue to have functional value in the everyday world of work and school groups. Buss (2000), in summarizing some of the ways we can hope to increase human happiness in a manner that is consistent with our evolutionary design, included a suggestion concerning the evolved mechanisms responsible for competition, mechanisms that have reproductive benefits but also produce personal costs. This proposed resolution involves the substitution of another evolved mechanism: cooperation. When members of a coalitional group work together to solve a shared problem, making use of the strategy of reciprocity rather than competition, a situation of mutual benefit is created. Within both school and work settings, research often has been conducted to test the effectiveness of groups that are organized in different ways. In particular, there has been a focus on the functioning of groups that operate in a competitive or a cooperative fashion.

There is consistent evidence for the benefits that follow from cooperative activities in the classroom. For example, cooperative learning programs have been found to lead to reductions in intergroup hostility (as well as fostering academic achievement; Slavin & Cooper, 1999). When classmates or workmates interact as equal participants in the accomplishment of shared goals, they shift away from the more typical competitive system that rewards individual achievement. Instead, they form a new kind of coalition that forges new alliances and breaks down the barriers across previous groups.

In organizational psychology, there has been a longstanding interest in the processes that follow when there is an emphasis on forging bonds between workers operating in groups. An effort to explore the benefits of cooperative groups originally developed within social psychology. In 1963, French concluded that healthier organizations could best be developed by "increasing the power of low status workers via decentralization, modifying conventional appraisal systems, and enabling cohesive and cooperative work groups to develop" (p. 39). Current approaches within organizational psychology focus on the ways in which cohesive work teams can foster organizational effectiveness through increased performance and improved quality of decision making (Guzzo & Dickson, 1996). In general, it has been found that self-directed team structures are an effective means of improving both organizational productivity and employee attitudes. That is, benefits accrue to the workers themselves as well as to the organization.

Because barriers between groups (at school and the work place) can weaken as a result of cooperation, group categorizations easily can shift when there are changes in cues related to shared identity. That is, intergroup bias follows more from the tendency to engage in a high level of social categorization rather than an inevitable tendency to categorize on such fixed premises as race. From this framework, racial en-

coding is seen as a by-product of inferential processes designed to simplify social reasoning. As a means to demonstrate that racial encoding is a by-product of coalitional encoding (i.e., social categorization based on shared identity), empirical work has been conducted showing that when race loses its predictive power concerning coalitional alliances (shared identity), the tendency to encode race as a socially relevant cue drops drastically (Kurzban, Cosmides, & Tooby, 2003).

Psychopathology in School and Work

Psychopathology in school and work settings takes a number of forms. The ones we focus on here are those that are relevant from an evolutionary standpoint. First, we will consider the negative outcomes that follow from a circumstance that was not present in our evolutionary past (extreme power differentials) and for which we have no evolutionary design (or adaptive defense). Second, we will consider a process (group aggression directed to outsiders or marginal group members) that was adaptive in our evolutionary past but is strikingly maladaptive in contemporary society. In school and work situations, it takes the form of bullying or harassment.

First, there are harmful processes that commonly occur in hierarchical organizational structures that would not have been present in our distant evolutionary past. Specifically, risk of morbidity and mortality increase in larger organizational structures in which there are extreme differentials between the power and resources of those at the top and those at the bottom (Wilkinson, 1996). In the subsistence-level environments that characterized our distant evolutionary past, such extremes would not have existed. In short, we are talking about a situation present today for which we have no evolutionary design.

Some of the most relevant information on this topic is available in work organizations. The classic Whitehall study (e.g., Marmot et al., 1991) was concerned with the health outcomes of individuals in a large civil service structure within the United Kingdom. Although all individuals in the organization received sufficient compensation and benefits to assure coverage of their health care and basic needs, they nonetheless showed a health pattern that mirrored their position within the hierarchy. At all ages, morbidity and mortality was significantly higher among those who occupied lower positions in the status hierarchy. Although low status is generally associated with poorer health outcomes, such outcomes are significantly greater in states or counties characterized by high income inequality than those characterized by low income inequality (Kahn, Wise, Kennedy, & Karachi, 2000; Wilkinson, 1996). Acting to disconfirm rival explanations, it has been observed that education, occupation, and income do not explain the relationship between status and health (Singh-Manoux, Adler, & Marmot, 2003).

Second, research has been conducted in both school and work settings on aggression directed to those who are viewed as outsiders to the group (or that occupy a marginal position within the group). In essence, we are talking about group bullying, a process where one individual—cheered on by others—or a group of individuals aggress against, harass, or terrorize an individual who lacks the power to defend himself or herself (Juvonen & Graham, 2001; Olweus, 2003; Prasad, Mills, Elmes, & Prasad, 1997).

The prevalence of victimization of those who are seen as outsiders is far too common to be considered an anomaly. Such processes reflect an evolutionary design to defend the group (or the group norms) against those seen as a source of threat. Bullying or harassment serves as a form of exclusion from the group. The power of threatened exclusion is indicated by the frequency with which it is reported as a strong fear (Baumeister & Tice, 1990; Caporael & Brewer, 1991). Although the defense of the group against actual threat may be seen as adaptive, defense of group norms or values by the exclusion or humiliation of those who do not fit in is not (Stephan, Ybarra, & Bachman, 1999). In contemporary life, bullying serves no useful function and produces long-term harm (Juvonen & Graham, 2001; Olweus, 2003).

In work environments, bullying is also a continuing problem. It has been pointed out that it is one of the greatest obstacles to creating and maintaining a diverse workforce (Prasad et al., 1997). That is, efforts to incorporate members of ethnic minorities into groups occupied by White Anglo workers are often impeded by the informal group processes in which those individuals are subject to incessant harassment and derogation.

Retirement

As there have been great changes in human longevity across the course of evolution, it is unclear whether or not adaptations reasonably could have evolved to serve the interests of the elderly. In addition, it is unclear the extent to which adaptations reasonably could evolve among the elderly (at least, among postmenopausal females) in that natural selection operates as a result of the replication of genes. However, it is probable that the involvement of postmenopausal women in child care would allow the possibility of gene replication to the extent their actions increased the reproductive success of younger kin. In support of this notion, it has been observed that within high-risk populations (low-income Black families living in inner-city environments) children fare better when there is a grandmother present in the home. Although this

finding is subject to a variety of interpretations, it does suggest a means by which investment in the care of grandchildren by postmenopausal women may serve to pass on the adaptive motivation to provide care for younger kin (Wilson et al., 1995).

Recreation and Play

Everyday Adaptations in Recreation and Play

The primary focus of evolutionary psychology on recreation has been with the play styles of the young. However, sex-typed play styles among children often continue into adult recreational activities.

The observed sex differences between children in play styles mirror the reproductive demands on males versus females in adult life (Geary, 1999). Greatest attention has been given to rough-and-tumble play, a style of play that young boys show beginning at about three years of age. Girls, in turn, rarely show this style of play. Of particular interest is the fact that these differences are associated with prenatal exposure to high levels of androgen (Breedlove, 1992). The aggressive play style of boys (rough-and-tumble play) occurs at an age when children are unlikely to produce real harm to each other and is associated with genuine positive affect rather than anger; for example, rough-and-tumble play is associated with elevations in levels of dopamine (Panksepp, 1993). Even though rough-and-tumble play discontinues in early adolescence, young adult males continue to show a physically competitive style with friends that affectively mirrors that shown in rough-and-tumble play among young boys. That is, aggressive encounters during games are accompanied by shared laughter (Palmer, 1993).

Girls, on the other hand, are more likely to engage in play that makes use of maternal activity—patterns that are less likely to occur if they are exposed to high levels of androgen prenatally (as, for example, occurs if they have experienced congenital adrenal hyperplasia; Berenbaum & Hines, 1992; Leveroni & Berenbaum, 1998). Play among girls is also more likely to involve the forging of cooperative bonds that involve shared intimacy and social support (Geary, 1999).

These sex-typical play activities, in turn, allow practice in activities that have traditionally been relevant for sex-typed behavior in adulthood. That is, they focus on dominance-related competitive activity among males and parenting activity among females (activities that were relevant for reproductive success in our evolutionary past). Although these processes may be amplified by cultural norms, they are also influenced by hormonal responses that set up the child for sexually dimorphic interest patterns. In traditional cultures, such processes may be seen as adaptive. However, within contemporary Western civilizations, their utility has decreased.

Pathology in Recreation and Play

Many types of problems can be identified in connection with adult recreation and play. As one example, one can think of the ways in which sporting activities (either as participants or as observers) can lead to extremes of uncontrolled aggression (e.g., Tenenbaum, Stewart, Singer, & Duda, 1996). In addition, the heavy focus on competition within and between leagues creates the possibility for high levels of stress among all those who lost as participants or fans. Team loss, in turn, leads not only to reductions in self-esteem (e.g., Hirt, Zillman, Erickson, & Kennedy, 1992) but also to declines in levels of testosterone among males (Bernhardt, Dabbs, Feldman, & Luttar, 1998). As an extreme example of risk among audiences of competitive sports, hospital admissions for myocardial infarction increased by 25 percent following a major loss in a sporting event (England's loss of the World Cup in football to Argentina in 1998; Carroll, Ebrahim, Tilling, MacLeod, & Davey Smith, 2002). This phenomenon may be thought of as reflecting the risks that arise when play styles of the young (which have built-in safeguards) are culturally perpetuated into adulthood without associated safeguards.

A more pervasive example of problems associated with recreation follows from one of the most ubiquitous and passive sources of recreation—watching TV. Problems arise in connection with the evolved mechanism for social comparison. In our daily lives, we associate with a relatively small number of people with whom we compare ourselves—sometimes favorably, sometimes unfavorably. However, we live in a much more extensive world through the lens of television. Within that illusory world (as pointed out by Buss, 2000), we see endless images of people who are more attractive than we or who are more successful than we (or who can also be seen as more attractive and/or more successful than our partners). As has been demonstrated empirically (Gutierres, Kenrick, & Parch, 1999; Kenrick et al., 1994), we respond to such images by becoming less satisfied not only with ourselves but also our partners. Feelings of personal failure generated by media images, in turn, may lead to increases in levels of depression (as suggested by Nesse & Williams, 1994). In addition, mass media carry the possibility of reducing our social connections with others—thus extending further the isolation that exists in contemporary times in comparison with our evolutionary past.

CONCLUSIONS

In this chapter we hope to have shown the ways in which evolutionary psychology can contribute to our understanding of the normative and pathological processes that occur in everyday life. Evolutionary thought offers its greatest contribution through the ways in which it accounts for some common occurrences that are so clearly maladaptive in the present day world—the ways in which we make ourselves ill with competitive strivings that rarely allow us to feel satisfied, with continuous conflict with subgroups within our own societies, or various shifting enemies in other countries, or with persistent, nagging jealousies about our romantic partners.

Evolutionary psychology has moved away from early reliance on speculation as to what might have been to experimental tests of its tenets. That is, evidence is provided when privileged learning or selective perception can be shown in ways that are consistent with the presence of an adaptation. Support is particularly strong when evidence is provided for the continuing privileged status of an adaptation, even when it is not functional in today's world and cannot easily be explained by other theoretical perspectives.

Our evolutionary design also allows us some less-conflicted adaptations, however. These include the maintenance of positive bonds with kin (who will have a penchant for coming to our aid even when we can not always get along), the possibility of establishing close friendships that provide trustworthy sources of support, and the capability for creating cooperative relationships in work or school groups that allow the entire group to benefit as a result of the collective action of all. It also allows us to design interventions that prevent some of the more negative consequences that follow from our evolutionary design. For example, interventions that assist parents in obtaining resources (economic, social, and cognitive) may be particularly effective in fostering parental investment in their at-risk offspring. Only when we have the full picture of our biological design can we make use of its intricacies not only to enhance our science but also to improve our quality of life.

REFERENCES

Albarracin, D., Repetto, M. J., & Albarracin, M. (1997). Social support in child abuse and neglect: Support functions, sources, and contexts. *Child Abuse and Neglect, 21,* 607–615.

Baron-Cohen, S. (Ed.). (1997). *The maladapted mind.* East Sussex, UK: Psychology Press.

Baumeister, R. F., & Tice, D. M. (1990). Anxiety and social exclusion. *Journal of Social and Clinical Psychology, 9,* 165–195.

Belsky, J., Steinberg, L., & Draper, P. (1991). Childhood experience, interpersonal development, and reproductive strategy: An evolutionary theory of socialization. *Child Development, 62,* 647–670.

Berenbaum, S. A., & Hines, M. (1992). Early androgens are related to childhood sex-typed toy preferences. *Psychological Science, 3,* 203–206.

Bernhardt, P. C., Dabbs, J. M., Jr., Feldman, J. A., & Luttar, C. D. (1998). Testosterone changes during vicarious experiences of winning and losing among fans at sporting events. *Physiology and Behavior, 65,* 59–62.

Bjorklund, D. F., & Pellegrini, A. D. (2000). Child development and evolutionary psychology. *Child Development, 71,* 1687–1708.

Bock, W. J. (2000). Explanatory history of the origin of feathers. *American Zoology, 40,* 478–485.

Boukydis, C. Z., & Burgess, R. L. (1982). A physiological response to infant cries: Effects of temperament of infant, parental status, and gender. *Child Development, 53,* 1291–1298.

Bowlby, J. (1969). *Attachment.* New York: Basic Books.

Breedlove, S. (1992). Sexual differentiation of the brain and behavior. In J. Becker, S. Breedlove, & D. Crews (Eds.), *Behavioral endocrinology* (pp. 39–68). Cambridge, MA: MIT Press.

Bruer, J. T., & Greenough, W. T. (2001). The subtle science of how experience affects the brain. In D. B. Bailey, J. T. Bruer, F. J. Symons, & J. W. Lichtman (Eds.), *Critical thinking about critical periods* (pp. 209–232). Baltimore: Paul H. Brookes Publishing.

Bugental, D. B., & Beaulieu, D. A. (2003). A bio-social-cognitive approach to understanding and promoting the outcomes of children with medical and physical disorders. In R. Kail (Ed.), *Advances in child development and behavior* (Vol. 31, pp. 129–164). New York: Academic Press.

Bugental, D. B., & Grusec, J. E. (in press). Socialization processes. In N. Eiserberg (Vol. Ed.), *Handbook of child psychology.*

Bugental, D. B., & Happaney, K. (2004). Predicting infant maltreatment in low-income families: The interactive effects of maternal attributions and child status at birth. *Developmental Psychology, 40,* 234–243.

Burnham, T. C., Chapman, J. F., Gray, P. B., McIntyre, M. H., Lipson, S. F., & Ellison, P. T. (2003). Men in committed, romantic relationships have lower testosterone. *Hormones and Behavior, 44,* 119–122.

Buss, D. M. (1989). Sex differences in human mate preferences: Evolutionary hypotheses tested in 37 cultures. *Behavioral and Brain Sciences, 12,* 1–49.

Buss, D. M. (1992). Mate preference mechanisms: Consequences for partner choice and intrasexual competition. In J. H. Barkow, L. Cosmides, & J. Tooby (Eds.), *The adapted mind* (pp. 249–266). New York: Oxford University Press.

Buss, D. M. (1999). *Evolutionary psychology.* London: Allyn & Bacon.

Buss, D. M. (2000). The evolution of happiness. *American Psychologist, 55,* 15–23.

Buss, D., Larsen, R., Westen, D., & Semmelroth, J. (1992). Sex differences in jealousy: Evolution, physiology, and psychology. *Psychological Science, 3,* 251–255.

Caporael, L. R., & Brewer, M. B. (1991). Reviving evolutionary psychology: Biology meets society. *Journal of Social Issues, 47,* 187–195.

Carroll, D., Ebrahim, S., Tilling, K., MacLeod, J., & Davey Smith, G. (2002). Admissions for myocardial infraction and World Cup football. *British Medical Journal, 325,* 1439–1442.

Cosmides, L., & Tooby, J. (1992). Cognitive adaptations for social exchange. In J. Barkow, L. Cosmides, & J. Tooby (Eds.), *The adapted mind* (pp. 163–228). New York: Oxford University Press.

DeCasper, A. J., & Fifer, W. P. (1987). Of human bonding: newborns prefer their mothers' voices. In J. Oates & S. Sheldon (Eds.), *Cognitive development in infancy* (pp. 111–118). Hillsdale, NJ: Erlbaum.

DeSteno, D., Bartlett, M. Y., Braverman, J., & Salovey, P. (2002). Sex differences in jealousy: Evolutionary mechanism or artifact of measurement? *Journal of Personality and Social Psychology, 83,* 1103–1116.

Dewsbury, D. A. (1999). The proximate and the ultimate: Past, present and future. *Behavioural Process, 46,* 189–199.

Dornbusch, S. M., Carlsmith, J. M., Bushwall, S. J., Ritter, P. L., Leiderman, H., Hastorf, A. H., et al. (1985). Single parents, extended households, and the control of adolescents. *Child Development, 56,* 326–341.

Dunbar, R. I. (1982). Adaptation, fitness, and the evolutionary tautology. In B. C. R. Betrtram, T. H. Clutton-Brock, R. I. M. Dunbar, D. I. Rubenstein, & R. W. Wrangham (Eds.), *Current problems in sociobiology* (pp. 9–28). Cambridge, UK: Cambridge University Press.

Ellis, B. J. (1992). The evolution of sexual attraction: Evaluative mechanisms in women. In J. H. Barkow, L. Cosmides, & J. Tooby (Eds.), *The adapted mind* (pp. 267–288). New York: Oxford University Press.

Ellis, B. J., McFadyen-Ketchum, S., Dodge, K. A., Pettit, G. S., & Bates, J. E. (1999). Quality of early family relationships and individual differences in the timing of pubertal maturation in girls: A longitudinal test of an evolutionary model. *Journal of Personality and Social Psychology, 77,* 387–401.

Emde, R. N., Biringen, Z., Clyman, R. B., & Oppenheim, D. (1991). The moral self of infancy. Affective core and procedural knowledge. *Developmental Review, 11,* 251–270.

Fernald, A., Taeschner, T., Dunn, J., Papousek, M., DeBoyson-Bardles, B., & Fukui, J. (1989). A cross-language study of prosodic modifications in mother's and father's speech to preverbal infants. *Journal of Child Language, 16,* 477–501.

Field, T. M., Cohen, D., Garcia, R., & Greenberg, R. (1984). Mother-stranger face discrimination by the newborn. *Infant Behavior and Development, 7,* 19–25.

Figueredo, A. J., Corral-Verdugo, V., Frias-Armenta, M., Bachar, K. J., White, J., McNeill, P. L., et al. (2001). Blood, solidarity, status, and honor: The sexual balance of power and spousal abuse in Sonora, Mexico. *Evolution and Human Behavior, 22,* 295–328.

Fink, B., & Penton-Voak, I. (2002). Evolutionary psychology of facial attractiveness. *Current Directions in Psychological Science, 11,* 154–158.

Fleming, A. S. (1990). Hormonal and experiential correlates of maternal responsiveness in human mothers. In N. A. Krasnegor & R. S. Bridges (Eds.), *Mammalian parenting: Biochemical, neurobiological, and behavioral determinants* (pp. 184–208). Oxford, UK: Oxford University Press.

Fleming, A. S., Corter, C., Franks, P., Surbey, M., Schneider, B., & Steiner, M. (1993). Postpartum factors related to mother's attraction to newborn infant odors. *Developmental Psychobiology, 26,* 115–132.

Fleming, A. S., Corter, C., Stallings, J., & Steiner, M. (2002). Testosterone and prolactin are associated with emotional responses to infant cries in new fathers. *Hormones and Behavior, 42,* 399–413.

Flinn, M. V., Quinlan, R. J., Decker, S. A., Turner, M. T., & England, B. G. (1996). Male-female differences in effects of parental absence on glucocorticoid stress response. *Human Nature, 7,* 125–162.

French, J. R. P. (1963). The social environment and mental health. *Journal of Social Issues, 19,* 39–56.

Gabarino, J. (1977). The price of privacy in the social dynamics of child abuse. *Child Welfare, 56,* 565–575.

Geary, D. C. (1998). *Male, female: The evolution of human sex differences.* Washington, DC: American Psychological Association.

Geary, D. C. (1999). Evolution and developmental sex differences. *Psychological Science, 8,* 115–120.

Geers, A., & Moog, J. (1987). Predicting spoken language acquisition of profoundly hearing-impaired children. *Journal of Speech and Hearing Disorders, 52,* 84–94.

Gilbert, P. (1998). Evolutionary psychopathology: Why isn't the mind designed better than it is? *British Journal of Medical Psychology, 71,* 353–373.

Gilbert, P. (2001). Depression and stress: A biopsychosocial exploration of evolved functions and mechanisms. *Stress: The International Journal of the Biology of Stress, 4,* 121–135.

Goren, C. C., Sarty, M., & Wu, P. Y. (1975). Visual following and pattern discrimination of face-like stimuli by new born infants. *Pediatrics, 56,* 544–549.

Gray, P. B., Kahlenberg, S. M., Barrett, E. S., Lipson, S. F., & Ellison, P. T. (2002). Marriage and fatherhood are associated with lower testosterone in males. *Evolution and Human Behavior, 23,* 193–201.

Gutierres, S. E., Kenrick, D. T., & Partch, J. J. (1999). Beauty, dominance, and the mating game: Contrast effects in self-assessment reflect gender differences in mate selection. *Personality and Social Psychology Bulletin, 25,* 1126–1134.

Guzzo, R. A., & Dickson, M. W. (1996). Teams in organizations: Recent research on performance and effectiveness. *Annual Review of Psychology, 47,* 307–338.

Hagen, E. H. (1999). The functions of postpartum depression. *Evolution and Human Behavior, 20,* 325–359.

Harlow, H. F. (1973). *Learning to love.* Oxford, UK: Ballantine.

Harris, C. N. (2003). A review of sex differences in sexual jealousy, including self-report data, psychophysiological responses, interpersonal violence, and morbid jealousy. *Personality and Social Psychology Review, 7,* 102–128.

Hirt, E. R., Zillman, D., Erickson, G. A., & Kennedy, C. (1992). Costs and benefits of allegiance: Changes in fans' self-ascribed competencies after team victory versus defeat. *Journal of Personality and Social Psychology, 63,* 724–738.

Inamura, Y., Nakan, Y., Ohta, Y., & Kondo, H. (1999). Lifetime prevalence of schizophrenia among individuals prenatally exposed to atomic radiation in Nagasaki city. *Acta Psychiatrica Scandinavica, 100,* 344–349.

Jensen, P. S., Mrazek, D., Knapp, P. K., Steinberg, L., Pfeffer, C., Schowalter, J., et al. (1997). Evolution and revolution in child psychiatry: ADHD as a disorder of adaptation. *Journal of the American Academy of Child & Adolescent Psychiatry, 36,* 1672–1681.

Johnson, M. H., Dziurawiec, S., Ellis, H. D., & Morton, S. (1991). Newborns' preferential tracking of face-like stimuli and its subsequent decline. *Cognition, 40,* 1–21.

Juvonen, J., & Graham, S. (2001). *Peer harassment in school: The plight of the vulnerable and victimized.* New York: Guilford Press.

Kahn, R. S., Wise, P. H., Kennedy, B. P., & Karachi, I. (2000). State income inequality, household income, and maternal mental and physical health: Cross sectional national survey. *British Medical Journal, 321,* 1311–1315.

Kenrick, D. T., Neuberg, S. L., Zierk, K. L., & Krones, J. M. (1994). Evolution and social cognition: Contrast effects as a function of sex, dominance, and physical attractiveness. *Personality and Social Psychology Bulletin, 20,* 210–217.

Ketelaar, T., & Ellis, B. J. (2000). Are evolutionary explanations unfalsifiable? Evolutionary psychology and Lakatosian philosophy of science. *Psychological Inquiry, 11,* 1–21.

Kitamura, C., Thanavishuth, C., Burnham, D., & Luksaneeyanawin, S. (2002). Universality and specificity in infant-directed speech: Pitch modifications as a function of infant age and sex in a tonal and non-tonal language. *Infant Behavior and Development, 24,* 372–392.

Kurzban, R., Cosmides, L., & Tooby, J. (2001). Can race be erased? Coalitional computation and social categorization. *Proceedings of the National Academy of Sciences, 98,* 15387–15392.

Lamond, A. I., & Earnshaw, W. C. (1998). Structure and function in the nucleus. *Science, 280,* 547–553.

Leahy, R. L. (2002). Pessimism and the evolution of negativity. *Journal of Cognitive Psychotherapy, 16,* 295–316.

Leveroni, C. L., & Berenbaum, S. A. (1998). Early androgen effects on interest in infants: Evidence from children with congenital adrenal hyperplasia. *Developmental Neuropsychology, 14,* 321–340.

Marks, I. M., & Nesse, R. M. (1994). Fear and fitness: An evolutionary analysis of anxiety disorders. *Ethology and Sociobiology, 15,* 247–261.

Marmot, M. G., Davey Smith, G., Stansfield, S., Patel, C., North, F., & Head, J. (1991). Health inequalities among British civil servants: The Whitehall II study. *Lancet, 337,* 2487–1393.

Maurer, D., & Salapatek, P. (1976). Developmental changes in the scanning of faces in young infants. *Child Development, 47,* 523–527.

Mayr, E. (1961). Cause and effect in biology. *Science, 134,* 1501–1506.

Nesse, R. M., & Williams, G. C. (1994). *Why we get sick.* New York: New York Times Books.

NiParko, J. K. (2004). Speech, language, and reading skills after early cochlear implantation. *Journal of the American Medical Association, 291,* 2378–2380.

Olweus, D. (2003). Social problems in school. In A. Slater & G. Bremner (Eds.), *An introduction to developmental psychology* (pp. 434–454). Malden, MA: Blackwell.

Ostrom, J. H. (1974). Archaeopteryx and the origin of flight. *Quarterly Review of Biology, 49,* 27–47.

Ostwald, P. E. (1963). *Soundmaking: The acoustic communication of emotion.* Oxford, UK: Charles C. Thomas.

Palmer, C. T. (1993). Anger, aggression, and humor in Newfoundland floor hockey: An evolutionary analysis. *Aggressive Behavior, 19,* 167–173.

Panksepp, J. (1993). Rough and tumble play: A fundamental brain process. In K. MacDonald (Ed), *Parent-child play: Descriptions and implications* (pp. 147–184). Albany: State University of New York Press.

Prasad, P., Mills, A., Elmes, M., & Prasad, A. (Eds.). (1997). *Managing the organizational melting pot: Dilemmas of workplace diversity.* Thousand Oaks, CA: Sage.

Rutter, M., & O'Connor, T. G. (2004). Are there biological programming effects for psychological development? Findings from a study of Romanian orphans. *Developmental Psychology, 40,* 81–94.

Scarr, S., & Salapatak, P. (1970). Patterns of fear development during infancy. *Merrill-Palmer Quarterly, 16,* 53–90.

Shepard, R. (1992). The perceptual organization of colors: An adaptation to regularities in the terrestrial world? In J. Barkow, L. Cosmides, & J. Tooby (Eds.), *The adapted mind* (pp. 495–532). New York: Oxford University Press.

Singh-Manoux, A., Adler, N. E., & Marmot, M. G. (2003). Subjective social status: Its determinants and its association with measures of ill-health in the Whitehall II study. *Social Science and Medicine, 56,* 1321–1333.

Skarin, K. S. (1977). Cognitive and contextual determinants of stranger fear in six- and eleven-month-old infants. *Child Development, 48,* 537–544.

Slavin, R. E., & Cooper, R. (1999). Improving intergroup relations: Lessons learned from cooperative learning programs. *Journal of Social Issues, 55,* 647–663.

Stephan, W. G., Ybarra, O., & Bachman, G. (1999). Prejudice toward immigrants. *Journal of Applied Social Psychology, 11,* 2221–2237.

Symons, D. (1992). On the use and misuse of Darwinism in the study of human behavior. In J. Barkow, L. Cosmides, & J. Tooby (Eds.), *The adapted mind* (pp. 137–162). New York: Oxford University Press.

Tenenbaum, G., Stewart, E., Singer, R. N., & Duda, J. (1996). Aggression and violence in sport: An ISSP position stand. *International Journal of Sport Psychology, 27,* 229–236.

Tinbergen, N. (1963). On aims and methods of ethology. *Zeitschrift für Tierpsychologie, 20,* 410–463.

Tooby, J., & Cosmides, L. (1992). The psychological foundation of culture. In J. Barkow, L. Cosmides, & J. Tooby (Eds.), *The adapted mind* (pp. 19–136). New York: Oxford University Press.

Trivers, R. (1974). Parent-offspring conflict. *American Zoologist, 14,* 249–264.

Turnbull, H. R. (1986). Incidence of infanticide in America: Public and professional attitudes. *Issues in Law and Medicine, 2,* 363–389.

Walker, P. L. (2001). Bio-archeological perspective on the history of violence. *Annual Review of Anthropology, 30,* 573–596.

Wilkinson, R. G. (1996). *Unhealthy societies.* New York: Routledge.

Williams, G. C. (1966). *Adaptation and natural selection.* Princeton, NJ: Princeton University Press.

Wilson, M., & Daly, M. (1994). The psychology of parenting in evolutionary perspective and the case of human filicide. In S. Parmigiani & F. S. von Saal (Eds.), *Infanticide and parental care* (pp. 73–134). London: Academic Publishers.

Wilson, M. N., Greene-Bates, C., McKim, L., Simmons, F., Askew, T., Curry-El., J., et al. (1995). African American family life: The dynamics of interactions, relationships, and roles. In M. N. Wilson (Ed.), *African-American family life: Its structural and ecological aspects* (pp. 5–21). San Francisco, CA: Jossey-Bass.

Zebrowitz, L. (1997). *Reading faces.* Boulder, CO: Westview.

Zebrowitz, L. A., Kendall-Tackett, K. A., & Fafel, J. (1991). The influence of children's facial maturity on parental expectations and punishments. *Journal of Experimental Child Psychology, 52,* 221–238.

CHAPTER 9

Cognitive Theories

DAVID J. A. DOZOIS, PAUL A. FREWEN, AND ROGER COVIN

CLINICAL COGNITIVE THEORIES

The essence of cognitive theories is capsulated in what Epictetus (c. A.D. 101) stated centuries ago when he wrote *The Enchiridion:* "Men are disturbed not by things, but by the view which they take of them" (Epictetus, c. A.D. 101/ 1955). From their inception, contemporary cognitive theories of personality and psychological functioning have adopted the position that one's idiosyncratic thoughts profoundly influence one's affect and behavior.

The purpose of this chapter is to examine the main clinical cognitive theories and to discuss their application to everyday functioning. We begin by highlighting the main theoretical assumptions of two prominent cognitive therapeutic models: Aaron T. Beck's cognitive therapy (CT) and Albert Ellis's rational emotive behavioral therapy (REBT). Although the models advanced by these theorists differ in some fundamental ways, they share the view that an individual's beliefs affect his or her interpretation and response to various life circumstances, thereby contributing to emotional adjustment or maladjustment. Following an overview of the fundamental theoretical underpinnings of CT and REBT, we address factors that relate to the development of core beliefs and schemata and briefly consider possible relationships between neurobiological and cognitive functioning. Next, we discuss some of the boundaries of these theories and summarize the empirical evidence that pertains to these models. We conclude this chapter with a discussion of the application of cognitive theories to understanding everyday functioning.

Acknowledgments: During the preparation of this chapter, David J. A. Dozois was supported by a Young Investigator Award from the National Alliance for Research on Schizophrenia and Depression (jointly funded by the Institute of Neurosciences, Mental Health, and Addiction of the Canadian Institutes of Health Research) and an intermediate researcher fellowship from the Ontario Mental Health Foundation. Paul A. Frewen and Roger Covin were supported by the Social Sciences and Humanities Research Council of Canada.

Specifically, we illustrate how cognition influences social interactions and relationships, determination and perseverance in work and school, one's choices and ability to function in recreational activities, and one's capability to enjoy or cope with retirement.

STATEMENT OF THE THEORIES

There are many different clinically oriented cognitive theories (Dobson, 2001; Mahoney, 1995), and a review of the many distinctions and nuances of each of these theories is beyond the scope of this chapter. However, at the most general level, each of the cognitive theories share three fundamental hypotheses: (1) that cognition affects emotion and behavior; (2) that cognition can be monitored and changed; and (3) that by altering cognitions, one can exert desired behavioral and emotional change (Dobson & Dozois, 2001). Considering that they are the most theoretically comprehensive and widely applied therapeutic modalities, coupled with the fact that Beck's approach has been subject to the most elaborate empirical scrutiny, we have chosen here to focus solely on the theoretical precepts of the cognitive restructuring models (i.e., CT and REBT; see Dobson & Dozois, 2001; Dobson, Backs-Dermott, & Dozois, 2000). These theories have garnered the greatest support in both the scholarly and the therapeutic communities, and, despite originating in attempts to understand psychopathology and personality problems, they also have important implications for understanding everyday-normative psychological functioning.

Beck's Cognitive Theory and Therapy

Beck's cognitive model (Beck, 1963, 1964, 1967; Beck, Emery, & Greenberg, 1985; Beck, Rush, Shaw, & Emery, 1979; Clark, Beck, & Alford, 1999) purports that an individual's emotions and behaviors are influenced by his or her perception or cognitive appraisal of events. Three main levels of cognition are emphasized in this theory: (1) schemata,

(2) information processing and intermediate beliefs (including dysfunctional rules, assumptions, and attitudes), and (3) automatic thoughts.

Schemata are defined as "relatively enduring internal structures of stored generic or prototypical features of stimuli, ideas, or experience that are used to organize new information in a meaningful way thereby determining how phenomena are perceived and conceptualized" (Clark et al., 1999, p. 79). In other words, a self-schema is a well-organized and consolidated perceptual set that forms the basis of core beliefs about self. Schematic organization is adaptive insofar as it facilitates the efficient processing of information. This efficiency entails a bias toward attending to, encoding, and retrieving schema-consistent information at the expense of information that is not consistent with the schema. Thus, previous experience and knowledge structures influence the processing of novel stimuli, and, to use the phraseology of Jean Piaget (1954, cited in Flavell, 1985), assimilation dominates over accommodation. As such, schematic organization becomes maladaptive when the core content of the self-schema is negative.

According to Beck, the development and structure of a maladaptive self-schema is presumed to occur during early childhood, but its activity usually remains dormant until it is later triggered by adverse circumstances (see Beck et al., 1979; Robins & Hayes, 1993). Once activated, the schema then proceeds to influence the filtering, encoding, storage, retrieval, and interpretation of information in a schema-congruent fashion. For example, an individual who is susceptible to depression may have a latent core belief that he or she is worthless and unlovable. This belief system may be particularly salient and affect subsequent information processing once it has been triggered by certain life circumstances (e.g., peer or partner rejection). Once activated, the individual with depression may then selectively attend to and recall information that is consistent with this negative view of self (e.g., paying attention to cues that are suggestive of unlovability and disqualifying information that does not fit with that expectation and belief). To provide another illustration, consider the cognitive functioning of aggressive youth. These individuals tend to exhibit a hostile attribution bias that influences how they process ambiguous stimuli regarding the intention of others (Crick & Dodge, 1994; Mash & Dozois, 2003). When the intention of an adverse social event is obvious (the harm caused was clearly intentional or clearly accidental), aggressive youths often respond in the same way as do less-aggressive children. However, in situations where intention is ambiguous, aggressive youth rely on their schemata to interpret situations, which results in attributions that harm was caused intentionally.

Although schemata have been discussed in the literature as synonymous with dysfunctional beliefs and underlying assumptions (Freeman, Pretzer, Fleming, & Simon, 1990), theoretical revisions and subsequent empirical research have contributed to a clearer differentiation of these constructs (Beck, 1996; Clark et al., 1999; Ingram & Kendall, 1986; Ingram, Miranda, & Segal, 1998; Teasdale, 1996). Ingram et al. (1998), for instance, note that the schema construct encompasses not only cognitive propositions (i.e., the actual content of information that is stored in memory; namely, core beliefs and assumptions), but also the organization and structure of that information (cf. Dozois & Dobson, 2001a). The core beliefs that are organized within an individual's self-system are "understandings that are so fundamental and deep that [individuals] often do not articulate them" (J. S. Beck, 1995, p. 15). These understandings often can be expressed as unconditional evaluations (e.g., "I am incompetent"; "I am bad"; "I am unlovable"; "I am defective"). Using terminology from cognitive experimental psychology, Teasdale (1996) has described this level of meaning as an *implicational code,* which represents higher-order meanings synthesizing information stemming separately from sensory, propositional, and bodily affective cues (Teasdale & Barnard, 1993).

Information-processing biases and intermediate beliefs make up the next level of cognition (Beck et al., 1979; J. S. Beck, 1995; Clark et al., 1999). These biases often take the form of selective attention or enhanced memory for information that is schema-consistent, but they also are represented as faulty interpretations, *if . . . then . . .* statements, and inaccurate causal attributions. For example, a person may engage in all-or-nothing thinking in which he or she evaluates personal qualities or situations in absolutist terms (e.g., an A student receiving a lower-than-expected grade may regard him- or herself as a complete failure). A description of some common dysfunctional beliefs is listed in Table 9.1. Dysfunctional attitudes may also be represented as *if . . . then . . .* statements. According to the self-worth contingency model (Kuiper & Olinger, 1986), individuals are unlikely to feel as though their self-worth is compromised as long as they perceive that they are meeting their personal criteria for defining it. For instance, the rule "If I am not approved by everyone, then I am not worthwhile," although dysfunctional in and of itself, nevertheless is not assumed to result in feelings of worthlessness as long as the individual continues to feel accepted. Once this conditional requirement for defining self-worth is violated, however, he or she may be more likely to succumb to depression.

Finally, automatic thoughts refer to the stream of cognitions that all people have throughout the waking day. These thoughts are not accompanied by direct conscious delibera-

TABLE 9.1   Commonly Observed Cognitive Distortions

Label	Description
Dichotomous thinking	Things are seen in terms of two mutually exclusive categories with no shades of gray in between, for example, believing that one is either a success or a failure and that anything short of a perfect performance is a total failure.
Overgeneralization	A specific event is seen as being characteristic of life in general rather than as being one event among many, for example, concluding that an inconsiderate response from one's spouse shows that she does not care, despite her having showed consideration on other occasion.
Selective abstraction	One aspect of a complex situation is the focus of attention, and other relevant aspects of the situation are ignored, for example, focusing on the one negative comment in a performance evaluation received at work and overlooking a number of positive comments.
Disqualifying the positive	Positive experiences that would conflict with the individual's negative views are discounted by declaring that they do not count, for example, disbelieving positive feedback from friends and colleagues and thinking, "They're only saying that to be nice."
Mind reading	The individual assumes that others are reacting negatively without evidence that this is the case, for example, thinking, "I just know he thought I was an idiot!" despite the other person's having behaved politely.
Fortune-telling	The individual reacts as though his or her negative expectations about future events are established facts, for example, thinking, "He's leaving me, I just know it!" and acting as though this is definitely true.
Catastrophizing	Negative events that might occur are treated as intolerable catastrophes rather than being seen in perspective, for example, thinking "Oh my God, what if I faint!" without considering that, whereas fainting may be unpleasant and embarrassing, it is not terribly dangerous.
Minimization	Positive characteristics or experiences are treated as real but insignificant, for example, thinking, "Sure, I'm good at my job, but so what, my parents don't respect me."
Emotional reasoning	Assuming that emotional reactions necessarily reflect the true situation, for example, deciding that because one feels hopeless, the situation must really be hopeless.
Should statements	The use of *should* and *have-to* statements to provide motivation or control behavior, for example, thinking, "I shouldn't feel aggravated. She's my mother, I have to listen to her."
Labeling	Attaching a global label to oneself rather than referring to specific events or actions, for example, thinking, "I'm a failure!" rather than "Boy, I blew that one!"
Personalization	Assuming that one is the cause of a particular external event when, in fact, other factors are responsible, for example, assuming that a supervisor's lack of friendliness is a reflection of her feelings about the client rather than realizing that she is upset over a death in the family.

Note. From *Clinical Applications of Cognitive Therapy,* by A. Freeman, J. Pretzer, B. Fleming, & K. M. Simon. © 1990. Reprinted with permission from Plenum Publishers.

tion or volition; instead, they arise associatively (and almost spontaneously) as different aspects of one's core belief system are activated via external environmental cues. Automatic thoughts are considered cognitive by-products because they stem directly from core beliefs/schemata in interaction with the environment. For example, an individual who is passed in the corridor at work without a colleague's salutation may have the automatic thought, "She doesn't like me," perhaps stemming from a core belief of being unlovable or undesirable. Similarly, someone with a self-schema focused on incompetence may have the thought, "I will never be able to do this," when faced with a novel task.

Although cognition is the primary focus of Beck's theory, the model does not simply state that cognitions cause emotions and behaviors. Instead, it is acknowledged that these

variables are interrelated, and several cognitive models have been advanced to characterize this interaction (e.g., Bower, 1981; Fielder, 1996; Forgas, 1995; Teasdale, 1996). The complex interplay among cognitive and affective systems also has received increasing attention in recent adaptations of Beck's model (e.g., Beck, 1996; Teasdale & Barnard, 1993), although Beck maintains that "the nature and function of information processing (i.e., the assignment of meaning) constitutes the key to understanding maladaptive behavior" (Alford & Beck, 1997, p. 11).

Another important axiom of Beck's model is that of content specificity (Alford & Beck, 1997; Clark et al., 1999). Specifically, distinctive cognitive vulnerabilities (i.e., a predisposition to make certain kinds of distortions and to focus on particular maladaptive meanings about oneself, the world, and future goals; also known as the cognitive triad) are purported to relate to specific clinical syndromes. For example, individuals who are depressed are theorized to have negative automatic thoughts that focus principally on themes of personal loss, deprivation, and failure (Beck et al., 1979). In contrast, anxiety themes center on thoughts about the world being dangerous, the future being uncertain, and the self being inadequate (Beck et al., 1985). Individuals with anxiety problems, for instance, tend to overestimate the probability of risk while simultaneously underestimating their resources for coping with threats. On the other hand, an individual who exhibits features of paranoid personality disorder believes that people cannot be trusted and perceives others as malevolent, abusive, and deceitful. Someone who has dependent personality disorder has a view of self as weak, helpless, and incompetent and has beliefs such as, "I need constant support and encouragement from others to survive and be happy" (see Beck, Freeman, & Associates, 2003).

With the use of research methodologies adapted from cognitive experimental psychology, a number of compatible information-processing models have been advanced and refined using Beck's original theory as the foundation (e.g., Bower, 1981; Ingram, 1984, 1990; Kuiper, Derry, & MacDonald, 1982; Teasdale, 1997; Teasdale & Barnard, 1993). Although the main tenets of his theory have been well supported by the research literature (Beck, 1991, 1993; Clark et al., 1999; Haaga, Dyck, & Ernst, 1991; Dobson & Kendall, 1993), Beck recently has expanded aspects of his theory to incorporate incoming evidence from experimental cognitive science (see Alford & Beck, 1997; Beck, 1996; Clark et al., 1999). In this way, Beck's theory has remained an open system, and not one that simply assimilates information that is consistent with the theory while ignoring incompatible data. Instead, Beck's theory has been revised in order to accommodate the growing empirical database associating personality characteristics with aspects of cognition and emotion.

Consistent with the major tenants of Beck's cognitive theory of psychological functioning, cognitive therapy aims to help clients shift from unhealthy appraisals to more realistic and adaptive appraisals using Socratic dialogue and behavioral experiments. Treatment is highly collaborative and involves designing specific learning experiences to teach clients how to monitor automatic thoughts; understand the relationships among cognition, affect, and behavior; examine the validity of automatic thoughts; develop more realistic and adaptive cognitions; and alter underlying beliefs, assumptions, and schemata (Dobson & Dozois, 2001).

Ellis's Rational Emotive Behavior Therapy

The basic theory and practice of REBT, which represented the first of the cognitive-behavioral therapies, was formulated by Albert Ellis more than four decades ago (Ellis, 2004). Ellis (1962, 1999) has argued that, when faced with unfavorable life circumstances, human beings make themselves feel frustrated, disappointed, and miserable and behave in self-defeating ways, mainly because they construct irrational beliefs about themselves and their situations. Conversely, Ellis believes that individuals can generate adaptive feelings and behaviors by adopting rational and functional thoughts (Ellis, 1999). At the crux of this conceptualization is the ABC model of human disturbance, which states that the consequences (C) of life events (e.g., symptomatology, negative affect) are not contingent upon the activating event (A) per se but are mediated by one's beliefs (B) about these experiences (Dryden & Ellis, 2001). Irrational beliefs are purported to underlie and maintain emotional disturbance, although cognition, emotion, and behavior are viewed as interrelated phenomena (Dryden & Ellis, 2001; Ellis, 1993, 1999).

In addition to being acquired in childhood through the teachings of caregivers, Ellis also contends that humans have a biological predisposition to think irrationally (Ellis, 1993, 1999). As such, irrational beliefs are actively challenged and confronted in REBT: the "therapist strongly believes in a rigorous application of the rules of logic, straight thinking, and of scientific method to everyday life. He or she ruthlessly uncovers the most important elements of irrational thinking . . . and energetically encourages clients to take more reasonable channels of feeling and behaving" (Ellis, 1999, p. 73; see also Ellis, 2004). This innate irrationality is believed to be modifiable because of a second biological tendency that humans have for metacognition (i.e., thinking about thinking).

Ellis (1991) identified a number of distinctive irrational beliefs that may contribute to emotional disturbance. As displayed in Table 9.2, these beliefs are considered maladaptive because they are expressed in absolutist terms and held onto rigidly as needs, demands, and evaluative statements rather than as more flexible preferences, wishes, or desires (Dryden & Ellis, 2001; Walen, DiGiuseppe, & Dryden, 1992). Ellis contends that, due to the presence of these absolutist demands (so-called musts), individuals who are psychologically disturbed also exhibit a number of cognitive errors and distortions (Dobson et al., 2000; Dryden & Ellis, 2001). In addition, Ellis noted that people typically reaffirm their irrational beliefs by steadfastly adhering to "core musturbatory philosophies" despite any objective evidence to affirm their validity (Ellis, 1999, p. 91).

Since his original proposal (Ellis, 1962), Ellis has made some modifications to his theory. For example, he now acknowledges that it is not simply the irrational propositions (e.g., words, phrases) that people use that contribute to feelings of dysphoria and negative affect but the basic meaning and core philosophy that underlies each of these statements

TABLE 9.2 Irrational Ideas Related to Emotional Disturbance

- It is necessary for me "to be loved or approved by virtually every significant other person in [my] community" (Ellis, 1962, p. 61).
- In order to be worthwhile, I "should be thoroughly competent, adequate, and achieving in all possible respects" (p. 63).
- Some people are bad or wicked and "should be severely blamed and punished" (p. 65).
- It "is awful and catastrophic when things are not the way" I would like them to be (p. 69).
- Unhappiness is due to external circumstances, and "people have little or no ability to control their sorrows and disturbances" (p. 72).
- If "something is or may be dangerous or fearsome [I] should be terribly concerned about it and should keep dwelling on the possibility of its occurring" (p. 75).
- It is better for me "to avoid than to face certain life difficulties and self-responsibilities" (p. 78).
- I need someone who is stronger than I to rely and be dependent on (p. 80).
- My "past history is an all-important determiner of [my] present behavior . . . because something once strongly affected [my] life, it should indefinitely have a similar effect" (p. 85).
- I should "become quite upset over other people's problems and disturbances" (p. 85).
- There "is invariably a right, precise, and perfect solution to [my] problems and . . . it is catastrophic if this perfect solution is not found" (p. 87).

Note. From *Reason and Emotion in Psychotherapy* by A. Ellis © 1991.

that is the prime denigrator of their sense of self-worth (Ellis, 1999).

Summary

The broad conceptualizations underlying Beck's and Ellis's therapies are similar in many respects. Although the approach to therapy is quite distinct (e.g., Ellis believes that irrational beliefs should be attacked and refuted, whereas Beck engages in collaborative empiricism and guided discovery to help clients evaluate the validity of their thinking), they share a focus on present cognition (the here and now) and the idea that cognitive change is an essential ingredient for therapeutic change. Beck and Ellis also agree that dysfunctional cognition contributes to psychological distress.

Beck's theory (e.g., Beck, 1963, 1964; Beck et al., 1979; Beck et al., 1985), however, extends beyond simply associating particular thoughts with particular emotions and is instead presented as a coherent and comprehensive system of self-relevant knowledge representation composed of automatic thoughts, intermediate beliefs, schemata, and (more recently) modes (Beck, 1996). Although the more recent writings of Ellis (1999) have focused more explicitly on an individual's core philosophies, his theory is not articulated as a comprehensive effort to represent all forms of the interaction among thought, feeling, and action. Thus, although Ellis believes that individuals' personal core philosophies of so-called musterbation pervade their thinking, he has consis-

tently focused on the effects of irrational beliefs (which essentially comprise Beck's level of intermediate beliefs, rules, and assumptions; see J. S. Beck, 1995; Freeman et al., 1990). As such, Ellis's model appears to represent a broad-based theory of personality and psychological functioning, one that is a less comprehensive and empirically driven than Beck's model. A further example of this point is that Ellis's model does not evoke the principle of content specificity but instead stands merely on the more general assumption that irrational thoughts lead to psychological distress and misery. Whereas Beck hypothesizes further that different psychological problems are associated with different sets of core beliefs, Ellis's model is vague in this regard. Given that Beck's cognitive theory is better elaborated and has stimulated far greater research attention than Ellis's REBT (both in terms of basic theoretical and clinical-applied research), we devote more of our discussion to Beck's theory in subsequent sections of this chapter. We also focus on the notion of schemata and core beliefs, although we discuss other levels of the cognitive taxonomy when warranted.

DEVELOPMENTAL CONSIDERATIONS

Empirical tests of cognitive theories generally have sought to answer the question, "If an individual has core belief *x*, how will he or she probably react to life event *y*?" Considerable evidence suggests that individuals' characteristic sets of core beliefs about self and others do indeed predict their future interpretations, behavior, and affective responses to life events. However, to circumvent the potential epistemological problem of infinite theoretical regress, further validation of cognitive theory rests equally on an explanation of how people come to develop their core beliefs in the first place. Although this question has historically received less theoretical emphasis in the writings of Beck and Ellis, whose theories underscore the influence of current cognitive factors for psychological functioning, both of their models assume that core beliefs or irrational thoughts develop primarily as a result of prior experiential learning (in interaction with temperament), especially learning that takes place during early childhood (Beck et al., 1979; J. S. Beck, 1995; Clark et al., 1999; Dryden & Ellis, 2001; Ellis, 1999).

Parenting styles and the quality and type of early caregiver bonding, for example, are thought to be foundational to the development of core beliefs about self and others (Ingram, 2003). Viewed from the perspective of attachment theory (Bowlby, 1988), children form internal working models of relationships as they interact with their caregivers, which are internalized cognitive representations of the meaning, function, and value of social relationships. Securely attached children, who have supportive and affectionate relationships with their caregivers, learn self-efficacy, emotional understanding, and self-regulatory skills, thereby leading to a positive core belief about self. In addition, securely attached children come to expect compassion, goodwill, and sincerity from others, in turn contributing to favorable beliefs about the value of relationships (Bowlby, 1988). In contrast, children who are insecurely attached perceive a lack of emotional support from their caregiver, come to view others as equally unsupportive, uncaring, or unaffectionate, and consider themselves isolated, vulnerable, and unworthy (e.g., Bowlby, 1980).

Consequently, internal working models formed via attachment relationships are assumed to represent the primary cognitive underpinnings of adult core beliefs related to self and others. In other words, children are thought to assimilate later interpersonal events into their predominate schema or internal-working model for relationships, forming a memory structure for relationships that over time become increasingly consolidated and resistant to change. Attachment and cognitive theories share the focal developmental assumption that the particular types of early life experiences a young individual is exposed to partially determine the specific set of core beliefs that he or she will eventually hold concerning self and others. These core beliefs then define an organizing framework through which subsequent experiences are interpreted. According to cognitive theories, core beliefs also constitute the basis for determining which particular stressful experiences an individual will be vulnerable to in the future (Ingram et al., 1998; Ingram & Price, 2001).

Young and his colleagues (1990, 1999; Young, Klosko, & Weshaar, 2003) have been prominent in further expanding cognitive theory from a developmental perspective. Young distinguishes five different types of developmental settings in which a child might be raised and theorizes that each of these diverse environments may foster a discernable number of distinctive core beliefs, which he terms *early maladaptive schemata* (EMS). When an individual is abused, regularly deprived of emotional affection, or exposed to familial interactions that are emotionally detached, cold, and rejecting, he or she is more likely to develop core beliefs that his or her needs for security, stability, nurturance, empathy, and acceptance are unlikely to be reliably met. Young termed this belief set *Disconnection and Rejection,* and theorized that an individual raised in this type of environment may believe that he or she is unwanted, inferior, unlovable, and socially isolated. Such an individual may interpret later interpersonal rejection or social stress as further justification that his or her core beliefs are accurate, resulting in depression or social anxiety.

A second EMS described by Young represents core beliefs related to *Autonomy and Performance.* Individuals regarded as autonomous and performance impaired consider themselves unequipped to cope independently even with life's day-to-day challenges. This belief system is thought to have developed as a result of a childhood upbringing that either failed to reinforce or that undermined a child's personal confidence and perceived competence (e.g., parents' harsh criticism). Individuals endorsing these particular core beliefs may feel vulnerable and become dependent upon others to cope with everyday responsibilities and stressors.

A third set of EMS described by Young et al. (2003) involves *Impaired Limits,* which are thought to develop in the context of parental overpermissiveness and lack of discipline. Individuals endorsing this set of core beliefs may perceive themselves as grandiose, superior, and entitled to power and control over others. Therefore, these individuals may have low frustration tolerance (cf. Dryden & Ellis, 2001) and may be less inhibited in their expression of aggressive emotion. This lack of inhibition often results in oppression of, and domination over, more timid and less self-assured peers, whereas it may result in social rejection by assertive individuals.

A fourth EMS discussed by Young is *Other-directedness,* which relates to beliefs concerning the need for affection and approval. Individuals who endorse other-directed beliefs consider their own needs secondary to those of others and believe that their individual needs are best met by fulfilling the wishes and desires of others. Young et al. (2003) theorize that typical families of origin that generate this pattern of core beliefs include those in which self-preoccupied parents focus on their personal needs, neglect the needs of their children, and cultivate a family dynamic in which their children are able to gain acceptance only by suppressing their own needs and pleasing their parents. In subsequent years, such an individual likely would submit to others in times of disagreement, primarily to avoid conflict, abandonment, and personal feelings of guilt and self-criticism. Additionally, these persons may attempt to compensate for a perceived lack of a true identity by excessively seeking reassurance.

A fifth and final set of EMS described by Young et al. (2003) relates to *Overvigilance and Inhibition.* Individuals with this set of core beliefs are disdainful of risk taking, spontaneity, and positive emotional expressiveness. These individuals often believe that it is safer, wiser, and more commendable to act in accordance with ethics and logical rule-based directives for attaining achievement. This belief set is thought to be cultivated in demanding, rigid, and disciplinary family environments where falling in line and avoiding mistakes are rewarded as opposed to explorative, creative, and pleasure-seeking behaviors. Adhering to this set of core beliefs may culminate in excessive uncertainty about one's capability in handling unpredictable events and result in fear of taking risks because one might make a mistake and be disapproved of.

Although research generally supports Young's conceptual differentiation among these five classes of core beliefs and EMS (e.g., Glaser, Campbell, Calhoun, Bates, & Petrocelli, 2002; Lee, Taylor, & Dunn, 1999; Schmidt, Joiner, Young, & Telch, 1995), no studies have yet documented their prevalence in association with distinctive parenting styles and practices. In general, considerable debate revolves around the strength of associations linking parenting practices and children's personality development (Havlerson & Wampler, 1997). However, an initial representative body of findings continues to accumulate. For example, McCranie and Bass (1984) found that parental overcontrol during childhood was associated with core beliefs related to dependency and self-criticism in adulthood. Other researchers have found that perceived insecurity in parental attachment as an adult is associated with endorsement of dysfunctional attitudes related to dependency and performance evaluation (Roberts, Gotlib, & Kassel, 1996; Whisman & Kwon, 1992; Whisman & McGarvey, 1995). Perceptions of maternal care also have been associated with indexes of positive and negative self-thinking (e.g., Ingram, Overbey, & Fortier, 2001) and information-processing biases (Ingram & Ritter, 2000). Moreover, these associations at least partially may be driven by children's internalization of parental attitudes and behaviors. For example, researchers have found a relatively close correspondence on indexes of negative and positive self-cognition between depressed mothers and their offspring (Garber & Flynn, 2001; Jaenicke et al., 1987; Radke-Yarrow, Belmont, Nottelmann, & Bottomly, 1990; Taylor & Ingram, 1999).

It is important to note, however, that cognitive theories do not propose that early experiential learning is fully deterministic, but that instead they posit that core beliefs are malleable to some extent on the basis of subsequent learning (e.g., that which is learned can be unlearned). Over the course of cognitive development, greater metacognitive control over one's automatic thoughts and interpretations is enabled compared with the rudimentary thinking of the younger child (Bartsch & Estes, 1996; Kuhn, 1999). A concerted effort to counteract one's original way of thinking, coupled with supportive real-life experiences, can remodel early thinking styles and replace, or at least compete with, prior core beliefs for an individual's conscious attention. Such a concerted effort exemplifies the major focus of cognitive restructuring therapies.

BIOLOGICAL/PHYSIOLOGICAL RELATIONSHIPS

One measure of the breadth and utility of a scientific theory is its ability to explain phenomena not only within the pur-

view of its primary subject matter but also that resulting from outside its foundational base. Although the transportability of psychological constructs such as automatic thoughts and irrational core beliefs to neurobiological terminology might have been unfathomable in recent decades, and indeed remains a difficult theoretical problem, progress in the cognitive and affective neurosciences is steadily fusing the theoretical void between psychological and biological approaches to the study of mood and personality (Kandel & Squire, 2001). Although biological approaches are not central to either of their work, Beck's and Ellis's theories are broadly compatible with a psychobiological perspective on the nature of mood and personality. From the perspective of cognitive theories, physiological variables of import include studies that have examined the influence of cognitive restructuring on emotional-behavioral functioning at the neural level as well as neurobiological theories of knowledge representation, especially as applied to understanding the self and personality.

Both Beck and Ellis acknowledge that the uniquely human capacity for rationality likely evolved much later in our biological lineage and, accordingly, that the remnants of an irrational and more primal emotional or drive-based form of information processing still characterizes much of our thought. Indeed, Ellis's theory explicitly assumes that individuals have a biological predisposition to be irrational (Dryden & Ellis, 2001; Ellis, 1999), which may entail acting primarily in accordance with intellectual faculties based in unconscious associative conditioning (Sloman, 1996; see also Beck, 1996). Our additional human capacity to employ a logical rule-based knowledge system (working memory) and self-govern the direction of our actions, however, awards us some level of freedom over these biological predispositions. Indeed this is the central platform upon which Beck's and Ellis's therapies are based. From the cognitive perspective, psychological insight and well-being are best gained when one is able to regulate one's moods and exert a level of executive control over one's more irrational mind via top-down cortical processing: "The brain of *Homo sapiens* has apparently evolved adaptability to provide not only for planning, selecting appropriate memories, and so forth, but also for overriding the more primitive cognitive-affective-behavioral patterns when these are perceived to be maladaptive" (Alford & Beck, 1997, p. 71).

Greater use of this higher-order cortical control over our moods and behavioral responses may indeed be one of the primary neurobiological outcomes of cognitive restructuring therapies. For example, two recent studies have examined brain metabolic changes before and after a cognitive-behavioral intervention for a psychological disorder. Goldapple et al. (2004) examined the neural effects of cognitive therapy of depression (Beck et al., 1979) using positron-emission tomography (PET) and found pre- versus posttreatment changes in metabolic activity in multiple brain areas, including those known to be implicated in memory and executive functions (e.g., changes were found in hippocampal and parahippocampal regions, cingulate cortex, and frontal cortex in addition to parietal and temporal regions). Interestingly, Goldapple et al. found that some of these neural changes were unique to, or in a different direction from, regional metabolic changes observed with antidepressant pharmacotherapy. Goldapple et al. conjectured that a top-down (cortical-limbic) therapeutic mechanism may have been active in the cognitive-therapy intervention, whereas a bottom-up (limbic-cortical) mechanism may have mediated antidepressant symptom reduction. Furmark et al. (2002) also reported a neuroimaging investigation of the effects of a cognitive-behavioral intervention for social phobia using PET. Compared to pretreatment, following cognitive-behavioral therapy (CBT), reduced blood flow was observed in multiple brain areas (including bilaterally in the amygdala, hippocampus, areas of the temporal cortex, periaqueductal gray, and right cerebellum) during public speaking. Other physiological indexes also have shown sensitivity to pre- versus postchanges associated with cognitive restructuring interventions. Joffe, Segal, and Singer (1996), for instance, found that the normalization of blood thyroid-hormone levels was associated with clinical response to cognitive therapy for depression. These studies reveal that cognitive restructuring therapies directly impact neural functioning.

A second way that cognitive and psychobiological theories intersect involves the ways in which they conceptualize knowledge representation that occurs in the mind-brain. Ellis's theory is less relevant in this regard as it is not derived upon a formal model of knowledge representation. Beck's theory, in contrast, expressly proposes that self and personality-relevant information (e.g., core beliefs) are stored in the mind as schemata. The schema construct also has been conceptualized in network terminology as a specific constellation of self-referent information distributed across information-processing nodes (e.g., Bower, 1981; Ingram, 1984; Teasdale & Barnard, 1993), which, in connectionist systems, are conceived of as neuronal populations.

Although still in their infancy, psychobiological models of self and personality knowledge representation are similar in discernable ways to those proposed by schema models. LeDoux (2002) has advanced one of the most well-articulated theories of self-representation from a psychobiological perspective. In brief, LeDoux conceptualizes that individual differences in personality are derived from analogous between-individual variation in neural-network connections. Moreover, these connections are regarded as developing not only on the basis of programmed genetic influence but also via the individual's experiences (i.e., through neural plasticity). Variation in the organization of connections among neurons is believed to strongly influence, and in turn be influenced by, the processing of subsequent stimuli, especially self-relevant and emotional events. Most influential in this top-down process is the operation of neural convergence zones (e.g., in prefrontal, posterior parietal, and medial temporal cortex and hippocampus), the description of which is strikingly similar to Teasdale and Barnard's (1993) conceptualization of implicational codes in the context of synthesizing self-relevant meanings from information across multiple sensory and verbal-propositional modalities. Information stored in convergence zones not only directly influences subsequent sensory (e.g., attentional) processing but also frequently forms the contents of working memory and thus can influence subsequent perception and experience through its involvement in executive functions.

BOUNDARIES OF THE THEORIES

Cognitive theories are comprehensive, but some boundaries and limitations exist in their explanatory capacity. Notwithstanding the fact that Beck's theory continues to be refined (cf. Beck, 1996), two conceptual issues warrant discussion: (1) cross-culture generalizability and (2) the construct of the schema.

Cultural differences in the definition and construal of self have been the source of recent theoretical and empirical scrutiny (Heine, Lehman, Markus, & Kitayama, 1999; Hong, Morris, Chiu, & Benet-Martinez, 2000; Markus & Kitayama, 1994; Parkes, Schneider, & Bochner, 1999; Singelis, 1994). Researchers uniformly have proclaimed that self-psychology must take into account these cultural discrepancies if researchers are to understand accurately the nature of this construct. Unfortunately, cognitive theory has lagged behind in its accommodation of such recommendations. In particular, several assumptions of the cognitive model of self generalize poorly to other cultures. First, cognitive theories postulate that information that is consistent with the content of the self-schema is processed efficiently. Furthermore, the attributes and beliefs underlying the self-schema are conceptualized to be relatively stable. However, cross-cultural research has challenged the generalizability of these assumptions. For example, North Americans tend to consider internal features, such as traits and attributes, central to self-definition, whereas individuals living in Eastern cultures regard their social roles and obligations to the group as critical to self-definition (Markus & Kitayama, 1994). Hence, information related to the self is believed to be processed less efficiently than information about the self in relation to the group. This issue was exemplified in a recent experiment by Wagar and Cohen (2003) who found that Asian Canadians processed information about the collectivist self more efficiently than the traditional personal self.

In addition, the stability of internal attributes can vary across cultures. Some Eastern cultures engender what is referred to as a *contextualized self,* meaning that self-concepts are qualified by contextual factors such as time, place, and roles (e.g., "I am smart at school"; Markus & Kitayama, 1991; Parkes et al., 1999). In contrast, the self-schema is conceptualized by cognitive theory to be a relatively stable construct. In North America, core beliefs and assumptions are generally consistent across time and place because of the tendency to encode and process information in a schema-consistent fashion. This process may, however, be unique to Westerners, as those with a contextualized self typically hold several different self-beliefs depending on the context at hand. These cultural differences pose problems for cognitive theories because their tenets are not commensurate with a transient, group-oriented self-schema.

A second assumption of the cognitive model that may not generalize well to all cultures is the belief that positive self-regard should correlate positively, and self-criticism negatively, with mental health. Following their extensive review of the literature, Heine et al. (1999) concluded that the need for a positive self-view is a product of North American culture that does not generalize to Japanese culture. In Japanese culture, children are taught to focus on their weaknesses to aid self-improvement, whereas the elaboration of positive self-content is discouraged in favor of being modest and enhancing group relations. In fact, the cognitive understanding of vulnerability to depression may be quite incompatible with Japanese culture. Kitayama, Markus, and Kurokawa (1991, as cited in Markus & Kitayama, 1994) found that the response time for self-description among Japanese participants was much slower than that of U.S. participants, especially for positive self-attributes. One interpretation of this finding is that the Japanese participants possessed a poorly consolidated positive self-schema, which is believed to be a potential vulnerability marker for depression (Dozois & Dobson, 2001a, 2001b). Yet, as Heine et al. (1999) concluded, "what contributes to mental health may vary importantly across cultures, and this cultural variance may well extend beyond self-esteem to other characteristics of psychological well-being that have been identified in the Western literature" (p. 786).

Another limitation of cognitive theory is that it relies on a construct (schema) that is difficult to measure, define, and conceptualize (Fiske & Linville, 1980). For example, there is no consensus regarding how best to assess the structure and content of the self-schema. Attempts to measure or infer the structure of the self-schema have included questionnaires (e.g., Dysfunctional Attitude Scale [DAS]; Weissman & Beck, 1978), memory-recall tasks (MacDonald, Kuiper, & Olinger, 1985), reaction-time tasks (Derry & Kuiper, 1981), priming paradigms (Segal & Vella, 1990), card sorts (Linville, 1985; Showers, 1992), multidimensional scaling (DeSteno & Salovey, 1997), and distance-scaling tasks (Dozois & Dobson, 2001a). These various strategies, however, may not be assessing the same construct (Campbell, Assanand, & DiPaula, 2003).

In terms of conceptual issues, the self-schema has been described as a construct composed of both verbal and non-verbal components (Brewin, 1989; Teasdale & Barnard, 1993); yet virtually all attempts to assess and measure the self-schema utilize adjectives, making them highly verbal or linguistic. Brewin (1989) proposed that memory representations often can be unconscious and not open to introspective thought (see also Teasdale & Barnard, 1993). Similarly, core beliefs and assumptions contained within the self-schema may not be represented exclusively in a verbal format and may not be completely accessible to conscious thought. Instead, the content and organization of the schema is necessarily inferred or interpreted in light of the pattern of output from lower-level subsystems (Teasdale, 1996). As a consequence, a complete understanding of self-schematic content may not be objectively possible.

EVIDENCE RELATED TO COGNITIVE THEORIES

Notwithstanding their limitations, considerable evidence has supported the main tenets of the cognitive theories. As previously noted, the central axioms of clinical cognitive theories as a general class include that (1) cognition affects emotion and behavior, (2) that cognition can be monitored and changed, and (3) that by altering cognitions, one can exert desired behavioral and emotional change. Although the role of cognition as a mediator between stimulus and response at one time was questioned (e.g., during the behaviorism era), this fact is no longer sensibly disputed (for review, see Dobson & Dozois, 2001). Myriad studies from clinical science, cognitive experimental psychology, and social psychology have demonstrated that individuals tend to filter information and respond to stimuli and situations in a way that is consistent with a mediating or moderating role for preexisting attitudes, assumptions, and expectations (e.g., Olson, Roese, & Zanna, 1996; Tversky & Kahneman, 1974). In addition, considerable advances have been made to isolate some of the fundamental constituent cognitive processes that determine individual differences in personality and mood, such as those involved in selective attention, memory, and judgment (e.g., Williams, Watts, MacLeod, & Mathews, 1997).

Accordingly, our review of the evidence bearing on cognitive theories focuses on data pertaining more directly to the clinical cognitive models described previously, which include Beck's notion that there are distinctive levels of cognition that work in synchrony to impact emotional and behavioral responses and Beck's idea that different emotional experiences or personality problems can be characterized by a unique set of core beliefs and automatic thoughts (i.e., content specificity). The assumption that, by restructuring irrational (Ellis, 1962) and maladaptive belief systems (Beck et al., 1979), one can positively affect emotional well-being and behavioral patterns is also discussed within the context of the CT and REBT psychotherapy-process literature.

Levels of Cognition

Based initially on his clinical observations, Beck was the first theorist to distinguish among different levels of cognition, each of which was purported to relate to emotional distress. Beck (1967) originally organized his theoretical constructs in a three-tiered cognitive hierarchy composed of automatic thoughts, processing biases and intermediate beliefs, and cognitive schemata. Over time, Beck's theory has been increasingly informed by the areas of cognitive experimental psychology and social cognition, but an important precedent for evaluating these cognitive mechanisms has involved increased conceptual clarity and operationalization of the constructs proposed.[1] Ingram (Ingram & Kendall, 1986; Ingram et al., 1998) suggested, for example, that there are four main components of the cognitive taxonomy: the structures, content, operations, and products of cognition. *Cognitive structure* refers to the internal representation and organization of information in memory that, together with cognitive content (e.g., core beliefs) make up the schema. *Cognitive operations* are defined as the processes of the schema and include such variables as attention, encoding, retrieval, and interpretation of incoming stimuli. Finally *cognitive products* (i.e., automatic thoughts) are assumed to stem from the interaction of schemata and information processing.

Research accumulating since Beck's original proposals continues to support the view that the mind is best conceptualized in terms of different levels of cognitive analysis. Much of this research has been devoted to understanding the cognitive underpinnings of depression and anxiety. For example, studies show that an increased frequency of negative automatic self-statements, and increased endorsement of various dysfunctional belief sets concerning affiliation and achievement, commonly accompany depression and anxiety (e.g., Beck & Perkins, 2001; Dozois, Covin, & Brinker, 2003). Furthermore, several studies have revealed affective biases in information processing, such as attention and memory (for reviews, see Clark et al., 1999; Dobson & Dozois, 2004; Haaga et al., 1991; Williams, Mathews, & MacLeod, 1996).

One of the criticisms of cognitive theory, however, has been that the cognitive factors purported to causally affect mood actually fluctuate with one's affective state and thus may be caused by emotion (e.g., Barnett & Gotlib, 1988; Coyne & Gotlib, 1983). For example, when individuals are depressed, they tend to show attentional biases toward and recall biases for negative material, although this information processing appears to improve once depression remits (e.g., Dozois & Dobson, 2001b). In addition, studies that compare previously depressed individuals to never-depressed controls tend not to distinguish between groups on the basis of cognitive products and processes (for review, see Ingram et al., 1998). In contrast, studies that have used an emotional challenge or prime (e.g., the induction of negative moods) prior to cognitive assessment more consistently have demonstrated differences between individuals with a history of depression and those who have never been depressed (Miranda & Persons, 1988; Miranda, Persons, & Byers, 1990; Persons & Miranda, 1992; Segal & Ingram, 1994; Solomon, Haaga, Brody, Kirk, & Friedman, 1998). Such studies have advanced the understanding of mood-congruent information-processing biases and support the concept of stable cognitive structures that may become activated with changes in mood states.

The schema construct, although the most central in Beck's theory, historically has been one of the most difficult to define and study (Segal, 1988). However, a number of novel assessment methodologies have been developed to operationalize this construct for empirical study. Several priming and reaction-time studies demonstrate that individuals likely organize self-relevant content in memory as a well-consolidated and interconnected network of associations. For example, Rogers, Kuiper, and Kirker (1977) documented that information processed in terms of its self-reference (e.g., "Describes you?") produces superior recall relative to information evaluated according to its semantic (e.g., "Means the same as *x*?"), structural (e.g., "Small letters?"), or phonemic (e.g., "Rhythmic?") properties. These results indicate that self-referent processing promotes a deeper level of encoding and yields a stronger and more elaborate memory trace than does information that is not self-referent (for review, see Symons & Johnson, 1997). Other measures of information processing used to infer the existence of self-schemata include card-sorting tasks (e.g., Linville, 1985), the implicit-association task (e.g., Gemar, Segal, Sagrati, & Kennedy, 2001), and prime-target-relatedness tasks (e.g., Segal, Gemar, Truchon, Guirguis, & Horowitz, 1995), although each of these measures necessarily confounds process-method variance with self-schema assessment. Another recent approach that may hold promise is the psychological-distance-scaling task (Dozois & Dobson, 2001a), which operationalizes self-schema assessment in terms of a computation of interstimulus distances among adjective stimuli having to do with self-representation. Studies reveal that negative information is well consolidated in the self-schemata of individuals with anxiety and depressive disorders, whereas positive information is less well organized specifically in depression (Dozois & Dobson, 2001a). This task also reveals that negative self-structures are stable across time, irrespective of symptom improvement (Dozois & Dobson, 2001b), and may become more consolidated with increasing episodes of depression (Dozois & Dobson, 2003) and levels of dysphoria (Dozois, 2002).

Content Specificity

The content-specificity hypothesis suggests that different emotional experiences or personality problems can be distinguished on the basis of unique sets of core beliefs and automatic thoughts. Research in experimental psychopathology generally has supported the content-specificity hypothesis (e.g., Beck, Brown, Steer, Eidelson, & Riskind, 1987; Hankin, Abramson, Miller, & Haeffel, 2004; Westra & Kuiper, 1997). Studies that have investigated this proposition in depression and anxiety have produced mixed results (Beck & Perkins, 2001). Given the high degree of comorbidity, as well as the theoretical overlap between these constructs, such studies have produced a very conservative test of the content-specificity model. Novel measures that better differentiate among types of negative automatic thoughts (e.g., among panic, depression, worry, somatic preoccupation, and social fear-related thoughts; see Woody, Taylor, McLean, & Koch, 1998) may hold more promise in future tests of the content specificity of cognitive products. Westra and Kuiper (1997), for instance, tested participants' self-descriptiveness ratings on several adjectives sampled from the depression, anxiety, bulimia, and personality literature. Endorsement ratings provided support for the content-specificity hypothesis. Specifically, partial correlations revealed that dysphoria was uniquely associated with adjectives pertaining to loss, failure, and hopelessness, whereas the themes in anxiety centered on threat and stigmatization. These researchers also found

content-specificity effects for selective attentional biases in dysphoria, anxiety, and bulimia using a visual probe-detection task and enhanced memory performance for domain-specific adjectives on an incidental recognition measure (but in dysphoric and bulimic groups only).

Cognitive Restructuring

Although distinct in their approach, Beck's and Ellis's therapies seek to positively impact emotional well-being and behavior by restructuring irrational and maladaptive belief systems, which is the unifying principle upon which all cognitive-behavioral therapies rest (Dobson, 2001). Accordingly, this assumption forms the pivotal platform upon which the validity of cognitive theories can be tested via psychotherapy process research. Although researchers disagree on the specific change processes that take place over the course of successful cognitive therapy, it is generally agreed that they are cognitive in nature (for reviews, see Barber & DeRubeis, 1989; Elkin, Pilkonis, Docherty, & Sotsky, 1988; Hollon, DeRubeis, & Evans, 1987; Robins & Hayes, 1993; Whisman, 1993).

A number of studies directly have examined changes in cognitive variables over the course of cognitive therapy. For example, several studies have found that pretreatment measures of dysfunctional attitudes, attributional style, hopelessness, and cognitive bias predict the level of subsequent symptom reduction in cognitive therapy for depression (e.g., DeRubeis et al. 1990; Miller, Norman, & Keitner, 1990; Rector, Bagby, Segal, Joffe, & Levitt, 2000). Some of the most interesting theoretical findings in this regard are those of Tang and DeRubeis (1999). These researchers evaluated therapy process by reviewing audiotaped sessions of cognitive therapy and demonstrated that nonlinear substantial reductions in depressive symptoms (sudden gains) were preceded by significant cognitive shifts, such as when patients identified or corrected a maladaptive core belief or schema or adopted a new belief or schema.

Additional support for cognitive mediation of symptom reduction has been found in the form of an increased reduction in negative cognition with cognitive interventions relative to pharmacotherapy. For example, cognitive interventions are associated with greater reductions in dysfunctional attitudes related to need for social approval, hopelessness cognitions, low self-concept, and cognitive bias (e.g., Rush, Beck, Kovacs, Weissenburger, & Hollon, 1982; Whisman, Miller, Norman, & Keitner, 1991). However, these findings have not been replicated uniformly (e.g., Moore & Blackburn, 1996; Simons, Garfield, & Murphy, 1984).

Pharmacotherapy interventions also reduce symptomatic cognition (e.g., the frequency of negative automatic thoughts), but cognitive interventions may uniquely alter associations between transient mood fluctuations and schema activation. In a test of this hypothesis, Segal, Gemar, and Williams (1999) administered a self-report measure of negative beliefs and attitudes concerning self (i.e., the DAS) to patients who had successfully completed either CT or antidepressant treatment. This scale was administered to the full sample of posttreatment patients both before and after a negative-mood-induction procedure. Segal et al. found that individuals who received antidepressant medication, while not differing from individuals who received CT in a neutral mood state, showed more elevated DAS scores than those who received CT after the negative-mood-induction procedure. Furthermore, the degree of elevation in dysfunctional attitudes between neutral and negative moods predicted the probability of depressive relapse six months later. These results suggest that cognitive interventions do indeed alter certain crucial cognitive patterns.

PREDICTIONS FOR EVERYDAY FUNCTIONING

Having discussed the tenets, correlates, limitations, and evidence of cognitive theories, we conclude this chapter with a descriptive account of their predictions for everyday functioning in four domains: relationships, work, recreation, and retirement. Common to each of these domains is the operation of a self-schema replete with core beliefs, assumptions, and cognitive distortions that allow for an idiosyncratic approach to viewing the world. Consistent with cognitive theory, we also would maintain that the influence of the self-schema on everyday functioning will be apparent only to the extent that its underlying content is activated. This section illustrates that self-schemata alone do not impact thoughts, emotions, and behaviors, but rather it is the dynamic interaction of environment and underlying cognition that determines functioning in these domains.

Relationships

Interpersonal relationships have played a prominent role in cognitive theories (Beck, 1983, 1988). As outlined previously, there are some aspects of the self-schema that are positive and healthy and other components that are more negative and maladaptive. Empirical research has demonstrated, for instance, that a desire for connectedness to others is a healthy style of interaction, whereas dependency on others is problematic (Rude & Burnham, 1995). Thus, the structure and content of the self-schema largely determines whether one's behavior will be healthy or maladaptive. If the core content of one's self-schema reflects a connectedness approach to interpersonal interactions, one would not routinely look for cues of rejection or abandonment, nor would one regularly engage in irrational thinking about the interpersonal behaviors of others. Individuals with a *dependent self-schema,* on the other hand, would have more problematic interpersonal relationships because their core beliefs and assumptions foster cognitive biases that result in the misinterpretation of interpersonal behaviors and cues. To illustrate, a woman with a core belief that she is unlovable might misinterpret the cancellation of a date inferring that "He must not love me" rather than attempting to find out whether this automatic thought has any validity. Such mind reading (see Table 9.1) would be detrimental to the relationship because it precludes the use of open communication, which is a necessary feature of any relationship. Such irrational thinking also may lead to behaviors that ultimately impair relationships (e.g., being clingy and excessively seeking reassurance), thereby producing self-fulfilling prophecies and strengthening the consolidation of dependency content in memory.

Aside from dependency schemata are other dysfunctional beliefs (e.g., having rigid and irrational beliefs about maintaining independence and control) that can create interpersonal stress (Alden & Bieling, 1996; Bieling & Alden, 2001; Nelson, Hammen, Daley, Burge, & Davila, 2001). Alden and Bieling (1996) found that individuals who exhibited a high need for independence and control (an autonomous schema) also tended to be cold and interpersonally distant from others. As opposed to the dependent self-schema, a person with an *autonomous self-schema* would interpret cues of interpersonal intimacy and connection as threatening, which would result in an entirely different set of interpersonal problems.

Preconceived ideas about the general nature of intimate relationships (which likely stem from early modeling) also may impact day-to-day relationship functioning. For instance, individuals in couple relationships may believe that they are not being loved and cared for by their partners when, in reality, the problem may stem from a misperception of behavioral cues. One individual may have grown up in a home where love was demonstrated through physical affection; his or her partner may have been brought up to believe that love should be demonstrated through works. In such a scenario, miscommunication obviously would result if each individual showed and responded to his or her own definition of what the expression of love entails. Beck (1988) has written about a number of other cognitive biases that interfere with healthy relationship functioning (e.g., tunnel vision, mind reading, jumping to conclusions, etc.). The following excerpt illustrates how one's own biases can affect subsequent interactions in a relationship:

> Karen, an interior designer, described how she came home one day flushed with excitement and eager to discuss some good news with her husband, Ted. She has just been awarded a lucrative contract. . . . But when she started to tell Ted about this unexpected success in her career, he seemed distant and uninvolved. She thought, "*He doesn't really care about me. He's only interested in himself.*" Her excitement evaporated. Instead of celebrating with him, Karen went into another room and poured herself a glass of champagne. Meanwhile, Ted—who was feeling somewhat dejected that day because of a setback in his career—had the thought, "*She doesn't really care about me. She's only interested in her career.*" (Beck, 1988, p. 15)

In this example, both Karen and Ted may then jump to conclusions about the cause of this behavior, attributing it to internal flaws (e.g., he is selfish). A negative mind-set about one's partner may then produce other biases in attention and memory. For example, Karen may start to see only the faults in Ted rather his more redeeming features. Moreover, the very traits that excited her about Ted when their relationship began may now be looked at through a lens of negativity, contributing to further dissolution of the relationship.

Self-schemata not only guide one's thoughts, emotions, and behaviors during the course of a particular relationship but also impact expectations and attitudes toward relationships in general. Past experiences with rejection, for example, can consolidate negative content in the self-schema and lead to cognitive distortions that create trepidation or, worse, avoidance of interpersonal relationships. For example, overgeneralization (see Table 9.1) of past negative interpersonal experiences might lead a person to believe that future relationships also will be disastrous. This prediction could lead to avoidance of interpersonal intimacy or, conversely, compel the individual with a dependent self-schema to cling tightly to future romantic partners.

Work

The motive to express competency and achieve success is common to many individuals (Markus & Kitayama, 1991). Beck (1983; Clark et al., 1999) postulated that some individuals exhibit a personality mode that is oriented toward achievement goals. One positive feature of having an *achievement-oriented schema* is that it fosters motivation in individuals to succeed in their respective careers. Harboring the belief that achieving success at work is an important component of self-definition can have many positive outcomes. For example, this type of self-schema can motivate a person

to work very hard (behavior), which produces a sense of pride (affect), especially if the hard work translates into success, and leads the person to believe that he or she is competent (cognitive). Of course, such beliefs (e.g., "I am a competent worker") serve to engender a sense of self-efficacy and confidence to perform well again, which further consolidates the self-schema in a cyclical fashion. To the extent that self-worth is contingent upon success, however, individuals with an achievement-oriented self-schema may become dysphoric and be forced to revise their perception of competence when they encounter failure experiences. Similarly, viewing success as a necessity rather than a desire also would negatively impact an individual who fails to meet these expectations (see Table 9.2; Dryden & Ellis, 2001).

J. S. Beck (1995) noted that people may engage in compensatory strategies to prevent a negative core belief (e.g., "I am incompetent") from becoming realized (see also Young et al., 2003). For example, an individual might decide to exert an excessive amount of effort at work to avoid future setbacks (an overcompensation strategy). Conversely, an individual might take on an overwhelming amount of work so that possible failures can be explained away by the sheer volume of work (e.g., "It was too much for anyone to do") and not by his or her internal ability (a self-handicapping strategy). Another person might respond to failure by focusing on something new that will reestablish a sense of competency (a mood-repair strategy).

It is not to be assumed that all people with an achievement-oriented schema will fall into a maladaptive pattern of functioning following a failure experience. The types of dysfunctional beliefs contained within the schema, as well as one's coping ability, are just two of many factors that will determine how an individual will respond to difficulties at work. For instance, other factors that might mitigate a failure experience include self-efficacy and the belief that one's circumstances are changeable. Children who believe that competence is equivalent to capacity (i.e., that you either have a given skill or you do not) tend to give up following a failure experience. In contrast, children who are more incremental theorists (i.e., believing that competence is acquired in a step-by-step fashion) will continue to persevere through hardship because failure is appraised as feedback rather than as an end product (see Sternberg & Kolligian, 1990).

Recreation

Cognitive theories have not made explicit predictions for the functioning of individuals in recreational activities, yet it is possible to surmise how the self-schema might impact this life domain based on their premises. Given that the content of an individual's self-schema will often determine his or her behavior, it is expected that the type of recreational activities an individual chooses to engage in may also be influenced (at least to some extent) by this construct. For instance, if an individual considers him or herself to be an intellectual, he or she might be motivated to validate this self-view by reading, attending lectures, and visiting museums. However, these behaviors also could be determined by the presence of dysfunctional core beliefs in the schema. If a core belief is negative (e.g., "I am stupid"), then the person could be using compensatory strategies to prevent such a belief from being validated. Consequently, the individual might selectively choose to read material that he or she is confident in comprehending or take friends to museums to demonstrate knowledge and augment feelings of self-worth.

It is conceivable that the recreational activities of an individual also may stem from self-schematic beliefs that are ostensibly unrelated to the activity itself. For example, imagine that through early attachment experiences an individual develops the core belief that he or she is unlovable. In order to deal with this underlying self-belief, the person may use athletics to garner attention and admiration from others. Such a need for attention and approval might manifest itself through other recreational activities such as acting, painting, singing, and writing.

Not only might underlying beliefs guide the thoughts, behaviors, and emotional experiences of individuals in recreational activities, but an extreme imbalance in self-schema content could create either a relative avoidance of or an overinvolvement with recreational activities. An individual with an extreme achievement-based self-schema might concentrate most of his or her time on excelling at work, at the expense of engaging in leisure activities. To use a clinical example, individuals with obsessive-compulsive personality disorder often have automatic thoughts related to achievement (e.g., "I must do something productive rather than waste time going for a walk"; see Beck et al., 2003). The opposite type of imbalance involves spending too much time in recreational pursuits. An individual who exhibits the dysfunctional attitude "If other people like me, it shows that I am lovable" may spend an inordinate amount of time socializing. In this case, this person's self-worth is contingent upon other people's admiration, which leads to overcompensating behaviors that focus heavily on recreational activities. This interpersonal style is characteristic of individuals with histrionic personality disorder who believe that they have to be loved by everyone and actively seek attention and approval (Beck et al., 2003).

Thus, cognitive theory can help predict preferred recreational activities and the extent to which they are utilized.

However, cognitive theory also might be helpful in predicting the extent to which an individual enjoys or experiences a given activity. For example, a person with a core belief related to negative social consequences (e.g., "I am inadequate"; "I am stupid") might not enjoy social activities because the activation of the self-schema would result in scanning the environment for rejection cues. Another possibility is that the person's actual behavior or performance in a recreational activity will be adversely affected by his or her underlying beliefs (e.g., "I am a failure"). For instance, during a hockey game, one player might evaluate his or her performance positively, whereas another player offers a negative self-evaluation, despite the fact that both performances are equal. Such evaluations will reflect the functioning of the self-schema and might inevitably lead to self-fulfilling prophecies, which would further consolidate different content sets within the self-schema.

Retirement

The vast majority of cognitive-theory research is conducted with younger adults, and cognitive theories rarely outline predictions for self-schema functioning in the elderly. Thus, a paucity of theory and research are available with which to understand the impact that late-life events, such as retirement, have on behavior, thoughts, and feelings. Given that self-schemata are postulated to be stable constructs that impact psychological experience across the person's life, it may be assumed that the self-schemata of elderly adults resemble those of their youth. Although the self-schema will undergo some changes and modifications due to accommodation, it is possible that some of the core features of the self-schema remain relatively stable across the life span. Elderly persons, however, tend to confront different life experiences than do individuals in early adulthood, which may activate different components of the self-schema. For example, an individual with an achievement-oriented self-schema who is forced to retire might be motivated to pursue postretirement activities that promote a sense of accomplishment and productivity. If an individual believes that self-worth is contingent upon being employed, then long periods of inactivity accompanying forced retirement may result in frustration and depression.

CONCLUSION AND FUTURE DIRECTIONS

As this review has demonstrated, clinical cognitive theories have provided the foundational springboard for a compelling array of research investigations: studies that have examined the various levels of cognition in psychopathology, developmental precursors to the self-schema, the neurobiological correlates of cognitive change, the specificity of cognitive content to different psychological problems, and the cognitive mechanisms underlying treatment change. In addition, cognitive theories (Beck's model, in particular), have continued to evolve in a synergistic manner with existing research. Although the self-schema has been (and likely always will be) difficult to verify empirically, novel methodologies continue to be developed to facilitate our understanding of this construct.

The paucity of literature in some of the areas that we have reviewed in this chapter suggests a number of interesting avenues for future research. For example, in recent years we have witnessed exciting data on the neurobiological changes that take place in cognitive therapy (Goldapple et al., 2004). Further research is needed to examine the interface among therapy outcome, cognitive mechanisms of change, and neural processes. Similarly, research continues to advance in the area of attachment, and we now have a more comprehensive understanding of the possible origins of self-schemata. This research is, however, in its own early stages of development, and more empirical work is necessary to better understand the relationship between parent-child interactions and the consolidation of self-schemata. Clearly, more research also is needed to determine the cultural boundaries of cognitive theories. Finally, although considerable research already has been conducted in cognitive science and social cognition, another interesting line of investigation would involve studying the impact of core beliefs (and other levels of the cognitive taxonomy) in everyday functioning.

NOTE

1. REBT has had a significant impact on the field of psychotherapy and has been applied to a number of clinical problems. However, its empirical status is more dubious (Haaga & Davison, 1989, 1995). Ellis's theory and therapy have not been studied as extensively as Beck's (Ellis, 2004). Although there may be several reasons for this discrepancy (Ellis, 2003), a central problem has involved the conceptual ambiguity regarding the main constructs of REBT and the lack of methodological rigor in existing studies (Haaga & Davison, 1989, 1995).

REFERENCES

Alden, L. E., & Bieling, P. J. (1996). Interpersonal convergence of personality constructs in dynamic and cognitive models of depression. *Journal of Research in Personality, 30,* 60–75.

Alford, B. A., & Beck, A. T. (1997). *The integrative power of cognitive therapy.* New York: Guilford Press.

Barber, J. P., & DeRubeis, R. J. (1989). On second thought: Where the action is in cognitive therapy for depression. *Cognitive Therapy and Research, 13,* 441–457.

Barnett, P. A., & Gotlib, I. H. (1988). Psychosocial functioning and depression: Distinguishing among antecedents, concomitants, and consequences. *Psychological Bulletin, 104,* 97–126.

Bartsch, K., & Estes, D. (1996). Individual differences in children's developing theory of mind and implications for metacognition. *Learning & Individual Differences, 8,* 281–304.

Beck, A. T. (1963). Thinking and depression. I. Idiosyncratic content and cognitive distortions. *Archives of General Psychiatry, 9,* 36–46.

Beck, A. T. (1964). Thinking and depression. II. Theory and therapy. *Archives of General Psychiatry, 10,* 561–571.

Beck, A. T. (1967). *Depression: Causes and treatment.* Philadelphia: University of Pennsylvania Press.

Beck, A. T. (1983). Cognitive therapy of depression: New perspectives. In P. J. Clayton & J. E. Barrett (Eds.), *Treatment of depression: Old controversies and new approaches* (pp. 265–290). New York: Raven Press.

Beck, A. T. (1988). *Love is never enough.* New York: Harper and Row.

Beck, A. T. (1991). Cognitive therapy: A 30-year retrospective. *American Psychologist, 46,* 368–375.

Beck, A. T. (1993). Cognitive therapy: Past, present, and future. *Journal of Consulting and Clinical Psychology, 61,* 194–198.

Beck, A. T. (1996). Beyond belief: A theory of modes, personality, and psychopathology. In P. M. Salkovskis (Ed.), *Frontiers of cognitive therapy* (pp. 1–25). New York: Guilford Press.

Beck, A. T., Brown, G., Steer, R. A., Eidelson, J. I., & Riskind, J. H. (1987). Differentiating anxiety and depression: A test of the cognitive content-specificity hypothesis. *Journal of Abnormal Psychology, 96,* 179–183.

Beck, A. T., Emery, G., & Greenberg, R. L. (1985). *Anxiety disorders and phobias: A cognitive perspective.* New York: Basic Books.

Beck, A. T., Freeman, A., & Associates. (2003). *Cognitive therapy of personality disorders* (2nd ed.). New York: Guilford Press.

Beck, A. T., Rush, A. J., Shaw, B. F., & Emery, G. (1979). *Cognitive therapy of depression.* New York: Guilford Press.

Beck, J. S. (1995). *Cognitive therapy: Basics and beyond.* New York: Guilford Press.

Beck, R., & Perkins, T. S. (2001). Cognitive content-specificity for anxiety and depression: A meta-analysis. *Cognitive Therapy and Research, 25,* 651–663.

Bieling, P. J., & Alden, L. E. (2001). Sociotropy, autonomy and interpersonal model of depression: An integration. *Cognitive Therapy and Research, 25,* 167–184.

Bower, G. H. (1981). Mood and memory. *American Psychologist, 36,* 129–148.

Bowlby, J. (1980). *Attachment and loss: Vol. 3. Loss: Sadness and depression.* New York: Basic Books.

Bowlby, J. (1988). *A secure base: Parent-child attachment and healthy human development.* New York: Basic Books.

Brewin, C. (1989). Cognitive change processes in psychotherapy. *Psychological Review, 96,* 379–394.

Campbell, J. D., Assanand, S., & DiPaula, A. (2003). The structure of the self-concept and its relation to psychological adjustment. *Journal of Personality, 71,* 115–140.

Clark, D. A., Beck, A. T., & Alford, B. A. (1999). *Scientific foundations of cognitive theory and therapy of depression.* New York: Wiley.

Coyne, J. C., & Gotlib, I. H. (1983). The role of cognition in depression: A critical appraisal. *Psychological Bulletin, 94,* 472–505.

Crick, N. R., & Dodge, K. A. (1994). A review and reformulation of social information-processing mechanisms in children's social adjustment. *Psychological Bulletin, 115,* 73–101.

Derry, P. A., & Kuiper, N. A. (1981). Schematic processing and self-reference in clinical depression. *Journal of Abnormal Psychology, 90,* 286–297.

DeRubeis, R. J., Evans, M. D., Hollon, S. D., Garvey, M. J., Grove, W. M., & Tuason, V. B. (1990). How does cognitive therapy work? Cognitive change and symptom change in cognitive therapy and pharmacotherapy for depression. *Journal of Consulting & Clinical Psychology, 58,* 862–869.

DeSteno, D. A., & Salovey, P. (1997). The effects of mood on the structure of the self-concept. *Cognition and Emotion, 11,* 351–372.

Dobson, K. S. (Ed.). (2001). *Handbook of cognitive-behavioral therapies* (2nd ed.). New York: Guilford Press.

Dobson, K. S., Backs-Dermott, B. J., & Dozois, D. J. A. (2000). Cognitive and cognitive-behavioral therapies. In C. R. Snyder & R. E. Ingram (Eds.), *Handbook of psychological change: Psychotherapy processes and practices for the 21st century* (pp. 409–428). New York: Wiley.

Dobson, K. S., & Dozois, D. J. A. (2001). Historical and philosophical bases of the cognitive-behavioral therapies. In K. S. Dobson (Ed.), *Handbook of cognitive-behavioral therapies* (2nd ed., pp. 3–39). New York: Guilford Press.

Dobson, K. S., & Dozois, D. J. A. (2004). Attentional biases in eating disorders: A meta-analytic review of Stroop performance. *Clinical Psychology Review, 23,* 1001–1022.

Dobson, K. S., & Kendall, P. C. (1993). *Psychopathology and cognition.* New York: Academic Press.

Dozois, D. J. A. (2002). Cognitive organization of self-schematic content in nondysphoric, mildly dysphoric, and moderately-severely dysphoric individuals. *Cognitive Therapy and Research, 26,* 417–429.

Dozois, D. J. A., Covin, R., & Brinker, J. K. (2003). Normative data on cognitive measures of depression. *Journal of Consulting and Clinical Psychology, 71,* 71–80.

Dozois, D. J. A., & Dobson, K. S. (2001a). Information processing and cognitive organization in unipolar depression: Specificity and comorbidity issues. *Journal of Abnormal Psychology, 110,* 236–246.

Dozois, D. J. A., & Dobson, K. S. (2001b). A longitudinal investigation of information processing and cognitive organization in clinical depression: Stability of schematic interconnectedness. *Journal of Consulting and Clinical Psychology, 69,* 914–925.

Dozois, D. J. A., & Dobson, K. S. (2003). The structure of the self-schema in clinical depression: Differences related to episode recurrence. *Cognition and Emotion, 17,* 933–941.

Dryden, W., & Ellis, A. (2001). Rational emotive behavior therapy. In K. S. Dobson (Ed.), *Handbook of cognitive-behavioral therapies* (2nd ed., pp. 295–348). New York: Guilford Press.

Elkin, I., Pilkonis, P. A., Docherty, J. P., & Sotsky, S. M. (1988). Conceptual and methodological issues in comparative studies of psychotherapy and pharmacotherapy. I: Active ingredients and mechanisms of change. *American Journal of Psychiatry, 145,* 909–917.

Ellis, A. (1962). *Reason and emotion in psychotherapy.* New York: Stuart.

Ellis, A. (1991). *Reason and emotion in psychotherapy.* New York: Citadel.

Ellis, A. (1993). Reflections on rational-emotive therapy. *Journal of Consulting and Clinical Psychology, 61,* 199–201.

Ellis, A. (1999). Early theories and practices of rational emotive behavior therapy and how they have been augmented and revised during the last three decades. *Journal of Rational-Emotive and Cognitive Therapy, 17,* 69–93.

Ellis, A. (2003). Reasons why rational emotive behavior therapy is relatively neglected in the professional and scientific literature. *Journal of Rational-Emotive and Cognitive-Behavior Therapy, 21,* 245–252.

Ellis, A. (2004). Why rational emotive behavior therapy is the most comprehensive and effective form of behavior therapy. *Journal of Rational-Emotive and Cognitive-Behavior Therapy, 22,* 85–92.

Epictetus. (1955). *The enchiridion.* (G. Long, Trans.). New York: Promethean Press. (Original work published circa A.D. 101)

Fielder, K. (1996). Explaining and simulating judgment biases as an aggregation phenomenon in probabilistic, multiple-cue environments. *Psychological Review, 103,* 193–214.

Fiske, S. T., & Linville, P. W. (1980). What does the schema concept buy us? *Personality and Social Psychology Bulletin, 6,* 543–557.

Flavell, J. H. (1985). *Cognitive development* (2nd ed.). Englewood Cliffs, NJ: Prentice Hall.

Forgas, J. P. (1995). Mood and judgment: The affect infusion model (AIM). *Psychological Bulletin, 117,* 39–66.

Freeman, A., Pretzer, J., Fleming, B., & Simon, K. M. (1990). *Clinical applications of cognitive therapy.* New York: Plenum Press.

Furmark, T., Tillfors, M., Marteinsdottir, I., Fischer, H., Pissiota, A., Langstrom, B., et al. (2002). Common changes in cerebral blood flow in patients with social phobia treated with citalopram or cognitive-behavioral therapy. *Archives of General Psychiatry, 59,* 425–433.

Garber, J., & Flynn, C. (2001). Predictors of depressive cognitions in young adolescents. *Cognitive Therapy and Research, 25,* 353–376.

Gemar, M. C., Segal, Z.V , Sagrati, S., & Kennedy, S. J. (2001). Mood-induced changes on the Implicit Association Test in recovered depressed patients. *Journal of Abnormal Psychology, 110,* 282–289.

Glaser, B. A., Campbell, L. F., Calhoun, G. B., Bates, J. M., & Petrocelli, J. V. (2002). The Early Maladaptive Schema Questionnaire–Short Form: A construct validity study. *Measurement & Evaluation in Counseling & Development, 35,* 2–13.

Goldapple, K., Segal, Z., Garson, C., Lau, M., Bieling, P., Kennedy, S., et al. (2004). Modulation of cortical-limbic pathways in major depression: Treatment-specific effects of cognitive behavior therapy. *Archives of General Psychiatry, 61,* 34–41.

Haaga, D. A. F., & Davison, G. C. (1989). Slow progress in rational-emotive therapy outcome research: Etiology and treatment. *Cognitive Therapy and Research, 13,* 493–508.

Haaga, D. A. F., & Davison, G. C. (1995). An appraisal of rational-emotive therapy. In M. J. Mahoney (Ed.), *Cognitive and constructivist psychotherapies: Theory, research and practice* (pp. 74–86). New York: Springer.

Haaga, D. A. F., Dyck, M. J., & Ernst, D. (1991). Empirical status of cognitive theory of depression. *Psychological Bulletin, 110,* 215–236.

Halverson, C. F., & Wampler, K. S. (1997). Family influences on personality development. In R. Hogan & J. A. Johnson (Eds.), *Handbook of personality psychology* (pp. 241–267). San Diego, CA: Academic Press.

Hankin, B. L., Abramson, L. Y., Miller, N., & Haeffel, G. L. (2004). Cognitive vulnerability-stress theories of depression: Examining affective specificity in the prediction of depression versus anxiety in three prospective studies. *Cognitive Therapy and Research, 28,* 309–345.

Heine, S., Lehman, D. R., Markus, H. R., & Kitayama, S. (1999). Is there a universal need for positive self-regard. *Psychological Review, 106,* 766–794.

Hollon, S. D., DeRubeis, R. J., & Evans, M. D. (1987). Causal mediation of change in treatment for depression: Discriminating between nonspecificity and noncausality. *Psychological Bulletin, 102,* 139–149.

Hong, Y., Morris, M. W., Chiu, C., & Benet-Martinez, V. (2000). Multicultural minds: A dynamic approach to culture and cognition. *American Psychologist, 55,* 709–720.

Ingram, R. E. (1984). Toward an information-processing analysis of depression. *Cognitive Therapy and Research, 8,* 443–447.

Ingram, R. E. (1990). Depressive cognition: Models, mechanisms, and methods. In R. E. Ingram (Ed.), *Contemporary psychological approaches to depression* (pp. 169–195). New York: Plenum Press.

Ingram, R. E. (2003). Origins of cognitive vulnerability to depression. *Cognitive Therapy and Research, 27,* 77–88.

Ingram, R. E., & Kendall, P. C. (1986). Cognitive clinical psychology: Implications of an information processing perspective. In R. E. Ingram (Ed.), *Information processing approaches to clinical psychology* (pp. 3–21). London: Academic Press.

Ingram, R. E., Miranda, J., & Segal, Z. V. (1998). *Cognitive vulnerability to depression.* New York: Guilford Press.

Ingram, R. E., Overbey, T., & Fortier, M. (2001). Individual differences in dysfunctional automatic thinking and parental bonding: Specificity of maternal care. *Personality & Individual Differences, 30,* 401–412.

Ingram, R. E., & Price, J. M. (Eds.). (2001) *Vulnerability to psychopathology: Risk across the lifespan.* New York: Guilford Press.

Ingram, R. E., & Ritter, J. (2000). Vulnerability to depression: Cognitive reactivity and parental bonding in high-risk individuals. *Journal of Abnormal Psychology, 109,* 588–596.

Jaenicke, C., Hammen, C. L., Zupan, B., Hiroto, D., Gordon, D., Adrain, C., et al. (1987). Cognitive vulnerability in children at risk for depression. *Journal of Abnormal Child Psychology, 15,* 559–572.

Joffe, R., Segal, Z., & Singer, W. (1996). Change in thyroid hormone levels following response to cognitive therapy for major depression. *American Journal of Psychiatry, 153,* 411–413.

Kandel, E. R., & Squire, L. R. (2001). Neuroscience: Breaking down scientific barriers to the study of brain and mind. *Annals of the New York Academy of Sciences, 935,* 118–135.

Kuhn, D. (1999). Metacognitive development. In L. Balter & C. S. Tamis-LeMonda (Eds.), *Child psychology: A handbook of contemporary issues* (pp. 259–286). Philadelphia: Psychology Press.

Kuiper, N. A., Derry, P. A., & MacDonald, M. R. (1982). Self-reference and person perception in depression: A social cognition perspective. In G. Weary & H. L. Mirels (Eds.), *Integrations of clinical and social psychology* (pp. 79–103). Oxford, UK: Oxford University Press.

Kuiper, N. A., & Olinger, L. J. (1986). Dysfunctional attitudes and a self-worth contingency model of depression. In P. C. Kendall (Ed.), *Advances in cognitive-behavioral research and therapy* (Vol. 5, pp. 115–142). New York: Academic Press.

LeDoux, J. E. (2002). *Synaptic self: How our brains become who we are.* New York: Viking.

Lee, C. W., Taylor, G., & Dunn, J. (1999). Factor structure of the Schema Questionnaire in a large clinical sample. *Cognitive Therapy and Research, 23,* 441–451.

Linville, P. W. (1985). Self-complexity and affective extremity: Don't put all of your eggs in one cognitive basket. *Social Cognition, 3,* 94–120.

MacDonald, M. R., Kuiper, N. A., & Olinger, L. J. (1985). Vulnerability to depression, mild depression, and degree of self-schema consolidation. *Motivation and Emotion, 9,* 369–379.

Mahoney, M. J. (Ed.). (1995). *Cognitive and constructive psychotherapies: Theory, research, and practice.* New York: Springer.

Markus, H. R., & Kitayama, S. (1991). Culture and the self: Implications for cognition, emotion, and motivation. *Psychological Review, 98,* 224–253.

Markus, H. R., & Kitayama, S. (1994). A collective fear of the collective: Implications for selves and theories of self. *Personality and Social Psychology Bulletin, 20,* 568–579.

Mash, E. J., & Dozois, D. J. A. (2003). Child psychopathology: A developmental-systems perspective. In E. J. Mash & R. A. Barkley (Eds.), *Child psychopathology* (2nd ed., pp. 3–71). New York: Guilford Press.

McCranie, E. W., & Bass, J. D. (1984). Childhood family antecedents of dependency and self-criticism: Implications for depression. *Journal of Abnormal Psychology, 93,* 3–8.

Miller, I. W., Norman, W. H., & Keitner, G. I. (1990). Treatment response of high cognitive dysfunction depressed patients. *Comprehensive Psychiatry, 30,* 62–71.

Miranda, J., & Persons, J. B. (1988). Dysfunctional attitudes are mood-state dependent. *Journal of Abnormal Psychology, 97,* 76–79.

Miranda, J., Persons, J. B., & Byers, C. N. (1990). Endorsement of dysfunctional beliefs depends on current mood state. *Journal of Abnormal Psychology, 99,* 237–241.

Moore, R. G., & Blackburn, I. M. (1996). The stability of sociotropy and autonomy in depressed patients undergoing treatment. *Cognitive Therapy and Research, 20,* 69–80.

Nelson, D. R., Hammen, C., Daley, S. E., Burge, D., & Davila, J. (2001). Sociotropic and autonomous personality styles: Contributions to chronic life stress. *Cognitive Therapy and Research, 25,* 61–76.

Olson, J. M., Roese, N. J., & Zanna, M. P. (1996). Expectancies. In E. T. Higgins & A. W. Kruglanski (Eds.), *Social psychology: Handbook of basic principles* (pp. 211–238). New York: Guilford Press.

Parkes, L. P., Schneider, S. K., & Bochner, S. (1999). Individualism-collectivism and self-concept: Social or contextual? *Asian Journal of Social Psychology, 2,* 367–383.

Persons, J. B., & Miranda, J. (1992). Cognitive theories of vulnerability to depression: Reconciling negative evidence. *Cognitive Therapy and Research, 16,* 485–502.

Radke-Yarrow, M., Belmont, B., Nottelmann, E. D., & Bottomly, L. (1990). Young children's self-conceptions: Origins in the natural discourse of depressed mothers and their children. In D. Chicchetti & M. Beeghly (Eds.), *The self in transition: Infancy to childhood* (pp. 345–361). Chicago: University of Chicago Press.

Rector, N. A., Bagby, R. M., Segal, Z. V., Joffe, R. T., & Levitt, A. (2000). Self-criticism and dependency in depressed patients treated with cognitive therapy or pharmacotherapy. *Cognitive Therapy and Research, 24,* 571–584.

Roberts, J. E., Gotlib, I. H., & Kassel, J. D. (1996). Adult attachment security and symptoms of depression: The mediating roles of dysfunctional attitudes and low self-esteem. *Journal of Personality and Social Psychology, 70,* 310–320.

Robins, C. J., & Hayes, A. M. (1993). An appraisal of cognitive therapy. *Journal of Consulting and Clinical Psychology, 61,* 205–214.

Rogers, T. B., Kuiper, N. A., & Kirker, W. S. (1977). Self-reference and the encoding of personal information. *Journal of Personality and Social Psychology, 35,* 677–688.

Rude, S. S., & Burnham, B. L. (1995). Connectedness and neediness: Factors of the DEQ and SAS dependency scales. *Cognitive Therapy and Research, 19,* 323–340.

Rush, A. J., Beck, A. T., Kovacs, M., Weissenburger, J., & Hollon, S. D. (1982). Comparison of the effects of cognitive therapy and pharmacotherapy on hopelessness and self-concept. *American Journal of Psychiatry, 139,* 862–866.

Schmidt, N. B., Joiner, T. E., Young, J. E., & Telch, M. J. (1995). The Schema Questionnaire: Investigation of psychometric properties and the hierarchical structure of a measure of maladaptive schemas. *Cognitive Therapy and Research, 19,* 295–321.

Segal, Z. V. (1988). Appraisal of the self-schema construct in cognitive models of depression. *Psychological Bulletin, 103,* 147–162.

Segal, Z. V., Gemar, M., Truchon, C., Guirguis, M., & Horowitz, L. M. (1995). A priming methodology for studying self-representation in major depressive disorder. *Journal of Abnormal Psychology, 104,* 205–213.

Segal, Z. V., Gemar, M., & Williams, S. (1999). Differential cognitive response to a mood challenge following successful cognitive therapy or pharmacotherapy for unipolar depression. *Journal of Abnormal Psychology, 108,* 3–10.

Segal, Z. V., & Ingram, R. E. (1994). Mood priming and construct activation in tests of cognitive vulnerability to unipolar depression. *Clinical Psychology Review, 14,* 663–695.

Segal, Z. V., & Vella, D. D. (1990). Self-schema in major depression: Replication and extension of a priming methodology. *Cognitive Therapy and Research, 14,* 161–176.

Showers, C. (1992). Compartmentalization of positive and negative self-knowledge: Keeping bad apples out of the bunch. *Journal of Personality and Social Psychology, 62,* 1036–1049.

Simons, A. D., Garfield, S. L., & Murphy, G. E. (1984). The process of change in cognitive therapy and pharmacotherapy for depression: Changes in mood and cognition. *Archives of General Psychiatry, 41,* 45–51.

Singelis, T. M. (1994). The measurement of independent and interdependent self-construals. *Personality and Social Psychology Bulletin, 20,* 580–591.

Sloman, S. A. (1996). The empirical case for two systems of reasoning. *Psychological Review, 119,* 3–22.

Solomon, A., Haaga, D. A. F., Brody, C., Kirk, L., & Friedman, D. G. (1998). Priming irrational beliefs in recovered-depressed people. *Journal of Abnormal Psychology, 107,* 440–449.

Sternberg, R. J., & Kolligian, J., Jr. (Eds.). (1990). *Competence considered.* New Haven, CT: Yale University Press.

Symons, C. S., & Johnson, B. T. (1997). The self-reference effect in memory: A meta-analysis. *Psychological Bulletin, 121,* 371–394.

Tang, T. Z., & DeRubeis, R. J. (1999). Sudden gains and critical sessions in cognitive-behavioral therapy for depression. *Journal of Consulting and Clinical Psychology, 67,* 894–904.

Taylor, L., & Ingram, R. E. (1999). Cognitive reactivity and depressotypic information processing in children of depressed mothers. *Journal of Abnormal Psychology, 108,* 202–210.

Teasdale, J. D. (1996). Clinically relevant theory: Integrating clinical insight with cognitive science. In P. M. Salkovskis (Ed.), *Frontiers of cognitive therapy* (pp. 26–47). New York: Guilford Press.

Teasdale, J. D. (1997). The relationship between cognition and emotion: The mind-in-place in mood disorders. In D. M. Clark & C. G. Fairburn (Eds.), *Science and practice of cognitive behaviour therapy* (pp. 67–93). Oxford, UK: Oxford Medical Publications.

Teasdale, J. D., & Barnard, P. J. (1993). *Affect, cognition, & change: Re-modeling depressive thought.* Hillsdale, NJ: Erlbaum.

Teasdale, J. D., Segal, Z. V., & Williams, J. M. G. (1995). How does cognitive therapy prevent depressive relapse and why should attentional control (mindfulness) training help? *Behavioral Research and Therapy, 33,* 25–39.

Tversky, M., & Kahneman, D. (1974). Judgement under uncertainty: Heuristics and biases. *Science, 185,* 1124–1131.

Wagar, B. M., & Cohen, D. (2003). Culture, memory, and the self: An analysis of the personal and collective self in long term memory. *Journal of Experimental Social Psychology, 39,* 468–475.

Walen, S. R., DiGiuseppe, R., & Dryden, W. (1992). *A practitioner's guide to rational-emotive therapy* (2nd ed.). Oxford, UK: Oxford University Press.

Weissman, A. N., & Beck, A. T. (1978, April). *Development and validation of the Dysfunctional Attitude Scale: A preliminary investigation.* Paper presented at the annual meeting of the American Educational Research Association, Toronto, Ontario.

Westra, H. A., & Kuiper, N. A. (1997). Cognitive content specificity in selective attention across four domains of maladjustment. *Behavior Research and Therapy, 35,* 349–365.

Whisman, M. A. (1993). Mediators and moderators of change in cognitive therapy of depression. *Psychological Bulletin, 114,* 248–265.

Whisman, M. A., & Kwon, P. (1992). Parental representations, cognitive distortions, and mild depression. *Cognitive Therapy and Research, 16,* 557–568.

Whisman, M. A., & McGarvey, A. E. (1995). Attachment, depressotypic cognitions and dysphoria. *Cognitive Therapy and Research, 19,* 633–650.

Whisman, M. A., Miller, I. W., Norman, W. H., & Keitner, G. I. (1991). Cognitive therapy with depressed inpatients: Specific effects on dysfunctional cognitions. *Journal of Consulting and Clinical Psychology, 59,* 282–288.

Williams, J. M., Mathews, A., & MacLeod, C. (1996). The emotional Stroop task and psychopathology. *Psychological Bulletin, 120,* 3–24.

Williams, J. M. G., Watts, F. N., MacLeod, C., & Mathews, A. (1997). *Cognitive psychology and emotional disorders* (2nd ed.). Chichester, UK: Wiley.

Woody, S. R., Taylor, S., McLean, P. D., & Koch, W. J. (1998). Cognitive specificity in panic and depression: Implications for comorbidity. *Cognitive Therapy and Research, 22,* 427–443.

Young, J. E. (1990). *Cognitive therapy for personality disorders.* Sarasota, FL: Professional Resources Press.

Young, J. E. (1999). *Cognitive therapy for personality disorders: A schema-focused approach* (3rd ed.). Sarasota, FL: Professional Resource Press.

Young, J. E., Klosko, J. S., & Weshaar, M. E. (2003). *Schema therapy: A practitioner's guide.* New York: Guilford Press.

CHAPTER 10

Existential and Humanistic Theories

PAUL T. P. WONG

AN INTEGRATIVE, MEANING-CENTERED APPROACH

Existential and humanistic theories are as varied as the progenitors associated with them. They also are separated by philosophical disagreements and cultural differences (Spinelli, 1989, 2001). Nevertheless, they all share some fundamental assumptions about human nature and human condition that set them apart from other theories of personality. The overarching assumption is that individuals have the freedom and courage to transcend existential givens and biological/environmental influences to create their own future. Second, they emphasize the phenomenological reality of the experiencing person. Third, they are holistic in their focus on the lived experience and future aspirations of the whole person in action and in context. Finally, they attempt to capture the high drama of human existence, the striving for survival and fulfillment in spite of the human vulnerability to dread and despair.

This particular perspective raises several questions relevant to the struggles and challenges faced by all people: What is the point of striving toward a life goal when death is the inevitable end? How can people find meaning and fulfillment in the midst of failures, sufferings, and chaos? How can they realize their potential and become fully functioning? What is the primary, unifying motivation that keeps them going in spite of setbacks and difficulties?

Generally, European existentialists (e.g., Biswanger, Heidegger) tend to be pessimistic in their emphasis on the negative existential givens, such as the dread of nothingness and the anxiety about meaninglessness. American humanistic psychologists (e.g., Maslow, Rogers), on the other hand, tend to be optimistic in their focus on the positive existential givens, such as growth orientation and self-actualization.

The meaning-centered approach integrates both points of view. Thus, personality dynamics stem from the conflict between negative and positive existential givens. The choices individuals make in resolving the inner conflict result in different personalities. The structure of personality is viewed primarily as a life story situated in a particular context. The human story is about the lived experience of individuals searching for meaning and fulfillment in a world that is beyond comprehension and control.

The present chapter reviews the historical roots of existential and humanistic theories and critiques the major existential and humanistic models before articulating the meaning-centered approach as a reformulated existential-humanistic theory. The chapter then presents the empirical evidence and discusses the practical implications of the meaning-centered approach.

Reasons for reformulating the existential-humanistic theories include:

1. To provide a more balanced and realistic view of the human condition by recognizing the ongoing conflicts between the positive and negative existential givens.
2. The need of a common existential-humanistic theory capable of explaining both the best and worst of human behaviors.
3. The need to clarify and operationalize important existential and humanistic concepts.
4. To reframe the crucial issues of existential, humanistic psychology in terms of the human struggle for survival and fulfillment in a chaotic and difficult world.
5. To facilitate rapprochement between qualitative and quantitative research traditions.
6. To bridge the gaps between existential, humanistic, and transpersonal psychology by making goal striving for meaning and significance the common foundation.

STATEMENT OF THE THEORIES

Historical Background

Philosophical Roots

Existential psychology is based on existential philosophy. Its philosophical roots can be traced to the works of Søren

Kierkegaard (1813–1855), Friedrich Nietzsche (1844–1900), Karl Jaspers (1883–1969), Edmund Husserl (1859–1938), and Martin Heidegger (1889–1976). Husserl (1913/1962), founder of phenomenology, emphasizes that knowledge begins with subjective human experience, thus rejecting scientific realism and mind-body dualism. Phenomenology seeks to describe and clarify the immediate experience with everyday language rather than with scientific vocabulary.

Bearing a clear mark of Husserl's influence, Heidegger's (1962) philosophy of existence (ontology) is sometimes characterized as existential-phenomenological. His most influential concept is *being-in-the-world*. The person has his or her being or existence in the world, and the world has its existence as experienced and disclosed by the being. The world changes as the person's ideas about it change. The person and the human world are one because they cannot exist apart from each other.

Existentialism as a popular movement in Europe began right after the end of World War II. Its main proponents are two French intellectuals: Jean-Paul Sartre (1905–1980) and Albert Camus (1913–1960). Existentialism is concerned with the ontological issues of human existence, such as freedom, responsibility, and authenticity. Even though human existence is devoid of ultimate meaning, individuals can create meaning and live authentically through the choices they make.

In spite of his dark and pessimistic view of life, Jean-Paul Sartre also affirms the limitless possibilities of individual freedom. To Sartre, freedom is the fountain of hope, the foundation of all human values. Freedom constitutes us as human beings. Freedom, not biology, is our destiny. Through the exercise of freedom, we can transcend our genes, our past history, and the environment. Our capacity to choose how we exist determines what kind of people we will become. Thus, the existential dictum (Sartre 1946).

Psychological Roots

Two Swiss psychiatrists were primarily responsible for applying philosophical phenomenology to psychotherapy and psychology. Ludwig Biswanger, influenced by Martin Heidegger and Martin Buber, was the first self-declared existential analyst. He has been able to apply Heidegger's concept of being-in-the-world to psychotherapy (Biswanger, 1958). Medard Boss (1963), a friend of Heidegger, was director of the Institute of Daseinsanalytic Therapy. He has had considerable impact on U.S. humanistic psychology. An entire issue of *The Humanistic Psychologist* (Craig, 1988) was devoted to Boss.

Biswanger believes that the truth about human existence cannot be acquired through experimentation and intellectual exercise; it only can be revealed through the phenomenological methods of describing lived experiences. To study the person as a whole and gain a complete understanding of human existence, we need to include three levels, or three regions, of the conscious experience: (a) Umwelt (the biological world)—our sensations about our body and the physical world around us, such as pleasure and pain, warmth and cold; (b) Mitwelt (the social world)—our social relations, community, and culture, including how we feel and think about others; (c) Eigenwelt (psychological world)—the subjective, phenomenological world of personal meaning, such as our awareness of the special meaning something holds and our understanding of the experience itself.

The experience of being in the world points to the experience of nonbeing or nothingness. The dread of nothingness is one of the existential givens. However, this negative given may be mitigated by the positive existential given of yearning to realize one's new possibilities. This desire is captured by the concept of *being-beyond-the-world* through transcending the world in which one lives. Transcendence refers to the capacity to transcend time and space of the present world by transporting oneself to the future. It entails the capacity to choose one's future in spite of the constraints from the present and past. Transcendence entails more than imagination and creative symbolism; it involves making courageous choices, designing one's own world, and taking actions to fulfill one's full potentiality.

To choose the possibilities for change is to live an authentic life and become fully human. On the other hand, when individuals avoid the risk of change and choose to remain where they are, then they are living an inauthentic existence. Individuals are free to choose either kind of life. However, authenticity does not automatically mean self-actualization because the project of becoming fully human is fraught with difficulty. Therefore, the existential guilt of failing to fulfill all possibilities is always with us. Part of the difficulty in the human project is due to ground of existence, which limits our freedom. The concept of *ground of existence* represents conditions of "thrownness," which constitute one's destiny. One can still live an authentic life by achieving the possibilities within the limitations due to thrownness. These early existential psychologists clearly recognize the dialectical dynamics of inner conflict: the negative existential givens of anxiety, dread, guilt, and despair as well as the positive existential givens of freedom, responsibility, and transcendence. The concept of being-in-the-world can be understood as person-in-context because it encompasses the person's biological, psychological, existential, and spiritual needs as well as the social/cultural context.

European Existential-Phenomenological Psychotherapy

Ernesto Spinelli (1989, 1997) and Emmy van Deurzen (1988, 1997) are among the leaders in existential psychotherapy in Europe today. Both are strongly influenced by existential-phenomenological philosophy. Cooper (2003) has provided a more detailed description of the British school of existential analysis and more recent developments.

Emmy van Deurzen's approach to existential therapy is to enable people to (a) become more authentic, (b) broaden their understanding of themselves and their future, and (c) create something worth living in the present. These therapeutic goals are achieved through clarifying the clients' assumptions, values, and worldviews, exploring what is meaningful to them, and empowering them to confront existential givens and personal limitations with honesty and authenticity. Similarly, for Ernesto Spinelli (1989), the therapeutic goal is "to offer the means for individuals to examine, confront, and clarify and reassess their understanding of life, the problems encountered throughout their life, and the limits imposed upon the possibilities inherent in being-in-the-world" (p. 127). This goal can be achieved through adopting an attitude of empathy and neutrality, using descriptive questioning to clarify their present experience, and facilitating their discovery of their own meanings in spite of the existential givens. Spinelli's latest book (1997) focuses on dialogues and encounters in therapeutic relationships and presents several case studies.

Both Spinelli and Van Deurzen implicitly recognize the positive existential givens, such as the quest for meaning, authenticity, and fulfillment of potentiality in spite of the negative existential givens. Healthy personality development requires (a) confronting and accepting negative existential givens, (b) living with conflicts and limitations, and (c) affirming the possibilities of authentic living and personal growth. However, Spinelli (2001) does not accept actualization as an inevitable tendency of the self and points out that both wholeness and incompleteness are aspects of lived experience.

Logotherapy and Existential Analysis

Different from other European existential psychologists, Viktor Frankl (1905–1997) was the first to emphasize positive existential givens. This is remarkable because personally he experienced more horrors and sufferings than any of the other existential philosophers and psychologists. Frankl spent 1942 to 1945 in Nazi concentration camps. His parents, brother, and wife all were murdered in Nazi death camps. According to his own account (Frankl, 1984), he developed logotherapy and existential analysis, known as the Third Vi-

ennese School of Psychotherapy, in 1938 out of his dissatisfaction with psychoanalysis. Frankl studied with both Freud and Adler. He accepted Freud's concept of unconsciousness but considered the will to meaning as more fundamental to human development than the will to pleasure. Existential analysis, similar to psychoanalysis, is designed to bring to consciousness and enhance the "hidden" logos. Existential analysis refers to the specific therapeutic process involved in helping people discover their meaning in life. "Logotherapy regards its assignment as that of assisting the patient to find meaning in his life. Inasmuch as logotherapy makes him aware of the hidden logos of his existence, it is an analytical process" (Frankl, 1984, p. 125). However, in Frankl's writing, the two terms are used either interchangeably or together as a unified name.

Logotherapy was put to a severe test in a very personal way when Frankl was incarcerated in Nazi concentration camps. "This was the lesson I had to learn in three years spent in Auschwitz and Dachau: those most apt to survive the camps were those oriented toward the future, toward a meaning to be fulfilled by them in the future" (Frankl, 1985, p. 37). This observation strengthened his belief that the primary human motivation is the *will to meaning.*

Logotherapy is a distinct branch of the existential-humanistic school of psychotherapy because of its focus on positive meaning and the human spirit (Wong, 2002b). What sets Frankl apart from Rollo May and Irvin Yalom (2000) is his unconditional affirmation of life's meaning, including the ultimate meaning. The main objective of logotherapy is twofold: facilitate clients' quest for meaning and empower them to live responsibly, regardless of their life circumstances. Logotherapy literally means "healing or therapy through meaning." It comes from the Greek word *logos,* which may mean "the word," "meaning," or "God's will" (Fabry, 1994). Most people do not realize that logotherapy is actually a spiritually oriented approach toward psychotherapy. "A psychotherapy which not only recognizes man's spirit, but actually starts from it may be termed *logotherapy.* In this connection, *logos* is intended to signify 'the spiritual' and beyond that 'the meaning'" (Frankl, 1986, p. xvii). Frankl (1986) proposes that "three factors characterize human existence as such: man's spirituality, his freedom, his responsibility" (p. xxiv). According to Frankl's dimensional ontology (Frankl, 1986), human beings exist in three dimensions: somatic, mental, and spiritual. Spirituality is the uniquely human dimension. However, these different dimensional entities must be understood in their totality, because a person is a unity in complexity.

Specific versus Ultimate Meaning

According to Frankl (1967, 1984, 1986) there are two levels of meaning: (a) the present meaning, or meaning of the moment, and (b) the ultimate meaning, or supermeaning. Frankl believes that it is more helpful to address specific meaning of the moment, of the situation, rather than talking about meaning of life in general because ultimate meanings exist in the suprahuman dimension, which is "hidden" from us. Each individual must discover the specific meanings of the moment. Only the individual knows the right meaning specific to the moment. The therapist can also facilitate the quest and guide them to those areas in which meanings can be found (Fabry, 1994; Frankl, 1984, 1986).

Meaning versus Value

Values are abstract meanings based on the lived experiences of many, many individuals. Frankl (1967, 1986) believes that these values can guide our search for meaning and simplify decision making. Traditional values are the examples of the accumulation of meaning experiences of many individuals over a long period of time. However, these values are threatened by modernization. Even with the loss of traditional values, individuals can still find meaning in concrete situations. According to Frankl (1967), "Even if all universal values disappeared, life would remain meaningful, since the unique meanings remain untouched by the loss of traditions" (p. 64).

Values may lie latent and need to be awakened and discovered. For example, in the camp, prisoners were degraded and treated as nonentities. Most of them became demoralized and behaved like animals. However, some prisoners were able to maintain their dignity and a sense of self-worth. Frankl (1984) commented that, "The consciousness of one's inner value is anchored in higher, more spiritual things, and cannot be shaken by camp life. But how many free men, let alone prisoners, possess it?" (p. 83).

Basic Tenets of Logotherapy

The logotherapeutic tenets include freedom of will, the will to meaning, and the meaning of life (Frankl 1967, 1969, 1986).

1. Freedom of will: Frankl (1978) realizes that, "Human freedom is finite freedom. Man is not free from conditions. But he is free to take a stand in regard to them. The conditions do not completely condition him" (p. 47). Frankl believes that although our existence is influenced by instincts, inherited disposition, and environment, an area of freedom is always available to us. "Everything can be taken from a man, but . . . the last of the human freedoms—to choose one's attitude in any a given set of circumstances, to choose one's own way" (Frankl, 1963, p. 104). Therefore, we all have the freedom to take a stand

toward the deterministic conditions, to transcend our fate. With freedom comes responsibility. Frankl (1984) differentiates between responsibility and responsibleness. The former comes from possessing the freedom of will. The latter refers to exercising our freedom to make the right decisions according to the demands of life.

2. Will to meaning: This is "the basic striving of man to find meaning and purpose" (Frankl, 1969, p. 35). The will to meaning is possible because of the human capacity of self-transcendence: "Being human is being always directed, and pointing to something or someone other than oneself: to a meaning to fulfill or another human being to encounter, a cause to serve or a person to love" (Frankl, 1978, p. 35). Self-transcendence allows people to be free from the confines of time and space. They are able to move from what they are toward what they "ought to be" or "should be." Self-transcendence is essential for finding happiness because fulfillment is a by-product of meaning: "Only to the extent to which man fulfils a meaning out there in the world, does he fulfil himself" (Frankl, 1969, p. 38).

3. Meaning of life: For Frankl (1963), "The meaning of our existence is not invented by ourselves, but rather detected" (p. 157). It is an "Aha!" experience, a moment of awareness and awakening akin to enlightenment. How do we answer the existential question: "Is life as a whole meaningful or meaningless?" On the one hand, Frankl avoids giving an abstract answer to such general existential questions; on the other hand, he affirms the potential for meaningfulness for every human being in all situations. Frankl (1984) suggests three ways of finding meaning: "According to logotherapy, we can discover this meaning in life in three different ways: (1) by creating a work or doing a deed; (2) by experiencing something or encountering someone; and (3) by the attitude we take towards unavoidable suffering" (p. 133).

Attitudinal values are especially important in situations of unavoidable suffering. Frankl (1969) claims: "This is why life never ceases to hold meaning, for even a person who is deprived of both creative and experiential values is still challenged by a meaning to fulfil, that is, by the meaning inherent in the right, in an upright way of suffering" (p. 70).

Existential Frustration and Noogenic Neurosis

Existential frustration is a universal human experience because the quest for meaning can be blocked by external circumstances as well as by internal hindrances. When the will to meaning is frustrated, one may develop noogenic neurosis or existential vacuum. "Noogenic neuroses have their origin not in the psychological but rather in the 'noological' (from the Greek *noos* meaning mind) dimension of human existence" (Frankl, 1984, p. 123). Therefore, other forms of psychotherapy would not be adequate, and logotherapy is specifically appropriate in dealing with existential neuroses.

Existential vacuum refers to a general sense of meaninglessness or emptiness, as evidenced by a state of boredom. It is a widespread phenomenon of the twentieth century as a result of industrialization, the loss of traditional values, and dehumanization of individuals. Most people may experience existential vacuum without developing existential neurosis. Many people feel that life has no purpose, no challenge, no obligation, and they try to fill their existential vacuum with materials things, pleasure, sex, power, or busy work, but they are misguided (Frankl, 1984). "The feeling of meaninglessness not only underlies the mass neurotic triad of today, i.e., depression-addiction-aggression, but also may eventually result in what we logotherapists call a 'noogenic neurosis'" (Frankl, 1986, p. 298). Existential vacuum is not a neurosis or disease. In fact, it may make us aware of our own emptiness and trigger a quest for meaning. The therapist can empower and challenge the clients to fill their inner emptiness. Logotherapy can supplement psychotherapy in psychogenic cases and somatogenic neurosis because "by filling the existential vacuum, the patient will be prevented from suffering further relapses" (Frankl, 1984, p. 130).

Suffering and Tragic Triad

Frankl (1984) reasons that, "If there is a meaning in life at all, then there must be a meaning in suffering. Suffering is an ineradicable part of life, even as fate and death" (p. 88). Suffering is not a necessary condition for meaning, but suffering tends to trigger the quest for meaning. Frankl (1967) observes that the Homo sapiens is concerned with success, whereas the Homo patiens (the suffering human being) is more concerned about meaning. Frankl (1963, 1984) has observed through his own experience and his observation of prisoners and clients that people are willing to endure any suffering if they are convinced that this suffering has meaning. However, suffering without meaning leads to despair.

Quest for meaning is more likely to be occasioned by three negative facets of human existence: pain, guilt, and death. Pain refers to human suffering, guilt to the awareness of our fallibility, and death to our awareness of the transitoriness of life (Frankl, 1967, 1984). These negative experiences make us more aware of our needs for meaning and spiritual connection. Neuroses are more likely to originate from our attempt to obscure the reality of pain, guilt, and death as existential facts (Frankl, 1967, 1984). Logotherapy provides

an answer to the tragic triad through attitudinal values and tragic optimism (Frankl, 1984):

> I speak of a tragic optimism, that is, an optimism in the face of tragedy and in view of the human potential which at its best always allows for: (a) turning suffering into a human achievement and accomplishment; (2) deriving from guilt the opportunity to change oneself for the better; and (3) deriving from life's transitoriness an incentive to take responsible action. (p. 162)

The Positive Existential Psychology of Viktor Frankl

Frankl is unabashedly positive, emphasizing human strengths without downplaying the difficulties inherent in human existence. He discovered in concentration camps that "some of our comrades behaved like swine while others behaved like saints. Man has both potentialities within himself; which one is actualized depends on decisions but not on conditions" (Frankl, 1984, p. 157). He believes that "it is possible to say yes to life in spite of all the tragic aspects of human existence" (p. 17). "Man is capable of changing the world for the better if possible, and of changing himself for the better if necessary" (p. 154). Therefore, "life is potentially meaningful under any conditions, be they pleasurable or miserable" (Frankl, 1986, p. 301). This affirmation of meaning is the foundation of logotherapy. However, Viktor Frankl's impact extends far beyond logotherapy and psychotherapy. He deserves to be recognized as the father of positive psychology. His positive triad—meaning, optimism, and spirituality—have become the major research areas for several disciplines, such as psychology, medicine, management, and education, as attested by Batthyany and Guttmann's (2005) annotated bibliography of research on meaning and purpose.

American Existential Psychology

Existential psychology was introduced to the United States by Rollo May (1909–1994). The early history of existential psychology in the United States can be found in May, Angel, and Ellenberger (1958) and May (1961). May acknowledges the influence of Husserl, Heidegger, Merleau-Ponty, Biswanger, William James, Paul Tillich, and R. D. Laing. May plays a key role in bridging between European existentialism and American psychology. Influenced by European existential philosophers and psychologists, May (1950) focuses on anxiety as an inevitable given in human existence and recognizes a prevailing sense of meaninglessness as a major problem for modern age.

May (1965) clarifies Husserl's concept of intentionality and makes it the central piece of human consciousness. Intentionality provides the structure which gives meaning to human experience, and it underlies the process of planning and decision making between several alternatives. All human beings are confronted with a basic choice between ontological anxiety and ontological guilt. The former refers to choosing the future in spite of fear of the unknown and difficulties ahead. The latter refers to choosing the status quo and familiar past practices; it will bring ontological guilt because of a felt sense of missed opportunity. One can achieve authenticity by having the courage to embark on an unknown future.

May (1953) is concerned about the loss of traditional values and a sense of personal dignity as the sources of anxiety:

> The upshot is that the values and goals which provided a unifying center for previous centuries in the modern period no longer are cogent. We have not yet found the new center which will enable us to choose our goals constructively, and thus to overcome the painful bewilderment and anxiety of not knowing which way to move. Another root of our malady is our loss of the sense of the worth and dignity of the human being. (p. 49)

Following Heidegger, May (1961) later points out that the main source of anxiety and conflict comes from the self-consciousness of the "I am" experience in the world and the awareness of the state of nonbeing or nothingness. Paradoxically, in order to affirm or preserve their sense of self, they need to give up part of their self-centeredness by reaching out to others. Similarly, in order to overcome the anxiety of nonbeing, they need to have the courage to develop new possibilities. Freedom and courage enable individuals to rise above their anxiety and personal issues. "Freedom is man's capacity to take a hand in his own development. It is our capacity to mold ourselves" (May, 1953, p. 138). The challenge is to live each moment with freedom and responsibility. Although freedom enables one to rise above personal problems, the exercise of freedom also can become a source of anxiety. In the absence of traditional values as consistent guides, the individuals are thrown on their own to make the right decisions. "Courage is the capacity to meet the anxiety which arises as one achieves freedom. It is the willingness to differentiate, to move from the protecting realms of parental dependence to new levels of freedom and integration" (May, 1953, p. 192).

Courage is paradoxical. In *Courage to Create,* May (1994) elaborates on the concept of courage, which means the capacity to choose to be authentic, to move forward and create a new future in spite of one's shadow or "daimonic." Courage is the best expression of authenticity and is at the very heart of the creative process, which always involves existential encounters with anxiety and fear. The authentic individuals are free to create because they have the courage to confront and

accept their self-doubts and anxiety. Freedom means the liberty to choose, to design one's own future, in spite of inherent limitations, which May (1999) calls destiny. May is able to shift from determinism to destiny by recognizing our capacity for freedom and intentionality in spite of internal and external limitations. To May, destiny means both thrownness and the daimonic.

The Greek word *daimon* is generally translated as "demon." To May (1969), a daimon is anything that can limit one's freedom, such as sex, anger, and power. Basically, a daimon is any natural function that has the potential to take control of the whole person. When the daimonic system is out of balance and not integrated with the self, it can disrupt normal functioning and drives the person to engage in evil deeds. For example, to achieve a sense of personal significance and alleviate feelings of powerlessness, one may be bent on seeking power through violent means. Therefore, we are capable of both good and evil. May's (1982) belief in the dark or sinister side of human nature sets him apart from Carl Rogers's humanistic psychology.

Agreeing with Paul Tillich (1952) and Viktor Frankl (1986), May (1953) believes that religion can play a positive role in endowing life with meaning:

> We define religion as the assumption that life has meaning. Religion, or lack of it, is shown not in some intellectual or verbal formulations but in one's total orientation to life. Religion is whatever the individual takes to be his ultimate concern. One's religious attitude is to be found at that point where he has a conviction that there are values in human existence worth living and dying for. (May, 1953, p. 180)

In his last book, *The Cry for Myth,* May (1992) continues to lament the loss of values in the modern age and emphasizes the need for individuals to exercise their will to create their own values by which to live. In the absence of religion and God, myths may provide "guiding narratives" to make sense of our own lives and help us live authentically. His existential psychology is clearly dialectical. We are both free and determined, good and evil, alive and dead. It is through confronting and integrating the opposites that we discover meaning and authenticity.

Irwin Yalom is another influential American existential psychologist. Like May, he believes that we can live meaningfully when we confront death anxiety and other existential givens. Yalom (1980) lists four existential givens relevant to psychotherapy: the inevitability of death, the freedom to choose how we live, our sense of ultimate aloneness, and the obvious meaninglessness of life in the face of the previous three givens. These givens create a lot of anxiety, and many psychological problems arise from our defense mechanisms in coping with existential anxiety. The objective of psychotherapy is to help clients confront their fears and anxieties by engaging in life courageously and creatively.

American Humanistic Psychology

Abraham Maslow (1908–1970)

One of the widely circulated stories about the emergence of the humanistic psychology movement is that it began in the early 1950s, growing out of a mailing list kept by Abraham Maslow (1908–1970) of psychologists dissatisfied with psychoanalysis and behaviorism. His landmark publication *Motivation and Personality* in 1954 provided a major impetus to the movement. Abraham Maslow and Carl Rogers are considered founders of humanistic psychology. Historically, a number of key figures have directly and indirectly influenced the development of humanistic psychology. Among them are Carl Jung, William James, Gordon Allport, Henry Murray, Erich Fromm, and Max Wertheimer. These individuals, though different from one another in their approaches to psychology, all share the same view in their opposition to treating human beings as things or animals determined by biological and environmental forces.

Humanistic psychology also has its roots in existential philosophy. The existential tenet that human beings are free and responsible for their existence is readily incorporated into the humanistic movement, which focuses on the personal worth and growth potential of individuals. Different from European existential philosophers and psychologists, humanist psychologists emphasize the positive existential givens: the creative, spontaneous, and self-actualizing tendency of human beings. Generally, humanistic psychologists tend to have a very optimistic view of the human condition.

Abraham Maslow (1961) rejected the European emphasis on despair, anxiety, and death. He was clearly the first positive psychologist because he suggested that existentialism might provide a "push toward the establishment of another branch of psychology, the psychology of the fully evolved and authentic self and its ways of being" (p. 56). This new branch of psychology would switch the focus away from the psychopathology of the average person to the authentic, self-actualized person (Maslow, 1964). He coined the term the *Third Force* to describe the existential-humanistic approach.

Maslow probably is best known for his theory of a hierarchy of needs, which consists of five levels: (a) physiological needs, (b) safety and security needs, (c) the need for love and belonging, (d) esteem needs, and (e) the need for self-actualization. The first four needs are categories of deficient needs or D-motives, because people are motivated to fill the deficiency in these needs. Self-actualization motives, such as the search for truth and beauty, represent lived experiences at the "being" level and can be called the B-values or B-motives. Maslow (1964) believes that the unifying and holistic motivational principle is to pursue higher needs when lower needs are sufficiently satisfied.

In his last book *The Farther Reaches of Human Nature* (1971), Maslow expanded the list of B-motives, which now includes the following: truth, goodness, beauty, wholeness, aliveness, uniqueness, perfection, completion, justice, simplicity, richness, effortlessness, playfulness, and self-sufficiency. It is worth noting that the motive to achieve wholeness or oneness involves dichotomy-transcendence and synergy. *Dichotomy-transcendence* refers to acceptance, integration, or transcendence of opposites and contradictions. *Synergy* refers to the transformation of oppositions into unity. His holistic, integrative thinking is similar to Carl Jung's concept of individuation, which involves the integration of opposite aspects of the personality. He is opposed to the atomistic, dichotomous thinking prevalent in academe. In his later years, Maslow (1970) believed that it is possible to integrate experiential subjectivity with experimental objectivity and "integrate the healthily animal, material, and selfish with the naturalistically transcendent, spiritual, and axiological" (p. 5).

His theory of human motivation has become the basis of a growth-oriented personality theory, which emphasizes on the inner push toward self-actualization and peak experiences, which are common to those who are fully self-actualized. Peak experiences can be described by B-values: mystical, transcendental, and experiential, similar to the Zen concept of enlightenment. They include a sense of joy, wonder, and ecstasy, which changes people's view of themselves and the world around them. However, Maslow (1970), in the last year of his life, realized the danger of seeking peak experiences as the highest good of life without considering the criteria of right and wrong. Such people "may become not only selfish but also evil. My impression, from the history of mysticism, is that this trend can sometimes wind up in meanness, nastiness, loss of compassion, or even in extreme sadism" (p. 3).

Self-actualized people are those who have realized their full potentials and become fully human. Their personality is healthy, balanced, and integrated. They are at peace with themselves and with others. They are loving, creative, realistic, ethical, compassionate, interested in helping others, and interested in fighting against injustice. They demonstrate the best of humanity as described by the B-values. They are not only fully functioning but also transcendental and spiritual. But only a few can become fully self-actualized. Some of the historical figures identified by Maslow as self-actualized persons include Albert Einstein, Abraham Lincoln, and William James.

Maslow is exclusively interested in self-actualization as a universal motive. His optimistic view of the positive human potential raises these questions: Why are there so few self-actualized persons? Why do so many people who have all of their D-needs satisfied continue to lead a life of self-indulgence and self-aggrandizement at the expense of others? In his later years, Maslow recognized that his self-actualized friends were "prima donnas" who were self-centered and could not work together. "Maslow strived to believe the best about the potentialities of human beings, but like Jung and many others, ultimately had to admit that the darker, weaker side of people could never be eliminated" (Friedman & Schustack, 2003, p. 330). Maslow's main contribution to existential-humanistic psychology is his emphasis on the positive existential givens and the transcendental, spiritual level of human existence. This higher level of consciousness is evolved biologically. His recognition of biological determination further sets him apart from European existential psychologists.

Carl Rogers (1902–1987)

Carl Rogers is probably the most influential humanistic psychologist. His personality theory is basically phenomenological because of his emphasis on the phenomenological field of the experiential person. He is existential because of his focus on the importance of freedom, responsibility, and authenticity. Most of all, he is humanistic because of his belief in personal dignity and human potential for growth. His biggest contribution is his dual-emphasis on self-directed growth and conditions for healthy personality. There has been a large amount of research on his revolutionary hypothesis that "a self-directed growth process would follow the provision and reception of a particular kind of relationship characterized by genuineness, nonjudgmental caring, and empathy" (Raskin & Rogers, 1995, p. 128).

Along with Carl Jung and Maslow, Rogers believes in the absence of external forces: individuals would choose to be healthy, to be independent, and to further the optimal development. However, different from Maslow, who reserves the need for self-actualization to the highest level of personality development attainable by a few, Rogers considers the actualizing tendency as the universal, inherent, underlying motivation to enhance the experiencing organism. Rogers is holistic and integrative. He posits that the organismic actualizing tendency involves the whole organism; therefore, it includes the need for drive reduction, pleasure-seeking, autonomy, and personal growth. There is an innate urge pushing every individual toward becoming fully functioning and realizing their full potential.

Rogers's Self Theory.   The "self" evolves from the perceptual field through a process of differentiation: the result of interaction with the world, especially the evaluational interaction with significant others. The self is described as "the organized, consistent, conceptual gestalt composed of perceptions of the characteristics of the 'I' or 'me' and the perceptions of the relationships of the 'I' or 'me' to others and to various aspects of life, together with the values attached to these perceptions" (Rogers, 1959, p. 200).

Rogers's theory of personality is described in his 1951 book, *Client-Centered Therapy,* and following are some main points relevant to our current discussion. Each individual exists in a personal world, a phenomenological field. The individual, as an organized whole, reacts to "reality" as experienced and perceived. Every organism has the basic actualizing tendency to strive to meet all his needs and enhance the experiencing organism. Therefore, behavior is always goal-directed and purposive. Because behavior is reaction to reality as perceived, the best way to understand behavior is from the internal frame of reference of the individual himself. In order words, we need to focus on the phenomenological world of the clients and let them disclose and discover the meanings of their inner experiences.

The self-structure is an organized yet fluid, consistent conceptual pattern of perceptions of the self and the values attached to these concepts. These values can be either directly experienced by the organism through the organismic valuing process or introjected from significant others. Healthy personality develops where there is congruence between their actual sense of who they are and who they feel they should be. A healthy person has the courage to become one's self without worrying about what other people's expectations in terms of "shoulds" or "oughts." This is essentially the existential concept of being an authentic person. Psychological maladjustment results when one's life experiences are inconsistent with the self-structure and are not assimilated. Whenever there is a discrepancy between the person's perception of self (an ideal self) and real life experiences (a real self), there will be problems of adjustment and personal growth. Existential anxiety arises when individuals do not accept themselves the way they are and pretend to be someone else in order to conform to other people's expectations. Incongruence often results from the needs for positive regard from others. When parents say, "We will love you only when you behave well," they in fact set up conditions of worth. In order to receive parents' conditional positive regards, children become other-oriented and alienated from their basic nature.

Rogers (1961) observes that maladjustment or psychopathology can occur when people are not aware of their own rationality and inner voices because of their defenses or distorted self-concept; as a result, they make decisions that are inconsistent with the dictates of their organismic evaluations. The organismic valuing process in individuals enables them to make value judgments and choices based on their sensory and visceral experiences and organismic processing of situations. Rogers (1977) believes that people are naturally rational and responsible, and they are "capable of evaluating the outer and inner situation, understanding herself in its context, making constructive choices as to the next steps in life, and acting on those choices" (p. 15).

Those who trust in their own organismic valuing process become fully functioning because their self-concept would be congruent with their experience based on their own innate evaluation (Rogers, 1959). Somehow, this organismic valuing process has the capacity to guide people in making the right choices for their lives and facilitate their self-actualizing tendency. The fully functioning individuals represent mental health, mature personality, and self-actualization because they are free from defenses, open to new experiences, and able to live authentically. They also express their feelings freely, accept their own weaknesses, act independently, and live "the good life" (Rogers, 1961).

Conditions for Healthy Personality.   Rogers has a very optimistic view of human nature. He believes that "the core of man's nature is essentially positive" (Rogers, 1961, p. 73) and that human beings are naturally growth oriented. They are free agents motivated and guided by the universal actualizing tendency and the organismic valuing process. They are responsible and free agents, capable of choosing and designing their own futures in a constructive, healthy way. To Rogers, the human infant is an example of congruence and genuineness. Unfortunately, conditions of worth and distorted self-concept may result in alienation from one's true nature and in departure from self-actualization.

There are so many maladjusted people because of the lack of an ideal childhood and a trusting, supportive environment. Later, Rogers (1977) blamed society for reinforcing behaviors that are "perversions of the unitary actualizing tendency" (p. 248). The problem for pathology is socialization and society. Based on his client-centered counseling, he has discovered that the therapist can provide certain conditions that help remove the conditions of worth and restore the organismic valuing process so that individuals can become fully functioning (Rogers, 1957). The necessary and sufficient conditions for healing and wholeness are the following:

Unconditional positive regard: This means accepting the clients regardless of the nature of their struggles, without judgment or condemnation. This will undo the harm of conditional positive regard and expose them to the healing power of acceptance, openness, and trust that comes from unconditional love.

Empathy: This means that the counselor is fully present with the clients, trying to understand the their inner struggles and their world of meanings. It can be very therapeutic when the clients experience someone listening to them, understanding them, and caring about how they think and feel.

Genuineness (congruence): This means that the counselor is genuine and congruent and the therapeutic relationship is an honest, genuine one. It means that the counselor really possesses the attitude of unconditional positive regard and empathy and that this reality is communicated to the clients throughout their encounters and interactions. This kind of relationship will help restore a sense of trust in people.

Together, these attitudes will provide a safe environment for clients to (a) explore and experience aspects of self that have been hidden or distorted, (b) recognize the blocks to personal growth, and (c) regain a sense of direction and courage to move forward with courage, openness, and self-trust. Rogers also believes that these core conditions for healing and personal growth can be applied to home, school, work, and community. His message on the need to treat people with respect and dignity and to create a healthy environment is much needed in the present climate of ruthless competition, brutal conflicts, and unethical manipulation of people as instruments.

However, in today's culture, with daily news on corporate scandals, cutthroat competitions, and widespread violence and terror, many are wondering: (a) How could people born with good nature and growth orientation be so mean and destructive? (b) How many people can we really trust? (c) Where can we find fully functioning individuals? (d) Is it possible for anyone to practice the three Rogerian values consistently in all human encounters on a daily basis?

Blaming the society and culture for all our social ills and personal problems only creates additional questions: (a) Because society is consisted of people, what makes them create a toxic culture of dehumanization and oppression? (b) If people are indeed as free and growth oriented as Rogers has theorized, why can they not exercise their agency and responsibility to follow their organismic valuing process and transcend the less than ideal environment? (c) Why do people need counseling in order to get back on the track of self-actualization?

In light of the horrors of genocides and the depravity of massacre of innocent children, it becomes increasingly difficult to square Rogers's optimistic view of human nature with the daily news events and our own life experiences. Still, Rogers's ideas are powerful. Providing a safe and positive environment is more likely to bring out the best in children and adults than providing an unsafe and toxic environment. The biggest challenge is how can we bring up a new generation of young people, workers, and leaders who would internalize the values articulated by Rogers so that they can be fully functioning and help create a healthy society.

Space will not allow me to discuss the more recent developments in humanistic psychology, but the interested reader is referred to Schneider, Bugental and Pierson (2001) and Cain and Seeman (2001). Suffice it to say that the most important development is the field of transpersonal psychology, which considers spirituality as the new frontier for humanistic psychology. It is also noteworthy that "existential and transpersonal disciplines have similar concerns. Both emphasize a practical focus on those matters of deepest life importance, especially the causes and relief of suffering and what it means to live fully" (Walsh, 2001, p. 609). Some of the leading figures in transpersonal psychology are Ken Wilber (1997, 1998), Stanislave Grof (1993, 1998), Roger Walsh (1999, 2001), and A. H. Almaas (1988, 1996).

LIMITATIONS AND CHALLENGES OF THE THEORIES

The major models of existential and humanistic psychology previously discussed demonstrate the scope, depth, and relevance of this particular approach to personality. I have already critiqued these models. Some of the main limitations and challenges of humanistic and existential psychology identified at the Old Saybrook 2 Conference (Warmoth, 2001, p. 651) include: romanticizing the past, naïveté about the goodness of human nature, avoidance of scientific rigor, rejection of positivist psychology, fragmentation within humanistic-existential-transpersonal psychology, and failure to articulate a common theory. Some of the challenges are elaborated here.

Basking in Past Glories

Many existentially oriented psychologists still bask in the glory of their illustrious masters and are reluctant to accept any changes. Loyalty to a theoretical tradition means carrying the philosophical baggage from the past and discouraging innovation. Although the philosophical concepts, which inspired existential-humanistic psychology, are rich and powerful, their ambiguity, underlying assumptions, and metaphoric expressions make communication with psychologists difficult. Although appreciating the contribution of European existentialism in deepening our understanding of the human condition, Gordon Allport (1961) critiqued the European style of philosophizing and writing. He proposed that American psychology clarify and empirically test the existential concepts.

Failing to Develop a Scientific Body of Knowledge

Existential-humanistic psychology has been criticized often for failing to develop a scientific body of knowledge. This is probably one of the main hindrances to wider acceptance by mainstream psychology. In his assessment of humanistic psychology, Csikszentmihalyi (2001) wonders whether "the rejection of the hegemonic sway of scientific methodology, which is perfectly understandable given the 'dustbowl empiricism' in force when the founders were writing, has served humanistic psychology well in the long run" (pp. xv–xvi). He proposes: "To join the parade and influence its direction and pace, one must show that one can follow the tune. In less metaphorical terms, sustained good work needs to be done" (p. xvi).

Many in the existential-humanistic tradition continue to reject the positivist psychology and experimental research. For example, Van Kaam (1966) believes that "experiences such as responsibility, dread, anxiety, despair, freedom, love, wonder, or decision cannot be measured or experimented with. . . . They are simply there and can only be explicated in their givenness" (p. 187). Such an antireductionist and antiexperimental attitude prevents them not only from doing quantitative research but also from recognizing relevant experimental research supporting existential-humanistic principles. For example, scientific studies of the personal projects, goal seeking, and personal meaning (Wong & Fry, 1998) provide plenty of empirical support of the central tenet on the importance of meaning to mental health and well-being, yet these studies were seldom recognized by existential, humanistic psychologists. It is important to remember that what makes research humanistic is not its research methods but its perspective toward human behavior and experience (Polkinghorne, 1982).

Carl Rogers consistently has insisted on the importance of objective, scientific proof. He is in favor of testing hypotheses deduced from existential-humanistic principles through experimental research. That is why there is a large body of scientific research on Rogers's theory. We need a rapprochement between quantitative, experimental research and qualitative, phenomenological study. There is no reason why we cannot embrace both the natural science and human science in studying the complex human condition. All kinds of research methods can be used, depending on their appropriateness. Broadly speaking, the subject matter of psychology consists of both the lived phenomenological experiences of individuals and the behavioral manifestations and neurological correlates that can be objectively observed and measured. Therefore, a complete understanding of lived experience needs to include neurophysiological mapping and cognitive-behavioral measures. Thus, the main challenge is to develop and articulate new paradigms and new research agendas for existential-humanistic psychology.

Providing Polarized Views of Human Nature

Allport (1961) critiqued European existentialism for being too preoccupied with existential anxiety, anguish, and despair. Even freedom has a negative undertone because of the anxiety it generates. American existential-humanistic psychologists, such as Rogers and Maslow, tend to have a very optimistic view. Both biases have been shaped by the different cultural experiences and ideologies prevailing in the Old and the New Worlds. The mainland United States has been spared the devastations Europe endured through the two World Wars. The new-frontier, can-do American attitude coupled with the Judeo-Christian values of faith and human dignity further contribute to the optimistic worldview of American humanistic psychology.

However, a realistic understanding of human nature requires us to recognize both the good and dark sides of humanity. Rollo May hits the right note when he says that human beings are capable of both good and evil. Viktor Frankl also strikes the right balance when he says that people need to develop a sense of tragic optimism. Mahoney and Mahoney (2000) propose that challenges facing humanistic psychology "include the crisis of hope and the quest for meaning (both of which must address the problems of death and the potential 'evil' or 'dark sides' of humanity)" (pp. 659–660).

THE INTEGRATIVE MEANING-CENTERED APPROACH

Existential and humanistic psychologists are at a crossroads. They are confronted with the fundamental existential crisis: the security of the status quo (ontological guilt) or the risk of venturing into uncharted territories (ontological anxiety). I have chosen the latter because that is being authentic. The meaning-centered approach to personality represents my attempt to bridge the gaps between existential, humanistic, and transpersonal disciplines through the unifying construct of meaning. It is also an attempt to overcome some of the limitations discussed earlier. Clearly, the concept of meaning plays a vital role in all the existential-humanistic models. The phenomenological psychologists focus on meaning because they believe that human beings respond to the meanings of events and not events themselves. Viktor Frankl and other existential analysts make the important claim that it is the will to meaning that characterizes us as human beings. The humanistic psychology is built on the foundation of existential-phenomenological psychology. Transpersonal psychology is interested in the meaning of spirituality.

Elsewhere (Wong, 2004a), I have pointed out that the existential-humanist psychology for the twenty-first century as I envision it should be "the mature, positive psychology of how to live and die well in spite of the conflicts and tensions that pervade human existence" (p. 1). I have identified four major themes for the integrative existential psychology:

1. Human nature and human existence: What is a human being? What does it mean to exist and live as a human being? What sets us apart from infrahuman animals? What are the unique human characteristics and potentials that enable us to rise above the laws of the jungle?

2. Personal growth and actualization: What is human potential? How can we fulfill our potential? How can we become authentic and fully functioning? How can we maintain a passion for living when things are not going well? How can we function fully, develop our full potential, and remain optimistic in an uncertain and oppressive environment?

3. The dynamics and structure of personality: What are the underlying dynamics of human motivations? What are the positive and negative existential givens and how do they interact? What is the structure of human existence in all its complexity and duality?

4. The human context and positive community: What are the external forces that shape the phenomenological field and the human condition? What are the social and cultural forces contributing to war and violence? What needs to be done to create a safe, trusting, and caring community conducive to human growth?

In order to address the previous questions and develop the kind of compassionate, positive, and pragmatic existential-humanistic psychology for the twenty-first century, we need to step out of the long shadows of Kierkegaard, Heidegger, Husserl, and Sartre and develop a more inclusive and more scientific identity. The present meaning-centered approach does not see any contradiction between the holistic, phenomenological study of the whole person and the quantitative experimental research on specific psychological attributes and processes because both approaches are needed to enrich our understanding of human existence. Life is full of paradoxes, puzzles, and mysteries; no single approach can answer all the questions. Therefore, we need creative, innovative methods to illuminate the seemingly incomprehensible, inexplicable wonders and horrors of human existence.

The following are a set of assumptions and propositions that can be subjected to empirical research and hypothesis-testing. It is hoped that an open-minded approach will encourage systematic, rigorous research to build a body of scientific knowledge regarding the four major themes pertaining to human existence.

Basic Assumptions and Postulates

1. Humans are bio-psycho-social-spiritual beings: The center of self is spiritual because it encompasses the defiant human spirit, the core values and beliefs, and the deep-seated yearning for meaning, fulfillment, and transcendence.

2. Humans are meaning-seeking and meaning-making creatures living in a world of meaning. They seek cognitive and existential understanding of events through causal attributions and existential attributions (Wong & Weiner, 1981). They create meaning through choices, actions, and commitments to certain life goals. They live and operate in the human world of meaning (Adler, 1958). Bruner (1990) points out that without meaning, "we would be lost in a murk of chaotic experience and probably would not have survived as a species in any case" (p. 56).

3. Humans are moral agents capable of making moral choices because of their innate conscience, spiritual awareness, and socialization (May, 1953).

4. Humans have two primary motivations: (a) to survive and (b) to find meaning and happiness. The survival instinct makes the meaning quest possible, whereas the intentional goal striving for meaning and happiness provides the reasons for survival in difficult times (Wong, 1998b).

5. Humans are hardwired for community and spirituality (Adler, 1964; Frankl, 1986). Love God and love others are major sources of meaning (Wong, 1998b) that transcend selfish interests.

6. The overriding personal structure is fluid and narrative in nature (Gergen, 1985; Sarbin, 1986). Each individual life is a story (McAdams, 1993; Schank, 1990).

7. The overriding dynamics of personality stem from conflicts between opposing forces within the person. This is because humans are dialectical systems consisting of both negative and positive existential givens. The negative existential givens (e.g., meaninglessness, despair, fear of death) are counteracted by positive existential givens (e.g., quest for meaning, the defiant human spirit, and faith in God or higher power). The dialectical process is an essential part of human beings as psychological agents (Rychlak, 1998).

8. The dynamics of personality also stem from conflicts between needs and life goals, which compete for attention and allocation of limited resources.

9. Humans have the freedom and responsibility to choose their own future, even though such freedom often is limited by external and internal constraints.

10. Humans are capable of personal growth and actualization when they choose to live authentically, responsibly, and pursue life goals that transcend self-interest.

11. Healthy personality is likely to develop when there is a healthy balance between positive and negative existential givens and between competing needs and life goals.

12. Humans are capable of self-destruction and disintegration when they choose to live inauthentically, irresponsibly, and pursue self-centered life goals.

13. Humans are capable of evil when they overreact to negative existential givens. For example, those who ruthlessly pursue power as their life goal may be overreacting to feelings of helplessness and vulnerability (Fromm, 1973).

14. Pathology is likely to develop when negative existential givens far exceed positive givens or when one is fixated on only one life goal or one human need.

15. Human freedom is possible because of our capacity to transcend biological, environmental, and historical influences. It is also because of our capacity for imagination, intentionality, self-distancing, and self-transcendence.

16. All humans have the courage to do what is right and meaningful, to live authentically, and to pursue their dreams. Existential courage stems from self-transcendence, the defiant human spirit, and a sense of moral agency.

17. Positive, healing conditions (trusting, supporting, and caring) bring out the best in humanity because they strengthen the positive existential givens and weaken the negative givens; negative, toxic conditions (oppressive, suspicious, and fearful) bring out the worst in humanity because they strengthen the negative givens and weaken the positive givens.

18. The principle of reinforcement, both direct and vicarious, plays an important role in influencing one's values, habits, attitudes, actions, and the choice of life goals.

These 18 principles are part of the existential-humanistic psychology and mainstream psychology. Reviewing empirical evidence of each of the previous postulates would be beyond the scope of this chapter. Some of the research support can be found in the section "Research in Support of and against the Theories." However, the best test of any psychological theory needs to be based on four criteria: (a) Self-validation—Does it resonate with my lived experience? (b) Intersubject validation—Is there intersubject agreement regarding the lived experience? (c) Historical cross-validation—Is it consistent with the historical, collective lived experience of humanity? (d) Empirical cross-validation—Is it supported by qualitative and quantitative research? The reformulated existential-humanistic theory will be judged according to these four criteria.

Types of Personality

From the perspective of a meaning-centered approach, personality structure can be described both in terms of functional components and in terms of narrative structures. The components are variables that can be quantified and measured; they include cognitive schemata, attitudes, traits, interpersonal styles, values, beliefs, and personal meaning systems. The narrative structures are organized as life stories with their leitmotifs, plots, casts of characters, roles, conflicts, and crises. Personality as a life story can be studied through personal documents, life histories, psychobiography, phenomenology, and other narrative tools. The narrative structures of personality can be described in terms of themes, typologies, metaphors, and myths.

However, an existential theory of personality is primarily a dynamic, motivational theory because what ultimately shape personality development are internal dynamics, both conscious and unconscious. These dynamics are mostly related to conflict between positive and negative existential givens. The following illustrate how various types of personality can be derived and described in terms of these existential dynamics.

The Dynamics of Pursuing Different Sources of Meaning

This can be studied through Wong's Personal Meaning Profile (1998b), which identifies seven sources of meaning: achievement, relationship, intimacy, religion, self-acceptance, self-transcendence, and fair treatment. Personality can be measured either by the overall profile or by the dominant source of meaning. For example, those whose lives are devoted almost exclusively to religion can be classified as the religious type. Similarly, those who are consumed by achievement can be classified as the ambitious type.

The Dynamics of Conflict between Negative and Positive Existential Givens

This is another way of providing a typology of personality. For example, Wong's existential model of tragic optimism (Leung, Vroon, Steinfort, & Wong, 2003; Wong, 2004b) encompasses both negative existential givens and positive existential givens. The negative existential givens are measured by the realistic pessimism of accepting the "valley" experiences of human existence and the dark side of human nature. The positive existential givens are measured by idealistic optimism consisting of: affirmation of meaning, faith in God, self-transcendence, and existential courage. As a result, we have four types of personality:

1. *Pessimists:* They are high in pessimism and low in optimism. They tend to be vulnerable to depression and helplessness. They have poor self-concept and give up readily. They also have low levels of subjective well-being.
2. *Tragic heroes:* They are high in both pessimism and optimism. They remain hopeful even when the situation looks hopeless. They stay the course, keep the faith, and remain confident about the future in spite of setbacks, overwhelming odds, and self-doubts. Their resolve and courage come from baptism by fire.
3. *Pollyannas:* They are low in pessimism and high in optimism. They tend to see the glass as half full and underestimate the seriousness of presenting problems; they tend to epitomize the benefits of positive illusions. But there are limits to their optimism, which may unravel in conditions of unrelenting and uncontrollable traumas, such as the Nazi death camps.
4. *Followers:* They are low in both pessimism and optimism. They are not optimistic about their own future because, as conformists, they have surrendered their future to their bosses out of fear. However, they are not very pessimistic because they know that their submission to the leadership will at least earn them some security in terms of meeting their basic needs.

The Dynamics of Different Combinations of Motivations

The motivation for personal meaning (PM) and the motivation for social interest (SI) can be combined to yield four types of personality:

1. Hi PM and Hi SI: The *actualizers/heroes* seek to live authentically and fulfill their calling. Their personal meaning is self-transcendent and derives from their sense of mission to serve others. Their passion for their mission leaves

little room for selfish gains. They do not only seek glory and power; they are on a mission to serve a higher purpose. They seek truth, justice, goodness, and beauty, whatever the cost. They are Abraham Lincoln, Vincent van Gogh, Beethoven, Leo Tolstoy, Feodor Dostoevsky, Albert Schweitzer, Martin Luther King Jr., and Henri Nouwen. The world became a better place because of their sacrifices.

2. Hi PM Lo SI: The *terminators/deceivers* seek to achieve their personal ambitions without any regard for others. Their personal meaning is based solely on their blind ambition for power and fame. They resort to any means to further their personal ambitions, which include deception, manipulation, and merciless destruction of their opponents. Many politicians, corporation CEOs, and religious leaders can be so described. Psychopaths and tyrants also belong to this destructive personality type.

3. Lo PM Hi SI: The *devotees/activists* have a low sense of personal meaning that is reflected in the fact that they do not really know who they are and what to do with their lives. But they do have some interest in larger social causes. As a result, they avoid having to make personal decisions for their own lives by getting deeply involved in some sort of political, religious, or activist organizations. They are likely candidates to be cult members and political groupies.

4. Lo PM Lo SI: The *escapists/victims* find life devoid of meaning, and they have no interest in others. They generally escape freedom and responsibility through addiction or pleasure seeking. They tend to be aimless drifters who survive on a series of temporary jobs and government assistance. Acting as victims, they blame others, bad luck, and circumstances for their misery.

The Dynamics of Pursuing Different Levels of Needs

Maslow's *hierarchy model of needs* represents the ideal or rational progression through the different levels of needs. However, it needs to be complemented by a *conflict model of needs*. I propose that under many conditions, different levels of human needs compete for immediate attention, and individuals may choose to bypass a lower-level need in order to meet a higher-level need. For example, many have risked and lost their lives in pursuing the ideal of freedom by trying to escape from totalitarian states. Some people may choose to be fixated at a lower level of needs instead of the ideal of self-actualization. For example, many individuals squander their lives in drug addiction in spite of their professional success.

This conflict model also predicts that for various reasons—such as early childhood experience, traumatic experience, past reinforcement history, or ideology—some individuals may become fixated at one specific level to the point of being consumed by it. This selective, overblown fixation at one level at the expense of other levels is similar to Rollo May's daimonics and may result in following extreme types of personality:

1. The *sacrificial actualizers* would give up everything, including their lives, in order to realize their dreams and fulfill their mission. They include the starving artists, religious zealots, martyrs, terrorists, and revolutionaries. They have the same all-consuming passion, the same selfless dedication but totally different outcomes. It all hinges on the choices one makes. If we strive to achieve the B-values proposed by Maslow, we are likely to make a positive contribution to humanity. However, if we strive for power and domination (Fromm 1973), whether in the name of nationalism (Hitler), ideology (Stalin), or religion (Osama bin Laden), we are likely to have a negative impact on society.

2. The *status seekers* would do anything to make a name for themselves and gain respect. They constantly seek recognition and publicity. They are likely to be the vanity-consumers, social-ladder climbers, impersonators, and hypocrites who consistently make themselves look better than they really are.

3. The *anxious clingers* have a desperate need for love and attachment. They would give up everything for acceptance and intimacy. Paradoxically, they go from one failed relationship to another because they love too much.

4. The *safety fanatics* are so overly anxious about personal safety and future security that they give up many opportunities in order to play safe. The recluse millionaire Howard Hughes is an extreme example. Their concern for physical safety may generalize to matters of personal security. For example, safety-conscious individuals tend to be conformists and compromisers to avoid confrontation. They have the habit of saving for the rainy days. Given a choice, they consistently choose status quo over new adventures.

5. The *hedonists* devote their life to pursuing physical pleasures. They live to eat rather than eat to live, and their stomach is their God. They also are obsessed with sex not as an expression of intimacy but as a recreation. Sexual exploits become their way of finding happiness and personal significance.

The previous conceptual analysis shows that the meaning-centered approach to personality can generate innovative research ideas on personality and provide fresh insights into maladaptive as well as healthy behaviors. For example, both constructive and destructive behaviors can be predicted based on the 18 postulates. Systematic research is needed to find out how external variables and personality traits interact to predict the likely pattern of meaning quest. Culture, socialization and reinforcement history are likely to have an influence on the selection of life goals, sources of meaning, and pathways to meaning. The meaning-centered approach to personality has broad implications for research and applications. It shows that an exciting new vista will open up once we dare to step out of the shadow and stand on the shoulders of the giants in existential-humanistic psychology.

RESEARCH IN SUPPORT OF AND AGAINST THE THEORIES

Much of the research support for existential, humanistic psychotherapy can be found in Schneider et al. (2001) and Cain and Seeman (2001). Empirical support for logotherapy and existential analysis appears in a special anthology edited by Batthyany and Levinson (2005) to celebrate the 100th birthday of Viktor Frankl. Empirical support for meaning-centered counseling can be found in Wong (1998c).

As stated earlier regarding failure to build a scientific body of knowledge, many of the concepts and principles of existential, humanistic psychology are too ambiguous or imprecise to be tested empirically. Therefore, scientific support for existential and humanistic theories are either weak or nonexistent. But it also means that there is no clear scientific evidence against existential and humanistic theories.

However, when we move on to the reformulated existential-humanistic theory, we enter into a very different terrain of research. There has been rather extensive research on the role of meaning in personal, motivation, and life-span development (Reker & Chamberlain, 2001; Wong & Fry, 1998). A meaning-centered approach to personality has a broad base of empirical support and goes beyond Emmons's (1986) personal goal-striving approach to personality. Space limitation only allows me to highlight a few areas.

The Positive Role of Meaning in Happiness and Subjective Well-Being

Viktor Frankl (1969) has consistently stated that happiness will elude us if we directly pursue it, but it will come in through the back door if we pursue meaning in life. There are now literally hundreds of studies that support Frankl's existential insights (Batthyany & Guttmann, 2005). We now know that meaning is an essential component of happiness

and well-being (Ryff, 1989; Ryff & Keyes, 1995) and that happiness is an essential component of personal meaning (Wong, 1998b). Researchers have reached the consensus that the good life of happiness and fulfillment cannot be found in wealth and possessions and that it can be found only through living a meaningful life. Such a life would entail helping others, setting long-term life goals, enjoying good relationships, having a religious faith, seeking spiritual experiences, making a contribution to society, and having a philosophy of life (Diener, 2000; Myers, 1992, 2000). This existential view of happiness also can explain why people find contentment and fulfillment even when they are suffering (Wong, 2004b). Ryan and Deci (2001) differentiated between hedonic and eudaimonic happiness. Only the latter can be considered mature, authentic happiness because it is not dependent on circumstances or physical pleasures.

The Positive Role of Meaning in Overcoming Adversities

Research is accumulating that affirmation of positive meaning plays a key role in enduring and overcoming adversities. Several meaning-based processes are involved in the humans' heroic effort to survive and thrive in the midst of stress and trauma. These processes include meaning management to repair shattered assumptions (Janoff-Bulman, 1999), the existential coping of acceptance and finding positive meaning in suffering (Wong & Reker, 2005), developing a sense of coherence (Antonovsky, 1987), maintaining a sense of tragic optimism (Wong, 2004b), and contributing to posttraumatic growth (Leung et al, 2003; Tedeschi, Park, & Calhoun, 1998).

The Positive Role of Meaning in Death Acceptance

Existential philosophers and psychologists, such as Heidegger, Jaspers, Sartre, and May, have long emphasized the centrality of death anxiety in human existence. Feifel (1959) proposed that research on the meaning of death and dying could deepen our understanding of the development of mature and authentic personality in confronting and incorporating death concept. Since then, much research has been done on death attitudes. Most relevant to the meaning-centered approach is recent research on both death acceptance and death anxiety. Wong and his associates (Wong, Reker, & Gesser, 1994) have found that accepting one's mortality (i.e., neutral death acceptance) is beneficial because it reduces death fear and motivates people to make something of their lives before it is too late. Similarly, the belief in an afterlife (i.e., approaching-death acceptance) may also ease one's dread of nonexistence. Wong also has found that life review (Wong, 1995) and meaning contribute to successful aging and death acceptance (Wong, 1999).

The Positive Role of Meaning in Goal Striving and Achievement

Humans are purposeful and goal oriented (Klinger, 1998). The importance and benefits of personal projects (Little, 1998) and goal striving (Emmons, 1986) have been well documented. Wong (1998a) has further demonstrated that the meaning one attributes to university education is positively related to academic achievement. These findings suggest that the quest for meaning and personal significance is not an ambiguous concept because it can be investigated in terms of pursuit of specific life goals and projects. In sum, the meaning-centered approach is evidence-based and represents the positive, existential psychology, which transforms suffering and death into human strengths.

PREDICTIONS FOR EVERYDAY FUNCTIONING

Given that the meaning-centered approach to personality focuses on the real-life drama of surviving and thriving in the context of adversities, suffering, and death, it is clearly relevant to everyday functioning. I will briefly highlight applications of meaning-based principles to the following domains:

Family Life

The family as a social institution is unraveling with high divorce rates, domestic violence, and out-of-control teens. The existential approach predicts that family life is more likely to be healthy if the following four principles are implemented:

1. Create a safe and trusting environment by adopting the three Rogerian values of genuineness, empathetic understanding, and unconditional acceptance (trust). Good relationships between family members are likely to follow in such a home environment.
2. Encourage deeper understanding of self and other family members in order to establish more realistic expectations and discover more meaningful ways of relating. "The existential approach involves an encounter between persons who are jointly taking risks in a shared exploration of the realities of the family members' experience and expectation of each other. This requires a true openness and honesty in the search for new, meaningful, and freer pattern of behavior and relationships" (Haldane & McCluskey, 1982, p. 124).

3. Emphasize both personal and collective responsibility for own behavior and for other family members. The pursuit of individual freedom without regard for others is at the root of many familial and social problems. Parents need to teach their children that there are consequences for their actions.
4. Promote joint projects in order to promote family cohesiveness (Lantz, 1996). Similarly, couples need to have shared values and life goals so that they will not be pulling constantly in opposite directions.

School and Education

The teacher can facilitate classroom learning by practicing the three Rogerian attitudes (Rogers & Freiberg, 1993). The most essential value is genuineness because the teacher can get connected with the learner only when the teacher enters into the encounter without any facade. An attitude of unconditional acceptance and trust is important because it communicates to the learners the facilitator's trust in their worth and capacity as human beings. Empathetic understanding also enhances self-initiated learning because when students feel that they are understood for their own point of view and are not being judged, they are more eager to learn.

The teacher also can motivate students with materials that are both challenging and meaningful with respect to fulfilling students' potential. Students develop their strengths through overcoming difficulties and solving problems. Students are more likely to be motivated when they understand that the information and skills they acquire are important for their survival and success in fulfilling their career goals (Wong, 1998a).

Work

The same Rogerian core conditions also apply to work situations. Encounter groups (Rogers, 1970) have been run in various organizations to create a safe and trusting environment. In such a positive climate, workers are more likely to find work meaningful and become authentic in relating to others (Wong, 2002a).

Maslow's model of hierarchy of needs has been widely accepted by human resources managers but seldom practiced. However, it can be predicted that workers are more likely to be motivated when their work provides opportunities for meeting all five levels of needs. More recent research has shown that workers' need for meaning and spirituality is important for productivity and job satisfaction (Wong, 2002a; Wong & Gupta, 2004).

Retirement

Retirement represents a major life transition. To those whose self-identity and personal meaning have been defined by their work, retirement would mean more than just a loss of status and income. The key to a productive retirement is to rediscover the meaning for living. Individuals are more likely to enjoy their retirement and experience successful aging if they engage in the following:

1. Spend some time in life review and reflect on the meaning of their lives (Wong, 1995; Wong & Watt, 1991). They may gain a deeper self-understanding and become better prepared for the dwindling opportunities that come with aging.
2. Explore opportunities for personal growth in terms of wisdom, maturity, and spiritual transformation (Wong, 1989, 1998d, 1999) because this is the only area that is relatively free from the limiting effect of aging.
3. Continue to pursue one's life mission, though in a gradually diminished capacity. One may retire from formal employment, but one does not need to retire from one's vocation and mission. As long as health permits, retirees need to continue to do work related to their calling. It may mean volunteer work, part-time employment, or self-initiated projects.

Recreation

From the meaning-centered perspective, other than work, recreation offers the most opportunities to discover personal meaning and contribute to human fulfillment. At a certain level, work and play become the same. There are two types of recreation:

1. Sensation-seeking activities include extreme sports, traveling, going to theaters, listening to music, and so forth. These activities enrich our lives through the experiential value of finding meaning, according to Frankl (1984).
2. Creative activities include painting, writing poetry, playing music, carpentry, or doing something for others. These activities express and discover ourselves through creative value of finding meaning, according to Frankl (1984). Creative recreational activities often develop into a career or lifelong calling.

CONCLUSION

Because the meaning-centered approach to personality addresses fundamental issues of human existence, it stands to reason that this particular approach is relevant to all the major domains of life and helpful to people in their daily struggles. It also provides new insights into a wide range of personalities, from the healthy to the destructive types. Thus, this theoretical framework is a promising way to study people both at their best and at their worst.

The reformulated existential-humanistic theory is dialectical because the underlying motivation is based on the conflict between negative and positive existential givens as well as between competing life goals. Motivation stems from both the tension of conflict (Mahoney & Mahoney, 2001) and the choices one makes. Healthy personality results from balancing and integrating conflicting forces, whereas the destructive personality often results from obsession with a single ambition for power. This dialectical view is similar to Csikszentmihalyi's (1996, 2000) description of dialectic tension between contradictory forces in creative individuals and to Fromm's (1941, 1999) concept of dialectical humanism, which emphasizes the human capacity to transcend opposing forces between biological drives and societal pressures.

Research on the positive triad of meaning, optimism, and spirituality in the context of negative existential givens and negative circumstances encompasses the entire range of lived experience. This inclusive research agenda expands the frontier of positive psychology (Seligman & Csikszentmihalyi, 2000), which is still predicated on the false dichotomy that positivity is good and negativity is bad (Seligman, 2002). The integrative reformulated existential-humanistic psychology also realizes Bugental's (1981) prophetic vision: "The existential point of view speaks of man's condition in a fashion that transcends the dichotomy of pathology and health" (p. 17). More importantly, the current focus on the human quest for meaning and fulfillment is able to circumvent philosophical divides and brings existential-humanistic psychology back to mainstream psychology. Finally, the conception of personal meaning as socially constructed (Gergen, 1999; Wong, 1998b) will shed light on the development of personality in different cultural contexts. Leong and Wong (2003) have shown that the meaning of optimal functioning is dependent on the values and beliefs of different cultures. The meaning-based existential-humanistic theory hopefully will contribute to a multicultural perspective of personality functioning and appeal to the international psychology community.

REFERENCES

Adler, A. (1958). *What life should mean to you.* New York: Capricorn Books.

Adler, A. (1964). *Social interest: A challenge to mankind.* New York: Capricorn Books.

Allport, G. (1961). Commentary on earlier chapters. In R. May (Ed.), *Existential psychology* (pp. 93–98). New York: McGraw-Hill.

Almaas, A. H. (1988). *The pearl beyond price: Integration of personality into being—An object relations approach.* Berkeley: Diamond Books.

Almaas, A. H. (1996). *The point of existence: Transformations of narcissism in self-realization.* Berkeley: Diamond Books.

Antonovsky, A. (1987). *Unraveling the mystery of health: How people manage stress and stay well.* London: Jossey-Bass.

Batthyany, A., & Guttmann, D. (2005). *Annotated bibliography of research on meaning and purpose.* Phoenix, AZ: Zeig, Tucker & Theissen.

Batthyany, A., & Levinson, J. (Eds.). (2005). *Anthology of Viktor Frankl's logotherapy.* Vienna: Viktor Frankl Institute.

Binswanger, L. (1958). The existential analysis school of thought. In R. May, E. Angel, & H. Ellenberger (Eds.), *Existence* (pp. 191–213). New York: Basic Books.

Boss, M. (1963). *Psychoanalysis and Daseinsanalysis.* New York: Basic Books.

Bruner, J. (1990). *Acts of meaning.* Cambridge, MA: Harvard University Press.

Bugental, J. F. T. (1981). *The search for authenticity* (Rev. ed.). New York: Irvington.

Cain, D. J., & Seeman, J. (Eds.). (2001). *Humanistic psychotherapies: Handbook of research and practice.* Washington, DC: American Psychological Association.

Cooper, M. (2003). *Existential therapies.* London: Sage.

Craig, E. (Ed.). (1988). Psychotherapy for freedom: The Daseinsanalytic way in psychology and psychoanalysis. *The Humanistic Psychologist, 16*(Spring).

Csikszentmihalyi, M. (1996). *Creativity: Flow and the psychology of discovery and invention.* New York: HarperCollins.

Csikszentmihalyi, M. (2000). *Beyond boredom and anxiety.* San Francisco: Jossey-Bass.

Csikszentmihalyi, M. (2001). Preface. In K. J. Schneider, J. F. T. Bugental, & J. F. Pierson (Eds.), *The handbook of humanistic psychology* (pp. xv–xvii). Thousand Oaks, CA: Sage.

Diener, E. (2000). Subjective well-being: The science of happiness and a proposal for a national index. *American Psychologist, 55,* 34–43.

Emmons, R. A. (1986). Personal strivings: An approach to personality and subjective well-being. *Journal of Personality and Social Psychology, 51,* 1058–1068.

Fabry, J. (1994). *The pursuit of meaning* (New rev. ed.). Abilene, TX: Institute of Logotherapy Press.

Feifel, H. (Ed.). (1959). *The meaning of death.* New York: McGraw-Hill.

Frankl, V. E. (1963). *Man's search for meaning: An introduction to logotherapy.* New York: Pocket Books.

Frankl, V. E. (1967). *Psychotherapy and existentialism: Selected papers on logotherapy.* New York: Washington Square Press/Pocket Books.

Frankl, V. E. (1969). *The will to meaning: Foundations and applications of logotherapy.* New York: World Publishing.

Frankl, V. E. (1978). *The unheard cry for meaning: Psychotherapy and humanism.* New York: Simon & Schuster.

Frankl, V. E. (1984). *Man's search for meaning* (Rev. ed.). New York: Washington Square Press/Pocket Books.

Frankl, V. E. (1985). *The unheard cry for meaning: Psychotherapy and humanism* (New ed.). New York: Simon & Schuster.

Frankl, V. E. (1986). *The doctor and the soul: From psychotherapy to logotherapy* (Rev. ed.). New York: Vintage.

Friedman, H. S., & Schustack, M. W. (2003). *Personality: Classic theories and modern research* (2nd ed.). Boston: Allyn & Bacon.

Fromm, E. (1941). *Escape from freedom.* New York: Farrar & Rinehart.

Fromm, E. (1973). *The anatomy of human destructiveness.* New York: Holt, Rinehart & Winston.

Fromm, E. (1999). *Man for himself: An inquiry into the psychology of ethics* (New ed.). London: Routledge.

Gergen, K. J. (1985). The social constructionist movement in modern psychology. *American Psychologist, 40,* 266–75.

Gergen, K. J. (1999). *An invitation to social constructionism.* London: Sage.

Grof, S. (1993). *The holotropic mind: The three levels of human consciousness and how they shape our lives.* San Francisco: HarperCollins.

Grof, S. (1998). *The cosmic game: Explorations of the frontiers of human consciousness.* Albany, NY: SUNY Press.

Haldane, D., & McCluskey, U. (1982). Existentialism and family therapy: A neglected perspective. *Journal of Family Therapy, 4,* 117–132.

Heidegger, M. (1962). *Being and time.* New York: Harper and Row.

Husserl, E. (1962). *Ideas: General introduction to pure phenomenology* (W. R. B. Gibson, Trans.) New York: Collier Books. (Original work published 1913)

Janoff-Bulman, R. (1999). Rebuilding shattered assumptions after traumatic life events. In C. R. Synder (Ed.), *Coping: The psychology of what works* (pp. 305–323). New York: Oxford University Press.

Klinger, E. (1998). The search for meaning in evolutionary perspective and its clinical implications. In P. T. P. Wong & P. S. Fry (Eds.), *The human quest for meaning: A handbook of psychological research and clinical application* (pp. 27–50). Mahwah, NJ: Erlbaum.

Lantz, J. (1996). Stages and treatment activities in family logotherapy. *The International Forum for Logotherapy, 19,* 20–22.

Leong, F. T. L., & Wong, P. T. P. (2003). Optimal functioning from cross cultural perspectives. In W. B. Walsh (Ed.), *Counseling psychology and optimal human functioning* (pp. 123–150). Mahwah, NJ: Erlbaum.

Leung, M. M., Vroon, E. J., Steinfort, T., & Wong, P. T. P. (2003, August). *Tragic optimism: Validation of a new measurement of the construct.* Poster presented at the American Psychological Association Convention, Toronto, Ontario.

Little, B. R. (1998). Personal project pursuit: Dimensions and dynamics of personal meaning. In P. T. P. Wong & P. S. Fry (Eds.), *The human quest for meaning: A handbook of psychological research and clinical application* (pp. 193–212). Mahwah, NJ: Erlbaum.

Mahoney, M. J., & Mahoney, S. (2001). Living within essential tensions: Dialectics and future development. In K. J. Schneider, J. F. T. Bugental, & J. F. Pierson (Eds.), *The handbook of humanistic psychology* (pp. 659–665). Thousand Oaks, CA: Sage.

Maslow, A. H. (1943). A theory of human motivation. *Psychological Review, 50,* 370–96.

Maslow, A. H. (1954). *Motivation and personality.* New York: HarperCollins.

Maslow, A. H. (1961). Existential psychology: What's in it for us? In R. May (Ed.), *Existential psychology* (pp. 49–57). New York: McGraw-Hill.

Maslow, A. H. (1964). *Toward a psychology of being.* Princeton, NJ: Van Nostrand.

Maslow, A. H. (1970). *Motivation and personality* (2nd ed.). New York: Harper and Row.

Maslow, A. H. (1971). *The farther reaches of human nature.* New York: Viking.

May, R. (1950). *The meaning of anxiety.* New York: Ronald Press.

May, R. (1953). *Man's search for himself.* New York: Norton.

May, R. (Ed.). (1961). *Existential psychology.* New York: McGraw-Hill.

May, R. (1965). Intention, will, and psychotherapy. *The Journal of Humanistic Psychology, 5,* 202–209.

May, R. (1969). *Love and will.* New York: Norton.

May, R. (1982). The problem of evil: An open letter to Carl Rogers. *Journal of Humanistic Psychology, 22,* 10–21.

May, R. (1992). *The cry for myth.* New York: Norton.

May, R. (1994). *Courage to create.* New York: Norton.

May, R. (1999). *Freedom and destiny.* New York: Norton.

May, R., Angel, E., & Ellenberger, H. (Eds.). (1958). *Existence.* New York: Basic Books.

May, R., & Yalom, I. (2000). Existential psychotherapy. In R. J. Corsini & D. Wedding (Eds.), *Current psychotherapies* (6th ed., pp. 273–302). Itasca, IL: F. E. Peacock.

McAdams, D. P. (1993). *The stories we live by: Personal myths and the making of the self.* New York: Guilford Press.

Myers, D. G. (1992). *The pursuit of happiness.* New York: Avon Books.

Myers, D. G. (2000). *The American paradox: Spiritual hunger in an age of plenty.* New Haven, CT: Yale University Press.

Polkinghorne, D. E. (1982). What makes research humanistic? *Journal of Humanistic Psychology, 22,* 47–54.

Raskin, N. J., & Rogers, C. R. (1995). Person-centered therapy. In R. J. Corsini & D. Wedding (Eds.), *Current psychotherapies* (5th ed., pp. 128–161). Itasca, IL: F. E. Peacock.

Reker, G. T., & Chamberlain, K. (Eds.). (2000). *Exploring existential meaning: Optimizing human development across the life span.* Thousand Oaks, CA: Sage.

Rogers, C. R. (1951). *Client-centered therapy: Its current practice, implications, and theory.* Boston: Houghton Mifflin.

Rogers, C. R. (1957). The necessary and sufficient conditions of therapeutic personality change. *Journal of Consulting Psychology, 21,* 95–103.

Rogers, C. R. (1959). A theory of therapy, personality and interpersonal relationships, as developed in the client-centered framework. In S. Koch (Ed.), *Psychology: A study of science* (pp. 184–256). New York: McGraw-Hill.

Rogers, C. R. (1961). *On becoming a person.* Boston: Houghton Mifflin.

Rogers, C. R. (1970). *Encounter groups.* New York: Harper and Row.

Rogers, C. R. (1977). *Carl Rogers on personal power.* New York: Delacorte.

Rogers, C. R., & Freiberg, H. J. (1993). *Freedom to learn* (3rd ed.). New York: Merrill.

Ryan, R. M., & Deci, E. L. (2001). To be happy or to be self-fulfilled: A review of research on hedonic and eudemonic well-being. In S. Fiske (Ed.), *Annual review of psychology* (Vol. 52, pp. 141–166). Palo Alto, CA: Annual Reviews.

Rychalk, J. F. (1988). *The psychology of rigorous humanism* (2nd ed.). New York: New York University Press.

Ryff, C. D. (1989). Happiness is everything, or is it? Explorations on the meaning of psychological well-being. *Journal of Personality and Social Psychology, 57,* 1069–1081.

Ryff, C. D., & Keyes, C. L. M. (1995). The structure of psychological well-being revisited. *Journal of Personality and Social Psychology, 69,* 719–727.

Sarbin, T. R. (Ed.). (1986). *Narrative psychology: The storied nature of human conduct.* New York: Praeger.

Sartre, J. P. (1946). Existentialism is a humanism. Retrieved April 5, 2005, from http://www.marxists.org/reference/archive/sartre/works/exist/sartre.htm

Schank, R. (1990). *Tell me a story.* New York: Scribner's.

Schneider, K. J., Bugental, J. F. T., & Pierson, J. F. (Eds.). (2001). *The handbook of humanistic psychology.* Thousand Oaks, CA: Sage.

Seligman, M. E. P. (2002). *Authentic happiness: Using the new positive psychology to realize your potential for lasting fulfillment.* New York: Free Press.

Seligman, M. E. P., & Csikszentmihalyi, M. (2000). Positive psychology: An introduction. *American Psychologist, 55,* 5–14.

Spinelli, E. (1989). *The interpreted world: An introduction to phenomenological psychology.* London: Sage.

Spinelli, E. (1997). *Tales of un-knowing: Therapeutic encounters from an existential perspective.* London: Duckworth.

Spinelli, E. (2001). A reply to John Rowan. In K. J. Schneider, J. F. T. Bugental, & J. F. Pierson (Eds.), *The handbook of humanistic psychology* (pp. 465–471). Thousand Oaks, CA: Sage.

Tedeschi, R., Park, C. L., & Calhoun, L. G. (Eds.). (1998). *Posttraumatic growth: Positive change in the aftermath of crisis.* Mahwah, NJ: Erlbaum.

Tillich, P. (1952). *The courage to be.* New Haven, CT: Yale University Press.

Van Deurzen, E. (1988). *Existential counselling in practice.* London: Sage.

Van Deurzen, E. (1997). *Everyday mysteries: Existential dimensions of psychotherapy.* London: Routledge.

Van Kaam, A. (1966). *Existential foundations of psychology.* Pittsburgh, PA: Duquesne University Press.

Walsh, R. (1999). *Essential spirituality: The seven central practices to awaken heart and mind.* New York: Wiley.

Walsh, R. (2001). Authenticity, conventionality and angst: Existential and transpersonal perspectives. In K. J. Schneider, J. F. T. Bugental, & J. F. Pierson (Eds.), *The handbook of humanistic psychology* (pp. 609–619). Thousand Oaks, CA: Sage.

Warmoth, A. (2001). The Old Saybrook 2 report and the outlook for the future. In K. J. Schneider, J. F. T. Bugental, & J. F. Pierson (Eds.), *The handbook of humanistic psychology* (pp. 649–657). Thousand Oaks, CA: Sage.

Wilber, K. (1997). *The eye of spirit: An integral vision for a world gone slightly mad.* Boston: Shambhala.

Wilber, K. (1998). *The marriage of sense and soul: Integrating science and religion.* New York: Random House.

Wong, P. T. P. (1989). Successful aging and personal meaning. *Canadian Psychology, 30,* 516–525.

Wong, P. T. P. (1995). The adaptive processes of reminiscence. In B. Haight & J. D. Webster (Eds.), *Reminiscence: Theory, research methods, and applications* (pp. 23–35). Washington, DC: Taylor & Francis.

Wong, P. T. P. (1998a). Academic values and achievement motivation. In P. T. P. Wong & P. S. Fry (Eds.), *The human quest for meaning: A handbook of psychological research and clinical application* (pp. 261–292). Mahwah, NJ: Erlbaum.

Wong, P. T. P. (1998b). Implicit theories of meaningful life and the development of the Personal Meaning Profile (PMP). In P. T. P. Wong & P. Fry (Eds.), *The human quest for meaning: A handbook of psychological research and clinical applications* (pp. 111–140). Mahwah, NJ: Erlbaum.

Wong, P. T. P. (1998c). Meaning-centered counselling. In P. T. P. Wong & P. Fry (Eds.), *The human quest for meaning: A handbook of psychological research and clinical applications* (pp. 395–435). Mahwah, NJ: Erlbaum.

Wong, P. T. P. (1998d). Spirituality, meaning, and successful aging. In P. T. P. Wong & P. Fry (Eds.), *The human quest for meaning: A handbook of psychological research and clinical applications* (pp. 359–394). Mahwah, NJ: Erlbaum.

Wong, P. T. P. (1999). Meaning of life and meaning of death in successful aging. In A. Tomer (Ed.), *Death attitudes and the older adult* (pp. 23–35). London: Brunner/Mazel.

Wong, P. T. P. (2002a). Creating a positive, meaningful work place: New challenges in management and leadership. In B. Pattanayak & V. Gupta (Eds.), *Creating performing organizations* (pp. 74–129). New Delhi, India: Sage.

Wong, P. T. P. (2002b). Logotherapy. In G. Zimmer (Ed.), *Encyclopedia of psychotherapy.* New York: Academic Press.

Wong, P. T. P. (2004a). Editorial: Existential psychology for the 21st century. *International Journal for Existential Psychology and Existential Psychotherapy, 1,* 1–3.

Wong, P. T. P. (2004b, July). *Finding hope in the midst of suffering and death.* Presidential address given at the 3rd Biennial International Meaning Conference, Vancouver, British Columbia.

Wong, P. T. P., & Fry, P. S. (Eds.). (1998). *The human quest for meaning: A handbook of psychological research and clinical applications.* Mahwah, NJ: Erlbaum.

Wong, P. T. P., & Gupta, V. (2004). The positive psychology of transformative organizations. In V. Gupta (Ed.), *Transformative organization* (pp. 341–360). New Delhi, India: Sage.

Wong, P. T. P., & Reker, G. T. (2005). The development of Coping Schema Inventory. In P. T. P. Wong & L. Wong (Eds.), *Handbook of a multicultural perspective of stress and coping.* New York: Springer.

Wong, P. T. P., Reker, G. T., & Gesser, G. (1994). Death attitude profile-revised: A multidimensional measure of attitudes toward death. In R. A. Neimeyer (Ed.), *Death anxiety handbook: Research, instrumentation, and application* (pp. 121–148). Washington, DC: Taylor & Francis.

Wong, P. T. P., & Watt, L. (1991). What types of reminiscence are associated with successful aging? *Psychology and Aging, 6,* 272–279.

Wong, P. T. P., & Weiner, B. (1981). When people ask why questions and the heuristics of attributional search. *Journal of Personality and Social Psychology, 40,* 650–663.

Yalom, I. D. (1980). *Existential psychotherapy.* New York: Basic Books.

CHAPTER 11

Constructivist Theories

JONATHAN D. RASKIN

Constructivism reflects not so much a singular psychological theory but rather a group of related theories. However, despite some important differences, constructivist theories posit similar central assumptions about human functioning. At the root of all constructivist theories is the assumption that human beings—on their own and through their relationships with one another—create meaningful mental frameworks of understanding, which they use to comprehend themselves, others, and the surrounding world (Gergen, 1994; Hayes & Oppenheim, 1997; Lyddon, 1995; Mahoney, 1988; Raskin & Bridges, 2002; Rosen, 1996; Sexton, 1997). Generally, constructivist theories hold that people do not have unfettered access to the world in itself but only indirect access to that world via humanly invented understandings (Chiari & Nuzzo, 1996a; Mahoney, 1991; Neimeyer, 1997; Raskin, 2002). When people believe they are using their senses to map an external world, they are instead only arranging or rearranging the mental structures they use to make sense of ongoing experience (Efran & Fauber, 1995; Efran, Lukens, & Lukens, 1990; Kenny & Gardner, 1988). Consequently, constructivists follow in the long intellectual tradition of philosophical skepticism, arguing that what people regard as true depends not so much on external reality but on their constructed assumptions.

Constructivist theories do not simply provide a model for comprehending personality and psychopathology but also function as metatheories applicable to knowledge systems in general (Mahoney, 1988). Constructivists reflexively apply their theories not only to their psychotherapy clients but also to themselves because they regard all knowledge systems—those employed by personality and psychopathology researchers as well as those used by clients to understand their everyday relationships—as ever-changing human inventions designed not to provide access to the world as it is but to pragmatically help people successfully make sense of and

Acknowledgment: The author thanks Laurie Ann Morano for her assistance in gathering research materials for this chapter.

live life (Neimeyer & Raskin, 2000b). As such, in the clinical realm constructivist psychotherapists conceptualize psychopathology (the problems in living that clients bring into the consulting room) as deeply tied to how people meaningfully anticipate life experiences (Neimeyer & Raskin, 2000a). Therapy involves helping people revise or replace even the most deeply held constructions when these constructions are judged to no longer work satisfactorily (Ecker & Hulley, 1996; Efran et al., 1990; Epting, 1984; Eron & Lund, 1996; Mahoney, 2003; McNamee & Gergen, 1992; Neimeyer & Mahoney, 1995). Importantly, constructivist psychologists identify the theories that they and their colleagues use to understand personality and psychopathology as useful constructions not to be mistaken for reality itself. In other words, constructivists consider not only their clients' ways of looking at the world as constructions but all theories of personality and psychopathology (including their own) as constructions, too (Neimeyer & Mahoney, 1995; Neimeyer & Raskin, 2000a).

This chapter reviews constructivist perspectives on personality and psychopathology. Three approaches to constructivism receive attention—personal constructivism, radical constructivism, and social constructionism. The chapter presents a summary of these constructivist theories, including explicit attention to developmental and physiological considerations. Discussion of theoretical boundaries among constructivist theories and between constructivist and nonconstructivist theories occurs, followed by a review of evidence for and against constructivist theories. Finally, the chapter offers predictions for family life, school, work, retirement, and recreation based on constructivist perspectives.

STATEMENT OF THE THEORY

Historical Antecedents

Although use of the term *constructivism* is relatively new, "constructivism is a perennial in the history of ideas"

(Mahoney, 2003, p. 212). The ancient philosophies of Lao Tzu, Buddha, and Heraclitus all contain constructivist themes (Mahoney, 2003), whereas the more recent philosophies of Giambattista Vico, Immanual Kant, and Hans Vaihinger directly influenced constructivist psychology (Mahoney, 2003; Neimeyer & Bridges, 2003). Vico questioned both empiricist and rationalist philosophies by analyzing popular myths and fables as a way to highlight the humanly invented presumptions upon which knowledge was built (Mahoney, 2003; Mancuso, 2000; Neimeyer & Bridges, 2003). He argued "human knowing must be understood as a process of construction that takes place in social and historical contexts" (Mahoney, 2003, p. 214). Later, Kant's distinction between *noumena* (things themselves) and *phenomena* (personal experience)—combined with his emphasis on how the mind organizes experience based on its structure—readily anticipated constructivist theories (Mahoney, 2003; Neimeyer & Bridges, 2003). More recently came Vaihinger's philosophy of "as if," in which he advanced the idea that people create and employ *explanatory fictions* to make sense of things and then live "as if" these fictions were true (Mahoney, 2003; Neimeyer & Bridges, 2003; Warren, 1998). Space limitations prevent further elucidation, but many other influences can be found in constructivist theories, among them the work of William James, John Dewey, George Herbert Mead, Alfred Korzybski, Friedrich Hayek, Fedric Bartlett, and Alfred Adler (Bredo, 2000; Mahoney, 2003; Neimeyer & Bridges, 2003; Warren, 1998; Watts & Phillips, 2004).

Classifying Constructivist Theories

Constructivist theories often seem confusing and abstract to newcomers. First, much constructivist scholarship fails to make itself accessible to the uninitiated. Jargon and "epistobabble" sometimes shroud constructivism in an impenetrable haze (Neimeyer, 1997). Second, as already mentioned, constructivism encompasses a number of related but somewhat diverse theories. This often makes it difficult to know precisely what the term refers to. However, Chiari and Nuzzo's categorization of constructivist theories into two broad types, epistemological and hermeneutic, can be quite helpful in making sense of different constructivist theories (Chiari & Nuzzo, 1996b). Chiari and Nuzzo's categorization scheme, summarized next, is employed throughout this chapter to highlight aspects of the three types of constructivism overviewed: personal constructivism, radical constructivism, and social constructionism.

Epistemological Constructivism

Epistemological constructivists believe in an external world independent of human constructions. However, they contend that human perception does not provide direct access to it. Rather, people only know the world obliquely via how they construe it. The accuracy of constructs remains indeterminate because humans cannot step outside their constructions to access the world as it is (Chiari & Nuzzo, 1996b). This does not mean that epistemological constructivists never concern themselves with accurate knowledge. It is simply that for them, what counts as accurate knowledge is always defined within the confines of the construct systems that people use to imbue events with meaning. In other words, what gets regarded as true stems not simply from people passively perceiving external reality but from the meaningful frameworks that people actively invent and employ to organize and comprehend their experiences. Multiple constructions of the same thing often prove effective in different ways, and those considered true often vary depending upon one's momentary goals and desires.

Hermeneutic Constructivism

Hermeneutic constructivists go further than their epistemological counterparts by blurring the distinction between knower and known. Instead of dividing the world into subjective and objective components, hermeneutic constructivists argue that knower and known cannot be separated. Rather, they mutually specify one another as people who collectively negotiate socially shared constructions (Chiari & Nuzzo, 1996b). The ways people collaborate within the social realm through communally agreed upon (and often tacitly accepted) ways of talking about themselves and their surroundings shape a common social reality. From a hermeneutic constructivist view, different cultures often have widely contrasting notions about knowledge, truth, and human identity because over the course of their unique relational histories they have generated and come to live by quite different societal constructions. The socially constructed origins of a given culture's accepted knowledge usually remain obscure to its members. This is why culturally relative local truths often seem universally true and right to those who hold them. However, from a hermeneutic perspective, there are as many knowledge systems as there are social groups.

Limited Realism

Limited realists, in contrast to hermeneutic and epistemological constructivists, maintain that external reality exists and can be known directly, even though they grant that correspondence between human knowledge and the world often remains imperfect. Constructivist theories diverge from limited realism in that they try to move past the traditional distinction between realism and idealism by adopting the position that the structure and organization of the knower are indivisible from what is known (Chiari & Nuzzo, 1996b). Despite their differences, what makes both epistemological and hermeneutic varieties types of constructivism is their insistence that human knowledge does not mirror nature and that people actively create—sometimes alone, sometimes in concert with one another—the knowledge schemes they use to meaningfully understand themselves and their surroundings.

Personal Constructivism

Personal constructivism (also known as personal construct psychology, or PCP) contends that people organize their experiences in order to psychologically anticipate and make sense of the ongoing flow of everyday life. Its practitioners conceptualize people as personal scientists testing out meaningful hypotheses they have devised to understand themselves, others, and the world. The theory originated in the pioneering work of clinical psychologist George Kelly, who comprehensively introduced it in his two-volume 1955 magnum opus, *The Psychology of Personal Constructs* (Kelly, 1955/1991a, 1955/1991b). In the 50 years since, personal constructivists have made significant contributions to the clinical literature by elaborating upon Kelly's unique approach to personality, psychopathology, and psychotherapy (Fransella, 2003).

Basic Theory

At its core, personal constructivism posits the person as an active creator of psychological meanings. These meanings are unique to each person, and, according to Kelly's (1955/1991a) central principle of *constructive alternativism,* there are an infinite number of these meanings (i.e., coherent ways to make sense of things) possible. In personal constructivism, the meanings created—called personal constructs—are bipolar dimensions, each consisting of a mental idea or symbol and its perceived opposite (Kelly, 1970, 1955/1991a). An individual's personal construct system consists of a finite number of hierarchically organized personal constructs (Kelly, 1970, 1955/1991a). Personal construct psychologists have devoted a great deal of time and effort to eliciting and mapping personal constructs. Kelly (1955/1991a) himself originally developed the Repertory Grid—an idiographic form of assessment designed to elicit and measure personal constructs—as a method for helping ascertain the personal meanings of clients or research participants. A substantial amount

of Repertory Grid research has been generated since Kelly first introduced the grid 50 years ago. Interested readers are referred to recent sources that introduce and overview the Repertory Grid (Fromm, 2004; Jankowicz, 2003).

Behavior as an Experiment

Personal construct psychologists conceptualize people as personal scientists actively testing their constructs by applying them in everyday circumstances (Kelly, 1969, 1955/1991a, 1955/1991b). One's constructions are confirmed if they allow for effective navigation through life's obstacles. They are disconfirmed and in need of revision or replacement if they do not. Thus, rather than seeing people as the deterministic by-products of internal drives (psychoanalysis), environmental manipulation (behaviorism), or some combination of environmental and internal rumblings (cognitive behaviorism), personal constructivists maintain that people freely generate their own actions in accordance with how they construe events (Kelly, 1969). This diverges from more deterministic approaches to personality theory, in which behavior is generally assumed to be the product of efficient causation, a passive, often mechanistic, human response to internal processes, external occurrences, or some combination of both. Kelly, rather playfully, tweaked his more experimentally inclined colleagues by suggesting that behavior is not the dependent variable to be monitored and measured in response to independent variable manipulations. Instead, behavior is the independent variable itself, an active and intentional effort to put one's personal constructs to the test. In other words, rather than an end product, behavior is an experiment, a way of testing one's constructed hypotheses (Kelly, 1969). This active view of the person is central to personal constructivism.

Role Relationships

Because (1) people actively create meaningful hypotheses to live by and (2) there are an infinite number of hypotheses that can be generated, it becomes clear that (a) different people's construct systems reveal very different ways of meaningfully understanding life, self, and relationships, and (b) if one wishes to understand another person, one must grasp that person's unique way of construing things (Kelly, 1955/1991a, 1955/1991b). Personal construct psychologists take a *credulous approach* in this respect, accepting at face value the accounts clients convey to them (Epting, 1984; Viney, 1996; Winter, 1992). In so doing, personal construct therapists endeavor to understand how their clients construe events and in turn therapists form what Kelly referred to as *role relationships* with clients. Through these role relationships, therapists come to genuinely comprehend their clients' ways of construing (Faidley & Leitner, 1993; Leitner & Faidley, 1995). This opens possibilities for encouraging clients to test new ways of meaningfully anticipating ongoing experience.

For example, take the hypothetical constructs of Doug and Glenn. Both say they are happy, but until we know how Doug and Glenn perceive the opposite of being happy, we know little about their personal meaning systems. In his construct system, Doug defines the opposite of happy as "not in a relationship," whereas Glenn defines it as "tied down." Thus, *happy* means something quite different to each of them. Doug's serial dating and Glenn's tendency to move from place to place, which may have previously seemed inexplicable, make more sense when their personal ways of construing events are understood. By credulously accepting and coming to understand Doug and Glenn's unique ways of construing, a psychotherapist can develop some good ideas for helping each of them try out alternative constructions. Doing so might allow Doug and Glenn to expand and revise their meaningful ways of understanding themselves and their relationships in potentially new and expansive ways.

Core Constructs and Selfhood

Because personal constructs are organized in a hierarchical fashion, some constructs are more central to one's identity than others. Core constructs are those that are most important to one's sense of self (Kelly, 1955/1991a). Not surprisingly then, core constructs are the most difficult to change. However, unlike classically humanistic conceptions of selfhood, personal constructivism sees the self as ultimately a construction rather than an innate essence with which one must be consistent (Epting & Amerikaner, 1980). Therefore, psychotherapy becomes an arena in which people can examine and, even though it is often difficult, revise their sense of self. Fixed-role therapy, in which one is asked to play the role of someone who construes things quite differently for a designated period of time in order to test out alternative constructions, marks one very powerful way of doing this. It is the only major clinical technique Kelly introduced. Further attention to fixed-role therapy specifically and personal construct psychotherapy more generally lies beyond the purview of this chapter, though a number of sources provide excellent summations (Epting, 1984; Kelly, 1955/1991a; Viney, 1996; Winter, 1992).

Psychopathology

In personal constructivism, psychopathology (i.e., problems in living) occurs when one's ways of construing become ineffective. Instead of conceptualizing psychopathology in terms of categorical disease entities (such as those in the *DSM*), personal constructivists prefer to define it in terms of ways one's construct system is currently inadequate in accounting for life events (Johnson, Pfenninger, & Klion, 2000; Raskin & Epting, 1993; Raskin & Lewandowski, 2000; Winter, 1992). Several examples of how Kelly (1955/1991a, 1955/1991b) conceptualized problematic construing are as follows:

- *Tight or loose construing: Tight construing* occurs when one's constructs are applied too rigidly, yielding unwavering predictions; this may make one's life quite predictable but can also lock one into unhelpful ways of making sense of events from which escape seems impossible. Clients labeled as obsessive-compulsive often construe in an overly tight manner, leaving little room for alternative hypotheses or revisions to their meaning systems. By contrast, *loose construing* occurs when one's constructs fail to provide reliable predictions; creativity depends on one's ability to apply one's constructions to a wider range of elements without worrying too much about making reliable and consistent predictions. However, if one's constructions become too loose, then one's meaning system breaks down; psychotic, disorganized behavior can be seen as the product of extremely loose construing.

- *Constriction or dilation. Constriction* occurs when one narrows one's perceptual field in order to avoid evidence that might invalidate one's current ways of construing. For example, Jason might constrict his focus to prevent himself from encountering evidence that his wife is cheating on him. In so doing, his construction of his wife as devoted remains unchallenged. *Dilation* occurs when one expands one's construct system in order to reorganize it at a higher level of abstraction, without necessarily having given much thought to the way these more abstract constructs apply. For example, when Jason discovers his wife's infidelity, he may try to make sense of it by employing more general constructions about what constitutes love; however, because until now he has not had much reason to flesh out his constructions of love (especially as they pertain to his own marriage), he finds himself with few new insights into his current difficulties.

- *Threat and hostility.* Sometimes, our core constructions let us down. This is known as *threat.* Jason's cheating wife experiences threat when her core constructions of herself as a loyal spouse are called into question; after all, her most central self-constructions have been invalidated, threatening longstanding ways she has understood her own identity. *Hostility,* on the other hand, occurs when one tries to force events to fit with one's constructions. Jason exhibits hostility when he refuses to revise constructions pertaining to his wife's fidelity in the aftermath of her affair. For example, he may place all the blame on the man with whom his wife has cheated, refusing to revise constructions of his marriage despite strong evidence that this may be necessary.

Epistemological or Hermeneutic?

Classifying personal construct psychology using Chiari and Nuzzo's (1996a, 1996b) distinction between epistemological and hermeneutic constructivism is no easy task. Extensive debate in the last decade has focused not so much on whether PCP exemplifies epistemological or hermeneutic constructivism but more on whether PCP is best deemed epistemological constructivism or limited realism (Bohart, 1995; Chiari & Nuzzo, 1996a; Noaparast, 1995; Raskin, 2001; Stevens, 1998; Warren, 1998; Weihs, 2004). Those arguing in favor of PCP as limited realism have held that some constructions are indeed better than others because some constructions better conform to the shape of the real world. These personal construct psychologists generally have been critical of efforts to steer PCP in a more explicitly constructivist direction. Instead, they have advocated quite strongly that personal construct psychology should remain wary of the broader constructivist movement in psychology, lest PCP be weakened and theoretically watered down by what they see as a dangerous march toward antirealism (Chiari, 2000; Noaparast, 1995; Stevens, 1998; Warren, 1998).

Although much discussion has addressed the epistemological constructivism-limited realism issue, more recent scholarship has taken up the epistemological versus hermeneutic constructivism distinction. PCP, with its emphasis on knowing external reality only indirectly through a set of personal constructs outside of which one can never step, can be readily considered an epistemological constructivism (Chiari, 2000; Chiari & Nuzzo, 1996a; Raskin, 2002). After all, most PCP literature maintains the distinction between knower and known but holds that knowers only get at the known indirectly by means of their personal constructs. However, efforts to push PCP in a more hermeneutic constructivist direction recently have begun (Chiari & Nuzzo, 2004; Domenici, 2004). Interestingly, the authors of such efforts generally have incorporated radical constructivist and social constructionist literature quite extensively in developing their arguments. They suggest that personal construct psychologists should move beyond the traditional distinction between knower and known in order see what might ensue should personal constructivism more readily embrace the idea that knower and known mutually specify one another. As such, advocates of PCP as hermeneutic constructivism have increasingly incorporated aspects of radical constructivism and social constructionism, which are discussed next.

Radical Constructivism

Radical constructivism is best exemplified in the theories of Ernst von Glaserfeld and Humberto Maturana. Though different in certain respects (outlined in the following sections), both von Glaserfeld and Maturana's theories share a common assumption, namely that people are closed systems (Efran & Fauber, 1995; Kenny & Gardner, 1988; Mahoney, 1991; Maturana, 1988; Maturana & Varela, 1992; Raskin, 2002; von Glaserfeld, 1984, 1995b). This simple assertion has significant implications. By contending that living organisms are structurally closed, radical constructivists maintain that all an organism ever has direct contact with is its own internal processes. More plainly, nothing inside ever gets outside and nothing outside ever gets inside. Another way of saying this is that organisms respond to their own internal structure much more so than they do to external goings-on. This is significant because it moves radical constructivism away from the presumption that perception accurately maps an outside world. To the radical constructivist, people never directly contact the world. Instead, human perception is viewed as something adaptive that helps an organism survive. Yet, whereas perception may be adaptive, it never provides contact with external reality. Rather, living organisms come in contact only with their own internal structures. The idea that one's structure determines experience more so than external reality is easily demonstrated; after all, outside events trigger only internal changes if an organism is structurally sensitive to relevant stimulation. For example, dogs are structurally responsive to certain odors to which human beings are not. The different olfactory structures of dogs and humans are the key here; to argue about whether dogs or people perceive more accurately is to miss the point because external events underdetermine an organism's response to them. The organism's internal structure is inseparable from how and what it experiences. Therefore, the smell response of a dog is determined by the way its olfactory system is built much more than it is by odors in and of themselves. By contending that living organisms are perceptually closed, radical constructivists advance the notion that the structure of the knower, not the known itself, is central to the manner in which organisms meaningfully construe events.

Von Glaserfeld's Theory

Von Glaserfeld (1995b) bases much of his theory on the work of Jean Piaget, contending that North American psychology has downplayed the constructivism inherent within Piaget's scholarship by conceptualizing cognitive development as a maturational progression toward not only more abstract thinking but also more accurate reality contact. By contrast, von Glaserfeld's (1995b) ideas about Piagetian concepts like *assimilation* and *accommodation* hinge upon his radical constructivist commitment to the notion of people as closed systems in contact only with their own processes, never with external reality. To von Glaserfeld (1995b), assimilation and accommodation occur when people bump into the external world and an internal response is produced. Sometimes when this occurs, people's internal mental structures—responsive to specific kinds of external stimulation but structurally closed—are thrown off balance. People assimilate or accommodate to regain their equilibrium. When people assimilate, they take the internal response that is produced by external stimulation and make sense of it in a manner consistent with their current mental schemes for understanding. When people accommodate, they change their current schemes in response to the internal stimulation. Von Glaserfeld's (1984, 1995b) emphasis on the structurally closed nature of human experience means he attributes accommodation to the failure of one's mental schemes rather than to the direct impact of external reality. More broadly, assimilation and accommodation refer simply to internal processes of self-organization designed to help people adapt to, rather than accurately perceive, their environments. Neither necessarily produces, nor is designed to produce, greater correspondence between mental schemes and the outside world. The ongoing processes of assimilation and accommodation may indeed lead to more satisfying and productive mental schemes, but because people are closed systems they can only judge their revised schemes in terms of increased effectiveness rather than accuracy.

Not surprisingly, von Glaserfeld (1995b) conceptualizes people as operating within their own private realities. Even when people communicate, they never come into direct contact with each other's realities. A person simply responds to the way in which his or her internal mental structure is impacted by another's words, an impact predicated much more on the structure of said person's mental schemes than on the words themselves. In a radical constructivist approach, language and communication become much more about social negotiation and coordination than they do about accurate conveyance of meaning because the latter is rejected as a possibility. Maturana's theory, to which we turn next, speaks even more directly to the issues of language and social coordination that radical constructivists raise.

Maturana's Theory

Maturana's constructivism grows from his work as a biologist studying the nature of consciousness (Maturana, 1988; Maturana & Varela, 1992). He builds his theory around the central concept of *autopoiesis,* which holds that living organisms create and sustain their own systemic processes in order to perpetuate their ongoing existence and survival (Efran & Lukens, 1985; Maturana & Varela, 1992). He also posits *structure determinism,* the idea that how an organism perceives itself and its surroundings is determined by its physiological and psychological structure (Efran & Lukens, 1985; Maturana & Varela, 1992; Simon, 1985). The world looks a certain way to the human eye not because the human eye captures the world as it is but because the human eye is built to respond in particular ways to specific kinds of stimulation. The same environmental stimulation of human and cat eyes produces somewhat different perceptual experiences for people and their feline companions. In the dark, the cat eye responds to stimulation the human eye does not; hence, cats see more effectively at night. Human eyes, due to their high concentration of cones on the fovea, respond more extensively to color stimulation compared to cat eyes. Cat and human eyes evolved not to help cats and humans directly perceive things as they are but to adapt to and survive within their environments.

The environmental triggers to which we respond are determined by how our perceptual organs are built; even though the environment triggers perceptual responses, what we experience in the end is primarily a product of our own internal structure (Maturana & Varela, 1992; Simon, 1985). Given the radical constructivist commitment to living organisms as closed systems, neither human or cat eyes provide more or less accurate reality perception. They simply provide experiences consistent with their structural responses to current surroundings. Though people generally think they are mapping external reality when they see, smell, taste, and touch, all they are doing is experiencing their own structurally determined internal processes (Efran & Lukens, 1985; Maturana & Varela, 1992). Lived experience involves the ongoing process of structural change in response to triggers from one's external surroundings. Thus, people are forever evolving their psychological and physiological structure as a means of adapting to environmental stimulation. This ongoing process, which continues until some sort of disintegrating event leads to the death of the organism, has no particular purpose or direction other than the ongoing survival of the organism.

Related to autopoiesis is the idea of *structural coupling,* whereby two or more autopoietic systems collaborate with each other to form a unity of their own (Maturana & Varela, 1992). Structural coupling happens at both biological and interpersonal levels. For example, at the biological level a group of cells collectively constitutes a specific body organ. The individual cells are both unities unto themselves and part of a larger unity—for example, a functioning liver. At the interpersonal level, the area often of greatest interest to psychologists, human beings enhance their own likelihood of survival by structurally coupling with each other to form communities. These are called *third-order couplings,* and they are highly dependent upon communication among their members (Maturana & Varela, 1992). This is why language becomes so important in radical constructivism (Efran & Fauber, 1995; Efran et al., 1990; Maturana, 1988). Whereas many organisms communicate within what Maturana calls *linguistic domains,* human beings differ from most other organisms because they create genuine languages that allow them not only to communicate with each other but also to reflexively consider their own communicative processes (Maturana, 1988; Maturana & Varela, 1992). Importantly, languages exist not to reflect reality but to help community members in the ongoing process of social coordination (Maturana, 1988). Thus, people use language to develop accounts that they believe will best enhance the ongoing maintenance of their communities. Maturana uses the term *explanatory domain* in referring to the many competing ways community members talk about and make sense of life (Maturana & Varela, 1992). There are many explanatory domains: scientific perspectives, religious beliefs, political ideologies, philosophical positions, and so on (Maturana & Varela, 1992). None of these explanatory domains tells us about an objective reality. Instead, explanatory domains are unique to the communities of people that create them. People adopt those explanatory domains that they think allow them the most effective ongoing adaptation to their surroundings. Yet explanatory domains do not map an external world. Like one's basic perceptual processes, explanatory domains forever remain structurally closed creations of third-order (i.e., social) unities (Efran & Lukens, 1985; Kenny & Gardner, 1988; Maturana, 1988). They provide a means of organizing experience and surviving within a particular context, but they never provide contact with any world beyond their own boundaries. Psychologically speaking, people understand their own processes from within the confines of those processes themselves.

Psychopathology

Michael Mahoney's (2003) constructive therapy reflects radical constructivist ideas about maintaining equilibrium within one's meaning-making system. He refers to core ordering processes (COP), which are "deeply abstract processes that are central to our psychological experiencing" (Mahoney, 2003, p. 49). People experience psychopathology (less ominously referred to by Mahoney as *problems*) when perturbations throw their core-ordering processes off balance. Problems "are expressions of a living system's attempts to protect itself and to pursue directions that feel immediately satisfying. What this means, among other things, is that prob-

lems are often attempts at solutions" (Mahoney, 2003, p. 45). People who seek therapy often do so because their current solutions are not working especially well. Mahoney (2003) distinguishes problems from *patterns* and *processes.* Problems are specific instances in which a person encounters difficulty—for example, when Steve gets fired from his job at Taco World for insubordination. Patterns are broader themes that cut across many aspects of a person's life. Whereas getting fired from Taco World constitutes a specific problem, in therapy Steve may find himself examining larger patterns, such as why he has difficulty sustaining constructive relationships with peers, relatives, and coworkers. Processes involve immediate experiencing; Steve's moment-to-moment lived interactions with his therapist occur at a process level. Examining patterns and processes is often essential to resolving problems and reestablishing equilibrium in one's day-to-day life.

Jay Efran builds a related, but somewhat different, radical constructivist framework for comprehending psychopathology (Efran & Cook, 2000; Efran & Fauber, 1995; Efran et al., 1990). Tying his approach explicitly to Maturana's theorizing, Efran sees problems in living as arising from language and the resulting reflexivity it affords people. As such, "psychotherapeutic problems are fundamentally issues of self-reference" (Efran et al., 1990, p. 26). That is, people experience problems when they get stuck talking about themselves and their lives in particular ways. This is limiting but does not warrant blame because, in keeping with Maturana's radical constructivism, how a person experiences life is determined by the person's current structure. The key to therapeutic change thus becomes relating to clients in ways that disrupt their current structure and lead to its reorganization. Although a person's structure is continually in a state of evolution as the person goes through life experiences, neither client nor therapist can know when, whether, or how a particular experience will change it. When Lynn and her therapist decide Lynn should spend a night on the town as a way to feel better after a recent breakup, it may or may not work out as expected. Even if Lynn's structure changes, the direction such changes take cannot be predicted with certainty. To everyone's dismay, Lynn may feel more depressed after the night out rather than less. Efran's approach infuses a great deal of creativity into the therapeutic process. Each client-therapist dyad must generate its own ways of communicating about the client's problems until it stumbles upon one that initiates desired changes in the client's structure and experience. Efran's perspective perhaps explains why psychotherapy researchers, despite massive research efforts, continue to encounter extensive difficulty predicting therapeutic outcomes:

[P]sychotherapy *triggers* changes in clients, but the kinds of changes that occur are a function of the structure of the client and the nature of the client-therapist coupling. The therapist does not unilaterally determine how, when, or if a particular client will change in a particular direction. Neither does the client. (Efran et al., 1990, pp. 63–64)

Epistemological or Hermeneutic?

Radical constructivism, with its emphasis on organisms as structurally closed systems, often appears to lend itself to ready classification as an epistemological form of constructivism (Raskin, 2002). After all, epistemological constructivists accept the idea of an external world (or *medium,* in Maturana's terms) that organisms dwell within but never come in contact. Thus, to the extent that radical constructivism advances a view of people as isolated within their own private realities, it adheres to the epistemological constructivist tradition (Raskin, 2002). At the same time, with its emphasis on communication (however imperfect), radical constructivism supports the hermeneutic constructivist idea that knower and known mutually specify each other (Chiari & Nuzzo, 2004; Raskin, 2002). Though von Glaserfeld (1995b), in keeping with epistemological constructivism, remains skeptical about whether interpersonal communication ever allows a person to step out of her own constructions and into someone else's, his theory nevertheless suggests that how people use their personal constructions to talk with one another is critical to social activity. This seems, at the very least, a step in a hermeneutic direction (Chiari & Nuzzo, 2004).

Admittedly, Maturana appears to move more readily toward hermeneutic constructivism than does von Glaserfeld. He does so by advancing the idea of third-order couplings. In third-order couplings, people collectively form social unities from which spring various explanatory domains—the ways of talking about things central to negotiating a communally shared sense of reality. In the end, socially shared realities form the foundations from which people linguistically explain, justify, and persuade others to adopt certain points of view. The way knower and known discursively shape one another is primary to Maturana's radical constructivism, making it easy to view his theory as residing squarely within the hermeneutic constructivist camp.

Social Constructionism

Scholars of social construction typically prefer the term *social constructionism* to *social constructivism* in order to differentiate their emphasis on relational and social processes from the more internalized, private meaning systems stressed by their constructivist colleagues (Gergen, 1994; McNamee, 2004). A central theme of social constructionism is that lived experience cannot be traced primarily to external reality or to individually created meanings. Instead, it is the product of ongoing social coordination and communication between people—what social constructionists refer to as *joint action* (Shotter, 1993). In this respect, social constructionists typically have criticized what they perceive as psychology's excessive focus on individuals instead of on context and relationships (Burr, 1995). Though there have been many influences on and directions from which social constructionism developed, the approach presented herein most reflects the work of Kenneth Gergen (1985, 1991, 1994).

Basic Theory

Social constructionism challenges the traditional belief within psychology (and Western culture more generally) that people have stable, coherent personalities characterized by a potentially measurable set of innate psychological traits (Gergen, 1985, 1991). Social constructionism instead builds from the assumption that all knowledge, whether about our psychological makeup or the world in which we live, is something that people create together as they relate to one another and their surroundings (Gergen, 1994). The ideas people share about personality and what constitutes it are socially agreed upon constructions whose interpersonally negotiated origins people overlook. Thus, in thinking about self and personality, psychologists often stress an essential and universal human nature. By contrast, social constructionists see personality and selfhood as relationally constructed creations designed to account for and make sense out of human activity. As such, they prefer the term *identity* to *self* because identity implies something that shifts based on contextual circumstances (Gergen, 1994). Like radical constructivism, social constructionism emphasizes that how people talk about things structures the reality they come to experience as true (Burr, 1995; Gergen, 1994).

Multiphrenic Selves

Social constructionism rejects a view of people as having stable selves that remain constant across time and situations. Social constructionists prefer to talk about *multiphrenic selves,* which are the many different identities a person has across numerous life contexts (Gergen, 1991). For example, Alison's work identity is that of the collegial and easygoing colleague. At home, however, her identity is more that of a doting mom. In each of these circumstances, her behavior and "personality" are very different. At work, she behaves in a very lackadaisical manner, allowing her coworkers to complete important projects without her input. At home, however, she behaves in more hands-on ways with her children, such as completing their homework for them lest they do a poor job. It is not that Alison is being true to herself in one context and disingenuous in another. Rather, Alison's identity is constituted differently in various life situations by her relationships and by the conditions in which she functions. Hopefully this example highlights that in social constructionism, identity is not located inside the person. Rather, identity springs from the relational patterns that occur within a given set of circumstances. It varies from situation to situation based on the ongoing interplay of person, context, and relationships. It is out of these relationships, not a set of enduring traits, that shared understandings about self and world emanate.

Discourse and Warranting Voice

Because the reality we experience grows from how we talk to one another in relationships, language plays a critical role in social constructionism (Burr, 1995). Identity is constituted in language (Gergen, 1994). In other words, how we come to know ourselves is indelibly tied to the ways we meaningfully construct, in conjunction with those around us, understandings through language. In Western culture the language of agency, freedom, and selfhood shapes how we define ourselves. People see themselves as making choices, taking responsibility for their actions, and living according to their inner characters. They do so not because these are necessarily true aspects of an eternal human nature but because such ways of talking about people have engulfed them throughout their lives.

Though critics suggest otherwise (Held, 1995; Mackay, 2003b), social constructionists contend that the ways people learn to talk about personhood constrain (rather than dictate) how people understand themselves. In other words, identities, although constituted in language, are not determined (Paris & Epting, 2004). As an example, consider high school, a time in which a number of socially constructed identities are available for people to choose from. Although the identity a person establishes in high school is constituted within some clearly established parameters (i.e., cool kid, jock, nerd, cutup, etc.), the manner in which a given person appropriates from within these parameters is up to him or her. Importantly, these parameters are not set in stone; they are always contestable and evolve over time as people continually coordinate their boundaries and meanings. In this regard, social constructionism espouses a relativist perspective in which it refuses to privilege knowledge developed in one context over knowledge developed in another (Gergen, 1994).

In social constructionism, there are always alternative ways of talking about the same thing, none of which can be judged outside of a socially constructed perspective. Social constructionists refer to the many different ways of talking as *discourses* (Burr, 1995). People vie for influence through competing discourses. People *warrant voice* when they are able to get others to accept and live according to their preferred discourses (Burr, 1995; Gergen, 1989). Power relations become important within social constructionism; language is seen not as descriptive but as prescriptive. For example, when President Bush called Senator Kerry a flip-flopper during the 2004 presidential election, he was not simply describing his opponent but was intimating that the electorate take a specific course of action come Election Day.

Psychopathology

Not surprisingly, social constructionists reject the view of psychopathology as internal dysfunction. They conceptualize psychological problems as something produced within the context of particular relationships (McNamee & Gergen, 1992). For example, imagine a father and teenage son eating dinner in a restaurant. The son suddenly gets up and throws his plate of spaghetti at the wall and storms out the door. An individualistic perspective might hypothesize that the son has an anger-management problem, such as intermittent-explosive disorder. However, social constructionists look at the son's behavior not unto itself but within the father-son relationship. Perhaps the father has just informed the son that he is disinheriting him. This surely places the son's spaghetti throwing within context, most readily grasped not by looking at the son alone but by understanding the dynamic interplay between him and his father. Human behavior cannot be meaningfully understood in isolation but rather must be explored as it occurs within context and relationships. Thus, there might be a problem between father and son worth attending to, but social constructionists deem it unwise to locate any such problem as primarily internal to one of them. To the social constructionist all meaning making, psychopathology included, is socially constructed. Within current mental health practice, the discourse of individualized pathology has come to dominate, making the relational emphasis of social constructionism appear less obvious (Gergen & McNamee, 2000). Even so, a variety of authors have explored social constructionist alternatives to individualized psychopathology and developed some interesting clinical strategies (Gergen & McNamee, 2000; McNamee & Gergen, 1992).

Epistemological or Hermeneutic?

With its emphasis on knower and known as inextricably tied, social constructionism falls most readily into the hermeneutic constructivist camp. Social constructionists reject the idea of an isolated knower who indirectly accesses the world. Instead, knower and known are inseparable and mutually specifying. In this regard, social constructionism challenges traditional conceptions of psychology quite directly by insisting that psychology's struggles to isolate aspects of personality in laboratory settings by controlling for context are misguided (Burr, 1995). People only can be understood in the settings in which they live and all understandings psychologists develop are merely social constructions, themselves. Although psychological constructions often prove useful, they are merely one of many socially negotiated ways of understanding.

DEVELOPMENTAL CONSIDERATIONS

Radical constructivism, with its Piagetian influences, stresses how the evolution of cognitive and physiological structures throughout development plays a vital role in how people construe themselves and their surroundings. However, constructivist researchers often have been wary to endorse clear-cut developmental stages because doing so (1) encourages a view of children as in a transitional period prior to becoming fully formed adults rather than as people in their own right (Epting, 1988) and (2) often overlooks significant idiographic developmental disparities by insisting development unfolds in invariant sequences (Becvar, 2000). Both personal and radical constructivists instead conceptualize development as the ongoing process of enhancing the complexity of one's meaning system. In this vein, it even has been suggested that viewing any given domain from a constructivist worldview is, in and of itself, the developmental outcome of ever-increasing cognitive complexity (Botella & Gallifa, 1995).

Personal constructivists have taken a great deal of interest in personality development. From their perspective, personality development occurs as the person, through sociality, successively revises his or her core role constructs in the course of interpersonal relationships (Anderson, 1990). As mentioned previously, role relationships occur when people effectively construe one another's constructions (Leitner & Faidley, 1995). Personality development results as a person revises or refines his or her core role in response to changing patterns of role relating. For example, Tim's core constructs—developed as he related throughout his childhood to his parents—portray him as an aloof and cold person. However, his core constructs evolve when he goes to college and begins to form new relationships with peers. In these relationships, Tim comes to experience his core role somewhat differently. His aloofness becomes understood, by both him and his friends, as shyness, and—rather than cold—he comes

to construe himself as kind, even if sometimes reserved. Consequently, Tim finds himself behaving in warm and affectionate ways he never thought possible of an aloof person. Thus, personality development occurs as Tim successively revises his core role by way of his relationships to others. It becomes a process tied not only to Tim's constructions of himself but also to how he is construed by people with whom he forms role relationships.

Social constructionists push the envelope further. They leave behind PCP's notion of sociality (the idea that people effectively construe each other's constructions to form relationships) because they feel it remains too wedded to the idea that individuals in relationships maintain their own idiosyncratic constructions, even when successfully relating to one another. In its place, social constructionism posits development as entirely relational, with identity constituted within social context. Identity does not develop from individuals evolving their own private meaning structures. On the contrary, it is the communal product of ongoing engagement and interaction with others. It involves mastering what McNamee and Gergen (1992, p. 1) refer to as the "forestructures of understanding" employed within one's social context (Becvar, 2000). That is, "each of us is born into and assimilates preexisting forms of language in a culturally created linguistic system. In the process of socialization we learn to speak in accepted ways and simultaneously to adopt the shared values and ideology of our language system" (Becvar, 2000, p. 71). The social realm dictates the parameters within which people come to meaningfully understand themselves and their world.

Mascolo, Pollack, and Fischer (1997) put forward a constructivist theory of development with the goal of moving beyond the individual versus social dichotomy described previously. They feel social constructionism relies too heavily on the sociocultural to explain development (Mascolo et al., 1997). At the same time, they remain uncomfortable with approaches that see development as primarily interiorized and innate. In an effort to resolve this dilemma, they recommend an *epigenetic systems* perspective in which a person's psychological structure (i.e., constructions) "are formed neither innately nor through environmental forces, but rather through the relations among biological, cognitive, and social activity at multiple levels" (Mascolo et al., 1997, p. 45). Though they do not cite him, their developmental approach brings to mind Maturana's (1988) radical constructivism to the extent that biological, psychological, and social activity constitute interacting unities in ongoing relation to one another. According to Mascolo et al. (1997), constructive epigenetic conceptions of development insist on "the inseparability of the biological and behavioral subsystems that compose the individual's functioning and the sociocultural systems in which that functioning is embedded" (p. 45).

BIOLOGICAL/PHYSIOLOGICAL RELATIONSHIPS

Constructivist scholars have examined biological/physiological relationships in a number of ways. Kelly (1955/1991b) noted that biological/physiological versus psychological/mental is a construct dimension that, although often useful, need not limit people by dichotomously dividing their thinking about human functioning. Three examples of how constructivists have addressed biological/physiological relationships are briefly presented in the following sections.

Structure and Change

Maturana's radical constructivism advances the idea that human psychological functioning stems from human biological structure (Maturana, 1988; Maturana & Varela, 1992). Thus, his theory elegantly portrays the delicate relationship between human psychology and the biological platform upon which it is based. His explicit incorporation of concepts like autopoiesis and structure determinism make clear that the worlds we experience are constructions shaped in good measure by our physiology. After all, we are only sensitive to those changes in our surroundings to which our physiology is responsive. Although other constructivist theories, compared to Maturana's, have not attended as readily to biological foundations of human construction, Maturana's ideas about physiological structure can readily be incorporated into a more general constructivist approach. Based on Maturana's work, it is clear that research into how human biological structure influences human meaning making holds an important place in constructivist theory.

Embodied Knowing

Another way to think about biological/physiological aspects of constructivism, besides using Maturana's structure determinism, is by examining the role of embodiment in human knowing. Those interested in embodiment often approach constructivism from a hermeneutic point of view. They challenge notions of personhood that posit the self as separate from, but contained within, the body. For example, Trevor Butt (2004) combines the philosophy of Merleau-Ponty with Kelly's personal constructivism and Gergen's social constructionism. In so doing, he rejects the idea of "selves inside bodies" and its implicit dualism in which nonembodied selves are masters over mechanical and passive bodies. Instead, Butt (2004) argues that knowledge and action stem from active and embodied engagement with the world. That is, knowing is not primarily a cognitive activity separate from our bodies. Self and body are inseparably intertwined as a "body-subject" (p. 126). As body-subjects, people "interact with the world, both finding and constructing meaning within it" (p. 98). People become a form of motion, freely engaging the world through their embodied experience of it (Butt, 2004). In this conception, the body's physiological parameters again take a prominent position within constructivist theory.

Medical Model as Construction

In the clinical realm, constructivist scholars often have criticized physiological approaches to psychiatry and psychology with close ties to the medical model (Faidley & Leitner, 1993; Honos-Webb & Leitner, 2001; Neimeyer & Raskin, 2000a; Raskin & Epting, 1993). Rather than seeing the problems clients bring to psychotherapy as manifestations of internal (typically biological) pathologies, constructivists generally have approached client problems as failed efforts at meaning making. Because constructivist practitioners often emphasize the idiographic aspects of human experience, they sometimes find themselves limited by the nomothetic categories of the *DSM* (American Psychiatric Association, 2000). This does not mean that they never employ said categories, but rather, in keeping with constructive alternativism, they see the *DSM* simply as one among many possible ways to construe client problems (Raskin & Lewandowski, 2000). Consequently, *DSM* categories do not play a very large role in most constructivist therapies because these categories generally say more about the meaning-making frameworks held by those treating clients than they do about those held by the clients themselves (Neimeyer & Raskin, 2000a). Additionally, constructivist therapists directly question the medical model's presumption that similar symptoms can be organized into constellations and labeled as disorders that share common underlying etiologies (Neimeyer & Raskin, 2000a). On the contrary, constructivist therapists believe that the same symptoms can have very different meanings to different clients. Further, although physiological structure clearly plays a role in how persons construct meaning, it should be clear by now that identifying disorders based on the presumption that "normal" people's structures yield meanings more closely corresponding to reality than "abnormal" people's does not fit very well within a constructivist orientation.

BOUNDARIES OF THE THEORY

Theoretical Boundaries

The theoretical boundaries of constructivist theories are difficult to pinpoint, perhaps because constructivist theories themselves are so diverse. Whereas personal construct psychology is often seen as sharing much in common with cognitive or humanistic theories (Epting & Leitner, 1992), social constructionism is regularly identified as being antagonistic to cognitive and humanistic approaches (Burr, 1995). Whereas personal construct psychologists tend to see people as active agents possessing a strong degree of self-determination (Epting & Leitner, 1992; Holland, 1970), radical constructivists like Maturana highlight how much of human experience is structure determined (Efran & Lukens, 1985; Maturana, 1988). Whereas the more explicitly constructivist approaches accentuate the importance of individual and private meanings (von Glaserfeld, 1984, 1995b), more overtly social constructionist perspectives underscore the constituting power of socially invented meanings (Gergen, 1994). Because of the many different emphases across types of constructivism, identifying clear-cut boundaries remains tricky. However, two presumptions that appear to cut across all constructivist theories are that they (1) emphasize the centrality of humanly devised ways of understanding and (2) remain skeptical that said understandings carve nature at its joints.

Loosening Boundaries of the Culture-Person Construct

Culture plays a key role in constructivist theory and always has. When Kelly published personal construct psychology, he explicitly discussed the importance of culture. In attending to the import of cultural factors on psychological functioning, Kelly was ahead of his time, observing way back in 1955 that "a failure to understand cultural controls may make the therapist insensitive to the disruptive nature of some of the client's anxieties" (Kelly, 1955/1991a, p. 125). From a personal construct perspective, person versus culture is just another construct dimension—one sometimes helpful, sometimes not. Social constructionism takes things further, highlighting how people are constituted within the sociocultural settings in which they live. Culture is not an external force that affects isolated individuals. On the contrary, in the spirit of hermeneutic constructivism, person and culture are mutually specifying (Gergen, 1994).

Personal constructivism and von Glaserfeld's radical constructivism sometimes seem to overemphasize individuality, whereas social constructionism occasionally appears to reduce everything to the sociocultural. However, Maturana's (1988) radical constructivism offers a graceful way to tack back and forth between social and individual. It does so by positing the social, including culture, as a "third-order unity"—something that functions as a self-sustaining entity but which is also constructed out of individual unities (i.e., people). One of radical constructivism's most valuable contributions is that, by positing different unities across different explanatory

domains, it provides a means to readily span multiple levels of analysis (cellular/biological, individual/personal, cultural/social) in a theoretically coherent manner. In this way, the boundaries of the person-culture construct are both stretched and challenged.

EVIDENCE IN SUPPORT OF AND AGAINST THE THEORY

A fair amount of criticism has been leveled at constructivist theories. Constructivism has been critiqued for being anti-realist, antiscientific, and relativistic (Held, 1995; Mackay, 2003b; Matthews, 1998; McCarty & Schwandt, 2000; Parker, 1999). Opponents see constructivism as endangering long-held ideas about knowledge, truth, and scientific inquiry by contending that people never access the world, only their constructions. They feel this allows for an "anything goes" relativism in which any perspective is as good as another as long as you believe it. Constructivists generally respond by arguing that constructivism does not result in "anything goes" relativism because what "goes" depends on a person's constructions. That is to say, human constructions inevitably constrain what goes (Edwards, Ashmore, & Potter, 1995; Gergen, 1994; Raskin, 2001; Raskin & Neimeyer, 2003). Consequently, in constructivist theories "anything goes" is not an option because people never step outside the points of view they inhabit. People have no choice but to abide by their beliefs, even if those beliefs emanate from how they make sense of things. For example, constructivists can (and do!) believe in the value of scientific constructions while still maintaining that such constructions are human understandings, not truth itself. Nevertheless, ongoing debate continues about the relative merits of constructivist thinking. A recent exchange in *Theory and Psychology* highlights more fully the ongoing debate over the theoretical coherence of constructivist theories (Mackay, 2003a, 2003b; McNamee, 2003; Raskin & Neimeyer, 2003), as do many of the chapters in Phillips (2000).

Despite the criticisms, there is substantial evidence that constructivism offers a great deal to clinical practice. Significant scholarship outlining ways to incorporate constructivism into assessment and psychotherapy has appeared in the last few years (Ecker & Hulley, 1996; Efran et al., 1990; Eron & Lund, 1996; Mahoney, 2003; McNamee, 1996; Neimeyer & Mahoney, 1995; Neimeyer & Raskin, 2000a; Winter, 1992). When it comes to psychotherapy research, constructivist theorists are skeptical of "horserace comparisons" of different therapies because all too often these comparisons fail to account for the interpersonal subtleties that make up a prime ingredient of all effective therapies (Neimeyer &

Bridges, 2003). At the same time, constructivists are quick to point out empirical support for the experiential and humanistic processes used in constructivist therapies (Neimeyer & Bridges, 2003). Yet they remain cautious about therapy-effectiveness research, especially in lieu of findings suggesting that researcher allegiance to the therapies tested accounts for the bulk of differential effectiveness results (Neimeyer & Bridges, 2003; Wampold, 2001).

PREDICTIONS FOR EVERYDAY FUNCTIONING

Family Life

Perspectives on family life are reflected in a number of constructivist approaches to therapy (Eron & Lund, 1996; White & Epston, 1990). One particularly well-developed example of a constructivist perspective on family life is seen in the narrative solutions therapy of White and Epston (1990). Narrative solutions therapy, in keeping with the premises of constructivism, maintains that presenting problems reflect meaningful constructions created and sustained within the context of family interactions (White & Epston, 1990). Family members both personally construe the meaning of what is going on and also partake in family interactions that grow from a shared family construction of the problem. White and Epston (1990) give the example of "Sneaky Poo," a case in which a young boy named Nick was brought to therapy by his parents, Sue and Ron, in order to eliminate an encopresis problem in which Nick picked up and smeared his own feces throughout the house. As a result, Ron experienced shame and avoided having others over to the house, Sue felt deeply miserable, and Nick was labeled as the source of the problem (i.e., a boy afflicted with a mental disorder residing within him).

Narrative solutions therapy encourages families to *externalize the problem,* a technique in which the problem is not seen as residing within any particular family member. Instead of attributing problems to internal dysfunctions inside people, the problem is talked about as its own objective entity, one that typically outsmarts family members in a manner that perpetuates the ongoing occurrence of each family member's reactions. That is, the problem requires certain responses on the part of each family member in order to sustain itself. By externalizing, "the problem becomes a separate entity and thus external to the person or relationship that was ascribed as the problem" (White & Epston, 1990, p. 38). This renders the problem "less fixed and restricting" (p. 38) because it is no longer a permanent attribute inside a person but rather a separate entity that encourages specific kinds of responses

from family members—responses they can resist once aware of them. Nick, Ron, and Sue externalized their family encopresis problem as Sneaky Poo, an entity that invited each of them to respond in particular ways. Externalizing allowed Nick, Ron, and Sue to map their family problem and gain new perspectives on it. They each came to see how Sneaky Poo got the best of them: Ron by avoiding others outside the family, Sue by sinking into depression and misery, and Nick by playing with his waste. Once aware of Sneaky Poo's demands, Nick, Ron, and Sue became able to think about exceptions—times when they did not give into the requirements of the problem. For example, Nick was able to identify times when Sneaky Poo did not talk him into playing with his feces, whereas Sue was able to recall an instance in which she turned on the stereo in response to Sneaky Poo instead of feeling miserable. As they externalized the problem, the family began to pay closer attention to their own behavior and resist the requirements of the problem. As each of them did this, the Sneaky Poo problem dissolved, and new patterns of family interaction began to emerge (White & Epston, 1990).

School

Constructivism has been applied extensively to education from PCP (Shapiro, 1994), radical constructivist (von Glaserfeld, 1995a), and social constructionist perspectives (Gergen, 1995). From a PCP view, education requires teachers to take into account the personal constructions of students and to come to a shared view—via sociality—about the material being learned (Shapiro, 1994). This differs somewhat from the radical constructivist approach. For radical constructivists, knowledge can never be transferred from teacher to learner because people are closed systems that never come into contact. Thus, effective teaching involves creating disequilibriums within students that leads them to change their internal ways of understanding (Tobin, 1993). Radical constructivist education involves exposing students to new information and experiences that produce internal perturbations. Students then assimilate and accommodate in response to these changes, often revising the internal schemes they employ in order to help them make sense of what they encounter (Tobin, 1993; von Glaserfeld, 1995a). Importantly, teachers do not impute knowledge; they merely provide the context in which students can devise viable ways of understanding new experiences. Although teachers provide the learning context designed to create internal perturbations within students' meaning systems, they do not dictate the solutions students construct to help them regain their equilibrium. Learning is a personal, private task, and there are an infinite number of ways for students to effectively adapt their mental schemes. This is why students respond to the same learning experience in different ways and often draw different—but, depending on their goals, equally effective—conclusions.

Social constructionism takes a somewhat different approach. For Gergen (1994), knowledge is always a social invention. Therefore, it does not reside in individual minds but is inevitably a product of ongoing discursive relationships. Knowledge advocated by those warranting the most voice has the greatest influence. In the classroom setting, teachers usually warrant the most voice and are thus charged with filling their students with knowledge. Gergen moves away from this manner of thinking about education. Instead he sees teaching as a relational process in which students become better skilled at utilizing various knowledge discourses, which they draw on to achieve practical goals (Gergen, 1995). Although both radical constructivist and social constructionist approaches to education certainly have been criticized (Phillips, 2000), their influence in the area of education nevertheless has been extensive (Gergen, 1995; Shapiro, 1994; Tobin, 1993; von Glaserfeld, 1995a).

Work

Constructivist theorists have begun explicating strategies for career counseling, and recent efforts have been made to integrate constructivist and objectivist vocational approaches (Chen, 2003). An important theme for constructivists is that career counseling can be enriched by (1) moving beyond traditional notions of self as stable, rational, and reliably measurable and (2) conceptualizing career decisions as one component of a person's larger task of constructing a meaningful life (Constantine & Erickson, 1998; Peavy, 1996). Constructivist career counseling does not rely on vocational assessments designed primarily around matching people to careers based on interests and aptitudes. Career decisions instead become part of a larger meaning-making process within therapy (Constantine & Erickson, 1998; Peavy, 1996). Constructivist career counseling downplays standardized assessments and emphasizes activities that help clients explore and engage their own emerging constructions about self as it relates to career. Though constructivist career counselors often use traditional career assessment when they believe doing so will stimulate clients to examine their own career-related meanings, they also import constructivist techniques such as the Repertory Grid, fixed-role therapy, narrative-solutions letter writing, and so forth (Constantine & Erickson, 1998; Neimeyer, 1992; Peavy, 1996).

Retirement and Aging

Constructivist themes are found in narrative gerontology research, which focuses on how understandings of aging are personally and socially constructed and then reflected in the meaningful stories people tell about aging (Kenyon, Clark, & de Vries, 2001). Retirement is simply one event within the aging process, a process taken up in recent years by social constructionists Kenneth and Mary Gergen. Since 2001, they have published an Internet newsletter called "Positive Aging." The newsletter regularly updates subscribers about research and information related to aging, all with a social constructionist flavor. When it comes to retirement, the Gergens lament dominant social constructions that espouse a deficit-and-decline perspective (Gergen & Gergen, 2001). They note how "for many, retirement becomes essentially a 'door to death.' Self-esteem and sense of empowerment may decline, depression is invited, and engaged activity may suffer" (Gergen & Gergen, 2001). Their newsletter fosters alternative conversations about aging and retirement, with the goal of constituting new identities for the retired and elderly: "By moving beyond practices of repair and prevention, to emphasize growth-enhancing activities, practitioners . . . contribute to the societal reconstruction of aging" (Gergen & Gergen, 2001).

Recreation and Leisure

There does not appear to be a great deal of research about recreation from a constructivist perspective. Botterill (1989) adopted a personal construct perspective on tourism. Using conversations and the Repertory Grid, he examined the evolving personal constructs of a client before and after the client visited Japan (Botterill, 1989). He advocated that vacations be seen as affording travelers opportunities to actively evolve their personal constructs. He contrasted this with what he saw as the causally determined " 'ping-pong ball' model of the tourist, who is conceived as a mindless object responding blindly to the stimuli of the environment" (Botterill, 1989, p. 281). Thus, from Botterill's (1989) view, tourists actively revise their constructs in unique ways rather than being impacted in some universal fashion by sights seen.

More recently, Watkins (2000) examined leisure meanings in general. He compared behavioral, cognitive, individual constructivist, and social constructionist paradigms for studying leisure meanings. He concluded that behaviorist approaches see leisure meanings as excessively dictated by environment, whereas cognitive approaches overemphasize leisure meanings as innate and fixed (Watkins, 2000). Although Watkins (2000) identified some distinct advantages to constructivist and social constructionist approaches to leisure meanings, he also noted common criticisms, namely that constructivism makes leisure meanings too private and individualistic, whereas constructionism produces too much relativism. In the end, he advocated for an "experientialist" approach to leisure meanings. According to Watkins "the experientialist paradigm draws from and complements the cognitivist's and individual constructivist's concern with the inner content of experience, as well as the behaviorist's and social constructivist's concern with the outer structuring of experience" (2000, p. 104). This allows for "descriptions of difference and change in leisure meanings that can be compared and contrasted in terms of their complexity of experience" (p. 104). Interestingly, what Watkins (2000) calls an experientialist approach to leisure meanings seems to echo hermeneutic constructivist efforts to move beyond the person-object dichotomy and to conceive of knower and known as mutually specifying each another.

CONCLUSION

Constructivist theories offer a variety of different perspectives on how people meaningfully develop ways of understanding ongoing experience. All postulate that meaning frameworks are humanly invented templates rather than mirrors on an external reality. Because this common theme runs through all varieties of constructivism, it is not surprising that efforts to bridge the differences across constructivist theories have begun (Raskin & Bridges, 2004). Constructivist theories offer practitioners and researchers alike a great deal of theoretical and applied flexibility. The reflexivity of constructivist theories allows ideas and strategies from any and all other theoretical orientations to be incorporated into research and practice. At the same time, it discourages the intellectual rigidity that at times has set in among theorists who thought they had a stranglehold on truth. With their theoretical sophistication and many implications for research and practice, it is anticipated that constructivist theories will continue to influence psychology and related disciplines in the coming years.

REFERENCES

American Psychiatric Association. (2000). *Diagnostic and statistical manual of mental disorders* (4th ed., Text Rev.). Washington, DC: Author.

Anderson, R. (1990). Role relationships and personality development. *Early Child Development and Care, 55,* 81–88.

Becvar, D. S. (2000). Human development as a process of meaning making and reality construction. In W. C. Nichols, M. A. Pace-Nichols, D. S. Becvar, & A. Y. Napier (Eds.), *Handbook of family development and intervention* (pp. 65–82). New York: Wiley.

Bohart, A. C. (1995). Configurationism: Constructivism from an experiential perspective. *Journal of Constructivist Psychology, 8,* 317–326.

Botella, L., & Gallifa, J. (1995). A constructivist approach to the development of personal epistemic assumptions and worldviews. *Journal of Constructivist Psychology, 8,* 1–18.

Botterill, T. D. (1989). Humanistic tourism? Personal constructions of a tourist: Sam visits Japan. *Leisure Studies, 8,* 281–293.

Bredo, E. (2000). Reconsidering social constructivism: The relevance of George Herbert Mead's interactionism. In D. C. Phillips (Ed.), *Ninety-ninth yearbook of the National Society for the Study of Education: Part 1. Constructivism in education: Opinions and second opinions on controversial issues* (pp. 127–157). Chicago: National Society for the Study of Education.

Burr, V. (1995). *An introduction to social constructionism.* London: Routledge.

Butt, T. (2004). *Understanding people.* Houndmills, UK: Palgrave Macmillan.

Chen, C. P. (2003). Integrating perspectives in career development theory and practice. *The Career Development Quarterly, 51,* 203–216.

Chiari, G. (2000). Personal construct theory and the constructivist family: A friendship to cultivate, a marriage not to celebrate. In J. W. Scheer (Ed.), *The person in society: Challenges to a constructivist theory* (pp. 66–78). Giessen, Germany: Psychosozial-Verlag.

Chiari, G., & Nuzzo, M. L. (1996a). Personal construct theory within psychological constructivism: Precursor or avant-garde? In B. M. Walker, J. Costigan, L. L. Viney, & B. Warren (Eds.), *Personal construct theory: A psychology for the future* (pp. 25–54). Melbourne: Australian Psychological Society Imprint Series.

Chiari, G., & Nuzzo, M. L. (1996b). Psychological constructivisms: A metatheoretical differentiation. *Journal of Constructivist Psychology, 9,* 163–184.

Chiari, G., & Nuzzo, M. L. (2004). Steering personal construct theory towards hermeneutic constructivism. In J. D. Raskin & S. K. Bridges (Eds.), *Studies in meaning 2: Bridging the personal and social in constructivist psychology* (pp. 51–65). New York: Pace University Press.

Constantine, M. G., & Erickson, C. D. (1998). Examining social constructions in vocational counselling: Implications for multicultural counseling competency. *Counselling Psychology Quarterly, 11,* 189–199.

Domenici, D. J. (2004, June). *Perspectives and possibility: Exploring and expanding hermeneutic constructivism.* Paper presented at the 11th Biennial Conference of the North American Personal Construct Network, Memphis, TN.

Ecker, B., & Hulley, L. (1996). *Depth-oriented brief therapy.* San Francisco: Jossey-Bass.

Edwards, D., Ashmore, M., & Potter, J. (1995). Death and furniture: The rhetoric, politics and theology of bottom line arguments against relativism. *History of the Human Sciences, 8,* 25–49.

Efran, J. S., & Cook, P. F. (2000). Linguistic ambiguity as a diagnostic tool. In R. A. Neimeyer & J. D. Raskin (Eds.), *Constructions of disorder: Meaning-making frameworks for psychotherapy* (pp. 121–144). Washington, DC: American Psychological Association.

Efran, J. S., & Fauber, R. L. (1995). Radical constructivism: Questions and answers. In R. A. Neimeyer & M. J. Mahoney (Eds.), *Constructivism in psychotherapy* (pp. 275–304). Washington, DC: American Psychological Association.

Efran, J. S., & Lukens, M. D. (1985, May/June). The world according to Humberto Maturana. *Family Therapy Networker, 9*(3) 23–28, 72–75.

Efran, J. S., Lukens, M. D., & Lukens, R. J. (1990). *Language, structure, and change: Frameworks of meaning in psychotherapy.* New York: Norton.

Epting, F. R. (1984). *Personal construct counseling and psychotherapy.* New York: Wiley.

Epting, F. R. (1988). Journeying into the personal constructs of children. *International Journal of Personal Construct Psychology, 1,* 53–61.

Epting, F. R., & Amerikaner, M. (1980). Optimal functioning: A personal construct approach. In A. W. Landfield & L. M. Leitner (Eds.), *Personal construct psychology: Psychotherapy and personality* (pp. 55–73). New York: Wiley-Interscience.

Epting, F. R., & Leitner, L. M. (1992). Humanistic psychology and personal construct theory. *Humanistic Psychologist, 20,* 243–259.

Eron, J. B., & Lund, T. W. (1996). *Narrative solutions in brief therapy.* New York: Guilford Press.

Faidley, A. F., & Leitner, L. M. (1993). *Assessing experience in psychotherapy: Personal construct alternatives.* Westport, CT: Praeger.

Fransella, F. (Ed.). (2003). *International handbook of personal construct psychology.* Chichester, UK: Wiley.

Fromm, M. (2004). *Introduction to the Repertory Grid Interview* (rev. ed.). New York: Waxman Münster.

Gergen, K. J. (1985). The social constructionist movement in modern psychology. *American Psychologist, 40,* 266–275.

Gergen, K. J. (1989). Warranting voice and the elaboration of the self. In J. Shotter & K. J. Gergen (Eds.), *Texts of identity* (pp. 70–81). London: Sage.

Gergen, K. J. (1991). *The saturated self: Dilemmas of identity in contemporary life.* New York: Basic Books.

Gergen, K. J. (1994). *Realities and relationships.* Cambridge, MA: Harvard University Press.

Gergen, K. J. (1995). Social construction and the education process. In L. P. Steffe & J. Gale (Eds.), *Constructivism in education* (pp. 17–39). Hillsdale, NJ: Erlbaum.

Gergen, K. J., & McNamee, S. (2000). From disordering discourse to transformative dialogue. In R. A. Neimeyer & J. D. Raskin (Eds.), *Constructions of disorder: Meaning-making frameworks for psychotherapy* (pp. 333–349). Washington, DC: American Psychological Association.

Gergen, M., & Gergen, K. J. (2001). Focal commentary: The new aging. *The Positive Aging Newsletter.* Retrieved March 18, 2005, from http://www.taosinstitute.net/resources/pa1.html

Hayes, R. L., & Oppenheim, R. (1997). Constructivism: Reality is what you make it. In T. L. Sexton & B. L. Griffin (Eds.), *Constructivist thinking in counseling practice* (pp. 19–40). New York: Teachers College Press.

Held, B. S. (1995). *Back to reality: A critique of postmodern theory in psychotherapy.* New York: Norton.

Holland, R. (1970). George Kelly: Constructive innocent and reluctant existentialist. In D. Bannister (Ed.), *Perspectives in personal construct theory* (pp. 111–132). London: Academic Press.

Honos-Webb, L., & Leitner, L. M. (2001). How using the DSM causes damage: A client's report. *Journal of Humanistic Psychology, 41*(4), 36–56.

Jankowicz, D. (2003). *The easy guide to repertory grids.* Chichester, UK: Wiley.

Johnson, T. J., Pfenninger, D. T., & Klion, R. E. (2000). Constructing and deconstructing transitive diagnosis. In R. A. Neimeyer & J. D. Raskin (Eds.), *Constructions of disorder: Meaning-making frameworks for psychotherapy* (pp. 145–174). Washington, DC: American Psychological Association.

Kelly, G. A. (1969). Ontological acceleration. In B. Maher (Ed.), *Clinical psychology and personality: The selected papers of George Kelly* (pp. 7–45). New York: Wiley.

Kelly, G. A. (1970). A brief introduction to personal construct psychology. In D. Bannister (Ed.), *Perspectives in personal construct psychology* (pp. 1–30). San Diego, CA: Academic Press.

Kelly, G. A. (1991a). *The psychology of personal constructs: Vol. 1. A theory of personality.* London: Routledge. (Original work published 1955)

Kelly, G. A. (1991b). *The psychology of personal constructs: Vol. 2. Clinical diagnosis and psychotherapy.* London: Routledge. (Original work published 1955)

Kenny, V., & Gardner, G. (1988). Constructions of self-organizing systems. *The Irish Journal of Psychology, 9,* 1–24.

Kenyon, G. M., Clark, P. G., & de Vries, B. (Eds.). (2001). *Narrative gerontology: Theory, research, and practice.* New York: Springer.

Leitner, L. M., & Faidley, A. F. (1995). The awful, aweful nature of role relationships. In R. A. Neimeyer & G. J. Neimeyer (Eds.), *Advances in personal construct theory* (Vol. 3, pp. 291–314). Greenwich, CT: JAI Press.

Lyddon, W. J. (1995). Forms and facets of constructivist psychology. In R. A. Neimeyer & M. J. Mahoney (Eds.), *Constructivism in psychotherapy* (pp. 69–92). Washington, DC: American Psychological Association.

Mackay, N. (2003a). On "just not getting it": A reply to McNamee and to Raskin and Neimeyer. *Theory and Psychology, 13,* 411–419.

Mackay, N. (2003b). Psychotherapy and the idea of meaning. *Theory and Psychology, 13,* 359–386.

Mahoney, M. J. (1988). Constructive metatheory: I. Basic features and historical foundations. *International Journal of Personal Construct Psychology, 1,* 1–35.

Mahoney, M. J. (1991). *Human change processes.* New York: Basic Books.

Mahoney, M. J. (2003). *Constructive psychotherapy.* New York: Guilford Press.

Mancuso, J. C. (2000). Claiming Giambattista Vico as a narrativist/constructivist. *Karl Jaspers Forum,* Target Article 33. Retrieved July 28, 2004, from http://www.douglashospital.qc.ca/fdg/kjf/33-TAMAN.htm

Mascolo, M. F., Pollack, R. D., & Fischer, K. W. (1997). Keeping the constructor in development: An epigenetic systems approach. *Journal of Constructivist Psychology, 10,* 25–49.

Matthews, W. J. (1998). Let's get real: The fallacy of postmodernism. *Journal of Theoretical and Philosophical Psychology, 18,* 16–32.

Maturana, H. R. (1988). Reality: The search for objectivity or the quest for a compelling argument. *The Irish Journal of Psychology, 9,* 25–82.

Maturana, H. R., & Varela, F. J. (1992). *The tree of knowledge: The biological roots of human understanding* (Rev. ed.; R. Paolucci, Trans.). Boston: Shambhala.

McCarty, L. P., & Schwandt, T. A. (2000). Seductive illusions: Von Glasersfeld and Gergen on epistemology and education. In D. C. Phillips (Ed.), *Constructivism in education: Opinions and second opinions on controversial issues* (pp. 41–85). Chicago: National Society for the Study of Education.

McNamee, S. (1996). Psychotherapy as social construction. In H. Rosen & K. T. Kuehlwein (Eds.), *Constructing reality: Meaning-making perspectives for psychotherapists* (pp. 115–137). San Francisco: Jossey-Bass.

McNamee, S. (2003). Bridging incommensurate discourses: A response to Mackay. *Theory and Psychology, 13,* 387–396.

McNamee, S. (2004). Relational bridges between constructionism and constructivism. In J. D. Raskin & S. K. Bridges (Eds.), *Studies in meaning 2: Bridging the personal and social in constructivist psychology* (pp. 37–50). New York: Pace University Press.

McNamee, S., & Gergen, K. J. (Eds.). (1992). *Therapy as social construction.* London: Sage.

Neimeyer, G. J. (1992). Personal constructs in career counseling and development. *Journal of Career Development, 18,* 163–173.

Neimeyer, R. A. (1997). Problems and prospects in constructivist psychotherapy. *Journal of Constructivist Psychology, 10,* 51–74.

Neimeyer, R. A., & Bridges, S. K. (2003). Postmodern approaches to psychotherapy. In A. S. Gurman & S. B. Messer (Eds.), *Essential psychotherapies: Theory and practice* (2nd ed., pp. 272–316). New York: Guilford Press.

Neimeyer, R. A., & Mahoney, M. J. (Eds.). (1995). *Constructivism in psychotherapy.* Washington, DC: American Psychological Association.

Neimeyer, R. A., & Raskin, J. D. (Eds.). (2000a). *Constructions of disorder: Meaning-making frameworks for psychotherapy.* Washington, DC: American Psychological Association.

Neimeyer, R. A., & Raskin, J. D. (2000b). On practicing postmodern therapy in modern times. In R. A. Neimeyer & J. D. Raskin (Eds.), *Constructions of disorder: Meaning-making frameworks for psychotherapy* (pp. 1–14). Washington, DC: American Psychological Association.

Noaparast, K. B. (1995). Toward a more realistic constructivism. In R. A. Neimeyer & G. J. Neimeyer (Eds.), *Advances in personal construct theory* (Vol. 3, pp. 37–59). Greenwich, CT: JAI Press.

Paris, M. E., & Epting, F. R. (2004). Social and personal construction: Two sides of the same coin. In J. D. Raskin & S. K. Bridges (Eds.), *Studies in meaning 2: Bridging the personal and social in constructivist psychology* (pp. 3–35). New York: Pace University Press.

Parker, I. (1999). Against relativism in psychology, on balance. *History of the Human Sciences, 12,* 61–78.

Peavy, R. V. (1996). Constructivist career counselling and assessment. *Guidance and Counseling, 11,* 8–14.

Phillips, D. C. (Ed.). (2000). *Ninety-ninth yearbook of the National Society for the Study of Education: Part 1. Constructivism in education: Opinions and second opinions on controversial issues.* Chicago: National Society for the Study of Education.

Raskin, J. D. (2001). On relativism in constructivist psychology. *Journal of Constructivist Psychology, 14,* 285–313.

Raskin, J. D. (2002). Constructivism in psychology: Personal construct psychology, radical constructivism, and social constructionism. In J. D. Raskin & S. K. Bridges (Eds.), *Studies in meaning: Exploring constructivist psychology* (pp. 1–25). New York: Pace University Press.

Raskin, J. D., & Bridges, S. K. (Eds.). (2002). *Studies in meaning: Exploring constructivist psychology.* New York: Pace University Press.

Raskin, J. D., & Bridges, S. K. (Eds.). (2004). *Studies in meaning 2: Bridging the personal and social in constructivist psychology.* New York: Pace University Press.

Raskin, J. D., & Epting, F. R. (1993). Personal construct theory and the argument against mental illness. *International Journal of Personal Construct Psychology, 6,* 351–369.

Raskin, J. D., & Lewandowski, A. M. (2000). The construction of disorder as human enterprise. In R. A. Neimeyer & J. D. Raskin (Eds.), *Constructions of disorder: Meaning-making frameworks for psychotherapy* (pp. 15–40). Washington, DC: American Psychological Association.

Raskin, J. D., & Neimeyer, R. A. (2003). Coherent constructivism: A response to Mackay. *Theory and Psychology, 13,* 397–409.

Rosen, H. (1996). Meaning-making narratives: Foundations for constructivist and social constructionist psychotherapies. In H. Rosen & K. T. Kuehlwein (Eds.), *Constructing realities: Meaning-making perspectives for psychotherapists* (pp. 3–51). San Francisco: Jossey-Bass.

Sexton, T. L. (1997). Constructivist thinking within the history of ideas: The challenge of a new paradigm. In T. L. Sexton & B. L. Griffin (Eds.), *Constructivist thinking in counseling practice, research, and training* (pp. 3–18). New York: Teachers College Press.

Shapiro, B. L. (1994). *What children bring to light: A constructivist perspective on children's learning in science.* New York: Teachers College Press.

Shotter, J. (1993). *Cultural politics of everyday life: Social constructionism, rhetoric and knowing of the third kind.* Toronto, Ontario: University of Toronto Press.

Simon, R. (1985, May/June). A frog's eye view of the world. *Family Therapy Networker, 9*(3), 33–43.

Stevens, C. D. (1998). Realism and Kelly's pragmatic constructivism. *Journal of Constructivist Psychology, 11,* 283–308.

Tobin, K. (Ed.). (1993). *The practice of constructivism in science education.* Washington, DC: AAAS Press.

Viney, L. L. (1996). *Personal construct therapy: A handbook.* Norwood, NJ: Ablex.

von Glaserfeld, E. (1984). An introduction to radical constructivism. In P. Watzlawick (Ed.), *The invented reality: How do we know what we believe we know? Contributions to constructivism* (pp. 17–40). New York: Norton.

von Glaserfeld, E. (1995a). A constructivist approach to teaching. In L. P. Steffe & J. Gale (Eds.), *Constructivism in education* (pp. 3–15). Hillsdale, NJ: Erlbaum.

von Glaserfeld, E. (1995b). *Radical constructivism: A way of knowing and learning.* London: Falmer Press.

Wampold, B. E. (2001). *The great psychotherapy debate: Models, methods, and findings.* Mahwah, NJ: Erlbaum.

Warren, B. (1998). *Philosophical dimensions of personal construct psychology.* London: Routledge.

Watkins, M. (2000). Ways of learning about leisure meanings. *Leisure Studies, 22,* 93–107.

Watts, R. E., & Phillips, K. A. (2004). Adlerian psychology and psychotherapy: A relational constructivist approach. In J. D. Raskin & S. K. Bridges (Eds.), *Studies in meaning 2: Bridging the personal and social in constructivist psychology* (pp. 267–289). New York: Pace University Press.

Weihs, K. D. (2004). A conversation with personal construct psychology [Review of the book *Philosophical dimensions of personal construct psychology*]. *Journal of Constructivist Psychology, 17,* 69–75.

White, M., & Epston, D. (1990). *Narrative means to therapeutic ends.* New York: Norton.

Winter, D. A. (1992). *Personal construct psychology in clinical practice: Theory, research and applications.* London: Routledge.

PART THREE

MID-RANGE THEORIES

CHAPTER 12

Role Motivation Theories

JOHN B. MINER

INTRODUCTION

My thought in introducing the subject of role motivation theory is to provide certain data derived from the theory, and thus emblematic of the type of ideas it can generate. These data are given in Table 12.1 and Table 12.2; they deal with findings from four studies, two of which utilize entrepreneurs as subjects and two involving managers. The former are longitudinal in nature and draw upon follow-up analyses to establish criterion relationships; the latter are concurrent.

These are all the data I know of that compare the Miner Sentence Completion Scales (MSCSs) with various self-report measures using similar constructs. The MSCSs represent the preferred procedure for measuring the constructs of role motivation theory and thus are projective in nature. Projective techniques such as the MSCSs unearth both conscious and unconscious motives, but with a heavy emphasis on the latter; self-report measures deal entirely with the conscious level. Projective techniques accomplish their measurement processes by eliciting typical samples of cognitive, emotional, and perceptual content in response to ambiguous, or as in the case of the MSCSs more content-focused, stimuli that are then analyzed to determine meanings and motives. In contrast, self-report indexes insert meanings and motives into multiple-choice alternatives so that responses are predetermined and channeled into what the investigator is looking for. In the first instance the really difficult work begins after a response occurs, whereas in the latter instance it occurs in the item-development phase. Errors in projective measurement tend to occur because of failures in interpretation; errors in self-report measurement are usually attributable to inappropriate item specification.

Projective techniques are said to measure implicit motives and self-report approaches self-attributed motives. According to this distinction the two types of motives are quite different in origin and yield substantial cross-method disparities. Meyer (1996) provides the following definitions and theoretical elaborations:

Implicit motivations are viewed as being more unconscious and physiologically related, as developing earlier in life and not requiring language and verbal mediation to solidify, and as being more strongly associated with long-term spontaneous behavioral trends. In contrast, self-attributed motives are understood as having different historical antecedents and as being better predictors of conscious choices and immediate, situationally defined behaviors. . . . Cross-method disagreement is thus not a question of test invalidity. Rather it is a phenomenon that can lead to a more refined identification of people and more accurate behavioral predictions. (Meyer, 1996, p. 575)

The cross-method disagreement has been hypothesized to result in a correlation between projective and self-report measures of essentially .00, and early data supported that conclusion (McClelland, Koestner, & Weinberger, 1989). However, more recent and comprehensive findings suggest a small positive relationship (Spangler, 1992). Other results that focused more specifically on the MSCSs yield this same positive conclusion (Miner & Raju, 2004), and indeed that is what the data of Tables 12.1 and 12.2 indicate, with median intercorrelations of .11 and .12, respectively.

Thus, one thing that can be learned from these tables is that correlations between projective and self-report measures are indeed low as expected and accordingly that it matters which type of measure is used to validate role motivation theory. The theoretical approach of choice involves some type of projective index because the theory posits that unconscious (implicit) motives are crucial.

In both Tables 12.1 and 12.2 criterion relationships are given for both projective techniques and self-report measures, and in both instances the median value is higher for projectives and the number of significant findings is higher as well. Yet what is really meaningful here is the comparison of the Table 12.1 data with those of Table 12.2: the comparison under theoretically congruent conditions with theoretically noncongruent conditions. In the former instance the projective technique correlations average .35 with 85 percent significant at $p < .05$ or better and values as high as .59 with

TABLE 12.1   Correlations between Projective Techniques and Self-Report Measures and Criteria (Plus Intercorrelations) Involving Similar and Overlapping Constructs for Theoretically Congruent Situations

Measures	Criterion correlations — Follow-up success as entrepreneur	Intercorrelations (a)	Intercorrelations (b)	Summaries — Median correlation	Summaries — No. with $p<.05$
Study 1: Buffalo, NY area entrepreneurs (N = 100) (Miner, 1997)	Achievement motivation				
Projective techniques					
MSCS—Form T					
(a) Total score	.42**			.30	2 (100%)
(b) Self-achievement subscale	.18*				
Self-report measures					
(c) Lynn Achievement Motivation Questionnaire	.14	.17	.19	.10	0 (0%)
(d) Elizur Achievement Motivation Index	.09	.14	−.04		
(e) Ghiselli SDI—Need for Occupational Achievement	.10	.08	−.03	.11 for intercorrelations	
Desire to innovate					
Projective techniques					
MSCS—Form T					
(a) Total score	.42**			.43	2 (100%)
(b) Personal innovation subscale	.44**				
Self-report measures					
(c) Rowe/Mason DSI—Conceptual	−.01	.17	.21*	.13	1 (33%)
(d) Slocum/Hellriegel PSQ—Intuition	.13	.14	.36**	.18 for intercorrelations	
(e) Ghiselli SDI—Initiative	.22*	.19	.15		
Desire to avoid risks					
Projective techniques					
MSCS—Form T					
(a) Total score	.42**			.43	2 (100%)
(b) Avoiding risks subscale	.44**				
Self-report measures					
(c) Shure/Meeker Risk Avoidance Scale	−.10	.01	.07	−.10	0 (0%)
				.04 for intercorrelations	

Measures	Criterion correlations — Entrepreneurial propensity score	Criterion correlations — Business plan grade	Criterion correlations — Follow-up behavior as entrepreneur	Intercorrelations (a)	Intercorrelations (b)	Summaries — Median correlation	Summaries — No. with $p<.05$
Study 2: SUNY/Buffalo graduate students in entrepreneurship (N = 159) (Miner, 1997)	Achievement motivation						
Projective techniques							
MSCS—Form T							
(a) Total score	.59**	.38**	.41**			.395	5 (83%)
(b) Self-achievement subscale	.45**	.11	.27*				
Self-report measures (None available)							
Desire to innovate							
Projective techniques							
MSCS—Form T							
(a) Total score	.59**	.38**	.41**			.395	6 (100%)
(b) Personal innovation subscale	.44**	.24**	.33**				
Self-report measures							
(c) Rowe/Mason DSI—Conceptual	.14	.13	.12	.07	.12	.125	1 (17%)
(d) Slocum/Hellriegel PSQ—Intuition	.01	.08	.23*	−.02	.12	.095 for intercorrelations	

(continued)

TABLE 12.1   *(Continued)*

		Criterion correlations			Intercorrelations		Summaries	
	Measures	Entrepreneurial propensity score	Business plan grade	Follow-up behavior as entrepreneur	(a)	(b)	Median correlation	No. with $p<.05$
	Desire to avoid risks Projective techniques MSCS—Form T							
	(a) Total score	.59**	.38**	.41**			.26	3 (50%)
	(b) Avoiding risks subscale	.05	.14	−.04				
	Self-report measures (c) Shure/Meeker Risk Avoidance Scale	−.21**	−.05	−.17	−.01	.30**	−.17 .145 for intercorrelations	1 (33%)

		Criterion correlations		Intercorrelations		Summaries	
		Management appraisals				Median correlation	No. with $p<.05$
	Measures	Performance	Potential	(a)	(b)		
Study 3: Business managers from a single firm (N = 420) (Miner, 1965)	Power motivation Projective techniques MSCS—Form H						
	(a) Total score	.24*	.43**			.265	4 (100%)
	(b) Imposing wishes subscale	.29**	.24*				
	Self-report measures (c) Kuder Preference Record-Vocational-Supervisory Scale	.14**	.24**	.45**	.32**	.19 .385 for intercorrelations	2 (100%)

		Composite success score	Intercorrelations		Summaries	
			(a)	(b)	Median correlation	No. with $p<.05$
Study 4: Human Resource Managers from varied firms (N = 101) (Miner, 1977)	Power motivation Projective techniques MSCS—Form H					
	(a) Total score	.28**			.195	1 (50%)
	(b) Imposing wishes subscale	.11				
	Self-report measures (c) Ghiselli SDI—Supervisory ability	.18*	.26**	NS	.08	1 (33%)
	(d) Ghiselli SDI—Need for power	.08	NS	NS	.11 (est.) for intercorrelations	
	(e) Kuder Preference Record-Vocational-Supervisory Scale	.08	.38**	.12		

Summary of summaries		
Projective techniques	.35	85%
Self-report measures	.10	31%
Intercorrelations	.11	

Note. MSCS = Miner Sentence Completion Scale.
The Composite Success Score criterion reflects the position level attained in the hierarchy ($r = .80$) and the income from that position ($r = .71$).
The three criteria are all significantly related (at $p < .05$) in the range .22 to .54.
Lynn Achievement Motivation Questionnaire (Lynn, 1969); Elizur Achievement Motivation Index (Elizur, 1984); Ghiselli SDI = Self Description Index (Ghiselli, 1971); Rowe/Mason DSI = Decision Style Inventory (Rowe & Mason, 1987); Slocum/Hellriegel PSQ = Problem Solving Questionnaire (Slocum & Hellriegel, 1983); Shure/Meeker Risk Avoidance Scale (Shure & Meeker, 1967); Kuder Preference Record-Vocational-Supervisory Scale (Miner, 1977).
*$p < .05$.
**$p < .01$.

TABLE 12.2   Correlations between Projective Techniques and Self-Report Measures and Criteria (Plus Intercorrelations) Involving Similar and Overlapping Constructs for Theoretically Noncongruent Situations

	Measures	Criterion correlations: Follow-up success as entrepreneur	Intercorrelations (a)	Intercorrelations (b)	Summaries: Median correlation	Summaries: No. with $p<.05$
Study 1	Power motivation					
	Projective techniques					
	MSCS—Form H					
	(a) Total score	.21*			.19	1 (50%)
	(b) Imposing wishes subscale	.17				
	Self-report measures					
	(c) Rowe/Mason DSI—Directive	.16	.18	.25*	.085	1 (25%)
	(d) Slocum/Hellriegel PSQ—Thinking	−.08	.16	.24*	.15 for intercorrelations	
	Ghiselli SDI—					
	(e) Supervisory ability	.01	.03	−.06		
	(f) Need for power	.22*	.14	.05		
	Affiliation motivation					
	Projective techniques					
	MSCS—Form P					
	(a) Total score	.24*			.155	1 (50%)
	(b) Providing help subscale	.07				
	Self-report measures					
	(c) Rowe/Mason DSI—Behavioral	−.09	.20*	.15	.085	0 (0%)
	(d) Slocum/Hellriegel PSQ—Feeling	.08	.08	.24*	.17 for intercorrelations	
	(e) Fiedler's LPC Score	.09	−.09	.19		
	(f) Elizur Work Values Questionnaire— Social Values Items	.10	.30**	.02		

	Measures	Criterion correlations: Entrepreneurial propensity score	Criterion correlations: Business plan grade	Criterion correlations: Follow-up behavior as entrepreneur	Intercorrelations (a)	Intercorrelations (b)	Summaries: Median correlation	Summaries: No. with $p<.05$
Study 2	Power motivation							
	Projective techniques							
	MSCS—Form H							
	(a) Total score	.11	.14	.12			.115	1 (17%)
	(b) Imposing wishes subscale	.17*	−.06	−.01				
	Self-report measures							
	(c) Rowe/Mason DSI— Directive	.07	−.07	−.07	.05	−.07	−.07	1 (17%)
	(d) Slocum/Hellriegel PSQ—Thinking	.09	−.21*	−.13	.15	.17*	.10 for intercorrelations	
	Affiliation motivation							
	Projective techniques							
	MSCS—Form P							
	(a) Total score	.08	.02	.42**			.11	2 (33%)
	(b) Providing help subscale	.14	.06	.31*				
	Self-report measures							
	(c) Rowe/Mason DSI— Behavioral	−.21*	−.01	−.10	−.06	.02	−.05	2 (33%)
	(d) Slocum/Hellriegel PSQ—Feeling	−.09	.21*	.13	.06	.29**	.04 for intercorrelations	

Summary of summaries	Median correlation	No. with $p<.05$
Projective techniques	.135	37%
Self-report measures	.02	19%
Intercorrelations	.12	

Note. Fiedler's LPC Score = Least Preferred Coworker Score (Fiedler, 1967); Elizur Work Values Questionnaire (Elizur, 1984).
*$p < .05$.
**$p < .01$.

numerous findings in the .40s. In the situation where role motivation theory does not anticipate many sizable criteria relationships, these correlations are much lower and much less frequently significant as well; they top out in the low .20s. Thus, it is not only the difference between projective and self-report measurement, unconscious versus conscious, that matters but the difference between research situations where a theoretical fit, or congruence, exists between the individual's predominant motives and the work context. What this theoretical fit means requires considerable elaboration, and this is the subject to which I now turn.

EARLY DEVELOPMENTS

Role motivation theory has been a continually evolving project since the first article was published (Miner, 1960a). Actually, its more remote origin was a book presenting the various strategic factors that seemed to cause World War II soldiers to be discharged prematurely. This book drew upon government records and follow-up data to construct a schema, illustrated with case histories, that set forth the influences contributing to failure. Among these were factors such as personality, family, the immediate group, military organization, conflicting values, and situational stress (Ginzberg, Miner, Anderson, Ginsburg, & Herma, 1959).

Role Motivation Training

This schema, derived from the military materials, was subsequently expanded and extrapolated into the company context to produce a management-development program aimed at arousing managerial motivation among members of a company research and development department. This course, taught by the author, had as its objective that the managers who were exposed to it would be induced to think of themselves as managers primarily and scientists only secondarily. The training served to present a role model as manager and to provide a way to behave in accordance with that model by teaching the managers how to diagnose the causes of subordinate performance problems and appropriate treatments to apply to specific types of causes.

The underlying rationale comes from psychoanalytic theory, and the idea was to aid in the development of a type of ego ideal. Assuming that some of the managers were responding to managerial tasks with avoidance behavior occasioned by anxiety produced in their jobs, the schema for dealing with ineffective performance was presented first as a way of managing subordinates and then as an approach to understanding their own performance failures. Specifically,

phobic reactions to the managerial situation were addressed. Thus course participants were given something very similar to psychoanalytic interpretations of their unconscious motives in the hope that this might help them handle the anxiety aroused in the managerial role.

Evaluations comparing those who took the course with a control group who did not indicated that the training produced a substantial increase in managerial motivation (see Miner, 1960a, 1965). This course came to be known as managerial role motivation training.

Framework of the Training

Over numerous presentations the original course expanded considerably. The schema of strategic factors presented came to take the following form, and company cases were developed to illustrate the operation of these factors:

Intelligence and job-knowledge problems
    Insufficient verbal ability
    Insufficient special ability
    Insufficient job knowledge
    Defect of judgment or memory
Emotional problems
    Frequent disruptive emotion: anxiety, depression, anger, excitement, shame, guilt, jealousy
    Neurosis: with anxiety, depression, anger predominating
    Psychosis: with anxiety, depression, anger predominating
    Alcohol and drug problems
Motivational problems
    Strong motives frustrated at work: pleasure in success, fear of failure, avoidance motives, dominance, desire to be popular, social motivation, need for attention
    Unintegrated means used to satisfy strong motives
    Low personal work standards
    Generalized low work motivation
Physical problems
    Physical illness or handicap, including brain disorders
    Physical disorders of emotional origin
    Inappropriate physical characteristics
    Insufficient muscular or sensory ability or skill
Family-related problems
    Family crises: divorce, death, severe illness
    Separation from the family and isolation

Predominance of family considerations over job demands

Work-group problems

    Negative consequences of group cohesion

    Ineffective management

    Inappropriate managerial standards or criteria

Organizational problems

    Insufficient organizational action

    Placement error

    Organizational overpermissiveness

    Excessive spans of control

    Inappropriate organizational standards and criteria

Society-related problems

    Applications of legal sanctions

    Other enforcement of societal values, including the use of inappropriate value-based criteria

    Conflict between job demands and cultural values: equity, freedom, moral and religious values

Problems related to the work situation

    Negative consequences of economic forces

    Negative consequences of geographic location

    Detrimental conditions in the work setting

    Excessive danger

    Problems inherent in the work itself (Miner, 1985)

This framework is to be used in diagnosing the causes of ineffective performance in accordance with a stepwise process of control:

Step 1—Establish role requirements through some type of organizational, group, or individual process.

Step 2—Establish standards of acceptable behavior relative to these requirements.

Step 3—Measure performance against these standards.

Step 4a—If no unacceptable deviations from standards are noted, take no action.

Step 4b—If unacceptable deviations from standards are noted, diagnose the causal factors contributing to these unacceptable deviations and take appropriate corrective action (Miner, 1988).

These steps are applied to self-diagnosis and corrective action in the context of problems related to the work situation and specifically under problems inherent in the work itself; thus they are at the end of the schema presentation.

Development of the Training Evaluation Instrument

The training evaluation requirement presented a need to obtain some instrument that could be used to measure motivation to manage. Because the literature appeared to contain nothing that could be used for this purpose, initial efforts were devoted to adapting the Kuder Preference Record to fulfill the need. This turned out to be fruitful, but the validities, though significant, were too low to warrant continuing along this path (Miner, 1960b). Falling back on my early training, I created a sentence completion instrument intended initially to measure the characteristics of good managers as defined by the management appraisals conducted within the company and based on my own observations of managers considered to be the better performers; thus the theory underlying the measure was of a grounded nature (Locke, 2001) and restricted to this one company. This was the theory behind what became the MSCS-Form H as presented in the introduction.

That instrument and its theory were developed by writing a host of possible stems then selecting the actual items to use after comparing the responses of a sample of good company managers with a group of not-so-good managers. Accordingly, theory development was an after-the-fact, inductive process based on a reading of the particular items that survived this kind of item analysis. The components of the theory were abstracted from a conceptual grouping of these items, in much the same way that the factors that emerge from factor analysis are labeled.

The rationale behind these conceptual factors was that managers were evaluated in relation to informal role prescriptions with which they either behaved congruently or noncongruently, and thus in the first instance they were judged to be effective or in the latter case were considered ineffective. This formulation regarding roles took a strictly psychological, as opposed to a sociological, tack in dealing with role behavior and thus factored in a sizable individual difference component (see Ashforth, 2001).

HIERARCHIC ROLE MOTIVATION THEORY

The hierarchic theory assumes a hierarchic organizational form and associated managerial role requirements. In line with these role prescriptions, certain motive patterns if held are expected to generate judgments of effective performance. These roles and their matching motives are as follows:

1. Positive relations with authority   →   Favorable attitude to superiors

2. Competing with peers   →   Desire to compete

3. Imposing wishes on → Desire to exercise power
   subordinates

4. Behaving assertively → Desire to assert oneself

5. Standing out from the → Desire to be distinct and
   group   different

6. Performing routine → Desire to perform routine
   administrative   duties responsibly (Miner,
   functions   1993)

To the extent responses to sentence completion stems follow the theory, a manager is expected to possess the motive pattern indicated. To the extent responses inconsistent with the theory are given, lack of motivation is assumed, extending to avoidance motivation; the latter may result from anxiety and guilt, with the result that motives are driven to the unconscious level. Yet negative emotion may persist should the attempted avoidance fail to achieve its goals.

Rationales

The rationales as to why the six motive patterns contribute to judgments of effective and ineffective performance as they do can be established with some certainty.

Favorable Attitudes Upward

In hierarchies, managers are typically expected to behave in ways that do not provoke negative reactions from their superiors; ideally they will elicit positive responses. Managers must be in a position to represent their groups upward in the organization and to obtain support for their actions at higher levels. This requires a good relationship between manager and superior. It follows that managers should have a generally positive attitude toward those holding positions of authority over them if they are to meet this particular role requirement. If managers do, in fact, like and respect their bosses, it will be much easier to work with the superiors in the numerous instances where cooperative endeavor is necessary. Any tendency to generalized hatred, distaste, or anxiety in dealing with people in positions of authority will make it extremely difficult to meet managerial job demands. Interactions with superiors either will be minimal or will be filled with so much negative feeling that the necessary positive reactions and support cannot possibly be attained.

Competitiveness Laterally

Insofar as peers are concerned, there is a strong competitive element built into managerial work. This is a function of the pyramidal nature of hierarchic organizations, with fewer and

fewer positions present as one ascends the managerial hierarchy. Managers must compete for scarce rewards both for themselves and for their groups; somebody wins and somebody loses. If managers do not compete, they may very well lose ground as they and their functions are relegated to lower and lower status levels. Without competitive behavior, promotion is unlikely. Thus, managers must characteristically strive to win for themselves and their groups and accept such challenges as managers at a comparable level may introduce. On occasion, challenges may come from below, particularly from among one's own subordinates. In order to meet the competitive role requirement, a person should be favorably disposed toward engaging in competition. Managers should ideally enjoy rivalry of this kind and be motivated to seek it whenever possible. If they are unwilling to fight for position, status, advancement, and their ideas, they are unlikely to succeed. It may well be that such a manager will be ignored so consistently that the whole unit disappears from the organization chart or is merged into or subordinated to some other unit. Any generalized tendency to associate unpleasant emotion, such as anxiety and depression, with performance in competitive situations almost surely will result in behavior that falls short of role demands.

Power Downward

Managers in a hierarchy interact downward as well as upward and horizontally. Here the need is to exercise power over subordinates and direct their behavior in a manner consistent with organizational objectives. Managers must tell others what to do when this becomes necessary and enforce their words with appropriate use of positive and negative sanctions. The individual who finds such behavior difficult and emotionally disturbing, who does not wish to impose upon others or believes it is wrong to utilize power, would not be expected to meet this particular role requirement. On the other hand a more favorable attitude toward this type of activity, perhaps even an enjoyment of exercising power, should contribute to successful performance as a manager. In the typical situation subordinates must be actively induced to perform in a manner conducive to attaining organizational goals, and the person placed in a position of authority over them ideally desires to behave in ways intended to achieve this objective.

Asserting Oneself

Up to the early 1970s this was referred to as the *masculine role*. The change in name was introduced because it became increasingly evident that many women possess this type of motivation at a high level, and thus a label that appeared to indicate a characteristic of males only was misleading. However, the conceptual foundation involved is the traditional male or father role as it existed in the United States during and prior to the 1950s. Although this masculinity-femininity aspect of motivation is less frequently noted in the literature of the 1960s and beyond, there are significant exceptions; see, for example, Ghiselli (1971) and Hofstede (1980). Clearly, changing gender-role patterns have had a significant impact over the years. Thus it is important to emphasize that the discussion of assertiveness here extends back to gender norms and expectations of an earlier period. This is the motive pattern, and role requirement, with which the theory is concerned. It appears to be less manifest today than in the past.

Taking, then, this pattern of a prior period, there appears to be considerable similarity between the requirements of the managerial role and the more general demands of the masculine, father role. Both sets of expectations emphasize taking charge, making decisions, taking disciplinary action when necessary, and protecting other members of the group (family). Thus, one of the more common role requirements of the managerial job is that the incumbent behave in this essentially masculine manner. In fact a major means of demonstrating masculinity has been to assume a position of managerial responsibility. When women are appointed to managerial positions, these same role expectations apply. Those individuals who prefer more characteristically feminine behavior patterns, irrespective of their sex, and those who become upset or disturbed at the prospect of behaving in this masculine manner would not be expected to possess the type of motivation that contributes to managerial success. The job appears to require an individual who obtains pleasure from performing as prescribed by this culturally defined male role and who is therefore highly motivated to act in accordance with this particular behavior model. The behavior involved may well give the appearance of being somewhat macho.

Distinctiveness

The managerial job requires a person to behave in ways differing in a number of respects from the behavior of others in the same face-to-face group. An incumbent must in this sense stand out from the group and assume a position of high visibility. Managers cannot use the actions of the people with whom they are most frequently associated, their subordinates, as guides for their behavior. Rather, they must deviate from the immediate group and do things that inevitably will invite attention, discussion, and perhaps criticism from those who report to them. The managerial role requires that an individ-

ual assume a position of considerable importance insofar as the motives and emotions of other people are concerned. When this prospect is viewed as unattractive, when the idea of standing out from the group, of behaving in a different manner, and of being highly visible elicits feelings of unpleasantness, then behavior appropriate to the role will occur much less often than would otherwise be the case. It is the person who enjoys being at the center of attention and who prefers to deviate to some degree from others in a group who is most likely to meet the demands of the managerial job in this area. Such a person will wish to gain visibility and will have many of the characteristics of a good actor. Certainly a manager is frequently on stage.

Conscientiousness

Here the basic concern is with communication and decision-making processes needed to get the work out and to keep on top of routine demands. The things that have to be done must actually be done. These functions range from constructing budget estimates to serving on committees, to talking on the telephone, to filling out employee rating forms and salary-change recommendations. There are administrative requirements of this kind in all managerial work, although the specific activities will vary somewhat from one situation to another. To meet these prescriptions, managers must at least be willing to face this type of routine, and ideally they will gain some satisfaction from it. If, on the other hand, such behavior is consistently viewed with apprehension or loathing, a person's chances of success in management would appear to be considerably less. A desire to put off or avoid the various more-or-less standard administrative duties of the managerial job can result in considerable deviation from role requirements.

Generalizing to Bureaucracies

With its origins in the workings of a single-company managerial role motivation theory in the early years had a somewhat fuzzy domain. With additional research in other organizations (Miner, 1965; 1977), it became increasingly evident that the real domain of the theory was Weber's bureaucracy (see Weber, 1968). Thus, it was defined to explain the successes and failures of managers working in bureaucratic organizations. When managers' motives were aligned with the informal role requirements specified and their success level was measured in terms of hierarchic criteria such as management appraisals, promotions, compensation, and the like, positive correlations should result. When congruency of this type was lacking, with nonmanagers or in organizations that were not of the bureaucratic form, the theory would not be expected to work very well at all.

LATER DEVELOPMENTS

The early period dealt only with the hierarchic theory and with Form H of the MSCS. Later, beginning in the 1970s, other organizational forms became part of the theoretical domain (Miner, 1977). The upshot of this expansion was the statement of a set of four hypotheses:

1. In hierarchic systems, managerial motivation should be at a high level in top management, and it should be positively correlated with other managerial success indexes; managerial motivation should not differentiate in these ways within other types of systems.
2. In professional systems, professional motivation should be at a high level among senior professionals, and it should be positively correlated with other professional success indexes; professional motivation should not differentiate in these ways within other types of systems.
3. In task systems, task (achievement) motivation should be at a high level among task performers (entrepreneurs, for example), and it should be positively correlated with task success indexes; task motivation should not differentiate in these ways within other types of systems.
4. In group systems, group motivation should be at a high level among emergent leaders, and it should be positively correlated with other group-determined success indexes; group motivation should not differentiate in these ways within other types of systems (Miner, 1982).

Professional Theory

The literature, especially that of a sociological nature, provided much more input to the professional theory (see hypothesis 2). Again, however, role requirements were specified and matching motives were established with the objective of indicating what is required for effective performance in professional roles within professional systems:

1. Acquiring knowledge   →   Desire to learn and acquire knowledge
2. Acting independently   →   Desire to exhibit independence
3. Accepting status   →   Desire to acquire status
4. Providing help   →   Desire to help others

5. Exhibiting professional commitment   →   Value-based identification with the profession (Miner, 1993)

These motive patterns are measured with the MSCS-Form P that operates in much the same manner as Form H, but with completely independent stems. The rationales as to why these 5 motive constellations contribute to judgments of different types regarding professional performance follow.

Knowledge Acquisition

In the professions the essence of the work is that technical expertise be developed, transmitted, and used in the service of clients, patients, students, or other users of professional services. Accordingly, to do professional work well a professional must want to learn what needs to be learned to provide an expert service. Those who do not want to acquire knowledge, or who find doing so distasteful for some reason, will fall short of others' performance expectations. Their work is likely to be lacking in the key ingredient of professional expertise.

Independence

Professionals have a personally responsible relationship with clients that often requires independent action based on their own best professional judgment. It is necessary to determine what the best interests of the client are and then act to serve those interests, even if the client wants something else. Similarly, pressures from other interested parties and in support of social norms must be subordinated to the professional's own independent judgment. Only in this way will professional expertise be brought to bear fully. Professionals who find it difficult to act independently, or are afraid to do so, run the risk that their special knowledge will not be used. Becoming dependent on others with lesser knowledge or for some reason not to use their knowledge in the interest of the client practically ensures that professional services will be provided at a level below capacity.

Status Acquisition

The provision of professional services to clients is predicated on client recognition of the professional's expert status. Professionals must take steps to achieve and retain status in the eyes of users and potential users of their services. Without this the services simply will go unused, no matter how effective they might have been. Consequently, professionals who are embarrassed at promoting themselves or find such activities distasteful are unlikely to have successful careers. Research and/or publication are one means to status acquisition. In the professions it is common practice to seek status among professional colleagues initially; this in turn is subsequently transmitted to the client population.

Helping

The professional-client relationship is central to any professional practice. In that relationship the professional is expected to assist the client in achieving desired goals or in some instances what from a professional perspective is in the client's best interest, even if not consciously desired. As a consequence, a professional must want to help others. In certain professions this role requirement is recognized by the designation *helping profession.* However, helping in some form is inherent in all professions.

Those who are unmotivated to help others lack something as professionals. Although this type of motivation is usually interpreted in terms of a desire to serve others, it may just as often reflect a desire to serve oneself. This latter process is inherent in the concept of helping power (McClelland, 1975), whereby an individual satisfies certain types of power motives by assuming a role where clients are dependent on him or her for assistance.

Professional Identification

Professional careers are intended to be of a lifelong nature. There is a substantial investment in training, and this is expedient only if the individual is to utilize this training over many years. Thus, there must be a strong emotional tie to the profession that keeps members in it. This is achieved through value-based identification. This professional commitment also serves to keep members responsive to the profession's ethical norms. Without such an identification, individuals may leave the profession in search of greater opportunities prior to the time the training investment is recovered, and they may also act in unprofessional ways, perhaps to the point of being expelled from the profession. Professional identification or commitment is a crucial ingredient in the profession's survival (Blau, Tatum, & Ward-Cook, 2003).

Task Theory

Task-role motivation theory takes its cue from McClelland's (1961) achievement motivation formulations. However, it places greater emphasis on the concept of role than McClelland did, and it deals with five distinct motive patterns derived from the McClelland achievement situation rather than his

single achievement need. Role prescriptions were matched with motive patterns to predict effective performance as measured by entrepreneurial criteria (see hypothesis 3).

1. Achieving as an individual → Desire to achieve through one's own efforts
2. Avoiding risks → Desire to avoid risks
3. Seeking results of behavior → Desire for feedback on performance
4. Personally innovating → Desire to introduce innovative solutions
5. Planning and setting goals → Desire to plan and establish goals (Miner, 1993)

Form T of the MSCS is the measure used to identify the motive patterns, again with a new set of stems. In essence this is a sentence completion index of achievement motivation. Rationales for the operation of the five motivational measures follow.

Self-Achievement

The key consideration here is being able to attribute success, or failure, to personal causation, the concept of individual responsibility. Entrepreneurs must be pulled into the task situation continually so that they do not simply avoid pressures and anxieties involved by escaping from the work context. The major source of this pull is an intrinsic desire to achieve through one's own efforts and ability and to experience the enhanced self-esteem that such achievement permits—to be able to say "I did it myself." Good team members who are highly cooperative and prefer to share the credit for accomplishments tend to lack this intense desire to achieve through one's own efforts and accordingly lack the drive that makes a task system dynamic and growing.

Risk Avoidance

McClelland emphasized a moderate degree of risk taking, whereas task theory stresses risk avoidance. Raynor (1974), however, endorsed the task theory explanation, as did Atkinson (1977) subsequently. Risk taking may result in an entrepreneur being forced out of the entrepreneurial situation because of business failure. To avoid this, and to continue to experience a sense of self-achievement, the entrepreneur attempts to minimize risk. There is ample evidence that a major reason for small-company failure is the adoption of a strategic stance that places the entire company at high risk, frequently in connection with some large-scale new venture that puts the company as currently constituted on the line (Richards,

1973). The argument that effective entrepreneurs must avoid risks does not mean that they do not take what others perceive as risks, however. Uncertainty exists in the eyes of the beholder; to be successful, entrepreneurs must avoid it to the degree possible, wherever they see it. Yet the ideal situation for an entrepreneur is one where others perceive that a high degree of risk exists, and thus high rewards are warranted, and the entrepreneur with his or her knowledge sees practically no risk at all.

Feedback

Entrepreneurs desire some clear index of the level of their performance. They do not enjoy being unsure whether they have performed well or not. Feedback on the level and results of one's performance is necessary in order to attribute any degree of success (or failure) to one's efforts. It is crucial to know whether one has succeeded or failed, and feedback is the means to that end. An individual who is lacking in the desire for performance feedback is inevitably less concerned about achievement as well. An entrepreneur must be motivated to actively seek out results-oriented feedback in terms of measures such as profitability, productive output, wastage, course grades, and the like if a sense of self-achievement is to be attained.

Innovation

For entrepreneurs the pull of individual achievement operates only to the extent the individual can attribute personal causation. Original, or novel, or creative, or innovative approaches have a distinctive quality that makes it easier to identify them as one's own and thus to take personal credit for them. Those who wish to forego innovation give up this opportunity for attaining a sense of self-achievement. Thus a desire to introduce innovation is consistent with the concept of achieving through one's own efforts, and experiencing approval for doing so.

Planning and Goal Setting

Effective entrepreneurship requires a desire to think about the future and anticipate future possibilities. Entrepreneurs must be pulled by the prospect of anticipated future rewards (expectancies) and therefore must approach their work with a strong future orientation. There needs to be a desire to plan, to set goals that will signify personal achievement, and to plot paths to goal achievement. This implies a minimal expectation, or fear, of future failure. Without this type of future orientation, the gleam in the entrepreneur's eyes tends to dull

and the motivational incentive of striving for a future goal is lost. The entrepreneurial organization loses power.

I should note that a related effort that uses the MSCS measures and deals with entrepreneurship (Miner, 1997) is not in reality an instance of role motivation theory. The theory involved there establishes an entrepreneurial typology of personal achievers, real managers, expert idea generators, and empathic supersalespeople, thus expanding the domain of entrepreneurship, but does not rely upon the role motivation dynamic.

Group Theory

Group theory, although established as a theoretical entity, has not been operationalized with a sentence completion or any other type of measure; nor has it been tested. The theory derives from the literature on organization development and autonomous work groups and predicts in the same manner as the previously noted theories (see hypothesis 4). The roles and motive patterns are again quite different and would require a completely new instrument. The theory is applicable to group organizations such as legislative branches, town meetings, and independent work units.

1. Interacting with peers effectively → Desire to interact socially and affiliate with others
2. Gaining group acceptance → Desire for continuing belongingness in a group
3. Positive relations with peers → Favorable attitudes toward peers
4. Cooperating with peers → Desire to have cooperative/ collaborative relationships
5. Acting democratically → Desire to participate in democratic processes (Miner, 1993)

The rationales involved here follow.

Affiliation

Group members are required to spend considerable time interacting with others in order to make and obtain implementation of decisions. It thus becomes necessary that they enjoy affiliative relationships and the use of social skills to exert influence and minimize nonproductive conflict. In essence this is the need for affiliation that McClelland and Burnham (1976) discuss. In the more clinical terminology, group members need to be sociophilic; to the extent they are sociophobic, group interaction will be damaged.

Belongingness

Group members must maintain identification with the group both to facilitate participation in group processes and to make them responsive to group-administered sanctions, including the threat of expulsion. Accordingly, a desire not merely for social interaction but for acceptance and a sense of belongingness in the group is required. Without this, members simply may leave the group when things do not go their way, and they are less likely to support the group's decisions because rejection for not doing so is of little concern.

Favorable Attitudes Laterally

Just as in hierarchic systems, favorable attitudes upward are required to facilitate hierarchic communication; in group systems, favorable attitudes toward group members, or potential group members, are required to facilitate the essential communications with peers. These positive attitudes should take such forms as belief in others, trust, consideration, and mutual respect. Where favorable attitudes toward peers are lacking because of other reference groups, strong status consciousness, or whatever other reason, necessary communications may fail to occur.

Cooperation

Group systems require that members work together closely. Competition can disrupt communications and lead to withholding of needed information, even to group disintegration. As a result, group members must eschew competition in favor of cooperative, collaborative relations and must gain satisfaction from doing so. The case for collaboration in organizations, and against competition, has been argued strongly by Kraus (1980). The key consideration is what type of organization one is dealing with: hierarchic or group.

Democratic Process

In group systems the primary method of getting things done is some variant of the power-equalized, democratic process, including open expression of ideas and views and the use of democratic procedures such as the vote to reach decisions. For these processes to function effectively, members must be favorably disposed toward them and desire to contribute to their effective operation. Strong authoritarian views, impatience with lengthy debate, and the like may operate to thwart the democratic process in groups.

On Motive Patterns

Five, or in one case six, patterns represent the motive patterns for each theory. Presumably there are more such patterns in each instance. Those patterns noted are intended to represent the more important ones within each theoretical domain, however. In most multiple-predictor research, adding variables beyond five or six has not increased the explained variance in the criterion to any meaningful degree. Thus, there seems little reason to extend the theories beyond their present scopes, assuming of course that the motive patterns noted do in fact account for substantial criterion variance.

Because of the way they are derived, the motive patterns of role motivation theory cannot be assumed to represent unitary needs or values. The role motivation theories are not need theories in the sense of Maslow's (1954) need hierarchy theory. The reason this is true is that the motive patterns derive from role requirements. Anything of a motivational nature that fits or matches the role requirement is included in the pattern. The result is that the motive patterns typically contain a constellation of motives; different people meet the same role requirement in different ways, and it may even be that the same person does so in different ways at different points in time.

Thus, the favorable attitudes to authority of the hierarchic theory may be part of a wider positive feeling toward all people, a manifestation of unresolved positive transference in the sense envisioned by psychoanalytic theory, a consequence of strong heterosexual or homosexual drives depending on the gender mix of superior and subordinate, and so on. Similarly, the desire to learn and acquire knowledge of the professional theory may be broad, extending to practically all knowledge, or narrowly specific to a particular professional specialty, or anything in between. The desire may stem from a pervasive curiosity, the symbolic significance of the particular knowledge constellation for the individual, a need to prove oneself strong by being omniscient, or some other motive. The key factor to be emphasized is that role requirements may be met in multiple ways, and for purposes of role motivation theory it does not matter exactly how. The relevant consideration for theory is the degree of role requirement–motive pattern match only.

A point related to motive patterns is that they, and the role requirements that determine them, may well not be conscious. For various reasons the types of motives discussed may be held out of consciousness. The motives operate and they serve to predict events, but the person cannot tell you much about them; not infrequently, the existence of the motives is completely denied. A manager, for instance, may possess the strong desire to exercise power posited by hierarchic role motivation theory while at the same time be concerned about being viewed as dictatorial. One way of dealing with the dilemma thus created is to continue to seek gratification of the power motive while making its presence entirely unconscious. When asked, such a person may very well deny any interest in exercising power over others and thus imposing his or her wishes on them.

On Organization Types

The role motivation theories deal not just with motives but with motives in the context of organizational forms. Thus they are mesotheories (House, Rousseau, & Thomas-Hunt, 1995). In view of the fact that these theories must predict person-organization fit or congruence (see Tinsley, 2000) if there is to be a match between role prescriptions and role behavior, a measure of the four organization types was clearly needed.

Consequently, Oliver (1982) has developed an instrument in the form of the Oliver Organization Description Questionnaire for this purpose. This questionnaire that measures the four organizational types—hierarchic, professional, task, and group—has been used in research (Wilderom & Miner, 1991) and has been shown to be effective in distinguishing the domains and contexts of the role motivation theories. A fifth type of organizational form, as yet unmeasured, has also been proposed with reference to the network form (Vicere, 2002). Whether this is distinct from the hierarchic form out of which it arises is an open question at this time (see DiMaggio, 2001). In any event we should recognize that the four types represent only a distillation of forms that predominate at the present time; other forms have existed in the past as Weber (1968) notes, and other forms are likely to exist in the future as the network development suggests.

On Leadership

Leadership came to the role motivation literature in Miner (2000) and was further developed in Miner (2002). The idea was that leaders in different organizational contexts are completely different kinds of people whose motivational patterns must mesh with the role requirements of their organization types if they are to prove effective. The hypothesis involved is as follows:

> Leadership roles take different forms in different organizational contexts and require different types of people to perform in these roles effectively—people whose motives are strongly congruent with the particular organizational type involved; thus leadership careers vary in important ways with the organizational forms in which they occur. (Miner, 2002, p. 318)

Leadership may be viewed as a gradually increasing type of career identification through which an individual assumes a set of institutionalized roles seen to be personally compatible. The leaders of hierarchic organizations are in reality those given the roles of top management, whereas managers below that level are best considered to be playing some kind of preleadership role. The leaders of professional organizations are of an intellectual elite nature, and their status may be bestowed either in a cosmopolitan or local context. The leaders of task systems, such as entrepreneurial leaders (Gupta, MacMillan, & Surie, 2004), are lead entrepreneurs (Ensley, Carland, & Carland, 2000) who are growth oriented. The leaders of group systems are emergent based on group norms and tend to be elected in some manner.

Leadership careers operate in the same way as other careers: leadership is first established, then leadership persistence occurs, and ultimately a full-blown career emerges (Foti & Miner, 2003). Congruent careers of any type can be expected to be predicted with higher correlation coefficients than other relevant criteria of role motivation theory. Theory considers the role requirements, against which leaders match their inherent motive patterns, as prototypes that are formed in organization-specific terms by the majority of observers (including the leaders themselves and their followers). These cognitive prototypes (Lord, 1985) are defined as being institutionalized, thus widely held to be legitimate, and also informal in nature. Institutionalization may be illustrated with the executive (hierarchic theory), legislative (group theory), and judicial (professional theory) branches of government; it is best defined in terms of Scott's (2001) theory. The informal aspects involved follow from Zenger, Lazzarini, and Poppo's (2002) elaboration.

A recent meta-analysis of the leadership literature reports that the so-called Five-Factor Theory is quite effective in predicting leader emergence and performance (Judge, Bono, Ilies, & Gerhardt, 2002). However, a study of the literature included in the analysis clearly indicates that it concentrates primarily on hierarchic management and that it makes little if any use of projective techniques and unconscious measurement. Thus, it lacks inclusiveness both as to the type of leadership and as to the measure used, concentrating largely on self-report instruments. Yet, I have argued that unconscious processes are role motivation theory's major concern and show in the introduction and in Miner and Raju (2004) that they can yield quite discrepant results.

It is widely held that theories that set forth constructs at one level, such as the individual, dyad, group, or organizational, should be tested using constructs at that level. Yet rarely are levels within the individual considered. Motives specified at the unconscious or implicit level should be tested at that level as well. Thus, to consider the research on the Five-Factor Theory relevant for role motivation theory is inappropriate; it mixes levels.

RESEARCH EVIDENCE

Organizational Forms

Substantial evidence is available regarding the types of organizational forms hypothesized by role motivation theory. Despite earlier predictions regarding the demise of bureaucracy and the ascension of alternatives to hierarchy, organizations of the type considered by the hierarchic theory clearly remain abundant today (Leavitt, 2003; Russell, 2001). Professional organizations can be distinguished from bureaucracies in a number of respects (Golden, Dukerich, & Fabian, 2000) and create their own career progressions (Baruch & Hall, 2004). Schoonhoven and Romanelli (2001) do an excellent job of differentiating task organizations from other forms, whereas a sizable literature has arisen accentuating the role of growth orientation in entrepreneurial firms (Delmar, Davidsson, & Gartner, 2003; Wiklund & Shepherd, 2003). The separate identity of group systems is well established by studies in this domain (Shaw, Duffy, & Stark, 2000; Taggar, Hackett, & Saha, 1999). Thus the distinctive nature of the four types seems well established, although other forms may exist as well.

Motive Patterns

Of the three role motivation theories where motive patterns have been investigated, the hierarchic theory has received the most research attention. This is reflected in the meta-analyses that have been conducted on it (Carson & Gilliard, 1993; Eagly, Karau, Miner, & Johnson, 1994; Nathan & Alexander, 1985) and in the qualitative reviews that have appeared over the years (Adler & Weiss, 1988; Cornelius, 1983; Latham, 1988). Both these forms of feedback on the research evidence, insofar as the hierarchic theory is concerned, are consistently positive. Major summaries for the early years are contained in Miner (1965, 1977); see also the introduction. Miner (1993) extends the time period substantially.

Research on the motivational aspects of the professional and task theories is less extensive but is growing. Those with a particular interest in the professional theory should consult Miner, Crane, and Vandenberg (1994), which deals with arbitrators and lawyers. Task theory has reached a point where it has elicited a meta-analysis (Collins, Hanges, & Locke,

2004). However, though the results are significant and positive, they do not draw upon data from studies 1 and 2 in Table 12.1 (Miner, 1997), nor do they cite Osborne (2003). Those studies would raise their average correlations considerably. All of the research results reported to this point provide consistent support for the role motivation theories.

A stocktaking of the results overall (Miner, 1993) may be used to embellish upon this conclusion. Some 57 studies yield 92 criterion relationships with 92 percent being significant and in the theoretically hypothesized direction. Outside the theory's domain, as in Table 12.2, there are 28 studies and 59 criterion relationships, and 100 percent are either nonsignificant or significant in a negative direction. These results run up to 1993 and contain findings for all three role motivation theories, with the lowest number of relationships being 13 for the professional theory. To these figures should be added the data presented in Tables 12.1 and 12.2, which does yield a few significant noncongruent correlations resulting from the way in which the samples were constituted. Also, Osborne (2003) and some data on the hierarchic theory from China (Chen, Yu, & Miner, 1997; Ebrahimi, 1999) continue to support the theory.

Evidence exists as well with regard to the leadership theorizing that is supportive (Miner, 2002). Furthermore the research with regard to leadership careers indicates that congruent correlations ranging from .41 to .75 (median .58) are obtained. The median for nine noncongruent correlations is .11 (Foti & Miner, 2003, p. 96).

The recent literature provides considerable endorsement for role motivation theorizing from qualitative reviewers (Rauch & Frese, 2000; Shane, Locke, & Collins, 2003; Yukl, 2002). These reviews tend to focus on one or the other of the theories consistent with the focus of the review, but all are positive. Vecchio (2003) indicates that the research results from role motivation theorizing have been consistently supportive of the position that different kinds of people are drawn to different organizational systems.

The Dark Side

If all this sounds too good to be true, it is; although role motivation theory itself has been largely free from criticism, the same cannot be said for the various MSCS measures. On this score there have been concerns. The problems seem to revolve around the projective nature of the tests and the fact that as such they do not operate in the same manner as self-report tests. Projective measurements came to organizational behavior from clinical psychology and in the process brought both its positive advantages and its negative stereotypes with it. The controversy often has been intense in both domains (for an example of what is happening in clinical psychology currently, cf. Hibbard, 2003; Lilienfeld, Wood, & Garb, 2000).

Against this background, criticisms often have been entered, and replies extended, on some five grounds. This literature is summarized in Miner (1993), and a comprehensive response is provided there. The criticisms are as follows:

1. Construct validity is lacking.
2. Reliability is lacking.
3. Role motivation training teaches the theory.
4. The decline (in motivation to manage during the 1960s) is questionable.
5. Gender effects are widespread.

The construct validity issue appears to have been occasioned by the fact that, as shown in Tables 12.1 and 12.2, projective and self-report tests often do not correlate well. Given that implicit motives differ from self-attributed ones (McClelland et al., 1989), this is to be expected and should not reflect on construct validity.

With regard to reliability, there have been diverse concerns. With regard to scorer reliability, figures above .90 have been attained consistently for both the MSCS total scores and the subscales (see Miner, 1993), although it may take considerable checking against experienced scorers to achieve this result. Test-retest reliability averages .86 for the total scores and .20 lower for the subscales, commensurate with the differences in the number of items. Internal consistency reliability is nonexistent; however, it is not appropriate as an index of the effectiveness of tests of the MSCSs' type (see Streiner, 2003).

Research on the effects of managerial role motivation training in producing increases in motivational scores indicates that teaching the theory is not a factor in this finding (see Miner, 1993).

The decline appears to have been a very real phenomenon closely associated with student activism. It has been documented with a variety of measures and by a number of investigators (Miner, 1974).

The gender concern applies only to the MSCS-Form H and appears to reflect that the employment culture of the 1950s when the instrument was developed was very different from that of today. Older respondents with experience in the earlier culture have no problems, but some of the younger generation do. Here there may well be an affect on the acceptability of certain items, although validity seems to remain unchanged. Perhaps a revised instrument more closely at-

tuned to the current world should be introduced; this, however, has not yet been done.

Managerial Role Motivation Training

The effectiveness of the training undertaken as the hierarchic theory first emerged is of considerable interest in its own right, but it also bears on the construct validity of the MSCS-Form H. This training has been utilized often, with both students and managers (see Miner, 1977). The results indicate increases in managerial motivation in 96 percent of the 24 experimental groups studied, with none of the 11 control groups showing a significant improvement. Clearly the training does have the expected effect on motivation to manage (Miner, 1993).

Furthermore, an analysis of promotions across a five-year time period after completing the training found that among those managers who stayed with the company 86 percent were subsequently promoted, whereas the promotion rate for a control group who had no training was 57 percent; 10 percent of the controls were in fact demoted. Among those managers who separated during the five years, 69 percent of the trained experimental group were recommended for rehire by their superiors, against 30 percent of the untrained controls. Clearly the training does produce substantial change of the type desired.

Similar changes in the motivational patterns of the other role motivation theories have not been attained, although research with achievement motivation training by others suggests that task motivation is capable of being affected (see McClelland & Winter 1969).

CONCLUSIONS

Role motivation theory seems to have worked well within its established domains. Questions arise, however, regarding the possibilities for expansion. Could the present theories be brought to bear in explaining motivation and behavior beyond the organization-specific domains that have been studied to date? Could the role motivation approach be extended to other sets of role prescriptions? Basically the underlying concept is that roles become established in the thinking of a substantial segment of the population; these roles may well be at least partially unconscious, then they are used to evaluate the role behavior of those who come to perform in these roles, and those whose existing motives match well with the parts they are expected to play are judged to play the part well.

This suggests for one thing that other roles beyond the organizational might be equally susceptible to study with this approach—family roles such as that of parent, and student roles for instance. Also, the current roles might be expanded beyond their existing domains. There has been some success in extending the task theory to evangelical religions (Osborne, 2003); perhaps this type of extension could be taken even further.

Whether a more general theory of personality might be created using these types of generalizations, of either the underlying theoretical approach or of the existing theories, is an open question at present. That will take some new theory and much new research.

REFERENCES

Adler, S., & Weiss, H. M. (1988). Recent developments in the study of personality and organizational behavior. *International Review of Industrial and Organizational Psychology, 3,* 307–330.

Ashforth, B. E. (2001). *Role transitions in organizational life: An identity-based perspective.* Mahwah, NJ: Erlbaum.

Atkinson, J. W. (1977). Motivation for achievement. In T. Blass (Ed.), *Personality variables in social behavior* (pp. 25–108). Hillsdale, NJ: Erlbaum.

Baruch, Y., & Hall, D. T. (2004). The academic career: A model for future careers in other sectors? *Journal of Vocational Behavior, 64,* 241–262.

Blau, G., Tatum, D. S., & Ward-Cook, K. (2003). Correlates of professional versus organizational withdrawal cognitions. *Journal of Vocational Behavior, 63,* 72–85.

Carson, K. P., & Gilliard, D. J. (1993). Construct validity of the Miner Sentence Completion Scale. *Journal of Occupational and Organizational Psychology, 66,* 171–175.

Chen, C. C., Yu, K. C., & Miner, J. B. (1997). Motivation to manage: A study of women in Chinese state-owned enterprises. *Journal of Applied Behavioral Science, 33,* 160–173.

Collins, C. J., Hanges, P. J., & Locke, E. A. (2004). The relationship of achievement motivation to entrepreneurial behavior: A meta-analysis. *Human Performance, 17,* 95–117.

Cornelius, E. T. (1983). The use of projective techniques in personnel selection. *Research in Personnel and Human Resources Management, 1,* 127–168.

Delmar, F., Davidsson, P., & Gartner, W. B. (2003). Arriving at the high-growth firm. *Journal of Business Venturing, 18,* 189–216.

DiMaggio, P. (2001). *The twenty-first century firm: Changing economic organization in international perspective.* Princeton, NJ: Princeton University Press.

Eagly, A. H., Karau, S. J., Miner, J. B., & Johnson, B. T. (1994). Gender and motivation to manage in hierarchic organizations: A meta-analysis. *Leadership Quarterly, 5,* 135–159.

Ebrahimi, B. (1999). Motivation to manage in China: Implications for strategic HRM. *Asia Pacific Business Review, 5*(3/4), 204–222.

Elizur, D. (1984). Facets of work values: A structural analysis of work outcomes. *Journal of Applied Psychology, 69,* 379–389.

Ensley, M. D., Carland, J. W., & Carland, J. C. (2000). Investigating the existence of the lead entrepreneur. *Journal of Small Business Management, 38*(4), 59–77.

Fiedler, F. E. (1967). *A theory of leadership effectiveness.* New York: McGraw-Hill.

Foti, R. J., & Miner, J. B. (2003). Individual differences and organizational forms in the leadership process. *Leadership Quarterly, 14,* 83–112.

Ghiselli, E. E. (1971). *Explorations in managerial talent.* Pacific Palisades, CA: Goodyear.

Ginzberg, E., Miner, J. B., Anderson, J. K., Ginsburg, S. W., & Herma, J. L. (1959). *Breakdown and recovery.* New York: Columbia University Press.

Golden, B. R., Dukerich, J. M., & Fabian, F. H. (2000). The interpretation and resolution of resource allocation issues in professional organizations: A critical examination of the professional-manager dichotomy. *Journal of Management Studies, 37,* 1157–1187.

Gupta, V., MacMillan, I. C., & Surie, G. (2004). Entrepreneurial leadership: Developing and measuring a cross-cultural construct. *Journal of Business Venturing, 19,* 241–260.

Hibbard, S. (2003). A critique of Lilienfeld et al.'s (2000) "The scientific status of projective techniques." *Journal of Personality Assessment, 80,* 260–271.

Hofstede, G. H. (1980). Culture's consequences: International differences in work-related values. Beverly Hills, CA: Sage.

House, R., Rousseau, D. M., & Thomas-Hunt, M. (1995). The meso paradigm: A framework for integration of micro and macro organizational behavior. *Research in Organizational Behavior, 17,* 71–114.

Judge, T. A., Bono, J. E., Ilies, R., & Gerhardt, M. W. (2002). Personality and leadership: A qualitative and quantitative review. *Journal of Applied Psychology, 87,* 765–780.

Kraus, W. A. (1980). *Collaboration in organizations: Alternatives to hierarchy.* New York: Human Sciences Press.

Latham, G. P. (1988). Human resource training and development. *Annual Review of Psychology, 39,* 545–582.

Leavitt, H. J. (2003). Why hierarchies thrive. *Harvard Business Review, 81*(3), 96–102.

Lilienfeld, S. O., Wood, J. M., & Garb, H. N. (2000). The scientific status of projective techniques. *Psychological Science in the Public Interest, 1,* 27–66.

Locke, K. (2001). *Grounded theory in management research.* Thousand Oaks, CA: Sage.

Lord, R. G. (1985). An information processing approach to social perceptions, leadership, and behavioral measurement in organizations. *Research in Organizational Behavior, 7,* 87–128.

Lynn, R. (1969). An achievement motivation questionnaire. *British Journal of Psychology, 60,* 529–534.

Maslow, A. H. (1954). *Motivation and personality.* New York: Harper and Row.

McClelland, D. C. (1961). *The achieving society.* Princeton, NJ: Van Nostrand.

McClelland, D. C. (1975). *Power: The inner experience.* New York: Irvington.

McClelland, D. C., & Burnham, D. H. (1976). Power is the great motivator. *Harvard Business Review, 54*(2), 100–110.

McClelland, D. C., Koestner, R., & Weinberger, J. (1989). How do self-attributed and implicit motives differ? *Psychological Review, 96,* 690–702.

McClelland, D. C., & Winter, D. G. (1969). *Motivating economic achievement.* New York: Free Press.

Meyer, G. J. (1996). The Rorschach and MMPI: Toward a more scientifically differentiated understanding of cross-method assessment. *Journal of Personality Assessment, 67,* 558–578.

Miner, J. B. (1960a). The effect of a course in psychology on the attitudes of research and development supervisors. *Journal of Applied Psychology, 44,* 224–232.

Miner, J. B. (1960b). The Kuder Preference Record in management appraisal. *Personnel Psychology, 13,* 187–196.

Miner, J. B. (1965). *Studies in management education.* New York: Springer.

Miner, J. B. (1974). *The human constraint: The coming shortage of managerial talent.* Washington, DC: BNA Books.

Miner, J. B. (1977). *Motivation to manage: A ten year update on the "Studies in Management Education" research.* Eugene, OR: Organizational Measurement Systems Press.

Miner, J. B. (1982). The uncertain future of the leadership concept: Revisions and clarifications. *Journal of Applied Behavioral Science, 18,* 293–307.

Miner, J. B. (1985). *People problems: The executive answer book.* New York: Random House.

Miner, J. B. (1988). *Organizational behavior: Performance and productivity.* New York: Random House.

Miner, J. B. (1993). *Role motivation theories.* London: Routledge.

Miner, J. B. (1997). *A psychological typology of successful entrepreneurs.* Westport, CT: Quorum.

Miner, J. B. (2000). Testing a psychological typology of entrepreneurship using business founders. *Journal of Applied Behavioral Science, 36,* 43–69.

Miner, J. B. (2002). The role motivation theories of organizational leadership. In B. J. Avolio & F. J. Yammarino (Eds.), *Transformational and charismatic leadership: The road ahead* (pp. 309–338). Oxford, UK: Elsevier Science.

Miner, J. B., Crane, D. P., & Vandenberg, R. J. (1994). Congruence and fit in professional role motivation theory. *Organization Science, 5,* 86–97.

Miner, J. B., & Raju, N. S. (2004). Risk propensity differences between managers and entrepreneurs and between low- and high-growth entrepreneurs: A reply in a more conservative vein. *Journal of Applied Psychology, 89,* 3–13.

Nathan, B. R., & Alexander, R. A. (1985). An application of meta-analysis to theory building and construct validation. *Academy of Management Proceedings, 45,* 224–228.

Oliver, J. E. (1982). An instrument for classifying organizations. *Academy of Management Journal, 25,* 855–866.

Osborne, G. (2003). *Are apostles entrepreneurs: The need for achievement as a common trait between entrepreneurs and apostles in the International Coalition of Apostles (ICA).* Unpublished doctoral dissertation, Regent University, Virginia Beach, VA.

Rauch, A., & Frese, M. (2000). Psychological approaches to entrepreneurial success: A general model and an overview of findings. *International Review of Industrial and Organizational Psychology, 15,* 101–141.

Raynor, J. O. (1974). Future orientation in the study of achievement motivation. In J. W. Atkinson & J. O. Raynor (Eds.), *Motivation and achievement* (pp. 121–154). New York: Wiley.

Richards, M. D. (1973). An exploratory study of strategic failure. *Academy of Management Proceedings, 33,* 40–46.

Rowe, A. J., & Mason, R. O. (1987). *Managing with style: A guide to understanding, assessing, and improving decision making.* San Francisco, CA: Jossey-Bass.

Russell, C. J. (2001). A longitudinal study of top-level executive performance. *Journal of Applied Psychology, 86,* 560–573.

Schoonhoven, C. B., & Romanelli, E. (2001). *The entrepreneurship dynamic: Origins of entrepreneurship and the evolution of industries.* Stanford, CA: Stanford University Press.

Scott, W. R. (2001). *Institutions and organizations.* Thousand Oaks, CA: Sage.

Shane, S., Locke, E. A., & Collins, C. J. (2003). Entrepreneurial motivation. *Human Resource Management Review, 13,* 257–279.

Shaw, J. D., Duffy, M. K., & Stark, E. M. (2000). Interdependence and preference for group work: Main and congruence effects on the satisfaction and performance of group members. *Journal of Management, 26,* 259–279.

Shure, G. H., & Meeker, J. P. (1967). A personality attitude schedule for use in experimental bargaining studies. *Journal of Psychology, 65,* 233–252.

Slocum, J. W., & Hellriegel, D. (1983). A look at how managers' minds work. *Business Horizons, 26*(4), 58–68.

Spangler, W. D. (1992). Validity of questionnaire and TAT measures of need for achievement: Two meta-analyses. *Psychological Bulletin, 112,* 140–154.

Streiner, D. L. (2003). Starting at the beginning: An introduction to coefficient alpha and internal consistency. *Journal of Personality Assessment, 80,* 99–103.

Taggar, S., Hackett, R., & Saha, S. (1999). Leadership emergence in autonomous work teams: Antecedents and outcomes. *Personnel Psychology, 52,* 899–926.

Tinsley, H. E. A. (2000). The congruence myth: An analysis of the efficacy of the person-environment fit model. *Journal of Vocational Behavior, 56,* 147–179.

Vecchio, R. P. (2003). Entrepreneurship and leadership: Common trends and common threads. *Human Resource Management Review, 13,* 303–327.

Vicere, A. A. (2002). Leadership and the networked economy. *Human Resource Planning, 25*(2), 26–33.

Weber, M. (1968). *Economy and society.* New York: Bedminster.

Wiklund, J., & Shepherd, D. (2003). Aspiring for, and achieving growth: The moderating role of resources and opportunities. *Journal of Management Studies, 40,* 1919–1941.

Wilderom, C. P. M., & Miner, J. B. (1991). Defining voluntary groups and agencies within organization science. *Organization Science, 2,* 366–378.

Yukl, G. (2002). *Leadership in organizations.* Upper Saddle River, NJ: Prentice Hall.

Zenger, T. R., Lazzarini, S. G., & Poppo, L. (2002). Informal and formal organization in new institutional economics. *Advances in Strategic Management, 19,* 277–305.

CHAPTER 13

Vocational Interests

K. S. DOUGLAS LOW AND JAMES ROUNDS

VOCATIONAL INTERESTS: BRIDGING PERSON AND ENVIRONMENT

Interests provide a natural springboard to understanding how the individual develops and functions in a dynamic, continuous, and reciprocal process of interaction with his or her environment. Since Frank Parson's (1909) pioneering work of matching people's traits with work conditions, the interaction between person and environment has been the heuristic background principle for vocational interest research (Rounds & Tracey, 1990). Parson (1909) provided one of the first statements describing the person-environment relationship by advocating the importance of matching individual capabilities and characteristics with demands of the work environment. Today, the subject of person-environment interaction in interest research is best represented by J. L. Holland's (1958, 1973, 1997) theory of vocational personalities and work environments.

The present chapter begins by reviewing Holland's theoretical formulations. We proceed to a discussion of interest development, focusing in particular on person-environment transactions that promote continuity and change of interests across the life course. This is followed by an examination of the boundaries of Holland's theory focusing on the cross-cultural generalizability of Holland's model and its limitations in describing the world of work. We then move to evaluate Holland's claim that interest inventories are in effect personality inventories and propose that interests and personality traits can be understood through their different motivational roles in human behavior. Finally, the chapter concludes with a discussion of the contribution interests make to school, work, retirement, leisure, and well-being.

HOLLAND'S THEORETICAL FORMULATIONS

The most dominant model in vocational psychology (Day & Rounds, 1998), Holland's (1958, 1997) theory of vocational

personalities and work environments is premised on a match between individuals and occupations. Central to Holland's (1997, pp. 2–5) theory is the assumption that most individuals can be categorized into one of six personality types: Realistic (R), Investigative (I), Artistic (A), Social (S), Enterprising (E), and Conventional (C). Each of the six types consists of clusters of personality and behavioral repertories and is defined by vocational and avocational preferences, life goals and values, self-beliefs, problem-solving style, competencies, and personality characteristics. The RIASEC personality types are described in Table 13.1.

Today, the RIASEC personality types are found in most interest inventories, such as the Strong Interest Inventory (SII) (Harmon, Hansen, Borgen, & Hammer, 1994) and the unisex edition of the American College Testing (ACT) interest inventory (Swaney, 1995). The RIASEC scales reference many kinds of occupations and represent what Kuder (1977) and Guilford, Christensen, Bond, and Sutton (1954) referred to as "basic generalized dimensions." Also known as general interests, these interest dimensions are the broadest of three levels of generality within interest scales (Rounds, 1995). At the next level of generality are basic interests, which are usually characterized by a shared property of the activity (e.g., Selling, Teaching, Technical Writing) and are often implied in the objects of interest (Mathematics, Physical Science, Religion). Grouped by theoretical rationales (as in the case of the RIASEC scales), statistical clustering techniques, or a combination of both, general interest scales and basic interest scales contain items with homogeneous content. At the lowest level of generality, occupational interests comprise a circumscribed set of work activities that are dissimilar in character and that reference a specific occupation (e.g., psychologist, lawyer). The 1994 SII contains 211 occupational scales (occupational scales are empirically derived, heterogeneous scales composed of items that discriminate workers in specific occupational groups from people in general).

A second assumption of Holland's theory is that there are six model environments that parallel the six personality

TABLE 13.1 Holland's Personality Types and Salient Characteristics

	Realistic	Investigative	Artistic	Social	Enterprising	Conventional
Adjectival descriptors	Hardheaded Unassuming Practical Dogmatic Reserved Uninsightful	Analytical Intellectual Curious Scholarly Open Broad interests	Open Nonconforming Imaginative Intuitive Sensitive Creative	Agreeable Friendly Understanding Sociable Kind Extroverted	Extroverted Dominant Adventurous Enthusiastic Persuasive Energetic	Conforming Conservative Unimaginative Inhibited Practical-minded Methodical
Life goals	Inventing apparatus or equipment Becoming outstanding athlete	Inventing valuable product Theoretical contribution to science	Becoming famous in performing arts Publishing stories Original painting Musical composition	Helping others Making sacrifices for others Competent teacher or therapist	Being community leader Expert in commerce	Expert in finance Producing a lot of work
Competencies	Technical	Scientific	Arts	Social and interpersonal	Leadership and sales Management	Business and clerical

Note. Adapted from Holland, Powell, & Fritzsche (1994).

types: Realistic (R), Investigative (I), Artistic (A), Social (S), Enterprising (E), and Conventional (C). According to Holland (1976, p. 534), "the character of an environment emanates from the types [of people] which dominate that environment." For example, a realistic environment is populated by realistic types of people. Herein is perhaps Holland's most important contribution. A major methodological issue in person-environment fit research has been the lack of commensurate measures of the person and the environment (Edwards, 1991); person-environment measures are often at different levels of generality and/or encompass different dimensions. In Holland's model, the person and the environment are described in commensurate ways. The link between the individual's personality and the environmental context is direct: The individual's personality is manifested as preferences for work activities, and work environments are described in terms of the people who work in them and the activities they perform. Thus, it becomes possible to assess the environment in the same terms that individuals are assessed. A simple way to do this is to describe the environment in terms of the percentage of the different RIASEC types. Holland's model, therefore, allows people and environments to be mapped in the same interest space. Both persons and work settings can be described with RIASEC codes. Typically, people and environments are described with three-letter codes, with the first letter code being most descriptive. For example, electricians are characterized by RIC and newspaper editors are characterized by AES.

A third assumption is that individuals search for environments that allow them to use their skills and abilities and express their interests and values. Realistic types seek Realistic environments. Investigative types seek Investigative en-

vironments and so forth. Environments attract people with certain characteristics, and environments are shaped by the people who inhabit them.

The final major assumption of Holland's (1997) theory is that "behavior is determined by an interaction between personality and environment" (p. 4). In other words, outcomes are a function of the degree of similarity (i.e., congruence) between Holland personality types and environmental types. Knowledge of personality types and information on composition of the environment can be used to forecast educational and vocational behaviors, including choice of major field of study and occupation, job success and satisfaction, and job changes. People find environments reinforcing and satisfying when environmental patterns resemble their personality patterns. This situation makes for stability of behavior as individuals' complementary actions are rewarded and reinforced. Conversely, incongruent interactions stimulate change in human behavior; incongruent individuals are influenced by the dominant environment to change in the direction of congruency. When placed in an incongruent environment, a person will seek a new and congruent environment by remaking or leaving the present environment or by changing personal behavior and perceptions. The person and the environment thus interact in a reciprocal process.

Holland's structural hypothesis, called the *calculus assumption,* is a cornerstone for the congruence and consistency assumption. As shown in Figure 13.1, the personality types and environments are related to each other in a circular fashion (Holland calls his model a hexagon). Similar to circumplex models in personality, such as Kiesler's (1983) or Wiggins's (1982) interpersonal circle, the physical proximity between types reflects the closeness of their conceptual re-

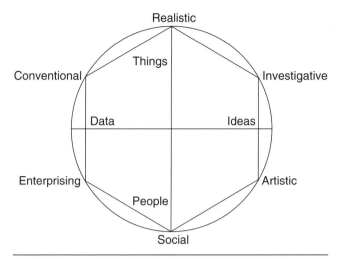

Figure 13.1 Holland's circular model of interests with Prediger's People-Things and Data-Ideas dimensions.

lationships. Because of the circular nature of Holland's RIASEC model, it is expected that the correlations decrease as the scales move farther away from each other. In other words, one would expect the correlation between the Realistic scale and the Investigative scale to be larger than the correlation between the Realistic scale and the Artistic scale, which would be larger than the correlation between the Realistic scale and the Social scale. Similarly, because the scales theoretically comprise a circular structure, one would expect that the correlation between the Realistic scale and the Conventional scale would be approximately as large as the correlation between the Realistic and Investigative scale.

Three secondary assumptions of Holland's theory—consistency, differentiation, and identity—define the clarity of the RIASEC types and environments. *Consistency* is generally defined as the similarity among the personality types according to the RIASEC circular ordering of types shown in Figure 13.1. A common operational definition of high point codes uses the highest two or three scores chosen from six RIASEC scores to represent an individual's interest profile. The RIASEC profile is categorized as high, middle, or low consistency according to the adjacency of the types. For example, a Realistic-Investigative pattern is highly consistent due to their consecutive ordering on the circle. Conversely, a Realistic-Social pattern is of low consistency because they are diametrically opposed. *Differentiation* refers to how clearly and coherently defined are the individuals and environments. An individual with well-differentiated interests would have a RIASEC type that is clearly elevated above the other five types. Similarly, a well-differentiated environment is dominated by a single type, whereas an undifferentiated environment would produce a uniform RIASEC profile with

an even balance of types. Finally, *identity* provides an estimate of the clarity and stability of the goals, interests, and talents of an individual. When applied to an environment, identity is defined by the clarity of organizational goals, tasks, and rewards. Holland (1997) suggests that consistency, differentiation, and identity probably represent the same concept: clarity, focus, and definition of the personality types and environments.

DEVELOPMENT OF INTERESTS

Reflective of the pragmatic focus of interests in facilitating the fit between individuals and their occupations, Holland's theory affords little attention to the issue of development. With its historical emphasis on practical utility, the focus of interest research largely has centered on the construction, validation, and interpretation of psychometric scales and instruments. Although interest assessment now constitutes a major portion of psychological testing within the United States, this dustbowl empiricism tradition within interest research may have impeded the development of theory and research to address the role of interests in life course development (Dawis, 1991). Nonetheless, a survey of both theory and research suggests that (1) interests demonstrate a high level of continuity across the life course, but (2) they maintain a dynamic quality as well.

Interest Continuity

The idea that interests are stable dispositional attributes is central to all considerations of the construct—especially its primary purpose in matching the individual with the environment—because large fluctuations in interests over short periods of time would limit their use for predictive purposes. The focus on facilitating fit between person and environment means that the empirical focus of interest development has largely centered on students between middle adolescence (ages 15 or 16) and beginning of adulthood (ages 21 or 22), the period in which most people make concrete decisions regarding educational plans and occupational choice and entry. The small body of literature on children's interests focuses primarily on aspirations. Studies indicate that children are able to articulate their aspirations from as young as age four (Trice & Rush, 1995) and are relatively stable (Gottfredson, 1981; Trice, 1991). Researchers (e.g., Tracey & Ward, 1998) have also found these aspirations tend to reflect children's perceptions of the masculinity/femininity of specific occupations.

Qualitative (Campbell, 1971; Strong, 1955; Swanson, 1999) and quantitative (Low, Yoon, Roberts, & Rounds, in press) reviews of longitudinal studies indicate an impressive stability of adults' interests over time. Results of test-retest studies using various versions of the SII (Harmon et al., 1994) demonstrate robustness in interest stability across long time periods, both in scores for single persons over time (profile correlations; Swanson & Hansen, 1988) and in the relative placement of individuals within a group (rank-order correlations; Strong, 1951).

In a meta-analytic review of 66 longitudinal studies, Low et al. (in press) estimated the stability of interests at different life stages. Interests were observed to be relatively stable, even at early adolescence. Stability estimates for the age periods (i.e., ages 12–13.9, ages 14–15.9, and ages 16–17.9) prior to graduation from high school remained unchanged during the period ($\rho_{12-13.9} = .55$, $\rho_{14-15.9} = .57$, $\rho_{16-17.9} = .58$) as evidenced from 95 percent confidence intervals that overlapped each other to large degrees. During the college years, interest stability increased dramatically to .67. The estimates for the age periods after ages 18 to 21.9 were $\rho_{22-24.9} = .70$, $\rho_{25-29.9} = .83$, $\rho_{30-34.9} = .72$, and $\rho_{35-40} = .64$. Although estimates continue to fluctuate after the college years, the apparent peak at ages 25 to 29.9 must be qualified by a comparatively smaller sample and a confidence interval with great overlaps with the intervals of the preceding and subsequent age categories. Results thus suggest that the actual peak occurred during college years (ages 18–21.9) and subsequently plateaud for the next two decades. The findings of the Low et al. study—graphed as an age trajectory—allow us to speculate about possible person-environment transactions responsible for the pattern of interest development during life course.

A reasonable expectation is that adolescents' interests become progressively more stable with age, in part because of cognitive maturity, accumulated exposure to vocational information, and increased mastery of their environments. However, contrary to expectations, the stability of adolescents' interests remained consistent for the entire period prior to graduation from high school. This lack of change may be a reflection of how schools structure the opportunities for involvement in new and different activities. There are limited opportunities for youths in U.S. schools to observe and participate in adult activities (Task Force on Education of Young Adolescents, 1989), and instructional practices are frequently removed from social contexts. Without an adequate understanding of workplace roles and demands, and befitted of the ability to choose or manipulate their environments, there is little internal or external press toward crystallization of adolescents' interests.

Interest stability increased markedly at ages 18 to 22—the period in which most individuals in the United States transitioned from high school into college or the workforce—during which time many decisions about career choice and entry are made. With fewer environmental constraints, people are more able to choose the contexts, such as courses, work, leisure activities, and social relationships, that are better aligned with their interests. In that way, these experiences serve to deepen the characteristics that lead people to those experiences in the first place, resulting in an elaboration and subsequent stabilization of the interest dispositions being shaped by experience. After the period between ages 18 and 22, the adolescent formally enters the stages of adulthood. The increased commitments to other life roles at adulthood, such as being a spouse, a parent, and/or caregiver (Levinson 1986), affect the latitude an individual has in changing occupations. A person's talents, expectations, irreversible choices, and credentials also restrict the range of movement he or she has after entry into the workforce (Holland, 1997). Interests, therefore, increase in stability within a small window of time, after which the constancy of workplace environments limits the frequency of new experiences as well as curtails further elaboration of fit between the individual and the environment.

To provide a benchmark to assess the relative stability of interests, Low et al. (2004) compared the stability of personality traits to interests. Personality traits, as typified by the Five-Factor Model (FFM), are widely assumed to be developmental antecedents to the formation of interests (e.g., Costa, McCrae, & Holland, 1984; Swanson, 1999). A popular position (Lent, Brown, & Hackett, 1994) within the field of career development further explicates the personality-interest relationship by suggesting that personality traits shape how individuals perceive their task competencies and the outcomes of these efforts and in the process increase individuals' affinities for certain activities that over time become interests. Personality traits should be as stable, if not more stable, than interests if the personality traits are indeed the precursors of interests. However, when stability estimates of interest are compared to the stability estimates of personality traits reported in Roberts and DelVecchio's (2000) study, interests were consistently more stable than personality traits across the entire period examined (age 12 to age 40; see Figure 13.2). At adolescence, interests evidenced higher stability ($\rho_{\text{interest}} = .55$, cf. $\rho_{\text{personality}} = .47$) and outpaced the stability of personality traits through the college years ($\rho_{\text{interest}} = .64$, cf. $\rho_{\text{personality}} = .51$) and the first decade of adulthood ($\rho_{\text{interest}} = .70$, cf. $\rho_{\text{personality}} = .57$). Personality traits approximated interests in stability (both $\rho = .62$) only with the advent of middle age (i.e., age 40). Beyond possessing a level of continuity similar to traits and abilities, interests were remarkably stable during adolescence, which is perhaps the most

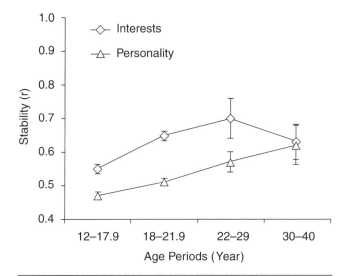

Figure 13.2 Comparison between interest stability and personality consistency across age group. T-bars indicate 95% confidence intervals for each age group. From Low, Yoon, Roberts, & Round, in press.

volatile life-course transition that is characterized by numerous social, cognitive, and biological changes.

A number of normative person-environment transactions may be responsible for the differences in stability between interests and personality traits. There is substantial evidence that both the person and the environment play important roles in promoting continuity and change of personality traits. Parallel continuities in child-rearing practices and children's behaviors (e.g., Cairns & Hood, 1983) suggest an important connection between the socialization environment and the continuity of personality traits. Conversely, a number of studies have found changes in personality traits to be associated with environmental experiences in young adulthood (Pals, 1999), midlife (Roberts & Chapman, 2000), and old age (Tower & Kasl, 1996). Personality traits are posited to change in response to contingencies, modeling of others, and through receiving persistent feedback that contradicts closely held views of self (Roberts & Caspi, 2003).

It is likely that the greater familial and societal emphasis on future job choice (i.e., interests) than on future working styles (i.e., personality) provides environmental pressures that accelerate the crystallization of interests over personality traits. From the time they are able to speak, children are frequently asked what careers or occupations they would like to have as adults ("What do you want to be when you grow up?"), whereas it is highly unlikely that they will be asked about their aspired adult personality traits. Apart from real-life exposure, a child also is inundated from a very young age with cultural imagery of occupations through the media and other sources (Wright et al., 1995). Children are able to

articulate their aspirations from as young as age four (Trice & Rush, 1995). In contrast, children are much less able to describe themselves with trait terms (Rholes, Ruble, & Newman, 1990).

By influencing one's environmental preferences and subsequently the range of experiences an individual has, interests play an important role within the person-environment transactions responsible for promoting change and continuity of personality traits. As a major determinant of career choice and entry (Fouad, 1999), interests play a pivotal role in the range and type of roles a person undertakes, as well as the social interactions and behavioral reinforcements. Much of an individual's waking time is spent at work, or in preparation for work, and work settings constitute substantial portions of the environments afforded by communities. An individual's status in society is largely determined by his or her occupation (Dornbusch, Glasgow, & Lin, 1996). Sociological surveys indicate that a large number of interpersonal ties are formed in work (Marks, 1994), and employees are especially likely to have ties to others who occupy the same job (Ibarra, 1995). Finally, interests may be influential in which traits are developed and refined over time. For example, Roberts, Caspi, and Moffitt (2003) identified job characteristics that were related to longitudinal changes in personality even after controlling for prework personalities. They found job characteristics circumscribed by interests—occupational attainment, availability of resource power, financial security, and the opportunity to work independently—lead to changes in personality traits, such as positive/negative emotionality, dominance, conscientiousness, and traditionalism.

Interest Change

Interests are stable internal dispositions that guide agentic behaviors in individuals' responses to the environment. At the same time, the relationship between interests and environment is likely a bidirectional one. Evidence indicates that interests, although largely stable across the life course, change in response to pressures in the environment. People change their interests in response to the positive and negative environmental reinforcements they receive. The most direct form of explicit contingency is in parents' influences on their children's interests. Parents shape their children's interests by controlling the type of activities the children are exposed to, and through their interactions, they influence their children's perceptions of appropriate careers. For example, parents with strong academic efficacy for their child would discourage consideration of occupational pursuits relying heavily on manual labor (Bandura, Barbaranelli, Caprara, & Pastorelli, 2001). Similarly, teachers influence interest development by reinforcing aptitudes for certain skills or subjects or by making certain subjects more enjoyable to learn.

Change in interests also are likely triggered by the assimilation of new role demands, by watching others and ourselves, as well as by responding to feedback from those around us. Meir and Navon (1992), for instance, found newly employed bank tellers shift toward conventional profiles after half a year of employment. The tellers' level of congruence was in turn highly associated with their supervisors' evaluation of their performance. Nauta, Epperson, and Kahn (1998) also point to the presence of role models in increasing the participation of women in nontraditional occupational fields. Social and cultural forces are also powerful influences, affecting barriers and supports to goal fulfillment as well as determining what individuals construe as important. Their effects are evidenced in differences in the types of interests expressed across gender (Betz & Schifano, 2000), racial/ethnic groups (Leong, 1995), and socioeconomic status (Bandura et al., 2001). There is also evidence (Blustein, Phillips, Jobin-Davis, Finkelberg, & Roarke, 1997) that macrolevel factors such as economics and public policy contribute to the development of interests. The context of family, friends, and community play a critical role in influencing a person's interests. Deci and Ryan (1991), for example, characterized interests as the thread that connects "the self to external and internal experiences" (p. 241). When we think of what we like to do and the people we like to be with, we take into account past and present situations where we have encountered successes and failures and make predictions about the likelihood of future success in different environments. Interests play an assimilatory role in connecting individuals' beliefs of their capabilities and self-attributes, the affordances of their environment, and the likely outcomes of different courses of action.

BIOLOGICAL RELATIONSHIPS

Behavioral genetics studies indicate that genetic factors play a part in the development of interests. For example, Moloney, Bouchard, and Segal (1991) examined the interests of monozygotic and dizygotic twins reared apart across an interval of 10 years. The mean correlation of monozygotic twins for vocational interests was .50, with heritability estimates of .41, .66, .50, .52, .50, and .38, respectively, for Holland's RIASEC typology, indicating a balance between consistency and change. Moloney estimated that 40 percent to 50 percent of interest consistency was attributable to genetic influences, a result that was subsequently replicated in a study by Lykken, Bouchard, McGue, and Tellegen (1993). These estimates were somewhat lower compared to findings on personality traits (Plomin & Caspi, 1999) and cognitive abilities (Finkel, Pedersen, McGue, & McClearn, 1995). Taken with findings (Betsworth et al., 1994; Moloney et al., 1991) that environmental influences, particularly nonshared environmental effects, exert more influence than do genetic effects, some researchers (e.g., Lykken et al., 1993; Swanson, 1999) have proposed that interests develop from the precursor traits that are closer to the genetic level (i.e., personality, intelligence). Nonetheless, the higher stability of interests compared to personality traits suggests a more complex relationship between different individual difference domains. It is likely that genetic factors delineate the limits on the potential of all characteristics, but the specificity of their contribution to behaviors is determined by the interplay between different facets of individuality, such as abilities, personality traits, and interests, with the environments they exist in.

BOUNDARIES OF HOLLAND'S MODEL

Holland's RIASEC typology provides a simple heuristic for explaining the matching process between person and environment. Its popularity is evidenced in its widespread applications across diverse settings. Most interest inventories have been revised to yield scores comparable to Holland codes, and comprehensive lists of occupational titles associated with each Holland RIASEC code are available in the *Dictionary of Holland Occupational Codes* (Gottfredson & Holland, 1996) and in the U.S. Department of Labor's O*NET database (U.S. Department of Labor, 1998). The American College Testing Program has expanded upon the Holland model by organizing 23 groups of occupations, or job families, into the spatial model of RIASEC types as a world of work map (Prediger 1982; Swaney, 1995). Despite its dominant position, a number of researchers (e.g., Tinsley, 2000; Tracey & Rounds, 1995, 1996) have questioned the adequacy of Holland's model in representing the world of work.

Two kinds of RIASEC models are customarily considered (Armstrong, Hubert, & Rounds, 2003). The first model, a circular order model, specifies that the types order in a circular fashion of R-I-A-S-E-C. This is similar to Guttman's (1954) quasi-circumplex model. The quasi-circumplex is a less restrictive model because it allows for unequal distances between adjacent types in a circular structure. In comparison, a second model, the circulant, is more restrictive due to the constraint that distances between adjacent types must be equal (e.g., RI, IA, AS). With a few exceptions (e.g., Rounds & Tracey, 1993; Tracey & Rounds, 1993), most studies generally have focused on testing the quasi-circumplex model instead of the circulant model.

Since Holland identified the RIASEC structure, researchers have pursued two approaches to investigating the structure of interests. The first approach involves evaluation of the generalizability of the RIASEC model across measures and diverse groups. Because of the use of interest inventories in guidance and counseling, it has been important to demonstrate that Holland's model is applicable to diverse groups in the United States. With clearly differing socialization and opportunity, men and women seem obvious candidates to differ in their responses to the world of work. However, this does not seem to hold true, according to a meta-analysis by Rounds and Tracey (1993). When they evaluated the circulant model-data fit, they found that the model accounted for 76 percent of the variance among 31 samples of women and for 76 percent of the variance among 31 samples of men. In addition, Anderson, Tracey, and Rounds (1997) examined 14 SII matrices, and found that the fit of the RIASEC data to both quasi-circumplex and circulant models to be similar for both men and women.

Other groups that might be expected to hold different world views are ethnic and racial minorities within the United States. Studies on structural fit with U.S. ethnic/racial minorities have been less clear. Although Rounds and Tracey's (1996) metastructural analysis found a better fit with data from 73 U.S. White samples than with data from 20 U.S. ethnic/racial samples, other large-sample studies (e.g., Day, Rounds, & Swaney, 1998; Fouad, Harmon, & Borgen, 1997) have found no differences in Holland's quasi-circumplex model for ethnic/racial groups. Armstrong et al. (2003), however, have rekindled the debate on ethnic/racial differences in model-fit. They studied large samples of African American, Asian American, Caucasian American, and Hispanic American high school students and employed adults who completed either the ACT Interest Inventory (Swaney, 1995) or the SII (Harmon et al., 1994). Results indicated that a quasi-circumplex model was a good fit with all samples; however, the circulant model may be more appropriate for Asian Americans and Caucasian Americans than for other groups. These results suggested that distinctions made between Holland's types may be less salient for some minority groups and that additional work is needed to produce interest measures with improved structural validity.

On the other hand, evidence over the lack of fit of Holland's model outside the United States is less ambiguous. In a meta-analysis of 76 RIASEC matrices from 18 countries, Rounds and Tracey (1996) found the fit of the international samples to be significantly lower compared to U.S. White samples. Fifteen of the 18 countries failed to fit Holland's quasi-circumplex model, and potential moderators such as per capita gross national product and cultural values of individualism-collectivism and masculinity-femininity did not explain model-fit differences between countries. More recently, similar poor RIASEC model fit has been reported by investigators studying samples from Bolivia (Glidden-Tracey & Parraga, 1996), China (Liu & Rounds, 2003), Japan (Tracey, Watanabe, & Schneider, 1997), Singapore (Soh & Leong, 2001), and South Africa (du Toit & de Bruin, 2002). One exception is that the RIASEC model fits well in Iceland (Einarsdóttir, Rounds, Ægisdóttir, & Gerstein, 2002).

The second approach to the structure of interests focuses on developing elaborations of Holland's model and alternative ways to represent the RIASEC types. The factor analytic approach to describing the interest domain has yielded a variety of models, including Jackson's (1977) 29 primary- and 8 second-order factor model, Kuder's (1977) 16-factor model, and Rounds and Dawis (1979) 14-factor model for men and 13-factor model for women. To accommodate these factor analytic models within Holland's circumplex, Tracey and Rounds (1995) have proposed a concentric circle model, recently discussed by Rounds and Day (1999) as the vocational interest circle. Two three-dimensional models, the spherical model (Tracey & Rounds, 1996) and the Strong Ring (Armstrong, Smith, Donnay, & Rounds, 2004) have been proposed that build on Holland's typology. These structural elaborations are described in more detail in a following paragraph.

In line with Wiggins's (1982) suggestion that personality types within circumplex models are in reality fuzzy sets or prototypes of characteristics, Tracey and Rounds (1995) demonstrated that there was no empirical superiority between carving 6 scale points (as in Holland's model) and 8, or even 5 or 10 points, on the circular interest model. In other words, the defining feature of interests is not the number of categories but the circular nature. The number of interest categories is thus arbitrary because the number of points on a circle is infinite. Depending on context and utility, the circle can be divided into any number of components and scales. For example, simple models are useful for identifying broad areas of exploration for an adolescent, whereas more differentiated models are more relevant in aiding a middle-aged worker in his or her choice of specialized training. As shown in Figure 13.3, interests, therefore, can be described as a series of concentric circles of varying complexity. The innermost circle is the simplest, delineating, for example, Prediger's (1982) two dimensions of People-Things and Data-Ideas. Prediger's model is subsequently circumscribed by Holland's RIASEC model, which in turn is bounded by a more complex model. In that way, model complexity increases with distance from the circle, and each successive circle is described by more differentiated interests.

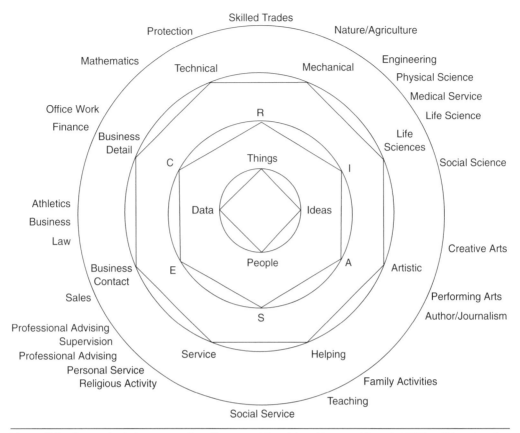

Figure 13.3 Concentric circle representation of interests. Adapted from Tracey and Rounds (1995) and Rounds and Day (1999).

There is no reason why the ideal vocational interest structure would have only two dimensions, and a three-dimensional representation of the RIASEC types has been suggested (Gottfredson & Holland, 1996; Roe & Klos, 1969; Tracey & Rounds, 1996). A number of dimensions (see Tracey & Rounds, 1996), such as status, sex-type, socioeconomic status, level of training, occupational level, level of difficulty and responsibility, and level of task complexity have been suggested to account for individual differences in occupational preferences. Tracey and Rounds (1996) argued that all these variables are highly related and can be represented by a common construct, which they termed *prestige*. According to Tracey and Rounds, the third dimension of prestige lies orthogonal to the other two dimensions of the circular model, in effect creating a spherical representation of interests. The spherical model has received some empirical support (Tracey, 2002).

Armstrong et al. (2004) argue that the categories of Holland's RIASEC typology have limited applicability as they are too general, are overly abstract, and group together a wide range of occupations with notable differences. Using the Basic Interest scales in the SII (Harmon et al., 1994), they

developed a hierarchical model with three levels of aggregation: 99 individual occupational titles were grouped into 19 occupational clusters, which were subsumed by 9 basic interest factors—each representing interest categories used in everyday language (i.e., Social Service, Influencing, Service Arts, Protective, Business, Health Services, Skilled Labor, Arts, and Analytical). Using multidimensional scaling and property vector fitting techniques, they derived a three-dimensional ringlike structure, called the Strong Ring. The first dimension (Persuasion versus Problem Solving) was found to differentiate interests in persuasion and negotiation and interests that involve preferences for scientific investigation and technical applications. The second dimension (Structured versus Dynamic) contrasted interest in working environments that have clearly defined activities and responsibilities with environments that are more flexible and allow for creative expression. The third dimension (Social Service versus Solitary Work) represented a range of interests in occupations that involve working with others in a helping or teaching capacity to occupations that involve a preference for autonomous work with little social interaction. Although there are several differences when compared to Holland's model, the Strong Ring clearly builds on the foundation of Holland's interest theory.

ARE INTERESTS SIMPLY ANOTHER ASPECT OF PERSONALITY?

A major centerpiece of Holland's theory is his assertion that interests are more than individuals' liking, indifference, or disliking of certain activities but are "another aspect of personality," representing "the expression of personality in work, school subjects, hobbies, recreational activities, and preferences" (Holland, 1997, p. 8). Interest inventories, surmised Holland (1958, 1973, 1997), are thus functional equivalents of personality inventories. In this section, we evaluate Holland's claim through the empirical and theoretical convergences between interests and personality traits. We then argue that contemporary motivation theories are a better explanatory model for interests.

The widespread acceptance of Holland's RIASEC typology and the FFM as frameworks for organizing the interest domain and the personality domain, respectively, have made the correlation of their respective scales a natural starting point for investigating the interest-personality link. Recent meta-analyses of these correlation studies (Barrick, Mount, & Gupta, 2003; Larson, Rottinghaus, & Borgen, 2002) indicate some degree of association between interests and personality, especially between enterprising interest and extraversion (both studies $\rho = .41$) and between artistic interest and openness ($\rho_{Barrick} = .39$, $\rho_{Larson} = .48$). In addition, studies have demonstrated links between social interest and extraversion (Costa et al., 1984), investigative interest and openness (Costa et al., 1984), social interest and agreeableness (Tokar, Fisher, & Subich, 1998), conventional interest and conscientiousness (Gottfredson, Jones, & Holland, 1993), and enterprising interest and emotional stability (De Fruyt & Mervielde, 1997). There is little evidence of any association between realistic interest and FFM traits.

Despite overlaps between measures, the evidence does not support Holland's claim of equivalence between interest and personality measures. The highest meta-analytic correlations between RIASEC and FFM scales rarely exceed .30, and none exceed .50 (Barrick et al., 2003; Larson et al., 2002). The modest correlations have led to some skepticism about the overlap between interests and personality (e.g., Dawis, 1991; Waller, Lykken, & Tellegen, 1995). Dawis (1991) noted that interests and personality traits are most commonly measured through the use of structured self-report instruments, and the level of correlation of scales between instruments is not much different from that of scales within these instruments. He proposed that the apparent overlaps between interests and personality traits are attributable to rating bias, especially that caused by acquiescence. Waller et al. (1995) argue that the correlations are due to people's perceptions of the prerequisite personality traits for certain occupations. In that light, interests and personality traits should be treated separately because individuals' job perceptions and self-perceptions are discrete psychological entities.

Yet, interests clearly share many qualities attributed to personality traits. As stable dispositional tendencies, they are both associated with initiating and maintaining purposive behavior. Given that a person's daily behaviors are not random and can be seen as "organized by a set of strivings whose goals are typically pursued in the form of temporally extended life tasks and personal projects" (Craik, 2000, p. 243), the relationship between interests and personality traits can be best explicated through an examination of their roles in individuals' goal striving and goal attainment. Broadly speaking, a person's interests reflect his or her preferences for behaviors, situations, contexts in which activities occur, and the outcomes associated with the preferred activities (Rounds, 1995). In other words, when people look for environments that will optimize their chances of attaining their goals, they are motivated by their interests. Personality traits, on the other hand, appear to affect how a person copes with, or adapts to, an environment. McCrae and Costa (1999), for instance, argue that personality traits are central to problem solving, influencing the ability to make strategic alliances and to compete with others for resources. In that way, personality traits influence individuals' behaviors toward adaptive functioning in an environment after the environment has been selected.

There is support within the empirical literature for differentiating interests and personality traits in terms of their motivational processes. Although both constructs are shown to be associated with job satisfaction, they do so through different pathways. In investigations of the contributions of interest to satisfaction, researchers typically use the degree of congruence between individuals' interests and their occupations. Correlation studies (e.g., Assouline & Meir, 1987; Morris, 2003) have, in general, found weak to moderate associations between congruence and satisfaction. In essence, how appropriate a person's chosen environment is in meeting his or her needs is predictive of how satisfied the person is within that environment. People are motivated by their interests to seek out environments where they can engage in activities they like and interact with people who are like them.

Studies on the link between personality traits and satisfaction, on the other hand, have focused on the direct correlations between different traits and satisfaction. FFM traits, such as emotional stability (Magnus, Diener, Fujita, & Pavot, 1993), extraversion (Watson & Clark, 1997) and conscientiousness (Organ & Lingl, 1995), are shown to correlate with job satisfaction. Indeed, recent meta-analyses (Judge, Heller, & Mount, 2002) reported moderate correlations between these three personality traits with job satisfaction. These results suggest that personality traits influence job satisfaction through their influences on the coping strategies and level of task accomplishment as well as one's sensitivity to stimuli within a prespecified context.

Interests and personality traits are also related to different outcomes. Interests are robust predictors of occupational membership (Fouad, 1999). Conversely, there is limited evidence for personality traits as valid predictors of occupational membership criteria. Meta-analyses have demonstrated that two FFM traits, conscientiousness and emotional stability, correlate moderately ($\rho = .2-.3$) with performance measures across almost all jobs (e.g., Barrick, Mount, & Judge, 2001). Compound traits made up of combinations of FFM dimensions (e.g., customer service orientation) are found to correlate even higher with job performance (ρ of about .40; Hough, 2003). In comparison, the relationship between interests and performance is much less pronounced. For instance, a meta-analysis by Hunter and Hunter (1984) reported a mean correlation of .10.

As predictors of occupational membership, interests initiate and energize behaviors toward achieving goals. Given the association between interest congruence and occupational tenure, interests are also responsible for the persistence and maintenance of these behaviors. Personality traits, as represented by the FFM, do not cover as wide a range of motivational processes as interests. Conscientiousness and emotional stability affect the probability of success in attaining goals but are by themselves not necessary for the process. People who are conscientious and emotionally stable tend to perform better and receive more environmental reinforcements. In other words, personality traits can be conceived as an individual's efficiency in striving toward his or her goals. Taken together, personality traits moderate the process of goal striving and attainment. As the basic tendencies of human nature, personality traits do not provide any reference points toward which human action can be directed. Interests, on the other hand, have overt endpoints that are associated with positive emotional states (Silvia, 2001). Similarly, Fryer (1931) described interests as the objects and activities that stimulate pleasant feelings. As such, a person finds satisfaction in an environment that matches his or her interests. Interests initiate and maintain goal-oriented activity; personality traits affect the potential for success.

PREDICTIONS FOR EVERYDAY FUNCTIONING

There have been several recent reviews of research relating to Holland's theory (Spokane, Meir, & Catalano, 2000; Tinsley, 2000). Although researchers agree on the contributions of Holland's model, the perspectives vary over the applicability of congruence to understanding individuals' functioning in different life domains. In this section, we evaluate some of the same research, focusing in particular on meta-analytic reviews of the literature.

School

Interests are related to choice of a major and academic adjustment. Studies (e.g., Lapan, Shaughnessy, & Boggs, 1996) have found that interests of high school students are predictive of their choice of college majors. Surveys (e.g., Hansen & Sackett, 1993; Holland, 1985) on college undergraduates have, in turn, consistently found a high degree of fit between their interest profiles and their majors. Moreover, educational environments act to accentuate students' interests over time. College students in different Holland environments tended to become more like their environments. For example, Smart (1997) found students in enterprising majors to report higher personal growth in career and leadership, social majors to report more educational and social growth, and artistic majors to report more artistic and cultural growth than students outside their Holland-typed majors.

Results on the outcomes of interest congruence in educational settings are less robust; most findings were consistent with theoretical predictions, but a small number of studies (e.g., Chartrand, Camp, & McFadden, 1992) found no significant effects on a variety of criterion variables. In general, college students whose interests were congruent with their majors encountered fewer problems in adjusting to college life (Walsh & Russell, 1969), had higher self-esteem (Leonard, Walsh, & Osipow, 1973), were more academically adjusted (Walsh, Spokane, & Mitchell, 1976), and had better academic performances (Reutefors, Schneider, & Overton, 1979) than their noncongruent peers.

Workplace

Interests are highly reliable predictors of occupational membership, tenure, and job satisfaction and performance. In Fouad's (1999) review, she reports that "somewhere between 40 percent and 60 percent of individuals are in occupations that may be predicted from their inventory results" (p. 202). Furthermore, the predictive ability of interests remains robust across long periods of time. Strong (1943), for example, reported hits rates as high as 78 percent in the prediction of occupational membership based on interest scores obtained 5 to 18 years prior. Representative-sample studies using census data report a similar trend; most changes in careers are characterized by transitions within the same RIASEC type (e.g., Gottfredson, 1977).

In addition to initiating behavior, interests also influence individuals' likelihood to persist in their jobs. Interest congruence is associated with longer occupational tenure (Gottfredson & Holland, 1990), and individuals in incongruent occupations are more likely to contemplate changing their jobs (Vaitenas & Wiener, 1977). Moreover, when these changes do occur, they tended to move in the direction of greater congruence (Oleski & Subich, 1996). Morris (2003) reported a meta-analysis of 17 studies with tenure as the criterion and reported a mean congruence-tenure correlation of .13 after correcting for sampling error.

Many studies have focused on the association between interest congruence and job satisfaction. Studies across a diversity of occupational settings have found a weak to moderate correlation between congruence and satisfaction. Barge and Hough (1988) reviewed 18 such studies and reported a median correlation of .31 between interests and satisfaction. A number of meta-analytic reviews (Assouline & Meir, 1987; Morris, 2003; Tranberg, Slane, & Ekeberg, 1993) have been conducted on the literature and have found somewhat lower associations between congruence and satisfaction. Tranberg and colleagues limited their review to only studies that have been published ($k = 17$) and reported a mean correlation of .20 and a 95 percent confidence interval (CI) from $-.06$ to .45. An almost identical estimate of .21 (95% CI $= -.09$ to .51) was reported by Assouline and Meir's (1987) meta-analysis, which was based on 53 correlations and included unpublished theses. In a recent meta-analysis of 76 correlations, Morris (2003) obtained a mean correlation of .24, with a 95 percent CI from .03 to .45, after correcting for sampling error and scale reliability. Taken together, there is support for congruence as a contributor to job satisfaction.

The link between congruence and satisfaction may not be as unequivocal as indicated by the meta-analytic estimates. Because most incumbents are likely to express satisfaction with their work, many researchers (e.g., Campbell, 1971; Rounds, McKenna, Hubert, & Day, 2000) have proposed that the restriction of range in people's self-reports of satisfaction may be responsible for the lack of significant findings in some congruence-satisfaction studies. In addition, the manner in which congruence is evaluated often has been cited as a likely confound affecting the magnitude and significance of correlations between congruence and outcome variables. Morris (2003) aggregated 75 studies by the complexity of

their congruence indexes into three categories. Contrary to previous assertions (e.g., Camp & Chartrand, 1992), the meta-analytic estimates were the lowest for the most sophisticated indexes ($\rho = .10$), followed by the crudest indexes ($\rho = .17$). Indexes at the moderate or middle level of complexity evidenced the highest mean correlation with satisfaction ($\rho = .27$).

Given the person-centered focus of interest research, there is comparatively less research on the relationship between interests and the degree to which an employee is regarded by others as satisfactory. Although there are occasional negative findings, studies (e.g., Fritzsche, Powell, & Hoffman, 1999; Tziner, Meir, & Segal, 2002) generally have demonstrated low and significant correlations between congruence and performance ratings across a variety of occupational groups. Barge and Hough (1988) reviewed the findings of 11 studies and report correlations ranging from .01 to .40, with a median correlation of .20. An earlier meta-analysis by Hunter and Hunter (1984) reported a mean congruence-performance rating correlation of .10.

Some researchers (see Cardy & Dobbins, 1994) suggest that performance ratings may not be an accurate measure of actual performance and are instead heavily influenced by the personal-social relationships between supervisor and subordinate rather than the output of the subordinate in question. Indeed, correlations tended to be higher between congruence and objective indexes of worker productivity. In Barge and Hough's (1988) review, for instance, congruence-productivity correlations were found to be higher than performance rating correlations, with a median correlation of .33 (cf., .20). In the same vein, Morris (2003) reported a much higher meta-analytic estimate for the correlation between task performance ($\rho = .31$), proficiency in which incumbents perform the activities important for their jobs, compared to contextual performance ($\rho = .13$), extra-task proficiency that contributes to organizational, social, and psychological environment.

Leisure and Retirement

Leisure is perceived as relatively self-determined, discretionary activities (see Howe & Rancourt, 1990). Individuals' leisure interests correlate highly with their reported vocational interests (Hansen & Scullard, 2002). Kerby and Ragan (2002) demonstrated that the leisure activities of older adults can be classified into nine categories. The pattern of relationships between these nine categories in Euclidean space coincided with Holland's circular model, suggesting that nonwork activities (and environments) share a similar structure as occupational activities. Indeed, people in congruent occupations perceived their leisure activities as an extension of the type of activities they did at work (Melamed & Meir, 1981). Conversely, leisure activities are also a source of mastery and self-fulfillment experiences not available at the workplace. As such, individuals engaging in congruent leisure activities are more satisfied with their jobs and reported better psychological and physical health (Melamed, Meir, & Samson, 1995).

Retirement from work constitutes one of the most important later life events, and the fluidity of the transition is associated with a wide variety of health variables (see Kim & Moen, 2002). There is evidence (Herzog, House, & Morgan, 1991; Kim & Moen, 2002) indicating that retirees who are engaged in activities of their choice are more satisfied with their lives and remain in better psychological and physical health. Moreover, the sense of personal control is implicated in older adults' overall well-being (Rodin, Timko, & Harris, 1985). Researchers (e.g., Bronfenbrenner, 1995) also have advocated the importance of locating transitions within the context of retirees' environments and social relationships. The notion of choice and personal control within the context of one's environments is the central theme of interest congruence. Fitting a person's attributes to an appropriate environment extends beyond the workplace. Given the availability and good psychometrics of interest inventories, interests can help identify postwork environments that are most conducive to the optimal functioning of older adults.

General Well-Being

The research on the link between interests and individuals' well-being is relatively sparse. As noted in our review of congruence research on college students, interest-congruent individuals tended to have fewer life and academic adjustment issues (Walsh & Russell, 1969; Walsh et al., 1976) and reported higher self-esteem (Leonard et al., 1973). In a unique study, Celeste, Walsh, and Raote (1995) found significant differences on eight Minnesota Multiphasic Personality Inventory (MMPI) subscales between congruent, incongruent, and moderately congruent groups of male ministers. Congruent ministers evidenced better psychological adjustment than moderately congruent ministers, who were in turn better adjusted than ministers whose interests were incongruent with their profession.

The implications of interests on psychological and physical well-being become more obvious when examining work and health. Role conflict and ambiguity—postulated by Holland (1997) to be consequences of a diffuse identity—are tied to illness precursors and illness (Caplan & Jones, 1975). Perceptions that one's career development is inadequate—a potential manifestation of incongruence—increase the incidence of psychological distress and poor health, especially cardiovascular disease (Catalano, Dooley, Wilson, & Hough, 1993). Moreover, a lack of congruence between individuals' interests and their occupations is also implicated in an increase in the amount of stress felt at work (Sutherland, Fogarty, & Pithers, 1995). Work stress is significantly associated with poorer physical and psychological functioning (Lerner, Levine, Malspeis, & D'Agostino, 1994). Stress experienced at the workplace also negatively influences spousal relationships (Kelloway, & Barling, 1995) and parent-child interactions (Crouter & Bumpus, 2001), leading to poor familial outcomes.

Holland's notion that "birds of a feather flock together" implied that incongruent individuals are likely to be dissimilar to their coworkers. There is robust evidence (see McPherson, Smith-Lovin, & Cook, 2001) that people are more likely to form meaningful relationships with others who are similar to them. Many studies of the workplace (e.g., Ibarra, 1995) found that the support networks formed are shaped not just by the composition of the organization but even more strongly by the organizational demography at an individual's own level and job title. We expect incongruent workers to have reduced social networks and thus are less likely to enjoy the health-promoting benefits of social ties (Berkman, 1995). Moreover, a lack of satisfying work relationships also is connected with more negative affect at work (Bunnk, Doosie, Jans, & Hopstaken, 1993) and poorer physical and mental health (Repetti, 1993).

CONCLUSION

Interests are more than just a person's preference of an occupation or work environment. When we think about our interests, we also are thinking of critical features of different environments and the behaviors entailed in those environments. In defining the environmental affordances, interests constitute the means of attaining our goals. Human action is energized and directed toward attaining and maintaining environments best suited to fulfill individuals' needs. In that sense, interests describe the means and environments in which people can function optimally. The degree of congruence between one's interests and environment has wide-ranging implications on one's well-being in multiple life domains. The importance of interests in life decisions go beyond the initial career choices and affect an individual's success and satisfaction across the entire life course.

REFERENCES

Anderson, M. Z., Tracey, T. J. G., & Rounds, J. B. (1997). Examining the invariance of Holland's vocational interest model across sex. *Journal of Vocational Behavior, 50,* 349–364.

Armstrong, P. I., Hubert, L., & Rounds, J. B. (2003). Circular uni-dimensional scaling: A new look at group differences in interest structure. *Journal of Counseling Psychology, 50,* 297–308.

Armstrong, P. I., Smith, T. J., Donnay, D. A. C., & Rounds, J. B. (2004). The Strong ring: A basic interest model of occupational structure. *Journal of Counseling Psychology, 51,* 229–313.

Assouline, M., & Meir, E. I. (1987). Meta-analysis of the relationship between congruence and well-being measures. *Journal of Vocational Behavior, 31,* 319–332.

Bandura, A., Barbaranelli, C., Caprara, G. V., & Pastorelli, C. (2001). Self-efficacy beliefs as shapers of children's aspirations and career trajectories. *Child Development, 72,* 187–20.

Barge, B. N., & Hough, L. M. (1988). Utility of biographical data for the prediction of job performance. In L. M. Hough (Ed.), *Literature review: Utility of temperament, biodata, and interest assessment for predicting job performance* (ARI Research Note 88–020). Alexandria, VA: U.S. Army Research Institute.

Barrick, M. R., Mount, M. K., & Gupta, R. (2003). Meta-analysis of the relationship between the five-factor model of personality and Holland's occupational types. *Personnel Psychology, 56,* 45–74.

Barrick, M. R., Mount, M. K., & Judge, T. A. (2001). Personality and performance at the beginning of the new millennium: What do we know and where do we go next? *International Journal of Selection and Assessment, 9,* 9–31.

Berkman, L. F. (1995). The role of social relations in health promotion. *Psychosomatic Medicine, 57,* 245–254.

Betsworth, D. G., Bouchard, T. J., Cooper, C. R., Grotevant, H. D., Hansen, J. C., Scarr, S., et al. (1994). Genetic and environmental influences on vocational interests assessed using adoptive and biological families and twins reared apart and together. *Journal of Vocational Behavior, 44,* 263–278.

Betz, N. E., & Schifano, R. S. (2000). Evaluation of an invention to increase realistic self-efficacy and interest in college women. *Journal of Vocational Behavior, 56,* 35–52.

Blustein, D. L., Phillips, S. D., Jobin-Davis, K., Finkelberg, S. L., & Roarke, A. E. (1997). A theory-building investigation of the school-to-work transition. *The Counseling Psychologist, 25,* 364–402.

Bronfenbrenner, U. (1995). Developmental ecology through space and time: A future perspective. In P. Moen, G. H. Elder, & K. Luscher (Eds.), *Examining lives in context: Perspectives on the ecology of human development* (pp. 599–647). Washington, DC: American Psychological Association.

Bunnk, B. P., Doosie, B. J., Jans, L. G. J. M., & Hopstaken, L. E. M. (1993). Perceived reciprocity, social support, and stress at work: The role of exchange and communal orientation. *Journal of Personality and Social Psychology, 65,* 801–811.

Byrne, D. (1997). An overview (and underview) of research and theory within the attraction paradigm. *Journal of Social and Personal Relationships, 14,* 417–431.

Cairns, R. B., & Hood, K. E. (1983). Continuity in social development: A comparative perspective on individual differences

prediction. In P. B. Baltes & O. G. Brim Jr. (Eds.), *Life-span developmental psychology* (Vol. 5, pp. 301–358). New York: Academic Press.

Camp, C. C., & Chartrand, J. M. (1992). A comparison and evaluation of interest congruence indices. *Journal of Vocational Behavior, 41,* 162–182.

Campbell, D. P. (1971). *Handbook for the Strong Vocational Interest Blank.* Stanford, CA: Stanford University Press.

Caplan, R. D., & Jones, J. W. (1975). Effects of workload, role ambiguity and type A personality on anxiety, depression, and heart rate. *Journal of Applied Psychology, 60,* 713–719.

Cardy, R. L., & Dobbins, G. H. (1994). *Performance appraisal: Alternative perspectives.* Florence, KY: South Western.

Catalano, R., Dooley, D., Wilson, G., & Hough, R. (1993). Job loss and alcohol abuse: A test using data from the Epidemiologic Catchment Area project. *Journal of Health and Social Behavior, 34,* 215–225.

Celeste, B. L., Walsh, W. B., & Raote, R. G. (1995). Congruence and psychological adjustment for practicing male ministers. *Career Development Quarterly, 43,* 374–384.

Chartrand, J. M., Camp, C. C., & McFadden, K. L. (1992). Predicting academic adjustment and career indecision: A comparison of self-efficacy, interest congruence, and commitment. *Journal of College Student Development, 33,* 293–300.

Costa, P. T., McCrae, R. R., & Holland, J. L. (1984). Personality and vocational interests in an adult sample. *Journal of Applied Psychology, 69,* 390–400.

Craik, K. H. (2000). The lived day of an individual: A person-environment perspective. In W. B. Walsh, K. H. Craik, & R. H. Price (Eds.), *Person-environment psychology: New directions and perspectives* (pp. 233–266). Mahwah, NJ: Erlbaum.

Crouter, A. C., & Bumpus, M. F. (2001). Linking parents' work stress to children's and adolescents' psychological adjustment. *Current Directions in Psychological Science, 10,* 156–159.

Dawis, R. V. (1991). Vocational interests, values, and preferences. In M. D. Dunnette & L. Hough (Eds.), *Handbook of industrial and organizational psychology* (Vol. 2, 2nd ed., pp. 833–872). Palo Alto, CA: Consulting Psychologists Press.

Day, S. X., & Rounds, J. (1998). The universality of vocational interest structure among racial/ethnic minorities. *American Psychologist, 53,* 728–736.

Day, S. X., Rounds, J., & Swaney, K. (1998). The structure of vocational interests for diverse racial-ethnic groups. *Psychological Science, 9,* 40–44.

Deci, E. (1971). Effects of externally mediated rewards on intrinsic motivation. *Journal of Personality and Social Psychology, 18,* 105–115.

Deci, E., & Ryan, R. (1991). A motivational approach to self: Integration in personality. In R. Dienstbier (Ed.), *Perspectives on motivation. Nebraska Symposium on Motivation.* Lincoln: University of Nebraska Press.

De Fruyt, F., & Mervielde, I. (1997). The five-factor model of personality and Holland's RIASEC interest types. *Personality and Individual Differences, 23,* 87–103.

Dornbusch, S. M., Glasgow, K. L., & Lin, I. C. (1996). The social structure of schooling. *Annual Review of Psychology, 47,* 401–402.

du Toit, R., & de Bruin, G. P.(2002). The structural validity of Holland's R-I-A-S-E-C model of vocational personality types for young black South African men and women. *Journal of Career Assessment, 10,* 62–77.

Edwards, J. (1991). Person-job fit: A conceptual integration, literature review and methodological critique. *International Review of Industrial and Organisational Psychology, 6,* 283–358.

Einarsdóttir, S., Rounds, J., Ægisdóttir, S., & Gerstein, L. H. (2002). The structure of vocational interests in Iceland: Examining Holland's and Gati's RIASEC models. *European Journal of Psychological Assessment, 18,* 85–95.

Finkel, D., Pedersen, N. L., McGue, M., & McClearn, G. E. (1995). Heritability of cognitive abilities in adult twins: Comparison of Minnesota and Swedish data. *Behavior Genetics, 25,* 421–431.

Fouad, N. A. (1999). Validity evidence for interest inventories. In M. L. Savickas & R. L. Spokane (Eds.), *Vocational interests: Meaning, measurement, and counseling use* (pp. 193–209). Palo Alto, CA: Davies-Black.

Fouad, N. A., Harmon, L. W., & Borgen, F. H. (1997). Structure of interests in employed male and female members of U.S. racial-ethnic minority and nonminority groups. *Journal of Counseling Psychology, 44,* 329–345.

Fritzsche, B. A., Powell, A. B., & Hoffman, R. (1999). Person-environment congruence as a predictor of customer service performance. *Journal of Vocational Behavior, 54,* 59–70.

Fryer, D. (1931). *The measurement of interests.* New York: Henry Holt.

Glidden-Tracey, C. E., & Parraga, M. I. (1996). Assessing the structure of vocational interests among Bolivian university students. *Journal of Vocational Behavior, 48,* 96–106.

Gottfredson, G. D. (1977). Career stability and redirection in adulthood. *Journal of Applied Psychology, 62,* 436–445.

Gottfredson, G. D., & Holland, J. L. (1990). A longitudinal test of the influence of congruence: Job satisfaction, competency utilization, and counterproductive behavior. *Journal of Counseling Psychology, 37,* 389–398.

Gottfredson, G. D., & Holland, J. L. (1996). *Dictionary of Holland occupational codes* (3rd ed.). Odessa, FL: Psychological Assessment Resources.

Gottfredson, G. D., Jones, E. M., & Holland, J. L. (1993). Personality and vocational interests: The relation of Holland's six interest dimensions to five robust dimensions of personality. *Journal of Counseling Psychology, 40,* 518–524.

Gottfredson, L. (1981). Circumscription and compromise: A developmental theory of occupational aspirations. *Journal of Counseling Psychology, 28,* 545–580.

Guilford, J. P., Christensen, P. R., Bond, N. A., & Sutton, M. A. (1954). A factor analysis study of human interests. *Psychological Monographs, 68*(4).

Guttman, L. (1954). A new approach to factor analysis: The radex. In P. R. Lazarsfeld (Ed.), *Mathematical thinking in the social sciences.* Glencoe, IL: Free Press.

Hansen, J. C., & Sackett, S. A. (1993). Agreement between college major and vocational interests for female athlete and non-athlete college students. *Journal of Vocational Behavior, 43,* 298–309.

Hansen, J. C., & Scullard, M. (2002). Psychometric evidence for the Leisure Interest Questionnaire and analyses of the structure of leisure interests. *Journal of Counseling Psychology, 49,* 331–341.

Harmon, L. W., Hansen, J. C., Borgen, F. H., & Hammer, A. L. (1994). *Strong Interest Inventory: Applications and technical guide.* Stanford, CA: Stanford University Press.

Herzog, A. R., House, J., & Morgan, J. (1991). Relation of work and retirement to health and wellbeing. *Psychology of Aging, 6,* 202–211.

Holland, J. L. (1958). A personality inventory employing occupational titles. *Journal of Applied Psychology, 42,* 336–342.

Holland, J. L. (1973). *Making vocational choices: A theory of careers.* Englewood Cliffs, NJ: Prentice Hall.

Holland, J. L. (1976). Vocational preferences. In M. D. Dunnette (Ed.), *Handbook of industrial and organizational psychology* (pp. 521–570). Chicago: Rand-McNally.

Holland, J. L. (1985). *The self-directed search professional manual.* Odessa, FL: Psychological Assesment Resources.

Holland, J. L. (1997). *Making vocational choices: A theory of vocational personalities and work environments* (3rd ed.). Odessa, FL: Psychological Assessment Resources.

Holland, J., Powell, A, & Fritzsche, B. (1994) *Professional user's guide for the Self-Directed Search.* Odessa, FL: Psychological Assessment Resources.

Hough, L. (2003). Emerging trends and needs in personality research and practice: Beyond main effects. In M. Barrick & A. M. Ryan (Eds.), *Personality and work.* San Francisco: Jossey-Bass.

Howe, C. Z., & Rancourt, A. M. (1990). The importance of definitions of selected concepts for leisure inquiry. *Leisure Sciences, 12,* 395–406.

Hunter, J. E., & Hunter, R. E. (1984). Validity and utility of alternative predictors of job performance. *Psychological Bulletin, 96,* 72–98.

Ibarra, H. (1995). Race, opportunity, and diversity of social circles in managerial networks. *Academy of Management Journal, 38,* 673–703.

Jackson, D. N. (1977). *Manual for the Jackson Vocational Interest Survey.* Port Huron, MI: Research Psychologists Press.

Judge, T. A., Heller, D., & Mount, M. K. (2002). Five-factor model of personality and job satisfaction: A meta-analysis. *Journal of Applied Psychology, 87,* 530–541.

Kelloway, E. K., & Barling, J. (1995). Stress, control, well-being, and marital functioning: A causal correlational analysis. In G. P. Keita & J. J. Hurrell (Eds.), *Job stress in changing workforce* (pp. 241–251). Washington, DC: American Psychological Association.

Kerby, D. S., & Ragan, K. M. (2002). Activity interests and Holland's RIASEC system in older adults. *International Journal of Aging and Human Development, 55,* 117–139.

Kiesler, D. J. (1983). The 1982 interpersonal circle: A taxonomy for complementarity in human transactions. *Psychological Review, 90,* 185–214.

Kim, J., & Moen, P. (2002). Retirement transitions, gender, and psychological well-being. *Journal of Gerontology, 57,* 212—222.

Kuder, G. F. (1977). *Activity interests and occupational choice.* Chicago: Science Research Associates.

Lapan, R., Shaughnessy, P., & Boggs, K. (1996). Efficacy expectations and vocational interests as mediators between sex and choice of math/science college majors: A longitudinal study. *Journal of Vocational Behavior, 49,* 277–291.

Larson, L. M., Rottinghaus, P. J., & Borgen, F. (2002). Meta-analyses of Big Six interests and Big Five personality factors. *Journal of Vocational Behavior, 61,* 217–239.

Lent, R. W., Brown, S. D., & Hackett, G. (1994). Toward a unifying social cognitive theory of career and academic interest, choice, and performance. *Journal of Vocational Behavior, 45,* 79–122.

Leonard, R. L, Walsh, W. B., & Osipow, S. H. (1973). Self-esteem, self-consistency, and second vocational choice. *Journal of Counseling Psychology, 20,* 91–93.

Leong, F. T. L. (1995). *Career development and vocational behavior of racial and ethnic minorities.* Hillsdale, NJ: Erlbaum.

Lerner, D., Levine, S., Malspeis, S., & D'Agostino, R. B. (1994). Job strain and health-related quality of life in a national sample. *American Journal of Public Health, 84,* 1580–1585.

Levinson, D. J. (1986). A Conception of Adult Development. *American Psychologist, 41,* 3–13.

Liu, C., & Rounds, J. (2003). Evaluating the structure of vocational interests in China. *Acta Psychologica Sinica, 35,* 411–418.

Low, K. S. D., Yoon, M., Roberts, B. W., & Rounds, J. B. (in press). *The stability of interests from early adolescence to middle adulthood: A quantitative review of longitudinal studies.* Psychological Bulletin.

Lykken, D. T., Bouchard, T. J., Jr., McGue, M., & Tellegen, A. (1993). Heritability of interests: A twin study. *Journal of Applied Psychology, 78,* 649–661.

Magnus, K., Diener, B., Fujita, F., & Pavot, W. (1993). Extraversion and neuroticism as predictors of objective life events: A longitudinal analysis. *Journal of Personality and Social Psychology, 65,* 1046–1053.

Marks, S. R. (1994). Intimacy in the public realm: The case of co-workers. *Social Forces, 72,* 843–858.

McCrae, R. R., & Costa, P. T. (1999). A five-factory theory of personality. In L. A. Pervin & O. P. John (Eds.), *Handbook of personality: Theory and research* (pp. 139–153). New York: Guilford.

McPherson, M., Smith-Lovin, L., & Cook, J. M. (2001). Birds of a feather: Homophily in social networks. *Annual Review of Sociology, 27,* 415–444.

Meir, E. I., & Navon, M. (1992). A longitudinal examination of congruence hypotheses. *Journal of Vocational Behavior, 41,* 35–47.

Melamed, S., & Meir, E. I. (1981). The relationship between interests-job incongruity and selection of avocational activity. *Journal of Vocational Behavior, 14,* 310–325.

Melamed, S., Meir, E. I., & Samson, A. (1995). The benefits of personality-leisure congruence: Evidence and implications. *Journal of Leisure Research, 27,* 25–40.

Moloney, D. P., Bouchard, T. J., Segal, N. L. (1991). A genetic and environmental analysis of the vocational interests of monozygotic and dizygotic twins reared apart. *Journal of Vocational Behavior, 39,* 76–109.

Morris, M. A. (2003). A meta-analytic investigation of vocational interest-based job fit, and its relationship to job satisfaction, performance, and turnover. *Dissertation Abstracts International, 64,* 2428.

Nauta, M. M., Epperson, D. L., & Kahn, J. H. (1998). A multiple groups analysis of predictors of higher level career aspirations among women in science and engineering. *Journal of Counseling Psychology, 45,* 483–496.

Oleski, D., & Subich, L. M. (1996). Congruence and career change in employed adults. *Journal of Vocational Behavior, 49,* 221–229.

Organ, D. W., & Lingl, A. (1995). Personality, satisfaction, and organizational citizenship behavior. *Journal of Social Psychology, 135,* 339–350.

Pals, J. L. (1999). Identity consolidation in early adulthood: Relations with ego-resiliency, the context of marriage, and personality change. *Journal of Personality, 67,* 295–329.

Parson, F. (1909). *Choosing a vocation.* Boston: Houghton Mifflin.

Plomin, R., & Caspi, A. (1999). Behavioral genetics and personality. In L. A. Pervin & O. P. John (Eds.), *Handbook of personality: Theory and research* (2nd ed., pp. 251–276). New York: Guilford Press.

Prediger, D. J. (1982). Dimensions underlying Holland's hexagon: Missing link between interests and occupations? *Journal of Vocational Behavior, 21,* 259–287.

Repetti, R. L. (1993). The effects of workload and the social environment at work on health. In L. Goldberger & S. Bresnitz (Eds.), *Handbook of stress* (pp. 368–385). New York: Free Press.

Reutefors, D. L., Schneider, L. J., & Overton, T. D. (1979). Academic achievement: An examination of Holland's congruence, consistency, and differentiation predictions. *Journal of Vocational Behavior, 14,* 181–189.

Rholes, W. S., Ruble, D. N., & Newman, L. S. (1990). Children's understanding of self and other: Developmental and motivational aspects of perceiving persons in terms of invariant dispositions. In R. M. Sorrentino & E. T. Higgins (Eds.), *Handbook of motivation and cognition: Foundations of social behavior* (Vol. 2, pp. 369–407). Hillsdale, NJ: Erlbaum.

Roberts, B. W., & Caspi, A. (2003). The cumulative continuity model of personality development: Striking a balance between continuity and change in personality traits across the life course. In R. M. Staudinger & U. Lindenberger (Eds.), *Understanding human development: Lifespan psychology in exchange with other disciplines* (pp. 183–214). Dordrecht, Netherlands: Kluwer.

Roberts, B. W., Caspi, A., & Moffitt, T. (2003). Work experiences and personality development in young adulthood. *Journal of Personality and Social Psychology, 84,* 582–593.

Roberts, B. W., & Chapman, C. (2000). Change in dispositional well-being and its relation to role quality: A 30-year longitudinal study. *Journal of Research in Personality, 34,* 26–41.

Roberts, B. W., & DelVecchio, W. F. (2000). The rank-order consistency of personality from childhood to old age: A quantitative review of longitudinal studies. *Psychological Bulletin, 126,* 3–25.

Rodin, J., Timko, C., & Harris, S. (1985). The construct of control: Biological and psychosocial correlates. *Annual Review of Gerontology and Geriatrics, 5,* 3–55.

Roe, A., & Klos, D. (1969). Occupational classification. *Counseling Psychologist, 1,* 84–92.

Rounds, J. (1995). Vocational interests: Evaluating structural hypotheses. In D. Lubinski & R. V. Dawis (Eds.), *Assessing individual differences in human behavior: New concepts, methods and findings* (pp. 177–232) Palo Alto, CA: Davies-Black.

Rounds, J., & Dawis, R. V. (1979). Factor analysis of Strong Vocational Interest Blank Items. *Journal of Applied Psychology, 64,* 132–143.

Rounds, J., & Day, S. X. (1999). Describing, evaluating, and creating vocational interest structures. In M. L. Savickas & A. R. Spokane (Eds.), *Vocational interests: Meaning, measurement, and counseling use* (pp. 103–133). Palo Alto, CA: Davies-Black.

Rounds, J., McKenna, M. C., Hubert, L., & Day, S. X. (2000). Response: Tinsley on Holland: A misshapen argument. *Journal of Vocational Behavior, 56,* 205–215.

Rounds, J., & Tracey, T. J. (1990). From trait-and-factor to person-environment fit counseling: Theory and process. In W. B. Walsh & S. J. Osipow (Eds.), *Career counseling: Contemporary topics in vocational psychology* (pp. 1–44). Hillsdale, NJ: Erlbaum.

Rounds, J., & Tracey, T. J. G. (1993). Prediger's dimensional representation of Holland's RIASEC circumplex. *Journal of Applied Psychology, 78,* 875–890.

Rounds, J., & Tracey, T. J. G. (1996). Cross-cultural structural equivalence of RIASEC models and measures. *Journal of Counseling Psychology, 43,* 310–329.

Ryan, R. M. (1982). Control and information in the intrapersonal sphere: An extension of cognitive evaluation theory. *Journal of Personality and Social Psychology, 43,* 450–461.

Ryan, R. M., & Deci, E. L. (2000). Self-determination theory and the facilitation of intrinsic motivation, social development, and well-being. *American Psychologist, 55,* 68–78.

Silvia, P. J. (2001). Interest and interests: The psychology of constructive capriciousness. *Review of General Psychology, 5,* 270–290.

Smart, J. C. (1997). Academic sub-environments and differential patterns of self-perceived growth during college: A test of Holland's theory. *Journal of College Student Development, 38,* 68–72.

Soh, S., & Leong, F. T. L (2001). Cross-cultural validation of Holland's theory in Singapore: Beyond structural validity of RIASEC. *Journal of Career Assessment, 9,* 115–132.

Spokane, A. R., Meir, E. I., & Catalano, M. (2000). Person-environment congruence and Holland's theory: A review and reconsideration. *Journal of Vocational Behavior, 57,* 137–187.

Strong, E. K. (1943). *The vocational interests of men and women.* Stanford, CA: Stanford University Press.

Strong, E. K. (1951). Permanence of interest scores over 22 years. *Journal of Applied Psychology, 35,* 89–91.

Strong, E. K. (1955). *Vocational interests 18 years after college.* Minneapolis: University of Minnesota Press.

Sutherland, L., Fogarty, G., & Pithers, R. (1995). Congruence as a predictor of occupational stress. *Journal of Vocational Behavior, 46,* 292–309.

Swaney, K. B. (1995). *Technical manual: Revised unisex edition of the ACT Interest Inventory (UNIACT).* Iowa City, IA: ACT, Inc.

Swanson, J. H., & Hansen, J. C. (1988). Stability of vocational interests over 4-year, 8-year, and 12-year intervals. *Journal of Vocational Behavior, 33,* 185–202.

Swanson, J. L. (1999). Stability and change in vocational interests. In M. L. Savickas & R. L. Spokane (Eds.), *Vocational interests: Meaning, measurement, and counseling use* (pp. 135–158). Palo Alto, CA: Davies-Black.

Task Force on Education of Young Adolescents. (1989). *Turning points: Preparing American youth for the 21st century.* Washington, DC: Carnegie Council on Adolescent Development.

Tinsley, H. E. A. (2000). The congruence myth: An analysis of the efficacy of the person-environment fit model. *Journal of Vocational Behavior, 56,* 147–179.

Tokar, D. M., Fischer, A. R., & Subich, L. M. (1998). Personality and vocational behavior: A selective review of the literature, 1993–1997. *Journal of Vocational Behavior, 53,* 115–153.

Tower, R. B., & Kasl, S. V. (1996). Depressive symptoms across older spouses: Longitudinal influences. *Psychology and Aging, 11,* 683–697.

Tracey, T. J. G. (2002). Personal Globe Inventory: Measurement of the spherical model of interests and competence beliefs. *Journal of Vocational Behavior, 60,* 113–172.

Tracey, T. J., & Rounds, J. (1993). Evaluating Holland's and Gati's vocational interest models: A structural meta-analysis. *Psychological Bulletin, 113,* 229—246.

Tracey, T. J., & Rounds, J. (1995). The arbitrary nature of Holland's RIASEC types: A concentric-circles structure. *Journal of Counseling Psychology, 42,* 431–439.

Tracey, T. J. G., & Rounds, J. (1996). The spherical representation of vocational interests. *Journal of Vocational Behavior, 48,* 3–41.

Tracey, T. J. G., & Ward, C. C. (1998). The structure of children's interests and competence perceptions. *Journal of Counseling Psychology, 45,* 290–303.

Tracey, T. J. G., Watanabe, N., & Schneider, P. L. (1997). Structural invariance of vocational interests across Japanese and American cultures. *Journal of Counseling Psychology, 44,* 346–354.

Tranberg, M., Slane, S., & Ekeberg, E. (1993). The relation between interest congruence and satisfaction: A meta-analysis. *Journal of Vocational Behavior, 42,* 253–264.

Trice, A. D. (1991). Stability of children's career aspirations. *Journal of Genetic Psychology, 152,* 137–139.

Trice, A. D., & Rush, K. (1995). Sex-stereotyping in four-year-olds' occupational aspirations. *Perceptual and Motor Skills, 81,* 701–702.

Tziner, A., Meir, E. I., & Segal, H. (2002). Occupational congruence and personal task-related attributes: How do they relate to work performance? *Journal of Career Assessment, 10,* 401–412.

U.S. Department of Labor. (1998). *O*NET 98: Data dictionary.* Washington, DC: U.S. Government Printing Office.

Vaitenas, R., & Wiener, Y. (1977). Developmental, emotional, and interest factors in voluntary mid-career change. *Journal of Vocational Behavior, 11,* 291–304.

Waller, N. G., Lykken, D. T., & Tellegen, A. (1995). Occupational interests, leisure time interests, and personality. In D. Lubinski & R. V. Dawis (Eds.), *Assessing individual differences in human behavior: New concepts, methods, and findings* (pp. 233–259). Palo Alto, CA: Davies-Black.

Walsh, W. B., & Russell, J. H. (1969). College major choice and personal adjustment. *Personnel and Guidance Journal. 47,* 685–688.

Walsh, W. B., Spokane, A. R., & Mitchell, E. (1976). Consistent occupational preferences and academic adjustment. *Research in Higher Education, 4,* 123–129.

Watson, D., & Clark, L. A. (1997). Extraversion and its positive emotional core. In R. Hogan, J. Johnson, & S. Briggs (Eds.), *Handbook of personality psychology* (pp. 767–793). San Diego, CA: Academic Press.

Wiggins, J. S. (1982). Circumplex models of interpersonal behavior in clinical psychology. In P. C. Kendall & J. N. Butcher (Eds.), *Handbook of research methods in clinical psychology* (pp. 183–221). New York: Wiley.

Wright, J. C., Huston, A. C., Truglio, R., Fitch, M., Smith, E., & Piemyat, S. (1995). Occupational portrayals on television: Children's role schemata, career aspirations and perceptions of reality. *Child Development, 66,* 1706–1718.

Young, G., Tokar, D. M., & Subich, L. M. (1998). Congruence revisited: Do 11 indices differentially predict job satisfaction and is the relation moderated by person and situation variables? *Journal of Vocational Behavior, 52,* 208–223.

CHAPTER 14

Positive and Negative Affect: Bridging States and Traits

PAUL J. SILVIA AND JOHN B. WARBURTON

Even when viewed with the generous eye of history, psychology's neglect of emotions for most of the last century is surprising. Emotions were reduced to activation and arousal, rejected as mere fictions, or simply ignored (see Duffy, 1934; Oatley, 2004). But inner subjective experience is difficult to deny (Seager, 2002); it was only a matter of time before psychologists applied the hard-nosed spirit of behavioral research to the problems posed by human emotions. The result of their research efforts is an explosion of research on emotional experience. The study of emotions has never been more popular. It is seen in the formation of journals and organizations, in the priorities of funding agencies, and in the ceaseless flow of books and articles about emotional life. The study of emotions is now maturing into an overarching area of psychology, one that speaks to fundamental concerns of clinical, social, personality, developmental, and cognitive psychologists.

This chapter explores positive and negative affect as aspects of immediate experience and as aspects of enduring qualities of people. One branch of research, associated with emotion psychology, has studied the dynamics of momentary emotional experience. This is the study of the causes and consequences of transient moods and emotional states (Ekman, 1992; Lazarus, 1991). Another branch of research, associated with personality psychology, has studied enduring dispositions related to emotions. This is the study of the many predispositions to experience an emotion, such as trait anxiety, neuroticism, and positive and negative affectivity (see Watson, 2000). As Cronbach (1957) contended long ago, psychology should be able to integrate individual differences with situational processes. In the first part of this chapter, we review emotions, moods, and the dynamics of momentary feelings. In the second part of this chapter, we review traits relevant to positive and negative affect. Studying positive and negative affect at situational and dispositional levels provides a richer understanding of the psychology of emotional experience.

POSITIVE AND NEGATIVE AFFECT AS MOMENTARY STATES

One class of research investigates positive and negative affect as momentary states, as aspects of immediate experience. This domain examines the nature and structure of emotional experience, how thoughts and feelings affect each other, and how people express and control their emotions. When thinking about the momentary experience of positive and negative affect, it is helpful to distinguish between emotions and mood (Watson, 2000). In the first part of this section, we will describe classic and modern theories of emotion and mood. In the second part of this section, we will review how people regulate their moods and emotions.

Emotions

What is an emotion? This old question, like many old questions, has many answers. Nearly all modern theories of emotion define emotions as coherent sets of components—no single feature of an emotion is sufficient. Roseman (2001), for example, defines emotions as syndromes of expressions, physiology, phenomenology, behaviors, and goals. Similarly, Scherer (2001) proposes that emotions consist of cognitive, motivational, expressive, physiological, and experiential components. Ekman (1992) adds coherence between the emotion's components, rapid onset and brief duration, and unbidden occurrence; other researchers would add appearance in early life and adaptive functions across the life span as defining features of emotions (Izard, 1977; Izard & Ackerman, 2000).

Emotions have many features that suggest they are innate. Since Darwin (1872/1998), the evolutionary evidence has stimulated a lot of thought about the adaptive functions of emotions (Brehm, 1999; Keltner & Gross, 1999; Oatley & Jenkins, 1992). People generally experience emotions that are appropriate to the situations that face them (Roseman & Smith, 2001); emotions arise automatically in response to adaptive crises (LeDoux, 1996), and some emotions have patterns of activation that prepare the body for action (Levenson, 1992). Parrott (2001) points out that functional views of emotions can go too far. Emotions can have maladaptive and counterproductive effects as well. He suggests that the issue is not if emotions are functional but rather when an emotion is functional. Emotions are probably functional in a narrow sense, such as adaptive for earlier environments or adaptive on average.

Basic Emotions

Theories of emotions split into two approaches. The *basic-emotions approach,* historically traced to Silvan Tomkins (1962, 1963), proposes a small group of distinct emotions (see Ekman, 1992). Basic emotions are universal, evolved mechanisms for dealing with fundamental adaptational tasks. Each emotion has a distinct facial expression (Ekman, 1993), physiological signature (Levenson, 1992), and biosocial function (Izard & Ackerman, 2000). The basic-emotions approach emphasizes emotions as psychobiological categories instead of points on dimensions. Happiness and sadness, for instance, are seen as qualitatively different emotion systems, not as opposing points on a dimension of valence. In this sense, basic emotions do not have opposites.

Theories of basic emotions disagree about exactly which emotions should be considered basic, and they have been sharply criticized for that reason (Ortony & Turner, 1990). The disagreement is not as troublesome as it might seem. The different lists of basic emotions reflect different taxonomic starting points. Some basic-emotion theories use universal facial expressions as their gold standard (Ekman, 1992); others use biological systems (Panksepp, 1998). The different lists follow from the different criteria of basicness. Furthermore, basic-emotion theories agree on a small group of emotions. Most basic-emotion theories include happiness, sadness, fear, anger, shame, and disgust; others include contempt, interest, surprise, and guilt (see Ekman, 1992; Izard, 1977).

Emotion psychologists commonly refer to *positive emotions* and *negative emotions,* but this distinction is not central to theories of emotions (see Fredrickson, 1998). There are many senses in which an emotion can be positive or negative: The subjective experience can be pleasant or unpleasant, the emotion can motivate prosocial or antisocial activity, or the events giving rise to the emotion can be beneficial or harmful (see Parkinson, 1995; Tomkins, 1962). As Lazarus (2001, p. 62) contends, "dividing discrete emotions into two types, negative and positive, obscures their individual substantive qualities and the complex relational meanings inherent in

each." This is probably why the terms *positive* and *negative emotions* are used casually by emotion psychologists. This highlights a difference between mood and emotion: Positive and negative moods are real psychological categories, but positive and negative emotions probably are not (cf. Griffiths, 1997).

Appraisal Theories of Emotions

Another group of theories, usually called *appraisal theories,* offers a different approach to the nature of emotion (Lazarus, 1991; Roseman, 2001; Scherer, 2001; Smith & Ellsworth, 1985). Appraisal theories contend that emotions come from evaluations of events. People continuously appraise events in the world for their significance for goals and well-being. Events appraised as relevant to the person are evaluated in additional detail. Emotions result from these patterns of evaluation, known as *appraisal structures,* of which we will have more to say later. The appraisal approach is thus a cognitive approach to emotions because emotions are traced to evaluations of events. It would be a mistake, however, to equate appraisal processes with conscious, deliberate reasoning. No appraisal theory assumes that appraisals are necessarily, or even primarily, conscious and controlled (Roseman & Smith, 2001). Appraisals can occur consciously and deliberately, but appraisal processes are primarily automatic and nonconscious. The environment can change quickly—to be useful, appraisals need to be fast (Lazarus, 2001).

It is important to appreciate the subjectivity inherent in the appraisal approach. Strictly speaking, events themselves do not cause emotions (see Lazarus, 2001). This subjectivity enables the appraisal approach to explain some of emotion psychology's hard questions. Roseman and Smith (2001) describe seven fundamental questions about emotions that appraisal theories can address:

1. How can we account for the differentiated nature of emotional response?

2. How can we explain individual and temporal differences in emotional response to the same event?

3. How can we account for the range of situations that evoke the same emotion?

4. What starts the process of emotional response?

5. How can we explain the appropriateness of emotional responses to the situations in which they occur?

6. What accounts for irrational aspects of emotions?

7. How can developmentally and clinically induced changes in emotion be explained?

If emotions are caused by events, it is hard to explain why an event evokes different emotions in different people (question 2) and why diverse events cause the same emotion (question 3). These questions are easily handled when one assumes that subjective evaluations of events cause emotions. If different people appraise the same event differently, then different emotions will result. If diverse events—such as unexpected car trouble, losing a favorite book, and having a manuscript rejected—are appraised similarly, then people will experience similar emotions.

Most appraisal research focuses on the structure of appraisal, the evaluations that collectively constitute the emotion. Each emotion has a unique appraisal structure composed of a set of appraisal components; this makes emotions different (question 1). As in any active area, there are a lot of theories of appraisal structure. These theories disagree in some respects, but their overall agreement is remarkably high (see Ellsworth & Scherer, 2003). As an example, Table 14.1 lists how three appraisal theories describe the appraisal structure of anger (Lazarus, 1991; Roseman, 2001; Scherer, 2001). The three theories agree on the appraisal components central to anger (see Kuppens, Van Mechelen, Smits, & De Boeck, 2003). All of them assume anger involves (1) appraising an event as incongruent with a goal or motive, (2) appraising an agent (typically another person) as blameworthy for the event, and (3) appraising one's potential to cope with the event as high, such as through self-assertion or aggression. The theories differ in some subtle ways. Lazarus and Scherer predict that an event is appraised as relevant to a goal before

it is appraised as incongruent; Roseman predicts that approach goals, not avoidance goals, are implicated in anger; and Scherer predicts that the event must be appraised as inconsistent with external social standards. This pattern of overlap is typical for appraisal theories, which usually agree on a central set of components but disagree about whether extra components are necessary.

Emotions, then, arise from the unfolding of sets of appraisal components. Some emotions have simple appraisal structures. Interest's structure, for example, consists of two appraisals: an appraisal of something as new, unexpected, or complex, and an appraisal of one's ability to comprehend the new, complex thing (Silvia, in press-a, in press-b, 2005). Other emotions have intricate appraisal structures. The appraisal structure of shame in Scherer's (2001) model, for instance, involves appraising an event as (1) relevant, (2) caused by the self, (3) urgent, (4) involving bad outcomes, (5) committed through negligence, and (6) inconsistent with personal standards.

Another way of viewing appraisal structures is to distill the set of components into a single theme. Lazarus (1991, 2001) advocates thinking of emotions in terms of holistic appraisals, known as *core relational themes*. An emotion's core relational theme "is a terse synthesis of the separate appraisal components into a complex, meaning-centered whole" (Lazarus, 2001, p. 64). Some of these themes are shown in Table 14.2. Lazarus further suggests that people can appraise events thematically without making the individual appraisals. For example, people might appraise an event as meaning they are making reasonable progress toward the realization of a goal instead of appraising an event as (1) relevant to the self, (2) congruent with a goal, and (3) likely to continue (Lazarus, 1991). Making one thematic appraisal is presumably faster and more efficient. There is little research, however, that tests how and when appraisals are compiled into thematic units.

The appraisal position implies that there are a lot of emotions, many more than are posited by the basic-emotions approach. If each emotion is defined by a unique appraisal structure, then the number of emotions is defined by the number of psychologically coherent combinations of appraisals.

TABLE 14.1   Components in the Appraisal Structure of Anger: Comparing Three Theories

Lazarus (1991)	Roseman (2001)	Scherer (2001)
Relevant to a goal	Inconsistent with a motive	Unexpected event
Incongruent with a goal	Blockage of an approach goal	Relevant to a goal
Ego-involvement (preserve or enhance the self)	High control potential	Inconsistent with a goal
Blaming an agent for the event	Caused by another person	Intentionally caused by another person
High coping potential		High coping potential
Expecting a positive outcome of the instrumental action		Inconsistent with external/social standards

Note. Adapted from Lazarus (1991), Roseman (2001), and Scherer (2001). In Lazarus's model, the first four components are seen as necessary and sufficient for anger; the remaining components facilitate anger. For Scherer's model, the components for rage/hot anger (versus irritation/cold anger) are listed.

TABLE 14.2   Some Emotions and Their Core Relational Themes

Emotion	Core Relational Theme
Sadness	Having experienced an irrevocable loss
Happiness	Making reasonable progress toward the realization of a goal
Anger	A demeaning offense against me and mine
Shame	Failing to live up to an ego-ideal

Note. Adapted from Lazarus (1991, 2001).

Scherer (2001) has suggested a multidimensional appraisal space defined by the intersection of each dimension of appraisal. Some regions represent modal emotions such as sadness, happiness, fear, and anger; nearby regions have the variants on the modal emotions; and some infrequent combinations of appraisals are subtle, complex states that lack natural language descriptors (see Ellsworth & Scherer, 2003).

Essentially all theories of appraisal contend that appraisals cause emotional experience (question 4; Roseman & Evdokas, 2004). How this happens is the study of the process of appraisal (Smith & Kirby, 2001). Appraisal theories assume that the process of evaluating events is continuous. When an emotion arises, the process of appraisal continues in search of changes in the situation. This is known as *reappraisal* (Lazarus, 2001). Reappraisal explains why an angered person does not remain angry indefinitely. Emotions abate, amplify, or transform into other emotions as a result of reappraisal. Perceiving a threat can arouse anxiety; reappraising the events may reveal that the threat was averted, thus reducing anxiety and creating relief (Lazarus, 1991).

A controversy in the study of appraisal processes is whether appraisals occur sequentially or simultaneously. Some theories argue that some appraisals unfold serially at several levels (Scherer, 1999, 2001). Other theories propose that events are appraised holistically as core relational themes or that appraisals are executed in parallel (Lazarus, 2001; Roseman & Smith, 2001). There is not much research on this topic, in part because there is little research on appraisal processes in general. Nevertheless, Scherer makes a strong theoretical case for a sequential process of appraisal. He points out that some appraisals are logically prior to others. For example, people must appraise that something significant and relevant has happened before they can appraise whether the event violates personal or social standards. Likewise, people must appraise something as new and relevant before appraising whether they have the resources to cope with it. In these cases, the early appraisals provide the information needed to make the later appraisals. Sequential hypotheses are hard to test; appraisals happen fast. Research on rapid changes in facial expressions associated with appraisals may clarify this problem (Kaiser & Wehrle, 2001).

Comparing Basic-Emotion and Appraisal Approaches

The differences between basic-emotion theories and appraisal theories are subtle but significant. The appraisal approach rejects the view of emotions as discrete categories or as qualitatively different psychobiological systems. Instead, the appraisal approach construes emotions as organizations of components. In a basic-emotions model, there are a small number of emotions. Proposing a new basic emotion is a big deal because the emotion needs to have a distinct facial expression that appears across cultures, distinctive patterns of physiological activity, and other markers of an evolved psychobiological system. For this reason, proposals of new emotions tend to be controversial, such as Rozin and Cohen's (2003) suggestion that confusion is a basic emotion (Ellsworth, 2003; Hess, 2003). In an appraisal model, in contrast, there are a lot of emotions. Asserting a new emotion is relatively easy so long as a distinct pattern of appraisal can be identified.

At the same time, the disagreements between basic-emotion theorists and appraisal theorists are not as grave as some of their arguments would suggest. They agree that emotions enable flexible adaptations to changing circumstances; that emotions have motivational, expressive, subjective, and physiological components; and that emotions show coherence among their components. Moreover, many basic-emotion theories would agree with the appraisal theorists about the role of appraisal processes in causing emotional experience, although they usually posit nonappraisal causes as well (e.g., Izard, 1993). Their genuine disagreements aside, basic-emotion theories and appraisal theories could be seen as complementary because they emphasize different aspects of emotion. Appraisal theories focus on the causes of emotional experience, the processes that underlie appraisals, and how related emotions differ (Roseman & Smith, 2001). Basic-emotion theories focus on facial expressions, cross-cultural similarities, and biological substrates. Collectively, they provide a richer understanding of emotion.

Facial and Vocal Expressions of Emotions

People do not blankly experience emotions. Although usually viewed as internal states, emotions have powerful relations to overt expressions. A huge literature examines expressive signals, particularly facial and vocal expressions of emotion (see Ekman & Rosenberg, 1997; Johnstone & Scherer, 2000; Keltner & Ekman, 2000). Emotion psychologists view the expressive aspects of emotions—such as changes in posture, facial muscles, and the voice—as components of an emotion, not as effects of an emotion (Izard, 1977; Scherer, 2001). A facial expression of happiness, for example, is part of what it is to be happy, not a separate consequence of an internal state of happiness. The expressive aspects of emotions highlight their fundamentally interpersonal nature because communicating to others is a central feature of emotional expressions (Parkinson, 1995).

The basic-emotion approach and the appraisal approach, not surprisingly, disagree about how to interpret facial expressions of emotion. The basic-emotion approach emphasizes holistic, prototypical expressions of emotion. Universal facial expressions are hallmarks of basic emotions. A few emotions—sadness, happiness, anger, surprise, disgust, fear, and, possibly, contempt—have pancultural prototypical expressions (Ekman, 1993; Ekman & Friesen, 1986; Izard, 1971). These expressions are thought to be automatically activated as part of the unfolding of the emotion's affect program (Ekman, 1992). Neurological research on spontaneous facial expressions is consistent with this claim (Rinn, 1984).

The appraisal approach, in contrast, emphasizes the components of facial expressions instead of patterns of expression. As before, the basic-emotions approach suggests a holistic analysis and the appraisal approach suggests a componential analysis. Appraisal researchers suggest that components of an expression, such as the raising or lowering of the eyebrows, have a specific meaning associated with a specific appraisal (Kaiser & Wehrle, 2001; Smith & Scott, 1997). For example, raising the eyebrows and upper eyelids reflects appraisals of novelty and unexpectedness (Pope & Smith, 1994). This is an intriguing idea because it suggests that facial movements over time can be used to infer dynamic changes in appraisal. The mapping of appraisals onto facial movements is still nascent, but it could emerge as a major perspective on the meaning of facial expressions.

Apart from its theoretical appeal, the study of facial expressions has provided tools for studying emotions in infants (e.g., Camras et al., 2002; Scherer, Zentner, & Stern, 2004). Without expressive markers of emotion, studying emotions in preverbal children would be extraordinarily challenging. The Facial Action Coding System is a popular method for measuring emotional expressions (see Ekman & Rosenberg, 1997). This system codes specific action units on the face. Prototypical emotion expressions are defined by sets of action units. Other systems code holistic facial expressions, consistent with the view of emotion expressions as coordinated sets of expressive movements.

Vocal expressions of emotion involve many of the same issues as facial expressions (Johnstone & Scherer, 2000). Like facial expressions, vocal expressions of emotion appear to be pancultural. Some dimensions of vocal expression— such as the rate, volume, and pitch of speech—are reliable markers of emotional states. Furthermore, people can recognize emotions from speech, even when semantic information is removed. In one study (Banse & Scherer, 1996), professional actors portrayed 14 emotions by speaking sentences of meaningless utterances. People then listened to the sentences and judged the speaker's emotion. Hot anger (78 percent), boredom (76 percent), and interest (75 percent) were recognized most accurately; disgust (15 percent) and

shame (22 percent) were recognized least accurately. Confusions of emotions were systematic rather than random. For example, vocal expressions of interest were most often confused with happiness, and expressions of boredom were most often confused with sadness.

Processing Emotion Expressions

People are experts at processing emotional expressions. Facial expressions of emotion appear to grab attention automatically (Stenberg, Wiking, & Dahl, 1998), and people automatically identify the expressions. Automatic identification is shown by studies that present emotional faces subliminally. When emotional expressions are presented outside of awareness, people still extract the emotional meaning of the face. One line of research shows that people nonconsciously mimic emotional expressions that are presented subliminally (Dimburg, Thunberg, & Elmehed, 2000). Despite being unaware of seeing an emotional face, people's own facial muscles moved in accord with the expression that was presented. Subliminal happy and sad faces activate different brain areas (Killgore & Yurgelun-Todd, 2004) and prime emotional concepts, indicating that the emotional meaning was processed automatically (Soldat & Sinclair, 2001).

There is controversy over whether certain facial expressions are particularly potent. Some experiments show that negative facial expressions, particularly expressions of threat, are processed differently (Schupp et al., 2004). Fox and her colleagues have found that angry faces grab attention because they are detected more efficiently (Fox et al., 2000). Angry faces also hold attention because people take longer to disengage attention from them (Fox, Russo, Bowles, & Dutton, 2001; Fox, Russo, & Dutton, 2002). Sad faces also seem relatively potent. In visual search paradigms, people detect sad faces faster than other faces (Eastwood, Smilek, & Merikle, 2001). Furthermore, sad faces are more distracting than happy and neutral faces (Fenske & Eastwood, 2003). But, at the same time, happy faces have advantages. When people are shown faces and asked to identify the emotion, people identify happy faces faster than neutral and negative faces (Leppänen & Hietanen, 2003; Leppänen, Tenhunen, & Hietanen, 2003). Research is still sorting out how people process emotional faces. The diverse findings make this one of emotion psychology's most active and intriguing areas.

Mood

Moods differ from emotions in some key ways; Table 14.3 lists some central differences. First, moods are less intense than emotions. Moods are the affective quality of experience,

TABLE 14.3   Central Differences between Moods and Emotions

Moods	Emotions
Mild	Intense
Objectless and vague	Refer to specific events
Sustained	Brief
No motivational or physiological implications	Stable motivational and physiological implications
Cyclical	Episodic
Positive or negative	Differentiated and discrete

the frame of mind (Morris, 1989). They are probably experienced constantly, even though people may only consciously reflect on their moods sporadically (Parkinson, Totterdell, Briner, & Reynolds, 1996). Second, moods lack objects. Emotions, as responses to interpretations of events, have objects: People are happy, sad, or angry about something. Moods, in contrast, are psychologically diffuse. People in a good mood are simply happy; the positive feeling is not attached to specific objects or events (Gendolla, 2000). Third, moods last longer than emotions. Full-blown emotions are measured in seconds, whereas moods can persist for hours (Ekman, 1992). Fourth, moods serve different psychological functions. Unlike emotions, moods do not rapidly mobilize the body for action or for expressive communication. As a result, moods lack the physiological and expressive markers of emotions (Gendolla, Abele, & Krüsken, 2001). Fifth, baseline moods are cyclical—people's baseline moods shift reliably over the course of the sleep-wake cycle (Watson, 2000). Emotions, in contrast, arise erratically as a result of appraised events. Finally, mood has a simpler structure than emotions. Emotions are differentiated, either by basic-emotion systems (Ekman, 1992) or by patterns of appraisal (Scherer, 2001). There are a lot of emotions, but moods are basically positive or negative (Watson, 2000).

Measuring Mood

Moods are easy to measure. Indeed, the simplicity of mood measurement surely contributes to the enormous popularity of mood research. Watson (2000) argued that self-reports are the ideal way to measure moods. As conscious affective states, moods are best described with reports of conscious experience. The most popular format for self-reported mood is to give people a list of affective words and ask them to indicate how much they are experiencing each affective state. The Positive and Negative Affect Schedule (PANAS; Watson, Clark, & Tellegen, 1988) has 10 positive adjectives (e.g., *interested, proud, active*) and 10 negative adjectives (e.g.,

nervous, upset, scared). The Brief Mood Introspection Survey (BMIS; Mayer & Gaschke, 1988) has eight positive (e.g., *happy, caring, lively*) and eight negative adjectives (e.g., *sad, tired, gloomy*). Participants can be instructed to report on their current mood or on their mood over various time intervals, such as during the past day, week, or year.

The Experience of Mood in Daily Life

One of the most intriguing areas of mood research is the study of mood in everyday life. Instead of inducing moods in the laboratory or asking people to remember past moods, researchers can measure how people are feeling at the moment several times a day; this is known as *experience sampling.* This enables insight into the dynamics of mood in real situations, thus obviating problems associated with retrospective reports and the low ecological validity of experiments. The development of experience-sampling methods arose from the convergence of new technologies and the maturation of statistical methods for longitudinal and multilevel data (Fleeson, in press). Modern experience-sampling research lends participants handheld computers for one or more weeks. The researcher can beep the participant at fixed or random times. The participants then complete questions about their current mood, what they are doing, who they are with, and so forth. Because an enormous amount of data can be collected on a single person, researchers can look at within-person trends over time.

Experience-sampling research has revealed daily cycles in the experience of positive and negative moods (see Watson, 2000, chap. 4). Over the course of the day, positive and negative affect show different trajectories. Positive mood is lowest upon waking; it increases over the course of the day and then declines as the body prepares for sleep. Negative mood, in contrast, is relatively stable throughout the day. Apart from an increase upon waking, negative mood shows little change (Clark, Watson, & Leeka, 1989). Watson (2000) proposes that these diurnal patterns in positive and negative mood reflect the sleep-wake cycle. Consistent with this claim, the same mood patterns appear regardless of the actual hour of waking. Furthermore, positive mood over the course of the day correlates strongly (nearly .80) with body temperature (Watson, Wiese, Vaidya, & Tellegen, 1999), which is affected by the biological systems that control sleep.

Effects of Mood on Cognitive Processes

A massive literature explores how moods affect cognitive processes (see Clore, Gasper, & Garvin, 2001; Fiedler, 2001; Forgas, 1995; Gendolla, 2000; Isen, 2000). The best-known effect is *mood-congruent judgment,* in which the content of thought matches the mood's valence (Mayer, Gaschke, Braverman, & Evans, 1992). In this effect, positive and negative moods bias judgments in the direction of the mood. For example, happy people rate their lives as more satisfying and their chances of success as better, relative to people in neutral and negative moods (see Gendolla, 2000; Schwartz, 1990). Mood-congruent judgment is a robust, reliable, and general effect, but—like all interesting effects—it has important boundary conditions. People may discount the mood as a source of information if their attention is called to the mood or its cause. For instance, positive moods are no longer biased judgments of life satisfaction when people were asked about the sunny weather; presumably people noticed the real source of their good moods (Schwartz & Clore, 1983). In other studies, simply telling people that their moods will bias their judgments caused people to correct for their moods (Gendolla & Krüsken, 2002a).

Given the rich, pervasive effects of mood on judgment, it is not surprising that many theories have been advanced. Some theories assume that positive and negative moods evoke different processing styles (Mackie & Worth, 1989). Positive moods are thought to reduce cognitive capacity, presumably by activating extensively associated positive knowledge, or to induce heuristic processing, a relatively effortless form of reasoning. In contrast, negative moods are thought to induce systematic information processing, possibly because the mood signals that something is wrong (Schwartz, 1990). Later experiments failed to support this view. Bless et al. (1996) found that people in happy moods were more likely to rely on schemata and general knowledge structures; they were processing differently, not less. Some researchers thus suggest that positive moods foster top-down processing and that negative moods foster bottom-up processing (Clore & Colcombe, 2003; Clore et al., 2001). Other theories suggest that positive and negative moods operate through similar mechanisms. One perspective, the mood-as-input model, asserts that moods have flexible effects on cognition (Martin & Stoner, 1996). If moods offer information, then the meaning of their information should depend on contextual factors, such as the person's goals or the task at hand. Although this model does not describe the specific mechanisms by which moods affect cognition, it makes interesting predictions about how positive and negative moods interact with situational factors. Debates about how, when, and why moods affect cognition will not be settled soon.

Although judgment gets the most attention, many cognitive processes are affected by moods. Positive and negative moods affect other higher-order processes, such as the categorization of objects. People are more likely to categorize

objects based on valence when feeling emotional (Niedenthal, Halberstadt, & Innes-Ker, 1999). One set of experiments asked people to say which of two words (e.g., *sunbeam, speech*) best fit a target word (e.g., *joke*). One option reflected an emotion-based categorization (*joke, sunbeam*); the other option reflected a taxonomic categorization (*joke, speech*). Happy and sad people were more likely to pair words based on emotional meaning than on taxonomic similarity. Positive moods also promote broad, inclusive categorizations of objects and social groups (Isen, 2000; Isen & Daubman, 1984). This may stem from an effect of positive mood on divergent thought processes, in which happy people can see creative and unusual associations between objects (Isen, Daubman, & Nowicki, 1987).

Simple perceptual processes, like identifying words and faces, also are influenced by mood states. People are faster to name words that match their current mood relative to mismatched words (Niedenthal, Halberstadt, & Setterlund, 1997; Niedenthal & Setterlund, 1994); relative to sad people, happy people could identify words like *happy* and *joy* faster. Similarly, people in a positive mood are faster at recognizing happy faces (Leppänen & Hietanen, 2003). Moods thus broadly affect cognition, ranging from effects on lower-order perceptual processes to effects on higher-order reasoning and judgment.

Mood Effects without Mood

Are feelings necessary for mood to affect cognition? This seems like a heretical question in light of the vast literature on mood and judgment, but it is plausible. Manipulating people's moods affects more than just subjective experience; it also affects the accessibility of emotional knowledge. When people listen to cheerful music, for example, two things typically happen: their mood becomes more positive and semantic knowledge about happiness (e.g., memories, typical causes and effects of being happy) becomes more salient (Niedenthal et al., 1997). Perhaps the effects of mood on judgment stem from the priming of emotional knowledge, not from the change in subjective experience. Because mood manipulations have two effects, it is unclear if subjective experience is the real cause of mood effects on cognition. Innes-Ker and Niedenthal (2002) thus tested whether emotional experience was necessary. Some participants were induced into happy, sad, or neutral moods; other participants completed a priming task that primed concepts related to happiness, sadness, or neutrality. Then people completed a judgment task designed to elicit mood-congruent judgment. People who felt happy and sad showed the classic mood-congruent judgment effect; people who were primed with *happy* and *sad* did not.

This suggests that subjective feelings are essential for mood effects (see Niedenthal, Rohmann, & Dalle, 2003).

Other studies, however, find that merely priming emotion concepts can replicate mood effects. Soldat and Sinclair (2001; Soldat, Sinclair, & Mark, 1997) found that affective cues—bright and subdued colors, happy and sad facial expressions—affected judgments without affecting subjective experience. In one experiment, participants read a series of persuasive arguments on a computer screen. A happy or serious face appeared briefly (13 milliseconds) before each argument. The affective faces did not affect people's subjectively experienced moods, but they did affect how people processed the message. In another experiment, reading arguments on blue paper (a sad cue) caused deeper processing, relative to reading arguments on red paper (a happy cue). The affective cues had the same effects that mood manipulations had in prior research.

In short, sometimes affective information can replicate the effects of affective states. Some theories of mood expect this to happen. The affect-as-information model (Clore et al., 2001) assumes that emotional states and primed emotion concepts carry the same information, so they could have the same effects on cognition. For example, both a sad mood and a sad informational cue (e.g., a frowning face) could inform the person that things are amiss. Other theories do not expect widespread effects of affective cues on cognition. If moods affect cognition because people use subjective experience as information, then subjective experience should be necessary for mood effects (see Niedenthal et al., 2003). This is one of the many intriguing issues that research on mood and social cognition has not yet settled.

Effects of Mood on Motivation and Action

How do moods affect motivation and action? Because moods lack inherent motivating properties, one would think that they are irrelevant to energizing for action. The mood–behavior model (Gendolla, 2000), however, outlines how positive and negative moods affect motivational arousal in situations calling for effort. In a clever line of research, Gendolla and his colleagues (2001) show how mood states affect physiological measures of effort. None of their studies find direct effects of mood on motivational arousal, consistent with the view of moods as diffuse (see Table 14.3). For example, inducing positive and negative moods does not affect cardiovascular and electrodermal activity (Gendolla et al., 2001). Instead, moods affect motivation through two indirect pathways. First, moods can affect people's appraisals of confidence and task difficulty through mood-congruent judgment processes. People in a positive mood are less energized for easy tasks,

relative to people in a negative mood, because they appraise the task as relatively easy and hence needing less motivation. For difficult tasks, in contrast, people in positive moods are more energized, relative to people in negative moods, because they are more optimistic about success (Gendolla & Krüsken, 2001, 2002b, 2002c). Second, moods can create incentives by influencing affect-regulation motives. For example, tasks can become more important if they offer opportunities to improve a bad mood, and higher importance can affect effort (Gendolla & Krüsken, 2002b).

Affect

The meaning of affect is less clear than the meanings of emotions and moods. Some researchers use *affect* as a convenient superordinate term. In this usage, affect can refer to full-blown emotions, to sustained moods, to information about preferences, and to affective dispositions that involve emotions and moods. The phrase *affective science* is an example of this usage (e.g., Davidson, Scherer, & Goldsmith, 2003). Scientific research on any aspect of moods, emotions, and feelings—experiments on mood and judgment, cross-cultural studies of facial expressions, computational modeling of appraisal architectures, longitudinal analyses of temperament, and linguistic studies of emotion words—would fall under affective science. A superordinate category is useful because a lot of research areas do not fit easily into mood or emotion. For instance, people remember emotional words better than neutral words (D'Argembeau & Van der Linden, 2004), but the words are not affecting moods or emotions.

Other researchers use *affect* to denote diffuse positive and negative feelings that are less intense and more obscure than emotions and moods (see Batson, Shaw, & Oleson, 1992; Watson, 2000). In this usage, affect is seen as simple and atavistic. Vaguely experienced feelings that arise from facial feedback or from subliminal exposure to pictures would qualify as affect. Some researchers even suggest that affect can occur nonconsciously (Berridge & Winkielman, 2003). We have implicitly used the first meaning of *affect* in this chapter. There is merit to both sides, and it is best to avoid what Abelson (1995) called "a case of the reallies." Questions such as "Is affect really a superordinate category?" and "Is affect really a diffuse state different from mood?" are usually unproductive compared to questions about causes, effects, and relationships.

Regulating Affective States

Theories of emotion and mood can give the impression that people are passive recipients of experience. To the contrary, emotion research is vitally interested in how people actively shape, control, and regulate their feelings. This is the study of *emotion regulation.* People constantly try to change how they are feeling, be it getting out of a bad mood, suppressing giggles and smiles, controlling anxious feelings, or trying to seem suitably somber. Some theories even claim that all adult emotions are regulated to some degree (Tomkins, 1962). Regulating negative feelings is the prototype of emotion regulation, but people also regulate positive feelings. Sometimes people seek neutral and negative moods, such as when interacting with strangers or people in power, when expecting conflict, or when trying to enhance concentration (Erber, 1996; Parkinson et al., 1996).

Emotion regulation involves two components: monitoring one's emotional state and using strategies to change the emotion (Parkinson et al., 1996). Monitoring requires noticing and labeling an affective state and assessing changes in the state over time (Silvia, 2002a, 2002b). Using strategies involves enacting behaviors that are intended to influence emotions in the desired direction. Emotion regulation thus can go awry for several reasons. Problems with monitoring one's feelings can arise when people lack the skills to label emotions or when people simply do not pay attention to their subjective experience. Problems with strategies arise when people's ideas about how their emotions work are wrong. For example, many people do not know that exercise is better than eating for regulating a bad mood (Thayer, 2001).

Several studies have classified the strategies people use to change their moods. In this research, people are asked to describe how they deliberately change their moods. The following list is a sample of these strategies:

Think positively.

Exercise.

Meditate.

Have a cup of coffee.

Spend some time alone.

Think about people who are worse off than me.

Buy something for myself.

Listen to music.

Use drugs.

Watch TV.

Tell someone how I am feeling.

The number of strategies is remarkable. In their research, Parkinson et al. (1996) found more than 200 mood-regulation strategies. To simplify the data, researchers have sought underlying dimensions through factor analysis. Thayer, Newman, and McClain (1994), for example, collected strategies used

to change bad moods, increase energy, and reduce tension. They found six factors: active mood management; seeking pleasurable activities; passive mood management; support, ventilation, and gratification; direct tension reduction; and withdrawal-avoidance. A three-factor model, however, also represented the data. Parkinson et al. (1996) argued that studies of the structure of mood-regulation strategies have not replicated each other, in part because researchers sample different kinds of strategies and use different underlying theories of mood.

Gross (1998) proposed a general model of the nature and consequences of emotion regulation. This model divides emotion-regulation strategies into two categories. First, people can try to control their emotions through *antecedent-focused* strategies. These methods control emotions on the front end by controlling the appraisal processes that give rise to emotions. An example of an antecedent-focused strategy is reappraisal. People may prevent or stifle negative feelings by reappraising the situation in ways that defuse the negative emotional response. Second, people can use *response-focused* strategies. These methods control emotions on the back end by modifying aspects of a fully experienced emotional state. An example of response-focused control is expressive suppression. People may control an emotion by suppressing all outward expression of the emotion, such as by inhibiting their facial expressions and trying to look natural.

The distinction between reappraisal and expressive suppression is important because these methods have different consequences for memory and for social interaction. Richards and Gross (2000) found that the emotion-regulation strategies have different effects on memory. They reasoned that expressive suppression requires more attention than reappraisal. Reappraisal only needs to be done once, so it should require relatively little time and attention. For example, at the start of a disturbing film, people simply can tell themselves that it is fictional, thus reducing negative emotions. Expressive suppression, in contrast, requires more time and attention because people must continuously monitor their expressions for slips in inhibition. In several experiments, people who controlled their emotion with expressive suppression had worse memory for emotional events. People who controlled their emotion with reappraisal, however, did not show impaired memory. This shows intriguing cognitive consequences of controlling one's feelings.

Other experiments show social effects of emotion regulation (Butler et al., 2003). Because inhibiting expressions is distracting and preoccupying, social interactions should be less pleasant and more stressful when one person is trying to regulate emotional expressions. Pairs of female strangers were asked to discuss a distressing topic. In some conditions, one person was told to regulate their emotion during the interaction. The two methods of regulation had different consequences for the regulator and for her partner. Inhibiting expressions caused the regulator to feel more distracted and to have higher blood pressure, consistent with the effort needed to monitor and control one's facial and postural movements continuously. Moreover, the regulator's partner had higher blood pressure, reflecting the stress that emotion inhibition puts on an interaction. The regulator's partner also reported less rapport and less interest in future interactions. Reappraising, in contrast, did not have these negative social effects.

POSITIVE AND NEGATIVE AFFECT AS DISPOSITIONAL TRAITS

Thus far, we have described positive and negative affect as aspects of momentary experience. The concepts of positive affect and negative affect are also fundamental to understanding enduring individual differences. These dispositional traits, the focus of personality psychology, describe and define a person's tendency toward reacting to events in a patterned and predictable manner. Theories of personality structure are, by virtue of the complicated nature of human personalities, quite complex. A full discussion of personality theories is outside of the scope of this chapter, so we will focus on the role of positive and negative affect within broader models of personality structure. Despite great variability in the number and type of dimensions, many theoretical systems include concepts related to positive and negative affect. We thus turn to the role of affect in prominent theories of personality. Table 14.4 gives an overview of these theories.

Eysenck's PEN Model

In his early attempts to describe the fundamental characteristics that define a person, Hans Eysenck (1947, 1952) used factor analysis to create a hierarchical taxonomy with three main superfactors. According to this model (Eysenck, 1990), Psychoticism, Extraversion, and Neuroticism (PEN) are the fundamental traits that serve as the most basic components of personality. Each superfactor in this system is a hierarchically organized set of covarying behaviors, habits, and factors that describe a person's biologically based traits (Eysenck & Eysenck, 1985). These characteristics are viewed as dimensional constructs, and individual differences are assumed to result from combinations of the three superfactors.

The personality superfactor of extraversion refers to a broad range of behavioral characteristics that arise from genetically determined levels of cortical activation. People high in Extraversion (as opposed to introversion) have lower cortical arousal and thus are prone to seek out social experiences and to be sensitive to environmental rewards, which are often social in nature. As a result, Extraversion is associated with social interest and frequent experience of positive affect. Although the direction of causation is complex (Diener & Larsen, 1993; Fleeson, Malanos, & Achille, 2002), a tendency to experience positive affect, to approach social situations, and to value social rewards are all central to Extraversion. Within Eysenck's framework, experiencing positive affect is a chief component of Extraversion.

Neuroticism, the second of the PEN model superfactors, is related to an person's tendency toward negative emotions. Levels of Neuroticism stem from genetically determined activation thresholds of the sympathetic nervous system (Eysenck, 1967, 1990), which is responsible for the fight-or-flight response to potentially dangerous stimuli. Because of their lower activation thresholds, people high in Neuroticism have sympathetic nervous systems that are frequently aroused. As a result, neurotic people tend to experience negative affect in the face of minor stressors. Relative to people who are more emotionally stable, neurotic people are easily upset; negative emotional states become the norm.

Most analyses of Eysenck's PEN model have supported the inclusion of Extraversion and Neuroticism as fundamental components of personality (Eysenck, 1967, 1990). Indeed, the characteristics that give rise to the acronym PEN are sometimes shortened to the two-factor E-IN model (Extroversion-Introversion, Neuroticism; Eysenck, 1991). Although critics of this system have suggested that other traits belong elsewhere or are necessary in the superordinate tier—including impulsivity (Gray, 1981; Revelle, 1997), intelligence, and social attitudes (Cattell, Eber, & Tatsuoka, 1970)—the strong empirical support for the Extraversion and Neuroticism superfactors continues to lend credence to these constructs as fundamental to understanding human traits.

The Five-Factor Model

A similar system for representing individual differences, proposed by Costa and McCrae (1992), has added to the enormous research literature on extraversion and neuroticism. This system focuses on the Big Five personality factors—Neuroticism, Extraversion, Openness to Experience, Agreeableness, and Conscientiousness—and is known as the Five-Factor Model (FFM) of personality. This model, like the PEN model, organizes personality characteristics into hierarchical domains composed of facets. The five domains are assumed to have environmental as well as genetic determinants (Bergeman et al., 1993; Jang, McCrae, Angleitner, Riemann, & Livesley, 1998; Loehlin, McCrae, Costa, & John, 1998) and to be normally distributed (McCrae & John, 1992). Tests of this model have shown that the five factors remain stable over time (Soldz & Vaillant, 1999) and appear in many cultures (McCrae & Costa, 1997). These findings provide further evidence for the inclusion of positive and negative affect as part of personality structure.

As in Eysenck's model, the description of Extraversion in the FFM closely follows the concept of positive affect. High Extraversion is characterized by increased experience of positive emotions, social activity, and orientation to exciting stimuli. With such positively valenced affective and behavioral characteristics at its core, Extraversion has been defined as "a trait characterized by a keen interest in other people and external events, and venturing forth with confidence" (Ewen, 1998, p. 289). This view, with positive affect as a fundamental component of the Extraversion trait, closely follows the view of Extraversion within the PEN model. Similarly, the concept of Neuroticism in the FFM is closely related to negative affective tendencies. Within this framework, Neuroticism has been broadly defined as a tendency to experience negative affect, and it is composed of facets that describe proneness to depression, anxiety, shame, and hostility (Costa & McCrae, 1992). People high in Neuroticism experience a broad variety of negative emotions, including vulnerability to psychopathology.

Although the theoretical frameworks of Eysenck (1990) and Costa and McCrae (1992) are strikingly similar in their reliance on Extraversion and Neuroticism as superordinate factors of personality, there is some disagreement about the necessity of the final three factors in the FFM (Eysenck, 1991, 1992). Proponents of Eysenck's model suggest that Openness, Agreeableness, and Conscientiousness may be mixtures of personality facets that are hierarchically subsumed under the three superfactors of the PEN model and that the reformulation of the PEN model into the FFM is unnecessary and overly complicated (Eysenck, 1991, 1992). For our purposes, it is important to point out that Extraversion and Neuroticism are central in both models of personality.

The BIS–BAS Model

To connect emotions with neurobiological systems, some theories have posited separate approach and withdrawal systems that underlie action and emotion. Based on Gray's (1972, 1994) influential theory of personality, such theories suggest that Extraversion and Neuroticism result from two neurological systems—the Behavioral Approach System (BAS) and the Behavioral Inhibition System (BIS)—that respond to cues of reward and punishment, respectively. The BAS—also known as the behavioral activation system (Fowles, 1987) and behavioral facilitation system (Depue & Collins, 1999)—is responsible for orientation to stimuli, approach behavior, and attention to rewards. When this system is activated by environmental cues, an organism shows approach behavior and experiences positive affect (Gray, 1994). The BIS, in contrast, is responsible for inhibition, withdrawal behavior, and negative affects like anxiety (Gray, 1994). Despite some dissension (Carver, 2004), most theories agree that the BAS generates positive affect and the BIS generates negative affect.

Neuroscience research suggests that the neural circuitry underlying these systems is at least partially localized. Incentives (which trigger the approach behaviors and positive affect typical of BAS activation) predict higher relative activity in the left prefrontal area of the cortex (Harmon-Jones & Allen, 1997; Sobotka, Davidson, & Senulis, 1992), whereas threat cues (which trigger the withdrawal behaviors and negative affect typical of BIS activation) predict higher relative activity in the right prefrontal area (Sobotka et al., 1992). BIS–BAS models presume that people vary, due to biological circumstances, in their sensitivity to these two independent systems. Long-term sensitivity to each system could explain tendencies toward experiencing positive or negative affect. That is, personality may be largely determined by differential sensitivity to the BIS and the BAS and the resultant tendency to experience predominantly negative or positive affect (Carver & White, 1994).

Cloninger's Biosocial Model

Similar affective concepts appear in Robert Cloninger's temperamental theory of personality (1986, 1991). Although developed to explain severe forms of psychopathology, Cloninger's theoretical framework, like those described previously, posits concepts that are closely related to positive and negative affect. According to this framework, personality is defined by components of temperament, a set of response biases that are largely biologically determined, and character, a set of environmentally determined ways of relating the self to the outside world (Cloninger, Svrakic, & Przybeck, 1993).

Fundamental to this biosocial model of personality are the dimensions of Novelty Seeking and Harm Avoidance (Cloninger, 1986, 1991; Cloninger et al., 1993), which are presumed to be genetically based (Heath, Cloninger, & Martin, 1994). Similar to the PEN, FFM, and BIS–BAS theories, these components of temperament in Cloninger's model of

TABLE 14.4   Concepts of Positive and Negative Affect Represented in Major Theories of Personality

Model	Main theorists	Positive affect	Negative affect	Other traits
PEN	Eysenck	Extraversion	Neuroticism	Psychoticism
FFM	Costa & McCrae	Extraversion	Neuroticism	Openness, Agreeableness, Conscientiousness
BIS–BAS	Gray	Behavioral Approach	Behavioral Inhibition	
	Fowles	Behavioral Activation	Behavioral Inhibition	
	Depue	Behavioral Facilitation	Behavioral Inhibition	
Biosocial	Cloninger	Novelty Seeking	Harm Avoidance	Reward Dependence
PA–NA	Tellegen, Watson, & Clark	Positive Affectivity	Negative Affectivity	

personality relate closely to the dispositional tendency to experience positive or negative affect. The dimension of Novelty Seeking is a tendency to encounter and approach novel stimuli (Cloninger, 1986); it resembles Extraversion and BAS sensitivity. People high in Novelty Seeking are therefore likely to encounter rewards and experience positive affect. The dimension of Harm Avoidance involves sensitivity to threat cues and subsequent withdrawal. As with Neuroticism and BIS sensitivity, this characteristic is closely related to the experience of negative affects such as anxiety (Cloninger, 1986). In a study of the relationship between temperament and emotionality, Novelty Seeking positively predicted positive emotionality, whereas Harm Avoidance negatively predicted positive emotionality (Cloninger, Bayon, & Svrakic, 1998).

Positive and Negative Affectivity

So far we have reviewed models of personality that include traits relevant to positive and negative affect. A different approach to emotion traits comes from research on the structure of emotional experience. Although not rooted in general theories of personality structure, this research has reached the same conclusions about the centrality of positive and negative affect in personality. Watson, Clark, and Tellegen have proposed two independent biobehavioral systems, known as positive affectivity and negative affectivity (Tellegen, 1985; Watson, 2000; Watson & Tellegen, 1985; Watson et al., 1999). These traits are dispositional versions of positive and negative mood; state and trait affect are assumed to have the same psychological structure. These traits have strong associations with Extraversion and Neuroticism. Positive Affectivity correlates positively with Extraversion and negatively with Neuroticism; Negative Affectivity correlates positively with Neuroticism and negatively with Extraversion (see Watson, 2000, chap. 6).

Many of the models have incorporated emotional qualities into their definitions of Extraversion and Neuroticism, but Tellegen (1985) argued that these traits were more aptly renamed as *positive emotionality* and *negative emotionality*. According to this theory, general positive affect and general negative affect are not subsumed as components of broader factors or superfactors but rather themselves are fundamental dimensions of personality (Tellegen, 1985; Watson & Clark, 1984). Watson (2000) makes a strong case for positive and negative affect as the central cores of Extraversion and Neuroticism. This is not controversial for Neuroticism—essentially all models view Neuroticism as a disposition for negative emotions. But it is controversial to claim that Extraversion is fundamentally a disposition for positive emotions. Most models of Extraversion include gregariousness, dominance, and experience seeking as important components (Eysenck, 1990). Nevertheless, Watson and Clark (1997) found that positive affectivity was the central component of Extraversion. After controlling for positive affectivity, other components of Extraversion (such as dominance and gregariousness) no longer correlated with each other. This suggests that Extraversion, like Neuroticism, is fundamentally an affective trait.

Conceptual Similarities

Our review of dispositional positive and negative affect has revealed striking similarities between different theories of personality. First, all of the models of personality structure have included something like positive and negative affect. The terms vary somewhat, as Table 14.4 shows, but the essential meanings of the traits are similar. Second, these theories connect positive and negative affect to psychobiological systems. Dispositional affect is assumed to be rooted in traits with high heritabilities and clear physiological substrates. None of the theories assumes a strong learned or environmental component of dispositional positive and negative affect.

Some theories imply biological substrates through research on heritability and stability; other theories explicitly claim that these are biological systems (Gray, 1994; Watson, 2000). Finally, all of these theories take a macrolevel approach to affect. Not much attention is paid to specific, discrete emotions like fear, sadness, guilt, interest, and happiness. Instead, dispositional affect is modeled as broad positive and negative feelings (cf. Watson, 2000). This is not a problem—the massive literature shows that this approach has validity—but it would enrich the study of emotion traits to examine dispositions for specific emotions.

CONCLUSION

The study of positive and negative affect has become a sophisticated and interdisciplinary part of psychological science. This massive field of psychology moves fast; there is too much research to cover in one chapter, or even in one handbook. Nevertheless, we have tried to identify the ideas and themes that have proved to be of enduring interest to the field. Positive and negative affect should be viewed from two levels: the level of momentary experience and the level of enduring individual differences. The first part of this chapter examined positive and negative affect as states, the province of emotion psychology. We examined different theories of emotions, the cognitive processes that cause emotions, and how people express and process emotions. Then we considered mood, particularly its effects on cognitive processes. The second part of this chapter examined positive and negative affect as traits, the province of personality psychology. Many theories assume that positive and negative affect are fundamental components of personality structure. The convergence of different models on positive and negative affect suggests the centrality of emotional experience to the study of personality.

REFERENCES

Abelson, R. P. (1995). *Statistics as principled argument.* Hillsdale, NJ: Erlbaum.

Banse, R., & Scherer, K. R. (1996). Acoustic profiles in vocal emotion expressions. *Journal of Personality and Social Psychology, 70,* 614–636.

Batson, C. D., Shaw, L. L., & Oleson, K. C. (1992). Differentiating affect, mood, and emotion: Toward functionally-based conceptual distinctions. In M. S. Clark (Ed.), *Review of personality and social psychology* (Vol. 13, pp. 294–326). Newbury Park, CA: Sage.

Bergeman, C. S., Chipuer, H. M., Plomin, R., Pedersen, N. L., McClearn, G. E., Nesselroade, J. R., et al. (1993). Genetic and environmental effects on openness to experience, agreeableness, and conscientiousness: An adoption/twin study. *Journal of Personality, 61,* 159–179.

Berridge, K. C., & Winkielman, P. (2003). What is an unconscious emotion? (The case for unconscious "liking"). *Cognition and Emotion, 17,* 181–211.

Bless, H., Clore, G. L., Schwartz, N., Golisano, V., Rabe, C., & Wölk, M. (1996). Mood and the use of scripts: Does a happy mood really lead to mindlessness? *Journal of Personality and Social Psychology, 71,* 665–679.

Brehm, J. W. (1999). The intensity of emotion. *Personality and Social Psychology Review, 3,* 2–22.

Butler, E. A., Egloff, B., Wilhelm, F. H., Smith, N. C., Erickson, E. A., & Gross, J. J. (2003). The social consequences of expressive suppression. *Emotion, 3,* 48–67.

Camras, L. A., Meng, Z., Ujiie, T., Dharamsi, S., Miyake, K., Oster, H., et al. (2002). Observing emotion in infants: Facial expression, body behavior, and rater judgments of responses to an expectancy-violating event. *Emotion, 2,* 179–193.

Carver, C. S. (2004). Negative affects deriving from the behavioral approach system. *Emotion, 4,* 3–22.

Carver, C. S., & White, T. L. (1994). Behavioral inhibition, behavioral activation, and affective responses to impending reward and punishment: The BIS/BAS scales. *Journal of Personality and Social Psychology, 67,* 319–333.

Cattell, R. B., Eber, H. W., & Tatsuoka, M. M. (1970). *Handbook for the 16 PF.* Champaign, IL: Institute for Personality and Ability Testing.

Clark, L. A., Watson, D., & Leeka, J. (1989). Diurnal variation in the positive affects. *Motivation and Emotion, 13,* 205–234.

Cloninger, C. R. (1986). A unified biosocial theory of personality and its role in the development of anxiety states. *Psychiatric Developments, 3,* 167–226.

Cloninger, C. R. (1991). Brain networks underlying personality development. In B. J. Carroll & J. E. Barrett (Eds.), *Psychopathology and the brain* (pp. 183–208). New York: Raven Press.

Cloninger, C. R., Bayon, C., & Svrakic, D. M. (1998). Measurement of temperament and character in mood disorders: A model of fundamental states as personality types. *Journal of Affective Disorders, 51,* 21–32.

Cloninger, C. R., Svrakic, D. M., & Przybeck, T. R. (1993). A psychobiological model of temperament and character. *Archives of General Psychiatry, 50,* 975–990.

Clore, G. L., & Colcombe, S. (2003). The parallel worlds of affective concepts and feelings. In J. Musch & K. C. Klauer (Eds.), *The psychology of evaluation* (pp. 335–369). Mahwah, NJ: Erlbaum.

Clore, G. L., Gasper, K., & Garvin, E. (2001). Affect as information. In J. P. Forgas (Ed.), *Handbook of affect and social cognition* (pp. 121–144). Mahwah, NJ: Erlbaum.

Costa, P. T., Jr., & McCrae, R. R. (1992). Normal personality assessment in clinical practice: The NEO Personality Inventory. *Psychological Assessment, 4,* 5–13.

Cronbach, L. J. (1957). The two disciplines of scientific psychology. *American Psychologist, 12,* 671–684.

D'Argembeau, A., & Van der Linden, M. (2004). Influence of affective meaning on memory for contextual information. *Emotion, 4,* 173–188.

Darwin, C. (1998). *The expression of the emotions in man and animals* (3rd ed.). New York: Oxford University Press. (Original work published 1872)

Davidson, R. J., Scherer, K. R., & Goldsmith, H. H. (Eds.). (2003). *Handbook of affective sciences.* New York: Oxford University Press.

Depue, R. A., & Collins, P. F. (1999). Neurobiology of the structure of personality: Dopamine, facilitation of incentive motivation, and extraversion. *Behavioral and Brain Sciences, 22,* 491–517.

Diener, E., & Larsen, R. J. (1993). The experience of emotional well-being. In M. Lewis & J. Haviland (Eds.), *Handbook of emotions* (pp. 405–415). New York: Guilford Press.

Dimburg, U., Thunberg, M., & Elmehed, K. (2000). Unconscious facial reactions to emotional facial expressions. *Psychological Science, 11,* 86–89.

Duffy, E. (1934). Emotion: An example of the need for reorientation in psychology. *Psychological Review, 44,* 184–198.

Eastwood, J. D., Smilek, D., & Merikle, P. M. (2001). Differential attentional guidance by unattended faces expressing positive and negative emotion. *Perception and Psychophysics, 65,* 352–358.

Ekman, P. (1992). An argument for basic emotions. *Cognition and Emotion, 6,* 169–200.

Ekman, P. (1993). Facial expression and emotion. *American Psychologist, 48,* 384–392.

Ekman, P., & Friesen, W. V. (1986). A new pan-cultural facial expression of emotion. *Motivation and Emotion, 10,* 159–168.

Ekman, P., & Rosenberg, E. L. (Eds.). (1997). *What the face reveals.* New York: Oxford University Press.

Ellsworth, P. C. (2003). Confusion, concentration, and other emotions of interest: Commentary on Rozin and Cohen (2003). *Emotion, 3,* 81–85.

Ellsworth, P. C., & Scherer, K. R. (2003). Appraisal processes in emotion. In R. J. Davidson, K. R. Scherer, & H. H. Goldsmith (Eds.), *Handbook of affective sciences* (pp. 572–595). New York: Oxford University Press.

Erber, R. (1996). The self-regulation of moods. In L. L. Martin & A. Tesser (Eds.), *Striving and feeling* (pp. 251–275). Mahwah, NJ: Erlbaum.

Ewen, R. B. (1998). *Personality: A topical approach.* Mahwah, NJ: Erlbaum.

Eysenck, H. J. (1947). *Dimensions of personality.* London: Routledge.

Eysenck, H. J. (1952). *The scientific study of personality.* New York: Macmillan.

Eysenck, H. J. (1967). *The biological basis of personality.* Springfield, IL: Thomas.

Eysenck, H. J. (1990). Biological dimensions of personality. In L. A. Pervin (Ed.), *Handbook of personality* (pp. 244–276). New York: Guilford Press.

Eysenck, H. J. (1991). Dimensions of personality: 16, 5, or 3?—Criteria for a taxonomic paradigm. *Personality and Individual Differences, 12,* 773–790.

Eysenck, H. J. (1992). Four ways five factors are not basic. *Personality and Individual Differences, 13,* 667–673.

Eysenck, H. J., & Eysenck, M. W. (1985). *Personality and individual differences: A natural science approach.* New York: Plenum Press.

Fenske, M. J., & Eastwood, J. D. (2003). Modulation of focused attention by faces expressing emotion: Evidence from flanker tasks. *Emotion, 3,* 327–343.

Fiedler, K. (2001). Affective influences on social information processing. In J. P. Forgas (Ed.), *Handbook of affect and social cognition* (pp. 163–185). Mahwah, NJ: Erlbaum.

Fleeson, W. (in press). Using experience-sampling and multilevel linear modeling to study person-situation interactionist approaches to positive psychology. In A. D. Ong & M. van Dulmen (Eds.), *Handbook of methods in positive psychology.*

Fleeson, W., Malanos, A. B., & Achille, N. M. (2002). An intra-individual process approach to the relationship between extraversion and positive affect: Is acting extraverted as "good" as being extraverted? *Journal of Personality and Social Psychology, 83,* 1409–1422.

Forgas, J. P. (1995). Mood and judgment: The affect infusion model (AIM). *Psychological Bulletin, 117,* 36–66.

Fowles, D. C. (1987). Application of a behavioral theory of motivation to the concepts of anxiety and impulsivity. *Journal of Research in Personality, 21,* 417–435.

Fox, E., Lester, V., Russo, R., Bowles, R. J., Pichler, A., & Dutton, K. (2000). Facial expressions of emotion: Are angry faces detected more efficiently? *Cognition and Emotion, 14,* 61–92.

Fox, E., Russo, R., Bowles, R., & Dutton, K. (2001). Do threatening stimuli draw or hold visual attention in subclinical anxiety? *Journal of Experimental Psychology: General, 130,* 681–700.

Fox, E., Russo, R., & Dutton, K. (2002). Attentional bias for threat: Evidence for delayed disengagement from emotional faces. *Cognition and Emotion, 16,* 355–379.

Fredrickson, B. L. (1998). What good are positive emotions? *Review of General Psychology, 2,* 300–319.

Gendolla, G. H. E. (2000). On the impact of mood on behavior: An integrative theory and a review. *Review of General Psychology, 4,* 378–408.

Gendolla, G. H. E., Abele, A. E., & Krüsken, J. (2001). The informational impact of mood on effort mobilization: A study of cardiovascular and electrodermal responses. *Emotion, 1,* 12–24.

Gendolla, G. H. E., & Krüsken, J. (2001). The joint impact of mood and task difficulty on cardiovascular and electrodermal reactivity in active coping. *Psychophysiology, 38,* 548–556.

Gendolla, G. H. E., & Krüsken, J. (2002a). Informational mood impact on effort-related cardiovascular response: The diagnostic value of moods counts. *Emotion, 2,* 251–262.

Gendolla, G. H. E., & Krüsken, J. (2002b). The joint effect of informational mood impact and performance-contingent incentive on effort-related cardiovascular response. *Journal of Personality and Social Psychology, 83,* 271–283.

Gendolla, G. H. E., & Krüsken, J. (2002c). Mood, task demand, and effort-related cardiovascular response. *Cognition and Emotion, 16,* 577–603.

Gray, J. A. (1972). The psychophysiological basis of introversion–extraversion: A modification of Eysenck's theory. In V. D. Nebylitsyn & J. A. Gray (Eds.), *The biological bases of individual behavior* (pp. 182–205). New York: Academic Press.

Gray, J. A. (1981). A critique of Eysenck's theory of personality. In H. J. Eysenck (Ed.), *A model for personality* (pp. 246–277). Berlin, Germany: Springer.

Gray, J. A. (1994). Personality dimensions and emotion systems. In P. Ekman & R. J. Davidson (Eds.), *The nature of emotion* (pp. 329–331). New York: Oxford University Press.

Griffiths, P. E. (1997). *What emotions really are: The problem of psychological categories.* Chicago: University of Chicago Press.

Gross, J. J. (1998). The emerging field of emotion regulation: An integrative review. *Review of General Psychology, 2,* 271–299.

Harmon-Jones, E., & Allen, J. J. B. (1997). Behavioral activation sensitivity and resting frontal EEG asymmetry: Covariation of putative indicators related to risk for mood disorders. *Journal of Abnormal Psychology, 106,* 159–163.

Heath, A. C., Cloninger, C. R., & Martin, N. G. (1994). Testing a model for the genetic structure of personality: A comparison of the personality systems of Cloninger and Eysenck. *Journal of Personality and Social Psychology, 66,* 762–775.

Hess, U. (2003). Now you see it, now you don't—The confusing case of confusion as an emotion: Commentary on Rozin and Cohen (2003). *Emotion, 3,* 76–80.

Innes-Ker, Å., & Niedenthal, P. M. (2002). Emotion concepts and emotional states in social judgment and categorization. *Journal of Personality and Social Psychology, 83,* 804–816.

Isen, A. M. (2000). Positive affect and decision making. In M. Lewis & J. M. Haviland-Jones (Eds.), *Handbook of emotions* (2nd ed., pp. 417–435). New York: Guilford Press.

Isen, A. M., & Daubman, K. A. (1984).The influence of affect on categorization. *Journal of Personality and Social Psychology, 47,* 1206–1217.

Isen, A. M., Daubman, K. A., & Nowicki, G. P. (1987). Positive affect facilitates creative problem solving. *Journal of Personality and Social Psychology, 52,* 1122–1131.

Izard, C. E. (1971). *The face of emotion.* New York: Appleton.

Izard, C. E. (1977). *Human emotions.* New York: Plenum Press.

Izard, C. E. (1993). Four systems of emotion activation: Cognitive and noncognitive processes. *Psychological Review, 100,* 68–90.

Izard, C. E., & Ackerman, B. P. (2000). Motivational, organizational, and regulatory functions of discrete emotions. In M. Lewis & J. M. Haviland-Jones (Eds.), *Handbook of emotions* (2nd ed., pp. 253–264). New York: Guilford Press.

Jang, K. L., McCrae, R. R., Angleitner, A., Riemann, R., & Livesley, W. J. (1998). Heritability of facet-level traits in a cross-cultural twin sample: Support for a hierarchical model of personality. *Journal of Personality and Social Psychology, 74,* 1556–1565.

Johnstone, T., & Scherer, K. R. (2000). Vocal communication of emotion. In M. Lewis & J. M. Haviland-Jones (Eds.), *Handbook of emotions* (2nd ed., pp. 220–235). New York: Guilford Press.

Kaiser, S., & Wehrle, T. (2001). Facial expressions as indicators of appraisal processes. In K. R. Scherer, A. Schorr, & T. Johnstone (Eds.), *Appraisal processes in emotion* (pp. 285–300). New York: Oxford University Press.

Keltner, D., & Ekman, P. (2000). Facial expression of emotion. In M. Lewis & J. M. Haviland-Jones (Eds.), *Handbook of emotions* (2nd ed., pp. 236–249). New York: Guilford Press.

Keltner, D., & Gross, J. J. (1999). Functional accounts of emotions. *Cognition and Emotion, 13,* 467–480.

Killgore, W. D. S., & Yurgelun-Todd, D. A. (2004). Activation of the amygdala and anterior cingulate during nonconscious processing of sad versus happy faces. *NeuroImage, 21,* 1215–1223.

Kuppens, P., Van Mechelen, I., Smits, D. J. M., & De Boeck, P. (2003). The appraisal basis of anger: Specificity, necessity, and sufficiency of components. *Emotion, 3,* 254–269.

Lazarus, R. S. (1991). *Emotion and adaptation.* New York: Oxford University Press.

Lazarus, R. S. (2001). Relational meaning and discrete emotions. In K. R. Scherer, A. Schorr, & T. Johnstone (Eds.), *Appraisal processes in emotion* (pp. 37–67). New York: Oxford University Press.

LeDoux, J. (1996). *The emotional brain.* New York: Simon & Schuster.

Leppänen, J. M., & Hietanen, J. K. (2003). Affect and face perception: Odors modulate the recognition advantage of happy faces. *Emotion, 3,* 315–326.

Leppänen, J. M., Tenhunen, M., & Hietanen, J. K. (2003). Faster choice-reaction times to positive than to negative facial expressions. *Journal of Psychophysiology, 17,* 113–123.

Levenson, R. W. (1992). Autonomic nervous system differences among emotions. *Psychological Science, 3,* 23–27.

Loehlin, J. C., McCrae, R. R., Costa, P. T., Jr., & John, O. P. (1998). Heritabilities of common and measure-specific components of the Big Five personality factors. *Journal of Research in Personality, 32,* 431–453.

Mackie, D. M., & Worth, L. T. (1989). Cognitive deficits and the mediation of positive affect in persuasion. *Journal of Personality and Social Psychology, 57,* 27–40.

Martin, L. L., & Stoner, P. (1996). Mood as input: What we think about how we feel determines how we think. In L. L. Martin & A. Tesser, (Eds.), *Striving and feeling* (pp. 279–301). Mahwah, NJ: Erlbaum.

Mayer, J. D., & Gaschke, Y. N. (1988). The experience and meta-experience of mood. *Journal of Personality and Social Psychology, 55,* 102–111.

Mayer, J. D., Gaschke, Y. N., Braverman, D. L., & Evans, T. W. (1992). Mood-congruent judgment is a general effect. *Journal of Personality and Social Psychology, 63,* 119–132.

McCrae, R. R., & Costa, P. T., Jr. (1997). Personality trait structure as a human universal. *American Psychologist, 52,* 509–516.

McCrae, R. R., & John, O. P. (1992). An introduction to the 5-factor model and its applications. *Journal of Personality, 60,* 175–215.

Morris, W. N. (1989). *Mood: The frame of mind.* New York: Springer.

Niedenthal, P. M., Halberstadt, J. B., & Innes-Ker, Å. H. (1999). Emotional response categorization. *Psychological Review, 106,* 337–361.

Niedenthal, P. M., Halberstadt, J. B., & Setterlund, M. B. (1997). Being happy and seeing "happy": Emotional state mediates visual word recognition. *Cognition and Emotion, 11,* 403–432.

Niedenthal, P. M., Rohmann, A., & Dalle, N. (2003). What is primed by emotion concepts and emotion words? In J. Musch & K. C. Klauer (Eds.), *The psychology of evaluation* (pp. 307–333). Mahwah, NJ: Erlbaum.

Niedenthal, P. M., & Setterlund, M. B. (1994). Emotion congruence in perception. *Personality and Social Psychology Bulletin, 20,* 401–410.

Oatley, K. (2004). *Emotion: A brief history.* Malden, MA: Blackwell.

Oatley, K., & Jenkins, J. M. (1992). Human emotions: Function and dysfunction. *Annual Review of Psychology, 43,* 55–85.

Ortony, A., & Turner, T. J. (1990). What's basic about basic emotions? *Psychological Review, 97,* 315–331.

Panksepp, J. (1998). *Affective neuroscience.* New York: Oxford University Press.

Parkinson, B. (1995). *Ideas and realities of emotion.* London: Routledge.

Parkinson, B., Totterdell, P., Briner, R. B., & Reynolds, S. (1996). *Changing moods: The psychology of mood and mood regulation.* London: Longman.

Parrott, W. G. (2001). Implications of dysfunctional emotions for understanding how emotions function. *Review of General Psychology, 5,* 180–186.

Pope, L. K., & Smith, C. A. (1994). On the distinct meanings of smiles and frowns. *Cognition and Emotion, 8,* 65–72.

Revelle, W. (1997). Extraversion and impulsivity: The lost dimension? In H. Nyborg (Ed.), *The scientific study of human nature* (pp. 189–212). New York: Elsevier.

Richards, J. M., & Gross, J. J. (2000). Emotion regulation and memory: The cognitive costs of keeping one's cool. *Journal of Personality and Social Psychology, 79,* 410–424.

Rinn, W. E. (1984). The neurophysiology of facial expression: A review of the neurological and psychological mechanisms for producing facial expressions. *Psychological Bulletin, 95,* 52–77.

Roseman, I. J. (2001). A model of appraisal in the emotion system: Integrating theory, research, and applications. In K. R. Scherer, A. Schorr, & T. Johnstone (Eds.), *Appraisal processes in emotion* (pp. 68–91). New York: Oxford University Press.

Roseman, I. J., & Evdokas, A. (2004). Appraisals cause experienced emotions: Experimental evidence. *Cognition and Emotion, 18,* 1–28.

Roseman, I. J., & Smith, C. A. (2001). Appraisal theory: Overview, assumptions, varieties, controversies. In K. R. Scherer, A. Schorr, & T. Johnstone (Eds.), *Appraisal processes in emotion* (pp. 3–19). New York: Oxford University Press.

Rozin, P., & Cohen, A. B. (2003). High frequency of facial expressions corresponding to confusion, concentration, and worry in an analysis of naturally occurring facial expressions of Americans. *Emotion, 3,* 68–75.

Scherer, K. R. (1999). On the sequential nature of appraisal processes: Indirect evidence from a recognition task. *Cognition and Emotion, 13,* 763–793.

Scherer, K. R. (2001). Appraisal considered as a process of multilevel sequential checking. In K. R. Scherer, A. Schorr, & T. Johnstone (Eds.), *Appraisal processes in emotion* (pp. 92–120). New York: Oxford University Press.

Scherer, K. R., Zentner, M. R., & Stern, D. (2004). Beyond surprise: The puzzle of infants' expressive reaction to expectancy violation. *Emotion, 4,* 389–402.

Schupp, H. T., Öhman, A., Junghöfer, M., Weike, A. I., Stockburger, J., & Hamm, A. O. (2004). The facilitated processing of threatening faces: An ERP analysis. *Emotion, 4,* 189–200.

Schwartz, N. (1990). Feelings as information: Informational and motivational functions of affective states. In E. T. Higgins & R. M. Sorrentino (Eds.), *Handbook of motivation and cognition* (Vol. 2, pp. 527–561). New York: Guilford Press.

Schwartz, N., & Clore, G. L. (1983). Mood, misattribution, and judgments of well-being: Informative and directive functions of affective states. *Journal of Personality and Social Psychology, 45,* 513–523.

Seager, W. (2002). Emotional introspection. *Consciousness and Cognition, 11,* 666–687.

Silvia, P. J. (2002a). Self-awareness and emotional intensity. *Cognition and Emotion, 16,* 195–216.

Silvia, P. J. (2002b). Self-awareness and the regulation of emotional intensity. *Self and Identity, 1,* 3–10.

Silvia, P. J. (in press-a). *Exploring the psychology of interest.* New York: Oxford University Press.

Silvia, P. J. (in press-b). Cognitive appraisals and interest in visual art: Exploring an appraisal theory of aesthetic emotions. *Empirical Studies of the Arts.*

Silvia, P. J. (2005). What is interesting? Exploring the appraisal structure of interest. *Emotion, 5,* 89–102.

Smith, C. A., & Ellsworth, P. C. (1985). Patterns of cognitive appraisal in emotion. *Journal of Personality and Social Psychology, 48,* 813–838.

Smith, C. A., & Kirby, L. D. (2001). Toward delivering on the promise of appraisal theory. In K. R. Scherer, A. Schorr, & T. Johnstone (Eds.), *Appraisal processes in emotion* (pp. 121–138). New York: Oxford University Press.

Smith, C. A., & Scott, H. S. (1997). A componential approach to the meaning of facial expression. In J. A. Russell & J. M. Fernandez-Dols (Eds.), *The psychology of facial expression* (pp. 229–254). Cambridge, UK: Cambridge University Press.

Sobotka, S. S., Davidson, R. J., & Senulis, J. A. (1992). Anterior brain electrical asymmetries in response to reward and punishment. *Electroencephalography and Clinical Neurophysiology, 83,* 236–247.

Soldat, A. S., & Sinclair, R. C. (2001). Colors, smiles, and frowns: External affective cues can directly affect responses to persuasive communications in a mood-like manner without affecting mood. *Social Cognition, 19,* 469–490.

Soldat, A. S., Sinclair, R. C., & Mark, M. M. (1997). Color as an environmental processing cue: External affective cues can directly affect processing strategy without affecting mood. *Social Cognition, 15,* 55–71.

Soldz, S., & Vaillant, G. E. (1999). The Big Five personality traits and the life course: A 45-year longitudinal study. *Journal of Research in Personality, 33,* 208–232.

Stenberg, G., Wiking, S., & Dahl, M. (1998). Judging words at face value: Interference in a word processing task reveals automatic processing of affective facial expressions. *Cognition and Emotion, 12,* 755–782.

Tellegen, A. (1985). Structures of mood and personality and their relevance to assessing anxiety, with an emphasis on self-report. In A. H. Tuma & J. D. Maser (Eds.), *Anxiety and the anxiety disorders* (pp. 681–706). Hillsdale, NJ: Erlbaum.

Thayer, R. E. (2001). *Calm energy: How people regulate mood with food and exercise.* New York: Oxford University Press.

Thayer, R. E., Newman, J. R., & McClain, T. M. (1994). Self-regulation of mood: Strategies for changing a bad mood, raising energy, and reducing tension. *Journal of Personality and Social Psychology, 67,* 910–925.

Tomkins, S. S. (1962). *Affect, imagery, consciousness: Vol. 1. The positive affects.* New York: Springer.

Tomkins, S. S. (1963). *Affect, imagery, consciousness: Vol. 2. The negative affects.* New York: Springer.

Watson, D. (2000). *Mood and temperament.* New York: Guilford Press.

Watson, D., & Clark, L. A. (1984). Negative affectivity: The disposition to experience aversive emotional states. *Psychological Bulletin, 96,* 465–490.

Watson, D., & Clark, L. A. (1997). Extraversion and its positive emotional core. In R. Hogan, J. Johnson, & S. Briggs (Eds.), *Handbook of personality psychology* (pp. 767–793). San Diego, CA: Academic Press.

Watson, D., Clark, L. A., & Tellegen, A. (1988). Development and validation of brief measures of positive and negative affect: The PANAS scales. *Journal of Personality and Social Psychology, 54,* 1063–1070.

Watson, D., & Tellegen, A. (1985). Toward a consensual structure of mood. *Psychological Bulletin, 98,* 219–235.

Watson, D., Wiese, D., Vaidya, J., & Tellegen, A. (1999). The two general systems of affect: Structural findings, evolutionary considerations, and psychobiological evidence. *Journal of Personality and Social Psychology, 76,* 820–838.

CHAPTER 15

Explanatory Style and Well-Being

DEBORAH WISE AND JOHAN ROSQVIST

Imagine that you face some sort of adversity, such as failing a test, losing your wallet, or even being the victim of a violent attack. When faced with difficult experiences, people naturally attempt to understand the causes of these events, how these events will impact other aspects of their lives, and the extent to which these events will persistently impact their lives. Explanatory style refers to this habitual manner of explaining the causes and impact of adverse events. Explanatory style is important because it impacts our reactions to challenging experiences. Because explanatory style impacts our attempts to cope with ordinary and adverse life circumstances, it influences life satisfaction and, more broadly, subjective well-being.

THEORIES OF EXPLANATORY STYLE

Theories of explanatory style have changed dramatically over time. The learned helplessness model (e.g., Maier & Seligman, 1976; Overmier & Seligman, 1967; Seligman, 1968; Seligman, Maier, & Geer, 1968; Seligman & Meyer, 1970) yielded the attributional reformulation of the learned helplessness model, a theory of explanatory style (Abramson, Seligman, & Teasdale, 1978). Other theories of explanatory style, such as the hopelessness theory of depression (Abramson, Metalsky, & Alloy, 1989) and concepts of dispositional optimism (Carver & Scheier, 2003, 1998), are based on this previous theoretical work but depart from the attributional reformulation of the learned helplessness model in important ways. A brief review of these theories will be presented to provide a foundation with which to explore the impact of explanatory style on well-being.

Learned Helplessness Model

Theories of explanatory style are based upon research on learned helplessness. Learned helplessness was first observed in laboratory experiments in which animals were placed in situations and subjected to aversive outcomes that were in-

dependent of their responses (e.g., Maier & Seligman, 1976; Overmier & Seligman, 1967; Seligman, 1968; Seligman et al., 1968; Seligman & Meyer, 1970). For example, a dog that was exposed to painful shocks without opportunities for escape or avoidance responded by passively enduring the shocks (Maier & Seligman, 1976). Researchers hypothesized that helplessness is a learned behavior and that when animals are placed in situations in which outcomes are independent of their efforts, the animals conclude that future efforts will be useless. Learned helplessness includes motivational, cognitive, and behavioral components.

Researchers hypothesized that similar processes may function in human beings, and they applied the theory of learned helplessness to human behavior. People were exposed to unescapable events, such as aversive tones and insoluble problems (Hiroto & Seligman, 1975). Researchers found that, similar to animals, when people were exposed to situations in which outcomes were independent of their efforts, they thought that they were powerless to affect future outcomes, and consequently they stopped trying to change their situations. In this respect, learned helplessness became a self-fulfilling prophesy; without effort, a person's situation is likely to remain the same. It was proposed that the processes that lead to learned helplessness also lead to depression (Seligman, 1973).

Attributional Reformulation of the Learned Helplessness Model

In a critique of the learned helplessness model, Abramson, Seligman, and Teasdale (1978) noted that this model failed to account for variability among reactions to uncontrollable events. The learned helplessness model failed to distinguish between uncontrollable situations that are universal and specific to certain people, between uncontrollable situations that are general across experiences and specific to a single experience, and between outcomes that are chronic and acute. Moreover, the learned helplessness model failed to account for loss of self-esteem, one component of depression. A reformulation of the learned helplessness theory was offered that incorporated attribution theory to address these inadequacies.

In this reformulation, causal attributions play a fundamental role in functioning after an uncontrollable event (Abramson et al., 1978). Causal attributions occur along three dimensions: internal versus external, stable versus unstable, and global versus specific. In the first dimension, internal attributions relate to factors relevant to that person, whereas external attributions refer to other factors, such as other people or luck. In the second dimension, stable attributions suggest factors that endure over time, whereas unstable attributions are short-lived. In the third dimension, global attributions involve a wide range of one's experiences, whereas specific attributions are constrained to that circumstance. For example, imagine that John, a college student, failed his first examination in Psychology 100. If he attributes his failure to internal causes, he may think, "This is my fault," whereas if he attributes his failure to external causes, he may think, "The teacher's test was unfair, and that is why I failed." If John thinks that his failure is due to stable causes, he may think, "I will never pass a test in this class," whereas if he thinks that his failure is due to unstable causes he may think, "Although I did not do well on this test, I will perform better on the next test." Finally, if John believes that his failure reflects global causes, he may think, "Because I failed this exam, I will probably fail all of my tests in all of my classes," whereas if he believes that his failure reflects specific causes, he may think, "This failure may impact my grade in this class, but I can work hard and do better on the next test and in my other classes."

As you can imagine in John's case, his causal attributions are linked to his emotional, cognitive, and motivational processes (Abramson et al., 1978). If John's attributions are internal, he is likely to have self-esteem deficits. If John's attributions are stable, his perceptions of helplessness are likely to persist over time. If John's attributions are global, then he will likely experience long-lasting learned helplessness. These perceptions of helplessness are likely to yield feelings of sadness and diminish his motivation to change his situation.

When faced with an uncontrollable event coupled with a vague situational explanation for the cause of this event, explanatory style affects one's response to that event (Peterson & Seligman, 1984). Explanatory style refers to a habitual manner of explaining the causes of positive and negative experiences. There is evidence to suggest that one's manner of explaining the causes of events does persist over time. In a study using a content analysis of writing samples taken at two times more than 50 years apart, explanatory style for negative events appeared to persist across the life span, whereas explanatory style for positive events did not (Burns & Seligman, 1989).

Individuals may have pessimistic or optimistic explanatory styles (Buchanan & Seligman, 1995; Peterson & Seligman, 1984). Explanatory style for negative events is independent of explanatory style for positive events. A pessimistic explanatory style involves making internal, stable, and global attributions for negative events and making external, unstable, and specific attributions for positive events. On the other hand, an optimistic explanatory style involves making external, unstable, and specific attributions for negative events and internal, stable, and global attributions for positive events.

Because explanatory style is impacted by experience and influences how a person reacts to future experiences, pessimistic explanatory style may be a risk factor for poor functioning (Peterson & Seligman, 1984). Individuals who blame themselves for negative experiences, think that these experiences will endure over time, and believe that these experiences will impact many domains of their lives are likely to experience depression (e.g., Gladstone & Kaslow, 1995; Joiner & Wagner, 1996; Sweeney, Anderson, & Bailey, 1986). However, optimistic explanatory style is associated with well-being (Peterson & Steen, 2002). Individuals with optimistic explanatory styles demonstrate motivation, achievement, physical well-being, and lower depression (Buchanan & Seligman, 1995; Peterson & Steen, 2002).

Hopelessness Theory of Depression

The hopelessness theory of depression evolved from the reformulated attributional theory of learned helplessness (Abramson, Metalsky, & Alloy, 1989). Similar to the reformulated attributional theory of learned helplessness, the hopelessness theory of depression is a diathesis-stress model. In cognitive diathesis-stress models, a pessimistic explanatory style is a risk factor that, when coupled with exposure to a stressful situation, contributes to the onset and maintenance of depression. However, unlike the reformulated attributional theory of learned helplessness, in the hopelessness model of depression, the role of internal attributions is deemphasized. Instead, theorists hypothesized that stable and global explanations for negative events yield hopelessness. Hopelessness is the expectation that regardless of one's efforts, future outcomes will be aversive, pervasive, and will negatively impact many aspects of one's life. Hopelessness about the future, rather than perceptions of helplessness, constitutes a proximal and sufficient cause of a subtype of depression, called hopelessness depression.

Theory of Dispositional Optimism

Dispositional optimism is another phenomenon relevant to explanatory style (Carver & Scheier, 1998, 2003). Dispositional optimism is exemplified by the colloquialism "every cloud has a silver lining" because optimists expect that good generally will occur when confronting problems across important life domains (Tomakowsky, Lumley, Markowitz, & Frank, 2001). Whereas explanatory style is composed of three dimensions (internality, stability, and globality) for how to understand causes of events, dispositional style instead emphasizes generalized expectancies for future outcomes. In this sense, based on the theory of dispositional optimism, optimists generally expect that good will prevail over bad. Dispositional optimism is similar to explanatory style in that it represents a relatively stable system for understanding oneself, the world, and the future. Unlike pessimists in the learned helplessness model, dispositional optimists assume that situations and circumstances always will work out for the best.

Concepts of optimism and pessimism are based on how people approach life experiences. Optimists expect good things to happen or generally believe that problems in living will resolve themselves and good outcomes will result (Isaacowitz & Seligman, 2001, 2003). Dictionary definitions of optimism include the belief that good ultimately prevails over evil and the tendency to take the most hopeful view of matters (Agnes, 2003). Conversely, people who are prone to pessimistic styles expect that things will not work out or that bad outcomes will occur (Reivich & Gillham, 2003). Dictionary definitions of pessimism include the belief that the evil in life outweighs the good and the tendency always to expect the worst (Agnes, 2003). Given that these two disparate stances are polar opposites, it is more realistic to suggest that more commonly people blend both perspectives rather than espousing one style or the other (Peterson & Park, 1998). However, there is support for the notion that people favor one dispositional style in terms of future expectations and tend to use one style more than the other in novel, future situations (e.g., Gohm & Clore, 2002). In other words, people may possess a default disposition that favors either optimism or pessimism, but such a default will fall somewhere along the spectrum of possible blends. Although having an entirely pessimistic or optimistic approach may be statistically rare, these anchor points form weights for whether a person tends more toward one style of coping or the other. Understanding explanatory style affords greater insight into how people may fair when faced with atypical life circumstances such as surgery or losing a close friend.

Carver and Scheier (1998, 2003) posited that expectancy-value models largely influence people's motivations when it comes to projecting desires into the future. They suggested that people imagine desired end states, or goals, when they look into the future and that they strive to obtain these goals. Goals can be positive or negative; positive goals are those that people work toward obtaining, and negative goals are those that people try to prevent, diminish, escape, or avoid. Inherently, in a hedonistic fashion, people are driven by desire to obtain positive outcomes and to avoid negative or punishing outcomes. Hedonism is the tendency to maximize what feels good and to minimize what feels bad; by definition, hedonism is the doctrine that pleasure is the principal good (Agnes, 2003). Hence, people seek out what feels good and avoid what is experienced as bad. In short, the more desired an outcome is for an individual, the more that person will covet it and work for it; the value of an outcome is intimately tied to the importance or desirability of the particular end state.

The key to people's effort in pursuing desired outcomes rests with their belief, or expectation, that they will succeed in obtaining or reaching a specified goal (Peterson & Stunkard, 1992). When they expect to be able to reach the goal, they will try harder in their efforts to achieve this objective. When people expect that goals are attainable, they also persist in the face of adversity, both for long durations and with strong intensity. The belief that objectives will be reached drives people to work continually toward goals, even when they are not being immediately reinforced for doing so; delay of gratification is enhanced by the expectation that gratification will be obtained. Should people, instead, believe they are not likely to obtain their goal, they may put forth little or no effort toward goals; after all, if a goal is not obtainable (and if that were true), why attempt to reach it? If people do not expect to be rewarded, then they are unlikely to strive for their goals.

When people believe that goals are not attainable, they will be unlikely even to start pursuing goals, and they are likely to give up the pursuit of goals quickly should they start at all. Doubt, which is a common topic in research on anxiety and depression, tends to impede both overt and covert behaviors both prior to and during goal-oriented activity (e.g., Peterson & Stunkard, 1992). Common sense and principles of conservation suggest that people are unlikely to want to waste energy, as it may be required later for other, important needs that are perhaps more likely to be gratified. This principle actually has basic survival value; over eons of evolution, it was important for survival to have energy to act when it really mattered, as in the case of running from a predator (Barlow, 1991a, 1991b). Wasting energy on activities that did not directly feed, fuel, and protect the species was dropped from many behavioral repertoires aimed at survival. On an evolutionary and developmental level, this leads people to discontinue tasks that do not directly or immediately help the person. If there is no discernible more immediate value, then the person will not expend energy toward actions believed to yield no tangible benefits. Over time, it might have led people to make quick estimations of which tasks and goals were possible prior to taking any action, so that little or no energy was wasted, leaving the largest possible energy reserves for more crucial times. In modern times—where people are, for the most part, at the top of the food chain, have most if not all of their basic needs met, and have true excesses in life—creative, critical, and meaningful thinking is much more important than simply reacting with immediate, indiscriminate conservation or spending of energy (e.g., Paterson, 1997a, 1997b). Purposeful planning and acting serves to address modern-day threats better than reactivity; for example, collected and focused thinking and responding serves a person going through a job performance review or evaluation better than running from this conceivably threatening meeting or avoiding it all together, especially if the goal is promotion or remaining employed.

Nonetheless, people's expectancy, or belief in being able to reach the goal, is still largely responsible for shaping responses employed in reaction to goals or targets. This concept of expectancy is closely tied to optimism and pessimism, and it is reflective of confidence or doubt in whether a goal is attainable. Confidence, a reflection of optimistic expectations, breeds action, whereas doubt, a reflection of pessimistic expectations, fosters faltering and weak action or inaction. This makes common sense and also follows the human hedonistic principle.

Confidence or doubt in expectations also can be generalized (i.e., broad and nonspecific) or focused (i.e., narrow and specific; Carver & Scheier, 1998, 2003). With strong beliefs in the notion that good will prevail, one can readily imagine or picture a positive dispositional style, which may be something akin to a positive personality, positive traits, and broad and pervasive positive patterns and styles of interacting with the world. Optimists take a global stance of confidence and persistence, whereas pessimists tend to exhibit a hesitant and doubtful style. These dispositional stances have broad implications for how people cope with experience, especially when it comes to stressors. In studies of anxiety and depression, individuals with these symptoms often demonstrate catastrophic thinking, including predicting disasters and negative outcomes without much actual or convincing evidence to support such negative expectations (e.g., Peterson & Park, 1998). In such instances, people commonly tend to base their reasoning on how things feel. Therefore, people may use emotional reasoning, or ex-consequentia reasoning, to decide on courses of action. Using emotional reasoning, if things

feel bad, situations often are reified into being bad and (because of hedonism) then are avoided or escaped from (Arntz, Rauner, & van den Hout, 1995). These generalized cognitive styles are what Carver and Scheier (1998, 2003) referred to when they suggested that dispositional style pertains to entire lives, because people demonstrate a pervasive, relatively stable pattern of reasoning that tends to be either positive or negative.

FACTORS THAT IMPACT ATTRIBUTIONS

Explanatory style is not created in a vacuum. Instead, several factors shape the development of optimistic or pessimistic explanatory styles, including personal characteristics, such as temperament or gender, modeling by parents, interactions with teachers and through exposure to media, and unusual experiences, such as traumatic events.

Personal Characteristics

Temperament

People differ in some inherent, psychobiological fashion in virtually all domains. This broad human diversity lends clues to underlying processes and mechanisms of individual functioning. For instance, although some people are readily aroused or activated by small amounts of stimulation (e.g., softer sounds, sights, smells, tastes, and tactile information), others need strong stimulation (e.g., skydiving) to feel anything (Otto, Jones, Craske, & Barlow, 1996). Moreover, although some people truly are novelty (stimulation) seeking, others are as distinctly harm (stimulation) avoidant. Similar to personality styles, temperament models afford the ability to scrutinize underlying dimensions on which people differ. For example, the difference between those who seek versus those who avoid stimulation is based on whether stimulation itself is seen and experienced as rewarding or punishing. Cloninger (1987) reported that behavioral inhibition (i.e., escape and avoidance patterns of behavior, similar to prototypical pessimist response patterns) occurs in direct response to signals and expectations of punishment or nonreward. Behavioral activation, on the other hand, occurs in response to novel (excitatory) cues and signs of reward or relief from punishment. Four dimensions of temperament are proposed to exist, namely novelty seeking (positive affect/emotionality and approach behaviors, which may include anger and irritability to overcome obstacles blocking goals), harm avoidance (fear, distress, and negative emotionality, producing behavioral inhibition to novelty), reward dependence (desire for social acceptance/inclusion), and (attentional) persistence/

self-regulatory capacity and control (e.g., Heath, Cloninger, & Martin, 1994; Rothbart, Posner, & Hershey, 1995; Stallings, Hewitt, Cloninger, Heath, & Eaves, 1996).

Broadly defined, temperament refers to one's natural disposition or one's nature (Agnes, 2003). Natural disposition, or nature, refers to a given individual's variations in underlying neural, excitatory, and inhibitory systems. These systems are designed and used for basic survival of the species, making temperament and personality functional in the sense of supporting survival behaviors through regulating a blend of approach and avoidance behaviors for goals and safety (Barlow, 2002).

In simpler terms, an exemplar of inhibition is a defensive system of being quiet and shy around unfamiliar people, being cautious when approaching new scenarios, and being tense. Being uninhibited would take on opposite characteristics and is not a defensive system per se but is instead a system geared at attaining goals. On a deeper, biophysiological level, these behavioral markers are supported by underlying, covert behaviors. Although they activate primarily during stressful times, such behaviors also will respond to perceived stress and include such responses as an accelerated heart rate, pupil dilation, increased muscular tension, and the release of a variety of stress-related hormones and chemicals (e.g., norepinephrine, cortisol, endorphins; Barlow, & Craske, 2000). This kind of biological reaction is survival oriented and is intimately tied to perceptions of danger and fear reactions. As suggested, perceptions of threat are very much driven by expectations, another element closely related to and driven by the phenomenon of optimistic and pessimistic explanatory style. Temperament, therefore, is closely related to the how one perceives and interacts with the world. Optimistic and pessimistic explanatory style may reflect stimulus seeking and stimulus-avoidance behavioral patterns, which are part of temperamental systems of coping. Differences in temperament, much like personality differences and optimistic and pessimistic explanatory style, are closely related to diverse ways of trying to cope with life demands and to the efficiency and effectiveness of these different explanatory styles. Vulnerability to negative temperaments, just like with pessimistic explanatory style, appears to be related to expectations of failures and subsequent withdrawals through emotional coping, as opposed to active problem solving.

Gender Differences

Given that women exhibit higher rates of anxiety- and depression-related disorders than do men (i.e., Nolen-Hoeksema & Girgus, 1995; Sachs-Ericsson & Ciarlo, 2000), some researchers have examined the link between gender dif-

ferences and explanatory style. Studies of gender differences in mean levels of explanatory style have yielded mixed results; research findings range from no gender differences in the relationship between attributional style and depression (Whitley, Michael, & Tremont, 1991) to significant gender differences between attributional style and depression (Boggiano & Barrett, 1991; Johnston & Page, 1991). However, discrepancies exist even among studies in which robust differences between men and women have been found. In one study, women were more likely than men to report both a pessimistic explanatory style and depressive symptoms (Boggiano & Barrett, 1991). Contrary to these findings, in another study, compared to women, men reported higher levels of pessimistic explanatory style (Johnston & Page, 1991). Given these mixed results, it may be that gender-related differences in rates of anxiety and depressive disorders reflect differences in styles of coping with stress rather than differences in explanatory style; women may employ more help-seeking behaviors than do men.

Some researchers have sought to explore gender differences in explanatory style across childhood (Nolen-Hoeksema & Girgus, 1995; Nolen-Hoeksema, Girgus, & Seligman, 1992). In both cross-sectional studies and longitudinal studies, explanatory style among boys and girls changed over time (Nolen-Hoeksema & Girgus, 1995). The correlation between explanatory styles and depression increased with age (Nolen-Hoeksema et al., 1992). Moreover, significant gender differences emerged over time. Among preadolescent children, boys' explanations for negative events were more pessimistic than girls' explanations, and there were no gender differences in explanations for positive events (Nolen-Hoeksema & Girgus, 1995). This may explain why preadolescent boys are more likely to be depressed than preadolescent girls (Nolen-Hoeksema et al., 1992). However, although boys in the fourth, sixth, and eighth grades were more pessimistic and depressed than same-aged girls, between the eighth and tenth grades, girls became more pessimistic and more depressed than boys (Nolen-Hoeksema & Girgus, 1995). However, the reasons for these gender-based changes in explanatory style during childhood are unclear.

It is likely that pessimistic explanatory style for negative events operates in different personality domains for men and women. Unlike men, women reported a significant discrepancy between actual and ideal self-perceptions, and this discrepancy was significantly correlated with pessimistic explanatory style (Boggiano & Barrett, 1991). Among women, concerns about their health, personal problems, future options, and impressions on others were associated with pessimistic explanatory style for negative events (Bunce & Peterson, 1997). However, among men, perceptions of shyness, unease in social situations, preference for remaining in the margins in social situations, lack of conformity to rules and regulations, and difficulty with task completion were associated with pessimistic explanatory style for negative events. In other words, women who reported deficits in personal well-being and men who reported deficits in interpersonal skills were likely to have a pessimistic explanatory style.

Modeling

Children learn about themselves and the world through processes of observational learning, also called modeling (Bandura, 1977). They observe others' behaviors and the outcomes of their actions, and this impacts their expectations regarding future reinforcements or punishment. In this respect, modeling impacts how children explain experiences to themselves, and, therefore, modeling can shape explanatory style. Parents, teachers, and media are important sources of modeling and may, therefore, have a significant impact on children's explanatory style.

Family

Although it seems clear that certain styles of interacting with the world seem to be due in part to genetic disposition, such as temperament, such variance toward poor coping cannot clearly be parceled out from familial modeling of negative expectancy, hesitancy, doubt, and correspondingly poor or negative behavioral tendencies. Vicarious learning (e.g., Cormier & Nurius, 2003; Domjan, 1993) is especially strong within primary relationships because the models observed hold important social power as parental units. Indeed, modeling is one of the most important ways in which people, and especially children, learn new behaviors and skills. When poor or maladaptive coping is modeled, a child might observe others' efforts not leading to fruition and thereby begin to expect that one has no control over their lives or that bad things are prevalent in the world. Poor coping probably will not just be overtly modeled but will likely also be further engrained by negative (catastrophic) verbal reactions to failure (e.g., "the world isn't fair, and it will never change!"). This negative expectation might be especially strong if the child considers engaging in those behaviors estimated, through past observation and learning, to be nonproductive, unfruitful, and perhaps even punishing.

People tend to avoid actions until they have observed others doing them first, and people tend to avoid behaviors that they believe will not be reinforced or will be punished (Sturmey, 1996). In this fashion, they may conclude—with-

out actual evidence of what would occur if they performed a given task—that they will not be successful, and they, therefore, will not engage in the task. Following this line of reasoning, people understand that they are fine when they do not engage in the goal/target behavior because the negative outcome predicted or expected does not occur, at least not at that immediate moment. Unfortunately, this is a conclusion reached in the absence of evidence, even beyond what they might have observed modeled by parents and, therefore, expect to be true and absolute in the world. That is, they really do not know what would happen for them unless they engage in the task of obtaining that goal. Yet, they may have observed a deficient or poor example of problem solving, and a more adaptive method of problem solving may have yielded a more satisfactory outcome. If so, then observational learning could have allowed the individual to reach different conclusions and, as a result, may have led to different behaviors (e.g., action versus nonaction, persistence versus giving up). The power of modeling vis-à-vis the influence of genes needs to be carefully weighed, as implications for correction of the latter may leave individuals with an even more pessimistic outlook for success and positive change. Genes are commonly interpreted to be much more deterministic than flexible and adjustable (Sturmey, 1996).

Pessimists are likely to give up readily and quickly because their expectancy of actual success is low, and, therefore, it is likely that a child growing up with a pessimistic parent or parents will regularly observe two common types of events. First, pessimistic parents likely will not take on many challenging or demanding tasks because they believe they will not reach goals, either due to personal shortcomings or inherent unfairness in the world (i.e., it is bad and evil). As part of regular child rearing, they also probably will try to diminish suffering in their offspring. Unfortunately, they may approach this desire to protect their children from an unjust and difficult life through instructing their children about what is not possible in the world, according to their own experiences with living and trying to succeed in life. Whether intentionally or merely modeling pessimistic explanatory style through their own behaviors, parents inadvertently may send the message that most of life is too hard, too difficult, and too unfair and that trying to achieve is a waste of energy. The coping strategy of choice, therefore, becomes one of avoidance of or escape from challenge and adversity. This is understandable from the pessimistic perspective because in such a view problems simply are not conquerable and working to solve problems is seen as hopeless, painful, and perhaps even stupid. In short, the approach is one avoiding what feels bad. Unfortunately, avoidance and escape breed a life of suffering and inaccurate reasoning skills that commonly lead to negative self-fulfilling prophecies.

Conversely, coping responses include the ability to adapt to stressors and deal with anger, frustration, fear, and other standard life experiences. Common coping responses typifying the optimist are: acceptance of adversity, positively reframing genuine difficulty, and a focus on active problem solving in response to challenging situations (i.e., no avoidance or escape, both cognitively and behaviorally; Gohm & Clore, 2002). Ironically, pessimistic explanatory styles support the idea that effort should not be expended unless success is guaranteed. Of course, this need for guarantees, or control over outcomes, is not realistic. Additionally, it is clear that a mastery stance, in which one believes that individuals are always successful in obtaining goals and perform perfectly every time from the first time, reduces self-efficacy both in the individual and also in observers. Not modeling flexibility and adaptability in coping with stressors has clear, deleterious effects on children and may negatively shape and influence their future adulthood expectancies through diminished flexibility, lack of persistence, and low self-efficacy (Shatte, Seligman, Gillham, & Reivich, in press). Indeed, people with a pessimistic explanatory style tend to deny the existence of, and typically distance themselves from, problems, commonly through such maladaptive means as substance abuse or other avoidance strategies (Carver, Meyer, & Antoni, 2000). However, avoiding problematic circumstances often only makes them worse than if they were addressed.

In anxiety research, this kind of real-life, probably fixable problem is often referred to as a *Type 1 problem* (Dugas, & Ladouceur, 2000). Type 1 problems are exemplified by real-life, here-and-now issues that many people face in the course of living, such as paying bills, meeting deadlines, and other issues that are accessible to active problem solving. On the other hand, *Type 2 problems* are future-oriented fears about problems that may arise but have not done so and may never arise. Obviously, this kind of future-oriented, potential problem is less available to here-and-now problem solving and plays a significant role in heightening anticipatory anxiety. Type 2 problems also tend to promote negative rumination and inaction that might solve an imagined problematic situation if it ever arose. Catastrophizing, a common element representative of a poor coping stance, is in essence the same phenomenon as anticipatory anxiety (Dugas, Gagnon, Ladouceur, & Freeston, 1998). In both cases, average probabilities are ignored in favor of far more unlikely and negative outcomes, which again typifies the negative worldview that a person with a pessimistic explanatory style maintains to support the belief in evil and badness. Type 1 and Type 2 problems are common to generalized anxiety disorder (GAD)

and other anxiety disorders, as well as depression, and are commonly addressed through active problem solving and habituation to distress (Dugas et al., 1998; Leger, Ladouceur, Dugas, & Freeston, 2003; Wells & Carter, 1999).

A second type of event that a child may observe in a pessimistic parent is that this parent is less likely to follow through and persist in trying to obtain goals, especially if the task requires flexibility, persistence, and increased effort without immediate payoffs or positive results. Therefore, parents with a pessimistic explanatory style are likely to model inconsistency and, ultimately, give up and retreat in a self-protective, self-soothing manner. Parents with a pessimistic explanatory style are unlikely to label accurately that they may not have tried hard enough, for long enough, or in flexible enough ways and instead are likely to suggest that the world is unfair and biased against them. Ironically, this sends an extremely poor and inaccurate message to the child; that is, the world is broadly (globally) unfair, and this is true now and will remain so in the future (stable), and the power for obtaining goals or affecting change rests with power or sheer luck in the world (external), not within the person. In fact, the internal view held by the pessimist is one of being flawed and disabled. Should people with a pessimistic explanatory style occasionally be successful in obtaining desired outcomes, they are likely to attribute chance or luck (unstable) variables to such outcomes, which does not challenge their otherwise negative worldview of themselves as ineffectual or flawed, weak, and powerless (Peterson, Seligman, Yurko, Martin, & Friedman, 1998). Schunk, Hanson, and Cox (1987) demonstrated that observing a coping model versus a mastery model led to increased self-efficacy, skill level, and training performance. Given how pessimists generally interact with life, it appears unlikely they will exhibit and demonstrate a coping model, thereby teaching their children to be self-doubting, to see themselves as possessing few effective skills, and to withdraw from challenge and difficulties. Indeed, what they may transmit through modeling ineffectual coping is a generalized negative (pessimistic) expectancy about the self and the world (Alloy et al., 2001; Johnson & Kliewer, 1999).

Teachers

Clearly, children's attributions about their successes and failures are impacted by interactions with important people in their lives. Children spend much of their time in school settings, where teacher feedback about their classroom performance shapes their explanatory style (Dweck, 2002; Dweck, Davidson, Nelson, & Bradley, 1978; Heyman, Dweck, & Cain, 1992; Mueller & Dweck, 1998).

Teacher criticism for academic failures is associated with children's pessimistic explanatory style (Heyman, Dweck, & Cain, 1992). In a study in which kindergarten children role-played situations in which they received criticism from teachers, 39 percent of the children displayed learned helplessness behaviors, including negative affect, negative opinions about their project, reluctance to participate in future projects, and negative internal, stable, and global judgments about themselves.

Not only does criticism contribute to pessimistic explanatory style, but praise for attributes that are perceived to be fixed also may contribute to a pessimistic explanatory style (Mueller & Dweck, 1998). Fifth-grade children who were praised for intelligence, an attribute that was perceived to be a fixed trait, valued performance over learning and demonstrated learned helplessness in response to challenges or failures. Children who were praised for intelligence made internal attributions for their failures and were less likely to enjoy tasks, persist at tasks, and perform tasks well than were children who were praised for their effort. In sum, teachers' feedback may shape children's beliefs about their intelligence, thereby impacting their motivation and level of achievement (Dweck, 2002).

Media

Repeated mass media exposure may facilitate pessimistic explanatory style by overemphasizing the stable and global nature of environmental threat (Peterson & Steen, 2002). Given the threats of terrorism that have reverberated throughout the media recently, this possibility is not difficult to imagine. We have been told repeatedly that elusive terrorists may be anywhere and that the threat they pose will last into the foreseeable future. Attributions of helplessness and hopelessness may stem from these gloomy pronouncements.

The overemphasis of perceptions of helplessness in the media is not new. A 1977 content analysis of newscasts on major broadcasting networks revealed that perceptions of helplessness were modeled in 71 percent of the news items (Levine, 1977).

What is the impact of media messages that emphasize threat? Among adults, amount of exposure to television was related to perceptions of societal problems, and perceptions of societal problems were related to anger and depressive symptoms (McNaughton-Cassill & Smith, 2002).

In the aftermath of the attacks of September 11, 2001, in which many Americans were repeatedly exposed to news stories that emphasized global and stable threat and our collective helplessness to change this outcome, symptoms of distress peaked in the short term (Ahern, Galea, Resnick, &

Vlahow, 2004; Niles, Wolf, & Kutter, 2003). Among respondents to a random-digit-dial telephone survey conducted four months after September 11, watching a greater amount of television during the week after September 11 was associated with symptoms similar to post-traumatic stress disorder (Ahern et al., 2004).

However, just because media messages of stability and globality of threat are pervasive, does that mean that watching television engenders a pessimistic explanatory style? Although it is possible that exposure to mass media violence may engender perceptions of stable and global environmental threat, the impact of these factors on explanatory style has yet to be examined.

Traumatic Events

Consistent with the diathesis-stress models of explanatory style, traumatic events make up one type of stressor that may contribute to pessimistic explanatory style. By definition, traumatic events are stressors that involve threats to the physical integrity of the self or others and engender fear, helplessness, or horror (American Psychiatric Association, 1994). If people blame themselves for traumatic events and perceive the impact of events to be pervasive and permanent, they may be more likely to have a pessimistic explanatory style. Therefore, researchers hypothesized that early traumatic events, such as a parent's death, could produce a pessimistic explanatory style (Peterson & Seligman, 1984).

Indeed, several studies suggest that the experience of traumatic events, such as child maltreatment, is associated with pessimistic explanatory style (Bunce, Larsen, & Peterson, 1995; Cerezo-Jimenez & Frias, 1994; Gold, 1986; Kaufman, 1991). Children ages 8 to 13 with histories of chronic physical and emotional abuse were more likely to manifest a pessimistic explanatory style than nonabused controls (Cerezo-Jimenez & Frias, 1994). Abused children in this sample perceived punishments to be unpredictable and reported low self-esteem and sadness. Similarly, in a community sample of 103 sexually abused and 88 nonabused women, the sexually abused group was more likely to have a pessimistic explanatory style (Gold, 1986). In another study, college students with histories of traumatic stressors were more likely to report a pessimistic explanatory style than students without histories of traumatic stressors (Bunce, Larsen, & Peterson, 1995). Clearly, exposure to traumatic events and pessimistic explanatory style appear to be correlated.

Peterson et al. (2001) conducted a series of experiments to see if pessimistic explanatory style increased the risk of exposure to traumatic events. They hypothesized that pessimistic explanatory style leads to perceptions of helplessness and poor problem-solving behaviors, which contribute to risky behaviors, thereby increasing the likelihood of exposure to traumatic accidents. As predicted, pessimistic explanatory style was associated with exposure to potentially traumatic events, such as motor vehicle accidents, fires, and serious injuries. Moreover, college students and patients hospitalized for accidents reported engaging in risky behavior to reduce bad moods. In sum, these findings suggest that exposure to traumatic events is associated with pessimistic explanatory style, and pessimistic explanatory style increases the risk of exposure to potentially traumatic events.

FACETS OF WELL-BEING

Explanatory style can have a significant and prolonged impact on well-being. Although pessimistic explanatory style can negatively impact several facets of well-being, including physical health, academic and career achievement, and mental health functioning, such as symptoms of depression and anxiety, optimistic explanatory style may serve as a protective factor.

Health and Coping Styles (Hardiness)

Pessimists explain past failures in global terms (Carver & Scheier, 1998, 2003). This tendency means that failure and being ineffectual, in terms of the person's understanding of causality and individual influence on outcome, span across most, if not all, aspects of life. A pessimistic stance suggests that outcomes will be bad across most life domains, and a person is and will remain unable to affect outcomes. Therefore, there may be little or no incentive for action to prevent bad things from happening; after all, not only will action require effort, but, from the pessimistic perspective, it is unlikely to resolve problems, and the bad will still outweigh the good in the end anyway, so why try? The hopelessness theory of depression follows this line of negative emotional coping closely (Peterson & Park, 1998).

Pessimistic explanatory style unfortunately, but expectedly, impacts the pessimists' health status and health-related behaviors (Carver, Lehman, & Antoni, 2003). Because pessimists expect bad things to happen, they are more prone to experience negatively valenced emotional states, such as anxiety, guilt, anger, sadness, despair, and hopelessness (Isaacowitz & Seligman, 2003). These states are positively correlated with negative well-being and poor health status (Brennan & Charnetski, 2000; Jason, Witter, & Torres-Harding, 2003; Tomakowsky et al., 2001). This appears to be true whether the person faces ordinary life circumstances or more acute and serious threats to well-being and personal health. In either case, people with pessimistic explanatory styles exhibit and experience more personal distress compared to people with an optimistic explanatory style. This distress contributes in important but deleterious ways to a stress-diathesis model of health and subjective well-being. In the eyes of many researchers and clinicians alike, pessimism represents a fundamental antithesis to personal health, well-being, and optimal functioning (Carstensen, Charles, Isaacowitz, & Kennedy, 2003).

On the other hand, optimism is a protective factor that serves to enhance and further fuel individual hardiness, which is the capacity to withstand and rise to challenges (Sweetman, Munz, & Wheeler, 1993). Hardiness further affects perceptions of quality of life because it relates to expectations, and thus behaviors, to improve living circumstances (Peterson & Stunkard, 1992). Hardiness is positively correlated with optimism because optimists tend to engage in behaviors related to hardiness, such as acceptance of circumstances, active problem solving, and appreciation of support. Even in the face of common health stressors, such as childbirth, optimism appears to boost people's resistance to depressive symptoms (Carver, 2004).

Optimism also appears to improve coping with life-threatening health concerns (Carver et al., 2003). When faced with invasive surgeries, such as coronary artery bypass surgery, optimists exhibit less hostility, anger, and depression prior to surgery and demonstrate clearer happiness with their care, support, and life, even when faced with recovery from serious medical interventions, than do pessimists (Scheier et al., 1999). Compared to pessimists, optimists simply seem to exhibit greater life satisfaction, even when dealing with serious health risks and threats to personal well-being (Spencer et al., 1999). The expectation that good will prevail and that it will all be worth it in the end seems to help individuals with an optimistic explanatory style cope with challenging experiences. Acceptance of stressful events produces less anger, and when mixed with the belief that things will work out for the better, optimism facilitates effective coping and well-being.

Across many health-related problems, such as infertility and in vitro fertilization, optimism promotes the idea that much can be learned from difficult experiences (Carver & Gaines, 1987). This idea is part of an active problem-solving approach in which the person affected by health problems tries to integrate the experience into an existing, positive worldview for use in future problem solving. It is through this same approach that civil engineers learn to build better bridges through carefully analyzing bridges that fall down and incorporating this knowledge into future engineering endeavors. They do not ignore or suppress failure; instead, they embrace this information and use it to build better bridges in the future (Petroski, 1992). Optimists are adept at using fallen bridges to inform them about what to do next time to optimize future outcomes. For them, one failure does not signal future failures; instead, it might even signal the elimination or at least the diminishment of future failures through using what can be gleaned to better cope with future problems. Optimists do not necessarily look at adversity as problematic, but instead they see adversity as challenges to be met, learned from, and adapted to. This does not have to mean that an optimist necessarily seeks out failure, or tries to produce failure experiences, but instead that they are not opposed to having adversity occur because it is viewed as additional opportunity for human growth and development, instead of further proof of personal shortcomings or flaws.

Achievement

Explanatory style may inform reactions to current and future academic successes and failures (Peterson & Barrett, 1987). Attributing academic successes to luck and failures to lack of intelligence reflects a pessimistic explanatory style, and attributing academic successes to personal skill and failures to lack of effort reflects an optimistic explanatory style. Pessimistic explanatory style may contribute to motivation deficits, whereas optimistic explanatory style may lead to persistence in the face of adversity resulting in higher achievement. Studies of the relationship between explanatory style and achievement have yielded mixed results.

Among several studies, the relationship between pessimistic explanatory style and achievement is robust (Nolen-Hoeksema, Girgus, & Seligman, 1986; Nolen-Hoeksema & Girgus, 1995; Peterson & Barrett, 1987; Yu & Seligman, 2002). College students who attributed negative academic events to internal, stable, and global causes did more poorly in their classes than did students who attributed negative academic events to external, unstable, and specific causes, even after depressive symptoms and initial ability were controlled (Peterson & Barrett, 1987). Moreover, pessimistic explanatory style appeared to be a self-fulfilling prophesy; students with negative explanatory style were less likely to have specific academic goals and were less likely to seek academic advising, variables that also were associated with poor grades. Similarly, in a study of school children, pessimistic explanatory style was associated with poor achievement on the California Achievement Test battery (Nolen-Hoeksema et al., 1986). Schoolchildren with pessimistic explanatory style tended to display learned helplessness behaviors, such as giving up easily when challenged (Nolen-Hoeksema &

Girgus, 1995). These results were replicated among Chinese children among whom pessimistic explanatory style was associated with academic achievement and school conduct problems (Yu & Seligman, 2002).

Poor achievement also may serve as a stressor that, when accompanied by pessimistic explanatory style, facilitates depressive symptoms. After receiving poor grades, fifth- and sixth-grade children with pessimistic explanatory style were more likely to exhibit depressive symptoms than were children with optimistic explanatory styles, even after controlling for initial symptom levels (Hilsman & Garber, 1995).

Some studies suggest that the impact of explanatory style persists beyond school. Among life-insurance salespeople, agents with an optimistic explanatory style sold more insurance and remained with the company longer than did agents with a pessimistic explanatory style (Seligman & Schulman, 1986).

Contrary to results of previously described studies, other researchers have found an association between pessimistic explanatory style and high achievement. Among college juniors and seniors beginning a marketing degree program, students who endorsed pessimistic explanatory styles performed better in classes than students with optimistic explanatory styles (LaForge & Cantrell, 2003). Similarly, among law students, compared to their optimistic counterparts, students with pessimistic explanatory style achieved higher grades (Satterfield, Monahan, & Seligman, 1997). Researchers hypothesized that in some contexts, students can use a pessimistic explanatory style to their advantage; by discounting successes and focusing on personal failures, skepticism may be an advantage to individuals in these highly demanding academic environments.

A couple of studies have not borne out the association between explanatory style and achievement. Among college athletes, there was no significant association between explanatory style and academic achievement (Hale, 1993). However, these results may be due to the fact that in this study, general measures of attributions were employed, rather than attributions specific to the domains being measured. Another study failed to find a relationship between explanatory style and performance among medical residents (Hershberger, Zimmerman, Markert, Kirkham, & Bosworth, 2000). However, there was a highly restricted range of explanatory style and performance among participants, thereby making significant results unlikely.

Overall, it is likely that explanatory style has significant implications for school and work achievement. However, to clarify the relationship between explanatory style and achievement, future studies should incorporate measures of attributions that are specific to the domains being measured. In addition, it would be helpful to measure achievement across different training and work settings to determine if certain types of explanatory style provide situation-specific benefits.

Mental Health Functioning

Depression

According to diathesis-stress models of depression, pessimistic explanatory style in the context of stressful experiences increases the risk of depression. The internal, stable, and global explanations for less than desirable aspects of life that make up a pessimistic explanatory style are significant risk factors for depression due to the inherent negative-valenced thinking style central to both phenomenon. Consistent with diathesis-stress models of depression, the correlation between pessimistic explanatory style and depression is robust (Gladstone & Kaslow, 1995; Joiner & Wagner, 1995; Sharpley & Yardley, 1999; Sweeney et al., 1986). In meta-analytic reviews of the association between explanatory style and depressive symptoms, pessimistic explanatory style was associated with higher levels of depressive symptoms among adults (Sweeney et al., 1986), adolescents, and children (Gladstone & Kaslow, 1995; Joiner & Wagner, 1995). The association between explanatory style and depression also has been shown among older adults, ages 65 to 80 (Sharpley & Yardley, 1999).

Among several studies, explanatory style mediated the relationship between stressors and symptoms of depression. Pessimistic explanatory style interacts with stressors to predict symptoms of depression in school-aged children (Hilsman & Garber, 1995) and adults (McKean, 1994; Metalsky, Abramson, Seligman, Semmel, & Peterson, 1982; Metalsky, Halberstadt, & Abramson, 1987).

Longitudinal investigations of the association between pessimistic explanatory style and depression suggest that this association persists over time (Nolen-Hoeksema, Girgus, & Seligman, 1986, 1992; Peterson & Seligman, 1984). For example, in a five-year longitudinal study of third-grade children, pessimistic explanatory style predicted depression (Nolen-Hoeksema et al., 1986, 1992). Moreover, the severity of pessimistic explanatory style increased during the course of depressive episodes, and these pessimistic explanatory styles persisted even after the cessation of depressive episodes.

Given the strong association between pessimistic explanatory style and depression, interventions have been developed to prevent pessimistic explanatory style and promote optimistic explanatory style. Cognitive behavioral interventions that emphasize challenging pessimistic cognitions have been associated with decreases in pessimistic explanatory style and depression (Gillham, Reivich, Jaycox, & Seligman, 1995; Jaycox, Reivich, Gillham, & Seligman, 1994; Seligman et al., 1988; Seligman, Schulman, DeRubeis, & Hollon, 1999). The Penn Resiliency Program is one such program designed to prevent depressive symptoms among at-risk middle-school children. In this program, children learn to challenge pessimistic cognitions and to develop social problem-solving skills. Compared with a control group, children in the prevention program reported significantly fewer depressive symptoms and conduct problems (Jaycox, Reivich, Gillham, & Seligman, 1994). At a two-year follow-up, children who had completed the program were more likely to show optimistic explanatory style and less likely to show depressive symptoms compared to children in the control group (Gillham et al., 1995). Optimistic explanatory style mediated the relationship between stressors and depressive symptoms.

Anxiety

How one makes sense of experiences largely determines whether an individual will go on to develop an inordinate amount of anxiety and inaccurate reactivity that can lead to perceiving threats in benign circumstances (Craske, 1999). Reacting with fear in truly dangerous situations remains important and has a strong survival value. Still, how one reacts to fear during real danger largely determines whether the fear will be useful or whether it will hinder positive coping and survival. Cognitive evaluation of cause and effect appears pivotal to the experience of anxiety (Emmelkamp, Bouman, & Scholing, 1992).

Clearly, there are acknowledged genetic/biological and environmental contributions to many, if not most, anxiety phenomena, but it remains useful to explore how explanatory style might moderate clinical anxiety. After all, explanatory style is based upon people's understanding of the causes and the impact of their experiences and their perceptions of the power that they have to influence outcomes. Because not all people exposed to traumatic experiences go on to develop post-traumatic stress disorder (PTSD; Foa, 2000), it is useful to investigate whether domains such as internality, stability, and globality influence the development, the maintenance, and the worsening of such conditions.

In an attempt to understand how anxiety influences optimism and pessimism, and vice versa, PTSD is a useful syndrome for evaluation because avoidant coping style is one of the fundamental aspects of PTSD. This common PTSD coping style is similar to the emotion-focused coping style typically used by the pessimist, who avoids distress through sleeping, eating, drinking, and engaging in other attempts at withdrawal, distancing, or self-blame (Gray, Pumphrey, &

Lombardo, 2003). Rather than the optimistic acceptance and integration of experiences into existing life models, the pessimist (and PTSD sufferer) frequently employs active denial to cope with stress, forcing a negative change to schematic understanding of self, others, and the world.

People cope with traumatic information through assimilation, accommodation, or overaccommodation (Resick & Schnicke, 1993). Assimilation is the process by which people distort information to match current beliefs about themselves and the world, for example, by denying the experience of a traumatic event. This is the process that occurs when rape survivors question whether or not a sexual assault actually occurred. Accommodation is the process by which people alter beliefs about themselves and the world to cope with stressful events. Accommodation is an adaptive response to a traumatic experience; for example, a rape survivor may acknowledge that a rape occurred and view this as evidence that some men are rapists. Overaccommodation is the process by which people make extreme distortions of beliefs about the self and the world. A rape survivor who engages in overaccommodation may not only acknowledge that a rape occurred but view this as evidence that all men are rapists. Processes of overaccommodation yield perceptions of being unable to personally affect change (i.e., internalizing: "I screwed up, and I can't fix it!"), perceptions that traumatic events will happen again (i.e., stable: "Oh my God, what a fool I have been, I've been thinking life is safe, but I was wrong. It's really bad, and unless I'm much, much more careful this will happen again!"), and perceptions that broadly evil prevails (i.e., global: "All driving/men/other stimulus are dangerous!"). In other words, the process of overaccommodation yields thoughts that are similar to a pessimistic explanatory style. In sum, individuals who suffer from PTSD may expect bad things to happen, may perceive that they are unable to stop bad things from occurring in the future, and may experience environmental threats as pervasive. Interestingly, maladaptive schemata and beliefs about oneself, the world, and the future are prototypical targets in PTSD treatment, suggesting significant overlap with negative expectations experienced in pessimism (Resick & Schnicke, 1993).

Overall, PTSD is characterized by reexperiencing, avoidance, and hyperarousal symptoms following a traumatic event (APA; *DSM–IV,* 1994). PTSD is often comorbid with depression, and similar variables may yield both disorders (Kessler, Sonnega, Bromet, Hughes, & Nelson, 1995; O'Donnell, Creamer, & Pattison, 2004). The comorbidity between PTSD and depression is not surprising given that many symptoms of depression, such as decreased interest in activities, sleep difficulties, irritability, and heightened startle response, are also symptoms of PTSD. Given the linkages between PTSD and depression and the robust relationship between pessimistic explanatory style and depression, many researchers have examined the relationship between pessimistic explanatory style and PTSD.

Internal attributions regarding sexual abuse have been associated with depression, lower self-esteem, anxiety, and PTSD (Gold, 1986; Mannarino & Cohen, 1996a, 1996b; Morrow, 1991; Taska & Feiring, 2000; Wolfe, Sas, & Wekerle, 1994; Wyatt & Newcomb, 1990). These have been identified across several studies. Compared with women without histories of childhood sexual abuse, women with histories of sexual abuse were more likely to manifest symptoms of depression and low self-esteem than were the nonabused group (Gold, 1986). Moreover, internal attributions mediate the relationship between abuse-related factors, such as duration and types of psychological coercion, and psychological adjustment (Wyatt & Newcomb, 1990).

Similarly, internal attributions regarding sexual abuse have been associated with distress among children. In a study of 90 sexually abused children ages 6 through 16, internal attributions significantly contributed to PTSD, even after controlling for age, gender, and nature of the sexually abusive experiences (Wolfe et al., 1994). Among 77 sexually abused children from ages 7 through 12, self-blame was related to self-reported depression, anxiety, and self-esteem problems (Mannarino & Cohen, 1996a, 1996b). Among 98 children who had been sexually or physically abused, pessimistic explanatory style was associated with depressive symptoms, and the interaction between pessimistic explanatory style and type of abuse predicted PTSD symptoms (Runyon & Kenny, 2002).

Internal attributions regarding other types of traumatic events also have been associated with PTSD. Among adolescent survivors of a sinking ship, internal causal attributions for this experience were associated with post-traumatic stress symptoms (Joseph, Brewin, Yule, & Williams, 1993). Pessimistic explanatory style also was associated with PTSD among military veterans (McCormick, Taber, & Kruedelbach, 1989).

Although many studies have shown an association between general explanatory style and PTSD, some studies suggest that attributions specific to a traumatic experience are associated with PTSD symptoms more than explanatory style (Feiring, Taska, & Chen, 2002; Gray et al., 2003). In other words, it may be attributions regarding a particular event rather than a general style of understanding the world that are associated with PTSD symptoms.

Contrary to these results, some studies suggest that pessimistic explanatory style is associated with depression but not with PTSD symptoms. Among adult survivors of the

Northridge, California, earthquake, pessimistic explanatory style mediated the relationship between disaster exposure and depressive, but not PTSD, symptoms (Greening, Stoppelbein, & Doctor, 2002). Moreover, among 158 survivors of motor vehicle accidents, internal attributions were associated with lower rather than higher levels of PTSD (Hickling, Blanchard, Buckley, & Taylor, 1999). This may be because in the case of natural disasters or motor vehicle accidents, internal attributions may increase perceptions of control and decrease a survivor's sense of helplessness.

In sum, pessimistic explanatory style has been associated with poor mental health functioning, as indicated by symptoms of anxiety and depression. Facets of pessimistic explanatory style, particularly internal attributions for traumatic events, are associated with post-traumatic stress symptoms. Stable and global perceptions of threat also have been associated with PTSD.

MEASUREMENT OF EXPLANATORY STYLE

Assessment strategies long have been used to measure human behaviors. Although this information has a multitude of important clinical uses, the overarching question that measuring human behavior tries to answer is, "Why do people do what they do?" Understanding what factors contribute to behaviors provides critical information about antecedents, organismic variables, response patterns, and consequences. In this Stimulus-Organism-Response-Consequence framework (S-O-R-C; Cormier, & Nurius, 2003), the assessment data provide the capacity to predict the conditions that produce responses. From prediction flows the beginnings of control and, thereby, change. Beyond measuring the presence or absence of some concept, like optimism and pessimism, assessment is pivotal to try also to understand reasons for responses to situational stimuli.

In this sense, researchers and clinicians have wondered why some people see the glass as half full while others see it as half empty; in other words, how could one measure, and perhaps predict and begin to modify, explanatory style and ultimately well-being. Because personal explanatory style influences coping style, whether people are life-engaged and problem solving or withdrawn and self-blaming, several measures have been developed to assess explanatory style.

Adult Measures of Explanatory Style

Measures of explanatory style among adult populations include self-report questionnaires and content analysis of pre-existing speech and text. Self-report measures designed to assess various facets of explanatory style include the Attributional Style Questionnaire (ASQ; Peterson et al., 1982), the Cognitive Styles Questionnaire (CSQ; Abramson et al., 1998), and the Life Orientation Test (LOT; Scheier & Carver, 1985).

The ASQ (Peterson et al., 1982) was the first assessment instrument that specifically gauged explanatory style. Participants are presented with 12 hypothetical good and bad events and asked to write about the major cause of each event. Participants then are asked to rate the internality, stability, and globality of these explanations on a seven-point Likert scale. The ASQ yields scores on internal attributions for positive events, internal attributions for negative events, stable attributions for positive events, stable attributions for negative events, global attributions for positive events, and global attributions for negative events. Due to modest reliability of these subscales, composites of these scores, which have satisfactory reliability, typically are used (e.g., Peterson et al., 1982). The composite negative explanatory style includes the summation of internal, stable, and global scores for negative events; the composite positive explanatory style includes the summation of internal, stable, and global scores for positive events; the total score subtracts the negative composite score from the positive composite score. Test-retest reliability of the ASQ suggests that explanatory style is fairly stable across time. Golin, Sweeny, and Schaffer (1981) found that for positive events, an undergraduate-student sample produced test-retest reliability coefficients of .66 for internality, .56 for stability, and .51 for globality. For negative events, the test-retest correlations were .47 for internality, .61 for stability, and .65 for globality. Construct validity ranged from .48 to .71 (Schuman, Castellon, & Seligman, 1989). For a comprehensive overview of how the ASQ has been used in investigating the phenomenon of depression, see Sweeney, Anderson, and Bailey's (1986) review.

Two expanded ASQs exist, and are worth noting. Both are known as the Expanded Attributional Style Questionnaires (E-ASQ; Metalsky et al., 1987; Peterson & Villanova, 1988). These two measures are more heavily loaded for negative events and more reliably produce information about how pessimists understand and make sense of their world and experiences. Because neither polls for reactions to positive events, these instruments have limited generalizability. Only information about negative explanatory style for negative events is gathered, but if critical information with a focus on the pessimistic, hopeless style is desired, these instruments may be useful. The ASQ is considered to be a psychometrically sound measure, with modest reliabilities of Cronbach's alpha ranging from .44 to .70. Attributional style also appears to be a stable variable of personality, with test-retest correlations ranging from .57 to .70. The construct and criterion validity has been supported by several studies (e.g., Metalsky et al., 1982). Criterion validity was investigated by examining the extent to which the ASQ predicts causal explanations occurring spontaneously. Correlations between the spontaneous explanations and the relevant scales on the ASQ ranged from .19 ($p < 0.10$) to 0.41 ($p < 0.001$) (Metalsky et al., 1982).

To provide clearer indexes of internalizing, stabilizing, and globalizing domains and behavioral tendencies, Abramson, Metalsky, and Alloy (1998) developed the CSQ. This instrument specifically measures the trend toward inferring stable and global causes, negative consequences, and negative characteristics about the self. Information regarding the reliability and validity of this measure has not yet been published.

Content Analysis of Verbatim Explanations (CAVE; Peterson, Bettes, & Seligman, 1985) is a flexible method for considering causal explanations in spontaneous, unprompted writing and speaking to measure explanatory style. Like the ASQ, this method relies on extracting content and rating this content along the dimensions of internality, stability, and globality. Explanatory style assessed using the CAVE method has been established as reliable, consistent, and valid and, more importantly, has made it possible to evaluate these dimensions without formal measures by analyzing samples of speech and writing (Peterson, Schulman, Castellon, & Seligman, 1992).

The Minnesota Multiphasic Personality Inventory-2 (MMPI-2; Butcher, Dahlstrom, Graham, Tellegen, & Kaemmer, 1989) has been scored in a particular way to gauge explanatory style (Colligan, Offord, Malinchoc, Schulman, & Seligman, 1994). Colligan et al. (1994) used approximately half of the items in the original MMPI that referred to bad or good events and applied the CAVE technique to rate each response on the domains of internality, stability, and globality. Explanatory style for bad events (e.g., "I cannot do anything well") is strongly associated with the depressive subscale (De) of the MMPI-2.

Responses to the Thematic Apperception Test (TAT; Morgan & Murray, 1935), a fantasy-based measure in which people are asked to provide stories and explanations to pictorial stimuli, also have been subjected to the CAVE scoring technique. Measures of stability and globality have been obtained from fantasy content (e.g., Peterson & Park, 1995). In short, this suggests that causal explanations can be found readily by analyzing the people's stories and fantasies.

Scheier, Carver, and Bridges (1994) developed the Life Orientation Test–Revised (LOT–R), an abbreviated version of the LOT (Scheier & Carver, 1985). The LOT–R measure assesses for differences inherent to how optimists and pessimists evaluate cause and effect in both good and bad situations and circumstances. Both the LOT–R and LOT produce continuous distribution scores, resulting in a normal distribution. Unlike what one might expect from a measure of polar opposite concepts, the distribution produced is not bimodal (suggesting that people are either optimists or pessimists but not a blend). Instead, most people display a blend of optimistic and pessimistic capacities (Scheier et al., 1994). Explanatory style at any particular juncture is highly dependent upon Stimulus-Organism-Response-Consequence (S-O-R-C; Cormier & Nurius, 2003) contributions and may be hard to predict. However, the LOT–R exhibits good psychometric qualities, such as good internal consistency (Cronbach's alpha in .70s to .80s) and test-retest stability. The LOT–R is highly correlated with the original LOT, which comes as no great surprise because there is extensive overlap between the two measures (Scheier et al., 1994).

Child Measures of Explanatory Style

Few measures of explanatory style have been developed for children. Among these measures, the Children's Attributional Style Questionnaire (CASQ; Kaslow, Tannenbaum & Seligman, 1978), the Children's Attributional Style Questionnaire–Revised (CASQ–R; Kaslow & Nolen-Hoeksema, 1991), and the Children's Attributional Style Interview (CASI; Conley, Haines, Hilt, & Metalsky, 2001) are used to assess dimensions relevant to the diathesis-stress model of depression; the Life Optimism Test (LOT; Scheier et al., 1994) and Youth Life Orientation Test (YLOT; Ey et al., in press) are used to assess dispositional optimism.

The CASQ (Kaslow et. al., 1978) is the most widely used measure of explanatory style in children (Reivich & Gillham, 2003). The CASQ is a 48-item measure used to assess children's causal attributions of positive and negative events. Children ages 8 to 14 are presented with 24 positive and 24 negative hypothetical events and are asked to choose between two explanations for these events. Subscales reflect internal versus external attributions, stable versus unstable attributions, and global versus specific attributions for positive and negative events separately. The test-retest reliability with combined subscales for positive and negative events is adequate. Internal consistencies for this measure range from moderate to low, particularly for the negative event subscales (e.g., Conley et al., 2001; Hilsman & Garber, 1995; Nolen-Hoeksema et al., 1992).

The CASQ–R (Kaslow & Nolen-Hoeksema, 1991) is a shortened version of the CASQ that is comprised of 24 items derived from the original measure. This measure is less reliable than the CASQ, with moderate internal consistency and fair test-retest reliability (Thompson, Kaslow, Weiss, & Nolen-Hoeksema, 1998). However, this shorter measure can be useful in time-limited situations.

The CASI (Conley et al., 2001) is a measure of attributional style for children ages five and older. The CASI in an interactive interview that consists of 16 events, 8 of which are positive and 8 of which are negative. These positive and negative events are divided evenly between events that are interpersonal in nature, involving families and peers, and events that are achievement oriented in nature, involving cognitive tasks, classroom situations, and sports and arts activities. After each situation is presented, children are asked to describe their causal attributions and to rate the internality, stability, and globality of these attributions on continuous sliding scales. The CASI has demonstrated good internal consistency.

The LOT–R is a 10-item inventory that measures generalized optimism and pessimism (Scheier et al., 1994). Although the LOT–R was normed on adult populations, this measure has been applied to adolescents aged 15 to 18 years. Among inpatient adolescents, this measure has good internal consistency and one-week test-retest reliability (Goodman, Knight, & DuRant, 1997).

The YLOT, based on the LOT–R, was developed to assess dispositional optimism among elementary school-aged children (Ey et al., in press). The YLOT is a 12-item self-report measure of children's optimism and pessimism. Children in the third through the sixth grades are asked to rate the personal applicability of optimistic and pessimistic statements on a four-point Likert scale. On the YLOT, an optimism score, a pessimism score, and a total optimism score are yielded. The YLOT has acceptable internal consistency and one-month test-retest reliability.

SUMMARY

Given the association between explanatory style and several facets of well-being, including physical health and hardiness, levels of academic and career achievement, and the presence of depression, and anxiety, it is important to measure explanatory style in clinical contexts. Understanding the internal, stable, and global cognitive distortions that people make is essential to challenging these unhelpful thoughts. People with pessimistic explanatory styles likely will view adverse events as being their own fault (i.e., internal) and will believe that they will not be able to affect the outcome in the same or a similar situation in the future (i.e., stable) because the world is generally unfair, bad, and evil (i.e., global). When good

things happen to people with pessimistic explanatory styles, they unfortunately discount these experiences as being based on actions other than their own (i.e., cause is external), as single experiences that will not be repeated (i.e., the event is unstable), and as flukes in an otherwise evil world (i.e., chance specific to only the event). When good things happen to people with an optimistic explanatory style, however, they tend to understand these experiences in internal, stable, and global ways; in other words, they believe they caused the outcome, that they will continue to be successful, and that they will be successful in other, perhaps novel, life experiences. Further, optimists explain bad events in terms of external, unstable, and specific variables, making negative life experiences have less deleterious effects on their otherwise positive expectancy values and explanatory style. Large components of cognitive-behavioral therapy (CBT) approaches are based on challenging faulty and irrational thinking styles (Emmelkamp, 1994). Understanding explanatory style helps to identify thought-based problems to target in treatment. Furthermore, appreciating the personal history that shaped that style of reasoning may heighten both the therapist's and the client's empathy for their particular explanatory style.

FUTURE AREAS FOR RESEARCH

Several questions have yet to be adequately addressed in research on explanatory style. Pessimistic explanatory style has been shown to have a deleterious impact on various domains of functioning, including an association with symptoms of depression (i.e., Gladstone & Kaslow, 1995; Joiner & Wagner, 1995; Sharpley & Yarley, 1999; Sweeney et al., 1986) and anxiety (i.e., McCormick et al., 1989; Runyon & Kenny, 2002). Therefore, it is important to better understand processes and outcomes of optimistic and pessimistic explanatory style across the life span.

Although researchers have investigated explanatory style for one's own experiences, few studies have investigated the role of explanatory style in understanding others' behaviors. It is unclear whether attributions regarding personal experiences and the experiences of others are correlated. Discrepancies between attributions for one's own and others' experiences may have implications for mental health functioning. Thus, these types of attributions should be examined in future investigations.

In addition, although explanatory style may be pervasive across situations, situational cues may evoke responses that are divergent from what would be predicted given a person's explanatory style. Environmental contingencies can significantly impact situation-specific attributions. For example, in the middle of a bank robbery, an optimist may manifest pessimistic beliefs. Therefore, in measures of explanatory style, it would be helpful to anchor optimistic and pessimistic beliefs not only to general and theoretical circumstances but also to actual life experiences to learn about changes in optimistic and pessimistic beliefs across situations and time. As previously described, research on child sexual abuse shows that trauma-specific attributions are better predictors of functioning than are general explanatory style (Feiring et al., 2002; Gray et al., 2003). Similarly, the most robust findings regarding the relationship between explanatory style and achievement are based on studies in which achievement-oriented cognitions are assessed (Peterson & Barrett, 1987). Therefore, both situation-specific and general-explanatory style should be assessed in future studies.

Moreover, given the pervasive impact of media on mental health functioning and the violent images that are commonly displayed on television, research on the impact of mass media on explanatory styles is outdated. It is important to understand not only the impact of these images on mental health functioning but also the process by which these images impact mental health functioning. Does explanatory style impact how we process information presented in the mass media? Does mass media influence our explanatory style? These questions have been largely ignored up to this point. Additionally, the potential impact of new technologies on explanatory style has yet to be investigated. For example, it is possible that explanatory style may be related to Internet exposure and that Internet exposure may impact the development of explanatory style. These issues should be addressed in future investigations.

Finally, although pessimistic explanatory style has been linked to deleterious mental and physical health outcomes, it is possible that pessimistic explanatory style may be a protective factor in certain circumstances. In a couple of studies, there was evidence of an association between pessimistic explanatory style and high achievement among college juniors and seniors beginning a marketing degree program (LaForge & Cantrell, 2003) and among law students (Satterfield et al., 1997). Given that it is possible that some aspects of pessimistic explanatory style may be adaptive in certain circumstances, understanding the types of pessimistic beliefs that facilitate adaptive functioning as well as the types of circumstances in which these beliefs present an advantage would be helpful.

Explanatory style has particular implications for physical and mental health functioning, two major indices of well-being. Given the association between explanatory style and well-being, it is of pivotal importance to better understand the development and maintenance of pessimistic and opti-mistic explanatory styles and the implications for these explanatory styles in specific circumstances and across the life span. This knowledge can be used to improve primary, secondary, and tertiary prevention programs to increase the likelihood of individual well-being in social, occupational, and academic domains of functioning.

REFERENCES

Abramson, L. Y., Metalsky, G. I., & Alloy, L. B. (1989). Hopelessness depression: A theory-based subtype of depression. *Psychological Review, 96,* 358–372.

Abramson, L. Y., Metalsky, G. I., & Alloy, L. B. (1998). Untitled, unpublished manuscript, University of Wisconsin, Madison.

Abramson, L. Y., Seligman, M. E., & Teasdale, J. D. (1978). Learned helplessness in humans: Critique and reformulation. *Journal of Abnormal Psychology, 87,* 49–74.

Agnes, M. E. (2003). *Webster's New World Dictionary.* New York: Pocket Books.

Ahern, J., Galea, S., Resnick, H., & Vlahow, D. (2004). Television images and probable posttraumatic stress disorder after September 11: The role of background characteristics, event exposures, and perievent panic. *Journal of Nervous & Mental Disease, 192,* 217–226.

Alloy, L. B., Abramson, L. Y., Tashman, N. A., Berrebbi, D. S., Hogan, M. E., Whitehouse, W. G., et al. (2001). Developmental origins of cognitive vulnerability to depression: Parenting, cognitive, and inferential feedback styles of the parents of individuals at high and low cognitive risk for depression. *Cognitive Therapy & Research, 25,* 397–423.

American Psychiatric Association. (1994). *Diagnostic and statistical manual of mental disorders* (4th ed.). Washington, DC: Author.

Arntz, A., Rauner, M., & van den Hout, M. (1995). "If I feel anxious, there must be danger": Ex-consequentia reasoning in inferring danger in anxiety disorders. *Behaviour Research and Therapy, 33*(8), 917–925.

Bandura, A. (1977). *Social learning theory.* New York: General Learning Press.

Barlow, D. H. (1991a). Disorders of emotion. *Psychological Inquiry, 2*(1), 58–71.

Barlow, D. H. (1991b). Disorders of emotions: Clarification, elaboration, and future directions. *Psychological Inquiry, 2*(1), 97–105.

Barlow, D. H. (2002). *Anxiety and its disorders: The nature and treatment of anxiety and panic* (2nd ed.). New York: Guilford Press.

Barlow, D. H., & Craske, M. G. (2000). *Mastery of your anxiety and panic (MAP-3): Client workbook for anxiety and panic: Client workbook for anxiety and panic* (3rd ed.). San Antonio, TX: Graywind/Psychological.

Boggiano, A. K., Barrett, M. (1991). Gender differences in depression in college students. *Sex Roles, 25,* 595–605.

Brennan, F. X., & Charnetski, C. J. (2000). Explanatory style and immunoglobulin A (IgA). *Integrative Physiological and Behavioral Science, 35*(4), 251–255.

Buchanan, G. M., & Seligman, M. E. P. (1995). *Explanatory Style.* New York: Erlbaum.

Bunce, S. C., Larsen, R. J., Peterson, C. (1995). Life after trauma: Personality and daily life experiences of traumatized people. *Journal of Personality. 63,* 165–188.

Bunce, S. C., & Peterson, C. (1997). Gender differences in personality correlates of explanatory style. *Personality & Individual Differences, 23,* 639–646.

Burns, M., & Seligman, M. E. (1989). Explanatory style across the life span: Evidence for stability over 52 years. *Journal of Personality and Social Psychology, 56,* 471–477.

Butcher, J. N., Dahlstrom, W. G., Graham, J. R., Tellegen, A., & Kaemmer, B. (1989). *Minnesota Multiphasic Personality Inventory-2 (MMPI-2): Manual for administration and scoring.* Minneapolis: University of Minnesota Press.

Carstensen, L. L, Charles, S. T., Isaacowitz, D. M., & Kennedy, Q. (2003). Life-span personality development and emotion. In R. J. Davidson, H. H. Goldsmith, & K. Scherer (Eds.), *The Handbook of Affective Sciences* (pp. 726–744). Oxford, UK: Oxford University Press.

Carver, C. S. (2004). Negative affects deriving from the behavioral approach system. *Emotion, 4,* 3–22.

Carver, C. S., & Gaines, J. G. (1987). Optimism, pessimism, and postpartum depression. *Cognitive Therapy and Research, 11,* 449–462.

Carver, C. S., Lehman, J. M., & Antoni, M. H. (2003). Dispositional pessimism predicts illness-related disruption of social and recreational activities among breast cancer patients. *Journal of Personality and Social Psychology, 84,* 813–821.

Carver, C. S., Meyer, B., & Antoni, M. H. (2000). Responsiveness to threats and incentives, expectancy of recurrence, and distress and disengagement: Moderator effects in early-stage breast cancer patients. *Journal of Consulting and Clinical Psychology, 68,* 965–975.

Carver, C. S., & Scheier, M. F. (1998). *On the self-regulation of behavior.* New York: Cambridge University Press.

Carver, C. S., & Scheier, M.F. (2003) Optimism. In C. R. Snyder & S. J. Lopez (Eds.), *Handbook of positive psychology* (pp. 231–243). Oxford, UK: Oxford University Press.

Cerezo-Jimenez, M. A., Frias, D. (1994). Emotional and cognitive adjustment in abused children. *Child Abuse & Neglect, 18*(11), 923–932.

Cloninger, C. R. (1987). A systematic method for clinical description and classification of personality variants: A proposal. *Archives of General Psychiatry, 44,* 573–588.

Colligan, R. C., Offord, K. P., Malinchoc, M., Schulman, P., & Seligman, M. E. P. (1994). CAVEing the MMPI for an optimism-pessimism scale: Seligman's attributional model and the assessment of explanatory style. *Journal of Clinical Psychology, 50,* 71–95.

Conley, C. S, Haines, B. A., Hilt, L. M., & Metalsky, G. I. (2001). The Children's Attributional Style Interview: Developmental tests of cognitive diathesis-stress theories of depression. *Journal of Abnormal Child Psychology, 29,* 445–463.

Cormier, S., & Nurius, P. S. (2003). *Interviewing and change strategies for helpers: Fundamental skills and cognitive behavioral interventions* (5th ed.). Pacific Grove, CA: Brooks/Cole-Thomson Learning.

Craske, M. G. (1999). *Anxiety disorders: Psychological approaches to theory and treatment.* Boulder, CO: Westview.

Domjan, M. (1993). *The principles of learning and behavior* (3rd ed.). Belmont, CA: Brookes/Cole.

Dugas, M. J., Gagnon, F., Ladouceur, R., & Freeston, M. H. (1998). Generalized anxiety disorder: A preliminary test of a conceptual model. *Behaviour Research and Therapy, 36,* 215–226.

Dugas, M. J., & Ladouceur, R. (2000). Treatment of GAD: Targeting intolerance of uncertainty in two types of worry. *Behavior Modification, 24,* 635–657.

Dweck, C. S. (2002). Messages that motivate: How praise molds students' beliefs, motivation, and performance (in surprising ways). In J. Aronson (Ed.)., *Improving academic achievement: Impact of psychological factors on education* (pp. 37–60). San Diego, CA: Academic Press.

Dweck, C. S., Davidson, W., Nelson, S., & Bradley, E. (1978). Sex differences in learned helplessness: II. The contingencies of evaluative feedback in the classroom and III. An experimental analysis. *Developmental Psychology, 14,* 268–276.

Emmelkamp, P. M. G. (1994). Behavior therapy with adults. In A. E. Bergin & S. L. Garfield (Eds.), *Handbook of psychotherapy and behavior change* (4th ed.). New York: Wiley.

Emmelkamp, P. M. G., Bouman, T. K., & Scholing, A. (1992). *Anxiety disorders: A practitioner's guide.* Chichester, UK: Wiley.

Ey, S., Hadley, W., Allen, D. N., Palmer, S., Klosky, J., Deptula, D., et al. (in press). A new measure of children's optimism and pessimism: The Youth Life Orientation Test. *Journal of Child Psychology and Psychiatry.*

Feiring, C., Taska, L., & Chen, K. (2002). Trying to understand why horrible things happen: Attribution, shame, and symptom development following sexual abuse. *Child Maltreatment, 7,* 26–41.

Foa, E. B. (2000). Psychosocial treatment of posttraumatic stress disorder. *Journal of Clinical Psychiatry, 61,* 43–48.

Gillham, J. E., Reivich, K. J., Jaycox, L. H., & Seligman, M. E. P. (1995). Prevention of depressive symptoms in schoolchildren: Two-year follow-up. *Psychological Science, 6,* 343–351.

Gladstone, T. R. G., & Kaslow, N. J. (1995). Depression and attributions in children and adolescents: A meta-analytic review. *Journal of Abnormal Child Psychology, 23,* 597–606.

Gohm, C. L., & Clore, G. L. (2002). Four latent traits of emotional experience and their involvement in well-being, coping, and attributional style. *Cognition and Emotion, 16*(4), 495–518.

Gold, E. R. (1986). Long-term effects of sexual victimization in childhood: An attributional approach. *Journal of Consulting and Clinical Psychology, 54,* 471–475.

Golin, S., Sweeney, P. D., & Schaeffer, S. J. (1981). The causality of casual attributions in depression: A cross-legged panel correlational analysis. *Journal of Abnormal Psychology, 90,* 14–22.

Goodman, E., Knight, J. R., & DuRant, R. H. (1997). Use of the Life Optimism Test among adolescents in a clinical setting: A report of reliability testing. *Journal of Adolescent Health, 21,* 218–220.

Gray, M. J., Pumphrey, J. E., & Lombardo, T. W. (2003). The relationship between dispositional pessimistic attributional style versus trauma-specific attributions and PTSD symptoms. *Journal of Anxiety Disorders, 17,* 289–303.

Greening, L., Stoppelbein, L., Doctor, R. (2002). The mediating effects of attributional style and event-specific attributions on postdisaster adjustment. *Cognitive Therapy & Research, 26,* 261–274.

Hale, B. D. (1993). Explanatory style as a predictor of academic and athletic achievement in college athletes. *Journal of Sport Behavior, 16,* 63–75.

Heath, A. C., Cloninger, C. R., & Martin, N. G. (1994). Testing a model for the genetic structure of personality: A comparison of the personality systems of Cloninger and Eysenck. *Journal of Personality and Social Psychology, 66,* 762–775.

Hershberger, P. J., Zimmerman, G. L., Markert, R. J., Kirkham, K. E., & Bosworth, M. F. (2000). Explanatory style and the performance of residents. *Medical Education, 34,* 676–678.

Heyman, G. D., Dweck, C. S., & Cain, K. M. (1992). Young children's vulnerability to self-blame and helplessness: Relationship to beliefs about goodness. *Child Development, 63,* 401–415.

Hickling, E. J., Blanchard, E. B., Buckley, T. C., & Taylor, A. E. (1999). Effects of attribution of responsibility for motor vehicle accidents on severity of PTSD symptoms, ways of coping, and recovery over six months. *Journal of Traumatic Stress, 12,* 345–353.

Hilsman, R., & Garber, J. (1995). A test of the cognitive diathesis-stress model of depression in children: Academic stressors, attributional style, perceived competence, and control. *Journal of Personality and Social Psychology, 69,* 370–380.

Hiroto, D. S., & Seligman, M. E. (1975). Generality of learned helplessness in man. *Journal of Personality & Social Psychology, 31,* 311–327.

Isaacowitz, D. M., & Seligman, M. E. P. (2001). Is pessimism a risk factor for depressive mood among community dwelling older adults? *Behaviour Research and Therapy, 39,* 255–272.

Issacowitz, D. M., & Seligman, M. E. P. (2003). Cognitive styles and psychological well-being in adulthood and old age. In M. Bornstein, L. Davidson, C. L. M. Keyes, K. Moore, & The Center for Child Well-Being (Eds.), *Well-being: Positive development across the lifespan* (pp. 449–475). Mahwah, NJ: Erlbaum.

Jason, L. A., Witter, E., & Torres-Harding, S. (2003). Chronic fatigue syndrome, coping, optimism and social support. *Journal of Mental Health, 12*(2), 109–118.

Jaycox, L. H., Reivich, K. J., Gillham, J., Seligman, M. E. P. (1994). Prevention of depressive symptoms in school children. *Behaviour Research & Therapy, 32,* 801–816.

Johnson, P. D., & Kliewer, W. (1999). Family and contextual predictors of depressive symptoms in inner-city African American youth. *Journal of Child and Family Studies, 8*(2), 181–192.

Johnston, M. A., & Page, S. (1991). Subject age and gender as predictors of life stress, attributional style, and personal adjustment. *Canadian Journal of Behavioural Science, 23,* 475–478.

Joiner, T. E., & Wagner, K. D. (1995). Attribution style and depression in children and adolescents: A meta-analytic review. *Clinical Psychology Review, 15,* 777–798.

Joseph, S. A., Brewin, C. R., Yule, W., & Williams, R. (1993). Causal attributions and post-traumatic stress in adolescents. *Journal of Child Psychology & Psychiatry & Allied Disciplines, 34,* 247–253.

Kaslow, N. J., & Nolen-Hoeksema, S. (1991). *Children's Attributional Style Questionnaire–Revised (CASQ–R).* Unpublished manuscript, Emory University, Atlanta, GA.

Kaslow, N. J., Tannenbaum, R. L., & Seligman, M. E. P. (1978). *The KASTAN: A children's attributional style questionnaire.* Unpublished manuscript, University of Pennsylvania, Philadelphia.

Kaufman, J. (1991). Depressive disorders in maltreated children. *Journal of the American Academy of Child & Adolescent Psychiatry, 30,* 257–265.

Kessler, R. C., Sonnega, A., Bromet, E., Hughes, M., & Nelson, C. B. (1995). Posttraumatic stress disorder in the national comorbidity study. *Archives of General Psychiatry, 52,* 1048–1060.

LaForge, M. C., & Cantrell, S. (2003). Explanatory style and academic performance among college students beginning a major course of study. *Psychological Reports, 92,* 861–865.

Leger, E., Ladouceur, R., Dugas, M. J., & Freeston, M. (2003). Cognitive-behavioral treatment of generalized anxiety disorder among adolescents: A case series. *Journal of the American Academy of Child & Adolescent Psychiatry, 42*(3), 327–330.

Levine, G. F. (1977). Learned helplessness and the evening news. *Journal of Communication, 27,* 100–105.

Maier, S. F., & Seligman, M. E. (1976). Learned helplessness: Theory and evidence. *Journal of Experimental Psychology: General, 105,* 3–46.

Mannarino, A. P., & Cohen, J. A. (1996a). Abuse-related attributions and perceptions, general attributions, and locus of control in sexually abused girls. *Journal of Interpersonal Violence, 11,* 162–180.

Mannarino, A. P., & Cohen, J. A. (1996b). A follow-up study of factors that mediate the development of psychological symptomatology in sexually abused girls. *Child Maltreatment, 1,* 246–260.

McCormick, R. A., Taber, J., & Kruedelbach, N. (1989). The relationship between attributional style and post-traumatic stress disorder in addicted patients. *Journal of Traumatic Stress, 2,* 477–487.

McKean, K. J. (1994). Using multiple risk factors to assess the behavioral, cognitive and affective effects of learned helplessness. *Journal of Psychology, 128,* 177–183.

McNaughton-Cassill, M. E., & Smith, T. (2002). My world is OK, but yours is not: Television news, the optimism gap, and stress. *Stress & Health, 18,* 27–33.

Metalsky, G. I., Abramson, L. Y., Seligman, M. E. P., Semmel, A., & Peterson, C. (1982). Attributional styles and life events in the classroom: Vulnerability and invulnerability to depressive mood reactions. *Journal of Personality & Social Psychology, 43,* 612–617.

Metalsky, G. I., Halberstadt, L. J., & Abramson, L. Y. (1987). Vulnerability to depressive mood reactions: Toward a more powerful test of the diathesis-stress and causal mediation components of the reformulated theory of depression. *Journal of Personality and Social Psychology, 52,* 386–393.

Morgan, C. D., & Murray, H. A. (1935). A method for investigating fantasies. *Archives of Neurology and Psychiatry, 34,* 289–306.

Morrow, K. B. (1991). Attributions of female adolescent incest victims regarding their molestation. *Child Abuse and Neglect, 15,* 477–483.

Mueller, C. M., & Dweck, C. S. (1998). Praise for intelligence can undermine children's motivation and performance. *Journal of Personality & Social Psychology, 75,* 33–52.

Niles, B. L., Wolf, E. J., & Kutter, C. J. (2003). Posttraumatic stress disorder symptomatology in Vietnam veterans before and after September 11. *Journal of Nervous & Mental Disease, 191,* 682–684.

Nolen-Hoeksema, S. (1995). Epidemiology and theories of gender differences in unipolar depression. In M. V. Seeman (Ed.), *Gender and psychopathology* (pp. 63–87). Washington, DC: American Psychiatric Association.

Nolen-Hoeksema, S., & Girgus, J. S. (1995). Explanatory style and achievement, depression, and gender differences in childhood and early adolescence. In G. M. Buchanan & M. E. P. Seligman (Eds.), *Explanatory style* (pp. 57–70). Hillsdale, NJ: Erlbaum.

Nolen-Hoeksema, S., Girgus, J. S., & Seligman, M. E. (1986). Learned helplessness in children: A longitudinal study of depression, achievement, and explanatory style. *Journal of Personality & Social Psychology, 51,* 435–442.

Nolen-Hoeksema, S., Girgus, J. S., & Seligman, M. E. (1992). Predictors and consequences of childhood depressive symptoms: A 5-year longitudinal study. *Journal of Abnormal Psychology, 101,* 405–422.

O'Donnell, M. L., Creamer, M., & Pattison, P. (2004). Posttraumatic stress disorder and depression following trauma: Understanding comorbidity. *American Journal of Psychiatry, 161,* 1390–1396.

Otto, M. W., Jones, J. C., Craske, M. G., & Barlow, D. H. (1996). *Stopping anxiety medication: Panic control therapy for benzodiazepine discontinuation: Therapist guide.* Boulder, CO: Graywind.

Overmier, J. B., & Seligman, M. E. (1967). Effects of inescapable shock upon subsequent escape and avoidance responding. *Journal of Comparative & Physiological Psychology, 63,* 28–33.

Paterson, R. (1997a). *The changeways core programme trainer's manual.* Vancouver, British Columbia: Changeways.

Paterson, R. (1997b). *Relaxation programme trainer's manual.* Vancouver, British Columbia: Changeways.

Peterson, C., & Barrett, L. C. (1987). Explanatory style and academic performance among university freshman. *Journal of Personality & Social Psychology, 53,* 603–607.

Peterson, C., Bettes, B. A., & Seligman, M. E. P. (1985). Depressive symptoms and unprompted causal attributions: Content analysis. *Behaviour Research and Therapy, 23,* 379–382.

Peterson, C., Bishop, M. P., Fletcher, C. W., Kaplan, M. R, Yesko, E. S., Moon, C.H., et al. (2001). Explanatory style as a risk factor for traumatic mishaps. *Cognitive Therapy and Research, 25,* 633–649.

Peterson, C., & Park, C. (1995). *Implicit and explicit explanatory styles in the lifecourse of college-educated women.* Unpublished manuscript, University of Michigan, Ann Arbor.

Peterson, C., & Park, M. (1998). Learned helplessness and explanatory style. In D. F. Barone, M. Hersen, & V. B. Van Hasselt (Eds.), *Advanced personality* (pp. 287–310). New York: Plenum Press.

Peterson, C., Schulman, P., Castellon, C., & Seligman, M. E. P. (1992). The explanatory style scoring manual. In C. P. Smith (Ed.), *Handbook of thematic analysis.* New York: Cambridge University Press.

Peterson, C., & Seligman, M. E. (1984). Causal explanations as a risk factor for depression: Theory and evidence. *Psychological Review, 91,* 347–374.

Peterson, C., Seligman, M. E. P., Yurko, K. H., Martin, L. R., & Friedman, H. S. (1998). Catastrophizing and ultimate death. *Psychological Science, 9*(2), 127–130.

Peterson, C., Semmel, A., von Baeyer, C., Abramson, L. Y., Metalsky, G. I., & Seligman, M. E. P. (1982). The attributional style questionnaire. *Cognitive Therapy and Research, 6,* 287–299.

Peterson, C., & Steen, T. A. (2002). Optimistic explanatory style. In C. R. Snyder & S. J. Lopez (Eds.), *Handbook of positive psychology* (pp. 244–256). London: Oxford University Press.

Peterson, C., & Stunkard, A. J. (1992). Cognates of personal control: Locus of control, self-efficacy, and explanatory style. *Applied and Preventive Psychology, 1,* 111–117.

Peterson, C., & Villanova, P. (1988). An expanded attributional style questionnaire. *Journal of Abnormal Psychology, 97,* 87–89.

Petroski, H. (1992). *To engineer is human: The role of failure in successful design.* New York: Vintage Books.

Reivich, K., & Gillham, J. (2003). Learned optimism: The measurement of explanatory style. In S. J. Lopez & C. R. Snyder (Eds.), *Positive psychological assessment: A handbook of models and measures* (pp. 57–74). Washington, DC: American Psychological Association.

Resick, P. A., & Schnicke, M. K. (1993). *Cognitive processing therapy for rape victims: A treatment manual.* Newbury Park, CA: Sage.

Rothbart, M. K., Posner, M. I., & Hershey, K. L. (1995). Temperament, attention, and developmental psychopathology. In D. Cicchetti & D. J. Cohen (Eds.), *Developmental psychopathology: Vol. 1. Theory and methods* (pp. 315–340). Oxford, England: Wiley.

Runyon, M. K., & Kenny, M. C. (2002). Relationship of attributional style, depression, and posttrauma distress among children who suffered physical or sexual abuse. *Child Maltreatment, 7,* 254–264.

Sachs-Ericsson, N., & Ciarlo, J. A. (2000). Gender, social roles, and mental health: An epidemiological perspective. *Sex Roles, 43,* 605–628.

Satterfield, J. M., Monahan, J., & Seligman, M. E. P. (1997). Law school performance predicted by explanatory style. *Behavioral Sciences and the Law, 15,* 95–105.

Scheier, M. F., Carver, C. S., & Bridges, M. W. (1994). A reevaluation of the life orientation test. *Journal of Personality & Social Psychology, 67,* 1063–1078.

Scheier, M. F., Carver, S. (1985). Optimism, coping, and health: Assessment and implications of generalized outcome expectancies. *Health Psychology, 4,* 219–247.

Scheier, M. F., Matthews, K. A., Owens, J. F., Schulz, R., Bridges, M. W., Magovern, G. J., Sr., et al. (1999). Optimism and rehospitalization following coronary artery bypass graft surgery. *Archives of Internal Medicine, 159,* 829–835.

Schuman, P., Castellon, C., & Seligman, M. E. P. (1989). Assessing explanatory style: The content analysis of verbatim explanations and the attributional style questionnaire. *Behaviour Research and Therapy, 27,* 505–512.

Schunk, D. H., Hanson, R., & Cox, P. D. (1987). Peer-model attributes and children's achievement behaviors. *Journal of Educational Psychology, 79*(1), 54–61.

Seligman, M. E. (1968). Chronic fear produced by unpredictable electric shock. *Journal of Comparative & Physiological Psychology, 66,* 402–411.

Seligman, M. E. (1973). Fall into helplessness. *Psychology Today, 7,* 43–48.

Seligman, M. E, Castellon, C., Cacciola, J., Schulman, P., Luborsky, L., Ollove, M., et al. (1988). Explanatory style change during cognitive therapy for unipolar depression. *Journal of Abnormal Psychology, 97,* 13–18.

Seligman, M. E., Maier, S. F., & Geer, J. H. (1968). Alleviation of learned helplessness in the dog. *Journal of Abnormal Psychology, 73,* 256–262.

Seligman, M. E., & Meyer, B. (1970). Chronic fear and ulcers in rats as a function of the unpredictability of safety. *Journal of Comparative & Physiological Psychology, 73,* 202–207.

Seligman, M. E., & Schulman, P. (1986). Explanatory style as a predictor of productivity and quitting among life insurance sales agents. *Journal of Personality & Social Psychology, 50,* 832–838.

Seligman, M. E. P., Schulman, P., DeRubeis, R. J., & Hollon, S. H. (1999). *Prevention & Treatment, 2,* 1–22.

Sharpley, C. F., & Yardley, P. (1999). The relationship between cognitive hardiness, explanatory style, and depression-happiness in post-retirement men and women. *The Australian Psychologist, 34,* 198–203.

Shatte, A. J., Seligman, M. E. P., Gillham, J. E., & Reivich, K. (in press). The role of positive psychology in child, adolescent, and family development. In R. E. Lerner, F. Jacobs, & D. Wertlieb (Eds.), *Promoting positive child, adolescent, and family development: A handbook of program and policy innovations.* Thousand Oaks, CA: Sage.

Silverman, R. J., Peterson, C. (1993). Explanatory style of schizophrenic and depressed outpatients. *Cognitive Therapy & Research, 17,* 457–470.

Spencer, S. M., Lehman, J. M., Wynings, C., Arena, P., Carver, C. S., Antoni, M. H., et al. (1999). Concerns about breast cancer and relations to psychosocial well-being in a multi-ethnic sample of early stage patients. *Health Psychology, 18,* 159–168.

Stallings, M. C., Hewitt, J. K., Cloninger, C. R., Heath, A. C., & Eaves, L. J. (1996). Genetic and environmental structure of the tri-dimensional personality questionnaire: Three or four primary temperament dimensions. *Journal of Social Psychology, 70,* 127–140.

Sturmey, P. (1996). *Functional analysis in clinical psychology.* Chichester, UK: Wiley.

Sweeney, P. D., Anderson, K., & Bailey, S. (1986). Attributional style in depression: A meta-analytic review. *Journal of Personality & Social Psychology. 50,* 974–991.

Sweetman, M. E., Munz, D. C., & Wheeler, R. J. (1993). Optimism, hardiness, and explanatory style as predictors of general well-being among attorneys. *Social Indicators Research, 29,* 153–161.

Taska, L., & Feiring, C. (2000, January). *Why do bad things happen? Attributions and symptom development following sexual abuse.* Paper presented at the Conference on Responding to Child Maltreatment, San Diego, CA.

Thompson, M., Kaslow, N. J., Weiss, B., & Nolen-Hoeksema, S. (1998). Children's Attributional Style Questionnaire–Revised:

Psychometric examination. *Psychological Assessment, 10,* 166–170.

Tomakowsky, J., Lumley, M. A., Markowitz, N., & Frank, C. (2001). Optimistic explanatory style and dispositional optimism in HIV-infected men. *Journal of Psychosomatic Research, 51,* 577–587.

Wells, A., & Carter, K. (1999). Preliminary tests of a cognitive model of generalized anxiety disorder. *Behaviour Research and Therapy, 37,* 585–594.

Whitley, B. E., Michael, S. T., & Tremont, G. (1991) Testing for sex differences in the relationship between attributional style and depression. *Sex Roles, 24,* 753–758.

Wolfe, D. A., Sas, L., & Wekerle, C. (1994). Factors associated with the development of posttraumatic stress disorder among child victims of sexual abuse. *Child Abuse and Neglect, 18,* 37–50.

Wyatt, G., & Newcomb, M. (1990). Internal and external mediators of women's sexual abuse in childhood. *Journal of Consulting and Clinical Psychology, 58,* 758–767.

Yu, D. L, & Seligman, M. E. P. (2002). Preventing depressive symptoms in Chinese children. *Prevention and Treatment, 5,* 1–39.

Zimmerman, M., Coryell, W., Corenthal, C., & Wilson, S. (1986). Dysfunctional attitudes and attribution style in healthy controls and patients with schizophrenia, psychotic depression, and nonpsychotic depression. *Journal of Abnormal Psychology. 95,* 403–405.

CHAPTER 16

Hardiness: The Courage to Be Resilient

SALVATORE R. MADDI

Over the last 25 years, hardiness has emerged in psychology as a pattern of attitudes that facilitates turning stressful circumstances from potential disasters into growth opportunities (Maddi, 1994, 1998, 2002). These attitudes of hardiness constitute the courage and motivation to face and transform stressors, rather than to deny or to catastrophize, and to avoid or strike out against them, and are especially essential in our changing, turbulent times (Maddi, 1998, 2002). What follows is a conceptual and empirical analysis of hardiness.

THE CONCEPTUALIZATION OF HARDINESS AS EXISTENTIAL COURAGE

The recent resurgence of an emphasis on positive psychology (e.g., Seligman & Csikszentmihalyi, 2000) is welcome and has spurred relevant theorizing and research. Thus far, the foundation stone of this movement has been happiness, as featured in optimism (e.g., Peterson, 2000; Seligman, 1991) and a sense of subjective well-being (e.g., Diener, 2000; Diener, Suh, Lucas, & Smith, 1999). Although meant to counteract preoccupations in psychology with such characteristics as low self-esteem and assertiveness and high depression, anxiety, and anger, the emphasis on happiness is problematic in that it does not fully appreciate the inherently stressful nature of living well (Maddi, 2002, 2004).

Life as Stressful Enough to Require Courage

Indeed, living is reasonably conceptualized as the ongoing experience of stressful circumstances. In general, these stressful experiences are part of what it means to interact with the events, people, circumstances, norms, and requirements we all encounter everyday. As children, we go from ineptly lying in our cribs and in our parent's arms, to crawling around and walking clumsily into things. Soon, we must learn to delay gratifications and take others into account. As we grow older, we leave the safe house we were born into, go to school,

begin to learn abstract matters, and start interacting with peers and adults outside of our family. Before we know it, we are struggling to find our special talents, figure out whom to relate to intimately, deepen our interests into a career, and somehow become an independent, responsible adult. As the years go by, we find ourselves trying to deepen and value, or change and reconsider, our choices of career, loved ones, and community commitments. And, when we grow older, we increasingly have to deal with retirement from work, the health problems we and those around us experience, and our children's difficulties as they grow up. What is important in all this is the recognition that the normal developmental process that takes us from birth to death is full of stressful circumstances.

Added to these normal stressful circumstances are the stresses that are not developmentally predictable. As you are driving home, you may get into an accident that kills someone or injures you. When you least expect it, you may lose your job as your company downsizes or merges. Your spouse may have met someone else and insists on a divorce. These are just a few examples of major stresses that are not developmentally inevitable. There are also minor, but nonetheless stressful, circumstances that are not developmentally predictable. An example might be finding out that your friend snubbed you by not telling you about, or inviting you to, an exciting party he or she gave. Or, you get passed over for a pay raise even though you were expecting it. Add relatively unexpected stresses to those that are developmentally predictable, and you are pushed even further toward a conceptualization of life as quite a stressful phenomenon.

It is the inherently stressful nature of living that provokes the recognition that happiness may not be a sufficient basis for defining positive psychology. Indeed, it may be more instructive to study courage as the strength to face stressful circumstances directly (rather than denying or catastrophizing them) and be motivated to cope with them by doing the hard work of turning them from potential disasters into growth opportunities (rather than avoiding or striking out against them).

Interestingly enough, courage has not been broadly emphasized in psychology, either in theorizing or research. Virtually the only theoretical emphasis on courage is in existential psychology (e.g., Binswanger, 1963; Frankl, 1960; Maddi, 1998; May, 1958; Tillich, 1952). That position assumes that every experience in life is a decision to move toward the future (by experiencing the unknown) or the past (by preserving what is already known). These decisions may involve actual actions, mental elaborations on experience, or both. Future-oriented decisions are the best, as they lead to growth and development through the processing of new experience, but they also provoke anxiety because the outcome cannot be predicted in advance. And, if the outcome is not immediately advantageous, that will likely arouse sadness or even anger. It is important developmentally for the anticipatory anxiety not to stifle projecting oneself into the future and for the possible resulting sadness or anger not to stifle efforts to turn what seems like a failure into a learning experience instead. Thus, in order to be able to choose the future regularly and learn from the result, one has to develop the courage to tolerate and not give into anxiety, sadness, and anger.

Needless to say, courage is also considered useful in facing and coping with the stressful circumstances that are imposed on us in unexpected ways, rather than provoked by our own decisions. This is relevant to all of us, and the paradigm is resilience. It is clear that under imposed conditions that are extremely stressful—even cataclysmic—most people experiencing them get undermined in performance and health, but there is a minority that manages to survive and even thrive (e.g., Bonanno, 2004). Examples of this resilience range from developing an admirable, professional career, despite humble beginnings, to emerging as a hero in life-threatening catastrophes. Such resilience under imposed stresses has been attributed not only to social support (e.g., Baumeister & Leary, 1995) but to courage as well (Maddi, 1988).

Sometimes stressors cannot be transformed, having the status of givens (Khoshaba & Maddi, 2004). Ready examples of such givens are physical limitations that are inborn or the result of accidents or illnesses. A relatively minor example is being a short, slight male growing up in a gang-ridden neighborhood where physical strength is a basis for adequacy and acceptance. A more extreme example is having become paralyzed from the waist down due to an accident. Resilience in such cases involves finding a compensatory approach to living that makes it acceptable. The slight youngster and the crippled person might try especially hard to develop their minds and go on to become academics or professionals. This kind of compensatory resilience has also been explained not only through social support (e.g., Baumeister & Leary, 1995) but through courage as well (e.g., Maddi, 1988).

The Attitudes of Hardiness as Existential Courage

Building on existential psychology, the attitudes of hardiness are conceptualized as the three Cs of commitment, control, and challenge (Kobasa, 1979; Maddi, 1988; Maddi & Kobasa, 1984). If you are strong in commitment, you believe that stresses are best dealt with by staying involved with the people and events going on around you. In this way, you expect to find the most meaning and fulfillment. Pulling back into isolation and alienation seems like a waste of time. If you are strong in control, you believe that it is best to struggle to have an influence on the outcomes affecting you, however difficult this may be. In this way, you expect to make a difference in your own life, so letting yourself sink into passivity and powerlessness when stresses mount seems foolish. If you are strong in challenge, you believe that stresses and changes are normal and provide a basis for learning from your experiences, whether they are positive or negative. In this way, you expect to grow in wisdom and capability. Wistfully wishing for easy comfort and security seems unrealistic to you.

Although commitment, control, and challenge share certain qualities, they are conceptualized as three attitudes, which, though related, are hardly the same thing. Nonetheless, it is all three together that constitute existential courage, or hardiness (Maddi, 2002). To understand this conceptualization, let us consider what it would be like to have only one hardiness attitude but not the other two.

Expressing the current preoccupation with the importance of the control attitude, some psychologists have suggested that it is this attitude that fully defines hardiness. People high in control, but low in commitment and challenge, would want to determine outcomes but not waste time and effort learning from experience or feeling closely involved with people, things, and events. In that these people would be riddled with impatience, irritability, isolation, and bitter suffering whenever control efforts fail, we see something like the type A behavior pattern, with all of its physical, mental, and social vulnerabilities. Such people also would be egotistical, seeing themselves as better than the others and as having nothing more to learn. There is surprisingly little to call hardiness in this orientation.

Now imagine people high in commitment but simultaneously low in control and challenge. They would be completely enmeshed with the people, things, and events around them, never thinking to have an influence through, or to reflect on, their experience of their interactions. They would have little individuality, and their sense of meaning would be completely given by the social institutions and interaction patterns within which they would lose themselves. Such people would be extremely vulnerable whenever any but the most trivial changes were imposed on them. There is certainly little to call hardiness here.

Finally, imagine people who, though high in challenge, are simultaneously low in control and commitment. They would be preoccupied with novelty, caring little for the well-being and coherence of others, things, and events around them and not imagining that they could have a continuing influence on anything. They might appear to be learning constantly, but this would be trivial by comparison with their investment in the thrill of novelty per se. They would resemble adventurers (Maddi, 1970) and could be expected to engage in games of chance and risky activities for the excitement they bring. Once again, there is little of hardiness in this.

Conceptually, it is only with the confluence of all three Cs that one's experiences and actions express hardiness as existential courage. In everyday life, and even when stresses mount precipitously, a hardy person remains involved with the people, things, and events of life, continues to try to influence ongoing outcomes, and learns by the resulting experiences in order to grow in capability and wisdom for the future.

THE DEVELOPMENT OF HARDINESS

Courage is not inborn, according to the existentialists. This stance is well expressed by Nietzsche's (1968, p. 254) exclamation, "Whatever does not kill me makes me stronger." Unfortunately, existentialism has little else to say about the conditions leading to the development of courage. But, once existential courage was concretely defined as hardiness, it seemed natural to consider relevant developmental conditions (Maddi & Kobasa, 1984).

Several ways in which parents and significant others can instill hardiness in youngsters have been identified (Maddi, 1988, 1994, 1996b). One way is to expose children to rich and diverse experiences, such as by taking them to lots of places and having them interact with others. Another way is to show love and respect for the children as budding individuals by rewarding them when they show initiative or individuality. A third way is to teach the value of vigorous symbolization, imagination, and judgment directly (by rewarding their expressions of these cognitive capabilities) and by example (by the significant others expressing these cognitive capabilities themselves). The overall aim of these three ways of instilling hardiness in youngsters is to help them realize that growing up involves finding one's own way in life and that this process is fully supported and encouraged by one's significant others.

A final way of encouraging the development of hardiness is for significant others to freely impose limits based on their own life trajectories (Maddi, 1970). This may seem paradoxical, or even contradictory, with those already mentioned, but actually it is not. If the youngsters are simultaneously experiencing a richness of experience, love, and respect for their own individuality, and encouragement to think and learn on their own, then having to recognize that the significant others are individuals in their own right fits in with this. Then, in imposing limits, significant others do not seem spiteful or insecure but rather are just the people they have evolved into. In this way, they can actually appear as models for the development of the youngsters but not as people to be slavishly imitated in their concrete ways. Further, that the significant others are who they are, though are loving nonetheless, encourages the youngsters to find constructive ways of interacting with them rather than just withdrawing or striking out. This is a developmental impetus for compensating well when confronted with the givens, or facticity, that all of us encounter in life.

Although it is natural for hardiness levels to be developed in early life, this does not mean that learning in adulthood is irrelevant. What is important here is to consider how an adult with a low level of hardiness can improve this essential existential courage. This question was addressed when, after cataclysmic upheaval at Illinois Bell Telephone resulting from the breakup of the old Bell system, we were asked to supplement our research activities there with providing help for the employees overwhelmed with stress. This led to an initial hardiness training program (Maddi, 1987) that has been refined and elaborated over the years.

As to format, the general approach used now involves a series of weekly meetings between small groups of trainees and a trainer, with the interaction guided by a workbook. The workbook (Khoshaba & Maddi, 2004) includes descriptive narrative, inspirational examples, exercises, and checkpoints, all aimed at helping trainees engage in transformational coping, social assistance and encouragement, and self-care in reaction to the stressful circumstances they are encountering and using the feedback from these efforts to deepen the hardiness attitudes of commitment, control, and challenge. The rationale behind this approach is for the trainees to be supervised, encouraged, and aided as they go through the process of dealing effectively with stressors and recognizing that they can and are doing this so that when the training is over they will have deepened their courage, motivation, and skills to continue this process on their own.

BIOLOGICAL BASES AND INFLUENCES OF HARDINESS

What motivates human beings? The answers to this question have tended to concern primarily biological and social needs.

In contrast, the conceptualization of hardiness as existential courage emphasizes a consideration of psychological or cognitive needs as they motivate the search for life's meaning (Maddi, 1967, 1970, 1988, 2002).

Defining Human Motivation in Terms of Biological Needs

When biological needs are considered paramount, the underlying assumptions are that survival is the primary concern and that humans are not dramatically different in this from lower forms of animals. The typical needs emphasized are for food, water, and safety. It is also common for research done on animals lower on the phylogenetic scale to be extrapolated explanatorily to the human level.

The picture of the human being that emerges when biological needs are considered primary and exclusive is as essentially simple, materialistic, and selfish (Maddi, 1996a). From the beginning of life, the primary (or inherent) drives lead us to want the volume of food and water that will satisfy our cravings and the level of safety that permits us to feel comfortable. As we become adults, we develop secondary (or learned) drives that lead us to strive for the level of income and status that provides what will regularly satisfy the primary drives. So, our motivations to work, engage in family life, enter politics, and so forth, hark back to what is needed to satisfy regularly our biological needs for food, water, and safety.

Life's meaning is fairly obvious in this explanatory approach, and even apparently complex activities are reduced to their relevance for primary need satisfaction. According to this view, when push comes to shove, we will become obviously selfish and even aggressive in order to obtain primary-need satisfaction. When we appear altruistic, it is because that behavior is, under the existing circumstances, likely to further ensure biological need satisfaction.

Defining Human Motivation in Terms of Social Needs

To be sure, there are social implications (e.g., altruism) in many approaches to understanding motivation as spurred by biological needs. Some emphases, however, make social needs even more basic, less derivative. These primarily social approaches tend to consider contact, communication, and solidarity as basic experiences needed by human beings if they are to feel satisfied (Maddi, 1996a). If there is no one to touch or smell, talk to, or feel bonded to, you are isolated, tense, and unhappy.

Usually, these social approaches see precedents for human socializing in the interactions that can be observed in species lower on the phylogenetic scale. Not surprisingly, almost anything that constitutes contact and communication between humans is regarded as satisfying the basic social needs. And, defining ourselves as part of our group is also considered a basic satisfaction. Advocates of these approaches emphasize the value of traditional societies and cultures over the modern-day situation, which appears too individualistic and isolated for the necessary satisfaction of social needs.

The meaning of life in these predominantly social approaches is caught up in moment-to-moment, day-to-day interactions, however repetitive and predictable they may be. Indeed, there is comfort in social predictability. You know who you are through your interactions with those around you. As you are one of them, you find satisfaction in the repeated, regular interactions that constitute your social solidarity. You may even carry this solidarity to the point of rejecting others who are not part of your group. There is little motivation, after all, to find out more about outsiders if your social needs are already well satisfied by your ongoing interactions within your own group.

What About the Quest for Meaning?

Conceptualizing motivation as essentially biological or social does not lead easily to an emphasis on humans as searchers for life's meaning, whose sense of fulfillment is enhanced by a continual process of learning, no matter where it may lead. Rather, the assumption of biological needs as paramount leads toward a relatively simple sense of life's meaning as physical survival and comfort. Further, the assumption of social needs as paramount leads toward an equally simple sense of life's meaning as social interaction comprising solidarity with one's group.

Why, then, do some humans even bother being writers of fiction or fact, researchers, philosophers, historians, poets, artists, and world travelers? Why do some humans struggle incessantly to speculate beyond what they know or be creative about changing the way of things? Are such activities easily and compellingly explained merely as efforts to satisfy primary biological or social needs? Not in a compelling way. These activities suggest the presence of a quest for meaning that is just as pervasive as the search for biological and social security.

Psychological or Cognitive Needs

Elaborating on the existential emphasis, Maddi (1967, 1970) has proposed that the pervasive quest for meaning in humans involves the underlying mental needs for symbolization, imagination, and judgment. These mental needs are fueled by the requirements of the uniquely large, complex brain cortex at the human level.

Symbolization involves abstracting constructs from our observations that help us to determine the similarities and differences among these experiences. Once we have constructs, we can think about and communicate observations without actually experiencing them. Words are, in this sense, constructs. If someone were to come into the room and say, "Fire! Fire!" we would all know what was meant and what should be done, even without experiencing flames and smoke. The process of abstracting constructs from observation is an important part of developing meaning because it takes us beyond mere sensory experience into understanding.

Also involved in developing meaning, imagination is a process of combining and recombining constructs in our minds in a manner that leads to previously unanticipated similarities and differences (Maddi, 1967, 1970). As it is primarily constructs that are being reshuffled, imagination may lead us far beyond mere observations. Consistent with this view, William James (1890) once called creativity "the electric sense of analogy." What he meant was that the imaginative process of bringing a construct, which arose from one set of observations, to bear on another construct commonly associated with a second set of observations can irrevocably change how we understand that second set of observations. Clearly, meaning can be changed and deepened through the exercise of imagination. Indeed, the end result of exercising imagination is having ideas about change.

Yet another cognitive process that contributes meaning is judgment (Maddi, 1967, 1970). This involves evaluating observations and constructs in a manner that leads us to have a point of view about them. The most generic expressions of judgment are ethical and preferential. Ethical judgment leads to evaluations about what is good or bad, whereas preferential judgment yields evaluations of what is liked or disliked. But, there are also other forms of judgment that lead to comparative evaluations less influenced by what is ethical or preferred.

Evolution and Ubiquity

In what sense are symbolization, imagination, and judgment expressive of a mental need? One answer is evolutionary. Once the big, elaborate human cortex evolved, the design dictated its functioning. The enormous information-processing capacity of the human brain could not lie fallow, so new information was continually sought and was its own reward. The more we engage in symbolization, imagination, and judgment, the greater is the amount of information our brains are processing. Another answer involves ubiquity. After all, words are the result of symbolization, and all individuals and cultures have elaborate languages seemingly far more elab-

orate than the communication bases available to other species. The fruits of elaborate imagination, such as stories, myths, art, and philosophy, are also ubiquitous across individuals and cultures. The same is true for the fruits of judgment, which appear in all human societies in the form of norms and laws delineating what is mandatory and what is preferential.

The Role of Hardiness

If the human brain requires a continual influx of information, then there is motivational pressure to keep exercising the mental capacities of symbolization, imagination, and judgment. It is not likely that we could rest easily as soon as we have a few constructs, ideas about change, and ethical or preferential judgments. Rather, we are engaged in an ongoing process of developing new ways of understanding and influencing our experiences. This is what the existential psychologists mean by choosing the future, rather than the past, in the ongoing decision-making process that expresses the quest for meaning.

As indicated earlier, the paradox in all this is that the pressure of mental needs toward choosing the future, and vigorously expressing symbolization, imagination, and judgment in order to keep bringing new information, arouses the stress and anxiety of unpredictability and possible failure. One role of existential courage, or hardiness, is to make this situation tolerable so that vigorous pursuit of meaning and the future can go forward. In this regard, hardiness is regarded as moderating the capability of new or stressful experiences to arouse negative emotions and physiological signs of strain. Needless to say, this moderating function of hardiness is also important with regard to stressful circumstances imposed on people by outside forces rather than those resulting from their own future-oriented decision making. In this additional role, hardiness lends the moderation of negative emotions and physiological strain that facilitates facing the stressor and doing the hard work of turning it from a potential disaster into a growth opportunity instead.

BOUNDARIES OF HARDINESS

Defined as an operationalization of existential courage, hardiness emphasizes the attitudes of commitment, control, and challenge. Although hardiness is regarded as a ubiquitous, essential feature for effective performance, conduct, and health under stress, it is not synonymous with other features that facilitate this fullness of life. Indeed, hardiness is conceptualized as a personality disposition, with the emphasis on individual differences in it as they affect performance, conduct, and health. And, as mentioned before, the theoretical underpinnings of hardiness are existential psychology rather than behaviorism, psychoanalysis, or biological reductionism.

Hardiness as a Particular Personality Disposition

The present emphasis on positive psychology (Seligman & Csikszentmihalyi, 2000) features happiness, in the forms of personality dispositions of optimism (Peterson, 2000; Seligman, 1991) and subjective well-being (Diener, 2000). Clearly, as courage, hardiness is not the same as happiness. Under usual circumstances, it might be expected that hardiness and optimism or subjective well-being would be positively related in the sense that successful struggle with problems through courage would result in happiness. But, circumstances might be problematic or unresolved enough that hardiness and optimism or subjective well-being might show little relationship. Also, these happiness measures could reflect complacency or denial, which would be different from hardiness as a courage measure.

Nor is hardiness the same as religiousness, though both include courage and ways of finding meaning. Religiousness is typically based on a God figure and an unchangeable credo of acceptable and unacceptable values and actions. In contrast, hardiness, in its existential base, emphasizes finding one's own way, struggling with uncertainties and obstacles, and thereby building meaning. Although measures of religiousness and hardiness should show a positive relationship, there are various reasons why this relationship might not be strong. For example, religiousness can vary from strong efforts to improve living to more passively accepting that decisions and power are in God's hands. This attitude of deferral to a higher power is not consistent with hardiness.

Among personality dispositions proposed in psychology, the two that would appear most similar to hardiness are ego strength (Barron, 1963) and self-efficacy (Bandura, 1977). But, where ego strength derives from psychoanalytic thinking and self-efficacy from behaviorism, hardiness has its roots in existential psychology. The writings on ego strength and self-efficacy seem to emphasize getting ahead rather than searching for meaning, whereas hardiness has the opposite emphasis. The theoretical framework of these three personality dispositions suggests that, though they are similar, hardiness is not the same as the other two.

Coping, Social Support, and Self-Care

Clearly, coping style is relevant to one's performance, conduct, and health under stress. Nonetheless, the concrete con-

text of making decisions and implementing actions involved in coping is not completely the same as the attitudes of hardiness, or courage. When one has to address significantly stressful circumstances, this brings into relevance not only concrete coping strategies but also whether one has the courage or hardiness to carry them out under pressure. The attitudes of hardiness are not the same as the actions involved in coping. But, it is expected (Khoshaba & Maddi, 2004; Maddi, 2002) that hardiness encourages and motivates coping strategies that are transformational (in which stressful circumstances are approached as problems to be solved) rather than regressive (in which stressors are denied or catastrophized and avoided or attacked).

Having social support available is frequently regarded as important in maintaining and enhancing performance, conduct, and health under pressure (Khoshaba & Maddi, 2004; Maddi, 2002). Although this also is considered true for hardiness, it is an internal set of attitudes rather than the actions of others around you. As such, hardiness and social support are not the same thing. But, the conceptualization of hardiness (Khoshaba & Maddi, 2004; Maddi, 2002) includes the courage and motivation to interact with significant others by giving them assistance and encouragement (rather than competition or overprotection) and expecting the same back from them. This predicts a positive relationship between social support and hardiness.

Self-care, in such forms as relaxation exercises, sound nutrition, and physical exercise, has also been considered important in maintaining and enhancing performance and health under stress (Khoshaba & Maddi, 2004; Maddi, 2002). Once again, the attitudes of hardiness, or courage, are clearly not the same as the specific facilitative actions involved in relaxing, eating, and exercising. Nonetheless, it is theorized that these facilitative actions are often not carried out unless the person has the attitudes of hardiness that provide courage and motivation. There should be a positive relationship between hardiness and self-care.

EMPIRICAL EVIDENCE CONCERNING HARDINESS

More than twenty years have gone by since the original conceptualization of hardiness as an attitudinal factor important in providing the courage and motivation to be resilient under stressful conditions. In the ensuing years, there has been active interplay between theorizing, researching, and practicing, which has elaborated and consolidated hardiness into an established component of the ongoing process whereby stressful circumstances are turned from potential disasters into growth opportunities instead.

The Discovery of Hardiness

The prevailing message of the 1970s to avoid stressful change lest it kill you seemed too extreme. At that time, Maddi (1965) was studying regularly creative people who emerged as very interested in, and in pursuit of, change. It seemed hard for him and his research team to believe that these creative people were trying to commit suicide. The resulting motivation to study individual differences in reactions to stressful circumstances is what led this research team in 1975 to begin a 12-year longitudinal study of managers at Illinois Bell Telephone (IBT). At that time, it was rumored that the federal regulation of telephone service was coming to an end in order to encourage the competition that has led to our present telecommunications industry. AT&T's status as a federally regulated monopoly would be ended, and the divestiture of its subsidiary companies (such as IBT) would be mandated.

The lower-, middle-, and upper-level managers in the IBT study were tested psychologically and medically every year from 1975 through 1986. In 1981, the cataclysmic deregulation and divestiture took place and is still regarded as the largest upheaval in corporate history. In barely a year, IBT decreased its workforce almost by half. As an example of the upheaval, one manager reported that he had had 10 supervisors in one year and that neither they nor he knew what they were supposed to do.

Over the years of this longitudinal study, several data analyses demonstrated that a pattern of attitudes that we identified as the three Cs of commitment, control, and challenge, or hardiness, moderated the stress-illness relationship. In her dissertation, Kobasa (1979) found through a retrospective design that among managers, all of whom were high in stresses, those who showed the hardiness attitudes experienced fewer mental and physical illness symptoms. Subsequent IBT studies with prospective designs (Kobasa, Maddi, & Courington, 1981; Kobasa, Maddi, & Kahn, 1982; Kobasa, Maddi, & Puccetti, 1982) showed that hardiness attitudes, along with social support and physical exercise, did indeed predict fewer stress-related illnesses, despite the fact that inherited vulnerabilities increase the risk of such illnesses.

In the ongoing attempt to learn more about stress management at IBT, two additional studies contributed to the larger picture of hardiness. In one study (Kobasa, Maddi, Puccetti, & Zola, 1986), hardiness, social support, and physical exercise were compared in their stress-management effectiveness. Among managers who were all above the sample median in stresses, hardiness was roughly twice as effective in decreasing the subsequent risk of illnesses than were social support and exercise. Of particular interest was the synergistically beneficial effect of these three stress-buffering variables: Managers with two stress buffers did somewhat better than those with only one, but those with all three buffers did remarkably better than those with only two.

The other study was Khoshaba's dissertation (Khoshaba, 1990; Khoshaba & Maddi, 1999), which concerned the early development of hardiness. A subsample of managers selected to be either very high or very low in hardiness were interviewed blind concerning their early life experiences. Content analyses of their statements showed that, by comparison with the others, the managers high in hardiness remembered not only a disruptive, stressful early family life but also that they were selected by their parents to be successful nonetheless, accepted that role, and worked hard to justify being the family's hope.

The confluence of the previously mentioned and other studies done at IBT are summarized in the hardiness model (Maddi, 2002; Maddi & Kobasa, 1984), shown here as Figure 16.1. This model includes the well-accepted view (e.g., Cannon, 1929; Selye, 1976) that stressful circumstances (whether acute or chronic) provoke bodily arousal, or strain (often called the fight-or-flight reaction), which, when too intense or prolonged, depletes the person's resources sufficiently to lead to breakdown in performance, conduct, and/or health. Also, when breakdowns occur, they will tend to be along the lines of inherited vulnerabilities. This sinister process can be moderated by hardy beliefs, which provide the courage and motivation to engage in hardy social support, hardy coping, and hardy health practices. In particular, the combination of hardy beliefs, social support, and coping decreases the stressfulness of the circumstances being experienced, which minimizes the likelihood of excessive strain leading to breakdown. Also, the combination of hardy beliefs, social support, and health practices decreases the strain level resulting from stressful circumstances, in that way minimizing the likelihood of breakdown.

Ongoing Research on Hardiness

Literature searches reveal that there have been more than 600 hardiness references over the last 20 years. Also, the various editions of the Personal Views Survey (PVS) measure of hardiness have been translated into 15 Asian, European, and Middle Eastern languages, to say nothing of the numerous countries that use it in English. There also have been several reviews of hardiness research (e.g., Funk, 1992; Maddi,

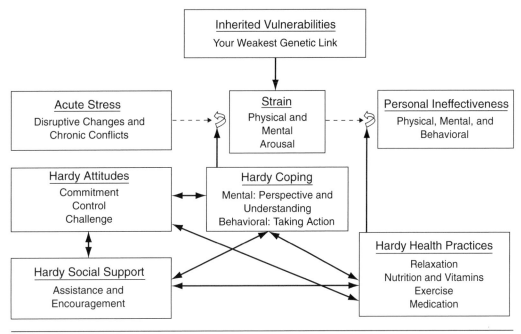

Figure 16.1   The hardiness model for performance and health enhancement. © Copyright 1986–2004 by Hardiness Institute.

1990; Orr & Westman, 1990; Ouellette, 1993). A summary of the main trends in hardiness research follows.

Measurement and Conceptual Criticisms

The initial measure of hardiness, the PVS, involved a combination of existing scales that had emerged in the IBT studies as differentiating managers who responded resiliently to the company upheavals by comparison with those who did not. In addition, early hardiness studies tended to utilize self-report measures of dependent variables concerning health and performance. The combination of these factors led to two criticisms based on inconsistent results in some early studies.

In particular, a measurement criticism that arose early on was that the commitment, control, and challenge components of hardiness did not consistently show the positive intercorrelations that had been predicted. With undergraduate samples, the challenge component of the PVS sometimes tended to be uncorrelated to commitment, control, or both (Funk & Houston, 1987; Ganellen & Blaney, 1984; Hull, Van Treuren, & Virnelli, 1987). In contrast, however, all three Cs continued to show a sufficient, reliable positive interrelationship consistent with their being considered part of an overall entity (Maddi, 1997). The problem was finally identified as due to several items in the original measure of challenge, which were being interpreted differently by working adults and college students. Once these and other items were deleted or rephrased, the next (PVS II, PVS III) and current (PVS III-R)

editions of the hardiness measure regularly yield 3C scores that are positively intercorrelated not only in samples of working adults and college students but of high school students as well (Maddi, 1997; Maddi & Hess, 1992; Maddi & Khoshaba, 2001b; Maddi, Wadhwa, & Haier, 1996). Further, recent research shows that the best psychometric summarization of hardiness test responses is that commitment, control, and challenge are positively intercorrelated components nested under a higher-order hardiness factor (Maddi, Harvey, et al., 2004; Sinclair & Tetrick, 2000). This is, of course, consistent with hardiness theory.

The other criticism that arose early on is both methodological and conceptual, contending that the hardiness may be no more than a negative indicator of neuroticism or negative affectivity (e.g., Costa & McCrae, 1992; Funk & Houston, 1987; Ganellen & Blaney, 1984; Hull et al., 1987). That hardiness findings cannot be explained away like this is indicated by a study (Maddi & Khoshaba, 1994) in which hardy attitudes and an accepted measure of negative affectivity were entered into a regression analysis as independent variables in the attempt to predict the clinical scales of the Minnesota Multiphasic Personality Inventory (MMPI) as dependent variables. With the effects of negative affectivity controlled, hardiness was still a pervasive negative predictor of MMPI clinical scale scores. Further undermining the criticism are the results of a study (Maddi, Khoshaba, Persico, et al., 2002) involving the NEO-FFI measure of the Five-Factor Model (Costa & McCrae, 1992) showing that hardiness was not only negatively related to Neuroticism but also positively related to all of the other four factors, despite that the five factors are orthogonal to each other. Also, the five factors taken together accounted for only about 35 percent of the variance of hardiness. Putting the results of these studies together indicates the unlikelihood that hardiness is no more than the opposite of negative affectivity or neuroticism.

Health, Performance, and Conduct Studies

By now, results supporting and extending those at IBT showing that hardiness is helpful in maintaining or enhancing performance and health under stresses have been reported for people engaged in various occupations, activities, and life circumstances. These results are quite consistent with the conceptualization of hardiness as the existential courage for dealing with difficult circumstances. For example, hardiness is associated with satisfaction with one's work and a minimum of stress-related illness symptoms among groups as diverse as bus drivers (Bartone, 1989), fire fighters (Giatras, 2000), and lawyers (Kobasa, 1982). Also, hardiness is a negative predictor of burnout in nurses who work in intensive care units or hospices (Keane, Ducette, & Adler, 1985; McCranie, Lambert, & Lambert, 1987; Pagana, 1990; Rich & Rich, 1987; Topf, 1989). Among the elderly, hardiness is associated with remaining active rather than becoming passive and dependent (Magnani, 1990). Similarly, hardiness is a positive predictor of quality of life in serious illness sufferers (Okun, Zantra, & Robinson, 1988; Pollock, 1989; Pollock & Duffy, 1990).

Several studies in a military context fit here as well. For example, Bartone and Snook (1999) found that hardiness was the best predictor of leadership behavior over the four years of demanding training among a cohort of cadets at the U.S. Military Academy at West Point. In Israel, hardiness levels in male and female military personnel predicted successful graduation from grueling officer-training and combat-training programs (Florian, Milkulincer, & Taubman, 1995; Westman, 1990). Also, Bartone, Ursano, Wright, and Ingraham (1989) showed that the mental and physical health of military personnel assisting over a period of time with a tragic air disaster was maintained in those who were high in hardiness. Further, hardiness measured before soldiers departed on peacekeeping or combat missions overseas showed a negative relationship with post-traumatic stress and depression disorders following life-threatening experiences (Bartone, 1999).

There are also research results supporting the value of hardiness as existential courage in stressful circumstances that are more commonplace or less dramatic. For example, Lifton, Seahy, and Bushke (2000) have shown that hardiness, measured as students arrived at college, predicted better than SAT scores or rank in high school graduating class who would remain in school two years later. Studying adults engaged in entrepreneurial consulting work, Maddi, Harvey, et al. (2004) found that hardiness was positively correlated with billable hours measured over the ensuing year. Billable hours is a clear financial indicator of an entrepreneur's effectiveness in obtaining and retaining clients through being an effective consultant. Further, among senior Army officers attending a year of advanced training, hardiness was negatively related to experiences of depression and anger (Maddi, Brow, Khoshaba, & Vaitkus, 2004). Similar results have been found in the context of non-life-threatening culture shock for U.S. employees on two-year work missions in China (Atella, 1989). Although most employees tended to decrease in performance and health during the first six months abroad, those with high hardiness levels recovered more quickly and completely over the next year and a half than did the others (Atella, 1989). Similarly, hardiness predicts rapidity and extent of cultural assimilation and life adequacy among Asian immigrants to the United States (Kuo & Tsai, 1986).

Hardiness also has been studied with regard to performance in sports. Maddi and Hess (1992) measured hardiness levels of male, high school, varsity basketball players in the summer and obtained on them the objective statistics accumulated by their coaches throughout the ensuing season. Hardiness predicted six out of seven indexes of performance in the expected direction, showing that even among players good enough to be on the varsity team, hardiness influenced excellence of performance. The only index not predicted by hardiness was free-throw percentage, which summarizes performance in the only period of relative calm (low stress) in an otherwise tumultuous game. Also, Lancer (2004) has found that among young women competing for and in Olympic synchronized swimming in the year 2000, hardiness levels predicted not only who would make the team but also how well they would perform in the world competition.

The studies summarized thus far have emphasized performance and health, showing the importance of hardiness in this and supporting its conceptualization as courage and motivation. If hardiness is indeed the courage and motivation to face and deal with stressful circumstances, then it also should decrease the likelihood of poor conduct, which often can be construed as taking the easiest rather than the best way out of difficulties. One relevant study (Maddi et al., 1996) involved the relationship of hardiness to alcohol and drug use among high school graduates about to enroll in college. Whereas a family risk-factor index was positively correlated with self-report of whether alcohol and drugs had been tried, it was hardiness that was negatively correlated with self-report of the frequency with which alcohol and drugs were used. As to more objective measurement, drug use assessed through urine screens correlated negatively with hardiness. Although only a beginning, this study suggests that hardiness protects against not only health and performance breakdowns but poor conduct as well.

Construct Validation Studies

There is also by now an accumulation of studies that are best considered relevant to construct validation, as they test implications of the hardiness model concerning mechanisms whereby the courage and motivation brought by hardy attitudes can maintain and enhance performance, conduct, and health despite stressful circumstances. In a basic study along these lines (Maddi, 1999), working adults wearing pagers completed a short questionnaire concerning what they were doing, with whom, and how they felt about it every time they were paged (which was 10 times at random during each of three consecutive days). They had completed the hardiness measure a month before the pager study. The higher their hardiness level, the more workers reported that their activities were enjoyable, interesting, important, and self-determined. Hardiness also was correlated positively with openness to experience and feelings of support from others. Overall, these findings support the validity of the hardiness measure and suggest that it is well considered an indication of existential courage.

Further evidence that, as expected, hardiness is associated with openness to experience and imaginativeness is also available (Maddi, Harvey, et al., 2004). In one sample, hardiness showed a negative relationship to repressive style as measured by the combination of manifest anxiety and social desirability that has become accepted (Weinberger, Schwartz, & Davidson, 1979). In another sample, hardiness showed a negative correlation with right-wing authoritarianism. And, in a third sample, hardiness was positively related to imaginativeness as measured by the Unusual Uses Test, a well-known index of creativity.

There are also several studies testing the contention that one way hardiness protects against stress-related breakdowns is by providing the courage and motivation to bring about effective or transformational coping (i.e., turning stressful circumstances from potential disasters into growth opportunities instead) and minimize self-limiting or regressive coping (i.e., protecting against stressful circumstances by denying and avoiding them). In an analysis of variance design, one study (Maddi, 1999) considered the effects of stressful event content and hardiness and the interaction of the two on transformational and regressive coping. Although stressful event content had a main effect, such that work stressors more regularly elicited transformational coping than did personal life stressors, hardiness had an interaction effect that accelerated this tendency. As to regressive coping, stressful event content was not a factor, but hardiness decreased the likelihood of this self-limiting reaction. Another coping study (Maddi & Hightower, 1999) showed that, in three samples that varied in the content and intensity of stressors, hardiness was consistent in a positive association with transformational coping and in a negative association with regressive coping.

Evidence is also accumulating concerning other mechanisms whereby hardiness protects against the undermining effects of stressors. It appears that hardiness is not only associated positively with transformational and negatively with regressive coping but also positively with socially supportive interactions (Maddi, Harvey, et al., 2004). In addition, studies support the tendency of hardiness to (1) promote the view of life as less stressful (Rhodewalt & Zone, 1989), (2) have a more vigorous immune response (e.g., Okun et al., 1988), (3) show less physiological arousal to stressors (Allred & Smith, 1989; Contrada, 1989), and (4) be more conscientious about health practices (e.g., Weibe & McCallum, 1986). All in all, evidence is accumulating that hardiness facilitates perceptions of and behaviors toward stressors that facilitate facing and transforming stressful circumstances in order to solve problems and thereby grow.

Comparative Analytic Studies

Hardiness is emerging as a personality disposition that helps in maintaining and enhancing performance, conduct, and health under stressful circumstances. There are certainly other dispositions that make similar claims. The time has come to assess the relative effectiveness of these various dispositions. Useful in this approach is comparative analytic studies (Maddi, 1996b) in which two or more relevant dispositions are compared in their effects on dependent variables that are conceptually relevant to the dispositions involved.

One relevant study (Maddi & Hightower, 1999) compared hardiness and optimism in their effects on transformational and regressive coping across three samples. Across these samples, hardiness and optimism showed moderate positive correlations with each other. Then, the effectiveness comparison was done by entering hardiness and optimism as independent variables in multiple regression analyses so as to determine the influence that each variable, purified of the effects of the other, had on coping style. Involving undergraduates with a wide range of everyday stressors as participants, the first two samples differed in the tests used to assess transformational and regressive coping styles. The results, however, were the same: By comparison with optimism, hardiness was a more powerful influence on coping in general and especially in the avoidance of regressive coping. Using the same approach, the third sample involved women who had breast lumps and were arriving at a specialty clinic for diagnosis of whether or not they had cancer. Under this life-threatening stressor, optimism finally energized as having close to as many coping efforts as did hardiness, but it was still true that only hardiness was a negative predictor of regressive coping efforts. Taken together, these three samples show that hardiness operates as expected with regard to coping and that, by comparison, optimism may be laced with naive complacency.

Another relevant study (Maddi, Brow, et al., 2004) utilized the same approach to compare the relative effectiveness of hardiness and religiousness in protecting against depression and anger. Hardiness and religiousness showed a moderate positive correlation in a sample of senior Army officers. Then, hardiness and religiousness were entered as independent variables in multiple regression analyses in order to determine the relationship of each, purified of the effects of the other, on depression and anger variables. Results indicated that only hardiness had main effects and that these showed a negative relationship of this variable with depression and anger variables. A few interaction effects emerged, suggesting that religiousness is negatively related to depression and anger only when hardiness is low. These results suggest that hardiness may be more effective than religiousness in helping people deal with stressors without falling apart or becoming aggressive. Needless to say, more studies need to be done taping other populations and measures of religiousness before definite conclusions can be reached.

Once the results of more comparative analytic studies become available, it will be possible to reassess available theorizing concerning dispositions expected to have a positive influence on performance and health in order to develop a more comprehensive framework. In this, hardiness needs to be compared not only to optimism and religiousness but to such variables as subjective well-being, ego strength, and self-efficacy as well.

Effectiveness of Hardiness Training

The first evaluation of hardiness training took place following the catastrophic upheaval at IBT. In a waiting-list control study (Maddi, 1987), IBT employees undergoing hardiness training decreased in anxiety, depression, physical illness symptoms, and blood pressure and increased in hardy attitudes and job satisfaction. These beneficial changes had persisted at the six-month follow-up. When employees who had

been on the waiting-list comparison group then underwent hardiness training, they, too, showed the same change pattern. Another study with working adults (Maddi, Kahn, & Maddi, 1998) showed that all the components of hardiness training improved mental and physical states, along with hardy attitudes, though transformational coping and social assistance and encouragement produced greater changes than did self-care practices.

Thus far, there is one study (Maddi, Khoshaba, Jensen, et al., 2002) on the effects of hardiness training with high-risk students in a community college. In this study, hardiness training was compared with a standard student enrichment approach (involving such matters as time management and writing, computer, and study skills), controlling for teacher effectiveness and gender. Also, both hardiness training and the standard student enrichment approach were regular credit courses at the school. Results showed that, by comparison with the standard student enrichment approach, hardiness training not only produced a greater increase in the three Cs at the end of the training but also greater increases in GPA and retention level after one year.

Although more studies are needed in order to reach definitive conclusions, it appears that hardiness training is effective in maintaining and enhancing performance and health under stresses. Once again, it also will be useful to compare hardiness training to other forms of stress-management training in terms of their relative effectiveness.

Current Measurement and Training Resources

As to hardiness measurement, the latest and best test is the Personal Views Survey III-R (PVS III-R), an 18-rating-scale-item questionnaire that can be administered either in hard-copy form or on the Internet (Maddi & Khoshaba, 2001b). This test regularly yields commitment, control, and challenge scores that show moderate positive intercorrelation and substantial correlation with total hardiness score. Further, the test has adequate reliability and validity and does not show sex, age, or ethnic differences (Maddi, Harvey, et al., 2004). Also available is the HardiSurvey III-R, a 65-rating-scale-item questionnaire that also is available in hard copy or on the Internet (Maddi & Khoshaba, 2001a). This test supplements the hardy attitudes measured by the PVS III-R with the other resistance resources of transformational coping and social assistance and encouragement and the vulnerability factors of stress, strain, and regressive coping. Results on this test are combined into a comprehensive report with recommendations.

There also is now a refined and elaborated hardiness-training program built around a workbook (Khoshaba & Maddi, 2004) that is appropriate for adults and college students. The components of the training program involve the skills of transformational coping, social assistance and encouragement, relaxation, nutrition, and physical exercise. Some or all of these components may be used in the training program. With regard to all skills, trainees are taught how to use feedback obtained through their efforts to deepen their hardy attitudes of commitment, control, and challenge.

PREDICTIONS FOR EVERYDAY FUNCTIONING

What are the implications of hardiness theory and research for how people conduct their lives? In general, scrutiny is necessary regarding how the aspects of everyday life can provoke stressful circumstances and how people can address these stresses in a manner that resolves them and contributes to resilience and growth.

Family Life

A predominant thing about families is that their members are tied to each other in a more permanent manner than is true in other relationships. In one's family of origin, the tie is not only social but also genetic. One's family of reference begins with a marriage contract and continues to solidify through the genetic ties involving those who are conceived and born.

But, the closeness and importance of family ties, and the difficulty in breaking them, does not mean that the ongoing interactions of family members will be always harmonious. Indeed, there are many relational pressures that can easily arouse stress. Parents worry about whether their children will grow up well and struggle to steer them in the right directions. Children fear that they will be stifled or embarrassed by their parents and may keep their secrets to themselves. And, children wonder whether they or their siblings will be the favorites or the most successful and can fall easily into invidious competition.

It is easy for family members to fall into conflictful relationships that fester and get worse rather than improve. Unless one is careful and dedicated, this sinister process can lead to denial and avoidance or even catastrophizing and striking out. It takes a special, concerted, continuing effort to improve the relationship by resolving the conflict and replacing it with a pattern of giving and getting assistance and encouragement. This takes the kind of social interaction and coping skills practiced in our hardiness training program. But, this hard work will not be done consistently unless there is the courage provided by the hardy attitudes. This is especially true because the family member who initiates conflict resolution must unilaterally start the process by giving assistance and encouragement, regardless of accumulated resentment and apprehension.

The person strong in the courage of hardiness will try hard to empathize with and appreciate family members, even if they do not start out reciprocating. Further, the hardy family member will try to find ways to help the others reach their goals and fulfill their responsibilities in such ways as being a sounding board, taking up the slack, and giving space as needed. Once that facilitative pattern continues, it becomes more difficult for the other family member not to feel grateful and reciprocate. Soon, conflict will have been resolved and replaced with a mutual pattern of assistance and encouragement. The bond between these family members will continue to deepen as they help each other to develop and reach their goals. Hardy people can certainly influence the goals and directions of their family members in a process based on mutual appreciation and respect rather than an overly narrow sense of what is worthwhile in others.

Work or School

The main thing about work and school functioning is carrying out activities so as to reach goals that are of both social and personal significance. The process involves encountering circumstances that can be stressful insofar as they are not entirely predictable and require you to stretch beyond your habits and conveniences. Most people spend the largest proportion of their waking time in school and at work.

Work and school functioning involves not only personal development and goal attainment but also interaction with others in this process. These are often significant others in the sense that at work, they are team members, supervisors, or subordinates and at school, they are classmates, teachers, or club members. Although not as primary and unchangeable as those with family members, these relationships with others at work or in school are nonetheless important in one's development, goal attainment, and sense of intimacy. And, social norms for behavioral appropriateness operate, if anything, even stronger in work and school relationships than they do among family members.

Nonetheless, people low in hardiness often fall into disregard and competition with others at work or in school. Frequently, this disregard and competition is subtle so as not to appear socially inappropriate, but sometimes it is even open. Also, others who appear to be advancing well can arouse self-rejection in those around them who are low in hardiness. In general, those low in hardiness also will appear less directed, being unable to tackle difficult problems and learn in the process.

Those high in the courage of hardiness will show a very different pattern at work or school. They are likely to show directionality and progress in their own activities, turning stressful circumstances from potential disasters into opportunities for growth, development, and success. They will be quite able to shoulder the danger involved in taking unavoidable risks on the path to reaching their goals. In this process, they will work well with others around them, helping them and accepting help from them so that everyone wins. If someone else achieves promotion or gets the highest grade, the people high in hardiness will not feel defeated but rather will appreciate the other's accomplishment and continue their own efforts to learn and achieve.

Retirement

It is characteristic of those low in hardiness to look forward to retirement because work is for them typically fraught with undermining stresses and uncertainties that seem imposed on them by others. Because of this, they may feel some initial relief when retirement occurs. But, as time goes on, they will tend to feel a growing absence of meaning because they cannot come up with what would be worth doing, and things go from bad to worse. The nightmare of retirement may lead them toward various destructive attempts to deny and avoid, such as alcoholism or gambling.

In contrast, those high in hardiness will be sufficiently involved with their work that they will not hope for retirement unless they become ill in some way. After all, their hardiness will have led them over the years to find work that is challenging enough to be fulfilling and growth inducing. If their health is good, they will search out ways to continue working rather than retire.

But, recognizing that ceasing to work is an inevitability, those high in the courage of hardiness will have begun making plans for their retirement years before it actually takes place. Once retirement occurs, these plans may lead them to take up activities that always had seemed interesting though had not been carried out before. Perhaps they will try artwork, writing, or traveling, particular sports activities, political involvement, or altruistic efforts—whatever seems interesting, provocative, and a learning experience. Nor will they sink into social isolation, instead making sure that they service their existing relationships and build new ones as a function of their new activities.

Recreation

Recreation is the alternative to developmental, goal-directed activities of work or school. People low or high in hardiness are both likely to engage in recreational activities. But, those low in hardiness (i.e., without courage) may spend less time or more time in recreation than is common for those high in this characteristic. For those low in hardiness, work or school may seem so overwhelmingly stressful that they will deny and avoid, leading them to engage in more enjoyable activities. Many of them will seek out recreational activities with which they are familiar and that seem easy and unthreatening. Others will seek out such risky situations that there is nothing they can do to influence the outcome except to hope that they are lucky. But, among people low in hardiness, some will be so preoccupied with failing and being rejected due to the massive stressfulness of work or school requirements that they may not be able to imagine engaging in recreational activities at all. For them, to do something recreational is tantamount to ensuring failure in the work or school tasks that already seem too formidable.

In contrast, people high in the courage of hardiness will be able to take a break from the developmental process of engaging fully in work or school tasks. After all, these tasks, though formidable, will not seem overwhelming to them, and they will see recreation as a way of rebuilding their personal resources for successful task performance at work or school. As they are not overwhelmed by work or school, they can formulate a balanced life that, overall, is the most satisfying. When they take a break, the recreational activities they are likely to find most satisfying are those that are complicated and unusual enough to provoke them to learn, even though there is much less at stake than in work or school activities. So, they will want recreational activities that are not merely repetitive and that require mastery and provoke development. Although this may involve some risk-taking, this will be restricted to a moderate level in which mastery can be achieved readily through concentrated effort. This will not include games of chance where there is little or no way or influencing the outcome.

REFERENCES

Allred, K. D., & Smith, T. W. (1989). The hardy personality: Cognitive and physiological responses to evaluative threat. *Journal of Personality and Social Psychology, 56,* 257–264.

Atella, M. (1989). *Crossing boundaries: Effectiveness and health among Western managers living in China.* Unpublished doctoral dissertation, University of Chicago.

Bandura, A. (1977). Self-efficacy: Toward a unifying theory of behavior change. *Psychological Review, 84,* 191–215.

Barron, F. (1963). *Creativity and psychological health.* Princeton, NJ: Van Nostrand.

Bartone, P. T. (1989). Predictors of stress related illness in city bus drivers. *Journal of Occupational Medicine, 31,* 657–663.

Bartone, P. T. (1999). Hardiness protects against war-related stress in Army reserve forces. *Consulting Psychology Journal, 51,* 72–82.

Bartone, P. T., & Snook, S. A., (1999, May). *Cognitive and personality factors predict leader development in U.S. Army cadets.* Paper presented at the 35th International Applied Military Psychology Symposium (IAMPS), Florence, Italy.

Bartone, P. T., Ursano, R. J., Wright, K. M., & Ingraham, L. H. (1989). The impact of a military air disaster on the health of assistance workers: A prospective study. *Journal of Nervous and Mental Diseases, 177,* 317–328.

Baumeister, R. F., & Leary, M. R. (1995). The need to belong: Desire for interpersonal attachments as a fundamental human motivation. *Psychological Bulletin, 117,* 497–529.

Binswanger, L. (1963). *Being-in-the-world: Selected papers of Ludwig Binswanger.* New York: Basic Books.

Bonanno, G. (2004). Loss, trauma, and human resilience: Have we underestimated the human capacity to thrive after extremely aversive events? *American Psychologist, 51,* 72–82.

Cannon, W. B. (1929). *Bodily changes in pain, hunger, fear and rage.* New York: Appleton.

Contrada, R. J. (1989). Type A behavior, personality hardiness, and cardiovascular responses to stress. *Journal of Personality and Social Psychology, 57,* 895–903.

Costa, P. T., Jr., & McCrae, R. R. (1992). *Revised NEO Personality Inventory (NEO-PI-R) and NEO Five-Factor Inventory (NEO-FFI) professional manual.* Odessa, FL: Psychological Assessment Resources.

Diener, E. (2000). Subjective well-being: The science of happiness and a proposal for a national index. *American Psychologist, 55,* 34–43.

Diener, E., Suh, E., Lucas, R. E., & Smith, H. L. (1999). Subjective well-being: Three decades of progress. *Psychological Bulletin, 125,* 276–302.

Florian, V., Milkulincer, M., & Taubman, O. (1995). Does hardiness contribute to mental health during a stressful real life situation? The roles of appraisal and coping. *Journal of Personality and Social Psychology, 68,* 687–695.

Frankl, V. (1960). *The doctor and the soul.* New York: Knopf.

Funk, S. C. (1992). Hardiness: A review of theory and research. *Health Psychology, 11,* 335–345.

Funk, S. C., & Houston, B. K. (1987). A critical analysis of the Hardiness Scale's validity and utility. *Journal of Personality and Social Psychology, 53,* 572–578.

Ganellen, R. J., & Blaney, P. H. (1984). Hardiness and social support as moderators of the effects of life stress. *Journal of Personality and Social Psychology, 47,* 156–163.

Giatras, C. D. (2000). *Personality hardiness: A predictor of occupational stress and job satisfaction among California fire service personnel.* Unpublished master's thesis, California State University, Long Beach.

Hull, J. G., Van Treuren, R. R., & Virnelli, S. (1987). Hardiness and health: A critique and alternative approach. *Journal of Personality and Social Psychology, 53,* 518–530.

James, W. (1890). *The principles of psychology.* Boston: Henry Holt.

Keane, A., Ducette, J., & Adler, D. (1985). Stress in ICU and non-ICU nurses. *Nursing Research, 34,* 231–236.

Khoshaba, D. M. (1990). *Early antecedents of hardiness.* Unpublished doctoral dissertation, Illinois School of Professional Psychology.

Khoshaba, D. M., & Maddi, S. R. (1999). Early experiences in hardiness development. *Consulting Psychology Journal, 51,* 106–116.

Khoshaba, D. M., & Maddi, S. R. (2004). *HardiTraining: Managing Stress for Performance and Health Enhancement.* Newport Beach, CA: Hardiness Institute.

Kobasa, S. C. (1979). Stressful life events, personality, and health: An inquiry into hardiness. *Journal of Personality and Social Psychology, 37,* 1–11.

Kobasa, S. C. (1982). Commitment and coping among stress resistance among lawyers. *Journal of Personality and Social Psychology, 42,* 707–717.

Kobasa, S. C., Maddi, S. R., & Courington, S. (1981). Personality and constitution as mediators of the stress-illness relationship. *Journal of Health and Social Behavior, 22,* 368–378.

Kobasa, S. C., Maddi, S. R., & Kahn, S. (1982). Hardiness and health: A prospective study. *Journal of Personality and Social Psychology, 42,* 884–890.

Kobasa, S. C., Maddi, S. R., & Puccetti, M. (1982). Personality and exercise as buffers in the stress-illness relationship. *Journal of Behavioral Medicine, 4,* 391–404.

Kobasa, S. C., Maddi, S. R., Puccetti, M., & Zola, M. (1986). Relative effectiveness of hardiness, exercise, and social support as resources against illness. *Journal of Psychosomatic Research, 29,* 525–533.

Kuo, W. H., & Tsai, Y. (1986). Social networking, hardiness, and immigrant's mental health. *Journal of Health and Social Behavior, 27,* 133–149.

Lancer, K. (2000, June). Hardiness and Olympic women's synchronized swim team. Paper presented for invited presentation at the University of Nevada, Las Vegas.

Lifton, D. E., Seahy, S., & Bushke, A. (2000, Summer). Can student hardiness serve as an indicator of likely persistence to graduation? Basic results from a longitudinal study. *Academic Exchange Quarterly, 4,* 73–81.

Maddi, S. R. (1965). Motivational aspects of creativity. *Journal of Personality, 33,* 330–347.

Maddi, S. R. (1967). The existential neurosis. *Journal of Abnormal Psychology, 72,* 311–325.

Maddi, S. R. (1970). The search for meaning. In M. Page (Ed.), *Nebraska symposium on motivation* (pp. 137–186). Lincoln: University of Nebraska Press.

Maddi, S. R. (1987). Hardiness training at Illinois Bell Telephone. In J. P. Opatz (Ed.), *Health promotion evaluation*. Stevens Point, WI: National Wellness Institute.

Maddi, S. R. (1988). On the problem of accepting facticity and pursuing possibility. In S. B. Messer, L. A. Sass, & R. L. Woolfolk (Eds.), *Hermeneutics and psychological theory: Interpretive perspectives on personality, psychotherapy, and psychopathology*. New Brunswick, NJ: Rutgers University Press.

Maddi, S. R. (1990). Issues and interventions in stress mastery. In H. S. Friedman (Ed.), *Personality and disease* (pp. 121–154). New York: Wiley.

Maddi, S. R. (1994). The Hardiness Enhancing Lifestyle Program (HELP) for improving physical, mental, and social wellness. In C. Hopper (Ed.), *Wellness lecture series* (pp. 1–16). Oakland: University of California/HealthNet.

Maddi, S. R. (1996a). Existential psychotherapy. In S. J. Lynn & J. P. Garske (Eds.), *Contemporary psychotherapies* (2nd ed., pp. 191–219). Columbus, OH: Charles Merrill.

Maddi, S. R. (1996b). *Personality theories: A comparative analysis* (6th ed.). Prospect Heights, IL: Waveland Press.

Maddi, S. R. (1997). Personal Views Survey II: A measure of dispositional hardiness. In C. P. Zalaquett & R. J. Woods (Eds.), *Evaluating stress: A book of resources* (pp. 293–310). New York: New York University Press.

Maddi, S. R. (1998). Creating meaning through making decisions. In P. T. P. Wong & P. S. Fry (Eds.), *The human quest for meaning*. Mahwah, NJ: Erlbaum.

Maddi, S. R. (1999). The personality construct of hardiness, I: Effects on experiencing, coping & strain. *Consulting Psychology Journal, 51,* 106–116.

Maddi, S. R. (2002). The story of hardiness: Twenty years of theorizing, research, and practice. *Consulting Psychology Journal, 54,* 173–185.

Maddi, S. R. (2004, August). *The other positive psychology: The courage of hardiness under stress.* Invited address to the convention of the American Psychological Association, Honolulu, HI.

Maddi, S. R., Brow, M., Khoshaba, D. M., & Vaitkus, M. (2004). The relationship of hardiness and religiousness to depression and anger. Manuscript submitted for publication.

Maddi, S. R., Harvey, R. H., Khoshaba, D. M., Lu, J. L., Persico, M., & Brow, M. (2004). The personality construct of hardiness, III: Relationships with repression, innovativeness, authoritarianism, and performance. Manuscript submitted for publication.

Maddi, S. R., & Hess, M. (1992). Hardiness and success in basketball. *International Journal of Sports Psychology, 23,* 360–368.

Maddi, S. R., & Hightower, M. (1999). Hardiness and optimism as expressed in coping patterns. *Consulting Psychology Journal, 51,* 95–105.

Maddi, S. R., Kahn, S., & Maddi, K. L. (1998). The effectiveness of hardiness training. *Consulting Psychology Journal, 50,* 78–86.

Maddi, S. R., & Khoshaba, D. M. (1994). Hardiness and mental health. *Journal of Personality Assessment, 63,* 265–274.

Maddi, S. R., & Khoshaba, D. M. (2001a). *HardiSurvey III-R: Internet instruction manual.* Newport Beach, CA: Hardiness Institute.

Maddi, S. R., & Khoshaba, D. M. (2001b). *Personal Views Survey III-R: Internet instruction manual.* Newport Beach, CA: Hardiness Institute.

Maddi, S. R., & Khoshaba, D. M. (2005). *Resilience at work.* New York: Amacom.

Maddi, S. R., Khoshaba, D. M., Jensen, K., Carter, E., Lu, J. L., & Harvey, R. H. (2002). Hardiness training for high-risk undergraduates. *NACADA Journal, 22,* 45–55.

Maddi, S. R., Khoshaba, D. M., Persico, M., Lu, J. L., Harvey, R. H., & Bleecker, F. (2002). The personality construct of hardiness, II: Relationships with measures of psychopathology and personality. *Journal of Research in Personality, 36,* 72–85.

Maddi, S. R., & Kobasa, S. C. (1984). *The hardy executive: Health under stress.* Homewood, IL: Dow Jones-Irwin.

Maddi, S. R., Wadhwa, P., & Haier, R. J. (1996). Relationship of hardiness to alcohol and drug use in adolescents. *American Journal of Drug and Alcohol Abuse, 22,* 247–257.

Magnani, L. E. (1990). Hardiness, self-perceived health, and activity among independently functioning older adults. *Scholarly Inquiry for Nursing Practice: An International Journal, 4,* 171–184.

May, R. (1958). Contributions of existential psychotherapy. In R. May, E. Angel, & H. F. Ellenberger (Eds.), *Existence: A new dimension of psychiatry and psychology.* New York: Basic Books.

McCranie, E. W., Lambert, V. A., & Lambert, C. E., Jr. (1987). Work stress, hardiness, and burnout among hospital staff nurses. *Nursing Research, 36,* 374–378.

Moos, R. H. (1993). *Coping response inventory.* Odessa, FL: Psychological Assessment Resources.

Nietzsche, F. (1968). *The will to power* (W. Kaufman, Ed.). New York: Vintage.

Okun, M. A., Zantra, A. J., & Robinson, S. E. (1988). Hardiness and health among women with rheumatoid arthritis. *Personality and Individual Differences, 9,* 101–107.

Orr, E., & Westman, M. (1990). Hardiness as a stress moderator: A review. In M. Rosenbaum (Ed.), *Learned resourcefulness: On coping skills, self-control, and adaptive behavior* (pp. 64–94). New York: Springer-Verlag.

Ouellette, S. C. (1993). Inquiries into hardiness. In L. Goldberg & S. Bresnitz (Eds.), *Handbook of stress: Theoretical and clinical aspects* (2nd ed., pp. 77–100). New York: Free Press.

Pagana, K. D. (1990). The relationship of hardiness and social support to student appraisal of stress in an initial clinical nursing situation. *Journal of Nursing Education, 29,* 255–261.

Peterson, C. (2000). The future of optimism. *American Psychologist, 55,* 44–55.

Pollock, S. E. (1989). The hardiness characteristic: A motivating factor in adaptation. *Advances in Nursing Science, 11,* 53–62.

Pollock, S. E., & Duffy, M. E. (1990). The Health-Related Hardiness Scale: Development and psychometric analysis. *Nursing Research, 39,* 218–222.

Rhodewalt, F., & Zone, J. B. (1989). Appraisal of life change, depression, and illness in hardy and non-hardy women. *Journal of Personality and Social Psychology, 56,* 81–88.

Rich, V. L., & Rich, A. R. (1987). Personality hardiness and burnout in female staff nurses. *Image, 19,* 63–66.

Seligman, M. E. P. (1991). *Learned optimism.* New York: Knopf.

Seligman, M. E. P., & Csikszentmihalyi, M. (2000). Positive psychology: An introduction. *American Psychologist, 55,* 5–14.

Selye, H. (1976). *The stress of life* (2nd ed.). New York: McGraw-Hill.

Sinclair, R. R., & Tetrick, L. E. (2000). Implications of item wording for hardiness structure, relation with neuroticism, and stress buffering. *Journal of Research in Personality, 34,* 1–25.

Tillich, P. (1952). *The courage to be.* New Haven, CT: Yale University Press.

Topf, M. (1989). Personality hardiness, occupational stress, and burnout in critical care nurses. *Research in Nursing and Health, 12,* 179–186.

Weibe, D. J., & McCallum, D. M. (1986). Health practices and hardiness as mediators in the stress-illness relationship. *Health Psychology, 5,* 435–438.

Weinberger, D. A., Schwartz, G. E., & Davidson, R. J. (1979). Low anxious, high anxious, and repressive coping styles: Psychometric patterns and behavioral and physiological responses to stress. *Journal of Abnormal Psychology, 88,* 369–380.

Westman, M. (1990). The relationship between stress and performance: The moderating effect of hardiness. *Human Performance, 3,* 141–155.

CHAPTER 17

Sensation Seeking, Risk Taking, and Fearlessness

GENEVIEVE L. Y. ARNAUT

OVERVIEW

Sensation seeking refers to individual differences in preferred and/or optimal levels of arousal and stimulation. Marvin Zuckerman conducted much of the seminal work in this area, and in his 1994 book he defined sensation seeking as "a trait defined by the seeking of varied, novel, complex, and intense sensations and experiences, and the willingness to take physical, social, legal, and financial risks for the sake of such experience" (Zuckerman, 1994, p. 27).

In this chapter, I provide an overview of research on sensation seeking since Zuckerman's (1994) publication, tying it into fearlessness and risk taking. Doing justice to this topic would require another book; thus, my approach has been to select several topics of interest and discuss representative and/or important studies in each area. Although research has indicated that sensation seeking is associated with various forms of psychopathology, such as bipolar disorder and antisocial personality disorder (Zuckerman, 1994), my focus is on sensation seeking as a normal trait dimension and its relevance in daily functioning.

I begin with an abbreviated overview of prior research in order to put more recent results in context. After discussing the construct of sensation seeking and its relationship with personality theories, I address assessment and cross-cultural issues. Next, I look at various categories of risk-taking behaviors in adults and adolescents and the relationship between risk taking and fearlessness. Finally, I look at some more positive aspects of sensation seeking, such as its role in life satisfaction and stress.

SENSATION-SEEKING COMPONENTS AND CORRELATES

Factor analytic studies have suggested that sensation seeking comprises four components (Zuckerman, 1994): (1) *thrill and adventure seeking* (TAS): a desire to engage in sports or phys-

ically risky activities that produce physiological sensations; (2) *experience seeking* (ES): seeking novel and unconventional intellectual and sensory experiences; (3) *disinhibition* (Dis): seeking sensation through uninhibited social activities; and (4) *boredom susceptibility* (BS): intolerance of repetition or boring people.

As Haynes, Miles, and Clements (2000) noted, evidence for the four-factor structure has been found across gender and culture (e.g., in U.S., English, and Australian samples), although some studies have suggested some problems with the test items. As Zuckerman (1994) has summarized, higher scores on sensation seeking are associated with risk-taking behaviors (e.g., in sports, driving, and sexual activity), substance abuse, vocational choice, and aesthetic preference. Males typically score higher than females on sensation-seeking measures (TAS and Dis but not ES). Scores on sensation seeking typically decrease with age, peaking in late adolescence or the early twenties. As will be seen in the next section, information processing and cognitive styles may also be correlated with sensation seeking.

ORIGINS AND PHYSIOLOGY OF SENSATION SEEKING

Sensation seeking appears to be a trait rooted in physiology and heredity. In fact, Zuckerman (1994) indicated that almost 60 percent of sensation seeking is accounted for by heritability. An interesting recent study on the relationship between child-rearing practices and self-esteem by Keltikangas-Järvinen, Kivimäki, and Keskivaara (2003) has some bearing on this issue. Although these authors did not look at sensation seeking specifically, they found virtually no relationship between novelty seeking and child rearing in a longitudinal study of males, suggesting that novelty seeking may be more rooted in temperament than child-rearing practices.

In his extensive review of the psychophysiology of sensation seeking, Zuckerman (1990) wrote of his belief that differences in sensation seeking reflected inherited differences in the central nervous system. Although results were not always consistent, findings across the many studies reviewed indicated that stimulus factors of novelty, intensity, and stimulus significance were consistently associated with different responses in high and low sensation seekers. High sensation seekers tended to give stronger *orienting responses* to novel, interesting stimuli of moderate intensity, whereas low sensation seekers tended to show defensive responses (e.g., increased heart rate). High sensation seekers also were more responsive to stimuli of varying, and particularly high, intensity. Zuckerman (1994, 1999) suggested that genetic factors impact sensation seeking by influencing the activity and sensitivity of systems regulated by the catecholamines dopamine and norepinephrine as well as monoamine oxidase.

Assuming a biological basis for sensation seeking, we may expect to see associated sensory and cognitive differences. For example, Zuckerman (1994) reported several studies showing that the performance of low sensation seekers was disrupted more by a distraction than was the performance of high sensation seekers. Research on stimulus intensity also has shown relatively consistent results. For example, Brocke, Beauducel, John, Debener, and Heilemann (2000) replicated the commonly found positive correlation between sensation seeking and augmenting/reducing evoked potentials in healthy controls. That is, when stimulus intensity increased, high sensation seekers responded with a marked increase in components of evoked potentials (called an *augmenting disposition* or *high-level intensity dependence*) as compared with low sensation seekers. This is part of the orienting response referred to earlier.

Noting that such studies do not tell about the subjective experience of the perceiver, however, Neely, Lundström, and Björkvist (2002) were interested in the possibility that judgments of intensity may play an important role in sensation seeking. A total of 12 Swedish undergraduate participants (all women, age unspecified) took the Sensation Seeking Scale Form V (SSS-V, described later) and were divided into low and high sensation-seeking groups. A vibration stimulus (a sound from a helicopter presented together with a whole-body vibration) was started at low intensity and gradually increased. The dependent measure was time (i.e., time elapsed before a participant stopped the stimulus to identify one of three levels of specified unpleasantness on three different trials).

Neely et al. (2002) found that high sensation seekers exposed themselves for approximately twice as long to a stimulus before reporting the same level of subjective unpleasantness as those in the low sensation seeking group. There appeared to be a ceiling effect in that some of the high sensation seek-

ers went beyond the time limit without reporting maximum unpleasantness. The authors reported that "High Sensation Seekers consistently allowed themselves to be exposed to a more physically intense stimulus than Low Sensation Seekers did while reporting equal ratings of subjective unpleasantness" (p. 710). As the authors noted, such results may have many implications; for example, high sensation seekers may expose themselves to more dangerous stimuli in work environments.

Turning toward cognitive aspects of sensation seeking, Kohler (1996) assessed 100 undergraduates on measures of risk-taking behavior (using the SSS-V), locus of control, and critical thinking skills. Results indicated a multiple correlation of .29 between the criterion of risk taking and the predictors gender, locus of control, and critical thinking. Gender was most predictive: Without gender, the multiple correlation was greatly reduced (.10), which Kohler took to mean that there was essentially no relationship between sensation seeking and critical thinking. As is typical, men had higher sensation-seeking scores than women. Kohler believed that the absence of a relationship between sensation seeking and critical thinking indicated that inaccurate risk assessment did not play a role in what the author referred to as *self-defeating behaviors*. This common finding will be seen again in our discussion of risk-taking and driving behaviors.

THE CONSTRUCT OF SENSATION SEEKING AND ITS PLACE IN PERSONALITY THEORY

It is virtually impossible to separate a discussion of the construct of sensation seeking from the manner in which it is operationalized. However, for ease of discussion, I have made a rather artificial distinction between these topics. I first consider how sensation seeking is conceptualized and how it fits into larger theories of personality before considering in the next section how it is assessed.

Some theorists have discussed characteristics that may be similar to sensation seeking or that may make up components of sensation seeking. For example, novelty seeking is one of four primary dimensions of temperament identified by Cloninger (1987) as enduring individual differences, in addition to harm avoidance, reward dependence, and persistence. In fact, some authors use novelty seeking and sensation seeking interchangeably (e.g., Wills, Windle, & Cleary, 1998). Zuckerman and Cloninger (1996) reported a high correlation (.68) between Zuckerman's impulsive sensation seeking scale and Cloninger's novelty seeking scale.

Some researchers talk about risk taking or "risk proneness" (e.g., Raffaelli & Crockett, 2003), with no clear discussion of how this may be related to sensation seeking.

However, a study by Trimpop, Kerr, and Kirkcaldy (1999) suggests that sensation seeking and risk taking should not be confused. They looked at the relationship between a global measure of risk-taking behavior, an arousal-seeking measure, desire for control, and the SSS-V in Canadian men aged 16 to 29. Of interest for the present discussion was the finding that two factors of recklessness and risk taking (on the global measure of risk taking) correlated positively with sensation seeking. However, the subscales on the SSS-V and the factors on the risk-taking inventory did not totally overlap, suggesting that sensation seeking and risk taking are correlated but not synonymous. Similarly, Zuckerman (1994) identified willingness to take risks as only part of the definition of sensation seeking. Risk (appraised likelihood of a negative outcome) itself was not the essential motivator, but risk was tolerated for the sake of experience.

Evidence for a separate personality dimension of sensation seeking comes from a comprehensive effort to distinguish among current personality theories. Zuckerman, Kuhlman, Joireman, Teta, and Kraft (1993) compared several structural models of personality. They noted that authors of structural models for personality generally agree on two basic factors: Extraversion-Introversion (E-IN) and Neuroticism (N). H. J. Eysenck (1967) added only Psychoticism (P) and viewed other factors as components of the three primary factors. Costa and McCrae's (1992a) Big Five included three more factors: Agreeableness, Conscientiousness, and Openness to Experience. In an alternative five-factor model, Zuckerman et al. added three components—Impulsive Unsocialized Sensation Seeking, Aggression-Hostility, and Activity—to Sociability and Neuroticism-Anxiety.

Zuckerman et al. (1993) modified an earlier personality inventory to become the Zuckerman-Kuhlman Personality Questionnaire Third Edition, Revised (ZKPQ-III-R), which measured Impulsive Sensation Seeking (ImpSS), Neuroticism-Anxiety (N-A), Aggression-Hostility (Agg-Host), Activity (Act), and Sociability (Sy). Undergraduates took the Eysenck Personality Questionnaire, Revised (EPQ-R; Eysenck & Eysenck, 1975), followed by the ZKPQ-III-R a week later, and then the Revised NEO Personality Inventory (NEO-PI-R; Costa & McCrae, 1992b) a week later. Results of a factor analysis indicated that Extraversion and Neuroticism were similar across all three models. When factors were limited to three, a model very similar to Eysenck's results emerged (i.e., three factors labeled *E, N,* and *P*). In a four-factor model, Psychoticism appeared to be identified with Conscientiousness and ImpSS, and Agreeableness and Aggression-Hostility formed a separate fourth factor. Activity did not emerge as a separate dimension. Comparing Zuckerman et al.'s system with Costa and McCrae's system, ImpSS and Agg-Host were associated with Conscientiousness and Agreeableness.

Further discussion of personality models is beyond the scope of the present chapter, but the importance of these results for the present discussion is that this analysis provided evidence that sensation seeking, at least as it is defined on the ZKPQ-III-R, may be a basic dimension of personality. In the next two subsections, we will look more specifically at two personality dimensions that have been associated with sensation seeking: curiosity and extraversion.

Curiosity

Wentworth and Witryol (2003) defined curiosity as "the desire to learn more" (p. 281) and noted that curiosity had the capacity to energize and direct behavior. Novelty seeking biases the direction toward which curiosity aims, and curiosity is enhanced by the novelty, complexity, and uncertainty of stimuli. As Wentworth and Witryol noted, curiosity, exploration, and novelty seeking are important features of cognitive growth across the life span, and curiosity plays an important role in the nature and amount of what is learned. Given that sensation seeking and curiosity appear to share a tendency toward exploratory behaviors and a desire for novel stimulation, the question arises as to whether curiosity is associated with sensation seeking.

Daniel Berlyne wrote extensively about curiosity, and in 1954 he distinguished perceptual curiosity, "which leads to increased perception of stimuli" (p. 180), and epistemic curiosity, or a "drive to know" (p. 187). In addition, Berlyne (1960) identified two types of exploratory behavior (diversive and specific) associated with curiosity. Adopting this definition of curiosity, Litman and Spielberger (2003) noted that in previous research the TAS and ES subscales of sensation seeking loaded on an Experience Seeking factor, as opposed to an Information Seeking factor, when curiosity, novelty experiencing, and sensation seeking scales were examined. They subsequently conducted a study in which one purpose was to determine whether their measure of epistemic curiosity was associated with sensation seeking.

Litman and Spielberger (2003) administered the TAS and ES subscales of the SSS (form unidentified) to 739 undergraduates, aged 18 to 65 (546 women, 193 men; mean age = 23.6) as well as a curiosity questionnaire and some additional personality measures. A factor analysis showed a single curiosity construct with two major dimensions consistent with epistemic and perceptual curiosity. In addition, small but significant positive correlations were found between the epistemic curiosity scale and subscale scores and sensation-seeking scores. The authors concluded that epistemic curiosity was relatively independent of sensation seeking but that epistemic curiosity at least to some extent involves seeking sensory stimulation. Because the purpose of Litman and

Spielberger's (2003) study was to develop a scale to measure epistemic curiosity rather than perceptual curiosity, the relationship between sensation seeking and perceptual curiosity was unfortunately unexplored.

Evidence for the relationship between epistemic curiosity and sensation seeking comes also from an unusual study conducted by Schroth and McCormack (2000). These authors were interested in whether sensation seeking and need for achievement would provide useful heuristics with which to interpret cross-cultural phenomena. They recruited 378 participants (127 males, 251 females; mean age = 24.8) from 14 countries in the California State University International Program and compared them with a U.S. college sample from a previous study. Using the SSS-V, they found that foreign males had higher scores on ES but lower TAS, Dis, BS, and total sensation-seeking scores when compared with their U.S. counterparts. Foreign-born women scored higher on ES and lower on TAS, Dis, and total sensation-seeking scores than their U.S. counterparts (with no difference on the BS subscale).

Foreign men and women had higher scores on work, mastery, and competitiveness than their U.S. counterparts. Reminiscent of the distinction between epistemic and perceptual curiosity and the small but positive link between sensation seeking and epistemic curiosity in Litman and Spielberger's (2003) study, Schroth and McCormack (2000) concluded that low scores on TAS, Dis, and BS subscales suggested the foreign students "were serious young scholars who sought experiences not available at home. This finding does not fit the stereotype of sensation seekers in search of dangerous activities, parties, and so forth. . . . Instead, the study-abroad students' high scores on the Experience Seeking subscale suggest that their needs consist of seeking new experiences through the mind and senses by traveling abroad" (p. 534).

As noted previously, prior research indicated a link between the experience-seeking facet of curiosity and aspects of sensation seeking. The two studies just discussed suggest that there also may be some relationship between sensation seeking (particularly ES) and desire for knowledge. This is certainly an area meriting further study, given the link between curiosity and cognitive growth (Wentworth & Witryol, 2003). An additional implication is that all sensation seekers are not alike; those high on ES and low on other subscales may desire experiences of a particular sort, which may not involve risk.

Extraversion

Another area in which sensation seeking might be hypothesized to play a role is in relation to extraversion and shyness. Intuitively, individuals high on sensation seeking might be expected to be more extraverted and less shy. Indeed, as Aluja, García, and García (2003) noted, the proneness to high stimulating activities that is a component of sensation seeking also can be attributed to extraverted and impulsive individuals. As noted previously, sensation seeking has been found to be related to Extraversion and Psychoticism. Aluja et al. (2003) investigated the relationship between the NEO measures of Openness to Experience (O) and Extraversion (E) and the SSS-V. They administered the SSS-V and the NEO-PI-R to 1,006 undergraduate nonpsychology students (367 males, 639 females; aged 17 to 52; mean age = 22) in Spain. E and O scores were strongly related to sensation seeking, and correlations between SSS total scores and total E and total O scores were very similar for both scales. Of the extraversion components, E5-Excitement-Seeking was the most related to sensation seeking total scores and the subscale scores. The authors noted, however, that sociable components did not share common variance, so "excitement-seeking people can be sociable as well as unsociable" (Aluja et al., 2003, p. 678). Overall, E-5 Excitement seeking and O4-Actions and O1-Fantasy "allow for the successful classification of 85 percent of higher and lower sensation seekers" (p. 679). Therefore, as with curiosity, the ES subscale appears to be the most strongly related aspect of sensation seeking in terms of extraversion.

Noting that scores on shyness scales have been shown to be negatively correlated with extraversion, and given the previous findings that sensation seeking and extraversion are related, Crozier and Birdsey (2003) looked at sensation seeking and birth-order position as related to shyness. They included birth order because Zuckerman (1994) reported results indicating that there was a tendency for firstborns and only children to be higher in sensation seeking, perhaps due to having exclusive attention of parents and receiving more varied stimulation. Because the latter results came only from an unpublished study, Crozier and Birdsey tested this factor further.

A British sample of 250 undergraduates in England, aged 18 to 52 (96 males, 154 females; mean age = 22 years) took a shyness scale and the SSS-V as well as reporting on gender and birth order. Results indicated a significant negative relationship between shyness and sensation seeking (i.e., higher levels of sensation seeking were associated with lower levels of shyness), which was explained by the correlation between the Dis subscale and shyness. An interesting finding was that there was no difference in shyness among firstborn and later-born children, which the authors suggested might reflect the large influence of genetics on sensation seeking.

Bohlin, Bengtsgård, and Andersson (2000) took a different approach to the topic of shyness and looked at social inhibition, or a general tendency to withdraw versus approach when faced with unfamiliar stimulation. Associated with, but distinct from, social inhibition is overfriendliness, or a lack of normal reserve in social encounters. In an initial study not concerned with sensation seeking, these authors assessed Swedish children, aged seven and eight. Socially inhibited children were rated by their parents as having more internalizing problem behaviors and lower social competence as compared with low-inhibited children. In addition, children who were low in social inhibition (referred to as *low-inhibited children*) and who also had high scores on overfriendliness were rated as showing more problem behaviors than did low-inhibited children having lower scores on overfriendliness (problem behaviors included attention but also externalizing and internalizing behaviors).

Bengtsgård and Bohlin (2001) conducted a 2-year follow-up with 45 children and reported that social inhibition and overfriendliness appeared stable over the 2-year period. Based on a structured play and conversation period (with a stranger who gave brief responses to any questions by the child for 5 minutes and then asked neutral questions for 5 minutes), observers rated social inhibition using a revised version of a shyness scale and a 5-point overfriendliness scale. A 10-item thrill-seeking subscale of sensation-seeking behavior was adapted from Russo's work (see following), and some other measures (e.g., parental reports) were used.

Results indicated that thrill seeking was negatively correlated with social inhibition. Further, the overfriendly group scored higher on thrill seeking and hyperactivity than did the low-overfriendly and low-inhibited group. The authors noted that only the low-overfriendly and low-inhibited group appeared confident. Thus, although thrill seeking may be beneficial if it is associated with low social inhibition, it also may contribute to socioemotional problems if it is associated with hyperactivity and overfriendliness.

ASSESSING SENSATION SEEKING

Having discussed evidence for the construct of sensation seeking, I will turn now to the assessment of sensation seeking. Many, if not most, researchers who investigate sensation seeking have used the Sensation Seeking Scale Form V, or SSS-V, developed by Zuckerman (for a complete discussion, see Zuckerman, 1994).

The SSS-V developed out of a series of SSS forms, beginning with Form I in 1964. Factor analyses of Form II suggested four factors corresponding to the components listed previously, and with several iterations of items and factor analyses, Form V emerged in 1978. The SSS-V contains 40 forced-choice items, 10 for each subscale. For example,

Item 1 asks the respondent to choose between the statements: "I like 'wild' uninhibited parties," and "I prefer quiet parties with good conversation." Zuckerman (1994) provided a range of estimates of internal reliability for the total score of .83 to .86, with a range of reliabilities for the subscales from .56 to .82. A Form VI using three-point answer scales also was developed, but the SSS-V has remained the most widely used instrument.

Several authors (e.g., Arnett, 1994; Gilchrist, Povey, Dickinson, & Povey, 1995) have commented that some of the terms in the original SSS-V were outdated (e.g., "swingers," "hippies"). However, as Zuckerman (1996) pointed out, these items were revised, and the revisions were included in Zuckerman's (1994) book. The scale was not renormed because these appeared to be minor changes, but Zuckerman (1996) noted that subsequent studies showed equivalent subscale means and standard deviations.

An additional scale rooted in Zuckerman's model is the Zuckerman-Kuhlman Personality Questionnaire, now in a third and revised edition, ZKPQ-III-R (see previous discussion of Zuckerman et al., 1993). The ZKPQ-III-R is a broader measure of personality than the SSS-V, and, as noted previously, Impulsive Sensation Seeking (ImpSS) is only one component of personality that is assessed. The items were designed to reflect the Experience Seeking subscale of the SSS-V. Zuckerman (1996) found that the ImpSS correlated with the four subscales of the SSS-V at about .43 to .45 and at .70 with the SSS-V total score. Zuckerman suggested that researchers interested in an overall sensation-seeking measure combined with impulsivity should use this new scale. Advantages are that the scale is brief (19 items), does not refer to specific behaviors, and has updated terms.

A point of confusion arises because some authors say that they are measuring sensation seeking, yet they do not use standard measures or definitions. For example, Slater (2003a, 2003b) developed his own two-item measure for use with adolescents. Oishi, Schimmack, and Colcombe (2003) used part of the extraversion scale in the NEO-PI. Ang and Woo (2003) used a scale generated by the self-report form of the Behavior Assessment System for Children (BASC). Wood and Cochran (1995) titled their article "Sensation-Seeking and Delinquent Substance Use: An Extension of Learning Theory," yet they operationalized sensation seeking with a combination of scales to measure impulsivity, thrill seeking, and desire for immediate gratification. Zuckerman (1994) provided information about comparability of measures with the SSS; unless studies have indicated equivalence, it is probably not safe to assume comparability.

Perhaps the most comprehensive alternative to the SSS-V has been developed by Jeffrey Arnett, author of the Arnett

Inventory of Sensation Seeking (AISS; Arnett, 1994). Arnett emphasized the need for novelty and intensity of stimulation in his definition of sensation seeking and characterized sensation seeking as a "predisposition . . . which may be expressed in a variety of ways depending on other aspects of the individual's personality and (especially) depending on how the socialization environment guides, shapes, or suppresses that predisposition" (p. 290).

Besides wanting to measure more directly this definition of sensation seeking, Arnett (1994) designed the AISS to address what he identified as four shortcomings of the SSS-V. First, he believed the forced-choice format of the SSS-V could be frustrating and perplexing if neither choice applied to a respondent. Second, some items contained physical activities in which older adults might be less likely to participate due to reduced physical strength (e.g., mountain climbing). Third, in early versions of the SSS-V, some of the terms were dated (as noted previously, these have been changed). Finally, the SSS-V contains items asking about drug and alcohol use and sexual behavior, which often are criterion measures in studies that investigate sensation seeking; thus, the high correlations between sensation seeking and these behaviors may reflect commonality of items rather than a separate association.

To address these issues, the AISS (a) focused on novelty and intensity, (b) had Likert-scale responses, (c) included items that were not intrinsically age-related, (d) did not refer to illegal or norm-breaking behaviors, and (e) contained two theoretically derived subscales, Novelty and Intensity.

Arnett (1994) conducted two exploratory studies with the AISS. In the first study, 116 high school students (54 boys, 62 girls) aged 16 to 18 completed the AISS, the SSS-V, and a 16-item adolescent-risk-behavior questionnaire developed by Arnett. Results indicated that the AISS was correlated significantly with several indices of risky driving behavior, casual sexual encounters, marijuana use, and some illegal activities. Scores on the SSS-V were correlated only with driving while intoxicated and with marijuana use. Arnett reported an overall correlation of .41 between the AISS and SSS-V, with correlations ranging from .08 to .47 between the AISS and SSS subscales. He also noted that, "In every case, the AISS was correlated more strongly with risk behavior than was the SSS" (Arnett, 1994, p. 292). The Intensity subscale of the AISS was correlated more strongly with risk behavior than was the Novelty subscale, and, consistent with earlier research, boys had higher total scores and Intensity subscale scores than girls. Internal reliability was reported to be .70 for the total scale and .64 and .50 for the Intensity and Novelty subscales, respectively.

In Arnett's (1994) second study, 139 high school students (67 boys, 72 girls; aged 16 to 18) and 38 of their parents (aged 41 to 59) took the AISS and the Aggression subscale of the California Psychological Inventory (CPI; Gough, 1987). The adolescents also answered the risk questionnaire described previously. Results indicated that the AISS was correlated with risky driving behaviors, casual sex, and illegal drug use. Adolescents had higher total and subscale scores than adults, particularly for the Intensity subscale. Arnett also compared parents to their own children and found that the age differences were significant for the total scale and the Intensity subscale but not for the Novelty subscale. For adolescents, but not for adults, sensation seeking was significantly correlated with scores on the Aggression subscale of the CPI. Finally, both adolescent and adult males scored higher on sensation seeking than did their female counterparts, with the exception of the Novelty subscale for adolescents. It was unclear why Arnett used adolescents in his study, but these initial results were promising.

Haynes et al. (2000) conducted confirmatory factor analyses to analyze the SSS-V and the AISS factor structures. They administered the SSS-V and the AISS to 822 undergraduates (615 females, 204 males, 3 unspecified gender), aged 18 to 72 (mean age = 24.8), in the United Kingdom. Discussion of specifics of the analyses is beyond the scope of the current chapter, but the general methodology was to split the sample in half and test the factor structures proposed by the respective authors. The models were then modified and reestimated using the second sample.

Haynes et al. (2000) concluded that "neither of the models is wholly adequate as proposed by the authors" (p. 835). For the SSS-V, subscales were tested separately. Although initial fit for most subscales was said to be adequate, the model was modified by allowing the unique variances of specific items on subscales to correlate; fit subsequently improved. The authors suggested that the magnitude of these correlations indicated that the subscales may not be unidimensional but may be measuring another trait. The authors attempted to develop a revised scale by removing items related to alcohol and drug use and omitting items thought to be no longer culturally relevant. Sixteen of the original items were left, and the model was not satisfactory.

As for the AISS, Haynes et al. (2000) believed that, compared with the SSS-V, it was more culturally relevant with a preferred response format (which they supported by noting that more returned AISS forms were usable than SSS-V forms [778 versus 748]), but they noted that in the first analysis of the AISS, seven items did not load adequately on their respective factors. When these items were removed, fit improved. The authors suggested that these seven items did not load on factors because Arnett did not use factor analysis to develop the scale. They also noted that this also could explain the relatively low reliabilities noted by other authors (e.g., Arnett, 1994; Roth, 2003). It should be pointed out that the sample Haynes et al. used was disproportionately female, which could have influenced the results.

Ferrando and Chico (2001) compared translated versions of the SSS-V and the AISS in a Spanish sample (448 undergraduates; 326 females, 112 males, 10 unspecified gender; mean age = 22.61). They indicated that their results suggested that both scales measured essentially the same dimension; the correlation between the two scales was .72, and the subscales of the AISS correlated as much or more with the SSS-V subscales than the SSS-V subscales did with each other. The authors suggested that if both scales are measuring the same scales, then the issue is when to choose one over the other. Noting that the SSS-V had better reliabilities and a clearer factor structure than the AISS, but it had a clear, logical theoretical structure and worked well at the subscale level, they concluded, "Without wanting to decide in favour of one scale or the other, our opinion is that both the AISS and the SSS-V are improvable" (Ferrando and Chico, 2001, p. 1132).

Roth (2003) pointed out that, in spite of the fact that Arnett (1994) criticized other researchers for focusing primarily on risk behaviors, Arnett did so as well. Yet Arnett's definition of sensation seeking indicated that socialization could influence an individual high in sensation seeking to choose many behavioral expressions of the trait. Thus, Roth conducted a study intended to explore the criterion-related validity of the AISS by using a criterion other than risk behavior: willingness toward occupational change, measured as duration of current employment and intention to change the workplace. The study was conducted with 205 public utility employees aged 21 to 60 (46 percent males, 54 percent females) in Leipzig, Germany. Participants completed a German version of the AISS, inventories measuring social desirability and achievement motivation, and questions about their employment.

Social desirability did not appear to influence scores on the AISS. Using logistic regression, Roth (2003) found that younger age, higher scores on the Intensity subscale, and higher achievement motivation significantly predicted intention to change the workplace. Only age emerged as a significant predictor of short duration of present employment. Internal reliabilities for the total scale and Intensity and Novelty subscales were .61, .53, and .52, respectively. Roth believed his study provided evidence of criterion-related validity of the AISS in that sensation seeking was associated with work-related behaviors and not just risky behaviors.

Before leaving the topic of measurement, it is important to note that the SSS was developed for adolescent and adult populations. Russo et al. (1991) developed a preliminary

Sensation-Seeking Scale for Children (SSSC) for preadolescents. They tested 126 normal children (aged 7 to 12) and 176 clinic-referred (CLR) boys (aged 7 to 12). Parents of the latter group also completed the adult SSS. Results indicated that the SSSC was reliable and valid for both normal and CLR children. Interestingly, similar to Arnett's (1994) results, there was some support for familial transmission for CLR participants: A significant positive correlation was found between sensation-seeking scores of CLR boys and their mothers. In addition, sensation seeking showed associations with conduct problems. Boys with conduct disorder appeared to seek stimulation from their environments due to boredom. Although boys with anxiety disorders did not have low sensation-seeking scores relative to other CLR boys, boys who were anxious and who exhibited conduct disorder appeared to be less susceptible to such sensation stimulation seeking.

Russo et al. (1993) later revised the SSSC, and they standardized and validated it on a community sample of 660 elementary- and middle-school children (aged 9 to 15) and 168 clinic-referred boys (aged 9 to 24). Factor analysis of the combined samples yielded three unique factors that were different from the four factors traditionally found for adults. The factors were identified as Thrill and Adventure Seeking, Drug and Alcohol Attitudes, and Social Disinhibition. The authors reported that psychometric indices of reliability and validity were acceptable, but test-retest reliability was only moderate. The SSSC distinguished boys with conduct disorder from clinic controls but not from boys in the community sample.

Factor structures may also differ in adolescent populations. Michel et al. (1999) found a different factor structure for adolescents as compared with adults, using an abbreviated French version of the SSS with 40 items. The scale retained the forced-choice format and produces the same four subscale scores and an overall score as the SSS-V. A total of 278 French adolescents took part in the first year of study; 104 of these completed two testings in two additional years (mean age = 17.5 in the third year of study; gender distribution unknown). Results indicated a three-factor solution in the first year that remained stable over the two subsequent years. The three factors were identified as TAS, Dis, and Nonconformism (NC), which the authors believed to be similar to the results found by Russo et al. (1993). It might be noted that, even if the subscale had the same name as an adult subscale, the items were not necessarily the same (e.g., for adolescents, the use of alcohol or drugs also appeared to be related to illegal activities).

Taken together, these results indicate that the nature or manifestations of sensation seeking may differ in child and adolescent samples and/or French samples, and they point to the importance of considering factors such as age and culture when assessing individuals on this dimension. In the next section, we will consider cross-cultural comparisons.

CULTURAL FACTORS

The concept of sensation seeking not only has received factor-analytic support, as noted previously, it also has cross-cultural support. In addition to indicating consistent and reliable differences in sensation seeking within various cultural groups, research has shown differences across cultural groups (e.g., Eastern cultures and Spanish samples have tended to show lower scores). However, as Zuckerman (1994) noted, results are sometimes not comparable when scales are translated because researchers modify, add, and delete items. When results are compared, the nature and direction of these differences are sometimes unexpected. For example, in an early study, Berkowitz (1967) gave a Thai version of the SSS to 328 Thai college students (commerce, teacher training, and undergraduate students) and 89 Buddhist monks. Results indicated that, as in most countries, Thai males had higher sensation-seeking scores than Thai females. Thai students scored lower than U.S. students had in an earlier study by Zuckerman and colleagues. Monks studying at a Buddhist institute scored lower than Thai students. Although this latter result has face validity in that it might be expected that Buddhist monks would have a quiet life and score low in sensation seeking, it is curious for an unusual reason: In Thailand, most men become monks for a short period of time to bring merit to their families, and thus most monks are young men who are ordained for a few months and who then return to the secular world. If this was characteristic of the monk sample, it is curious that they scored lower than the Thai students.

Magaro, Smith, Cionini, and Velicogna (1979) gathered a sample of 211 Italians (101 males, 110 females; aged 15 to 72) and administered the SSS-IV and other personality and attitude measures. They compared results with data from previous studies and found that Italian females scored higher than Thai or Japanese female college students and were more similar to U.S. female college students. Interestingly, the opposite was found for Italian males, who scored lower than U.S. college males, with scores that were more similar to Thai and Japanese males. Unlike results in many other studies, Italian males and females did not differ in sensation-seeking scores. Sensation-seeking scores decreased with age for males only but not for females. The authors speculated that this result may have been due to the effects of education because education accounted for a larger proportion of variance in the SSS (10 percent) than did age for females, whereas for males age was more important. They concluded that either high sensation-seeking women seek education or males and females are differentially affected by exposure to education. A factor analysis indicated that high sensation seeking was associated with open-mindedness and youth, although the relationship was more complex for females (education, occupation, and political orientation also loaded highly).

In a more recent study, Wang et al. (2000) gave the SSS-V to a Chinese sample composed of 322 individuals (204 females, 118 males; aged 15 to 65; mean age = 29). The authors looked at factor loadings and individual item loadings and found four main factors consistent with those identified by Zuckerman, particularly TAS, ES, and Dis (although this is perhaps unsurprising, given that the SSS-V includes subscales designed to test these four factors). Age effects for TAS and ES were replicated (i.e., scores decreased with age), and some gender effects also were found (men generally scored higher on TAS and Dis, but only at age 40 to 49 on BS, and never on ES). Interestingly, intercorrelations between subscales were low, thus suggesting that for this sample the total score did not measure a broad sensation-seeking trait. Overall, the Chinese sample scored lower on the total score and on ES and BS subscales as compared with English culture-based studies.

Using a sample of adolescent boys in Singapore, Ang and Woo (2003) replicated the common relationship found for U.S. adolescents (discussed later) between sensation seeking and behavior problems. They assessed 143 grade-7 boys using the Behavior Assessment System for Children (BASC). Both self-report and teacher ratings were used, and sensation seeking was measured by a scale on the self-report form. Results indicated that sensation seeking was related significantly to hyperactivity, delinquency, and attitude toward school (i.e., greater dissatisfaction) but not to aggression.

Because cross-cultural differences have been noted (e.g., differences in level of sensation seeking, different gender effects), in the ensuing discussion I will note when a sample is from a country other than the United States. In addition, as will be seen later, even in the United States, cultural and ethnic differences must be taken into account, and thus I will note the demographics of samples when they were provided by researchers. Let us turn next to behavioral correlates of sensation seeking, beginning first with one of the most commonly reported correlates: risky behaviors.

RISKY BEHAVIORS IN ADULTHOOD

As noted previously, individuals who score high on sensation-seeking scales typically engage in more risky behaviors than do individuals who score low on sensation seeking. In this section, we will first look specifically at one activity that has been studied frequently in this context—driving behavior—before turning to sports, gambling, and aggression.

Driving Behaviors

Heino, van der Molen, and Wilde (1996) investigated whether a need for stimulation influences perceived risk in a study that was unique in two ways: First, the authors measured actual driving behavior rather than reported behavior, and, second, they measured three aspects of risk (behavioral, cognitive, and physiological). In a Canadian sample with a mean age of 25 years, 21 male sensation seekers and 21 male sensation avoiders followed another car at either free-following distance (i.e., the driver chose the distance) or a prescribed following distance. Three measures of target risk were taken: time-headway (a behavioral measure of the time lapse in seconds from the time the rear bumper of a car in front passed a certain point until the front bumper of a following car passed the same point), verbal risk ratings (a cognitive measure using a 7-point scale), and heart rate variability (a physiological measure).

Results indicated that sensation avoiders preferred a longer following distance, but there was no difference between groups in verbal risk ratings or heart rate. The prescribed following distance resulted in shorter time-headway, reflected in increase in experienced risk at both cognitive and physiological levels; the effect was largest for the sensation avoiders group. Heino et al. (1996) concluded that differences in sensation seeking primarily were related to differences in overt behavior and that individuals high in sensation seeking did not evaluate their behavior as being more risky than did those low in sensation seeking.

In an article published the following year, Jonah (1997) reviewed 40 articles on risky driving (which, by the way, is not an item on the SSS). Of 18 studies that reported statistics on drinking and driving, all but 5 studies indicated positive relationships such that as sensation seeking increased, reported driving while impaired (DWI) arrests increased. In addition, reported and/or convicted DWI offenders had higher sensation-seeking scores. Few studies looked at SSS subscales, but in one that did, the Dis subscale appeared to be correlated most strongly with drinking and driving. As with most studies on sensation seeking, the relationship generally was stronger among men than women and appeared to decline with age. Jonah indicated that there was some evidence to suggest that the sensation seeking–risky driving relationship was direct for men and mediated by alcohol for women. Jonah also noted that perceived risk of collision while drinking and driving appeared to mediate the relationship between sensation seeking and impaired driving; that is, as noted by Heino et al. (1996), in the same situation, individuals high in sensation seeking appeared to perceive less risk than did individuals low in sensation seeking.

Looking at 15 studies in which relationships between sensation seeking and other risky driving behaviors (e.g., driving speed, breaking laws, not using seat belts, unsafe passing, aggressiveness) were reported, Jonah (1997) found that all studies showed a positive correlation between sensation seeking and risky driving, especially for men. Again, high sensation seekers appeared to perceive less danger than did low sensation seekers. In these studies, the TAS subscale typically was related most strongly to risk driving. In 18 studies in which relationships between sensation seeking and consequences of risky driving were reported, high sensation seekers were more likely to experience collisions and violations than were low sensation seekers. Again, the TAS subscale appeared to be most strongly related with these consequences. The relationship was stronger with observed or reported driving behaviors than with traffic violations or collisions.

Jonah (1997) noted that these relationships were seen in many countries, including Canada, the United States, the United Kingdom, the Netherlands, Sweden, Norway, and Finland. Characteristically, the relationships were stronger in men than women and appeared to decrease with age in many studies. Typical correlations were in the range of .3 to .4 (accounting for 10 to 15 percent of variance). Jonah hypothesized that the actual relationship between sensation seeking and risky driving is higher than this but that lack of uniform operationalization of sensation seeking (e.g., using different scales or subsets of SSS) may have lowered these estimates.

Probably most important among these results is the consistent finding that risk perception may mediate the relationship between sensation seeking and risky driving. Jonah (1997) hypothesized that this may occur because higher sensation seekers perceived themselves as having superior driving skills, or they may accept the risk to experience some thrill and, if no negative consequences ensue, they subsequently perceive lower risk. Alcohol also may serve as a disinhibitor because risky behaviors increased even if participants in some studies just thought they had been given alcohol when in fact they had not.

An interesting suggestion offered by Jonah (1997) was that such findings may indicate that individuals who score high on sensation seeking could benefit from an educational program to reduce driving risk. However, in Kohler's (1996) study of cognitive aspects of sensation seeking discussed previously, the author offered an opinion that if sensation seeking is primarily biologically based, as Zuckerman (1990,

1994) suggested, then "to offer cognitive strategies as remediation or rehabilitation tools for these persons seems futile" (Kohler, 1996, p. 490). In addition, the accuracy of self-report in any widespread programmatic attempt to assess sensation seeking (such as in a driver's education context) likely would diminish over time as consequences of accuracy became obvious to the general public, thereby obviating any benefits of such programs.

Since Jonah's (1997) review, some additional studies have been conducted, of which two will be discussed here. For example, Jonah and colleagues (Jonah, Thiessen, & Au-Yeung, 2001) carried out a study of the relationship between sensation seeking and self-reported risky and aggressive driving as well as looked at the probability that individuals high on sensation seeking would adapt to an antilock braking system by driving in a more risky manner. Participants were 120 male and 159 female students in Canada (mean age = 25). They took the SSS-V and a questionnaire about their driving habits, which included a question about how they would respond to antilock brakes. Consistent with prior research, high sensation seekers reported engaging in more risky driving behaviors than did low sensation seekers. One new finding was that high sensation seekers reported more aggressive behavior while driving. The Dis subscale was related most strongly to risky driving, aggression, and behavioral adaptation. High sensation seekers reported that they would be more likely to engage in risky driving behaviors with an antilock braking system (i.e., to adapt their driving behaviors), suggesting that safety features may not compensate for risky driving in this population.

The final study we will consider was conducted by Rosenbloom (2003b), who was interested in whether mortality salience (i.e., awareness of inevitable mortality) would change risky driving in high and low sensation seekers. A total of 120 students in Israel (45 males, 75 females; aged 20 to 33; mean age = 24.6) took the SSS-V; two weeks later they saw either a frightening driving movie or a nature movie and then took an Inventory of Risk Taking designed for this study. In line with prior research, a significant main effect was found for sensation seeking, such that high sensation seekers reported higher risk taking in driving than low sensation seekers. In addition, a significant interaction was found between mortality salience and sensation seeking: The low sensation seekers in the mortality salience condition (i.e., those who saw the frightening movie) reported significantly lower risk taking than did the low sensation seekers in the nonmortality salience condition (i.e., the nature movie), whereas the high sensation seekers reported similar driving in both conditions. In fact, results indicated a nonsignificant trend for high sensation seekers to be even riskier in the mortality salience

condition, especially in reports of speeding. Rosenbloom hypothesized that mortality salience activated those high in sensation seeking to respond in an extreme mode, which may act as an anxiety buffer.

Thus far, results consistently have indicated that high sensation seekers may perceive less risk in given situations than do low sensation seekers, which may lead them to drive in more risky fashions. Subsequent to the study just cited, Rosenbloom (2003a) looked at risk in more general terms, citing Zuckerman's (1994) hypothesis that high sensation seekers value the rewards of a risky activity more than low sensation seekers do (i.e., the sensation of arousal outweighs the probability of a negative outcome). To study this question, 75 students in Israel (55 males, 20 females; aged 20 to 27; mean age = 22.6) took the SSS-V and an Inventory of Risk Evaluation apparently developed for this study. Two weeks later they took the Inventory of Risk Taking developed for the prior study. Consistent with past studies, a significant negative correlation was found between sensation seeking and risk evaluation, such that high sensation seekers estimated risk to be lower than did low sensation seekers. In addition, Rosenbloom found a significant positive correlation between sensation seeking and risk taking, in that high sensation seekers were also willing to take more risks than were low sensation seekers. What was new in this study was the finding of a significant interaction between sensation seeking and risk taking and risk evaluation: High sensation seekers were higher in risk taking than in risk evaluation, and low sensation seekers were higher in risk evaluation than in risk taking.

Rosenbloom (2003a) hypothesized that the more high sensation seekers evaluate an activity as dangerous, the more they will be ready to engage in it due to the sense of pleasure it provides, whereas the more low sensation seekers evaluate an activity as dangerous, the more they will tend to avoid it. High sensation seekers do appear to evaluate risks differently than do low sensation seekers, but in this study they still differentiated between more and less dangerous situations as well as did low sensation seekers. Rosenbloom hypothesized that the key to understanding the underestimation of risks and attraction to danger in high sensation seekers risks may be control: High sensation seekers may underestimate risk on one hand and overestimate their own skills and abilities on the other hand, which may provide a sense of control in dangerous situations.

Sports

Recent research continues to show that scores on sensation seeking are related to choice of sports activities. For example,

Jack and Ronan (1998) administered the SSS-V as well as a measure of impulsiveness to 166 New Zealanders (119 males, 47 females; aged 13 to 76; mean age = 29) who regularly participated in one of eight sports disciplines. The authors divided the sports into a high-risk category (hang gliding, mountaineering, skydiving, and automobile racing) and a low-risk category (swimming, marathon running, aerobics, and golf). Jack and Ronan replicated the common finding that younger participants had higher sensation-seeking scores. The total sensation-seeking score differentiated between high- and low-risk sport participants, with high sensation-seeking participants choosing high-risk sports and low sensation-seeking participants choosing low-risk sports. In addition, those who participated in high-risk sports scored significantly higher on all SSS subscales than did the low-risk participants.

Looking next at impulsivity, Jack and Ronan (1998) concluded that sensation seeking appeared to be integrated within a broader trait called Impulsiveness–Sensation Seeking, because those with high sensation-seeking scores also scored significantly higher on Impulsiveness and Boredom Susceptibility than did those scoring low on sensation seeking. A significant positive correlation was found between total sensation-seeking and subscale scores and impulsiveness. Interestingly, individuals in different sports groups did not differ on impulsiveness. Thus, the authors concluded that impulsiveness may be more related to sensation seeking than to participation in sports.

Gambling

At an intuitive level, an activity such as gambling, with its inherent mixture of risk and arousal, would appear to attract those high on sensation seeking. However, as McDaniel and Zuckerman (2003) noted, research has been mixed: high sensation seeking has been correlated with betting levels, behavioral intentions, gambling frequency, variety of gambling forms, attitudes about gambling, and loss of control. However, some studies have shown no link between sensation seeking and gambling frequency, related physiological arousal, and/or diagnostic inventories for pathological gambling.

McDaniel and Zuckerman (2003) conducted a telephone survey to investigate Impulsive sensation seeking and various forms of gambling with the first community-based sample as part of a larger state-funded study on the commercial viability of horse racing. A total of 790 respondents (56 percent female, 44 percent male; 68 percent White, 25 percent African American; aged 18 to 87; mean age = 42) answered a series of questions about gambling activities, including forms, frequency, and interest, as well as responding to the ImpSS.

Results indicated that only 28 percent of participants had not gambled at all in the prior year (of those who did gamble, the lottery was the most frequent form). Participants high on sensation seeking showed greater levels of gambling interest, and males showed more interest than females. Those high on sensation seeking also showed a greater range of gambling behaviors as did males in comparison with females. McDaniel and Zuckerman suggested that the increased variety in gambling behaviors made sense because it was a strategy to avoid repetition. In sum, the influence of impulsivity and/or sensation seeking appeared to vary depending on gambling form and the gender of the gambler.

Aggression

A final risky behavior worthy of note is aggression. Joireman, Anderson, and Strathman (2003) noted that prior research showed that individuals who scored high on sensation seeking reported being less affiliative, nurturant, and deferent, lower in self-control and superego functioning, more paranoid, less satisfied in relationships, and more aggressive; in sum, they had "trouble regulating themselves and relating to others" (p. 1289). They conducted a series of studies to look at the relationship between sensation seeking and aggression specifically.

In a first study, 176 undergraduate psychology students (133 women, 36 men, 7 unspecified gender; 88 percent Caucasian; median age = 18) took a questionnaire measuring their ability to consider future consequences (CFC) and the ZKPQ. Results indicated that those who were higher on their ability to consider future consequences scored lower on Aggression-Hostility and ImpSS. In addition, there was significant positive correlation between ImpSS and Aggression-Hostility. In a second study, 206 introductory psychology students (75 males, 130 female, 1 unspecified genders; 87 percent White; median age = 19) took the CFC scale as well as an aggression questionnaire and the SSS-V. The best predictor of physical aggression was Dis from the SSS-V, and the best predictor of verbal aggression was BS.

In a third study, 516 psychology undergraduates (161 men, 130 women, 45 unspecified gender; 81 percent White; median age = 19) took the same measures as were administered in the prior study, with the addition of an 8-item Impulsivity measure from the ZKPQ. Results again showed that the Dis subscale was the best predictor of physical aggression, and impulsivity also was positively related. These relationships appeared to be mediated by hostility and anger. For verbal aggression, the BS subscale was again the best predictor. Verbal aggression was associated with impulsivity and was negatively related to ES.

In a final study, 179 participants from Study 3 were asked to imagine that they were watching a movie while hooked up to heart rate and blood pressure monitors. When asked to imagine further that the experimenter acted rudely, all participants expressed aggression when there were few consequences for their actions. For those who were low in their tendency to consider future consequences, more aggression was displayed if a future (rather than an immediate) interaction was expected; for individuals high in their ability to consider future consequences, more aggression was displayed if an immediate (rather than future) interaction was expected.

Joireman et al. (2003) concluded that "sensation seeking may affect aggression via hostile cognition and anger or via attraction to aggression-eliciting situations . . . [and] different forms of aggression may reflect a need for different types of sensation seeking" (p. 1300). For example, disinhibition predicted physical aggression, whereas boredom susceptibility predicted verbal aggression.

Overall, recent studies of adults uphold prior findings that sensation seeking is positively associated with participation in risky sports, a greater variety of gambling activity, and physical and verbal aggression.

RISKY BEHAVIORS IN THE TWENTIES

Before turning from adulthood to adolescence, it is worth mentioning a study relating to risk that spans the adolescent-adult gap. Arnett (1998) noted that risky behavior continues into the twenties and sometimes increases during this decade. Yet little research on this period of life has been conducted, even though the rate of automobile accidents and fatalities are almost as high in this decade as they are in the teens, and the rate is higher if the accidents are alcohol related. In addition, Arnett noted that the rate of sexually transmitted diseases (STDs) and the rate of alcohol and illicit drug use are higher in the early twenties, although crime rates decrease. One reason for this may be that marriage is associated with a decline in substance use, and the twenties is a time when many people get married (Arnett noted that longitudinal research suggests a causal relationship). In addition, prior research has shown mixed results regarding the association between religiosity and substance use or sexual activity, Therefore, Arnett conducted a study to look at the prevalence of reckless behavior in the twenties, specifically with respect to driving, substance use, and sexual activity. In addition, he looked at the relationship between sensation seeking, religiosity, and risk behavior, and he was interested in whether sensation seeking and religiosity were possible mediators of the marriage effect for driving and substance use.

In Arnett's (1998) study, 140 participants aged 21 to 28 (94 percent White; 60 percent single; 53 percent male) took the AISS and answered a questionnaire about frequency of risk behaviors. Age was found to be correlated with religiosity, marriage, and being a parent. Older participants were less likely to report binge drinking and had fewer sexual partners. Sensation seeking was negatively related to religiosity and having children, and it was positively related to most types of reckless behavior in all three areas of risk (driving, sex, and substance use). Arnett concluded that "risk behavior is widespread among this population" (p. 315) and noted that the finding that risk behaviors were significantly correlated suggested they may constitute a "syndrome." (That is, if an individual takes risks in one area, he or she is likely to take risks in other areas.)

Compared with religiosity and marital status, sensation seeking showed the strongest and broadest relationships to risk behaviors (i.e., in magnitude or association and types of behaviors), having positive relationships with risky driving, substance use, and risky sexual behavior. Arnett (1998) hypothesized that a key motivation in the teens and twenties appears to be the pleasure of novel and intense sensations and that religiosity may both cause and reflect a lower propensity for risk behaviors. In fact, religious participation is lowest in the twenties (lower than in teens or later in life), which may contribute to a high prevalence of risk. Individuals scoring higher on sensation seeking were less likely to be married or to have children, and Arnett suggested that "risk behavior in the twenties is rooted in part in delays in taking on the role commitments of marriage and parenthood" (p. 317).

RISKY BEHAVIORS IN ADOLESCENCE

Perhaps because scores on sensation-seeking measures consistently have been found to decrease with age, adolescent populations have been studied frequently. In this section, we will consider three areas of risky behaviors that have been studied in adolescents: substance use, sexual behaviors, and attraction to violent media.

Substance Use

Although most studies included in this chapter have been conducted since 1994, we will begin this section by looking at earlier research to provide a basis for discussion. Bachman, Johnston, and O'Malley (1981) noted that, with regard to substance use, "the kinds of young people most 'at risk' tend to remain much the same, while the kinds and amounts of substances used shift somewhat from year to year" (p. 67).

However, because aggregate level data had been used previously, even though a decrease in marijuana use and increase in perceived risk of such use had been identified, no causal links were possible. Thus, Bachman, Johnston, O'Malley, and Humphrey (1988) looked at individual level data collected as part of the Monitoring the Future project (surveys of nationally representative samples of high school seniors since 1975).

Using data from 1976 to 1986, Bachman et al. (1988) analyzed measures of marijuana use, perceived risks, and personal disapproval of marijuana use. In each class of seniors, those who perceived a great risk in regular marijuana use also reported little actual marijuana use during the previous year, and use increased as perceived risk decreased. The authors concluded that "(a) a very strong association exists between perceived risk and rate of self-reported use of marijuana, and (b) that this pattern of association has not changed much, especially since 1980" (p. 104). Such findings are reminiscent of the association between perceived risk and driving behavior reported previously, but no information about the relationship between sensation seeking and substance use can be gleaned from Bachman et al.'s work.

A year later, Andrucci, Archer, Pancoast, and Gordon (1989) noted that high sensation-seeking scores were related to higher levels of drug abuse among college students as well as chronic drug abuse, and, in fact, the SSS was typically more a powerful predictor of drug use than the MMPI Psychopathic Deviate (Pd) scale or the MacAndrew Alcoholism (MAC) scale. To assess for similar relationships in adolescents, they administered the MMPI (version not identified), the SSS (form not identified), and a scale to measure drug experimentation to 123 high school students (51 male, 72 female; aged 14 to 18; 94 White). Results indicated that the most consistent and significant associations with adolescent drug use were found for sensation seeking, particularly ES, Dis, and total SSS score. The authors suggested that adolescents may be unwilling to disclose accurate information about drug use and therefore "personality measure scores, particularly SSS results, may help to provide useful probability statements concerning the individual likelihood of drug experimentation (as well as drug abuse)" (p. 264).

Simon, Stacy, Sussman, and Dent (1994) administered the ImpSS subscale of the ZKPQ-III and a questionnaire about drug use prevalence to 120 high school students (approximately half male; 44 percent Latino, 41 percent White, 15 percent other [e.g., Asian, African American]). For males, sensation seeking was correlated with alcohol use and number of drugs used. For females, sensation seeking was correlated with all drug items except marijuana. For Latino participants, sensation seeking was related to all drug use as well as number of drugs used, but for White participants, none of the drug use items were related to sensation seeking (although when results were broken down into categories of sensation seeking, some association was seen at low to moderate levels of drug use). The authors hypothesized that, because drug use was higher in White participants overall, "among the White students, drug use does not provide the high sensation seeker with sufficient stimulation to warrant further drug use" (p. 671). These results certainly indicate that cultural factors should be taken into account when studying drug use and sensation seeking.

Wood and Cochran (1995) were interested in the relationship between sensation seeking and substance use in adolescents. However, unlike other authors, they operationalized sensation seeking as impulsivity (using the CPI impulsivity scale), thrill seeking (using their own scale with 6 items), and desire for immediate gratification (using a 4-item scale). These items were administered to nearly 1,600 male and female high school students (aged 15 to 21). Results indicated that for each substance use category (using tobacco, drinking alcohol, getting drunk, smoking marijuana/hashish, using hard drugs), thrill-seeking and impulsivity variables significantly increased the probability of use. Those with high scores on immediate gratification were more likely to engage in drug use than in alcohol use. The authors concluded that for adolescents, two intrinsic rewards serve as reinforcements that promote further substance use: risky, law-breaking behavior ("getting away with it") and pleasurable physiological effects. This suggestion appears to go against previous findings that high sensation seekers perceive risk as lower than do low sensation seekers (however, an atypical measure of sensation seeking was used, which might have impacted results). The authors also suggested that substance use was mediated by personality factors such as impulsivity, attraction to thrill seeking, and demand for immediate gratification.

Curran, White, and Hansell (2000) followed 1,201 New Jersey adolescents (89 percent White; no other demographic information included) longitudinally. Because studies such as Andrucci et al.'s (1989) indicated increased levels of substance use associated with higher levels of Dis and ES, Curran et al. administered those SSS subscales. In cross-sectional and longitudinal tests for a proposed interaction between sensation seeking and peer influences on marijuana use, they found no effect in longitudinal analyses and in only one of two cross-sectional analyses. Individuals high on ES were more likely to be problem marijuana users. In one cross-sectional analysis, Dis interacted with peer use, but it accounted for only 0.2 percent of explanatory variance in a hierarchical regression. In sum, results did not indicate a large relationship between sensation seeking and drug use. Instead, peer drug use and depression best predicted problem "hard" drug use, whereas motivations to use with others and disinhibition best predicted problem marijuana use.

It is not clear why Curran et al. (2000) found results counter to so many prior studies. Noting that Curran et al. emphasized regular drug use rather than experimentation, Slater (2003b) attempted to replicate their work with modified scales. Slater hypothesized that peer pressure might be an important factor and might influence experimentation differently than use. Slater also looked at perceptions of risk. A total of 3,127 middle and junior high school students (about half male; 79 percent White, 14 percent African American, 3 percent Latino; median age = 14) in 10 small towns and rural communities in the United States completed several measures: a two-item sensation-seeking measure (asking about enjoyment of risk taking), a questionnaire about marijuana and cigarette use (measured by an item asking how often marijuana was used in the past month and the type of user the respondent considered him- or herself to be), and measures of school and family alienation, harm perception, peer pressure, and perceived peer behavior.

Slater's (2003b) results indicated two significant interactions: (a) between perceived peer pressure and sensation seeking for marijuana use and (b) between sensation seeking and perceived peer substance use for marijuana cigarettes. That is, a combination of perceived peer pressure and sensation seeking was important for use, and neither was a risk factor by itself. Interestingly, personal aspirations inconsistent with marijuana use appeared protective for high sensation seekers. Thus, this study indicates that several factors besides sensation seeking may impact substance use: peer pressure and personal aspiration. This study is one of the few that has identified a protective factor such as personal aspiration that can moderate the influence of sensation seeking.

A final study will be considered. Kahler, Read, Wood, and Palfai (2003) studied 868 college students at two northeastern universities, one rural and one urban. Sample A was 65 percent women, 87 percent White (no other ethnic group predominated), with a mean age of 18.7. Sample B was 55 percent women, 72 percent White and 16 percent Asian/Pacific Islander (no other ethnic group predominated), with a mean age of 18.8. All participants took the ZKPQ. Results indicated that male gender, White ethnicity, and greater impulsive sensation seeking were associated with greater alcohol use. In fact, White ethnicity and ImpSS accounted for a third of the variance.

Because these factors are traits that precede entry to college and that are not shaped by the environment, Kahler et al. (2003) assumed that these characteristics influenced the environments chosen by the students. That is, the students selected environments in which alcohol use is encouraged.

However, it was unclear whether the desire to drink more alcohol influenced the choice of environments or whether the students drank more once they found themselves in certain environments. The authors suggested it is possible that individuals predisposed to heavy alcohol use may be socially reinforced for drinking by the activities and peers they choose.

Looking at these studies overall, several trends emerge. First, except in one study in which no relationship emerged, sensation seeking is consistently related with adolescent substance use, and adolescents and young adults who score high on sensation seeking may perceive less risk than do individuals scoring low on sensation seeking. However, this relationship may be impacted by factors such as culture and/or ethnicity, peer pressure and social environment, and personal aspiration.

Violent Media

An area of risk that has not been studied in as much depth as substance use is violent media. In an early study measuring need for activation using a novelty experiencing scale, Donohew, Palmgreen, and Duncan (1980) found that individuals with a high need for activation responded differently to messages than did individuals with a low need for activation. They concluded that messages that elicited arousal and affective response were more attractive to those with a high need for activation, and messages that were less arousing than desired produced negative affect.

Such results are suggestive of a relationship between arousing messages and sensation seeking. Looking more specifically at sensation seeking, Krcmar and Greene (1999) sampled 381 junior and senior high school students (aged 11 to 18) and 343 college students (aged 18 to 25). Of the total sample, 57 percent were women, 89 percent were White, and 8 percent were African American. Participants took the SSS-V and a measure of television viewing habits as well as indicating participation in risk behaviors. Results were somewhat complex. For males (and for females to a lesser extent), higher scores on the Dis subscale were related to more exposure to contact sports and realistic crime shows, whereas higher scores on ES (and TAS to a lesser extent) were associated with less exposure to violent drama, contact sports, and real-crime shows. Looking more closely, two patterns seemed to emerge. The first, which the authors described as *behavioral disinhibition,* indicated all four sensation-seeking subscales (especially Dis) were related to actual risk behaviors (drinking and criminal activities) but not to exposure to television violence. In the second category, labeled *high risk seeking,* ES and BS were related positively to serious risk-taking activities (drug use and drinking and driving) and negatively to contact sports, real-crime shows, and drinking.

In sum, it did not appear that high sensation seekers watched more violent television but rather that "television violence does not generally appear to compensate for exposure to real risk-taking" (Krcmar and Greene, 1999, p. 39).

In contrast, Aluja-Fabregat (2000) found stronger relationships between sensation seeking and exposure to violent media. Several personality measures, including the junior version of the Sensation Seeking Scale (SSS/J), were completed by 470 eighth-grade students (mean age = 13.6) along with a questionnaire asking about viewing of and interest in violent films. The Dis and TAS subscales of the SSS/J were associated with viewing of violent films in boys as were ES and TAS subscales in girls. Boys who watched more violent films are rated by their teachers as being more aggressive and excitable.

Slater (2003a) suggested that Krcmar and Greene's (1999) failure to find a relationship between ES and violent-media use may reflect the fact that "experience seeking is a dimension that measures interest in novel situations and experiences—and violent television is hardly novel" (p. 106). In addition, prior results may have been confounded with gender, given that males are typically higher in sensation seeking. Using the same sample of 3,127 eighth graders described previously for a substance-use study, Slater also administered items measuring alienation from peers, school, and family as well as aggressiveness and anger. Violent-media use was measured as frequency of viewing action movies or videos, use of computer or video games that included weapons, and visiting Internet sites promoting violence. He found that sensation seeking predicted the use of violent-media content, after controlling for gender. In fact, sensation seeking accounted for nearly 12 percent of variance after gender and Internet use were controlled. Measures of aggression were also predictive when sensation seeking and gender were controlled. Finally, alienation predicted some action or violent-film viewing as well. Sensation seeking was more predictive of a composite media measure (including all media types), which Slater suggested supported the interpretation that high sensation seekers were obtaining vicarious excitement and arousal. However, considering Krcmar and Greene's (1999) results, it is possible that as media become more violent, such forms become less novel, and, therefore, youths high in sensation seeking may look for a greater variety of stimulating media.

Other Risk-Taking Behaviors

Prior authors have indicated associations between early childhood personality characteristics and adolescent participation in risky behaviors. For example, Block, Block, and Keyes (1988) reported that undercontrol in childhood and adolescence was linked to adolescent substance use, and Caspi,

Henry, McGee, Moffitt, and Silva (1995) found that lack of control in early childhood predicted externalizing behaviors in adolescence, including drug use. Schwartz, Snidman, and Kagan (1996) reported that ratings of inhibition levels at 21 or 31 months were correlated with parent and self-reports of externalizing and aggressive behaviors at age 13.

Looking at risk proneness, Raffaelli and Crockett (2003) administered a risk proneness inventory (six self-report items assessing attraction to and tendency to engage in potentially risky behaviors) to 443 respondents (about half female; mean age = 13.3; 34 percent Black, 24 percent Hispanic, 42 percent other). The participants also reported on sexual experience. Results indicated that lower self-regulation and higher risk proneness were positively associated with sexual risk taking (defined as whether an adolescent had sex and the probability that first sex occurred before age 15) four years later. Risk proneness dropped to a trend when contextual factors were taken out (autonomous decision making and negative peer pressure). The authors concluded that poor self-regulators were more at risk. This research supports prior findings that characteristics associated with sensation seeking are associated with sexual risk taking. However, risk taking and sensation seeking are not one and the same.

Looking at more general risk measures, Rolison and Scherman (2002) were interested in relationships between risk involvement, locus of control, and sensation seeking (SSS-V). For 171 undergraduates (74 percent female, 26 percent male; aged 18 to 21; mean age = 19.2; 72 percent White), significant predictors of risk frequency were total SSS score and total perceived-risk score (accounting for 41 percent of variance). In terms of subscales, Dis and total perceived-risk scores were significant predictors of risk frequency (accounting for 50 percent of variance). Locus of control did not correlate with anything. The authors stated that sensation seeking was a more significant predictor than perceived risk. Perceived risk was negatively correlated with risk involvement, and perceived risks affected risk taking more than perceived benefits.

In sum, sensation seeking in adolescents mirrors findings in adults: High perceived risk is associated with decreased involvement in risky behaviors, and perceived risk is lower for youths high in sensation seeking.

FEARLESSNESS

Before leaving the topic of risky behaviors, let us briefly look at the relationship between fearlessness, anxiety, and sensation seeking. Much of the work on fearlessness has been conducted in relation to psychopathy and antisocial personality disorder (e.g., Lykken, 1995; Raine, 1996) rather than sensation seeking. Some research has suggested that fearlessness may influence vocational choice in adults. For example, Fannin and Dabbs (2003) surveyed 195 urban male firefighters (mean age = 37.9 years) and found that preference for firefighting over emergency-medical-service work was predicted in part by fearlessness.

In children, research has indicated that fearlessness (measured by approach toward a cabinet from which gorilla sounds were emanating and time spent near mother) at age one-and-a-half and two years was associated with conduct problems at age eight (Shaw, Gilliom, Ingoldsby, & Nagin, 2003). In a study by van Goozen, Snoek, Matthys, van Rossum, and van Engeland (2004), reduced startle responses were correlated with disruptive behavior disorder. The authors interpreted this as supporting the theory that fearlessness is important in explaining individual differences in antisocial behavior. In one of the few studies to consider both need for stimulation and fearlessness, Raine, Reynolds, Venables, Mednick, and Farrington (1998) looked at the relationship between fearlessness, stimulation seeking, and body size at age 3 and later aggressive and nonaggressive forms of antisocial behavior at age 11. Results indicated that childhood analogs of stimulation seeking and fearlessness at age 3 characterized children who were aggressive at age 11.

Results such as these, along with studies indicating that sensation seeking is correlated with behavior problems in adolescence, suggest that future investigations of fearlessness and its relation to sensation seeking would be beneficial. In fact, it is somewhat surprising that such research has not been conducted. Perhaps this is because prior research does not suggest that high sensation seeking is necessarily correlated with reduced levels of anxiety or fear. Studies cited previously suggest that high sensation seekers perceive less risk in situations than do low sensation seekers, which may lead them to behave in a more risky fashion. However, if their riskier behavior then raises perceived risk, high sensation seekers would not be expected to experience less anxiety overall than low sensation seekers; that is, their behavior may differ, but their overall level of anxiety may be unaffected. In this regard, Zuckerman (1994) stated, "To the extent there is any relationship between anxiety and sensation seeking, it is a low one between thrill and adventure seeking and fear. Anxiety [and thus perhaps fearlessness] has little or nothing to do with other forms of sensation seeking" (p. 71).

STRESS, LIFE SATISFACTION, AND HUMOR

As is evident from the previous discussion, sensation seeking has been correlated with risky and sometimes potentially destructive behaviors (e.g., criminal activities, substance abuse, aggression). However, some positive correlates of sensation seeking also have been identified. For example, research has shown that sensation seeking actually can provide a buffer against some forms of stress. As noted previously, Rosenbloom (2003b) suggested that the extreme responses of high sensation seekers in life-threatening situations may in fact act as an anxiety buffer.

Smith, Ptacek, and Smoll (1992) noted that some prior researchers have found correlations between negative life events and measures of psychological distress in those low on sensation seeking but not in those who score high in sensation seeking. Noting that prior research in this area was cross-sectional and used self-report measures, these authors set about to conduct a study that did not include such limitations. A total of 425 high school students (237 boys, 188 girls) aged 13 to 18 took several inventories to measure their perception of life events, their sports experience, athletic coping skills, mental health, student injury expectancies, and sensation seeking (SSS-IV). Injuries were assessed by coaches to develop a measure of exposure-corrected time loss, and coaches also rated athletic ability and performance.

Smith et al.'s (1992) results indicated that life stress was negatively related to a measure of well being only for those scoring low on sensation seeking. Sensation-seeking scores were not related to psychological distress, injury expectancies, or athletic ability. Those with high scores on sensation seeking identified more major negative general life events than those with low sensation-seeking scores, but they did not have more injuries. The authors believed that their results were "consistent with Zuckerman's (1979) suggestion that high sensation seeking may constitute a protective factor against life stress because of the greater ability of high sensation seekers to tolerate increases in arousal elicited by negative life change" (p. 1022). Further, low sensation seekers may experience an "above-optimal level of arousal" when they are under high stress, which may constitute a contributing factor to injuries (p. 1022). Smith et al. concluded that high sensation seeking appeared to be a buffer against stress rather than a vulnerability factor. They also noted that those high on sensation seeking had better coping skills, but those skills did not appear to mediate the influence of sensation seeking on stress-injury relation.

Although sensation seeking may have a buffering effect against the negative effects of stress, it does not appear to have a role in promoting life satisfaction. Oishi, Schimmack, and Diener (2001) noted that, although there is ample evidence for a strong link between sensation seeking and preference for high-arousal physical pleasures, no research had tested whether physical pleasure was related to daily satisfaction for those high in sensation seeking. In a first study, these researchers asked 152 undergraduate students (79 male) to keep a daily diary for 52 days, in which the participants assessed daily physical pleasure on a 7-point scale and daily social-life satisfaction on a 10-point scale. Long-term life satisfaction was measured with the Satisfaction with Life Scale (SWLS; Diener, Emmons, Larsen, & Griffin, 1985), and sensation seeking was measured using part of the extraversion scale on the NEO-PI. Oishi et al. found that, on average, physical pleasure was positively associated with social-life satisfaction, but the size of the effect varied depending on level of sensation seeking such that the social life satisfaction of high sensation seeking participants was more dependent on physical pleasure than that of low sensation seeking participants. However, sensation seeking did not moderate the role of average daily physical pleasure on long-term well-being.

In a second study, Oishi et al. (2001) asked 141 undergraduates (41 male, 100 female) to keep a 23-day daily diary and to measure daily life satisfaction on a nine-point scale. In this case, the daily satisfaction of high sensation seekers was found to be more dependent on physical pleasure than that of low sensation seekers. The authors concluded that physical pleasure was a stronger indicator of daily satisfaction among high sensation seekers than among low sensation seekers. In sum, high sensation seekers appeared to experience more pleasure in their social life and to have higher levels of daily satisfaction when they had more physical pleasure.

Oishi, Schimmack, and Colcombe (2003) extended these findings by looking at the role of excitement in measures of life satisfaction. With 151 undergraduates (41 males, 110 females; no other demographics provided), they measured life satisfaction and sensation seeking as they did in the prior study as well as frequency of excitement in the prior month using five-point scales. No direct effect of sensation seeking was found on satisfaction, but results did indicate a positive association between excitement and satisfaction. In addition, the researchers found an interaction between sensation seeking and excitement such that for high sensation seekers higher excitement was related to considerably more satisfaction (a difference of 7.34 points on a 35-point scale), whereas for low sensation seekers more excitement led to only a little more satisfaction (4.30 points). In sum, although there was no effect of sensation seeking on long-term well-being, the authors concluded "chronic accessibility of excitement could be important, because sensation seekers based their life satisfaction judgments more heavily on the frequency of excitement than did non-sensation seekers" (p. 243).

Finally, a study by Lourey and McLachlan (2003) suggests that high sensation seekers perceive more humor in life than do low sensation seekers. They administered the AISS and two humor questionnaires to 186 undergraduate students in Australia (117 females, 69 males; aged 18 to 47; mean age = 22.6). Results indicated that high sensation seekers saw humor in a wider variety of situations and displayed more overt humor in these situations. Novelty was related to perceived funniness, and Intensity was related to overt expressions of humor. The authors concluded that perceiving events as funny offered novel stimulation, whereas displaying expressions of humor offered more intense stimulation.

CONCLUSION

As the previous review demonstrates, sensation seeking is a robust trait that is associated with both negative and positive behaviors and outcomes. Past research has repeatedly demonstrated the prevalence of risky behaviors in high sensation seekers. Hence, future research addressing potential protective factors that might mediate the influence of sensation seeking (such as personal aspiration) would be beneficial. Similarly, the impact of educational programs on behaviors associated with sensation seeking has not been well studied. Additional positive correlates of sensation seeking might be identified. Finally, looking at various ways in which separate components of sensation seeking might be expressed or satisfied (e.g., experience seeking might be fulfilled through intellectual or physical activities) might help to identify subcategories of sensation seekers who act in different ways, depending upon their predominant needs for stimulation.

REFERENCES

Aluja, A., García, Ó., & García, L. (2003). Relationships among extraversion, openness to experience, and sensation seeking. *Personality and Individual Differences, 35,* 671–680.

Aluja-Fabregat, A. (2000). Personality and curiosity about TV and films violence in adolescents. *Personality and Individual Differences, 29*(2), 379–392.

Andrucci, G. L., Archer, R. P., Pancoast, D. L., & Gordon, R. A. (1989). The relationship of MMPI and sensation seeking scales to adolescent drug use. *Journal of Personality Assessment, 53*(2), 253–266.

Ang, R. P., & Woo, A. (2003). Influence of sensation seeking on boys' psychosocial adjustment. *North American Journal of Psychology, 5*(1), 121–136.

Arnett, J. (1994). Sensation seeking: A new conceptualization and a new scale. *Personality and Individual Differences, 16*(2), 289–296.

Arnett, J. J. (1998). Risk behavior and family role transition during the twenties. *Journal of Youth and Adolescence, 27*(3), 301–320.

Bachman, J. G., Johnston, L. D., & O'Malley, P. M. (1981). Smoking, drinking, and drug use in American high school students: Correlates and trends, 1975–1979. *American Journal of Public Health, 71,* 69–69.

Bachman, J. G., Johnston, L. D., O'Malley, P. M., Humphrey, R. H. (1988). Explaining the recent decline in marijuana use: Differentiating the effects of perceived risks, disapproval, and general lifestyle factors. *Journal of Health and Social Behavior, 29*(1), 92–112.

Bengtsgård, K., & Bohlin, G. (2001). Social inhibition and over-friendliness: Two-year follow-up and observational validation. *Journal of Clinical Child Psychology, 30*(3), 364–375.

Berkowitz, W. R. (1967). Use of the sensation-seeking scale with Thai subjects. *Psychological Reports, 20,* 635–641.

Berlyne, D. E. (1954). A theory of human curiosity. *British Journal of Psychology, 45,* 180–191.

Berlyne, D. E. (1960). *Conflict, arousal, and curiosity.* New York: McGraw-Hill.

Block, J., Block, J. H., & Keyes, S. (1988). Longitudinally foretelling drug usage in adolescence: Early childhood personality and environmental factors. *Child Development, 59,* 336–355.

Bohlin, G., Bengtsgård, K., & Andersson, K. (2000). Social inhibition and overfriendliness as related to socioemotional functioning in 7- and 8-year-old children. *Journal of Clinical Child Psychology, 29*(3), 414–423.

Brocke, B., Beauducel, A., John, R., Debener, S., & Heilemann, H. (2000). Sensation seeking and affective disorders: Characteristics in the intensity dependence of acoustic evoked potentials. *Neuropsychobiology, 41,* 24–30.

Caspi, A., Henry, B., McGee, R. O., Moffitt, T. E., & Silva, P. A. (1995). Temperamental origins of child and adolescent behavior problems: From age three to age fifteen. *Child Development, 66,* 55–68.

Cloninger, C. R. (1987). A systematic method for clinical description and classification of personality variants. *Archives of General Psychiatry, 44,* 573–588.

Costa, P. T., Jr., & McCrae, R. R. (1992a). Four ways five factors are basic. *Personality and Individual Differences, 13,* 653–665.

Costa, P. T., Jr., & McCrae, R. R. (1992b). *NEO-PI-R: Revised NEO Personality Inventory (NEO-PI-R).* Odessa, FL: Psychological Assessment Resources.

Crozier, W. R., & Birdsey, N. (2003). Shyness, sensation seeking and birth-order position. *Personality and Individual Differences, 35,* 127–134.

Curran, G. M., White, H. R., & Hansell, S. (2000). Personality, environment, and problem drug use. *Journal of Drug Issues, 30*(2), 375–406.

Diener, E., Emmons, R. A., Larsen, R. J., & Griffin, S. (1985). The Satisfaction with Life Scale. *Journal of Personality Assessment, 49*(1), 71–75.

Donohew, L., Palmgreen, P., & Duncan, J. (1980). An activation model of information exposure. *Communication Monographs, 47,* 295–303.

Eysenck, H. J. (1967). *The biological basis of personality.* Springfield, IL: Charles C. Thomas.

Eysenck, S. B. G., & Eysenck, H. J. (1975). *Manual of the Eysenck Personality Questionnaire.* San Diego, CA: Educational and Industrial Testing Service.

Fannin, N., & Dabbs, J. M., Jr. (2003). Testosterone and the work of firefighters: Fighting fires and delivering medical care. *Journal of Research in Personality, 37*(2), 107–115.

Ferrando, P. J., & Chico, E. (2001). The construct of sensation seeking as measured by Zuckerman's SSS-V and Arnett's AISS: A structural equation model. *Personality and Individual Differences, 31,* 1121–1133.

Gilchrist, H., Povey, R., Dickinson, A., & Povey, R. (1995). The Sensation Seeking Scale and its use in a study of the characteristics of people choosing "adventure holidays." *Personality and Individual Differences, 19,* 513–516.

Gough, H. G. (1987). *Manual for the California Psychological Inventory.* Palo Alto, CA: Consulting Psychologists Press.

Haynes, C. A., Miles, J. N. V., & Clements, K. (2000). A confirmatory factor analysis of two models of sensation seeking. *Personality and Individual Differences, 29,* 823–839.

Heino, A., van der Molen, H. H., & Wilde, G. J. S. (1996). Differences in risk experience between sensation avoiders and sensation seekers. *Personality and Individual Differences, 20*(1), 71–79.

Jack, S. J., & Ronan, K. R. (1998). Sensation seeking among high- and low-risk sports participants. *Personality and Individual Differences, 25,* 1063–1083.

Joireman, J., Anderson, J., and Strathman, A. (2003). The aggression paradox: Understanding links among aggression, sensation seeking, and the consideration of future consequences. *Journal of Personality and Social Psychology, 84*(6), 1287–1302.

Jonah, B. A. (1997). Sensation seeking and risky driving: A review and synthesis of the literature. *Accident Analysis and Prevention, 29*(5), 651–665.

Jonah, B. A., Thiessen, R., & Au-Yeung, E. (2001). Sensation seeking, risky driving and behavioral adaptation. *Accident Analysis and Prevention, 33,* 679–684.

Kahler, C. W., Read, J. P., Wood, M. D., & Palfai, T. P. (2003). Social environmental selection as a mediator of gender, ethnic, and personality effects on college student drinking. *Psychology of Addictive Behaviors, 17*(3), 226–234.

Keltikangas-Järvinen, L., Kivimäki, M., & Keskivaara, P. (2003). Parental practices, self-esteem and adult temperament: 17-year follow-up study of four population-based age cohorts. *Personality and Individual Differences, 34,* 431–447.

Kohler, M. (1996). Risk-taking behavior: A cognitive approach. *Psychological Reports, 78,* 489–490.

Krcmar, M., & Greene, K. (1999). Predicting exposure to and uses of television violence. *Journal of Communication, 49*(3), 24–45.

Litman, J. A., & Spielberger, C. D. (2003). Measuring epistemic curiosity and its diversive and specific components. *Journal of Personality Assessment, 80*(1), 75–86.

Lourey, E., & McLachlan, A. (2003). Elements of sensation seeking and their relationship with two aspects of humor appreciation—Perceived funniness and overt expression. *Personality and Individual Differences, 35,* 277–287.

Lykken, D. T. (1995). *The antisocial personalities.* Hillsdale, NJ: Erlbaum.

Magaro, P., Smith, P., Cionini, L., & Velicogna, F. (1979). Sensation-seeking in Italy and the United States. *The Journal of Social Psychology, 109,* 159–165.

McDaniel, S. R., & and Zuckerman, M. (2003). The relationship of impulsive sensation seeking and gender to interest and participation in gambling activities. *Personality and Individual Differences, 35,* 1385–1400.

Michel, G., Mouren-Siméoni, M.-C., Perez-Diaz, F., Falissard, B., Carton, S., & Jouvent, R. (1999). Construction and validation of a sensation seeking scale for adolescents. *Personality and Individual Differences, 26,* 159–174.

Neely, G., Lundström, R., & Björkvist, B. (2002). Sensation seeking and subjective unpleasantness ratings of stimulus intensity. *Perceptual and Motor Skills, 95,* 706–712.

Oishi, S., Schimmack, U., & Colcombe, S. J. (2003). The contextual and systematic nature of life satisfaction judgments. *Journal of Experimental Social Psychology, 39,* 232–247.

Oishi, S., Schimmack, U., & Diener, E. (2001). Pleasures and subjective well-being. *European Journal of Personality, 15,* 153–167.

Raffaelli, M., & Crockett, L. J. (2003). Sexual risk taking in adolescence: The role of self-regulation and attraction to risk. *Developmental Psychology, 39*(6), 1036–1046.

Raine, A. (1996). Autonomic nervous system factors underlying disinhibited, antisocial, and violent behavior: Biosocial perspectives and treatment implications. In C. F. Ferris & T. Grisso (Eds.), *Understanding aggressive behavior in children—Annals of the New York Academy of Sciences* (Vol. 794, pp. 46–59). New York: New York Academy of Sciences.

Raine, A., Reynolds, C., Venables, P. H., Mednick, S. A., & Farrington, D. P. (1998). Fearlessness, stimulation-seeking, and large body size at age 3 years as early predispositions to childhood aggression at age 11 years. *Archives of General Psychiatry, 55*(8), 745–751.

Rolison, M. R., & Scherman, A. (2002). Factors influencing adolescents' decision to engage in risk-taking behavior. *Adolescence, 37*(147), 586–596.

Rosenbloom, T. (2003a). Risk evaluation and risky behavior of high and low sensation seekers. *Social Behavior and Personality, 31*(4), 375–386.

Rosenbloom, T. (2003b). Sensation seeking and risk taking in mortality salience. *Personality and Individual Differences, 35,* 1809–1819.

Roth, M. (2003). Validation of the Arnett Inventory of Sensation Seeking: Efficiency to predict the willingness towards occupational chance, and affection by social desirability. *Personality and Individual Differences, 35,* 1307–1314.

Russo, M. F., Lahey, B. B., Christ, M. A, Frick, P. J., McBurnett, K., Walker, J. L., et al. (1991). Preliminary development of a sensation seeking scale for children. *Personality and Individual Differences, 12*(5), 399–405.

Russo, M. F., Stokes, G. S., Lahey, B. B., Christ, M. A., McBurnett, K., Loeber, R., et al. (1993). A sensation seeking scale for children: Further refinement and psychometric development. *Journal of Psychopathology & Behavioral Assessment, 15*(2), 69–86.

Schroth, M. L., & McCormack, W. A. (2000). Sensation seeking and need for achievement among study-abroad students. *The Journal of Social Psychology, 140*(4), 533–535.

Schwartz, C. E., Snidman, N., & Kagan, J. (1996). Early childhood temperament as a determinant of externalizing behavior in adolescence. *Development & Psychopathology, 8*(3), 527–537.

Shaw, D. S., Gilliom, M., Ingoldsby, E. M., & Nagin, D. S. (2003). Trajectories leading to school-age conduct problems. *Developmental Psychology, 39*(2), 189–200.

Simon, T. R., Stacy, A. W., Sussman, S., & Dent, C. W. (1994). Sensation seeking and drug use among high risk Latino and Anglo adolescents. *Personality and Individual Differences, 17*(5), 665–672.

Slater, M. D. (2003a). Alienation, aggression, and sensation seeking as predictors of adolescent use of violent film, computer, and website content. *Journal of Communication, 53*(1), 105–121.

Slater, M. D. (2003b). Sensation-seeking as a moderator of the effects of peer influences, consistency with personal aspirations, and perceived harm on marijuana and cigarette use among younger adolescents. *Substance Use & Misuse, 38*(7), 865–880.

Smith, R. E., Ptacek, J. T., & Smoll, F. L. (1992). Sensation seeking, stress, and adolescent injuries: A test of stress-buffering, risk-taking, and coping skills hypotheses. *Journal of Personality and Social Psychology, 62*(6), 1016–1024.

Trimpop, R. M., Kerr, J. H., & Kirkcaldy, B. (1999). Comparing personality constructs of risk-taking behavior. *Personality and Individual Differences, 26,* 237–254.

Van Goozen, S. H. M., Snoek, H., Matthys, W., van Rossum, I., & van Engeland, H. (2004). Evidence of fearlessness in behaviorally disordered children: A study on startle reflex modulation. *Journal of Child Psychopathology and Psychiatry, 45*(4), 884–892.

Wang, W., Wu, Y.-X., Peng, Z.-G., Lu, S.-W., Yu, L., Wang, G.-P., et al. (2000). Test of sensation seeking in a Chinese sample. *Personality and Individual Differences, 28,* 169–179.

Wentworth, N., & Witryol, S. L. (2003). Curiosity, exploration, and novelty-seeking. In M. H. Bornstein, L. Davidson, C. L. M.

Keyes, & K. Moore (Eds.), *Well-being: Positive development across the life course—Crosscurrents in contemporary psychology* (pp. 281–294). Mahwah, NJ: Erlbaum.

Whiteside, S. P., & Lynam, D. R. (2001). The Five Factor Model and impulsivity: Using a structural model of personality to understand impulsivity. *Personality and Individual Differences, 30,* 669–689.

Wills, T. A., Windle, M., & Cleary, S. D. (1998). Temperament and novelty seeking in adolescent substance use: Convergence of dimensions of temperament with constructs from Cloninger's theory. *Journal of Personality and Social Psychology, 74,* 387–406.

Wood, P. B., & Cochran, J. K. (1995). Sensation-seeking and delinquent substance use: An extension of learning theory. *Journal of Drug Issues, 25*(1), 173–193.

Zuckerman, M. (1979). *Sensation seeking: Beyond the optimal level of arousal.* Hillsdale, NJ: Erlbaum.

Zuckerman, M. (1990). The psychobiology of sensation seeking. *Journal of Personality, 58*(1), 313–345.

Zuckerman, M. (1994). *Behavioral expressions and biosocial bases of sensation seeking.* New York: Cambridge University Press.

Zuckerman, M. (1996). Item revisions in the Sensation Seeking Scale Form V (SSS-V). *Personality and Individual Differences, 20*(4), 515.

Zuckerman, M. (1999). *Vulnerability to psychopathology: A biosocial model.* Washington, DC: American Psychological Association.

Zuckerman, M., & Cloninger, C. R. (1996). Relationships between Cloninger's, Zuckerman's, and Eysenck's dimensions of personality. *Personality and Individual Differences, 21*(2), 283–285.

Zuckerman, M., Kuhlman, D. M., Joireman, J., Teta, P., & Kraft, M. (1993). A comparison of three structural models for personality: The Big Three, the Big Five, and the Alternative Five. *Journal of Personality and Social Psychology, 65*(4), 757–768.

PART FOUR

SPECIAL APPLICATIONS

CHAPTER 18

Personality and the Transformational Leader

RAM ADITYA

Historically, leadership has been the subject of much awe, speculation, and research. Over the centuries, our planet has witnessed an enormous variety of political leaders. The last century also saw several thousands of studies on leadership.

In the current state of the art, through the several decades of empirical and theoretical research on the topic, a precise definition of leadership still appears elusive. Indeed, as eminent political scientist and historian James McGregor Burns (1978) noted in his opening statement, it is no doubt "puzzling that after centuries of experience with rulers as power wielders, with royal and ecclesiastical and military authority, humankind should have made such limited progress in developing propositions about *leadership* . . ." (p. 23). Despite the voluminous body of knowledge, barely a handful of theoretical postulations have been developed (Aditya, House, & Kerr, 2000; House & Aditya, 1997). Among the most influential models is that proposed by Burns (1978) in his seminal treatise on leadership. His notion of *transforming leadership* quickly found favor with organizational behavior scholars, notably Bass (1985) and Tichy and Devanna (1986), whose conceptual models of transformational leadership for small groups and organizations spawned a whole new stream of research in a field that had reached something of an intellectual plateau.

However, there is not a great deal of empirical research on personality factors in transformational leadership—and perhaps for good reason. Leadership by itself is a complex and multifaceted construct that does not lend itself readily to empirical evaluation. The multiplicity of definitions of the term *leadership* certainly reflects this state of affairs. Even the narrower term *transformational leadership* does not enjoy consensus in definition.

This chapter begins with a historical overview of the evolution of leadership theory in modern scientific inquiry, followed by a discussion of Burns's (1978) theory of transforming leadership and the role of personality in his definition of the transforming leader. Next is a discussion of Bass's (1985) and Tichy and Devanna's (1986) adaptation of Burns's

(1978) theory to small groups and organizational contexts. Their "business" version differs in some ways from Burns's theory; these aspects are highlighted along with implications for the role of personality in the business version. The work of Bass, Sashkin, Burke, and their associates in operationalizing the construct for empirical research is described in the next section along with empirical findings on the relation between personality factors and transformational leadership. In conclusion, some general comments are offered on the study of leadership in the context of social science inquiry, its implications for transformational or transforming leadership, and some directions for future research.

It is useful to note that Burns (1978) uses the term *transforming leadership,* although he also uses the term *transformational* occasionally. However, the label *transforming* is predominant in his writing. As the organizational theorists' definition of transformational leadership differs in some marked respects from Burns's construct, I use the term *transforming* to refer to Burns's theory and the term *transformational* for the other models that originated from Burns's theory.

HISTORICAL OVERVIEW OF LEADERSHIP RESEARCH

In the initial empirical and theoretical studies of leadership during the first half of the twentieth century, *leadership* and *leader* were viewed synonymously, focusing on physical characteristics of the leader, such as appearance, energy level, height, and gender and on psychological characteristics such as intelligence, achievement motivation, authoritarianism, and need for power. Although individual studies produced large effects, they failed to replicate. As a result, early reviews of the accumulated empirical literature (e.g., Gibb, 1947; Jenkins, 1947; Stogdill, 1948) served to focus attention on other variables that might be of importance. Scholars turned to leader behaviors rather than physical or psychological traits, their enthusiasm fueled by the fact that behaviors, unlike psychological traits, are directly observable. Over the next three decades, the "behavioral school" took root and thrived at three centers of research—Harvard (e.g., Bales, 1954), Ohio State University (e.g., Stogdill & Coons, 1957), and the University of Michigan (e.g., Kahn & Katz, 1953; Likert, 1961; Mann, 1965). Two categories of behaviors emerged as orthogonal dimensions of leadership from these studies: people-oriented behaviors and task-oriented behaviors. However, these dimensions failed to produce consistent results in the prediction of organizational performance, and the late 1960s saw the birth of new perspectives in leadership that sought to specify situational variables that might interact with behaviors in predicting performance outcomes (e.g., Fiedler, 1967, 1971; Fiedler & Garcia, 1987; Hersey & Blanchard, 1982; House, 1971; Vroom & Yetton, 1973). These theories of leadership came to be called *contingency theories*. Fiedler's contingency theory, for instance, proposed *situational favorableness* (later termed *situational control*) as moderating the relationship between leader behaviors and leader effectiveness. Specifically, the theory states that task-oriented leaders will be more effective in very favorable or very unfavorable situations, whereas relationship-oriented leaders will be more effective in moderately favorable situations. House's (1971) path-goal theory proposed that leadership effectiveness (specifically, follower satisfaction and follower performance) depended on the interaction of leader behaviors; several situational moderators such as task structure, role ambiguity, and job autonomy; follower characteristics such as dependence, ability, and locus of control; as well as other variables such as follower expectancies. A meta-analysis of the research on path-goal theory by Wofford and Liska (1993) revealed, among other things, that support for the theory depended on the measuring instruments used.

Vroom and Yetton's (1973) decision-process model, more conducive to practical applications than academic research, proposed a decision tree with contingency questions at each node that would lead the path toward a specific type of decision. Their decision model has received some support, primarily in field studies. Another contingency theory, called the *situational leadership theory* (Hersey & Blanchard, 1982), specified four leadership styles: telling, selling, participating, and delegating. The appropriateness of one or the other style is believed to depend on the followers' "maturity" levels, or the extent to which followers are prepared to handle the tasks of the group. Fiedler and Garcia's (1987) cognitive-resource theory focused on cognitive processes in decision making. Empirically derived, its primary finding was that the relationships of intelligence and experience with performance are moderated by a situational variable: *stress;* under condi-

tions of low stress, intelligence correlated better with performance, whereas under conditions of high stress, experience, rather than intelligence, better predicted performance.

In the 1970s, interest in leadership traits returned with renewed vigor when Stogdill (1974), updating his 1948 review, qualified his previous conclusions on the potential for unearthing universal leadership traits. Further, House and Baetz (1979) pointed out that if studies of adolescents and children were omitted from Stogdill's (1948) review, some consistent results regarding leadership traits and follower perceptions emerge. Specifically, they highlighted the role of intelligence, prosocial assertiveness, self-confidence, energy/activity, and task-relevant knowledge in determining leadership effectiveness. Achievement motivation (McClelland, 1961) also became an important constituent of leadership models. Close on its heels followed power and affiliation motives. McClelland's (1975) leader-motive profile theory proposed that effective leaders will be higher in need for power than in need for affiliation, accompanied, however, by a concern for the moral use of power. House's (1977) model of charismatic leadership incorporates the traits of self-confidence, strong need for power, conviction in the moral correctness of the leader's beliefs, propensity to take risks, and perseverance in the face of opposition as markers of leadership effectiveness. The moral component in the use of power in contributing to follower welfare has been recognized by other writers as well (e.g., Winter & Barenbaum, 1985).

Although all these models of leadership treated the follower group as a single entity, a new approach that focused on dyadic relationships between followers and leaders was the vertical dyadic linkage (VDL) model (Dansereau, Graen, & Haga, 1975), later to become known as the leader-member exchange (LMX) model through the work of Graen and his associates (e.g., Graen & Cashman, 1975; Graen, Liden, & Hoel, 1982; Graen, Scandura, & Graen, 1986; Graen & Uhl-Bien, 1995). Essentially, this model recognizes the formation of two groups within the followers based on their relationships with the leader: an *in-group* that enjoys a close relationship with the leader, is privy to information not shared with others, and has special privileges and an *out-group* that typically is involved in a task-oriented relationship with the leader and is left out of the information grapevine regarding opportunities for advancement. Another new perspective on the leadership process, the implicit leadership theory (ILT; Lord, Binning, Rush, & Thomas, 1978; Lord & Maher, 1991; Rush, Thomas, & Lord, 1977), looked at leadership in terms of the perceptions of followers. ILT draws attention to follower expectations in the emergence of leadership.

House's (1977) theory of charismatic leadership gave way to a number of theories that focused on extraordinary levels of follower performance: Burns's (1978) transforming leadership, adapted by Bass (1985) into his model of transformational leadership, and the visionary theories of Bennis and Nanus (1985), Kouzes and Posner (1987), Sashkin (1988), and others. These theories focus on top leadership and leader attributes and behaviors at an emotional or symbolic level rather than at the physical level.

Other concepts in leadership are receiving increasing attention as well. One such is *distributed leadership,* of which at least three forms are discernible in the literature: *delegated leadership* (e.g., Elderkin & Bartlett, 1993; Schlender, 1995); *coleadership,* first proposed by Bales (1954, p. 320); and *peer leadership* (e.g., Bowers & Seashore, 1966).

The leadership theories outlined previously are elaborated in Aditya et al. (2000) and addressed in greater detail in House and Aditya (1997). Here, in keeping with the focus of this chapter, I turn to a deeper analysis of the conceptual and empirical foundations of transformational leadership and the role of personality in the transformational leader.

TRANSFORMING LEADERSHIP

Leadership, noted Burns (1978, p. 2), is "one of the most observed and least understood phenomena on earth." He asserted, however, that the current intellectual muddle with regard to leadership is a fairly recent development, noting that scholars had attended to the problems of rulers and their subjects for at least two millennia. A wealth of literature on "rulership" was available well before the advent of modern science and its reductionist methods of inquiry. Thus, the concept of leadership "dissolved into small and discrete meanings" (p. 2), with one study turning up some 130 definitions of the term. In Burns's view, a serious failing in the evolution of leadership thought was the bifurcation of the literatures on leadership and followership, with little effort to integrate the two. From a broader perspective, there was nothing to distinguish the Gandhis from the Hitlers, although the distinction would be obvious intuitively to a lay person. A basic problem in our approach to understanding leadership, argues Burns, is that modern-day theorizing about leadership focuses too much on the personality "cult" and the private lives of leaders, "as though their sleeping habits, eating preferences, sexual practices, dogs, and hobbies carry messages of profound significance. . . . [Indeed,] if we know all too much about our leaders, we know far too little about *leadership*" (p. 1).

Burns's (1978) seminal work helped build a philosophical base for understanding the leadership phenomenon. At the core of his thesis was that there were basically two types of leadership: transactional leadership and transforming leadership.

In *transactional leadership,* leaders initiate an exchange of rewards for services, with both rewards and services being defined broadly to include economic, political, or psychological realms. Each party to the exchange may be equally conscious of the other's power resources and motivations. Their objectives usually are not similar enough to be enduring but are related enough to enable a successful exchange of rewards and services. The continuation of the leader-follower relationship, then, depends on the continued need for the resources provided by the other party. Transactional leadership, in Burns's incisive analysis of political systems at work, is reflected in the opinion leadership strategies followed by many political leaders to gain short-term ends. Indeed, it is seen in almost every other facet of life in the United States. It is reflected in the power play of street gang leaders in the way they hold their group together with brute force and psychological pressures; in the bureaucracy of explicitly formulated rules and procedures that often are instituted between leaders and their subjects; in the conflict-resolution tactics adopted by organizational leaders, party leaders, and government leaders; and in the "trading" that goes on among members of the free legislature as individual goals and motives are reconciled.

In contrast, transforming leaders capitalize on followers' motivations to achieve higher ends; leaders engage followers in ways that raise both to higher levels of motivation and morality. Thus, in the course of transforming leadership, followers are groomed to become leaders, and leaders move on to become moral agents. Their individual purposes, even if separate at the start, become fused along the way, with power resources being employed not to match one against the other but to support a common purpose. For all the linkage, however, leaders can still be distinguished from followers in a number of ways. Leaders, not followers, create the circumstances for communication and exchange. The leader is more skillful at deciphering followers' motives and relative power bases than they are at evaluating his. The transforming leader is always a step ahead of followers in maintaining the communication network and exchange in the group and in other ways facilitating the movement of the group toward the common goal.

The Moral Imperative

Clearly, moral concerns play a vital role in Burns's (1978) notion of leadership and, especially so, in transforming leadership. Early in his exposition of the construct, Burns distinguishes leadership from "naked power wielding" such as that of Mte'sa, king of Uganda, and Adolf Hitler: "Hitler, once he gained power and crushed all opposition, was no leader—he was a tyrant. A leader and a tyrant are polar opposites" (p. 2). These rulers displayed the kind of absolute power that turned their subjects into mere objects. Their subjects, indeed, could be better described as victims, whose power bases and motives were so completely disregarded or overridden by their rulers as to become virtually nonexistent. In turn, this form of power wielding dehumanized the rulers as well. But to Burns, there is nothing intellectually challenging about these power wielders, horrifying as it is to hear of their acts of brutality. Their stature does not even bring them within the realm of leadership. On the other hand, it is the way that some leaders weave their way through the contracts in social exchange with their followers to achieve a common purpose while elevating themselves and the followers to higher levels of being that Burns finds fascinating. Both types of rulership involve issues of power; the crux of the distinction between leaders and naked power wielders seems to lie in the role of morals and ethics. Burns traces a route from Plato's exposition of needs and wants, through the role of values in the histories created by rulers in various regions of the world, the relevance of conflict to the emergence of leadership as well as of barbarism, and the influence of Freudian superego to make the case for the inherence of morality in the leadership process. As with many other things, stages can be identified in moral development in leadership. It is common to find leaders who take a "law-and-order" approach toward the maintenance of social order for its own sake. This is the level of social contract morality (p. 42). It is at the highest stage of moral development, reflected in near-universal principles of ethics and justice involving human rights and dignity of the individual, that the opportunity for rare and creative leadership is to be found. Thus, Burns lays a foundation of morality for leadership in general and distinguishes transactional and transforming leadership in terms, among others, of stages in moral development.

Other Aspects of Transforming Leadership

Although the moral aspect is emphasized in laying the foundations of the transforming leader, Burns noted a number of other ingredients that went into creating such a leader. The transforming leader had to be, as noted previously, an intellectual leader; intellectual leadership, Burns noted, involves the use of values to achieve a conscious purpose. In this respect, intellectual leadership is transforming.

In addition, the transforming leader also had to be a reformer and a revolutionary who could understand the dynamics of conflict in the process of change. Reform leadership, however, included moral considerations by definition, and this imposes restrictions on the leader with regard to the means the leader employs to achieve moral ends. At the same time, the leadership role implies that the means employed must be successful, or the leadership status cannot be maintained.

Transforming leaders would no doubt also possess characteristics that bordered on "charisma." Burns mourned, however, the multifarious connotations of the term that detracted from its usefulness in expressing precisely his notion of this quality in transforming leadership. Burns chose the term *heroic* leadership in place of *charismatic*. He noted that heroic leadership is not simply a characteristic of the leader; it is a feature of the relationship between leader and followers. Heroic leaders, he explained, arise usually in times of extreme crises, when traditional systems of conflict resolution have broken down. Heroic leaders would be driven by ideas and ideologies that offer new paradigms of thought to resolve existing conflict and elevate the follower to new and higher levels of morality.

TRANSFORMATIONAL LEADERSHIP: BASS (1985)

Bass's (1985) work on transformational leadership has been very influential in contemporary organizational literature on leadership. However, two major differences exist between the conceptualizations of Bass (1985) and Burns (1978), as elaborated later.

The Issue of Morality

Burns's (1978) transforming leader was one who engaged with others in a manner that elevated both respectively to "higher levels of motivation and morality" (p. 19). His classification of four historical figures provides further insight into his conceptualization of leadership:

> . . . Woodrow Wilson, Mahatma Gandhi, Nikolai Lenin, and Adolf Hitler—the first two of these leaders in my sense, the third a leader whose theory of leadership had a fatal flaw, the fourth an absolute wielder of brutal power—we can compare the origins and development of four men who took different routes to power and exercised power in different ways. We will note in these cases and others that authoritarian rulers can emerge from relatively benign circumstances and democratic leaders from less benign ones. (Burns, 1978, p. 27)

In adapting the concept of transforming leadership from the political arena of Burns to the small group and organization setting, Bass (1985) virtually removes the central aspect of morality from the description of his transformational leader, choosing to focus only on motivational needs. Bass (1985) represents Burns's (1978) concept of transformational leadership thus:

> For Burns, the transformational leader also recognizes these existing needs in potential followers [referring to an aspect of transactional leadership] but tends to go further, seeking to arouse and satisfy higher needs, to engage the full person of the follower. Transformational leaders can attempt and succeed in elevating those influenced from a lower to a higher level of need according to Maslow's (1954) hierarchy of needs. (Bass, 1985, p. 14)

Conspicuous by its absence in the previous representation is the morality ingredient of Burns's (1978) transforming leader. Bass devotes a brief mention at the end of his book to the issue of morality. According to Bass (1985, p. 182): "For Burns, transformational leadership is moral if it deals with the true needs of the followers as defined by the followers based on informed choice." In fact, for Burns, morality plays an important role in leadership—its presence distinguishing leaders from naked power wielders and its level serving to delineate transactional from transformational leaders. Thus, for Burns (1978), morality is at the core of leadership, whether transactional or transforming. Immoral rulership constitutes naked power wielding:

> Leadership is a process of morality to the degree that leaders engage with followers on the basis of shared motives and values and goals—on the basis, that is, of the followers' "true" needs as well as those of leaders: psychological, economic, safety, spiritual, sexual, aesthetic, or physical. . . . Ultimately, the moral legitimacy of transformational leadership, and to a lesser degree transactional leadership, is grounded in *conscious choice among real alternatives.* Hence leadership assumes competition and conflict, and brute power denies it. (p. 36)

Without moral sense, then, there could be no transformational leadership. According to Bass (1985, pp. 182–183), Hitler was a transformational leader who was immoral. Burns's Hitler was no leader at all, simply "an absolute wielder of brutal power" (Burns, 1978, p. 36). Morality is a flavoring in Bass's (1985) model of transformational leadership; for Burns (1978), it is an essential ingredient. This move away from the moral aspect in the organizational model is understandable. Neither organizational theorists nor organizational "leaders" are comfortable with the issue of morality—practitioners probably because it is "not practical" in the world of business and academics because the ingredient would not be of much appeal to practitioners.

The issue of morality is the second of three points of distinction that Bass (1985, pp. 20–22) enumerates between his model of transformational leadership and that of Burns (1978). For Bass, unlike for Burns, Germany was "transformed" by Hitler, even if the transformation did not morally elevate the people of that nation or Hitler himself. This aspect of Bass's model is, in this author's opinion, the only real distinction between Bass's and Burns's perspectives on transformational leadership. Bass mentions two other distinguishing features that are not borne out by a close examination of Burns's (1978, p. 22) work. First, Bass (1985, p. 22) claims that his addition of the clause "expanding our portfolio of needs and wants" to "altering our need level" as a transformational strategy represents a change from Burns's position. Burns refrained from defining transforming leadership in simplistic and precise-sounding statements, preferring to elaborate on the concept through illustrations and discussion. It is not clear that Bass's statement well represents Burns's perspective; even if it does, the addition of "expanding" to "altering" does not change the meaning significantly enough to qualify as a distinguishing feature. Bass does not elaborate on this point. The other distinguishing aspect he lists is that his model, based on conceptual and empirical study, views transformational leadership as coexisting in leaders: "Most leaders do both but in different amounts" (Bass, 1985, p. 22). In contrast, "He [Burns] sees transformational leadership as the opposite end of a single continuum from transactional leadership" (Bass, 1985, p. 22). It is not clear at all that the two statements represent mutually exclusive positions, except in the case of a leader being at one or the other extreme end of the continuum or exhibiting high (or low) levels of both leadership styles. Furthermore, Burns (1978) provides ample indication that transactional and transforming leadership may be necessary for the leader to be effective: "Both forms of leadership can contribute to human purpose. If the *transactions* between leaders and followers result in realizing the individual goals of each, followers may satisfy certain wants, such as food or drink, in order to realize goals higher in the hierarchy of values, such as aesthetic needs" (Burns, 1978, p. 426). By implication, transformational leadership may in fact require transactional leadership behaviors to be effective. Moreover, to Burns, it is not as if transforming leadership is at some rare and exalted level: "So defined, leadership—especially transforming leadership—is far more pervasive, widespread—indeed, common—than we generally recognize" (Burns, 1978, p. 426). Acts of leadership are not restricted to "presidential mansions and parliamentary assemblies" but pervade all walks of life and may be found in the behaviors of parents, teachers, village elders, preachers, as well as political party officials (Burns, 1978, p. 426). To Burns, "The chief monitors of transactional leadership are *modal values,* that is, values of means—honesty, responsibility, fairness, the honoring of commitments—without which transactional leadership could not work. Transformational leadership is more concerned with *end-values,* such as liberty, justice, equality. Transforming leaders 'raise' their followers up through levels of morality, though insufficient attention to means can corrupt the ends" (Burns, 1978, p. 426).

That said, there is a more conspicuous difference between Bass's perspective and Burns's theory on transforming leadership: the role of charisma. Bass discusses charisma foremost in developing his model of transformational leadership; Burns not only touches on this aspect last in his discussion of transforming leadership but actually shies away from the term, as noted earlier, preferring the phrase heroic leadership instead. Bass asserts that organizational theorists as well as practitioners had ignored charisma but would find it relevant to transformational leadership. However, he as well as other empirical researchers have had trouble distinguishing charismatic leadership from inspirational leadership.

The Element of Charisma

Introduced into the sociological literature by Weber (1947), charisma is yet another construct that has eluded precise definition, inseparable as it appears to be from the relationship between leaders and their followers as well as from situational factors. A leader's charisma evokes in followers intense emotional and cognitive identification with the leader. This may be the result, in part, of the leader's personal characteristics, follower characteristics, and environmental conditions. However, the literature on the nature and dynamics of charisma is sparse and ambiguous. For instance, Bass (1985, p. 36) cites a study by Lodahl (1982) as support for the contention that charisma of a leader depends on the personality of followers as well as that of leaders. In this study, Lodahl (1982) is reported as finding that the "Moonies" (followers of the charismatic leader Rev. Sun Myung Moon) revealed higher levels of "feelings of helplessness, cynicism, distrust of political action, and less confidence in their own sexual identity, their own values and in the future" than members of a control group (Bass, 1985, p. 36). From this report, however, it cannot be conclusively determined whether these characteristics of the followers gave rise to leader charisma or whether these were the result of indoctrination by the leader by virtue of his charismatic personage. The latter explanation in fact seems more plausible.

Downton (1973), clarifying the concept of charisma, noted that since Weber's introduction of the term in his theoretical exploration of authority, the term has become notorious for

its misuse in leadership theory. In Weber's (1947) formulation, charisma was not just in the person of the leader but resided in the relationship between the leader and the led. That relationship is characterized by a psychological readiness on the part of the follower to obey the leader, a devotion born of distress and enthusiasm. Yet, the charismatic leader's authority does not stem from the follower's consent or what French and Raven (1959) would call legitimate power but from the personal magnetism of the leader. Much of the confusion arising from Weber's (1947) discussion of charisma, in Downton's (1973) view, has to do with the integration of the social and psychological dimensions of charisma. In particular, and of prime relevance to the context of transformational leadership, Downton (1973, pp. 235–236) draws a distinction between charismatic and inspirational leadership in the literature. Whereas Emmett (1958) would associate charisma with providing inspiration rather than exerting a hypnotic and mystic hold over followers, Downton (1973) prefers to retain the core of Weber's (1947) conceptualization of charisma. Downton's (1973) view is that whereas charisma implies the provision of inspiration to followers, inspirational leadership need not necessarily involve a charismatic relationship.

Barbuto (1997), like House (1977), views charismatic leaders as those who enjoy the loyalty and unquestioning obedience of their followers. He contends that transformational leadership should be distinct, conceptually and empirically, from charismatic leadership, noting that whereas transformational leaders empower followers to become problem solvers functioning independently of the leaders' supervision, charismatic leaders focus on personal loyalty and obedience to keep followers weak and dependent. However, whereas Bass (1985) embraces charisma and inspirational motivation foremost in his concept of transformational leadership, Barbuto (1997) calls for taking charisma out of the domain of transformational leadership altogether, retaining inspirational leadership in its place.

Prior to Barbuto (1997), however, Gardner (1990) had called for exclusion of charisma from the notion of leadership in general: "To the extent that the word *charisma* has any use at all in serious contemporary discussions of leadership, it should probably be confined to leader-constituent relationships in which the leader has an exceptional gift for inspirational, nonrational communication, and the followers' response is characterized by awe, reverence, devotion, or emotional dependence" (pp. 35–36).

Boal and Bryson (1988) introduced a new dimension to the discussion of charisma, drawing on House's (1977) specification of charisma in terms of its effects on followers. Taking a phenomenological-structural approach, Boal and Bryson

(1988) argued that charismatic leadership creates—or helps create, even if only temporarily—unusually powerful correspondence between feelings, behavior and cognitions, and the consequences of behavior among the followers. They also proposed that there were two forms of charismatic leadership: that which is crisis produced and that which is visionary. Butterfield (1988), however, objects to this classification of charismatic leadership, observing that there is nothing charismatic about a crisis situation in which a leader emerges just by virtue of being at the right place at the right time. To Butterfield, visionary leadership alone is worth pursuing conceptually and empirically as a part of charismatic leadership. Unlike Barbuto (1997), Butterfield (1988) does not see a need to remove charisma from the notion of transformational leadership, although he has maintained that charisma is practically impossible to measure (Butterfield, 1972, 1988).

Graham (1988), on the other hand, takes issue with the inclusion of charisma in the measurement of transformational leadership. He observes that transformational leadership should be about fostering follower autonomy rather than the follower dependence that House's (1977) definition of charisma suggests.

In Bass's view, a good part of charisma may lie in the personality of the leader. Bass (1985, p. 45) notes that a universal trait of the charismatic leader is self-confidence and self-esteem. Self-esteem may be helpful in resolving conflicts without defensiveness and in maintaining the trust and loyalty of followers (Hill, 1976; reported in Bass, 1985, p. 45).

In addition to self-confidence and self-esteem, according to Bass (1985), charismatic leaders also are possessed of a strong sense of self-determination. In psychological terms, this may be described as a highly internal locus of control. House (1977) offered seven propositions about the role of charisma in the leadership of complex organizations. Charismatic leaders display, besides self-confidence, qualities of dominance; have a need for influence; have a deep conviction in the moral correctness of their paths; create the impressions of competence and successful outcomes; are more likely to articulate ideological goals; have high expectations of, and confidence in, their followers; and arouse motives in the followers that are relevant to their ideological goals.

However, in Bass's view, charisma by itself is not sufficient for transformational leadership; individual consideration and intellectual stimulation are other factors critical to the transformation process (Bass 1985, pp. 51–52). His arguments here are somewhat unclear. On the one hand, he states, "Even when successful as leaders, charismatics may fail to have a transforming or inspirational influence on followers" (p. 51). Elsewhere, on the other hand, he defines

inspirational leadership as being a "subfactor within charismatic leadership behavior" (p. 62).

TICHY AND DEVANNA'S (1986) THREE-ACT DRAMA

Drawing upon Burns's notion of transformation in leadership as well as Zaleznik's (1977) distinction between managers and leaders, Tichy and Devanna (1986) redefined leadership in the organizational context. Following Bass (1985), they called their brand of leadership as "transformational" leadership. If Bass barely touched on the issue of morality in his tome, Tichy and Devanna (1986) saw fit to ignore the role of morality altogether in theirs. To them, transformational leadership is about change, innovation, and entrepreneurship. More importantly, they believe that transformational leadership is a systematic and purposeful behavioral process that can be learned. Of course, this would seem to imply that personality has little to do with transformational leadership. This perspective is certainly consistent with the early empirical research on leadership "traits" reviewed by Stogdill (1948) but not with the more recent return to emphasis on personal characteristics in the neocharismatic tradition (Aditya et al., 2000; House & Aditya, 1997). Tichy and Devanna (1986, p. 29) characterize transformational leadership as a three-act drama. Act I is recognizing the need for revitalization. The notion of revitalization at first glance appears like a contingency that is appropriate only when things are not going well, but one may argue that in today's rapidly changing environment, maintaining status quo is by itself a prescription for failure. The need for revitalization, therefore, is created today as a matter of course. The need for adaptation to a changing environment has become a given. The task of the transformational leader in Act I is not simply recognizing the need for change but adopting a set of behaviors that will make the organization's internal environment less resistant to impending change. A key strategy is to make central players in the organization dissatisfied with the status quo (Tichy & Devanna, 1986, p. 30).

Act II of the drama is creating a vision and mobilizing commitment to that vision. Unless a critical proportion of employees in the organization buy into that vision created by the leader, the chances of bringing about change are minimal. Tichy and Devanna (1986, p. 30) note that, "Each leader must develop a vision and communicate it in a way that is congruent with the leader's philosophy and style." Implied in this view is the idea that the personality of the leader is less important than the act of creating a vision and communicating it appropriately. Although this is a "politically correct" perspective in today's context of nondiscrimination and human rights, it underplays the role of personality in the creation of vision and in the ability to communicate the vision to followers. Are visionaries born or made? It is a challenging question, to say the least. A second, equally important question is: Can all great visionaries be or become great communicators as well?

Act III of the transformational leadership drama, in Tichy and Devanna's drama, is institutionalizing change. This is the operational aspect of the "organizational transformation" that is central to the concept of transformational leadership. This act begins with the systematic and carefully planned destruction of old ways of working and creating a sustainable new paradigm that not only will engage and stimulate organizational members to adopt their redefined roles but also will make them feel comfortable and secure doing it. What does this entail for the transformational leader's personality? What kind of personality can deal with the psychological challenges created by the organization for individual employees? This would be a central issue for empirical study.

EMPIRICAL STUDIES OF PERSONALITY AND TRANSFORMATIONAL LEADERSHIP

Burns's (1978) concept of transforming leadership, although it laid the foundation for academics in other disciplines to create their own brand of the construct, did not give rise to empirical research. On the other hand, researchers in management and organizational behavior, organizational psychology, and educational psychology have picked up on the notion of transformational leadership—transforming leadership without the base of morality as the underlying central point of distinction—for study in its application to institutional and organizational outcomes.

EXPLORING THE ROLE OF PERSONALITY IN TRANSFORMATIONAL LEADERSHIP

The foregoing discussion brought out some differences in conceptualization of transforming, or transformational, leadership that have implications for the study of personality factors as predictor variables. Whereas Burns left the role of personality somewhat open to speculation, organizational theorists (e.g., Bass, 1985; Tichy & Devanna, 1986) took the concept definitively into the realm of behavior. Such a move served a desirable purpose from the perspective of organizational theorists; it brought transformational leadership within the reach of all, at least theoretically, because behav-

iors can be taught and learned. Trainability has immediate appeal in the disciplines of organizational psychology and management. Organizational research often has been guided by considerations of political correctness and marketability of concepts in the social milieu of our times.

However that may be, scholars also have examined the role of personality in transformational leadership, theoretically and empirically. Shortly after Bass's (1985) publication, Kuhnert and Lewis (1987) offered a constructive/developmental analysis of transactional and transformational leadership in an attempt to explain how personality might influence these leadership styles. In so doing, they drew from Kegan's (1982) six stages of adult development to identify two levels of transactional leadership.

According to their model, the three stages of leadership—lower-order transactional, higher-order transactional, and transformational leadership—represent Stages 2, 3, and 4, respectively, of Kegan's (1982) typology. In taking this perspective, Kuhnert and Lewis (1987) diverge conceptually from Bass's (1985) model, according to which the same leaders engage in both transactional and transformational leadership, albeit to different degrees.

According to Kuhnert and Lewis (1987), lower-order transactional leaders view their interpersonal world of relationships through the lens of their personal goals and agendas. They tend to evaluate the behavior of others in relation to whether or not these behaviors advance their personal goals. At this stage of their own adult development, lower-order transactional leaders deal with followers largely in terms of concrete contractual agreements that further their personal goals. They are incapable of participating in mutual experiences and shared perceptions needed for higher-order transactions involving exchange of obligations and interpersonal connections.

When Stage 2 leaders can reflect on their interests and goals concurrently with those of others, they move to the higher stage of interpersonal transactions, where transactional agreements move from concrete issues such as work time and extrinsic rewards toward more abstract transactions involving mutual support, interpersonal expectations, mutual obligations, and intrinsic rewards. A noteworthy aspect of the higher-order transactional leader is the dependence on mutual respect that is shared with followers. In contrast, when leaders develop to Stage 4 of Kegan's model, they are no longer dependent on a mutual sense of obligation and respect. Leaders now operate from a subjective frame of reference involving their internal values. They thus are able to transcend agendas and divided loyalties to engage followers in the pursuit of societal or organizational goals.

Speculating on the more traditionally studied personality traits with respect to his model of transformational leadership, Bass (1985, pp. 176–177) notes that whereas the transactional leader may give in to a need for affiliation, the transformational leader, to be able to "confront the present with the drive to influence its transformation," needs to be able to withstand social affiliative pressures while at the same time being bold enough to institute change. At the same time, the task of intellectually stimulating followers would require the leader to be reflective and introspective, whereas transactional leaders would find it more important to be sociable. Energy level may be another aspect of the transformational leader's personality because the process of instituting changes in the status quo requires much extra effort on the part of the leader.

Transformation implies field independence and originality in the transformational leader, Bass argues, and also the need for power and achievement (as opposed to values of conformity and equity and the need for affiliation in the transactional leader). Long-term orientation in vision and an internal rather than external locus of control also may be enhancing attributes of a transformational leader.

In an interesting examination of attachment styles (Ainsworth, Blehar, Waters, & Wall, 1978; Griffin & Bartholomew, 1994) and transformational leadership, Popper, Mayseless, and Castelnovo (2000) hypothesized that individuals who have experienced a secure attachment style (versus uncertain or avoidant attachment styles) would be more apt to engage in a transformational leadership style in later life. In the first of three studies, the investigators had six team commanders in a regular officers' course in the Israel police rate a total of 86 male cadets, 25 to 35 years old with 12 years of schooling, who were nearing the end of their training program. The cadets were rated on a Hebrew version of Bass's (1985) Multifactor Leadership Questionnaire (MLQ), validated by Abraham (1992) to measure transformational leadership, and Bartholomew's Relationship Questionnaire (RSQ; Griffin & Bartholomew, 1994), which measures attachment style using four classifications—secure, preoccupied (ambivalent), fearful, and dismissing. They obtained strong positive correlations between secure attachment style and each of the three dimensions of transformational leadership that constituted the 1985 version of the MLQ (charisma, .36; individualized consideration, .45; intellectual stimulation, .27) as well as with the overall transformational leadership score (r = .43). In addition, they also obtained negligible or strong negative correlations with the other three attachment styles.

Responding to a need to overcome correlated measures biases evident in the methodology of their first study, Popper et al. (2000) conducted a second study in which attachment style was assessed through self-reports of the participants. This study employed 85 male cadets, with a mean age of 20 years, in three platoons undergoing an officers' course in the Israeli military. A different measure of attachment style was used, which combined and adapted items from Griffin and Bartholomew's (1994) RSQ, Hazan and Shaver's (1987) questionnaire, and the Adult Attachment Scale (Collins & Read, 1990). Also included was a measure of social desirability (Marlowe & Crowne, 1964). As anticipated, attachment-style scores were found to be correlated with social desirability. After adjusting for the influence of this factor, however, the researchers obtained results similar to those of Study 1, although the correlations were somewhat lower in magnitude. Interestingly, the zero-order correlations were even smaller, supporting suspicions of a strong bias due to correlated measures in Study 1.

In their third study, the researchers obtained leadership ratings from subordinates rather than from superiors, as done in the first two studies. They used a short, updated version of the MLQ. They also used an additional 15-item measure of attachment styles created by Mikulincer, Florian, and Tolmacz (1990) and tested extensively in Israeli settings. The results of the third study substantively replicated those of the first two studies.

Atwater and Yammarino (1993) examined leader intelligence, conformity, coping style (both emotional and behavioral), decision style as measured by the Myers-Briggs Type Inventory (MBTI), and athletic experience as predictors of transformational and transactional leadership. They studied two ratings of leadership: one by the focal leaders' superiors and the other by their subordinates because there is some evidence to show that these two ratings may be different. Their study included 99 male and 8 female college squad leaders (juniors and seniors) in training at a U.S. military academy. The subordinates in the sample were 1,235 freshmen who reported to the squad leaders; the other participants were 11 military officers who supervised the squad leaders.

The focal leaders had completed the Sixteen Personality Factors Test (16PF; Cattell, Eber, & Tatsuoka, 1980) approximately two years prior to becoming squad leaders in the program and the MBTI approximately six months prior. Strength scores from the MBTI (Myers & McCaulley, 1986) were used for their regression analyses. The Constructive Thinking Inventory (CTI; Epstein & Meier, 1989) was used to assess coping style. The number of varsity sports played by the leaders, averaged across semesters, constituted the measure of athletic experience. A modified form of Bass and Avolio's (1990) MLQ, called the Multifactor Officer Questionnaire (Yammarino & Bass, 1990), was created for military applications and adapted for administration to superiors and subordinates.

Noteworthy in their findings is that ratings of transformational and transactional leadership behaviors correlated .84 for subordinates and .70 for superiors, indicating a high level of empirical correlation between the two constructs as measured by the Multifactor Officer Questionnaire. That said, personal attributes of leaders were found to account for 28 percent of the variance in subordinate ratings of transformational leadership (33 percent for transactional leadership). In particular, emotional coping was negatively correlated with transformational leadership ratings ($r = -.25$, $p \leq .05$, 95 percent Confidence Interval [CI] $-.06$ to $-.42$) and also the thinking/feeling dimension ($r = -.29$, $p \leq .01$, 95 percent CI $-.11$ to $-.45$). The former result indicates that those scoring high on emotional stability might in fact be seen as less of a transformational leader than those scoring low on this measure. Atwater and Yammarino (1993) explained this result with the argument that the emotional coping measure contains an element of sensitivity: emotional stability presumes a certain degree of insensitivity to others' opinions. Understandably, then, subordinate ratings of transformational leadership may be reflective of their insensitivity aspect of the leaders' personality. The results for the thinking/feeling dimension of the MBTI suggest that, contrary to previous findings that leaders are predominantly "thinking" types (e.g., Osborn & Osborn, 1986), they may be perceived as less of a leader by their subordinates than are those who are "feeling" types.

Results also indicated that intelligence was positively related to subordinate perceptions of transformational leadership ($r = .20$, $p \leq .05$, 95 percent CI .01 to .38). A fourth predictor of subordinate perceptions of transformational leadership was athletic experience ($r = .30$, $p \leq .01$, 95 percent CI .12 to .46). Results were similar for subordinate perceptions of transactional leadership but differed from superior perceptions of either transformational or transactional leadership. Where superior ratings were concerned, behavioral coping, conformity, and thinking/feeling type emerged as predictors of transformational leadership, with correlations of .22 ($p \leq .05$, 95 percent CI .03 to .39), .22 ($p \leq .05$, 95 percent CI .03 to .39), and $-.30$ ($p \leq .01$, 95 percent CI $-.12$ to $-.46$), respectively. Similar results were obtained in the case of transactional leadership ratings by superiors.

In a correlational study of personality and transformational leadership in an organizational context, Dubinsky, Yammarino, and Jolson (1995) collected data from self-reports of 174 sales personnel (34 sales managers and 140 sales persons) in a multinational medical firm. All sales managers were male. Transformational leadership was measured with the MLQ (Bass & Avolio, 1989). Predictor variables examined were: emotional coping (9 items) and behavioral coping (12 items; Epstein & Meier, 1989); abstract orientation (18 items; Hendrick, 1990); innovation (13 items) and risk taking (12 items) from the Jackson Personality Inventory (Jackson, 1974); use of humor (6 items; Howell & Avolio, 1993); and experience (3 items: length of service in organization, length of service in current job, and level of education). Reliability coefficients of three of the scales (behavioral coping, abstract orientation, and risk taking) ranged from .53 to .67; that of the others ranged from .77 to .95. Unlike the Atwater and Yammarino (1993) study, this analysis focused on the four individual dimensions of transformational leadership and examined zero-order correlations as well as third-order partial correlations after controlling for the three experience variables (organizational tenure, job tenure, and education level). The four dimensions of transformational leadership examined were charismatic leadership (10 items), inspirational leadership (7 items), intellectual stimulation (10 items), and individualized consideration (10 items).

Only one personal attribute—abstract orientation—was strongly and consistently related to all of the dimensions of transformational leadership in the raw correlations (charismatic leadership, $-.36$; inspirational leadership, $-.42$; intellectual stimulation, $-.45$; and individualized consideration, $-.41$; all p's $\leq .05$). This attribute retained its relationship in the partial correlations controlling for the experience variables, with correlations of $-.34$, $-.40$, $-.38$, and $-.39$ with the four transformational leadership dimensions, respectively.

Education level had statistically detectable moderate zero-order correlations with charismatic leadership ($r = -.26$, $p \leq .10$, 95 percent CI .09 to $-.55$) and inspirational leadership ($r = -.24$, $p \leq .10$, 95 percent CI .11 to $-.53$), a somewhat smaller correlation with individualized consideration ($r = .17$, ns., 95 percent CI $-.18$ to .48), and a small correlation with intellectual stimulation ($r = -.08$, ns., 95 percent CI .27 to $-.41$). Risk taking exhibited small to moderate correlations with the four transformational leadership dimensions (charismatic leadership, .21, ns., 95 percent CI $-.14$ to .51; inspirational leadership, .18, ns, 95 percent CI $-.17$ to .49; intellectual stimulation, .25, $p \leq .10$, 95 percent CI .10 to .54 ; and individualized consideration, .21, ns., 95 percent CI $-.14$ to .51) and maintained these relationships in the third-order analysis with values of .25 ($p \leq .10$, 95 percent CI $-.10$ to .54), .21 (ns., 95 percent CI $-.14$ to .51), .22 (ns., 95 percent CI $-.13$ to .52), and .23 (ns, 95 percent CI .12 to .53) for the four transformational leadership dimensions, respectively. Due to sample size restrictions in the number of focal leaders studied ($N = 34$), the previous relationships merit further investigation with larger samples.

A later study by Ross and Offermann (1997) examined self-confidence, dominance, and the need for change as predictors of transformational leadership using, however, an early version of the MLQ (Bass, 1985) with three dimensions—charismatic leadership, intellectual stimulation, and individualized consideration—instead of four. In addition to the variables mentioned previously, Ross and Offermann also looked at a number of attributes based on the work of Clover (1988, 1990): nurturance, pragmatism, masculine and feminine attributes, criticalness, and aggression. Focal leaders in the study were 40 (35 male and 5 female) commissioned officers at the U.S. Air Force Academy. Each leader had approximately 120 cadets in his or her squadron, and a total of 4,200 cadets provided the subordinate ratings of transformational leadership, whereas three direct subordinates closest to each leader provided data on the personal attributes, all of which were measured using the Adjective Checklist (ACL; Gough & Heilbrun, 1983). Reported coefficient alphas for the ACL scales used in this study ranged from .56 to .83. Transformational leadership was measured using 16 items (charismatic leadership, 9; individualized consideration, 4; intellectual stimulation, 3). Coefficient alphas ranged from .82 to .95 for the three scales. These items were administered as part of a routine survey given to cadets. On account of high intercorrelations among the three factor scores ($r = .91$ to .94), these scores were combined to form a single transformational leadership score. Also, scores from all subordinates of a leader were summed up to yield the transformational leadership score.

The results of this study are worth noting, especially for some findings that run counter to previously hypothesized relationships. Of the three attributes proposed as primary predictors (with positive correlations) of transformational leadership—self-confidence, dominance, and need for change—only self-confidence emerged as a significant predictor ($r = .53$, $p \leq .01$, 95 percent CI .26 to .72). The other two had small effects (dominance, .16, ns., 95 percent CI $-.16$ to .45; need for change, .17, ns., 95 percent CI $-.15$ to .46). Dominance became a sizable predictor if self-confidence was entered first in the regression analysis but not otherwise. Need for change remained insignificant, regardless of order of entry.[1]

The addition of variables from Clover's (1988) set—masculine and feminine attributes, pragmatism, nurturance, criticalness, and aggression—boosted the explanatory power of their regression model from .41 to .67 of the variance explained in the dependent variable. Self-confidence, criticalness, and aggression emerged as significant individual predictors. In the raw correlations, however, nurturance had the highest correlation with transformational leadership scores (r

$= .69$, $p \leq .01$, 95 percent CI .48 to .82) followed by pragmatism ($r = .62$, $p \leq .01$, 95 percent CI .38 to .78), self-confidence ($r = .53$, $p \leq .01$, 95 percent CI .26 to .72), feminine attributes ($r = .52$, $p \leq .01$, 95 percent CI .25 to .72), aggression ($r = -.50$, $p \leq .01$, 95 percent CI $-.22$ to $-.70$), and criticalness ($r = -.48$, $p \leq .01$, 95 percent CI $-.20$ to $-.69$).

Need for change lends itself at an intuitive level as a predictor of transformational leadership because such leaders are theorized to be change agents (Gough & Heilbrun, 1983). The results of the Ross and Offermann (1997) study strongly run counter to this expectation. They also run counter to the expectations of Bass (1985), House (1977), and others of dominance as a characteristic of charisma and thus being predictive of transformational leadership. It would appear that feminine attributes and a nurturing role go much farther in follower perceptions of a transformational leader than do dominance or need for change. Aggression was actually strongly but negatively correlated with perceptions of transformational leadership, all the more interesting because the focal leaders in the sample were predominantly male. Not clear from Ross and Offermann's report, however, is the proportion of men and women among the raters in the sample. Gender effects in leadership as well as leader perceptions merit further study.

In a much larger investigation involving 253 senior executives of a highly diversified global corporation and their direct subordinates, Church and Waclawski (1998) examined individual differences in problem-solving styles and decision-making styles in relation to transformational leadership. Unlike other studies reported here, this study used a self-other feedback instrument called the Leadership Assessment Inventory (LAI; Burke, 1991) to assess transformational leadership. The LAI evaluated leadership by measuring the extent to which a leader is oriented toward the long term rather than the short term. Based on the transformational-transactional framework, the LAI measured five elements of Burke's (1979, 1986, 1990) model of leadership: establishing purpose, inspiring followers, determining direction, influencing followers, and making things happen. Problem-solving styles were assessed using the Kirton Adaptation Inventory (KAI; Kirton, 1991, 1992), a 33-item instrument that generated a score ranging from 32 to 160. High scorers were labeled as *innovators*: risk takers who may bend or break rules in trying out new solutions and generating new ideas. By contrast, low scorers were *adapters*: individuals who stick to tried and tested methods in finding safe solutions to problems. Finally, decision styles were assessed with the MBTI, described earlier.

Church and Waclawski (1998) obtained leadership scores both from leaders and from subordinates' ratings of the leaders. Consistent with prior findings, self-reports of leaders produced a stronger profile of transformational leadership than that indicated by subordinate ratings, with correlations between the two ratings ranging from .09 to .36 for the five individual elements in the LAI.

KAI scores yielded moderate to strong zero-order correlations with all LAI elements of leadership as rated by subordinates, with the exception of inspiring followers (determining direction, .44, $p \leq$ .001, 95 percent CI .33 to .53; influencing followers, .31, $p \leq$ .001, 95 percent CI .19 to .42; establishing purpose, .27, $p \leq$ .001, 95 percent CI .15 to .38; making things happen, .23, $p \leq$ .01, 95 percent CI .11 to .34). The correlation with inspiring followers was small ($r =$ .10, ns., 95 percent CI $-$.02 to .22). The correlation of KAI scores with transformational leadership overall (LAI total) scores was .42 ($p \leq$ .001, 95 percent CI .31 to .52). Additionally, the LAI total score was correlated .23 ($p \leq$ .001, 95 percent CI .11 to .34) with the sensing dimension of the MBTI.

In one study to examine predictors of consolidated business unit performance, Howell and Avolio (1993) obtained data that showed positive, small to moderate correlations of locus of control with the three dimensions of transformational leadership measured by Bass and Avolio's (1990) MLQ-Form 10. This instrument has three scales to measure, respectively, charisma (7 items), intellectual stimulation (6 items), and individualized consideration (6 items). Locus of control was measured with 13 items from Rotter's (1966) scale, selected on the basis of high loadings on the political control factor, following reports of multidimensionality in the original 24-item scale (Gurin, Gurin, & Morrison, 1978; Mirels, 1970). Participants were 78 managers from the top four levels of a large Canadian financial institution, aged 29 to 64. The vast majority were male, and all were White.

In Howell and Avolio's (1993) analysis, locus of control correlated .19 (ns., 95 percent CI $-$.03 to .40) with charisma, .25 ($p \leq$ .05, 95 percent CI .03 to .45) with intellectual stimulation, and .33 ($p \leq$ .01, 95 percent CI .12 to .51) with individualized consideration. They also had measured support for innovation as a moderator variable in the relationship between leadership style and unit performance. In a partial least squares (PLS) analysis, locus of control was found to explain 3, 6, and 11 percent of the variance in charisma, intellectual stimulation, and individualized consideration, respectively, without the moderator variable. At high levels of the moderator (that is, support for innovation), the variance explained dropped to 0, 2, and 0 percent, respectively, for the three dimensions; at low levels of support for innovation, the variance explained went up to 25, 0, and 24 percent for the three

dimensions, respectively. Thus, the relationship between locus of control and intellectual stimulation appeared to be relatively unaffected by support for innovation, whereas the relationships of locus of control with charisma and individualized consideration appear to fluctuate strongly with changes in support for innovation.

In a dissertation study of elementary school principals, McGrattan (1997) examined the relation between personality types assessed by the MBTI (Myers & McCaulley, 1986) and transformational leadership as measured by the Nature of School Leadership questionnaire developed by Leithwood (1992). The MBTI is a widely used instrument for personality profiling on four bipolar dimensions based on Carl Jung's theory of personality: introvert-extrovert (I/E), sensate-intuitive (S/N), thinking-feeling (T/F), and judging-perceiving (J/P). A predominance of one or the other characteristic in each dimension gives rise to a total of 16 combinations, or personality "types." The MBTI is a commercialized instrument used more in counseling research and practice than in organizational research or selection procedures and is used by organizations and other groups for a variety of other less legally sensitive applications. The Nature of School Leadership questionnaire is based on the theoretical framework of transformational leadership adapted to the K−12 education context. Its application largely has been limited to graduate research. It consists of 50 statements about the leader, on each of which the subordinates would be required to rate his or her agreement on a 6-point scale ranging from 1 (strongly disagree) to 6 (strongly agree). The leader behaviors assessed are classified into eight classes unequally grouped into four categories: purpose, people, strengthening school culture, and building collaborative structures. Internal consistency reliabilities of all eight subscales ranged from .76 to .92. The high intercorrelations among subscale scores indicate a unidimensional scale. McGrattan (1997) found no statistically significant difference between the 16 groups of participants (categorized on the basis of their MBTI profiles) in transformational leadership scores. However, on converting the MBTI scores into continuous scores and running a multiple regression analysis, McGrattan found the thinking/feeling dimension to have a significant correlation with transformational leadership scores, with a standardized beta value of $-$.28, suggesting that transformational leaders tended to be "thinkers" rather than "feelers."

In another dissertation study of 25 secondary principals from Christian schools in the middle region of the United States, Koehler (1992) examined personality correlates of transformational leadership as measured by the Leadership Practices Inventory (LPI; Posner & Kouzes, 1988). The personality traits were assessed through the California Psychological Inventory, Revised (CPI-R; Gough, 1989). LPI scores are obtained from two sets of ratings, from LPI-Self and LPI-Other questionnaires, administered to the leader and to subordinates, respectively. The LPI measures leadership behaviors on five dimensions: (1) challenging existing procedures, (2) inspiring a shared vision, (3) enabling others to act, (4) modeling the way, and (5) encouraging the heart.

The CPI-R is a 462-item instrument consisting of 23 factor scales, each containing between 28 and 58 items. In addition to the scales, three structural measures address interpersonal orientation (external to internal), normative perspective (norm favoring to norm questioning), and realization (lower to higher levels). In summarizing the results of his analyses, Koehler (1992) concluded that principals who scored high on transformational leadership, among other things, (1) value affiliation, fellowship, social contact, and rapport with others; (2) have a broad set of interests, are not necessarily concerned with upward mobility in their organizations, are norm questioning, although they are likely to observe rules except when under pressure to conform; (3) are sincere, dependable, and trustworthy individuals with strong views and an internal orientation to self-advancement; and (4) are perceptive and attuned to the needs of others.

These conclusions confirm Burns's thesis in very general terms; however, contrary to Bass's (1985) speculations on differential personality characteristics of transformational versus transactional leaders, Koehler's study found transformational leaders value social affiliations and rapport with other and that they are not concerned with advancing their position in their organizations. Of course, these results may be explained away by the fact that (a) Koehler did not use Bass's MLQ measure and (b) the school context may not provide a valid indication regarding upward-mobility concerns in business organizations. The first of the reasons is certainly an issue of more general import in leadership and behavioral research: conclusions often depend on the measures used and, often less apparent and recognized, on the methodology adopted.

Even focusing only on Bass's (1985) model of transformational leadership 15 years after the MLQ was first introduced, Judge and Bono (2000) were led to conclude that "[d]espite the research support, it is unclear whether this theory is a trait or behavioral theory of leadership." They set out to answer the question using the Revised NEO Personality Inventory (NEO-PI-R; Costa & McCrae, 1992) and the MLQ-Form 5X. This version of the MLQ replaced the MLQ-Form 5R (for a review of the MLQ, see Aditya, 2003).

The participants in their study were current or past attendees of community leadership programs throughout the U.S. Midwest that were affiliated with the National Association

for Community Leadership (listwise N = 169). Surveys containing both MLQ and NEO-PI-R were mailed to the leaders. In addition, MLQ data were obtained from the leaders' supervisors and subordinates whenever possible. From their analyses, consistent with Koehler's findings noted previously, Agreeableness emerged as the strongest personality predictor of transformational leadership (r = .27, p ≤ .01, 95 percent CI .12 to .40) overall and with each of the individual dimensions as well (idealized influence, .28, 95 percent CI .13 to .41; inspirational motivation, .21, 95 percent CI .06 to .35; intellectual stimulation, .24, 95 percent CI .09 to .38; individualized consideration, .23, 95 percent CI .08 to .37; all p's ≤ .05, two tailed).

Extraversion emerged as the next strongest predictor of transformational leadership overall (r = .22, p ≤ .01, 95 percent CI .07 to .36), with positive small-to-moderate correlations with each of the individual dimensions (idealized influence, .22, p ≤ .05, 95 percent CI .07 to .36; inspirational motivation, .24, p ≤ 05, 95 percent CI .09 to .38; intellectual stimulation, .14, p ≤ .01, 95 percent CI −.01 to .28; and individualized consideration, .19, p ≤ .05, 95 percent CI .04 to .33). Openness to Experience had a comparable association with overall transformational leadership scores (r = .20, p ≤ .01, 95 percent CI .05 to .34) and with the individual dimensions (idealized influence, .18, p ≤ .05, 95 percent CI .03 to .32; inspirational motivation, .22, p ≤ .05, 95 percent CI .07 to .36; intellectual stimulation, .10, ns., 95 percent CI −.05 to .25; individualized consideration, .21, p ≤ .05, 95 percent CI .06 to .35). The other two personality factors—Neuroticism and Conscientiousness—did not come across as significant predictors.

Sampling 418 individuals in business courses across the United States, Pillai, Williams, Lowe, and Jung (2003) examined voter perceptions of leader personality and leadership potential of presidential candidates running for the U.S. presidency. They collected data on voter perceptions on three personality variables—proactivity, need for achievement, and emotional empathy—along with other variables, two weeks prior to the 2000 U.S. presidential election as well as data on actual voting behavior two weeks after the election. Following Bateman and Crant (1993, p. 103), they defined proactivity as a dispositional construct that addresses the degree to which the rater takes action to influence his or her environment. Proactivity was assessed by means of a 17-item scale developed by Latack (1986). Need for achievement (McClelland, 1985) has been proposed as a characteristic of transformational leaders (Bass, 1985). A four-item measure addressing opportunity to satisfy the need for achievement (Medcof & Wegener, 1992) was used in this study. Emotional empathy, proposed by several authors as an influential variable in leadership, was evaluated using a 10-item subscale of the original 30-item measure developed by Mayer, Caruso, and Salovey (1999). The short version addresses empathic suffering, positive sharing, and feeling for others. Charisma[2] and transformational leadership were treated as separate constructs and measured with different scales. Charisma was assessed with the 8-item charisma scale from a version of the MLQ (Bass & Avolio, 1991). Transformational leadership was measured with a 23-item instrument developed by Podsakoff, MacKenzie, Moorman, and Fetter (1990). This measure addresses six leadership behaviors—articulating a vision, proving an appropriate model, fostering the acceptance of group goals, high performance expectations, individualized support, and intellectual stimulation.

Pillai et al. (2003) ran two separate sets of analyses with the data, one coded for each of the candidates, George W. Bush and Al Gore. In both sets of analyses, the zero-order correlations indicated strong linear relationships between the three personality variables (proactivity, need for achievement, and emotional empathy) and the two leadership variables (transformational leadership and charisma), although none of the correlations for Gore were higher than those for Bush. Correlations ranged from .37 (95 percent CI .28 to .45) to .60 (95 percent CI .53 to .66) for Gore, and between .54 (95 percent CI .47 to .60) and .66 (95 percent CI .60 to .71) for Bush (all p's ≤ .01).

It is interesting to note from their reported results that a number of correlations, representing relationships other than those noted previously, also were less for Gore than for Bush. For example, perceptions of transformational leadership correlated .49 (95 percent CI .41 to .56) with intent to vote and .40 (95 percent CI .31 to .49) with actual voting behavior, respectively, for Bush; the corresponding correlations for Gore were .38 (95 percent CI .29 to .46) and .20 (95 percent CI .10 to .30). Likewise, perceived charisma correlated .49 (95 percent CI .41 to .56) and .37 (95 percent CI .27 to .46) with intent to vote and actual voting, respectively, for Bush; the corresponding values for Gore were .37 (95 percent CI .28 to .45) and .21 (95 percent CI .11 to .31). Beyond a passing comment with regard to empathy and leadership perceptions, Pillai et al. (2003) do not offer an explanation for this general trend in their results. Although we may expect mean scores on the variables to be lower for Gore than for Bush (assuming the veracity of election outcomes as a reflection of voter perceptions), there is no real reason to expect that the relationship between variables (with the exception, perhaps, of the correlation between intent and actual voting behavior, under the assumption stated earlier) would be any different across candidates unless there is a moderator variable at work.

A Note on Construct Operationalization

Langford (2003) has reported a series of studies comparing the predictive validity of Shafer's (1999) 30-bipolar-item measure of the Big Five personality markers to an abridged 15-item measure, a 5-item scale clustering all of the 60 adjectives in the original 30-item measure, and a 5-item bipolar global measure. Langford's sample consisted of 122 managers and 233 subordinates from a wide range of organizations. Among the correlations he examined were those with the six elements of Podsakoff's Transformational Leadership Behavior Inventory (TLI; Podsakoff et al., 1990) mentioned earlier. Although the different versions produced similar results in general, some differences could be observed as well. Interestingly, Agreeableness had significant correlations with three of the six transformational leadership dimensions: intellectual stimulation, articulating a vision, and having high expectations of followers. The correlations of each with the Agreeableness scores from the four measurement versions (30-item, 15-item, 5-item clustered, and 5-item bipolar global, in that order) were as follows: intellectual stimulation: −.19 (95 percent CI −.06 to −.31), −.18 (95 percent CI −.05 to −.30), −.08 (95 percent CI .05 to −.21), and −.09 (95 percent CI .04 to −.21), respectively; articulating a vision: −.27 (95 percent CI −.15 to −.38), −.23 (95 percent CI −.11 to −.35), −.13 (95 percent CI 0 to −.25), and −.22 (95 percent CI −.10 to −.34), respectively; and having high expectations: −.28 (95 percent CI −.16 to −.39), −.22 (95 percent CI −.10 to −.34), −.19 (95 percent CI −.06 to −.31), and −.21 (95 percent CI −.08 to −.33), respectively. Additionally, Conscientiousness correlated with having high expectations: .28 (95 percent CI −.16 to −.39), .26 (95 percent CI −.14 to −.38), .24 (95 percent CI −.12 to −.36), and .20 (95 percent CI −.07 to −.32), respectively, with the four measurement versions.

Substantively, the results for Agreeableness run counter to Bass's (1985) expectations but are consistent with the findings of Koehler (1992) and Judge and Bono (2000) described earlier. Although the "one-minute" versions seem to be yielding surprisingly comparable results with respect to the longer versions, the correlations with intellectual stimulation highlight the fact that they may not always do so. Further, there is empirical evidence (e.g., Wofford & Liska, 1993), as mentioned earlier, that choice of measures determines results in leadership research.

Transformational Leadership and Follower Personality

Two studies provide information on the relationship between transformational leadership and follower personality. In one exploratory study, Singer and Singer (1986) sampled 87 male undergraduates at a university in New Zealand. Participants described their ideal leader using the MLQ (Bass, 1985) and also completed Edwards's (1959) Achievement, Affiliation, and Succorance subscales as well as a single-item measure of conformity. Affiliation correlated .26 (95 percent CI .05 to .45) with charisma, .19 (95 percent CI − .02 to .39) with individualized consideration, and .19 (95 percent CI − .02 to .39) with the transformational factor overall. Achievement orientation correlated .16 (95 percent CI − .05 to .36) with intellectual stimulation and .17 (95 percent CI − .04 to .37) with the transformational factor overall. The single item rating on conformity correlated .18 (95 percent CI − .03 to .38) with intellectual stimulation. Notwithstanding the fact that the situation was an imaginary one for the participants, the results offer some directions for further research.

In a more recent field study, Shin and Zhou (2003) examined the relationship between transformational leadership and follower creativity, among other variables, in Korean settings. Using Korean versions of all measures, they administered the MLQ-Form 5X-Short (Bass & Avolio, 1995) and a 13-item measure of creativity (Zhou and George, 2001), among other measures, to a sample of 333 employees and 77 supervisors from six established firms and 40 new ventures in a variety of industries. Although the employees rated their supervisors on leadership attributes and on their own values of conservation and intrinsic motivation, the supervisors rated the employees on creativity. Transformational leadership of supervisors correlated .22 (95 percent CI 0 to .42) with subordinate creativity. It is to be noted, however, that creativity was viewed here as an outcome rather than as a personality trait.

CONCLUSION

Leadership research has moved in emphasis over the last several decades from personal characteristics to behavior to contingencies and contextual variables as predictors of leadership, finally homing in again on personal factors—only this time, with more sophisticated measures of personality and more complex constructs such as charisma that have proved themselves elusive in definition and measurement. This perennial search for predictors is due largely to the fact that none of the classes of predictors studied have yielded consistent results in isolation. It is becoming increasingly clear that better results may be obtained by studying all major variables simultaneously, to look at composite predictors by means of multiple regression analyses. Multiple regression procedures have been adopted by some researchers to address

a number of variables simultaneously within a class of predictors, such as personal characteristics (e.g., Atwater & Yammarino, 1993) or cognitive structures in implicit leadership theories (e.g., Lord, Foti, & DeVader, 1984). More comprehensive models to predict leadership may be possible to test by including variables across several classes—behavioral, personal, and contextual—to make up a full regression model. Of course, such a study would be prohibitive in terms of financial, material, and time resources required.

A limitation mentioned by Church and Waclawski (1998, p. 120) is worth noting for its relevance to all organizational research but especially for its salience in field studies of leadership: "[A]lthough the universe of assessment instruments is full of alternative measures (e.g., those that measure the Big Five dimensions of personality, those that conceptualize transformational and transactional leadership as two independent dimensions instead of one, etc.), field research of the type presented here is often constrained by (a) what the client organization wants and feels comfortable using and (b) what the practitioner/researcher prefers and feels comfortable using."

However, regardless of the measure used, it is pertinent to note that much of leadership research is conducted using questionnaire measures that obtain self-ratings or ratings by others. Especially in empirical research on transformational leadership, ratings typically are obtained from subordinates and superiors. It is important to keep in mind, in interpreting results from these studies, that scores from the measures of transformational leadership may be reflective more of the raters' implicit theories of leadership rather than of the leaders themselves.

More than a quarter of a century after Burns (1978) published his insightful ideas on leadership, his construct of transforming leadership is perhaps the most widely used concept in leadership theory and research. However, his original notion of transforming leadership is buried in a multitude of definitions that leave the leadership field in no state of consensus. In all this confusion, however, Burns's emphasis on morality as a pinion of the construct appears to have disappeared.

Although we seem to have today a great accumulation of research on transformational leadership, our understanding of the construct in theory and research has been muddled by a multitude of definitions and operationalizations. Likewise, there are several versions of the Big Five personality traits and also of other personality variables studied. Under the circumstances, the relation of personality to transformational leadership must, at best, remain tied to specific definitions of transformational leadership and personality traits as reflected in the measures used to study the relationships.

NOTES

1. In the case of nonsignificant (ns) correlations reported here, the reader may find it useful to consider, besides the CI values, the counternull statistic (Rosenthal, Rosnow, & Rubin, 2000; Rosnow & Rosenthal, 1996). The counternull of a statistically nonsignificant effect size r gives the upper limit (in terms of magnitude) of r from which the reported effect is statistically indistinguishable. An approximation of the counternull is easily obtained from a simple Fisher's z transformation of the observed effect, which is doubled and then converted back to r.

2. Pillai et al. (2003) use the term *attributed charisma* to the charisma construct, thereby creating the impression that the other variables of interest here (transformational leadership, proactivity, need for achievement, and emotional empathy) are somehow "real." In fact, all these variables, as measured in this study, represent voter perceptions—and to that extent, attributions.

REFERENCES

Abraham, J. (1992). Management, according to the transformational leadership paradigm and its effect on organizational outcomes. Unpublished doctoral dissertation, Israel Institute of Technology, Haifa.

Aditya, R. N. (2003). Leadership. In J. C. Thomas (Ed.), *Comprehensive handbook of psychological assessment: Vol. 4. Industrial and organizational assessment* (pp. 216–239). New York: Wiley.

Aditya, R. N., House, R. J., & Kerr, S. (2000). Theory and practice of leadership: Into the new millennium. In C. L. Cooper & E. A. Locke (Eds.), *Industrial and organizational psychology: Linking theory and practice* (pp. 130–165). New York: Blackwell.

Ainsworth, M. D. S., Blehar, M., Waters, E., & Wall, S. (1978). *Patterns of attachment: A psychological study of strange situations.* Hillsdale, NJ: Erlbaum.

Atwater, L. E., & Yammarino, F. J. (1993). Personal attributes as predictors of superiors' and subordinates' perceptions of military academy leadership. *Human Relations, 46*(5), 645–668.

Bales, R. F. (1954). In conference. *Harvard Business Review, 32*(2), 44–50.

Barbuto, J. E., Jr. (1997). Taking the charisma out of transformational leadership. *Journal of Social Behavior and Personality, 12*(3), 689–697.

Bass, B. M. (1985). *Leadership and performance beyond expectations.* New York: Free Press.

Bass, B. M. (1995). Theory of transformational leadership redux. *Leadership Quarterly, 6,* 463–478.

Bass, B. M., & Avolio, B. J. (1989). *Manual: The multifactor leadership questionnaire.* Palo Alto, CA: Consulting Psychologists Press.

Bass, B. M., & Avolio, B. J. (1990). *The multifactor leadership questionnaire.* Palo Alto, CA: Consulting Psychologists Press.

Bass, B. M,. & Avolio, B. J. (1991). *The multifactor leadership questionnaire.* Palo Alto, CA: Consulting Psychologists Press.

Bass, B. M., & Avolio, B. J. (1995). *MLQ multifactor leadership questionnaire* (2nd ed.). Redwood City, CA: Mind Garden.

Bateman, T. S., & Crant, J. M. (1993). The proactive component of organizational behavior. *Journal of Organizational Behavior, 14,* 103–118.

Bennis, W., & Nanus, B. (1985). *Leaders: The strategies for taking charge.* New York: Harper and Row.

Boal, K. B., & Bryson, J. M. (1988). Charismatic leadership: A phenomenological and structural approach. In J. G. Hunt, B. R. Baliga, H. P. Dachler, & C. A. Schriesheim (Eds.), *Emerging leadership vistas* (pp. 11–28). Boston: Lexington Books.

Bowers, D. G., & Seashore, S. E. (1966). Predicting organizational effectiveness with a four-factor theory of leadership. *Administrative Science Quarterly, 11,* 238–263.

Burke, W. W. (1979). Leaders and their development. *Group and Organizational Studies, 4,* 273–280.

Burke, W. W. (1986). Leadership as empowering others. In S. Srivastva (Ed.), *Executive power* (pp. 51–77). San Francisco: Jossey-Bass.

Burke, W. W. (1990). *The leadership report* (3rd ed.). Pelham, NY: Warner Burke.

Burke, W. W. (1991). *The Leadership Assessment Inventory* (Rev. ed.). Pelham, NY: Warner Burke.

Burns, J. M. (1978). *Leadership.* New York: Harper and Row.

Butterfield, D. A. (1972). Leadership and organizational effectiveness. In P. Mott (Ed.), *The characteristics of effective organizations* (pp. 117–149). New York: Harper and Row.

Butterfield, D. A. (1988). Welcome back charisma. In J. G. Hunt, B. R. Baliga, H. P. Dachler, & C. A. Schriesheim (Eds.), *Emerging leadership vistas* (pp. 67–72). Boston: Lexington Books.

Cattell, R., Eber, H., & Tatsuoka, M. (1980). *Handbook for the 16PF.* Champaign, IL: Institute for Personality and Ability Testing.

Church, A. H., & Waclawski, J. (1998). The relationship between individual personality orientation and executive leadership behaviour. *Journal of Occupational and Organizational Psychology, 71,* 99–125.

Clover, W. H. (1988). *Personality attributes of transformational AOCs.* Paper presented to the U.S. Air Force Academy, Colorado Springs, CO.

Clover, W. H. (1990). Transformational leaders: Team performance, leadership ratings, and firsthand impressions. In K. E. Clark & M. B. Clark (Eds.), *Measures of leadership* (pp. 171–184). West Orange, NJ: Leadership Library of America.

Collins, N. L., & Read, S. J. (1990). Adult attachment, working models, and relationship quality in dating couples. *Journal of Personality and Social Psychology, 58*(4), 644–663.

Costa, P. T., Jr., & McCrae, R. R. (1992). *Revised NEO Personality Inventory (NEO-PI-R) and NEO Five-Factor Inventory (NEO-FFI) professional manual.* Odessa, FL: Psychological Assessment Resources.

Dansereau, F., Graen, G. B., & Haga, W. (1975). A vertical dyad linkage approach to leadership in formal organizations. *Organizational Behavior and Human Performance, 13,* 46–78.

Downton, J. V., Jr. (1973). *Rebel leadership.* New York: Free Press.

Dubinsky, A. J., Yammarino, F. J., & Jolson, M. A. (1995). An examination of linkages between personal characteristics and dimensions of transformational leadership. *Journal of Business and Psychology, 9*(3), 315–335.

Edwards, A. L. (1959). *Edwards Personal Preference Schedule.* New York: Psychological Corp.

Elderkin, K. W., & Bartlett, C. A. (1993). *General Electric: Jack Welch's second wave* (A). Harvard Business School, case number: 9–391–248.

Emmett, D. (1958). *Function, purpose and powers.* New York: Macmillan.

Epstein, S., & Meier, P. (1989). Constructive thinking: A broad coping variable with specific components. *Journal of Personality and Social Psychology, 57*(2), 332–350.

Fiedler, F. E. (1967). *A theory of leadership effectiveness.* New York: McGraw-Hill.

Fiedler, F. E. (1971). Validation and extension of the contingency model of leadership effectiveness: A review of empirical findings. *Psychological Bulletin, 76,* 128–148.

Fiedler, F. E., & Garcia, J. E. (1987). *New approaches to effective leadership: Cognitive resources and organizational performance.* New York: Wiley.

French, J. R. P., and Raven, B. H. (1959). The bases of social power. In D. Cartwright (Ed.), *Studies in social power* (pp. 150–167). Ann Arbor, MI: Institute for Social Research.

Gardner, J. W. (1990). *On leadership.* New York: Free Press.

Gibb, C. A. (1947). The principles and traits of leadership. *Journal of Abnormal and Social Psychology, 42,* 267–284.

Gough, H. G. (1989). The California psychological inventory. In C. S. Newmark (Ed.), *Major psychological assessment instruments* (Vol. 2, pp. 67–98). Boston: Allyn & Bacon.

Gough, H. G., & Heilbrun, A. B. (1983). *The Adjective Checklist manual.* Palo Alto, CA: Consulting Psychologists Press.

Graen, G., & Cashman, J. F. (1975). A role-making model of leadership in formal organizations: A developmental approach. In J. G. Hunt & L. L. Larson (Eds.) *Leadership Frontiers* (pp. 143–165). Kent, OH: Kent State University Press.

Graen, G. B., Liden, R. C., & Hoel, W. (1982). Short notes: Role of leadership in employee withdrawal process. *Journal of Applied Psychology, 67*(6), 868–872.

Graen, G. B., Scandura, T., & Graen, M. R. (1986). A field experimental test of the moderating effects of growth need strength on productivity. *Journal of Applied Psychology, 71,* 484–491.

Graen, G. B., & Uhl-Bien, M. (1995). Relationship-based approach to leadership: Development of leader-member exchange (LMX) theory of leadership over 25 years: Applying a multi-level multi-domain perspective. *Leadership Quarterly, 6*(2), 219–247.

Graham, J. W. (1988). Transformational leadership: Fostering follower autonomy, not automatic followership. In J. G. Hunt, B. R. Baliga, H. P. Dachler, & C. A. Schriesheim (Eds.), *Emerging leadership vistas* (pp. 73–79). Boston: Lexington Books.

Griffin, D. W., & Bartholomew, K. (1994). The metaphysics of measurement: The case of adult attachment. In K. Bartholomew & D. Perlman (Eds.), *Advances in personal relationships* (Vol. 5, pp. 17–52). London: Jessica Kingsley.

Gurin, P., Gurin, G., & Morrison, B. M. (1978). Personal and ideological aspects of internal and external control. *Social Psychology, 41,* 275–296.

Hazan, C., & Shaver, P. (1987). Romantic love conceptualized as an attachment process. *Journal of Personality and Social Psychology, 52,* 511–524.

Hendrick, H. W. (1990). Perceptual accuracy of self and others and leadership status as functions of cognitive complexity. In K. E. Clark and M. B. Clark (Eds.), *Measures of leadership* (pp. 511–519). West Orange, NJ: Leadership Library of America.

Hersey, P., & Blanchard, K. (1982). *Management of organizational behavior: Utilizing human resources.* Englewood Cliffs, NJ: Prentice Hall.

Hill, N. (1976). Self-esteem: The key to effective leadership. *Administrative Management, 31*(8), 24.

Hough, L. (1992). The "Big Five" personality variables—Construct confusion: Description versus prediction. *Human Performance, 5,* 139–155.

House, R. J. (1971). A path goal theory of leader effectiveness. *Administrative Science Quarterly, 16,* 321–338.

House, R. J. (1977). A 1976 theory of charismatic leadership. In J. G. Hunt & L. L. Larson (Eds.), *Leadership: The cutting edge* (pp. 189–207). Carbondale: Southern Illinois University Press.

House, R. J., & Aditya, R. N. (1997). The social scientific study of leadership: *Quo Vadis? Journal of Management, 27*(3), 409–473.

House, R. J., & Baetz, M. L. (1979) Leadership: Some empirical generalizations and new research directions. *Research in Organizational Behavior, 1,* 341–423.

Howell, J., & Avolio, B. J. (1993) Transformational leadership, transactional leadership, locus of control, and support for innovation: Key predictors of consolidated-business-unit performance. *Journal of Applied Psychology, 78,* 891–902.

Jackson, D. N. (1974). *Personality Research Form manual: PRF-Form E.* Goshen, NY: Research Psychologists Press.

Jenkins, W. O. (1947). A review of leadership studies with particular reference to military problems. *Psychological Bulletin, 44*, 54–79.

Judge, T. A., & Bono, J. E. (2000). Five-factor model of personality and transformational leadership. *Journal of Applied Psychology, 85*(5), 751–765.

Kahn, R. L., & Katz, D. (1953). Leadership practices in relation to productivity and morale. In D. Cartwright & A. Zander (Eds.), *Group dynamics.* New York: Harper and Row.

Kegan, R. (1982). *The evolving self: Problem and process in human development.* Cambridge, MA: Harvard University Press.

Kirton, M. J. (1991). *KAI response sheet.* Highlands, UK: Occupational Research Centre.

Kirton, M. J. (1992). *KAI feedback summary.* Highlands, UK: Occupational Research Centre.

Koehler, C. D. (1992). *Personality traits associated with transformational leadership styles of secondary principals in Christian schools.* Unpublished doctoral dissertation, Kent State University, Kent, OH.

Kouzes, J. M., & Posner, B. Z. (1987). *The leadership challenge: How to get extraordinary things done in organizations.* San Francisco: Jossey-Bass.

Kuhnert, K. W., & Lewis, P. (1987). Transactional and transformational leadership: A constructive/developmental analysis. *Academy of Management Journal, 12*(4), 648–657.

Langford, P. H. (2003). A one-minute measure of the Big Five? Evaluating and abridging Shafer's (1999a) Big Five markers. *Personality and Individual Differences, 35*, 1127–1140.

Latack, J. C. (1986). Coping with job stress: Measures and future directions for scale development. *Journal of Applied Psychology, 71*, 377–385.

Leithwood, K. (1992). The move toward transformational leadership. *Educational Leadership, 49*(5), 8–12.

Likert, R. (1961). *New patterns of management.* New York: McGraw-Hill.

Lodahl, A. (1982). Crisis in values and the success of the Unification Church. Unpublished master's thesis, Cornell University, Ithaca, NY.

Lord, R. G., Binning, J. F., Rush, M. C., & Thomas, J. C. (1978). The effects of performance cues and leader behavior on questionnaire ratings of leadership behavior. *Organizational Behavior and Human Performance, 21*(1), 27–39.

Lord, R. G., Foti, R., & DeVader, C. (1984). A test of leadership categorization theory: Internal structure, information processing, and leadership perceptions. *Organizational Behavior and Human Performance, 34*, 343–378.

Lord, R. G., & Maher, K. J. (1991). *Leadership and information processing: Linking perception and performance.* Boston: Unwin Hyman.

Mann, F. C. (1965). Toward an understanding of the leadership role in formal organization. In R. Dublin (Ed.), *Leadership and productivity.* San Francisco: Chandler.

Marlowe, D., & Crowne, D. P. (1964). *The approval motive.* New York: Wiley.

Maslow, A. (1954). *Motivation and personality.* New York: Harper & Row.

Mayer, J. D., Caruso, D. R., & Salovey, P. (1999). Emotional intelligence meets traditional standards for an intelligence. *Intelligence, 27*, 267–298.

McClelland, D. C. (1961). *The achieving society.* New York: Van Nostrand Reinhold.

McClelland, D. C. (1975). *Power: The inner experience.* New York: Irvington.

McClelland, D. C. (1985). *Human motivation.* Glenview, CA: Scott Foresman.

McGrattan, R. J. (1997). *The relationship between personality traits and transformational leadership among North Carolina elementary public school principals.* Unpublished doctoral dissertation, East Tennessee State University, Johnson City. (UMI No. AAM9726833)

Medcof, J. W., & Wegener, J. G. (1992). Work technology and the need for achievement and nurturance among nurses. *Journal of Organizational Behavior, 13*, 413–423.

Mikulincer, M., Florian, V., & Tolmacz, R. (1990). Attachment styles and fear of personal death: A case study of affect regulation. *Journal of Personality and Social Psychology, 58*, 273–280.

Mirels, H. L. (1970). Dimensions of internal versus external control. *Journal of Consulting and Clinical Psychology, 36*, 40–44.

Myers, I., & McCaulley, M. (1986). *Manual: A guide to the development and use of the Myers-Briggs Type Indicator.* Palo Alto, CA: Consulting Psychologists Press.

Osborn, T., & Osborn, D. (1986). Leadership profiles in Latin America: How different are Latin American managers from their counterparts? *Issues and Observations, 6*, 7–10.

Pillai, R., Williams, E. A., Lowe, K. B., & Jung, D. I. (2003). Personality, transformational leadership, trust, and the 2000 U.S. presidential vote. *The Leadership Quarterly, 14*, 161–192.

Podsakoff, P. M., MacKenzie, S. B., Moorman, R. H., & Fetter, R. (1990). Transformational leader behaviors and their effects on followers' trust in leader, satisfaction, and organizational citizenship behaviors. *Leadership Quarterly, 1*, 107–142.

Popper, M., Mayseless, O., & Castelnovo, O. (2000). Transformational leadership and attachment. *Leadership Quarterly, 11*(2), 267–289.

Posner, B. Z., & Kouzes, J. M. (1988). Development and validation of the Leadership Practices Inventory. *Educational and Psychological Measurement, 48*, 483–496.

Rosenthal, R., Rosnow, R. L., & Rubin, D. B. (2000). *Contrasts and effect sizes in behavioral research: A correlational approach.* Cambridge, UK: Cambridge University Press.

Rosnow, R. L., & Rosenthal, R. (1996). Computing contrasts, effect sizes, and counternulls on other people's published data: General procedures for research consumers. *Psychological Methods, 1*, 331–340.

Ross, S. M., & Offermann, L. R. (1997). Transformational leaders: Measurement of personality attributes and work group performance. *Personality and Social Psychology Bulletin, 23,* 1078–1086.

Rotter, J. B. (1966). Generalized expectancies for internal versus external locus of control of reinforcement. *Psychological Monographs: General and Applied, 80*(609).

Rush, M. C., Thomas, J. C., & Lord, R. G. (1977). Implicit leadership theory: A potential threat to the internal validity of leader behavior questionnaires. *Organizational Behavior and Human Performance, 20,* 93–110.

Sashkin, M. (1988). The visionary leader. In J. A. Conger & R. A. Kanungo (Eds.), *Charismatic leadership: The elusive factor in organizational effectiveness* (pp. 122–160). San Francisco: Jossey-Bass.

Sashkin, M., & Burke, W. W. (1990). Understanding and assessing organizational leadership. In K. E. Clark & M. B. Clark (Eds.), *Measures of leadership* (pp. 297–325). Greensboro, NC: Center for Creative Leadership.

Schlender, B. (1995). What Bill Gates really wants. *Fortune Magazine, 131*(1), 34–36.

Shafer, A. B. (1999). Brief bipolar markers for the Five Factor Model of Personality. *Psychological Reports, 84,* 1173–1179.

Shin, S. J., & Zhou, J. (2003). Transformational leadership, conservation, and creativity: Evidence from Korea. *Academy of Management Journal, 46,* 703–714.

Singer, M. S., & Singer, A. E. (1986). Relation between transformational vs transactional leadership preference and subordinates' personality: An exploratory study. *Perceptual & Motor Skills, 62*(3), 775–780.

Stogdill, R. M. (1948). Personal factors associated with leadership: A survey of the literature. *Journal of Psychology, 25,* 35–71.

Stogdill, R. M. (1974). *Handbook of leadership: A survey of theory and research.* New York: Free Press.

Stogdill, R. M., & Coons, A. E. (1957). Leader behavior: Its description and measurement. Columbus: Ohio State University, Bureau of Business Research.

Tichy, N. M., & Devanna, M. A. (1986). *The transformational leader.* New York: Wiley.

Vroom, V. H., & Yetton, P. W. (1973). *Leadership and decision-making.* Pittsburgh, PA: University of Pittsburgh Press.

Weber, M. (1947). *The theory of social and economic organization,* New York: Free Press.

Winter, D. G., & Barenbaum, N. B. (1985). Responsibility and the power motive in women and men. In A. J. Stewart & M. B. Lykes (Eds.), *Gender and personality* (pp. 247–267). Durham, NC: Duke University Press. (Reprinted from *Journal of Personality, 53,* 335–355)

Wofford, J. C., & Liska, L. Z. (1993). Path-goal theories of leadership: A meta-analysis. *Journal of Management, 19,* 857–876.

Yammarino, F., & Bass, B. (1990). Long-term forecasting of transformational leadership and its effects among naval officers. In K. E. Clark and M. B. Clark (Eds.), *Measures of leadership* (pp. 151–169). West Orange, NJ: Leadership Library of America.

Zaleznik, A. (1977). Managers and leaders: Are they different? *Harvard Business Review, 55*(3), 67–68.

Zhou, J., & George, J. M. (2001). When job dissatisfaction leads to creativity: Encouraging the expression of voice. *Academy of Management Journal, 44,* 682–696.

CHAPTER 19

Person-Environment Fit and Performance

JOHN F. BINNING, JAMES M. LEBRETON, AND ANTHONY J. ADORNO

INTRODUCTION

The lexical hypothesis in trait-based personality psychology maintains that clues to meaningful regularities in human behavior can be found in the analysis of natural language terms used to describe others' behavior (John, Angleitner, & Ostendorf, 1988). To provoke thought about the theme of this chapter, we propose an extension of this hypothesis to common idioms and suggest that many of them capture a natural tendency to view an individual's behavior relative to the specific environmental or situational demands impinging on him or her. For example, when we use phrases such as, "a fish out of water," "in the right place at the right time," "a round peg in a square hole," "a bull in a china shop," "going against the grain," "barking up the wrong tree," "bending over backward," "bite off more than you can chew," "get the lay of the land," "you're in over your head," "know your way around," "make hay while the sun shines," "you are out of your element," "shape up or ship out," or "strike while the iron is hot," we are referring in some way to the efficacy of one's conduct given certain environmental circumstances. These common sayings share reference to someone confronting specific environmental demands and either being "fit" to deal successfully with the circumstances or not. In this chapter we systematically examine how person-environment (P-E) fit, the importance of which is reflected naturally in these and many other idiomatic expressions, can be coherently conceptualized, so that it can be more fruitfully studied scientifically and its links to important life consequences can be discovered.

Psychological science has embraced the concept of P-E fit, despite its many construct labels and variety of conceptual forms, because the study of P-E fit makes explicit that which is implicit to all theoretical paradigms in scientific psychology, that effective explanations of human functioning concurrently must conceptualize person characteristics, situational characteristics, and the nature of their interaction. Even the "environment-skewed" forms of behaviorism posit operant relationships that capture an organism's relationship with en-

vironmental contingencies, and "person-skewed" forms of humanism stress at least phenomenological regard for a person's understanding of their environment. Generally speaking, P-E fit is the dominant conceptual paradigm in psychology (Schneider, 2001; Walsh, Craik, & Price, 2000), or at least the "paradigm par excellence for psychology" (Dawis, 2000, p. 180).

Substantial research and theory on P-E fit has been produced by vocational counseling and industrial/organizational psychologists. Two prominent theoretical frameworks are Holland's (1997) Realistic, Investigative, Artistic, Social, Enterprising, Convention (RIASEC) model linking vocational interests with career outcomes and Dawis and Lofquist's (1984) theory of work adjustment (TWA) linking personal values and abilities with career outcomes. Although these two perspectives have had considerable impact on the study of P-E fit, and have perhaps unduly dominated conceptual advances in this area, other approaches and applications of P-E fit concepts have emerged (e.g., Kristof, 1996; Schneider, 1987; Walsh, Craik, & Price, 1992, 2000; Wapner, Demick, Yamamoto, & Minami, 2000). In addition, several qualitative and meta-analytic empirical reviews of P-E fit concepts and methodology have been published in the past decade or so (Edwards, 1991; Kristof, 1996; Tinsley, 2000; Tranberg, Slane, & Ekeberg, 1993; Verquer, Beehr, & Wagner, 2003). Given this, we will not focus on reviewing the P-E fit literature per se. Rather, the focus of this chapter is the explication of an integrative framework designed to help (1) clarify the conceptual boundaries of the myriad P-E fit concepts that have been proposed and researched over the years, (2) highlight and organize extant P-E fit research, even research not explicitly labeled as such, and (3) provide heuristic stimulation for future integrative P-E fit research. In this chapter we have purposely chosen a broad perspective in an attempt to integrate all P-E fit concepts advanced to date, with a clear emphasis on the role of the social-organizational environment in P-E fit formulations. We also describe some of the representative theoretical and applied research efforts that concomitantly conceptualize and assess person and environment attributes and model the nature of their interactions.

WHAT IS PERSON-ENVIRONMENT FIT?

Origin of the Person-Environment Fit Concept

The notion of person-environment fit can be traced back to Plato's *The Republic,* where he discussed assigning people to jobs based on their personal attributes (Tinsley, 2000). A similar historical vein runs through ancient Chinese use of civil service examinations to match people to jobs (Bass & Barrett, 1981). Heightened interest in P-E fit might well be traced to Charles Darwin, who in 1859 published his seminal *Origin of the Species;* among its other monumental effects on our world, this work made the concept of organism-environment fit widely known. Central to Darwin's influential theory was his proposal about the "survival of the fittest," a concept he co-opted from a contemporary evolutionary psychologist and philosopher, Herbert Spencer. Social Darwinism has directly influenced formal thought in many scientific disciplines, and the concept of person-environment fit has appeared in myriad forms throughout academic and popular literature for the past 150 years. Although Darwin focused on organisms' environmental fit vis-à-vis the survival of their offspring, the concept has been generalized to refer generally to an organism's viability within a specific set of environmental circumstances. Modern psychology's embrace of the P-E fit paradigm is often traced directly to Kurt Lewin's (1935) well-known social psychological formulation—B = f(P, E)—where behavior is a function of person and environment (Schneider, 2001).

Defining Person-Environment Fit

Whether referred to by terms such as adaptation, adjustment, compatibility, congruence, convergence, correspondence, exchange, fit, holistic, interaction, interdependence, match, overlap, reciprocal causality, similarity, transactional, or even polemically cast as the person-situation debate or the nature-nurture controversy, the fundamental premise of the P-E fit perspective is that explaining human behavior and consequent instrumental outcomes of such requires a substantive understanding of (1) the person and their unique constellation of relevant personal attributes, (2) the relevant aspects of the environment in which behavior is being exhibited, and (3) the relevant processes by which the two interact with each other. Fit implies that certain combinations of person characteristics and situational characteristics yield substantively different, and by implication better or more favorable, outcomes than

other combinations. Conversely, *misfit* yields less favorable outcomes. Different theoretical orientations emphasize and more explicitly conceptualize these three explanatory loci differently, but all three are necessary for understanding and prediction.

We propose a working definition, such that in its broadest conceptual sense, P-E fit refers to the extent to which an individual engages in, or otherwise has the potential to engage in, situationally functional comportment when interacting with specific environmental demands in order to survive and flourish, either literally or relative to particular social standards. Functional comportment certainly can involve exhibiting overt behaviors (e.g., speaking out on an important issue at a city council meeting or pursuing a hit-and-run driver until police arrive to take over the pursuit). It also can involve not exhibiting behavior (e.g., sitting still and quiet during the city council meeting while another citizen makes the same point in a more compelling way or fighting the impulse to pursue the fleeing felon in order to lend support to the victim). Hence the functional quality of the behavior, or lack thereof, depends on critical aspects of the specific situation and is always evaluated vis-à-vis specific environmental demands or circumstances.

We want to note that the previous examples clearly emphasize the instrumental nature of overt behavior (or refrainment from such), because traditional conceptions of P-E fit focused on how people navigated behaviorally through their physical and social environments. In the current analysis, we deliberately use the term *comportment* to suggest that there may be considerable utility in generalizing the conception of *behavior* to include less overt responses to environmental stimuli, such as emotional and physiological reactions, as well as various cognitions and judgments (cf. Heckhausen & Schulz, 1995; Izard, 1993). The dramatic increase in theory and research on affective and cognitive processes, which are both independent and dependent variables of interest, has widened the conceptual space within which environmentally appropriate comportment can be viewed. For example, the extent to which an individual labors emotionally in the completion of a task, although covert and generally unobservable, can be viewed as a meaningful antecedent or consequence of certain environmental conditions and can be logically tied to conceptions of P-E fit (Grandey, 2000). Emotional labor occurs when an individual behaves overtly in a way that is inconsistent with his or her covert felt emotions. Two customer service employees might behave identically when interacting with a rude customer, and therefore during that given slice of time be "equally fit," but one may experience more intense negative emotional reactions and subsequent emotional exhaustion, thus leading to disrupted subsequent performance, illness, job dissatisfaction, and so forth. These differences in emotional labor reflect meaningful differences in P-E fit, distinct from the overt behavior used to deal directly with interpersonal task demands. It is important to emphasize, however, that whereas covert processes and reactions to environmental circumstances are important aspects of a full P-E fit analysis, their import is determined primarily by the role they play in helping to understand and predict overt behavior necessary for organizational functioning. This distinction parallels that between primary control and secondary control in Heckhausen and Schulz's (1995) theory of life-span development, where control through acting directly on the environment has primacy over intraindividual ways of controlling one's relationship with the environment. The organizational parallel is that, as we discuss later, in exchange relationships with members, organizations are ultimately dependent on patterns of members' overt behaviors and relatively less concerned about covert processes.

"Natural" versus Socially Constructed Environments

Another important distinction in the framework presented here is that between "natural" environments and "socially constructed" environments. Naturally occurring environments can place real life-and-death demands on people in that they present circumstances that are involuntarily experienced, and literal survival is contingent on whether the individual exhibits the comportment required for survival in the situation. When an avalanche destroys an expedition's base camp and planned return route, the more "fit" climbers, within the limits of their personal resources, improvise alternative life-support measures and an effective route home, whereas their less "fit" counterparts become discouraged and disoriented and are subsequently memorialized by others. When tornado warning sirens sound, some people take immediate shelter, others continue their normal routine, and nature decides who is more fit.

In socially constructed environments (e.g., schools, work organizations, social clubs, retirement communities), literal survival is seldom the relevant outcome, and relatively voluntary exposure to environmental circumstances is generally the rule. In social environments, the more fit individuals are the ones whose comportment meets the *social demands* or *expectations* relevant to the situation and makes it possible to successfully "navigate" through myriad interpersonal circumstances. Social expectations can take many forms, including formal or informal agendas, formal or informal roles, and behavioral scripts, or standard operating procedures and policies (Hofmann, Morgeson, & Gerras, 2003; R. Hogan & Roberts, 2000; Porter, Lawler, & Hackman, 1975; Schlenker,

Britt, Pennington, Murphy, & Doherty, 1994; Weick, 1995). In modern human enterprise, these expectations generally translate into questions of whether an individual can (a) exhibit "acceptable" behaviors, (b) refrain from "unacceptable" behaviors, or (c) otherwise benefit from the opportunities presented in the immediate environment that are (d) viewed by some "dominant coalition" whose evaluations and opinions carry more weight via formal and/or informal authority or social power. We want to emphasize that these evaluations are generally relative to, or aligned with, the demands for behavior that are instrumental in achieving consensually valued goals or outcomes. In other words, the fundamental sociometric standard by which the "value" of behavior is judged is its role in helping some collectivity achieve a desired goal or objective. In modern society, one's offspring can be viewed as one's valued contributions to individual, group, and collective goal achievement. Those individuals who can exhibit behaviors that enhance the likelihood that they will function in good standing within a specific environment are said to be better fit than those whose behaviors lack instrumentality or those who actually obstruct goal attainment.

The relationships between individuals and their social environments, rather than being naturally imposed, are more usefully viewed as economic- and social-exchange relationships (Cropanzano, Rupp, & Byrne, 2003; Dabos & Rousseau, 2004; Rhoades & Eisenberger, 2002). *Economic-exchange relationships* are built largely to sustain quid pro quo interchanges of basic goods and supplies. *Social-exchange relationships* are more socioemotionally substantive and generally involve more personal investment by the parties to the relationship. For the purposes of this chapter, we plan to use the term *organization* very broadly to refer to socially constructed environments, as well as their respective parts. It is important, therefore, to keep in mind that many of the propositions advanced here are intended to apply to virtually any type of socially constructed environment (e.g., vocations, work organizations, nonwork organizations, teams and work groups, and individual jobs or organizational roles), not just industrial or business organizations. In this chapter, we focus on conceptualizing the fit between people and the social systems in which they function, which are in turn continually posing behavioral expectations surrounding their members' involvement.

The Plethora of Fit Concepts

The scientific literature is replete with assorted conceptualizations of P-E fit. As mentioned earlier, the RIASEC and TWA models are widely known, and Schneider's (1987) attraction-selection-attrition (ASA) model is increasingly so.

Muchinsky and Monahan (1987) introduced the distinction between supplementary versus complementary fit. Kristof (1996) elaborated this distinction by delineating two types of complementary fit. There is consistent reference to some variation of *desire-supply fit* versus *abilities-demands fit* (Converse, Oswald, Gillespie, Field, & Bizot, 2004; Tinsley, 2000). There also is frequent reference to the environmental level with which fit is examined (e.g., person–national-culture fit, person-vocation fit, person-organization fit, person-group fit, or person-job fit). Myriad other conceptualizations abound in the broader person-environment literature (cf. Wachs & Plomin, 1991; Walsh et al., 1992, 2000). This plethora of P-E fit concepts, although reflective of the complexity of the P-E fit paradigm, in our view is approaching the point of diminishing scientific returns and is engendering conceptual confusion in the P-E fit literature. Even a casual review of recent literature demonstrates a general lack of agreement about how to conceptualize P-E fit. Gati (2000) calls for more attention to the implications of various fit distinctions on P-E fit research, and we strongly concur. Therefore, before proceeding, it is important to clarify the conceptual boundaries of these different dimensions of fit and to integrate them into a single conceptual framework.

A FRAMEWORK FOR DISTINGUISHING PERSON-ENVIRONMENT FIT CONSTRUCTS

We propose a framework where P-E fit is conceptualized at multiple nomological levels (cf. Embretson, 1983; Lubinski, 2000; Margenau, 1950). Nomological Level I is the broadest and most abstract, designed to conceptualize four fundamental relationships that exist between people and their socially constructed environments (i.e., organizations) and thus define four fundamental facets of P-E fit. Level I is the most distal relative to actual behavior and environmental conditions. Level II moves nomologically in a more behaviorally specific direction and expands these four fit relationships by showing how human behavioral contributions to organizations as well as environmental circumstances can be organized into specific domains of human functioning. Level II can be viewed at three levels of behavioral specificity (i.e., Level IIA, IIB, and IIC described later). Level III is the most behaviorally specific and describes specific systems of person and environmental constructs in order to facilitate an integrative view of psychological science as it applies to P-E fit.

Person-Environment Fit at Nomological Level I

We propose that all P-E fit issues can be organized into the framework portrayed in Figure 19.1. This presents the broad-est and most general dimensions of P-E fit and will help us clarify the distinctions between desire-supply fit versus ability-demand fit as well as supplementary and complementary fit mentioned earlier. We begin this examination by emphasizing that the core of every person-organization relationship is a reciprocal exchange portrayed as dual fit relationships (FR) 1 and 2 in Figure 19.1. This dual fit between the organization's and the person's lower-order requisites and lower-order supplies is tantamount to the economic exchange relationship mentioned earlier.

Before proceeding, it is important to address the general issue of personifying organizational environments. Throughout this chapter, we deliberately have chosen to describe organizations in anthropomorphic ways. We decided to use this language in order to facilitate the presentation of our conceptual framework for P-E fit. We recognize the view that organizations do not cognize (James, Joyce, & Slocum, 1988), nor do they have needs or desires or the like. However, research does suggest that individuals share cognitive-affective experiences and that these experiences may appropriately be conceptualized as group or organizational phenomena (George, 1990; George & James, 1993). There is evidence that people personify organizations naturally and react to these cognitions (cf. Rhoades & Eisenberger, 2002; Slaughter, Zickar, Highhouse, & Mohr, 2004), and by describing organizations this way, we believe that the essence of social exchange as a basis for P-E fit is usefully accentuated. Our anthropomorphic description of organizations should be interpreted as scientific shorthand for cognitive-affective phenomena shared among organizational members and/or the characteristics (e.g., priorities, goals, needs, etc.) of an organizational leader that "trickle down" and are internalized by an organization's members. We encourage the interested reader to peruse a special issue of *Academy of Management Review* (vol. 24, no. 2) on collective constructs and multilevel theorizing about social collectivities. We call special attention to the paper by Morgeson and Hofmann (1999) for an effective analysis of the issues. Having established this proviso, we now turn to an examination of each of the four fit relationships, starting with the two relationships involving the fit between lower-order requisites.

Lower-Order Requisites and Supplies

Organizations fundamentally require attainment of valued outcomes necessary for survival and continued functioning (e.g., securing capital, creating and maintaining workforces, memberships, or enrollments, generating desirable goods or services, etc.). The outcomes necessary for survival are closely tied to the attainment of outcomes central to the or-

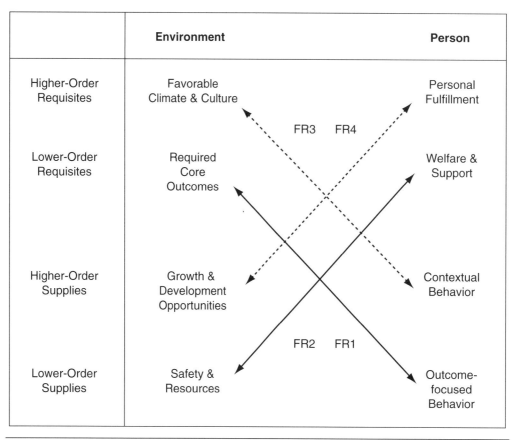

Figure 19.1   Facets of P-E fit in socially constructed environments: Level I.

ganization's core mission. In fact, organizations must attain these basic outcomes, and to do so requires members to exhibit patterns of behavior that lead to this attainment. This dimension of fit is portrayed as FR1 and represents the sine qua non of P-E fit in that without this aspect of fit the organization cannot continue to exist and, in a sense, the value of other aspects of P-E fit becomes moot. FR1, in the common parlance of the P-E fit literature, is referred to as *ability-demand fit*. Interestingly, this ability-demand concept generally is used in reference to what the organization demands from its members, with relative neglect of what the members' lower-order requisites demand as their reciprocal share of the dual exchange. Because of this neglect of person demands, and because it connotes a nomologically and psychologically myopic conception of P-E fit, we recommend the abandonment of the ability-demand terminology as it has been used in the literature to date. What an organization "demands" from its members is outcome-directed behavior (i.e., job performance, task behavior), not abilities, per se. Note that *task behavior* should be viewed broadly to include any behavior required to make the organization perform its basic functions (e.g., from operating production equipment in a factory, to

suturing a laceration in an emergency room, to transporting libations for a fraternity social event). In nomological contrast, abilities, along with a host of other psychological constructs, are behavioral potentials or predictive surrogates for what the organization demands (i.e., effective behavior) and as such are best conceptualized at a different nomological level, namely Level II in the framework being proposed here. This important distinction between effective behavior and the potential for such is something to which any parent or acquaintance of an underachiever surely will attest and reflects the long-standing distinction between aptitude/ability and performance! Performance results from the appropriate matching of aptitudes and abilities with environmental stimulus conditions (cf. Dawis & Lofquist, 1984).

The other part of the fundamental lower-order dual exchange (i.e., person demands) is the organizational member's requirement that the organization provide environmental conditions that promote and maintain their physical security and well-being as well as at least rudimentary institutional support for required task behavior. This is portrayed as FR2. Organizational members require that the organization provide an environment that ensures literal survival and insulation from unreasonable physical or psychological harm. Organizations do differ in their safety climate (Hofmann, & Morgeson, 1999; Hofmann et al., 2003), and this form of variation in FR2 may explain important aspects of P-E fit. It also is intriguing to expand the domain of this fit relationship to include safety from psychological harm. Given that the most common forms of workplace violence are not physical (Binning & Wagner, 2002), this may be an especially important area for fit research. In addition, members require that the organization provide at least basic support for their efforts to attain organizationally valued goals and outcomes in the form of basic tools, information, supplies, equipment, and support services. The importance of members' perceptions of this support on various outcome variables has been demonstrated empirically (Rhoades & Eisenberger, 2002). FR2 explicitly recognizes the fact that functional exchanges require something from both parties (i.e., P and E). Dawis (2000) advocates the use of the term *requirements* to capture the fact that both the person and the environment require something of each other, thus emphasizing the symmetry of the P-E relationship.

Characterizing Poor Lower-Order Fit

Poor P-E fit can occur in FR1 or FR2 or both. A faulty FR1 occurs when an organizational member fails to exhibit the task (i.e., outcome-directed) behaviors required to achieve outcomes critical for continued organizational (or subunit) functioning. In work organizations, this represents employee performance deficiencies. These deficiencies can take the form of exhibiting counterproductive behaviors or refraining from exhibiting productive behaviors (cf. Binning & Wagner, 2002). Similarly, in nonwork organizations, poor FR1 involves members engaging in patterns of behavior that obstruct or limit organizational goal attainment or otherwise threaten the organization's attainment of core mission outcomes (e.g., a priest treating parishioners inappropriately, a country-club treasurer embezzling membership dues, or a telephone fundraising volunteer badmouthing the host charity). Poor FR2 occurs when an organization fails to provide adequately for members' safety and/or does not provide the basic resources required for the employee to engage in task behavior. In work organizations, this can take the form of an organization noticeably not providing safety equipment, requiring employees to work in conditions known to threaten their physical or psychological health, or not maintaining production equipment so that frequent breakdowns limit piecerate compensation rates. These failures to provide for basic needs erode trust and threaten the basic exchange relationship between employees and employers (Kramer, 1999). Simi-

larly, in nonwork organizations, poor FR2 involves the organization failing to provide basic safety and resource support to its members (e.g., a country club without lifeguards or security personnel, a municipal government whose water supply has toxic levels of sulfites, or a community social organization that never schedules any dances or other social events).

We need to emphasize that the dual-exchange process requires that over time both FR1 and FR2 be properly maintained and balanced. Poor fit in either or both relationships will tend the organization toward entropy. Acute imbalances do occur, and they sometimes capture national media attention, as in the Enron debacle, domestic sweatshop operations, or the 2004 Los Angeles Lakers' failure to win the NBA championship. Often, poor FR1 is associated with poor FR2, but it is possible to have periods of time with very good fit in one and not in the other relationship. For example, an organization may include members who can and do perform basic tasks with considerable acumen, and yet, if the organization ceases providing necessary security or resources, the enterprise either will be motivated to undertake an adjustment or likely will disintegrate. For example, the convenience store around the corner may very well have personable and capable sales representatives, but they are quitting and refusing to come to work because of a series of armed robberies and no steps to install security cameras or protective cages for employees. To summarize, the fundamental nexus between an organization and its members is the fit between the organization's need to achieve valued outcomes and the patterns of task-focused behavior the members contribute to such ends. The dual lower-order exchange is completed by the organization providing safety and requisite resources to satisfy employees' basic requisites for security and support of required activities. The various individual differences that help explain and predict patterns of task behavior, conceptualized as abilities, as well as myriad other psychological constructs, are scientific summaries for behavioral potential, and can be used to assist in creating good P-E fit.

FR1 and FR2 represent the match between lower-order requisites of both organizations and members and the extent to which each supply what is needed by the other. We propose that fit relationships between organizations and members also exist at a higher level. The basic distinction between lower-order and higher-order human requisites is well established and generally accepted, even if controversy surrounds the specific nature of their arrangement (e.g., Alderfer, 1972; Herzberg, 1974; Maslow, 1970). Dawis & Lofquist (1984) contend that curricula of medieval universities reflected a basic distinction between the servile and liberal arts: the former involving manual and exertive activities undertaken to satisfy basic needs and, by implication, the latter associated with aesthetic pursuits characterized by intellectual, spiritual, and contemplative activities. In simple terms, people need basic security and support, but they also generally desire some form of higher-order personal fulfillment. Recently, Schneider, Hanges, Smith, and Salvaggio (2003) presented empirical evidence that is consistent with this distinction. Their multisample confirmatory factor analyses yielded six distinct dimensions of job attitudes, including satisfaction with security, pay, work group, job fulfillment, work fulfillment, and empowerment. Others go so far as to contend that work situations are unique in their being able to provide satisfaction of human needs at all levels (e.g., Dawis & Lofquist, 1984; Roe, 1956).

We are proposing here an organizational parallel. We believe that an organization's higher-order requisites (parallel to an individual's desire for personal fulfillment) can be summarized as a desire for a favorable organizational climate and culture, characterized by order and civility. In general, functional organizations desire day-to-day conditions that are positive, enriching, enjoyable, and socioemotionally fertile for members. Whereas it is not absolutely imperative that these conditions exist, especially during short time frames, we suggest that organizations generally desire this state of affairs, and research has demonstrated empirically the functional benefits of favorable organizational climates (e.g., Gelade & Ivery, 2003). The conceptualization of higher-order requisites for both organizations and its members creates another basis for dual exchange comprising two fit relationships. These higher-order fit relationships are portrayed as FR3 and FR4 in Figure 19.1 and together are tantamount to the social exchange relationship mentioned earlier. Social exchange relationships are built around attachments, loyalties, perceived obligations, commitments, and personal identifications that members feel for their organizations, which are ostensibly based on some form of reciprocation by organizations.

Higher-Order Requisites and Supplies

FR3 is the match between an organization's desire for a favorable socioemotional climate and culture and the members' behaviors, valued norms, and beliefs about appropriate conduct that contribute to that climate and culture. Behaviors that contribute to a favorable climate and culture can be distinguished from more core task- or outcome-directed behaviors in that they generally are not explicitly proscribed and, therefore, are to a larger degree discretionary on the part of organization members (Motowidlo & Van Scotter, 1994). In fact, these behaviors variously are referred to as discretionary, extrarole, or peripheral and often are characterized as *organiza-*

tional citizenship. We concur with others that the broader class of behavior is best described as *contextual* (e.g., Goodman & Svyantek, 1999; Organ, 1997). Organization members supply contextual behaviors to help satisfy an organization's desire for a favorable climate and culture by voluntarily exhibiting behaviors that mutually benefit others (e.g., offering unsolicited assistance to coworkers, maintaining cordiality, exhibiting civility during conflict, not complaining about trivial problems, describing the organization in favorable terms to others, stimulating innovative ways of improving the organization versus gossiping about others, yelling at someone during a disagreement, sexually harassing a coworker, or stifling creativity via blatant malingering) and that generally make involvement in the organization more enriching, pleasurable, tolerant, and hospitable.

FR4 is the match between a member's desire for higher-order personal fulfillment and the organization's provision of opportunities for such fulfillment. This aspect of fit is what often has been referred to in the P-E fit literature as *desire-supply fit,* where desires are variously conceptualized as growth needs, goals, interests, preferences, or values (Tinsley, 2000). This terminological complexity portends the fact that personal fulfillment is clearly psychologically complex and, consequently, the conceptualization of this fit relationship will be complex. Generally speaking, we are using the term *personal fulfillment* to subsume such requisites as emotional support, affiliation, esteem, opportunities to manifest abilities and personality traits, and so forth. Bronfenbrenner and Ceci (1994) list six developmental outcomes that "represent the actualization of potentials" (p. 569), and they include directing and controlling one's own behavior, acquiring knowledge and skill, establishing and maintaining mutually rewarding relationships, and modifying and constructing one's own physical, social, and symbolic environment. We suggest that personal fulfillment even can involve organizational members' preferences for types of organization climate and culture, as reflected in the nature of supervisory practices or values (Van Vianen, 2000). Many of these qualities characterize high-performance work systems (Barling, Kelloway, & Iverson, 2003; Pfeffer, 1998), which have been shown to impact individual and organizational outcomes. Let it suffice for now that organizations vary considerably in how well they provide for the satisfaction of their members' higher-order requisites. Some specific forms of FR4 will become more apparent when we move to the next nomological level.

Characterizing Poor Higher-Order Fit

As was the case for FR1 and FR2, poor P-E fit can occur in FR3 or FR4 or both. A poor FR3 occurs when an organizational member fails to exhibit the contextual behaviors required to achieve a favorable climate and culture. In work organizations, this historically involved employees treating each other uncivilly, but this was often distinguished from performance. Increasingly, organizations are melding some aspects of contextual behavior into explicit definitions of job performance. Contextual behavior deficiencies can take the form of exhibiting passively or covertly counterproductive behaviors or refusing to exhibit productive interpersonal behaviors. Similarly, in nonwork organizations, poor FR3 involves members engaging in patterns of behavior that obstruct or limit the quality of the organization's climate and culture (e.g., a church's secretary constantly complaining about how boring the job is, a country-club member maliciously gossiping about another member, or a PTA officer criticizing someone's child in public). Poor FR4 occurs when an organization fails to provide adequately for members' needs for personal fulfillment. In work organizations, this can take the form of an organization noticeably not providing challenging assignments, learning opportunities, appropriate autonomy, or recognition of achievements. Similarly, in nonwork organizations, poor FR4 involves the organization failing to provide its members with opportunities for interpersonal interaction, social recognition, and awareness raising (e.g., a country club with "unexciting" facilities and boring events, a municipal government whose city council stifles free expression and disagreement, or a community social organization that minimizes members' involvement in event planning and participation). Given the complexity of personal fulfillment noted earlier, these examples merely scratch the surface of potential ways that FR3 and FR4 can be conceptualized, much less managed and maintained.

When poor fit in any of the four fit relationships develops, both individuals and organizations usually are motivated to adjust the fit. Of course, people differ and organizations differ in their tolerance of poor fit (i.e., flexibility or resilience) as well as in their reactions to poor fit (i.e., change self or change other) and in their tolerance for duration of poor fit and adjustment processes (i.e., perseverance).

Complementary versus Supplementary Fit

One last clarification is in order before we move to another nomological level. As we mentioned earlier, Muchinsky & Monahan (1987) introduced the concept of supplementary fit and stated that it exists when a person "supplements, embellishes, or possess characteristics which are similar to other individuals in an environment" (p. 269). Supplementary fit, originally defined as members of the organization sharing similar characteristics, is an example of members sharing similar profiles of attributes, or person-person fit (Van Vianen, 2000). One way to envision this form of fit would be to think of a "different" Figure 19.1 for each member of an organization. Supplementary fit refers to when the "Person" column (i.e., personal fulfillment needs, security and support needs, patterns of task and contextual behavior) for a target person (e.g., prospective new employee or member) is similar or identical to that for other organization members. Of course, this similarity can be viewed from any nomological level (i.e., Level I, Level II, or Level III) and often is evoked in the context of member knowledge, skill, ability, and other personal attribute (KSAO) profiles. Hence, supplementary fit, as originally conceived, actually is fit between organization members, defined as attribute similarity, rather than the environment, per se.

In the most articulated literature review and model of person-organization fit to date, Kristof (1996) distinguished between two aspects of complementary fit versus supplementary fit. The two forms of complementary fit in Kristof's framework referred to person and organization demands and supplies for such commodities as psychological and financial resources, interpersonal opportunities, and so forth, and as such reflect FR1 and FR3 collapsed together and FR2 and FR4 collapsed together. These higher-order versus lower-order aspects of fit, both from the organization's and from the person's perspectives, have very different implications for organizational as well as individual psychological functioning, and therefore we believe they should be distinguished from each other.

Kristof (1996) went on to reconceptualize supplementary fit to include "the relationship between the fundamental characteristics of an organization and a person" (p. 3). Similarly, Kristof-Brown (2000) defined supplementary fit as "when two entities (i.e., person and organization) share similar characteristics, and because of that similarity are compatible" (p. 642). Examples provided of characteristics that people and organizations might share include, "the culture, climate, values, goals, and norms" (Kristof, 1996, p. 3). This notion of supplementary fit (as shared characteristics between an organization and its members) requires personifying organizations along psychological dimensions conceived of as human individual differences (e.g., values as well as other KSAOs). Although we see heuristic value in this personification as discussed previously, we do want to point out that Kristof's definition of supplementary fit is conceptually asymmetrical because it is limited logically to more behaviorally abstract constructs that are less behaviorally specific. In other words, it is much easier to characterize an organization's values, goals, or norms as isomorphic with specific members' values, goals, or norms than to do so with certain abilities or skills, for instance. In fact, it is conceptually incoherent to personify an organization in very specific construct terms (e.g., reference to an organization's "lower back strength" or "fine motor dexterity"). For this reason, we endorse the original conceptualization of supplementary fit as similarity in the attribute profiles of organization members. Of course, some theorists take the position that in social organizations, the environment is the people comprising the organization, and therefore, if the people really do make the place (R. Hogan & Roberts, 2000; Schneider, 1987), then supplementary fit can be viewed as similarity between people in their FR1, FR2, FR3, and FR4 profiles at nomological Level I.

Although the people in the organization clearly represent the preeminent aspect of the social environment, we caution against neglecting other aspects of the environment, such as physical, cognitive, and affective demands posed by specific tasks and activities. We believe that fit between profiles of member personal attributes is best viewed at nomological Level II because of the greater psychological depth and the flexibility to conceptualize environmental demands associated with other people (e.g., interpersonal demands such as smoothing conflict between two coworkers) versus environmental demands tied directly to certain tasks or activities (e.g., physical demands such as having to climb a 200-foot ladder with 110 pounds of equipment) it affords.

To summarize the proposed model at nomological Level I, P-E fit involves four dual exchange relationships rather than the two most commonly targeted (i.e., ability-demand and desire-supply). The dual lower-order fit relationships are tied directly to individual and organizational performance. Higher-order fit relationships generally have a more indirect, albeit potentially quite potent, impact on individual and organizational functioning because of their linking organizational and personal states of functioning associated with longer-term comfort and resilience, freedom from undue angst, and general growth and favorable development. We believe the dichotomous fit taxonomy commonly referred to in the P-E fit literature is conceptually deficient and should, therefore, be replaced with the four fit relationships presented in Figure 19.1. We do want to point out that Level I of the current framework shares some features (e.g., organization and individual contributions and requirements) with the individual-organization interaction model proposed by Porter et al. (1975). But important differences exist as well (e.g., collapsing lower-order and higher-order resources together, conceptualizing person contributions as *skills and energies,* and not distinguishing between task versus contextual behavior). Despite what we consider to be some significant con-

ceptual gaps in their framework, we do encourage those interested in P-E fit to read their rich and substantive treatment of the topic.

Person-Environment Fit at Nomological Level II

A closer examination of the fit relationships previously described will help to refine our conceptualization of P-E fit. To enhance the analysis of these fit relationships we propose a framework for Level II that can be used to organize conceptions of task and contextual behavior, the personal attributes that underlie such behavior, and environmental circumstances relevant to the behavior. Level II is introduced in Figure 19.2. Level II delineates relatively distinct domains of human functioning. Figure 19.2 depicts the three *fundamental domains* of functioning, and these make up Level IIA. Level IIB comprises three additional domains created by the intersection of the fundamental domains. Finally, Level IIC is created from the intersection of all six previous domains. Each aspect of Level II will now be discussed.

Nomological Level IIA: Cognitive, Affective, and Physical Functioning

The foundation of nomological Level II is the explication of the three fundamental functional domains in which people interact with their environment—*physical, cognitive,* and *affective.* People possess physical, cognitive, and affective systems that manifest themselves in measurable individual differences in behavior and reactions. The cognitive and affective systems play executor roles (albeit different roles; cf. Izard, 1993; Judge & Larsen, 2001) in processing environmental information and combine with the physical system to act on the environment. As we will discuss later, we propose viewing environments as manifesting demands for functioning in each of these domains.

A significant chapter in the history of psychological theory and research had as its focus the identification and measurement of human enduring attributes in these fundamental domains. Dawis (2000) goes so far as to contend that "the identification and measurement of human capabilities and requirements has been the defining task of psychology since its inception in the Wundtian laboratory era" (p. 182). He goes on to suggest four areas of study, namely sensation-perception, cognition, affect (or emotion), and psychomotor response. We advance the current framework as more nomologically coherent and exhaustive but readily recognize the conceptual convergence.

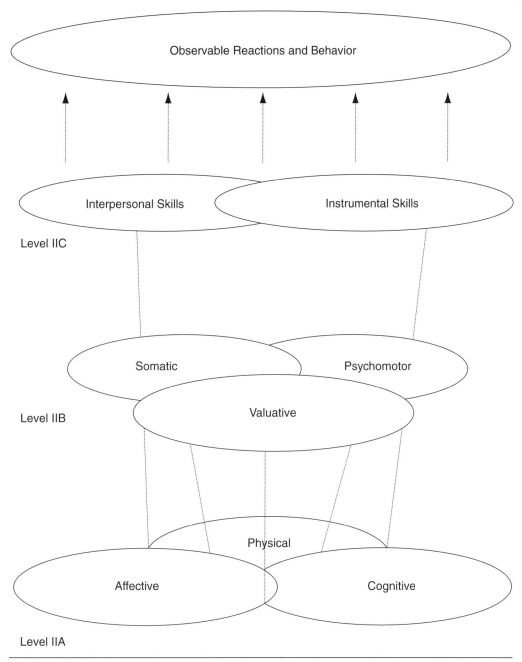

Figure 19.2   Domains of human functioning: Levels IIA, IIB, and IIC.

The triarchic view of human functioning advanced thus far is intended to be an organizing framework for myriad construct systems proposed by social and behavioral scientists over the years. We readily recognize that the boundaries between domains are fuzzy and prone to idiosyncratic interpretation depending on one's scientific and theoretical predilections. We do assert that it is possible to map most, if not all, conceptions of psychological and behavioral functioning onto this framework. For example, affective and cognitive functioning can be meaningfully distinguished (cf. Ekman, 1992; Izard, 1992), but they clearly interact. Affect is motivational—providing cues for attraction and repulsion, whereas cognition is knowledge-based—involving learning, memory, symbol manipulation, and language. However, because affect is motivational and cognition underlies person-environment transactions, their interaction is common, leading to affective-cognitive structures (Izard, 1993). Some representative cross-domain construct systems will be reviewed in our discussion of nomological Level III.

Nomological Level IIB: Psychomotor, Valuative, and Somatic Functioning

Level II can be viewed at each of three levels of specificity, and all three levels (i.e., Levels IIA, IIB, and IIC) are elaborated in Figure 19.2. The elaboration of Level II is based on the premise that the three fundamental domains of functioning (Level IIA) interact, and their interactions create interstitial construct domains (Level IIB). In turn, constructs at the fundamental and the interstitial levels "cooperate" to create hybrid behavioral constellations. The *interstitial domains* can be thought of as domains of functioning where two fundamental domains combine or interact. More specifically, the intersection of the cognitive and physical domains is commonly referred to as *psychomotor* functioning. This domain involves the coordination of physical movement and cognitively processed information. Exemplar constructs in this domain include gross motor coordination, fine finger dexterity, control precision, and complex reaction time, all involving the visual/perceptual processing of information coordinated with physical movements.

We call the intersection of the cognitive and affective domains the *valuative* domain (cf. Wapner & Demick, 2000). Constructs in this domain involve evaluative cognitive judgments combined with affective reactions. Exemplar constructs in this domain include general and specific attitudes, beliefs, values, preferences, interests, and job satisfaction, which is increasingly being conceived of as a construct with both affective and cognitive components (Brief & Weiss, 2002; Judge & Larsen, 2001; Schleicher, Watt, & Greguras, 2004).

Finally, we call the intersection between physical and affective functioning, the *somatic* domain. Somatic functioning involves interactions between the physical and affective systems and has received relatively more attention from psychiatric and clinical professionals to explain pathogenic symptomology (e.g., psychosomatic disorders or emotion-based physical ailments). Health psychologists and, more generally, psychologists interested in "positive psychology" (e.g., Diener, Suh, Lucas, & Smith, 1999; Seligman & Csikszentmihalyi, 2000) are beginning actively to conceptualize individual differences relevant to "mind-body" relations and physical-affective resilience. Links between affective, cognitive, and physical functioning are beginning to be demonstrated empirically (e.g., Cohen, 1996; Cohen, Tyrrell, &

Smith, 1993; Schaubroeck, Jones, & Xie, 2001; Zeier, Brauchli, & Joller-Jemelka, 1996). An exemplar in this relatively infant construct domain is stress hardiness.

Nomological Level IIC: Instrumental and Interpersonal Knowledge and Skills

This level represents constructs often referred to as knowledge domains and skills. As such, these constructs are more experiential and learned than many of the Level IIA and Level IIB constructs. Specifically, we propose two broad classes of knowledge/skill constructs—instrumental and interpersonal—hereafter referred to for simplicity merely as skills. *Instrumental skills* are constellations of learned knowledge-based behavior patterns, resulting from the joint operation of fundamental and interstitial constructs at Levels IIA and IIB. Instrumental skills involve active manipulation of data and things in one's immediate environment for the purpose of performing a task or otherwise enhancing task performance (e.g., welding pieces of tubular steel together according to strict specifications, landing a big fish after adroitly luring it onto a hook, skiing slalom without incurring bodily harm, ad infinitum). Although constructs in all six domains can operate in determining instrumental skills, these skills generally are saturated with physical, psychomotor, and cognitive functioning.

Interpersonal skills are constellations of learned knowledge-based behavior patterns, resulting from the joint operation of fundamental and interstitial constructs at Levels IIA and IIB that involve active manipulation of social interactions with people in one's immediate environment for the purpose of performing a task or otherwise enhancing task performance (e.g., delivering a stellar lecture to a group of students, counseling a couple to better understand their relationship difficulties, striking up a mutually enjoyable conversation with someone in an airport, ad infinitum). Although constructs in all six domains can operate in determining interpersonal skills, these skills generally are saturated with affective, attitudinal, and cognitive functioning. Together, instrumental and interpersonal skills constitute the characteristic ways the people engage their environment in order to "get things done." This distinction overlaps conceptually with the common portrayal of tasks involving interactions with people, data, and things (Fine & Wiley, 1971; U.S. Department of Labor, 1977), although we are collapsing *data* and *things* into the instrumental skills category. The breadth and depth of skills in these two broad skill categories are determined by one's complement of individual differences that can be conceptualized at nomological Level IIB and Level IIA. The distinction between source versus surface traits is relevant here (Binning, LeBreton, & Adorno, 1999; R. Hogan, 1991). Level IIC is closest to the nomological "surface," whereas Level IIA is nomologically deeper and functions more as a source for certain behavioral regularities.

Person-Environment Fit at Nomological Level III

Each of the domains of functioning previously described has spawned numerous theoretical construct systems to describe individual differences in patterns of behavior, some of which are landmarks in the history of psychological science. For example, Binet's Intelligence or Spearman's g in the cognitive domain, Freud's id or neuroticism in the affective domain, and Sheldon's somatotypes or Fleishman's trunk strength in the physical domain (albeit less well known, but equally exemplifying) represent exemplar constructs in various theoretical attempts to identify enduring individual differences in how people function in each domain. A sample of other notable constructs in these fundamental domains includes quantitative, verbal, and spatial (cognitive abilities); need for achievement, self-esteem, positive affectivity, and trait anxiety (affective traits); and cardiovascular stamina, physical height, somatotype, lower back strength, and physical attractiveness (physical attributes).

Of the interstitial construct domains, the psychomotor and valuative domains have received the most attention in the past. Fleishman's (1972) taxonomy of psychomotor abilities is the dominant framework in this area. High-profile construct systems in the valuative domain include taxonomies of values (Dawis & Lofquist, 1984; O'Reilly, Chatman, & Caldwell, 1991; Rokeach, 1973), vocational interests (Holland, 1997), and facets of job satisfaction (Dawis & Lofquist, 1984; Smith, Kendall, & Hulin, 1969). As we mentioned earlier, there has been relatively less systematic taxonomic work in the somatic domain, but the increased interest in health psychology, the positive psychology movement, and links between emotional functioning and physical health and somatic complaints is fueling research in this area.

Cross-domain construct systems also are emerging, some of which incorporate mechanisms to explain environmental contingencies. A variety of theories of personality explicitly posit the role of cognitive-affective structures in determining characteristic behavior patterns (e.g., Epstein, 1994; Mischel, 2004; Mischel & Shoda, 1995; Paulhus & Martin, 1987). Perhaps the best example of a cross-domain theory that also explicitly incorporates person and environment characteristics is Walter Mischel's cognitive-affective personality system (CAPS). This theory posits individual differences in

cognitive-affective mediating units (e.g., expectancies, beliefs, encodings) and the manner in which these units interact with psychological features of situations. Of particular interest are the hypothesized individual differences in *if . . . then . . .* situation-behavior relations. Each person is thought to possess unique cognitive-affective units that link situational characteristics with reliable patterns of reactions and behavior. The CAPS theory of personality shows real promise in explaining behavioral variance in typical patterns of behavior in myriad social situations. If effectively combined with information about physical, psychomotor, and cognitive abilities, it could increment predictions of performance in many work and nonwork contexts.

Other cross-domain work includes the relatively new construct of emotional intelligence, which has a core conception involving the cognitive awareness of emotion and the skills to regulate affective reactions, and it is distinct from personality constructs (Goleman, 1995; Law, Wong, & Song, 2004). Dawis and Lofquist's (1984) TWA explicitly posits the combined development of abilities across cognitive and psychomotor domains concomitantly with valuative (i.e., values and needs) attributes. Another example of cross-domain theory and research is the posited relationships between physical attributes and personality constructs. Judge and Cable (2004) recently proposed that physical height relates to career success via self-esteem and social esteem. Similar research has examined links between physical attractiveness and aspects of personality and interpersonal functioning (Hosada, Stone-Romero, & Coats, 2003). Another cross-level research focus involves examining interactions between personality traits and interpersonal skills (e.g., Witt & Ferris, 2003). The central issue here is that the proposed framework can be used to organize theoretical constructs both in terms of what Embretson (1983) calls construct representation as well as nomothetic span. In other words, reliable individual differences in each domain can be identified, and the network of their empirical relationships can be delineated. Coherent nomological mapping of constructs and their relations, for both people and their environments, will enhance our understanding of P-E fit.

Thus far, we have examined P-E fit at the level of environmental exchange (Level I), and the domains of psychological functioning (Level II) that are evoked in such exchange, and some specific construct systems within the different domains of functioning (Level III). In the next section we will integrate the three by discussing how each of the four fit relationships (i.e., FR1, FR2, FR3, and FR4) has been examined psychologically in the research literature.

THE PSYCHOLOGY OF PERSON-ENVIRONMENT FIT

Each of the four fundamental fit relationships involves the perception and interpretation of one's own and others' contributions to the exchange. These perceptions and interpretations are determined by the psychological attributes of the parties involved. In the following sections we discuss the four fit relationships in the context of a sample of representative psychological literature relevant to each, in an initial attempt to demonstrate how the psychological research literature can be integrated around P-E fit concepts.

Representative Psychological Research on Fit Relationship 1

The extent to which organizational members engage in task behaviors that lead to the attainment of organizationally valued outcomes is the heart of what traditionally has been described in the industrial/organizational literature as individual job performance. Binning and Barrett (1989) defined performance as a domain of behavior-outcome units. By implication, they showed that traditional notions of human resource selection system validity are largely about the quality of decisions regarding this dimension of fit. They also suggested that the effective delineation of requisite member behaviors (i.e., the specification of performance domains, an organization's lower-order requisites) is dependent on a priori explicit delineation of valued organizational outcomes.

It is important to distinguish between work behavior and job performance to highlight the importance of interpreting a behavior's value (i.e., whether it qualifies as performance) relative to specific environmental circumstances and social standards (Tett & Burnett, 2003). The basic point here is that a given behavior (or constellation of behaviors) may be quite effective in one context, but quite ineffective in another, and that P-E fit, especially in socially constructed environments, is relative to local social standards. In work organizations this may take the form of a supervisor's evaluations, a team's consensus impressions of another member's effectiveness, or the aggregate of 360-degree feedback about an employee's work contributions. Of course this basic logic can be generalized to any person's involvement in any type of organization. In a country club this may take the form of the dominant evaluative theme about someone that is growing on the club's member grapevine or, in the case of a retirement community, the director's opinions about the civility of a community member. One important implication of this inevitable social interpretation process is that the ultimate success of attempts to create effective or optimal P-E fit is often, if not generally,

dependent on these social interpretations of behavior. Dysfunctional perturbations in these social interpretations (e.g., a supervisor who rates an otherwise outstanding performer as poor because of feeling threatened and harboring inexplicable personal dislike or deliberately false rumors being spread about a club member) create forms of P-E misfit that are not directly tied to whether the individual can achieve valued organizational outcomes, independent of certain individuals in the social system. Moreover, poor fit can morph rapidly into good fit upon the reassignment of the supervisor or the public exoneration of the gossip victim. This social mediation of the more formal P-E relationship adds a significant layer of "error" to any P-E fit formulation or intervention.

In work organizations, formal human resource management attempts to enhance FR1 take the general form of either (a) personnel selection, (b) employee training and development, or (c) job design, depending on the assumptions about people guiding the intervention. In many nonwork organizations, attempts to enhance (or maintain) FR1 take the form of (a) member recruitment and selection (e.g., accepting only the "right kinds" of members), (b) member socialization and indoctrination (e.g., stringent initiation rituals), and (c) differential task or project assignments (e.g., having the political fundraiser reception at the home of the wealthiest member). Numerous analytic frameworks for delineating behavioral requirements, as well as individual difference requirements, have been proposed in the professional literature (Borman, Hanson, & Hedge, 1997; Guion, 1991; Lubinski, 2000).

Representative Psychological Research on Fit Relationship 2

It is interesting to note that historically, FR1 garnered greater emphasis by management and organizational scholars well into the twentieth century. Early industrial organizations notoriously neglected FR2, taking the general form of relatively less concern for employee safety and welfare compared to the organization's requisites. Economic conditions being what they generally were, employee lower-order–need strength was relatively stronger, and thus many employees endured poorer work conditions than generally would be tolerated today. With the increased awareness of workplace abuses (e.g., Max Weber's bureaucratic social reform) and the advent of workplace democratization, the Quality of Work Life movement, and human relations organizational theory (e.g., Argyris, 1957, 1964), as well as federal legislation designed to improve working conditions (e.g., Fair Labor Standards Act of 1938; Occupational Safety and Health Administration), FR2 came under increasing scrutiny during the latter half of the twentieth century.

FR2, the extent to which an organization's members receive adequate security and basic support, often has been considered the purview of operations management rather than psychologists. However, research on the psychological implications of disruptions of this fit can be gleaned from the psychological literature. Research on performance constraints exemplifies how an organization's failure to provide members with adequate resources to support their task performance can affect FR1, as well as members' reactions to organizational membership (Peters, O'Connor, & Rudolf, 1980). Performance constraints can be overt and obvious such as not having sufficient raw materials to continue normal production or contractual restrictions on productive activities. Tett and Burnett (2003) discuss situational constraints that have their effects more covertly. They propose the existence of situation constraints on *trait expression.* Specifically, they suggest that all situations possess cues that make the expression of some traits more "relevant" than others. A situational characteristic that restricts cues for the expression of a particular trait is considered a constraint. These constraints act indirectly on task behavior by restricting the expression of trait-driven behavior that may be particularly relevant to the performance of specific tasks. Situational constraints can act directly on task behavior (Level I) or on the evocation of specific traits relevant to task behavior (Level II).

The last decade has seen a burgeoning research literature on organizational support theory that explicitly examines the social exchange between organizations and their employees and the variables that affect employee feelings of commitment, loyalty, and welfare (Rhoades & Eisenberger, 2002). In a recent meta-analytic review, three areas of organizational support (i.e., fairness, supervisory support, and rewards and favorable job conditions) were found to predict perceived organizational support, which was in turn shown to relate to various outcomes such as job satisfaction, commitment, and performance, and in another study positive organizational support was associated with lower levels of employee deviance (Colbert, Mount, Harter, Witt, & Barrick, 2004). Employee perceptions of an organization's justice and support even can be moderated by the structure of the organization (Ambrose & Schminke, 2003).

Another line of research that can be viewed from the perspective of FR2 is research on job stress and burnout, especially when these result from work in high-risk occupations. Burnout (and its component emotional exhaustion, detachment and cynicism, and feelings of reduced efficacy) results from people chronically experiencing overwhelming demands, such as role overload (e.g., too many demands with too few resources), and other forms of poor work conditions that represent threats to one's welfare (Maslach, Schaufeli, & Leiter,

2001). It clearly has been demonstrated that prolonged exposure to work conditions that engender burnout leads to withdrawal (e.g., absenteeism, turnover) as well as to diminished performance. In this context we want to call attention to Maslach, Schaufeli, & Leiter's (2001) call for broadened conception of person-environment fit in the theory and research on burnout. They state that "the challenge is to extend the job-person paradigm to a broader and more complex conceptualization of the person situated in the job context" (p. 413). They posit six domains within one's work environment: workload, control, reward, community, fairness, and values. The suggestion that individual differences may exist in the perceived importance of these domains is a provocative call for psychologically substantive P-E fit research. We believe these domains involve both FR2 and FR4 delineated earlier and represent a heuristic broadening of P-E fit construct domains. In addition to expanding conceptions of the environment, work is being done to frame the burnout construct in "positive" psychological terms by positing *job engagement* as energy, involvement, and efficacy. Research has begun to show that burnout is related to *job demands,* whereas job engagement is related to *job resources* (Maslach, Schaufeli, & Leiter, 2001). We suggest that the latter is more relevant to FR2, whereas the former is more relevant to FR1.

There is a consistent and strong body of research evidence linking lack of organizational support to burnout, especially lack of supervisory support. This literature needs to be integrated with the literature previously cited on perceived organizational support. Maslach, Schaufeli, & Leiter (2001) suggest that the violation of the *psychological contract* (i.e., reciprocal exchange relationships) between an individual and their organization likely erodes the notion of reciprocity, a critical factor in maintaining well-being. The literature on psychological contracts between organizations and their employees (Dabos & Rousseau, 2004; Rousseau, 1995) clearly is relevant to FR2, although the multiple dimensions of these contracts and their relationships clearly are complex (Lambert, Edwards, & Cable, 2003). Finally, Brief and Weiss (2002) report an encouraging trend in that "threats to physical well-being are beginning to receive the attention they deserve" (p. 288). We hope this trend continues.

Representative Psychological Research on Fit Relationship 3

The systematic research in this area has increased dramatically in the past decade, due largely to the flattening and "unstructuring" of organizations, the concomitant increase in fuzzy or boundaryless jobs (Nelson, 1997), as well as the increased attention to psychological explanations for volitional behavior. A dominant research paradigm during the mid-twentieth century focused on identifying and developing measurement processes for cognitive, psychomotor, and physical abilities because of the focus on explaining and predicting task behaviors "imposed" by structured, relatively routine jobs with rigid behavioral boundaries. A premium was placed on predicting maximum performance differences, with the assumption that management pressure or technologically induced control would ensure this maximum performance. Changes in the nature of jobs and management philosophies, as well as the evolution of legal mandates about justifying and defending staffing decisions, have fueled considerable interest in psychological explanations for "typical" patterns of volitional employee behavior (e.g., personality traits, attitudinal constructs, affective bases for behavior). Early research in this new area focused on distinguishing between contextual and task behavior (Organ, 1988) as well as on the evaluation of contextual behavior. More recently, construct clarification continues. Its impact on various aspects of organizational functioning has been addressed (e.g., Cropanzano et al., 2003; Zellars, Tepper, & Duffy, 2002) as well as the cross-cultural generalizability of these findings (e.g., Hui, Lee, & Rousseau, 2004).

One line of research very specifically relevant to FR3 is the work on organizational climate as a social-cognitive construction (Zohar & Luria, 2004). Defined as "a socially construed and shared representation of those aspects of organizational environment that inform role behavior" (p. 322), *climate* can be viewed as facet-specific perceptual convergences about organizational events that mediate actual environmental characteristics and their relations to various outcomes. The role that managerial practices play in making coherent an organization's climate(s) is a fruitful nexus for integrating research from these two areas of psychological literature. More generally, conceptualizing climate perceptions as the result of negotiated agreements about the meaning of an environment and the symbolic interactionism implied by this view (Zohar & Luria, 2004) can provide an initial framework for examining this aspect of P-E fit.

At another level of analysis, empirical research is beginning to demonstrate the association between positive employee relations and organizational performance. For example, Fulmer, Gerhart, and Scott (2003) suggest that positive employee relations impact organizational functioning via enhanced collective worker quality, motivation, and productivity but also via "the existence of idiosyncratic and hard-to-imitate internal assets" (p. 968). Positive employee relations are viewed as strategic assets that enhance a firm's competitive advantage and are likely associated with lower incidence of employee deviance (Colbert et al., 2004). Aggregate jus-

tice perceptions also have been shown to impact organizational outcomes (Simons & Roberson, 2003) as well as the conditions comprising high-performance work systems (e.g., recognition of the uniqueness of human resources, investment in human capital, and human resource practices that emphasize employee participation). Barling et al. (2003) even have found that work conditions that favor personal fulfillment actually impact occupational safety. This implies the interaction between the fit relationships posited here. In sum, research results indicate that positive employee relations are associated with better organizational performance. Research is needed to link employee attitudes and behavior with organizational-level functioning by identifying the specific mechanisms that underlie these findings.

Representative Psychological Research on Fit Relationship 4

Starting in the middle of the twentieth century, concern for the role one's socioemotional environment plays in determining patterns of behavior and other reactions to work gained momentum. The relative neglect of this aspect of P-E fit likely crescendoed in the 1970s when widespread worker anomie was labeled the "blue-collar blues" or the "Lordstown Syndrome" and the Quality of Work Life movement took hold (Bass & Barrett, 1981). Theorists and practitioners with predilections ranging from humanism (e.g., Alderfer, 1972; Maslow, 1970), to human relations organizations (e.g., Argyris, 1957, 1964; McGregor, 1960), to job enrichment (e.g., Hackman & Oldham, 1980), to transformational leadership (e.g., Avolio, 1999), to total quality management (e.g., Deming, 1986) variously have embraced the general notion that people are driven to grow and "be more human" by seeking personal fulfillment, and environments that facilitate this growth are generally better for people. Of course, individual differences in the strength of growth and fulfillment needs have been proposed (e.g., Hackman & Oldham, 1980), but the general drive to function in a "higher quality" environment that allows some forms of personal growth and expression is commonly recognized. At a more macroorganizational level of analysis, Argyris (1957, 1964) was a major proponent of an interactionist perspective on this aspect of person-organization fit. His focus was on restructuring organizations to provide greater decision control and involvement in participatory management. Similarly, influential conceptualizations of job satisfaction were built on the notion that discrepancies between what an environment provides and what an individual desires explain valuative reactions to work (Beehr, 1996; Locke, 1976).

A full delineation of factors relevant to the psychology of personal fulfillment is beyond the scope of this chapter, but it is important to realize that research on certain facets of job satisfaction can provide rudimentary taxonomies for clarifying this aspect of P-E fit. Individual differences in needs for tangible rewards (Lawler & Jenkins, 1992), benefits (Gerhart & Milkovich, 1992), social relationships (Hackman, 1992), specific work activities (Hackman & Oldham, 1980), achievement opportunities (McClelland, 1961), and so forth, as well as research on adaptations to job dissatisfaction (Miller & Rosse, 2002) and research on subjective well-being (Diener et al., 1999; Diener, Scollon, & Lucas, 2003), can guide research and theory about this important aspect of P-E fit. Research in this latter area already is demonstrating that environments present different opportunities for trait expression, some of which foster well-being better than others (Brandstatter, 1994), and that pleasant affect results from engaging in behaviors consistent with one's natural trait dispositions (Moskowitz & Cote, 1995; Tett & Burnett, 2003). These findings may be tied to the "density" of behavior-contingent reinforcements offered by different environments and their relations to individual differences (Dawis & Lofquist, 1984; Diener, 1997). Characterizing environments in terms of demands for cognitive, affective, and physical functioning discussed earlier would move in the direction of identifying differences in P-E fit that may enhance our ability to achieve FR4.

CONCEPTUALIZING ENVIRONMENTS

Characterizing environments in psychologically meaningful ways may well be the Achilles' heel of P-E fit theory. Despite decades-long research programs to develop several well-known models of P-E fit, R. Hogan and Roberts (2000) go so far as to state that "situations have yet to be adequately conceptualized" (p. 3). We believe this is especially true when one considers all of the domains of functioning outlined earlier. A comprehensive taxonomy of environments would characterize the four reciprocal exchange fit relationships in terms of physical, psychomotor, cognitive, valuative, affective, somatic, interpersonal, and instrumental demands for functioning. Even relatively simple operationalizations can capture meaningful differences. For example, Diefendorff and Richard (2003) identified job differences in interpersonal demands by having incumbents describe their jobs and by having expert raters trichotomize based on interpersonal requirements.

Historically, two major schools of psychological research and theory have characterized the conceptualizing of orga-

nizational environments. First is the focus on the extent to which a given environment is congruent with one's vocational interests, preferences, values, or personality. The environment generally was viewed at a broad level of analysis as a vocation or career (i.e., P-vocation fit), rather than specific organizations (i.e., P-O fit) or jobs (i.e., P-J fit). The focus on these valuative constructs as environmental characteristics of choice is most notably reflected in Holland's RIASEC and Dawis and Lofquist's TWA and derives from a desire to explain such outcomes as career choice, job satisfaction, or tenure. Valuative dimensions (i.e., interstitial constructs combining cognitive and affective functioning) have been long thought to explain the lion's share of variance in decisions to seek out and stay employed in a given work environment.

The second major focus is the characterization of environments in terms of physical, psychomotor, and cognitive abilities, deemphasizing affective and affective-cognitive functioning. This abilities model dominated personnel-selection research and practice for much of the twentieth century; however, the characterization of environments was more an "implicit theory of fit" (Schneider, 2001). It was implicit in that work environments were routinely analyzed (via job and task analysis), and their demands were translated into requisite knowledge, skills, and abilities (KSAs). This often was done judgmentally and in accordance with a given job analyst's implicit theory of P-E relations, rather than a research- or theory-based taxonomy of environmental characteristics. Some more systematic models of P-E fit did emerge from this job analysis tradition that in effect taxonomized job environments (e.g., Dawis & Lofquist, 1984; Fine & Wiley, 1971; Harvey, 1991; Lopez, Kesselman, & Lopez, 1981; McCormick, Jeanneret, & Mecham, 1972; Peterson et al., 2001), but their adoption by most research and applied selection specialists was sporadic. During this same time frame, there always was a relatively "underground" movement to use job analysis as a basis for determining personality requirements, thus broadening the construct spectrum to include affective functioning. However, this trend did not enter mainstream selection research until the 1990s when renewed interest in emotions and affective functioning gained momentum (Brief & Weiss, 2002; Judge & Larsen, 2001) and conceptualizing person-organization fit was viewed as an important need (Judge & Ferris, 1992).

Another conceptual gap in the two schools previously described is the relative neglect of aversive environmental stimuli in determining reactions and behavior. The "valuative school" emphasized the role of preferences, values, and desires in determining P-E fit. In other words, the nexus of fit was between what persons desired and whether the environment satisfied that want. The "abilities school" emphasized whether individuals could, under maximum performance conditions, engage in the behaviors required by the organization. Both of these emphases neglects the systematic ways in which environments can affect people via aversive circumstances. The way that environments can engender negative affective reactions has been studied in the stress literature (e.g., Burke, Brief, & George, 1993), relying heavily on concepts such as role overload, conflict, or ambiguity. There has been little systematic research on the specific environmental characteristics that engender negative affect. One approach introduced by Bernardin (1987) assesses individual differences in negative reactions to specific job characteristics. Others are building on this approach and investigating the combined role of trait negative affectivity and job-specific negative affectivity in determining work outcomes (Adorno & Binning, 2001; Binning & Adorno, 2001; LeBreton, Binning, Adorno, & Melcher, 2004). Another approach focuses on daily hassles and how they affect functioning (e.g., Zohar, 1999). Systematically identifying how environmental conditions engender negative emotional reactions, in addition to how they satisfy individuals' needs and desires, may prove to be an especially useful perspective on P-E fit. In their review of research on affect in the workplace, Brief and Weiss (2002) concluded that, "What we do not have and need are theories that guide us in identifying specific kinds of work conditions and/or events (physical, social, or economic) associated with specific affective states" (p. 299).

Building on the Level II domains of functioning previously described, we suggest that environments can be conceptualized more explicitly in terms of demands for human functioning. Environments present circumstances that require behavior, and, therefore, these environmental circumstances can be conceived of in terms of the relative importance of each type of functioning. More specifically, on the environmental side of fit, the organization requires behavior from members (i.e., FR1 and FR3). As such, organizations present situational and environmental demands that require (or at least evoke) myriad forms of members' physical, psychomotor, cognitive, valuative, affective, somatic, instrumental, and interpersonal functioning. Continuing in the anthropomorphic vein discussed earlier, it is possible to conceptualize organizations as having physical, cognitive, and affective functioning systems (cf. Dawis & Lofquist, 1984), even if the specific behaviors and actions in each domain are different from those exhibited by individual members. In fact, the personification of organizations as humanlike entities underlies organizational support theory (Rhoades & Eisenberger, 2002) and research on organizational personalities (Slaughter et al., 2004). Therefore, a given P-E interaction often can be con-

ceptualized in commensurate terms of person functioning (e.g., performance in a beauty pageant requires physical attractiveness) or in terms of organization functioning (e.g., performance in a competitive enrollment or recruitment market requires that a university's facilities be physically attractive). In other circumstances it may be best to characterize organizations' needs for member behavior in terms of human functioning in critical domains.

INTEGRATING ACROSS NOMOLOGICAL LEVELS

In Figure 19.3 we arrange the fundamental fit relationships (Level I) and the domains of functioning (Level II) in such a way as to portray how they functionally relate and to facilitate seeing them in a conceptually integrative way. Moving from left to right, the supplies for the dual social exchange fuel the attainment of valued outcomes, but this attainment is mediated by the extent to which the supplies satisfy requisites. The four fit relationships discussed earlier involve fit between (a) patterns of behavior and judgments about that behavior vis-à-vis organizational functioning (i.e., FR1 and FR3) and (b) members' experience (i.e., perceptions, cognitions, and feelings) of the organization's supplies (i.e., FR2 and FR4). These patterns of behavior, the *patterns of experienced supplies,* and the person's outcomes from this interaction are nomologically undergirded by individual profiles of personal attributes. This results in five general construct links (CLs). We will briefly enumerate these links and then propose some research needed to clarify their role in P-E fit.

Together CLs 1, 2, 3, 4, and 5 represent the links between an individual's personal characteristics (i.e., psychological constructs) and their functioning (i.e., reactions and behavior) in a particular organizational environment. CL1 links specific profiles of cognitive, affective, physical, somatic, psychomotor, valuative, interpersonal, and instrumental attributes to specific patterns of task behavior. As mentioned earlier, this has been the focus of personnel and human resource selection for years, but there clearly has been greater emphasis on cognitive, physical, and psychomotor attributes, with only recent attention shifting to the role of affective, somatic, and valuative attributes. CL2 links underlying attributes to patterns of contextual behavior in an attempt to identify predictors of behaviors that demonstrate citizenship, loyalty, and discretionary civility that enhance and facilitate functioning in the organization. Not only are the boundaries of task and contextual behavior domains being clarified, research on which attributes underlie each class of behaviors is beginning to appear. CL3 links personal attributes to experienced lower-order security and basic well-being. Clearly there are indi-

Supplies   **Requisites**   **Outcomes**

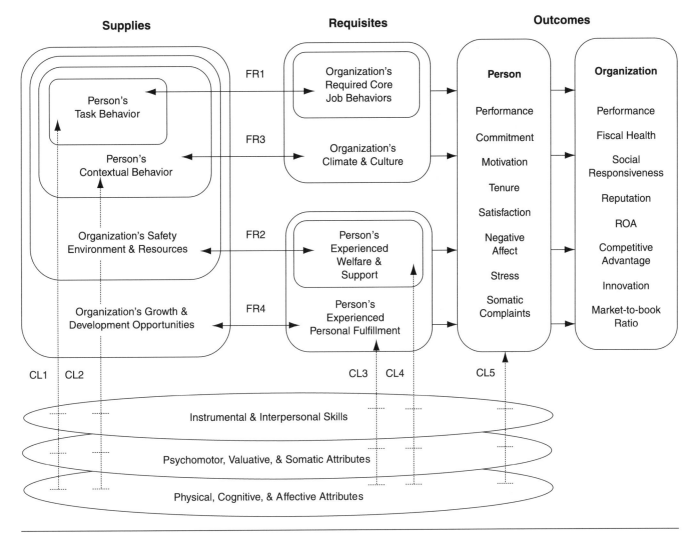

Figure 19.3   An integrative view of nomological Levels I and II.

vidual differences in how likely an individual is to experience security and support in different situations, but those situational characteristics that engender these experiences, and the psychological meaning of situational features, need to be better explored. Past theory and research has focused on how environmental characteristics affect personal reactions and outcomes, but CL3 represents how those situational factors interact with personal attributes to explain outcomes. Similarly, CL4 links profiles of personal attributes with experiences of higher-order fulfillment in the context of organizational membership. CL5 represents the psychological underpinnings of various reactions and outcomes to P-E fit. In other words, the psychological attributes and mechanisms by which different forms of fit (or misfit) engender different types of reactions from different individuals are portrayed in CL5.

The research literature is beginning to produce tests of these various construct links underlying P-E fit. For example,

Colbert et al. (2004) examined how personality traits of conscientiousness, emotional stability, and agreeableness interacted with employee perceptions of the work situation to predict workplace deviance. They found that when employees low in conscientiousness and emotional stability perceived that the organization did not provide developmental opportunities, they exhibited more deviant behavior (i.e., passive withholding of performance) compared to their more conscientious and emotionally stable coworkers. Similarly, when employees low in agreeableness perceived that the organization was not providing sufficient support, they engaged in more deviant behavior. It is interesting to note that these authors contend that "the study of situational perceptions suffers from the lack of an organizing taxonomy" (Colbert et al., 2004, p. 600). The framework presented here is an initial attempt to provide such an organized taxonomy of P-E fit constructs. In another recent study, Simmering, Colquitt,

Noe, and Porter (2003) demonstrated that personality interacts with person-organization autonomy fit to explain employee-initiated development. In other words, they proposed that the more conscientious employees would react to either too little or too much job autonomy by engaging in more self-development activities, compared to their less conscientious coworkers. They reasoned that the development of job skills and competencies would be viewed as a way to increase fit, either by increasing autonomy or by increasing self-confidence and subsequent need for autonomy. Taken together this recent research exemplifies how the combined study of environmental characteristics and interactions with specific psychological constructs can illuminate the complex P-E relationships.

SOME DIRECTIONS FOR FUTURE RESEARCH

We now turn to a brief outline of some testable research ideas framed within the model proposed here. In this section we advance a small sample of research agenda items to illustrate how the proposed framework can guide and organize empirical investigations of P-E fit.

Research Direction One

A reasonable initial test of the proposed framework would involve operationalizing each of the fit relationships and linking them empirically to outcomes. The framework proposed here suggests that all four aspects of fit are important for achieving desirable outcomes. A multivariate or meta-analytic test of whether each fit relationship increments outcome predictions would provide a summary initial test of this general proposition.

Research Direction Two

We call for more research focused on conceptually and empirically distinguishing between task behavior and contextual behavior and identifying how work behavior in these domains may be affected differentially by lack of fit. For example, as organizations shift from job-specific conceptualizations of demands to organization-level demands and a greater focus on broad categories of competencies rather than job-specific knowledge, skills, and abilities (Bowen, Ledford, & Nathan, 1991; Shippman, et al., 2001), fundamental notions of person-organization fit are modified. Competency models are likely to include psychological constructs at different nomological levels linked to outcomes at various individual and organizational levels. It is interesting to speculate that in organizations where competency models supplant more

traditional job analysis-based KSAO models, FR3 may be more important than FR1 for predicting certain outcomes, such as individual performance or organizational competitive advantage.

Research Direction Three

An example of how the framework can be used to guide microlevel investigations might involve the issue of affective functioning in reactions to job characteristics. As we mentioned earlier, relatively little research has focused on how jobs engender negative emotional reactions in incumbents. A specific focus on negative affective and valuative functioning could answer the following questions. How much variance can be explained by reliable individual differences in negative reactions to task characteristics in general versus identifying specific task characteristics that engender negative emotional reactions in certain people? If an incumbent labors emotionally in the performance of task behaviors, does that affect the performance of contextual behaviors? If an incumbent experiences negative emotions at work, but does not labor to suppress their display, how is the development of burnout affected? How do negative reactions differ when evoked by task performance versus lack of experienced welfare or personal fulfillment?

The list of unanswered questions about negative affective functioning is formidable, but research in this area clearly presents the potential for both theoretical and applied utility. For example, our research has demonstrated that predictions of turnover in customer service jobs is incremented by assessing not only trait-based negative affective functioning but also task-specific negative affectivity (Adorno & Binning, 2001; LeBreton et al., 2004). Research expanding this focus to include other outcomes clearly is needed.

Research Direction Four

Another direction for more microlevel investigation could pursue several issues raised by Lambert et al. (2003). They found that, when considering breach or fulfillment of psychological contracts, the direction of fit is important. Using polynomial regression they demonstrated how deficiencies versus excesses of various inducements can have differential effects on certain outcomes. We join these authors in calling for research on "a broader array of psychological contract terms to the extent the results reported" as well as expanding the set of "outcomes beyond satisfaction to include other affective and behavioral consequences of breach and fulfillment" (Lambert et al., 2003, p. 928).

Research Direction Five

Workplace violence and aggression are increasingly garnering research attention for a variety of reasons. FR2 links the organization's provision of safety to members' experience of welfare. In addition to physical safety, it is important to understand how "psychological safety" can be conceptualized and enhanced. In other words, what determines whether a given environment is experienced as "safe"? What types of enduring individual differences help explain different perceptions of environmental safety and interpersonal nurturance? The affective and interpersonal roots (i.e., CL4) of these experiences and their role in determining various outcomes is another area needing conceptual and empirical research.

SUMMARY AND CONCLUSIONS

We presented an integrative framework designed to clarify the conceptual boundaries between various constructs discussed in the P-E fit literature. The framework is broad and inclusive in order to integrate dimensions of P-E fit with dimensions of human functioning and to illustrate how environmental and psychological characteristics can be linked conceptually. We then reviewed selected research relevant to the major components of this framework to demonstrate how seemingly diverse topics can be viewed from this integrative perspective. Finally, a sample of ideas for how the framework can organize empirical research was offered to stimulate systematic examinations of P-E fit.

REFERENCES

Ackerman, P. L., & Heggestad, E. D. (1997). Intelligence, personality, and interests: Evidence for overlapping traits. *Psychological Bulletin, 121,* 218–245.

Adorno, A. J., & Binning, J. F. (2001). Reducing call center employee turnover. In N. L. Petouhoff (Ed.), *In action: Recruiting, training, and evaluating call center employees.* Alexandria, VA: American Society for Training and Development.

Alderfer, C. P. (1972). *Existence, relatedness and growth.* New York: Free Press.

Ambrose, M L., & Schminke, M. (2003). Organization structure as a moderator of the relationship between procedural justice, interactional justice, perceived organizational support, and supervisory trust. *Journal of Applied Psychology, 88,* 295–305.

Argyris, C. (1957). *Personality and organization: The conflict between system and individual.* New York: Harper & Brothers.

Argyris, C. (1964). *Integrating the individual and the organization.* New York: Wiley.

Avolio, B. J. (1999). *Full leadership development: Building the vital forces in organizations.* Thousand Oaks, CA: Sage.

Barling, J., Kelloway, E. K., & Iverson, R. D. (2003). High-quality work, job satisfaction, and occupational injuries. *Journal of Applied Psychology, 88,* 276–283.

Bass, B. M., & Barrett, G. V. (1981). *People, work, and organizations: An introduction to industrial and organizational psychology.* Boston: Allyn & Bacon.

Beehr, T. A. (1996). *Basic organizational psychology.* Boston: Allyn & Bacon.

Bernardin, H. J. (1987). Development and validation of a forced choice scale to measure job-related discomfort among customer service representatives. *Academy of Management Journal, 30,* 162–173.

Binning, J. F., & Adorno, A. J. (2001, April). *Personality and emotional labor as predictors of turnover in customer service call centers.* Paper presented at the annual conference of the Society for Industrial and Organizational Psychology, San Diego, CA.

Binning, J. F., & Barrett, G. V. (1989). Validity of personnel decisions: A conceptual analysis of the inferential and evidential bases. *Journal of Applied Psychology, 74,* 478–494.

Binning, J. F., LeBreton, J. M., & Adorno, A. J. (1999). Assessing personality. In R. W. Eder & M. M. Harris (Eds.), *The employment interview handbook.* Newbury Park, CA: Sage.

Binning, J. F., & Wagner, E. E. (2002). Passive-aggressive behavior in the workplace. In J. C. Thomas & M. Hersen (Eds.), *Handbook of mental health in the workplace.* Newbury Park, CA: Sage.

Borman, W. C., Hanson, M. A., & Hedge, J. W. (1997). Personnel selection. *Annual Review of Psychology, 48,* 299–337.

Bowen, D. E., Ledford, G. E., & Nathan, B. R. (1991). Hiring for the organization, not the job. *Academy of Management Executive, 5,* 35–51.

Brandstatter, H. (1994). Pleasure of leisure-pleasure of work: Personality makes the difference. *Personality and Individual Differences, 16,* 931–946.

Brief, A. P., & Weiss, H. M. (2002). Organizational behavior: Affect in the workplace. *Annual Review of Psychology, 53,* 279–307.

Bronfenbrenner, U., & Ceci, S. J. (1994). Nature-nurture reconceptualized in developmental perspective: A bioecological model. *Psychological Review, 101,* 568–586.

Burke, M. J., Brief, A. P., & George, J. M. (1993). The role of negative affectivity in understanding relations between self-reports of stressors and strains: A comment on the applied psychology literature. *Journal of Applied Psychology, 78,* 402–412.

Campion, M. A. (1983). Personnel selection for physically demanding jobs. *Personnel Psychology, 36,* 527–550.

Cohen, S. (1996). Psychological stress, immunity, and upper respiratory infections. *Current Directions in Psychological Science, 5,* 86–90.

Cohen, S., Tyrrell, D. A. J., & Smith, A. P. (1993). Negative life events, perceived stress, negative affect and susceptibility to the common cold. *Journal of Personality and Social Psychology, 64,* 131–140.

Colbert, A. E., Mount, M. K., Harter, J. K, Witt, L. A., & Barrick, M. R. (2004). Interactive effects of personality and perceptions of the work situation on workplace deviance. *Journal of Applied Psychology, 89,* 599–609.

Converse, P. D., Oswald, F. L., Gillespie, M. A., Field, K. A., & Bizot, E. B. (2004). Matching individuals to occupations using abilities and the O*NET: Issues and an application in career guidance. *Personnel Psychology, 57,* 451–487.

Cropanzano, R., Rupp, D. E., Byrne, Z. S. (2003). The relationship of emotional exhaustion to work attitudes, job performance, and organizational citizenship behaviors. *Journal of Applied Psychology, 88,* 160–169.

Dabos, G. E., & Rousseau, D. M. (2004). Mutuality and reciprocity in the psychological contracts of employees and employers. *Journal of Applied Psychology, 89,* 52–72.

Dawis, R. V. (2000). P-E fit as paradigm: Comment on Tinsley (2000). *Journal of Vocational Behavior, 56,* 180–183.

Dawis, R. V., & Lofquist, L. H. (1984). *A psychological theory of work adjustment.* Minneapolis: University of Minnesota Press.

Day, D. D., & Bedeian, A. G. (1995). Personality similarity and work-related outcomes among African-American nursing personnel: A test of the supplementary model of person-environment congruence. *Journal of Vocational Behavior, 46,* 55–70.

De Fruyt, F. (2002). A person-centered approach to P-E fit questions using a multiple-trait model. *Journal of Vocational Behavior, 60,* 73–90.

Deming, W. E. (1986). *Out of the crisis.* Cambridge: Massachusetts Institute of Technology, Center for Advanced Engineering Study.

Diefendorff, J. M., & Richard, E. M. (2003). Antecedents and consequences of emotional display rule perceptions. *Journal of Applied Psychology, 88,* 284–294.

Diener, E. (1997). Subjective well-being and personality. In D. Barone, M. Hersen, & V. Van Hasselt (Eds.), *Advanced personality.* New York: Plenum Press.

Diener, E., Scollon, C. N., & Lucas, R. E. (2003). The evolving concept of subjective well-being: The multifaceted nature of happiness. *Advances in Cell Aging and Gerontology, 15,* 187–219.

Diener, E., Suh, E. M., Lucas, R. E., & Smith, H. I. (1999). Subjective well-being: Three decades of progress. *Psychological Bulletin, 125,* 267–302.

Edwards, J. R. (1991). Person-job fit: A conceptual integration, literature review, and methodological critique. *International review of industrial/organizational psychology* (Vol. 6, pp. 283–357). London: Wiley

Edwards, J. R., & Rothbard, N. P. (1999). Work and family stress and well-being: An examination of person-environment fit in the work and family domains. *Organizational Behavior and Human Decision Processes, 77,* 85–129.

Ekman, P. (1992). Are there basic emotions? *Psychological Review, 99,* 550–553.

Embretson, S. (1983). Construct validity: Construct representation versus nomothetic span. *Psychological Bulletin, 93,* 179–197.

Epstein, S. (1994). Integration of the cognitive and psychodynamic unconscious. *American Psychologist, 49,* 709–724.

Fine, S. A., & Wiley, W. W. (1971). *An introduction to functional job analysis.* Washington, DC: Upjohn Institute for Employment Research.

Fleishman, E. A. (1972). On the relation between abilities, learning, and human performance. *American Psychologist, 27,* 1017–1032.

Fulmer, I. S., Gerhart, B., & Scott, K. S. (2003). Are the 100 best better? An empirical investigation of the relationship between being a "great place to work" and firm performance. *Personnel Psychology, 56,* 965–993.

Furnham, A. (2001). Vocational preference and P-O fit: Reflections on Holland's theory of vocational choice. *Applied Psychology: An International Review, 50,* 5–29.

Gati, I. (2000). Pitfalls of congruence research: A comment on Tinsley's "The Congruence Myth." *Journal of Vocational Behavior, 56,* 184–189.

Gelade, G. A., & Ivery, M. (2003). The impact of human resource management and work climate on organizational performance. *Personnel Psychology, 56,* 383–404.

George, J. M. (1990). Personality, affect, and behavior in groups. *Journal of Applied Psychology, 75,* 107–116.

George, J. M., & James, L. R. (1993). Personality, affect, and behavior in groups revisited: Comment on aggregation, levels of analysis, and a recent application of within and between analysis. *Journal of Applied Psychology, 78,* 798–804.

Gerhart, B., & Milkovich, G. (1992). Employee compensation: Research and practice. In M. D. Dunnette & L. M. Hough (Eds.), *Handbook of industrial/organizational psychology* (2nd ed.). Palo Alto, CA: Consulting Psychologists Press.

Goleman, D. (1995). *Emotional intelligence: Why it can matter more than IQ.* New York: Bantam.

Goodman, S. A., & Svyantek, D. J. (1999). Person-organization fit and contextual performance: Do shared values matter. *Journal of Vocational Behavior, 55,* 254–275.

Grandey, A. A. (2000). Emotion regulation in the workplace: A new way to conceptualize emotional labor. *Journal of Occupational Health Psychology, 5,* 95–100.

Guion, R. M. (1991). Personnel assessment, selection, and placement. In M. D. Dunnette & L. M. Hough (Eds.), *Handbook of industrial/organizational psychology* (2nd ed.). Palo Alto, CA: Consulting Psychologists Press.

Gustafson, S. B., & Mumford, M. D. (1995). Personal style and person-environment fit: A pattern approach. *Journal of Vocational Behavior, 46,* 163–188.

Hackman, J. R. (1992). Group influences on individuals in organizations. In M. D. Dunnette & L. M. Hough (Eds.), *Handbook of industrial/organizational psychology* (2nd ed.). Palo Alto, CA: Consulting Psychologists Press.

Hackman, J. R., & Oldham, G. R. (1980). *Work redesign.* Reading, MA: Addison-Wesley.

Hardy, G. E., Woods, D., & Wall, T. D. (2003). The impact of psychological distress on absence from work. *Journal of Applied Psychology, 88,* 306–314.

Harvey, R. J. (1991). Job analysis. In M. D. Dunnette & L. M. Hough (Eds.), *Handbook of industrial/organizational psychology* (2nd ed.). Palo Alto, CA: Consulting Psychologists Press.

Heckhausen, J., & Schulz, R. (1995). A life-span theory of control. *Psychological Review, 102,* 284–304.

Herzberg, F. (1974). Motivator-hygiene profiles: Pinpointing what ails the organization. *Organizational Dynamics, 3,* 18–29.

Hofmann, D. A., & Morgeson, F. P. (1999). Safety-related behavior as a social exchange: The role of perceived organizational support and leader-member exchange. *Journal of Applied Psychology, 84,* 286–296.

Hofmann, D. A., Morgeson, F. P., & Gerras, S. J. (2003). Climate as a moderator of the relationship between leader-member exchange and content specific citizenship: Safety climate as an exemplar. *Journal of Applied Psychology, 88,* 170–178.

Hogan, J. C. (1991). Physical abilities. In M. D. Dunnette & L. M. Hough (Eds.), *Handbook of industrial/organizational psychology* (2nd ed.). Palo Alto, CA: Consulting Psychologists Press.

Hogan, R. (1991). Personality and personality measurement. In M. D. Dunnette & L. M. Hough (Eds.), *Handbook of industrial/organizational psychology* (2nd ed.). Palo Alto, CA: Consulting Psychologists Press.

Hogan, R., & Roberts, B. W. (2000). A socioanalytical perspective on person-environment interaction. In W. B. Walsh, K. H Craik, & R. H. Price (Eds.), *Person-environment psychology: Models and perspectives* (2nd ed.). Mahwah, NJ: Erlbaum.

Holland, J. L. (1997). *Making vocational choices: A theory of vocational personalities and work environments* (3rd ed.). Odessa, FL: Psychological Assessment Resources.

Hollenbeck, J. R., Moon, H., Ellis, A. P. J., West, B. J., Ilgen, D. R., Sheppard, L., et al. (2002). Structural contingency theory and individual differences: Examination of external and internal person-team fit. *Journal of Applied Psychology, 87,* 599–606.

Hosada, M., Stone-Romero, E. F., & Coats, G. (2003). The effects of physical attractiveness on job-related outcomes: A meta-analysis of experimental studies. *Personnel Psychology, 56,* 431–462.

Howell, W. C. (1991). Human factors in the workplace. In M. D. Dunnette & L. M. Hough (Eds.), *Handbook of industrial/organizational psychology* (2nd ed.). Palo Alto, CA: Consulting Psychologists Press.

Hui, C., Lee, C., & Rousseau, D. M. (2004). Psychological construct and organizational citizenship behavior in China: Investigating generalizability and instrumentality. *Journal of Applied Psychology, 89,* 311–321.

Izard, C. E. (1992). Basic emotions, relations among emotions, and emotion-cognition relations. *Psychological Review, 99,* 561–565.

Izard, C. E. (1993). Four systems for emotion activation: Cognitive and noncognitive processes. *Psychological Review, 100,* 68–90.

James, L. R., Joyce, W. F., & Slocum, J. W. (1988). Organizations do not cognize. *Academy of Management Review, 13,* 129–132.

John, O. P, Angleitner, A., & Ostendorf, F. (1988). The lexical approach to personality: A historical review of trait taxonomic research. *European Journal of Personality, 2,* 171–203.

Judge, T. A., & Cable, D. M. (2004). The effect of physical height on workplace success and income: Preliminary test of a theoretical model. *Journal of Applied Psychology, 89,* 428–441.

Judge, T. A., & Ferris, G. R. (1992). The elusive criterion of fit in human resource staffing decisions. *Human Resource Planning, 154,* 47–67.

Judge, T. A., & Larsen, R. J. (2001). Dispositional affect and job satisfaction: A review and theoretical extension. *Organizational Behavior and Human Decision Processes, 86,* 67–98.

Kahana, E., Lovegreen, L., Kahana, B., & Kahana, M. (2003). Person, environment, and person-environment fit as influences on residential satisfaction of elders. *Environment and Behavior, 35,* 434–453.

Kramer, R. M. (1999). Trust and distrust in organizations: Emerging perspectives, enduring questions. *Annual Review of Psychology, 50,* 569–598.

Kristof, A. L. (1996). Person-organization fit: An integrative review of its conceptualizations, measurement, and implications. *Personnel Psychology, 49,* 1–49.

Kristof-Brown, A. L. (2000). Perceived applicant fit: Distinguishing between recruiters' perceptions of person-job and person-organization fit. *Personnel Psychology, 53,* 643–671.

Lambert, L. S., Edwards, J. R., & Cable, D. M. (2003). Breach and fulfillment of the psychological contract: A comparison of traditional and expanded views. *Personnel Psychology, 56,* 895–934.

Lauver, K. J., & Kristof-Brown, A. (2001). Distinguishing between employees' perceptions of person-job and person-organization fit. *Journal of Vocational Behavior, 59,* 454–470.

Law, K. S., Wong, C., & Song, L. J. (2004). The construct and criterion validity of emotional intelligence and its potential utility for management studies. *Journal of Applied Psychology, 89,* 483–496.

Lawler, E. E., III, & Jenkins, G. D. (1992). Strategic reward systems. In M. D. Dunnette & L. M. Hough (Eds.), *Handbook of industrial/organizational psychology* (2nd ed.). Palo Alto, CA: Consulting Psychologists Press.

LeBreton, J. M., Binning, J. F., Adorno, A. J., & Melcher, K. M. (2004). Importance of personality and job-specific affect for predicting job attitudes and withdrawal behavior. *Organizational Research Methods, 7,* 300–325.

Lewin, K. (1935). *Dynamic theory of personality.* New York: McGraw-Hill.

Livingstone, L. P., Nelson, D. L., & Barr, S. H. (1997). Person-environment fit and creativity: An examination of supply-value and demand ability versions of fit. *Journal of Management, 23,* 119–146.

Locke, E. A. (1976). The nature and causes of job satisfaction. In M. D. Dunnette (Ed.), *Handbook of industrial/organizational psychology.* Chicago: Rand McNally.

Lopez, F. M., Kesselman, G. A., & Lopez, F. E. (1981). An empirical test of a trait-oriented job analysis technique. *Personnel Psychology, 34,* 479–502.

Lubinski, D. (2000). Scientific and social significance of assessing individual differences: "Sinking shafts at a few critical points." *Annual Review of Psychology, 51,* 405–444.

Margenau, H. (1950). *The nature of physical reality.* New York: McGraw-Hill.

Maslach, C., Schaufeli, W. B., & Leiter, M. P. (2001). Job burnout. *Annual Review of Psychology, 52,* 397–422.

Maslow, A. H. (1970). *Motivation and personality* (2nd ed.). New York: Harper and Row.

McClelland, D. C. (1961). The achieving society. Princeton, NJ: Van Nostrand.

McCormick, E. J., Jeanneret, P. R., & Mecham, R. C. (1972). A study of job characteristics and job dimensions as based on the Position Analysis Questionnaire (PAQ). *Journal of Applied Psychology, 56,* 347–367.

McGregor, D. (1960). *The human side of enterprise.* New York: McGraw-Hill.

Miller, H. E., & Rosse, J. G. (2002). Emotional reserve and adaptation to job dissatisfaction. In J. M Brett & F. Drasgow (Eds.), *The psychology of work: Theoretically based empirical research.* Mahwah, NJ: Erlbaum.

Mischel, W. (2004). Toward an integrative science of the person. *Annual Review of Psychology, 55,* 1–22.

Mischel, W., & Shoda, Y. (1995). A cognitive-affective system theory of personality: Reconceptualizing situations, dispositions, dynamics, and invariance in personality structure. *Psychological Review, 102,* 246–268.

Morgeson, F. P., & Hofmann, D. A. (1999). The structure and function of collective constructs: Implications for multilevel research and theory development. *Academy of Management Review, 24,* 347–364.

Moskowitz, D. S., & Cote, S. (1995). Do interpersonal traits predict affect? A comparison of three models. *Journal of Personality and Social Psychology, 69,* 915–925.

Motowidlo, S. J., & Van Scotter, J. R. (1994). Evidence that task performance should be distinguished from contextual performance. *Journal of Applied Psychology, 79,* 475–480.

Muchinsky, P. M., & Monahan, C. J. (1987). What is person-environment congruence? Supplementary versus complementary models of fit. *Journal of Vocational Behavior, 31,* 268–277.

Nelson, J. B. (1997). The boundaryless organization: Implications for job analysis, recruitment, and selection. *Human Resource Planning, 4,* 39–49.

O'Reilly, C.A., III, Chatman, J., & Caldwell, D. F. (1991). People and organizational culture: A profile comparison approach to assessing person-organization fit. *Academy of Management, 34,* 487–516.

Organ, D. W. (1988). *Organizational citizenship behavior: The good soldier syndrome.* Lexington, MA: Lexington Books.

Organ, D. W. (1997). Organizational citizenship behavior: It's construct clean-up time. *Human Performance, 10,* 85–97.

Paulhus, D. L., & Martin, C. L. (1987). The structure of personality capabilities. *Journal of Personality and Social Psychology, 52,* 354–365.

Peters, L. H., O'Connor, E. J., & Rudolf, C. J. (1980). Situational constraints and work outcomes: The influence of a frequently overlooked construct. *Academy of Management Review, 5,* 391–397.

Peterson, N. G., Mumford, M. D., Borman, W. C., Jeanneret, P. R., Fleishman, E. A., Leven, K. Y., et al. (2001). Understanding work using the Occupational Information Network (O*NET): Implications for practice and research. *Personnel Psychology, 54,* 451–492.

Pfeffer, J. (1998). *The human equation: Building profits by putting people first.* Cambridge, MA: Harvard Business School Press.

Porter, L. W., Lawler, E. E., & Hackman, J. R. (1975). *Behavior in organizations.* New York: McGraw-Hill.

Roe, A. (1956). *The psychology of occupations.* New York: Wiley.

Rhoades, L., & Eisenberger, R. (2002). Perceived organizational support: A review of the literature. *Journal of Applied Psychology, 87,* 698–714.

Rokeach, M. (1973). *The nature of human values.* New York: Free Press.

Rousseau, D. M. (1995). *Psychological contracts in organizations: Understanding written and unwritten agreements.* Thousand Oaks, CA: Sage.

Saks, A. M., & Ashforth, B. E. (2002). Is job search related to employment quality? It all depends on the fit. *Journal of Applied Psychology, 87,* 646–654.

Schaubroeck, J., Jones, J. R., & Xie, J. L. (2001). Individual differences in utilizing control to cope with job demands: Effects on susceptibility to infectious disease. *Journal of Applied Psychology, 86,* 265–278.

Schleicher, D. J., Watt, J. D., & Greguras, G. J. (2004). Reexamining the job satisfaction-performance relationship: The complexity of attitudes. *Journal of Applied Psychology, 89,* 165–177.

Schlenker, B. R., Britt, T. W., Pennington, J., Murphy, R., & Doherty, K. (1994). The triangle model of responsibility. *Psychological Review, 101,* 632–652.

Schneider, B. (1987). The people make the place. *Personnel Psychology, 40,* 437–453.

Schneider, B. (2001). Fits about fit. *Applied Psychology: An International Review, 50,* 141–152.

Schneider, B., Goldstein, H. W., & Smith, D. B. (1995). The ASA framework: An update. *Personnel Psychology, 48,* 747–773.

Schneider, B., Hanges, P. J., Smith, D. B., & Salvaggio, A. N. (2003). Which comes first: Employee attitudes or organizational financial and market performance? *Journal of Applied Psychology, 88,* 836–851.

Schneider, B., Smith, D. B., & Goldstein, H. W. (2000). Attraction-selection-attrition: Toward a person-environment psychology of organizations. In W. B. Walsh, K. H Craik, & R. H. Price (Eds.) *Person-environment psychology: Models and perspectives* (2nd ed.). Mahwah, NJ: Erlbaum.

Seligman, M. E. P., & Csikszentmihalyi, M. (2000). Positive psychology: An introduction. *American Psychologist, 55,* 5–14.

Shippman, J. S., Ash, R. A., Battista, M., Carr, L., Eyde, L. D., Hesketh, B., et al. (2001). The practice of competency modeling. *Personnel Psychology, 53,* 703–740.

Simmering, M. J., Colquitt, J. A., Noe, R. A., & Porter, C. O. L. H. (2003). Conscientiousness, autonomy fit, and development: A longitudinal study. *Journal of Applied Psychology, 88,* 954–963.

Simons, T., & Roberson, Q. (2003). Why managers should care about fairness: The effects of aggregate justice perceptions on organizational outcomes. *Journal of Applied Psychology, 88,* 432–443.

Slaughter, J. E., Zickar, M. J., Highhouse, S., & Mohr, D. C. (2004). Personality trait inferences about organizations: Development of a measure and assessment of construct validity. *Journal of Applied Psychology, 89,* 85–103.

Smith, P. C., Kendall, L. M., & Hulin, C. L. (1969). *The measurement of satisfaction in work and retirement.* Chicago: Rand McNally.

Tett, R. P., & Burnett, D. D. (2003). A personality trait-based interactionist model of job performance. *Journal of Applied Psychology, 88,* 500–517.

Tinsley, H. E. A. (2000). The congruence myth: An analysis of the efficacy of the person-environment fit model. *Journal of Vocational Behavior, 56,* 147–179.

Tranberg, M., Slane, S., & Ekeberg, S. E. (1993). The relation between interest congruence and satisfaction: A meta-analysis. *Journal of Vocational Behavior, 42,* 253–264.

U.S. Department of Labor. (1977). *Dictionary of Occupational Titles* (4th ed.). Washington, DC: U.S. Employment Service.

Van Vianen, A. E. M. (2000). Person-organization fit: The match between newcomers' and recruiters' preferences for organizational cultures. *Personnel Psychology, 53,* 113–149.

Verquer, M. L., Beehr, T. A., & Wagner, S. H. (2003). A meta-analysis of relations between person-organization fit and work attitudes. *Journal of Vocational Behavior, 63,* 473–489.

Wachs, T. D., & Plomin, R. (Eds.). (1991). *Conceptualization and measurement of organism-environment interaction.* Washington, DC: American Psychological Association.

Walsh, W. B., Craik, K. H., & Price, R. H. (Eds.). (1992). *Person-environment psychology: Models and perspectives.* Hillsdale, NJ: Erlbaum.

Walsh, W. B., Craik, K. H., & Price, R. H. (Eds.). (2000). *Person-environment psychology: Models and perspectives* (2nd ed.). Mahwah, NJ: Erlbaum.

Wapner, S., & Demick, J. (2000). *Person-in-environment psychology: A holistic, developmental, systems-oriented perspective.* In W. B. Walsh, K. H Craik, & R. H. Price (Eds.), *Person-environment psychology: Models and perspectives* (2nd ed.). Mahwah, NJ: Erlbaum.

Wapner, S., Demick, J., Yamamoto, T., & Minami, H. (2000). *Theoretical perspectives in environment-behavior research: Underlying assumptions, research problems, and methodologies.* New York: Kluwer Academic/Plenum Publishers.

Weick, K. E. (1995). *Sensemaking in organizations.* Thousand Oaks, CA: Sage.

Witt, L. A., & Ferris, G. R. (2003). Social skill as moderator of the conscientiousness-performance relationship: Convergent results across four studies. *Journal of Applied Psychology, 88,* 809–820.

Zeier, H., Brauchli, P. & Joller-Jemelka, H. I. (1996). Effects of work demands on immunoglobulin A and cortisol in air traffic controllers. *Biological Psychology, 42,* 413–423.

Zellars, K. L., Tepper, B. J., & Duffy, M. K. (2002). Abusive supervision and subordinates' organizational citizenship behavior. *Journal of Applied Psychology, 87,* 1068–1076.

Zohar, D. (1999). When things go wrong: The effect of daily work hassles on effort, exertion, and negative mood. *Journal of Occupational and Organizational Psychology, 72,* 265–283.

Zohar, D., & Luria, G. (2004). Climate as a social-cognitive construction of supervisory safety practices: Scripts as proxy of behavior patterns. *Journal of Applied Psychology, 89,* 322–333.

CHAPTER 20

Subclinical Psychopaths

JAMES M. LEBRETON, JOHN F. BINNING, AND ANTHONY J. ADORNO

INTRODUCTION

"Jack" is a former CEO of a Fortune 500 multinational corporation. He is intellectually gifted and interpersonally charming. His Harvard MBA and charisma are, by most accounts, invaluable assets. Jack is able to discuss topics ranging from international politics, to sports, to poetry, to corporate finance. He has been described as having an agile mind and a larger-than-life personality. However, accompanying all of these strengths was a history of impulsive, irresponsible, and questionable behavior. Jack's conduct, along with his justifications for it, were consistent with a tendency for Jack to see himself as operating outside the legal and social rules that bind society. When confronted about his "questionable" behavior, Jack rarely demonstrated anything more than a superficial sense of remorse or regret, which often lacked emotional texture. Among the various accusations that surfaced regarding Jack's conduct were: (1) illegal drug use, (2) serial sexual promiscuity (including allegations of sexual harassment), and (3) inappropriate use of stockholder monies. Finally, the most dramatic accusation leveled against Jack was that he lied to stockholders and company executives regarding the threat of a hostile takeover by a competitor and used the so-called threat to justify his own takeover of the rival corporation.

Jack's executive board became increasingly concerned about his behavior and decision making and decided to conduct a series of informal interviews. When challenged by the board about the alleged wrongdoings, Jack responded that the allegations were simply attempts to "bring him down." During the board's inquiry, Jack rendered deceptive, manipulative, and/or inconsistent answers. Furthermore, his behavior often failed to align with his espoused values. For example, he purported to be a strong advocate of women's rights and opposed anything that resulted in the objectification of women; however, a number of women came forward to document his pattern of sexual harassment. When individuals came forth with accusations, he either redirected the dis-

cussion to an unrelated issue (e.g., stockholder satisfaction with his decisive leadership) or portrayed the accusers as having less than altruistic motives (e.g., wanting to take control of the company). The closest Jack ever came to admitting he lied to stockholders was his statement that, "Sometimes it is necessary to tell people 'what they want to hear,' even if it isn't entirely accurate."

After a time-consuming investigation, the board concluded that Jack lied during interviews, lied to stockholders in the days leading up to the takeover, lied about sexually harassing subordinate employees, and tried to obstruct the investigation at several different points in time. Ultimately, they recommended that Jack either resign or be terminated. Instead of expressing remorse and regret, Jack delivered a charismatic and persuasive speech to company stockholders. He argued that the real victims of this "corporate witch hunt" had been the stockholders. Although he superficially acknowledged that some of his behavior may have been "less than perfect," Jack emphasized that the investigation ultimately hurt the stockholders by distracting him from his true mission: to improve the company and make money for the stockholders. Although the board viewed Jack's speech as superficial and lacking any real sense of remorse, the stockholders were inspired by Jack's speech and his plans for the company's future. Ultimately, the stockholders offered such strong support for Jack that it was impossible for the board to fire him. Last year (after being offered an extremely lucrative retirement package) Jack retired and is in the process of writing an autobiography tentatively entitled *Jack's Way, the Right Way.*

Stories like this are becoming more and more common in U.S. society. Our newspapers are filled with stories with parallels about entertainers, athletes, and politicians. We are even beginning to see stories like these about "everyday" people: doctors, teachers, business owners, store workers, stockbrokers, religious leaders, and so forth. Common among these stories is a pattern of destructive, unethical, immoral, or even illegal behavior, coupled with superficial apologies (if any) that fail to convey a true sense of remorse and/or regret. These "offenders" typically possess an unrealistic and narcissistic sense of self-importance, believing that they are somehow above the social, moral, ethical, and legal principles that govern our society.

On the surface, few lay people (or psychologists) would label such individuals as clinical psychopaths; deviant, inappropriate, and counterproductive, yes; but psychopathic, no. Many people believe that psychopaths are deranged, serial criminals. Thus, it would stand to reason that clinical psychopaths would not be corporate, political, and religious leaders and certainly not teachers, gardeners, retail managers, students, spouses, and the myriad coworkers with whom we interact on a daily basis. Such an assessment is probably correct in most cases. This does not imply that clinical psychopaths do not exist in the general population, but that the base rate for such individuals is low. Given the rarity of clinical psychopathy, most research has been conducted in criminal or psychiatric settings. These individuals often have engaged in horrendous crimes and disturbing patterns of manipulation and deception. Clinical psychopaths are identified by symptoms such as: pathological lying, serial irresponsibility and impulsivity, lack of remorse, grandiose sense of self-worth, failure to accept responsibility for one's actions, superficial charm and charisma, manipulative and self-serving patterns of behavior, and adolescent and adult criminal behavior (Cleckley, 1976; Hare, 1999).

Although Jack might not be a clinical psychopath, comparing his story with these psychopathic symptoms reveals that he manifested a general pattern of behavior, affect, and cognition that is strikingly similar to those displayed by clinical psychopaths. As we will discuss, the primary difference between clinical and subclinical psychopathy is one of degree, not kind. Therefore, such individuals might appropriately be labeled *subclinical psychopaths* (Gustafson & Ritzer, 1995; Paulhus & Williams, 2002).

The purpose of the current chapter is to explore the concept of subclinical psychopathy and characterize how it might affect aspects of everyday life. We approach this chapter from an integrative social-cognitive perspective. As we will document, to date most of the research on subclinical (and clinical) psychopathy has focused largely on either overt behaviors (including documentation of those behaviors in case files) or conscious self-disclosures of behavior, affect, and cognition obtained via structured interviews or self-report surveys. We suggest combining such information with information regarding individuals' latent (i.e., unconscious) rationalizations and justifications for their behavior can lead to enhanced understanding and prediction of subclinical psychopathy. Before proceeding, it is important to be clear about the boundaries

of the subclinical psychopathy construct and how they differ from other toxic personality patterns.

Distinguishing Clinical and Subclinical Psychopathy

The difference is not in the types or categories of behavior, affect, interpersonal relationships, or rationalizations but instead in the degree, magnitude, or frequency of those behaviors and cognitions. Subclinical psychopaths do not differ from their clinical counterparts qualitatively (i.e., in the *types* or *kinds* of behaviors, affect, interpersonal relationships, and cognitions) in terms of their experiences, but they do differ quantitatively (i.e., in the *level, intensity,* or *frequency*) in those patterns of conduct (Gustafson & Ritzer, 1995). Clinical psychopathy is an all-encompassing pattern of aberrant and dysfunctional behavior, affect, and cognition that permeates multiple spheres or aspects of an individual's life (e.g., work, family, social). The individual is a clinically impaired, chronically dysfunctional employee, spouse, parent, and friend. They often are incapable of living among the general population and commonly end up in criminal or psychiatric institutions. Fortunately the base rate for clinical psychopathy is quite low, probably less than 1 percent of the general population (Hare, 1999).

In contrast, the subclinical psychopath experiences the same patterns of dysfunctional behaviors, affects, and cognitions; however, the pervasiveness and levels of impaired functioning are not as extreme because the individual manifests the symptoms at a commensurately lower level and rate. For example, whereas the clinical psychopath might make a career out of armed robbery, assault, and rape, the subclinical psychopath is likely to pursue less extreme (and less frequent) forms of antisocial behavior (e.g., inflating expense accounts, engaging in sexual harassment and other forms of interpersonal aggression). Although such an individual may be a less-than-ideal employee, spouse, parent, and friend, they are capable of maintaining relationships (albeit socioemotionally deficient ones) with others. Nevertheless, these relationships tend to be psychologically unhealthy, one-sided, volatile, and frustrating for others. A handful of empirical studies suggest that, although still a relatively infrequent phenomenon, subclinical psychopathy is much more common than its clinical counterpart, with base rates ranging from 5 percent to 15 percent in the general population (e.g., Gustafson & Ritzer 1995; Pethman & Earlandsson, 2002).

It is also worth noting that whereas some authors use terms such as *subcriminal psychopaths, noncriminal psychopaths, nonforensic psychopaths,* or *noninstitutionalized psychopaths* (cf. Forth, Brown, Hart, & Hare, 1996; Lilienfeld & Andrews, 1996; Widom, 1977), we recommend use of the term *sub-*

clinical psychopath to avoid the potential for conceptual confusion. For example, noncriminal psychopaths could refer to clinical psychopaths who have managed to avoid incarceration and/or a criminal record, or it could refer to individuals who display a pattern of behavior that is in some specific way "less severe" than their clinical counterparts.

Distinguishing Psychopathy from Other Toxic Personality Profiles

Before elaborating on the core symptoms or features of psychopathy, we want to review the conceptual fuzziness surrounding the psychopathy construct, especially as it relates to several other toxic personality profiles, including sociopathy, antisocial personality disorder (ASPD), and narcissistic personality disorder (NPD). Although some researchers use psychopathy and sociopathy interchangeably, others recommend that these terms should be used to distinguish the "triggers" or "causes" behind a lifelong pattern of deviant, antisocial, and often criminal behavior. The psychopath is believed to have been "born bad," whereas the sociopath is believed to have been "raised bad" (Lykken, 1995, 1998). Stated alternatively, some researchers argue that normal individuals who were not properly socialized should be labeled *sociopaths* to emphasize it was a lack of socialization that caused their deviant patterns of behavior and not some biological or genetic abnormality.

Arguably the greatest source of conceptual confusion surrounding the psychopathy construct stems from the changing and uncertain diagnostic criteria used to assess the ASPD described in the various editions of the American Psychiatric Association's *Diagnostic and Statistical Manual of Mental Disorders* (*DSM;* 1952, 1968, 1980, 1987, 1994, 2000). The overlap between psychopathy and ASPD has fluctuated, depending on which version of diagnostic criteria one used (Arrigo & Shipley, 2001; Hare, 1998; Hare, Hart, & Harpur, 1991; Lilienfeld, 1994). Reviewed in detail by Lilienfeld (1994) and Arrigo and Shipley (2001), the ASPD classification criteria have gone through a series of modifications and refinements, with some versions conforming quite closely to the Cleckley (1976) and Hare (1999) descriptions of psychopathy described later and other versions deviating substantially from those conceptualizations.

Central to the issue of equivalence between psychopathy and ASPD is the necessity of certain personality characteristics (e.g., egocentricity, irresponsibility, lack of remorse) and patterns of delinquent and antisocial behavior (e.g., lying, history of criminal conduct) in the diagnosis of ASPD. Earlier descriptions of ASPD (e.g., *DSM-II,* 1968) were fairly consistent with the Cleckley and Hare description of psychopathy,

emphasizing both *aberrant personality traits* and *delinquent behavior.* More recent descriptions (e.g., *DSM–III–R,* 1987; *DSM–IV,* 1994; *DSM–IV–TR,* 2000) placed little emphasis on personality traits instead focusing heavily on *antisocial and criminal behavior* (Arrigo & Shipley, 2001; Lilienfeld, 1994). This differential inclusion of personality traits has implications for the overlap between psychopathy and ASPD. For example, the majority of criminals diagnosed as psychopaths using the screening criteria from the Psychopathy Checklist–Revised (Hare, 1991) are also diagnosed as having ASPD using the *DSM–III* and *DSM–IV* criteria (50 percent to 80 percent); however, only a fraction of those diagnosed with ASPD would meet the criteria for being diagnosed as a psychopath (15 percent to 25 percent; Hare, 1985, 1999; Hart & Hare, 1997; Shipley & Arrigo, 2001). Thus, one must use caution when making inferences about psychopathy from research evidence based on ASPD to be sure that the diagnostic criteria were truly consistent with psychopathy.

The Cleckley and Hare conceptualization of psychopathy also overlaps with descriptions of narcissistic personality disorder (NPD; *DSM–IV,* 1994). Specifically, NPD and psychopathy share some traits (e.g., egocentricity, lack of empathy); however, NPD does not place a strong emphasis on antisocial or delinquent behaviors (e.g., lying, aggression, illegal behavior). The construct overlap between psychopathy, ASPD, and NPD is due in part to the overlap, and thus diagnostic comorbidity between ASPD and NPD. Psychopathy shares some narcissistic traits (e.g., egocentricity) with both NPD and ASPD while also sharing some affective deficiencies (e.g., lack of remorse) and antisocial behavior (e.g., deceitfulness) with ASPD.

Delimiting Subclinical Psychopathy

This overlap of several toxic personality profiles with the psychopathy construct has implications for the study of subclinical psychopathy. In the current chapter we use of the term *subclinical psychopathy* in a manner consistent with contemporary research conducted by Robert Hare and colleagues (Hare, 1991, 1999; Hare & Hare, 1997; Hare, Hart, & Harpur, 1991) to describe a personality profile marred with a constellation of *toxic personality characteristics* (including affective dysfunction), *delinquent behaviors* (including antisocial behavior), *dysfunctional interpersonal relationships* (including conning and manipulative interpersonal styles), and *atypical patterns of cognition* (including upwardly biased self-perceptions and downwardly biased perceptions of others). Subclinical psychopaths need not have an extensive criminal record, although many will have such records. Such individuals need not have been poorly socialized as children, although many will have lacked proper socialization. Thus, their personalities comprise both narcissistic and antisocial characteristics yielding aberrant patterns of affect, cognition, and behavior. Before reviewing these characteristics in greater detail, we provide a social-cognitive backdrop for our discussions of the theory and measurement of subclinical psychopathy.

PERSONALITY FROM A SOCIAL-COGNITIVE PERSPECTIVE

Social cognition is one of the most popular research paradigms in personality psychology (cf. Dweck & Leggett, 1988; Epstein, 1994; Fazio & Olson, 2003; Greenwald & Banaji, 1995; Hogan, 1991; James & Mazerolle, 2002; Kihlstrom, 1999; Mischel & Shoda, 1995). Social-cognitive theorists argue that in order to comprehensively assess a person's personality, we must capture both explicit and implicit social cognitions. *Explicit social cognitions* refer to the conscious (i.e., manifest, controlled) cognitions individuals have about their (and others') emotions, behavior, thoughts, needs, values, and attitudes and are accessible through conscious introspection and subsequent self-reports. Researchers interested in explicit social cognitions typically focus on measuring self-perceptions via self-report surveys or structured interviews (cf. Cattell, 1957; Costa & McCrae, 1992; Edwards, 1970; Goldberg, 1993; Greenwald & Banaji, 1995; Gustafson & Ritzer, 1995; Hare, 1991; Hogan, 1991; Hogan, Hogan, & Roberts, 1996; Jackson, 1984; Lanyon & Goodstein, 1997; Lilienfeld & Andrews, 1996; McClelland, Koestner, & Weinberger, 1989; McCrae & Costa, 1997; Winter, John, Stewart, Klohnen, & Duncan, 1998).

In contrast, *implicit social cognitions* refer to the unconscious (e.g., latent, automatic) cognitions individuals have about their (and others') emotions, behaviors, thoughts, needs, values, and attitudes. Because implicit social cognitions operate outside of conscious awareness, they are not introspectively available for an individual to explicitly self-disclose. As such, implicit social cognitions must be measured indirectly. Indirect measures neither inform the respondent of the construct being assessed nor require him or her to self-report explicitly on that construct (Greenwald & Banaji, 1995). Within the context of personality measurement, indirect measures of implicit cognitions include projective techniques such as the Thematic Apperception Test (TAT) and the Rorschach Inkblot Test (Lilienfeld, Wood, & Garb, 2000), implicit association tests (Greenwald & Banaji, 1995), or conditional reasoning tests (James, 1998). Researchers interested in implicit social cognitions employ such methods to supply information about a subject's unconscious thoughts and attitudes,

latent motives and values, and cognitive-affective structures underlying observable behavior (cf. Brewin, 1989; Epstein, 1994; Freud, 1959; Greenwald & Banaji, 1995; Hogan, 1991; James, 1998; Kihlstrom, Mulvaney, Tobias, & Tobis, 2000; McClelland et al., 1989; Murray, 1938; Westen, 1991, 1998; Westen & Gabbard, 1999; Winter et al., 1998).

There is growing awareness among researchers of the critical and interdependent roles that explicit and implicit cognitions have in determining behavior (cf. Brewin, 1989; Epstein, 1994; Fazio & Olson, 2003; Greenwald & Banaji, 1995; Hogan, 1991; James, 1998; James & Mazerolle, 2002; Kihlstrom, 1987, 1999; Kihlstrom et al., 2000; McClelland et al., 1989; Mischel & Shoda, 1995; Westen, 1991, 1998; Westen & Gabbard, 1999; Winter et al., 1998). Within the context of personality, McClelland et al. (1989) demonstrated that measures of implicit cognitions were better predictors of general behavior trends (operants), whereas measures of explicit cognitions were better predictors of attitudes and values (respondents). Their conclusions indicate that relying on both types of measures enhances researchers' ability to predict a variety of important criterion behaviors. Winter et al. (1998) hypothesized and found that explicit cognitions (i.e., self-reported personality) channeled the manifestation of one's implicit cognitions (i.e., latent motives assessed via the TAT) in an interactive way. Similar results have been obtained using conditional reasoning tests (Bing et al., 2004). These findings suggest that measures of implicit cognitions can increment predictions of important criterion behaviors. Such increments may accrue via additive models (i.e., main effects for both implicit and explicit) or via multiplicative models (i.e., implicit and explicit interactions).

The importance of both explicit and implicit cognitions for understanding personality has not yet been embraced by psychopathy researchers. We believe that theory, measurement, and practice concerning subclinical psychopathy can be vastly enhanced by including the role of implicit cognitions. In the remainder of this chapter, we plan to review important theory and research and build a case for this general thesis. To that end, in the remainder of this chapter we will: (1) review traditional conceptualizations of subclinical psychopathy, (2) review measures traditionally used to assess subclinical psychopathy, (3) examine how they fail to assess reliably individual differences in implicit cognitions, (4) propose a taxonomy of implicit cognitions relevant to psychopathy and describe how conditional reasoning can be used to assess these implicit cognitions, (5) present a model that integrates both implicit and explicit cognitions, and (6) illustrate how this integrative model could be used to derive testable research propositions about subpsychopathy in everyday life.

CORE FEATURES AND SYMPTOMS OF SUBCLINICAL PSYCHOPATHY

Though research on psychopathy can be traced to the early 1800s (Millon, Simonsen, & Birket-Smith, 1998), most researchers acknowledge that it was Cleckley's (1941) seminal book, *The Mask of Sanity* (now in its fifth edition, 1976) that provided the foundation for contemporary conceptualizations. More recently, Hare (1999) updated and refined the conceptualization in his book entitled *Without Conscience: The Disturbing World of Psychopaths among Us*. In this book he summarized nearly three decades of research on psychopathy, conducted primarily in psychiatric and prison settings, and identified the primary symptoms underlying a two-factor model of clinical psychopathy. According to Hare, one factor comprised symptoms associated with affective and interpersonal dysfunctions (sometimes labeled *aggressive narcissism;* Meloy, 1988), whereas the other factor comprised symptoms indicative of social and behavioral deviance.

For several decades Hare's two-factor theory was the dominant model of psychopathy. Recently, Cooke and Michie (2001) noted that most researchers agree that psychopathy comprises a diverse group of *behavioral, affective,* and *interpersonal* traits and hypothesized that a three-factor, hierarchical model better represented the psychopathy construct domain. They suggested that the interpersonal/emotional dimension should be partitioned into two separate dimensions and arranged in a hierarchical fashion with three first-order factors (i.e., behavioral, affective, and interpersonal aspects) loading on the second-order or "global" factor. Psychopathy still was conceptualized as a unitary concept; however, now it was described by a more complex hierarchical structure.

Building on this three-factor model, we label the global dimensions of subclinical psychopathy: (1) *arrogant and deceitful interpersonal style,* (2) *deficient affective experience,* and (3) *impulsive and irresponsible behavioral style.* Table 20.1 contains psychopathy symptoms recognized by Cleckley (1941) and later expanded by Hare (1991). These core symptoms are mapped into the two- and three-factor conceptualizations of clinical psychopathy as well as into recent frameworks (reviewed later) purporting to capture the subclinical variant of this toxic personality profile. In the interest of brevity we will use an abbreviation when referring to a subclinical psychopath (SCP). Using the three-factor model as a conceptual anchor, we briefly review the core symptoms associated with subclinical psychopathy.

Arrogant and Deceitful Interpersonal Style

A dominant characteristic of subclinical psychopathy is an all-encompassing, narcissistic, and grandiose sense of self-worth (Cleckley, 1976; Gustafson, 1999, 2000; Hare, 1991, 1999; Lilienfeld & Andrews, 1996). SCPs are egocentric and believe they are entitled to special consideration; they see themselves as superior individuals who do not need to conform to the rules of society; instead they prefer to live by their own personal code or ethos.

The SCP engages in active self-promotion and grandstanding while simultaneously criticizing anyone he or she sees as a potential rival or threat. In their eyes, their work is better than their coworkers', their athletic performance is better than their teammates', their ideas are better than their friends' and colleagues', and their parenting is better than their spouses'. The SCP sees himself or herself as smarter, funnier, braver, stronger, and more attractive. Such individuals discount as unimportant, trivial, or stupid, those activities in which they are incapable of excelling. Every aspect of an SCP's life is filtered through a cognitive prism of narcissistic self-enhancement.

Whereas some individuals see the SCP as arrogant, conceited, self-absorbed, and vain, to others the SCP is able to project a glib, charismatic, confident, convincing, and engaging public image. This glibness when combined with narcissism creates a potent interpersonal force: a dramatic and energized storyteller, often with themselves as the main character. As a result, SCPs can be extremely persuasive and charming, but this often requires the SCP to feign expertise in a particular subject area (e.g., art, economics, mathematics, music, poetry, politics, psychology). Although their lack of substantive knowledge on a particular topic is readily discernable by anyone with expertise in that area, they can glibly use cursory knowledge to tell interesting, if not improbable, stories that make a favorable first impression on an unsuspecting listener.

SCPs are comfortable and well practiced in the arts of deception, manipulation, insincerity, and lying (Cleckley, 1976; Gustafson, 1999, 2000; Hare 1991, 1999; Paulhus & Williams, 2002; Williams & Paulhus, 2004b). They have no difficulty being untruthful and insincere and rarely concern themselves with the prospect of being caught in such untruths. When caught, they are rarely embarrassed. Even after having a series of lies exposed, the SCP will not hesitate to make "promises" and "commitments" that he or she obviously has no intention of honoring. Their fluency with deception makes SCPs particularly adept at crimes such as impersonation, identity theft, fraud, and embezzlement. SCPs are able to justify such crimes by framing the world through a prism of narcissistic dominance: contests between the strong versus the weak, predators versus prey, and givers versus takers (Hare, 1999, p. 49). This cognitive framing of social interactions as dominance contests enables the SCP to justify winning at all costs. As such, the SCP is willing to lie, manipulate, deceive, cheat, steal, and even physically and emotionally harm others.

Deficient Affective Experience

SCPs are known for producing shallow and superficial emotional displays (Cleckley, 1976; Hare, 1999; Lilienfeld & Andrews, 1996; Williams & Paulhus, 2004b). The SCP is capable of expressing a variety of emotions; however, their expressions often lack emotional depth and texture. That is, they are capable of "going through the motions" of expressing a wide range of emotions, but the actual displays can be shallow and unconvincing. To the SCP, emotions are largely cognitive experiences; they have difficulty describing the physiological arousal and subjective affective appraisal that accompany such cognition.

As a result, SCPs rarely experience shame, guilt, remorse, or regret (Cleckley, 1976; Gustafson, 1999, 2000; Hare, 1999; Williams & Paulhus, 2004b). They are not concerned with the impact their behavior has on the emotional, financial, physical, social, or professional well-being of others. The careless and destructive ways they treat others are viewed as perfectly acceptable and appropriate. When, on rare occasion, SCPs verbalize remorse or guilt, their words are emotionally shallow and readily contradicted by future behavior (Hare, 1999). This lack of remorse is closely interwoven with their general lack of empathy (Gustafson, 1999, 2000; Hare, 1999). SCPs are restricted to largely intellectual connections with others, unable to bond at a deeper emotional level. They cannot "feel bad" about their actions because they cannot comprehend how their actions make others "feel." Their lack of empathy does not imply that they cannot maintain relationships with friends, spouses, or children. Rather, it implies that these relationships often will be one-sided, selfish, volatile, and rooted in conflict.

A related affective dysfunction is the general failure to experience anxiety or fear in situations that most individuals might find quite arousing (Cleckley, 1976; Hare, 1999). Thus, one reason that SCPs are able to engage in their antisocial, manipulative, and often dangerous behavior is that they do not experience trepidation over the consequences of their actions. In addition, they often take pride in their exploits. Acts of manipulation, deception, and aggression are rationalized as the psychopath's attempt to survive in a "dog-eat-dog" world and protect themselves against the hostile/malevolent intent of others (Hare, 1999). Specifically, SCPs are able to rationalize their exploitive acts by relying on a cognitive bias that filters the world through a prism of hostility and harmful intent (Hare, 1999; Lilienfeld & Andrews, 1996). In essence

they project their malevolent intent onto others and see others as "out to get them" or as potential "rivals," "enemies," or "threats." Such threats need to be dealt with swiftly and severely in order for the SCPs' continued "survival." Thus, experiencing remorse and guilt over their antisocial actions is inconceivable to the SCP because he or she does not see their actions as unacceptable or inappropriate but as effective interpersonal survival mechanisms.

Impulsive and Irresponsible Behavioral Style

Extending the description of characteristic behavior patterns, SCPs are impulsive and irresponsible. Their impulsivity has a largely narcissistic tone: they act because they "want to." Although SCPs prefer to describe their lifestyles as spontaneous, unstructured, and free-spirited, their behavior is often hasty and reckless and triggered by a whim with the sole purpose of immediate egocentric gratification (Cleckley, 1976; Hare, 1999). SCPs prefer to live moment-to-moment according to their own personal rules and standards and thus become frustrated and agitated when others try to impose structure or constraint on their behavior. Their impulsivity is driven by a constant need for excitement and stimulation or, alternatively, their tendency to experience boredom (Hare, 1999). To alleviate a sense of boredom, the SCP often turns to drugs, alcohol, promiscuous relationships, and/or various forms of delinquent behavior. The SCP will move from job to job and relationship to relationship in order to avoid the boredom and monotony he or she associates with "stability."

Such impulsivity causes SCPs to be irresponsible and unreliable (Cleckley, 1976; Gustafson, 1999, 2000; Hare, 1999; Lilienfeld & Andrews, 1996; Paulhus & Williams, 2002; Williams & Paulhus, 2004b). They routinely fail to honor their commitments, promises, and obligations both big and small. SCPs are more likely to have unstable patterns of work attendance and performance. They are more likely to forget, ignore, or be tardy for social engagements. They are more likely to be neglectful of friends and loved ones, especially children. Because they lack the capacity to empathize and experience guilt, SCPs are indifferent to the consequences and problems their irresponsibility causes for their friends, family, and coworkers (Hare, 1999). They do what they want, when they want, and with little regard for others.

This impulsivity and irresponsibility often results in SCPs having a difficult time articulating and achieving realistic long-term goals. Although their egocentricity makes them particularly adamant about their future successes, SCPs rarely have a feasible plan or the patience necessary for accomplishing those goals. They can visualize their future success but often cannot engage in the steps necessary to achieve their

TABLE 20.1 Framework for Comparing Different Conceptualizations of Subclinical Psychopathy

Cleckley (1941, 1976) and Hare (1991, 1999) psychopathy symptoms	Hare (1991)		Cooke & Michie (2001)		
	Interpersonal/ affective (aggressive narcissism)	Social deviance	Arrogant & deceitful interpersonal style	Deficient affective experience	Impulsive and irresponsible behavioral style
1. Glibness/superficial charm	X		X		
2. Grandiose sense of self-worth	X		X		
3. Need for stimulation/proneness to boredom		X			X
4. Pathological lying	X		X		
5. Conning/manipulative	X		X		
6. Lack of remorse or guilt	X			X	
7. Shallow affect	X			X	
8. Callous/lack of empathy	X			X	
9. Parasitic lifestyle		X			X
10. Poor behavioral controls		X			
11. Promiscuous sexual behavior					
12. Early behavioral problems		X			
13. Lack of realistic, long-term goals		X			X
14. Impulsivity		X			X
15. Irresponsibility		X			X
16. Failure to accept responsibility for own actions	X			X	
17. Many short-term marital relationships					
18. Juvenile delinquency		X			
19. Revocation of conditional release		X			
20. Criminal versatility					

(continued)

goals and accomplish their dreams (Cleckley, 1976; Hare, 1999). Desire for success combined with the SCPs' facility with manipulation and deception, often yields a proclivity toward parasitic relationships; they are particularly adept at using others for their own financial, personal, or professional gain (Hare, 1999). Such exploitive relationships come easy to the smooth-talking, confident SCP, who navigates through life without the burden of guilt or regret. Finally, like their clinical counterparts, SCPs have a tendency to engage in a wide range of aggressive antisocial behaviors (Cleckley, 1976; Gustafson & Ritzer, 1995; Hare, 1999; Lilienfeld & Andrews, 1996; Paulhus & Williams, 2002). These aggressive behaviors may take a variety of forms, including sexual harassment, intentional work slowdowns, threats, spreading rumors, theft, and showing up late for meetings (see also Buss, 1961; Folger & Baron, 1996).

In summary, what makes SCP such a toxic personality profile is the manifestation and synergistic integration of so many dysfunctional and counterproductive patterns of behavior, affect, and cognition. In isolation, each of the preceding symptoms is highly problematic; however, when many symptoms appear concurrently, the impact can be devastating to others. Although these symptoms have been studied in various forms since the early 1800s, it has been only in the last 30 years that reliable measurement tools have been developed for identifying clinical psychopaths, and only in the last 10 years have researchers seriously pursued identification of a subclinical profile.

A BRIEF REVIEW OF RESEARCH ON SUBCLINICAL PSYCHOPATHY

Although the most popular measure of clinical psychopathy has been the Psychopathy Checklist–Revised (PCL–R; Hare, 1991), self-report surveys have emerged as the methodology of choice among researchers exploring subclinical psychopathy. Later, we briefly review several SCP research programs that have relied on self-report inventories as their method of assessment. In each case, we link the authors' findings to the symptoms described earlier.

Gustafson and Ritzer (1995) used existing personality measures to create a profile of subclinical psychopathy. They labeled individuals with this personality profile *aberrant self-promoters* (ASPs) to emphasize their egocentric and antisocial tendencies. In contrast to the procedures described later that conceptualized SCP as a continuum, Gustafson and Ritzer's person-centered approach sought to identify a dichotomous set of "normal individuals" and "subclinical psychopaths" by examining the pattern of scores obtained across multiple personality inventories. Specifically, they asked individuals to complete a test battery measuring narcissism,

TABLE 20.1   *(Continued)*

Gustafson & Ritzer (1995)					Lilienfeld & Andrews (1996)								Williams & Paulhus (2004a)			
Narcissism	Socialization	Social desirability	Self-esteem	Self-report psychopathy	Machiavellian egocentricity	Social potency	Cold-heartedness	Carefree nonplanfulness	Fearlessness	Blame externalization	Impulsive nonconformity	Stress immunity	Antisocial behavior	Erratic lifestyle	Interpersonal manipulation	Callous affect
				X		X									X	
X			X	X	X											X
	X			X					X			X		X		
				X											X	
X				X	X										X	
				X			X				X				X	
				X			X		X						X	X
				X			X				X					X
	X			X							X			X		
				X												
	X			X									X			
								X								
	X			X				X						X		
				X								X		X		
				X									X			

socialization (i.e., antisocial tendencies), social desirability, self-esteem, and self-reported psychopathy. Table 20.1 maps these constructs into the symptoms identified by Hare (1991). Three different methods were used to divide their sample into a group of normal individuals and a group of ASPs. These diverse methods converged in their identification of ASPs, with agreement averaging more than 90 percent.

Gustafson and Ritzer (1995) found that, compared to normal individuals, ASPs had higher scores on the PCL–R (Hare, 1991), lower undergraduate grade point averages (symptoms: poor long-term planning, irresponsibility), greater numbers of parking violations (symptoms: antisocial and aggressive behavior, impulsivity), greater numbers of university judicial reprimands (symptoms: antisocial and aggressive behavior, irresponsibility), and a greater likelihood to report committing illegal acts (symptoms: antisocial and aggressive behavior, need for stimulation). Gustafson cross-validated her findings in a Swedish sample (see also Pethman & Erlandsson, 2002) and found that compared to normal individuals, and poorly socialized individuals, ASPs reported greater levels of conduct problems (symptoms: antisocial and aggressive behavior), such as property offenses, use of illegal drugs, vandalism, and violent offenses (Andershed, Gustafson, Kerr, & Stattin, 2002).

Extending the work of Gustafson and her colleagues, Russell (1996) compared the performance of ASPs to indi-

viduals scoring high on Machiavellianism (Machs) on a legislative game. He found that compared to Machs, ASPs were more likely to renege on bargains (symptoms: conning/manipulative, lying), be disliked by their fellow legislators, and sacrifice their constituents' interests to their own (symptoms: egocentric/grandiose, irresponsible, manipulative). In another study, D. LeBreton (1999) found that ASPs in authority positions could not recall accurately the performance of their "subordinates" unless the situation was set up to provide them with the opportunity for ego gratification (symptoms: egocentric/grandiose). Taken together, the results of Gustafson and her colleagues support the notion of a subclinical profile that is predictive of self-serving, antisocial, and ego-focused behavior.

Lilienfeld and Andrews (1996) developed the Psychopathic Personality Inventory (PPI). These researchers sought to assess the personality characteristics associated with SCP, avoiding questions about antisocial behaviors. Ambitious validation research yielded a measure comprising the eight subscales that we mapped into the symptoms identified by Hare (1991; see Table 20.1). Validity evidence included significant correlations between the PPI total score and ratings of drug abuse/dependence (symptoms: impulsivity, need for stimulation, antisocial and aggressive behavior), trustworthiness (symptoms: conning/manipulative, lying), antisocial personality disorder, and narcissistic personality disorder.

Overall, the PPI appears to be a psychometrically sound tool for assessing a wide range of personality characteristics typically associated with SCP.

Another research program using self-reports of SCP is being conducted by Delroy Paulhus and colleagues. Their research focuses on refining the factor structure of self-reported subclinical psychopathy and expanding the nomological network surrounding this construct. They examined the factor structure of the Self-Report Psychopathy Scale–Revised (SRP–R; Hare, 1985) in nonclinical samples. In an initial study, they determined that the SRP–R II maintained its predictive validity but that Hare's (1991, 1999) two-factor model did not cleanly emerge during factor analyses (Williams & Paulhus, 2004b). Recently, Williams and Paulhus (2004a) expanded the breadth of the psychopathy-related traits measured by the SRP–R II by adding new items and demonstrated moderate to strong fit between their data and a four-factor model containing the following factors: Antisocial Behavior, Erratic Lifestyle, Interpersonal Manipulation, and Callous Affect. They labeled the 40-item revised scale the SRP–R III. Table 20.1 maps these constructs onto the symptoms identified by Cleckley (1976) and Hare (1991, 1999).

In addition to examining and expanding the factor structure of the SRP–R, these authors have expanded the nomological network surrounding subclinical psychopathy. For example, Paulhus and Williams (2002) found that SRP–R total scores correlated positively with, but were not redundant with, subclinical narcissism (symptoms: egocentric/grandiose) and Machiavellianism (symptoms: conning/manipulative, glib/ charming). They also found that SCP correlates positively with extroversion, openness to experience, and negatively with agreeableness, conscientiousness, and neuroticism (for an extended review mapping the Big Five into psychopathy, see also Lynam, 2001). Williams and Paulhus (2004b) obtained a comparable pattern of correlations and also observed positive correlations with self-reports of bullying others (symptoms: antisocial and aggressive behavior), use of drugs (symptoms: antisocial and aggressive behavior, need for stimulation, impulsiveness, irresponsibility), minor and major crime (symptoms: antisocial and aggressive behavior, need for stimulation), and antiauthority misbehavior. In several unpublished papers, these authors reported that subclinical psychopathy was positively correlated with deviant sexual thoughts and behavior, likelihood to seek revenge after an evocative social interaction, and aggressive entertainment preferences (e.g., watching aggressive films, playing violent sports; see Nathanson, Williams, & Paulhus, 2004; Williams, Howell, Cooper, Yuille, & Paulhus, 2004; Williams, McAndrew, Learn, Harms, & Paulhus, 2001).

The research programs reviewed previously have led to refined measurement instruments (e.g., PPI, SRP–R III) and enhanced understanding of the nomological network surrounding SCP. Furthermore, all three programs of research have linked SCP to important criterion behaviors. As such, these programs have advanced our understanding of the structure and relationship between SCPs' explicit cognitions (i.e., conscious self-perceptions) and other constructs and criteria. Although self-perceptions are essential for a comprehensive understanding of an individual's personality (Hogan, 1991), the role of implicit cognitions also needs to be systematically examined.

MEASURING SUBCLINICAL PSYCHOPATHS' IMPLICIT COGNITIONS

A Note on Measuring Implicit Cognitions via Projective Techniques

The projective test most commonly used in clinical research on psychopathy is the Rorschach Inkblot Test (Gacono & Meloy, 1994; Meloy & Gacono, 2000). Although we are unaware of subclinical researchers employing the Rorschach, we see several serious obstacles to using projective techniques in general (e.g., TAT) and the Rorschach in particular. First, projective tests often demonstrate low empirical validity with correlations between projective techniques and behavioral criteria ranging from the .10s to the .20s and rarely exceeding .30 (cf. James & Mazerolle, 2002; Lilienfeld et al., 2000; Spangler, 1992). Second, the subjective nature of the testing and scoring process often yields low estimates of internal consistency and test-retest reliabilities for these techniques (Anastasi, 1982; James & Mazerolle, 2002; Lilienfeld et al., 2000; Nunnally, 1978). Finally, projective techniques tend to be difficult and time consuming to administer (James & Mazerolle, 2002). Consequently, theory and research concerning SCPs has not considered fully the roles of implicit cognitions in understanding the subclinical psychopathy construct.

The dearth of research on SCPs' implicit cognitions is not unique. Widespread integration of theory and research on implicit social cognitions across all areas of psychological theory has been limited by the lack of valid and reliable measurements systems (Greenwald & Banaji, 1995; James & Mazerolle, 2002). We believe that the assessment of subclinical psychopathy can be enhanced by including measures that assess the implicit rationalizations SCPs rely on to justify their narcissistic and antisocial patterns of behavior. Such an assessment when combined with traditional self-report inventories has the potential to increase dramatically our ability to understand and predict the behavior of SCPs. Taken together, this suggests new indirect measurement systems are needed that: (1) reliably assess implicit cognitions, (2) have strong criterion-related validity, and (3) can be applied to constructs such as subclinical psychopathy. Research on James's (1998) conditional reasoning measurement system suggests that it meets these criteria.

Measuring Implicit Cognitions via Conditional Reasoning

The conditional reasoning approach to measuring implicit cognitions is called such because the chosen "solution" to an inductive reasoning problem is conditional on the personality of the respondent (James, 1998). That is, the reasoning and inference processes evoked in day-to-day functioning differ systematically between SCPs and individuals with prosocial personalities. The conditional reasoning approach to measurement has been used to assess implicit social cognitions associated with several psychological constructs.

For example, James and colleagues (1998; James et al., in press) have used the Conditional Reasoning Test of Aggression (CRT-A) to measure the implicit biases that aggressive and antisocial individuals use to rationalize and justify their behavior. The CRT-A consists of 22 inductive reasoning problems developed from six forms of implicit rationalization described later. This test has demonstrated strong psychometric characteristics including mean uncorrected criterion-related validity coefficients exceeding .40 with a range of behavioral criteria. Furthermore, because respondents are not aware that personality characteristics are being inferred from their responses, conditional reasoning tests appear to be immune to faking or intentional response distortion (J. LeBreton, Barksdale, Burgess, & James, 2004). Instead, respondents believe that reasoning skills are the target of assessment. In fact, the items are bona fide inductive reasoning problems; however, the solutions to these problems are not based on intellectual aptitudes but instead on rationalizations and justifications that the respondent unknowingly uses to enhance the logical appeal of narcissistic and antisocial behaviors. As such, these problems have nonsignificant, near-zero correlations with proxy measures of general mental ability (e.g., SAT, ACT, GRE; James et al., in press).

Conditional reasoning taps implicit cognitions because people are motivated to believe that their behavior is rational, reasonable, logical, and appropriate. Of course these qualities are relative to one's favored standards, beliefs, and reasoning processes, and we propose that SCPs' favored standards, beliefs, and reasoning processes are far from rational, reason-

able, logical, and appropriate, relative to general conceptions of prosocial conduct. Instead their behavior is often unwarranted, too severe, irrational, overstated, and simply inappropriate. We assert that SCPs maintain a self-perception of rationality and propriety by implicitly relying on a unique set of justifications to enhance the logical appeal of their narcissistic and antisocial actions (Gustafson, 1999, 2000; James, 1998). By tapping into these implicit "conditional" differences in how SCPs justify their behavior, we capture variance that underlies differences in their typical behavior. These implicit biases may be conceptualized as one form of Freud's defense mechanism of *rationalization.* James (1998) referred to these implicit biases as *justification mechanisms* (JMs) to emphasize the critical role they play in justifying behavior that otherwise would be deemed as inappropriate or unwarranted. Justification comes from "rationalization," and mechanism comes from "defense mechanism." The basic idea is that individuals rely on these JMs to rationalize their psychopathic behavior. The rationalizations furnished by JMs provide a safeguard against potentially ego-threatening interactions and feedback from others.

JMs enable individuals to rationalize a grandiose sense of self-worth, thus insulating their egos from the social rejection and scorn engendered by their egocentric behavior and attitudes (e.g., "Others don't like me, not because I'm a bad person but because they are threatened by my greatness"). JMs enable individuals to rationalize not displaying empathy, guilt, or remorse, thus insulating their egos from the social stigma of not connecting with, or caring for, others (e.g., "It's not that I don't care about others, I don't care about my enemies; displaying emotions will be seen as a sign of weakness by my enemies"). JMs enable individuals to rationalize their antisocial behavior and violations of societal norms and values, thus insulating their egos from social disdain or disgust over their actions (e.g., "It's not that my behavior is inappropriate, I'm simply reacting to the mechanisms by which society tries to control us and obstruct our free will"; "Everyone manipulates to some degree"; "It takes courage to reject the routine monotony of everyday life").

An overview of the conditional reasoning process is portrayed in Figure 20.1 (adapted from J. LeBreton, 2002). As this figure suggests, people with different personality dispositions (e.g., subclinical psychopathy) unknowingly make use of a number of different cognitive biases when observing, interpreting, and reacting to people, situations, and events. James and Mazerolle (2002) presented nine general categories of cognitive bias (e.g., attributional biases). These biases are enduring patterns of thoughts, values, assumptions, and beliefs about people in general and about "how the world works." These worldviews are integral to patterns of person-

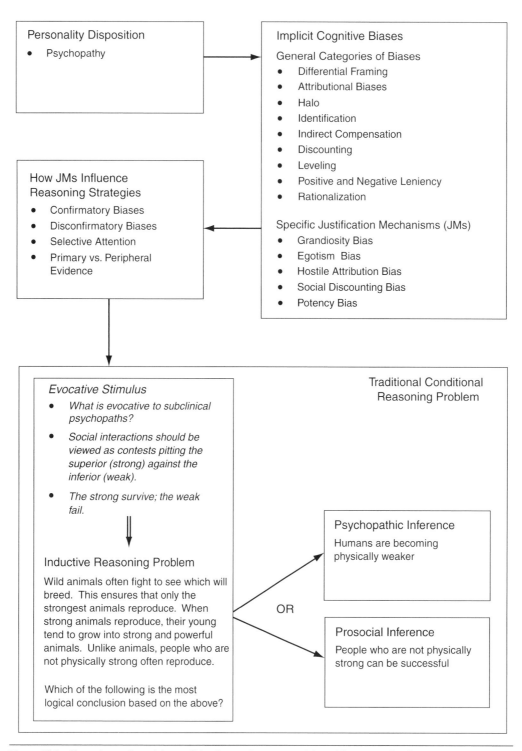

Figure 20.1 General overview of the conditional reasoning process. Adapted from *Use of Differential Framing to Measure Implicit Social Cognitions Associated with Aggression,* by J. M. LeBreton, 2002, an unpublished doctoral dissertation, University of Tennessee, Knoxville. Copyright © 2002 by the author and adapted with permission.

ality functioning and can be considered "signature" causes for patterns of intraindividual behavioral coherence (Mischel & Shoda, 1995). Associated with any specific constellation of these cognitive biases are specific ways of justifying the behavior that results, especially when explicitly called upon to do so (e.g., when the board asked Jack to justify his lying).

These JMs are "rational" explanations for behavior that allow the SCP, for example, to engage in otherwise unsavory conduct and avoid personally confronting the impropriety of such. These JMs enhance the rational appeal of dispositional or motive-based behavior by implicitly impacting the reasoning and analysis used by individuals to explain and justify responses to various situations and stimuli that by most accounts would be viewed as irrational or inappropriate. Stated alternatively, most SCPs do not have the (conscious) self-perception that their antisocial and narcissistic thoughts and behaviors are irrational, irresponsible, or inappropriate. In order to maintain the illusion that such thoughts and actions are in fact appropriate, SCPs engage in a form of (unconscious) rationalization. Because JMs operate outside the conscious awareness of SCPs, JMs must be assessed indirectly.

Although each JM may be traced back to one of the broad categories of implicit cognitive biases identified by James and Mazerolle (2002), each personality disposition will have a unique set of signature JMs. That is, SCPs are likely to evoke a unique set of JMs, compared to other personality profiles, to justify their behavior. These JMs impact the reasoning strategies used by individuals by shaping how they perceive, think, and analyze situations and their responses to these situations. Specifically, JMs implicitly impact cognitive processes such as perception (e.g., selective attention), information search strategies (e.g., confirmatory biases), reasoning, and causal inference (James & Mazerolle, 2002; LeBreton, 2002). We propose that SCPs rely on such JMs to enhance the logical appeal of their psychopathy-driven behavior and to provide a context for the self-perception of rationality, reasonableness, and appropriateness.

Based on our review of the conditional reasoning literature on aggression (James, 1998; James & Mazerolle, 2002), antisocial personality (Walton, 2004), and psychopathy (Gustafson, 1999, 2000), we identified an initial set of justification mechanisms that we believe offer a good starting point for researchers interested in understanding implicit cognitions of the SCP. The set of JMs presented in Table 20.2 is not exhaustive; different researchers might include other JMs or omit one or more of the JMs we have identified as relevant. Nevertheless, we offer these JMs as a reasonable starting point for individuals interested in understanding how SCPs justify, rationalize, and explain their toxic patterns of behavior and affect.

Hostile Attribution Bias

Take for example two individuals working on a report for their boss. Both individuals receive feedback from a coworker regarding some potential problems with the report.

TABLE 20.2   Justification Mechanisms for Subclinical Psychopathy

Social discounting bias: A tendency to call on socially unorthodox and frequently antisocial beliefs in interpreting and analyzing social events and relationships. People with this bias are disdainful of traditional ideals and conventional beliefs; they may be insensitive, unempathetic, and unfettered by social customs. They are often directly cynical or critical, with few subliminal channels for routing antisocial framing and analysis.

Egotism bias: A tendency to frame and reason from the standpoint that "what is right = what is right for me." Individuals with this bias frame the world through a prism of egocentric entitlement. They see situations and people as mechanisms for achieving their desires, irrespective of the consequences. Such egocentric framing and analysis results in cues or warnings toward patience, caution, concern, or prudence being discounted or ignored.

Grandiosity bias: A tendency to frame oneself as a superior being with a special destiny. Individuals with this bias grossly inflate perceptions and interpretations concerning their own abilities, accomplishments, and contributions while simultaneously deflating perceptions and interpretations of others' abilities, accomplishments, and contributions. People using this bias expect to be viewed as exceptional and superior to others, without ever providing the "proof" of such status.

Potency bias: A tendency to frame and reason using the contrast of strength vs. weakness. For example, people with a strong potency bias tend to frame others on a continuum ranging from (a) strong, assertive, powerful, daring, fearless, or brave to (b) weak, impotent, submissive, timid, compliant, conforming, or cowardly.

Hostile attribution bias: A tendency to see malevolent intention in the actions of others. Even benign or friendly acts may be seen as having hidden, hostile agendas designed intentionally to inflict harm. An especially virulent form of this bias occurs when benign or positive acts are attributed to selfish concerns and negative incentives.

Because an SCP often has a tendency to see hostile and malevolent intent in others (Hare, 1999; Lilienfeld & Andrews, 1996), he or she is likely to frame this feedback as overly critical, malicious, hostile, and combative. Furthermore, he or she suspects the coworker is trying to degrade and embarrass him or her. As a result, this individual may verbally assault the coworker and storm out of the room. On the other hand, the prosocial individual frames and interprets the feedback as helpful, considerate, developmental, supportive, and instrumental toward improving his or her performance. He or she likely would thank the coworker and adopt his or her suggestions for improving the report.

In this example, the SCP framed the comments of his or her coworker as critical and combative, whereas the prosocial individual framed these same comments as helpful and supportive. The disparity in how feedback was framed and evaluated represents an example of differential framing. *Differential framing* refers to the qualitative disparities in the meanings assigned to the same situations, attributes, or events by individuals with different personalities (James & Mazerolle, 2002; LeBreton, 2002). This initial framing was shaped further by another personality-related cognitive bias (i.e., an attributional bias). That is, the belief that the behavior of the coworker was malicious was shaped by a hostile attribution bias associated with aggressive/antisocial personality (Crick & Dodge, 1994). This bias may implicitly shape how the SCP responds if asked to justify his or her aggressive behavior (e.g., "My reaction was appropriate because my coworkers are all out to get me and I needed to defend myself"). Individuals who routinely call upon this bias to interpret situations, draw causal inferences regarding the behavior of others, and justify their own antisocial or aggressive behavior are said to have the JM of *hostile attribution bias* (Crick & Dodge, 1994; James, 1998).

Potency Bias

Recall that psychopaths frame the world through a prism of dominance and control (Hare, 1999). Such framing is at the heart of the *potency bias*. Individuals with a potency bias rationalize their narcissistic and antisocial behavior by implicitly framing and reasoning that social interactions are dominance contests that pit the weak against the strong, the prey against the predator, and the givers against the takers. Such individuals are constantly surveying their environments for opportunities to "win" against their weaker competitors. In explaining why they are deceptive and manipulative, someone with a potency bias might rely on rationales such as "rules are meant to be broken," "rules only apply to the weak," "a lie is only a lie if you get caught," "everyone lies to some degree," or "the only way to win is to play tough."

Social Discounting Bias

This bias (James et al., in press) is also relevant to understanding the SCP profile. The *social discounting bias* refers to "a tendency to call on socially unorthodox and frequently antisocial beliefs in interpreting and analyzing social events and relationships. People with this bias are disdainful of traditional ideals and conventional beliefs; they may be insensitive, unempathetic, and unfettered by social customs. They are often directly cynical or critical, with few subliminal channels for routing antisocial framing and analysis" (p. 143; James & Mazerolle, 2002).

Egotism Bias

The egotism bias refers to a tendency to frame and reason from the standpoint that "what is right = what is right for me" (Walton, 2004). Individuals with an egotism bias interpret and analyze the world through a prism of self-centered entitlement. The egotism bias is used by SCPs to justify their often impulsive, irresponsible, and reckless behavior. This is because the egotism bias is not necessarily linked to framing and reasoning stemming from an implicit sense of superiority or grandiosity but instead from the belief of "sovereignty and total selfishness" (Walton, 2004, p. 15) that is used to justify the immediate gratification of one's desires, even if such gratification requires impulsive, reckless, or dangerous actions. Thus, situations and people are framed and interpreted as the property and dominion of the SCP that should be used to his or her immediate advantage, irrespective of how one's behavior impacts others or themselves.

Grandiosity Bias

We combined several of the implicit assumptions identified by Gustafson (1999, 2000) to create a new JM we label the *grandiosity bias*. The grandiosity bias is a tendency for individuals to see themselves as superior human beings with special destinies (Gustafson, 1999, 2000). This bias stems from an implicit belief in the superiority and grandiosity of the SCP. Individuals with this bias tend to have grossly inflated self-perceptions concerning their abilities, accomplishments, and contributions while simultaneously having grossly deflated perceptions of others' abilities, accomplishments, and contributions. People with this bias expect others to view them as exceptional and superior (without ever providing the "proof" of such status; Gustafson, 1999, 2000). As such, situations will be interpreted through a filter that indicates others enjoy the opportunity to compliment superior people, and thus superior people should provide ample opportunity for others to provide such compliments (Gustafson, 1999, 2000).

Although both the egotism bias and the grandiosity bias share narcissistic qualities, they differ in subtle ways. The egotism bias is based not on framing and reasoning associated with an implicit sense of grandiosity but instead on the belief that the world is simply an extension of the self whose purpose is to supply the SCP with whatever he or she wants, whenever he or she wants it. In contrast, the grandiosity bias stems from the framing of the self as a special, superior individual with a special destiny. It is implicitly believed that others immediately recognize this special destiny (or would be receptive to its revelation). The grandiosity bias emphasizes how individuals rationalize inflated self-perceptions and deflated perceptions of others. They frame their work, efforts, and behavior as superior to others.

Returning to Figure 20.1, these JMs are believed to shape the types of reasoning strategies (i.e., processes) employed by SCPs; exemplars of such strategies are presented in the same figure. To illustrate, consider an SCP that implicitly relies on the JM of hostile attribution bias to rationalize his or her antisocial behavior. Use of this JM results in an individual unknowingly *selectively attending* to information that indicates others should not be trusted. Furthermore, he or she may engage reasoning strategies that *seek to confirm* this initial impression and thus justify aggressive behavior against this "untrustworthy" person. Finally, this JM also may direct this information to *discount salient information* (e.g., "This person has a reputation in our company for helping others") and *overemphasize tertiary information* (e.g., "I remember that this person got into a minor disagreement with a coworker nine months ago"; LeBreton, 2002).

JMs become the target of assessment in conditional reasoning tests (CRTs). Measurement of JMs is accomplished indirectly by asking respondents to solve inductive reasoning problems. An example of such a conditional reasoning problem is presented in the lower portion of Figure 20.1. Each problem starts with a situation or scenario thought to be evocative of the JMs used by SCPs. The scenario presented in the lower portion of Figure 20.1 focuses on social interactions as dominance contests between the "superior" psychopathic individual and "inferior" individuals. From this scenario, a reasoning problem was constructed.

This problem asks individuals to analyze information and draw an inference about reproductive outcomes among wild animals and among civilized people. This problem explains that wild animals often fight one another to determine which will breed and pass along their genes. It notes that when strong animals reproduce they tend to produce strong offspring. The problem then states that unlike wild animals, people who are not strong often reproduce. The respondent is then asked to make an inference concerning this information. One inference is based on psychopathic reasoning associated with the JM of potency bias (i.e., humans are becoming physically weaker). This solution is designed to be more logically appealing to SCPs than the solution based on prosocial reasoning (i.e., people who are not physically strong can be successful). The SCP is likely to disregard the prosocial inference as illogical and implausible because they equate "success" with strength and dominance. They believe it is impossible for a weak individual to be truly successful. In contrast, prosocial individuals will be drawn to the prosocial response because it allows everyone the opportunity to lead a successful, complete life, irrespective of strength or dominance. Like any good psychological test, CRTs contain multiple items and conclusions concerning an individual's construct status and are never based on the response to a single item.

To summarize how CRTs are constructed, inductive reasoning problems are written to evoke one or more reasoning strategies. These reasoning strategies are related to one or more JMs that are in turn related to a specific personality

disposition or motive (i.e., psychopathy). Although a fully validated conditional reasoning test of SCP has yet to be developed, we believe that the JMs in Table 20.2 present a good starting point for psychopathy researchers. Furthermore, a number of items already used to measure aggression (James & McIntyre, 2000) also could be used to measure aspects of SCP (see also the early work of Gustafson, 1999, 2000).

A SOCIAL-COGNITIVE MODEL OF SUBCLINICAL PSYCHOPATHY

As noted earlier, recent developments in social cognition have highlighted the important role that both explicit (i.e., conscious) and implicit (i.e., unconscious) social cognitions can play in understanding of important psychological phenomena, including attitudes and personality. One provocative line of research has examined how information from implicit and explicit personality measures may be combined to enhance synergistically the prediction of important criterion behaviors (McClelland et al., 1989; Winter et al., 1998). These integrations have relied on self-report personality surveys as the measure of explicit social cognitions and the TAT as the measure of implicit social cognition. Even with the generally poor psychometric characteristics of the TAT (Lilienfeld et al., 2000), researchers still were able to document that inclusion of both implicit and explicit measures led to enhanced prediction and understanding of a variety of important criterion behaviors.

Recently, Bing and his colleagues (Bing, 2002, 2003; Bing et al., 2001, 2004; Bing, Burroughs, Whanger, Green, & James, 2000; Bing & LeBreton, 2004) have developed and tested several models integrating information obtained from conditional reasoning tests (implicit cognitions) with information obtained from self-report surveys (explicit cognitions) to improve the prediction of a wide array of criterion behaviors. To date, integrative models for achievement motivation and aggression have been proposed and supported empirically. Drawing from these models, we propose the following as an integrative model of subclinical psychopathy that assimilates information obtained via self-report surveys with information obtained via conditional reasoning tests. We then rely on this integrative framework to derive a series of research propositions.

Integrative Model of Subclinical Psychopathy

Our model is presented in Table 20.3 and is a theoretical first cousin to Bing et al.'s (2000, 2004) integrative model of aggression. As will be described, our model explores conditions

TABLE 20.3   Proposed Integrative Model of Subclinical Psychopathy

		Self-report survey	
		Low psychopathy scores	High psychopathy scores
Conditional Reasoning Test	Justification mechanisms for psychopathy • Potency bias • Hostile attribution bias • Egotism bias • Socialization bias	Latent psychopaths • Do not see themselves as possessing psychopathic traits • Rely on psychopathy JMs to rationalize psychopathic behavior	Manifest psychopaths • See themselves as possessing psychopathic traits • Rely on psychopathy JMs to rationalize psychopathic behavior
	Prosocial values and reasoning • Properly socialized • Conventional values • Relationship-oriented	Prosocial individuals • Do not see themselves as possessing psychopathic traits • Rely on prosocial values and reasoning to guide their behavior	Hypercritical prosocials • See themselves as possessing psychopathic traits • Rely on prosocial values and reasoning to guide their behavior

where the explicit cognitions of an SCP are both congruent and incongruent with his or her implicit cognitions. To aid in our presentation, we bifurcate the subclinical psychopathy construct along both implicit and explicit lines. The left side of Table 20.3 represents a theoretical bifurcation of people into those who rely on prosocial cognition, affect, reasoning, and values versus those who rely on uniquely psychopathic justification mechanisms. Similarly, the right side of Table 20.3 represents a theoretical bifurcation of people into those who perceive themselves as prosocial versus those who perceive themselves as psychopathic. This 2 × 2 model yields four personality profiles, two of which represent variants on the SCP construct. We hasten to note that these bifurcations are theoretical in that both dimensions are conceptualized as continua (Bing et al., 2000, 2004). Thus, the four personality profiles are theoretical prototypes employed to guide our explanation of the model and should not be interpreted as representing four distinct categories or personality types.

As noted earlier, some of the JMs used to justify SCP were extracted from the literature on aggression and antisocial behavior. Similarly, some self-report surveys measuring SCP contain items that also tap aspects of aggressive and antisocial behavior. However, the SCP construct is broader than the aggression construct and includes personality traits such as narcissism, egocentricity, and affective impairments or dysfunctions. As such, different JMs are required to capture the implicit cognitions of the SCP, and additional self-report items are required to capture his or her explicit cognitions. Consequently, the integrative model for SCP is conceptually broader and potentially applicable to a wider range of criteria, including aggressive/antisocial behaviors, egocentric/narcissistic behaviors, and aberrant affective responses and impairments (e.g., lack of empathy).

Conditions of Congruency between Implicit and Explicit Cognitions

We will describe the two conditions where the explicit cognitions obtained via self-report surveys are congruent with an individual's implicit cognitions obtained via conditional reasoning tests.

Prosocials

The lower left cell in Table 20.3 represents individuals who self-report seeing themselves as having prosocial characteristics and whose implicit reasoning is rooted in prosocial values and beliefs (and thus do not need to rationalize their behavior); we refer to these individuals as *prosocials*. For these individuals, their self-attributed motives and latent motives/justifications are congruent with one another and guide them to engage in prosocial, cooperative, constructive, and helpful behaviors and enable them to have healthy and appropriate affective experiences. Such individuals have been properly socialized and rely on conventional values and norms to guide their reasoning. Prosocials do not view themselves as special, superior individuals or see others as potential enemies or rivals. Similarly, they generally frame aggressive and antisocial behavior as inappropriate and irrational.

Manifest Psychopaths

The upper right cell in Table 20.3 represents individuals who endorse items indicative of SCP on self-report surveys and whose implicit reasoning is based on JMs to justify psychopathic behavior; consequently, we refer to these individuals as *manifest psychopaths*. The self-attributed and latent motives/justifications of these individuals are congruent with one another; however, the congruence results in openly aberrant and deviant patterns of psychopathic behavior. Their toxic personality profile is further reinforced with implicit justifications to rationalize their counternormative behavioral tendencies. They openly acknowledge their deviant and antisocial behaviors (e.g., lying, manipulating, deceiving, and aggressing), their narcissistic worldviews and behaviors (e.g., egocentricity), and their affective "differences" (e.g., lack of concern for others); but, by relying on the JMs for psychopathy, they are able to rationalize these behaviors as perfectly logical, reasonable, normal, and appropriate.

Conditions of Incongruity between Implicit and Explicit Cognitions

We now turn to a description of the two conditions where one's explicit cognitions obtained via self-report surveys are incongruent with his or her implicit cognitions obtained via conditional reasoning tests.

Latent Psychopaths

The upper left cell in Table 20.3 represents individuals who self-report having prosocial characteristics but whose implicit reasoning is actually based on JMs to justify psychopathic behavior. Stated alternatively, these individuals believe themselves to be prosocial (e.g., helpful, friendly, altruistic, humble) but actually harbor the latent tendencies to rationalize being narcissistic, egocentric, aggressive, and antisocial; consequently, we refer to these individuals as *latent psychopaths*. Bing et al. (2000, 2004) found that aggressive individuals with such an incongruous pattern shied away from overt forms of deviance and aggression and instead gravitated toward more subtle (and passive) forms of aggression (cf. Binning & Wagner, 2002). Because the subclinical latent psychopath relies on some of the same JMs as aggressive individuals, we would predict a similar pattern of passive-aggressive behavior. Additionally, latent psychopaths have the self-perception of humility, self-constraint, and modesty but rely on JMs to justify narcissistic, self-serving, and egocentric patterns of behavior. Thus, this incongruent pattern likely would lead to less overt statements and actions suggestive of an exaggerated sense of personal entitlement. For example, compared to manifest psychopaths, latent psychopaths would be more likely to avoid public declarations of self-praise and aggrandizement, instead opting for more subtle (and covert) ways to "stroke their own ego" (e.g., leaving a memo containing positive feedback from a supervisor in an area frequented by coworkers).

Without empirical evidence we are hesitant to offer a definitive statement linking our two variants of SCP to a clinical counterpart. Nevertheless, we hypothesize that, compared to the latent SCPs, manifest SCPs are likely more similar to clinical psychopaths. Both groups of individuals readily acknowledge (i.e., self-report/disclose) their narcissistic and antisocial behavior, and both groups of individuals can readily generate explanations and rationalizations for this behavior (Cleckley, 1976; Hare, 1999). Additional research is needed in order to better understand the link between our proposed variants of SCP and their clinical counterpart.

Hypercritical Prosocials

The lower right cell in Table 20.3 represents individuals who self-report having psychopathic personality tendencies (e.g., high scores on the PPI) but whose implicit reasoning is rooted in prosocial values and beliefs; consequently, we refer to these individuals as *hypercritical prosocials*. Bing et al. (2000, 2004) suggested that in such an incongruity, latent prosocial tendencies dampen or inhibit the manifestation of aggressive behaviors. Similarly, we suggest that hypercritical prosocials avoid selfish, insensitive, narcissistic, and antisocial behaviors because their latent tendencies are rooted in prosocial norms and values. Instead these individuals tend to be overly friendly, cooperative, helpful, and altruistic (almost to a fault). Nevertheless, they self-report being self-absorbed, insensitive, uncaring, narcissistic, and antisocial; they are overly critical of themselves, likely feeling that they "never do enough" for others. Those with strong spiritual or religious beliefs may have a tendency to report that they are constantly sinning or behaving in an immoral or unethical manner.

To summarize, our model represents an integration of the implicit and explicit social cognitions of SCPs. This model acknowledges the potential incongruities between these two types of cognitions. We believe that combing information about an individual's self-perceptions with his or her latent cognitions may enhance our understanding of the psychopathy construct. In our final section, we present a set of research predictions developed using our integrative model of SCP.

PREDICTIONS FOR EVERYDAY FUNCTIONING

In this final section, we explore the implications of subclinical psychopathy in everyday life by deriving an initial set of testable research propositions linking subclinical psychopathy to aspects of everyday functioning, specifically work and family life. Our goal is to illustrate the utility of using our model, which integrates information about the implicit and explicit cognitions of the SCP, to derive testable research propositions not to derive an exhaustive list such propositions.

Subclinical Psychopathy and Work Life

Among industrial and organizational psychologists, job satisfaction is one of the most highly researched constructs (Judge, Heller, & Mount, 2002; Judge & Larsen, 2001; Judge, Thoresen, & Bono, 2001). Of particular importance to organizational researchers are the individual and organizational consequences of job satisfaction and job dissatisfaction. In an attempt to better understand the responses individuals have to job dissatisfaction, Farrell and colleagues (Farrell, 1983; Rusbult, Farrell, Rogers, & Mainous, 1988) developed a typology of responses that combined active versus passive responses with constructive versus destructive responses. Integrating these two dimensions yielded four unique response categories. According to Rusbult et al. (1988), the *exit* response was an active and destructive response wherein an individual withdrew from an organization by quitting, transferring, searching for a different job, or thinking about quitting. The *voice* response referred to taking active (and constructive) steps to try and improve the situation by engaging in active problem solving or speaking to others who might be able to help (e.g., coworkers, supervisors, union representatives). The *loyalty* response referred to a passive (but constructive) coping strategy that involved "optimistically" waiting for improvements, providing continued support to the organization, and "practicing good citizenship" (Rusbult et al., 1988, p. 601). Finally, the *neglect* response referred to a passive and destructive form of disregard for the organization by withdrawing effort, being absent, permitting mistakes, or using the company time (or resources) for personal matters.

We would like to note that whereas *voice* was defined in terms of a constructive response, it is possible to engage in a destructive voice response (e.g., spreading rumors, complaining, insubordination). Additionally, although neglect was described as a "destructive" response, it hardly seems that withholding citizenship behaviors (i.e., something that is not a core part of one's job description) is necessarily destructive; it may not be prosocial, but it is hardly antisocial. Thus, we expand their typology to include voice responses that are constructive (e.g., talking with a supervisor) and destructive (e.g., insubordination, gossip); we also expand their typology to include neglect responses that are constructive or at least neutral (e.g., withholding prosocial and organizational citizenship behaviors [OCBs]) and destructive (e.g., chronic tardiness, using company time/resources for personal matters).

We believe that the integrative model of subclinical psychopathy could be used to predict the likelihood that an individual would adopt a certain response style when faced with job dissatisfaction. We hasten to note that the narcissistic and entitled nature of SCPs likely will result in a main effect for both latent and manifest indicators of psychopathy, such that elevated psychopathy scores will be associated with deflated job satisfaction scores. Specifically, SCPs are likely to see themselves as always deserving more from their organizations. As such, they are likely to report being dissatisfied with their pay, supervision, coworkers, and so forth. Thus, we predict that as SCP scores (measured via self-report or conditional reasoning) increase, levels of job dissatisfaction also will increase. Stated formally:

Proposition 1: There is a main effect for subclinical psychopathy, assessed via self-reports, on general job satisfaction. Specifically, higher subclinical psychopathy scores will be associated with lower job satisfaction scores.

Proposition 2: There is a main effect for subclinical psychopathy, assessed via conditional reasoning tests, on general job satisfaction. Specifically, higher subclinical psychopathy scores will be associated with lower job satisfaction scores.

In addition to these main effects, we also predict an interaction such that, compared to the other prototypes, latent psychopaths will be more likely to respond to job dissatisfaction with destructive forms of neglect. These individuals self-report being prosocial, helpful, friendly, and altruistic. As such, they are likely to continue to report being good organizational citizens (and will manage their impressions around others who might be evaluating their OCBs). However, these individuals have a latent tendency toward egocentrism, entitlement, and antisocial behavior. As such, we predict that similar to the latent aggressive category described by Bing et al. (2000, 2004), these individuals (when experiencing job dissatisfaction) will engage in passive forms of counterproductive behavior that will be more difficult to document from an organizational perspective. For example, if confronted about elevated rates of absenteeism, the latent psychopath might respond "I am working so hard I've made myself sick." Such a response would be consistent with a self-perception of prosocial behaviors and would be difficult for an organization to dispute. Similarly, an employee might justify using company time to "surf the Web" by noting that some of the Web surfing was related to company business. Stated formally:

Proposition 3: There is an interaction between self-report and conditional reasoning measures of psychopathy in the prediction of responses to job dissatisfaction. Specifically, compared to the other types, latent psychopaths are more likely to respond to job dissatisfaction with destructive neglect.

In contrast, manifest psychopaths have both the explicit and the implicit motives that guide them toward narcissistic, aggressive, and antisocial behavior. They are more likely to see themselves as superior individuals who require extra resources and freedoms compared to their coworkers. When these extra perks are not bestowed upon them, manifest psychopaths are likely to respond in an active and maladaptive pattern. That is, they are likely to leave the organization in search of a company that will "appreciate" their unique skills and talents. Compared to other disgruntled, but prosocial, workers, manifest psychopaths want to get even with the organization that "disrespected and abused" them. As such, they are more likely to quit impulsively. When their decision to quit has been planned, they are more likely to avoid providing appropriate notice to their employer. These destructive forms of exit are consistent with the impulsive and irresponsible behavior that characterizes SCPs. When leaving the organization is not an option, manifest psychopaths may elect to engage in forms of destructive voice (e.g., yelling at coworkers, being insubordinate to a supervisor). Stated formally:

Proposition 4: There is an interaction between self-report and conditional reasoning measures of psychopathy in the prediction of responses to job dissatisfaction. Specifically, compared to the other types, manifest psychopaths are more likely to respond to job dissatisfaction by neglectful exit.

Proposition 5: There is an interaction between self-report and conditional reasoning measures of psychopathy in the prediction of responses to job dissatisfaction. Specifically, compared to the other types, manifest psychopaths are more likely to respond to job dissatisfaction by destructive voice.

In addition to job satisfaction, organizational commitment is another construct relevant to the study of subclinical psychopaths in organizations. Organizational commitment may take one of three forms. *Affective* or *attitudinal commitment* stems from an emotional attachment or bond that an individual has to an organization along with his or her identification and involvement with that organization. *Continuance commitment* stems from the apparent costs associated with exiting (i.e., turning over from) the organization. Finally, *normative*

commitment stems from the perceived "moral" obligation to stay with the organization (Dunham, Grube, & Castaneda, 1994; Mathieu & Zajac, 1990; Meyer, Stanley, Herscovitch, & Topolnytsky, 2002). These forms of commitment have been linked to a variety of organizational consequences, including job turnover. Interestingly, the correlations between commitment and turnover, although significant, are often only of a small to modest size. We believe that the integrative model described previously may be used to help explain these relatively weak correlations.

Due to the affective deficiencies associated with subclinical psychopathy, we predict that SCPs will not be able to develop or maintain the affective form of organizational commitment. Similarly, SCPs' increased thresholds for guilt make it unlikely they would experience the moral obligation to remain with the organization that underlies normative commitment. Finally, the impulsive nature of SCPs makes them less likely to concern themselves with the long-term "costs" associated with leaving an organization. Furthermore, relying on the JMs described previously, SCPs' decreased commitment and increased turnover are rationalized as reasonable responses to a controlling and manipulative organization. Thus, we predict main effects for subclinical psychopathy (measured using both self-reports and conditional reasoning tests) in the prediction of organizational commitment and job turnover. Stated formally:

Proposition 6: There is a main effect for subclinical psychopathy, assessed via self-reports, on measures of (a) affective, (b) normative and (c) calculative commitment, and (d) turnover. Specifically, higher subclinical psychopathy scores will be associated with lower commitment scores and increased likelihood of turnover.

Proposition 7: There is a main effect for subclinical psychopathy, assessed via conditional reasoning tests, on (a) affective, (b) normative and (c) calculative commitment, and (d) turnover. Specifically, higher subclinical psychopathy scores will be associated with lower commitment scores and increased likelihood of turnover.

In addition to these main effects, we believe that application of our integrative model may be used to explain the often small correlations between measures of organizational commitment and actual job turnover. Specifically, our understanding of actual job turnover may be improved when we consider how latent psychopaths and hypercritical prosocials might respond to questions concerning commitment and their potential for actual job turnover. Latent psychopaths have the self-perception of responsibility, loyalty, and reliability and thus are more likely to report increased levels of organizational commitment; however, compared to prosocials (who have similar self-perceptions), latent psychopaths are much more likely actually to turn over from a job. Similarly, hypercritical prosocials see themselves as unreliable and irresponsible and thus likely will self-report low levels of commitment; however, compared to manifest psychopaths (who have similar self-perceptions), hypercritical prosocials are much less likely actually to turn over from a job. Thus, by considering how the various prototypes in our model might respond to questions concerning commitment and their propensities for turnover, we might frame the latent psychopaths as "false positives" and hypercritical prosocials as "false negatives." That is, based solely on scores from a measure of organizational commitment, we would conclude erroneously that latent psychopaths are a low risk of turnover and hypercritical prosocials are a high risk for turnover. Removal of these individuals from the analysis should result in substantially stronger correlations between organizational commitment and turnover. Stated formally:

Proposition 8: Latent psychopaths' tendency to self-report higher levels of organizational commitment leads to a false conclusion that these individuals are a low turnover risk.

Proposition 9: Hypercritical prosocials' tendency to self-report lower levels of organizational commitment leads to a false conclusion that these individuals are a high turnover risk.

Proposition 10: Compared to the analyses using all workers, an analysis omitting scores from latent psychopaths and hypercritical prosocials will result in a stronger correlation between organizational commitment and turnover.

Subclinical Psychopathy and Family Life

We also believe that our integrative framework can be used to guide predictions about how the SCP behaves at home. For example, one of the dominant taxonomies of parenting styles was offered by Baumrind (1967, 1971, 1978). Her typology combined characteristics of demandingness and responsiveness. *Demandingness* refers to the extent that parents set high standards for their children or place controls on the child's behavior. *Responsiveness* refers to the extent that parents are caring, open, and receptive to their child. These two dimensions can be used to create a 2 × 2 parenting typology table. *Authoritative* parents are characterized by high levels of demandingness accompanied by high levels of responsiveness. *Authoritarian* parents are characterized by high levels of demandingness but an absence of care and responsiveness. *Permissive* parents are characterized by high levels

of responsiveness but low levels of demandingness. Finally, *neglectful* parents are characterized by low levels of both demandingness and responsiveness. Through her research program, Baumrind documented that the most "effective" style is the authoritative style. Children raised by an authoritative parent tend to be more socially responsible, have higher levels of achievement orientation, and have higher levels of self-esteem.

Our integrative framework can be used to generate predictions about the likelihood that an individual would adopt a certain parenting style. For example, latent psychopaths' self-reports indicate that they are caring, loving, altruistic people and thus are likely to report being "caring and responsive" parents. However, due to their latent tendency toward narcissism and antisocial behaviors, they fail to become actively involved with in their children's lives. They do not take the time to exercise control and discipline over their children and thus fail to set high standards and expectations for their conduct. Latent psychopaths rationalize that those who set boundaries or expectations for their children are trying to dominate and control them; thus, by not burdening the children with such controls, the children are free to express themselves and develop their own sense of appropriate conduct. In reality it is the latent psychopath who is not burdened with the responsibility of providing supervision and discipline for his or her child. Stated formally:

Proposition 11: Compared to the other prototypes in our model, latent psychopaths are more likely to adopt a permissive parenting style.

On the other hand, manifest psychopaths see themselves as superior, important individuals who should not be burdened with the responsibilities of everyday people. They openly acknowledge their superiority and feel that the rules of society simply do not apply. Compounding this manifest entitlement, their latent tendencies drive them toward narcissistic, entitled, and antisocial behavior. Thus, manifest psychopaths are likely to self-report (and reason) that it is not their job to watch their children every moment of the day. Manifest psychopaths will rationalize that they simply are too important and their time too valuable to be spent raising a child. Consequently, they are less likely to display any sense of care or responsiveness, nor are they likely to place any types of controls or demands on their children. Stated formally:

Proposition 12: Compared to the other prototypes in our model, manifest psychopaths are more likely to adopt a neglectful parenting style.

In addition to parenting styles, we also believe that subclinical psychopathy likely is linked to aspects of marital or relationship functioning. Given the manipulative nature of SCPs, along with their increased thresholds to guilt and remorse, we predict that SCPs are more likely to be unfaithful to a significant other (i.e., they are more likely to cheat on their partners; Cleckley, 1976; Hare, 1999). Both latent psychopaths and manifest psychopaths can easily justify such behavior using JMs such as the social discounting bias and the grandiosity bias. Using these biases, SCPs are able to attack traditional social institutions (e.g., marriage, monogamous relationships) as mechanisms used by society to hold back and control "superior" individuals from experiencing multiple "meaningful" relationships.

Manifest psychopaths are overtly narcissistic, unempathetic, and antisocial. Furthermore, these individuals have the JMs in place to justify these attitudes and actions. As such, they are more likely to engage in very public and overt forms of infidelity and unfaithfulness. They see no need to "hide" or "defend" their actions because they see themselves as entitled to do what they want when they want. In contrast, latent psychopaths have self-perceptions of humility, empathy, responsibility, and loyalty but, nevertheless, have the JMs in place to rationalize impulsive, narcissistic, and antisocial behavior (e.g., cheating). As such, we predict that latent psychopaths might still be unfaithful to their significant others, but this unfaithfulness takes a less public and more covert form. Thus, we predict two main effects for subclinical psychopathy (measured using both self-reports and conditional reasoning). We also predict an ordinal interaction between self-reports and conditional reasoning tests in the prediction of overt and covert instances of infidelity. Stated formally:

> Proposition 13: There is a main effect for subclinical psychopathy, assessed via self-reports, on instances of (a) overt and (b) covert infidelity. Specifically, higher subclinical psychopathy scores will be associated with increased instances of infidelity.
>
> Proposition 14: There is a main effect for subclinical psychopathy, assessed via conditional reasoning tests, on instances of (a) overt and (b) covert infidelity. Specifically, higher subclinical psychopathy scores will be associated with increased instances of infidelity.
>
> Proposition 15: Compared to the other prototypes in our model, manifest psychopaths are more likely to engage in overt acts of infidelity, and latent psychopaths are more likely to engage in covert acts of infidelity.

SUMMARY AND CONCLUSIONS

The purpose of the current chapter was to review the concept of subclinical psychopathy and offer predictions for how it might impact aspects of everyday functioning. After discussing the core symptoms or elements underlying subclinical psychopathy, we reviewed how the construct has been measured traditionally. We noted that traditional measurement techniques failed to capture reliably the rationalizations and justifications used (implicitly) by subclinical psychopaths to explain their aberrant patterns of affect, behavior, and interpersonal relationships. We addressed this limitation by proposing how the conditional reasoning approach could be used to measure these implicit rationalizations. We concluded by articulating a series of research propositions linking our new integrative model of subclinical psychopathy to work and family arenas. We hasten to note that our propositions were not exhaustive but rather illustrative of how our model might be used to enhance our understanding of subclinical psychopaths. Similar propositions could be derived for a number of research areas including:

- Subclinical psychopathy and executive/leadership derailment.
- Subclinical psychopathy and counterproductive behavior at work.
- Subclinical psychopathy and organizational citizenship behavior at work.
- Subclinical psychopathy and academic integrity at school.
- Subclinical psychopathy and bullying at school.
- Subclinical psychopathy and addictions (e.g., gambling, drugs).
- Subclinical psychopathy and perceptions of social support.
- Subclinical psychopathy and marital satisfaction.
- Subclinical psychopathy and general aggressive behavior.
- Subclinical psychopathy and racist or sexist behavior.

In conclusion, there has been a recent burst of research activity in the domain of subclinical psychopathy. We applaud these research efforts and note that the majority of this research has focused on measuring conscious self-perceptions concerning psychopathy. We suggest that our understanding of the subclinical psychopathy construct may be further enhanced by integrating these self-perceptions with the latent rationalizations used by subclinical psychopaths to justify their toxic patterns of behavior. We hope that the current chapter acts as a catalyst for such research.

REFERENCES

American Psychiatric Association. (1952). *Diagnostic and statistical manual of mental disorders*. Washington, DC: Author.

American Psychiatric Association. (1968). *Diagnostic and statistical manual of mental disorders* (Rev. ed.). Washington, DC: Author.

American Psychiatric Association. (1980). *Diagnostic and statistical manual of mental disorders* (3rd ed.). Washington, DC: Author.

American Psychiatric Association. (1987). *Diagnostic and statistical manual of mental disorders* (3rd ed., Rev.). Washington, DC: Author.

American Psychiatric Association. (1994). *Diagnostic and statistical manual of mental disorders* (4th ed.). Washington, DC: Author.

American Psychiatric Association. (2000). *Diagnostic and statistical manual of mental disorders* (4th ed., Text Rev.). Washington, DC: Author.

Anastasi, A. (1982). *Psychological testing* (5th ed.). New York: Macmillan.

Andershed, H. A., Gustafson, S. B., Kerr, M., Stattin, H. (2002). The usefulness of self-reported psychopathy-like traits in the study of antisocial behaviour among non-referred adolescents. *European Journal of Personality, 16,* 383–402.

Anderson, H. H., & Anderson, G. L. (1951). *An introduction to projective techniques.* Englewood Cliffs, NJ: Prentice Hall.

Arrigo, B. A., & Shipley, S. (2001). The confusion over psychopathy (I): Historical considerations. *International Journal of Offender Therapy and Comparative Criminology, 45,* 325–344.

Baumrind, D. (1967). Child care practices anteceding three patterns of preschool behavior. *Genetic Psychology Monographs, 75,* 43–88.

Baumrind, D. (1971). Current patterns of parental authority. *Developmental Psychology Monographs, 4*(1, pt. 2).

Baumrind, D. (1978). Parental disciplinary patterns and social competence in children. *Youth and Society, 9,* 239–276.

Baumrind, D. (1991). The influence of parenting style on adolescent competence and substance use. *Journal of Early Adolescence, 11,* 56–95.

Bing, M. N. (2002). *The integrative model of personality assessment for achievement motivation and fear of failure: Implications for the prediction of effort and performance.* Unpublished doctoral dissertation, University of Tennessee, Knoxville.

Bing, M. N. (2003). *Distinguishing clinical depression from malingering: A feasibility study.* Grant proposal to Office of Naval Research, Funding Number 50406, Groton, CT.

Bing, M. N., Burroughs, S. M., Davison, H. K., Green, P. D., McIntyre, M. D., & James, L. R. (2004). *The integrative model of personality assessment for aggression: Implications for personnel selection and predicting counterproductive workplace behavior.* Manuscript submitted for publication.

Bing, M. N., Burroughs, S. M., Whanger, J. C., Green, P. D., & James, L. R. (2000, August). The integrative model of personality assessment for aggression: Implications for personnel selection and predicting deviant workplace behavior. In J. LeBreton & J. Binning (Chairs), *Recent issues and innovations in personality assessment.* Symposium conducted at the 108th Annual Conference of the American Psychological Association, Washington, DC.

Bing, M. N., & LeBreton, J. M. (2004, June). *Distinguishing clinical depression from malingering: A feasibility study.* Presentation given to the Office of Naval Research and the U.S. Navy's Bureau of Medicine and Surgery program sponsors, San Diego, CA.

Bing, M. N., LeBreton, J. M., Migetz, D. Z., Vermillion, D. B., Davison, H. K., & James, L. R. (2001, April). The integrative model of personality assessment for achievement motivation and fear of failure: Implications for the prediction of effort, attribution, and performance. In J. LeBreton & J. Binning (Chairs), *Recent issues and innovations in personality assessment.* Symposium conducted at the 16th Annual Conference of the Society for Industrial and Organizational Psychology, San Diego, CA.

Binning, J. F., & Wagner, E. E. (2002). Passive-aggressive behavior in the workplace. In J. C. Thomas & M. Hersen (Eds.), *Handbook of mental health in the workplace* (pp. 457–476). Newbury Park, CA: Sage.

Bodholdt, R. H., Richards, H. R., & Gacono, C. B. (2000). Assessing psychopathy in adults: The psychopathy checklist–Revised and screening version. In C. B. Gacono (Ed.), *The clinical and forensic assessment of psychopathy: A practitioner's guide.* Mahwah, NJ: Earlbaum.

Brewin, C. R. (1989). Cognitive change processes in psychotherapy. *Psychological Review, 96,* 379–394.

Buss, H. (1961). *The psychology of aggression.* New York: Wiley.

Cattell, R. B. (1957). *Personality and motivation: Structure and measurement.* Yonkers-on-Hudson, NY: World Book Company.

Cleckley, H. (1941). *The mask of sanity.* St. Louis, MO: Mosby.

Cleckley, H. (1976). *The mask of sanity* (5th ed.). St. Louis, MO: Mosby.

Cooke, D. J., & Michie, C. (2001). Refining the construct of psychopathy: Towards a hierarchical model. *Psychological Assessment, 13,* 171–188.

Costa, P. T., Jr., & McCrae, R. R. (1992). *Revised NEO personality inventory (NEO-PI-R) and NEO five-factor inventory (NEO-FFI): Professional manual.* Odessa, FL: Psychological Assessment Resources.

Crick, N. R., & Dodge, K. A. (1994). A review and reformulation of social information-processing mechanisms in children's social adjustment. *Psychological Bulletin, 115,* 74–101.

Dunham, R. B., Grube, J. A., & Castaneda, M. B. (1994). Organizational commitment: The utility of an integrative definition. *Journal of Applied Psychology, 79,* 370–380.

Dweck, C. S., & Leggett, E. L. (1988). A social-cognitive approach to personality and motivation. *Psychological Review, 95,* 256–273.

Edwards, A. L. (1970). *The measurement of personality traits by scales and inventories.* New York: Holt, Rinehart, and Winston.

Epstein, S. (1994). Integration of the cognitive and psychodynamic unconscious. *American Psychologist, 49,* 709–724.

Farrell, D. (1983). Exit, voice, loyalty, and neglect as responses to job dissatisfaction: A multidimensional scaling study. *Academy of Management Journal, 26,* 596–607.

Fazio, R. H., & Olson, M. A. (2003). Implicit measures in social cognition research. *Annual Review of Psychology, 54,* 297–327.

Folger, R., & Baron, R. A. (1996). Violence and hostility at work: A model of reactions to perceived injustice. In G. R. VandenBos & E. Q. Bulatao (Eds.), *Violence on the job: Identifying the risks and developing solutions* (pp. 51–86). Washington, DC: American Psychological Association.

Forth, A. E., Brown, S. L., Hart, S. D., & Hare, R. D. (1996). The assessment of psychopathy in male and female noncriminals: Reliability and validity. *Personality & Individual Differences, 20,* 531–543.

Freud, S. (1959). *An outline of psychoanalysis.* New York: Norton.

Gacono, C. B., & Meloy, J. R. (1994). *Rorschach assessment of aggressive and psychopathic personalities.* Hillsdale, NJ: Erlbaum.

Goldberg, L. R. (1993). The structure of phenotypic personality traits. *American Psychologist, 48,* 26–34.

Greenwald, A. G., & Banaji, M. R. (1995). Implicit social cognition: Attitudes, self-esteem, and stereotypes. *Psychological Review, 102,* 4–27.

Gustafson, S. B. (1999, April). Out of their own mouths: A conditional reasoning instrument for identifying aberrant self-promoters. In P. Babiak (Chair), *Liars of the dark side: Can personality interfere with personality measurement?* Symposium conducted at the Thirteenth Annual Conference of the Society for Industrial and Organizational Psychology, Atlanta, GA.

Gustafson, S. B. (2000, April). Out of their own mouths II: Continuing support for the validity of a conditional reasoning instrument for identifying aberrant self-promoters. In S. Gustafson (Chair), *Personality in the shadows: A continuum of destructiveness.* Symposium conducted at the Fourteenth Annual Conference of the Society for Industrial and Organizational Psychology, New Orleans, LA.

Gustafson, S. B., & Ritzer, D. R. (1995). The dark side of normal: A psychopathy-linked pattern called aberrant self-promotion. *European Journal of Personality, 9,* 147–183.

Hare, R. D. (1985). A comparison of procedures for the assessment of psychopathy. *Journal of Consulting and Clinical Psychology, 53,* 7–16.

Hare, R. D. (1991). *The Hare psychopathy checklist–Revised.* Toronto, Ontario: Multi-Health Systems.

Hare, R. D. (1996). Psychopathy: A clinical construct whose time has come. *Criminal Justice and Behavior, 23,* 25–54.

Hare, R. D. (1998). Psychopaths and their nature: Implications for the mental health and criminal justice systems. In T. Millon, E. Simonsen, M. Birket-Smith, & R. D. Davis (Eds.), *Psychopathy: Antisocial, criminal, and violent behavior* (pp. 188–212). New York: Guilford Press.

Hare, R. D. (1999). *Without conscience: The disturbing world of the psychopaths among us.* New York: Guilford Press.

Hare, R. D., Hart, S. D., & Harpur, T. J. (1991). Psychopathy and the *DSM-IV* criteria for antisocial personality disorder. *Journal of Abnormal Psychology, 100,* 391–398.

Hart, S. D., & Hare, R. D. (1997). Psychopathy: Assessment and association with criminal conduct. In D. M. Stoff, J. Breiling, & J. D. Maser (Eds.), *Handbook of antisocial behavior* (pp. 22–35). New York: Wiley.

Hogan, R. (1991). Personality and personality measurement. In L. M. Hough & M. D. Dunnette, *Handbook of industrial and organizational psychology* (2nd ed., Vol. 2, pp. 873–919). Palo Alto, CA: Consulting Psychologists Press.

Hogan, R., Hogan, J., & Roberts, B. W. (1996). Personality measurement and employment decisions. *American Psychologist, 51,* 469–477.

Jackson, D. N. (1984). *Personality research form manual* (3rd ed.). Port Huron, MI: Research Psychologists Press/Sigma Assessment Systems.

James, L. R. (1998). Measurement of personality via conditional reasoning. *Organizational Research Methods, 1,* 131–163.

James, L. R., & Mazerolle, M. D. (2002). *Personality in work organizations: An integrative approach.* Sage.

James, L. R., & McIntyre, M. D. (2000). *Conditional reasoning test of aggression test manual.* San Antonio, TX: The Psychological Corporation. (also available from Knoxville, TN: Innovative Assessment Technology).

James, L. R., McIntyre, M. D., Glisson, C. A., Green, P. D., Patton, T. W., LeBreton, J. M., et al. (in press). Conditional reasoning: An efficient, indirect method for assessing implicit cognitive readiness to aggress. *Organizational Research Methods.*

Judge, T. A., Heller, D., & Mount, M. K. (2002). Five-factor model of personality and job satisfaction: A meta-analysis. *Journal of Applied Psychology, 87,* 530–541.

Judge, T. A., & Larsen, R. J. (2001). Dispositional affect and job satisfaction: A review and theoretical extension. *Organizational Behavior & Human Decision Processes, 86,* 67–98.

Judge, T. A., Thoresen, C. J., & Bono, J. E. (2001). The job satisfaction-job performance relationship: A qualitative and quantitative review. *Psychological Bulletin, 127,* 376–407.

Kihlstrom, J. F. (1987). The cognitive unconscious. *Science, 237,* 1445–1452.

Kihlstrom, J. F. (1999). The psychological unconscious. In L. A. Pervin & O. P. John (Eds.), *Handbook of personality: Theory and research* (2nd ed., pp. 424–442). New York: Guilford Press.

Kihlstrom, J. F., Mulvaney, S., Tobias, B. A., & Tobis, I. P. (2000). The emotional unconscious. In E. Eich, J. F. Kihlstrom, G. H. Bower, J. P. Forgas, & P. M. Niedenthal (Eds.), *Cognition and emotion* (pp. 30–86). New York: Oxford University Press.

Lanyon, R. I., & Goodstein, L. D. (1997). *Personality assessment* (3rd ed.). New York: Wiley.

LeBreton, D. M. (1999). *An investigation of behavioral accuracy and leniency: The roles of aberrant self-promotion, accountability, and opportunity for personal recognition.* Unpublished master's thesis, Virginia Polytechnic and State University, Blacksburg, VA.

LeBreton, J. M. (2002). *Use of differential framing to measure implicit social cognitions associated with aggression.* Unpublished doctoral dissertation, University of Tennessee, Knoxville.

LeBreton, J. M., Barksdale, C., Burgess, J. R. D., & James, L. R. (2004). *Measurement issues associated with Conditional Reasoning tests of personality: Deception and faking.* Manuscript submitted for publication.

Lilienfeld, S. O. (1994). Conceptual problems in the assessment of psychopathy. *Clinical Psychology Review, 14,* 17–38.

Lilienfeld, S. O. (1998). Methodological advances and developments in the assessment of psychopathy. *Behaviour Research and Therapy, 36,* 99–125.

Lilienfeld, S. O., & Andrews, B. P. (1996). Development and preliminary validation of a self-report measure of psychopathic personality traits in noncriminal populations. *Journal of Personality Assessment, 66,* 488–524.

Lilienfeld, S. O., Wood, J. M., & Garb, H. M. (2002). The scientific status of projective techniques. *Psychological Science in the Public Interest, 1,* 27–66.

Lykken, D. T. (1995). *The antisocial personalities.* Hillsdale, NJ: Earlbaum.

Lykken, D. T. (1998). The case for parental licensure. In T. Millon, E. Simonsen, M. Birket-Smith, & R. D. Davis (Eds.), *Psychopathy: Antisocial, criminal and violent behavior* (pp. 122–144). New York: Guilford Press.

Lynam, D. R. (2001). Psychopathy from the perspective of the five-factor model of personality. In P. T. Costa Jr. & T. A. Widiger (Eds.), *Personality disorders and the five-factor model of personality* (2nd ed., pp. 325–348). Washington, DC: American Psychological Association.

Mathieu, J. E., & Zajac, D. M. (1990). A review and meta-analysis of the antecedents, correlates, and consequences of organizational commitment. *Psychological Bulletin, 108,* 171–194.

McClelland, D. C., Koestner, R., & Weinberger, J. (1989). How do self-attributed and implicit motives differ? *Psychological Review, 96,* 690–702.

McCrae, R. R., & Costa, P. T., Jr. (1997). Personality trait structure as a human universal. *American Psychologist, 52,* 509–516.

Meloy, J. R. (1988). *The psychopathic mind: Origins, dynamics, and treatment.* Northvale, NJ: Aronson.

Meloy, J. R., & Gacono, C. B. (2000). Assessing psychopathy: Psychological testing and report writing. In C. B. Gacono (Ed.), *The clinical and forensic assessment of psychopathy: A practitioner's guide* (pp. 231–250). Mahway, NJ: Erlbaum.

Meyer, J. P., Stanley, D. J., Herscovitch, L., & Topolnytsky, L. (2002). Affective, continuance, and normative commitment to the organization: A meta-analysis of antecedents, correlates, and consequences. *Journal of Vocational Behavior, 61,* 20–52.

Millon, T., Simonsen, E., & Birket-Smith, M. (1998). Historical conceptions of psychopathy in the United States and Europe. In T. Millon, E. Simonsen, M. Birket-Smith, & R. Davis (Eds.), *Psychopathy: Antisocial, criminal, and violent behavior* (pp. 3–31). New York: Guilford Press.

Mischel, W., & Shoda, Y. (1995). A cognitive-affective system theory of personality: Reconceptualizing situations, dispositions, dynamics, and invariance in personality structure. *Psychological Review, 102,* 246–268.

Murray, H. A. (1938). *Explorations in personality.* New York: Oxford University Press.

Nathanson, C., Williams, K. M., Paulhus, D. L. (2004, May). *Don't get mad, get even: Psychopaths' reactions to interpersonal provocations.* Paper presented at the annual meeting of the American Psychological Society, Chicago.

Nunnally, J. C. (1978). *Psychometric theory* (2nd ed.). New York: McGraw-Hill.

Paulhus, D. L., & Williams, K. M. (2002). The dark triad of personality: Narcissism, Machiavellianism, and psychopathy. *Journal of Research in Personality, 36,* 556–563.

Pethman, T. M. I., & Erlandsson, S. I. (2002). Aberrant self-promotion or subclinical psychopathy in a Swedish general population. *The Psychological Record, 52,* 33–50.

Rusbult, C. E., Farrell, D., Rogers, G., & Mainous, A. G. (1988). Impact of exchange variables on exit, voice, loyalty, and neglect: An integrative model of responses to declining job satisfaction. *Academy of Management Journal, 31,* 599–627.

Russell, D. P. (1996). *Aberrant self-promotion versus Machiavellianism: A differentiation of constructs.* Unpublished master's thesis, Virginia Polytechnic and State University, Blacksburg, VA.

Shipley, S., & Arrigo, B. A. (2001). The confusion over psychopathy (II): Implications for forensic (correctional) practice. *International Journal of Offender Therapy and Comparative Criminology, 45,* 325–344.

Spangler, W. D. (1992). Validity of questionnaire and TAT measures of need for achievement: Two meta-analyses. *Psychological Bulletin, 112,* 140–154.

Walton, W. R. (2004). *Justification of antisocial behavior.* Unpublished doctoral dissertation, University of Tennessee, Knoxville.

Westen, D. (1991). Social cognition and object relations. *Psychological Bulletin, 109,* 429–455.

Westen, D. (1998). The scientific legacy of Sigmund Freud: Toward a psychodynamically informed psychological science. *Psychological Bulletin, 124,* 333–571.

Westen, D., & Gabbard, G. O. (1999). Psychoanalytic approaches to personality. In L. A. Pervin & O. P. John (Eds.), *Handbook of personality: Theory and research* (2nd ed., pp. 57–101). New York: Guilford Press.

Widom, C. S. (1977). A methodology for studying non-institution-alized psychopaths. *Journal of Consulting and Clinical Psychology, 45,* 674–683.

Williams, K. M., Howell, T., Cooper, B. S., Yuille, J. C., & Paulhus, D. L. (2004). Deviant sexual thoughts and behaviors: The roles of personality and pornography use. Poster presented at the annual meeting of the American Psychological Society, Chicago.

Williams, K. M., McAndrew, A., Learn, T., Harms, P., & Paulhus, D. L. (2001, August). *The dark triad returns: Entertainment preferences and anti-social behavior among narcissists, Machiavellians, and psychopaths.* Poster presented at the annual meet-ing of the American Psychological Association, San Francisco, CA.

Williams, K. M., & Paulhus, D. L. (2004a). Capturing the four-facet structure of psychopathy in non-forensic samples: The self-report psychopathy scale (SRP–III). Manuscript submitted for publication.

Williams, K. M., & Paulhus, D. L. (2004b). Factor structure of the self-report psychopathy scale (SRP–II) in non-forensic samples. *Personality and Individual Differences, 33,* 1520–1530.

Winter, D. G., John, O. P., Stewart, A. J., Klohnen, E. C., & Duncan, L. E. (1998). Traits and motives: Toward an integration of two traditions in personality research. *Psychological Review, 105,* 230–250.

CHAPTER 21

Organizational Climate, Personality Interactions, and Organizational Behavior

DANIEL J. SVYANTEK AND JENNIFER P. BOTT

The explanation of complex human behavior requires the consideration of person, contextual, and behavioral variables (Funder, 2001). The context in which an individual resides, as well as individual differences in personality, is related to the production of behavior. The behaviors exhibited in a situation have an adaptive function (Morris, 1988). The degree to which behavior is adaptive, however, is defined relative to the situational requirements. Therefore, understanding how personality affects everyday functioning requires an understanding of the context in which people reside. Understanding how contexts affect the production of behavior is a critical requirement for studying how individuals act when in groups and organizations. A primary contextual variable in organizations that influences how personality variables affect behavior is organizational climate.

This chapter will (1) describe the historical debate on the relative influence of dispositional and situational factors in personality psychology and the current consensus on this debate, (2) illustrate how this debate has played out in organizational research, and (3) offer some suggestions for investigating the joint effects of dispositional and situational factors in explaining organizational behavior.

PERSONALITY AND SITUATIONAL INFLUENCES ON BEHAVIOR

The mission of personality psychology is to account for the characteristic patterns of thoughts, emotions, and behaviors and the psychological mechanisms that generate these thought patterns (Funder, 2001). The most basic question for building a science of the person is "How can one identify and understand the psychological invariance that distinctively charac-

terizes an individual and that underlies the variations in thoughts, feelings, and actions that occur across contexts and over time?" (Mischel, 2004, p. 1).

This basic question of interest is concerned with the degree to which individuals function psychologically in terms of the processes that underlie stable individual differences in behavior and allow the explanation of intraindividual variability across situations (Mischel & Shoda, 1998). There are three primary theoretical approaches to personality (Fleeson, 2004; Mischel, 2004; Mischel & Shoda, 1998).

The Dispositional Model of Personality

The first approach is the dispositional or trait-theory approach to personality (Mischel & Shoda, 1998). This approach proposes the existence of broad, stable traits, factors, or behavioral dispositions as its basic units. Its fundamental goal is to characterize individuals in terms of a comprehensive, but finite and preferably small, set of stable dispositions that remain invariant across situations. These are distinctive for the individual and determine a wide range of important behaviors. The dispositional argument, therefore, proposes that behavior is determined by a person's traits and that a given individual will act similarly much of the time (Fleeson, 2004).

The dispositional approach is reflected in the Big Five (Funder, 2001; Mischel & Shoda, 1998). Currently, the Big Five model forms the common currency of personality research (Funder, 2001). This model proposes that five orthogonal factors can be used to describe personality: Neuroticism (emotional stability), Extraversion, Conscientiousness, Openness to Experience (intellect, openness), and Agreeableness (e.g., Costa & McCrae, 1985, 1988; Goldberg, 1993). The creators of the Big Five (Costa & McCrae) assert these personality traits are universal and biologically determined (McCrae, 2001; McCrae et al., 2000).

Acknowledgment: We would like to acknowledge and thank Aaron Holley for his work in compiling much of the list of articles used in the tables presented in this chapter.

This model and underlying theory (Five-Factor Theory) has its critics, most notably Jack Block. Block (1995, 2001) contends the orthogonal dimensions are not actually independent, as many empirical studies have found relatively high correlations between factors. In addition, Block claims there are problems both with the factor analysis used to arrive at five factors and with the lack of theoretical foundation for the model. According to Block's most current commentary, recent empirical work has uncovered two superfactors that should be examined more closely in future research. However, the issues Block raises do not involve the appropriateness of the dispositional approach but involve theoretical issues concerning the development of the small number of stable dispositions posited in this approach.

The dispositional approach to personality sees situational effects as error or noise (Mischel, 2004). Therefore, research is aggregated across situations to get the true score of personality's effects on behavior. This is consistent with the current predominant theory of personality in psychology. The basic qualities of the person are assumed to be independent of, and unconnected with, situations: Causal power for behavior is attributed to the person. Therefore, finding stable basic characteristics of the individual required taking out the variability introduced by different situations rather than focusing on this variability.

This view, however, has been criticized for an inability to predict behaviors across aggregated situations well. The behaviors of a sample of individuals observed in one situation has a correlation of $r = .40$ (accounting for about 16 percent of the variance in behavior) with their behavior in a second situation (Funder, 2001). Therefore, critics proposed that 84 percent of behavior was unaccounted for when a dispositional approach was used.

A Situational Model of Personality

The recognition that only 16 percent of the variance seemed to be accounted for by dispositional factors was initially misinterpreted. This led to the development of a situational model of personality. The basic situational model proposes that the immediate situation in which a person resides is the primary determinant of behavior (Fleeson, 2004). Therefore, an individual will act very differently on different occasions. Critics of the dispositional approach basically proposed that the remaining 84 percent of the variance unaccounted for in behavior by the dispositional model was due to the situation (Funder, 2001).

Research has not borne this out either, however. Whereas behavior of people observed in one situation has a correlation of $r = .40$ (accounting for about 16 percent of the variance

in behavior) with their behavior in a second situation, this correlation also represents the approximate size of some of the most important situational effects in social psychology (Funder, 2001). Therefore, a situational model of personality was no more effective in predicting behavior than the dispositional model was held to be.

The Interactional Model of Personality

The third approach to understanding and predicting behavior, therefore, is one in which the effects of both dispositional and situational elements are assessed. This approach is the interactional model of personality.

This approach is exemplified by the social-cognitive approach to personality (Mischel & Shoda, 1998). The social-cognitive approach construes personality as a system of mediating units (e.g., encodings, expectancies, and goals) and psychological processes that interact with the situation in which an individual resides. These psychological processes, or cognitive-affective dynamics, can be either conscious or unconscious. The key element of this model is that both situational and dispositional factors must be incorporated to understand how behavior is determined.

New research is showing that individuals exhibit stable patterns of cross-situational variability that characterize the individuals when behavior is examined in relation to situations in which this behavior occurs (Mischel, 2004). These stable patterns of person-situation interactions, in turn, hint at the organization of the underlying system that generates them. The focus of research shifts from a search for broad, situation-free trait descriptors (e.g., conscientiousness) to more situation-qualified characterizations of persons in contexts (e.g., conscientious people in the workplace). This means that dispositions must be understood as conditional and interactive with the situations in which they are expressed.

This view proposes that different situations will acquire different meanings for the same individual (Mischel, 2004). Therefore, there is no theoretical reason to expect the individual to display similar behavior in relation to different psychological situations unless they are functionally equivalent in meaning for them. The route to finding the invariance in personality requires taking account of the situation and its meaning for the individual and finding stable interactions illustrating the interplay between individuals and the situations.

Summary

This growing consensus in personality psychology is that the person-versus-situation debate about the causal determinants of behavior is no longer needed (Fleeson, 2004). The finding of large within-person variability is not a threat to the viability of traits, and traits are not a threat to the need to explain the considerable amounts of within-person variability using situations. Everyone routinely acts in a wide range of ways for the same behavior. A person's momentary behaviors can indeed vary widely, so when trying to predict behavior at a given moment, researchers should investigate psychological processes involving responses to situations. A person's averages over time, however, are similar, and when trying to describe and predict how a person acts on average, researchers also should use traits. Personality research should (a) use traits, (b) study the situational characteristics used to make distinctions among situations by people, and (c) be aware that there may be new personality variables discovered in the future.

DISPOSITIONAL AND SITUATIONAL MODELS IN ORGANIZATIONAL RESEARCH

Organizational research into the effects of dispositional and situational influences mirrors the debate in personality psychology. This is illustrated by describing some of the research efforts on dispositional and situational influences on organizational behavior.

Dispositional Approaches to Understanding Organizational Behavior

As mentioned previously, the dispositional approach is currently best represented as the Big Five: Neuroticism (emotional stability), Extraversion, Conscientiousness, Openness to Experience (intellect), and Agreeableness (e.g., Costa & McCrae, 1985, 1988; Funder, 2001; Goldberg, 1993).

Regardless of the issues surrounding the development of the Big Five, researchers within the field of industrial/organizational psychology have adopted this measurement for the investigation of many issues, including career success (e.g., Boudreau, Boswell, & Judge, 2001; Seibert & Kraimer, 2001), leadership (e.g., Judge & Bono, 2000), selection (e.g., Barrick & Mount, 1991; Hurtz & Donovan, 2000), organizational commitment (e.g., Allen & Meyer, 1990), and organizational citizenship behaviors (e.g., Organ & Ryan, 1995; Podsakoff, MacKenzie, Paine, & Bachrach, 2000).

Conscientiousness has been most consistently linked to job performance (Barrick & Mount, 1991, 1996; Hurtz & Donovan, 2000; Salgado, 1997). However, the relationship between these variables has been moderate at best: Meta-analytic results indicate a mean sample-weighted correlation of .13 (Salgado, 1997) to .26 (Barrick & Mount, 1996). In

the recent meta-analysis conducted by Hurtz and Donovan (2000) on explicit measures of the Big Five, the estimated true validity was .20. This validity was highest for sales positions (.26) and customer service jobs (.25).

Relationships between the other four variables of the Big Five have shown less consistent and weaker relationships with job performance (Barrick & Mount, 1991). However, in the Hurtz and Donovan (2000) meta-analysis, emotional stability was slightly predictive of sales jobs (.13), as was extraversion (.15). For customer service jobs, emotional stability (.12), agreeableness (.17), and openness (.15) were stable predictors, despite their lack of strength.

Therefore, it appears the Big Five is moderately predictive of overall job performance. Studies also have investigated the influence of the Big Five on other measures of performance, such as contextual performance (Borman & Motowidlo, 1993). Hurtz and Donovan (2000) examined the predictive validities of the Big Five for two aspects of contextual performance, job dedication and interpersonal facilitation. Again, Conscientiousness emerged as the strongest predictor (.15–.18), along with emotional stability (.13–.16) for task performance, job dedication, and interpersonal facilitation. For interpersonal facilitation, Agreeableness was also an important predictor (.17).

We have provided three tables that summarize findings from the literature for important organizational behaviors. Table 21.1 summarizes findings with respect to the validity of personality in the prediction of job performance. Table 21.2 summarizes findings related to the validity of personality as a predictor of training performance. Finally, Table 21.3 provides a summary of the validity of personality as a predictor of organizational citizenship behaviors. Each table indicates that personality predicts important organizational outcomes. For each organizational criterion, the average amount of variance accounted for by dispositional factors is similar to that found for the overall average variance accounted for by personality (cf. Funder, 2001). However, for each criterion, a significant and larger amount of variance still remains unexplained. In addition, in each table, there are nonsignificant findings for the effects of dispositional variables on the criteria.

Situational Approaches to Understanding Organizational Behavior

The basic situational model proposes that the immediate situation in which a person resides is the primary determinant of behavior (Fleeson, 2004). There are many situational variables to choose from in organizational research. We have chosen to investigate the effects of organizational climate as a

TABLE 21.1 Personality as a Predictor of Job Performance

Authors	Personality dimensions	Other variables	Criteria	Findings
Barrick & Mount (1991)[a]	Big Five and a sixth Miscellaneous dimension	Various occupations (professionals, police, managers, sales, and skilled/semiskilled)	Performance ratings and personnel data (e.g., turnover, salary level, tenure)	Conscientiousness predicted for all occupations, whereas extraversion predicted for sales representatives and managers. Conscientiousness predicted all three criteria.
Barrick, Mount, & Judge (2001)[b]	Big Five	Various occupations (see Barrick & Mount, 1991)	Work performance (supervisor ratings, objective performance), teamwork	Extraversion predicted for teamwork (.16), while Emotional Stability predicted for all jobs and teamwork (.22). Agreeableness only predicted teamwork (.34). Conscientiousness was a valid predictor across job criteria, including teamwork (.27).
Barrick, Stewart, Neubert, & Mount (1998)	Big Five using the Personal Characteristics Inventory (PCI)	Cognitive ability (Wonderlic Personnel Test)	Team performance, team viability, workload sharing, team communication, member flexibility, team conflict, social cohesiveness	Greater levels of mental ability and Conscientiousness was related to higher supervisor ratings of team performance; teams with higher levels of Extraversion and Emotional Stability had higher ratings of team viability; Agreeableness, Extraversion, and Emotional Stability were related to social cohesion.
Barrick, Stewart, & Piotrowski (2002)	Big Five using the Occupational Personality Questionniare	Motivation orientation	Performance ratings (mean of 9 dimensions)	Extraversion (.21), Conscientiousness (.26), and two aspects of motivation, status, and accomplishment striving, were significantly correlated with performance. Results also indicated that status and accomplishment striving mediate the relationship between Extraversion and Conscientiousness and Performance. Agreeableness, Emotional Stability, and Openness to Experience were not significantly related to performance and were not tested in the model.
Bradley, Nicol, Charbonneau, & Meyer (2002)	Surgency, Achievement, Adjustment, Dependability, Agreeableness, and Locus of Control (gathered from self, interviewer, and letters of reference)	Leadership	Performance scores from Basic Officer Training Course for the Canadian Military (measured at 3 time periods)	Locus of control (.15) was significantly related to the final, overall performance and instructors' ratings of leadership. Dominance (Time 1, self-report) was related to physical fitness grade (.39), military grade (.28), transformational leadership (.48), contingent reward (.42), peer ratings of transformational leadership (−.34), and management by exception (passive) peer ratings (−.34). Achievement was related to transformational leadership self-ratings (.40). Locus of control was related to management by exception (passive) self-ratings (−.30).
Brown, Mowen, Donavan, & Licata (2002)	Big Five, need for activity	Customer Service Orientation Surface Trait	Overall service worker performance	Conscientiousness was directly related to both self and supervisor ratings of performance. Agreeableness and the need for activity were negatively related to customer orientation and directly to performance. Emotional instability also indicated a reduction in customer orientation. Personality variables accounted for 39% of the variance in customer orientation (which is linked to performance).
Colquitt, Hollenbeck, Ilgen, LePine, & Sheppard (2002)	Openness to Experience	Efficiency with integration of verbal and computerized communication	Team decision-making performance	Teams that were more open to experience benefited the decision-making performance of teams using computerized communication. Efficiency in integration of verbal and computerized communication appeared to mediate the relationship between Openness to Experience and team decision-making performance.
Diefendorff, Brown, Kamin, & Lord (2002)	Agreeableness and Conscientiousness	Job involvement, and work centrality	Task performance	Job involvement was significantly related to task performance ratings. After controlling for work centrality, Conscientiousness, Agreeableness, and hours worked per week, job involvement continued to predict task performance.

(continued)

TABLE 21.1   (*Continued*)

Authors	Personality dimensions	Other variables	Criteria	Findings
Hurtz & Donovan (2000)[a]	Big Five	Various occupations (sales, customer service, managers, skilled/semiskilled)	Job proficiency, task performance, job dedication, interpersonal facilitation	Conscientiousness had the highest estimated true validity (.20), with highest validities for sales (.26) and customer service (.25). Emotional Stability and Extraversion had low but stable relationships with sales and managerial jobs, while Emotional Stability, Agreeableness, and Openness were related to customer service jobs. Conscientiousness and Emotional Stability were most predictive of job performance. Conscientiousness predicted task performance, job dedication, and interpersonal facilitation equally well (.15, −.18). Agreeableness and Emotional Stability were predictive of interpersonal facilitation.
LePine & Van Dyne (2001)	Big Five using the NEO	Cognitive ability	Task performance	None of the personality variables were correlated with task performance. Neuroticism was equally predictive of cooperative behaviors and task performance.
Mount, Barrick, & Stewart (1998)[a]	Big Five using the PCI	—	Overall performance, supervisor's ratings of interpersonal interactions	Conscientiousness (.26), Agreeableness (.21), and Emotional Stability (.18) had the highest true score validities. Emotional Stability and Agreeableness were more related to performance in teams, while Conscientiousness was related to nonteam performance. Agreeableness (.27) was the best predictor of interpersonal interactions, followed by Conscientiousness (.20) and Emotional Stability (.19).
Robertson, Baron, Gibbons, MacIver, & Nyfield (2000)	Conscientiousness using various measures in the Occupational Personality Questionnaire (OPQ)	Managerial work performance using the Inventory of Management Competencies	Current job performance, overall promotability	No relationship was found between Conscientiousness and current performance. A negative relationship was found between Conscientiousness and promotability (−.20).
Salgado (1997)[a]	Big Five	Various countries and occupations	Performance ratings and personnel data	Across job criteria and occupations, Conscientiousness has the highest predictive validity (.25, corrected for measurement error and range restriction), followed by Emotional Stability (.19).
Salgado (1998)[a]	Big Five	General Mental Ability (GMA)	Performance ratings and personnel data	Emotional Stability (.14) and Conscientiousness (.12) had the highest true score validity. These dimensions were also predictive across occupations and criteria. Conscientiousness and Emotional Stability accounted for an incremental amount of variance above and beyond GMA.
Witt, Burke, Barrick, & Mount (2002)	Agreeableness and Conscientiousness using the PCI	Various occupations	Job performance	Conscientiousness (.22) significantly predicted performance across 7 samples (occupations). Agreeableness (.15) predicted for jobs that involved cooperative interaction. The interaction between Conscientiousness and Agreeableness predicted for 5 samples, and these relationships were stronger for workers that scored around the mean or higher on Agreeableness.

[a]Meta-analytic results.
[b]Second-order meta-analytic results.

TABLE 21.2   **Personality as a Predictor of Training Performance**

Authors	Personality dimensions	Other variables	Criteria	Findings
Atwater (1992)	Emotional Stability and Expedience measured using the 16PF	Cognitive Ability (SAT scores), Practical Intelligence (Constructive Thinking Inventory)	Training performance grade issued by superior officers	The personality measures were not related to training performance ratings.

(*continued*)

TABLE 21.2 *(Continued)*

Authors	Personality dimensions	Other variables	Criteria	Findings
Barrick & Mount (1991)[a]	Big Five and a sixth Miscellaneous dimension	Various occupations (professionals, police, managers, sales, and skilled/semiskilled)	Training proficiency	Conscientiousness, Openness, and Extraversion predicted training proficiency.
Barrick, Mount, & Judge (2001)[b]	Big Five	Various occupations (see Barrick & Mount, 1991)	Training performance	Extraversion (.28) and Conscientiousness (.27) predicted training performance.
Driskell, Hogan, Salas, & Hoskin (1994)	Adjustment, Ambition, Sociability, Likeability, Prudence, Intellectance, and School Success using the Hogan Personality Inventory	Cognitive Ability using the ASVAB	Academic and nonacademic training performance criteria	Intellectance (.28), School Success (.28), and Ambition (.18) predicted academic training performance, while Prudence (−.18) predicted performance delinquency. A personality composite was created using Ambition, Intellectance, and School Success, which correlated .42 with academic performance.
Ferris, Bergin, & Gilmore (1986)	Measured using the 16PF	Mental ability	Training performance	Mental ability, Social Skill, Imagination, and Flexibility predicted training performance for flight attendants.
Ferris, Youngblood, & Yates (1985)	Extraversion, Anxiety, Corteria (tough poise), and Independence	Person-group fit	Training performance, attendance, turnover	None of the personality dimensions were related to training performance. Anxiety was related to attendance (−.34). A significant relationship between training performance and attendance was found for individuals with a high level of person-group fit. A significant negative relationship was found between training performance and turnover for the individuals in the low person-group fit group.
Hurtz & Donovan (2000)[a]	Big Five	Various occupations (sales, customer service, managers, skilled/semiskilled)	Training proficiency	Agreeableness and Extraversion predicted training performance.
Kabanoff & Bottger (1991)	Achievement, Deference, Autonomy, Affiliation, and Dominance using the Edwards Personal Preference Schedule	Torrence Tests of Creative Thinking	Performance on three tasks: project, reading reports, and presentation	Personality factors influenced who selected to participate in the creativity-training course and their performance in that course. Need for achievement is negatively related to performance on the project task (−.38), whereas autonomy is positively related to performance on the same task (.35). Personality did not predict any pre- or post-test gains in creative ability.
Nijenhuis & van der Flier (2000)	Neuroticism, Neurosomatism, and Extraversion	Dutch version of the General Aptitude Test Battery	Truck-driving training course proficiency: examination marks, professional attitude, practice skills	Extraversion predicted professional attitude. Neuroticism and Extraversion predicted practice skills (differential prediction for immigrants and minority group members).
Oakes, Ferris, Martocchio, Buckley, & Broach (2001)	16 PF subscales of Reasoning, Emotional Stability, Rule Consciousness, Sensitivity, Apprehension, Perfectionism, and Tension	Cognitive ability (measured using the Multiplex Control Aptitude Test, the Abstract Reasoning Test, Occupational Knowledge Test)	Skill acquisition (training performance)	Those with higher Reasoning and Apprehension scores performed better on the skill acquisition measure.
Salgado (1997)[a]	Big Five	Various countries and occupations	Training proficiency	Conscientiousness, Openness, and Agreeableness predicted training criteria.
Salgado (1998)[a]	Big Five	General mental ability (GMA)	Training ratings	For Army training performance, Emotional Stability had an estimated true validity of .45.
Savage & Stewart (1972)	Extraversion and Neuroticism using the Eysenck Personality Inventory	Name, number-comparison test, coding test	Training success indicated through speed and accuracy ratings; rated three times	There was a significant relationship between Extraversion and Time 1 rating (−.29) and Time 2 rating (−.34). There were no significant relationships between the three ratings and Neuroticism.

[a]Meta-analytic results.

TABLE 21.3   Personality as a Predictor of Organizational Citizenship Behaviors/Contextual Performance

Authors	Personality dimensions	Other variables	Criteria	Findings
Beatty, Cleveland, & Murphy (2001)	Big Five using the NEO	Strong versus weak situation	Intention to offer coworker help in job-performance situations; laboratory study	Neuroticism ($-.11$), Extraversion (.11), and Agreeableness (.14) were correlated with helping behavior. Neuroticism and Agreeableness appeared to be most influential in determining helping behaviors in a weak condition. The situation accounted for the greatest change in R^2 (.25 for all variables and situations) when personality, the situation, and the interaction between the two were entered into a regression.
Beatty, Cleveland, & Murphy (2001)	Big Five using the NEO	Strong versus weak situation	Intention to offer coworker help in job-performance situations; field study	Neuroticism ($-.36$) and Agreeableness (.24) were correlated with helping behavior. Neuroticism, Agreeableness, Conscientiousness, and Openness appeared to be most influential in determining helping behaviors in a weak condition. Only Neuroticism and the Conscientiousness by Situation interaction accounted for any variance in the regression results.
Bettencourt, Gwinner, & Meuter (2001)	Service orientation and Empathy	Job satisfaction, perceived organizational support and customer knowledge	Service-oriented OCBs with three dimensions: Loyalty, Service Delivery, and Participation	Personality variables better predicted service-delivery behaviors, whereas job attitudes predicted the loyalty dimension of service-oriented OCBs. In a second study, personality variables predicted 4% of variance to the prediction of loyalty, 20% of service-delivery and 8% of participation. Overall, it appears that personality variables are important in the prediction of service-delivery OCBs.
Borman, Penner, Allen, & Motow-idlo (2001)[a]	Conscientiousness, Agreeableness, Positive Affectivity, Extraversion, Negative Affectivity, Locus of Control, Collectivism, Other-Oriented Empathy, Helpfulness	None	Overall Citizenship Performance	Updated the Organ & Ryan (1995) meta-analysis; found a higher value for Conscientiousness (.24), Agreeableness (.13), and Positive Affectivity (.18). Other relationships uncovered Extraversion (.08), Negative Affectivity ($-.14$), Locus of Control (.16), Collectivism (.15), Other-Oriented Empathy (.28), and Helpfulness (.22). These relationships also were examined with self-reported data deleted.
Diefendorff, Brown, Kamin, & Lord (2002)	Agreeableness and Conscientiousness	Job involvement, and work centrality	OCB (five dimensions: Conscientiousness, Sportsmanship, Courtesy, Altruism, and Civic Virtue)	Job involvement was significantly related to ratings on Altruism, Civic Virtue, Sportsmanship, and Conscientiousness. Work centrality was correlated only with the Civic Virtue. After controlling for work centrality, Conscientiousness, Agreeableness, and hours worked per week, job involvement continued to predict OCB ratings of Altruism, Civic Virtue, and Conscientiousness. Gender interacted with OCBs and job involvement.
Fisher (2002)	Positive and Negative Affect	Affective (positive and negative) reactions at work, job satisfaction, organizational commitment	Intent to leave, helping behavior	Helping behavior was significantly related to positive affectivity (.41), positive affective reactions (.48), job satisfaction (.23), affective commitment (.33), and intention to leave ($-.19$). Positive and negative affectivity work through affective reactions and job satisfaction to influence affective commitment and helping behaviors.
Gellantly & Irving (2001)	Big Five using the NEO	Job autonomy	Five dimensions of OCB: Maintaining good working relationships, representing the organization to the public, persisting to reach goals, developing subordinates, and communicating effectively	Extraversion was significantly related to contextual performance (.20). Conscientiousness predicted of the variance in contextual performance (negative b weight), whereas Autonomy added incremental variance to Extraversion, Agreeableness, and Conscientiousness regressions. The interaction between Extraversion and Autonomy and Agreeableness and Autonomy was also significant.

(continued)

TABLE 21.3 *(Continued)*

Authors	Personality dimensions	Other variables	Criteria	Findings
Lee & Allen (2002)	Positive and Negative Affect	Job cognitions: intrinsic cognitions, procedural justice, pay cognitions and work-schedule load	OCB directed toward the individual (OCBI), OCB directed toward the organization (OCBO), workplace deviance behavior (WDB)	Positive affect predicted OCBI and OCBO. The facets of Negative affect predicted OCBI and WBD beyond the overall negative affect. For OCBI, job affect added a marginal amount of incremental variance beyond job cognitions. However, with respect to OCBO, job cognitions were more predictive than affect. Both job affect and job cognitions were predictive of WDB.
LePine, Erez, & Johnson (2002)[a]	Conscientiousness	Satisfaction, commitment, fairness, leader support	Overall OCB, Altruism, Courtesy, Conscientiousness, Civic Virtue, Sportsmanship	Overall OCB correlated moderately with Conscientiousness (.19, uncorrected population value, .23 corrected for unreliability). At the dimension level, Conscientiousness was related only to Altruism (.23 uncorrected, .2 corrected). Overall OCB had a greater relationship with the dimensions of OCB.
LePine & Van Dyne (2001)	Big Five using the NEO	Cognitive ability	Voice behavior, cooperative behavior, and task performance	Conscientiousness (.17), Extraversion (.14), Neuroticism (−.11), and Agreeableness (.18) were significantly related to cooperative behavior. Conscientiousness (.26), Extraversion (.30), Neuroticism (−.12), and Agreeableness (−.16) were significantly related to voice behavior. Conscientiousness, Extraversion, Neuroticism, and Agreeableness were predictive of cooperative behavior. Conscientiousness and Extraversion were more related to voice behaviors than task performance.
Miles, Borman, Spector, & Fox (2002)	Trait anger and affect	Organizational constraints, amount of work, interpersonal conflict at work	A combined measure of Citizenship Performance and the relative incidence of OCB, Counterproductive Work Behaviors (CWB)	Organizational constraints correlated significantly with negative emotions (.52 to .54) and positive emotions (−.23 to −.30). Regression analyses indicated that Environmental Constraints (workload, organizational constraints, interpersonal conflict) accounted for 11% of the variance in OCBs, whereas positive emotion accounted for an additional 13%. Environmental constraints accounted for 9% of the variance in CWB, trait anger accounted for an additional 9%, and negative emotion accounted for an additional 1%.
Motowidlo & Van Scotter (1994)	Work orientation, Dominance, Dependability, Adjustment, Cooperativeness, and Internal Control measured using the Assessment of Background and Life Experiences	Cognitive ability scores, training performance, task performance	Supervisor ratings of 16 dimensions of contextual performance	Personality variables predicted contextual performance better than task performance, as all six variables were significantly related to contextual performance. Work orientation had the highest relationship with contextual performance (.36), followed by Dependability (.31) and Internal Control (.26).
Neuman & Kickul (1999)	Conscientiousness, Extraversion, and Agreeableness measured using the NEO-PI-R	Covenantal relationship measured using the Supervisory Behavior Description Questionnaire, Index of Organizational Reactions, Organizational Commitment Survey	Five dimensions of OCBs: Altruism, Courtesy, Conscientiousness, Civic Virtue, Sportsmanship	The personality variables were significantly correlated with all five dimensions of OCB as well as with the covenantal relationship. Mediated regression analyses revealed that Agreeableness and Conscientiousness were partially mediated by the covenantal relationship. Extraversion was not predictive of OCBs or the covenantal relationship.
Organ & Ryan (1995)[a]	Conscientiousness, Agreeableness, Negative Affect, Positive Affect	Satisfaction, fairness, organizational commitment, leader supportiveness	Two dimensions of OCB: Altruism and Generalized Compliance	Attitudinal measures were more predictive of Altruism than personality variables; however, Conscientiousness almost reached the level of attitudinal measures. Conscientiousness had a higher sample-weighted mean estimate of the population correlation (.30) with Generalized Compliance.

(continued)

TABLE 21.3   *(Continued)*

Authors	Personality dimensions	Other variables	Criteria	Findings
Penney & Spector (2002)	Narcissism and Anger	Job constraints	Counterproductive work-place behaviors (CWB)	Narcissism was significantly related to Anger (.39) and counterproductive workplace behaviors (.27); Anger was also significantly related to CWB (.46). Regression analyses indicated that Anger mediated the relationship between Narcissism and CWB. Narcissism moderated the relationship between job constraints and CWB, such that in individuals who were high in Narcissism, there was a stronger relationship between job constraints and CWB.
Yilmaz & Hunt (2001)	Personal cooperativeness	Organizational commitment, trust, job satisfaction, shared values, communication quality, opportunistic behaviors, task interdependence, financial rewards, collectivist organizational norms, nonfinancial rewards, number of coworkers, age, education, organizational tenure	Salesperson cooperation	This study examined a complex model of salesperson cooperation. Results support the importance of task and personal factors (combined account for 30% of variance in salesperson cooperation). Organizational and relational factors accounted for 10% and 5% of the variance in cooperation. Task interdependence, personal cooperation, financial rewards, and norms contributed to these relationships. No significant relationships were found between number of coworkers, organizational commitment, and nonfinancial rewards and cooperation.

[a]Meta-analytic results.

model for the manner in which situational variables may impact organizational behaviors.

Organizational climate is a variable with a long history in organizational research. It has been used as an important contextual variable in the explanation of organizational behavior. The behaviors exhibited in a situation have an adaptive function (Morris, 1988). This degree to which behavior is adaptive, however, is defined relative to the situation. Therefore, understanding how contexts affect the production of behavior is a critical requirement for understanding how individuals act when in groups and organizations. A major reason for the formation of organizational climates is the creation of social order (Trice & Beyer, 1993). Organizational culture allows recurrent behavior patterns among people to develop within organizations. These patterns form the basis of predictable interactions within an organization.

Organizational climate influences behaviors within an organization by defining a strong situation (Mischel, 1977) for individuals residing within it. A strong situation provides people with generally accepted rules and guidelines for appropriate behavior. The rules that are present in strong situations constrain people from acting in a manner inconsistent with accepted conduct and behavior. Organizations develop values and norms to set parameters on the behaviors exhibited within an organization. Organizational climate acts to provide employees with information about what (1) behavioral styles

and (2) specific behaviors the organization in which they reside values.

The effects of organizational climate are particularly strong when the individual is motivated to adapt (Showers & Cantor, 1985). The ability to recognize and correctly adapt to the reality of organizational life is a critical component of career success (Sathe, 1985) in which managers are very motivated to understand the behaviors supported in their environment (Hannaway, 1989). Managers rely heavily on the information they receive from their social structure to infer appropriate behaviors and use this information to balance organizational goals and their personal career interests when making a decision (Hannaway, 1989; Svyantek, Jones, & Rozelle, 1991; Svyantek & Kolz, 1996). The constraints on the accepted range of behaviors within an organization create multiple organizational climates supporting responses for organizational criteria (e.g., decision making; Svyantek et al., 1991; Svyantek & Kolz, 1996). These constraints are created by, and reflect, the values and assumptions that make up an organizational climate.

Table 21.4 presents research literature that investigated the relationship between organizational climate and job performance. The literature presented in the table shows that organizational climate, like the dispositional variables presented in Tables 21.1, 21.2, and 21.3, is an effective predictor of job performance. However, the level of prediction is approxi-

TABLE 21.4   Relationship between Perceptions of Organizational Climate and Job Performance

Study	Sample characteristics	Climate measure	Performance measure	Results
Baer & Frese (2003)	Midsize German companies (N = 47)	Dimensions: climate for initiative and climate for psychological safety	Subjective measure of attainment and return on assets (ROA)	Both climates related to firm goal achievement and ROA. Climate for initiative moderated the relationship between process innovation and firm performance (both measures), whereas climate for psychological safety moderated the process innovativeness to ROA relationship.
Borucki & Burke (1999)	Retail organizations (N = 483 stores)	Service climate with two higher-order factors: Concern for Employees (6 dimensions) and Concern for Customers (4 dimensions)	Employee-rated service performance and customer-rated service performance; return on sales ratio (operating profit/loss as a percentage of total sales)	Path analysis revealed support for relationships between service climate and both types of service performance (similar magnitudes). Relationships between employee-rated service performance and store financial performance was significant (.17).
Burton, Lauridsen, & Obel (2004)	CEOs (N = 175)	Based on the competing-values concept (Quinn & Rohrbaugh, 1983); three dimensions: tension, resistance to change, and conflict	Return on assets (ROA)	Examined corporate-climate misfits with organizational strategy; in some cases, misfits resulted in lower ROA (e.g., a misfit included innovative strategies with high resistance, tension, and conflict from employees).
Carr, Schmidt, Ford, & DeShon (2003)	Meta-analysis of 15 studies with a total N of 3,136	Ostroff's (1993) classification scheme used: Affective, Cognitive, and Instrumental Climate	Not reported	No direct path from climate variables to job performance; the three climate dimensions worked through job satisfaction to influence job performance.
Day & Bedeian (1991)	Accountants (N = 483)	Organizational Climate Questionnaire (Litwin & Stringer, 1968)	Single-factor measure of performance relevant to accountants	Three significant interactions between climate dimensions and work orientation (warmth-support, reward, and accommodation): Highest performance for those with a high work orientation and positive climate perceptions; those with a high work orientation and negative climate perceptions had lowest performance.
Gelade & Ivery (2003)		General climate (average of seven dimensions); individual dimensions: leadership, local management, goal clarity, job enablers, coaching, job challenge, rewards	Average of standardized scores for sales against target, customer satisfaction, staff retention, and clerical accuracy	General climate had a .39 relationship with overall performance; climate was a partial mediator of the relationship between HRM practices (staffing level, overtime, professional development) and overall performance.
Kandis & Williams (2000)	Selected two companies: • Growth sector: electronic component manufacturer (N = 20) • Declining sector: knitwear manufacturer (N = 20)	Dimensions: supervisory style, coworkers, work motivation, employee competence, decision making, performance rewards	Average corporate performance over three years, average profit margin, average return on capital employed, sales growth	*Electronic components manufacturer*: strongest correlations between supervisory style and three performance measures (r range from .65–.69); *knitwear manufacturer*: only relationships between coworkers and performance variables (r range from .47–.69).
Lawler, Hall, & Oldham (1974)	Research and development firms (N = 21)	Five factors: Competent/Potent, Responsible, Practical, Risk-Oriented, Impulsive (bipolar adjectives)	Technical and administrative rated performance (single item each); overall performance (composite of 6 objective measures)	None of the climate dimensions were related to technical performance ratings; 3 of 5 dimensions were related to administrative performance and overall performance.
Ostroff (1993)	Secondary school teachers (N = 607)	Affective, Cognitive, and Instrumental higher-order factors of climate	Self-rated relative performance	Climate did not predict overall performance, nor did it interact with personal orientations to predict performance. When examining dimensions of the higher-order climate factors, innovation and participation had significant beta weights in the prediction of performance.

(continued)

TABLE 21.4   *(Continued)*

Study	Sample characteristics	Climate measure	Performance measure	Results
Patterson, Warr, & West (2004)	Manufacturing companies in the United Kingdom (N = 42)	Dimensions: involvement, autonomy, supervisory support, integration, employee welfare, skill development, effort, reflexivity, innovation and flexibility, outward focus, goal clarity, pressure to produce, quality, performance feedback, efficiency, formalization, tradition, employee affect	Productivity (financial value of net sales per employee) and profitability (profits before tax, controlling for company size)	The relationship between climate (supervisory support, effort, innovation and flexibility, quality, performance feedback, and formalization) and productivity was mediated by job satisfaction.
Potozsky & Ramakrishna (2002)	Information systems employees in software company (N = 163)	Climate for updating (innovation, creativity, up-to-date competencies)	Performance ratings (past and current)	No overall correlation between performance and climate. However, when examining models based on a median split on climate (high, low), a relationship between learning goal-orientation and self-efficacy with performance holds for perceived supportive climates; does not hold for low supportive climates.
Pritchard & Karasick (1973)	Two firms chosen: • national franchising chain (N = 46) • manufacturing (N = 30)	Dimensions: autonomy, conflict vs. cooperation, social relations, structure, level of rewards, performance-reward dependency, motivation to achieve, status polarization, flexibility and innovation, decision centralization, supportiveness	Overall job rating by management consultant (based on interviews with manager)	Climate was more related to managerial satisfaction than performance; significant interaction between need for dominance (personality) and status polarization on performance; such a stronger relationship between need for dominance and performance was found in a low status polarization climate.
Rogg, Schmidt, Shull, & Schmitt (2001)	Automobile dealerships (N = 351)	Dimensions: cooperation/coordination, customer orientation, employee commitment, managerial competence	Customer satisfaction: five dimensions: product loyalty, dealership loyalty, customer handling, service satisfaction, additional repairs needed	Structural equation modeling indicated that climate mediated the relationship between HR practices and customer satisfaction.
Singh & Dhillon (2004)	Staff reporters in Delhi, India (N = 100)	Organizational Climate Inventory dimensions: performance standards, communication flow, reward system, responsibility, conflict resolution, organizational structure, motivational level, decision-making process, support system, warmth, identity problem	Role efficacy/effectiveness	Stepwise regression indicated that role isolation, performance standards, writing attitudes, role overload, and reward system significantly predicted role efficacy. Performance standards were positively related to role efficacy (β = .28), whereas reward system was negatively related (β = −.23).
Smith-Crowe, Burke, & Landis (2003)	Two hazardous-waste worker samples: • 51 supervisors, 133 workers • 613 supervisors and workers	Dimensions: social and goal cues, task cues, punishment consequences, intrinsic reinforcement consequences, perception of management attitudes toward safety, perceived effects of required work pace on safety, perceived appropriateness of safety training	General safety performance scale	No significant moderation of safety knowledge, safety performance relationship by climate.
Suliman (2002)	Random selection of employees in 20 industrial companies (N = 783)	Dimensions: supervisory style, task characteristics, coworker relations, work motivation, employee competence, decision-making policy, performance-rewards relationship, pressure to produce, employee–immediate supervisor relationship, distributive justices, psychological contract, innovation climate, fairness	Self and supervisor performance ratings	The relationship between work climate and self and supervisory ratings of performance was partially mediated by organizational commitment. This relationship held for affective commitment, but no mediation was supported for continuance commitment.

(continued)

TABLE 21.4   *(Continued)*

Study	Sample characteristics	Climate measure	Performance measure	Results
Zohar (2000)	Production workers in a metal-processing plant; 534 workers divided into 53 work groups	Group safety climate: two dimensions: supervisory action and expectation	Microaccidents and accidents (lost-day injuries)	Both supervisory action and expectation predicted microaccidents ($\beta = -.47$ and $-.45$, respectively). Hierarchical linear modeling results indicated that supervisory action predicted injuries (T ratio $= -2.52$).
Zohar & Luria (2004)	81 platoons, composed of 2,024 soldiers	Safety climate strength and level using two dimensions: safety priority and mission priority	Injury rate over six months	No significant moderation by climate strength on the climate level to injury-rate relationship; climate level partially mediated relationship between supervisory patterns (i.e., transformational leadership, risk) and injury rate.

mately the same as that found for dispositional variables. Critics of the dispositional approach basically proposed that the remaining 84 percent of the variance unaccounted for in behavior by the dispositional model was due to the situation (Funder, 2001). The level of variance accounted for by organizational climate, however, does not approach 84 percent. Again, the level of variance accounted for by organizational climate is approximately equal to that of dispositional variables.

INTERACTIONAL MODELS IN ORGANIZATIONAL RESEARCH

These two approaches to the prediction of behavior, the situational and dispositional, reflect a deeper question about human behavior. This debate concerns whether the person performing a behavior or the situation in which the behavior occurs is the primary cause of a human behavior. However, research has consistently shown that the person-situation debate over whether consistencies in individuals' behavior are pervasive or broad enough to be meaningfully described in terms of personality traits is largely over (Funder, 2001). The long-standing dichotomy between the effect of the situation and the person on behavior is, therefore, a false dichotomy.

An understanding of the person, situation, and behaviors being performed are required for a clear understanding of human behavior (Funder, 2001). This is particularly important for organizational research. Organizational research, by definition, is the study of individuals in a particular type of context: the workplace. Therefore, although a simple point, organizational research into the determinants of workplace behavior must include both situational and dispositional variables to truly begin to understand the causes of important job behaviors such as task performance, organizational commitment, and contextual performance. Understanding organiza-

tional behavior, therefore, requires that an interactional model of personality be used in research.

We propose that there are two basic research approaches that may be used to conduct interactional studies of personality and situational effects in organizations. These are (1) person-organization fit studies and (2) the conduct of studies that explicitly incorporate measures of personality and the situation.

Person-Organization Fit as an Interactional Variable

Person-organization fit has been shown to be related to a number of organizational variables including (1) job-choice decisions by organizational applicants (Cable & Judge, 1996); (2) organizational attraction of applicants (Judge & Cable, 1997); (3) selection decisions made by recruitment interviewers (Cable & Judge, 1997); (4) employee job satisfaction, job tenure, and career success (Bretz & Judge, 1994); and (5) employees' level of task and organizational citizenship performance (Goodman & Svyantek, 1999). Person-organization fit has been defined as "the congruence between patterns of organizational values and patterns of individual values, defined here as what an individual values in an organization, such as being team-oriented or innovative" (Chatman, 1991, p. 459). The emphasis here is on the match of an individual's values, when considered along with the value system in a specific organizational context, and the potential effects that match (or lack of match) has on that individual's subsequent behavior and attitudes. Therefore, both situational and dispositional aspects are combined into one measure that, conceptually, represents an interaction between the two classes of situational and dispositional variables.

Researchers must decide how to measure person-organization fit. There are two related methods of doing this. Person-organization fit assessment involves collapsing two constructs into one measure as a predictor of some outcome.

The vast majority of person-organization fit studies have operationalized congruency by collapsing two or more measures into a single index. These profile similarity indices (PSIs) combine two sets of measures, or profiles, from corresponding entities (e.g., the ideal state and organization) into a single score intended to represent overall congruence (Cronbach & Glesser, 1953). Examples of this include the use of discrepancy scores and the use of correlations between observed culture and personal values (cf. O'Reilly, Chatman, & Caldwell, 1991).

Edwards (1993, 1994, 1995), however, suggests that PSIs should no longer be used in congruence research, such as person-organization fit. Instead, researchers should use polynomial equations containing measures of both entities (here the actual and ideal culture measurements) that typically are collapsed in PSIs (cf. Edwards, 1993, 1994; Edwards & Cooper, 1990; Edwards & Harrison, 1993; Edwards & Parry, 1993). The general approach suggested by Edwards (1993, 1994) offers several advantages over congruence indices currently in use. First, polynomial regression maintains the interpretability of the original component measures. Second, polynomial regression yields separate estimates of the relationships between component measures and the outcome. Third, polynomial regression provides a complete test of models underlying congruence indices, focusing not only on the overall magnitude of the relationship but also on the significance of individual effects, the validity of implied constraints, and the significance of higher-order terms. Finally, the approach proposed by Edwards (1993, 1994) may yield considerable increases in explained variance.

Goodman and Svyantek's (1999) findings were based on the use of Edwards's (1993, 1994) approach. The use of this method allowed interpretable patterns of results to be found for both actual and ideal measures of organizational climate. Therefore, we recommend that Edwards's approach be used when addressing issues of person-organization fit when investigating the interaction of situational and dispositional factors as defined by the construct of person-organization fit.

Measuring Both Situational and Dispositional Variables

One question to consider when conducting research based on an interactional model of personality is whether perceptions of organizational climate and measured dispositional variables or the match between individuals' perceptions of the current and ideal states (e.g., person-organization fit) is more helpful in predicting organizational behavior. At this point, the answer to this question is still unknown. It has been hypothesized that actual measures of organizational climate may be more predictive of performance measures than are perceived fit measures (Kristof, 1996). Therefore, it may be appropriate to include explicitly both situational and dispositional variables in research studies to assess how these variables affect organizational criteria.

Research studies incorporating both dispositional and situational variables have been conducted. For example, Schein and Diamonte (1988) found a relationship between three different personality variables and organizational characteristics. People who rated themselves as high on a personality characteristic were more likely to be attracted to an organization that was described as reflecting that characteristic. Similarly, it was found that organizational climate information and personality variables interact in a recruitment situation (Furlong & Svyantek, 1998). Personality variables were found to prime individuals to perceive and select organizational climates in which they will have a high probability of succeeding. Beatty, Cleveland, and Murphy (2001) studied the relationship between strong and weak situations and the Big Five personality variables. Their findings were that whereas Big Five personality variables did predict organizational citizenship performance variables, the variable with the highest R^2 value was the situation. Miles, Borman, Spector, and Fox (2002) used both situational and dispositional variables and found that situational variables and dispositional variables accounted for nearly the same amount of variance.

Perhaps the most interesting thing that the inclusion of both situational and dispositional variables in research allows is the study of the interaction between the situation and dispositional variables. We have conducted research (e.g., Svyantek & Philips, 2001) that indicates that understanding how personality interacts with the situation in the determination of organizational citizenship behaviors offers new insights into the explanation of organizational citizenship.

Organizational citizenship behaviors, or contextual performance (e.g., Borman & Motowidlo, 1993; Organ, 1997), refer to activities such as volunteering to carry out actions that are not formally part of the job, helping others, following organizational rules/procedures when personally inconvenient, endorsing and supporting organizational objectives, and persisting with extra effort to successfully complete one's task activities. Contextual-performance activities differ from task-performance activities in at least four important ways (Borman & Motowidlo, 1993). First, task activities contribute either directly or indirectly to the technical core of the organization; contextual activities, however, support the organizational, social, and psychological environment in which task performance occurs. Second, task activities vary between different jobs within the same organization; contextual activities, however, are common to many (or all) jobs. Third, task activities are role-prescribed and are behaviors that employees perform in exchange for pay; contextual behaviors are less role-prescribed. Finally, the important human characteristics for completing task activities are knowledge, skills, and abilities (KSAs). These KSAs usually covary with task proficiency. For contextual performance, the major source of variation is believed to be employee predispositions and volition. Behaviors such as volunteering, helping, and persisting are probably better predicted by volitional variables related to individual differences in motivational characteristics and predisposition (Borman & Motowidlo, 1993; Borman & Van Scotter, 1994) or person-organization fit (Borman, Hanson, & Hedge, 1997).

We examined the interaction between dispositional and situational variables in order to examine the effects of personality (using the IMAGES scale, a Big Five based personality measure; Saville & Holdsworth, 1993a), the situation (operationalized as organizational climate; Litwin & Stringer's [1968] Organizational Climate Questionnaire), and their interaction. This study was based on a survey on these variables of 221 members of an organization. Performance criteria information was gathered from the supervisors of these individuals.

Tables 21.5, 21.6, and 21.7 present the results of these analyses for task performance, OCB-Conscientiousness (organizationally focused citizenship behavior) and OCB-Altruism (individually focused citizenship behavior). Each table presents the results of two separate hierarchical multiple-regression analyses involving two steps. In the first step, all the personality variables were entered. The personality variables were entered first as a reflection of the dispositional model of personality. The situational variables were entered second to test the incremental effects of the situation on performance on these variables.

Inspection of the tables provides information relevant to the interactional approach to understanding organizational behavior. First, the analyses showed performance on tasks and the two forms of OCBs was affected differentially by the effects of situational and dispositional variables in the study.

Table 21.5 shows task performance was the least affected by personality and situational variables (overall model $R^2 = .140$). Table 21.5 also shows that the variance accounted for by personality variables ($R^2 = .061$) is approximately the same as that of the variance accounted for by situational variables ($R^2 = .079$) on task performance.

Table 21.6 shows the OCB-Conscientiousness variable was more affected by personality and situational variables than task (overall model $R^2 = .239$). Table 21.6 also shows that the variance accounted for by personality variables ($R^2 = .083$) is approximately half that of the variance accounted for by situational variables ($R^2 = .155$) on the OCB-Conscientiousness variable.

Table 21.7 shows that the OCB-Altruism variable was most affected by personality and situational variables (overall model $R^2 = .266$). Table 21.7 also shows that the variance accounted for by personality variables ($R^2 = .145$) was more than that of the variance accounted for by situational variables ($R^2 = .121$) on the OCB-Altruism variable.

These results are consistent with the proposal that behaviors such as volunteering, helping, and persisting are probably better predicted by volitional variables related to individual differences in motivational characteristics and predisposition (Borman & Motowidlo, 1993; Borman & Van Scotter, 1994) than is task performance. Second, these findings support the idea that OCB-Altruism and OCB-Conscientiousness are being differentially affected by personality variables in terms of variance accounted for by dispositional and situational factors.

Inspection of Tables 21.6 and 21.7 also shows that the constellation of variables predicting OCB-Conscientiousness and OCB-Altruism may be slightly different. Table 21.6 shows the significant personality and situational variables that predict OCB-Conscientiousness behavior.

Litwin and Stringer's (1968) Organizational Climate Questionnaire was used to describe important situational variables. Litwin and Stringer's measure assesses the shared beliefs and values of organizational members that constitute the per-

TABLE 21.5 Results of the Multiple Regression Analysis for the Effects of Personality and Organizational Climate on Task Performance

	R	R^2	F	Sig	df	R^2 change	F change	df	Sig
Step 1 Personality	.247	.061	2.28	.04	6,210	—	—	—	—
Step 2 OCQ	.374	.140	2.18	.01	15,201	.079	2.04	9,201	.04

Predictors (Step 2)	beta	t	Sig	Measure
Conflict	.158	2.24	.03	Situation

TABLE 21.6   Results of the Multiple Regression Analyses for the Effects of Personality and Organizational Climate on the OCB-Conscientiousness Scale

	R	R^2	F	Sig	df	R^2 change	F change	df	Sig
Step 1 Personality	.289	.083	3.18	.005	6,210	—	—	—	—
Step 2 OCQ	.489	.239	4.20	.001	15,201	.155	4.56	9,201	.001

Predictors (Step 2)	beta	t	Sig	Measure
Emotion	.138	2.137	.03	Person
Warmth	.337	3.88	.001	Situation
Standards	−.135	−1.98	.05	Situation

TABLE 21.7   Results of the Multiple Regression Analysis for the Effects of Personality and Organizational Climate on the OCB-Altruism Scale

	R	R^2	F	Sig	df	R^2 change	F change	df	Sig
Step 1 Personality	.380	.145	5.19	.001	6,210	—	—	—	—
Step 2 OCQ	.516	.266	4.85	.001	15,201	.121	3.68	9,201	.001

Predictors (Step 2)	beta	t	Sig	Measure
Achievement	.141	2.01	.05	Person
Emotion	.187	2.96	.03	Person
Gregariousness	.197	2.91	.04	Person
Warmth	.337	3.95	.001	Situation
Conflict	.127	1.95	.05	Situation
Standards	−.166	−2.49	.01	Situation

ceived work environment. The questionnaire is one of the better known surveys of its kind (Payne & Pugh, 1976). It consists of 50 items that assess 9 dimensions of climate. These nine dimensions are: (1) Structure (the feeling that employees have about the constraints in the group, how many rules, regulations, procedures there are; is there an emphasis on "red tape" and going through channels, or is there a loose and informal atmosphere); (2) Responsibility (the feeling of being your own boss; not having to double-check all your decisions; when you have a job to do, knowing that it is your job); (3) Reward (the feeling of being rewarded for a job well done; emphasizing positive rewards rather than punishment; the perceived fairness of the pay and promotion policies); (4) Risk (the sense of riskiness and challenge in the job and in the organization; is there an emphasis on taking calculated risks, or is playing it safe the best way to operate?); (5) Warmth (the feeling of general good fellowship that prevails in the work group atmosphere; the emphasis of being well liked; the prevalence of friendly and informal social groups); (6) Support (the perceived helpfulness of the managers and other employees in the group; emphasis on mutual support from above and below); (7) Standards (the perceived impor-

tance of implicit and explicit goals and performance standards; the emphasis on doing a good job; the challenge presented in personal and group goals); (8) Conflict (the feeling that managers and other workers want to hear different opinions; the emphasis placed on getting problems out in the open rather than smoothing them over or ignoring them); and (9) Identity (the feeling that you belong to a company and you are a valuable member of a working team; the importance placed on this kind of spirit).

Once again, the results for both analyses are presented in each table. When the OCQ dimensions define the situation, one personality variable (Emotion) and two situational variables (Warmth and Standards) significantly predict performance of this behavior. Warmth has the largest beta weight (.34): Both Emotion and Standards have beta weights of approximately the same magnitude (.14 and −.14, respectively). Table 21.7 shows the significant personality and situational variables that predict OCB-Altruism behavior. When the OCQ dimensions define the situation, three personality variables (Achievement, Emotion, and Gregariousness) and three situational variables (Warmth, Conflict, and Standards) significantly predict performance of this behavior.

Warmth has the largest beta weight again (.34), whereas the other five predictors have a range of similar magnitudes (absolute values from .13 to .20).

Once again, these results appear to be consistent with the proposal that, not only are behaviors such as volunteering, helping, and persisting probably better predicted by dispositional and volitional variables than is task performance, the different forms of OCB behavior are predicted by different sets of dispositional and situational variables. The prediction of OCB-Altruism behaviors is more complex than that of OCB-Conscientiousness behaviors. Again, OCB-Altruism probably is more volitional in nature: It is directed at helping other individual employees in the organization, and dispositional and situational variables may differentially impact this variable. OCB-Conscientiousness, however, is directed at the organization. Performance of these variables may seem as more closely a part of one's job, and the relative importance of situational and dispositional variables may differ.

We also were interested in investigating the possibility that individuals' personality variables interact with the situation in which they find themselves to show complex relationships between behavior and dispositional and situational variables. We limited ourselves to an investigation of this on the two OCB variables. Our exploratory analysis was performed by creating median splits on two variables, one personality and one situational variable. We believed this would give us a starting point for understanding the relationship of personality and situational differences on behavior by showing the degree to which individuals with the same personality characteristics were influenced by the situation on different variables.

The variables chosen were Emotion and Warmth. They were chosen because they both (a) predicted OCB-Conscientiousness and OCB-Altruism and (b) had the largest beta weights across both OCB variables when we inspected the regression analyses for the models with the OCQ dimensions defining the situation. The median split for the Emotion variable was calculated based on the individual employees' scores on the Emotion dimension. We attempted to get a more objective definition of the Warmth dimension than might be derived from separating employees based on their personal estimate. Therefore, the median split for Warmth was calculated using mean scores for departments within the organization and not on individual perceptions of Warmth.

A univariate ANOVA was conducted to test the effects of Emotion and Warmth on OCB-Conscientiousness and OCB-Altruism. In addition, the interaction between Emotion and Warmth was tested for each of the dependent variables.

The results for OCB-Conscientiousness showed (1) a significant main effect for Emotion ($F_{(1, 205)} = 5.37$, p $\leq$ .05)

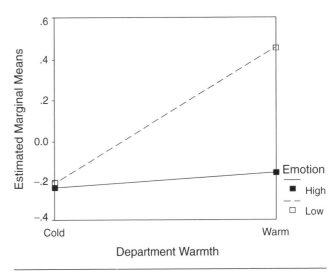

Figure 21.1   The interaction between Emotion and Warmth and OCB-Conscientiousness.

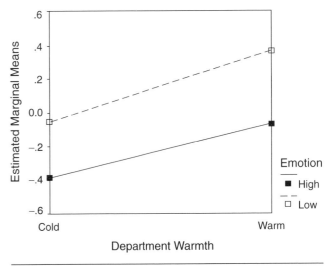

Figure 21.2   Main effects for Emotion and Warmth and OCB-Altruism.

with a partial eta-squared of .026, (2) a significant main effect for Warmth ($F_{(1, 205)} = 6.97$, p $\leq$ .01) with a partial eta-squared of .034, and (3) a significant interaction between Emotion and Warmth ($F_{(1, 205)} = 4.68$, p $\leq$ .05) with a partial eta-squared of .023. Figure 21.1 shows this interaction. This graph shows that individuals who are high on this scale perform about the same level of OCB-Conscientiousness behavior no matter what situation (Cold or Warm) is the context for this behavior. Individuals who are low on the Emotion scale, however, are much more affected by the situation in which they reside. Individuals who are low on this scale and in a department that is high on Warmth perform higher on the OCB-Conscientiousness scale than do low emotion individuals in a cold department.

The results for OCB-Altruism showed (1) a significant main effect for Emotion ($F_{(1, 205)}$ = 8.27, $p \leq .01$) with a partial eta-squared of .040 and (2) a significant main effect for Warmth ($F_{(1, 205)}$ = 7.46, $p \leq .01$) with a partial eta-squared of .036. There was no significant interaction between Emotion and Warmth. Figure 21.2 shows these main effects. Low scorers on the Emotion scale perform at a higher level than do those who score high on this scale. Individuals who are in a warmer department are more likely to perform OCB-Altruism behaviors than are people who reside in a colder department.

CONCLUSION

The growing consensus in personality psychology that the appropriate model for understanding how dispositional and situational variables act to determine behavior is an interactional model (Fleeson, 2004). The person-situation debate, concerning whether consistencies in individuals' behavior are pervasive or broad enough to be meaningfully described in terms of personality traits, can at last be declared about 98 percent over (Funder, 2001). The long-standing dichotomy between the effect of the situation and the person on behavior is a false dichotomy.

Rather, the study of the causes of behavior requires an understanding of the personality triad (Funder, 2001). The empirical study of personality properly has three elements: the person, the situation, and the behavior of interest. This is the personality triad referred to by Funder. Organizational research should be conducted that assesses all three aspects of this triad.

We have provided an example study (Svyantek & Phillips, 2001) that may serve as a guide to research in this area. This study measured (a) person variables using a Big Five type measure of personality, (b) situation variables using an organizational climate instrument, and (c) three different measures of performance. This study showed more complex findings than the standard study that assesses either personality or the situation by itself. This study showed the relationship between personality and situational causes of behavior differed in strength for different performance variables for the same set of subjects. In addition, an interaction was found between a dispositional and situational variable for one performance variable. The findings of (a) differential effects of personality and situation on various criteria and (b) the interactions of personality and situation variable for some criteria provide a much more complex picture of the causes of organizational behavior.

We, therefore, conclude with a call for always using an interactional approach to understanding organizational behavior. Without studying both the employee and the context in which he or she resides, we will always have less understanding than we could of why some individuals are high performers or good organizational citizens and others are poor performers and poor organizational citizens. We believe that the more complex studies necessitated by the interactional approach to personality offer a fascinating and interesting way of understanding the performance of individuals in the workplace that should be the guiding force of organizational research into the effects of personality on workplace behavior in the future.

REFERENCES

Allen, N. J., & Meyer, J. P. (1990). The measurement and antecedents of affective, continuance and normative commitment to the organization. *Journal of Occupational Psychology, 63*, 1–18.

Atwater, L. E. (1992). Beyond cognitive ability: Improving the prediction of performance. *Journal of Business and Psychology, 7*, 27–44.

Baer, M., & Frese, M. (2003). Innovation is not enough: Climates for initiative and psychological safety, process innovations, and firm performance. *Journal of Organizational Behavior, 24*, 45–68.

Barrick, M. R., & Mount, M. K. (1991). The Big Five personality dimensions and job performance: A meta-analysis. *Personnel Psychology, 44*, 1–25.

Barrick, M. R., Mount, M. K., & Judge, T. A. (2001). Personality and performance at the beginning of the new millennium: What do we know and where do we go next? *International Journal of Selection and Assessment, 9*, 9–30.

Barrick, M. R., Stewart, G. L., Neubert, M. J., & Mount, M. K. (1998). Relating member ability and personality to work-team processes and team effectiveness. *Journal of Applied Psychology, 83*, 377–391.

Barrick, M. R., Stewart, G. L., & Piotrowski, M. (2002). Personality and job performance: Test of the mediating effects of motivation among sales representatives. *Journal of Applied Psychology, 87*, 43–51.

Beatty, J. C., Jr., Cleveland, J. N., & Murphy, K. R. (2001). The relation between personality and contextual performance in "strong" versus "weak" situations. *Human Performance, 14*, 125–148.

Bettencourt, L. A., Gwinner, K. P., & Meuter, M. L. (2001). A comparison of attitude, personality, and knowledge predictors of service-oriented organizational citizenship behaviors. *Journal of Applied Psychology, 86*, 29–41.

Block, J. (1995). A contrarian view of the five-factor approach to personality description. *Psychological Bulletin, 117*, 187–215.

Block, J. (2001). Millennial contrarianism: The five-factor approach to personality description five years later. *Journal of Research in Personality, 35,* 98–107.

Borman, W. C., Hanson, M. A., & Hedge, J. W. (1997). Personnel selection. *Annual Review of Psychology, 48,* 299–337.

Borman, W. C., & Motowidlo, S. J. (1993). Expanding the criterion domain to include elements of contextual performance. In N. Schmitt & W. C. Borman (Eds.), *Personnel selection in organizations* (pp. 71–98). San Francisco: Jossey-Bass.

Borman, W. C., Penner, L. A., Allen, T. D., & Motowidlo, S. J. (2001). Personality predictors of citizenship performance. *International Journal of Selection and Assessment, 9,* 52–69.

Borman, S. J., & Van Scotter, J. R. (1994). Evidence that task performance should be distinguished from contextual performance. *Journal of Applied Psychology, 79,* 475–480.

Borucki, C. C., & Burke, M. J. (1999). An examination of service-related antecedents to retail store performance. *Journal of Organizational Behavior, 20,* 943–962.

Boudreau, J. W., Boswell, W. R., & Judge, T. A. (2001). Effects of personality on executive career success in the United States and Europe. *Journal of Vocational Behavior, 58,* 53–81.

Bradley, J. P., Nicol, A. A. M., Charbonneau, D., & Meyer, J. P. (2002). Personality correlates of leadership development in Canadian Forces officer candidates. *Canadian Journal of Behavioural Science, 34,* 92–103.

Bretz, R. D., & Judge, T. A. (1994). Person-organization fit and the theory of work adjustment: Implications for satisfaction, tenure, and career success. *Journal of Vocational Behavior, 44,* 32–54.

Brown, T. J., Mowen, J. C., Donavan, D. T., & Licata, J. W. (2002). The customer orientation of service workers: Personality trait effects on self- and supervisor performance ratings. *Journal of Marketing Research, 39,* 110–119.

Burton, R. M., Lauridsen, J., & Obel, B. (2004). The impact of organizational climate and strategic fit on firm performance. *Human Resource Management, 43,* 67–82.

Cable, D. M., & Judge, T. A. (1996). Person-organization fit, job choice decisions, and organizational entry. *Organizational Behavior and Human Decision Processes, 67,* 294–311.

Cable, D. M., & Judge, T. A. (1997). Interviewer's perceptions of person-organization fit and organizational selection decisions. *Journal of Applied Psychology, 82,* 546–561.

Carr, J. Z., Schmidt, A. M., Ford, J. K., & DeShon, R. P. (2003). Climate perceptions matter: A meta-analytic path analysis relating molar climate, cognitive, and affective state, and individual level work outcomes. *Journal of Applied Psychology, 88,* 605–619.

Chatman, J. A. (1991). Matching people and organizations: Selection and socialization in public accounting firms. *Administrative Science Quarterly, 36,* 459–484.

Colquitt, J. A., Hollenbeck, J. R., Ilgen, D. R., LePine, J. A., & Sheppard, L. (2002). Computer-assisted communication and team decision-making performance: The moderating effect of

openness to experience. *Journal of Applied Psychology, 87,* 402–410.

Costa, P. T., Jr., & McCrae, R. R. (1985). *The NEO Personality Inventory manual.* Odessa, FL: Psychological Assessment Resources.

Costa, P. T., Jr., & McCrae, R. R. (1988). From catalog to classification: Murray's needs and the five-factor model. *Journal of Personality and Social Psychology, 54,* 258–265.

Cronbach, L. J., & Glesser, G. C. (1953). Assessing the similarity between profiles. *Psychological Bulletin, 50,* 456–473.

Day, D. V., & Bedeian, A. G. (1991). Predicting job performance across organizations: The interaction of work orientation and psychological climate. *Journal of Management, 17,* 589–600.

Diefendorff, J. M., Brown, D. J., Kamin, A. M., & Lord, R. G. (2002). Examining the roles of job involvement and work centrality in predicting organizational citizenship behaviors and job performance. *Journal of Organizational Behavior, 23,* 93–108.

Driskell, J. E., Hogan, J., Salas, E., & Hoskin, B. (1994). Cognitive and personality predictors of training performance. *Military Psychology, 6,* 31–46.

Edwards, J. R. (1993). Problems with the use of profile similarity indices in the study of congruence in organizational research. *Personnel Psychology, 46,* 641–665.

Edwards, J. R. (1994). The study of congruence in organizational research: Critique and a proposed alternative. *Organizational Behavior and Human Decision Processes, 58,* 51–100.

Edwards, J. R. (1995). Alternatives to difference scores as dependent variables in the study of congruence in organizational research. *Organizational Behavior and Human Decision Processes, 64,* 307–324.

Edwards, J. R., & Cooper, C. L. (1990). The person-environment fit approach to stress: Recurring problems and some suggested solutions. *Journal of Organizational Behavior, 11,* 293–300.

Edwards, J. R., & Harrison, R. V. (1993). Job demands and worker health: Three-Dimensional reexamination of the relationship between person-environment fit and strain. *Journal of Applied Psychology, 78,* 628–648.

Edwards, J. R., & Parry, M. E. (1993). On the use of polynomial regression equations as alternatives to difference scores in organizational research. *Academy of Management Journal, 36,* 1577–1613.

Ferris, G. R., Bergin, T. G., & Gilmore, D. C. (1986). Personality and ability predictors of training performance for flight attendants. *Group & Organization Studies, 11,* 419–435.

Ferris, G. R., Youngblood, S. A., & Yates, V. L. (1985). Personality, training performance and withdrawal: A test of the person-group fit hypothesis for organizational newcomers. *Journal of Vocational Behavior, 27,* 377–388.

Fisher, C. D. (2002). Antecedents and consequences of real-time affective reactions at work. *Motivation and Emotion, 26,* 3–30.

Fleeson, W. (2004). Moving personality beyond the person-situation debate: The challenge and the opportunity of within-person variability. *Current Directions in Psychological Science, 13,* 83–87.

Funder, D. C. (2001). Personality. *Annual Review of Psychology, 52,* 197–221.

Furlong, M. A., & Svyantek, D. J. (1998). The relationship between organizational climate and personality: A contextualist perspective. *Journal of Psychology and Behavioral Sciences, 12,* 43–53.

Gelade, G. A., & Ivery, M. (2003). The impact of human resource management and work climate on organizational performance. *Personnel Psychology, 56,* 383–404.

Gellantly, I. R., & Irving, P. G. (2001). Personality, autonomy, and contextual performance of managers. *Human Performance, 14,* 231–245.

Goldberg, L. R. (1993). The structure of phenotypic personality traits. *American Psychologist, 48,* 26–34.

Goodman, S. A., & Svyantek, D. J. (1999). Person-organization fit and contextual performance: Do shared values matter? *Journal of Vocational Behavior, 55,* 254–275.

Hannaway, J. (1989). *Managers managing: The workings of an administrative system.* New York: Oxford University Press.

Hurtz, G. M., & Donovan, J. J. (2000). Personality and job performance: The Big Five revisited. *Journal of Applied Psychology, 85,* 869–879.

Judge, T. A., & Bono, J. E. (2000). Five-factor model of personality and transformational leadership. *Journal of Applied Psychology, 85,* 751–765.

Judge, T. A., & Cable, D. M. (1997). Applicant personality, organizational culture and organizational attraction. *Personnel Psychology, 50,* 359–394.

Kabanoff, B., & Bottger, P. (1991). Effectiveness of creativity training and its relation to selected personality factors. *Journal of Organizational Behavior, 12,* 235–248.

Kandis, P., & Williams, D. G. S. (2000). Organisational climate and corporate performance: An empirical investigation. *Management Decision, 38,* 531–540.

Kristof, A. L. (1996). Person-organization fit: An integrative review of its conceptualization, measurement, and implications. *Personnel Psychology, 49,* 1–49.

Lawler, E. E., III, Hall, D. T., & Oldham, G. R. (1974). Organizational climate: Relationship to organizational structure, process, and performance. *Organizational Behavior and Human Performance, 11,* 139–155.

Lee, K., & Allen, N. J. (2002). Organizational citizenship behavior and workplace deviance: The role of affect and cognitions. *Journal of Applied Psychology, 87,* 131–142.

LePine, J. A., Erez, A., & Johnson, D. E. (2002). The nature and dimensionality of organizational citizenship behavior: A critical review and meta-analysis. *Journal of Applied Psychology, 87,* 52–65.

LePine, J. A., & Van Dyne, L. (2001). Voice and cooperative behavior as contrasting forms of contextual performance: Evidence of differential relationships with Big Five personality characteristics and cognitive ability. *Journal of Applied Psychology, 86,* 326–336.

McCrae, R. R. (2001). Five years of progress: A reply to Block. *Journal of Research in Personality, 35,* 108–113.

McCrae, R. R., Costa, P. T., Jr., Ostendorf, F., Angleitner, A., Hrebickova, M., Avia, M. D., et al. (2000). Nature over nurture: Temperament, personality and life span development. *Journal of Personality and Social Psychology, 78,* 173–186.

Miles, D. E., Borman, W. E., Spector, P. E., & Fox, S. (2002). Building an integrative model of extra role work behaviors: A comparison of counterproductive work behavior with organizational citizenship behavior. *International Journal of Selection and Assessment, 10,* 51–57.

Mischel, W. (1977). The interaction of person and situation. In D. Magnusson and N. S. Endler (Eds.), *Personality at the Crossroads: Current Issues in Interactional Psychology.* Hillsdale, NJ: Erlbaum.

Mischel, W. (2004). Toward an integrative science of the person. *Annual Review of Psychology, 55,* 1–22.

Mischel, W., & Shoda, Y. (1998). Reconciling processing dynamics and personality dispositions. *Annual Review of Psychology, 49,* 229–258.

Morris, E. K. (1988). Contextualism: The world view of behavior analysis. *Journal of Experimental Child Psychology, 46,* 289–323.

Motowidlo, S. J., & Van Scotter, J. R. (1994). Evidence that task performance should be distinguished from contextual performance. *Journal of Applied Psychology, 79,* 475–480.

Mount, M. K., Barrick, M. R., & Stewart, G. L. (1998). Five-factor model of personality and performance in jobs involving interpersonal interactions. *Human Performance, 11,* 145–165.

Neuman, G. A., & Kickul, J. R. (1999). Organizational citizenship behaviors: Achievement orientation and personality. *Journal of Business and Psychology, 13,* 263–279.

Nijenhuis, J. T., & van der Flier, H. (2000). Differential prediction of immigrant versus majority group training performance using cognitive ability and personality measures. *International Journal of Selection and Assessment, 8,* 54–60.

Oakes, D. W., Ferris, G. R., Martocchio, J. J., Buckley, M. R., & Broach, D. (2001). Cognitive ability and personality predictors of training program skill acquisition and job performance. *Journal of Business and Psychology, 15,* 523–548.

O'Reilly, C. A., III, Chatman, J., Caldwell, D. F. (1991). People and organizational culture: A profile comparison approach to assessing person-organization fit. *Academy of Management Journal, 34,* 487–516.

Organ, D. W. (1997). Organizational citizenship behavior: It's construct clean-up time. *Human Performance, 10,* 85–97.

Organ, D. W., & Ryan, K. (1995). A meta-analytic review of attitudinal and dispositional predictors of organizational citizenship behavior. *Personnel Psychology, 48,* 775–800.

Ostroff, C. (1993). The effects of climate and personal influences on individual behavior and attitudes in organizations. *Organizational Behavior and Human Decision Processes, 56,* 56–90.

Patterson, M., Warr, P., & West, M. (2004). Organizational climate and company productivity: The role of employee affect and employee level. *Journal of Occupational and Organizational Psychology, 77,* 193–216.

Penney, L. M., & Spector, P. E. (2002). Narcissism and counterproductive work behavior: Do bigger egos mean bigger problems? *International Journal of Selection and Assessment, 10,* 126–134.

Podsakoff, P. M., MacKenzie, S. B., Paine, J. B., & Bachrach, D. G. (2000). Organizational citizenship behaviors: A critical review of the theoretical and empirical literature and suggestions for future research. *Journal of Management, 26,* 513–563.

Potozsky, D., & Ramakrishna, H. V. (2002). The moderating role of updating climate perceptions in the relationship between goal orientation, self-efficacy, and job performance. *Human Performance, 15,* 275–297.

Pritchard, R. D., & Karasick, B. W. (1973). The effects of organizational climate on managerial job performance and job satisfaction. *Organizational Behavior and Human Performance, 9,* 126–146.

Quinn, R. E., & Rohrbaugh, J. (1983). A spatial model of effectiveness criteria: Towards a competing values approach to organizational analysis. *Management Science, 29,* 363–377.

Robertson, I. T., Baron, H., Gibbons, P., MacIver, R., & Nyfield, G. (2000). Conscientiousness and managerial performance. *Journal of Occupational and Organizational Psychology, 73,* 171–180.

Rogg, K. L., Schmidt, D. B., Shull, C., & Schmitt, N. (2001). Human resource practices, organizational climate, and customer satisfaction. *Journal of Management, 27,* 431–449.

Salgado, J. F. (1997). The five factor model of personality and job performance in the European community. *Journal of Applied Psychology, 82,* 30–43.

Salgado, J. F. (1998). Big Five personality dimensions and job performance in Army and civil occupations: A European perspective. *Human Performance, 11,* 271–288.

Sathe, V. (1985). *Culture and related corporate realities.* Homewood, IL: R. D. Irwin.

Savage, R. D., & Stewart, R. R. (1972). Personality and the success of card-punch operators in training. *British Journal of Psychology, 63,* 445–450.

Schein, V. E., & Diamonte, T. (1988). Organizational attraction and the person-environment fit. *Psychological Reports, 62,* 167–173.

Showers, C., & Cantor, N. (1985). Social cognition: A look at motivated strategies. *Annual Review of Psychology. 36,* 275–305.

Singh, S. K., & Dhillon, P. K. (2004). Organizational and personal predictors of role effectiveness. *Journal of Management Research, 4,* 35–44.

Smith-Crowe, K., Burke, M. J., & Landis, R. S. (2003). Organizational climate as a moderator of safety knowledge–safety performance relationships. *Journal of Organizational Behavior, 24,* 861–876.

Suliman, A. M. T. (2002). Is it really a mediating construct? The mediating role of organizational commitment in work climate–performance relationship. *Journal of Management Development, 21,* 170–183.

Svyantek, D. J., Jones, A. P., & Rozelle, R. (1991). The relative influence of organizational decision frames on decision making. *Advances in Information Processing in Organizations, 4,* 127–145.

Svyantek, D. J., & Kolz, A. R. (1996). The effects of organizational frames and problem ambiguity on decision-making. *Journal of Business and Psychology, 11,* 131–150.

Svyantek, D. J., & Philips, J. (2001, June). *A cognitive-affective processing approach to organizational citizenship.* Paper presented at the meeting of the National American Psychological Society, Toronto, Ontario.

Trice, H. M., & Beyer, J. M. (1993). *The cultures of organizations.* Englewood Cliffs, NJ: Prentice Hall.

Witt, L. A., Burke, L. A., Barrick, M. A., Mount, M. K. (2002). The interactive effects of conscientiousness and agreeableness on job performance. *Journal of Applied Psychology, 87,* 164–169.

Yilmaz, G., & Hunt, S. D. (2001). Salesperson cooperation: The influence of relational, task, organizational and personal factors. *Journal of the Academy of Marketing Science, 29,* 335–357.

Zohar, D. (2000). A group-level model of safety climate: Testing the effect of group climate on microaccidents in manufacturing jobs. *Journal of Applied Psychology, 85,* 587–596.

Zohar, D., & Luria, G. (2004). Climate as a social-cognitive construction of supervisory safety practices: Scripts as proxy of behavior patterns. *Journal of Applied Psychology, 89,* 322–333.

CHAPTER 22

Gender, Personality, and Psychopathology

PAULA G. WILLIAMS AND HEATHER E. GUNN

It is often said that gender may be the single most important individual-difference factor, both with respect to self-concept and with respect to how we are perceived and treated by others in the social environment. Thus, consideration of gender and sex roles seems critical to a volume devoted to understanding the everyday functioning aspects of personality and psychopathology.

In this chapter, the key research issues related to how gender, personality, and psychopathology are interrelated are presented. First, the predominant gender differences in personality are reviewed. Both gender differences within traditional personality frameworks (e.g., the Five-Factor Model [FFM] and the interpersonal circumplex model) and research on gender-linked personality (i.e., masculinity and femininity) are considered. Additionally, recent attempts to integrate the study of gender-linked personality with the broader study of personality and individual differences are reviewed. Next, the predominant gender differences in psychopathology are outlined. The remainder of the chapter is devoted to understanding possible models that link gender, personality, and psychological adjustment. Specifically, the question of whether personality differences between males and females can explain gender differences in adjustment and psychopathology is addressed (i.e., Does personality mediate gender-psychopathology relations?). Also considered is the question of whether gender moderates personality-psychopathology relations (i.e., Are the links between personality and adjustment the same for males and females?). The latter includes consideration of the gender effects on some of the hypothesized pathways between personality and psychopathology (e.g., stress and coping). It is beyond the scope of this chapter to provide a comprehensive review of all aspects of gender in the personality-psychopathology realm; rather, the goal is to provide a useful overview of the key literature, provide a framework for considering the broader literature, and provide a look to the future.

With respect to definitions of key terms used in this chapter, *sex* is the term used to describe being biologically male or female; *gender* is a broader term that encompasses the psychological and social aspects of being male or female; and the term *sex role* refers to the behaviors and personality characteristics that are thought to be socialized within society based on being biologically male or female. Sex roles involve conceptions of masculinity and femininity that embody social practices that divide work, power, and social relations by gender (Rosenfield, 2000).

GENDER AND PERSONALITY

Gender-Linked Personality

A host of characteristics that include vocational interests, physical attributes, and personality traits have been ascribed to being male versus female. Taken together, these characteristics have been variously used to describe the multifaceted constructs *masculinity* and *femininity* (Lippa, 2001). Historically, the assessment of masculinity and femininity can be traced back to Terman and Miles (1936) and has its roots in the intelligence testing movement (for an in-depth account of history, see Ashmore, 1990). Measures of masculinity and femininity, such as the Bem Sex-Role Inventory (BSRI; Bem, 1974) and the Personal Attributes Questionnaire (PAQ; Spence, Helmreich, & Stapp, 1974), typically assess positive personality traits that are considered masculine and feminine. Masculine attributes are instrumental or agentic (i.e., involving personal accomplishments and achievement). Feminine attributes are expressive or communal (i.e., a focus on emotional expression, nurturance, and social connectedness). Thus, broadly speaking, masculinity or agency refers to a focus on the self and femininity or communion reflects a focus on others (Helgeson, 1994).

Masculinity/agency and femininity/communion, as assessed by the BSRI and the PAQ, are made up of largely socially desirable characteristics. In order also to assess the extremes (i.e., socially undesirable aspects) of agency and communion, an extended version of the PAQ was developed

(EPAQ; Spence, Helmreich, & Holahan, 1979). The extremes of agency and communion (i.e., unbalanced by the other sex-linked trait) have been termed *unmitigated agency* and *unmitigated communion*. Whereas agency and communion are independent constructs, unmitigated agency is, by definition, related to low communion and unmitigated communion is related to low agency (Helgeson, 1993, 1994; Helgeson & Fritz, 1999). Unmitigated agency (i.e., agency not mitigated by communion) refers to focus on the self to the exclusion of others, whereas unmitigated communion (i.e., communion not mitigated by agency) refers to focus on others to the exclusion of self-focus. Helgeson (1994) notes that although the EPAQ adequately captures the qualities of unmitigated agency, the socially undesirable feminine characteristics assessed do not adequately capture unmitigated communion. As such, she has developed a scale to assess unmitigated communion (Helgeson, 1993; Helgeson & Fritz, 1998).

Gender-Related Interests

Another approach to characterizing gender-related traits is with respect to vocational preferences and interests. This approach has utilized vocational/interest circumplex models, the axes of which have been labeled "People versus Things" and "Data versus Ideas" (Prediger, 1982). For example, women tend to prefer occupations that are focused on people (e.g., teacher), whereas men tend to prefer occupations focused on things (e.g., mechanic). Lippa (2001) argues that one historical problem with masculinity-femininity (M-F) scales is that they contained both personality factors as well as items that tapped gender-related interests, such as those noted previously. He suggests that a separate bipolar M-F individual difference factor might better capture the dimension related to these types of interests and preferences (e.g., occupations, hobbies, everyday activities). To this end, an approach to assessing this M-F factor termed *gender diagnosticity* (GD; Lippa & Connelly, 1990) was developed. This approach uses discriminant analyses of gender-linked interests to compute the probability that an individual is male or female. Interestingly, GD scores are more highly correlated with men's and women's self-assessed masculinity and femininity than are M (instrumentality, agency) or F (expressiveness, communion) measures (Lippa, 1991).

Gender Differences within the Broader Personality Frameworks

The Five-Factor Model (FFM) is a taxonomy that includes the major dimensions of personality that were derived using the lexical approach (i.e., factor analyses of personality descrip-

tors that occur in natural language). Although the Big Five have been designated by a variety of labels, in this chapter we use the dimensions assessed with the NEO-PI-R (Costa & McCrae, 1992), a commonly used instrument to assess the major personality traits. The five factors assessed with this instrument are Neuroticism, Extraversion, Openness to Experience, Agreeableness, and Conscientiousness. In considering gender differences in FFM traits, Corbitt and Widiger (1995) report that males score significantly lower than females in Agreeableness, on average, and make up the majority of individuals who score in the extreme low end of Agreeableness. Males also score in the highest range of excitement seeking (a facet of Extraversion) and have, on average, lower scores on the vulnerability and anxiety facets of Neuroticism compared to females. Females score, on average, higher than males on all facets of Neuroticism. These adult gender differences in FFM personality traits are consistent with studies of infant temperament: Female infants are rated higher in the fear dimension of infant temperament and male infants are rated higher in activity and high-intensity pleasure (Gartstein & Rothbart, 2003).

Interpersonal personality traits have been characterized in terms of the interpersonal mechanisms indexed by the dimensions dominant versus submissive and cold/hostile versus warm/friendly (Kiesler, 1983). Individual differences in interpersonal traits can be described by blends of these two dimensions, organized in a circular order that has come to be known as the interpersonal circumplex (Wiggins, 1982). There are substantial gender differences in the dominant-submissive dimension and the warm-cold dimension (Wiggins, 1991). However, the dimension that most strongly covaries with gender in the interpersonal circumplex is competitive-mistrusting versus deferent-trusting (a blend of the orthogonal coordinates described previously, with the octants often labeled as *arrogant-calculating/vindictive* and *unassuming-ingenuous/exploitable*) (Lippa, 2001). In a meta-analysis of gender differences in personality traits across a variety of models, Feingold (1994) concluded that males were higher than females on assertiveness, whereas females were higher than males on tender-mindedness.

Integration of Gender-Linked Personality and the Broader Personality Frameworks

Although conceptualization and assessment of masculinity and femininity suggest that the characteristics inherent in both constructs might be characterized with respect to broader models of personality, research on gender-linked personality developed largely independently from mainstream trait personality research (Lippa, 2001). Recently, however, attempts have been made to examine the interrelations between gender-related individual differences and the FFM and interpersonal circumplex. For example, the dominance and instrumentality that constitute conceptualizations of M are related to facets of Extraversion, Openness, and Neuroticism; the nurturance and expressiveness that constitute F are related to facets of Agreeableness, Conscientiousness, and Neuroticism (Lippa, 1995). Moreover, as described previously, these aspects (i.e., dominance versus submissiveness, warm-friendly versus cold-hearted) form the axes of the interpersonal circumplex. Indeed, Wiggins (1991) has characterized the interpersonal circumplex in terms of the metatheoretical concepts of agency and communion. Moreover, Wiggins and colleagues (Wiggins & Broughton, 1985; Wiggins & Holzmuller, 1981) have found the M and F scales of the BSRI to be essentially equivalent to standard measures of interpersonal dominance and nurturance. In examining relations between M and F and interpersonal problems, Lippa (1995) found that M is linked to being domineering and vindictive and F to being overly nurturing and exploitable as measured by the Inventory of Interpersonal Problems (Horowitz, Rosenberg, Baer, Ureno, & Villasenor, 1988). Gender diagnosticity (i.e., gender-related interests) is related to social dominance and authoritarianism in men, but not women (Lippa, 1995), but is largely unrelated to Five-Factor personality traits (Lippa, 1991).

With respect to unmitigated agency and unmitigated communion, unmitigated agency is associated with low Agreeableness, as well as low Conscientiousness and high Neuroticism within the FFM, and is captured by the arrogant-calculating (i.e., cold dominance) octant of the interpersonal circumplex (Helgeson & Fritz, 2000). Unmitigated communion, on the other hand, does not map as readily onto the interpersonal circumplex (Helgeson & Fritz, 1999), and the correlations with FFM traits (e.g., with Agreeableness) are accounted for by overlap with communion (Helgeson & Fritz, 1998). Thus, the unique aspects of unmitigated communion have yet to be adequately characterized within the broader personality models.

In general, the personality characteristics ascribed to being masculine and feminine map nicely onto the broader models of personality. As such, it is not surprising that the correlates of M and F with respect to psychological adjustment and psychopathology align with those of the corresponding aspects of the FFM and the interpersonal circumplex.

GENDER DIFFERENCES IN PSYCHOPATHOLOGY

Although it is beyond the scope of this chapter to provide a comprehensive account of gender differences in psychopa-

TABLE 22.1 Gender Differences in the Prevalence of *DSM-IV-TR* Diagnoses

Female prevalence	Male prevalence
Childhood anxiety disorders (ex. OCD)	Conduct disorder (childhood)
Major depressive disorder	Oppositional deviant disorder (childhood)
Rapid cycling bipolar disorder	Attention deficit disorder-hyperactive (childhood)
Bipolar II disorder	
Dysthymic disorder	Rumination (childhood)
Seasonal affective disorder	Learning disorders (all)
Adjustment disorders	Autistic & Asperger's disorders
Generalized anxiety disorder	Sleep terror disorder (childhood)
Panic disorders	Tourette's disorder
Post-traumatic stress disorder	Specific phobias (some)
Somatization disorder	Paraphilias
Conversion disorder	Gender identity disorder
Pain disorder	Substance abuse disorders (most)
Primary insomnia	Obstructive sleep apnea
Nightmare disorder	Sleepwalking disorder
Dissociative identity disorder	Schizophrenia
Depersonalization disorder	Delirium
Anorexia nervosa	Antisocial personality disorder
Bulimia nervosa	Narcissistic personality disorder
Borderline personality disorder	Mental retardation
Dependent personality disorder	
Histrionic personality disorder	

thology, some of the key differences are examined in this section. Table 22.1 lists the *Diagnostic and Statistical Manual of Mental Disorders,* fourth edition, text revision (*DSM-IV-TR;* American Psychiatric Association, 2000) diagnoses that are known to differ in prevalence by gender. Some of these differences first appear in childhood and persist into adulthood. For example, internalizing problems, especially anxiety disorders, are more common in girls, whereas externalizing problems, such as conduct disorder, are more common in boys. The gender difference in all anxiety disorders, except obsessive-compulsive disorder, continues into adulthood. Additionally, beginning in early adolescence, women have higher rates of depression. Men, on the other hand, have higher rates of antisocial personality disorder (APD) and substance-abuse disorders—disorders that have childhood externalizing problems as their precursors. Thus, the internalizing versus externalizing aspect of gender differences in psychopathology appears to be consistent from childhood to adulthood (Rosenfield, 2000).

Although many forms of psychopathology have personality correlates, the personality disorders are, by definition, related to personality traits. In this domain, there are notable gender differences, with men having higher rates of antisocial and narcissistic personality disorder and women having higher rates of borderline, histrionic, and dependent personality disorder. Moreover, women have higher rates of somatization disorder, which, although currently classified as a somatoform disorder, is typically of long duration and interpersonal in nature. Moreover, family studies have shown high rates of antisocial personality disorder in male relatives of female somatization patients (Lilienfeld, Van Valkenburg, Larntz, & Akiskal, 1986). These findings suggest that somatization disorder may be better categorized as a personality disorder (Williams, 2004). Indeed, females with family histories of antisocial personality disorder may be at risk for somatization disorder, histrionic personality disorder, and borderline personality. These findings have led to the hypothesis that cluster B personality disorders may represent variable expressions of a common diathesis, perhaps moderated by gender (Skodol, 2000). For example, some combination of temperament/personality and environmental risk factors for the development of chronic interpersonal problems may manifest themselves differently for males and females.

In considering gender differences in psychopathology, it is important to rule out reporting and treatment-seeking biases as the basis for the difference. This issue has been studied extensively in the case of the higher rate of depression among women versus men. Although there is now substantial evidence from community studies that the gender difference does not derive from women's greater tendency to seek treatment or admit to feelings of depression, self-reports of lifetime depression at least partially may be due to a gender difference in the accuracy of retrospective reporting (Kessler, 2000). Clearly, the issue of reporting and/or help-seeking behavior in gender differences in psychopathology needs continued study. Additionally, potential clinician bias in diagnosis (i.e., based on gender stereotypes) may also affect the reported prevalence rates by gender. This issue is of particular concern in accurate diagnosis of the personality disorders.

There is a vast literature devoted to understanding gender differences in psychological adjustment and psychopathology. Where gender differences exist, research has examined biological, psychological, and social factors and their interaction as potential explanations. We turn now to the interface of gender and personality in the etiology of psychopathology.

Personality as a Mediator of Gender-Psychopathology Relations

Given that there are gender differences in both personality and psychopathology, one hypothesis is that personality mediates the relation between gender and psychopathology (see Figure 22.1A). That is, to what extent are gender differences in psychopathology explained by gender differences in personality? In this regard, both gender-linked personality (i.e., M/agency and F/communion) and gender differences in the broader personality factors are considered.

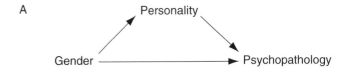

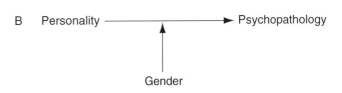

Figure 22.1   Models depicting potential relations between gender, personality, and psychopathology.

In the 1970s, the predominant theoretical perspective was that androgyny was related to superior psychological adjustment. Bem (1974, 1975) argued that individuals who were balanced in masculinity and femininity should have superior adjustment because they could better adapt to varying social circumstances. Subsequent refinement of this hypothesis led to the proposal that being high on both M and F (as opposed to simply balanced) was optimal for adjustment (Bem, 1977; Spence, Helmreich, & Stapp, 1975). Research on androgyny, however, has been fraught with methodological and theoretical shortcomings (Ashmore, 1990; for a discussion of the statistical problems with the androgyny literature, see also Holmbeck, 1989). Reviews of this literature (Markstrom-Adams, 1989) and meta-analyses (Bassoff & Glass, 1982; Whitley, 1983, 1984) conclude that masculinity (compared to androgyny and femininity) is the best predictor of measures of psychological adjustment. In examining multiple measures of psychological adjustment, Lippa (1995) found that although M was related to lower negative affectivity (a factor comprised of measures of neuroticism, depression, self-esteem, and interpersonal problems), it was also related to higher overbearingness, aggressiveness, and, for women, meanness. Femininity has been linked to high levels of eating psychopathology, whereas masculinity is associated with relatively healthy eating-related attitudes and behaviors (Meyer, Blissett, & Oldfield, 2001). In a study of gender-role and personality-disorder features, dependent traits were associated with higher femininity and lower masculinity, whereas antisocial traits were associated with higher masculinity (Klonsky, Serrita, Turkheimer, & Oltmanns, 2002).

Lippa (1995, 2001) notes that the association between masculinity and adjustment may be due, in part, to content overlap between measures (e.g., items such as *self-confident* in M scales and measures of self-esteem). On the other hand, low masculinity is associated with a range of clinician-diagnosed anxiety disorders (Shear, Feske, & Greeno, 2000), a finding that cannot be completely explained by measurement overlap. In general, findings from research on masculinity and femininity and psychological adjustment argue against the early hypothesis that androgyny should be related to better psychological adjustment.

As described previously, Helgeson (1994) has provided support for the notion that neither agency nor communion predicts psychological (or health) problems; rather, it is unmitigated agency and unmitigated communion that predict difficulties. For example, unmitigated communion predicts distress and poor disease control in adolescents with diabetes (Helgeson & Fritz, 1998), depression among coronary patients (Fritz, 2000), and poor adjustment to prostate cancer (Helgeson & Lepore, 1997). Unmitigated agency predicts alcohol and drug use (Snell, Belk, & Hawkins, 1987). Note that these findings are consistent with the overall pattern of women's higher rates of internalizing problems and men's higher rates of externalizing difficulties, though none of these studies directly examined mediation (i.e., whether gender-psychopathology relations drop to nonsignificant levels when gender-linked personality is controlled).

Helgeson and Fritz (2000) note that both unmitigated agency and unmitigated communion are associated with problem behavior and adjustment problems, though for different reasons. Unmitigated agency is linked to unwillingness to attend to relationships and a negative view of others, whereas unmitigated communion is related to a tendency to subjugate one's own needs to the needs of others and dependency on others for self-esteem.

As described previously, there are gender differences in the broader personality traits that make up the FFM and interpersonal circumplex model. Interestingly, specific tests of whether gender differences in personality explain gender differences in various psychopathologies do not routinely appear in the literature. Women's higher levels of neuroticism are an obvious possible mediator for the gender difference in mood disorders, given the strong link between neuroticism and anxiety and depression (Clark, Watson, & Mineka, 1994; Jorm et al., 2000). In one study examining this possibility, Goodwin and Gotlib (2004) found that when levels of neuroticism were statistically controlled, the gender difference in depression dropped, though still remained significant. On the other hand, when history of having any anxiety disorder is controlled, the gender difference in depression drops to marginally significant levels (Breslau, Chilcoat, Peterson, Schultz, 2000). Though additional research is needed, it ap-

pears that higher levels of neuroticism among women may at least partly explain women's higher levels of anxiety and depression compared to men. Because neuroticism is a risk factor for a variety of adjustment problems, examining this personality factor as a mechanism for women's higher rates of some adjustment problems and diagnoses, particularly those characterized by internalizing symptoms, seems warranted. Likewise, whether men's higher levels of some personality factors (e.g., excitement-seeking, low agreeableness) place them at risk for externalizing problems (e.g., antisocial behavior) deserves further scrutiny.

Gender as a Moderator of Personality-Psychopathology Relations

In the prior section, the possibility that personality mediates the relationship between gender and adjustment was explored. Another hypothetical model for the relations between gender, personality, and psychopathology is whether or not gender moderates the relationship between personality and psychological adjustment (Figure 22.1b). That is, is the strength of personality-psychopathology relations the same for men and women? For example, does neuroticism predict symptoms of anxiety and depression equally well for males and females? Given the overwhelming evidence that there are socialization differences between males and females, it seems likely that at least some temperament/personality characteristics may manifest themselves differently in men and women or present varying risks for psychopathology by gender. Unfortunately, interactions with gender appear to be rarely examined in studies linking personality to adjustment/psychopathology outcome measures. Studies of childhood temperament suggest that gender may moderate temperament-psychopathology relations. For example, Lengua, Sandler, West, Wolchik, and Curran (1999) found that negative emotionality predicted depression in boys but not in girls following the divorce of their parents. Similarly, Colder, Mott, and Berman (2002) found that high activity/low fear in infancy predicted escalating externalizing and internalizing symptoms and that high fear/low activity predicted escalating depression symptoms in boys but not in girls. These studies illustrate the importance of examining gender as a moderator of temperament risk for childhood behavior problems. In an example of testing gender as a moderator in the adult personality-psychopathology literature, Ruiz, Pincus, and Dickinson (2003) examined gender-interaction effects in a study of personality effects on alcohol use. Facets of Neuroticism, Conscientiousness, and Extraversion were associated with alcohol use and alcohol-related problems; however, gender did not moderate these effects (Ruiz, Pincus, & Dickinson, 2003).

Although examining gender by personality interactions is the soundest method for examining moderation, testing personality-psychopathology relations separately by gender is also informative. This approach has been more commonly used, particularly in studies of adjustment and psychopathology correlates of masculinity and femininity. For example, Lippa (1995) reports separate analyses by gender for the relations between M, F, and GD and measures of psychological adjustment. As described previously, gender diagnosticity was related to social dominance and authoritarianism in men but not in women; masculinity was related to meanness in women but not in men. These findings illustrate that both sex and personality (whether gender-linked or not) should be considered.

Gender Effects on Pathways between Personality and Psychopathology

Although the literature that has directly studied the moderating effects of gender on personality-psychopathology relations is small, we can examine the extent to which gender is related to the key pathways by which personality may affect psychological adjustment. In this section, we examine gender effects on some of the hypothesized mechanisms by which personality is linked to psychopathology. In particular, we consider gender differences in stress and coping and gender differences in physical health and functional disability.

Stress and Coping

One of the primary mechanisms by which personality differences may be related to psychopathology is via stress responses. Individual differences in the frequency of stressors (or stress exposure), stress appraisal and reactivity, and stress coping have all been associated with risk for both mental and physical health problems (e.g., Coyne & Downey, 1991; Kiecolt-Glaser, McGuire, Robles, & Glaser, 2002; Lovallo, 1997). To the extent that there are gender differences in stress and coping, this represents a potential mechanism for the relation between gender-linked personality and psychopathology. Additionally, gender differences in stress and coping suggest that gender may moderate this important pathway between personality and psychological adjustment.

A large literature has investigated gender and stress using a variety of methodologies. With respect to stress measurement, research has tended to focus on three types of stress: major life events, daily hassles, and laboratory stressors. To some extent, gender differences have been documented in each of these types of stress.

With respect to stress exposure, most research supports the view that women experience more life stress. In a meta-analytic review, Davis, Matthews, and Twamley (1999) found that women had higher rates of life stress compared to men. When severe, traumatic stress is considered, women also have higher stress exposure than do men. For example, rape and other forms of sexual trauma are more prevalent in women, and women are more often victims of domestic violence. Kessler (2000) notes that women's higher rate of traumatic stress fully explains the gender difference in post-traumatic stress disorder (PTSD) but does not completely account for the female excess in depression. Moreover, exposure to stressful life experiences is higher among people with a history of depression. The impact of stress on the onset of depressive episodes is stronger among people with a history of depression. Women are more likely than men to have a history of depression, which may explain findings regarding differential exposure and reactivity to stress.

In addition to major life stressors, women report more daily life hassles than men, which appears to at least partly explain women's higher levels of psychological distress. In a diary study of daily hassles and emotions, Almeida and Kessler (1998) found that women reported more frequent hassles, and this accounted for their higher levels of emotional distress. They did not find that women reported more prolonged distress (i.e., carryover effects). This finding challenges a prior hypothesis that women tend to ruminate about daily events, serving to amplify and prolong negative mood states (Nolen-Hoeksema, 1987). It is noteworthy that there are gender differences in the type of stressors that evoke distress; men report more stress related to financial problems, whereas women are more responsive to interpersonal stressors and family demands (Almeida & Kessler, 1998).

The prevailing hypothesis for women's higher rates of daily hassles is that women's marital and parenting roles contribute to greater stress exposure (Kiecolt-Glaser & Newton, 2001). In terms of time spent within the marriage, women tend to contribute more to domestic roles, whereas men tend to contribute less. In addition, it has been proposed that domestic chores and duties may make it more difficult for women to unwind when working outside the home, particularly among women with children. The inability to unwind and relax may play a role in disruption of important circadian rhythms, which may lead to negative health consequences and poorer mental health status (Frankenhaeuser, 1991).

Studies examining gender differences in self-reported major life events and daily stressors have been important in determining how naturally occurring stressors affect men and women differently. Laboratory stressors, on the other hand, have been central to examining how stressors directly affect physiological reactivity. As with other measures of stress, gender differences have emerged in response to laboratory stressors. Gender differences in physiological reactivity vary by the type of stressor used and by the type of response being measured. Overall, men appear to be more reactive to laboratory stressors (Kiecolt-Glaser & Newton, 2001; Traustadottir, Bosch, & Matt, 2003). However, when laboratory social-interaction tasks are utilized, women have been shown to be more reactive (Bloor, Uchino, Hicks, & Smith, 2004; Ennis, Kelly, & Lambert, 2001; Kiecolt-Glaser & Newton, 2001; Stroud, Salovey, & Epel, 2002).

Collectively, findings across studies of major life events, daily hassles, and laboratory stress tasks, seem to represent a salient pattern in agreement with the agency and communion literature. The types of stressors that most strongly affect men tend to have agency-related qualities (i.e., individual performance-based), whereas those reported by women tend to be communion-related (i.e., focus on others). This pattern is not only present in reported stress, but it is also evident in the literature on physiological responses to stress. Further, data from the laboratory and the field represent converging evidence that the same types of stressors that induce reactivity in the lab are also those that are associated with negative physiological outcomes in a naturalistic setting.

In addition to differences between males and females in stress exposure and reactivity, there are gender differences in stress-coping strategies. Studies examining preferred stress-coping strategies find that men tend to use problem-focused strategies, whereas women tend to use support-seeking and emotion-focused coping strategies (Ptacek, Smith, & Zanas, 1992). In a review of the biobehavioral stress responses in females, Taylor and colleagues (Taylor et al., 2000) characterize women as being more likely to tend and befriend in times of stress (as opposed to fight or flight, which the authors consider a characteristic male stress response). Tending (i.e., nurturing behavior) has been linked to oxytocin (a peptide). Oxytocin is also related to food satiety and is released at orgasm and during childbirth. Behaviorally, oxytocin is related to affiliative behavior, for example, pair bonding, peer bonding, and parental behavior. Women's greater tendency toward a tend-and-befriend response to stress, and the hypothesized release of oxytocin in this process, has been associated with reduced physiological responses to stress and quicker recovery in women (Taylor et al., 2000).

Recently, the role of oxytocin has received attention as a potentially important factor in the onset of depression in adolescent girls. Frank & Young (2000) describe animal research that demonstrates that the large, pubertal increase in oxytocin is related both to sexual behavior and to attachment in females but only to sex drive in males. They posit that a similar pubertal change occurs in adolescent humans and that the combination of increased desire for pair bonding among girls and increase only in sexual desire among boys sets the stage for distress among females. Specifically, when affiliative needs in adolescent girls are frustrated through real or symbolic breaches in affiliative bonds, the hormonal changes of puberty interact with interpersonal and romantic disappointments of adolescence to produce depressive symptoms and, in some cases, syndromal depression. Indeed, examination of the kinds of stressful events that seem to be associated with onset of depression in women suggests that many of these events represent breaches in affiliative bonds (Brown, Harris, & Hepworth, 1995).

These findings with respect to depression illustrate the potential moderating effect of gender: Males and females are hypothesized to experience a similar physiological change (in this case, oxytocin increase), but the behavioral manifestation of this change varies with gender, the results of which make females vulnerable to psychological distress. This example also highlights the potentially important, but often overlooked, role of genetic/biological factors in gender-related personality and behavior. Indeed, the animal research suggests that the female orientation toward others (i.e., communion) may, at least in part, be driven by genetically determined physiological processes.

In general, it seems that we find a similar pattern in the stress-buffering literature in relation to the agency and communion literature. Overall, it seems that the social networks play a key role in women's stress responses and psychological adjustment. Women's social networks are larger, and, although that may confer greater benefits from social support, it may also lead to increased interpersonal stress (Shumaker & Hill, 1991). Women appear to be more reactive than men when their social network is disrupted, however; social affiliations also play a role alleviating stress responses. Men, on the other hand, appear to be more negatively affected by achievement, work, or financial stressors, although it is not certain if positive occurrences in this area are associated with stress buffering.

Physical Health and Functional Disability

The interface of physical and mental health has become a topic of considerable interest in recent years. Physical health and psychopathology may be linked in several ways. Physical illness, particularly chronic illness, confers risks of mental health problems, especially depression. Premorbid psychopathology may place individuals at risk for subsequent physical health problems or poor adjustment to chronic illness (Taylor & Aspinwall, 1996). Additionally, both mental health and physical health problems may co-occur because of common physiological processes driving both (e.g., stress reactivity). A large body of research has been devoted to the study of personality effects on physical health. As described previously, gender-linked personality has been implicated in the development of both psychological adjustment problems and poor physical health outcomes. Thus, one potential mechanism by which gender may affect personality-psychopathology relations is via physical health and concomitant functional disability.

For example, there are reliable gender differences in perceived health. Women rate their overall health to be worse and report more physical symptoms than do men (National Center for Health Statistics [NCHS], 1994; Verbrugge, 1985; Williams & Wiebe, 2000). The gender difference in self-assessed health emerges in early adolescence and has been shown to be an antecedent risk factor for depressive symptoms (Williams, Colder, Richards, & Scalzo, 2002). There is much speculation that the reason that poor self-assessed health leads to depressed mood is functional disability. Specifically, individuals who assess their physical health to be poor may take measures to adopt the sick role, which leads to withdrawal from reinforcing life activities, setting the stage for low positive affect, and social isolation that makes one vulnerable to depressed mood. Consistent with this notion, women take more sick days from work, take more prescription and nonprescription medication, and make more physician visits (NCHS, 1994). Thus, to the extent that women have a greater propensity to become functionally disabled (i.e., to adopt the sick role) and to the extent that functional disability may be a pathway between personality and psychological adjustment, gender may play an important moderating role in personality-psychopathology relations.

Gender differences in sleep may also be an important consideration. The relationship between neuroticism and sleep problems has now been well documented (Gray & Watson, 2002). To the extent that women, either because of sex-role expectations (e.g., division of labor in childrearing) or personality (e.g., higher N)—or the interaction between the two—experience sleep disruption, they are at increased risk for a host of mental problems. Indeed, sleep disruption is often a precursor to depression (Ohayon & Roth, 2003) and sleep disruption may be the final common pathway to postpartum affective disturbance, such as mania (Wehr, Sack, & Rosenthal, 1987).

CONCLUSIONS AND FUTURE DIRECTIONS

In considering the relationship between personality and psychological adjustment, it is clear that the role of gender must be taken into account. This chapter has provided an overview of the vast literature on gender-linked personality (i.e., M/agency, F/communion) as well as gender differences in traditional personality traits. As often happens in the study of individual differences, independent lines of research have yielded a collection of gender-related personality descriptors that appear to be overlapping constructs, both in relation to each other and in relation to personality traits of the FFM and the interpersonal circumplex. Future research should consider the following question: Is it necessary to have a separate collection of gender-linked personality constructs or can these be more parsimoniously characterized within existing personality theories? Although there may be historical reasons why the study of gendered personality characteristics developed and evolved separately from the personality/individual-differences tradition within psychology, movement toward a common nomenclature would facilitate communication across these divisions of psychology that, in many ways, have common goals.

Beyond the exercise of outlining gender differences in personality and psychopathology, we have considered hypothesized models of the role gender might play in personality-psychopathology relations (Figure 22.1). Research on gender differences in personality certainly suggests that personality factors may mediate the relation between gender and psychological adjustment. Unfortunately, few studies have tested this hypothesis directly. Future research focused on explicating the mechanisms for gender differences in psychopathology should examine whether personality factors can account for these differences.

Additionally, the role of gender as a moderator in personality-psychopathology pathways has been underexamined. Several studies reviewed strongly suggest that the strength of relations between temperament/personality and psychology adjustment differ by gender. Future studies of personality and psychopathology should, where possible, include a sample balanced in gender and examine gender by personality interactions on key outcomes. Only in this way can we confidently conclude that findings regarding personality predictors of psychological adjustment apply equally to males and females.

The literature on gender effects on pathways between personality and adjustment suggests fruitful directions for future research. In particular, this literature would benefit from an increased focus on gender effects at the biological, social, developmental nexus of personality and psychopathology. Although explanations for sex differences in psychological and behavioral variables have long been the focus of research and debate (e.g., evolutionary versus sociocultural theories), examination of the interaction of physiological, social, and developmental processes has been lacking. For example, the behavior-genetic research that has become commonplace in the study of the traditional personality traits has been sorely lacking in the study of gendered personality. Moreover, there is preliminary evidence that there are gender differences in the contribution of genetic factors to personality (Brummett et al., 2003; Du, Bakish, & Hrdina, 2000). Relevant questions include: Are there genetic differences between males and females that result in different temperaments? Does genetically determined temperament manifest itself differently for males and females, and can this be explained by socialization differences? At what point in development are these differences first evident and why? What are the implications for prevention and treatment of psychological and behavioral difficulties?

Clearly, gender is a pivotal individual difference variable to be considered in understanding the role of personality in psychological adjustment. Not only are there significant gender differences in personality, but gender may be a critical moderator of how personality is manifest and of how (and whether) personality predicts psychopathology. Despite the impressive body of research that has accumulated on the interrelations among gender, personality, and psychological adjustment, there is still much we do not know. The routine consideration of gender in future studies of personality, emotion, stress, and psychological adjustment will ensure a better understanding of how and why being male versus being female affects the quality of our everyday lives.

REFERENCES

Almeida, D. M., & Kessler, R. C. (1998). Everyday stressors and gender differences in daily distress. *Journal of Personality and Social Psychology, 75,* 670–680.

American Psychiatric Association (2000). *Diagnostic and statistical manual of mental disorders.* (4th ed., text rev.). Washington, DC: Author.

Ashmore, R. D. (1990). Sex, gender, and the individual. In L. A. Pervin (Ed.), *Handbook of personality theory and research* (pp. 486–526). New York: Guilford Press.

Bassoff, E. S., & Glass, G. V. (1982). The relationship between sex roles and mental health: A meta-analysis of twenty-six studies. *Counseling Psychologist, 10,* 105–112.

Bem, S. L. (1974). The measurement of psychological androgyny. *The Journal of Consulting and Clinical Psychology, 42,* 155–162.

Bem, S. L. (1975). Sex role adaptability: One consequence of psychological androgyny. *Journal of Personality and Social Psychology, 31,* 634–643.

Bem, S. L. (1977). On the utility of alternative procedures for assessing psychological androgyny. *Journal of Consulting and Clinical Psychology, 45,* 196–205.

Bem, S. L. (1981). Gender schema theory: A cognitive account of sex typing. *Psychological Review, 88,* 354–364.

Bloor, L. E., Uchino, B. N., Hicks, A., & Smith, T. W. (2004). Social relationships and physiological function: The effects of recalling social relationships on cardiovascular reactivity. *Annals of Behavioral Medicine, 28*(1), 29–38.

Breslau, N., Chilcoat, H. D., Peterson, E. L., & Schultz, L. R. (2000). Gender differences in major depression: The role of anxiety. In E. Frank (Ed.), *Gender and its effects on psychopathology* (pp. 131–150). Washington, DC: American Psychiatric Press.

Brown, G. W., Harris, T. O., & Hepworth, C. (1995). Loss, humiliation and entrapment among women developing depression: A patient and non-patient comparison. *Psychological Medicine, 25,* 7–21.

Brummett, B. H., Siegler, I. C., McQuoid, D. R., Svenson, I. K., Marchuk, D. A., & Steffens, D. C. (2003). Associations among the NEO Personality Inventory, revised, and the serotonin transporter gene-linked polymorphic region in elders: Effects of depression and gender. *Psychiatric Genetics, 13,* 13–18.

Clark, L. A., Watson, D., & Mineka, S. (1994). Temperament, personality, and the mood and anxiety disorders. *Journal of Abnormal Psychology, 103,* 103–116.

Colder, C. R., Mott, J. A., & Berman, A. S. (2002). The interactive effects of infant activity level and fear on growth trajectories of early childhood behavior problems. *Development and Psychopathology, 14,* 1–23.

Corbitt, E. M., & Widiger, T. A. (1995). Sex differences among the personality disorders: An exploration of the data. *Clinical Psychology: Science and Practice, 2,* 225–238.

Costa, P. T., Jr., & McCrae, R. R. (1992). *Revised NEO Personality Inventory (NEO PI-R) and NEO Five-Factor Inventory (NEO-FFI): Professional manual.* Odessa, FL: Psychological Assessment Resources.

Coyne, J. C., & Downey, G. (1991). Social factors and psychopathology: Stress, social support, and coping processes. *Annual Review of Psychology, 42,* 401–425.

Davis, M. C., Matthews, K. A., & Twamley, E. W. (1999). Is life more difficult on Mars or Venus? A meta-analytic review of sex differences in major and minor life events. *Annals of Behavioral Medicine, 21*(1), 83–97.

Du, L., Bakish, D., & Hrdina, P. D. (2000). Gender differences in the association between serotonin transporter gene polymorphism and personality traits. *Psychiatric Genetics, 10,* 159–164.

Ennis, M., Kelly, K. S., & Lambert, P. L. (2001). Sex differences in cortisol excretion during anticipation of a psychological stressor: Possible support for the tend-and-befriend hypothesis. *Stress & Health: Journal of the International Society for the Investigation of Stress, 17*(4), 253–261.

Feingold, A. (1994). Gender differences in personality: A meta-analysis. *Psychological Bulletin, 116,* 429–456.

Frank, E., & Young, E. (2000). Pubertal changes and adolescent challenges: Why do rates of depression rise precipitously for girls between ages 10 and 15 years? In E. Frank (Ed.), *Gender and its effects on psychopathology* (pp. 85–102). Washington, DC: American Psychiatric Press.

Frankenhaeuser, M. (1991). The psychophysiology of workload, stress, and health: Comparison between the sexes. *Annals of Behavioral Medicine, 13,* 197–204.

Fritz, H. L. (2000). Gender-linked personality traits predict mental health and functional status following a first coronary event. *Health Psychology, 19,* 420–428.

Gartstein, M. A., & Rothbart, M. K. (2003). Studying infant temperament via the revised infant behavior questionnaire. *Infant Behavior & Development, 26,* 64–86.

Goodwin, R. D., & Gotlib, I. H. (2004). Gender differences in depression: The role of personality factors. *Psychiatry Research, 126*(2), 135–142.

Gray, E. K., & Watson, D. (2002). General and specific traits of personality and their relation to sleep and academic performance. *Journal of Personality, 70,* 177–206.

Helgeson, V. S. (1993). Implications of agency and communion for patient and spouse adjustment to a first coronary event. *Journal of Personality and Social Psychology, 64,* 807–816.

Helgeson, V. S. (1994). Relation of agency and communion to well-being: Evidence and potential explanations. *Psychological Bulletin, 116,* 412–428.

Helgeson, V. S., & Fritz, H. L. (1998). A theory of unmitigated communion. *Personality and Social Psychology Review, 2,* 173–183.

Helgeson, V. S., & Fritz, H. L. (1999). Unmitigated agency and unmitigated communion: Distinctions from agency and communion. *Journal of Research in Personality, 33,* 131–158.

Helgeson, V. S., & Fritz, H. L. (2000). The implications of unmitigated agency and unmitigated communion for domains of problem behavior. *Journal of Personality, 68,* 1031–1057.

Helgeson, V. S., & Lepore, S. J. (1997). Men's adjustment to prostrate cancer: The role of agency and unmitigated agency. *Sex Roles, 37*(3–4), 251–267.

Holmbeck, G. N. (1989). Masculinity, femininity, and multiple regression: Comment of Zeldow, Daugherty, and Clark's "Masculinity, femininity, and psychosocial adjustment in medical students: A 2-year follow-up." *Journal of Personality Assessment, 53,* 583–599.

Horowitz, L. M., Rosenberg, S. E., Baer, B. A., Ureno, G., & Villasenor, V. S. (1988). Inventory of interpersonal problems: Psychometric properties and clinical applications. *Journal of Consulting & Clinical Psychology, 56*(6), 885–892.

Jorm, A. F., Christensen, H., Henderson, A. S., Jacomb, P. A., Korten, A. E., & Rodgers, B. (2000). Predicting anxiety and depression from personality: Is there a synergistic effect of neuroticism and extraversion? *Journal of Abnormal Psychology, 109,* 145–149.

Kessler, R. C. (2000). Gender differences in major depression: Epidemiological findings. In E. Frank (Ed.), *Gender and its effects on psychopathology* (pp. 61–84). Washington, DC: American Psychiatric Press.

Kiecolt-Glaser, J. K., McGuire, L., Robles, T. E., & Glaser, R. (2002). Emotions, morbidity, and mortality: New perspectives from psychoneuroimmunology. *Annual Review of Psychology, 53,* 83–107.

Kiecolt-Glaser, J. K., & Newton, T. L. (2001). Marriage and health: His and hers. *Psychological Bulletin, 127*(4), 472–503.

Kiesler, D. J. (1983). The 1982 interpersonal circle: A taxonomy for complementarity in human transactions. *Psychological Review, 90,* 185–214.

Klonsky, E. D., Serrita, J. J., Turkheimer, E., & Oltmanns, T. F. (2002). Gender role and personality disorders. *Journal of Personality Disorders, 16,* 464–476.

Lengua, L. J., Sandler, I. N., West, S. G., Wolchik, S. A., & Curran, P. J. (1999). Emotionality and self-regulation, threat appraisal, and coping in children of divorce. *Development and Psychopathology, 11,* 15–37.

Lilienfeld, S. O., Van Valkenburg, C., Larntz, K., & Akiskal, H. S. (1986). The relationship of histrionic personality disorder to antisocial personality and somatization disorders. *American Journal of Psychiatry, 143,* 718–722.

Lippa, R. A. (1991). Some psychometric characteristics of gender diagnosticity measures: Reliability, validity, consistency across domains and relationship to the Big Five. *Journal of Personality and Social Psychology, 61,* 1000–1011.

Lippa, R. A. (1995). Gender-related individual differences and psychological adjustment in terms of the Big Five and circumplex models. *Journal of Personality and Social Psychology, 69,* 1184–1202.

Lippa, R. A. (2001). On deconstructing and reconstructing masculinity-femininity. *Journal of Research in Personality, 35,* 168–207.

Lippa, R. A., & Connelly, S. C. (1990). Gender diagnosticity: A new Bayesian approach to gender-related individual differences. *Journal of Personality and Social Psychology, 59,* 1051–1065.

Lippa, R. A., Martin, L. R., & Friedman, H. S. (2000). Gender-related individual differences and mortality in the Terman longitudinal study: Is masculinity hazardous to your health? *Personality & Social Psychology Bulletin, 26*(12), 1560–1570.

Lovallo, W. R. (1997). *Stress and health: Biological and psychological interactions.* Thousand Oaks, CA: Sage.

Markstrom-Adams, C. (1989). Androgyny and its relation to adolescent psychosocial well-being: A review of the literature. *Sex Roles, 21,* 325–340.

Meyer, C., Blissett, J., & Oldfield, C. (2001). Sexual orientation and eating psychopathology: The role of masculinity and femininity. *International Journal of Eating Disorders, 29,* 314–318.

National Center for Health Statistics. (1994). Vital and health statistics: Current estimates from the National Health Interview Survey, 1992. Series 10, No. 189. Washington, DC: U.S. Government Printing Office.

Nolen-Hoeksema, S. (1987). Sex differences in unipolar depression: Evidence and theory. *Psychological Bulletin, 101,* 259–282.

Ohayon, M. M., & Roth, T. (2003). Place of chronic insomnia in the course of depressive and anxiety disorders. *Journal of Psychiatric Research, 37,* 9–15.

Prediger, D. J. (1982). Dimensions underlying Holland's hexagon: Missing link between interests and occupations? *Journal of Vocational Behavior, 21,* 259–287.

Ptacek, J. T., Smith, R. E., & Zanas, J. (1992). Gender, appraisal, and coping: A longitudinal analysis. *Journal of Personality, 60,* 747–770.

Rosenfield, S. (2000). Gender and dimensions of the self. In E. Frank (Ed.), *Gender and its effects on psychopathology* (pp. 23–36). Washington, DC: American Psychiatric Press.

Ruiz, M. A., Pincus, A. L., & Dickinson, K. A. (2003). NEO PI-R predictors of alcohol use and alcohol-related problems. *Journal of Personality Assessment, 81,* 226–236.

Shear, M. K., Feske, U., & Greeno, C. (2000). Gender differences in anxiety disorders: Clinical implications. In E. Frank (Ed.), *Gender and its effects on psychopathology* (pp. 151–165). Washington, DC: American Psychiatric Press.

Shumaker, S. A., & Hill, D. R. (1991). Gender differences in social support and health. *Health Psychology, 10,* 102–111.

Skodol, A. E. (2000). Gender specific etiologies for antisocial and borderline personality disorders? In E. Frank (Ed.), *Gender and its effects on psychopathology* (pp. 37–58). Washington, DC: American Psychiatric Press.

Snell, W. E., Belk, S. S., & Hawkins, R. C., II. (1987). Alcohol and drug use in stressful times: The influence of the masculine role and sex-related personality differences. *Sex Roles, 16,* 359–373.

Spence, J. T., Helmreich, R. L., & Holahan, C. K. (1979). Negative and positive components of psychological masculinity and femininity and their relationships to self-reports of neurotic and acting out behaviors. *Journal of Personality and Social Psychology, 37,* 1673–1682.

Spence, J. T., Helmreich, R. L., & Stapp, J. (1974). The Personal Attributes Questionnaire: A measure of sex role stereotypes and masculinity-femininity. *JSAS Catalog of Selected Documents in Psychology, 4,* 43–44.

Spence, J. T., Helmreich, R. L., & Stapp, J. (1975). Ratings of self and peers on sex role attributes and their relation to self-esteem and conceptions of masculinity and femininity. *Journal of Personality and Social Psychology, 32,* 29–39.

Stroud, L. R., Salovey, P., & Epel, E. S. (2002). Sex differences in stress responses: Social rejection versus achievement stress. *Biological Psychiatry, 52,* 318–327.

Taylor, S. E., & Aspinwall, L. G. (1996). Psychosocial aspects of chronic illness. In P. T. Costa Jr. & G. R. VandenBos (Eds.), *Psychosocial aspects of serious illness: Chronic conditions, fatal diseases, and clinical care* (pp. 3–60). Washington, DC: American Psychological Association.

Taylor, S. E., Klein, L. C., Lewis, B. P., Gruenewald, T. L., Gurung, R. A. R., & Updegraff, J. A. (2000). Biobehavioral responses to stress in females: Tend-and-befriend, not fight-or-flight. *Psychological Review, 107*(3), 411–429.

Terman, L. M., & Miles, C. C. (1936). *Sex and personality: Studies in masculinity and femininity.* New York: McGraw-Hill.

Traustadottir, T., Bosch, P. R., & Matt, K. S. (2003). Gender differences in cardiovascular and hypothalamic-pituitary-adrenal axis responses to psychological stress in healthy older adult men and women. *Stress, 6*(2), 133–140.

Verbrugge, L. M. (1985). Gender and health: An update on hypotheses and evidence. *Journal of Health and Social Behavior, 26,* 156–182.

Wehr, T. A., Sack, D. A., & Rosenthal, N. E. (1987). Sleep reduction as a final common pathway in the genesis of mania. *American Journal of Psychiatry, 144,* 201–204.

Whitley, B. E., Jr. (1983). Sex-role orientation and self-esteem: A critical meta-analytic review. *Journal of Personality and Social Psychology, 44,* 765–778.

Whitley, B. E., Jr. (1984). Sex-role orientation and psychological well-being: Two meta-analyses. *Sex Roles, 12,* 207–225.

Wiggins, J. S. (1982). Circumplex models of interpersonal behavior in clinical psychology. In P. C. Kendell & J. N. Butcher (Eds.), *Handbook of research methods in clinical psychology* (pp. 183–221). New York: Wiley.

Wiggins, J. S. (1991). Agency and communion as conceptual coordinates for the understanding and measurement of interpersonal behavior. In W. M. Grove & D. Cicchetti (Eds.), *Thinking clearly about psychology: Vol. 2. Personality and psychopathology* (pp. 89–113). Minneapolis: University of Minnesota Press.

Wiggins, J. S., & Broughton, R. (1985). The Interpersonal Circle: A structural model for the integration of personality research. In R. Hogan & W. H. Jones (Eds.), *Perspectives in personality* (Vol. 1, pp. 1–41). Greenwich, CT: JAI Press.

Wiggins, J. S., & Holzmuller, A. (1981). Further evidence on androgyny and interpersonal flexibility. *Journal of Research in Personality, 15,* 67–80.

Williams, P. G. (2004). The psychopathology of self-assessed health: A cognitive approach to health anxiety and hypochondriasis. *Cognitive Therapy and Research, 28,* 629–644..

Williams, P. G., Colder, C. C., Richards, M. H., & Scalzo, C. A. (2002). The role of self-assessed health in the relationship between gender and depressive symptoms among adolescents. *Journal of Pediatric Psychology, 27,* 509–517.

Williams, P. G., & Wiebe, D. J. (2000). Individual differences in self-assessed health: Gender, neuroticism, and physical symptom reports. *Personality and Individual Differences, 28,* 823–835.

CHAPTER 23

A Classification of *DSM-IV-TR* Mental Disorders According to Their Relation to the Personality System

JOHN D. MAYER

PERSONALITY AND PSYCHOPATHOLOGY: SOME BACKGROUND

Personality can be regarded as an individual's pattern of psychological processes, including his or her motives, feelings, thoughts, and other major areas of psychological function. That is, the individual's personality is roughly synonymous with the major trends in his or her psychological, mental, functioning. These trends are expressed, in turn, through their influences on the individual's brain and body, conscious experience, and social behavior. The term *personality,* as employed here, is similar to the terms *psychological* and *mental* but emphasizes a person's general mental functioning and deemphasizes more specific processes such as those of sensation, perception, and other basic biopsychological and cognitive operations. These latter processes are relatively subsidiary, more circumscribed, or discrete and modular in their function, and although they help the personality system carry out its tasks, they remain relatively distinct from it.

Personality psychologists traditionally have studied both the strengths of the personality system and its weaknesses (O'Connor, 2002; Seligman & Csikszentmihalyi, 2000; Tellegen, 1994). If an individual's personality functioning becomes disturbed, that person is sometimes said to suffer from a mental disorder, such as a major depressive disorder, generalized anxiety disorder, or antisocial personality disorder, among many others. These disorders have been organized in the *Diagnostic and Statistical Manual of Mental Disorders (DSM)* published by the American Psychiatric Association. The *DSM* represents the scientific and legal approach to cate-

gorizing psychopathology in the United States. Its several editions have recorded the myriad ways in which human personality can become problematic—from declining function, to conflicts with society, to impairments that reach into and disturb bodily function. (The most recent editions of the *DSM* include: *Diagnostic and Statistical Manual of Mental Disorders,* third edition *[DSM-III],* 1980; *Diagnostic and Statistical Manual of Mental Disorders,* third edition, revised *[DSM-III-R],* 1994; *Diagnostic and Statistical Manual of Mental Disorders,* fourth edition *[DSM-IV],* 1994; *Diagnostic and Statistical Manual of Mental Disorders,* fourth edition with text revisions *[DSM-IV-TR],* 2000.) The most recent, the fourth edition with text revisions (*DSM-IV-TR*), is of telephone-book thickness and lists hundreds of disorders.

The *DSM* is primarily a medical-diagnostic document. The mental disorders it covers are not organized in a manner obviously relevant to personality psychology, except that it does describe an area termed *personality disorders.* Nor has the discipline of personality psychology developed a convincing means to organize the *DSM* disorders or to describe how such disorders relate to personality, although some connections have been made, particularly as regards the personality disorders (Costa & Widiger, 2002; Millon, 2002).

The standard field-wide outline of personality psychology is reflected in the discipline's personality's textbooks and reviews. That standard outline organizes the field by the different theories of personality: the psychodynamic, humanistic, psychobiological, and social-cognitive (Burger, 2000; Funder, 2001; Larsen & Buss, 2002). The *DSM-IV-TR,* on the other hand, employs a relatively pragmatic approach, deemphasizing any specific theoretical perspectives on psychopathology (Segal & Coolidge, 2001). This most recent edition has focused on making psychodiagnosis more reliable and valid than earlier approaches (Spitzer & Fleiss, 1974).

In personality psychology, a new field-wide framework is emerging that is more compatible with the *DSM-IV-TR* than

Acknowledgments: Zorana Ivcevic and Michael Faber read earlier drafts of this manuscript, and their comments led to a greatly strengthened chapter. I am also indebted to the editor, Daniel L. Segal, whose encouragement motivated me to attempt the project described here.

the older theoretical perspectives framework. This new approach is systems-oriented and draws on the original vision of personality psychology as an integrative discipline (Cloninger, 1996; Mayer, 2005a; Pervin, 2003). A specific example is the Systems Framework for Personality Psychology. It uses a pantheoretical approach to examine personality's parts, organization, and development (Mayer, 1998).

Seeking an integrated look at personality and psychopathology can reveal aspects of both. It can lead to a productive importing of methodological and conceptual tools from one area to the other (Sternberg & Grigorenko, 2001). This chapter introduces an organization of mental disorders found in the *DSM-IV-TR* and relates the disorders to personality using the Systems Framework for Personality Psychology (Mayer, 1994, 1998). Considerable compatibility is found between *DSM-IV-TR* and the Systems Framework for Personality in terms of how they define personality. At the same time, however, the *DSM* does not apply its definition of personality in a consistent or convincing way to its own diagnostic categories (e.g., Pfohl, 1999).

The "Background" section of this chapter briefly describes the evolution of the *DSM* classifications and then describes the Systems Framework for Personality. The section "A Comparison of the Personality Concept within Contemporary Personality Psychology and *DSM-IV*" examines the definition of personality in the *DSM* and the Systems Framework. In the section "Sorting of *DSM* Disorders in a Contemporary Personality Psychology Framework," a suggested regrouping of *DSM* disorders in relation to the personality system is proposed. The final section, "Discussion," elaborates how such a reclassification can illuminate issues of personality and psychopathology: Can current divisions of personality be useful in understanding *DSM* classifications? Does a discrete group of personality disorders really exist? If so, what distinguishes them?

BACKGROUND

The Diagnostic and Statistical Manual of Mental Disorders

Many descriptions of the *DSM* and its history already exist, so this section will present only a brief summary of this material. Psychiatric diagnosis arguably had its start in Ancient Mesopotamia and Egypt, where abnormal behavior was first recorded. These observations were then formalized as diagnostic categories and further developed with time (Segal & Coolidge, 2000; Veith, 1970).

Modern compendiums of psychiatric diagnoses are often dated to the systems of Kraepelin and Bleuler (Jablensky,

1995). The precursors of the U.S. *DSM* classification can be dated to a 1917 collaboration between the American Medical Association and the U.S. Bureau of the Census (American Psychiatric Association, 1994, p. xvii). This was then expanded into the *Standard Classified Nomenclature of Disease* during World War II (American Medical Association, 1942).

The first *DSM* was published in 1952. It had been expanded as a consequence of its extensive use in the Veteran's Administration following World War II. Four years before that, in 1948, the World Health Organization published diagnostic standards for mental disorders, in the *International Classification of Diseases (ICD-6)*, and since then there have been ongoing attempts to coordinate the classifications. Both the original 1952 edition of the *DSM* and its 1968 revision, *DSM-II*, were heavily influenced by psychodynamic conceptions of mental illness. Empirical studies of the *DSM*, however, were raising troubling issues as to the reliability and validity of the diagnostic categories (Spitzer & Fleiss, 1974).

In response to this, a new direction was taken for *DSM-III*. That volume was more empirically based, placed greater emphasis on behaviorally observable criteria over formulations of underlying personality processes, and included field studies of the reliability of diagnostic formulations. The *DSM-III* was also greatly expanded, containing far more diagnoses than ever before.

Like the *DSM-III*, the current *DSM-IV-TR* is heavily empirical. It intentionally steers clear of much discussion of the etiology or theoretical perspectives on disorders and focuses instead on their classification. It is organized into clusters of apparently related disorders. The more florid and obvious of these are coded on Axis I and include schizophrenic disorders, mood disorders, and disorders first usually diagnosed in infancy and childhood. Subtler, easier-to-miss disorders are coded on Axis II and it is there that the personality disorders are diagnosed (Nathan & Lagenbucher, 1999). Yet some disorders on Axis I, such as mood disorders, are also arguably disorders of personality or, at least, disorders of parts of personality (McDermut, Zimmerman, & Chelminski, 2003; Westen & Shedler, 1999).

The Systems Framework for Personality Psychology

The field of personality psychology is an area burgeoning with important contemporary research. The most current and comprehensive representations of this research represent it topically (Pervin & John, 1999). Such presentations occur without an accommodating framework that illustrates the interrelations among its topics. If one examines the majority of college textbooks in the area, they follow a theory-by-theory framework, proceeding through chapters or groups of chapters on the personality theories of the (mostly) early- to mid-twentieth century: psychodynamic, humanistic, trait, bioevolutionary, and social-cognitive perspectives. This framework shares little in common with research now carried out in the field, although good-faith efforts have been made to connect the two (Funder, 2002).

To fully integrate textbooks and research in the discipline of personality psychology likely requires a new field-wide framework. One such new framework is the Systems Framework for Personality Psychology (Mayer, 1994, 1998, 2005b). This framework builds on a vision of personality psychology as the discipline responsible for the integrated view of an individual. Human personality itself is viewed as the collective functioning of a person's major psychological subsystems—a person's motives, emotions, thoughts, the self, and so on. To create that integrated vision, personality is studied according to four topics that comprehensively encompass the field's concerns: (1) identifying personality, (2) analyzing personality's parts, (3) understanding personality organization, and (4) charting personality development.

The first topic, identifying personality, concerns personality's definition, boundaries, and relationships with other systems such as the body and outside social world. The general awareness of personality's position amid other systems of scientific study elucidates the scientific methods necessary to employ when examining it. Personality's position also determines some of the theoretical orientations likely to be of use (e.g., biological or social perspectives).

The second topic, analyzing personality's parts, examines the many relatively discrete parts of personality and their expressions. These parts run the gamut from an individual's basic urges and motivations, to the person's emotional style, to the unique mental models the individual may hold of him or herself. The parts further include the individual's mental abilities such as intelligence and creativity, the inner experience of consciousness, and the capacity for self-control.

The third topic is understanding personality organization. This topic examines both personality structure and dynamics. Personality structure concerns how personality's parts can be organized by, for example, the functional areas of which they are a part. For instance, one set of parts relates to an individual's emotionality; another set relates to the individual's cognitions. Recognizing distinct structural areas of emotion and cognition can be of assistance in keeping the parts straight. This structural organization will be of particular focus here because it can be used to group mental disorders according to the specific area of personality function they involve. For

example, mood disorders are specifically related to the individual's emotion system; mental retardation relates to the cognitive system. The topic of personality organization also concerns dynamic processes that lead to the expression of personality and its self-control, as might be involved in substance-abuse disorders. These dynamics help explain how personality operates as a whole.

The fourth systems topic, charting personality development, is concerned with understanding growth and change. It tracks the psychosocial tasks faced by the growing, developing individual and the personality's stability and possible changes across the life span. In regard to psychopathology, this topic pertains to why many disorders are characterized by a specific age of onset, how personality might have been impacted to bring about a mental disorder, and what treatments might be used to improve the problem, or work around it.

A COMPARISON OF THE PERSONALITY CONCEPT WITHIN CONTEMPORARY PERSONALITY PSYCHOLOGY AND *DSM-IV*

The *DSM-IV-TR* is a book of mental disorders although it contains a section on personality disorders. A mental disorder is described as "a clinically significant behavioral or psychological syndrome or pattern that occurs in an individual and that is associated with present distress . . . impairment . . . a significantly increased risk of suffering death . . . or an important loss of freedom" (American Psychiatric Association, 2000, p. xxxi).

For *DSM, mental disorder* is a broad concept, and personality disorders encompass a relatively narrow subset of those mental disorders—including only about a dozen diagnoses out of several hundred.[1] To understand the *DSM*'s treatment of personality, it helps to examine its section on personality disorders. The description of a personality disorder begins with an implicit definition of personality as "an enduring pattern of inner experience and behavior" (American Psychiatric Association, p. 685). It later notes that the personality pattern arises from areas of affectivity, cognition, interpersonal functioning, and impulse control. The *DSM*'s emphasis on patterns befits the purpose of its endeavor: to search for and identify patterns of pathology.

The Systems Framework for Personality Psychology employs quite similar definitions of personality. For example:

> Personality is the organized, developing psychological system within the individual that represents the collective action of that individual's major psychological subsystems. (Mayer, 2000)

This definition can be elaborated here as follows:

> Personality refers to an individual's pattern of psychological processes arising from motives, feelings, thoughts, and other major areas of psychological function. Personality is expressed through its influences on the body, in conscious mental life, and through an individual's social behavior.

Certainly the *DSM*'s conception of personality, with its attention to ongoing patterns, fits readily within the framework and is consistent with the general thrust of the discipline of personality psychology.[2] Yet, given the *DSM*'s definition of personality, its application of the term to only the narrow group of personality disorders appears quite limited. Certainly, for example, a dysthymic mood disorder, which gives rise to an enduring pattern of inner dysphoria and depression, might be a personality disorder, but it is not so labeled in the *DSM-IV* (Westen & Shedler, 1999).

The next section applies the views of personality shared by *DSM* and the Systems Framework for Personality in a methodical fashion to the *DSM* diagnostic categories. Doing so will help classify the disorders in a new fashion that can provide insight into personality, psychopathology, and their relation.

SORTING OF *DSM* DISORDERS IN A CONTEMPORARY PERSONALITY PSYCHOLOGY FRAMEWORK

In the previous section, the definitions of personality employed in the *DSM-IV-TR* and in the Systems Framework for Personality Psychology were described as quite similar. The *DSM,* however, does not apply the personality concept it employs in any consistent fashion. In this section, the *DSM* classification system is reenvisioned, with its disorders arranged according to a more comprehensive application of the personality concept. In this new approach, a great number of disorders will be classified according to the specific areas of personality they influence; another set of disorders will be grouped together because they appear to influence the whole personality.

The first step in the recategorization process was to collect representative disorders from *DSM-IV-TR.* Sixteen of the chapters of the *DSM-IV-TR* represent 16 different clusters of disorders. These clusters involve such disorders as (cluster 1) disorders usually first diagnosed in infancy, childhood, or adolescence, (cluster 5) schizophrenia and other psychotic disorders, and (cluster 16) personality disorders. Some of these clusters, such as (cluster 4) substance-related disorders,

describe relatively homogeneous groups of disorders whereas others of these clusters represent a diverse variety of disorders, such as the aforementioned cluster 1, disorders usually first diagnosed in infancy, childhood, or adolescence.

Table 23.1 lists these 16 clusters, and illustrates them with between three and nine constituent disorders. Those clusters that were particularly diverse or salient were typically represented with greater numbers of disorders. Those clusters that were more homogeneous and/or less observed were represented by fewer disorders. Cluster 3, mental disorders due to a general medical condition, was not represented because of the known, expressly organic conditions that account for them.

After the disorders were collected in Table 23.1, a group of them were identified that appeared to influence one or another specific areas of personality. The disorders, which are covered in the section "Specific Area Disorders of Personality," affected such distinct areas of personality as its emotions system, cognition, or social interaction. On the other hand, a second group of disorders appeared to influence the whole personality. Later, remaining disorders were examined and further categories were developed. The following sections describe these placements.

Specific Area Disorders of Personality

The assignment of mental disorders to specific areas of personality requires the initial division of personality into specific areas of function. It is always possible to divide a complex system such as personality in more than one way. Psychologists will be familiar with such divisions as the conscious, preconscious, and unconscious (Freud, 1917/1966); the id, ego, and superego (Freud, 1923/1960); and conation, affect, and motivation (Hilgard, 1980; Mayer, Chabot, & Carlsmith, 1997; Mendelssohn, 1971). Although multiple divisions of mind are possible, any division must meet adequate criteria for dividing personality. Minimally, it should (a) be few in number, (b) comprehensively divide the system, (c) employ distinct divisions, and (d) employ valid areas of personality (Mayer, 2003).

One division of personality that meets these criteria quite well is the systems set. The systems set divides personality into four areas: (a) an energy lattice corresponding roughly to motivation and emotion; (b) a knowledge works corresponding to the mental models of one's own self and models of the world as well as the intelligences that operate on them; (c) a social actor corresponding to automatically expressed social tendencies, role knowledge, attachments, and plans to

TABLE 23.1   List of *DSM* Groups of Mental Disorders Covered, with Specific Examples

DSM group	Mental disorders
1. Disorders usually first diagnosed in infancy, childhood, or adolescence	Attention deficit disorder, attention deficit hyperactivity disorder, communication disorders (e.g., stuttering, Tourette's disorder), conduct disorder, mental retardation, pervasive developmental disorders (e.g., Asperger's disorder, autistic disorder), reactive attachment disorder, learning disorder, elimination disorders (e.g., encopresis, enureses)
2. Delirium, dementia, amnestic, and other cognitive disorders	Amnestic disorder (due to a general medical condition), dementia: Alzheimer's, dementia: head trauma
3. Mental disorders due to a general medical condition	Not covered
4. Substance-related disorders	Alcohol abuse/dependence, cannabis abuse/dependence, hallucinogen abuse/dependence
5. Schizophrenia and other psychotic disorders	Catatonic schizophrenia, disorganized schizophrenia, paranoid schizophrenia, delusional disorder, schizoaffective disorder
6. Mood disorders	Bipolar disorder, major depressive disorder, cyclothymic disorder, dysthymic disorder
7. Anxiety disorders	Acute stress disorder, agoraphobia, generalized anxiety disorder, panic disorder
8. Somatoform disorders	Body dysmorphic disorder, conversion disorder, hypochondriasis, somatization disorder
9. Factitious disorders	Psychological factitious disorder, physical factitious disorder
10. Dissociative disorders	Dissociative fugue, depersonalization disorder, dissociative identity disorder
11. Sexual and gender identity disorders	Female orgasmic disorder, male erectile disorder, exhibitionism, pedophilia, gender identity disorder
12. Eating disorders	Anorexia nervosa, bulimia nervosa
13. Sleep disorders	Sleep terror disorder, breathing-related disorder, narcolepsy, hypersomnia, insomnia
14. Impulse-control disorders not elsewhere classified	Intermittent explosive disorder, kleptomania, pathological gambling
15. Adjustment disorders	Adjustment disorder with anxiety, adjustment disorder with depressed mood
16. Personality disorders	Obsessive-compulsive personality disorder, schizoid personality disorder, schizotypal personality disorder, avoidant personality disorder, dependent personality disorder, histrionic personality disorder, narcissistic personality disorder, paranoid personality disorder, passive-aggressive personality disorder,* antisocial personality disorder

*Diagnostic criteria provided by *DSM-IV-TR* for further study.

act; and (d) a conscious executive corresponding to awareness and self-control (Mayer, 2001).

The systems set arose from a process in which, first, roughly four hundred parts of personality were collected from nine different theoretical perspectives. Second, the parts were clustered together into roughly twenty groups based on functional considerations of personality as a whole (Mayer, 1995). Third, broad divisions were made among the clusters using the most proven distinctions among mental processes, such as those between conscious and unconscious, emotion and thought, and the like. The resulting structural division was formulated to meet the criteria of a good division of personality. It outperforms earlier structural divisions in organizing diverse traits by areas of personality described (Mayer, 2003). When judges classified personality change techniques of psychotherapy according to the areas of personality they most influenced using the systems set, a meaningful division similarly arose, again with adequate interjudge agreement (Mayer, 2003, 2004).[3]

Many disorders of the *DSM* clusters of disorders correspond to one of these four areas of personality. For example, mood and anxiety disorders fall within the energy lattice (motivation and emotion). Mental retardation and various cognitive disorders fall within the knowledge works. Factitious and communication disorders fall within the social actor. Finally, certain dissociative disorders fall within the conscious executive.

The systems set is a first division of personality, and there also exist blended areas (many personality traits fall within these blended areas). One important such blend is the self, which involves a combination of the conscious executive and self-related portions of the knowledge works. Many dissociative and depersonalization disorders concern the functioning of the self. A second blend is the enactor—an area depicting motives that are more-or-less expressed in a direct

TABLE 23.2   Mental Disorders Specific to Areas of Personality

I. Disorders of the conscious executive	Diagnosed in infancy, childhood [1*]: attention deficit disorder Dissociative disorders [10*]: dissociative fugue
I–II blend: Disorders of the self	Dissociative disorders [10*]: depersonalization disorder, dissociative identity disorder
II. Disorders of the energy lattice	Mood disorders [6*]: bipolar disorders, depressive disorders Anxiety disorders [7]: acute stress disorder, agoraphobia, generalized anxiety, panic disorder Sexual disorders [11*]: female orgasmic disorder, male erectile disorder Sleep disorders [13*]: sleep terror disorder
III. Disorders of the knowledge works	Diagnosed in infancy, childhood [1*]: mental retardation, pervasive developmental disorders (e.g., Asperger's disorder, autistic disorder), learning disorders Delirium, dementia [2*]: amnestic disorder (due to a general medical condition) Diagnosed in infancy, childhood [1*]: communication disorders (e.g., stuttering, Tourette's disorder)
II–IV blend: Disorders of the enactor	Personality disorders [16*]: obsessive-compulsive personality disorder Diagnosed in infancy, childhood [1*]: attention deficit hyperactivity disorder Sexual disorders [11*]: exhibitionism, pedophilia Impulse control disorders N.E.C. [14]: intermittent explosive disorder, kleptomania, pathological gambling
IV. Disorders of the social actor	Diagnosed in infancy, childhood [1*]: conduct disorder, reactive attachment disorder Factitious disorders [9]: psychological factitious disorder, physical factitious disorder

*Split category; some disorders assigned elsewhere.

social manner (e.g., blending the energy lattice and social actor). Here were included sexual exhibition and various impulse disorders. These are shown in Table 23.2. This is a provisional classification by the author, and a more definitive arrangement would require the use of a group of expert judges.

Disorders of Personality Adjustment and Adaptation

What Is a Personality Disorder?

It would be convenient if disorders of the whole personality corresponded to the *DSM*'s category of personality disorders, and this may be the case to some extent. It is common to point out that the personality disorders in *DSM* are of questionable reliability and difficult to distinguish from one an-

other (Coolidge & Segal, 1998; Westen & Shedler, 2000). Less commonly noted—but a potential contributing cause of the diagnostic difficulties in the category—is the fact that the definition of personality disorders itself is quite problematic.

Six criteria for a personality disorder are listed in the *DSM*. Of those, two are concerned with distinguishing mental disorders from normal mental processes and arguably apply to any disorder in the volume. These two criteria, A and C, state that personality disorders represent a pattern that: "(A) . . . deviates markedly from the expectations of an individual's culture . . . [and], (C) . . . leads to clinically significant distress or impairment in social, occupational, or other important areas of functioning" (American Psychiatric Association, 2000, p. 689).

Another of the criteria, D, is a developmental criterion that states that the disorder is of "stable and of long duration," that is, can be traced back to adolescence or early adulthood. This, too, could be seen to apply to many, though not all, disorders, including bipolar disorder, schizophrenia, mental retardation, the paraphilias, and so on. Two more criteria are the exclusionary rules included in almost all diagnoses. These include that the disordered pattern cannot be accounted for by (E) another mental disorder or by (F) a general medical condition (e.g., head trauma; American Psychiatric Association, 2000, p. 689).

That leaves one very interesting criterion that is unique to this group: That personality disorders are (B) "inflexible and pervasive across a broad range of personal and social situations" (American Psychiatric Association, 2000, p. 689).

Of inflexibility and pervasiveness, the inflexibility criterion appears to lack empirical support. The symptoms of personality disorders appear to be somewhat changeable. Some indirect evidence for this comes from the fact that measurement instruments show poor test-retest reliability for personality disorders over periods greater than six weeks (First et al., 1995; Zimmerman, 1994). More directly, developmental studies indicate greater flexibility of personality disorders than at first had been supposed (Shea & Yen, 2003).

Pervasiveness and Personality Disorders

The more distinctive criterion, then, is the pervasiveness of the disorder. That is, *DSM* distinguishes the personality disorders best when claiming that they span the whole personality system, relative to other disorders which influence more specific parts of mental life. Personality disorders appear to describe the individual's global aims, goals, and issues of living that, ultimately, permeate the person's entire psychology. To diagnose a personality disorder involves investigating such questions as: "What does the person wish for and fear?

. . . How does the person perceive and experience self and others, and how is he or she able to sustain . . . relationships?" (Westen & Shedler, 1999, p. 274).

This category might better be labeled *disorders of personality adaptation and adjustment* to emphasize that the disorders concern an individual's global adaptation to life as opposed to a focal problem in a specific psychological area, as is the case with the earlier-described *specific area disorders of personality*. The Systems Framework for Personality Psychology does, of course, represent personality as a system. There is an explicit recognition that an effect on one part of personality (e.g., moods) will influence another area (e.g., cognition). So the boundary between focal problems and general adaptation is a continuum; nonetheless, a need for a distinction on this basis seems implicit in the very notion of the personality disorders, at least as it is viewed here.

The disorders of personality adjustment and adaptation are identified here as follows:

> The individual's personality and its expression, although mostly functional, have globally adapted to a social niche or role that is personally sub-optimal, socially unrewarding, or socially disapproved of. The individual's urges, feelings, beliefs, and aims are generally functional and yet support a role which is negatively influencing the individual's internal mental status, and/or negatively impacting those around him or her.

A complete definition would then go on to add in the formulaic outline of a mental disorder (e.g., causes impairment, danger to the self or others, etc.).

Table 23.3 divides disorders of personality adjustment and adaptation into four areas: disorders of (1) internal personal adjustment, (2) social adjustment, (3) social relationships, and (4) social transgression. Each subtype has its own somewhat more specific description. For example, the mildest category is the disorders of social adjustment. These disorders correspond to adjustment disorders and can be described as occurring when an individual's psychological resources are committed to changing feelings, beliefs, or behavior to fit a new, or otherwise challenging, social environment.

For disorders of personal adjustment, the key feature is the presence of unusual, odd, or eccentric beliefs and behaviors that deviate from generally shared norms. For example, that reality is more tenuous in relation to how others perceive it (schizophrenic-spectrum disorders), or that reality is better or worse than how others see it (cyclothymic and dysthymic disorders).

Disorders of social relationships include as key the presence of beliefs such as that one is much more—or less—deserving than others or that one must dramatize one's needs or depend on others to maintain relationships.

TABLE 23.3   Mental Disorders of Global Personality Adjustment and Adaptation

Disorders of internal personal adjustment	Personality disorders [16*]: schizoid personality disorder, schizotypal personality disorder, avoidant personality disorder Mood disorders [6*]: cyclothymic disorder, dysthymic disorder
Disorders of social adjustment	Adjustment disorders [15]: adjustment disorder with anxiety, adjustment disorder with depressed mood Sexual and gender identity disorder [11*]: gender identity disorder
Disorders of social relationships	Personality disorders [16*]: dependent personality disorder, histrionic personality disorder, narcissistic personality disorder, paranoid personality disorder, passive-aggressive personality disorder**
Disorders of social transgression	Personality disorders [16*]: antisocial personality disorder Substance-related disorders [4]: alcohol abuse/dependence, cannabis abuse/dependence, hallucinogen abuse/dependence

*Represents a split category.
**Diagnostic criteria provided by *DSM-IV-TR* for further study.

Disorders of social transgression, which include both sociopathy and certain drug-abuse disorders, involve holding or living by socially sanctioned beliefs, such as that other people exist to be used or exploited (sociopathic) or that psychoactive drug use and abuse are a needed part of life (certain instances of substance abuse).

Further Categories

The disorders not yet covered can be encompassed in two further broad categories. The first of these, disorders of global personality malfunction, includes the degenerative disorders in which the illness affects multiple areas of function at once. These disorders represent a global type of organic and social deterioration rather than representing a functioning personality with problematic beliefs and aims. Included would be the schizophrenic disorders as well as certain organic-process disorders such as Alzheimer's disorder. They are shown in Table 23.4.

The final category is that of disorders linking the mind and the body. These would include somatoform disorders and certain sleep disorders, among others, shown in Table 23.5. When these two additional areas are included, all the disorders of the *DSM-IV-TR* represented in Table 23.1 are taken into account.

TABLE 23.4   Mental Disorders of Global Personality Malfunction

| Problems of general reality contact | Schizophrenia and other psychotic disorders [5]: catatonic schizophrenia, disorganized schizophrenia, paranoid schizophrenia, delusional disorder, schizoaffective disorder |
| | Delirium, dementia, and amnestic and other cognitive disorders [2*]: dementia, Alzheimer's; dementia, head trauma |

*Represents a split category.

TABLE 23.5   Mental Disorders Linking Personality and the Body

Disorders of under- or overcontrol of the body and its functions	Diagnosed in infancy, childhood [1*]: elimination disorders (e.g., encopresis, enureses)
	Eating disorders [12]: anorexia nervosa, bulimia nervosa
	Sleep disorders [13*]: breathing-related disorder, narcolepsy, hypersomnia, insomnia
Disorders of personality-body perception, communication, and understanding	Somatoform disorders [8]: body dysmorphic disorder, hypochondriasis, conversion disorder, somatization disorder

*Represents a split category.

DISCUSSION

Summary of Argument

In this chapter, the definition of personality employed in *DSM-IV-TR* and in the Systems Framework for Personality Psychology were compared, and they were found to be compatible. The great divergence of *DSM-IV-TR* from the Systems Framework for Personality Psychology is in how it applies the definition of personality to its own classification of mental disorders. Although *DSM* uses a fairly broad and general definition of personality, it does not use the concept of personality well in organizing its coverage. For example, dysthymic disorder, which plainly describes a type of impaired personality functioning, is not considered a personality disorder, though it might well be (Westen & Shedler, 1999).

In this chapter, a group of *DSM* disorders was sampled from 16 clusters corresponding to the 16 relevant chapters of the manual. These disorders then were divided into four broad new categories. The categories were: (1) mental disorders specific to areas of personality, (2) disorders of global personality adjustment and adaptation, (3) disorders of global personality malfunction, and (4) disorders linking personality and the body.

First are disorders of specific areas of personality. These are disorders that have as their primary influence a specific area of an individual's psychological (or personality, or men-

tal) function, such as the emotions area or cognitive area. Examples include mood disorders (affecting motivation and emotion) and mental retardation (affecting knowledge).

Second are disorders of general personality and personal adjustment. These are disorders that reflect global adjustments of an individual in the world that are either personally unsatisfying or disapproved of socially. Examples include many adjustment disorders, and the group of *DSM*-defined personality disorders, including those in which a person may violate ethical and moral principles or important legal boundaries.

Third are disorders of global personality malfunction. These are disorders that reflect the deterioration of function across several areas of personality. They include the schizophrenias and dementing illnesses such as Alzheimer's dementia.

Fourth are disorders linking personality and the body. These are disorders in which the interaction between personality and the body is disrupted in a way that causes personal distress and/or social impairment. They include somatoform disorders and some sleep disorders.

In one sense, these four categories can be thought of as superordinate to the 16 chapters that collectively organize all the disorders of the *DSM*. The 16 original *DSM* clusters fit into these four broad areas, but only imperfectly because some of the 16 clusters fall into one, two, or more categories and medical disorders leading to mental disorders were not covered here.

Implications for the Organization of the *DSM*

The present *DSM* segregates personality disorders on its own axis (labeled Axis II), separate from Axis I disorders. According to *DSM-IV-TR:*

> Axis II is for reporting Personality Disorders and Mental Retardation. It may also be used for noting prominent maladaptive personality features and defense mechanisms. (American Psychiatric Association, 2000, p. 28)

The *DSM* guidelines go on to note that the listing of personality disorders and mental retardation on a separate axis ensures that they will not be overlooked in comparison to the usually more florid Axis I disorders.

How might this viewpoint change given the present perspective? A revision that would in part approximate this approach would retain Axis I for disorders of specific areas of personality, and use Axis II for disorders of general personality. This would entail moving mental retardation, for example, from Axis II to Axis I (it does meet criteria for being florid in many cases and is hard to miss). In turn, certain quite general disorders, such as the schizophrenias, would be placed on Axis II. In essence, Axis II disorders would describe the general personality context within which more specific disorders would be operative. That is, Axis I might code a bipolar disorder in the context of an Axis II narcissistic personality disorder, much as it does now, but after this revision, it might also code mental retardation (Axis I) in the context of disorganized schizophrenia (Axis II), or generalized anxiety disorder (Axis I) in an adjustment disorder (Axis II), or factitious disorder (Axis I) in a person with a substance-abuse disorder (Axis II).

A number of alternatives also would be possible. Just to take one: The disorders of general personality malfunction, such as schizophrenia and other psychoses, might also be placed on their own new axis. Such a new placement would more clearly distinguish disorders that either (a) affect a part of personality or (b) are maladaptive and global but otherwise functional from (c) a globally malfunctioning mental system.

Conclusions: On Cross-Fertilizing the Fields of Psychopathology and Personality

The establishment of a personality-psychology approach to *DSM* can further foster bonds between personality psychology and abnormal psychology. Abnormal psychology can shed light on normal psychology by representing the extremes of behavior involved as well as by casting critical parts of personality (self-absorption, exploitative beliefs) in relief. At the same time, personality psychology can provide descriptive and explanatory models that are more helpful in better understanding aspects of psychopathology.

The twin literatures of personality psychology and abnormal psychology appear to map on to one another with remarkably little adjustment needed on either side. More specifically, the use of a transitional classification, as illustrated in this chapter, can align the *DSM* classification with personality approaches, with little further change than reorganizing the chapters/clusters of the *DSM*.

Creating a cross-classification between the Systems Framework for Personality Psychology and the *DSM* serves the important purpose of bringing together literatures in abnormal psychology and in standard personality psychology. For example, personality psychologists may be impressed to learn of the extensive research on distinguishing whether personality disorders are different in degree (dimensions) or kind (taxons) (e.g., Lenzenweger, 1999; Rothschild, Cleland, & Haslam, 2003).

The framework for personality employed here is systems based. It contains the basic idea that, yes, there are identifiable parts of personality, but they are only relatively independent of one another. Changing one part will cause the other parts to change as a consequence, because of their interrelations. So even those disorders that affect one area

(mood) also affect the whole personality. That can facilitate research into treatment and into how symptoms spread from one area to another—that is, how mood disorders affect thinking. Of course, people have been studying such relation for years (Forgas, 2001). The Systems Framework for Personality, however, provides a more systematic way to organize findings and to understand their implications.

Because of its systematic organizational properties, the Systems Framework for Personality Psychology also can integrate thinking across disciplines. For example, the systems set was recently employed to assign specific therapeutic techniques to parts of personality. These techniques included such examples as interpreting defense, helping the client through role playing, and systematic desensitization (Mayer, 2004). One could imagine juxtaposing these specific clinical treatments selected for the part of personality they influence, with the *DSM* disorders associated with the same areas of personality. The correspondences would allow for an inspection as to whether the treatments that affect a specific area of personality are used in an effective manner in addressing the disorders that disrupt those same functional areas. Similarly, personality traits have been divided according to the same functional areas of personality, and an inspection of the traits that correspond to a given area of personality might allow for better assessment of the given clinical pathology as well as for assessing its improvement with treatment (Mayer, 2003).

Finally, by placing personality amid neighboring systems, the Systems Framework for Personality makes clearer than before the degree to which, for example, disorders of personality adjustment and adaptation arise from conflict between the individual and society. By plainly specifying the location of the personality system and its surroundings, the framework makes clear that personality must compromise among biological possibilities, psychological needs, and social pressures. Some disorders are simply a consequence of a problematic compromise between biopsychological needs and the social situation. That compromise might appear warranted for the individual at some point in his or her life and yet appear less good at a later time—or at any time to those around the individual. Although some might say it is best to hide this social judgment in diagnosis, it has never been well hidden, and it is best to shed light on it in the long run. The Systems Framework for Personality Psychology does so plainly, so that the social assumptions regarding diagnoses can be examined and justified where necessary.

Overall, there is much to be gained by the cross talk between the disciplines of abnormal psychology and personality psychology. This chapter, and this volume more generally, represents a promising step toward better coordinating these areas.

NOTES

1. There is also a section on personality change due to a medical condition that is similar in its definition of personality to that of the section on personality disorders (American Psychiatric Association, 2000, p. 187).

2. Note also that the *DSM-IV* defines personality as involving inner experiences and social outcomes. Again, these are congruent with the systems-framework description of the collective function of major psychological subsystems. This collective function certainly brings about not only inner experience and social behavior but also—omitted by the *DSM*—psychological processes that are neither conscious nor expressed (Bargh & Ferguson, 2000; Kihlstrom, 1987; Niedenthal & Kitayama, 1994).

3. It is worth noting that there exists a striking resemblance between the four areas of the systems set and the *DSM*-specified areas of affect, cognition, interpersonal functioning, and impulse control. The correspondences are between *DSM*'s affect and the systems set's energy lattice, cognition and the knowledge works, interpersonal functioning and the social actor, and impulse control and the conscious executive.

REFERENCES

American Medical Association (1942). *Standard Nomenclature of Disease and Standard Nomenclature of Operations (SNDO)* (3rd ed.). Chicago, IL: Author.

American Psychiatric Association. (1980). *Diagnostic and statistical manual of mental disorders* (3rd ed.). Washington, DC: Author.

American Psychiatric Association. (1987). *Diagnostic and statistical manual of mental disorders* (3rd ed., rev.). Washington, DC: Author.

American Psychiatric Association. (1994). *Diagnostic and statistical manual of mental disorders* (4th ed.). Washington, DC: Author.

American Psychiatric Association. (2000). *Diagnostic and statistical manual of mental disorders* (4th ed., text rev.). Washington, DC: Author.

Bargh, J. A., & Ferguson, M. J. (2000). Beyond behaviorism: On the automaticity of higher mental processes. *Psychological Bulletin, 126,* 925–945.

Burger, J. M. (2000). *Personality* (5th ed.). Belmont, CA: Wadsworth.

Cloninger, S. (1996). *Personality: Description, dynamics, and development.* New York: Freeman.

Coolidge, F. L., & Segal, D. L. (1998). Evolution of the personality disorder diagnosis in the Diagnostic and Statistical Manual of Mental Disorders. *Clinical Psychology Review, 18,* 585–599.

Costa, P. T., Jr., & Widiger, T. A. (2002). *Personality disorders and the five-factor model of personality* (2nd ed.). Washington, DC: American Psychological Association.

First, M., Spitzer, R., Gibbon, M., Williams, J., Davies, J. B., Howes, M., et al. (1995). The structured clinical interview for DSM-III-R personality disorders (SCID-II). Part II: Multi-site test-retest reliability study. *Journal of Personality Disorders, 9,* 92–104.

Forgas, J. P. (Ed.). (2001). *Affect and social cognition.* Mahwah, NJ: Erlbaum.

Freud, S. (1960). *The ego and the id* (J. Riviere, Trans.). New York: Norton. (Original work published 1923)

Freud, S. (1966). *Introductory lectures on psychoanalysis* (J. Strachey, Ed. and Trans.). New York: Norton. (Original work published 1917)

Funder, D. C. (2001). *The personality puzzle.* New York: Norton.

Funder, D. C. (2002). Personality psychology: Current status and some issues for the future. *Journal of Research in Personality, 36,* 638–639.

Hilgard, E. R. (1980). The trilogy of mind: Cognition, affection, and conation. *Journal of the History of the Behavioral Sciences, 16,* 107–117.

Jablensky, A. (1995). Kraepelin's legacy: Paradigm or pitfall for modern psychiatry? *European Archives Psychiatry and Clinical Neuroscience, 245,* 186–188.

Kihlstrom, J. F. (1987). The cognitive unconscious. *Science, 237,* 1445–1452.

Larsen, R. J., & Buss, D. M. (2002). *Personality psychology: Domains of knowledge about human nature.* Boston: McGraw-Hill.

Lenzenweger, M. F. (1999). Deeper into the schizotypy taxon: On the robust nature of maximum covariance analysis. *Journal of Abnormal Psychology, 108,* 182–187.

Mayer, J. D. (1994). A system-topics framework for the study of personality. *Imagination, Cognition, and Personality, 13,* 99–123.

Mayer, J. D. (1995). A framework for the classification of personality components. *Journal of Personality, 63,* 819–877.

Mayer, J. D. (1998). A systems framework for the field of personality. *Psychological Inquiry, 9,* 118–144.

Mayer, J. D. (2000). *Personality psychology: A systems approach* (1st classroom test ed.). Boston: Pearson Custom Publishing.

Mayer, J. D. (2001). Primary divisions of personality and their scientific contributions: From the trilogy-of-mind to the systems set. *Journal for the Theory of Social Behaviour, 31,* 449–477.

Mayer, J. D. (2003). Structural divisions of personality and the classification of traits. *Review of General Psychology, 7,* 381–401.

Mayer, J. D. (2004). Classifying change techniques according to the areas of personality they influence: A systems framework integration. *Journal of Clinical Psychology, 60,* 1291–1315.

Mayer, J. D. (2005a). *Personality psychology: A systems approach* (3rd classroom test ed.). Boston: Pearson Custom Publishing.

Mayer, J. D. (2005b). A tale of two visions: Can a view of personality psychology help integrate psychology? *American Psychologist, 60,* 294–307.

Mayer, J. D., Chabot, H. F., & Carlsmith, K. (1997). Conation, affect, and cognition in personality. In G. Matthews (Ed.), *Cognitive science perspectives on personality and emotion* (pp. 31–63). Amsterdam: Elsevier Science.

McDermut, W., Zimmerman, M., & Chelminski, I. (2003). The construct validity of depressive personality disorder. *Journal of Abnormal Psychology, 112,* 49–60.

Mendelssohn, M. (1971). *Moses Mendelssohn: Gesammelte schriften jubilaumsausgabe (Band1: Schriften zur philosophie und asthetik).* Stuttgart, Germany: Friedrich Frommann Verlag (Gunther Holzboog).

Millon, T. (2002). Assessment is not enough: The SPA should participate in constructing a comprehensive clinical science of personality. *Journal of Personality Assessment, 78,* 209–218.

Nathan, P. E., & Lagenbucher, J. W. (1999). Psychopathology: Description and classification. *Annual Review of Psychology, 50,* 79–107.

Niedenthal, P. M., & Kitayama, S. (Eds.). (1994). *The heart's eye: Emotional influences in perception and attention.* San Diego, CA: Academic Press.

O'Connor, B. P. (2002). The search for dimensional structure differences between normality and abnormality: A statistical review of published data on personality and psychopathology. *Journal of Personality and Social Psychology, 83,* 962–982.

Pervin, L. A. (2003). *The science of personality* (2nd ed.). New York: Oxford University Press.

Pervin, L. A., & John, O. P. (Eds.). (1999). *Handbook of personality: Theory and research* (2nd ed.). New York: Guilford Press.

Pfohl, B. (1999). Axis I and Axis II: Comorbidity or confusion? In C. R. Cloninger (Ed.), *Personality and psychopathology* (pp. 83–98). Washington, DC: American Psychiatric Association.

Rothschild, L., Cleland, C., & Haslam, N. (2003). A Taxometric Study of Borderline Personality Disorder. *Journal of Abnormal Psychology, 112,* 657–666.

Segal, D. L., & Coolidge, F. L. (2000). Assessment. In *Encyclopedia of psychology* (pp. 264–272). Washington, DC: American Psychological Association.

Segal, D. L., & Coolidge, F. L. (2001). Diagnosis and classification. In M. Hersen & V. B. Van Hasselt (Eds.), *Advanced abnormal psychology* (2nd ed., pp. 5–22). New York: Kluwer Academic/Plenum Publishers.

Seligman, M. E. P., & Csikszentmihalyi, M. (2000). Positive psychology: An introduction. *American Psychologist, 55,* 5–14.

Shea, M. T., & Yen, S. (2003). Stability as a distinction between Axis I and Axis II disorders. *Journal of Personality Disorders, 17,* 373–386.

Spitzer, R. L., & Fleiss, J. L. (1974). A reanalysis of the reliability of psychiatric diagnosis. *British Journal of Psychiatry, 125,* 341–347.

Sternberg, R. J., & Grigorenko, E. L. (2001). Unified psychology. *American Psychologist, 56,* 1069–1079.

Tellegen, A. (1994). Foreword. In S. Strack & M. Lorr (Eds.), *Differentiating normal and abnormal personality* (pp. ix–xi). New York: Springer.

Veith, I. (1970). *Hysteria: The history of a disease.* Chicago: University of Chicago Press.

Westen, D., & Shedler, J. (1999). Revising and assessing Axis II, Part II: Toward an empirically based and clinically useful classification of personality disorders. *American Journal of Psychiatry, 156,* 273–285.

Westen, D., & Shedler, J. (2000). A prototype matching approach to diagnosing personality disorders: Toward DSM-V. *Journal of Personality Disorders, 14,* 109–126.

Zimmerman, M. (1994). Diagnosing personality disorders: A review of issues and research methods. *Archives of General Psychiatry, 51,* 225–245.

Author Index

Subject Index